ISBN 978-1-5279-3625-6
PIBN 10915623

1 MONTH OF
FREE
READING

at
www.ForgottenBooks.com

By purchasing this book you are eligible for one month membership to ForgottenBooks.com, giving you unlimited access to our entire collection of over 1,000,000 titles via our web site and mobile apps.

To claim your free month visit:
www.forgottenbooks.com/free915623

English
Français
Deutsche
Italiano
Español
Português

www.forgottenbooks.com

Mythology Photography **Fiction**
Fishing Christianity **Art** Cooking
Essays Buddhism Freemasonry
Medicine **Biology** Music **Ancient
Egypt** Evolution Carpentry Physics
Dance Geology **Mathematics** Fitness
Shakespeare **Folklore** Yoga Marketing
Confidence Immortality Biographies
Poetry **Psychology** Witchcraft
Electronics Chemistry History **Law**
Accounting **Philosophy** Anthropology
Alchemy Drama Quantum Mechanics
Atheism Sexual Health **Ancient History**
Entrepreneurship Languages Sport
Paleontology Needlework Islam
Metaphysics Investment Archaeology
Parenting Statistics Criminology
Motivational

64TH CONGRESS }
1st Session }

SENATE

{ DOCUMENT
{ No. 415

INDUSTRIAL RELATIONS

FINAL REPORT AND TESTIMONY

SUBMITTED TO CONGRESS BY THE

COMMISSION ON INDUSTRIAL RELATIONS

CREATED BY THE ACT OF
AUGUST 23, 1912

VOL. V

WASHINGTON
GOVERNMENT PRINTING OFFICE
1916

CONTENTS OF VOLUME V.

LATIONS AND REMEDIES,
TTLE, WASH.

———

r this subject, see pages 4414 to 4571)

———

COMMISSION ON INDUSTRIAL RELATIONS.

SEATTLE, WASH., *Monday, August 10, 1914—10 a. m.*

Present: Commissioners Commons (acting chairman), Lennon, O'Connell, and Garretson.

Acting Chairman COMMONS. The commission will come to order.

I will say to the witnesses and others that unfortunately several members of the commission have found it impossible to be here, and I have been selected to act as chairman in the absence of Mr. Walsh. Other members will be expected within a day or two, or are expected, and it is hoped that they will be here.

The Industrial Relations Commission was created by act of Congress to inquire into the general causes of industrial unrest, and to make recommendations to Congress, and to other legislative bodies, regarding such remedies as it may find advisable.

There is almost no specific limit to the field that should be covered by this commission in so far as it relates to the relations between employers and employees, and their relation to the general public.

The list of witnesses for Seattle covers almost all of the subjects which the commission is called upon to investigate.

The sessions of the commission are entirely informal. Witnesses are not sworn. The main object is to get such assistance as we can from the witnesses in understanding the main subjects that we have before us, and in giving recommendations based upon your practical experience and your knowledge of the conditions in the State of Washington.

Mr. Thompson, will you call your first witness?

Mr. THOMPSON. The Hon. Mr. Gill, please take the stand.

TESTIMONY OF HON. HIRAM C. GILL.

Mr. THOMPSON. Will you please give us your name?

Mr. GILL. Hiram C. Gill.

Mr. THOMPSON. Will you give your official position, please, in the city of Seattle?

Mr. GILL. I have been mayor of the city since the 4th day of March of this year; previously I was mayor from March, 1910, until March, 1911.

Mr. THOMPSON. March, 1911?

Mr. GILL. Yes, sir.

Mr. THOMPSON. How long have you lived in the city of Seattle?

Mr. GILL. Twenty-five years.

Mr. THOMPSON. Twenty-five years?

Mr. GILL. Yes, sir.

Mr. THOMPSON. What profession or occupation or business do you follow?

Mr. GILL. I am a lawyer by profession, and have been such except when I was mayor. I was a stenographer for the first three years.

Mr. THOMPSON. From your residence in the city of Seattle and your acquaintance with the general industrial conditions here, what in your opinion is the leading industrial work in Seattle and in the vicinity?

Mr. GILL. Oh, the various branches of lumbering are the leading industries here. Probably latterly the fishing industry more than it was—but the lumber has always been the dominating industry.

Mr. THOMPSON. In the city of Seattle itself what would be the industry—that, too?

Mr. GILL. Yes; that is included. Lumber probably employs more men right in the city, taking in the suburb of Ballard than anything else besides.

Mr. THOMPSON. As far as you know, what has been the general condition—what is the general condition of labor in the lumber industry in and around Seattle?

Mr. GILL. Well, it all has been depressed more or less the last several years, and is now. That is, logs have been way down, a great many mills are shut down, shingles particularly. I think they are picking up a little again just now lately, but there has been a great deal of depression. .

Mr. THOMPSON. Well, in particular with reference to the relationship which exists between the employer in the lumber industry and the employee, what would you say with reference to that?

Mr. GILL. Well, it has not been a satisfactory condition from the standpoint of the employee, particularly in the shingle business.

Mr. THOMPSON. Particularly in Chamberlin?

Mr. GILL. In shingling.

Mr. THOMPSON. Why do you make that statement?

Mr. GILL. Well, there was trouble over the wages between the men and the shingle-mill owners. You understand out at Ballard, there are probably more shingle mills than at any one place in the world, and that is where the shingles are mostly cut. That is in the city limits, and for a year or two there has been a continuous strike out there; it terminated a few months ago, but I think un-satisfactory to the employees, and there has always been a feeling of unrest there, I think; and there is throughout the State among the mill employees, particularly among the unskilled branches.

Mr. THOMPSON. Organized or unorganized?

Mr. GILL. They have an organization. The shingle weavers union has an organization for practically a comparatively unskilled trade, and it is not strong enough to absolutely dominate at all. And whatever hold they have on wages they have been compelled to fight for, and they have maintained them-selves, or they would not be getting the wages they do. And the fact that they could not reduce the wages of the employees, I think, has a great deal to do with the fact that a good many of the mills did shut down for quite a while.

Mr. THOMPSON. In the strikes which you say have occurred in the shingle industry here within the city limits of Ballard, what has been the general attitude of the city administration toward the preservation of peace at such times? What has been the nature of the strikes with reference to being peace-ful or disorderly?

Mr. GILL. My predecessor—there has been no strike nor trouble in Ballard since I took office this time. At that time I think my predecessor refused to furnish police, and all of the policing work was done by special deputy sheriffs furnished by the county sometimes, by the employees, or the men of the em-ployers. My own policy has been not to allow the police to interfere in any way on one side or another other than to preserve order on the streets. .

Mr. THOMPSON. In all of these cases where you say special deputy sheriffs were furnished by the county and in some cases by the employees—I under-stand by the last statement you mean that the employers hired men who were sworn in as deputy sheriffs?

Mr. GILL. I think that is true. Now, I don't want to say that positively. That was the general understanding. That is the understanding I had. I wasn't in office at that time, but merely knew superficially. I want you to under-stand my statements on these labor questions are just superficial general knowledge. I may be wrong on some of them. My understanding was that the mill companies designated these men, and that they were deputized by the sheriff. I think that is right.

Mr. THOMPSON. Generally, is that the method used here in handling strikes? For instance, do the employers hire outside agencies, such as the private de-tective agencies, or get protectors from other sources that are private, that some-times may be kept just as private detectives on the ground, and in other cases may be sworn in as deputy sheriffs?

Mr. GILL. I understand that that has been the practice of the county.

Mr. THOMPSON. Yes. So far as you know, has there ever been any objection to such a practice by the organized authorities, either of the city of Seattle, the county, or of the State, so far as you know?

Mr. GILL. Well, I don't—I think there has always been a good deal of ob-jection by everybody that thinks much of the rights of the ordinary citizen, to an employer of labor being able to hire men to perform police functions. I have got an objection myself, although I never said much about that. As mayor of the city, I would not tolerate it; that is, I would not deputize men as special police to run anybody's business.

Mr. THOMPSON. Has there ever been as far as you know—I rather imagine from your answer it has not been—but has any formal action ever been taken by the municipal authorities against the hiring of special guards by the employers?

Mr. GILL. Well, I could state only for myself. When I was mayor for the first time—I was elected in 1910—at that time there was a strike among the machinists and the shopmen. I was requested at that time to designate men as special policemen in various machine shops, which I refused to do. When I took office this last time there was a teamsters' strike on, and the city was maintaining some 50 special policemen and paying them. I didn't deem them necessary, and my chief of police and myself let them all out. The matter was settled up later on, and we have never had any more to do with it. But so far as the policy of the city government when I say I have been connected with it—I was councilman a good many years—it was always the policy of the city government during those times to refuse the employment of, or to allow employers of labor to designate their own men for police service. That is my policy—always will be. I don't believe in it.

Mr. THOMPSON. What would be your policy, Mr. Gill, in case a strike should occur in any important industry here and the employers should call on you for assistance to maintain order and to protect their property?

Mr. GILL. If the chief of police should say that he thought the police force was inadequate, and I agreed with him, I would try myself to name the special policemen and make the employers pay for them. That would be my idea if I could not get police force enough. Then I would ask the city government to let me name special policemen myself, and have them paid by the city. I would name them myself. I would not allow anybody else to name the policemen. That would be my policy if it ever came to that kind of situation.

Mr. THOMPSON. You say you never had any strikes during your term of office?

Mr. GILL. Yes; there was a teamsters' strike in existence when I came in office. That is all I ever had. The machinists' strike was on when I was first mayor.

Mr. THOMPSON. During all these strikes have the employers as such ever asked you to do more than to maintain order and protect property?

Mr. GILL. Well, in the machinists' strike the employers claimed that their property was being jeopardized and they thought I should police their premises for them; but when I investigated the matter I never found that the laboring men were doing anything that they hadn't the right to do, and that whatever abuses there were were always as much on one side as the other. We had an understanding as to what everybody should do, and we never had any more trouble. I never had any trouble with the strikers myself; they always seemed to me to be fair here in this city. We have never had anything that was serious.

Mr. THOMPSON. During those strikes, I take it, there was no destruction of the private property of the employers?

Mr. GILL. No, sir; never any destruction of private property in this city while I have been mayor in any strike that I can recall.

Mr. THOMPSON. Were there acts of violence committed during the strike?

Mr. GILL. Oh, of course, there are always street fights and fist fights between men. Take during the teamsters' strike there was a good deal of fighting—some men were beaten occasionally. Nobody could ever very well say on whom the blame could be laid. Just as many times it was the men hired by the team owners, the employers' association, as it was by the men themselves. The men employed to break this strike would go armed, and there would be bitter personal feeling, of course, between the men once in a while; but there never was, in my opinion, any violence which was sanctioned by the union strikers. I never could see that they sanctioned anything of the kind. A few hot-headed fellows would get out and fight. The same was true in the old machinists' strike. On the contrary, the shop owners used as much violence as anybody else. I remember one factory that undertook to turn a hose on a lot of employees in the street. They had a right to be in the street. They have used as much violence as the men have.

Mr. THOMPSON. What is your opinion from these two experiences which you state, with reference to the advisability or necessity of the employers using private guards?

Mr. GILL. I don't think they should be allowed to use them. I don't think any private individual should be given police authority to use in a fight where he is a party. I think the policemen should be impartial men, and I don't think an employer's policemen are impartial men any more than I think the labor men's policemen would be impartial. I don't think they should be allowed to use them while they are making a fight. They should be put on the same basis and fight it out.

Mr. THOMPSON. From your experience as mayor during these two strikes, what views have you with reference to the question of arbitration in industrial disputes and what experience as mayor have you had with that problem?

Mr. GILL. Well, that is a pretty broad question, the time is more or less limited.

Mr. THOMPSON. You did try to get these strikes submitted to arbitration, did you not?

Mr. GILL. How is that?

Mr. THOMPSON. You did try to get these strikes submitted to arbitration, did you not?

Mr. GILL. Well, this teamsters' strike was an illustration of what I think could generally be done. We have in this State a compulsory arbitration statute which is ineffective because it hasn't any penalty and is more or less a meaningless statute and does not amount to anything. In this teamsters' strike we had asked a body of men—I did, 12, I think, prominent business men around the town in all walks of life who had no interest one way or another—they were not employers of labor, because I didn't want them belonging to the employers' association, and they were not labor men. They took the matter up with the team owners and the striking teamsters and worked on it for quite a long while seeing what they could do in a perfectly voluntary manner. The strike was settled; both parties lived up to it in perfect good faith, and it worked admirably in that instance. They have had no more trouble. The teamsters themselves were just as willing, and more willing if anything, than the owners were, to settle. That has been my observation, that there are very few labor strikes nowadays which, if the employer will look at it in the light which he should under the legislation and developments of recent years, could not be settled without any trouble. My observation is that the employee is just as reasonable as the employer is. The trouble has been always for so many years that the employer could not get the idea in his head that anybody else had any intelligence or rights. They are getting over that idea. I believe they are going to realize that they are going to be treated as fairly as they treat the other men. It probably will be necessary to get legislation to compel arbitration where they won't arbitrate voluntarily. It is a hard thing to legislate on, and hard to enforce. I believe if anybody would try to deal with the situation and if the employers and employees tried to, they could settle most of them themselves.

Mr. THOMPSON. Mr. Gill, in your term of office as mayor of the city of Seattle have industrial disputes come up before you in an official way or a private way in which you have had to deal with them and which have not reached the strike stage?

Mr. GILL. I did not quite catch that last remark.

Mr. THOMPSON. Industrial disputes where there have not been strikes, have you had to deal with any of those cases, either as a private citizen or mayor?

Mr. GILL. No; I have not had to do that.

Mr. THOMPSON. What was done by the city in the industrial methods—that is, was not the question of relations between the employee and the employer considered; does the city exercise any supervision over that question in any shape or form?

Mr. GILL. No; only as to a part of it. That is, this city maintains and has for many years maintained a free employment bureau of its own—always has; that is about the only instance that we have had.

Mr. THOMPSON. Is that under the State law?

Mr. GILL. Of that we have control. We license employment agents—it has not worked very satisfactorily, yet it prevents a great many of the abuses. There is legislation pending now at the next election where there is an initiative bill forbidding private employment agents—probably unconstitutional, in my opinion, but the idea of that, though, was to put the employment of labor entirely in the hands of the city, I presume.

Mr. THOMPSON. Well, this employment agency you speak of now as being in the hands of the city, have you instances—are they run at the expense of the city?

Mr. GILL. Entirely at the expense of the city.

Mr. THOMPSON. Have you any detailed knowledge of the work it does, or would others speak of that?

Mr. GILL. Well, I know how it works. It furnishes thousands upon thousands of situations to both men and women. It has always worked very satisfactorily, so far as that is concerned. They can get the very best service the city can give, for nothing. But the trouble with the employment-agent situation, where the private employment agent cuts into it, is that a great many of the big employers of labor, their foremen, or somebody in them are dividing the money with the employment agents, and they will hire only through private employment agencies, because the employers are receiving the same service. That is why the city office can not be as effective as it might be.

Mr. THOMPSON. Is there anything specific which you would like to give the commission upon which you base that judgment, Mr. Gill?

Mr. GILL. No; I can not think of anything.

Mr. THOMPSON. What is your view of the bill which is to prohibit private employment agencies?

Mr. GILL. Oh, I never thought very seriously of it. It goes a long way in the direction of paternalism. There are abuses in private employment agencies, as there are abuses in everything. I do not think the bill is constitutional, myself, and for that reason I have not thought very seriously one way or the other. I do not think that it will amount to anything if it passes.

Mr. THOMPSON. That is all.

Commissioner LENNON. What wages are paid the city employees who work on the streets?

Mr. GILL. $2.75 is the minimum wage paid by the city. There are men in the street department who are paid, common labor, who are paid $3 a day, but the general run of men, labor, the wage is $2.75.

Commissioner LENNON. They work eight hours or more per day?

Mr. GILL. They work eight hours a day. They get two weeks a year vacation on pay.

Commissioner LENNON. Is there any rule or regulation of the city or any agreement with the employers which requires that they should be union men?

Mr. GILL. No; no requirement.

Commissioner LENNON. No requirement of that kind?

Mr. GILL. No, sir.

Commissioner LENNON. Is that the practice?

Mr. GILL. That is the practice by the city. Everything we have outside of the library department is civil service. The civil-service board has never made unionism or nonunionism a test of city employment, and consequently whatever they happen to be when the take the examination they remain. There are in the skilled departments, the light department particularly, a great many union men, probably more union than anybody else, I guess; that is simply because as a general rule they are better able to pass an examination than the others are.

Commissioner LENNON. Are there any large number of Asiatics in this city working in different industries?

Mr. GILL. You mean employed by the city?

Commissioner LENNON. No.

Mr. GILL. Employed by others?

Commissioner LENNON. Yes.

Mr. GILL. Yes; there are a lot of Japanese, a good many; they are not as a general rule employed in the skilled trades at all. They are restaurant men and domestic help, and a great many of them in the suburbs are getting to be vegetable gardeners, probably getting to control the vegetable gardening in and around the city.

Commissioner LENNON. Do you know whether or not they receive the standard wage where they are employed; that is, the wage that the American would receive?

Mr. GILL. No; I do not know. I do not think they are, however, although I noticed here a little while ago that the Japanese barbers are, a great many of them, applying for admission to the barbers' union. That matter was being very seriously considered by the union itself. The Japanese are, I think, willing to put their wages on a higher standard, as high a standard as anybody else. In those trades where they are skilled, I don't think they work for less than anybody else; they don't if they can help it.

Commissioner LENNON. You may have noticed in the eastern papers the reports of Hindus coming in just across the border. Has there been any attempt to land them here?

Mr. GILL. Practically no attempt. There are no Hindus here to speak of. There are just a very few. They have tried, and did try some time ago, to come in, but I think they were turned back; did not get in.

Commissioner LENNON. That is all.

Acting Chairman COMMONS. Mr. Garretson wants to ask some questions.

Commissioner GARRETSON. Do you believe that it is any greater inconsistency under our laws for laboring men to band themselves together as armed bands than it is for their employers to maintain armed bands?

Mr. GILL. No; I think if one is going to be allowed to maintain an armed band the other should. I don't think either of them should.

Commissioner GARRETSON. I agree with you.

Mr. GILL. If one should, both should.

Commissioner GARRETSON. You spoke as if you were somewhat of a believer in compulsory arbitration. When the arbitration becomes compulsory, isn't it a fact that it ceases to be arbitration and only becomes another form of a court?

Mr. GILL. Yes; that is what it would be, as I say. Now, I don't want to be misunderstood; I would simply say that if you had a compulsory arbitration statute it would help those who wanted to settle disputes by conciliation to settle them. I believe it can all be done practically, just as this little strike here was, by getting the people together themselves before an impartial body of men. I think most of them can be settled, and always could be, if people would try to do it.

Commissioner GARRETSON. Don't you really believe, then, that when you put it into those statutes in the form of law that what you would advocate is really conciliation?

Mr. GILL. That is what I say about that.

Commissioner GARRETSON. As against arbitration.

Mr. GILL. I want to make myself plain on that.

Commissioner GARRETSON. As against arbitration of compulsory form?

Mr. GILL. Yes; but you can't make a man conciliate with an ax. I want something to fall back on if people don't conciliate.

Commissioner GARRETSON. Well, then, it becomes really an industrial court, if it is compulsory. That is what it woud be, isn't that it?

Mr. GILL. Well, you may call it that.

Commissioner GARRETSON. It is only another form of legal tribunal.

Mr. GILL. It depends on the way the act is drawn.

Commissioner GARRETSON. Are you familiar with the old Erdman Act or the new Newlands Act, as applied to interstate employees of railways?

Mr. GILL. Yes; I understand that railroad act. I don't know about the new act.

Commissioner GARRETSON. Well, the new one has been in vogue since last July, I believe, and superseded the Erdman Act.

Mr. GILL. Yes.

Commissioner GARRETSON. It provides for conciliation first, and, if conciliation fails, then the energies of the administrators of the law are bent toward securing the consent of both parties to arbitrate, but there is nothing compulsory at any stage of the game.

Mr. GILL. No. Well, I don't—I may be a little dense—I don't understand the difference between conciliation which is compelled by law and an arbitration. You might want to call them something different.

Commissioner GARRETSON. There is no conciliation compelled by law.

Mr. GILL. I understand a conciliatory settlement to be one that is settled by the people themselves without reference to any legal enactment or any compulsion, and that when you can't get them to conciliate, why, then, you might enforce compulsory arbitration.

Commissioner GARRETSON. There has not been during the period in which the Erdman Act has been in vogue, covering a period from 1907 to the present time—it was dormant until that time—there has not been to exceed two instances in which conciliation was refused by either party—I mean the friendly service of the conciliators. It has not always. There are one or two instances where it failed. As, for instance, you are familiar with the engineers' trouble of late with the railroad companies?

Mr. GILL. Yes.

Commissioner GARRETSON. There you have a working of the act. They endeavored to conciliate, and the final result was that they secured the consent of both parties to arbitrate, although there is no compulsion on either party. Do you believe that that would be more desirable than compulsory arbitration would?

Mr. GILL. Yes; if they would get together, it certainly would.

Commissioner GARRETSON. Well, if they would not?

Mr. GILL. Well, I want to explain this much, that I don't really pretend to be very—possess a very deep knowledge in these matters, and I never hired anybody. I have simply got a superficial idea of how things could be adjusted. With me it has worked out. You have problems in the East which we don't have here. You don't use as much sense. You have got capitalists that can't recognize that there is anybody on earth but themselves. You have got employees that are ignorant. We have got a different class to deal with out here. My own personal opinion has been, as mayor of this city, that as long as the executive of the city wants to see these people treated fairly, and if the employer understands in the beginning that he has got to stand on his own bottom and make his own fight, that he will conciliate and join in arbitration, and that everything that ever comes up while I am mayor will be settled without any trouble. They will always fight and always refuse arbitration as long as the governing heads are elected and controlled only by one side, as they are mostly in the East. Out here they are not.

Commissioner GARRETSON. On the other hand, if the chief executive of the municipality, or of the State, as the case may be, was absolutely dominated by one interest or the other, it matters not which, then would not compulsory arbitration become a deadly weapon?

Mr. GILL. Yes, it would; unquestionably would.

Commissioner GARRETSON. Have you ever given any consideration, Mr. Mayor, to how limited the field is—the field of absolutely unbiased arbitrators on the part of the labor men?

Mr. GILL. No; I don't think they are limited in their choice out here at all.

Commissioner GARRETSON. How many men in your acquaintance can rise superior to their property interests in giving a verdict?

Mr. GILL. Well, I can get arbitrators who haven't any property interests, that is, who are affected by the particular industry involved in the strike. I don't mean a bunch of paupers.

Commissioner GARRETSON. Has it ever occurred to you that every employer of labor is himself disqualified for service as an arbitrator on the wage question?

Mr. GILL. Oh, no; I know lots of employers of labor that I regard as honest.

Commissioner GARRETSON. And so do I. But when it comes to raising the wage of some other employee when he thought it would react on his own men, then he might be honest and still not be desirous of doing that?

Mr. GILL. Oh, yes; if you are going to get down to a proposition that everybody that owns a dollar is a crook——

Commissioner GARRETSON. I know some men who don't own a dollar who are crooks.

Mr. GILL. That is all aside. I think that is taking too broad a view of the dishonesty of everybody, which I don't believe.

Commissioner GARRETSON. I have been seeking arbitrators for 30 years, and it is the outgrowth of my experience for that many years on the subject. When you take that phase of it and consider that every labor employer has a direct interest in the going wage, how many of them are qualified to act as arbitrators in industrial disputes that take in wages?

Mr. GILL. Oh, unquestionably the great body of them probably would be, you might say, disqualified by personal interest or prejudice; but there are a great many men in every municipality who have no relation of that kind who can settle these disputes. You don't need necessarily to get an employer of labor. You could get even a lawyer—he might arbitrate something—or a physician or a doctor or a minister. I had on this conciliation board of mine that kind of men mostly, because I didn't want the employers of labor. But we had no trouble in getting a body of men, very prominent people of all grades, and I think the labor men were perfectly satisfied after they got through that they acted fairly and impartially in their effort to settle the matter. It was a most important matter to settle.

Commissioner GARRETSON. Isn't it a fact that the labor man usually accepts the situation whether he is satisfied or not; isn't that the history of the movement?

Mr. GILL. My understanding is when a man is licked, whether a laboring man or a capitalist, he always accepts it. I always looked at it in that way.

Commissioner GARRETSON. Lots of men don't know when they are licked.

Mr. GILL. Most of them do.

Commissioner GARRETSON. It is not because of being licked when you accept an arbitration verdict.

Mr. GILL. We have feeble-minded homes for men who don't know when they are licked.

Commissioner GARRETSON. Do you look on the arbitration verdict as one to be accepted after you are licked? Arbitration is before it comes to war, while it is still hanging in the balance. If you are licked, the other side wouldn't arbitrate.

Mr. GILL. That is true.

Commissioner GARRETSON. I am speaking of the faith that underlies the acceptance of the verdict of the arbitration board.

Mr. GILL. You have given this thing a great deal more study than I have. I am really not qualified to say, looking at it from the standpoint of the employee along the lines you have suggested, whether I would as a matter of final analysis, and I had the enactment or not of compulsory arbitration—whether I would advise it or not. It simply has looked to me, as one who hasn't given this matter much study, but from the standpoint of the employee himself—and he is the man I generally think more of than the employer, because the employer can look out for himself better—in the final analysis where I could get these people together and settle—that is, where there is hope of settlement—that they should get together and settle. You can sometimes make a big employer settle if he thinks he has to.

Commissioner GARRETSON. The attitude of the employer himself toward that circumscribed field is something like this: In one case where the arbitration of a very large matter was proposed by a large railroad we took the position we would accept no employer of labor; we would accept no owner of stock of corporations or politician. Here is his interpretation: " My God, we wouldn't have nobody left but preachers and walking delegates." You can see where the field is narrowed to from the standpoint of the employer if you take the interested men out. If you study arbitration from that standpoint, as a party in interest in the arbitration naturally does, would it not narrow the field greatly?

Mr. GILL. Oh, yes; it narrows the field, but, then, everything has its limits. You elect your judges and you are narrowed down to lawyers. It might be better if we were not confined to that, but you have a good deal broader field in arbitrators than you have in judges. You have real estate men and insurance agents and things like that.

Commissioner GARRETSON. That is all, Mr. Chairman.

Acting Chairman COMMONS. Do you know whether there is any city or State supervision of employment offices?

Mr. GILL. Well, there are some State laws affecting it, although here we control them, in so far as they are controlled, by city ordinance. We supervise them in a measure.

Acting Chairman COMMONS. What is the extent of that supervision; are they required to pay license?

Mr. GILL. Our ordinance has this kind of provision: A man that is employed by a private employment agency must go to the place of the job and the employer must indorse on his slip, if they refuse him employment, why. They put it there, and we have a kind of record of it. If the man comes back—for instance, a crooked employment office sends him up to a job and there is no job—when he comes back, if he hasn't a job he can go to the employment agent, and he pays back the money. If he doesn't, we can revoke his license. It hasn't happened often that we have had to do that on account of this provision. The council passes on every license, and they can revoke the license.

Acting Chairman COMMONS. Who revokes the license?

Mr. GILL. The city council has the right of revocation.

Acting Chairman COMMONS. Do you have an officer or staff in charge of this supervision?

Mr. GILL. Yes, sir; it is a branch of the civil service department of the city. The secretary of the civil service board has supervision over that, and if he recommends to the council that the license be revoked, the council has that right. It is a measure of protection, and it saves a good many people from being robbed, as they are always; but still there are abuses that we can not get away from.

Acting Chairman COMMONS. Give us the name of the secretary.

Mr. GILL. A. H. Grout is secretary of the civil service board.

Acting Chairman COMMONS. A. H. Grout?

Mr. GILL. Arthur H. Grout; he can tell you in full—or Mr. Kenyon, his assistant.

Commissioner GARRETSON. He really exercises a jurisdiction as wide as the scope of the employment office?

Mr. GILL. Yes, sir.

Acting Chairman COMMONS. Who has charge of the city municipal employment office?

Mr. GILL. He has; he is secretary of the civil service board—Mr. Grout.

Acting Chairman COMMONS. Then the civil service commission is not only a civil service commission, but also an employment office?

Mr. GILL. Yes; the secretary is ex officio head of the employment office.

Acting Chairman COMMONS. Who is secretary of the civil service commission—the same man?

Mr. GILL. Mr. Grout, the same man.

Acting Chairman COMMONS. He is also head of the employment office?

Mr. GILL. Yes, sir.

Acting Chairman COMMONS. You spoke a moment ago apparently to the effect that the employment office was not quite as satisfactory as it might be. Did you have in mind any methods by which it could be improved?

Mr. GILL. No, sir; I haven't, for the simple reason I see the limitation in this way: Most of these large railroad companies employ men out of the city; most of the big mills—their men are coming and going all the time—they deal with private employment offices, I have always presumed, because somewhere is some boss who is getting part of the fee. That may be an unfair assumption, but that seems to me the hardest thing to combat and it limits our field of employment in that way.

Acting Chairman COMMONS. Does your civil service commission hold examinations for all employees of the city government?

Mr. GILL. Every employee of the city government except the hospital staff, the city treasurer's employees, and one city department, those are exceptions.

Acting Chairman COMMONS. Who is the officer that is responsible for holding those examinations; is that Mr. Grout here?

Mr. GILL. He has charge of them; yes, sir; under the direction of the board. The civil service board consists of three members.

Acting Chairman COMMONS. They are appointed?

Mr. GILL. They are appointed by the mayor and confirmed by the council, and they are at the head of the civil service commission. Theoretically, they hold the examinations, but it devolves upon the secretary.

Acting Chairman COMMONS. Does the municipality have any municipal utilities which it owns and operates, like waterworks and light plants?

Mr. GILL. It owns the water department and light and has a small asphalt plant and maintains its own city emergency hospital. That is all that the city owns, I think.

Acting Chairman COMMONS. Have they any interest in the street car system?

Mr. GILL. Oh, yes; we started on a street car system and own one line about 4 miles in length in the city and another about 9 miles in length which was given to the city if it would take charge of it, running out into a practically undeveloped territory at the south end of the city. It hasn't any connection up to the city yet, and we haven't got very far started on the street car proposition as yet.

Acting Chairman COMMONS. Are the employees under civil service?

Mr. GILL. Yes, sir.

Acting Chairman COMMONS. The old employees were taken over by the city at that time, or not?

Mr. GILL. No, sir.

Acting Chairman COMMONS. A new staff?

Mr. GILL. New men.

Acting Chairman COMMONS. Are they organized—have a union?

Mr. GILL. No, sir; I don't think so. The street car employees of the city have never been organized. Some years ago there was a very serious, long drawn out strike. That is about 8 or 10 years ago, and the men were beaten. Since that time they never have been organized.

Acting Chairman Commons. Do you have more unemployed in the winter than in the summer?

Mr. Gill. Yes, sir.

Acting Chairman Commons. Is it very much larger?

Mr. Gill. How is that?

Acting Chairman Commons. Is it very much larger?

Mr. Gill. Oh, yes; I think it increases very noticeably.

Acting Chairman Commons. Has the city undertaken in any way to provide for the unemployed in winter?

Mr. Gill. The city maintains a building out in the south suburb of the city where they are clearing a lot of land. Any man that goes to the city police station and reports he is broke or has no place to go or stay, they send him up there and let him sleep and eat, and let him work a couple of hours clearing land to pay for it. It maintains that all the time. No man need come to town and go hungry and have no place to sleep if he will report to the police station and be sent out. During last winter when the employment question got a little serious at one time the city appropriated some eight or ten thousand dollars, I think, that the street superintendent used in hiring men to clear some street slides at that time. They were given alternate days so as to make it cover a good many men. They got $2.75 a day, and that was used to relieve the situation. Outside of that all the city does is to maintain this place where any man can go and sleep and get something to eat.

Acting Chairman Commons. That is under your police department?

Mr. Gill. That is under the police department.

Acting Chairman Commons. Not under the civil-service department?

Mr. Gill. No, sir; not under the civil-service department.

Acting Chairman Commons. So that they are the ones that select these men for the jobs in the winter?

Mr. Gill. The occasion that I spoke of, that was rather an emergency proposition and really was an unlawful act. They had no right to employ anyone who wasn't a civil-service employee, but then the mayor and the street department simply went ahead and put these men to work. They had no right to do it theoretically, because they were not civil-service eligibles.

Acting Chairman Commons. The policy of the city seems to be to provide some opportunity for work every winter, and not only this emergency appropriation you mentioned, but also this other line?

Mr. Gill. The city always maintains a place out near one of the parks, which is being cleared up, where men may go and get a meal and sleep over night—sleep until he gets a job.

Acting Chairman Commons. Is that a kind of work that can be profitably done in winter?

Mr. Gill. There is no profit in it to the city, but it gives them work and makes them pay in a measure for what they get. It is profitable to the extent it is clearing land, which is needed.

Acting Chairman Commons. Is your winter so severe that the ground freezes?

Mr. Gill. The ground never freezes.

Acting Chairman Commons. It is possible to shift a good deal of construction work of the city into the winter?

Mr. Gill. Yes, sir; they can do that kind of work. The city maintains, for instance, the jail stockade. Men that get more than a five-day sentence are sent to the stockade, which is in one of the parks that is being cleared up. It is not being used as a park now, but it must be cleared up. Instead of the rock pile, they put them to clearing ground.

Acting Chairman Commons. You think the city does take care of the men in the winter?

Mr. Gill. Yes, sir; most any man who is down and out can always find some place he can sleep overnight and get a meal that will satisfy his hunger. We always do that.

Acting Chairman Commons. Would you think that would be preferable to place that under the head of the city employment office?

Mr. Gill. No, sir.

Acting Chairman Commons. You think it would be better to leave it to the police?

Mr. Gill. Yes, sir; leave it to the police.

Acting Chairman Commons. A man has to be a beggar to get a job, does he?

Mr., GILL. No, sir; he would not have to be a beggar. A man unfortunate enough to have to ask relief, simply has to go to the police department and state he has no place to sleep. In a great many cities of the country they go and report in that way and are allowed to lie on the cement floor, and here they are allowed to go to a decent bunk, and I would not say it was begging. It is a good deal better from the city's standpoint than to have them standing on the streets touching everybody that comes along for money and spending it for liquor.

Acting Chairman COMMONS. We can get this information from Mr. Kenyon, can we?

Mr. GILL. Yes; or Mr. Grout will give you the full information on the civil-service matter. Anybody in the police department will tell you all about the employment end of it.

Acting Chairman COMMONS. Whom would you get from the police department?

Mr. GILL. I think that Chief Griffith leaves the city to-night. He could probably get——

Acting Chairman COMMONS. Who would have charge of it in the police department?

Mr. GILL. Well, it is all right under the head. I would suggest Inspector Powers, Mike Powers, who is the inspector, and who would be chief in the absence of Chief Griffith leaving the city to-night.

Commissioner O'CONNELL. Who handles licenses in the city?

Mr. GILL. The saloon licenses and the employment licenses are granted by the city council by ordinance. All of the small peddling licenses and show licenses are issued, as a matter of course, by the comptroller, to whomever may pay him the money for them. But the saloons and employment licenses are kept strictly under the city council's office.

Commissioner LENNON. What is the city license for a saloon?

Mr. GILL. A saloon—$1,000.

Commissioner O'CONNELL. Does that cover all, like a bar in a hotel or restaurant?

Mr. GILL. Any bar which sells liquor must pay $1,000, and if a saloon in addition to that maintains a dining room in connection it pays an additional license of $250.

Commissioner O'CONNELL. How many licenses are there issued to saloons to sell liquor in Seattle?

Mr. GILL. The city charter limits the number to, I think it is, about 300. I have forgotten the exact number. That can never be exceeded. We have been running to the limit for a great many years. There can be no additional licenses.

Commissioner O'CONNELL. Are they issued in proportion to the number of citizens?

Mr. GILL. No; the number was fixed at an arbitrary figure by charter amendment several years ago. It can not be increased until the city has 500,000 population.

Commissioner O'CONNELL. What are the closing hours and opening hours of the saloons?

Mr. GILL. They close at 1 o'clock, except on Saturday, when they close at 12 o'clock; they open at 6.

Commissioner O'CONNELL. Are they open on Sundays, holidays, or election day?

Mr. GILL. They are open on holidays, but not on election days and Sundays.

Commissioner O'CONNELL. Are there any licenses issued in restricted districts, or are there any restricted districts?

Mr. GILL. There is no restricted district here now.

Commissioner O'CONNELL. How long since?

Mr. GILL. Since March, a little before March, 1911, when I retired. [Laughter.] It is a matter of local history. I was elected mayor——

Commissioner O'CONNELL. I must have struck an amusing spot.

Mr. GILL. It is understood better by the public in general than it is by you gentlemen. I was elected in March, 1910, as mayor of this city, on a platform to maintain a segregated district——

Commissioner O'CONNELL. Maintain it!

Mr. GILL. I was elected, and I was a believer in maintaining the district segregated, segregating these women. My opponent was not. I was elected. I maintained this district. Various complications arose, among others the fact that the women became eligible to vote, and I made a wrong start apparently with the chief of police, and I was recalled, and the mayor abolished the restricted district. He maintained the women mostly in the residence district of the city, and his successor also. In the meantime the State legislature passed what is known as one of these abatement acts, whereby there can be no such district maintained by any official; consequently we have no restricted district at the present time.

Commissioner O'CONNELL. Well, if there isn't any known restricted district, is there any other form of districting or method whereby such places are carried on?

Mr. GILL. Not as such. There is no such thing as a known house of prostitution in the city.

Commissioner O'CONNELL. Houses of assignation?

Mr. GILL. I am informed that there are some, and inevitably must be; but it is kept, whatever there is, under the present chief of police—I have been giving but very little attention to it. It is all handled by Mr. Griffith, and as the thing is recognized it does not exist at the present time in the residence district at all. But I presume there are a great many of these women living around in certain classes of hotels and places of that kind where they will always congregate.

Commissioner O'CONNELL. What licenses do the ordinary peddlers on the street pay?

Mr. GILL. Oh, they vary. The jewelry peddlers, for them I think the license is prohibitive, or something like $15 or $20 a day. These fish peddlers pay, I think, $10 a quarter. There is a varying and what I call an erratic schedule of peddlers' licenses in this city, and it is low as to necessaries and high as to jewelry and such things. The others are small.

Commissioner O'CONNELL. I understood you to say that when the women secured the vote here it rather changed the face of things in the city. Has it had an effect on cleansing the morals of the community politically and otherwise?

Mr. GILL. Yes; I think it has. I think it has. I don't want to say that the fact that the women had the vote was due to the fact that I was recalled, although I think a great many of them voted against me on that one issue of the restricted district. I ran the following year. I ran again against the man who beat me, and was beaten by Mayor O'Connell. This year I was elected. Now, speaking generally of their influence on the morals and things of that kind; why, I might be said to be prejudiced if I said I thought they had. I was elected this spring by a very large vote, and satisfied a great many women voters. But, as to what the effect has been generally I think it has been a very good effect. It has been a good effect on all officials. A great many officials can't do some things that they could do before women had the vote—morally, and in a great many other respects. It has been a good influence, and I wasn't a woman suffragist from the beginning, either.

Commissioner O'CONNELL. Are you now?

Mr. GILL. I am.

Acting Chairman COMMONS. Any questions?

Commissioner LENNON. Yes.

Acting Chairman COMMONS. Mr. Lennon.

Commissioner LENNON. I was just going to ask this question: Have the wage earners of the city, either organized or unorganized, given any expression as to their attitude as to the segregated district?

Mr. GILL. No; never have taken any attitude on it at all.

Acting Chairman COMMONS. Have they on the saloon license question, prohibition?

Mr. GILL. Never have.

Acting Chairman COMMONS. Has any investigation been made here, or any discussion respecting the increased cost of living among wage earners?

Mr. GILL. No; I don't think so, as organizations. I do not recollect of having heard anything of the kind; no.

Acting Chairman COMMONS. Respecting the increased cost of living in the last 10 or 15 years, has it been noticeable in this district?

Mr. GILL. Oh, yes; it has been noticeable. I can testify to that, and I think everybody else; but the fact that the cost of living has increased possibly proportionally, it has not increased as much here as in some other places, for the reason that the town was for a long time ahead of its buildings for people to live in, and rents were always high. And then there came rather a period of reaction when there were more buildings than there were people, and rents went down, and while other things may have been up rents were comparatively down.

Acting Chairman COMMONS. Who could give us the information on that question of rents?

Mr. GILL. Oh, you have a number of men here, I notice, that are subpœnaed from the various organizations, that, in my opinion, can give you as clear an idea along that line as anybody.

Acting Chairman COMMONS. Well, anybody who has made any investigation that would cover that?

Mr. GILL. No; there has never been any organized investigation of the question out here.

Acting Chairman COMMONS. I think that is all.

Mr. THOMPSON. One more question, Mr. Chairman.

Acting Chairman COMMONS. Mr. Thompson.

Mr. THOMPSON. Mr. Gill, in the case of a strike breaking out in the city, we will take it, that assumes large proportions, what view do you take of your duties and responsibilities so far as the use of the police is concerned?.

Mr. GILL. Simply that every policeman shall do his duty just as though he would be—as though there were no strike; simply enforce the city ordinances as to fighting and keep the streets clear as he would on an ordinary day when there was no strike on and attend to his business as a policeman without bias or prejudice one way or the other. As I say, if the situation got beyond control, where a mob got violent or anything of that kind, then I should simply, as I have the right to do under our city charter in case of an emergency—I have the right to appoint as many policemen as I want to on pay as city men until the next regular meeting of the city council. Unless the council indorses my action these men go out. It puts the ultimate responsibility onto the council, although I would have the right if they met and adjourned and threw my men out, I would declare an emergency the next day. That is the way I would handle it. I would expect the city policemen, of the city's own appointing, paid their $100 a month, to be city men and have them be unbiased and impartial and have them make arrests just exactly to the extent they would have to do.

Mr. THOMPSON. Apparently your experience here has been the same as that of the chief executives in cities elsewhere, as a sort of mediator or conciliator in the cases of industrial trouble. Would that fact, the fact that you are to act as such, influence you either consciously or unconsciously by your handling of the police?

Mr. GILL. I don't think so; no; I don't think so.

Mr. THOMPSON. What views do you take of chief executives of cities handling the police directly for the purpose of bringing about conciliation or arbitration where either of the parties don't want it?

Mr. GILL. Well, I have only had the one experience. Now, here was the way this teamsters' strike situation worked. The city was full of special policemen—there were 50 of them. The minute those 50 men were let out there was, in my opinion, better control of the whole situation than when they were in. They were men who didn't know police business. Some of them may have been biased one way, and some probably the other. It aggravated the situation rather than aided it, and the minute those men were out—and so far as that is concerned, except, as I say, in isolated instances where a couple of these men met and had a private fight of their own—we never had any disorder. And I never had any disorder to contend with on the part of labor unions in this city. They never violated any ordinances. They may have got out and claimed to do things which they had a right to do. The biggest man in the employers' association is a man that could not see the rights of the individual as against the manufacturing corporations under any conditions, nor don't want to, nor never will. But the ordinary kind of man will. And I have never had as much trouble yet here from the standpoint of violence, organized violence, turning the hose on the men—I never had anything from the men; it is the employer who wants that. And I have never had any trouble with organized labor. And from that standpoint I have never seen that they showed a disposition here to be violent. They wanted the things they have got a right to have, and that is all they have done to me.

Mr. THOMPSON. Take a case where there is a strike and the employer has hired private detectives or gun men or other people, and the strikers or employees are asking for protection against them. Take that case on the one side, and take it on the other side that the employer is asking for police protection against the destruction of his factory or property. Now, take it that either one of these people are asking for protection, and should not meet the views that, the city executive has of conciliation and arbitration. Do you believe that the executive would have the right to withhold the police force in order to enforce or persuade either side to agree to something that they didn't believe in?

Mr. GILL. Oh, he could not compulsorily do it. But I could do this, assuming that this state of facts existed, that some union was going to destroy some-body's property; I would put the whole police force down there to protect that property, assuming that condition to come about. But I don't assume the con-dition while I am mayor of this city where any employer of labor will have a lot of armed strike breakers, because I will disarm them and won't have them in there, nor will I have a lot of armed union men. I have never seen them try to arm, and I would not let them, nor I would not allow the employer to arm the men, nor I won't let him make his own men policemen. I will furnish the policemen to protect his property if his property is in danger, if I have to take everybody in town to protect it. I don't assume any condition of that kind ever will arise in Seattle. I have never seen anything that looked like it might ever.

Mr. THOMPSON. Neither would you give or withhold police force in order to induce either party to take any action you wanted to bring about—arbitration, for instance?

Mr. GILL. Why, I think the fact that I refused to maintain 50 men on the city's pay roll as special policemen here last spring had considerable to do in inducing people to get together in this little teamsters' strike. It wasn't, as a matter of fact, the team owners we had our difficulty with, it is what is known as the employers' association here, mostly big men who are absolutely nonunion, maintaining this employers' association. It was through them, that my prede-cessor put these men in as special policemen. As long as they can have all the special policemen they want and the taxpayers and the city care for them, they don't care much about settling things. And as soon as they can't, why they begin to feel conciliatory immediately. That is my experience.

Mr. THOMPSON. What theory did the employer have of the use of the police?

Mr. GILL. Why, he had the theory that if you let him, he will have his em-ployees for policemen paid by the city.

Mr. THOMPSON. Well, then, what would these police do, would they make attacks on strikers, would they protect property from destruction?

Mr. GILL. I think that is the assumption. I think back East they would prob-ably go out and shoot a lot of men.

Mr. THOMPSON. That is all, Mr. Chairman.

Acting Chairman COMMONS. Mr. Thompson, call your next witness?

Mr. THOMPSON. Hon. E. W. Olson.

TESTIMONY OF MR. E. W. OLSON.

Mr. THOMPSON. Will you please give your name to the reporter?

Mr. OLSON. Edward W. Olson.

Mr. THOMPSON. And your business address?

Mr. OLSON. Olympia.

Mr. THOMPSON. And your occupation or position?

Mr. OLSON. State labor commissioner.

Mr. THOMPSON. How long, Mr. Olson, have you been State labor commis-sioner?

Mr. OLSON. Since April 7, 1913.

Mr. THOMPSON. Is the commissioner appointed under some special act of the legislature creating that office?

Mr. OLSON. Under a special act creating the bureau of labor.

Mr. THOMPSON. When was that act passed, if you know; about?

Mr. OLSON. The act was passed in 1897.

Mr. THOMPSON. Well, is there any special commission that is appointed under an act of this State of recent date?

Mr. OLSON. An industrial commission?

Mr. THOMPSON. Yes.

Mr. OLSON. Yes; industrial welfare commission.

Mr. THOMPSON. Have you in your position as labor commissioner had any-thing to do with that commission?

Mr. OLSON. I am chairman of that commission.

Mr. THOMPSON. You may tell us, if you please, Mr. Olson, generally the scope and purpose of your department of labor?

Mr. OLSON. Of the bureau of labor?

Mr. THOMPSON. Yes.

Mr. OLSON. The scope of that department is to enforce all of the labor laws of the State, and to look after the welfare of the laboring people generally.

Mr. THOMPSON. How many inspectors have you to carry out the law of the State and into what divisions are they divided?

Mr. OLSON. I have an assistant, a lady assistant, to enforce the laws for women; five inspectors who go through the factories in the State, State factory inspectors; also two steamboat inspectors.

Mr. THOMPSON. Now, in a general way you can state, if you can offhand, the list—the laws of this State relating to industrial matters that come within the supervision of that bureau.

Mr. OLSON. All of the laws?

Mr. THOMPSON. Well, generally, the law, the child-labor law and so on.

Mr. OLSON. We have three statutes pertaining to child labor. Then we have the women's eight-hour law and several minor statutes pertaining to the welfare of women outside of the minimum-wage law. We have the 10-hour law for street car men and we have the mine inspectors' law for the inspection of coal mines. We have the eight-hour public work law for all contract labor that is employed on public works. It is impossible for me to here enumerate all of the minor laboring laws that we have.

Mr. THOMPSON. That is the general field?

Mr. OLSON. Yes; I would be glad to give the commission a copy of the laws.

Mr. THOMPSON. We would be very glad to have those. In your opinion, is the force that you have adequate to cause the various laws within your jurisdiction to be fulfilled and enforced?

(A pamphlet entitled " Labor Laws of the State of Washington," edition 1913, compiled by Edward W. Olson, commissioner of labor, was subsequently submitted in printed form.)

Mr. OLSON. I think in order to fulfill all of the functions of the bureau of labor it would be necessary at least to treble our force.

Mr. THOMPSON. In your opinion, from your experience as head of the bureau, are the laws here, with reference to the subject you have supervision of, generally lived up to or not?

Mr. OLSON. Beg pardon?

Mr. THOMPSON. Are the laws relating to industrial matters generally lived up to in this State, or not?

Mr. OLSON. As far as I can determine they are generally lived up to.

Mr. THOMPSON. Is that the report of your inspectors as they go around?

Mr. OLSON. That is the report of the inspectors as a general rule. We find violations under some of our laws, and it is almost impossible at times to enforce them.

Mr. THOMPSON. What laws, for instance?

Mr. OLSON. The eight-hour law for women is a very hard law to enforce, from the fact that it is impossible to get a woman to go on the witness stand against her employer, in many cases. We may subpoena them, but we find when they go on the witness stand that they use every effort to evade questions that are put to them and to protect the employer. This has generally been done in fear of discharge.

Mr. THOMPSON. What means do you take, then, to get the evidence in the case?

Mr. OLSON. We have no adequate means, because we can't do picket duty to get this evidence.

Mr. THOMPSON. Your force is not adequate?

Mr. OLSON. Our force is not adequate.

Mr. THOMPSON. Do you hold any executive sessions where witnesses are heard in private?

Mr. OLSON. We do wherever it is possible.

Mr. THOMPSON. And in cases of prosecution, of course you have to put the witnesses on the stand, or as commissioner of the bureau——

Mr. OLSON. We must put the witnesses on the stand.

Mr. THOMPSON. And bring an action in the ordinary courts?

Mr. OLSON. In the ordinary courts.

Mr. THOMPSON. And·in the trial of those cases you need the direct witnesses?

Mr. OLSON. The direct witnesses.

Mr. THOMPSON. The inspector is not permitted to speak except as to what he knows of his own knowledge, I take it?

Mr. OLSON. That is right.

Mr. THOMPSON. Are you a lawyer?

Mr. OLSON. I am not.

Mr. THOMPSON. With reference to the work of the commission which has established the minimum wage here, or is establishing minimum wages, what is the general scope and force of that commission, and how is it organized, and what does it do?

Mr. OLSON. The general scope?

Mr. THOMPSON. Yes.

Mr. OLSON. The general scope of that law is to create a living minimum wage for women and minors employed in the different industries of our State. And this wage is established by holding conferences that are called together by the commission, a conference for each industry. Did you want to know further about the scope of the work?

Mr. THOMPSON. Yes; go right ahead.

Mr. OLSON. Of our past work, is that of interest to the commission?

Mr. THOMPSON. Yes.

Mr. OLSON. Our first conference was called to order on, I think it was March 31 of this year, which was for the purpose of establishing a minimum wage and conditions of labor in the mercantile industry in this State. This conference was in session for about two days, and made a recommendation to the commission that a wage of $10 per week be established for women employed in that industry, and also other conditions of labor; all of which were adopted by the commission and put into effect on the 27th day of June. (See Olson Exhibit No. 1.)

The second conference was held in the month of May and was for the purpose of establishing a minimum wage in factories, the recommendation being made by that conference of $8.90 per week for women employed in that industry, and other conditions of labor also. These recommendations were adopted by the commission and became effective on the first of this month. (See Olson Exhibit No. 2.)

The third conference was held a few days after that, and was for the purpose of establishing a minimum wage in laundries. That conference recommended a wage of $8.50 for women employed in that industry, together with other conditions of labor. This wage was rejected by the commission on the ground that it was not a sufficient sum upon which a woman was able to live. Through the investigation made by the conference we had facts and figures that justified the commission in rejecting this recommendation. (See Olson Exhibit No. 3.)

A new conference was called which recommended to the commission the wage of $9 per week. And this was adopted, together with other conditions of labor recommended by the conference.

The fifth conference was· that of the telegraph and telephone industries, which recommended a minimum wage of $9 per week, which recommendation was also accepted by the commission and put into effect—or rather goes into effect on the 7th of next September.

Mr. THOMPSON. September 7 next?

Mr. OLSON. That covers the amount of work we have so far done. We have under investigation now the canning industry, the fruit picking industry, and several other occupations in which women are employed—office girls, hotel help, restaurant help, and so on.

Mr. THOMPSON. You may state, Mr. Olson, in your own way, how the commission is called to act upon this information and establish minimum wages? At whose instance, and what machinery did you use in carrying out the investigation; how you got your evidence, etc.?

Mr. OLSON. I might go back a little bit and state what the requirements of the law are in selecting these conferences. The law requires that an equal number of employees and employers shall sit in these conferences, together with one or more members representing the disinterested public. The commission is also authorized by that law to formulate rules and regulations governing the conduct of these conferences. And in these rules and regulations the commission decided to appoint three members representing the employers, three representing the public, and three representing the employees. The law requires that a member of the commission shall be chairman of these conferences. The member of the commission who is chairman of this conference does not vote on the questions submitted to the conference. In handling these conferences the cost of living is the main topic to be considered; although other questions are permitted to enter into the discussion.

Mr. THOMPSON. At whose instance are these conferences called to take up any particular industry? Does the commission itself pick out an industry, or do individuals request the commission to take an industry up?

Mr. OLSON. The law requires that the commission shall investigate the cost of living of women employed in different industries in the State. That was the first work of the commission, to investigate the different industries, and the cost of living; and in doing so the commission found that in nearly all of the industries in the State so far investigated the wages paid were not sufficient to cover the cost of living of a woman worker employed in these industries.

Mr. THOMPSON. Then the first investigations were undertaken by the commission itself?

Mr. OLSON. Yes.

Mr. THOMPSON. Now, in carrying on the work of investigation, take, for instance, the first one you made, the establishment of the minimum wage, the 10-hour day for women in mercantile establishments, how was that carried on, how many investigators did you have, what was the scope of their investigation?

Mr. OLSON. The commission did the main work of investigation, and also employed, I believe, five investigators in different parts of the State to enter into a comprehensive investigation of the cost of living and the conditions of labor and other things pertaining to that question.

Commissioner GARRETSON. Covering how long a period, Mr. Olson?

Mr. OLSON. How long a period?

Commissioner GARRETSON. How far back did you go—10, 12, or 15 years?

Mr. OLSON. No; that investigation was only for the present.

Commissioner GARRETSON. Only in the immediate present?

Mr. OLSON. Only in the immediate present.

Mr. THOMPSON. When you say the main part of the work was done by the commission, what do you want us to understand by that—that they made an investigation, or that they had hearings at which they sat, or what?

Mr. OLSON. This investigation was a personal investigation made by members of the commission, and also by employed investigators. In connection with that we held public hearings. We held 16 public hearings in the different parts of the State, some of them for employers and some for employees; this in order to get all of the information and data possible with the very least effort, because of the fact that our appropriation was not so large that we could employ very many investigators.

Mr. THOMPSON. Were the public hearings taken down in shorthand?

Mr. OLSON. Not in shorthand.

Mr. THOMPSON. Are there any public printed records of the results of these hearings—what was gotten there?

Mr. OLSON. No; there are none.

Mr. THOMPSON. That this commission could have the use of?

Mr. OLSON. No reports printed of these hearings.

Mr. THOMPSON. What individual work did the commissioners do, and how did they carry it on outside of the public hearings? You say they made individual investigations. Were different trades apportioned off for each commissioner, or how?

Mr. OLSON. To some extent; yes. The commissioners, the different commissioners residing in different parts of the State were expected to and did cover those parts as thoroughly as possible.

Mr. THOMPSON. And submit reports in writing?

Mr. OLSON. To some extent; yes.

Mr. THOMPSON. How would the commission get the benefit of the work of the man, the whole commission?

Mr. OLSON. The work of each member of the commission?

Mr. THOMPSON. Yes.

Mr. OLSON. That was brought about by employing a special investigator, Miss Gleason, or Oregon, secretary of the industrial welfare commission, who made a comprehensive survey of the State, taking into consideration also the data that had been secured by the other investigators and members of the commission, from all of which a report was compiled.

Mr. THOMPSON. And upon her survey she took into consideration the work of the commissioners and your other investigators, and you made these various findings?

Mr. OLSON. Yes.

Mr. THOMPSON. In these different industries?

Mr. OLSON. Yes.

Mr. THOMPSON. Could this commission be furnished with a copy of her report, her survey?

Mr. OLSON. I will send you one.

(A pamphlet entitled " Report of the Industrial Welfare Commission of the State of Washington," prepared by Caroline J. Gleason, dated Olympia, Wash., March, 1914, was subsequently submitted in printed form.)

Mr. THOMPSON. Now, in the act appointing this commission, it is stated it shall be unlawful to employ women or minors in any industry or occupation within the State of Washington under conditions of labor detrimental to their health or morals, or at wages which are not adequate to their maintenance. Has your commission, or has the commission so far made any finding as to what is detrimental to health or what is detrimental to morals?

Mr. OLSON. Any particular finding?

Mr. THOMPSON. Yes; I take it on the wage question you have made certain specific findings.

Mr. OLSON. Well, in order to be within our legal bounds, we have made particular findings which are to some extent embodied in our report.

Mr. THOMPSON. As to the health and morals proposition?

Mr. OLSON. Yes. The morals proposition, however, we did not cover, because that had no direct bearing on the establishing of the minimum wage.

Mr. THOMPSON. Well, in the question of the health proposition can you recall generally some of the findings that you have made on that phase of the question?

Mr. OLSON. Some of the findings that have been made?

Mr. THOMPSON. Yes; by your commission.

Mr. OLSON. It is rather hard for me to cite those here at the present time.

Mr. THOMPSON. Passing that subject for the moment, then—has your commission established a minimum wage for minors?

Mr. OLSON. Yes; minors under the age of 18?

Mr. THOMPSON. What is that minimum wage, or when was it established?

Mr. OLSON. We treated the question of minors in each industry separately, and so far we have established the same minimum wage of $6 per week for minors in all of the industries that we have covered.

Mr. THOMPSON. When was that put into effect?

Mr. OLSON. It went into effect at the time the minimum wage for women went into effect—the obligatory orders were issued at the same time.

Mr. THOMPSON. You have had no chance to study the results of the minimum wage for minors to any extent?

Mr. OLSON. We are now making a study of the effects of the minimum wage on both minors and women.

Mr. THOMPSON. Where are you beginning that study?

Mr. OLSON. We are beginning it all over the State.

Mr. THOMPSON. When do you think you will have it concluded?

Mr. OLSON. It will be a year before we conclude that.

Mr. THOMPSON. What difficulties in the administration of this commission, of your bureau, do you meet with generally? What are the most noticeable ones?

Mr. OLSON. We meet with a great many difficulties, difficulties that are unforeseen. I might be able to state them, but it would take a great deal of time.

Mr. THOMPSON. Take the general heads, so that we will know.

Mr. OLSON. Some of the great difficulties that we have had is in selecting the members from the employees' side for these conferences. As a rule, the girls whom we call on to serve on these conferences are very hesitant; they are afraid they may not be able to maintain their position if they properly represent the employees. We find that condition existing all the way through. That is one of the hardest problems that we have had to deal with in selecting the members of our conferences.

Mr. THOMPSON. Have you gotten around that difficulty in any respect?

Mr. OLSON. We have through a great deal of effort; we have found it necessary, sometimes, to interview as high as 30 or 40 girls before we find the ones we deem capable of representing their sister wage earners on these conferences.

Mr. THOMPSON. How about the penalty part of your law? Have you any difficulty with that?

Mr. OLSON. We have not found any difficulty with it so far, owing to the fact that we have had no occasion to enforce it. I rather think, though, that the penalty is not adequate to cover the situation.

Mr. THOMPSON. How generally is that true of the enforcement of the other labor laws under your bureau?

Mr. OLSON. I believe that is generally true of those, that the penalties are too small under all of our labor statutes. As a rule, it is hard to get any more than the minimum fine imposed in any case of violation.

Mr. THOMPSON. Have you brought many cases for the violation of the eight-hour law, and what has been the result in those cases generally?

Mr. OLSON. I am not certain as to the figures, but I believe we have brought as high as 60 cases in the last year and a half, out of which we have probably secured convictions in 75 per cent of those cases.

Mr. THOMPSON. What, so far as you have been able to ascertain, is the general attitude of the employers of this State toward the enforcement of the laws, of these laws?

Mr. OLSON. The general attitude of the employers toward the enforcement of the laws is very good. There are very few employers in the State who are trying to evade the law.

Mr. THOMPSON. Is there any defect in the administration or enforcement of the child-labor law that has come out so far in your investigation of its effect?

Mr. OLSON. Well, there are several defects in our child-labor laws. However, we are trying to remedy some of those defects through the authority given the minimum-wage commission.

Mr. THOMPSON. What are the most pointed defects that have come to your attention?

Mr. OLSON. Well, one of the greatest defects in our child-labor law is that it does not specify in particular all of the industries to which it should apply.

Mr. THOMPSON. Then, it does not apply generally?

Mr. OLSON. It is hard to get convictions under that statute, and especially in cases where the industry itself is not clearly defined; that is, the industry or establishment.

Mr. THOMPSON. Well, in a general way, what is the method of describing industries that are within the law? Are there excepted industries?

Mr. OLSON. There are some excepted industries, farm work, for instance.

Mr. THOMPSON. Is there any other industry that is excepted?

Mr. OLSON. No; not specifically, but it does not clearly define all of the industries that child-labor laws should cover. For instance, it is almost impossible to enforce the child-labor statute against theaters where children are employed on the stage. However, to some extent the juvenile court act covers that, at least they are trying to make it cover.

Mr. THOMPSON. How about selling newspapers on the street?

Mr. OLSON. That comes under the juvenile court act entirely.

Mr. THOMPSON. Did you make any investigation of the cannery industry of this State?

Mr. OLSON. I did.

Mr. THOMPSON. What did you find there? When was the investigation made?

Mr. OLSON. The investigation was made, I believe, on the 15th of August last, from the 15th to the 20th of last August. In company with a member of the welfare commission I made an investigation of these canneries. We covered 16 canneries in all; and this investigation was largely for the purpose of determining the status of the child-labor question as well as the woman-labor question; and in addition to that I also made an investigation of the employment of Chinese and Japs in these canneries.

Mr. THOMPSON. Well, with reference to women and children, what condition did you find there?

Mr. OLSON. In some cases we found the condition of labor of the women and children very deplorable. In other cases they were very good.

Mr. THOMPSON. When you say deplorable, what would we understand by that?

Mr. OLSON. So far as hours are concerned.

Mr. THOMPSON. So far as hours are concerned?

Mr. OLSON. Yes; and also the conditions under which they worked. These conditions varied in different canneries.

Mr. THOMPSON. Can you give the commission a general view as to some of the conditions that were objectionable?

Mr. OLSON. We found in some of the canneries women were required to work from 15 to 19 hours per day during the height of the canning season, and we found in some places where minors, under the ages of 14 and 16 years, were required to work as high as 15 hours a day.

Commissioner GARRETSON. Paid by the day, hour, or piece?

Mr. OLSON. We found that the women packing fish were paid by the piece. Some of these women were able to make $9 per day. They made all the way from $4.50 to $9 a day, packing flat cans of salmon by the piece. The children employed there were usually employed by the hour.

Commissioner O'CONNELL. How about sanitary conditions?

Mr. OLSON. As I said before, the sanitary conditions in some of the canneries are very good; in others very bad. I might say they run from one extreme to the other.

Commissioner O'CONNELL. Any inspection in regard to the health of the employees in connection with the cutting of the hands, disease, or in any way like that?

Mr. OLSON. I do not know. There is no inspection in that regard so far as I know.

Commissioner GARRETSON. What is the moral condition of the houses?

Mr. OLSON. The moral condition of the housing in some places was not of the best, but we did not find a great deal of that.

Commissioner O'CONNELL. Was there a proper segregation between the males and females?

Mr. OLSON. In all cases but one that I know of.

Commissioner O'CONNELL. In that instance they were compelled to use the same toilet?

Mr. OLSON. The same toilet; yes, sir. That, however, was remedied as soon as we called their attention to it.

Commissioner O'CONNELL. How about sleeping?

Mr. OLSON. Why, I found no case where the houses were not segregated. In some of the canning establishments they have bunk houses for the women as well as for the men—that is, not really bunk houses—they have bedsteads with four to six girls sleeping in a room—two or three beds in a room—and these houses are built of very rough lumber and are only intended for use during the period of the canning season.

Commissioner O'CONNELL. Do whole families go into the canning industry in the season—father, mother, and children?

Mr. OLSON. In some instances they did; not in a great many instances.

Commissioner O'CONNELL. Are the facilities for cooking in these houses good, or do they cook outside?

Mr. OLSON. They usually have a kitchen in connection with the house.

Commissioner O'CONNELL. Are there any of the camps where they have no houses and use tents?

Mr. OLSON. There were none brought to my notice.

Mr. THOMPSON. How young are the children employed in the industry?

Mr. OLSON. The youngest child that I found was 11 years of age.

Commissioner O'CONNELL. Male or female child?

Mr. OLSON. Male child. I was told there were some of an age less than 9, but I did not see them personally.

Commissioner O'CONNELL. What is the condition of the material being canned? Was it apparently being handled in a sanitary manner?

Mr. OLSON. Most of the fish in the canneries are canned by machines, and not handled by hand except to put the fish into the can. Some of the cans are handled by women, and are packed by hand. These women have gloves on, and I did not see any condition there that would be considered radically wrong. It is hard to make conditions pleasing to the eye, where they have a big lot of fish coming in, and have things look as though they are perfectly sanitary in all parts. There is bound to be more or less slush. However, we found some conditions that could have been remedied, to some extent at least.

Commissioner O'CONNELL. Have you fruit canneries?

Mr. OLSON. We have fruit canneries in the State.

Commissioner O'CONNELL. How about those?

Mr. OLSON. The conditions in the fruit canneries are quite good.

Commissioner O'CONNELL. As to sanitation and housing and segregation?

Mr. OLSON. They are quite good as far as I can see.

Commissioner GARRETSON. What are the hours?

Mr. Olson. The hours in the fruit canneries are a great deal the same as they are in the salmon canneries. They vary according to the amount of product they·bring in to have canned. I have not, however, noticed any· women employed in fruit canneries for more than 12 to 13 hours in the height of the season.

Commissioner Garbetson. Have you vegetable canneries?

Mr.᾿ Olson. Beg pardon?

Commissioner Garbetson. Have you vegetable canneries?

Mr. Olson. We have vegetable canneries, but they are run in connection with some of the fruit canneries.

Mr. Thompson.·With reference to the enforcement of the child-labor law, have you had any difficulty with that?

Mr. Olson. We have had some irregularity in issuing permits. The judges of the superior courts of the different counties of the State have been quite lax in issuing permits. In our investigation of the child-labor problem in one of the counties of the State we found that one of the judges had delegated this power to the county superintendent of schools, and he in turn had issued these permits promiscuously without any investigation.

Mr. Thompson. Does your bureau set up any standards, or does the law, upon which the certifications are issued?

Mr. Olson. Our department is not authorized under the law,· to do that. However, we do confer with the different judges of the superior courts in this matter ■henever cases arise, and·ask them to live up to certain standards in issuing these permits.

Mr. Thompson. I take it from what you say that the judge of the court issues the permit?

Mr. Olson. Yes, sir.

Mr. Thompson. What generally is the practice of the courts and judges with reference to ascertaining the age of the applicant?

Mr. Olson. Well, the court usually takes the word of the parents for that.

Mr. Thompson. Generally under oath or without?

Mr. Olson. No; not under oath.

Mr. Thompson. Not under oath?

Mr. Olson. No.

Mr. Thompson. What investigation do you make, or does your bureau make, as to whether or not in any case the facts are as stated in court? Do you have any check-up at all on the administration of the law?·

Mr. Olson. We haven't any check-up so far as that is concerned. Whenever we find a child-labor violation, of course, it is necessary for us to take the word of the child or the word of their parents or some one else as to their age. Usually we take it from the child, and I haven't found one case yet where the child has misrepresented.

Mr. Thompson. Then, when your inspector goes into a factory where children are employed, what is his method of making an investigation with reference to their ages?

Mr. Olson. What is his——

Mr. Thompson. Yes; what method of investigation does he make. Are the certificates all handed to him or on hand for him to investigate?

Mr. Olson. Yes, sir.

Mr. Thompson. Does he take the children apart and ask them their ages, or what does he do?

Mr. Olson. In some instances we found where the children hold the certificates, and others where they were left with the factory. In all cases we insist that the employer must have these certificates, so that we can investigate them.

Mr. Thompson. And generally one of your inspectors will go through the shop, is that the fact?

Mr. Olson. Yes, sir.

Mr. Thompson. And size up the children and those he considers look young——

Mr. Olson. He questions the children.

Mr. Thompson. With reference to the minimum-wage law for minors, how does the apprenticeship system which is in operation in this State affect that?

Mr. Olson. It will be hard for me to give a clear answer to you at this time, inasmuch as we are just working out the apprenticeship question. I might say this, however, that it was thought some time ago that the apprenticeship question might be the means of defeating the purpose of the law. I am absolutely convinced at this time that it is not, that it will not be the means of defeating the purpose of the law, but will rather be a benefit to it. In the mercantile establishments in this State, in which the law has been in effect since the 27th of June, and during that time the commission has issued something like 275 licenses to women to be employed as apprentices in all parts of the State. That is a very small per cent. We find, however, that it is necessary to reject a great many applications. I am not prepared at this time to say how many applications we have rejected during that time, but whenever we refuse these applications we find that the girls send them back and want us to reconsider them. That happens almost incessantly. Whenever we issue a license to a girl to work, say, for $7.50 or $9 a week and she fails to secure or hold the job at that wage, she immediately wants a reduction. That is the greatest problem we are up against in the apprenticeship question.

Mr. THOMPSON. What is the provision generally of the apprenticeship law as the commission has the right to enforce it?

Mr. OLSON. The provisions of it?

Mr. THOMPSON. Yes.

Mr. OLSON. The law gives the commission authority to issue to an apprentice a license designating the period of that apprenticeship, and the wage under which she may work.

Mr. THOMPSON. Are they related principally to—entirely to minors and women?

Mr. OLSON. No; the apprenticeship section does not relate to minors whatever. The law does not give the commission any authority to issue a license to a minor. However, in some instances we can make, and find it necessary to make, different rulings with reference to minors.

Mr. THOMPSON. Now, referring to the cannery proposition and fruit packing, those are seasonal occupations, of course?

Mr. OLSON. Yes; they are entirely seasonal.

Mr. THOMPSON. In either of those fields is the work that they there do generally their sole earnings for the year?

Mr. OLSON. No.

Mr. THOMPSON. Do the people that work in fish canneries rely upon the fish canneries for their total wage of the year?

Mr. OLSON. I haven't found any instances whereby I could say that it is. That employment goes hand in hand with a lot of other intermittent employment that we have in the State. As a matter of fact, this State is seething with intermittent employment. That is one of the great faults of our industrial life here, we have so much intermittent employment that men and women are not employed in the same industry but a short time, when they have to seek work in other lines.

Mr. THOMPSON. Has your commission given that any consideration, or have you any power?

Mr. OLSON. We are; but we have no power to remedy that situation.

Mr. THOMPSON. What appropriation does this commission have per year?

Mr. OLSON. Five thousand dollars per year, or ten thousand dollars for the biennium.

Mr. THOMPSON. That is all, Mr. Chairman.

Acting Chairman COMMONS. Mr. Lennon has a question.

Commissioner LENNON. Mr. Olson, has the enactment of the eight-hour day, even though not able to enforce it, has it had a general effect of reducing the hours of labor of women in the State of Washington?

Mr. OLSON. Yes, sir; it has. I don't want to leave this commission under the impression that the eight-hour law for women is not generally enforced.

Commissioner LENNON. No.

Mr. OLSON. Generally it is enforced.

Commissioner LENNON. Not thoroughly enforced?

Mr. OLSON. Not thoroughly enforced. I don't believe that there are any of our laws that are absolutely and thoroughly enforced.

Commissioner LENNON. Well, the experience with this law, where you go to make an investigation or inspection, for instance, where you have never been, where no inspection or investigation has ever been made, does your inquiry indicate that the enactment of the law has made some difference even in such a place?

Mr. OLSON. Oh, yes; yes, sir.

Commissioner LENNON. Mr. Olson, what have you to say regarding industrial or social unrest in the State of Washington that threatens in any way the social well-being of society or the continuity of civilized government? Do you know of any unrest that is dangerous in those ways?

Mr. OLSON. In the past few years we have had an unrest in this State that has been caused, or has come from various sources. As I said a little while ago, the great problem that we have before us in this State is the matter of unemployment which is caused by intermittent employment, Men secure work for two or three months in one class of employment, when they are required to find new fields. And they are constantly on the jump from one thing to another in order to make a living. This, however, is only general in certain industries.

The lumbering industry of this State is one of the largest that gives steady employment to men the year round. Our wheat fields, our canneries, and our fruit-packing and fruit-growing industries and hop-growing industries are those that give only intermittent employment to both men and women.

Then we have a peculiar condition surrounding us on the north as well as on the east. We have a very salubrious climate here, and in the wintertime a great many workmen flock in here from other sections of the country, from Montana—from the cold regions in Montana and from Alaska, from Oregon, from British Columbia. Last winter the problem of our unemployment was largely caused by the influx of laboring people from British Columbia. There was a period of depression over there in some of the industries, and men flocked from there here, and they naturally came to Seattle, the largest city in the State. When spring opens up they go out and find employment in some of the industries that give employment at that time. This employment is generally during the summer months, and we are back again to the same condition of unemployment in the wintertime.

Commissioner LENNON. Can you offer any suggestions to the commission as to what they might do to mitigate the evils of this irregular employment or to vitiate the unrest which is, in your opinion, not necessary for the advancement of civilization?

Mr. OLSON. I haven't anything to suggest in that regard that I think might be practical.

It is quite a hard problem. The only thing that I might say is that an effort should be made by the people of this State to get industries here that will fill up those periods of unemployment or give work to the people during those periods of unemployment. We require probably 50 per cent more people here in the summertime in these different industries than we do in the winter. In making figures on the question of employment throughout the State, covering only the factories—we are not tabulating them—I find that in the mills and workshops and factories in the State there are periods when we require 23 per cent more help than we do at other periods. In other words, we must have a surplus of 23 per cent of men in our mills and workshops. Those men are only employed a few months in the year.

Commissioner LENNON. Have you noticed whether or not an unrest which might be dangerous at times to the well-being of society is greater among organized than unorganized men and women?

Mr. OLSON. I should say that the social unrest is greatest among unorganized men. There we find conditions most deplorable. We have men in this State that are working for $1.50 a day and paying $1 a day board, or rather a little less than $1 a day board. But, of course, such cases are not very numerous, yet that condition exists to some extent. The organized laboring people of the State are commanding higher wages than that. There is not nearly as much social unrest there; but as it is organized, we probably see the effects of it more than we do among unorganized labor.

Commissioner LENNON. What opportunities are there now in the State of Washington for securing homesteads—getting land either under the homestead laws or for very small compensation?

Mr. OLSON. As far as I know there is very little opportunity, and where there is opportunity for a man to secure land, to secure a homestead, he would necessarily have to have considerable money in order to carry it through successfully. That has been my observation. Our land problem is a very deep one.

Commissioner LENNON. Not easy to get onto the land unless you have means, then?

Mr. OLSON. You must have means, and small means are not sufficient, such as they used to be.

Commissioner LENNON. How long have you been working under the compensation law in this State? How long has it been in operation?

Mr. OLSON. Workmen's compensation?

Commissioner LENNON. Yes.

Mr. OLSON. Since October, 1911.

Commissioner LENNON. Can you indicate to us as to the proportion under the compensation law that reaches the injured as compared with what it was under the old liability laws?

Mr. OLSON. I am not well enough conversant to give you a clear answer to that question. I know, however, that it is very much greater.

Commissioner LENNON. Prof. Commons tells me that there are men who are specially connected with that feature of the Government that can tell us.

Mr. OLSON. Yes.

Commissioner LENNON. That is all, as far as I am concerned.

Commissioner GARRETSON. You speak of the unrest of the organized and the unorganized. Has your experience been that the organized man finds means of expression and efforts to correct the causes of his unrest that the other man has not?

Mr. OLSON. That is precisely what I tried to convey.

Commissioner GARRETSON. In other words, the dangerous feature of the unrest of the organized man has a safety valve in his means of endeavoring to correct them that the other man has not?

Mr. OLSON. Yes; that is my belief.

Commissioner GARRETSON. Have you any birth-registration laws in the State?

Mr. OLSON. I am not conversant with that question. I rather think we have in different municipalities, but whether we have or not in the State at large, I don't know.

Commissioner GARRETSON. Has your investigation demonstrated anything as to whether or not the increase in wages within any given period has kept pace with the increased cost of living?

Mr. OLSON. I have some figures on that question which show that they have not; the increase in wages has not kept pace with the cost of living.

Commissioner GARRETSON. Has your commission any power to fix minimum wages or conditions of service for males of the adult age?

Mr. OLSON. Not males; no, sir.

Commissioner GARRETSON. Males of the adult age?

Mr. OLSON. No, sir.

Commissioner GARRETSON. You deal with minor males?

Mr. OLSON. Yes, sir.

Commissioner GARRETSON. And females of all ages?

Mr. OLSON. Yes, sir.

Commissioner GARRETSON. From your experience with the commission in the State of Washington, as long as it has existed, are your impressions favorable with the results that come from the existence of such law and the commission applying it as against the nonexistence of the law and the commission?

Mr. OLSON. I find that it will be necessary to see this law in effect for some time before I could adequately answer that question. However, at this time I think that there is good going to come from it.

Commissioner GARRETSON. You believe it exercises an influence that is desirable on behalf of that class of wageworkers who would exercise little influence on their own behalf?

Mr. OLSON. Yes; but not always to the one who does not exercise any influence on her own behalf. The inefficient worker is going to be thrown out of employment.

Commissioner GARRETSON. That naturally will follow on the application of such law. I think that is an economic fact. Do you believe, assuming for a moment that the existence of a commission of this character is desirable in a State, that those benefits would be added to by the existence of like commissions in all States and a close relationship between those commissions and an interchange of experience with each other and giving a chance to all to avail themselves of the experience of all.

Mr. OLSON. I think similar commissions in other States are absolutely necessary. I believe there should be commissions of this kind in every State if we are going to carry it out.

Commissioner GARRETSON. Do you believe a Federal commission similar in character, not necessarily exercising control but acting in accordance with and as a clearing house for such commissions, would produce beneficial results?

Mr. OLSON. I think such a Federal commission is absolutely necessary to gain the best results.

Commissioner GARRETSON. It furnishes the skeleton upon which the others hang?

Mr. OLSON. Yes, sir.

Commissioner GARRETSON. Is the harvesting of hops a great industry in this State?

Mr. OLSON. Yes, sir.

Commissioner GARRETSON. Have you made any investigation into the harvesting of the crop?

Mr. OLSON. The harvesting of the crop is not yet in progress.

Commissioner GARRETSON. Then you don't know what the abuses or absence of abuses may be in that direction, or whether like conditions exist here to what were cited as existing in other States?

Mr. OLSON. From what standpoint are you speaking?

Commissioner GARRETSON. Housing and hours and associated questions that go with them, just as they handle them in Canada.

Mr. OLSON. I made an investigation last year in one of the eastern Washington counties of certain conditions under which labor was performed in the field, and I find that the sanitary conditions are very bad, especially where they employ a large number of people. There is no preparation made whatever for these people coming there and they have to shift for themselves in the best way they can. Yet it is one of the conditions that I do not know how it is possible to remedy for years to come, because the industry can't stand to build these houses. It is one of the new and growing industries of the State, and we haven't any good market at the present time for fruit. This is the fruit industry that I am speaking of, and not the hop-growing industry. There are labor conditions that are deplorable in some of these sections.

Commissioner GARRETSON. Is the family engaged in that industry the same as it is in the eastern hop districts or is it the segregated individuals?

Mr. OLSON. I believe families are engaged in it to a great extent. I found it so in Yakima County. At the time of my investigation last year there were families who left home for a little recreation trip expecting to make some money during the vacation period in the fruit and hop fields. Some were disappointed and some were able to make wages.

Commissioner GARRETSON. Is your commission charged with the administration of the industrial insurance act of this State?

Mr. OLSON. No, sir.

Commissioner GARRETSON. It is not?

Mr. OLSON. No, sir; that is a different commission.

Commissioner GARRETSON. That is all.

Acting Chairman COMMONS. You spoke of increase in wages and the increased cost of living. Has that been published?

Mr. OLSON. The investigation of the increased cost of living—the figures I have were compiled by the Federal Government.

Acting Chairman COMMONS. You made no State investigation?

Mr. OLSON. No, sir; no State investigation has ever been made by our bureau.

Acting Chairman COMMONS. You are not able to state and have no way of stating whether those Federal figures apply to this State?

Mr. OLSON. They do; they apply to the Western States.

Acting Chairman COMMONS. Have you checked it up or tested it in any way to see whether they are. For example, would you say that the cost of living in this State in 17 years has increased 59 per cent?

Mr. OLSON. I could not. I have tried to test those figures, but it is impossible to do so, because I don't know upon what lines the Federal Government made its investigation, and it was made some time ago. However, I have made an investigation of the cost of living, but not in connection with wages; I haven't been able to reach that point yet. It is very difficult to get material from the past at the present time. The State bureau of labor in the past never made any investigation of that kind. It is something only recently undertaken, and what is being done now will not be of any material benefit until two or three years from now.

Acting Chairman COMMONS. So that your statement as to the increased cost of living and increased wages is based solely upon the Federal figures?

Mr. OLSON. Yes, sir.

Acting Chairman COMMONS. Not on your own investigation?

Mr. OLSON. Not on my own investigation.

Acting Chairman COMMONS. Has the question of the regulation of hours and the regulation of wages and the question of interstate competition arisen in this State as an objection?

Mr. OLSON. That is one of the great questions.

Acting Chairman COMMONS. In all industries?

Mr. OLSON. The manufacturing industries, they are more largely involved in that question than any other.

Acting Chairman COMMONS. The industries for which you have fixed wages seem to be the stores. They would not come in there, would they?

Mr. OLSON. Not to any great extent.

Acting Chairman COMMONS. Laundries?

Mr. OLSON. No, sir.

Acting Chairman COMMONS. Telephone and telegraph?

Mr. OLSON. No, sir.

Acting Chairman COMMONS. What is the number of women or minors in the industries which you have dealt with, or which exist in this State, which are affected by interstate competition.

Mr. OLSON. I would have to hazard a guess on that proposition, because, as I said before, there is not enough money in our appropriation to take a census of the State. We would naturally have to take a census of the entire State in order to get those figures.

Acting Chairman COMMONS. What are the main lines of manufacture in this State that come in competition with that of other States?

Mr. OLSON. The main line of manufacture?

Acting Chairman COMMONS. Yes, sir.

Mr. OLSON. There are a great many of them. The candy and cracker industry is one.

Acting Chairman COMMONS. With what State is that competing?

Mr. OLSON. It competes with a great many Eastern States—Illinois, Minnesota, and as far back as New York.

Acting Chairman COMMONS. Are there many establishments of that industry in this State—candy?

Mr. OLSON. They are quite numerous, small establishments, and we have a few large plants.

Acting Chairman COMMONS. What other industries in the State?

Mr. OLSON. Well, there are the manufacturers of small novelties and jewelry, and a great many such industries. I can't possibly enumerate them now, but I could if I had a little time to think.

Acting Chairman COMMONS. Could you furnish us a statement?

Mr. OLSON. There is our textile industry, our garment-making industry, our knitting works; they are in competition with the East.

Acting Chairman COMMONS. As a matter of fact, you have not fixed minimum wages for any industry of interstate competition?

Mr. OLSON. Oh, yes; we have.

Acting Chairman COMMONS. You mean what?

Mr. OLSON. In the factories.

Acting Chairman COMMONS. Has the regulation there affected all factories?

Mr. OLSON. Every factory in the State.

Acting Chairman COMMONS. You have placed a minimum there of——

Mr. OLSON. Eight dollars and ninety cents.

Acting Chairman COMMONS. Did you take into account in fixing the amount of that figure the cost of living in competing States?

Mr. OLSON. The law does not give us that authority. We base our minimum wage upon the cost of living in this State, regardless of other conditions.

Acting Chairman COMMONS. Did you make any study at all?

Mr. OLSON. To some extent we did.

Acting Chairman COMMONS. Did you consider whether or not your manufacturers would be placed at a disadvantage at the $8.90 rate in competition with other States?

Mr. OLSON. I am convinced that some of them are at a great disadvantage.

Acting Chairman COMMONS. What class of manufacturers?

Mr. OLSON. The candy-manufacturing industry, I think, has suffered much in that way. The cracker manufacturers, also. The freight rate out here also enters into that question, because I have had figures submitted to me showing a difference of 15 per cent over this wage scale as against manufacturing establishments in the East. An increase of 15 per cent; in other words, that product would cost 15 per cent more to manufacture here than it would in the East.

Acting Chairman COMMONS. That means solely the wages of the women employees?

Mr. OLSON. Yes, sir.

Acting Chairman COMMONS. That does not take into account the efficiency of the factory, or anything of that kind?

Mr. OLSON. No, sir; the factory is about as efficient here as it is in the East— those factories are. It is harder to get skilled help in this State, however, than it is in the East.

Acting Chairman COMMONS. And the freight rate from the East is so low that it does not offset the difference in wages?

Mr. OLSON. Yes, sir.

Acting Chairman COMMONS. There is a natural disadvantage of 15 per cent net in the candy industry?

Mr. OLSON. What I also had reference to was the cracker-manufacturing business.

Acting Chairman COMMONS. What is the net disadvantage?

Mr. OLSON. From 13 to 15 per cent.

Acting Chairman COMMONS. Taking the freight rate into account?

Mr. OLSON. Yes, sir.

Acting Chairman COMMONS. So that the difference in wages must be much greater than 15 per cent?

Mr. OLSON. Yes, sir; they are. In some of the cracker factories in the East I understand they employ female help for $4.50 as against $9 or $8.90 here.

Acting Chairman COMMONS. That is a difference of 100 per cent or more?

Mr. OLSON. And they work them in units in the cracker factories in all the larger establishments, and where we have 55 employed to a unit in the State of Washington, they have 50 to the unit back there. They employ less labor on the same output of their product.

Acting Chairman COMMONS. Does the general law regarding hours of labor fix the same standard of hours for all occupations of women, or is there a difference?

Mr. OLSON. The provisions of the eight-hour law control.

Acting Chairman COMMONS. Can the commission adjust the hours and make a difference?

Mr. OLSON. The law does not give us any authority to deal with hours as far as women are concerned.

Acting Chairman COMMONS. Could it make the hours longer in the canning industry in the height of the season, if it found it was not injurious to the health of the women, for a short period?

Mr. OLSON. We haven't determined the question yet whether or not the commission has the right to deal with hours in those industries not covered by the eight-hour law. That is a question that will have to be decided by the courts; the law is not clear on that point.

Acting Chairman COMMONS. You are speaking of the wages, are you?

Mr. OLSON. No, sir; the hours.

Acting Chairman COMMONS. Has the legislature enacted a uniform eight-hour law in all industries?

Mr. OLSON. Not in all industries; the canning and fruit-packing industries are excepted.

Acting Chairman COMMONS. That is the reason?

Mr. OLSON. Yes, sir.

Acting Chairman COMMONS. They are totally excepted?

Mr. OLSON. Yes, sir.

Acting Chairman COMMONS. And you have no authority, in certain industries where these abuses exist, to adjust them?

Mr. OLSON. And it is doubtful whether the welfare commission has authority to regulate hours in the industries exempted from the eight-hour law.

Acting Chairman COMMONS. The welfare commission regulates only wages?

Mr. OLSON. That is all; but it can regulate the hours of minors.

Acting Chairman COMMONS. Would it be advisable, in your judgment, to give to the welfare commission the power to regulate hours in season of the canning industries?

Mr. OLSON. I believe it would be well to have the welfare commission handle that question, as well as the question of wages, because they are closely related one to the other.

Acting Chairman COMMONS. You haven't had enough experience yet to know whether it would be difficult to enforce the minimum-wage law?

Mr. OLSON. I don't anticipate a great deal of difficulty, inasmuch as the employees will find it is to their advantage to aid us in enforcing the law, where the women under the eight-hour law do not. That is a matter of higher wages, and very few employees will hesitate in giving testimony against their employers when they are going to be financially benefited by it.

It is different with the eight-hour law, there she is likely to lose her job or have a cut in wages on account of a reduction in hours.

Acting Chairman COMMONS. Isn't she as likely to lose her job if she makes complaint regarding wages—as much as she is regarding hours?

Mr. OLSON. There is a chance that she will, yet at the same time the employer is placed in a different position than what he is under the eight-hour law.

Acting Chairman COMMONS. You have had no practical experience?

Mr. OLSON. We have had no practical demonstration.

Acting Chairman COMMONS. All you say is speculation so far on that question?

Mr. OLSON. Yes, sir.

Acting Chairman COMMONS. Do you enforce the law regarding safety and sanitation in factories, and so on?

Mr. OLSON. I do.

Acting Chairman COMMONS. What is the connection between your commission or department and the accident compensation commission in the matter of prevention of accidents?

Mr. OLSON. The law gives us no direct connection, except in the matter of the safeguarding of the plants. The Bureau of Labor is authorized under the law to put inspectors into the field to safeguard the machinery in different plants. The scope of that is limited, however.

Acting Chairman COMMONS. Which body keeps the statistics that would show whether or not there had been an improvement in that regard?

Mr. OLSON. The industrial insurance commission is better able to give those statistics than the bureau of labor is.

Acting Chairman COMMONS. But you enforce the law regarding safety?

Mr. OLSON. Yes, sir.

Acting Chairman COMMONS. And bring prosecutions?

Mr. OLSON. Yes, sir.

Acting Chairman COMMONS. Are there many prosecutions?

Mr. OLSON. We don't find any trouble in enforcing the safeguarding provisions of this law. The last report of the industrial insurance department shows only 2 per cent of the accidents caused in the mills and factories of this State were caused by lack of safeguarding. The employer, as a rule, does anything in the way of safeguarding that he is asked to do where it is possible to safeguard.

Acting Chairman COMMONS. Is that owing to the compensation law?

Mr. OLSON. I rather think it is.

Acting Chairman COMMONS. In the matter of employment offices, are there free employment offices in places other than Seattle?

Mr. OLSON. There are employment offices in all large cities—beg pardon, free?

Acting Chairman COMMONS. Yes; municipal employment offices?

Mr. OLSON. We have free employment offices in Tacoma and Spokane, and I don't know whether there is one in Everett now or not; there used to be.

Acting Chairman COMMONS. There is no State authority over them?

Mr. OLSON. No, sir; none whatever.

Acting Chairman COMMONS. Any system of connection between them?

Mr. OLSON. No, sir; none that I know of, except voluntary.

Acting Chairman COMMONS. Do you get reports from all of them or is there any central body?

Mr. OLSON. No central body whatever.

Acting Chairman COMMONS. No uniform method of keeping their records?

Mr. OLSON. There is not.

Acting Chairman COMMONS. Have you ever investigated these offices?

Mr. OLSON. To some extent. I have reports from them now that I have not yet been able to tabulate.

Acting Chairman COMMONS. Are you able to reach any decision, or have you a decision, with reference to the efficiency with which they are conducted?

Mr. OLSON. I have not. I rather think, from my general observation, that they are efficient. I can't come to any other conclusion but that they are quite efficient. However, they don't attract the class of labor that some of the private employment bureaus do; this probably from the fact that they don't receive the patronage of the large employers of the State.

Acting Chairman COMMONS. Do they make—I am speaking of outside of Seattle, because we will probably have some one here that can tell about Seattle—but do you know whether they make an effort to find the kind of men that employers want, or do they simply send to them anybody that comes along?

Mr. OLSON. I made an investigation of a lot of workmen in one of the road-construction camps in the mountains last week, and a great many of the men were sent there by the free employment bureau of Seattle, and I believe they sent the first ones on the list, the first ones that came along, regardless of the nature of the employment. At least the facts I gleaned there seemed to indicae that. I don't know how it is about skilled labor. However, there is some unskilled labor on these roads. I saw one man sent out as a blaster who had never seen gunpowder.

Acting Chairman COMMONS. Is it your idea that they send that type of employees—the first ones that come?

Mr. OLSON. It may be possible; I have no facts that would substantiate that theory.

Acting Chairman COMMONS. If so, it is not likely that the employers would patronize them?

Mr. OLSON. I could not say as to that, because I haven't any figures or facts.

Acting Chairman COMMONS. The only fact you have is this one you mentioned?

Mr. OLSON. Yes, sir.

Acting Chairman COMMONS. Was that public employment—public work?

Mr. OLSON. Yes, sir; that was public work.

Acting Chairman COMMONS. And they sent there men who were not fitted for that work?

Mr. OLSON. However, this was only one case I saw there; but I have seen other cases in other places.

Acting Chairman COMMONS. What other places?

Mr. OLSON. Well, in the sawmills and in the shingle mills.

Acting Chairman COMMONS. In the case of private employers?

Mr. OLSON. Yes, sir.

Acting Chairman COMMONS. Have they sent men not fitted for the work to private employers?

Mr. OLSON. Apparently so; but that is not alone true about the free employment agencies, that is probably more largely true of the private employment agents.

Acting Chairman COMMONS. How does it come that private agencies send in men not fitted for the work?

Mr. OLSON. I can't account for that except that they don't take the time to look into the matter—to investigate.

Acting Chairman COMMONS. Have the employers' associations established their own employment agencies for employing help?

Mr. OLSON. Yes; in some parts of the State.

Acting Chairman COMMONS. In what part of the State?

Mr. OLSON. I understand at Aberdeen the employers' associations have established agencies of their own.

Acting Chairman COMMONS. Is that lumber?

Mr. OLSON. Yes, sir.

Acting Chairman COMMONS. What other ones?

Mr. OLSON. Those are the only ones I know about.

Acting Chairman COMMONS. The rest of the employers depend upon private and public agencies as far as you know?

Mr. OLSON. Yes, sir.

Acting Chairman COMMONS. And neither endeavors to select the type of men that the employer specifically wants?

Mr. OLSON. Now, I wouldn't say that positively in all cases; but I have seen instances.

Acting Chairman COMMONS. So far as you have looked into it, it is so?

Mr. OLSON. Yes, sir.

Acting Chairman COMMONS. Any questions?

Commissioner LENNON. Yes, sir. If a child enters into an industry under the permit system or comes to the age where they can enter without such permission, what provisions have the State of Washington made for the continuation of schools or vocational schools or anything of that kind?

Mr. OLSON. No provision whatever. There was a bill introduced at the last session of the legislature for the purpose of establishing a continuation school; but it never emerged from the committee.

Commissioner LENNON. The matter is being discussed by your people, is it, and having consideration?

Mr. OLSON. To some extent.

Commissioner LENNON. Does the public-school system do anything along that line as to vocational training in Seattle or elsewhere in the State?

Mr. OLSON. I understand in the cities of Seattle, Spokane, and Tacoma— I am not certain as to Spokane, however, that they give some vocational training in regard to millinery work, and probably other lines. I do know that they do with reference to millinery.

Commissioner LENNON. That is all.

Acting Chairman COMMONS. Mr. Thompson, anything more?

Mr. THOMPSON. Just a few more questions. About how many workingmen are there in the State, if you know or have an estimate?

Mr. OLSON. I would have to hazard a guess, as there has never been a census taken except by the Federal Government, and I have gone to the census reports of the Federal Government and have not been able to find anything definite. I would say as a rough guess 400,000.

Mr. THOMPSON. What per cent, in your opinion, of those men are organized?

Mr. OLSON. I believe that there are about 25,000 men organized in the State of Washington.

Mr. THOMPSON. What, if any, efforts have been made, as far as you know, to prevent the organization of men in the various industries?

Mr. OLSON. In the last two years there has been an employers' association formed in the State of Washington to combat organized labor and the closed shop.

Mr. THOMPSON. Do some of the employers of this State shift their men for the purpose of preventing organization, as far as you know?

Mr. OLSON. I can't say positively; I have heard rumors of it.

Mr. THOMPSON. How about Gray Harbor district?

Mr. OLSON. I have heard rumors of them doing it there. However, so far as I have been able to investigate, I haven't gotten any facts in that case.

Mr. THOMPSON. Do you know whether there is any definite information abroad in that respect? Who would be apt to know?

Mr. OLSON. I could not point out anybody particularly that would know, because the rumor that has come to my ears has only been general.

Mr. THOMPSON. You say, if I remember correctly, that in fixing the minimum wage to be paid to these various women workers here in the State, that the element of the cost of living was largely considered?

Mr. OLSON. Yes, sir.

Mr. THOMPSON. Was that the only consideration?

Mr. OLSON. That was not the only consideration, but that was the main consideration. That was the one upon which the minimum wage is founded.

Mr. THOMPSON. What specific would you want to say about the establishment of this minimum wage for different industries, like $10 for mercantile establishments, $8.90 for manufacturing work, $9 for women working in laundries, and $9 for telegraph and telephone girls?

Mr. OLSON. To some extent, that is a matter of the difference of opinion of the different conferences. So far as the minimum wage established in mercantile establishments is concerned as against that established in factories, the facts that were brought out in those two conferences were, that there was a difference in the cost of living in those two industries—that the girl employed in a mercantile establishment required considerably more money for clothes than the one employed in a factory. Facts brought out in our laundry conference showed in some instances that a girl employed there needed more money for some things than the one employed in the mercantile establishments. However, it varied all down the line. For shoes, the girl working in the laundry required quite a bit more than the girl working in the mercantile establishment. That was rather a surprise to me, but these things were all gone over item by item, and, as I say, it might be to some extent a difference of opinion on the part of the different conferences in establishing the different wages. However, I think to a great extent they are logical.

Mr. THOMPSON. Can you file with this commission a statement of the various items which entered into the settlement of these different wages?

Mr. OLSON. I can.

Mr. THOMPSON. We will be pleased to have you do so.

Mr. OLSON. All right.

Acting Chairman COMMONS. Any questions?

Commissioner GARRETSON. Mr. Olson, if there were 25,000 organized workers in the State, and 375,000 were not organized, does the wage-fixing ability of the 25,000 exert a strong influence on the wage of the other 375,000?

Mr. OLSON. I think it does.

Commissioner GARRETSON. They are the real factor of strength in the wage fixing?

Mr. OLSON. There is no question about it.

Commissioner GARRETSON. That is all.

Commissioner O'CONNELL. Does that include the railroads of the State, the various brotherhoods, railroad brotherhoods?

Mr. OLSON. No; that does not include the railroad people of the State, because they have no locals in this State. I am merely speaking of those unions that have locals in the State.

Commissioner O'CONNELL. So there you lose almost 50 per cent of the organized force at once?

Mr. OLSON. Yes.

Commissioner GARRETSON. Is there any other industry of the State as closely organized as the railway employees?

Mr. OLSON. Yes; I think there is.

Commissioner GARRETSON. What branch?

Mr. OLSON. I think the printers and pressmen are as closely organized.

Commissioner GARRETSON. They are, I grant you, in the centers. Are they outlying?

Mr. OLSON. Well, they are if you include all of the railway men that are employed on logging railways, etc.

Commissioner GARRETSON. Well, I do not on logging railways. If you take the kind of labor that you speak of; the kind of employment I was referring to were the regular employees in the train movement and shop crafts.

Mr. OLSON. They might be weaker.

Commissioner O'CONNELL. Have you any idea as to the number of workmen that are employed in the transportation and mechanical forces in the railways of the State of Washington?

Mr. OLSON. I have not. I have not been able to get those figures.

Commissioner O'CONNELL. Do you think that they are organized to the extent of 98 per cent, both in the transportation and mechanical departments?

Mr. OLSON. They are very generally organized.

Commissioner O'CONNELL. You think there are about 25,000 organized. So far as your records show, do you think that can easily be doubled by putting in the railway people of the State?

Mr. OLSON. I have no idea how many railway people are employed in this State. On account of being interstate commerce it is hard to get those figures.

Commissioner GARRETSON. It is difficult to segregate them from interstate.

Acting Chairman COMMONS. Is this figure, 400,000, based on the census that was issued in the last month?

Mr. OLSON. I haven't seen a copy of that. Has it been delivered yet?

Acting Chairman COMMONS. Yes.

Mr. OLSON. Our department has not received it.

Acting Chairman COMMONS. Then of that 400,000, what number do you estimate are men and what women?

Mr. OLSON. I should say that we have 60,000 women employed in this State in all occupations.

Acting Chairman COMMONS. Three hundred and forty thousand, does that include agricultural labor and those in the seasonal industries, picking, and that kind of thing?

Mr. OLSON. Yes. That does not mean steady employment by any means to the 400,000.

Commissioner GARRETSON. Different individuals who labor?

Mr. OLSON. Yes.

Acting Chairman COMMONS. That is the maximum number of employees at any time?

Mr. OLSON. Yes, sir.

Commissioner GARRETSON. Or who are available for employment?

Mr. OLSON. Yes; that is it.

Acting Chairman COMMONS. That is sufficient. The commission - will" adjourn until 2 o'clock.

(And thereupon at 12.30 o'clock p. m. of this Monday, August 10, 1914, an adjournment was taken until 2 o'clock p. m. of the same day.)

AFTER RECESS—2 P. M.

Acting Chairman COMMONS. The commission will come to order. Mr. Thompson, call your next witness.

TESTIMONY OF DR. J. ALLEN SMITH.

Mr. THOMPSON. Dr. Smith, will you give your name, please?

Dr. SMITH. J. Allen Smith.

Mr. THOMPSON. Your address?

Dr. SMITH. 4510 Twenty-second Avenue Northeast, Seattle.

Mr .THOMPSON. And your business or profession?

Dr. SMITH. Professor of political and social science, State University, Seattle.

Mr. THOMPSON. How long have you been connected with the university?

Dr. SMITH. Seventeen years.

Mr. THOMPSON. And in this department?

Dr. SMITH. Seventeen years.

Mr. THOMPSON. Generally, for the information of the commission, what subjects do you personally take up in the pursuit of those two branches?

Dr. SMITH. My entire time and attention at present is given to political science. I have no work in any other field.

Mr. THOMPSON. But in your general university work and in your general study, Professor, you have covered the industrial field, I take it?

Dr. SMITH. I was formerly professor of economics, and gave most of my time to that one subject.

Mr. THOMPSON. Yes.

Dr. SMITH. But not recently.

Mr. THOMPSON. Have you followed the general industrial situation in this State and in the country in a general way?

Dr. SMITH. Only in a very general way, and then mostly with reference to political questions.

Mr. THOMPSON. Well, referring now, to Seattle and the State of Washington in the first instance, what in your view, or what views have you of the general economics and industrial situation in this vicinty?

Dr. SMITH. Well——

Mr. THOMPSON. I will· ask whether the relations between employers and employees are friendly, or where they have fallen down?

Dr. SMITH. I think the relation here is very much the same as you would find it in any other State where conditions are somewhat similar. In some lines it is friendly. But many of the large employers here in this State seem to be distinctly opposed to effective labor organizations. That is true, however, in other places as well.

Mr. THOMPSON. Are you familiar with the views or the grounds upon which they base their attitude?

Dr. SMITH. So far as I see, it is put on the same grounds as it is elsewhere— the alleged abuses of trades-unions. But, of course, it all comes back to the question of control—control of industry. I think that is one point upon which the whole controversy hinges.

Mr. THOMPSON. That is, the division of power?

Dr. SMITH. Yes, sir; the division of power between the employer and the employee and the general public.

Mr. THOMPSON. Have any questions come up here with reference to the restriction of output or limitation of work by the employee?

Dr. SMITH. What is your question?

Mr. THOMPSON. The question of limitation of output.

Dr. SMITH. Yes, sir.

Mr. THOMPSON. Or would all such questions be merged in the question of power?

Dr. SMITH. I think they all come back to this one question.

Mr. THOMPSON. Well, what would be your remedy for a controversy which hinges around, centers around that fact?

Dr. SMITH. If you will allow me to make a rather extended answer to that question.

Mr. THOMPSON. Do that.

Dr. SMITH. I would say that my remedy would be to give the worker larger control in industry. My reason for that is this: As I see it, the law practically recognizes the employer as in control of industry. Legally he is in control, though actually this control is limited, because of the activities of labor unions that are entirely outside the law. But, nevertheless, he has very great influence in the direction of determining the distribution of the income between employer and employee. Of course, his right to control industry is limited to some extent by legislation, here and everywhere else. But the laboring man has the feeling that governmental regulation of such matters may be unsatisfactory, for two reasons: In the first place, as lawyers know, the bulk, or at least a very large part, of the law relating to employer and employee comes down from a time when the employee had very little influence upon legislation. Consequently it does not fully recognize the rights and interests of the employee.

And another reason is this: This morning Mr. Olson said that in suits involving breaches of labor laws the minimum fines are assessed where convictions are obtained. I think that the law is not only administered too leniently but that the view taken by the Government itself too largely reflects the point of view of the employer, and it is hard for the laboring man to change the system because of the checks and restraints which characterize our whole political system in this country, under which the majority find it difficult to enact public opinion into legislation. This has the effect of making the laboring man realize the fact that the protection of his interests through State control is exceptionally difficult here in the United States, and so he naturally turns to the trade-union, entirely outside the law, as the most trustworthy source of relief. The trade-union is, you might say, an extra legal means by which the laboring man is seeking to get the protection which he feels he does not get at the present time in an adequate measure through the State.

Mr. THOMPSON. Relating to the law as you spoke of it, you have said that the system of government in this country, by means of the various checks and restraints that we have, makes it almost impossible for the laboring man to get an expression of his views.

Dr. SMITH. Yes, sir.

Mr. THOMPSON. What is your opinion as to whether or not the old common law as such——

Dr. SMITH. What is that?

Mr. THOMPSON. What is your opinion as to whether or not the old common law as such, coming out of an industrial situation wholly different from that which exists to-day——

Dr. SMITH. Yes, sir.

Mr. THOMPSON. In other words, relationship in the industry where master worked at the same bench with the men in many cases, do you think that common law itself is capable of reaching an adjustment of the rights and equities of the employees to-day?

Dr. SMITH. I think it would be, provided you had courts that were thoroughly in sympathy with the point of view of labor and thoroughly understood the problems that labor is up against. I think it largely fails because the courts do not sympathize with or fully understand the point of view of labor.

Mr. THOMPSON. You are familiar, of course, with law and jurisprudence?

Dr. SMITH. To some extent; yes, sir.

Mr. THOMPSON. Of course the old common law consisted of decisions and positions taken by the law wherein the memory of man runneth not to the contrary, and some of the old law relating to master and servant growing out of the early conditions might be perhaps appropriate to our present situation, where we have large factories and large industries like railroads?

Dr. SMITH. Yes, sir.

Mr. THOMPSON. If the common law would have to follow the beaten line of decisions coming down from that kind of civilization, do you believe, then, such law, even though fairly administered, would meet the present economic conditions?

Dr. SMITH. No, sir; not entirely. The laboring man has to look here, as in other countries, largely to the legislative power of the State to secure needed adjustment of laws to new conditions, and so many difficulties are encountered in securing readjustment, either through ordinary legislation or court decisions, that the laboring man does not get the relief at the hands of the State that he has a right to expect and which in some countries he has been getting.

Mr. THOMPSON. Have you any idea as to the specific form in which this relief might go, the form it might take in order to adjust some of this unrest and grievances which exist to-day?

Dr. SMITH. I think we have started in the right direction in this State in the case of the industrial insurance commission, which is based on the principle of protecting the laborer against the risks of industry.

Mr. THOMPSON. Do you think if the present courts had their power extended so that, say, in injunction cases where either of the parties came for an injunction in a labor dispute, the court would have a right to pass not only on the law of the case as it exists to-day, but might have the right to go into the merits of the industrial controversy and pass on that, would that be a help in your opinion?

Dr. SMITH. I would be afraid to extend the power of the courts in that direction until lawyers and judges as a whole are more in line, as far as their economic training is concerned, with the present condition of industry.

Mr. THOMPSON. What would be your opinion of a system of industrial courts not to be administered by lawyers, but to be administered by men who understood economics and business?

Dr. SMITH. I think if such courts were composed of laymen, business men and laboring men, and men other than lawyers and judges, they would be highly desirable.

Mr. THOMPSON. Of course, such courts would be a radical departure from our present system of government in this country, would it not?

Dr. SMITH. Yes, sir.

Mr. THOMPSON. And might be had to bring about?

Dr. SMITH. I don't know.

Mr. THOMPSON. A slow process?

Dr. SMITH. I don't know about the difficulty, but I think it would be very desirable.

Mr. THOMPSON. What would you think of the institution of a Federal industrial council, say with power to mediate and conciliate, and perhaps to arbitrate, if desired, by both sides?

Dr. SMITH. I think any move in that direction is desirable.

Mr. THOMPSON. And from your study of political and economic science, would that seem to be the line of least resistance and the next step—or what would you present to be the next step?

Dr. SMITH. Yes, sir; if you combine with that the taking over of the duty of investigation and publicity in connection with disputes. It seems to me that is the next and most important step at this time. If we could get all matters of dispute between employees and employer fully investigated and thoroughly aired before the public, that would be the best step to take at the present moment.

Mr. THOMPSON. I didn't state, but I meant to include that in my statement of such board. In your opinion, such council would be a good many steps in advance?

Dr. SMITH. I think it would.

Mr. THOMPSON. In your opinion, then, what else would you like to say, or have you in mind to say, with reference to the industrial unrest which exists and the causes which lead to it and the possible cure or remedy?

Dr. SMITH. I would like to make one comment on the reasons pointed out; in my opinion one of the causes of unrest peculiar to this country is the lack of control, either political or economic, on the part of the laboring man. So, naturally, I think, that one line along which it would be well to develop would be in the direction of a little more democracy. I think that would have an extremely good effect on both the laboring man and the employer. One of the reasons why the employer in this country is in some cases, especially in the case of the large employer, so unwilling to arbitrate or deal with the employee, is that he feels that when it comes to measuring strength with the employee, the latter is no match for him. More democracy, if it could be brought about, would weaken the power of resistance of the employer and make him more conciliatory. Also, on the part of the laboring man, it would give him a different attitude toward the Government. He would come to have more faith in its fairness and justice in all matters affecting labor.

Mr. THOMPSON. I take it the democracy you are speaking of now is political democracy rather than economic?

Dr. SMITH. Political democracy; yes.

Mr. THOMPSON. Now, where would you start out to get more democracy in our political make-up.

Dr. SMITH. I would suggest an easier method of amending the Constitution. Then we would be able to get at some of these other questions directly.

Mr. THOMPSON. Do you think that the principle of democracy might also be extended to industry itself?

Dr. SMITH. Yes; to some extent. I haven't thought of that in particular, but I believe that will come about in some measure.

Mr. THOMPSON. Well, in the field of collective bargaining, of course, the elements of democracy have more or less play.

Dr. SMITH. Yes, sir.

Mr. THOMPSON. And have you given that field any consideration?

Dr. SMITH. Yes, sir.

Mr. THOMPSON. As to its use and value in sounding problems of an industrial character?

Dr. SMITH. I feel that labor would have to be thoroughly organized in order to guarantee the success of the plan of collective bargaining. For that reason I would offer the freest possible opportunity on the part of labor to get together and act as a unit against the employer that is already a unit.

Mr. THOMPSON. When you say guarantee, what do you mean in that respect, to guarantee the collective bargaining?

Dr. SMITH. I mean the power practically to enforce it, because as it is now——

Mr. THOMPSON. As against the employer or against the employee?

Dr. SMITH. As against, I should say, both. I think that, logically, there goes along with that the idea that all workers must get together, otherwise the employer will have the advantage in the distribution of power. I can not see any other outcome than that labor will have to be fully organized if it is to hold its own in collective bargaining.

Mr. THOMPSON. In relation to the economic and political proposition, Doctor, do you believe that interstate competition has more or less to do with that problem?

Dr. SMITH. You mean such matters as were discussed here this morning?

Mr. THOMPSON. Yes.

Dr. SMITH. Certainly. It has a great deal to do with it.

Mr. THOMPSON. Well, do you believe that international competition has something to do, too, with that problem?

Dr. SMITH. It would, but for our tariff policy by which we guard against that, or attempt to at any rate. Its effect would be more pronounced under free trade, no doubt.

Mr. THOMPSON. Well, international forces have a good deal to do with the cost of living, don't they?

Dr. SMITH. Yes.

Mr. THOMPSON. The high cost?

Dr. SMITH. Yes, sir.

Mr. THOMPSON. Take, for instance, the present war.

Dr. SMITH. Very much.

Mr. THOMPSON. It has a material effect, I take it, on the price of foodstuffs, according to the market quotations?

Dr. SMITH. Yes, sir.

Mr. THOMPSON. Do you believe that anything could be done along that line in order to establish an equilibrium internationally?

Dr. SMITH. Establish what?

Mr. THOMPSON. An equilibrium or stability. Do you think that the workers of the country and of the world could do anything to help to bring about a stable situation?

Dr. SMITH. Stable in what respect?

Mr. THOMPSON. With regard to nations as well as with regard to interstate affairs.

Dr. SMITH. You mean so as to avoid collisions?

Mr. THOMPSON. Wars and the disturbance of economic conditions through wars.

Dr. SMITH. I think the remedy there, as the remedy must ultimately be, in the case of labor or any other problem we have, a matter of public opinion.

In that case possibly it would require a world public opinion. But if we can get a public opinion in any case that is clearly defined and thoroughly organized and well directed, I believe that it will accomplish its object.

Mr. THOMPSON. Of course, if we are correctly informed by the papers, labor has taken a very decided stand against the present war, for instance.

Dr. SMITH. Yes.

Mr. THOMPSON. In all the countries?

Dr. SMITH. Yes, sir.

Mr. THOMPSON. Recognizing, as they do thoroughly, that it has a very great effect——

Dr. SMITH. Yes, sir.

Mr. THOMPSON (continuing). On their economic conditions.

Dr. SMITH. Yes, sir.

Mr. THOMPSON. I am referring to that, as you stated you are professor of political science as well as economic science. Take the present war: Do you feel that an association, say, of the citizens of Germany and of England and of France and Austria, their people, if they come to this country, if they form an association together here, and speak to their respective peoples in Europe and state: " Here we live in friendship and in perfect accord "; do you think that it would have an influence on helping to determine that war or end it?

Dr. SMITH. I should think that the United States, being the one great neutral nation not having anything to do with this war in the Old World, any such move would have some moral effect; how much I don't know. Sometimes, of course, a very slight thing may change the whole course of history. Any organized protest against what is going on over there from a country such as this, where we have all nations represented—where, as you say, all do live side by side in the most friendly intercourse—would, I think, have a moral effect; but whether it would materially affect the attitude of the various foreign countries themselves in the present struggle is something to be determined by subsequent events.

Mr. THOMPSON. In referring to the question of collective bargaining, Doctor, what would you consider to be the elements that enter into that subject—I mean, take the question of responsibility—must it be mutual?

Dr. SMITH. I think that it would have to be mutual. I believe that when labor has its rights fully recognized in the law, labor will have more responsibility to assume than it assumes now. I believe that when a collective bargain is made both sides ought to be equally responsible.

Mr. THOMPSON. But you think that will come about through the fact that labor will ultimately——

Dr. SMITH. I think as labor gets more power labor will assume more responsibility, and will be willing to assume it.

Mr. THOMPSON. You think that labor as at present—under the present conditions—should assume a financial responsibility?

Dr. SMITH. I would not favor financial responsibility until labor has the power which, it seems to me, ought to go hand in hand with such responsibility.

Mr. THOMPSON. Referring to your last answer, Doctor, do you think if the financial responsibility were placed on unions to-day that it would tend to make them more responsible, or what effect do you think it would have on them?

Dr. SMITH. I think that inasmuch as the government in some localities is more or less opposed to the union such a policy would tend to disrupt and destroy it. That is why I would not want to see the union made financially responsible until it comes to possess the proportionate share of influence and power to which the importance of its interests would seem to entitle it.

Mr. THOMPSON. Have you made a study of public-service corporations and their methods?

Dr. SMITH. Not specially.

Mr. THOMPSON. Have you any views as to the organization of public-service employees, or employees of the State?

Dr. SMITH. You mean the public-service corporation employees?

Mr. THOMPSON. Like street car, electric light, or gas companies.

Dr. SMITH. My own belief is that public-service corporations should be required to submit their disputes with their employees to arbitration. I noticed some years ago in our street-car strike that we had to walk for about a week, although I think the franchise of that very company required the company to submit all matters of dispute to arbitration.

Mr. THOMPSON. What would you say with reference to Government employees?

. Dr. SMITH. I think that Government employees are in a somewhat different position from the employees of a private corporation.

Mr. THOMPSON. In what respect would his position be different from the private employee?

Dr. SMITH. There would be no question, in my opinion, about his right to organize; but I do think that in the case of Government employees the organization would have to submit to some restrictions not imposed on other employees. Take, for example, the postal employees. They naturally would not be permitted to inaugurate and carry out policies that an ordinary labor union might.

Mr. THOMPSON. Is your opinion based on some fundamental distinction you make between these two branches of service, or a sort of feeling you have?

Dr. SMITH. I haven't thought it out clearly, but I have in mind the relation which the employee bears to the employer and to the public. In one case the employer is the public, and in the other case a more or less regulated or unregulated private corporation. I think it is highly desirable, of course, to give labor in its dealings with unregulated private corporations, in many cases a monopoly, more freedom with reference to various policies of labor unions than would be given to employees working for the State itself.

Mr. THOMPSON. That is all, Mr. Chairman.

Commissioner GARRETSON. Doctor, do you believe that the system of finding for violation of law, for instance, the minimum wage law, or the eight-hour day law, is adequate in such event where the violation of the law, or the profit of the violation of the law exceeds the loss from the fine?

Dr. SMITH. I certainly do not. I think the fine must be heavy enough to discourage the offense.

Commissioner GARRETSON. Or else another penalty would have to be devised to make it effective?

Dr. SMITH. Yes.

Commissioner GARRETSON. Is it not true that under our system the employee, either industrially or legislatively, is compelled to fight against not only the employer, but capital itself concentrated in its hands—the power of capital?

Dr. SMITH. Yes; I think so.

Commissioner GARRETSON. That the only possible show that the employee would have to exercise any degree of influence is by a combination of the large number of human units for the purpose?

Dr. SMITH. That is my reason for saying that all labor must be combined so that capital can not play one part of it against the rest. Otherwise labor's influence, it seems to me, must be greatly weakened.

Commissioner GARRETSON. Counsel asked you a question with regard to your knowledge of jurisprudence. And he referred also to the growth of the common law, and I am only applying the common law of England—because our own is an outgrowth of it, or an appropriation of it—is not, in your opinion, the common law as it was, purely judge-made law?

Dr. SMITH. Yes; I would call it judge-made law. I do not know what lawyers would say about it. I would say more than that. I should say that during the time that it was crystallizing and becoming the common law, the judges did not in any sense represent the laboring class, but represented rather the ruling class.

Commissioner GARRETSON. That was exactly the next point I wanted to ask your opinion on. Is not the whole burden of that law evidence of the influence of the employer—and I am not using "influence" in the sense of improper—but one actually existant—the influence of the employer on the judiciary during the time of the building of the common law?

Dr. SMITH. I don't know that this influence was conscious, but the landlord class at that time largely controlled the State.

Commissioner GARRETSON. And the real burden was in favor of the master and against the man?

Dr. SMITH. Certainly. I think that is seen in all our common law, master and servant, etc.

Commissioner GARRETSON. If employers' associations should succeed in stamping out labor unions, in your opinion would the position of the individual laboring man be much better than it was under the English decisions in regard to the master and man?

Dr. SMITH. I think labor would be in an extremely unfortunate position if the labor unions should be completely crushed.

Commissioner GARRETSON. Has your experience .or investigation led you to form an opinion as to whether or not the clearly complete organization of men in any pursuit—I am speaking now of the healthy growth of an organization, not going in and taking immediate action—but where there have been complete organizations grown in any pursuit, and with that growth the power that comes from that organization, there has been a corresponding increase in the sense of responsibility on the part of the men that composed it?

Dr. SMITH. I think always, so far as I have been able to watch the working of unions, that has been noticeable. And it is perfectly natural that with the possession of power there should go the sense of responsibility.

Commissioner GARRETSON. Is it not really axiomatic that if a man has the material in him, putting the responsibility on him will develop it, bring it out?

Dr. SMITH. I think so.

Commissioner GARRETSON. And it would be unreasonable to suppose that it would not be the same; but the man is not impelled by the same motive, whether a member of a union or the administration of his property?

Dr. SMITH. Yes.

Acting Chairman COMMONS. I take it from what you have said you consider the establishment of the workmen's compensation or insurance commission in Washington as a step in the direction of eliminating the lawyer and judge and putting in the business man?

Dr. SMITH. Yes; in protecting the laboring man against the risks the old courts' decisions compelled him to assume.

Acting Chairman COMMONS. How has this system worked out according to your ideas? What would be the proper way for it to work out? Has it been effective in the sense you have in mind?

Dr. SMITH. I think the feeling is that the law does not go as far as it ought to. I believe that it has up to the present time been beneficial not only to the employee but to the employer as well. I think it should be revised and the scale of indemnities increased for various kinds of accidents.

Acting Chairman COMMONS. That is the only amendment you suggest, is it, in the scale of indemnities?

Dr. SMITH. Yes. Of course, there are many features that ought to be changed, but I think it is in the direction of giving labor a larger measure of damages. What I had in mind was its recognition of the principle that a trade ought to bear its own risk and not the individual worker.

Acting Chairman COMMONS. Has this law been effective in reducing accidents in this State?

Dr. SMITH. I could not say as to that, but I think it has, to some extent.

Acting Chairman COMMONS. Has there been the effect of making more burdensome on the employers of the State than similar lines in competing States?

Dr. SMITH. I have not given special attention to it, but from what I can see I think that the employers, as a whole, are very well satisfied with the law. I have not heard any serious complaint.

Acting Chairman COMMONS. Would you consider that the same principle should be, or that the State of Washington is now ready to extend that same principle of sickness insurance and occupational diseases; that it, has your experience with this law justified the principle sufficiently?

Dr. SMITH. Of course, we have not tried it sufficiently for one to have a final opinion with regard to it, but as to the general principle underlying it, I do not think there is any question.

Acting Chairman COMMONS. Have you investigated the sick-benefit system of private corporations in this State?

Mr. SMITH. No; not to any considerable extent. I know that such systems are in existence.

Acting Chairman COMMONS. That is all. Call your next witness.

Mr. THOMPSON. Earl Constantine.

TESTIMONY OF MR. EARL CONSTANTINE.

Mr. THOMPSON. Please give us your name.

Mr. CONSTANTINE. Earl Constantine.

Mr. THOMPSON. And your business address?

Mr. CONSTANTINE. 331 Lyon Building.

Mr. THOMPSON. And your position?

Mr. CONSTANTINE. Manager of the Employers' Association of Washington.

Mr. THOMPSON. Is that association over the whole State, or just confined in its workings to Seattle?

Mr. CONSTANTINE. It extends its field from the Columbia River on the south up to the British Columbia line on the north, and as far as the Cascades, overlapping only in a few cases.

Mr. THOMPSON. What is the membership, in round numbers, if you know, of the association?

Mr. CONSTANTINE. In factory membership—we have individual memberships, too, but in factory membership, about 600.

Mr. THOMPSON. What lines of industry does it take in, or what lines if any are excluded?

Mr. CONSTANTINE. It excludes none.

Mr. THOMPSON. Are the employers of the district covered by your association fairly well represented in the membership?

Mr. CONSTANTINE. Yes.

Mr. THOMPSON. What proportion of the employers of that district who are eligible to membership belong, if you know—about?

Mr. CONSTANTINE. It varies as to locality. In some cases it runs as high as 80 per cent; in other cases it would run as low even as 10 or 15 per cent.

Mr. THOMPSON. Where are the places where employers are best organized, and where is that territory the least best organized?

Mr. CONSTANTINE. I would say the best organized to-day outside the city of Seattle is what is known as the Grays Harbor country, taking in a number of small towns located on Grays Harbor.

Mr. THOMPSON. Is that territory right contiguous to Seattle?

Mr. CONSTANTINE. It is about sixty odd miles, I think, southwest of here; possibly a little bit more—it is a little bit more than that.

Mr. THOMPSON. Is there any one particular trade or industry which has a larger percentage of membership in your association than another?

Mr. CONSTANTINE. Possibly the lumber industry, that being our chief industry in the State.

Mr. THOMPSON. What are the objects and purposes of your association?

Mr. CONSTANTINE. Mainly, I would say, to act as an intelligence bureau on industrial matters for the benefit of its members; to act as advisor and counsel and assist with all difficulties or troubles, labor matters; next, I should say, to keep itself fully advised on modern legislation, and advise its members thereon and to lend such assistance as is within its power. Outside of that, the calls that come from our members for service and to see that the members are properly served.

Mr. THOMPSON. When you say that your association acts as an intelligence bureau, what would we understand by that, what are we to understand by it?

Mr. CONSTANTINE. Our mail daily brings us information from different members in different parts of the State as to conditions, industrial conditions. And we have our agents who are traveling throughout the State and they bring in information of their own.

Mr. THOMPSON. Well, what general field would this information cover, if it could be divided into classes of information?

Mr. CONSTANTINE. Labor and legislation in general.

Mr. THOMPSON. Would such organizations as unions be considered part of the information that you gather?

Mr. CONSTANTINE. Most certainly.

Mr. THOMPSON. Their existence and their work?

Mr. CONSTANTINE. Their work; their methods.

Mr. THOMPSON. Has your association got a constitution and by-laws?

Mr. CONSTANTINE. Yes, sir.

Mr. THOMPSON. Can you furnish the commission with a copy?

Mr. CONSTANTINE. Yes, sir.

(See Constantine Exhibit No. 1.)

Mr. THOMPSON. In your constitution and by-laws, does your association take any stand upon any particular phase of the industrial field?

Mr. CONSTANTINE. It takes the stand for the open shop as against the closed shop.

Mr. THOMPSON. Against the closed shop?

Mr. CONSTANTINE. Yes, sir.

Mr. THOMPSON. Are there any other matters upon which it takes a definite stand?

Mr. CONSTANTINE. It does not.

Mr. THOMPSON. When you say your association stands for the open shop as contrasted with the closed shop or union shop, what do you want the commission to understand by that action—I mean how far does it go?

Mr. CONSTANTINE. It goes this far: That our main principle of organization is we believe that a man has a right to take and sell his property, which in that case, in the case of labor, will be his brain and brawn, as he sees fit, and without the dictation of a third party.

Mr. THOMPSON. Will it go any further. I simply want to get your idea, is all. I understand what you say, but is that expressed in any particular attitude toward the organization of employees among your membership, other than just simply an open shop, so called?

Mr. CONSTANTINE. I fail to really grasp what your question is, if you will pardon me.

Mr. THOMPSON. I will put it more specifically, I don't want to ask you too direct. Is the open shop, as you state it, construed as in opposition to any organization of working men?

Mr. CONSTANTINE. No, sir; decidedly not. I don't know that the majority of our members—I don't know just what majority I would place it at, but the majority of the members of the employers' association do believe in organized labor.

Mr. THOMPSON. Do believe in it?

Mr. CONSTANTINE. They do believe in it, but they do not believe in having organizations to a point where they monopolize any particular plant or line of industry.

Mr. THOMPSON. What would be the facts upon which monopoly would be determined in an industry?

Mr. CONSTANTINE. When in a given plant the representative of the laboring men in that plant is able to walk in at any time and with such frequency as he may desire and upon such provocation as he may desire and tie up that plant for a given period of time. Or to use, in other words, hasty action or drastic action with reference to any plant. I might say that would be a monopoly.

Mr. THOMPSON. Of course, that might vary with the different trades?

Mr. CONSTANTINÉ. Yes, sir.

Mr. THOMPSON. If a man could walk into a plant and call out, say, 30 per cent of the workers, it might result in tying up that industry?

Mr. CONSTANTINE. Yes, sir.

Mr. THOMPSON. Would you consider the organization of 30 per cent of the workers such a monopoly as would create it a dangerous one?

Mr. CONSTANTINE. I will answer your question in this form: That given a certain plant and a plant where, say, there were three distinct lines of skilled labor that composed all the way from 90 to 100 per cent of the labor there employed, that the position of our members and our organization would be that in none of those three, any more than all three, should there be monopoly by organization. In other words, if a man should appear at the door of the plant or employment window and should show qualifications to perform services in an efficient manner and should show a character which is honest and commendable, and there should be a vacancy there, we ought to be able to give him employment despite the fact he does not belong to any union or pay tribute thereto.

Mr. THOMPSON. I do not wish to pursue you on that question, Mr. Constantine.

Mr. CONSTANTINE. That is all right; I am very glad to be here.

Mr. THOMPSON. What I want to get at as fully as you care to state is the view of your organization toward the question of organization?

Mr. CONSTANTINE. Yes, sir.

Mr. THOMPSON. Now, we have, for instance, to illustrate to you—in the past we have found associations which object to any organization which has more than 40 per cent of the workers of any class.

Mr. CONSTANTINE. Yes, sir.

Mr. THOMPSON. It becomes dangerous beyond that point?

Mr. CONSTANTINE. Yes, sir.

Mr. THOMPSON. They make it a percentage consideration and just simply have the open shop, that is all. Now, what, in so far as your association has gone into it, how far has it formulated any ideas in that respect?

Mr. CONSTANTINE. Well, that would be impossible for me, I think, to take and attempt to tell you what percentage of organized labor is a safe percentage to have. We do not figure it that way. There might be such a thing, I imagine, I can imagine such a thing as a very high percentage of organized labor, granting that the individuals in that percentage are men of intelligence and fair-minded, which would make the plant absolutely safe. But, following on the same thought and as voicing perhaps more my own personal opinions in the matter, I would believe in the closed shop when the same is based on a high standard of requirement for the laboring man to belong to that union, so that I know that that union's standard of efficiency is high. It thereby creates a closed market in which I am compelled to go to buy, because I must take and employ the most efficient labor if I am going to attempt to compete successfully in the market. But when the union in itself places absolutely no requirement on any man's joining the union—there are unions, of course, that have and require—in most cases unions make no requirement at all of ability and efficiency in accepting a man into their ranks, and we then do not grant them the power to monopolize a plant.

Mr. THOMPSON. Would it be fair to state that your association fears any organization; that is to say, when they hear that an organization of labor is attempted in any plant or industry, that it should be gotten rid of, because under present conditions such an organization or organizations are dangerous—would that be a fair statement of the position of your association?

Mr. CONSTANTINE. Well, I don't know just what you mean. You said any organization. Do you refer to some specific union?

Mr. THOMPSON. Well, assuming that you have got a lot of employers in your association.

Mr. CONSTANTINE. Yes, sir.

Mr. THOMPSON. And that an employer hears that there is an attempt being made in one of his factories to unionize the men. Would the attitude of your association be in advising that man, that he should limit the unionization of the men as much as possible and get rid of them?

Mr. CONSTANTINE. That is a hard question to answer. We have to treat every case on its own merits.

Mr. THOMPSON. Then there is no general rule?

Mr. CONSTANTINE. No. We usually send an investigator down to find what the conditions are in the plant and what situations have preceded that, before coming to some conclusion. We frequently have just as much trouble perhaps in making our own members see our light—I mean keeping them from going to the extreme, as we might in keeping them from not going far enough.

Mr. THOMPSON. In your opinion, now, personally, how do you view organizations of labor? Do you think that they lead to peace or do you think that they lead to strife in an industry?

Mr. CONSTANTINE. Organizations of labor, in my opinion, those that are based on open-shop principles, the history of the country in the past has shown that they lead to peace. And I have in mind the largest unions in the United States, and they are unions unfortunately that are not generally accepted as unions or looked on as unions by the public. I refer to the three large brotherhoods that control the labor on our railroads. Now, there are three large unions—I am speaking irrespective of the fact that one of the commissioners is an officer. I have put myself on record on that question time and again. There is a union that every employer in the country commends to-day. I understand that a man who enters, for instance, to-day as a locomotive engineer, is not eligible to membership in that brotherhood until he has had a certain period of apprenticeship. and when that period of apprenticeship has passed he is then eligible, and he no doubt is given an invitation to join, but it is optional as to whether he desires to join the brotherhood or not. I have lived in railroad communities where almost every neighbor of mine was a railroad man—engineer or fireman or so on—and their standard is exceptionally high, I should say the highest standard of labor in the country to-day. And there is absolutely no compulsion, however, placed upon the prospective candidate to join the union. And should he desire not to join the brotherhood, he could continue to pursue his labor in peace and to gain a livelihood for himself and for his family. Such a union has proven its worth. Such a principle has proven its worth, by the fact that the records show that all the way from 90 per cent up of the men eligible to it belong to the brotherhoods.

Mr. THOMPSON. If you were, as you are, advising this commission as to what you think is best, what would you advise them to recommend, that the organization of workingmen is a good thing to industry or not?

Mr. CONSTANTINE. With the open-shop principle connected with it, it is.

Mr. THOMPSON. Well would you make any statement of that character, or would you leave the question of organization out of consideration if you were on this commission?

Mr. CONSTANTINE. I have already committed myself here, that I believe in organization of labor, provided that it has the open-shop basis, and no coercion is used to get a man into the union or to prevent one that does not belong from securing a livelihood.

Mr. THOMPSON. Now, looking at the proposition from the standpoint of the employer, do you believe that the organization of workingmen is a good thing or not?

Mr. CONSTANTINE. I believe it is a good thing.

Mr. THOMPSON. Have you made any study—as you must have probably—of the economic and industrial situation around Seattle in the country where your association has its organization?

Mr. CONSTANTINE. Yes, sir.

Mr. THOMPSON. Is there a condition of unrest? I understand you have some views on that subject which you are ready to state to the commission?

Mr. CONSTANTINE. Yes, sir.

Mr. THOMPSON. You may go ahead and state them in your own way.

Mr. CONSTANTINE. There is undoubtedly a more or less general feeling of unrest in labor to-day. I think it is even perceptible to the average citizen. The causes for the same are no doubt varied.

Mr. THOMPSON. I didn't get your last answer.

Mr. CONSTANTINE. I say there are no doubt, of course, several causes for the unrest. It would be foolish and anything but truthful for me or anyone else to say that every employer has a standard that could be commended; I mean in his viewpoints toward labor or in his treatment of his own employees. We have black sheep among employers just as certainly as there are black sheep among laboring men. The unrest as it exists is partly of course in spots where there is such an employer who is unscrupulous. I believe it is only fair to say that the progress that we have made throughout the country in the last 20 years, particularly toward sanitation, toward safeguarding of machinery, toward care of the injured, toward providing, in other words, for the comfort and surroundings of the employee, and even providing for his increased return on his work, can not be attributable entirely to any one particular class of society, meaning labor. It is only fair to assume that a certain proportion of that movement comes on the part of the employer. In other words, it would be foolish for any economist to say that while labor has been progressing to a higher level that the employer on the other hand has been stagnating or falling down from the general levels of society. I think there is a general movement throughout the country. I traveled last year all over the United States for the purpose of studying that and no other purpose, and there is a general broadening of the viewpoints of the employer toward labor, toward matters of economics, sanitation, safeguarding of machinery, and all those things. I believe very firmly that the largest cause to-day for unrest, leaving out unemployment, which I shall touch upon, and a few other things of that kind, the largest cause of unrest to-day is the type of leadership in a very large number of unions and also very pointedly the kind of leadership that we find in the men who dictate the press of the labor unions.

Mr. THOMPSON. Well, from your study of industrial conditions in that trip you made around the country last year, did you arrive at any conclusion or any idea as to the improvements that could be made in the industrial situation which would relieve the unrest? More specifically, do you think that the question of the machinery that we have, either in the Government or in industry itself, is sufficient to meet the requirements?

Mr. CONSTANTINE. I don't know whether I am answering your question or not, but I wish to make this statement: It is a patent fact, and indisputable, of course, that the attitude of the manufacturer and the employer up to, say, 10 years ago was very much one of defense in matters of legislation. I believe that within the last 10 years there has been a gradually increasing and more and more perceptible movement of offensive, constructive effort on the part of the employer toward bettering labor conditions. And I believe that within the next 10 years we shall see much more of that. I happen to know that many employers' association, not only in the State of Washington but others are planning to take a more offensive part in legislation in the future, toward constructive work, toward remedying some of the abuses that now exist.

Mr. THOMPSON. During the last two years we have seen the breakdown of civil government in three of the great Commonwealths of this country because of the maladjustment of the relations of employer and employee. Have you any ideas as to any machinery that might be established, either by employers and employees themselves apart from the Government, or by the Government, which would assist and help in such cases as that and in other industrial disputes?

Mr. CONSTANTINE. Meaning arbitration?

Mr. THOMPSON. Meaning arbitration and conciliation.

Mr. CONSTANTINE. Yes. I don't see, of course, where the Federal Government would be of very much help to us in the majority of our industrial troubles, inasmuch as they are usually of a local nature. It might be that some such Federal board would have a natural tendency to set an example for the State legislatures. The question of arbitration between employer and employee in time of industrial strife is more and more on the increase, and my personal opinion is that arbitration, provided there were proper safeguards about it, as the mayor said this morning, and the personnel of the board was fair and was not partial either to employer or employee, will be eventually the solution of the question. Not the least important—the most important thing connected with arbitration is the fact that it gives publicity to the facts.

Mr. THOMPSON. Do you think that a Federal body, say, for instance, call it a Federal industrial council, from your view of the Federal Government as such, as contrasted with the State government, would have more influence toward conciliating than a State board would have?

Mr. CONSTANTINE. You mean if there was industrial trouble in the harbor at Seattle you could send us a Federal commission from Washington?

Mr. THOMPSON. Or a Federal commissioner, we will say, or mediator.

Mr. CONSTANTINE. Yes, sir.

Mr. THOMPSON. Would that be apt to have—the very fact that he represents the Federal Government—would that be apt to have more influence toward persuading the contending parties to enter into negotiation?

Mr. CONSTANTINE. I would say that it would have a good influence. It would tend toward settling the problems, although there are quite a few employers who look with some skepticism upon the general attitude of the Federal Government, particularly in the last several years.

Mr. THOMPSON. Of course that wouldn't necessarily affect that question at all, would it, just simply a Federal institution as such?

Mr. CONSTANTINE. Except that the element of the absence or presence of faith on the part of both parties in laying their case is important.

Mr. THOMPSON. I take it that absence of faith in all government does not exist to-day. Is there anything you care to say in reference to the formation of your association—conditions you have met and, more particularly, the teamsters' strike and the like here in Seattle?

Mr. CONSTANTINE. The mayor said this morning when he was inducted into office the teamsters' strike was nearly ended, and he made a statement that the employment of 45 policemen on the part of his predecessor was unjustifiable; and, therefore, having found it so, he discharged the men. The mayor is entitled to his opinion. However, the record shows approximately 300 cases of assault in a period of 11 months, and in every one of those cases the assault is directly attributable to the teamsters' strike—the slashing of horses, cutting of harness, destruction of automobile engines, ditching of wagons over the hill, the beating up of men, the use of firearms, and everything else—all of which occurred in the 12 months preceding the induction of the present mayor into office. That should be sufficient explanation—or excuse, at least—for his predecessor appointing those 45 men. All of these cases I have mentioned are to be found on the police records and court records of the city of Seattle. I shall present to the commission of the industrial—with the permission of the commission, I shall present an issue of the Weekly Messenger, the same being a weekly publication on the part of the employers' association, this of date April 11, which contains the presentation of our case to Mayor Gill's arbitration committee or investigation committee.

Mr. THOMPSON. Very much pleased to have it.

(The paper referred to, entitled "The Weekly Messenger," vol. 1, No. 13, dated April 11, 1914, published by the Employers' Association of Washington, Seattle, Wash., was submitted in printed form.)

Mr. Constantine. I should also like to attach to that a subsequent issue of the Weekly Messenger, dated April 25.

(The issue of the Weekly Messenger referred to, vol. 1, No. 15, dated April 25, 1914, was submitted in printed form.)

And just a word with reference to the teamsters' strike. The arbitration committee, as the mayor informed you this morning, was entirely disinterested. I am frank to say we were not entirely pleased with the personnel; probably the other side was not. You never could get both sides pleased. These men were public-spirited men—some doctors, some attorneys, some stockmen, insurance men, and educators, and ministers. They sat on the case for some three weeks. About a week prior to the filing of their decisions in the teamsters' strike—which is the most important strike that has taken place in Seattle in many years, affecting as it does the primary transportation—they called for a final statement on the part of both the teamsters' union and the team owners' association as to the final details of the statement on their part. In this issue of April 25 you will find the complete findings of this commission, including the two letters finally submitted by the union and by the employing team owners, and the findings of the commission are three, the first of which reads as follows:

"That the open-shop principle be hereafter fairly observed by both parties; that there shall never be any discrimination made by the employing team owners against a teamster because the latter may belong to a union; that no teamster shall ever discriminate against an employer because the latter may employ nonunion labor; and that efficiency shall at all times be the standard test for employment."

Since then, as the mayor says, both parties have gotten along very well. My last report of a month ago shows out of 40 new men employed 50 per cent of them had been men who had been on strike prior to that.

Mr. Thompson. Referring to the question of private detectives during the time of labor trouble, what is your opinion on that subject, if you have one, and what are the reasons back of it?

Mr. Constantine. I believe when a plant, or manufacturer, or employer is facing a condition where there is violence, or destruction of property actually going on or distinctly promised and approaching, or any danger of life and limb, that the employer is fully entitled to protection, even if it means doubling of the police force. I would not think violence should be countenanced on the part of the individual, or on the part of an organization any more than an individual.

Mr. Thompson. What would you say with reference to the right of an employer to hire private detectives?

Mr. Constantine. I don't think an employer would ever seek or think of suggesting the employment of private detectives if given full protection on the part of the public authorities.

Mr. Thompson. From your investigation of that subject, do you believe generally in the United States the employer does hire private detectives in labor disputes like strikes?

Mr. Constantine. I suppose there are places in the country where that is attempted more or less. In the State of Washington it is not countenanced.

Mr. Thompson. It is not countenanced?

Mr. Constantine. No, sir; it is rather rare, I would put it.

Mr. Thompson. The mayor, I think, testified this morning it had been done here.

Mr. Constantine. As I gather from the testimony of the mayor, he was referring to the Ballard strike here in the city, where the city is said to have not offered extra protection and the sheriff of the county swore in deputies and sent them out, and in some cases deputized employees of the employer.

Mr. Thompson. Take that case and the other cases which you say have existed in this country, do you believe in the principle of the employment by the employer of private guards or private detectives, or whatever you may call them, in time of strike and lockout?

Mr. Constantine. I think that basically it is not a good principle, but I think that the fact is-that generally the employer is not in position to get the protection he is entitled to, and that creates a condition where for the protection of life, as much as for the protection of property, he should have the right to take and deputize employees, or get them deputized, rather, to guard his plant.

Mr. THOMPSON. It has been said by some that this is the only country among civilized nations where such a condition is permitted; that in the old countries of Europe—France, Germany, England, and the like—private guards are not permitted at all.

Mr. CONSTANTINE. That is probably true, because the enforcement of law is much more observed.

Mr. THOMPSON. Would that be your reason for the difference?

Mr. CONSTANTINE. I believe so. I happen to have lived in Europe and know something about that.

Mr. THOMPSON. Is that all the reason you care to give, or is there anything else?

Mr. CONSTANTINE. I think that is sufficient.

Mr. THOMPSON. You have finished your own statement with reference to the question of unrest and conditions here in Seattle?

Mr. CONSTANTINE. I gave the main ones. Of course, there is the question of the unemployed, and that is due, to a very great extent, to the fact we have a very large amount of seasonal employment, and it is an unfortunate condition and could only be remedied did we have a large number of industries that could take this labor that is in the camps and fruit fields and farming in their regular period, and put them into a manufacturing plant; but our trouble is our industrial centers are very few, comparatively speaking.

Mr. THOMPSON. What is the general attitude, if you know, of the employers, or your association, toward witnesses who testified before the industrial commission? It has been stated here that the employees were being discharged when telling of the facts. What do you know about that?

Mr. CONSTANTINE. As far as my personal knowledge goes, and my personal feeling in the matter is that the employer would in no case—well, would in most cases—not object to an employee testifying in a matter that affected him or her so very directly. Now, we have again some black sheep in the flock, and I have had cases where I have had to go and talk to our members, where I have known that they would want to take and use their influence, and warned them against doing that—not for fear of the law but because we are trying to educate our members to a higher standard in some of these matters. We have a few that look upon those things not quite like we would like to have them.

Mr. THOMPSON. It follows from what you say that your association does not countenance such action?

Mr. CONSTANTINE. Absolutely not. I am not in position to take and mention specific cases, but I have several in mind.

Mr. THOMPSON. Does your association keep any track of employees who have been hired by the different employers of your association—keep any list of them, or anything of that kind, for any purpose?

Mr. CONSTANTINE. We do not run an employment bureau, I mean as a part of our work; it is simply incidental. We have calls every day on the part of employers seeking for employees to fill positions and we probably daily have calls on the part of employees seeking positions.

Mr. THOMPSON. But do you keep any list or record of employees?

Mr. CONSTANTINE. In other words, you want to know if we have a black-list? We do not.

Mr. THOMPSON. I didn't want to term it so.

Mr. CONSTANTINE. We do not have any blacklist. We do not countenance a blacklist.

Mr. THOMPSON. Is there any other statement you would like to make before this commission?

Mr. CONSTANTINE. Yes, sir. I think that one of the reasons that explains to a large extent why there are employers' associations and why they are growing in number as organizations and as members of organizations is the increasing activity which organized labor is taking in legislation. That activity assumes many different forms. It is to be found not only in the municipal affairs, but in particular I refer to State legislation. I am not speaking from hearsay, inasmuch as I had the privilege of representing the legislative bureau of the manufacturers at the last session of the legislature. With your permission—I imagine you want as many documents as you can get for information—I have here in my hand a form, three pages, that is an exact duplicate of the legislative pledge which is exacted, if possible, on the part of the labor unions from every man who is seeking election to the statehouse or State senate.

Mr. THOMPSON. I would like to have it filed.

(See Constantine Exhibit No. 2.)

Mr. CONSTANTINE. I would like to read part of this: "Joint legislative committee," and so on. It is addressed in the form of, a letter. If you will allow me the privilege of reading the first paragraph, it will cover the case:

"The joint legislative committee are anxious to inform their membership and the many voters of the State who look to them for guidance as to your attitude, if elected to the legislature, on the following issues, upon which these organizations have mutually agreed to support one another in securing the enactment of the legislation thereon.

"Your signature in the blank space below each measure outlined signifies that you approve of such legislation and will use your best endeavors to enact same into law in form as will effectually guard the interests of the masses of the people, whom the measure is aimed to benefit," and so on. "Failure to sign and return to the undersigned within 10 days will be construed as a negative answer. Your reply will be given the fullest possible publicity, in order that those interested may know your attitude toward these measures."

It is needless to say we do not believe in submitting to our candidates for the legislature a given number of measures in complete form and asking him to sign his name pledging himself to vote for those measures. If it pledged him on one measure, the influence there would not be so bad; but where there is a grouping together of good, bad, and indifferent, it is a significant fact. I have known of several cases in which a man perhaps not consciously but unthinkingly signs his name below the measure that is not good where, if he gave it sufficient thought, he would not support it. And in the gallery of the house and senate there stands regularly night and day an agent of that league with shorthand notes watching the actions of any one of their pledgees and checking up their members. It has actually been characterized by one of the members of the legislative session as "pulling the strings from the gallery of the house and senate." And those are the things that compelled the employers in the State of Washington and in other States of the country to organize themselves and keep very close tab on legislative matters.

Mr. THOMPSON. It has been stated by some of our witnesses that they believe in a thorough organization of both employers and employees, and the industrial council of England in investigating the matter made the same recommendations. Do you believe that fact? Do you believe it is best to have thorough organization of both employers and employees?

Mr. CONSTANTINE. I believe in organization for both sides.

Mr. THOMPSON. Wouldn't the organization of employers naturally come along with, concurrently, the organization of employees into unions;

Mr. CONSTANTINE. It is doing that to-day. It would be only natural it would.

Mr. THOMPSON. That is all, Mr. Chairman.

Commissioner O'CONNELL. How long has your employers' association been organized, did you say?

Mr. CONSTANTINE. About 12 years; originally under the name of the citizens' alliance, but under the present name changed name about 6 or 7 years ago.

Commissioner O'CONNELL. How long have you been secretary of it?

Mr. CONSTANTINE. Since March 1, 1914. Prior to that being secretary of the employers' association of Spokane; but my work there brought me very frequently into Seattle.

Commissioner O'CONNELL. What was your business before becoming secretary of the manufacturers' association?

Mr. CONSTANTINE. Instructor in the public high school.

Commissioner O'CONNELL. Instructor in the public high schools where?

Mr. CONSTANTINE. In the city of Spokane.

Commissioner O'CONNELL. How long were you instructor in the public high schools?

Mr. CONSTANTINE. Four years.

Commissioner O'CONNELL. Have you been a manufacturer?

Mr. CONSTANTINE. I have not.

Commissioner O'CONNELL. Before that what were you doing?

Mr. CONSTANTINE. I was in a publishing house in the city of Minneapolis.

Commissioner O'CONNELL. As a workman?

Mr. CONSTANTINE. Yes, sir.

Commissioner O'CONNELL. What was you working on?

Mr. CONSTANTINE. I had the getting out—the publication of post cards; that department.

Commissioner O'CONNELL. Post cards?

Mr. CONSTANTINE. Yes; view post cards.

Commissioner O'CONNELL. As a printer?

Mr. CONSTANTINE. No, sir; just in charge of that department.

Commissioner O'CONNELL. How long have you been in the United States?

Mr. CONSTANTINE. Thirteen years.

Commissioner O'CONNELL. You·are a citizen of the United States?

Mr. CONSTANTINE. Born a citizen.

Commissioner O'CONNELL. Born a citizen?

Mr. CONSTANTINE. Yes, sir.

Commissioner O'CONNELL. Is your association here connected with the National Manufacturers' Association or National Association of Manufacturers?

Mr. CONSTANTINE. Not connected with any association. We hold membership in what is known as the Federation of Employers' Association of the Pacific Coast. That takes in the coast from here to San Diego.

Commissioner O'CONNELL. That takes in all the employers' associations on the Pacific coast?

Mr. CONSTANTINE. Yes, sir.

Commissioner O'CONNELL. You say you have a number of individuals or firms?

Mr. CONSTANTINE. Yes, sir; we have individual memberships. Our membership is open to anyone who believes in the principle of the open shop.

Commissioner O'CONNELL. You take in individuals who may not be employers?

Mr. CONSTANTINE. Yes, sir.

· Commissioner O'CONNELL. What is the per cent of those that you have?

Mr. CONSTANTINE. Quite small; almost negligible.

Commissioner O'CONNELL. What value would an individual be to your manufacturers' association?

Mr. CONSTANTINE. He is of no direct value to us other than perhaps he forms one more agent of publicity. Simply gives him an opportunity to support the work in which he believes.

Commissioner O'CONNELL. You say your association does not keep any record of any kind of the individual workingmen?

Mr. CONSTANTINE. It does not.

Commissioner O'CONNELL. Does your individual membership keep any record?

Mr. CONSTANTINE. I am not in position to say. I do not know.

Commissioner O'CONNELL. If an association affiliated with your organization, from San Francisco, we will say, wrote to you here for information as to whether John Brown was a strike agitator, or something, in this city,·would you furnish him or seek to furnish him that information?

Mr. CONSTANTINE. I would furnish him that information.

Commissioner O'CONNELL. How would you go about doing it?

Mr. CONSTANTINE. By finding his former employer.

Commissioner O'CONNELL. You would not have any record in your office you could immediately refer to?

Mr. CONSTANTINE. No, sir; I would not.

Commissioner O'CONNELL. How many employees have you in your office?

Mr. CONSTANTINE. In the office?

Commissioner O'CONNELL. Yes, sir; here.

Mr. CONSTANTINE. We have five now.

Commissioner O'CONNELL. They are engaged in what sort of employment? What do they do?

Mr. CONSTANTINE. Two of them do general work; we send them out in the State to answer calls on the part of employers.

Commissioner O'CONNELL. What would the employer be calling for, for instance? Cite some case.

Mr. CONSTANTINE. Well, we have a case—for instance, a man even sends in sometimes to ask us whether his machinery is conforming possibly with certain regulations of the State. Now, you would expect a member would take and have sense enough to go to the state department and inquire, but instead of that they will take and ask us for it. Sometimes they have impending trouble coming up with their laborers and ask for a representative to consult with them.

Commissioner O'CONNELL. Now, if a member of your association in the city of Seattle or somewhere else in your jurisdiction has a strike, do you immediately proceed to take part as an association in that strike?

Mr. CONSTANTINE. No, sir; we do not.

Commissioner O'CONNELL. They first call upon you for services?

Mr. CONSTANTINE. Yes; and he must prove his case is good.

Commissioner O'CONNELL. What do you mean by a good case?

Mr. CONSTANTINE. That his side of the question is right and fair.

Commissioner O'CONNELL. Suppose the men rebel against what you are pleased to call the open shop; do you proceed to defend him in that position?

Mr. CONSTANTINE. We would.

Commissioner O'CONNELL. And when a strike occurred, to what extent would you go to defend him?

Mr. CONSTANTINE. In the first place, we would probably meet and give him advice based on other cases we have been close to, and give him such assistance in the matter of information, and so on, that would be of value to him.

Commissioner O'CONNELL. Seek to furnish him employees if his people went on strike?

Mr. CONSTANTINE. We do, sometimes.

Commissioner O'CONNELL. And trained men to guard his plant, possibly?

Mr. CONSTANTINE. We are not in touch with those. We don't keep in touch with any group of trained men for any purpose of that kind.

Commissioner O'CONNELL. Do you compensate the employer in any way for losses?

Mr. CONSTANTINE. No, sir; that is not our practice. We have had cases where members of our association have solicited our assistance where we have found that the facts in the case were that the only question involved was a question of wages, and we have absolutely refused to have any part in a situation of that kind.

Commissioner O'CONNELL. Does your association believe in collective bargaining?

Mr. CONSTANTINE. As an association?

Commissioner O'CONNELL. Yes.

Mr. CONSTANTINE. Well, they are not committed as an association on the question.

Commissioner O'CONNELL. Does it object to members—does your constitution or by-laws in any way object to that on the part of the members?

Mr. CONSTANTINE. No, sir; it does not.

Commissioner O'CONNELL. Does it prohibit in any way the membership signing contracts that only members of a certain union shall be employed?

Mr. CONSTANTINE. It does not.

Commissioner O'CONNELL. What do you mean by " open shop "?

Mr. CONSTANTINE. By the " open shop " I mean that the efficiency alone is the basis of employment.

Commissioner O'CONNELL. Efficiency?

Mr. CONSTANTINE. Efficiency—efficiency and desirability.

Commissioner O'CONNELL. That is to say that the employer shall have the right without question to hire and discharge at will?

Mr. CONSTANTINE. Yes, sir; exactly.

Commissioner O'CONNELL. Would it be a sufficient cause if one of your employers operating a shop should discover that one of his employees was a member of a union, to discharge him—and the employee felt that was not sufficient cause, would you support your member in that contention?

Mr. CONSTANTINE. That in itself would not be—I would not consider that, and the organization would not consider that cause for discharge. It is unfortunate, however, that in a very large number of cases where employees were discharged because of existing incompetency, that their fellow workmen assumed that the discharge was because of his connection with the union and not because of his lack of efficiency.

Commissioner O'CONNELL. Have you ever suspended or fined a member of your association for not complying with your laws?

Mr. CONSTANTINE. We have not.

Commissioner O'CONNELL. Have you ever had any charges preferred against one of your members for failure to comply with your laws?

Mr. CONSTANTINE. We have not; not during my incumbency.

Commissioner O'CONNELL. You spoke of a kind of union that you think ought to be organized, a high standard—a union of high standard.

Mr. CONSTANTINE. Yes, sir.

Commissioner O'CONNELL. And you cited an instance, I think, as an ideal of a high standard of union. I take it you infer from that they are operating under an open shop, and that they don't have strikes.

Mr. CONSTANTINE. No, sir.

Commissioner O'CONNELL. And don't boycott, and so on.

Mr. CONSTANTINE. No; I am better acquainted with their history than that.

Commissioner O'CONNELL. I didn't know but what it was because they didn't strike.

Mr. CONSTANTINE. No, sir; they sometimes make unreasonable demands in arbitration, and so on.

Commissioner O'CONNELL. You say that legislation has been going on for some years for the alleviation of the laboring people and public generally, and that that isn't due to any one particular phase of society, and that the employers' association and the employers are becoming interested, indicating, to me at least, that they have taken some part in the direction of having these laws passed. Will you cite to me one law in the State of Washington or in the United States that the employers have gone before the legislature to seek to enact, if the law was toward alleviation in any way?

Mr. CONSTANTINE. I cite to you the industrial insurance act of the State of Washington.

Commissioner O'CONNELL. That is immaterial, because that has been going on many years in all the States.

Mr. CONSTANTINE. You said in the State of Washington, and I mentioned a law of the State of Washington.

Commissioner O'CONNELL. You say you maintained a lobby at the State capital the same as the other side did.

Mr. CONSTANTINE. You didn't understand me.

Commissioner O'CONNELL. I am not using your exact words.

Mr. CONSTANTINE. What I said was they maintained a legislative bureau in the capital of the State—Olympia.

Commissioner O'CONNELL. Well, a rose by any other name.

Mr. CONSTANTINE. I am distinguishing between the two, that is why.

Commissioner O'CONNELL. For what purpose do you maintain that particular body at the State capital?

Mr. CONSTANTINE. It does not consist of any body; it consists of one man.

Commissioner O'CONNELL. Representing a number of bodies?

Mr. CONSTANTINE. Representing the employers of the State.

Commissioner O'CONNELL. Do you seek to influence legislation in any way?

Mr. CONSTANTINE. We seek to influence legislation by seeking a hearing before committees and presenting our facts.

Commissioner O'CONNELL. Have you appeared in opposition to all measures in which the representatives of organized labor have appeared at the State capital?

Mr. CONSTANTINE. No, sir; appeared only in some.

Commissioner O'CONNELL. In some?

Mr. CONSTANTINE. Yes, sir.

Commissioner O'CONNELL. Have you appeared in any there, in favor of them, that labor was standing for?

Mr. CONSTANTINE. Our organization was in favor of the minimum-wage law for women when it was before the session of the last legislature. We favored it. We only suggested two amendments, both of which the legislature incorporated.

Commissioner O'CONNELL. Did your association send out letters of any kind during the meeting of the State legislature to the members or others supposed to have influence with the legislature seeking to influence them in any way?

Mr. CONSTANTINE. Our bureau up there has never sent out any circular letter to the legislature. Never sent out a single circular to their own members. We propose at the next session to send out weekly bulletins, which may be public property.

Commissioner O'CONNELL. That will be for the purpose of what?

Mr. CONSTANTINE. Of advising our members of the status of particular measures in which they may be interested.

Commissioner O'CONNELL. They might fall into the hands of others which they might enlighten?

Mr. CONSTANTINE. They always do. We expect it would.

Commissioner O'CONNELL. You say your association is not opposed to collective bargaining. Under this idea of the so-called open shop, how could collective bargaining be successful if 30 per cent or 20 per cent of the people were organized and 70 per cent or 80 per cent were not organized?

Mr. CONSTANTINE. If, as I said a few minutes ago, in order to belong to the organized 30 per cent, a man would have to have a certain degree of efficiency as a prerequisite to membership in that 30 per cent, then he commands the labor market and I have to employ him because I must have efficiency in my plant, and in that you would find the strength of organized labor.

Commissioner O'CONNELL. Do you believe it is possible for a workingman, as an individual, to increase his wages, to reduce his hours, and to improve his condition of employment to-day?

Mr. CONSTANTINE. We have a large number of plants—a number of plants right here in the city of Seattle, open-shop plants, where the wages are higher by the way than the prevailing scale in the same line of work gotten by unions.

Commissioner O'CONNELL. How was that brought about—by the organized men?

Mr. CONSTANTINE. No, sir.

Commissioner O'CONNELL. How was it brought about?

Mr. CONSTANTINE. It was brought about because the modern manufacturer believes in efficient labor, and he is willing to pay for it.

Commissioner O'CONNELL. Is it possible for the individual to make our day? Would we get that to-day?

Mr. CONSTANTINE. We have plants in this State operating on the eight-hour schedule.

Commissioner O'CONNELL. How did that come about?

Mr. CONSTANTINE. Of course in some of the large industries where we are in a large competitive field, particularly with States farther east, like the metal trades and lumber business, it would be suicidal for those lines of business to take and put them on an eight-hour basis.

Commissioner O'CONNELL. Suppose that in the lumber business it was perfectly justifiable to work eight hours and that it was possibly a success, and that it was the best thing physically for the employee, and that the employer could get the best possible results from it, and yet he wouldn't care to reduce the hours of labor under those conditions—would it be possible for the individual employee to bring about a reduction of hours?

Mr. CONSTANTINE. I should not say so.

Commissioner O'CONNELL. What is there left for him to do then?

Mr. CONSTANTINE. It is to organize, as I said right here. Just so long as he grants the man who does not desire to organize the right to remain free, and not otherwise. I have one or two papers I would like to introduce into the record, if I may.

Commissioner O'CONNELL. Yes, sir.

Mr. CONSTANTINE. I have one or two papers I should like to introduce in the record, if I may.

Acting Chairman COMMONS. Yes.

Mr. CONSTANTINE. I should like to read one page briefly. Here is a letter, gentlemen of the commission, that is sent out by one of the local unions recently, and it reads as follows. This is addressed to some retailer [reading]:

STOP! LOOK! LISTEN!

INTERNATIONAL BROTHERHOOD OF ELECTRICAL WORKERS,
Local Union No. 77, Seattle, Wash.

DEAR SIR: Very recently a business man in Seattle who has more than $10,000 invested in an enterprise signed a contract for two years with "The Electric Co.," legally known as the Puget Sound Traction, Light & Power Co. This company some years ago was declared unfair to organized labor in Seattle and vicinity. This man claims he did not know this fact. His receipts dropped to such an extent that in a short time he would have been compelled to go out of business. He investigated and found the cause. He thereupon applied to the Central Labor Council of Seattle and vicinity, and an investigation was made by a committee of said council. He claimed he did not know the facts, and the committee, believing him, relieved him of further loss by a report, the gist of which was published in the Union Record and Seattle Herald of recent date. He will in the future stop, look, and listen.

Do you wish to be placed in the same predicament without the excuse he gave? You can not say you did not know—this informs you of the fact that the Puget Sound Traction, Light & Power Co. is unfair to organized labor.

If you are using this unfair product of this unfair company and your receipts are not coming up to your expectations you will know the cause of at least a part of the lack of income.

If you are contemplating using electric light and power, it would be advisable to sign a contract with the city of Seattle—your own plant—for light and power. Every user of city light in any business is known to Local Union No. 77, International Brotherhood of Electrical Workers. They send communications to the other 105 affiliated unions, representing about 60,000 population in this city and vicinity, and they are always on the job. A word to the wise is sufficient. Don't afterwards say "I did not know" (it was loaded).

Stop! look! listen! For city light, your own plant and property, call Main 8500, Local 56, and a solicitor will be sent to you.

Yours, truly,

LOCAL UNION NO. 77, I. B. E. W.

(See also Constantine Exhibit No. 3.

The witness also presented a newspaper, the Seattle Union Record, vol. 30, No. 16, dated Seattle, Wash., May 2, 1914.)

Commissioner LENNON. I suppose that having held the position in organized labor that I have I must be classed amongst the undesirables. Why is that so? What is there in my life, for instance, that makes me undesirable as a citizen or as an officer in organized labor?

Mr. CONSTANTINE. Mr. Lennon——

Commissioner LENNON. My life is known to the people of this country, in Seattle, as well as elsewhere.

Mr. CONSTANTINE. It would not be fair to take and accuse me of making a statement that every man who has held the position you have held is undesirable.

Commissioner LENNON. What makes the man undesirable? What are the things that he will do as an officer of the labor organization that makes him undesirable that is not good for organized labor? Answer that for me.

Mr. CONSTANTINE. It is unfortunate, but in my judgment very true, that frequently the agent, meaning the officer, agent of the union being employed, as he is, to safeguard the interests of his members, finds it necessary in his own eyes to do things which show him useful to the men he serves. The result of that is that he is looking always for something wrong, more so than looking for what is right.

Commissioner LENNON. That is never true with the employers?

Mr. CONSTANTINE. That is true in cases of employers, too.

Commissioner LENNON. Who fixes the qualifications for membership of the unions?

Mr. CONSTANTINE. I don't find that in many cases any fixing of qualification exists.

Commissioner LENNON. Where do unions recruit their membership?

Mr. CONSTANTINE. From the immediately surrounding territory, as a rule, and the incoming men from other centers.

Commissioner LENNON. Do they not recruit their membership from the people who are employed in their industry or in their trade or in their craft?

Mr. CONSTANTINE. To a certain extent; yes.

Commissioner LENNON. Well, if that is true——

Mr. CONSTANTINE. And to some extent, no.

Commissioner LENNON. Then they have to take as members people that the employers give work to? The labor organization, in other words, is the only organization in the world that has to take as members the people who are selected by somebody else?

Mr. CONSTANTINE. That is quite true; only I want to cite a case, for instance, to illustrate what I have in mind. Take the bricklayers' union, which is skilled labor. I might be a bricklayer in some small jerkwater town, and I might be laying up common brick which is entirely satisfactory for a town of that size, for the job I am working on; and then there may be a local bricklayers' union there, and it would not take very much service in laying up brick in a small town like that for me to become a member of the union. It may be that sometime after that I desire to move my residence to a large city; and I procure a transfer card, and I find myself into the membership of this large union where much of the work in the city is skilled; and, perhaps, let us say, within a week after I get to that union there is a call for bricklayers, and I am sent out, and I find myself up against a number of skilled bricklayers. Now, as a rule, in that union, it forces other competent men, members of the union, to take and keep their output down to mine to protect them.

Commissioner LENNON. If this alleged bricklayer that is incompetent comes from a nonunion town, and a man erecting a building in Seattle hires. him, what choice has the union as to the membership if they desire to maintain their organization?

Mr. CONSTANTINE. Is it essential that they have him as a member?

Commissioner LENNON. I am not arguing with you. That is not my province.

Mr. CONSTANTINE. I am not trying to do that; I am trying to get your ques-. tion, Mr. Lennon.

Commissioner LENNON. Will you admit as members of your organization, of the employers' organization, all the employers in a given industry?

Mr. CONSTANTINE. Provided they believed in open-shop rule.

Commissioner LENNON. Well, it would not be an open shop so far as the employers of the industry were concerned if everyone was in?

Mr. CONSTANTINE. Except we have not got—we are not in position to enforce upon the public that they buy all of their product from these particular manufacturers.

Commissioner LENNON. That is all.

Commissioner GARRETSON. You made the statement a moment ago that employers heretofore had been inactive in legislation; that the campaign of laboring men had gone on unopposed, but that for the future the manufacturers were going to take an aggressive position. Did I understand you correctly?

Mr. CONSTANTINE. I was speaking of legislation affecting the welfare of the employees at the time.

- Commissioner GARRETSON. What might be called social legislation?

Mr. CONSTANTINE. Yes; exactly.

Commissioner GARRETSON. I suppose you are familiar with the history of social legislation of this country?

Mr. CONSTANTINE. More or less.

Commissioner GARRETSON. How far back did the labor man of this country succeed in passing any social legislation?

Mr. CONSTANTINE. I made the statement, I think, to the effect that within the last 10 years the bulk of legislation of that nature has been passed.

Commissioner GARRETSON. Can you mention any specific act preceding that time?

Mr. CONSTANTINE. Not offhand.

Commissioner GARRETSON. Then, the activity of the labor man regarding social legislation did not adopt any particular form up until that time?

Mr. CONSTANTINE. Either that is part of the explanation, or the attempt had not been made as strong as it has been for the last 10 years.

Commissioner GARRETSON. How about the preceding 500 years to that time?

Mr. CONSTANTINE. Why, the attempt wasn't there as much as it has been in the last 10 years.

Commissioner GARRETSON. Preceding that 10 years has there ever been any record of legislation in any English-speaking country secured by labor outside of the factory acts of England?

Mr. CONSTANTINE. Not very much.

Commissioner GARRETSON. Then, the employer has had from the beginning of time virtually his innings, and now you assume labor has had 10 years, and you are going to start an aggressive campaign against it?

Mr. CONSTANTINE. Don't misquote me. I don't think you understood me. I said we are now becoming aggressive, working hand in hand with them, not against them.

Commissioner GARRETSON. Oh, hand in hand.

Mr. CONSTANTINE. Yes.

Commissioner GARRETSON. That is different. That is better than hand in pocket, isn't it? You spoke of this magnificent attitude of the railway brotherhood. I suppose you are familiar with the method of dealing of the railway brotherhoods with their employers?

Mr. CONSTANTINE. I am.

Commissioner GARRETSON. Are you aware of the fact you spoke of three brotherhoods? I don't know what grudge you had against the other one, because there are four of them.

Mr. CONSTANTINE. I am glad to include the fourth.

Commissioner GARRETSON. What?

Mr. CONSTANTINE. I am glad to include the fourth, and include more, too, if

Commissioner GARRETSON. Well, I didn't know but what you excepted the one that I belong to.

Mr. CONSTANTINE. That is probably the one that I forgot.

Commissioner GARRETSON. Are you aware of the attitude that these organizations, all four of them, take when they walk into the offices of their employers to determine wage?

Mr. CONSTANTINE. I have never been present at such an occasion.

Commissioner GARRETSON. Are you aware of the fact—I will take my own organization, called the Order of Railway Conductors—that when they walk into the general manager's office of the Northern Pacific Railway, you know who it assumes to deal for?

Mr. CONSTANTINE. For its members.

Commissioner GARRETSON. No, sir; for every conductor in the service of the Northern Pacific Railway.

Mr. CONSTANTINE. Well, that is good enough.

Commissioner GARRETSON. Members and nonmembers. We deal for every man on the line. Now, do you know the restriction we place on the man who is not a member? We are open shop, as you have quoted, but we don't let him work for less than we do. Are you aware of that?

Mr. CONSTANTINE. Yes, sir.

Commissioner GARRETSON. We sign an agreement for the company for every man who performs that service that he gets the stated rate of pay. Therefore a nonunion man is perfectly welcome to work there, but he can't work for less than the scale nor can he make any private agreement with the company. There is the position of those four brotherhoods on that basis. We do not recognize—are you aware of the fact that we do not recognize the right of the individual to deal for either his wage or conditions on a railway—the four brotherhoods?

Mr. CONSTANTINE. Why, I could not picture to myself where the 5 or 10 per cent would ever attempt to demand anything of the kind.

Commissioner GARRETSON. Oh, you have got the percentage too high; there are not near that many.

Mr. CONSTANTINE. Two per cent is closer to it.

Commissioner GARRETSON. It is closer.

Mr. CONSTANTINE. Yes, sir.

Commissioner GARRETSON. You used the phrase—I believe this was the phrase verbatim: "The man must be permitted to sell his property—that is, his brain and brawn—without the intervention of a third party." That is the attitude of your association?

Mr. CONSTANTINE. Yes, sir.

Commissioner GARRETSON. Don't that mean that you assert the right of the employer to buy his brain and brawn without the intervention of a third party?

Mr. CONSTANTINE. No; it does not.

Commissioner GARRETSON. Isn't that what it works out?

Mr. CONSTANTINE. No; it is not.

Commissioner GARRETSON. If you can keep him dealing on his own basis without the intervention of the third party, you won't need any aggressive—would you need any aggressive legislative campaign, hand in hand? Would you?

Mr. CONSTANTINE. I don't know if I exactly care to——

Commissioner GARRETSON. If you can keep him as an individual without the intervention of a third party, whether of his own class or not, you don't need any legislation to keep him under, do you?

Mr. CONSTANTINE. I don't know as I care to——

Commissioner GARRETSON. Oh, I would not want you to convict yourself.

Mr. CONSTANTINE. Yes, sir.

Commissioner GARRETSON. I suppose the slogan of your association is like that of many others—that you are engaged in upholding the God-given American right of a man to work when he wants to, regardless of what his wage is?

Mr. CONSTANTINE. It is his right, we believe, in that every man has the right to work as he chooses under conditions as he desires for such price as he desires.

Commissioner GARRETSON. And his right to remain unorganized?

Mr. CONSTANTINE. He has the right to remain unorganized; yes, sir; it is his privilege.

Commissioner GARRETSON. And then you immediately proceed to organize to see that he has the right to stay unorganized?

Mr. Constantine. Oh, we don't take and compel those who don't care to join us.

Commissioner Garretson. What is the difference between the boycott that you complain of on the part of the labor man in refusing to buy an article and the assertion of the right to hire and fire any man that you want to, regardless of cause, as long as he performs his work right? What is the difference between boycotting goods and boycotting humans?

Mr. Constantine. Because the boycott is frequently performed, most frequently, by parties that are not directly interested.

Commissioner Garretson. How is that?

Mr. Constantine. The boycott is most frequently practiced by the party that is not interested.

Commissioner Garretson. By the party that is not interested. They are at least interested to the extent that they don't want to buy the goods for a certain reason, whatever it may be.

Mr. Constantine. They are simply sent down by droves without knowing why they are going, and they are just simply going to damage this man's property.

Commissioner Garretson. But what has boycott got to do with damaging a man's property? It is refusing to buy property.

Mr. Constantine. That is what I mean; that is damaging.

Commissioner Garretson. If a man can't make a product that enough people want to use—to induce them to buy it—where does the speculative chance lie, with him or with them?

Mr. Constantine. When you boycott a product you naturally reduce the value of that product in the market.

Commissioner Garretson. And if it ought to be reduced, what then? I know a lot of properties that would be better off if their value was reduced.

Mr. Constantine. I am speaking of normal conditions. I am not speaking of abnormal conditions.

Commissioner Garretson. Oh! Has a man the right to refuse to purchase goods that don't suit him?

Mr. Constantine. He has.

Commissioner Garretson. If one under our laws—is it a crime for two men to do what one can legally do?

Mr. Constantine. It is.

Commissioner Garretson. Just in the boycott?

Mr. Constantine. No.

Commissioner Garretson. What laws? How does the conspiracy law read?

Mr. Constantine. The same thing is true in the monopolizing of manufacturing.

Commissioner Garretson. Don't the conspiracy act read that it is not a crime for men to do collectively what any of them can do individually lawfully?

Mr. Constantine. Well, it is just as unlawful to do it collectively as to do it individually.

Commissioner Garretson. Who has secured the decisions that exist, or the laws that exist in regard to boycott? Did you ever hear of the laborers trying to get them?

Mr. Constantine. To get laws against boycotting?

Commissioner Garretson. Yes.

Mr. Constantine. Why, of course not.

Commissioner Garretson. Sure not, and still they dominate legislation.

Mr. Constantine. Of course not.

Commissioner Garretson. Did you ever hear of labor trying to get further injunctional legislation enacted?

Mr. Constantine. No. I have heard of their trying to get class legislation enacted under the Clayton bill.

Commissioner Garretson. They have succeeded in some degree, haven't they?

Mr. Constantine. Yes, sir.

Commissioner Garretson. Have you ever had any request from nonunionized labor asking you to represent their rights?

Mr. Constantine. We have.

Commissioner Garretson. Could you file them with this commission?

Mr. Constantine. What do you mean?

Commissioner Garretson. Credentials that you are authorized to represent the unorganized laboring men of the Republic?

Mr. Constantine. I am speaking of individuals.

Commissioner Garretson. Oh, well, can you file any individual requests?

Mr. CONSTANTINE. We don't keep records of any, but we have had such records as the man coming in with tears streaming down his eyes, and telling his story, and that is a better record to carry in your mind than any record that you might have in black and white.

Commissioner GARRETSON. Yes. You heard about the man that had a million in his mind and lost his mind and went broke.

Mr. CONSTANTINE. It is not in the literature that I have read.

Commissioner GARRETSON. Well, I got it in the daily press that it was so.

Mr. CONSTANTINE. Maybe so.

Commissioner GARRETSON. Your position in regard to labor leaders being responsible for the present unrest—I suppose if that holds good at the present day, it ought to hold good throughout the most of the unrest of the ages, wouldn't it?

Mr. CONSTANTINE. I suppose so. It is probably a matter of degree. The degree is larger to-day.

Commissioner GARRETSON. How about the labor leaders preceding the French Revolution?

Mr. CONSTANTINE. I am not—I am more interested in present conditions than I am in that period.

Commissioner GARRETSON. There are people who have written that the security of the future lies in the history of the past. Were there any labor leaders then?

Mr. CONSTANTINE. There probably were.

Commissioner GARRETSON. Dead or alive?

Mr. CONSTANTINE. Well——

Commissioner GARRETSON. Under that régime would they have lasted?

Mr. CONSTANTINE. I don't know, sir.

Commissioner GARRETSON. Well, in regard to your position legislatively, do you spend any money in elections of candidates? Do you approve of it?

Mr. CONSTANTINE. We do not.

Commissioner GARRETSON. Do you make any effort to influence the make-up of committees of the State legislature?

Mr. CONSTANTINE. We do not.

Commissioner GARRETSON. Haven't any members under obligations to you by favors conferred or loans granted?

Mr. CONSTANTINE. Loans granted—no, sir.

Commissioner GARRETSON. You aren't in full sympathy, then, with some other manufacturers' associations?

Mr. CONSTANTINE. I imagine I would not be.

Commissioner GARRETSON. Do the labor unions in this State, through their labor lobby, exercise or endeavor to exercise—I won't put it exercise; I will put it endeavor to exercise—any greater or more legitimate influences than your association?

Mr. CONSTANTINE. I can only state at the last session they maintained all the way from 20 to 30 or more agents present at the legislature for a period of about two months. Now, as to just what influence those 20 to 30 had down there, I, of course, am not in a position to say.

Commissioner GARRETSON. How many did you maintain?

Mr. CONSTANTINE. I was down there alone, with two helpers in the office, and we went on the theory that where in the past the employers had everlastingly been down to the legislature in droves and had pestered the lives out of the legislators, that we would try to create a condition where the employers stayed away from the legislative session, except as some particular case came up which was of interest to him, and we advised them from our bureau and called them to Olympia as the case demanded.

Commissioner GARRETSON. Have they ever at any time in the history of legislation in the State of Washington—have employers ever compelled their employees to go to Olympia to give testimony with regard to the proposed legislation that was utterly opposed—where their testimony was opposed to the interests of labor in general?

Mr. CONSTANTINE. Not to my knowledge.

Commissioner GARRETSON. Have you ever endeavored to acquire knowledge of that subject?

Mr. CONSTANTINE. I should think that in my work, if there was anything of that kind going on, it would come to my knowledge before it would to anybody else's.

Commissioner GARRETSON. Well, if you haven't knowledge of that fact, let me commend you to a study of that subject.

Mr. CONSTANTINE. I have studied it for some time.

Commissioner GARRETSON. That is all, Mr. Chairman.

Acting Chairman COMMONS. Mr. Constantine, have you any knowledge of the enforcement of the factory-inspection laws in this State?

Mr. CONSTANTINE. Why, the factory-inspection laws, the enforcement of them, is in such cases, Mr. Chairman, dependent on the energy of the man who is administering them. I think that to-day the factory-inspection laws are being enforced probably more fully than ever before. Within the last six months there has been a very great movement on the part of both the metal trades and State labor commissioner, working jointly, to enforce the laws more fully, provide more safety devices on the machinery, and even it has gone to the extent where the State labor commissioner has created safety committees in a large number of factories. I think over two hundred-odd factories have safety committees of three employees, whose duty it is to watch the machinery in the plant and to make such recommendations as they think will make the working conditions safer.

Acting Chairman COMMONS. Your association has cooperated in that work?

Mr. CONSTANTINE. Our association has cooperated in that work. As soon as we heard that that was being done we wrote a letter to our members and approved of it and told them to assist in that.

Acting Chairman COMMONS. Do you approve of the class of men that have held office in the past years in the enforcement of labor laws?

Mr. CONSTANTINE. I have only been acquainted with the present incumbent and his predecessor. My judgment of both men is that they are men of high quality. We have differences on anything and everything except the enforcement of laws. We have always worked absolutely in harmony with them; never had any occasion to work any different. There has been no friction whatever between our association and the State labor commissioners.

Acting Chairman COMMONS. That is true also of these new laws that are being enacted under the head of minimum wage?

Mr. CONSTANTINE. The same thing would apply to those.

Acting Chairman COMMONS. Your association has cooperated?

Mr. CONSTANTINE. Exactly.

Acting Chairman COMMONS. Does your association include the metal trades?

Mr. CONSTANTINE. Yes, sir.

Acting Chairman COMMONS. That is a constituent part of the larger association?

Mr. CONSTANTINE. Yes, sir. In other words, we do not probably have all the metal trades members, but we have a majority of them—the large majority of them.

Acting Chairman COMMONS. I take it your position is that hitherto, up until recently, the laborers have used their political influence to get legislation bearing upon the employer—interfering with his business. Now that you consider that the employers are entitled to organize and defend themselves also, you are taking a step in advance of that, not only to defend yourselves against what you consider unfair acts, but you have actually gone ahead and taken the initiative in certain measures which you seem to be rightful in behalf of labor, either organized or unorganized?

Mr. CONSTANTINE. The condition in the State of Washington is very parallel to the condition, I would say, in the most of the States of the Union in the last 10 years. It is also true that when you swing a pendulum it is likely to swing one way more than it is best for all concerned. It has swung within the last several years, I would say, to a point where it has been disadvantageous to industry and business, and there is a feeling of fear on the part of industry to-day, both in the State of Washington and other States of the country, as we find it. And that is due in part to legislation enacted and in part to impending legislation, particularly such legislation as covers the eight-hour day, which is impending on November 4 in this State. It means, as I have said before, suicide to some of our industries that simply can not operate on an eight-hour day and compete with the competitive field. It would be only natural, then, that where any dispute of that kind exists there should be a large degree of hesitancy or fear on the part of the employer, and retrenchment. That retrenchment, perhaps, has been in part some of the unemployment existing to-day.

Acting Chairman COMMONS. Do you feel, for example, that the workmen's compensation law has put a burden on the employers of Washington higher than of other States?

Mr. CONSTANTINE. The compensation law generally is on an average a higher expense to the employer than the premiums paid previously to the insurance companies. However, in my judgment, practically every employer in the State of Washington is satisfied with the compensation law, and would not return to the old system, partly because all of the benefits of the act go directly to the hands of the man injured, or his widow and children, where formerly a large portion of them necessarily went into the hands of unscrupulous attorneys.

Acting Chairman COMMONS. Now, take interstate competition, is that true in that case also?

Mr. CONSTANTINE. That that is satisfactory?

Acting Chairman COMMONS. Yes.

Mr. CONSTANTINE. Yes; lumber is our main industry, and the lumbermen are satisfied with that.

Acting Chairman COMMONS. That is satisfactory to the lumber industry?

Mr. CONSTANTINE. Yes, sir. We, of course, have individual cases—individual manufacturers who would go back to the old basis—individual manufacturers who are not satisfied with the rates to-day, and so on. But, generally speaking, there is satisfaction—it is satisfactory to both employers and employees.

Acting Chairman COMMONS. Has your association taken up any other measures than this one, of which you have spoken, for the promotion of better industrial conditions?

Mr. CONSTANTINE. Well, I may mention off-hand, we had a measure drafted at the last session of the legislature to remedy some of the evils that exist in employment agencies. It was a remedial measure instead of a measure which was proposed by labor wanting to do away entirely with the fee agents. Our position was that employment agencies are to-day serving a purpose efficiently, and that our industry could not afford to do without them. We recognized, however, there were certain attending evils that had grown up in the trade in many years past, and that were wrong and should be remedied, and our measure was intended to remedy those.

Acting Chairman COMMONS. What is your knowledge and observation regarding the free employment offices in this State?

Mr. CONSTANTINE. The free employment offices generally are not used by the employer. That is true for several reasons. I will mention a few of them. We have in the city of Seattle several employment agencies that specialize in the kind of labor they supply. For instance, here is an agency that probably 90 per cent of its business is the supplying of labor for railroad construction, and here is another one that specializes in supplying labor for lumber camps, and the ordinary supply of labor for the metal trades, although the metal trades mostly employ their men directly. Now, these agencies become after years very well acquainted with the labor field of that particular trade. They know those men personally. They know whether they are fit and able or not, and as the result the employers in that line of business go to that particular agency in order to get their help. Now, such is the personality on the part of the employment agent and the man who is doing the work that it would be impossible in a public office, is impossible in a public office, to have that advantage, because of the frequent shiftings of the personnel in that office. The result is that while the agent in a public office may get to know his field for a year or two, why, it is likely that he may be either promoted out of business or be dropped out of office, and an ignorant man comes in there.

Acting Chairman COMMONS. What class of supervision do you propose for these private offices, by law, which you have originated?

Mr. CONSTANTINE. Well, where a man is sent out, for instance, to a job out of town without the employment agent being fully satisfied that the position really exists there, and the man is at a loss then for his fare to and from as well as his fee, we had a provision that not only would he be refunded his fare and refunded his fee, but there would be a case of misdemeanor, and action in court would rest. Although there were different abuses, we had them made misdemeanors and provided for legal redress on the part of the man injured.

Acting Chairman COMMONS. Your idea is if the private offices were abolished altogether, you would not have the assistance necessary in these public offices?

Mr. CONSTANTINE. No; it is not. My opinion is that if the private offices are abolished that there would be created more public offices, but at the same time I believe that organizations such as ours would be compelled to maintain free employment bureaus as an adjunct of their work. We would probably have to maintain an employment bureau where we would employ men without charge, without any fee. I believe that that would be one of the results of the abolishment of the regular employment agencies.

Acting Chairman COMMONS. That is, that you would be compelled to establish an employment office?

Mr. CONSTANTINE. Yes.

Acting Chairman COMMONS. Of the employers' association?

Mr. CONSTANTINE. Yes; and that would be true of other employers' organizations.

Acting Chairman COMMONS. Is there anything further you wish to say?

Mr. CONSTANTINE. No; nothing further that I know of.

Acting Chairman COMMONS. With regard to any of the other measures that your association has promoted?

Mr. CONSTANTINE. I have nothing particular just now to mention.

Acting Chairman COMMONS. Mr. Thompson, any questions?

Mr. THOMPSON. I have a question or two, Mr. Chairman. What has been the attitude of your association in regard to the enactment of the women's eight-hour law and child-labor law; did they furnish funds for carrying on the bureau of labor?

Mr. CONSTANTINE. My contact with legislation at Olympia is only since the last session of the legislature. I am not in position to answer the question. I wish I were.

Mr. THOMPSON. Well, did your association take any attitude on the subject of the eight-hour law for women?

Mr. CONSTANTINE. Well, so far as I know, from the records as I found them, no attitude has been taken at all in the matter. I believe that a larger number of employers were more fearful of the passage of such a measure at the time than history has proven that they were justified in.

Mr. THOMPSON. What attitude is your association taking to legislation now pending, with regard to the pending legislation for first aid?

Mr. CONSTANTINE. The pending legislation for first aid, or the initiative for first aid, is one which provides that the whole cost of the same shall devolve upon the employer. As I said a minute ago in answer to the chairman of the commission, the expense to the employer under the compensation act is higher to-day as a whole than the premiums that they paid to the insurance companies formerly. Now, the first aid as now proposed would be an additional burden to that cost on the part of the employer, and the estimates that we make show that that will run between 50 and as high as 100 per cent additional cost.

I think the attitude of most employers is that when we get first aid that some part of the expense of that first aid—it need not be a large part, but some part of the expense of that first aid should be contributed by the man who benefits from it, not so much because of the total fund it would create, because that would be negligible, but because of the fact that it brings in the element of responsibility and of cost and of care on the part of the employee which otherwise would naturally be absent to a great extent.

Acting Chairman COMMONS. Mr. Constantine, what is your proposed first aid? What do you mean by that; I don't understand it?

Mr. CONSTANTINE. That is attention to the injured in industry—sickness.

Acting Chairman COMMONS. Is it simply a provision that the employer shall pay the medical costs?

Mr. CONSTANTINE. Yes, sir; pay all the costs of first aid.

Acting Chairman COMMONS. Then it has not——

Mr. CONSTANTINE. It has not the waiting period provided; it provides for no waiting period.

Acting Chairman COMMONS. Well, isn't that cared for in the existing law?

Mr. CONSTANTINE. No; we don't have any first-aid feature to our compensation.

Acting Chairman COMMONS. It is simply compensation for time lost?

Mr. CONSTANTINE. It simply compensates for——

Acting Chairman COMMONS. And the injured pays his own medical expenses?

Mr. CONSTANTINE. Well, the compensation covers a variety of classes. There is the temporary total-disability class, temporary partial disability, permanent partial disability, and, of course, death cases. That covers those four classes in particular. I have some tables and reports I thought might be valuable.

Acting Chairman COMMONS. But it does not cover hospital and medical assistance?

Mr. CONSTANTINE. No; it does not.

Acting Chairman COMMONS. The employee pays for that himself?

Mr. CONSTANTINE. Yes, sir.

Mr. THOMPSON. I have in my hands, Mr. Constantine, a pamphlet entitled "Workmen's Compulsory Compensation System a Proved Failure and a Business Menace."

Mr. CONSTANTINE. Yes, sir.

Mr. THOMPSON. Apparently written by J. V. Paterson, president of the Seattle Construction & Dry Dock Co., Seattle, Wash. There is no date on that, but it is a statement of reasons against the compensation law.

Mr. CONSTANTINE. Yes, sir.

Mr. THOMPSON. Is the position taken by Mr. Paterson at the time he wrote that the same as the position he occupies to-day, and to what extent does that document express the opinion of a section of the employer class here, if you know?

Mr. CONSTANTINE. It perhaps expresses the opinion of a certain percentage. I would not say what percentage. But, as I said, generally speaking, the manufacturers approve the bill. That pamphlet was issued, I think, about two years ago. I don't know just what Mr. Paterson's position is to-day, although I am inclined to think it is about the same as it was at that time.

Mr. THOMPSON. Have you got extra copies, or could you furnish them?

Mr. CONSTANTINE. I could furnish them. I haven't got them in my office, but I will get them from Mr. Paterson.

Mr. THOMPSON. If you will, please, because this is only loaned to me. That is all, Mr. Chairman.

(The pamphlet referred to by Mr. Constantine, entitled "Workmen's Compulsory Compensation System, State of Washington," by J. V. Paterson, president Seattle Construction & Dry Dock Co., Seattle, Wash., was subsequently submitted in printed form.)

Mr. CONSTANTINE. Would you care, Mr. Chairman, for these blanks?

Mr. THOMPSON. Yes; if you will file them.

(The papers referred to, entitled "Bulletin No. 4, Statistical Review of the First Eighteen Months' Operation of the Workmen's Compensation Act," "Statement of Awards on Account of Injuries," year from October 1, 1912, to October 1, 1913, and "Statement of Accident Fund on October 1, 1913," all issued by the Industrial Insurance Commission of the State of Washington, were submitted in printed form.)

Acting Chairman COMMONS. Call your next.

TESTIMONY OF MR. GEORGE N. SKINNER.

Mr. THOMPSON. Mr. Skinner, give us your name, please.

Mr. SKINNER. George N. Skinner.

Mr. THOMPSON. Your business address?

Mr. SKINNER. 747 Central Building, Pier 3.

Mr. THOMPSON. Your business?

Mr. SKINNER. Wholesale lumber business and shipping. I operate some freight boats on the Sound.

Mr. THOMPSON. Do you also have the position of president of the Employers' Association of Washington?

Mr. SKINNER. Yes, sir.

Mr. THOMPSON. How long have you held that position, Mr. Skinner?

Mr. SKINNER. Since February.

Mr. THOMPSON. This year?

Mr. SKINNER. Yes, sir.

Mr. THOMPSON. Have you been a member of the board of directors or trustee before that time?

Mr. SKINNER. Yes, sir.

Mr. THOMPSON. For how long?

Mr. SKINNER. For some three years.

Mr. THOMPSON. How long have you been engaged in business in Seattle, Mr. Skinner?

Mr. SKINNER. About six years.

Mr. THOMPSON. Six years. From your position as an employer of labor here, and also as an official and officer of the Employers' Association of Washington, have you had occasion to study the industrial problems in this vicinity?

Mr. SKINNER. To some extent.

Mr. THOMPSON. What is your view of the unrest here? If there is any, what is its cause and what might be done to ameliorate it, lessen it?

Mr. SKINNER. Business conditions have more to do, I think, with the condition of unrest at the present time than anything else—lack of demand for help.

Mr. THOMPSON. Well, take the general situation apart from these few months past and take the general situation the last few years, as you have known it, the unrest.

Mr. SKINNER. We have had this same condition prevailing out here a great deal of the time during the last five years, particularly in the lumber business.

Mr. THOMPSON. Now, then, if business was fair, would there be no unrest industrially speaking; you think labor would be satisfied and there would be peace and harmony between employer and employee?

Mr. SKINNER. There would alwaye be more or less unrest on account of this being the big labor market of this section, the coming and going of a vast number of laborers to Alaska. People are induced to come here from all sections of the world expecting that they will find employment, and there is not enough employment even during normal conditions to employ everybody that comes here. It is like the immigrant coming to New York—they have to get away from New York before they get through. And here they go back east and south or different directions.

Mr. THOMPSON. Have you any views, Mr. Skinner, of the value and utility of the closed shop and the open shop as such?

Mr. SKINNER. Only from the experience that we have had in comparing conditions where ideal closed-shop conditions have prevailed; it has destroyed the industries and driven very largely the industries out of business.

Mr. THOMPSON. What industries have you in mind, Mr. Skinner?

Mr. SKINNER. Well, I have more particularly in mind the condition in San Francisco.

Mr. THOMPSON. You have been in business there?

Mr. SKINNER. What do you say?

Mr. THOMPSON. Have you made a study of conditions there?

Mr. SKINNER. Well, I have to some extent.

Mr. THOMPSON. Have you been in business there?

Mr. SKINNER. Through inquiry, and having been there, and so on.

Mr. THOMPSON. Have you ever worked a shop with the open shop?

Mr. SKINNER. My employment is entirely open shop. In fact, I never have asked, however, whether my people employed are union or nonunion men. In the boat business, that I am in, the engineers are pretty generaly organized, but I have never taken occasion to ask my office to employ only nonunion or union men. They are never taken into account.

Mr. THOMPSON. Have you any views as to the efficiency, comparative efficiency, of those two forms of organizations?

Mr. SKINNER. Well, I would assume that where employment is forced upon an employer, that the efficiency would naturally be lacking to some extent; personal effort—if that was entirely necessary to get the man the compensation that he thought was justly due him, he would be very apt to labor with a different idea in mind, and to better advantage.

Mr. THOMPSON. What view do you take of the organization of labor as such?

Mr. SKINNER. I believe in the organization of labor if the union is properly conducted.

Mr. THOMPSON. What suggestions have you to make to this condition, as to the way they should be organized so as to be properly conducted?

Mr. SKINNER. I think that the conduct of the labor unions should be entirely within the scope of the man that works, the man that is interested in his labor, and I think that they should be made responsible on both sides, and that both sides might have some of it.

Mr. THOMPSON. What form of responsibility? Have you given thought to that—what that might be?

Mr. SKINNER. The law should prescribe that anything that the labor unions entered into, if they entered into a contract with the employer, that they must carry it out or be penalized financially. They would have to organize, take out a charter, and pay a sufficient amount of capital to guarantee the enforcement of their contract, the living up to the contract.

Mr. THOMPSON. In other words, they should be incorporated?

Mr. SKINNER. Yes, sir.

Mr. THOMPSON. That is what you meant by taking out a charter?

Mr. SKINNER. Yes, sir.

Mr. THOMPSON. In your opinion, that would help a lot toward making labor more responsible?

Mr. SKINNER. I have no doubt that there are lots of things that laboring people do during disputes and times of trouble that they would not resort to if they were responsible.

Mr. THOMPSON. Have you in mind any specific thing they have done in times of trouble that because of lack of financial responsibility they would not have done otherwise?

Mr. SKINNER. You are all familiar, of course, with the methods that they have employed all over the country. We have had a recent exhibition right here in our teamsters' strike.

Mr. THOMPSON. What I want to get at——

Mr. SKINNER. Destruction of property.

Mr. THOMPSON. Destruction of property?

Mr. SKINNER. Destruction of property, and violence.

Mr. THOMPSON. That would be separate responsibility of private contract, of course.

Mr. SKINNER. That would be a part of the contract, wouldn't it?

Mr. THOMPSON. Well, hardly. I take it where you make a contract, agreeing to do certain things, a failure to carry out the contract would be, I think. Of course, if other things, if they did other things also, acts of violence like destruction of property and injury, that would bind still further by noncontractual liability, of course. Have you any idea as to what should be done in cases of breakdown of the civil law, like in Michigan and West Virginia, where they have had civil government absolutely broken down in the last two years because of the difference between employer and employee with regard to their relationship? What suggestion would you make in regard to that situation as a whole?

Mr. SKINNER. I think it is up to the police power of the State. I think that both the employer and the men are entitled to protection.

Mr. THOMPSON. That is after the trouble has arisen, if you have any such condition of civilization, or lack of it, that there is a conflict, what would you do or what would you suggest to prevent the coming of such a condition where troops have to come in and martial law has to be declared, or have you given any thought to that?

Mr. SKINNER. No, sir; I don't think I have.

Mr. THOMPSON. Have you heard the testimony of Mr. Constantine here?

Mr. SKINNER. Yes; but I can't hear readily enough to hear much of it. I could not understand much of it.

Mr. THOMPSON. Is there anything you would like to add to that which you did hear, as to what he said about your association or the general industrial situation in the city of Seattle?

Mr. SKINNER. I think Mr. Constantine covered the subject pretty thoroughly, and I am willing to subscribe to it. I am willing to subscribe to, I believe, all of it, because I know what his views are on all of these different subjects.

Mr. THOMPSON. And generally you are in accord with him?

Mr. SKINNER. Yes.

Mr. THOMPSON. Is that true also of the workmen's compensation law?

Mr. SKINNER. What is that?

Mr. THOMPSON. Is that true also of the workmen's compensation law in this State?

Mr. SKINNER. Yes; I was present when the compensation law was passed in Olympia, and we, the manufacturers of the State, were in favor of a compensation law, and argued for it before the committee.

Mr. THOMPSON. What was the stand or general attitude of the manufacturers and other employers on this eight-hour law for women, if you know? What opinion have you on that?

Mr. SKINNER. My impression is our own people did not offer any objection to it. We were not interested, our industry, at that time, in the employers' association.

Mr. THOMPSON. Have you got any opinion about the advisability of such legislation in industry?

Mr. SKINNER. I approve of it.

Mr. THOMPSON. Is that the general attitude of employers, as you follow them?

Mr. SKINNER. I think so, as far as mine are concerned.

Mr. THOMPSON. Have you any idea as to what might be done to assist and help the present machinery for the adjustment of industrial disputes? Do you think, for instance, such an institution as a Federal industrial council would help in preventing trouble? You heard what I said to Mr. Constantine about that.

Mr. SKINNER. I think a properly constituted arbitration board would be effective, without any prejudice.

Mr. THOMPSON. Is there anything else, Mr. Skinner, which you would like to say to the commission——

Mr. SKINNER. I don't know.

Mr. THOMPSON. Touching the industrial problems?

Mr. SKINNER. I don't know of anything in particular.

Acting Chairman COMMONS. Mr. Skinner, I think the Washington law on the compensation question is substantially an absolute insurance system, isn't it, in which the employers are required to contribute? Did your association favor that sort of an arrangement?

Mr. SKINNER. Yes, sir; we used our influence to get the law—we used our influence to have the law enacted.

Acting Chairman COMMONS. It has worked out satisfactorily, hasn't it, in that respect?

Mr. SKINNER. Yes; I think pretty generally.

Acting Chairman COMMONS. Has it brought about a reduction in the accidents; that is, the safeguards which the employers have installed in order to reduce the premiums they have to pay?

Mr. SKINNER. Well, I am not posted what the conditions are in that respect. I know that for a time, so far as the application that is made for relief was concerned, it was very much larger than had been reported. There were no records we could get at previously. Then, I think that for a time the experience was different; that the accidents were more limited. But I understand this year there is an increase again. To what extent I do not know, because I have not had the figures.

Acting Chairman COMMONS. In general, would you say that the employers of this State are satisfied with the law?

Mr. SKINNER. I think so, as a rule, and also with the movement to safeguard. There have been movements in the State during the past year to use extra precautions, put new safeguards on, and they have been generally in accord with that, so far as we know in our association. The metal trades have been very active; the employers of the metal-trade association here have been very active in helping to get for the commissioner of labor in the State the cooperation of all of the manufacturing industries in the State to put in these devices.

Acting Chairman COMMONS. Considerng the extent of unemployment that you have mentioned and the conditions here, would you think that there should be a better organization, a stronger central organization of employment offices, and that the offices should contribute or cooperate with each other in exchanging information? Have you thought of any way by which you could improve industrial conditions?

Mr. SKINNER. It would depend on so many things.

Acting Chairman COMMONS. Merely making the labor market more accessible—have you considered whether your association might properly take up and establish the employment offices and cooperate in that way?

Mr. SKINNER. I think our association would only be induced to undertake that provided the employment agencies were done away with and politics entered into the conduct of such employment agencies as was started by the State.

Acting Commissioner COMMONS. You are familiar with the employment offices that are conducted by the city around here?

Mr. SKINNER. Well, in a way. I never have had the same difficulty with the other employment agencies they had—private employment agencies. Just the other day we had a complaint that some people had gone in, and it had been represented to them that they could get work at a certain place, and five or six of them went down there and paid their fare and could not get positions and came back. I don't know whether that was intentional. I presume it was not. It is liable to happen with some of the private employment associations. I assume that the private employment agencies have to conduct this business in such a way that he gets his clientele and holds it in competition with the public and others in the same business. I assume that they are probably conducted in that way. Recently some of them have had their licenses—I understand some of their licenses have been taken away. They should be safeguarded and properly conducted.

Commissioner GARRETSON. Mr. Skinner, you spoke of making unions responsible by incorporating them and putting up bonds. Assume now for a moment that you entered into an agreement with your employees for a period of a year. That provided for a rate of wage and the other conditions that entered into an agreement of that kind with the ordinary union. That union put up a bond for the faithful carrying out and performance thereof. Would you hold that the employer also should put up a bond for the faithful performance of it, or would you hold that his business standing was a guaranty enough?

Mr. SKINNER. I think his credit would be subject to criticism by the union who are making that contract the same as the credit of the union would be by the employer who would expect that contract to be carried out.

Commissioner GARRETSON. Then you would look for the bond both ways?

Mr. SKINNER. Yes.

Commissioner GARRETSON. In the event of the failure, your failure in business, when half the period had been disposed of, would you hold with that guaranteed contract, in the event that the wage had risen, or the tendency were in that direction, that the unexpired period was an obligation of your firm?

Mr. SKINNER. I do not know that I just understand you.

Commissioner GARRETSON. If a contractor put up a bond to work at that rate for a year, and you held that contract and the bond payable therefor was guaranty therefor, if he failed in business, would that contract that he owns, in your opinion, be an asset of your firm?

Mr. SKINNER. Well, that depends.

Commissioner GARRETSON. If the labor market had gone up in the meanwhile, for instance, that would make it more valuable, wouldn't it, if it had an unexpired period to run?

Mr. SKINNER. It might. I haven't given that any thought.

Commissioner GARRETSON. Would you be willing to put up a bond big enough to guarantee payment of those men for the unexpired period after a failure that might occur?

Mr. SKINNER. Well, I think just as well as we would have to put up a bond to secure a contract of sufficient size. There should be security for the bond.

Commissioner GARRETSON. If your pay roll would be big enough it would take a good deal of money?

Mr. SKINNER. If he had a big pay roll he could probably afford to put up a big bond.

Commissioner GARRETSON. What is your experience? Is it your experience that the bigger the pay roll the greater the financial responsibility?

Mr. SKINNER. Not always; no, sir.

Commissioner GARRETSON. You state that you are favorable to organization if properly conducted. What would you consider an organization that is properly conducted?

Mr. SKINNER. We have had as members of our organization those who are doing business with labor unions under contract.

Commissioner GARRETSON. Well, I don't just understand that idea, and I want to understand it. If your employees organized completely—they may have been at it for a considerable period—but to-morrow they come in to you with a demand for an increased wage and better conditions, and you refuse, and they go on strike for the furtherance of their desire, in your opinion would that be a properly conducted labor organization?

Mr. SKINNER. I don't think they have any right to do any different than I would have any right to do—to destroy property or life or anything of that kind.

Commissioner GARRETSON. I am speaking particularly of a strike.

Mr. SKINNER. They can strike as much as they want; I do not see any reason why they can't strike.

Commissioner GARRETSON. That wouldn't be any reflection on the proper conduct of it?

Mr. SKINNER. I can't see that it would be. If a man does not want to work for a certain wage or under certain conditions, he certainly has a right to discontinue that employment.

Commissioner GARRETSON. Collectively?

Mr. SKINNER. Either that or separately.

Commissioner GARRETSON. Then you think and hold that a labor organization has a perfect right to carry the organization to a perfect sequence of what you might call coercing the employer, if your contracts were such you would have to yield?

Mr. SKINNER. That is the purpose of the organization, of the employers' association—to combat that very same condition. There is no reason why we should use coercion; I don't believe in coercion.

Commissioner GARRETSON. Oh, well, your employers' association is attempting to coerce labor unions into a different course of procedure in regard to the union shop.

Mr. SKINNER. No, sir; because labor unions constitute a very small portion of the labor that is employed in our State or in any other State, and there is no reason why the labor union should control, or any other labor, in that industry or any other industry. If they were the total number of employees in the labor union they might control them.

Commissioner GARRETSON. Does anybody but labor unions advocate the closed shop, as you speak of it?

Mr. SKINNER. I don't know of anybody.

Commissioner GARRETSON. Then your organization is formed to coerce union labor?

Mr. SKINNER. No, sir.

Commissioner GARRETSON. Oh! Coercion is one thing when done by the employee and another when it is done by the employer?

Mr. SKINNER. No, sir; it is for protection.

Commissioner GARRETSON. Coercion for protection?

Mr. SKINNER. Yes. I didn't say coercion at all; I do not believe in coercion on either side. I think we have got a free country, should have here, and I am not in favor of being told what I should do. I don't think the labor unions ought.

Commissioner GARRETSON. What is the courthouse built for, and the legislative halls, but to tell you what to do and to tell me what to do?

Mr. SKINNER. I don't think if only 8 per cent of the population are constituted with the authority to do that——

Commissioner GARRETSON. What is a church built for—what was the Bible written for?

Mr. SKINNER. To preach certain things.

Commissioner GARRETSON. To tell you and I what to do?

Mr. SKINNER. To advise us what to do.

Commissioner GARRETSON. It is for advice, instead of telling? That is all, Mr. Chairman.

Mr. SKINNER. People don't always carry out the dictates of the Bible.

Commissioner GARRETSON. Some of them have got coerced for not doing it.

Mr. SKINNER. No doubt about that.

Commissioner GARRETSON. If the theory is true, there is going to be a final job of coercion along the line.

Mr. THOMPSON. Is it not true that the employers' association was opposed to the first-aid provision presented by the commission composed of employees and employers?

Mr. SKINNER. Yes.

Mr. THOMPSON. And that same thing, I take it, was the reason back of the present opposition?

Mr. SKINNER. I don't hear you.

Mr. THOMPSON. The same reason actuating the employers' association in that case actuates them now?

Mr. SKINNER. The employers are not against the first aid to-day. The employers told them at the time this bill was passed—they made a suggestion that it was a pretty hard portion of the act to undertake at that time; that if they would allow it to go until later the employers would help frame such a subsitute for the bill or measure to attach to the bill as would be satisfactory to the employees and employers. But two years ago, when they started to undertake to pass a first-aid bill in the legislature there had not been sufficient experience with the law to enable us to get any data, and the result was they were asked to wait until this coming session, at which time I presume the employers will carry out their agreement to undertake to do what they agreed to do at that time and help draft a first-aid bill that will be satisfactory to both.

Mr. THOMPSON. Mr. Constantine said while on the stand that they opposed the first-aid provision on the theory that it required the employer to pay all, whereas, in his opinion, some portion of the burden should fall on the employee.

Mr. SKINNER. That was one of the reasons.

Mr. THOMPSON. Are there other reasons?

Mr. SKINNER. Yes; there were other reasons. There were hospitals maintained in connection with plants under different kinds of contracts.

Mr. THOMPSON. Take the position to-day; what would you say of it in that respect?

Mr. SKINNER. Well, I do not know that I have given much thought to it. I have given some thought to it. I don't believe I have my mind made up. I do not believe I am competent to express an opinion to-day. I haven't given it sufficient care and attention.

Mr. THOMPSON. Did the employees at the time of the passage of the original compensation law induce the legislature to reduce the scale of awards in case of different classes of injuries?

Mr. SKINNER. I don't believe that they took any part in any discussion of that kind before the committee. I was there at all of the meetings, and I don't remember any such.

Mr. THOMPSON. Was that a vital part of the working of the law?

Mr. SKINNER. I don't think they entered into that feature at all.

Mr. THOMPSON. It is a vital part of the law, is it not, Mr. Skinner, the question of the amount of the award?

Mr. SKINNER. Yes.

Mr. THOMPSON. And one that must be met by the contribution of all parties to the act?

Mr. SKINNER. Yes.

Mr. THOMPSON. Does the employers' association hire men for the Seattle Construction Co.?

Mr. SKINNER. No, sir.

Mr. THOMPSON. Do you know whether men hired by the company are asked whether they belong to unions or not?

Mr. SKINNER. I do not.

Mr. THOMPSON. That is all.

Acting Chairman COMMONS. Anything you care to add?

Mr. SKINNER. I don't think of anything.

Acting Chairman COMMONS. That is sufficient; much obliged.

The commission will not hold a session to-morrow afternoon, but we will meet to-morrow morning at 10 o'clock. The commission will now stand adjourned.

(Whereupon, at 4.45 o'clock p. m. of this Monday, August 10, 1914, an adjournment was taken until the following day, Tuesday, August 11, 1914, at the hour of 10 o'clock a. m.)

SEATTLE, WASH., *Tuesday, August 11, 1914—10 a. m.*

Present: Commissioners Commons (acting chairman), Lennon, O'Connell, and Garretson. W. O. Thompson, counsel.

Acting Chairman COMMONS. The commission will come to order.

Mr. Thompson, call the first witness, please.

Mr. THOMPSON. Mrs. McMahon.

TESTIMONY OF DR. THERESA S. McMAHON.

Mr. THOMPSON. Doctor, will you please give us your name?

Dr. McMAHON. Theresa S. McMahon.

Mr. THOMPSON. Your address?

Dr. McMAHON. 4026 Tenth NE.

Mr. THOMPSON. And your profession?

Dr. McMAHON. Teacher, political and social science department, University of Washington.

Mr. THOMPSON. How long have you been a teacher of political and social science?

Dr. McMAHON. Three years and a half.

Mr. THOMPSON. At this university?

Dr. McMAHON. Yes, sir.

Mr. THOMPSON. What were you doing before that; where were you instructor?

Dr. McMAHON. I was statistician for the Associated Charities of Chicago, and before that I gathered statistics for Hull House, and before that I was in school.

Mr. THOMPSON. In your work here in Seattle, have you had occasion to look into the general industrial situation?

Dr. McMAHON. Yes, sir; my subject is labor problems, so I have conducted a number of investigations with my students along the line of labor problems.

Mr. THOMPSON. Could you tell us briefly what you have done in that way; in what branches of industry you have examined?

Dr. McMAHON. Largely dealing with the labor of women and children. Last August I was appointed a member of the industrial welfare commission of the State, and I was assigned the term of four months, which did not give me very much opportunity to investigate. With the assistance of the students I investigated the employment of women and children in the State.

Mr. THOMPSON. Do I understand you were a member of the industrial commission?

Dr. McMAHON. Yes.

Mr. THOMPSON. And are you to-day?

Dr. McMAHON. No; my term expired the 1st of January, 1914; I was not reappointed.

Mr. THOMPSON. Well, what generally is the average term of the commissioners, four months or a longer period?

Dr. McMAHON. No; the first term expired the 1st of January, 1914. We were appointed, I think, July 31; the next term was a year and four months, or five months; the next, two years and the next three years. If I had been reappointed my term of office would have been for four years.

Mr. THOMPSON. In your study of industrial conditions around Seattle have you paid any attention to the question of emigration as affecting the relations between the employer and employee and the conditions of the worker?

Dr. McMAHON. The question of emigration is very much the same here as it is in other parts of the country. Wherever you have a large influx of workers, whether it is through emigration or whether the natural increase of the population, it has a tendency to lower wages. Of course, the more ignorant the emigrant, the less able is he to make a favorable contract with his employer. With us the emigration question up to the present time has been largely one of orientals. The more ignorant they are of our institutions and our customs the poorer the bargain they make. I have found in my investigations that just as soon as they become acquainted with our institutions they tend to demand more wages.

Mr. THOMPSON. Referring directly to the matter of your investigation, Doctor, you say you were connected mostly with the investigation in regard to women and children?

Dr. McMAHON. Yes, sir.

Mr. THOMPSON. Was that work in Seattle or other parts of the State, or all over the State?

Dr. McMAHON. Largely in Seattle. I carried on the investigation in Seattle for the commission.

Mr. THOMPSON. How was your investigation organized, what manner did you organize it, and how many assistants did you have, and how did they work?

Dr. McMAHON. I was allowed the sum of $100 to carry on the investigation. The commission thought that would be sufficient. Naturally, in order to get any material I had to have voluntary workers and work myself. As I was teaching in the university I found this very difficult to do. With the help of the students working in my department, I was able to go over the pay rolls of the principal industrial establishment in Seattle. In consulting the employer I was impressed with the fact that the question at issue would be one of apprenticeship. Practically all of the employers said they were willing that a minimum wage should be set, provided that a fair apprenticeship period were allowed. I thought, under the circumstances, it would be wise to look into the period of employment. We copied the pay rolls of the department stores, one box factory, two candy factories, two laundries, and a large mail-order house. We copied the names of all the girls on the pay roll the first week in October. We traced their term of employment back six months and inserted every new name that appeared. Every name that appeared on the pay rolls for six months was traced back one year. I wanted to find out how many girls were employed in the period of six months and what per cent of them worked more than one year, so as to see if the spirit of the law could be evaded if an apprenticeship period were allowed.

Mr. THOMPSON. As a result of that investigation what did you find with reference to the length of employment?

Dr. McMAHON. I found practically the same thing that the Massachusetts commission did—that practically the girls worked a comparatively short period. If you will pardon me, I have the figures here. I excluded from my tabulation the suit department because it is a seasonable trade and contained apprentices in dressmaking. The alteration, millinery, and restaurant departments were left out so as to make it a little fairer, since these departments are recognized as most susceptible to short periods of employment.

In department store No. 1 the records were valueless because the firm had been under new management only six months.

No. 2, exclusive of cloaks, suits, alteration, millinery, and restaurant departments, 60 per cent of the girls worked less than one year; 40 per cent one year or more. This was the best department store in the city in relation to the girls.

No. 3, 74 per cent of the girls worked less than a year and 26 per cent one year or more.

Massachusetts finds in one department store that 71.8 per cent of the girls worked less than one year, and 28.2 one year or more, getting practically the same results as I did.

I wish to say this about the department-store situation: Although my investigation dealt largely with the department stores, because more girls are employed in department stores than in any other line of work in the State, I did not find conditions as bad as in the factories. The wages are better. The reason the department stores receive more attention and are more sensitive to public opinion is that they deal directly with the consumer.

In a paper-box factory 88 per cent of the workers worked less than one year. None of this 88 per cent received $9.

Of the 12 per cent who worked one year or more only 14 per cent received $9 or more. Most of the girls in the factory received less than $5 per week. They rarely worked six days of the week. The average week was about five and one-half days or five days, depending upon the orders for boxes.

In the factories—the candy and cracker factories— 82 per cent of them worked less than one year. Seventy-two per cent of those who worked less than one year received less than $9. Eighteen per cent worked one year or more. Sixty per cent of these received less than $9.

The wages in the candy factories are very much as they are in the paper-box factories.

In the laundry, 80 per cent of the girls employed at the mangles during the six months which the investigation covered had worked less than six months. None of them received $9. Sixty-three per cent of all other workers in the other departments worked less than six months. Forty-three per cent of those girls in all other departments get $9 or more, showing that in the laundry you can make a distinct division between mangle work and work in other departments. The flux of workers among girls at mangles is very much greater.

In Massachusetts practically the same situation exists. In a Massachuetts laundry 92.9 per cent worked less than one year; 7.1 per cent worked one year or more.

I did this for the purpose of finding out whether the allowance of apprenticeship of six months or year would not defeat the entire spirit of the law, and I believe it will.

I think our rulings in this State are superior to the rulings made in Oregon. But the tendency on the part of the employers is to ask for an apprenticeship period, which, if granted, allows them to evade the spirit of the law entirely by discharging the girls when their apprenticeship period is over.

Apprenticeship laws have never been enforced since the old guild system. Only where you have a close organization of those interested in maintaining your apprenticeship has it been enforced. In the early nineteenth century the employers held that there was no need for apprenticeship, because with the division of labor much of the work was unskilled, and so the old apprenticeship laws were discarded at the request of the employers.

Since the division of labor has been carried on more minutely by virtue of scientific management we have the employers insisting that the apprenticeship system must be recognized in all industries. History shows that the employers have been inconsistent in their attitude.

The other phase of the question of the minimum-wage law is the one relative to age. The law in this State says that a girl is an adult as soon as she reaches the age of 16; before reaching that age she must get a legal permit to work. The minimum-wage law says she is not an adult until she is 18.

When child-labor laws are passed looking toward the prohibiting of the exploitation of children the employers are anxious to have the age 'limit made low. In minimum-wage laws they wish the age to be put just as high as possible.

The largest number of girls is available between the ages of 16 and 18. Many women marry before 20 years of age and leave the labor market. This is especially true in Washington, where women do not enter industry as workers to the same extent as in Eastern States.

I have found in our box factories and in our candy factories and mail-order houses that mostly all employees who were getting less than $9 were under 20 years of age. It is quite possible, it seems to me, to supply the demand for girl workers out of the available female labor supply of from 16 to 18 years—assuming the age limit can be enforced, which I doubt. The girl will lie about her age to hold her job. The mother will lie about the girl's age, and unless you have a very careful registration of births there is no way of enforcing it.

But assuming it can be enforced, it seems to me that the minimum-wage law puts a premium on child labor, and a girl of over 18 is going to find it very difficult to get a job. One of the most conscientious, honest, and frank employers I consulted when on the minimum-wage board, in whose establishment I found the best conditions, frankly said, when I asked, "What are you going to do?" said, "Let the girls go, and get girls under 18. I will admit it. The others may not."

One of the biggest problems in labor history is the substitution of child labor for adult labor. It has been taken up by Sidney and Beatrice Webb in England and others, and they found parents walked the streets while children can get employment.

It seems to me that legislation of this nature is merely aggravating the social problem. From my point of view the minimum-wage law as it is being passed all over the country has only one virtue. It is educating the public to the conditions that exist relative to women and child labor.

Mr. THOMPSON. Doctor, in case the minimum-wage law did not have any reference to age, providing that anybody in industry should pay at a certain rate, would that obviate your objection to the present law in the State?

Dr. McMAHON. Yes; I think when a child is in adult's work it ought to get adult's pay. As it is, there is no restriction to the number of children, according to the law; you can employ just as many as you like.

I found in the canneries boys competing with men in pushing heavy trucks. The boys could do it better than the men. The boss hurried the boys so that they ran with their trucks. A man would take, what he considered a reasonable gait, and if urged to hurry would probably quit work. Even then the boilers turned out the cans of salmon faster than the boys could take care of them. They never caught up with their job.

Mr. THOMPSON. Take the minimum-wage law as a general proposition; do you favor such a law?

Dr. McMAHON. I certainly do.

Mr. THOMPSON. What would be the provisions of such a law that would meet with your favor, and what would be the objections other than what you have already named of the age limit?.

Dr. McMAHON. I believe it would have to be a real minimum. For instance, we have a law relative to male workers in this city. The man is not told he has to have two weeks' experience before he can get the minimum wage. If he can't handle his shovel, he probably is discharged. I think the minimum wage ought to be fixed for unskilled labor. As far as the apprenticeship is concerned, from the experience of history, it seems to me that the training of the children will have to ultimately be taken over by our educational institutions.

Experience has taught us that we can't trust the employer to look after the interests of the children. As far as the blind-alley occupations are concerned, I think that children ought to be prohibited from following them. The immediate step, I think, ought to be an apprenticeship law, such as Wisconsin has, clearly defining what an apprenticeship is, and not including under it inexperienced workers whose only claim to apprenticeship is inexperience in handling goods.

, Mr. THOMPSON. Will you give us your reasons in favor of a minimum wage of the kind you believe in?

.. Dr. McMAHON. Industry is rapidly becoming so scientifically managed that you can clearly see that there are certain jobs that are more or less mechanical and that can be performed by anyone who is physically and mentally sound. Under those conditions you naturally have a large number of people competing for those jobs, and when they are out of a job their places are readily taken by others, either by immigrants who come over here or by people who live in the community. We have an oversupply of labor for the unskilled work. Those people are too weak to organize. I don't look forward to the time when we can organize all workers. When a man or woman is hungry his first thought is to get a job and it would be pretty hard to hold him in line and make a martyr of him for principle's sake. These unskilled workers are too weak to bargain themselves, so the State ought to step in and bargain for them.

Mr. THOMPSON. Referring to the effect and the employment of women 18 years and over by reason of the minimum wage law in this State, have you any concrete case where it has affected women over that age?

Dr. McMAHON. You mean the present enforcement of the law?

Mr. THOMPSON. Yes.

Dr. McMAHON. Yes; complaints come constantly to me. One, within the last day or two, by an organization coming in close contact with the girls, telling me that the girls had become panicky and were losing their places. I wanted a written statement, but the organization felt it could not afford to be involved and asked that I should not mention its name.

Mr. THOMPSON. Referring to the scale of wages that has been established here under this law in the different occupations, have you anything to say in regard to that.

Now, for instance, the wage of $10 for women in mercantile establishments that went into effect on July 27, last; also the wage of $8.90 for women in manufacturing work that went into effect on August 1; and $9 a week wage for girls in laundry work and telegraph and telephone operators.

Dr. McMAHON. I would like to say this, that in the department stores you can divide your workers into two broad classes, those girls who require skill, intelligence, and personality to sell the goods. Those girls go into the department store often without experience and draw wages of $10. There are other lines of work in the department stores. The sales girls are not as important from the viewpoint of the minimum wage as the cheap office girls. Much of the office work can be done by cheap help. Inexperienced saleswomen often get $9 or $10 per week, depending on the department in which they work. I found only five saleswomen in one large department over 18 years of age who had been employed by the firm one year or more who were not getting $9 or more per week.

Younger girls can be used for much of the office work, so that whether your minimum wage is fixed at seven, or eight, or nine, or ten dollars per week for adult workers the pay roll of the office force will be little affected.

Conditions are different in laundries. Laundries are not able to carry out the minute division of the work as in department stores and will have to depend largely on the fact that the girls will never be able to serve out their apprenticeship in order to avoid paying the fixed minimum wage for adults. Laundries can not use young girls.

Mr. THOMPSON. With reference to the $6 minimum established for minors, what is your view of that?

Dr. McMAHON. The fact that employers have to pay only $6 to girls under 18 and $10 to girls over 18 puts a big premium on child labor.

, Mr. THOMPSON. You have covered that, then, in your other statement?

Dr. McMAHON. Yes, sir.

Mr. THOMPSON. What condition did you find in the canning industry with reference to labor generally, not only labor of children and women, but of adults?

' Dr. McMAHON. Shortly after the minimum-wage commission was appointed Mr. Olson, the labor commissioner, and I made an investigation of the salmon canneries in the northern part of the State. The fish make a heavy run every four years, and we were fortunate enough to carry on the investigation in one of the heavy years. I do not know whether the commission has attempted to publish the results of the investigation, but I made a short synopsis of the result for the commission. Girls were employed moving and filling wooden trays with empty cans; wages, 20 cents. Trays were taken away on trucks by boys, filled, delivered to girls who stood at the head of the chute and slid the trays to the floors below, where the cans were filled with fish by older girls and women.

After the cans were filled and closed small children stacked them. Here.is where we found the large number of small children. Some were paid by the tray and others by the hour. The wages ranged from 10 to 15 cents an hour. Ages of the children ranged from 9 years to 14—many of them were illegally employed. Fifteen cents an hour is especially attractive, as the children worked long hours, thus making fairly good daily wages.

The work in can factories is done principally by boys and girls. We found but one can factory. The more skilled work fell to the girls from 16 to 19 years of age. Children were forced to work rapidly in order to keep up with the machinery. In several instances machinery had to be stopped as it belched.forth cans faster than the children could pick them up. Boys were quite generally employed in pushing trucks loaded with cans of salmon.

Mr. Olson was especially interested in the issuing of permits, I in the employment of women. The law says that boys under 14 and girls under 16 years of age must not work without permits. We found many violations of the child-labor law.

The reasons were given as follows: No apparent reason for the enforcement of the law, since permits were procured for the asking. I went over the permits issued by Whatcom County. I found two permits that did not even have the child's name on. The permit was issued to Mary Smith's niece or nephew.

Where we found violations of the law they were generally due to the inconvenience of getting the permit; when the county seat was in a different city. Under such circumstances we found 50 to 100 children working without permits. In one community where many children were employed in canneries no violations of the law were detected. This was true wherever the superintendent was given the power to issue permits. The children could run up after work and get their permit from the superintendent. When the judge failed to delegate this power, we found many violations.

Mr. THOMPSON. By superintendent you mean the superintendent of the cannery?

Dr. McMAHON. The superintendent of the schools.

Mr. THOMPSON. Oh.

Dr. McMAHON. When a cannery was located in a comparatively large city many children were employed. Canneries isolated from settled communities employed adults to do the work which was done by children in the large cities, showing that the children came in direct competition with the adults in the large cities. Occasionally men were found wheeling trucks of canned salmon from cannery to storehouse, but most often this work was done by boys, as I have told you before.

In one cannery the boys said they worked from 9.30 until 12 o'clock at night or 1 a. m. They were wheeling trays of salmon to the warehouse. The hours most often cited were from 6 a. m. to 7 p. m., with one-half hour for lunch.

Why are these children employed? The following reasons were given: First, the desire on the part of the canneries to get cheap labor; and, second, the willingness of parents to exploit their children because of the attractiveness of the wage. I believe that if an investigation were made it would be found that in but few instances do the parents need the wage of the children, because we found the parents working with the children, and many parents admitted it was not necessary for the children to work.

The cannery men gave as their reasons these: First, parents beg us to employ their children; second, social service on the part of the employers.who are willing to sacrifice their own interests in order to provide means for keeping the children off the streets and out of mischief.

Children are generally considered by the employers as being a nuisance in the canneries.

We often heard it said the women workers in canneries get high wages. The high wages are given in the packing of fish. They pack fish by hand and earn from $2 to $9 per day. The one girl alone who was able to make $9 a day said it was impossible for her to work for more than three weeks, and during that period she had to take frequent rests. The girls who are able to get high wages are pointed out with pride by the managers. They are.the pace setters, as we call them in industry. The girls said that the great difficulty in packing fish is that the wrists and the back give out. In one cannery the foreman said that rest intervals were provided for the girls. The girls said.these were forced rest periods of about 10 minutes, due to the clogging of the machinery or to the fact that fresh fish was not.butchered fast enough to keep up with the packers, or one department lagged behind the other. The packers were stopped until readjustments took place. Sometimes several days elapsed without such a rest period. At other times these rest periods came frequently. One of the.best packers in the plant gave as her reason for stopping her day's work at noon that so many stops occurred in the packing that day she could not make fair wages, and so she decided to take the remainder of the day off.

Wherever cans were filled by machinery, girls were paid a flat rate of 20 to 25 cents an hour.

When the eight-hour law for women came up before the legislature, I was requested to represent the girls. I had just come from Chicago, and, as a social worker, was asked to represent the girls before the joint committee of the house and senate. There I met the employers, who were well represented, making a plea that the canneries be exempted from the eight-hour law.

They said that if the eight-hour law applied to women in canneries they would discharge the girls and put in Chinamen. In going through the canneries it was evident there was no competition between the two classes of workers, the orientals and the girls; but on the contrary the complaint was made in practically every cannery that the oriental labor was becoming scarcer each year, and they found it absolutely necessary to employ white men in places formerly filled by orientals. This scarcity is due to a stricter enforcement of the Chinese-exclusion act. Whenever the question was asked as to whether the oriental or white men could be substituted for the girl packing fish, the answer invariably was that such a·move would be impracticable, as neither the oriental nor the white man possessed speed or dexterity of the female worker when it came to packing fish by hand.

With the exception of the women scraping and washing the fish the oriental and Indian women compete more often with juvenile labor than female adult labor. The women scraping and washing the fish do compete with the oriental and Indian man. These women get about 5 cents less an hour in canneries where Indian women were employed. This may be merely a coincidence. Canneries located in cities generally have no Indian labor supply to draw upon. The price of female labor in cities may have been higher because entering into competition with other industries in the community. If the labor supply is short, they often draw upon the Indian reservation for a considerable labor supply.

Women show little inclination to work in fish canneries for the same wage as in other industries. I think this is due to the disagreeable nature of the work. I doubt very much if the minimum wage, when it is fixed, will affect the women in canneries who get $2 a day for six days a week. The minimum wage would probably be less.

With a few exceptions the canning companies had taken little cognizance of the necessity of providing girls with sanitary washing and toilet facilities. Most of the canneries provide rough board privies located on the docks. Many of them were in a filthy condition. Often these privies were without locks or doors. The girls complained that those privies assigned to them were sometimes used by the men. This was the most common complaint in every cannery where flush toilets were not provided. The girls requested the minimum wage commission to better the sanitary conditions in canneries. After the fish have been cleaned by machinery, it is necessary for them to be scraped and washed. This is very disagreeable work, as the hands are constantly in water. The workers have to stand on a narrow plank in order to keep the feet dry. In most canneries this work is done by Chinese. It is done by Indian women only when near reservations. Examining the hands of some of these Indian women, they were found to be raw, and.ulcerous sores under the finger nails. These women work from 6 a. m. until 9 p. m., with one-half hour for lunch; wages, 20 cents per hour.

I hope that the commission will recommend that the cannery situation be investigated. I think that it is the worst condition.that we have in the State, and has received the least attention. I know nothing about the fruit canneries. I have not been through them.

I want to call the commission's attention to the contract in the canneries made with the Chinamen. I received some of this information from an oriental student who has worked in the canneries, from the employers themselves, and from the contract of which I have a printed copy.

Commissioner LENNON. Before leaving that subject, will you indicate whether or not you discovered anything with regard to the prevalence of tuberculosis among the girls in the canneries?

Dr. McMAHON. I had no way of determining. I asked a great many of the girls what they did when the canning season was over, and they said mostly housework.

I took the names of two or three girls in every cannery, hoping they would be of some assistance to the commission when I returned to Seattle. With one exception there was no response. The girl who answered my letter said that the girls were employed at housework during the winter and were not particularly interested in the industrial situation. The girls showed an unwillingness to give information that might involve them. My experience on the commission and watching the commission's work since convinces me that a girl is foolhardy to give any testimony or any information where her name is involved.

Mr. THOMPSON. What is the reason for that, Doctor?

Dr. McMAHON. Simply that she will be persecuted. The commission has the example of one of the girls who was called before the commission to act in behalf of the girls. She lost her position. I believe that the violation was brought up to court and the employer was fined. This experience makes me doubt the honesty of employers. They have not been honest with me in that many statements they have made proved false.

In going into one of the large department stores the employer wanted to convince me that the girls were satisfied; so he took me around to the different girls. "Jennie," he said, "how many times have I offered to promote you?" Jennie smiled and said, "Oh, a good many times—three or four times." So he said, "I will take you to some one else." He took me down the line with the same results. Finally I requested the privilege to ask the questions. "Jennie," I said, "if you were offered an increase in pay would you go over to department so-and-so?" "Sure I would." We did not go any further. But I felt that the employer was trying to give me an impression which was entirely false.

Another instance. At one of the conferences which I attended we asked if there were any employees in the audience. One of the girls got up and gave her testimony, describing to us the conditions in the industry in which she was employed. I was not on the commission very much longer. After my term expired I received a letter from an organization which deals with women in that city—"would I please do something for this girl; she had lost her job." I said I would do what I could. I spoke of the case in public as an illustration, showing that it was unwise for a girl to testify. It was taken up by the department of labor. Shortly after I received another letter from the same organization, asking if I would please call off the department of labor, that they were misinformed, the girl was merely laid off—that there was an oversupply of labor and the firm had to let some of the workers go and she happened to be one. I was not able to follow up that case and I do not know what became of it. But I think if a girl would testify before the commission as to the actual conditions, especially where she is showing that she has been unjustly treated, I can not see that her prospects of promotion would be very good even though she were not discharged.

Mr. THOMPSON. All right, Doctor.

Dr. McMAHON. Now, about these cannery contracts. We have a number of big Chinese contractors who agree to send Chinese to the canneries. They take the contract for canning the fish. Some of these Chinese contractors can't get enough Chinese, so they hire Japanese. The Japanese contractor has to agree to supply a certain number of Japanese for the work, and a fine of $50 for each man he fails to provide.

In case of sickness, idleness, or lay-off these Chinese workmen have to pay 25 cents an hour. They are paid only 15 cents an hour when they work. I have a printed copy here. I think the commission could get a similar one. It was given to me indirectly by our corporation counsel.

This reads: "If requested to work on Sunday or overtime the party of the second part shall do so at any time, under the directions of the Chinese foreman, the Japanese foreman, or the agent, or person in charge of the cannery, and if the second party shall refuse to work on Sunday or overtime, then the party of the first part shall have the right to deduct from all wages due to the party of the second part the sum of 25 cents per hour for each hour that the said party shall refuse to work on Sunday or overtime, and the same shall be deducted from the wages of the party of the second part at the end of the season."

, Acting Chairman COMMONS. Would you file it with the commission?

Dr. McMAHON. It is the only one I have, Prof. Commons. I will try to get you another one.

; Mr. THOMPSON. If you will let us have it, we will have it copied.

Dr. McMAHON. All right.

(The paper so presented was marked " McMahon Exhibit " and appears in full at the end of this subject.)

· Dr. McMAHON. The contractor charges an employment fee of $2 to $3 for each laborer employed. The Chinese contractor receives $9 to $12 a month for feeding the Chinese worker. Feeding is subcontracted to the bookman for $7 to $8. These bookmen feed their men for about $6 to $7. The food is extraordinarily poor, and the men are forced to buy canned food with their wages. There is a growing scarcity of Chinese labor. The young men absolutely refuse to put up with the conditions. The Japanese contractors have to put up large sums of money as security for the Japanese that they employ. The Japanese do not make as desirable workers as the Chinese; they are more independent; they are not as docile. They have to supplement the Chinese labor with the Hawaiians, Mexicans, and Filipinos.

The hours of work are often 19 hours a day for a period of three weeks. Often the Chinamen get but 3 hours sleep out of 24. White men never work more than 15 hours.

I have a statement here that was made by one of the employers of a cannery. He was one of the owners of a fish cannery. He said when they had a large run of fish he urged the contractor to get the Chinamen up earlier in the morning. The contractor said it was impossible, as they cried like babies. The cannery owner said he looked into the situation, and found that the men's hands were worn to the bone and their boots had to be cut off from their legs, they were so badly swollen. This occurred before the iron chink came into use.

On returning to Seattle I interviewed one of the biggest Chinese contractors. He said that the wages of the Chinese are going up, and they can't get them now without paying them $280 to $320 for the season. White men receive 25 cents an hour, and the oriental beside him, doing exactly the same work, gets 15 cents an hour. Invariably the answer was made to the question, " Why employ white men? " That Chinese were becoming scarcer because of the more rigid enforcement of the exclusion law.

The Americanized Chinese are unwilling to accept conditions that are accepted by the new arrivals. He also said no one can live up to the contract the employer imposes on them; it is too strong. · If you do not put up 2,000 cases of salmon, you have to pay $3.50 for each case you are short. That part of the contract is not enforced only when labor is plentiful and the rush is over. They must run two lines to fulfill the contract. If the machinery breaks down, they can not live up to the contract, although they are held responsible. The cannery people tried to enforce the contract. When fish are scarce, the contract does not hold. The contractor must pay the Chinamen in advance, often his season's pay. There is no danger of his running away, as he says Chinamen always keep their word. If the contractor just fills his contract, he loses money. If he puts up more fish than the contract calls for, he makes money. The labor cost is the main element, as the men are hired by the season.

I think that is about all unless you have some special questions on the cannery situation. One thing I want to mention is the reason why the men do not strike. There is a clause which you will notice in the contract which reads that in cases of strike any loss of time shall come out of their wages at the end of the season, so that the cannery owners are protected from striking workmen.

Mr. THOMPSON. Have you any remedy to suggest for the situation?

Dr. McMAHON. Yes; State ownership of the canneries. I believe that the fish belong to the people of the State. The cannery men pay nothing but a small tax for the fish. There is little expense involved in the canning of fish. They have just shacks in most cases, and there is not a great amount of machinery. I hope the time will come when the State takes the fish canneries over.

· Mr. THOMPSON. Assuming that the State owned the fish canneries, and there was a big catch of fish came in, how would you handle the labor problem in that case?

Dr. McMahon. By shifts. Employees could work in shifts; the machinery could be duplicated. According to the fish reports there are enormous profits in the business. The catches are small excepting once in four years. : Some of the canneries run only one out of four years. Cannery men can tell about how the fish are going to run. Many of the canneries are owned by large corporations. For instance, I found one of the canneries at Bellingham under the same management as one at Blaine, and another at Anacortes.

Mr. Thompson. You think the labor situation ought to be controlled by State legislation?

Dr. McMahon. I think the eight-hour law ought to apply to the canneries. I think the contract system ought to be looked into, and I do not see why legislation can't be passed relative to such contracts.

Mr. Thompson. These working conditions you speak about you testify that they relate to white workers as well?

Dr. McMahon. In most cases the white labor is employed directly by the canning company. In a few instances we found the girls were employed by the Chinese contractors. In one cannery the Chinese contractor had hired a woman to scour the country for female employees to take to the canneries.

Mr. Thompson. Referring, Doctor, to the apprenticeship law that you have just spoken of, have you made any study of apprenticeship as applied in industry to-day, under either unorganized trades or in trades that are organized?

Dr. McMahon. Yes, sir.

Mr. Thompson. Union rules and the like?

Dr. McMahon. I was fortunate enough to have one of the students who was working for a master's degree take up as her thesis subject child labor, and she worked in connection with the commission—that is, as long as I was on the commission.

She wrote to every union in the city and asked them for a copy of their apprenticeship rules, and went over them carefully.

This seemed to be the tendency—where your trade required considerable skill and your union was strong enough—there seemed to be some regulation of apprenticeship. Where your union was not strong the apprenticeship broke down—that is, the unions could not regulate the number of apprentices. Of course that has been true of history that the unions are losing out when it comes to the enforcement of apprenticeship agreements.

Mr. Thompson. Have you any idea as to how apprenticeships might be handled?

Dr. McMahon. Yes, sir; by the State.

Mr. Thompson. By the State?

Dr. McMahon. I can't see that there is any way out of it; that is, I think ultimately the State will have to educate for the trades and the professions.

Mr. Thompson. Well, do you mean to take care of it in what we ordinarily call vocational training of children and youth?

Dr. McMahon. Yes; and perhaps do as we do in school-teaching. For instance, we train teachers at the university. The students are sent to the city schools for a little experience—cadetting, as they say—under the teachers.

I don't know whether it is any help to the teachers or not, but I think some system will have to be worked out where they can get the practical side and the theoretical, but it will have to rest with the State in some way to see that the children are rightly trained.

Speaking of apprenticeship, I would like to call the commission's attention to the informal conferences that were held over the State to see what the employers thought of the situation. Those minutes are on file in the Olympia office. I would like to read two or three statements which show that the employers really agree with me.

Mr. Thompson. Go ahead, Doctor.

Dr. McMahon (reading). "If you are allowed "——

Acting Chairman Commons (interrupting). What minutes are these you are referring to?

Dr. McMahon. The commission decided to hold informal conferences over the State, one conference for employers and one for employees. We took up the laundry and mercantile establishments and factories. We generally held the conference for girls in the evening. They were not successful in many ways. For instance, at Everett, at the mercantile conference, the one held for mercantile establishments, one employer showed up. At Spokane we had a good attendance. At these conferences the secretary took the minutes. They were not taken in shorthand, but he wrote as rapidly as he could and got most of the testimony. These minutes ought to be on file. If not, I have a copy I should be very glad to allow your stenographer to copy, because I think they will be of great service to you when taking up the subject of the minimum-wage law.

"Question. If you are allowed a fair apprenticeship system, will the minimum wage affect your pay roll very much?

"Answer. It would some.

"Question. Suppose your pay roll were increased 15 per cent, would you want to reduce the wages of the higher-priced girls?

"Answer. That would be impossible, for they are too valuable to us.

"Question. Then you get them as cheap as you can, don't you?

"Answer. There is something in that. We are obliged to pay them high wages in order to hold them. Competition between merchants regulates that.

Another statement was made: "We are flooded with applicants all the time."

That is the most pitiful part of the employment of women.

In going over the books and going over files I saw there were thousands and thousands of girls who were applying for work in our department stores. I say department stores because I went into that industry more carefully, because of the criticisms aimed at them. I have heard girls pleading for jobs. One employer said: "They are glad to work part time in order to get on our list and to get a start."

Another one says: "There are carloads of them waiting to get in. You will find them in bunches."

Another one says, speaking of the notions department, the question was asked: "What proportion are still there at the end of six months?" He says, "About one-fourth."

"Question. If there were a minimum wage of $10, what would you do?" He says, "I think we would have to get some new people."

Another says: "The extreme worth of a great many girls is at $6 and $7 a week, and if the minimum wage is established these would be thrown out."

Another: "If you make a minimum wage at $9 and don't allow sufficient time for apprenticeship, it will turn out a tremendous amount of girls on the street, in my opinion. Suppose a term of apprenticeship was fixed at six months; at the end of that time a girl would have to be raised to the minimum, but we might refuse to pay her the minimum because she was not worth it, and she would be thrown out. The next merchant to whom she applied would look up her record, and she would not find a place anywhere."

You see they practically confirm beforehand what experience shows. The minimum wage has not worked anywhere, I think, on account of apprenticeship. Such is the complaint that is made in Australia and New Zealand. Girls have to pretend they are apprentices in order to get jobs.

Mr. THOMPSON. Referring to the issuance of permits to minors to work, you said you found that that was very lax here in the State—the issuance of them. Have you any ideas as to how in the administration of child-labor laws the permits issued to children might be checked up successfully?

Dr. McMAHON. Well, there seems to be a general feeling on the part of parents that a child ought to be employed during vacation. What I said concerning permits related to vacation time. I don't think that children under 14 years of age, or a higher age than that, should be allowed to be employed at all. I don't believe that a child should be employed because the parents need the money. I can't see any reason for a child being employed, unless it is for educational purposes of some kind.

I don't see how your permit system is going to work unless you specifically state the conditions under which children can work. For instance, take it in the city here, children are often excused from attendance at school because the parents need their assistance.

Miss Nellie Higgins carried on the investigation this winter. She interviewed all these children who had permits, and in comparing the statements of the wages of the family as filed with the superintendent of schools and the statements the children gave, she found they were contradictory. In many instances she found that the family had an income of as much as $90 a month. I don't believe in child labor at all.

Mr. THOMPSON. How would you take care of inefficient girls in industry where you have a minimum wage?

Dr. McMAHON. I can't see the force of the argument that the inefficient girl will be thrown out, unless our minimum wage is so high that it is going to attract girls from other places, which I think it might do.

For instance, if you are running a factory and you have got a large number of applicants, especially where you have a thousand or two or more of applicants than you need, you will pick out the very best girls you can. It seems to me that if minimum wage is fixed in all industries, and you have a fixed labor supply—assuming that new girls can not come in—you are going to try to get the best in all cases, whether the minimum is six or seven or eight or nine or ten dollars. If the minimum-wage law is going to attract girls from the East or from the States where the wage is not as high, then I think it would throw out the least efficient, but the employers are always picking out the best. Take, for instance, in Christmas time as many as 200 girls are taken on. What they do is to pick out the very best that they find. Some girls in the newly employed group are better than those steadily employed. They are retained and the older hands dismissed.

The fact that employers can take on 200 new girls at Christmas time without crippling their industry is pretty good proof that it is not a skilled trade.

Mr. THOMPSON. Doctor, in the course of your study of this problem, you are aware of the general economic conditions that exist in industry and with the unrest of the worker. Have you any suggestions to make to this commission as to what might be done to help or alleviate that situation?

Dr. McMAHON. I believe that there is a growing consciousness on the part of workers of the futility of laws. That is, we work for legislation, and by adding some loophole in the legislation its purpose is defeated. I think, perhaps, this is responsible for much of the unrest to-day. Low wages, unemployment, and labor laws are not enforced, or else they are so interpreted or so enforced as to defeat the end thay had in view. I think that there should be—I should recommend publicity for the first thing—that the facts should be given to the public. In fact, I am in favor of publicity of your books, of your department stores, and of your factories.

I believe that an industry is a public trust, and I think the public ought to know what is going on there. I believe that if we could get the facts and pass legislation accordingly, and enforce it, it would alleviate some of the unrest. I think though that the fact that so many of the working people feel that there is enough being produced—our storehouses are overflowing with products, we have good crops, and yet they can't get enough to keep soul and body together—even though they don't work it out in their own minds so that they know the exact reason, they feel that somewhere there is a great injustice. I believe that with the increased intelligence of the working people we are going to have increased social unrest.

Mr. THOMPSON. Well, Doctor, concretely, how would you go about providing a remedy for it? What would be the first thing you would do? Is there any governmental machinery or anything the workers can do, not Utopian, but something that is next at hand?

Dr. McMAHON Oh, as far as the commission is concerned?.

Mr. THOMPSON. Well, any ideas that come to your mind.

Dr. McMAHON. Well, first, I would have publicity. Second, I think we need organization of the labor market the country over. That must be followed, I think, by the organization of our industries, so as to prevent industries from carrying on work at periods of the year when it is not absolutely necessary, and so causing a great demand for labor at one period of the year and a small demand at other periods. After you have done this, I think, you will be in a position to get at some of the fundamental causes of unemployment. I don't believe that organization of the labor market is going to do away with unemployment; but I think that is the first step. We have got to get the situation in hand and to know the situation. I would say the organization of the labor market first. I believe in a national minimum-wage law, and that law must be worked out by students of the problem. The trouble with so much of our legislation is that we appoint commissions, and they are people who know absolutely nothing of labor history, people who are not well informed, whose hearts are in the right place, but who don't know and can't give the time to study it so as to provide effective legislation. And I think that these things must be worked out nationally. I believe that we will ultimately have a national minimum-wage law, and that we can remedy some of these defects that we are now confronted with, and which make many girls afraid of minimum-wage laws. I think the working people, as a whole, are afraid of minimum-wage laws.

Mr. THOMPSON. Doctor, in regard to the question of publicity and the like, do you believe that a national body, such as a Federal industrial council, with the power to investigate the conditions in industry and to give publicity to the facts ascertained by investigation, with the power to act as conciliators and mediators, where there is trouble, and arbitrators, where the parties agree, would that be a good method, in your opinion, to bring these forces into play that you say should be used?

Dr. McMAHON. I think that wherever there is industrial trouble, such as we have been having in the mines, a great deal would be gained by the commission investigation and giving the facts to the public. Just as soon as you would start to arbitrate as a commission, I would be a little skeptical about the influence that would be brought upon the commission in order to have that commission made up of members who would be favorable to the class that had the greatest power, and, under those conditions, I don't think arbitration would work.

Commissioner O'CONNELL. You think the commission would be all right if it were selected of human beings that would not be imposed upon then?

Dr. McMAHON. Well, I don't think that there are any intelligent people whose sympathies are not on one side or the other. I haven't found any.

Commissioner O'CONNELL. Intelligent people whose sympathies are not on one side or the other?

Dr. McMAHON. Yes.

Commissioner GARRETSON. The intelligent——

Dr. McMAHON (interposing). What I mean is this: You take a person with large property interests, naturally he would be biased. And you take a person who has not any property interests and he would be biased. Now, our mayor said yesterday that he could get people without any property interests. It is pretty hard to get anyone whose position professionally or otherwise is not related to one of the two classes. I don't believe that people are—I think people's opinions are very often largely guided by their economic interests.

Acting Chairman COMMONS. Mr. Lennon would like to ask you a question.

Commissioner LENNON. You were speaking of the breaking down of the apprenticeship system, and I understood you to say that you found employers recently taking the opposite position to which they used to take, and favorable to the apprenticeship system. Is that correct?

Dr. McMAHON. Yes, sir.

Commissioner LENNON. Are you aware of the fact that of the near 40 trades of the country that have rules and regulations regarding apprenticeship that in not a single one of the trades do the employers make use of the number that are allowed under the union rules?

Dr. McMAHON. I should have qualified my statement by saying that they wanted apprentices in the unskilled trades. I think that their attitude toward the skilled trades—that is, the attitude you speak of—is due to the fact that the regulation of apprenticeships is such that it would not allow abuse.

I think if the Wisconsin law is strictly enforced relative to apprenticeship the next cry will be that there is not sufficient opportunity for young people to learn the trades. That is, if you have got to teach the child the complete trade, it will affect the economic value of that child in the industry. That is, I believe that in the ordinary apprenticeship that the employer very often does not gain anything, or very little. It is questionable. It depends upon the trade.

Commissioner LENNON. I would like to ask your view regarding a certain line of testimony that has come before the commission very strongly, to the effect that in a number of industries in manufacturing the increase—the notable increase—in classes of employees is on the part of those that are highly skilled and that the more or less unskilled are becoming less in these industries all the time, whereas in the highly skilled and better paid workers are continually increasing. What is your view on that?

Dr. McMAHON. I don't believe it. I think that scientific management means the conduct of an industry with the greatest economy. And we know—take, for instance, I can give a good example from my experience in our department stores.

You take a department store in a small town in this State and the employee not only sells the goods but wraps the parcels and makes the change and does all of the work. The large department stores often employ 600 people. Now, if they have to pay this girl, we will say, $10 a week or $9 a week, in a large department store where they employ 600 girls they can carry out the division of labor to such an extent that this high-priced girl—we will say $9 is high wages, and it is a comparatively high wage—is kept busy at work that a' cheaper person could not do. The wrapping of the parcel is done by a girl; getting $6 a week, perhaps. Looking after the checks and the making òf change, and the division of labor there means that a cheaper girl can do the cheaper grades of work. The larger your establishment the more effectively' can this be carried out, which, of course, means that your smaller establishment can not compete as effectively as your large establishment where they draw upon the same trade.

Commissioner LENNON. You think that statement, then, is incorrect?

Dr. McMAHON. I would say it is incorrect.

Commissioner LENNON. It was made with very great emphasis by the representatives, for instance, of the Baldwin Locomotive Works, the Midvale Steel Co., the Link Belt Co., and with the insistence that for a dollar they had a greater value of product with the more and more highly skilled people employed than they had with the less skilled.

Dr. McMAHON. But wasn't the machinery changed in some way so that some of this unskilled work was done by machinery?

Commissioner LENNON. I just wanted to see what your observation had been. Is there any law in this State requiring the inspection of the food qualities of these salmon that are packed?

Dr. McMAHON. Yes, sir.

Commissioner LENNON. Is it a continuous inspection that is sufficient to protect the people?

Dr. McMAHON. The girls told me in one cannery that the fish smelled so bad that they had packed the Saturday before that it nauseated them so that they could hardly stand to work over it.

Commissioner LENNON. I wonder if I have bought any of that.

Dr. McMAHON. I haven't eaten any fish since I went to the cannery.

Commissioner LENNON. Well, I haven't wanted it very much. That is all.

Commissioner GARRETSON. Doctor, has your experience been that where public attention through any agency was attracted to an industry where conditions were virtually indefensible, that a better one followed?

Dr. McMAHON. Yes.

Commissioner GARRETSON. Do you believe that any greater power is wielded by the average labor union than the concentrating of public attention upon the evils that they complain of if those evils are indefensible?

Dr. McMAHON. I think you are right, sir.

Commissioner GARRETSON. Speaking of the apprenticeship system, has it appeared to you from investigation that whenever the apprenticeship system was of no value to the employer as a wage controller he had no use for it, but the moment it became a club by which the wage could be manipulated as against legislation that then he desired to use it?

Dr. McMAHON. Yes; I think all classes look out for their own financial interests.

Commissioner GARRETSON. And the employer is fully as active as a class as the employee can be?

Dr. McMAHON. Yes.

Commissioner GARRETSON. In that direction?

Dr. McMAHON. Yes; I think the only difference is that employers have the upper hand.

Commissioner GARRETSON. He has more power to carry this purpose to a conclusion in his favor?

Dr. McMAHON. Yes; and the more unemployed we have the greater that power is made.

Commissioner GARRETSON. Can there be free bargaining by a hungry man?

Dr. McMAHON. No, sir.

Commissioner GARRETSON. Hunger in itself constitutes duress. Can there be an unerring application of the child-labor law in which the age limit enters without a complete system of birth registration?

Dr. McMAHON. No, sir.

Commissioner GARRETSON. It is really basic on all legislation of that character?

Dr. McMAHON. Yes. Then you have got to have some one to enforce the law. Take in this State—we have one woman enforcing the law of this State relative to the women. A small appropriation—I don't remember what it is; I think $1,500—a small appropriation that allows her to go to some cities only once in a year, and I suppose some she can't get to at all. I think here in

Seattle there is work enough for two or three. When she enters a town they know she is there when she registers at the hotel, and of course she won't find many violations.

Commissioner GARRETSON. Because her presence—it is very possible that during her presence there that very many violations are covered up by collusion between employer and employee in many instances?

Dr. McMAHON. I don't doubt it.

Commissioner GARRETSON. In legislative matters has it been your experience that employers—I am speaking as a class and not of individuals—give their full and free support to social legislation that in its application means increased cost of operation?

Dr. McMAHON. I met the employers at the legislature when we worked for the eight-hour law. They were well represented; the girls were not. There were a few labor representatives—organized labor representatives—but I should say, as an offhand guess, that the employers had probably ten people to every one that represented the girls. Of course the employers had some girls representing them, too.

Commissioner GARRETSON. Then you have reason to believe that employers do require employees to go and give testimony in legislative matters that is really against the interests of the employees so testifying?

Dr. McMAHON. There is no doubt about it.

Commissioner GARRETSON. You heard it questioned yesterday?

Dr. McMAHON. Yes, sir.

Commissioner GARRETSON. Has your experience been that employers are apt to give full and free support to social legislation after they have been successful in pulling the teeth in the legislation?

Dr. McMAHON. Yes; they would rather have no legislation, but where there is bound to be some legislation they succeed in pulling the teeth almost every time.

Commissioner GARRETSON. They don't hesitate to avail themselves of the claim that they advocated such legislation. Rest periods in the canneries are deducted from the time paid for, are they?

Dr. McMAHON. No, sir. Those rest periods are with the pieceworkers, and they get so much for the cans or trays that they pack.

Commissioner GARRETSON. Then the worker pays for his own rest periods?

Dr. McMAHON. Certainly.

Commissioner GARRETSON. That is all. One minute. Let me ask one other question of the doctor. You spoke of the fact you do not believe child labor should be indulged in at all preceding a certain age. Do you hold the opinion that if the State assumes the right to pass legislation covering hours, conditions of labor, sanitation under which adults labor, that there is the accompanying obligation upon the State to assume, if necessary, the support of the child until it comes to the age where it can labor properly?

Dr. McMAHON. I certainly do.

Commissioner GARRETSON. And not stunt it?

Dr. McMAHON. I certainly do. I think it would be an economic gain for the community, both in dollars and cents, to take care of the child.

Commissioner GARRETSON. One is the direct opposite and associated with the other. That if the State fixes the conditions of labor it guarantees that the labor comes up to the age of competency uninjured by previous labor.

Dr. McMAHON. I believe the State is responsible for the child until the child reaches citizenship.

Commissioner O'CONNELL. I wanted to know something about the method, if there is any, of taking care of people in canneries during sickness.

Dr. McMAHON. In one cannery we found a matron who took care of the girls whenever they cut their hands. There is danger of poisoning the hands with the fish bones. She was there for the purpose of taking care of girls. That was the only cannery in which we found any attempt made to look out for the girls.

Commissioner O'CONNELL. No inspection of any kind at all on the part of the employers?

Dr. McMAHON. Not that we were conscious of.

Commissioner O'CONNELL. If the girl—the male or female—were taken sick and it was necessary to quit work?

Dr. McMAHON. Yes.

Commissioner O'CONNELL. By reason of some dangerous disease of some kind, what was done in the matter?

Dr. McMahon. We did not look into it. But in one case a man had been shot for breaking the fish laws relative to the traps, and the manager made the statement that he was in their hospital. The labor commissioner asked this question: "Do you have many people in the hospital?" and, if I remember correctly, he said he was the only one there at the time. We did not make it a point to ask the question. But this special cannery that had the hospital had unusually good conditions. The employer provided the girls with a hot dinner and the girls received as high wages as they did in any cannery— 25 cents an hour. It was the highest wage per hour we found in any cannery.

Commissioner O'Connell. Are the Americans and Asiatics separated?

Dr. McMahon. No; they work side by side.

Commissioner O'Connell. How about their living quarters?

Dr. McMahon. I don't know where the orientals stay in the cities. Most of the white people take care of themselves just as they would in a city of this size. Out in the country districts we found very few white men. The workers are principally Indians and orientals. The managers were white.

Girls were provided with bunk houses. We went through one bunk house, and it was nothing short of a fire trap. It was a two-story affair. There was a table in the kitchen, but no chairs were provided. On a table were a few loaves of bread, showing that the girls lived principally on luncheons. There was a stove. The girls had to do their own cooking. But the girls said when they worked such long hours they were so tired that they did not stop to cook. The bedrooms, which were upstairs, were partitioned off into small rooms, the partition not going to the ceiling. It was a fire trap in every sense of the word. In each room was, as I remember, two little beds and a dresser. This dresser consisted of a covered box, on which was bread and a few utensils, which indicated that the girls ate in their rooms. No chairs were provided anywhere. There were a few boxes standing around here and there. The whole place was insanitary and filthy. No provision was made for the care of the house or to see whether the girls were getting proper food. This cannery was some distance from any city.

Commissioner O'Connell. Were there males employed there?

Dr. McMahon. Yes. They told me that the moral conditions down there were very bad. I later met one of the girls who had lived right there in the community and worked in the cannery, and she said the moral conditions had been very bad. The cannery management made a rule that all girls had to be in the house at 10 o'clock. I don't know how strictly it was enforced, but this rule was made to meet the moral problem in this cannery.

Commissioner Garretson. Was this dormitory you speak of, where the girls were, segregated from the male dormitory?

D. McMahon. Yes; it was some distance away. I do not know where the white men stayed. We went through the oriental quarters, and the orientals had a much better place to stay than the girls. They provided their own. The girls' house was provided by the cannery management.

Commissioner O'Connell. About this matter that Attorney Thompson asked you, this proposed Federal board, with a view to looking into the difficulties of labor, mediating and conciliating and all that sort of thing, to bring about an amelioration of industrial unrest, you say that the people are so biased, either on one side or the other, that they would be afraid it would not operate? Am I to understand that you have lost faith in human nature, or are not the people big enough in this country of ours to assume such a position with fairness to all parties in interest through the entire country?

Dr. McMahon. Yes. And yet here is one point that I wanted to make clear: In an arbitration board of this kind it seems to me it is almost impossible to get people to serve on such a board who have no interest on one side or the other. If there are such disinterested people, is it not possible to control them in some other way, if they are people who are not economically free?

Acting Chairman Commons. Let me ask, Doctor, what kind of a board, what power are you considering in discussing this question?

Commissioner O'Connell. I was just going to ask that question.

Dr. McMahon. I think you asked the question of an arbitration board to arbitrate disputes between employer and employee.

Acting Chairman Commons. Compulsory arbitration?

Dr. McMahon. Compulsory arbitration.

Acting Chairman Commons. That is what you are talking about?

Dr. McMahon. That is what I was talking about.

Commissioner O'CONNELL. We are not talking about that. We are not considering the matter of compulsory arbitration at all. I do not know that anybody believes in that, the most radical on either side I don't think does. They may say so, but I do not think they do. But what we are trying to get at is a conciliation board, something to bring people together before they get to fighting, or even after they get to fighting, get them together; preferably before. Do you understand there is a law now under which railroad matters are handled in this way, that has power to prevent strikes, which brings them together, uses its great influence, great power to bring people together—the influence of the Government to bring people together—something of that kind, that would bring people together; if there were being appointed on that board to-day a dozen men of various walks of life, if you will, six from the man that has, and six from the man that has not? They may have equal powers, they may sit down at the round table together, invite in belligerents to sit in with them—nobody has any power to say do this or do that, but they conciliate and they appeal to men's reason, and to women's reason.

Dr. McMAHON. They are neither representing an entire class of employees or employers?

Commissioner O'CONNELL. If you will, neither or both.

Dr. McMAHON. Yes. I do not see why that should not work if they represent both evenly. I think that it would be a good thing, that is to show up persons to the other side, to show things they did not see before.

Commissioner O'CONNELL. Not so much a matter of showing up, not so much a matter of trying to make bad of one trouble and good of another, but the purpose of getting people to see each other's rights and wrongs, if there be any, and weaknesses, to bring people together in the first place, that is the purpose.

Dr. McMAHON. I do not see why it would not work well.

Commissioner O'CONNELL. Are not our troubles largely from the fact that we do not get together, we do not talk to each other, in some instances will not see each other, walking on one side of the street when we see him on the other side, if it is possible; going the other way when we see him coming down the street, the idea being to get people together. Our troubles, I think, and our unrest can be largely said to be because we do not get together. We do not see the other fellow's side of the question, his standard. The idea being, what we have in mind is not prepared, or even outlined, but we are trying to get from those with whom we come in touch in the various parts of the country what they think along that subject, and have them make suggestions along the line and give us advice and ideas as to something that might be formulated. What would you think of a board that was composed of business men, employers, and employees? In England, you know, they have a board that is composed of business men, employers, and employees, and so far as we learn they have accomplished wonders. And in our civilized country it seems as though we ought to be able to be big enough to do all the things that they have been successful in doing in other countries, and go still further in those matters. I think that is the idea of Mr. Thompson, that he was trying to get at. I did not want it to appear you were in opposition to it, because I do not think you quite understood.

Dr. McMAHON. No; the point I wanted to make was that there would be a tendency to attempt to get control over such a board—that is, for certain interests to get control over such a board. The capitalistic interests might get a man or men appointed on such a board. The employers might be more successful than employees. Isn't this one reason why working people are skeptical.

Commissioner O'CONNELL. People might be skeptical, yes; and probably in some instances in the past they have had some reason to be.

Dr. McMAHON. Yes.

Commissioner O'CONNELL. But I think that is only incidental. It is so small an amount as against the great things, that it ought to be overlooked; it ought to be forgotten, and we ought to make some progress in the other way. I do not think there would be anything accomplished in any direction that we are not going to have industrial unrest. I do not think anybody wants to get entirely rid of industrial unrest. I think that it would be a good thing. My personal belief is that we have got to have people, some of the minority. I don't think I look forward to the doing away entirely of industrial unrest or unrest of any kind. I do not suppose professors and doctors do. That is all.

Acting Chairman COMMONS. Dr. McMahon, your apprehension about these public bodies, is it based on your idea that simply employers are likely to get control of them?

Dr. McMAHON. No; I think that both sides would attempt to get control, but the employer class has in the past been more successful.

Acting Chairman COMMON. But you take our Labor Department—you take our Department of Laboi at Washington; you take the bureau of labor, the bureaus of labor statistics in this country—have you ever looked into the question as to what class is usually appointed to those positions? Is it not uually the representatives of the trades-unions?

Dr. McMAHON. Yes.

Acting Chairman COMMONS. Have you investigated that very fully?

Dr. McMAHON. Well, I have noted that. I have inquired on that point. Some of the union people feel that at times the weaker members are put in such positions, rather than the stronger.

Acting Chairman COMMONS. Have you investigated the matter to see whether trades-unions make an effort to have their representatives put in these positions?

Dr. McMAHON. It has been true here, I believe; they are represented.

Commissioner O'CONNELL. Have the trades-unions of this State endeavored to have their people put in these positions—labor departments and so on?

Dr. McMAHON. Yes, I think so.

Acting Chairman COMMONS. Well, would you consider it as injurious to the country that labor unions should control the departments as it would be if the employers should control these departments?

Dr. McMAHON. No, I do not. I do not think you will ever find that the working people will hold together for monopolistic purpose effectively for any length of time. They are too large a class.

Acting Chairman COMMONS. Well, why do you say that the weaker members are put forward, get the appointments? In what way? How does that come about?

Dr. McMAHON. That is the point that has been made by some of the representatives of labor to me when I have commented on the fact that a member of a trade-union had been put in a certain position. The member of the trade-union appointed is in sympathy with the employer or at least can be controlled by the employer. I think you will have examples of it before the end of the week. The best example that we have in mind is the industrial insurance commission. If I am rightly informed organized labor requested that the man who held the position representing organized labor be retained. He was the choice of organized labor. He was not retained but another member of organized labor was put in, whom I think did not have organized labor's support. As the bill was originally drawn, organized organized labor was to have a representative on the commission, but that part was eliminated from the bill; but the spirit has been lived up to and some member of organized labor has been on the commission ever since, but labor could not choose its own member.

Acting Chairman COMMONS. It appears, then, that the appointment is not made by the organization directly?

Dr. McMAHON. No. One of the weaker members of organized labor is appointed to a commission. This is not always true. It depends on who does the appointing. The employer tends to have his strongest people representing him.

Acting Chairman COMMONS. Is that your observation generally?

Dr. McMAHON. That has been my observation here; I haven't had much personal experience along that line except in this State, and I think I am fairly familiar with the leaders on both sides.

Commissioner O'CONNELL. Do I get what you mean by a weaker brother, the difference between conservatism and radicalism?

Dr. McMAHON. No; I would say the man who is most easily controlled. I think the average person has pretty weak knees. You will find such people in the ranks of organized labor, just as you find them everywhere. A weak-kneed person may have a good point of view; he may have the right point of view as far as organized labor is concerned, but he may not be able to withstand the pressure that is brought on him.

Commissioner O'CONNELL. How would that be ascertained before the appointment?

Dr. McMAHON. Why, I would put the responsibility on organized labor; let them pick out their own and then they won't feel that they had no voice in it. I think there is that danger.

Commissioner GARRETSON. Your idea is, Doctor, that a member of organized labor can, by his previous conduct under his employer, establish the fact that he will stand stronger for his convictions even though there may be considerable pressure brought to bear on him—not be subservient to a certain degree to the employer's interests?

Dr. McMAHON. Well, the fact that the employer is not willing that the labor union shall appoint their men looks a little bit as if they would be afraid they would appoint their strongest men.

Acting Chairman COMMONS. Then in the same way you would have the employers' association or organization select their own representative?

Dr. McMAHON. Yes.

Acting Chairman COMMONS. That means you would have neither appointed by the governor?

Dr. McMAHON. You mean when it comes to—I was thinking of the industrial insurance board.

Acting Chairman COMMONS. I was thinking of either the industrial insurance board, the minimum wage board, or an arbitration board, or any of these boards which tended to deal with the relations between employer and employee.

Dr. McMAHON. Why would neither be appointed?

Acting Chairman COMMONS. I am trying to get at how you are going to avoid these boards you are speaking of having this subtle underground influence you find which you think controls. The ordinary method I think as a rule is they are appointed by the governor, are they not?

Dr. McMAHON. Yes.

Acting Chairman COMMONS. And then if the governor appoints a weak brother, he does it at the behest of somebody, does he?

Dr. McMAHON. Well, it looks a little that way.

Acting Chairman COMMONS. Then how would you free the appointing power, or how would you eliminate this influence you speak of?

Dr. McMAHON. Well, I believe in holding the man who does the appointing responsible for his appointee. Of course that necessarily means you have to have some workable system of recall in order to hold them responsible. If the man who has the appointing power is in office for four years or a certain definite term and has no intention of running again, it is immaterial to him whether the public holds him responsible or not. I believe in the education of the people of the community by publicity, and I believe that publicity will be an important factor in holding the individual responsible for his appointee, but you have to have some tangible way of compelling him to be responsible.

Acting Chairman COMMONS. You think that the recall is all that is necessary?

Dr. McMAHON. Well, whether it is through recall or public opinion, we will have to have some way of some control over the man whom we hold responsible. It does not make any difference if I hold you responsible for a certain fact if you in no way are going to feel concerned for that responsibility.

Acting Chairman COMMONS. Are you familiar with the method of the selection of the industrial council?

Dr. McMAHON. No, sir.

Acting Chairman COMMONS. Are you familiar with the appointment of the Board of Mediation under the Newlands Act?

Dr. McMAHON. No, sir.

Commissioner GARRETSON. Your idea is that the members should be appointed, for instance, like the members of this commission were appointed. The bill provided the three labor members of this commission shall be representatives of organized labor. One of the representatives on this commission was supported by the largest labor body in the country, the A. F. of L., and one chosen by the four big brotherhoods of the railways, and they were appointed by the President, and they are undoubtedly responsible to those bodies. Is that your idea?

Dr. McMAHON. Certainly. If they are to represent organized labor or unorganied labor or capital, if they are to represent me, or to represent any class, I think that class ought to at least have the right to say who shall represent that class. I would hate to have somebody represent me and that somebody appointed in a haphazard way. I would want somebody that knew something about me to represent me.

Acting Chairman COMMONS. You heard the figure given yesterday about the number of wage earners in this State. Have you analyzed those figures yesterday as to the number that was organized?

Dr. McMahon. I asked the question after the conference yesterday morning of one of the labor leaders, and he estimated it to be something like 175,000 wage earners and about 50,000 organized. I suppose it was a rough guess.

Acting Chairman Commons. The commissioner of labor said 400,000 wage earners, and 25,000 organized.

Dr. McMahon. Yes, sir.

Acting Chairman Commons. So that you would say there is no statistics?

Dr. McMahon. No statistics available on the subject.

Acting Chairman Commons. So that you can't tell?

Dr. McMahon. We have a big influx of labor in the wintertime, due to the fact that the men come from Alaska, and then they go out again.

Acting Chairman Commons. What would be your method of having the unorganized labor represented on these bodies?

Dr. McMahon. I don't see how they can be represented unless they are represented by some one who is interested, especially interested in unorganized labor. I don't see how you can get them together to select their own representative.

Commissioner O'Connell. That would be the employer, then?

Dr. McMahon. You would have to have some one who is fairly on the side of the employee.

Commissioner O'Connell. I don't know of any one else but the employer.

Acting Chairman Commons. Would you say that apparently in this State there is anywhere from 90 per cent down to 60 per cent of unorganized wage earners? According to the figures given us yesterday, there would be about 6 per cent organized, and according to the figures you have just given, there would be about 25 per cent, I should think.

Dr. McMahon. With me it would be just a rough guess. My feeling about organized labor is this: I believe that organized labor has a stronger hold on the Pacific coast than it has farther east, and I think the reason for it is there hasn't been in our industries such a great demand for unskilled workers. I believe as time goes on that the tendency will be, if the development is practically the same as it has been in the past, for a decreasing proportion of workers to be organized.

Acting Chairman Commons. Decreasing?

Dr. McMahon. A decreasing number.

Acting Chairman Commons. Would you say in the appointment of these boards that the representatives of organized labor should be considered also as representatives of unorganized labor?

Dr. McMahon. No, sir. No; I do not think that they are always representatives of unorganized labor.

Acting Chairman Commons. On what ground do they not represent unorganized labor?

Dr. McMahon. Well——

Acting Chairman Commons. What instances have you in mind showing that they do not represent unorganized labor?

Dr. McMahon. I haven't any specific instances in mind in this State. In this State the labor unions have been instrumental in getting most of our labor legislation passed. The statement has been made to me by some eastern member of the organization that certain legislation was detrimental to unions in that the workers could get by legislation what the unions are organized to gain for them. Now, in this State the eight-hour law for women was initiated, brought up, and agitated by a woman who is head of the waitresses' union. It was taken up by organized labor, and that is true also of the minimum-wage law. There, again, the labor union instituted it. The labor unions in this State have taken the initiative. Now, in case you had a strong labor union which tended to be monopolistic in its character, I think the people on the outside might feel that they may not be fairly represented. That is organized labor's idea, it seems to me, to a certain extent, to protect the organized worker. I believe all workers should get into the organization.

Acting Chairman Commons. But you prophesy that a smaller and smaller proportion will be in the organization. So that according to that we will have to look for a larger and larger number not represented by those selected by organized labor.

Dr. McMahon. I think that organized labor is changing its attitude. As organized labor loses out I think it is beginning to find it has to represent the working people as a whole, and that is made clear by going into politics, and they then appeal to the working people as a whole. I believe when organized labor begins to find that it can not get by organization all it thinks is right and just, then it will go into politics. Then I think that they will come nearer representing labor as a whole; that is, they are acting as a mass. When speaking of organized labor perhaps I should have made it clear I have been thinking of trade organizations and not industrial organization. If the industrial idea can be realized of course they will be representative of the people as a whole.

Commissioner O'CONNELL. Is your ideal the industrial ideal of organization?

Dr. McMAHON. Yes, sir.

Commissioner O'CONNELL. What form of politics would you have labor organizations take up?

Dr. McMAHON. I believe in the labor party in politics representing the working classes, and while they have not been very successful in the past I think with the growing intelligence of the working people they will realize that their interests are common, and they will stand together just as the employers stand together.

Commissioner O'CONNELL. Do I understand you to say that your investigation showed that organized labor is growing less?

Dr. McMAHON. No, sir; I did not. That is my impression only. With the growing of these large industrial centers and the divisions of labor and the elimination of skill, it seems to me that the tendency would be, as the employers gain in power, with the concentration of wealth and the concentration of industry and large-scale production, that labor unionism is going to have rather a difficult road. I should point as an example to the steel workers.

Commissioner O'CONNELL. That is the general example everybody applies.

Dr. McMAHON. Yes, sir. In your monopolistic industries where it is carried on on a large scale and they carry out divisions of labor and employ unskilled workers we do not very often find that the labor union has been very successful in organizing the workers, and there is a tendency to large-scale production.

Commissioner O'CONNELL. You think the combination of capital is going on now, greater and greater all the time?

Dr. McMAHON. I certainly do.

Commissioner O'CONNELL. We haven't checked it by legislation at all?

Dr. McMAHON. Yes; but the ball rolls so much faster than the legislation.

Commissioner O'CONNELL. It is gathering speed on us?

Dr. McMAHON. Yes, sir.

Commissioner O'CONNELL. Do you believe in the organization of the employees in an industry as an organization, or the industry organized in which all belong?

Dr. McMAHON. I believe in an industrial organization in which all belong. I believe their working interests are very much the same. They may have to have divisions for the purpose of collective bargaining, but I believe the working people will have to stand together as a class politically.

Commissioner O'CONNELL. Then you are in perfect accord with the plan of the I. W. W.?

Dr. McMAHON. Not in their methods.

Commissioner O'CONNELL. Methods of organization?

Dr. McMAHON. Methods of reaching that organization.

Acting Chairman COMMONS. Have you paid attention to the organization of employment offices in this State?

Dr. McMAHON. Yes, sir. Last year one of our students wrote his master's thesis on employment offices. He got a permit from Mr. Grout, civil service commissioner, to go through the books of all private employment offices in the city. We haven't published it yet at the university; we haven't had the money.

Acting Chairman COMMONS. Did you have part in the investigation?

Dr. McMAHON. Yes, sir; he did the work with me.

Acting Chairman COMMONS. What is your own conclusions in the matter?

Dr. McMAHON. Practically the same conclusions were reached as Dr. Leiserson reached in his investigation in New York. The public employment office can not compete with the private employment office for a good many reasons. Your employer and your private employment offices are often in copartnership.

Acting Chairman COMMONS. What is your summing up of the efficiency of the public employment offices in this State?

Dr. McMAHON. I think that your private employment office has a financial motive only, while your public offices have as their motive services to the community. The two motives are entirely different, and that I think is one reason why your public offices fail in competing with private offices.

Acting Chairman COMMONS. In what way? Specify how does the public office fail.

Dr. McMAHON. Your public office attracts only unskilled workers. For instance, the women's employment office attracts household help, berry pickers, charwomen, or day workers. The complaint is made of the men's office that efficient help can not be secured. I think one reason for this is the lack·of office employees to carry on the work. For instance, in the men's office last year when we made the investigation there was but one man in the office. Now, all he could do when he got a job was to post it. There would be hundreds of men for that one job. There was no scientific method of management on account of lack of funds for that work.

Acting Chairman COMMONS. In other words, it does not make a definite effort to get the kind of people the employers want?

Dr. McMAHON. Not at all; it can't. Take, for instance, the women's employment office. One woman has charge of that, and she is.busy all day answering telephone calls and sending girls out. There is not adequate financial provision made for the support of the office.

Acting Chairman COMMONS. Is it your idea that the public office should try to get people that would satisfy the employers?

Dr. McMAHON. Yes, sir.

Acting Chairman COMMONS. In what sense would it differ from the private employment office?

Dr. McMAHON. You would have to eliminate your private office. For instance, Mr. Rice, in one case with another man went to a private employment office in order to get a position at one of the mills. He was charged a different rate than the man next to him. He said he probably looked a little more prosperous. I think there is no doubt that your employer and your employment office divides up the fee, which means nothing else but hiring your people at a lower wage. For instance, if the employment office charges a dollar and divides it with the employer, and in the course of a few days then man is discharged and another man is hired, it means lower pay roll for employer. Where the work is unskilled this method can be used. ·.I· have heard such instances given here. Whether they can be traced out and proven, I don't know. I don't doubt the statements are true. The history of employment has shown it to be true, and I think this is no exception.

Acting Chairman COMMONS. What is your idea of a remedy? .

Dr. McMAHON. To legislate private offices out of existence; that is, eliminate the fees. If you eliminate the fees you eliminate private offices carried on for gain. Trade-unions, I believe, can do the work more effectively.

Acting Chairman COMMONS. Your idea would be that employers' associations should run free offices?

Dr. McMAHON. If they want to run offices; yes, sir. They do now. You take, for instance, your department stores; they have their employment departments; they never advertise for workers. I don't believe they have advertised for a single worker.

Acting Chairman COMMONS. Do you think a public office could compete with a private office run by an employers' association if both were free?

Dr. McMAHON. It seems to me it wouldn't make very much difference. If you can compel private offices to keep records, if they want to render this service they ought to be in better position to know what kind of employees they want than the public office.

Acting Chairman COMMONS. Practically, that would drive the public office out of business.

Dr. McMAHON. Oh, no; I think not. For instance, in the department stores they wouldn't; in the lumbering industries to a certain extent. I think the lumbering industry has an office up at Everett. They did have a year or two ago; but there are a good many industries that could not afford it unless they had a general employers' employment office, which I don't think they would consider profitable. I think it would have to be a specific industry that had such an office.

Acting Chairman COMMONS. For the miscellaneous unorganized employee a public office would be desirable?

Dr. McMAHON. Yes, sir; I think so.

Acting Chairman COMMONS. The field would be divided among organized employers' associations which run their own offices?

Dr. McMahon. Yes, sir.

Acting Chairman Commons. And unorganized employers who would depend on the free public office?

Dr. McMahon. Yes; just as they do in Germany; but eliminate the fee. If we tried to eliminate all employment offices, the expense would be tremendous, and I am not sure the results would warrant the amount expended.

Acting Chairman Commons. Mr. Thompson, any questions?

Mr. Thompson. Just one other question: In your study of the industrial situation and trade-unions in this part of the country, have you made any particular investigation of collective bargaining, as such, between unions and employers?

Dr. McMahon. Well, if your unions are strong enough, they can bring about collective bargaining. In the copy of the contract they have sent me it is perfectly apparent that they had collective bargaining relative to certain points—apprenticeship and wages.

Mr. Thompson. Have you any idea as to how the contract so made might be carried out or might be enforced in case either party didn't wish to do it?

Dr. McMahon. Why, I think if your labor union is strong enough and your employers' association strong enough, they respect each other, and I think that mutual fear and respect would enforce it. It is only where one party is weaker than the other, I think, in carrying out the contract that you will find that it is not lived up to.

Mr. Thompson. How would you view any such thing as a penalty being placed on either of the parties in the nature of a fine?

Dr. McMahon. I don't think that would do, because a labor organization usually makes the best terms it can; it is not the terms that they consider exactly fair and just. If both sides considered they were fair and just at the time——

Acting Chairman Commons. Then, your view would be that the matter should be left to take its course in the natural development of the industry and of the organization of workers?

Dr. McMahon. Yes, sir.

Mr. Thompson. Have you any view as to the advisability of having trade-unions incorporated?

Dr. McMahon. Well, some of them are incorporated. I think that the great danger of incorporating them is making them liable, which I think would be a death blow to trade-unionism.

Mr. Thompson. That is all.

Acting Chairman Commons. Call your next witness.

Mr. Thompson. Mr. Ault.

(See letters filed in re testimony of Dr. McMahon, pp. 4563 to 4571.)

TESTIMONY OF MR. E. B. AULT.

Mr. Thompson. Give us your name.

Mr. Ault. E. B. Ault.

Mr. Thompson. And your business address.

Mr. Ault. Labor Temple.

Mr. Thompson. And your occupation.

Mr. Ault. I am editor and manager of the Seattle Union Record, the official organ of organized labor.

Mr. Thompson. The official organ?

Mr. Ault. Yes.

Mr. Thompson. What do you mean by official organ?

Mr. Ault. It is owned and controlled by the Central Labor Council, a delegate body representing practically all the unions in the city.

Mr. Thompson. How often is the paper issued?

Mr. Ault. Weekly.

Mr. Thompson. And what circulation generally has it got?

Mr. Ault. We print and distribute to subscribers sixty-five hundred copies per week.

Mr. Thompson. In a general way, what is the purpose of instituting the paper? To furnish the members with union news?

Mr. Ault. To furnish the members with news of labor movements in general, and educate them as to their rights under the law and as to suggested changes in the law that would benefit their condition.

Mr. Thompson. How long have you acted as editor of the paper?

Mr. AULT. Since April 7, 1913. I became editor coincident with Mr. Constantine becoming manager of the employers' association.

Mr. THOMPSON. Purely a coincidence?

Mr. AULT. Purely a coincidence; yes, sir.

Mr. THOMPSON. How long has the paper been in existence?

Mr. AULT. Sixteen years the 12th of last August.

Mr. THOMPSON. Prior to your becoming editor of this paper what were you doing?

Mr. AULT. A printer.

Mr. THOMPSON. And were you a member of the union—typographical union?

Mr. AULT. Yes, sir.

Mr. THOMPSON. How long have you been a member of the union?

Mr. AULT. Since October, 1901.

Mr. THOMPSON. Have you been living much in this part of the country?

Mr. AULT. Since becoming a member of organized labor, yes, sir. I came to Seattle in 1898.

Mr. THOMPSON. During these several years you have been a member of organized labor have you taken an active part in the work of organized labor?

Mr. AULT. Practically all the time: yes, sir.

Mr. THOMPSON. Have you been an officer of your union any part of the time?

Mr. AULT. Yes, sir; part of the time I have been an officer of my union.

Mr. THOMPSON. Now, during your work as an officer and with your membership in the organization have you made any study, general or specific, of industrial conditions?

Mr. AULT. Yes, sir.

Mr. THOMPSON. In Seattle and the country around here?

Mr. AULT. Yes, sir; I have, as far as lay in my power, studied that constantly all my life.

Mr. THOMPSON. Do you believe there are causes of industrial unrest existing in this country here?

Mr. AULT. Yes, sir.

Mr. THOMPSON. What, in your opinion, are they?

Mr. AULT. I think the main cause of industrial unrest is the lack of employment by a large proportion of the workers—available workers.

Mr. THOMPSON. Well, what is that due to, what are the conditions that bring that about?

Mr. AULT. Well, it is due to several—there are several reasons. The main reason, I take it, is that the worker is not able to repurchase his product. That is, it takes—that is, the sum received in wages by the average worker does not buy back products of the industry corresponding to the amount that the worker produces. I think that is the fundamental reason for unemployment.

Mr. THOMPSON. That reason is generally true of all people engaged in industry?

Mr. AULT. Of all people in all countries, as far as I know.

Mr. THOMPSON. That would apply even in the best organized crafts, would it not?

Mr. AULT. Yes; to a less degree. The better organized crafts have been able to secure a larger proportion of the products of their labor.

Mr. THOMPSON. What I mean is that that theory of unrest, while not saying it is not true, but it would be more of a general proposition not only the country over but the world over?

Mr. AULT. Yes, sir; that is true.

Mr. THOMPSON. It follows as a matter of necessity that the worker must get less if anybody else is to get any profit out of the industry?

Mr. AULT. Yes, sir.

Mr. THOMPSON. But more specifically or what nearer at hand would you say was the cause of the unrest here. Are there any other causes, in your opinion, that operate other than that cause?

Mr. AULT. It is perfectly true, as Mr. Constantaine said yesterday, that some of us who have reached some knowledge of the conditions under which the laboring classes labor are endeavoring to interest and lead the rest of the workers, who have not had the opportunity, to discover those conditions and know what those conditions are. I think there are agitators among the workers who attempt at all times to give the workers a knowledge of their rights, of the fact that they are abused under the present conditions and that they are entitled to a larger proportion of what they produce.

Mr. THOMPSON. Do you think that the workers in the canning industry in this State, as described by Dr. McMahon on the stand, require agitators to tell those workers that they have a hard time?

Mr. AULT. Yes, sir; I think they do. The workers in the canning industry are particularly and peculiarly subservient; they make no protest against these conditions; that is, no audible protest, no organized protest; they have no means of expressing any protest, and I think they do require agitation.

Mr. THOMPSON. Well, what I mean is: Do you think that the cause of their unrest would be the cause of an agitation which might be undertaken in their behalf?

Mr. AULT. Yes.

Mr. THOMPSON. Or whether it would be due to the conditions under which they work?

Mr. AULT. The conditions under which all of us work are the fundamental reasons that we agitate.

Mr. THOMPSON. What I want to get at, then, was not the voice which gives expression to the unrest, which we all recognize, of course, must go through certain avenues. Now, those are human beings that express themselves through the press or on the platform. But what, in your opinion, are the causes existing in this vicinity which would make the agitator—putting it in your own language—feel he should get up and start an agitation to make people dissatisfied?

Mr. AULT. Just such things as Mrs. McMahon spoke about in the canning industry—the long hours of labor—and the intermittent labor in the lumber industry, and, to a lesser degree, in all other industries, and the low wages, which are a general condition except in the better organized trades.

Mr. THOMPSON. For the benefit of the commission could you be a little more specific than that? For instance, we have the canning industry pretty well told; we have heard something of seasonal occupations, of the great amount of floating labor that comes here in the wintertime. Could you carry that out more specifically and give us some graspable condition?

Mr. AULT. I can't speak except in the most general terms with reference to the lumber industry, with which I am only acquainted by hearsay, and the same condition is true of our other largest industry, that of construction work, which takes in a large army of seasonal workers who work for usually a day of 10 hours, I believe; but they work for very low wages and under the most horrible sanitary conditions, and they are continuously going to and coming from the job. This movement is accelerated by the private employment offices, and, as has been stated before on the stand, the inference is general through the country here that there is collusion between some one in authority on these construction jobs and in the logging camp and in the mill and the private employment agent, whereby there is a rake-off from the fees that the men pay.

In addition to that the tendency to hire and fire men is accelerated by the fact that they charge more for board when the man stays less than a week out in the camp, and they charge 20 cents per day for hospital fee, so that the worker who works five days in any month is compelled to pay the full dollar required for the hospital fee, and if he is fired the next day and goes to another job he will be compelled to pay this hospital fee on the next job so that sometimes workers are compelled to pay four or five dollars a month in hospital fees. Those are all contributing causes to the unrest in this section.

Mr. THOMPSON. Take the question of this large amount of floating labor that comes here during the wintertime—that has been the condition in Seattle for a great number of years, has it not?

Mr. AULT. Yes, sir; as far as I can remember Seattle has been the mecca in the fall and winter months for the workers of the woods and construction workers.

Mr. THOMPSON. What remedy have you to suggest to the commission for that that would alleviate it in part or wholly?

Mr. AULT. There are a number of things which could be done to alleviate it and better it. One is better organization of the biggest industry in the State, the lumber industry. That is not necessarily a seasonal occupation in this country, because the winters are mild and there is no reasonable excuse for the logging and lumbering industries being seasonal occupations.

Mr. THOMPSON. What makes it such, if you know?

Mr. AULT. Why, the supply of labor; the fact that they can get all that they want at a given time, and there is this advantage in the summer months that they can work longer days than they can in the winter, the days are shorter in the winter. But a general reduction of the hours of labor in the logging camps and the industries generally, an eight-hour day would be a tremendous benefit to that industry and would solve in some small part this problem of seasonal employment.

Mr. THOMPSON. How, in your opinion, could this eight-hour day be best brought around?

Mr. AULT. In my opinion, the best way to bring it around is by organization of the workers involved. That would be the most effective way and the most certain way. At present we are engaged in an effort to bring it about through legislation.

Mr. THOMPSON. You are speaking now of lumbering generally?

Mr. AULT. Yes, sir.

Mr. THOMPSON. What organization is there, if any, now in that industry?

Mr. AULT. There is an organization styled the timber workers, which is composed, as I understand it, mainly of shingle weavers—men engaged in the manufacture and packing of shingles.

Mr. THOMPSON. Does that organization include also people that work in the forest?

Mr. AULT. It has jurisdiction to cover those workers and is attempting to organize them.

Mr. THOMPSON. You are not specifically acquainted with that industry, are you?

Mr. AULT. Not specifically; no, sir.

Mr. THOMPSON. What other remedy would you give for this state of industrial unrest which you say exists here?

Mr. AULT. Why, the only general remedy I could give is a radical reduction of the working day, so as to employ all available workers.

Mr. THOMPSON. Have you any industrial conflicts here. Are there many strikes of large or small degree?

Mr. AULT. They are fairly numerous; not so numerous, however, as in other places, and they haven't been particularly bitter; that is, in Seattle particularly.

Mr. THOMPSON. Has there been any trouble in adjusting those which have arisen?

Mr. AULT. Yes, sir; there has been trouble in all of them.

Mr. THOMPSON. Has there been much violence, if you know, and the destruction of property?

Mr. AULT. Not any appreciable violence or destruction of property.

Mr. THOMPSON. Have you any views as to the best method of adjusting industrial disputes where they arise, or any view as to how to prevent them from arising where there is organization or lack of organization, either way?

Mr. AULT. Well, the only method I know is by sufficient organization on the part of the workers to secure their demands.

Preferably, perhaps, through a show of power before a mediation board—conciliation board—but if necessary through a strike. I don't know of any way of avoiding strikes altogether. I don't know that it is desirable to avoid them altogether.

Mr. THOMPSON. Well, what part do you think this mediation board could play in the adjustment of the trouble between the employer and the employee?

Mr. AULT. I think in many instances a mediation board could on knowledge of trouble impending, get the conflicting parties together and perhaps bring about a settlement that would, while not satisfactory to either, avoid a conflict and would be a betterment of conditions for the workers, or probably in some cases hold what they are about to lose.

Mr. THOMPSON. Have you made a study of the subject of the mediation boards?

Mr. AULT. Only superficially.

Mr. THOMPSON. And their work?

Mr. AULT. Only superficially.

Mr. THOMPSON. Have you any conviction or idea as to how such a board could be constituted?

Mr. AULT. Well, I haven't really. I feel that such a board should be composed of equal numbers of the parties in interest.

Mr. THOMPSON. Your own union, the typographical union, is a believer in collective bargaining, is it not?

Mr. AULT. Yes, sir; and is very successful.

Mr. THOMPSON. They use that method extensively, I believe?

Mr. AULT. Altogether.

Mr. THOMPSON. What is your opinion as to the best method or any method that might be inaugurated for the purpose of helping those contracts to be carried out where both sides are concerned?

Mr. AULT. Well, the best method that I know of is an organization of all of the workers involved in the industry. And, on the other hand, the organization of the employers. Under such conditions the workers would be able to secure, when a contract had been entered into, the workers would be able to insure its observance.

Mr. THOMPSON. Where you say the workers would be able to insure its observance, do you mean on their part or on the part of the employers?

Mr. AULT. On the part of both. I think that the history of contractural relations between employer and employees will show that where there has been one violation of a contract on the part of the workers there have been a hundred violations on the part of the employer.

Mr. THOMPSON. Looking at this for the moment from the standpoint of the employers it is generally said, you hear it pretty often, that the employer feels that trades-unions do not live up to their contracts, and that there is more or less of a demand made that unions should either be incorporated or that they should give bonds, or that in some way they should be held responsible, definitely and financially, for agreements that they make. Have you heard that question raised?

Mr. AULT. Yes; I have heard that question raised.

Mr. THOMPSON. What is your view with regard to that matter?

Mr. AULT. I feel, speaking as a union man, that incorporation, or any form of financial liability on the individual members of organized labor, would be a great detriment to the progress of organized labor.

Mr. THOMPSON. Tell us more or less in detail your reasons why.

Mr. AULT. As, for instance, the case of the Danbury hatters, wherein the individual members of organized labor had been held responsible for losses incurred by a firm of manufacturers as the result of a boycott. Now, in a general fight of that kind the boycott is the only weapon that organized labor has. If the membership of organized labor, the individual membership of organized labor, can be held individually responsible for losses incurred by the employer, it means that labor must give up the only weapon that it has, and that when unions can do nothing for themselves they will naturally pass out of existence.

Mr. THOMPSON. In the troubles you have had out here, has there been any trouble over the policing of strikes or lockouts?

Mr. AULT. We have had——

Mr. THOMPSON. Or the employment of private agencies by the employer?

Mr. AULT. We have had some experience with that in the miners' strike at Renton, closed a short time ago; some firm furnished private guards to the employer, and they were deputized by the county sheriff. In another case in Ballard, in the shingle weavers' strike, a similar condition prevailed. There was more or less violence in both of those strikes, due almost entirely to the use of these guards. They picked fights and they got them when they picked them. And in Ballard, particularly, there were dynamite plants placed by one of these guards with the object of throwing odium on the union involved, but it was unsuccessful, because of the prompt action taken by the union in exposing the entire affair. But the attempt was there. And in the recent teamsters' strike there was an attempt to plant dynamite at the home of some of the strikers, but they made a mistake and got the dynamite planted 10 blocks away and that blew up.

Mr. THOMPSON. Well, have you opinions as to whether or not the law should take a hand in permitting or saying something about whether any class of the community should be permitted to hire private armed guards?

Mr. AULT. I think that the use of armed guards under private control is utterly indefensible, that if there is no law—I believe that it is an extralegal proceeding. There is no law that allows it, and if there is no law that prevents it, there should be a law.

Mr. THOMPSON. What would you say with reference to the argument which is stated pretty unanimously that the employer has to guard his works against destruction and prevent the property from being destroyed?

Mr. AULT. I can't think that that is true, in view of the fact that the employer has practically absolute control of the governing forces in city, State, and Nation.

Mr. THOMPSON. In this State, I understand, it was stated that when the mayor withdrew the 50 special armed guards that were placed there by the sheriff, that then the employers settled the trouble or agreed to arbitrate.

Mr. AULT. Well, that was a very——

Mr. THOMPSON. If that is so—I don't know, but it is stated that it is so— why was it that the employer was induced to settle, or why did he settle then when he had not before? What is your opinion on that?

Mr. AULT. There are a great many factors entering into that particular settlement.

Acting Chairman COMMONS. Mr. Ault, it is time for the commission to adjourn, and we will not meet again until to-morrow, on account of the funeral of Mrs. Wilson, the President's wife. Will you take the stand to-morrow at 10 o'clock?

Mr. AULT. Yes; I will be glad to.

Acting Chairman COMMONS. And begin at that point.

The commission will stand adjourned.

(And thereupon, at 12.30 o'clock p. m. Tuesday, August 11, 1914, an adjournment was taken until the following day, August 12, 1914, at 10 o'clock a. m.)

SEATTLE, WASH., *Wednesday, August 12, 1914—10 a. m.*

Present: Commissioners Commons (acting chairman), Lennon, Garretson, and O'Connell; also W. O. Thompson, counsel.

Acting Chairman COMMONS. The commission will come to order. Mr. Thompson, call your witness.

Mr. THOMPSON. Mr. Ault, take the stand.

TESTIMONY OF MR. E. B. AULT—Continued.

Mr. THOMPSON. I believe, Mr. Ault, you were stopped——

Mr. AULT. Why, I don't remember the question, and I would like to make a statement in respect to yesterday's testimony before proceeding with the examination. I was called up by a gentleman who styled himself president, I believe, of the association of employment agencies, who took exception to the testimony I gave yesterday in respect to collusion between employment offices and foremen or contractors or their agents. And he asked specific instances which I could not and can not give. The practice, or the assumption that the practice exists, however, is so general, and the conditions which make for such practice are so general and so generally accepted that we have made no particular effort as far as I know to get particular cases; but it is a generally accepted condition throughout the West that the employment offices, at least some of the employment offices, and some of the foremen have some method of dividing the employment fees, because there are bodies of workingmen going from job to job, from employment office back to the job constantly in such large numbers that the efficiency of the work must be impaired, and therefore there can be no other explanation except a division of the fees.

Commissioner O'CONNELL. Will you just designate who is the principal employment agent so that we can subpoena him?

Mr. AULT. The gentleman told me his name, but I could not understand it, the telephone wasn't working.

Commissioner O'CONNELL. Will you find out for us?

Mr. AULT. Yes, sir; we can find out.

Acting Chairman COMMONS. Get us his name and address.

Mr. AULT. Yes, sir; that is very easy, and maybe some of the other gentlemen here know it already.

Mr. THOMPSON. We ended yesterday's examination with some statement in regard to the teamsters' strike and the settlement of it. Prior to your testimony in that regard, Mr. Ault, you spoke of the fact that there had been some planting of dynamite here in Seattle by the employers, if I remember correctly?

Mr. AULT. I don't know that I said that. It was planted, I stated, in the effort to—oh, show that the strikers were—it was planted in an effort to cast odium on the strikers. That was the statement I made, I believe.

Mr. THOMPSON. That was planted, in your opinion, or according to the facts you have, by the employers, for that purpose, Mr. Ault?

Mr. AULT. I feel that the employers had knowledge of the condition; yes. I have no evidence to prove that, but that is my impression; that was the impression that was quite general through the city, I believe.

Mr. THOMPSON. That is, of course, a pretty serious charge.

Mr. AULT. Yes, sir.

Mr. THOMPSON. Would you want to be understood that they planted that with the idea of having an explosion occur, or just to be discovered and create public opinion?

Mr. AULT. In one case an explosion occurred, Mr. Thompson. In the case of the shingle weavers' strike in Ballard an explosion occurred. The dynamite was planted in that place where it would not do any particular harm to the plant, but the explosion occurred. In the other case the intention was that the men who—the dynamite was planted in the rear of what was presumed to be the home of a striking teamster, or a number of striking teamsters, in an effort to—and then was discovered—in an effort to prove that the teamsters were going to use dynamite.

Mr. THOMPSON. In regard to placing the responsibility for that, you have no specific evidence, you say?

Mr. AULT. I believe there is quite specific evidence in the matter of the shingle weavers planting at Ballard. The matter was in the courts, and for some reason or other the prosecuting attorney's office did not press the matter as thoroughly as we had hoped they would.

Mr. THOMPSON. Could you get the data and furnish this commission with it?

Mr. AULT. Why, I believe Mr. Brown who is to be called later has all of that matter.

Mr. THOMPSON. Now, with reference to the dynamite in the teamsters' strike in this city, is there any specific evidence that you have or could refer the commission to, which they could investigate?

Mr. AULT. We have only the evidence of the man who discovered the dynamite and implied in the confession that he made that another man who was well known in this country as a strike breaker, an agent for securing strike breakers, was implicated with him in the planting of the dynamite in an effort to throw suspicion on the teamsters' union. That confession is of record, I believe, in the county courthouse.

Mr. THOMPSON. Was there any prosecution of those two men?

Mr. AULT. I think that the man—I am not certain now—but I believe that the man who confessed served a six months' sentence, or was sentenced for six months. I think he is in jail now.

Mr. THOMPSON. Do you know how that confession was brought about?

Mr. AULT. By third-degree methods, I think, perhaps.

Mr. THOMPSON. I mean——

Mr. AULT. Careful questioning by the prosecuting attorney's office.

Mr. THOMPSON. Who unearthed the dynamite? Who reported it to the police? And if there was a prosecution, who was back of it, if you know?

Mr. AULT. Well, this man who confessed, as I remember, reported it to the sheriff's office, and the sheriff's deputies were suspicious and questioned the man closely, and he made a number of—his statements did not corroborate one another.

Mr. THOMPSON. Have you investigated, Mr. Ault, as to how it occurred that this man confessed to the sheriff as to what caused him to go to the sheriff after doing this thing and confessing it?

Mr. AULT. Well, his statement was that he went to the sheriff in an effort to show that the teamsters had dynamite planted here, and that he had discovered it, and he made the statement that the intention was to blow up some of the property of the members of the team owners' association.

Mr. THOMPSON. Who was the sheriff at that time?

Mr. AULT. The present sheriff, Sheriff Cudihee. This occurred only about six months ago.

Mr. THOMPSON. Do you know whether or not the employers' association of this city had something to do with causing the indictment and prosecution of these men?

Mr. AULT. No; I do not.

Mr. THOMPSON. Have you heard anything of that kind?

Mr. AULT. The only thing that I know positively is that they disclaimed any connection with the matter at the time it occurred.

Mr. THOMPSON. Did you personally make any investigation to see whether or not—to find out how the confession of this man was procured or how he came to make a confession to the sheriff?

Mr. AULT. No. The matter was looked on as though somebody's calculation had gone wrong, and the matter came out to our satisfaction, and we did not pay any more attention to it.

Mr. THOMPSON. Then so far as you actually know it might be that the unearthing of this dynamite planting, the apprehension of the men who did it, and their prosecution might have been at the hands of the employers' association of this city?

Mr. AULT. Yes; so far as I positively know.

Mr. THOMPSON. Referring to the question of specific remedies, Mr. Ault, in the industrial labor which you have spoken of more generally in your first testimony, what other remedies than those you have suggested, remedies that this commission has the legal power to take into consideration and which Congress of the United States have power to act on, would you suggest?

Mr. AULT. I think that a better organization of the labor distributing forces of the country might be accomplished through congressional action or through recommendation of this commission. That would tend to determine the actual number of wage workers in employment and out of employment at all times; something that is of vital importance to any constructive measure is to find out what the facts are. That is something that so far there apparently is no agency to cover.

Mr. THOMPSON. What sort of an agency would you have for that or would it include any other function than simply getting information?

Mr. AULT. Yes; I should think it would include as one of its functions the matter of furnishing employment and distributing the workers where there was work in case there was work and merely as a remedial measure.

Mr. THOMPSON. Then a system of Federal employment bureau or offices in the different cities and States of the Union working in cooperation with one another, keeping track of the matter of the labor market of the respective vicinities, and also keeping track of the labor supply and communicating back and forth, and working also in connection with State agencies, that, in your opinion, would be a good step?

Mr. AULT. That would be a good step to take, I think. I don't believe it would accomplish any great result in the matter of relieving the unemployed, because it is my firm belief from the data I have been able to gather that there is no possibility of employing all possible wage earners under the present conditions.

Mr. THOMPSON. In your opinion could the present conditions be changed radically?

Mr. AULT. Yes, sir.

Mr. THOMPSON. At any one time? I mean to say, considering the people, their ideas of industrial life, and so on, no radical change is possible, is it? You can't get the people to go with you on a radical change?

Mr. AULT. That, of course, I haven's absolutely determined for myself as yet. I feel it is possible, but perhaps hardly probable.

Mr. THOMPSON. I mean probable; we are dealing in probabilities, of course; we have to.

Mr. AULT. Yes, sir.

Mr. THOMPSON. With reference to any other thing which you think that the Federal Government could do to help at least in the line of progress along industrial and commercial fields.

Mr. AULT. I think perhaps the greatest thing that the workers need is some right, some method of enforcing their right to organize; that the Government take some steps to protect the workers in their right to organize and give them an opportunity to organize.

Mr. THOMPSON. Well, concretely, what would you recommend?

Mr. AULT. I would like to elaborate a little here.

Mr. THOMPSON. You can.

Mr. AULT. In this city, for instance, the Puget Sound Traction Light & Power Co. maintains an absolutely closed shop. No member of organized labor, if he is known to be a member of organized labor, can work for this company— that is, I speak of the operating department of the street railway. There are, I believe, one or two or half a dozen union men in the employment of the company in other positions, but in the operating department particularly there is every discrimination made against union men and I understand—this I can only speak of from secondhand information, men have told me who have worked for the company, that it is the practice of this company to every so often discharge a number of men and bulletin them as having been agitators or attempting to organize, whether there was any truth in the assertion or not. It was a method of keeping them in fear of any attempt to organize. There appears to be, according to the statements of these street car men to me, there appears to be no attempt to determine whether they have been agitators or not, but just a number of men who could be discharged were discharged, and it is the practice of the company to continually break in new men, so that perhaps 30 per cent of the working population of this city is now capable of running a street car in case of any disturbance. That right—that is, I believe, typical of a great many industries. That condition is true of the Seattle Construction & Dry Dock Co. The general manager of that company, Mr. J. V. Patterson, will not allow knowingly a union man to work in his plant. The metal trades association, I understand, have a very effective employment office which effectually disposes of all agitators. I think with that proposition it would be possible perhaps to withdraw from employers, who refused to allow their employers to organize, the protection of their property. That may sound a little funny at first, but in this State we have already done that in respect to the industrial insurance act. We have taken away from the employer all of the old common-law defenses in case of accident, in case he elects or refuses to come in under the industrial insurance act. In that case the old defenses of fellow servant and anything of that kind are removed, and an employee—or any employer who has not come under the industrial insurance act can go into court, and the employer has practically no defense. I think that some similar action might be taken in respect to the employer who will not allow his workers to organize and who will not deal or bargain collectively with his workers. I think there is more really involved than merely the right to organize. I think that they should be compelled to recognize the policy of collective bargaining and to bargain collectively. That I think would aid and probably work to the ultimate solution of the entire labor problem if such a policy was undertaken.

Mr. THOMPSON. Well, coming down to more detailed enactments, how would you do that? Would you simply say that the employer must permit his people to organize? Would you have any lines of organization that they might join?

Mr. AULT. I think that should be determined by the workers themselves, what their organization is, what their form of organization should be.

Mr. THOMPSON. Of course, in an insurance proposition, it is a State-wide matter.

Mr. AULT. Yes, sir.

Mr. THOMPSON. It relates not only to the employer who runs a factory or a store or a mill, but I take it—although I don't know your law in detail—it relates to everybody who is employed.

Mr. AULT. All in harzardous or partially hazardous occupations, that is all.

Mr. THOMPSON. Now, in the matter or organization, would you have it apply to all the States, to everybody employed, no matter in what service?

Mr. AULT. I should think so.

Mr. THOMPSON. And under that law, or in that law would you have any provision stating, for instance, that the members of a labor organization, any labor organization, should be denied the right to quit work because a man working for the same employer was not a member of their organization? Would you take that right away from the labor unions?

Mr. AULT. No; I would not. I think that is one of their fundamental rights.

Mr. THOMPSON. Yes. Well, now, assuming that your law then does not simply compel the employer to permit organization, and does not prevent the employees from refusing to work with anybody there, what would you do in case of rival organizations that were formed in the same factory, or in the case where some citizens of the United States—some American citizen, for reasons of his own, did not wish to join the organization?

Mr. AULT. Well, it would—that is a matter of detail which I will admit I haven't worked out in my own mind.

Mr. THOMPSON. Well, that would simply put industry so far as the workers are concerned, in the hands of those who would organize?

Mr. AULT. Yes, sir.

Mr. Thompson. And would be, as a matter of fact would be, a compulsion, indirect but still powerful, on the man and the worker who did not want to organize?

Mr. Ault. Yes, sir.

Mr. Thompson. How would you view that in the attitude of both the unions and employers who object to compulsory arbitration, where a great dispute is on; for instance, where a street car line may be tied up and citizens may be compelled to walk, and yet they say, "We won't submit to compulsory arbitration." How would you distinguish those two things one from the other?

Mr. Ault. As I say, I haven't worked out in my own mind the details of this proposition. It is a matter that occurred to me as a possible method of enforcing the right of the workers to organize. But I personally believe that it is the duty of every worker to organize. I see no, absolutely no method of the worker getting any control in industry, having anything to say in respect to his hours or conditions of employment, except through organization. And I feel that every worker is entitled to this right that he has. I have here a copy of the issue of the Weekly Messenger, official organ of the employers' association for August 1, 1914, in which they state in their concluding paragraph on their first page: "Our manufacturers must continue to realize that the most valuable machinery in the plant is the man or woman working in it, and that their health and happiness are productive of profits to both the employer and the employee." Now, we own that machinery. That is our capital that is invested, and we have the right to determine the conditions under which that machinery is used. And I see no effective way of doing that except through organization.

Mr. Thompson. Well, you are speaking, though, more directly of the fact the State should take a hand in that and compel organization.

Mr. Ault. No.

Mr. Thompson. I think everybody, apparently so far as we go and have gone, both the employer and the employee believe, do not question the right of the worker to organize.

Mr. Ault. That is true, Mr. Thompson, in testimony given, but in actual practice the reverse is true. They not only question the right of the employee to organize, but they prevent the possibility of him organizing.

Mr. Thompson. Well, what I probably should have stated is that they grant the theoretical right.

Mr. Ault. Yes.

Mr. Thompson. But they may reserve the personal right, that he don't want to deal with organization.

Mr. Ault. My proposal is an attempt at a practical proposition—to withdraw support, to withdraw Government support, to withdraw guaranties from an employer who actually in a concrete case refuses to allow his employees to organize.

Mr. Thompson. Well, such a law as you state would practically be the first step in the socialization of industry, would it not?

Mr. Ault. Probably that is true. At least in the democratization of the industry.

Mr. Thompson. Well, perhaps. With reference to that matter, do you think it is practicable to recommend to Congress the passage of such a law, when not more than 6 or 7 per cent of the workers of the country are organized—do you think there is enough public opinion back of it in this day and age to get it put into a law?

Mr. Ault. I would like to be a little clearer on that statement of 6 or 7 per cent of the workers being organized.

Mr. Thompson. Well, whatever per cent you agree——

Mr. Ault. I don't agree to that. I think that there is approximately 40 to 50 per cent of the workers susceptible to organization organized.

Mr. Thompson. Of course, I don't know on what you base that statement, but, as a matter of fact the workers of the country are more than 6 or 7 per cent, or possibly, at the outside, 10 per cent, as a matter of fact, organized.

Mr. Ault. Ten per cent of the population?

Mr. Thompson. Of the working population actually working. It may be there are a larger percentage of those who are subject to organization.

Mr. Ault. Three million.

Commissioner O'Connell. Of those who are capable of working?

Mr. Ault. Three million.

Mr. THOMPSON. Of those actually working?

Mr. AULT. Three million workers in the country.

Acting Chairman COMMONS. About 30,000,000 wage earners?

Mr. THOMPSON. About 30,000,000.

Commissioner O'CONNELL. That depends entirely upon what you figure as a wage earner.

Mr. AULT. That is the question.

Mr. THOMPSON. Understand, Mr. Ault, that it is the purpose of this commission, and we simply want to get from you and others practical suggestions that can be put in operation.

Mr. AULT. Yes; I recognize that.

Mr. THOMPSON. If we should recommend socialism, Congress will say that they can not do that; that that may be a very good propaganda, but it will not result in any practical effects. What other suggestions have you got, Mr. Ault, that this commission might recommend to Congress and which Congress, as society is now organized, might be willing to pass?

Mr. AULT. Well, I really believe that, as I say, the main proposition is to give the workers the right to organize. That is the first practical suggestion. If there is any possible practical way of enforcing the right of the workers to organize, I think that they will take care of most of these problems themselves. I think that they are altogether capable of taking care of their own problems if they can first be assured of the right to act collectively, as I said.

Mr. THOMPSON. Have you any more definite suggestion to offer as to how that might be brought about than you have already stated?

Mr. AULT. That is the only definite suggestion that I have in that respect.

Mr. THOMPSON. I might say to you if you get any other concrete views on that subject the commission will be pleased to receive anything you have to send to them in writing and make it a part of the record.

Mr. AULT. All right.

Mr. THOMPSON. Is there anything more, Mr. Ault, that you care to speak of?

Mr. AULT. Why, I want rather to emphasize the statement Dr. McMahon made yesterday with respect to the proportion of organized workers to unorganized workers in this State. As Mr. Olson said in his testimony, he was making a guess, and I am afraid he has hazarded a very wild guess. There are one hundred and sixty-five thousand and odd workers come under the industrial insurance act of this State. This comprises approximately 80 to 85 per cent of all the workers engaged in industry in this State. That would make a total working population of this State not more than 225,000 people.

The number of organized workers is not 25,000. We have 15,000 in Seattle. The railroad brotherhoods have nearly 15,000 themselves. There are more nearly 50,000 organized workers in the State than 25,000. So that the relative proportion is a great deal different from that that people who are otherwise uninformed would get from the testimony given. In this teamsters' strike—I have made a few notes of a number of things that I think should be touched on. In the teamsters' strike Mr. Constantine stated there had been 300 cases of arrest for violence. He failed to state also that there was only 1 conviction in those 300 cases. There were numerous convictions of strike breakers carrying arms, and of occasionally using them, but there was no instance where a striker was found carrying arms—not even found carrying arms. The matter of workers appearing before the minimum-wage commission and acting in their own interest or testifying in their own behalf: There was one young woman who was given permission by her employer to appear before the commission. Her testimony was distinctly favorable to a high minimum wage in the laundry industry and the result was she was discharged—or rather she was discharged, whether that was the result of her testimony or not is a matter of dispute. But be that as it may, the proprietor of that laundry was fined $100 in the justice court for his action in discharging this girl. The case is now before the superior court on appeal. This was the case of Miss Johanna Hilts. The teamsters' arbitration was not satisfactory to either party as far as I can gather.

The teamsters, I believe, have lived up absolutely to their part of the agreement. I don't believe there is any criticism even from the employers on that point. Some of the employers have not done as they agreed to do. Under the terms of the settlement the employers agreed to take back all the union men, employ them as fast as vacancies occurred. Instead of doing that, they have discriminated against some twenty-odd teamsters who are still in destitute circumstances because of the discrimination of the employers involved.

There is one other point that I want to bring out that I feel is the—that the solution of this proposition is the solution of the entire matter. The statement was made that in some industries in this State 23 per cent excess working population is required to handle the work in the rush season, in others as high as 50 per cent. That means—that is supplemented in a statement made by the secretary of the National Chamber of Commerce before the Indianapolis Cham-, ber of Commerce, some three or four months ago, I don't remember the exact date, in which he stated that the productive forces of this country had reached the point where they could supply the home market with 90 days' production. In 90 days' time each year. If that is true, there is certainly some radical remedy necessary to relieve such a condition. Something must be done to expand the home market or something must be done in the matter of dividing up the jobs so that all the workers may have the opportunity to work during those 90 days, or divide up those 90 days during the year. Those are all the notes I have made, Mr. Thompson.

Mr. THOMPSON. That is all, Mr. Chairman.

Acting Chairman COMMONS. Any questions, Mr. Lennon?

Commissioner LENNON. Were you here yesterday morning when Dr. McMahon was on the stand and Commissioner Garretson explained in asking questions as to their organization, what they meant by the open shop? Did you hear that?

Mr. AULT. Yes, sir; I heard that.

Commissioner LENNON. That is to say, as the railroad brotherhoods have collective bargaining, they do not insist on what is called the closed shop in so far as everybody must be a member of the brotherhood, but they do insist that there shall be no individual bargaining, that every one working in their particular line must come under the collective bargaining. Do you believe that that idea of the open shop would be objectionable to trade-unions generally?

Mr. AULT. As far as I know it would not. If that practice was general, I believe it would work out to the advantage of the trade-unions.

Commissioner LENNON. Now, in suggesting the idea of protecting the right to organize, you know something—perhaps you know more even than I do, for all I know—of the existing trade-union act in Great Britain, which recognizes certain practices that the unions are carrying out, and the work they participate in; recognizes the fact that the unions exist; that they picket and do certain other things, and in conjunction with the institution of the British Labor Council, a conciliatory body, a body for mediation purposes, recognizing by the nation that labor organization exist and that they have a right to exist. Do you believe that adapting this to American conditions, that the passage of a law by Congress of the United States on the line of the Great Britain union act and establishing a labor council to look after these interests generally, do you believe that would help in this country?

Mr. AULT. I am not very familiar with the trade act in England, but I believe such a condition would be of benefit to the workers. I believe that the recognition by the Government of the right to organize would be a long step toward the workers themselves taking up the opportunity to organize.

Commissioner LENNON. That is all I desire to ask.

Acting Chairman COMMONS. Any questions, Mr. O'Connell?

Commissioner O'CONNELL. Do you know whether there are any laws that are controlling these employment agencies—State laws or municipal laws?

Mr. AULT. There are State laws and some municipal ordinances.

Commissioner O'CONNELL. They are licensed, are they?

Mr. AULT. They pay a license of $100, I believe; I am not certain as to that, and the law provides that they inform the applicant for work whether there is a strike on at the place where the job is, and other details of that matter, and providing for the return of the fee in case the work is not found as represented.

Commissioner O'CONNELL. Do they make a practice of furnishing men to take the place of strikers?

Mr. AULT. I could not say generally, but some of them do that.

Commissioner O'CONNELL. Have you observed that they specialized their business here, some providing railroad men exclusively, and others lumbermen?

Mr. AULT. Yes; to quite a large extent that is true.

Commissioner O'CONNELL. Some of them make a specialty of supplying female labor?

Mr. AULT. Yes; a large number of them.

Commissioner O'CONNELL. Are there any inspectors or investigations as to the methods they adopt in employing female labor?

Mr. AULT. The city maintains a special agent for employment offices, who investigates all complaints and has general supervision over the employment offices. He is a very conscientious and earnest worker. I don't know how much he can do; he is alone.

Commissioner O'CONNELL. Have there been any charges of white slavery in connection with their employment?

Mr. AULT. Not that I know of.

Commissioner O'CONNELL. We have discovered in some instances where we have investigated that such has been the case.

Mr. AULT. Yes, sir. I know of nothing specific in that connection in this country.

Commissioner O'CONNELL. You will get the name of one who is considered to be the leader of the employment agents in the city, or if they have an association, the name of the president.

Acting Chairman COMMONS. We have it.

Commissioner O'CONNELL. Have they an association?

Mr. AULT. That is what I understand. A gentleman called me up this morning, stating that he was president of the association. I could not get his name over the telephone.

Acting Chairman COMMONS. Any questions, Mr. Garretson?

Commissioner GARRETSON. Are you aware of the fact that as far back as 1895 or 1897 a Federal act was passed making it an offense to discharge a man for membership in the labor union?

Mr. AULT. No, sir; I must admit that I am not.

Commissioner GARRETSON. Are you aware of the fact that the act was declared unconstitutional by the lowest grade of Federal judge, and there was no legal process in effect whereby it could be gotten to the Supreme Court to determine whether or not it was constitutional?

Mr. AULT. No, sir; not knowing the other fact, I naturally wouldn't know the sequence.

Commissioner GARRETSON. You are not familiar, then, with the provisions in the original act?

Mr. AULT. No, sir.

Commissioner GARRETSON. Affecting interstate employees?

Mr. AULT. No, sir.

Commissioner GARRETSON. In which that proviso was incorporated, and the decision was made by Judge Evans in a north Kentucky district?

Mr. AULT. That was in 1905?

Commissioner GARRETSON. The act was in 1895 or 1897.

Mr. AULT. I was a very, very young man at that time. I haven't studied the railroad situation particularly.

Commissioner GARRETSON. I am a very young man myself, but I was there when it was passed. Your belief is there are too many men for the jobs that exist?

Mr. AULT. Yes, sir.

Commissioner GARRETSON. There is not enough jobs to go around?

Mr. AULT. There is not enough jobs to go around; that is my belief.

Commissioner GARRETSON. But you do believe that the machinery that was cited to you, of a comprehensive system of employment agencies, combined as intelligence agencies, acting in conjunction with and under a certain degree of supervision of a Federal agency, naturally the Department of Labor, would at least succeed in getting the number of people—succeed in connecting the number of jobs that there are with the number of men that could fill them?

Mr. AULT. Yes; I think so; and in addition it would show the number of excess men there were, which is of vital importance.

Commissioner GARRETSON. We would know even if we could not feed them?

Mr. AULT. If we could learn the number we might take some steps to feed them.

Commissioner GARRETSON. In your personal contact with laboring men—not necessarily labor men, but laboring men, regardless of union or nonunion—have you ever found one who didn't regard the piling up of a colossal fortune in the hands of an individual as positive proof of the injustice of the present industrial system?

Mr. AULT. I have met a few who had hopes they would become pilers of colossal fortunes themselves—a very few.

Commissioner GARRETSON. They were perfectly willing to tolerate them if they were doing the piling?

Mr. AULT. That was the idea exactly.

Commissioner GARRETSON. But they did not approve of it in the hands of others?

Mr. AULT. No.

Commissioner GARRETSON. Then it was another question as an ethical proposition?

Mr. AULT. Yes; as an ethical proposition.

Commissioner GARRETSON. That is all.

Acting Chairman COMMONS. You stated yesterday in answer to some question that you were a socialist?

Mr. AULT. I have been a member of the Socialist Party for a great number of years; yes.

Acting Chairman COMMONS. Are you a member now?

Mr. AULT. Yes.

Acting Chairman COMMONS. Is your paper the official organ of trade-unions or of the socialists?

Mr. AULT. My paper is the official organ—it is not my paper—it is the official organ and the property of the Central Labor Council of Seattle. It is not a Socialist paper in any sense of the word. It is a trade-union paper, advocating the policies laid down by the American Federation of Labor.

Acting Chairman COMMONS. How do you distinguish in this State and in Seattle trades-unionism from socialism?

Mr. AULT. Well, socialism is—or rather the Socialist Party is—a political party to secure the enactment through legislation of certain economic theories, but the trades-union movement is an organization of wageworkers for the immediate amelioration of conditions of wageworkers, bettering of all kinds of conditions of wageworkers in so far as possible.

Acting Chairman COMMONS. Is it your judgment that a large proportion of trades-unionists are Socialists, also, like yourself, in this locality?

Mr. AULT. Well, a very large number are. I wouldn't say as to proportions, but a large number are also Socialists.

Acting Chairman COMMONS. So large it dominates the trades-union movement in your election?

Mr. AULT. No; I do not believe that the question of socialism entered into my election. I was, I think, selected because I had some experience in newspaper work and am able to get out a newspaper that was satisfactory to the majority of the membership.

Commissioner GARRETSON. Was there any understanding, Mr. Ault, at the time that you entered into that service, that you would not utilize the paper in the carrying on of socialistic propaganda?

Mr. AULT. That was not questioned at all. I do not consider that a trades-union paper, except in so far as the membership of organized labor may themselves discuss economic questions, is a vehicle for the furtherance of socialism. I think—I believe that it is a distinct disadvantage to any trade-union to become affiliated with any political party.

Acting Chairman COMMONS. But do you publish articles socialistic in their character?

Mr. AULT. There have been occasions, I presume, when that has occurred; yes.

Acting Chairman COMMONS. Speaking of the collective bargaining proposition, or rather the policy of the unions, would you consider that the boycott was an essential right of organized labor?

Mr. AULT. I can't conceive of any condition or any method of depriving labor of the boycott if they use it intelligently. I think that that is an essential right. I believe I have as an individual a personal right not to buy where I don't want to buy.

Acting Chairman COMMONS. Does that in your own mind go as far as what is known as the secondary boycott?

Mr. AULT. Yes; I think so.

Acting Chairman COMMONS. What do you understand by the secondary boycott?

Mr. AULT. The secondary boycott, as I understand it, is where the trade involved asks the assistance of all other workers in refraining from purchasing the articles produced by the merchant or the——

Acting Chairman COMMONS. For example—give an example of some case.

Mr. AULT. Well, for an example, the recent strike of the metal polishers in the Indian motorcycle factory, where the metal polishers——

Acting Chairman COMMONS. Where is that?

Mr. AULT. That is Springfield, Mass.

Acting Chairman COMMONS. Take a Seattle example.

Mr. AULT. Well, we haven't—I don't know that we have found it necessary particularly to use it in Seattle, unless, perhaps, in respect to the electrical workers.

Acting Chairman COMMONS. You have a central body?

Mr. AULT. Yes.

Acting Chairman COMMONS. Of all the trades?

Mr. AULT. Yes.

Acting Chairman COMMONS. Has that ever declared, or recently declared or assisted any of the local members of the associated unions?

Mr. AULT. Oh, yes.

Acting Chairman COMMONS. In refusing to patronize?

Mr. AULT. Well, on an appeal from a local union it is the practice to consider the—to secure an adjustment, if possible, calling all the parties in the controversy into council in an effort to secure an amicable settlement. In case that is unsuccessful, the council will declare for itself whether that firm is unfair or fair to organized labor. The members govern themselves accordingly, I believe. Not very generally—sometimes.

Acting Chairman COMMONS. So a secondary boycott with you means really a sympathetic boycott, where other unions join in to assist the union that is aggrieved?

Mr. AULT. Yes; that is my impression. Perhaps I am not correct technically, but that is the impression I have had of it.

Acting Chairman COMMONS. Well, as is suggested to me, take the hatters' case, was that boycott extended here in Seattle?

Mr. AULT. Yes, I think that it was; yes, we refused to buy, and still refuse to buy the hats produced under unfair conditions.

Acting Chairman COMMONS. What is the method of boycotting that—or the Buck's stove—did the organizations here go to dealers in hats and endeavor to get them to cease?

Mr. AULT. We endeavored to get them to handle only union made hats, which was determined by the use of the hat workers' union label.

Acting Chairman COMMONS. And if they refused to concede, would you go further and boycott their stores?

Mr. AULT. No; that never occurred in the hatters' case particularly.

Acting Chairman COMMONS. That never occurred?

Mr. AULT. We refused to purchase from them, that was all. They were posted as having no union hats, and we refused to purchase from them, but there was no official action taken in that case.

Acting Chairman COMMONS. Was there an agreement at all amongst the unions that you should refuse to patronize any hatter's store here that dealt in these?

Mr. AULT. No.

Acting Chairman COMMONS. How about the Buck's stove?

Mr. AULT. We used every means in our power to let our own membership know that the Buck's Stove & Range Co. was unfair, and to urge them not to purchase a Buck's stove and range.

Acting Chairman COMMONS. And did you visit the dealers in the Buck's stoves here?

Mr. AULT. That was before my time in active participation in central labor council affairs. I could not say definitely.

Acting Chairman COMMONS. I take it you speak for the organized labor of the city. You hold that it is an essential and important right to maintain this second class, which I would call the secondary boycott instead of the sympathetic boycott?

Mr. AULT. Yes; I think in a great many instances we are unable to bring any effective pressure to bear on an employer except through this form of discrimination that we may make.

Acting Chairman COMMONS. You have never practiced it, however, in Seattle, or in this State, that you know of?

Mr. AULT. Well, understand me correctly. We are constantly striving to educate our membership to the fact that they are violating their obligations, that they are discriminating against themselves, unless they purchase only union-made products. These are determined by the use of the union label. In cases where there are—where particularly flagrant violations of union—or rather particularly flagrant discriminations against unions occur, we have published the fact that these certain firms have made these discriminations and urged our membership not to purchase their products.

Acting Chairman COMMONS. Well, take any local stores in this town, have you declared any boycotts against any local stores?

Mr. AULT. Yes, sir.

Acting Chairman COMMONS. What, for example?

Mr. AULT. We declared the Bon Marché unfair at one time.

Acting Chairman COMMONS. What was the reason?

Mr. AULT. They refused to deal with the clerks' union. At the time we declared them unfair they refused to allow the clerks to organize in their store.

Acting Chairman COMMONS. What other cases in this town?

Mr. AULT. Well, the Puget Sound Traction, Light & Power Co. has been declared unfair by organized labor because of their refusal to allow more than 50 per cent of their employees in the construction department to organize. They were willing to agree that 50 per cent of their employees should organize, but that not one of those 50 per cent might be advanced in position, and that there never should be more than 50 per cent organized. We could not naturally accept such an agreement as that, and we refused to. Not being able to secure any better conditions, we declared them unfair.

Acting Chairman COMMONS. And what other cases?

Mr. AULT. Well, there are numerous cases coming up, little affairs where a single union is involved, that calls on the assistance of other unions, and those are always taken up and adjusted to the best of our ability. If they are not adjusted, why we refuse to patronize those firms.

Acting Chairman COMMONS. Are there any other unions that have brought up grievances to this council?

Mr. AULT. Any other unions?

Acting Chairman COMMONS. Yes; local unions—any local cases? You have spoken of the clerks and of the street car employees.

Mr. AULT. No; not the street car employees. The construction workers and the linemen.

Acting Chairman COMMONS. The shopmen?

Mr. AULT. That is the linemen.

Acting Chairman COMMONS. That is the electrical workers?

Mr. AULT. Yes, sir.

Commissioner GARRETSON. I saw men this morning patroling in front of a local tailor shop.

Mr. AULT. Yes.

Commissioner GARRETSON. With a card across their breasts with the proprietor's name, and in big letters the words, "He is unfair."

Mr. AULT. They haven't—that is, a tailor's fight of their own. They haven't asked the assistance of organized labor in that matter.

Commissioner GARRETSON. It is individuals banded together and acting, is it?

Mr. AULT. Yes, sir—that is, it is the tailors' union, I presume.

Commissioner GARRETSON. Oh.

Mr. AULT. But they haven't asked the assistance of the rest of organized labor. The same is true of the—the same has been true of the culinary crafts at various times. They usually settle their own affairs, though.

Acting Chairman COMMONS. You mean the——

Mr. AULT (interposing). Cooks and waiters.

Acting Chairman COMMONS. You mean by that waiters and cooks?

Mr. AULT. Cooks and waiters; yes.

Acting Chairman COMMONS. Has there been any sympathetic strikes on, or have they been declared at all by them?

Mr. AULT. Yes; the Hollywood Lunch was declared unfair a year or so ago.

Acting Chairman COMMONS: As far as your knowledge goes, what has been the outcome of these local boycotts?

Mr. AULT. The outcome has been a successful settlement, as a rule, the recognition of the union, the right of collective bargaining, and the management thoroughly satisfied with the conditions after they had tried them.

Acting Chairman COMMONS. Is that true in the case of the Bon Marché?

Mr. AULT. The Bon Marché settlement was not entirely successful from the workers' standpoint in that the clerks are not yet organized. But the Bon Marché management recognizes the right of the clerks to organize, and it is up to the clerks now to do their part.

Acting Chairman COMMONS. Is that true in the case of the traction company?

Mr. AULT. The traction company is still unfair to organized labor. They will not allow any of their men to organize under any circumstances.

Acting Chairman COMMONS. Then, apparently it has been successful in one instance and not successful in the other?

Mr. AULT. Yes.

Acting Chairman COMMONS. You mentioned three instances. What was the third? I have forgotten. Practically it is an equal balance, then?

Mr. AULT. It is about an even break. There has been constant progress in the securing of enactments—agreements in this State—without the recourse to either the strike or the boycott.

Acting Chairman COMMONS. Do the unions of this locality consider it an esstential thing to obtain the right to quit work in case a nonunion man is employed?

Mr. AULT. So far as my knowledge goes all of the unions affiliated with the American Federation of Labor do not require the closed-shop conditions. The larger number do, I believe, and in this city the general sentiment is that the workers should have the right to quit work—that is, the organized worker should quit unless all of the men are organized.

Acting Chairman COMMONS. Do you call that the closed shop?

Mr. AULT. We call it the union shop. It is not the closed shop, because every worker is open to become a member of organized labor. We make no discrimination.

Acting Chairman COMMONS. Have there been strikes here—quitting work on account of the employment of nonunion men in the establishment?

Mr. AULT. I do not remember of any specific instance.

Acting Chairman COMMONS. You do not know that they have gone out in a case of that kind?

Mr. AULT. No; I do not know of any specific instance.

Acting Chairman COMMONS. Or that they have threatened the employers with a strike if they kept nonunion men?

Mr. AULT. Well, I do not know of any specific instance of that. I do not know that it has been necessary.

Acting Chairman COMMONS. But they all consider that is essential?

Mr. AULT. We consider that that is essential. I believe that is the general sentiment of the labor movement of this city. We consider it essential that, in case we have our work with a firm, that our members only should be employed.

Acting Chairman COMMONS. Well, do you consider, then, that the employer has the right to refuse to employ union men?

Mr. AULT. Yes; if he can get along without them.

Acting Chairman COMMONS. Would you call that a blacklist?

Mr. AULT. You mean the employer refusing to hire union men?

Acting Chairman COMMONS. Yes.

Mr. AULT. No; not where it is done by an individual employer against an entire body of men. But where an association of employers will keep a list of certain agitators discriminating against certain individuals then I consider that a blacklist.

Commissioner O'CONNELL. If the employer would use that as a reason why he would not employ them, because a man did belong to the union?

Mr. AULT. Yes.

Commissioner O'CONNELL. Specifically state that; would you consider that a blacklist?

Mr. AULT. We would consider that a blacklist.

Commissioner O'CONNELL. Where he communicated to other parties that he had done that?

Mr. AULT. Really that is what in my opinion constitutes a blacklist, where he communicates to other parties. A man can not get very far in blacklisting on his own account. I realize that in a great many industries it is not easy to build up a working force that is wholly satisfactory to the employer, and that he will discriminate against some men because he does not like them,

because he can not work with them. That will be done under almost any conditions. But where he communicates with corporations and with some other
employer, that is an attempt to prevent that man from securing work at all,—
that, I consider, is a blacklist.

Acting Chairman COMMONS. That is what you would have legislation probibit?

Mr. AULT. Yes; I think that would be desirable for the legislature to prohibit it.

Acting Chairman COMMONS. If the legislature should prohibit that, should
it not also prohibit boycotting and sympathetic strikes—prohibit the unions
from quitting work where the employer had nonunion men?

Mr. AULT. I would like to make a statement. I consider the best method of
arriving at all of these conclusions is through the organization of the workers
determining their own condition. I have not a great deal of faith in legislative
enactments. My impression is that ordinary labor legislation is entirely unenforced unless there is an effective trades-union or some sort of union organization to back it up and see that it is enforced.

Acting Chairman COMMONS. Then, according to that you would permit the
employers to blacklist by law?

Mr. AULT. I do not know of any particular advantage it would be to prevent
them from blacklisting by law. I do not know that they could be enforced.

Acting Chairman COMMONS. How would you enforce a law, then, that would
require you to engage in collective bargaining?

Mr. AULT. By withdrawing all protection in case of strike. In case of a
strike of any kind, let the workers and employers fight it out. If they are
unwilling to consider the right of the men to organize, let them rely on their
own resources to prevent them organizing. The use of the police power—of
course, our entire Government system is built up on the theory that the protection of property is the supreme thing.

Acting Chairman COMMONS. Well, if you took away the protection of the
police power, would you permit them to have their own private guards?

Mr. AULT. No; they should not be allowed any protection.

Acting Chairman COMMONS. Provided they did not have their guards deputized as sheriffs, you think they should protect themselves in self-defense;
would you prohibit that?

Mr. AULT. I would prohibit that. If they are so unreasonable as to refuse
to bargain collectively, they should not have any protection from the State.

Acting Chairman COMMONS. The printers' union have a rule, I understand,
requiring that matrices shall not be exchanged among printing offices? Or,
that when type is set up in one office it can not be used by another office for
the same work, but that it has to be set over again if it is taken up by another
office.

Mr. AULT. I am not certain that I can answer that question.

Acting Chairman COMMONS. You are a member of the printers' union?

Mr. AULT. I am a member of the printers' union.

Acting Chairman COMMONS. And you do not know whether there is such a
rule in the union or not?

Mr. AULT. I know that the practice is to discourage switching matter.

Acting Chairman COMMONS. Do you have a copy of the agreement of the
printers' union?

Mr. AULT. It can be procured; yes, sir. I haven't got a copy, but I can get
one. I am in this position: A job printer by trade and I am not as familiar
with the newspaper scale as I should be.

Acting Chairman COMMONS. In the job business would not the same thing
hold?

Mr. AULT. We are not allowed, under our agreement, to transfer matter
from one job-printing office to another job-printing office.

Acting Chairman COMMONS. That is, you have this rule in job offices?

Mr. AULT. Yes, sir.

Acting Chairman COMMONS. Is that true as applied to newspaper offices?

Mr. AULT. Yes.

Acting Chairman COMMONS. Well, suppose an employer refuses to make an
agreement with you in which you have that sort of a demand, would you have
the Government then take away his defense?

Mr. AULT. Well, as far as the printers are concerned, they have been able to
handle their situation very efficiently without any Government interference
one way or the other. We have fairly good conditions with them, and we have

fairly good relations with our employers. We have not had any trouble over this particular provision that I know of in any instance.

Acting Chairman COMMONS. So that that would be generally true if the right to organize was legalized?

Mr. AULT. I think so.

Commissioner O'CONNELL. There would not be any necessity for any other laws at all?

Mr. AULT. The reason I proposed this manner of action was that the right to organize might be enforced. It was a suggestion as to the manner in which the right to organize might be enforced. I believe everybody agrees we have a right to organize.

Acting Chairman COMMONS. Do you consider you have a right to organize?

Mr. AULT. Yes; I believe we have the right to organize.

Acting Chairman COMMONS. What is the main point, then, which prevents you from making that effective?

Mr. AULT. Why, just as——

Acting Chairman COMMONS. Isn't it simply what you stated at the beginning, that the employer refuses to hire a union man, blacklists the union man, that is the only reason why your right to organize is not effective?

Mr. AULT. Yes; that probably is the real reason. As I say, I do not know of any way of enforcing the right to organize. It is not a right, really, unless we can enforce it.

Acting Chairman COMMONS. Then you can not enforce the right to organize except by taking away the right from the employer to hire nonunion men, or to discharge union men; that is the only way you can make the right effective?

Mr. AULT. That is the only way I know of.

Acting Chairman COMMONS. So that, then, you would have the Government require employers to hire union men?

Mr. AULT. Well, that is a hard question. I think that it is a reasonable proposition that employers should be required to hire union men, but I realize also that it is not likely that that will ever be a Government enactment.

Acting Chairman COMMONS. If you should enforce it, it would take away all the rights that the union has to boycott, the sympathetic strike, and sympathetic boycott?

Mr. AULT. I do not believe sympathetic boycotts would be necessary if we had an effective and thorough organization. The sympathetic boycotts are used almost always in the interests of unions which are numerically weak—I mean in relation to the industry.

Acting Chairman COMMONS. And they are numerically weak because the employer will not hire union men?

Mr. AULT. Yes.

Acting Chairman COMMONS. So you get back to the proposition, Mr. Ault, you can not give them strength unless you take away from the employer his right to hire nonunion men?

Commissioner LENNON. Mr. Ault, would you be willing to concede exactly the same rights of organization to the employers as you demand for your workingmen?

Mr. AULT. Yes. I do not see any objection to the employers organizing. I think that perhaps it would be advantageous in developing a system of collective bargaining that the employers should be thoroughly organized.

Mr. THOMPSON. I would like to ask you a few questions here, Mr. Ault. Do you know of any crime which men have committed in the past, or in our present system in this country—of any crime which is on our statute books which takes away from the criminal the protection not only of his life but of his property?

Commissioner O'CONNELL. I did not get that.

Mr. THOMPSON. The question I asked was this: Does he know of any laws in this country, any criminal laws, which describe what crime is, from murder up or down, which take away from the criminal the protection for his life and protection for his property.

Mr. AULT. I can cite the instance of the employers who refused to come under the industrial insurance act in this State, the protection of their property is taken away from them.

Mr. THOMPSON. No.

Mr. AULT. Some protection, perhaps not all, but some protection is taken away from them.

Mr. THOMPSON. No. I would say, perhaps, being a lawyer I can possibly put you right on that.

38819°—S. Doc. 415, 64–1—vol 5——8

Mr. AULT. Yes.

Mr. THOMPSON. A number of the old rules of the common law are changed, the master and servant law and perhaps the assumption of risk, which are only parts of the law——

Mr. AULT. Yes.

Mr. THOMPSON. But the man has a right to have his property protected in case of riot, in case of anybody seeking to blow it up, in case of a man seeking to burn it; not only that, but he can not be enforced to pay any money in case persons are injured without trial in court.

Mr. AULT. That is true.

Mr. THOMPSON. Without trial in court by jury of his peers. But I know of no case in this country, or know of no case anywhere, where Anglo-Saxon jurisprudence reigns, in Canada, Australia, New Zealand, South Africa, England, in the last 500 years where a criminal has been deprived either of his right to life or his rights to property without what is called due process of law.

Mr. AULT. Well, Mr. Thompson——

Mr. THOMPSON. It used to be in the early days when a man, for instance, was declared, by act of Parliament, an outlaw—500 years ago—then anybody who met him on the street could take his life, or steal his property, or anything else.

Mr. AULT. If a burglar enters my house I can shoot him, too.

Mr. THOMPSON. If he enters your house?

Mr. AULT. Yes. I think that this—I can conceive of a condition, not being a lawyer I can't work out the technical details, but I can conceive of a condition where some of the safeguards that exist now for employers should be withdrawn in case they refuse to allow their employees to organize. Now, I do not make that as a sweeping statement, but I make that as a suggestion that might be considered by the commission as a method of enforcing the right to organize.

Mr. THOMPSON. Now, more specifically, what would you recommend? Do you think it would help the progress of society industrially if we should take away the protection of property of anybody, which would mean that we would permit people to burn and destroy wantonly; do you think that such a condition, such a law, would make for progress among men?

Mr. AULT. I think that is assuming that some of them want to burn and destroy.

Mr. THOMPSON. Giving them the privilege, the property would become outlaw property.

Mr. AULT. I do not think the assumption is a fair assumption.

Mr. THOMPSON. It is very pertinently said, why take away the protection of either unless we take away all that protection that is supposed to have some influence upon the employer. What would he fear? What would a man fear, have a right to fear, from the common knowledge of the history of men, in such a case?

Mr. AULT. For instance, in the street car——

Mr. THOMPSON. In other words, do you intend to use coercion on the employer to take away the protection?

Mr. AULT. For instance, in case of the street car company, which I have in mind, the present government in case of a strike will use the police power to enforce the laws on the running of the street cars in the streets. Now, I can conceive of a condition whereby those street cars will not be allowed to run through legal process because of the employer refusing to deal with his men in collective bargaining.

Mr. THOMPSON. What would you say about the street cars themselves, if they were housed in a barn with other property?

Mr. AULT. That is a line of demarcation that could be drawn.

Mr. THOMPSON. Then you would change it, then, to this, that you would have a law by which the Government would refuse to assist in carrying on the business?

Mr. AULT. That is the idea. That is the thing I had in mind.

Mr. THOMPSON. That is what now exists in the Colorado coal fields with the United States troops.

Mr. AULT. To a certain extent.

Mr. THOMPSON. When you say you have no confidence in law, in its enforcement, from your experience in this State with laws and your labor bureau, and from Commissioner Olson's work here, do you feel that the enforcement of laws is always curtailed and crippled?

Mr. AULT. I believe that Commissioner Olson does everything, and his assistants do everything they can to enforce the law. On the other hand they have nothing to work with, no appropriation, no funds, and they can not enforce the law. The prosecuting officials in the various counties who are charged with the enforcement of the law refuse to enforce the law, refuse to take any steps toward the enforcement of the law. That is what I mean. The women's eight-hour law is constantly violated throughout this State, in innumerable instances almost, because of the refusal of the prosecuting officers, because of the refusal of the women themselves to testify because of the fear of discharge. There is no method has yet been devised whereby workers will be protected in their right to avail themselves of any labor legislation except they are organized into some effective trades-unions.

Mr. THOMPSON. As I understood it, if I understood it correctly, your attitude was against laws being efficacious and helpful to the worker. Now, I would like to ask whether you or your association, the Central Labor Union, sought to have the eight-hour law passed?

Mr. AULT. Yes. If I was understood that way, I was understood wrong. I do
• not want it to be inferred that the law—that laws can not be depended on. They are of advantage. They are of advantage in the establishing of conditions of public opinion at a given time; in establishing a condition, the condition of public opinion. Now, if we pass an eight-hour law, which we are endeavoring to do, that will be an assertion that the public of the State of Washington believes that eight hours is long enough for any man, woman, or child to work. But that law can not be enforced unless we have an organization to see that it is enforced in its detail.

Mr. THOMPSON. Well, as far as Commissioner Olson has funds, so far as he has investigators employed, have they been able to enforce the law in any degree?

Mr. AULT. Yes. The law has been of advantage in that it has been enforced in some degree.

Mr. THOMPSON. Wouldn't your attitude on that proposition be rather not opposition to laws, but the request for more laws, so that actual provision will be made for the enforcement of such laws as the eight-hour law?

Mr. AULT. I want this thoroughly understood. My attitude is not opposition to the laws or to law. My attitude is that the workers can not and should not depend upon the law solely.

Mr. THOMPSON. In regard to the number of union men in this State, are there any sources of information that are at your disposal by which you could ascertain the number of men?

Mr. AULT. I think that can be ascertained within one or two thousand.

Mr. THOMPSON. In regard to the figures you have given, 15,000 men in Seattle and 15,000 railway men, are those estimates from just glancing over the field generally or have you some basis of fact on which to base them?

Mr. AULT. We have the basis of the per capita tax paid by the individual members. It can be determined within, as I say, within one or two thousand at the very outside.

Mr. THOMPSON. To what extent do you believe in carrying out the principle of the boycott, that is, would you limit it to the action of the unions themselves, allied together, organized people, or would you seek to impose the boycott on nonunion people, and how would you seek to do that?

Mr. AULT. The principle effect of a boycott is the education of the—well, the boycott, if it is effective at all, must be used in every way possible. I believe in getting the assistance of all classes who are sympathetic with the issue involved. The main method of enforcing the boycott that I have ever known is the publication of the facts in relation to the controversy involved, and the public has determined its purchasing in accordance with the facts as shown.

Mr. THOMPSON. Will you be in favor of any form of coercion to compel third parties, not union people, but the public generally, to help in the boycott?

Mr. AULT. Do you mean legal coercion, or any form?

Mr. THOMPSON. Coercion by the people who carry on the boycott, by the union people or others who may carry it on.

Mr. AULT. I see no reasonable objection to my refusing to purchase from a man whom I know is supporting practically a firm which is at war with some of my fellow unionists, if that is what you mean.

Mr. THOMPSON. How far would you carry that; would you have the plumber refuse to repair the plumbing in the house of a man who bought goods that were unfair?

Mr. AULT. That is something of a ridiculous question because of its impossibility, the impossibility of carrying a boycott to that extent.

Personally, if you want my personal view on it, I should say yes, but it is not possible.

Mr. THOMPSON. Then, as far as you are concerned, if that could be done you believe in doing it?

Mr. AULT. Yes, sir.

Mr. THOMPSON. And that would be what you would advocate as a plan of action by the union?

Mr. AULT. That is probably substantially what I am trying to educate the organized workers into doing—is to use all of the legal weapons that they have to secure better conditions.

Mr. THOMPSON. That is all, Mr. Chairman.

Commissioner O'CONNELL. I just want to ask a question. We seem to have gotten into a legal proposition here in this boycott. Is it not a fact that every human being is constantly boycotting every opportunity? We differentiate between where we will eat dinner. Is that not in itself a boycott against the place where we do not eat?

Mr. AULT. I consider it such.

Commissioner O'CONNELL. If we go to buy a suit of clothes we differentiate between the places we buy. We may go to a dozen different places. We may tell our friends that the place we were in didn't suit us at all and that we found the best place and the cheapest place in some other place, and isn't that a boycott?

Mr. AULT. That is as much a boycott as I know of.

Commissioner O'CONNELL. If our esteemed friend, the counsel, wouldn't choose to go to dinner with another counsel for some reason or other, would it not be evidence of some sort of boycott in his own mind?

Mr. AULT. I should think so. A discrimination certainly.

Commissioner O'CONNELL. So that in every step, however innocent, we are innocently boycotting somebody?

Mr. AULT. That would be my opinion; certainly.

Commissioner O'CONNELL. Now this question of blacklisting. I think counsel probably got your impression wrong, your nonbelief, in law. The same rights—you would be willing to grant to the employer the same protection under the law that you ask for yourself, but you want the law equally and fairly administered?

Mr. AULT. That is the position exactly. The law—the enforcement of the law—has been in the hands of the opponents of labor.

Commissioner O'CONNELL. And you want the laws that are on our statute books enforced, not laws that are made by some individual person?

Mr. AULT. That is it exactly.

Commissioner O'CONNELL. At his will and behest, and you want the wageworkers to have the protection under the law that the other person has under the law, the employer or wealthy person under the law?

Mr. AULT. Yes, sir; exactly.

Commissioner O'CONNELL. You want the law so that you can get quick action under the law because you are a poor man as the rich man gets under the law?

Mr. AULT. Certainly.

Commissioner O'CONNELL. In other words, you don't want the law, because of your inability to carry your case from court to court, that the very law itself under the action of the law will simply make it impossible for you to get justice because of your inability to carry it through. You want the courts so arranged that the law can be speedily carried out. After all that is what you have in mind with regard to the question of law. You have no opposition to law, and organized labor, as you understand it, has no opposition to law?

Mr. AULT. Certainly not.

Commissioner O'CONNELL. But organized labor has found it necessary to band themselves together for the purpose of seeing that the laws when they are enacted are enforced?

Mr. AULT. Yes, sir.

Commissioner O'CONNELL. All the laws that have been enacted for the alleviation of the working people, as well as of laboring conditions and covering the employment of children and women and the conditions of employment and safety appliances and all of that, if it were not for organized labor these laws would be a dead letter on the statute books?

Mr. AULT. If it were not for organized labor these laws would not exist, in my estimation.

Commissioner O'CONNELL. Well, but after they do exist?

Mr. AULT. They would all be dead letters, certainly.

Acting Chairman COMMONS. That is all, Mr. Ault.   Call your next witness.

Mr. THOMPSON. Mr. Brown.

TESTIMONY OF MR. J. G. BROWN.

Mr. THOMPSON.. Mr. Brown, will you please give us your name?

Mr. BROWN. J. G. Brown.

Mr. THOMPSON. Your business address?

Mr. BROWN. 202 Maynard Building.

Mr. THOMPSON: And your position?

Mr. BROWN. President of the International Union of Timber Workers.

Acting Chairman COMMONS. Mr. Brown, could you speak a little louder? We find it difficult to hear what you say.

Mr. THOMPSON. Now state again your position.

Mr. BROWN. President of the International Union of Timber Workers.

Mr. THOMPSON. What workmen does that organization embrace?

Mr. BROWN. It embraces all men employed in and around sawmills, logging camps, shingle mills, and all other woodworking industries and woodworking factories and plants.

Mr. THOMPSON. Well, sash and door mills?

Mr. BROWN. Well, not particularly—where it don't infringe on other organizations.

Mr. THOMPSON. What other organizations?

Mr. BROWN. Well, the carpenters' union takes in some of the men working in sash and door factories. The glaziers, for instance, take in the glaziers.

Mr. THOMPSON. You don't——

Mr. BROWN. We don't extend over that. There isn't any organization but what finds a time when it possibly overlaps onto some other one.

Mr. THOMPSON. How old an organization is yours?

Mr. BROWN. Well, as an international union of timber workers it is only about 2 years old, but it is the outgrowth of the old International Union of Shingle Weavers which was organized about 10 or 11 years ago.

Mr. THOMPSON. Are these unions, or were the old ones, or is the present one affiliated with any labor body?

Mr. BROWN. Yes; they were both affiliated with the American Federation of Labor and the various State bodies of the American Federation of Labor.

Mr. THOMPSON. Where is the principal membership of your organization?

Mr. BROWN. Here on Puget Sound; and I think perhaps in Everett we have the largest membership of any one locality.

Mr. THOMPSON. About how many members have you, if you care to state, in your organization?

Mr. BROWN. I think about 8,000.

Mr. THOMPSON. And that is the country over?

Mr. BROWN. Yes; but the most of them are here on Puget Sound.

Mr. THOMPSON. Have you got a constitution and by-laws printed?

Mr. BROWN. Yes, sir.

Mr. THOMPSON. Would you be willing to furnish the commission with a copy?

Mr. BROWN. Be glad to.

Mr. THOMPSON. We will be pleased to have you.

Mr. BROWN. I haven't got one with me.   I can get one.

Mr. THOMPSON. You can send one to the commission.   What is the general purpose and object or objects of your association?

Mr. BROWN. Well, to improve the conditions of the men, promote fraternal relations, and shorten the hours of labor and increase wages and remuneration.

Mr. THOMPSON. Well, it is the same as that of all the other unions affiliated with the American Federation of Labor, is that right?

Mr. BROWN. Exactly.

Mr. THOMPSON. How long have you been connected with this organization?

Mr. BROWN. Since it first started, about—we had a few local unions that were affiliated directly with the American Federation of Labor, and those local unions having a sufficient number to justify it, were brought together by delegate representatives, and they organized the international union. I think it is about 14 years ago since the union that I was particularly connected with was organized.

Mr. THOMPSON. Well, from your experience in this line of industry with your organization, what have you got to say as to the general conditions in that industry, conditions of the workingmen?

Mr. BROWN. I believe the conditions in the lumber industry are the worst they are in any industry in America.

Mr. THOMPSON. Now, Mr. Brown, will you please tell us your reasons for making that statement?

Mr. BROWN. Well, the wages are the lowest, the hours are as long, the conditions are as bad under which men have to work as that of any other industry generally, or worse, in America, I think.

Mr. THOMPSON. Well, would you care, Mr. Brown, to go more into specific detail in that regard? What are the wages, what are the hours in the different branches of your trade?

Mr. BROWN. I have here a reproduction of a cut taken from the American Lumberman. It is published in Chicago and, I think, the recognized, one of the recognized, authorities of the lumber industry—that is, the employers., In the issue of May 30, I think this year, showing the attractiveness of the lumber industry for investors, they produce figures presumably taken, alleged to be taken, from the census of 1910, in which they show the number of men employed in the lumber industry and the amount of wages paid them.

That cut is supposed to represent the number of men employed [indicating]. The next is the steel industry, which is about, I should judge, one-fifth less. These bags down here [indicating] are supposed to represent the wages and, because of the fact that there are a fifth more men employed in the lumber industry, you see there is about a fifth less wages gotten. The value of the products. according to the same authority, is represented as somewheres near the sum of about fifty or sixty million dollars more for the steel products. I should say, if that is correct, that the conditions must be worse in the lumber industry than they are in the steel industry, so far as the wages are concerned, so far as the amount of that proportion of the products going to the worker.

Mr. THOMPSON. Would you be willing to file that with the commission?

Mr. BROWN. Yes, sir.

(The paper so presented was marked "Document Serial No. 430, August 12, 1914, Witness Brown."

The paper referred to, an illustration, was submitted in printed form.)

Mr. THOMPSON. Well, could you give us some definite information or details with reference to the situation here in Washington?

Mr. BROWN. Yes, sir. Here in Washington, in the logging camps, I think the men are imposed on perhaps more than in any other branch of the industry. The industry in a general way has three departments. They might be classified as the shingle department and the lumber mill department and the logging camp department, where they get out the logs out of the woods. In the sawmill department, of course, come other branches and subdivisions, like planing mills, box factories, and tank factories, and that sort of thing. I think the shingle mill department is the best organized. There the highest percentage of skill is required. I should imagine there is 90 per cent of the men employed in that branch of the industry who are organized. Their hours of labor, however, are the same as those in the other branches—that is, in the sawmill department—that is, 10 hours a day. The wages are a great deal better. The lowest wages for any of the hazardous occupations in the shingle department are $3.50 a day; that is union wages. The nonhazardous occupation in the shingle mill pays a somewhat less wage. I don't think there is anyone works in the shingle department that does not get as high as $2.50 a day.

In the sawmills the wages are miserably low. The conditions of employment are not good. The men are victimized by employment-office men to the very last degree, I think. I know one, as an illustration, I know of one sawmill on Grays Harbor—the Grays Harbor country—where they used to have a standing order with employment offices in Portland and in Tacoma and in Seattle for men. I don't know whether there was any collusion between the employers and any of the foremen of the company or not, but I know there was always a place found for these men. They went down there in any quantities it was possible for the employment-office man to secure. Naturally, after they got down there a place had to be made for them if it did not already exist. The upshot of that was that men worked a very short time sometimes, because of the bad conditions. They got small wages. They had to pay hospital dues, paid their board, and other things of that sort. Frequently the other mills of Grays Harbor, where conditions were a little better, used to rely upon the floaters that drifted away from this plant to recruit their labor from. I think the common laborer in this particular plant was getting about $26 a month and board. Now, if they happen to be married men they were allowed $10 a month in place of their board. If they wanted to stay at home, they were allowed $10 a month. If, however, they laid off one or two days they were charged board at the rate of $20 a month. That board amounted to $10 a month if you didn't take it, and $20 a month if you did. The frequent changing of men always required the payment of a month's hospital dues. The men might work in two or three of those mills during the same month and have to pay hospital dues in each one of them.

Some mills have a practice if men work four days, some only one day, some five days, they pay their monthly hospital dues, which run from 50 cents to $1, most of them $1 a month. These men were usually advanced their fare when they went down to this plant by the employment agent. He would take their baggage as security that this money would be paid back that was advanced—their fee and their fare. When they got down there they worked out their board as they went along, their hospital dues, and their employment-agency fee, and their fare down there, and then they got a chance to change their clothes. I hold in my hand some time statements from a mill down in Centralia, a sawmill.

Mr. THOMPSON. Would you mind reading those, if you care to?

Mr. BROWN. Yes; I would just as soon. This is the Eastern Railway & Lumber Co., Centralia, Wash., 730——

Acting Chairman COMMONS. Mr. Brown, will you turn them in as exhibits?

Mr. BROWN. Yes, sir.

Acting Chairman COMMONS. Will you kindly let the reporter number them for identification?

(See Brown exhibit.)

Commissioner LENNON. Before leaving the subject of sawmills tell us the wages paid to the different men that work in the different sawmills.

Mr. BROWN. Yes; I am just getting at that.

Commissioner LENNON. All right.

Mr. BROWN. These are common wages—wages for common laborers. Here is the one I started on: Eastern Railway & Lumber Co. pay-roll statement: Name, A. Kesler; worked 45 hours; wages, $1.50, less 10 per cent.

Commissioner O'CONNELL. For 45 hours?

Mr. BROWN. What?

Commissioner O'CONNELL. For 45 hours?

Mr. BROWN. Well, he got at the rate of $1.50 a day; that means a 10-hour day. That means four days and a half. He got $1.50 a day less 10 per cent.

Commissioner O'CONNELL. What was that?

Mr. BROWN. Well, that would be 15 cents off from $1.50.

Commissioner O'CONNELL. No; but why?

Mr. BROWN. Well, I don't know why. They have that marked this way. There is his wages stated on the slip. Then down here at the bottom it says: "Less 10 per cent," and that 10 per cent is subtracted.

Commissioner LENNON. What rule causes all that?

Commissioner O'CONNELL. What is it for, do you know, Mr. Brown?

Mr. BROWN. Well, I think it is cheaper labor.

Commissioner GARRETSON. Who gets the 10 per cent, the employer?

Mr. BROWN. The man who owns the mill; the employer; yes.

Commissioner GARRETSON. He declares a dividend on wages?

Mr. BROWN. Yes. That is all it says. Instead of stating the wages at $1.35, which would be the same, they give him $1.50 a day and then subtract 10 per cent. That makes his wages $1.35.

Commissioner O'CONNELL. That is frenzied financiering.

Mr. BROWN. Then here is another one where a man worked; this man has six children. This man's name is——

Commissioner O'CONNELL. Mr. Brown, before you get away from that there, is there any method whereby we can get what that means? Is there some one subpœnaed here from the lumber interests who would know anything about why that is—that reduction, I mean, of 10 per cent?

Mr. BROWN. I suppose there is nobody here.

Commissioner O'CONNELL. Any of the employment agencies?

Mr. THOMPSON. Where is that mill?

Mr. BROWN. Centralia.

Commissioner GARRETSON. The name of the corporation.

Mr. BROWN. Eastern Railway & Lumber Co. I have just been down there. These boys went on a strike here a few days ago, and that is how the matter was brought to my attention, and I got hold of these statements at that time. Now, on the 1st of May their wages was reduced; they were told that the wages would be reduced 10 per cent, and they took this form of carrying it out.

Commissioner O'CONNELL. Then they gave notice of reduction of wages, and then when they went to pay off they made the reduction from what they had formerly agreed to pay?

Mr. BROWN. Yes.

Commissioner O'CONNELL. Is that the idea?

Mr. BROWN. No; no. They agreed to pay this; they had been paying them— from last year I think the average wages there were about $2.25. On the 8th of September they cut the wages from 25 cents to $1 a day, according to the different class of men. Then on May 1 they notified them that times were so hard that they would have to cut wages again 10 per cent, and it seems their statements are according to the rate that was paid after the first cut last September, less 10 per cent. I don't know why that is. That is rather new to me, but that is the way it works out. Here is a man who worked 244 hours at a rate of $1.75 a day. From that is deducted 10 per cent and $1 for hospital dues. At the same time that this company reduced the pay last September they raised the price of wood that they sell to their employees and to others 25 cents a load. Those are samples of the others. None of them run above $1.75 less 10 per cent; that was the wages paid, I think, for common labor in that mill.

Commissioner LENNON. They are all from the same mill?

Mr. BROWN. Yes; they are all from the same mill; these are.

Mr. THOMPSON. Mr. Brown, are these conditions which you speak of in connection with that mill typical of the conditions in this vicinity in all mills?

Mr. BROWN. I think they are. I don't think there are any places where they are any worse than the two I have cited. I don't know of any, and there are some where they are better. Take at Everett, for instance, where the men are to some extent, perhaps 50 per cent, organized, and the wages for common labor about $2.50 a day. There has been no effort to cut the wages of those men in any department. But in this place, Centralia, there has been a very backward movement. The employers resist the attempt to organize. Most of these men have come out there from Missouri, men who have lived in agricultural communities, and it seems as though they take advantage of their non-resistance or timidity or something and cut them down until they have them down to a margin as low as a dollar and thirty-five cents a day. The per cent of skilled men in sawmills is very small. In a sawmill employing 100 men the only skilled men would be the engineer, the filer, the head sawyer, the edger man, and perhaps a head planer. That is about all the really skilled men that would be required around a sawmill.

Commissioner LENNON. What do those skilled men get?

Mr. BROWN. Well, there is no fixed scale of wages. Band-saw filers get as high as $12 to $14 a day. They get as low as $5, depending on the size of the mill and the amount of work required.

Mr. THOMPSON. Referring to the statement again, Mr. Brown, that you read off. Are those conditions typical in Buckley?

Mr. BROWN. Well, there are no sawmills in Buckley now that I know of.

Mr. THOMPSON. Well, I mean of labor in use in Buckley.

Mr. BROWN. Well, there is no sawmill at Buckley that I know of now, or shingle mill, either.

Mr. THOMPSON. How about Cosmopolis?

Mr. BROWN. Yes, sir; that is one of the mills I was speaking of. That was the first one I mentioned.

Mr. THOMPSON. That includes the Gray Harbor country?

Mr. BROWN. Cosmopolis is one of the towns that makes up what is called the Gray Harbor country.

Mr. THOMPSON. How about Aberdeen?

Mr. BROWN. At Aberdeen the conditions of employment are a little better. I think wages are as low as a dollar and seventy-five cents a day. They haven't the mess-house feature; that is, where they board all the men as they do in Cosmopolis. They pay them so much a day and let them board where they like.

. Mr. THOMPSON. You can go ahead, Mr. Brown.

Mr. BROWN. In the logging camps the wages are a little better, because there is a higher per cent of skill required than there is in the sawmills. However, for common labor I don't think the wages are very much higher, perhaps 25 cents a day higher, than they are in the sawmills. One of the biggest logging camps on Grays Harbor pays $2 a day for common labor. They charge $5.25 a week for board at that mill, and deduct the hospital dues from each month or a fraction of a month that the man works there. The worst thing I find that the men in the logging camps have to contend with is the bad conditions. There is one logging camp on Grays Harbor where they have a bunk house with room in the bunk house for about 50 persons. Those men sleep in wooden bunks; those bunks are double tiers running clear around the building. Those bunk houses have only one window in one end of them. A man would have to light a lamp to read in the middle of the day. They have a big stove in the center of that, and the only other comfort is a bench that runs around on a level with the lower bunk. A man can sit on those benches, or perhaps have a box or something of that sort to sit on if they want to sit around the table and play cards or something of that character. They have stoves, and in the periods of the year when it is raining the stoves are hung all about with wet clothing. That is their only method that these loggers and woodmen have of drying their clothes. The men naturally in the bunks have to inhale the steam that comes off of these drying clothes. In the wintertime or fall of the year the men keep the door open in order that they can be more comfortable from the heat of the stoves. When the fire dies out that makes a sudden change in the temperature. They are victims of colds and other diseases that come from that—rheumatism and the like of that. They work these men in the fall and winter all of the daylight there is. In the summer time they work them about 12 hours a day. The start out from the bunk house at 6 o'clock, presumably; frequently it is 20 minutes to 6. They walk anywhere from 20 rods to a mile and a half to their work. They reach their work and leave at 6 o'clock at night and have to go that distance back home on their own time. They theoretically work one way on the company's time and the other way on their own time. It frequently happens that what is theoretically 10 hours is stretched into a 12-hour day, sometimes even longer than that. Those long hours of employment, the uncertainty of it, and the bad conditions under which they live are the main complaints that the loggers have. They resent very bitterly this compulsory payment of hospital fees. But speaking further about the insanitary conditions: It usually happens that 25 or 30 feet from the bunk house is the cookhouse, and the cookhouses usually have a habit of throwing all their garbage and empty cans and everything right out of the window. In the hot time of the summer that not only makes a bad odor but attracts swarms of flies, and presumably the idea is they convey disease to a greater or less extent. Of course, the work in the logging camps is in the open and healthful, and that, perhaps, is one reason why they are not the victims of diseases that they otherwise would be.

The shingle weavers tried for a long while to get out of the payment of these hospital dues. I remember I was in Willapa Harbor, and the shingle weavers took that matter up with the employers and asked them to let the union provide for their own members. They explained at that time as a reason why they could not do that that the casualty insurance company with whom they then insured—that was before the passage of the workmen's compensation law in this State—required that every mill guarantee first-aid treatment to all their employees. The only way they were in position to guarantee that was by seeing that every one of their employees carried this hospital insurance, and in order to make certain of that they attended to it themselves.

Commissioner O'CONNELL. Are they still continuing the hospital insurance?

Mr. BROWN. Yes, sir. We haven't taken the matter up. I don't know what the excuse is now, but that was the reason then. The members of organized labor, the direct legislation league, and others introduced a first-aid bill in the last legislature. The provisions of that bill were that the employer and employee should each stand half of the cost of that first aid. The employers were very bitterly opposed to it, and it failed to pass. Now we have a first-aid law among these initiative measures that we are trying to get submitted to the voters of this State this fall. That measure will require the employer to pay the whole of the first-aid insurance cost.

Mr. THOMPSON. How are the conditions at these camps with reference to the kind of food supplied and toilet arrangements?

Mr. BROWN. Well, they don't usually have much of any toilet arrangements. They turn the man loose and let him choose any part of the property he wants that is not otherwise occupied.

Mr. THOMPSON. How about the food?

Mr. BROWN. Well, the food generally is fair. The food is fairly good; it is of a substantial nature; it is good, nutritious food. Usually fair in quality and quantity.

Commissioner O'CONNELL. Follow up, Mr. Thompson, the bunking facilities and beds. What about that?

Mr. BROWN. There has been an improvement in some of those bunks. Now, most of the places in Grays Harbor they have iron beds with springs, a cheap quality of mattress. The men have to carry their own bedding; they carry it around with them from place to place. They rent these bunks to the men, and charge them 25 cents a month for the use of these bunks in the bunk house.

Commissioner GARRETSON. For what period?

Mr. BROWN. Each month.

Commissioner GARRETSON. Each month?

Mr. BROWN. Yes, sir; 25 cents each month.

Commissioner O'CONNELL. Are there some of these bunk houses where they have no mattresses, and simply throw straw or hay in them?

Mr. BROWN. Yes, sir; some of them; and it used to be general. Some of them are just wooden affairs, wooden bottoms, and the wall constitutes one side, and they have a board nailed on the other side, and divisions between them. They just fill them with straw, and frequently the men choose to use boughs of the trees. The straw usually attracts too much vermin and things of that sort.

Commissioner O'CONNELL. Whose duty would it be to turn the straw over, or change it occasionally?

Mr. BROWN. I think that would be the logger's duty. Most of the camps even now have no caretaker. They are simply camps—there are some camps where conditions are good, but very few, very few.

Commissioner O'CONNELL. These camps have horses and mules in them, camped around?

Mr. BROWN. Yes, sir; they usually have.

Commissioner O'CONNELL. What is the condition comparatively between the horses and human beings, as to bunking arrangements?

Mr. BROWN. Well, the beds are always made for the horses, the other fellows have to make their own beds, if they are made. Usually these men are tired out, and have no chance to, or care or desire to improve their conditions. They just come in and sleep. Nearly all of these camps are infested with bedbugs, some of them have fleas, and some of them are lousy. One camp down on Grays Harbor—the men last summer went out and slept out doors out in the woods, rather than tolerate the conditions in the bunk house. They would take their bed and go out and sleep on the ground in the woods. They did that for quite a period of time to get rid of the bedbugs.

Mr. THOMPSON. Are there any strikes now in the lumber industry in this State?

Mr. BROWN. Well, there is a strike on down in Centralia where the men are working for the Eastern Railway & Lumber Co.

Mr. THOMPSON. What is the basis of the strike?

Mr. BROWN. They have asked a restoration of 10 per cent, the last cut in wages.

Mr. THOMPSON. How many men are involved in the strike?

Mr. BROWN. About a hundred and twenty-five.

Mr. THOMPSON. How long has it been on?

Mr. BROWN. Since the 2d or 3d of this month.

Mr. THOMPSON. Has there been any effort made to reach a settlement there?

Mr. BROWN. Yes, sir; the men went and organized at the time they went out on a strike. At the time this dissatisfaction arose they appointed from among their number a committee to go and see the foreman and tell him that they wanted a restoration of this 10 per cent last cut. That was on Saturday, I think, of August 1. They told him they would give him until August 3, that would be Monday, for an answer. On the 3d of August one of the members of the committee went to the foreman and asked him if he had his answer ready. The foreman appeared not to know what he was talking about, and he asked him, "What are you talking about?" He said, "About this 10 per cent increase in wages." "You fellows will get no increase in wages; you can go to hell, all of you."

So they quit, and after a day or two formed a union.

Mr. THOMPSON. Have there been any negotiations between the men since they have organized and the company, that you know of?

Mr. BROWN. The company expressed a willingness to see a committee, or desired to see a committee from among their members, and they selected five and they went; down, and the company told them that the men could return to work. if they wanted to and there would be no discrimination against them because of their membership in the union; but that there could be no increase in the wages because they were paying as much as they could afford to pay at that time. That company operates, I think, under as favorable conditions as any other in the State. They have their own logging camp, and thereby get whatever profit comes from handling the raw material; they are at a junction point where they have all kinds of railroad connections—there are five or six transcontinental lines that pass right through there—they have all the local trade there is in that part of the country; I think they are as favorably situated to pay good wages as any I know of, if a person would judge from observation.

Mr. THOMPSON. Have any of your officials had any dealings with the company?

Mr. BROWN. How is that?

Mr. THOMPSON. Have any of your officials had any dealings with this company with regard to' the strike?

Mr. BROWN. Oh, I had some very brief dealings with them. I went down with the men, down on the picket line. The company said they were going to start up one morning, and they did start up. At noon the men thought they would go down on the picket line and see if they could induce any of the men to quit. As we went down there, perhaps 75 men, we approached the company's property, and I learned afterwards the owner and president of the company came out and said it must be understood we were not to trespass on the company's property. I asked them to define exactly where the company's property extended to, and he showed me, and we went out on the railroad track. He then started out to make a speech to the men, and warned them against following any labor leader because, for those who had done it, he said, it usually resulted in disaster, and I replied that the men did not have much to lose, because the men were only getting a dollar fifty-seven cents a day in the majority of cases taking his advice, and they could not lose very much by experimenting in some other direction. The men seemed to be pretty well satisfied, and we had a few words back and forth, not entirely of a complimentary nature. That is about the only time the company and any official of our organization have come in contact.

Mr. THOMPSON. Is there a general depression in the lumber industry in this section of the country?

Mr. BROWN. Yes, sir; I think there is.

Mr. THOMPSON. Do you think that would have anything to do with the reduction in wages?

Mr. BROWN. It hasn't had anything to do with the reduction of wages in the organized portion of it. The employers naturally avail themselves of the flooded labor market to reduce wages where they can. Last fall they reduced wages in the logging camps of Grays Harbor from $2.50 to $2 a day. This spring they raised the price of board in one camp particularly from 75 cents to 90 cents a day, and the men went on strike at that camp, and they went on strike at noon, I think, and the employers' association began sending men down to take their places the next morning " after making a full investigation of the affair."

Commissioner GARRETSON. Has there been any corresponding decrease in the price of the output in the lumber mills?

Mr. BROWN. No, sir; I don't think so. There has been perhaps some, but the prices haven't been very good, but I don't know that their market quotations are any less. I think in some particulars they are more this year than they were last. The demand, however, I think has been less.

Mr. THOMPSON. Has there been any introduction of the speeding-up process in the lumber and logging camps? Have men been offered bonuses to speed up and the work done this year been taken as a basis for the minimum wage the next year?

Mr. BROWN. I could not say generally as to that.

Mr. THOMPSON. Or has the amount of work done been made the minimum for the amount of work to be done the next season?

Mr. BROWN. Yes; I think that is the general practice of the employer, to take the highest work done by anyone as a standard toward which they endeavor to get all to come up to. Out here in the camps between here and Everett this spring I was told they started the men on the minimum-wage basis and offered them bonuses if they would get out a certain amount of logs, a certain number of feet of logs, as they were measured; and later on having shown that the men could do a considerable amount more than the minimum that had been established, they cut off the bonuses and then required as a condition of employment that the men should do what they had previously shown was possible for them to do when they were getting the bonus. .·

In the shingle mills the piecework system, I think, has been employed more than in any other place. The men have been able to preserve their relative wages, but it is none the less a very disagreeable thing for them. They introduced about 10 years ago into this country a new kind of shingle machine called an upright. When that machine was first introduced the men who first worked on it found it possible to cut about 20,000 a day after some little experience and some little practice. There have been a few improvements in the machine since then; men have become more proficient in their use, and they have been more generally introduced. There are some mills now that won't hire a man, however, that can't cut on an average 45,000 a day. That is more than twice what the first men were able to do after some experience.

Mr. THOMPSON. In your experience has the tariff, the raising of the tariff on shingles, had anything to do with the wages of the men?

Mr. BROWN. Well, I think perhaps it has this year, from the fact that there has been a lack of demand for the shingles. That is the situation here in this State, and naturally this limited market had to be divided with the shingles that come in from British Columbia. I don't think, as a general thing, as a general proposition, that the tariff cuts any figure. I don't think the wage cost or labor cost, as a general thing, is any less in British Columbia than it is in Washington.

Mr. THOMPSON. Would putting on the tariff, or an increasing of the tariff, increase the value of stumpage here and affect wages in that way?

Mr. BROWN. I could not say whether it increases the value of the stumpage or not. The stumpage rates are higher here than in British Columbia.

Mr. THOMPSON. What per cent of the men, if you know, use the hospital during the month?

Mr. BROWN. Well, I don't know. The shingle weavers very rarely use it. Most of the shingle weavers belong to different fraternal orders that provide insurance, and they prefer, since they have to pay it in both places, they prefer to take their services from the lodge that they belong to—the Eagles, and Elks, and Moose, and that sort of thing.

Mr. THOMPSON. Take the case of Centralia, where the men's wages were reduced 10 per cent. Was there any statement made to the men by the company that they would have to operate more cheaply on the labor proposition or shut down, and were the men given an opportunity to accept reduced wages and continue work or have the industry closed down? Do you know about that?

Mr. BROWN. They were notified last May—I think on the 29th of April each employee received a printed circular stating that the conditions in the lumber business at that plant had been so bad that the company could not longer operate at a profit or pay the wages they had been paying, and therefore the company was confronted with the alternative of either being compelled to reduce wages or close the plant, and they decided they would reduce the wages, and beginning the 1st of May the wages would be reduced 10 per cent. I don't think the men had any option on the matter at all, further than to accept the 10 per cent reduction or quit.

Mr. THOMPSON. With what field does this section here compete in the lumber market?

Mr. BROWN. How is that?

Mr. THOMPSON. What competition has the lumber market here?   · ′ ′

Mr. BROWN. All of the mills in this part of the country are in one competitive field; the same market is open to all of them; all of them have the same rate on the railroads. The mills in Seattle would be in—except for local conditions, what little local trade they would get—there would be no advantage whether the mill was located here or at Centralia, as to their being able to market their product, or at Everett or anywhere else.

Mr. THOMPSON. Have you got your mills classified as to districts here?

Mr. BROWN. No, sir.   .

⁹, Mr. THOMPSON. Is there such a thing as southern mills and northern mills?

Mr. BROWN. No, sir; our district is north of the California line. They are not very accurately divided, but we have three districts. District No. 1 includes all of this territory west of the Missouri River and north of the California line, or what would be parallel with the California line.

Mr. THOMPSON. I have a question presented here that the party requests that the question be asked. If there is no objection to that I will put it to you in that way. I don't understand what it means:

Does the lumber industry in this section have to compete with the southern mills?

Mr. BROWN. Oh, I suppose it is like the factories all over this section. It is like the jurisdiction of the different unions, one laps over the other in some places. There is no active competition.

Mr. THOMPSON. What do you understand is meant by southern mills?

Mr. BROWN. The mills in Louisiana, down in the cypress field; that is an entirely different timber. They manufacture shingles out of cypress and yellow pine. The timber here is cedar, fir, and spruce.

Mr. THOMPSON. Does this timber here compete with that?

Mr. BROWN. I suppose in some measure.

Mr. THOMPSON. Do you know what effect that competition has had on the profits of the business or mills here?

Mr. BROWN. I have never seen any particular complaint or any particular reference made to it; it is hardly ever mentioned.

Mr. THOMPSON. Would it affect some mills in this section more than others?

Mr. BROWN. Well, I presume it might.

Mr. THOMPSON. Well, take the Centralia mill; would that suffer more on account of this competition than other mills that pay better wages that you have spoken of?

Mr. BROWN. I could not see why it should. They make all classes of lumber—rough and finished lumber—and all that sort of thing. I could not see any reason why they should be subject to any greater competition.

Mr. THOMPSON. You have made a study of the industrial situation; what remedy have you to suggest to the commission that the commission could recommend to Congress or the various States that they could adopt which would help in any degree?

Mr. BROWN. Well, I think as a State proposition, I think it will be a general help to the men in the lumber industry if they succeed in passing this bill to do away with the fee employment offices here in this State. I think the fact that the employer knows by merely telephoning to an industrial center he can get other men on the next train it makes him less patient with the men for any reason, be it frivolous or important, and he discharges the men because he knows he can get more to take their place very readily. That is one reason why the men change around so much. On the other hand, the fact that a man knows he can go and buy a job probably makes him less likely to stay in one place. I think that will be very helpful if that law is adopted and is pronounced constitutional. I am very largely of the same opinion as Mr. Ault—that if some measure could be brought about whereby the men could be protected in their right to organize, that would have a more helpful effect than any one thing that could be done. There are so many mills here where they will not simply allow the men to organize at all. Some mills even compel men to sign a statement before entering their employ, and they require them to sign a statement that they are not now, and will not during their employment with the firm, become a member of any labor organization.

Mr. THOMPSON. Could you give us a list of those mills?

Mr. BROWN. Well, I can give you one mill.

Mr. THOMPSON. Can you get us a form of the statement required?

Mr. BROWN. I am not sure that I can. The matter came to my attention two or three years ago, and I got a copy of the statement which the men were required to sign. The only way, I suppose, that could be furnished is from the company's office.

Mr. THOMPSON. Can you name the company?

Mr. BROWN. Yes, sir; the Stimson Mill Co. here in Seattle.

Mr. THOMPSON. What?

Mr. BROWN. The Stimson Co. here in Seattle; they require that, and on the statement made to me by some of the employees I took the matter up with the labor commissioner here in this State. He wrote back to me and told me he would take the matter up with the attorney general and see if anything could be done to cause that company to rescind on that proposition. The attorney general rendered an opinion that the company was violating no law by requiring the men to sign such a statement, and so nothing further could be done.

. Mr. THOMPSON. Have you any further recommendation you think would help in the solution of these problems? That is all.

Mr. BROWN. Well, I believe that a Federal board, Federal commission that would make inquiry into these conditions, and give them publicity, act as an intelligence bureau, and that would act as a conciliation board, some department of it, bring men together, employers and employees together, where there was an industrial dispute on, that they will all be helpful.

Mr. THOMPSON. Such a council, for instance, as they have in England, the Industrial Council?

Mr. BROWN. I am not very familiar with the Industrial Council. If it is such as I understand it to be, that is along the lines that I have in mind.

Mr. THOMPSON. Are you acquainted with the Industrial Workers of the World, Mr. Brown?

Mr. BROWN. Yes; some.

Mr. THOMPSON. What relations do you have with them, if any?

Mr. BROWN. We do not have very pleasant relations with them.

Mr. THOMPSON. Well, do you meet in the organization of this industry that you work in?

Mr. BROWN. How is that?

Mr. THOMPSON. Do your two organizations meet in the organization of the lumber industry?

Mr. BROWN. Well, I do not think they have any organization.

Mr. THOMPSON. Why do you say that your relations are not friendly? .

Mr. BROWN. Well, they have organizations in the industry, and then they have members scattered around, individual members. It seems to be a part of their program to try and defeat the organization, and in that respect they become very capable allies of the employers in defeating our efforts to organize.

Mr. THOMPSON. You have had some serious strikes in this country, haven't you?

Mr. BROWN. Yes; we had a strike—about the most serious strike we have had has been in the shingle department, out here in Ballard, which is a suburb of Seattle.

Mr. THOMPSON. How about questions of violence in that strike, or those strikes?   . '

Mr. BROWN. Out in Ballard we had a strike there in 1906 that lasted for several months. The employers, on the plea that there was violence there being committed, secured an injunction against us. I have forgotten all the things that they did prohibit us from doing, pretty nearly everything that we wanted to do. The injunction was never—could never be brought to a hearing. Whenever we made an attempt to secure a hearing on the injunction it was postponed upon the request of the attorney for the plaintiffs. When the strike was over the plaintiffs' attorney asked for a dismissal of the injunction, and it was done. The case never came on for a hearing. Last year we had a strike out there. I think there was perhaps 15 or 20 men arrested on some—some union men and some nonunion men. We were not very successful in securing the arrest of the nonunion men. I think one of our men was a man who happened to belong to a union, was convicted of assault. However, it did not grow out of the strike. It was some personal family matter, I think. And that is about the only cases there were that came in—the justice court. There was some dynamite exploded out there one night, and we endeavored to secure the arrest of the proprietors of one of the mills out there for exploding the dynamite. We had affidavits from five or six of his employees showing he engineered the thing. We were not able to secure his arrest, however. We got one of his leading strikebreakers arrested. The prosecuting attorney claimed that the same evidence would come on in the hearing of his case as would in the hearing of the other case; that the one trial would. be made a test. This man's case was tried in the justice court. The men, whose affidavits we had, when they were put on the stand, absolutely denied their affidavits. I do not know just what their reasons were for denying them, but it was a coincidence at least that these men had left the employ of this company, were reemployed by the company, and their material circumstances took on a marked improvement. We tried to get the prosecuting attorney—the justice, when he was trying the case, asked this man after they had read the affidavits, asked the man: "You now say all that is untrue?" "Absolutely untrue," he said. The justice said: "You step over here; I will look into your case a little further." He insisted he should be held on a charge of perjury. I thought that was a pretty clear case. But when I went up to the prosecuting attorney's office in an effort to press the proposition, he said it was almost impossible to secure a conviction. The man was subsequently released.

Mr. THOMPSON. Have you any views with reference to the employment of private detectives or private agencies by the employer in case of strikes, and also as to the use of the municipal police and State authorities?

Mr. BROWN. Last summer out in Ballard, the strike we had out there, the police came down there morning, noon, and night, usually one there all the time. They did not bother us. They seemed to act impartially, and we got along all right until finally a day or two before this dynamite was exploded the mill owners out there made application to the sheriff to have some of their employees, their watchmen and one thing and another, deputized. This sheriff did deputize a number of them. This man we had arrested for—that was arrested for exploding the dynamite, he was one of them. He made no bones about being a professional strike breaker. He was in the business. He hired men to break the strike of the coal miners out here at Renton. He made a business of hiring men out there. We got quite well acquainted with him later on when he came, after he had had a falling out with his employers out here in Ballard; he came and wanted to strike up a bargain with us whereby he would procure the necessary evidence to be able to convict this millman out here in Ballard. I went again up to the prosecuting attorney's office for some other advice, and they told me it was a dangerous thing to do, to hire anybody that way; that they did not think a conviction could be secured. So we dropped the matter.

Then the man then said he was—this man was trying to hire strike breakers for the coal mines in Colorado. Such men as that, the employment of such men at that time out there in Ballard—whatever trouble there was started from the time of their employment. It is my belief that the dynamite was exploded in order that a plausible pretext could be made for asking for the appointment of these deputies. These deputies were not appointed to avoid the trouble, but it seemed like it started then. I think that the start of that trouble out there was assisted and fostered by the employers. I believe that is usually the purpose of the employment of private guards and deputy sheriffs. I think many of the employers' associations have no other purpose in asking for troops, extra police force, and the appointment of deputies except to have those men partisan to their side to use either as strike breakers themselves or as helps to strike breakers.

Mr. THOMPSON. This same man that you spoke of that was involved in the dynamiting was involved in the teamsters' strike?

Mr. BROWN. The same man, but not convicted in either case. Mr. Ault, you remember, spoke about one man confessing This man who made the confession said that this other man, Semple by name, was implicated with him; that he, Semple, had made the dynamite plant. Semple was again arrested, but, I think, not proved guilty.

Mr. THOMPSON. That is all, Mr. Chairman.

Acting Chairman COMMONS. The commission will stand adjourned until 2 o'clock.

Mr. Brown, you will resume the stand at 2 o'clock.

(Whereupon, at 12.30 o'clock p. m. of this Wednesday, August 12, 1914, the commission took an adjournment until 2 o'clock p. m. of the same day.)

AFTER RECESS—2 P. M.

Present: Commissioners Commons (acting chairman), Lennon, Garretson, and O'Connell; also W. O. Thompson, Esq., counsel.

Acting Chairman COMMONS. The commission will come to order. You may proceed, Mr. Thompson.

TESTIMONY OF MR. J. G. BROWN—Continued.

Mr. THOMPSON. I am through.

Acting Chairman COMMONS. Have you any questions to ask of Mr. Brown, Mr. O'Connell?

Commissioner O'CONNELL. Yes.

Acting Chairman COMMONS. Mr. Brown, Mr. O'Connell has some questions.

Commissioner O'Connell. Mr. Brown, I want to get at something as to the method of employing people in these mills and logging camps. Are the men largely secured from these employment agencies?

Mr. Brown. Yes. I think they are except in—well, even in the cities, even the men who are employed in the city here I think they are largely secured from employment offices—private employment offices.

Commissioner O'Connell. Do you suppose there is any collusion between the employers and those agencies in the matter of securing men because of the fees charged?

Mr. Brown. Well, I haven't the positive proof, but there are many circumstances that point to that. For instance, there have been one or two cases of where their licenses have been revoked. For instance—this does not apply to a mill, but it is along the same lines—there was an employment office in Spokane named Mayko Bros. Employment Office; they furnished men for a construction camp on the Chicago, Milwaukee & St. Paul road. The men were employed near Ritzville. There was only a hundred men employed there when the crew was filled up. This concern sent out 300 men there in one month. That would indicate that there was a change in less than every 10 days. They charged those men $2 each for the job, and each one of those men had to pay a dollar hospital dues besides their railroad fares. Some of them I presume were shipped out on the company's own lines. That matter was brought to the attention of the Spokane city council, the case was worked up by the men over there in Spokane, and the license of this concern was finally revoked.

Commissioner O'Connell. Does the State law cover these agencies as to compelling them to return the fees where work is not procured?

Mr. Brown. I do not believe there is any State law. I think Mr. Ault, when he testified there was a State law regulating employment offices, was mistaken. There was a bill introduced at the last session of the legislature requiring employment offices to post notices where a strike was on and men were to be secured to work in those places. And the matter was killed in the rules committee; died in the rules committee. I do not think there is any law at all, only such law as may be provided by the different municipalities. Now, this city has a law requiring that notice shall appear where there is a strike on. Now, we have run across that in several instances. They do not tell the men anything about it. They just give them a slip, have the ordinance printed on a slip, and it is filled in, a few blank spaces, and they stamp across the face of it, "Strike on"; and unless the man is looking for it, especially where he can not read the language, it is a downright deception, even though it does appear on there. They had a strike up in Everett this spring and we ran across any number of men who came up there, claiming no knowledge of the strike being on. At the same time this appeared stamped across the page "Strike on."

Commissioner O'Connell. I suppose that fulfills the requirement of the law?

Mr. Brown. It seemingly would. The city ordinance here requires the return of the fee, and I think it is fair when the job is secured through misrepresentation, but when that is marked across there they hold there is no misrepresentation for which the men can be held.

Commissioner O'Connell. Are there evidences of large numbers of these men being sent out to the camps and only working a few days, and being discharged or let go?

Mr. Brown. I know of a case of a man who went to a logging camp up here and asked for a job, and he was told to come to Seattle and secure employment through an agent, giving him the name. He came and got the job and went back and was put to work and worked three days and was discharged.

Commissioner O'Connell. Are there any laws requiring sanitary inspection of camps or inspection of boilers and machinery and wire-rope cables and so on?

Mr. Brown. Absolutely none. There is no law requiring an inspection of logging camps in this State.

Commissioner O'Connell. Are there any number of boiler explosions in these camps?

Mr. Brown. Well, there are some. There was one boiler explosion last year in a camp on Grays Harbor. Two or three men were killed. Men working there told me that the boiler had long been known to be absolutely past the point where a large pressure of steam was safe in it. I think some one told me it had been condemned for use in some factory or city work here where it had been used.

Commissioner O'CONNELL. Do the employers themselves have any inspection to see that the cables are properly kept up? If a strand becomes broken that they don't break entirely?

Mr. BROWN. I suppose if they saw a cable was going to break and do some damage that they would anticipate it and try to have it fixed, because when a cable starts to break in one strand it soon unravels and breaks very easily. No inspection of any kind is required. There is no man designated to do that class of work; it just happens, and if they see it some one of course stops it, and it is repaired.

Commissioner O'CONNELL. Now, about this hospital fee charge, this dollar a month, what do the men get in return for that?

Mr. BROWN. They just get hospital care in case they are hurt while at work.

Commissioner O'CONNELL. Do they get compensation for loss of time while they are injured?

Mr. BROWN. No, sir; no compensation at all. That is the only thing the contract implies—if you are hurt, a man gets a leg smashed or cut off he is loaded into the best conveyance at hand and shipped to the hospital that the arrangement is made with, and there he is treated until his leg is well. He gets no compensation, however.

Commissioner O'CONNELL. Are the hospitals at the camps?

Mr. BROWN. They don't have hospitals at any of the camps. I think that all of the men who are hurt in Grays Harbor section; that, I think, is the largest lumber section in this country, probably 3,000 men are employed, and there are 50 camps. When any of them are injured at those camps, from 25 to 50 miles away, they are brought to Aberdeen or Cosmopolis or Hoquiam.

Commissioner O'CONNELL. There are about 3,000 men in the camps?

Mr. BROWN. Yes, sir.

Commissioner O'CONNELL. They pay $3,000 a month for hospital fees?

Mr. BROWN. If they didn't change around, just take a dollar from each man. Sometimes one job may have three or four men during the month. In that event there will be $3 or $4 collected on that one job.

Commissioner O'CONNELL. Are those hospitals, the physicians that are there, employed exclusively for the men at these places?

Mr. BROWN. No, sir. The Aberdeen general hospital, I think, has a contract with most of the camps. The hospital arrangements are made between the doctors and the company; the men have absolutely no choice in the matter and nothing to say about it, and are never consulted as far as I know.

Commissioner O'CONNELL. If a man is taken with disease of some kind other than an accident, do they take care of him in that case and take him to the hospital?

Mr. BROWN. I think it would be purely optional with the company. The men working in logging camps are generally healthy and not very much sickness occurs among them because it is hard work and requires big, strong, healthy men to do the work. I think it would be purely optional with the company as to whether they got any hospital treatment in case of sickness or not.

Commissioner O'CONNELL. The men who follow the logging end of the business, do they, when the logging business is not active, go into the mills, and vice versa?

Mr. BROWN. No; the man who follows the logging usually has his—that is his calling. When there isn't any logging he doesn't work at all as a rule.

Commissioner O'CONNELL. Now, how much time in a year would a man in the logging business—how much work would he secure in a year?

Mr. BROWN. Well, I presume in an exceptionally good year he might figure on nine months, possibly nine and a half. The time that would be off for holiday periods and time when weather conditions would prevent operations would limit his work to, at least—would limit his work two months and a half out of the year. Now, if conditions were as they are, or have been here for the last five or six years, I don't believe the men have averaged over six or seven months in the year.

Commissioner O'CONNELL. What would be his average earnings for the year?

Mr. BROWN. Well, I would imagine they get—a man working seven months would probably get about $700, that is, in the skilled branches. If he worked in the unskilled branches with wages as they are now, he would not make much more than half of that.

Commissioner O'CONNELL. Now, what do they follow when they are not working at the logging business?

38819°—S. Doc. 415, 64–1—vol 5——9

Mr.-Brown. Well, the most of them congregate in town, and they become a problem for the municipalities to look after. I think here in Seattle last winter there was at one time perhaps 20,000 men. I think it is safe to say that 95 per cent of those men relied upon the lumber industry for their livelihood.

Commissioner O'Connell. In the commissary arrangements in these camps· do the companies sell all the things that they ordinarily buy outside of ·their regular keeping, like tobaccos, clothing, and liquors? Do they sell them? · :

Mr. Brown. No. I do not know of any camp where they sell intoxicating liquors. They generally have a commissary in each camp where the men· can buy tobacco and such clothing as they are likely to need in the camp, blankets and that sort of thing.

Commissioner O'Connell. Have you any idea as to what prices range in those camps—how they compare with city prices?

Mr. Brown. No; I have not. Well, even if the prices were the same, I should imagine the profit would be greater, because there would be no expense in the way of rent and other things that would have to be taken care of in a. gen-. eral merchandise store. They just have them in a rough shack where the men can go and get them.

Commissioner O'Connell. Do you have in your business what is called rust-ling cards or clearance cards?

Mr. Brown. No; not in very many cases. I think there are one or two places where they require references as to a man's previous employment.

Commissioner O'Connell. Is any physical examination of any kind re-quired?

Mr. Brown. No; no physical examination of any kind at all in any depart-ment.

Commissioner O'Connell. Do they make any distinction in the selection be-tween married men and single men?

Mr. Brown. Well, it frequently happens in cities like Seattle and Tacoma and Everett they hardly ever ask the question whether they are married or. single. But in a good many out-of-the-way places—I have in mind one mill particularly up here about 100 miles, they send in to our office sometimes for some of their shingle-mill help, and they always make the special request that the men be married men. The inference that we draw from that is that when they get them up there—they own all the houses, they own the store, and. everything—when they get the men up there they would get rent out of them. And they think, for instance, they are less likely to move for a trifling cause. On the other hand, at Cosmopolis, I think they rather put a premium on single men. They only allow them $10 out of the $20 usual rate charged for board in case they board at home.

Commissioner O'Connell. In some of the stories I have read of the logging camps in the Northwest by some of our famous writers they tell about a sort of cleaning up in the spring time, a general carousal on the part of the woods-men, a general beating up of each other until the king lives among them. Is that the custom that prevails now?

Mr. Brown. I don't think so. I didn't happen to be around when anything of that kind happened.

Commissioner O'Connell. You have read some of the stories?

Mr. Brown. I have read some of them. It is very interesting reading, but I never happened to be there.

Commissioner O'Connell. That is all.

Commissioner Lennon. Mr. Brown, what effort has your union made to enter into collective agreements in order to maintain conditions by these strikes in the lumber regions?

Mr. Brown. We have always held out; we have always advocated the trade agreement as the best method of adjusting the relations between the men and the employers. But I do not think we ever made a special effort to get the mills signed up until 1912. I interviewed something like 100 different mill companies, and our organizers interviewed as many more as they could, in an effort to secure a trade agreement. The provisions of the agreement, that we asked them to sign at that time were that the conditions that then prevailed should continue until March 1, 1914, at which time, or 30 days before the ex-piration of which time, a joint meeting should be held for the purpose of enter: ing into a new agreement to adjust such inequalities as might then exist. We were not, however, very successful in it. I think we got something in the neighborhood of 40 concerns to sign that agreement. Outside of the city of Everett there were not any very large concerns. The ones who signed outside of Everett were very small manufacturers and had very little influence in the industry generally. We only tried to do that in the shingle mills, because our organization at that time only included the shingle-mill workers in its ranks. The percentage of the number who signed was so small that we felt that it was neither a satisfactory arrangement for the men nor for ourselves. However, we.tried to get some of those who signed that agreement to call a meeting on the 1st of last February, or during the month of February, 30 days before it expired; but we were unable to get anyone to call such a meeting, and the contract.therefore expired. All of these contracts that we had signed at that time provided that in case of dispute—provided several preliminary stages by which they might be adjusted, and if they were not adjusted in this way they should finally be left to arbitration as a means for settling disputes.

Commissioner LENNON. Well, in undertaking to reach an agreement, do you believe that your representatives would fairly take into consideration the competition in the business and general conditions that prevail through the country, or would you be arbitrary and stand out for just what you could get?

Mr. BROWN. The conditions in the shingle department are nearly uniform. Such inequalities as exist in the matter of wages—for instance, some places they pay above the minimum scale, but in those places they are usually remote, and that disadvantage is offset by the advantage of being closer to the raw material. They get their timber cheaper. The conditions are fairly uniform in the shingle branch of the industry, and there is at present no competition in the shingle mills in this part of the country. They are all on about the same footing with the exception, perhaps, of a few. That might be slightly modified by saying that the mills in British Columbia, some of them, get their timber a little bit cheaper—somewhat cheaper.

Acting Chairman COMMONS. Mr. Thompson, have you anything more?

Mr. THOMPSON. I have a couple of questions here. With reference to the wages paid in your industry, seven or eight years ago there was a higher wage, was there not?

Mr. BROWN. Well, I think they were somewhat higher in the logging and sawmill branches. There has been no change, no general change in the wage scale in the shingle mills since 1907.

Mr. THOMPSON. How about the selling price of the product, has that remained stationery, or has it gone up or down?

Mr. BROWN. Well, that fluctuates. It has been up and it has been down.

Mr. THOMPSON. Generally, as compared with seven or eight years ago, how is it?

Mr. BROWN. Well, I think that the—1907 was an exceptional year. There was an embargo on among the railroads here, and shipment facilities were badly crippled, and as a consequence the price of all lumber products went up. The next spring when shipping conditions became more nearly normal, the prices went down, and I think it has been about the same since then as it was before. Possibly a little higher in some respects.

Mr. THOMPSON. Has the fact that there is another organization seeking to organize the workers in the lumber industry affected the attitude of the employers toward your organization?

Mr. BROWN. Well, I don't know. Outside of the shingle manufacturers—some of them we have had very friendly relations with for a long while—I have never yet met a man who in the logging and sawmill branches of the industry expressed a willingness to see his men organized in any kind of a union.

Mr. THOMPSON. In your organization, do you take in all branches of the workers—you do?

Mr. BROWN. All branches.

Mr. THOMPSON. Your union might be called an industrial union, might it not?

Mr. BROWN. Yes, sir.

Mr. THOMPSON. Are the different branches organized into different locals, or in some places are the members performing different work, in the same local?

Mr. BROWN. They are all in the same local, except it is provided that in case it would be any advantage for them to segregate for purposes of expediting business, they could do that. But up to this time they are all organized in mixed locals where all of the men in any branch of the industry may belong and do belong.

Mr. THOMPSON. Do you as an organization stand for the idea of collective bargaining—do you not?

Mr. BROWN. Yes, sir.

Mr. THOMPSON. Is that one of the instruments through which you expect to help the worker?

Mr. BROWN. Yes, sir.

Mr. THOMPSON. How about the other organizations in the field that are seeking to get these same workers into their organization?

Mr. BROWN. I think it is the policy of the Industrial Workers of the World—they are the only organization I know of that is professing to organize the men—I think they frankly proclaim a revolutionary program. They go on the theory that it is a continual war between the employers and the employees, and that any advantage they can take at any time is justifiable.

Mr. THOMPSON. Well, do you think the fact that such an organization having that program, has sought to organize the workers in your field, has helped your organization at all?

Mr. BROWN. No; I don't think it has. I haven't any reason for believing that it has. I rather think that the employers use every method they can to prevent organization by holding a club over the heads of the men. The Industrial Workers of the World have an equally effective weapon by pointing out the futility of organizing anything less than a revolutionary union. One discourages them, causes them to believe that they could not gain from organizing in any other union except theirs, and the employers prevent them from organizing by fear of discharge and other things.

Mr. THOMPSON. Referring to employment agencies, what would you do with the private agency, would you abolish them?

Mr. BROWN. Yes, sir.

Mr. THOMPSON. Or would you regulate them?

Mr. BROWN. I don't see that the private employment agent serves any necessary function. Down in Grays Harbor, for instance, the Grays Harbor Commercial Co., I think, hires their own men through a private employement office in Seattle, Tacoma, and Portland. The logging camps of Grays Harbor put in together, each camp puts in $15 a month, I understand, to maintain a free employment office in the city of Aberdeen. That secures all their men through that employment office. The city of Hoquiam as a city maintains a free employment office in that city. The free employment offices here in this city—I think the city will put on all the additional help that the patronage of that office will require. The facts of the matter are, employers don't send there for help, and consequently they can not furnish help that is not asked for.

Mr. THOMPSON. That is all, Mr. Chairman.

Commissioner GARRETSON. In the conduct of employment agencies is there any belief or evidence that somebody splits the money?

Mr. BROWN. Well, yes, sir; there is a widespread belief and some evidence. I think the fact that men are changed around for trifling causes or no cause aparently, that all men must be hired through private employment agencies, I think that is evidence that there is some sort of collusion between them.

Commissioner GARRETSON. If such a practice did exist wouldn't the entire influence of the man who was splitting his part out be used to retain the private employment agency as a means for securing men?

Mr. BROWN. Yes, sir; I think so.

Commissioner GARRETSON. He might urge other reasons, but that would be the actual one?

Mr. BROWN. They had a hearing down at Olympia, a joint hearing of the committee on labor—the joint house of representatives and senate, when this bill to abolish private employment offices and substitute public employment offices was up for consideration at the last session.

At that time the men who opposed the bill the most were not the employment agents themselves, but the loggers, the logging-camp owners and mill owners. There was only one, as I remember, only one proprietor of an employment office, that appeared in opposition to that measure, and the reasons advanced why these private employment offices should be maintained was that they specialized in their work. Now, as a matter of fact, they don't sepcialize particularly. Some men who may have an acquaintance, for instance, at the shingle mills do make a kind of specialty of shingle-mill employees, but they take the men for other positions all the time. They take the man's word for it all the time. If they want a saw filer—for instance, a man comes in and says he is a saw filer, that is enough, that is all the evidence that is required that he is a saw filer, and they take his money and turn him loose on the job. The same test could be applied in the public employment office, they would have to take a man's word for it in any event. It is only possible he might accept the position from the public employment office, even though he did not have the confidence in his ability that he would otherwise. By paying for the job, it would probably indicate he had confidence in his ability to hold the job. One of these employment offices here in Seattle—the question was asked this morning whether they were used as strike breakers or recruiting agencies for strike breakers. I can say one employment office here last year misrepresented the conditions at the Ballard strike so much that application was made to the city council to have their license revoked. It was found out upon investigation that their license expired in a very short time, and the evidence was so strong against them that they refused to renew their license. I would just like, if I might, to say just a few words not in response to any question; it is a matter I did not touch on this morning.

I spoke of high wages in the shingle mills, the shingle department. That was true, but rather a false impression might be gained of the amount of money that they get if it was not also stated they are very much like the logging camps. The time, the months during the year when this work can be done I don't believe has averaged over seven months, sometimes runs down to five months in a year. Another thing that should be stated about them is the extreme danger. I just cut out a clipping in a paper this morning, in this morning's paper, stating that out of a list of accidents numbering 2,119 that had been looked into by the bureau of labor in this State, 547 was the result of accidents on power-driven saws. Most of the accidents on saws in mills occur in shingle mills because there is where the workers have to come in close contact with the saws. We found in an investigation four or five years ago—investigating a thousand members—we found out that the year previous 15 per cent of those members had been incapacitated either through accident or through the injurious effect of cedar dust which they inhale in the cedar mills, and it is very injurious to the lungs, produces cedar asthma, and that sort of thing.

I just want to say a further word in connection with the difficulty we have in cooperating with the manufacturers. They proposed to raise the tariff on shingles in the year 1908, I believe. We were very much in hopes that if the price of shingles was raised, or if the tariff was lowered, we were told we would be thrown in competition with British Columbia, where orientals are very much employed in shingle mills, so that we got very busy in our endeavors, not only to keep the tariff where it was, but to secure an advance in it. We succeeded. We sent one $28 telegram that I remember of. I don't know just what influence that had, but, anyway, the tariff went up from 30 cents a thousand to 50 cents a thousand. We anticipated very prosperous times. There was not another year in the history of our organization when we had to make as hard a fight as we did then to maintain our scale of wages. The employers attacked us all over this part of the State. So that when the question of taking the tariff off this time was brought up some of our enthusiasm had died out. In the meantime, I remember talking to one man, and he pointed out that all the mills would move over into British Columbia if they took the tariff off of shingles. told him I would take it up at our meeting.

We had a meeting of the boys over at Ballard, and there was one of them said he thought he could move over into British Columbia nearly as easy as they could move the big mills, so that we didn't take any active part in keeping the tariff on shingles. As a matter of fact, I don't believe there is any advantage in the employment of oriental labor from the employers' standpoint. They have to have about twice as much machinery to produce the same amount of work, and that carries twice the overhead expense and twice the capacity of the mills, and twice the investment, and that sort of thing.

Commissioner O'CONNELL. Are orientals employed in the mills of this State?

Mr. BROWN. Not in the sawmills. Mr. Skinner, who is the head of the Fort Blakely mill, employs a large number in his mill at Fort Blakely, and there is another mill, the Crown Lumber Co., that employs a large number of orientals, mostly Japanese.

Commissioner O'CONNELL. Are they employed in logging?

Mr. BROWN. No, sir; not in this State.

Commissioner O'CONNELL. Why not?

Mr. BROWN. I think for the same reason they are not employed in British Columbia. There is the additional reason that there is not nearly as many here as there are there. They are physically unable to do the work required in the logging camps. Hardly any are employed in the logging camps in British Columbia.

Commissioner O'CONNELL. That is all.
ACTING CHAIRMAN COMMONS. That is all. Call your next, Mr. Thompson.
Mr. THOMPSON. Col. Blethen.

TESTIMONY OF COL. ALDEN J. BLETHEN.

Mr. THOMPSON. Colonel, will you give us your name?
Col. BLETHEN. Alden J. Blethen.
Mr. THOMPSON. And your business address?
Col. BLETHEN. Seattle.
Mr. THOMPSON. And you are publisher of the Seattle Times?
Col. BLETHEN. I am the president of the company, which is really the pub-
lisher, and the editor in chief.
Mr. THOMPSON. How long have you been head of that paper?
Col. BLETHEN. Eighteen years the 10th day of this month; eighteen years day
before yesterday.
Mr. THOMPSON. In your public capacity as a newspaper man you have had
occasion to keep pretty well in touch with industrial conditions around Seattle
and in Seattle, have you?
Col. BLETHEN. Yes, sir.
Mr. THOMPSON. In that touch which you have kept with industrial affairs
here, have you reached any opinion in regard to the industrial unrest which
exists, the causes which have led to it, if it does exist, and any ideas as to
how it might be remedied, in detail or in part?
(See Blethen exhibit.)
Col. BLETHEN. My observation as publisher is, I find unrest in industrial
conditions is based on the idea of idleness. Men employed are usually contented if not happy. We have but very little trouble with men when they are
employed. If they are not employed, necessarily the cost of living going on
the same as before, the ability to live is reduced, and they become unhappy,
and out of it grows agitation—street speaking by the I. W. W. [laughter]——
Commissioner LENNON. We will not have that.
Mr. THOMPSON. Now, Col. Blethen, in your view of the conditions in Seattle,
has there been a good deal of the idleness that you speak of which has led
to this trouble? What is the cause of the idleness, in your opinion?
Col. BLETHEN. Lack of employment. In other words, there have been more
men and women than could be employed to produce the product that could
be sold.
Mr. THOMPSON. Well, has that lack of employment been due to the fact
either that there are too many working people or, perhaps, have been to
are seasonal occupations around Seattle which employ the men at one time of
the year but do not keep them employed the whole year?
Col. BLETHEN. Undoubtedly that is true.
Mr. THOMPSON. To what extent would you say that the seasonal occupations
that exist around Seattle are responsible for the unemployment of a great
number of workers during a large part of the year?
Col. BLETHEN. To a very large degree. The industrial conditions in lumber,
which have been very carefully set forth by Mr. Brown, necessarily renders
idle an average for nearly half the time of a great body of men who are
employed the rest of the time.
Mr. THOMPSON. How would it be with reference to the workers who come
down in the winter time from Alaska?
Col. BLETHEN. Not so true of them, in my experience, because they have
generally done better. They have had higher wages or, perhaps, have been to
work for themselves. And I don't think that the return from Alaska during
the winter months has added very materially to the unemployed.
Mr. THOMPSON. How would you suggest, Col. Blethen, that we might remedy the unemployment arising from the seasonal occupations in Seattle?
Col. BLETHEM. I don't know how. I can't suggest any remedy. Our conditions
here are very favorable compared with the colder States. Although we have
a good deal of rain in the winter, we have no cold weather. We have on the
mountains some snow, and once in a while a little ice in the valleys, but
generally, so far as temperature is concerned, men could work the year
around. But conditions arise, either from overproduction or from rules and
regulations which are established by the manufacturer himself, so that it is
a fact that those engaged in the forests and in the lumber business and in the
products of lumber are not employed a very considerable portion of the year.

And they do not receive sufficient wages during the time they are employed to maintain them during the balance of the year. If we could find markets enough so we could keep all of these men employed for 12 months in 'the year, there would be no unrest as a rule. There are certain classes of people that are always uneasy. They don't want to work. But the great majority of people want to work and are happy when they do work.

Mr. THOMPSON. Well, Colonel, what can we do to help the situation? What can the city do? What can the employers do? What can the community as a whole do through the National Government, State government, or the municipality to help in that situation of enforced idleness apparently because of seasonal work?

Col. BLETHEN. I scarcely know how the regulations which have been adopted by the various unions can be improved by law. Take my own business, for example: Of course, we go on the year around. If we have any slackness in our business, it is in July and August and January and February, but not to that extent by any means that prevails in the East, where you have extreme heat in the summer and extreme cold in the winter. Our men receive, for example, $5 by day for seven hours' work; $5.50 by night. And there are other compensations. And they get quite uniformly steady employment. Our printers, our pressmen, our stereotypers—the men who work for the newspapers here—are among the very best in quality and manhood, in education and steadiness, that can be found anywhere. One of the interesting things that I have always tried to do—and I am now over 30 years in the business—is to make my employees happy, to make them contented, to get them to be home builders, because I find that a contented and happy man produces better work and more of it—so I am a little selfish. I find that the man who is a home builder is a great deal better than the man who to-day is here and in Portland next week. I find that by assisting men when they are ill, by sort of pensioning them when they get to be old, and helping them feel that they are a part and parcel of our institution, tends to make better men, to make for greater contentment, and we get better results.

Now, the laws of the State or the Nation could not help us as publishers. At least I don't see how they could. We have contentions every year or two. You know the publishers are brought together under demand of the typographical union, the pressmen's union, the stereotypers' union—all three unions—for a new scale and shorter hours and new things. We get together and scold each other half a dozen times or a dozen times, and then we get down to work—and as the result of conciliation I think we have never had two arbitrations in the 18 years I have been here. Matters are settled by conciliation, and everybody goes home happy. And then we try to benefit those who try to benefit themselves. Two men or two women sitting side by side at the Mergenthaler machines, one will produce 45,000, perhaps, in seven hours and a half, or 42,000 in seven hours, just as easily as the other will produce 35,000. We established a minimum product that they must make. No person that does not reach that would be retained. The union would not have them. We don't have to keep them. But when we come to a man or a woman who does this extra work just as naturally and just as easily as the man or the woman does the other, we pay those people a bonus—extra money for the extra work. And of course that is selfish. But it helps that man and woman to earn more, to get more, and to build a better home.

Mr. THOMPSON. Is that bonus, Colonel, based upon any regular systematic estimate of extra work?

Col. BLETHEN. No.

Mr. THOMPSON. Just as you may size it up from time to time?

Col. BLETHEN. Oh, no; it is measured by machines. They know exactly each day when they get through how many thousands they have set. And the difference between the amount which they must set under their contract in order to earn a day's wages and what they do set, is split and paid for by the thousands.

Mr. THOMPSON. I see. You take half and he takes half of the extra pay?

Col. BLETHEN. Yes, sir.

Mr. THOMPSON. Under that scheme, of course, it is the best thing for you to have the faster workers?

Col. BLETHEN. Yes.

Mr. THOMPSON. It would reduce the average cost of your production?

Col. BLETHEN. It makes that man a better man. He gets a better home, and he likes to stay in Seattle; he don't want to go away.

Mr. THOMPSON. Of course you have collective bargaining with these different unions?

Col. BLETHEN. Yes; necessarily.

Mr. THOMPSON. Do you believe in the theory of collective bargaining?

Col. BLETHEN. We get better results out of the union as handled by the men than we get out of unorganized labor. The men are under control. They are expected to come up to a standard. They can not go to the foreman and complain that they are being treated badly. They must go to the union and deal with the union officials, and they must take it up, and they must go to the executive board, and if they have a wrong the committee will take it up with them. The result is that the general character of the union men who work for us is higher than the nonunion men I employed when I first started in Kansas City where I had a nonunion office.

Mr. THOMPSON. Then I easily gather from what you say that you believe in organized labor?

Col. BLETHEN. I do when controlled by the men. When controlled by the walking delegate—no. The agitator is bad.

Mr. THOMPSON. And from your idea, Colonel, you believe it is a good thing for the employer as well as for the employee?

Col. BLETHEN. Absolutely.

Mr. THOMPSON. Now, you say you draw the line at the walking delegate or the agitator? Explain in detail what you mean by that.

Col. BLETHEN. I mean to say the man who uses his mouth to get a living rather than his hands, and who is employed to go among other men of his own profession, and stir them up to believe that they are working too many hours—not getting pay enough—who is here for a week, and then somewhere else next week, has not the vital interest of the men at heart that the home builder, the regular man, the executive officers of the union have.

Mr. THOMPSON. Of course, these different unions that you deal with—the typographical union, the stereotypers' union, the pressmen's union—all have agents representing them who do not work at the trade.

Col. BLETHEN. Oh, I presume so, but we never see them. We enter into a contract once a year, or once in two years, or sometimes four years, and that is the end of it. We deal entirely with our own men.

Mr. THOMPSON. But you know that they have these agents?

Col. BLETHEN. Oh, yes.

Mr. THOMPSON. Who are watching their interests?

Col. BLETHEN. I presume so.

Mr. THOMPSON. That is true all over the United States that these locals you speak of—unions you speak of?

Col. BLETHEN. Well, in the Typographical Union, the president of the union, the secretary of the union, and the executive committee here look after the interests of these men so thoroughly that they do not need any help.

Mr. THOMPSON. Are these men that you speak of engaged in typesetting or in presswork?

Col. BLETHEN. Oh, yes; both. They are a part of our establishment. Every one of them, I think, holds positions on the papers of this city.

Mr. THOMPSON. Well, has the Typographical Union got any agent in this city who is located here all the time to look after the business of the Typographical Union, not only among the newspapers but among the job plants?

Col. BLETHEN. Well, if they have, I don't know. We do not deal with them enough so that I know them. I have only met them occasionally.

Mr. THOMPSON. Wouldn't your judgment be that there is such a man here?

Col. BLETHEN. Oh, I presume there is. But if there be, I do not see him enough, Mr. Thompson, to know. The president of the union knows, and I would be glad to give you his name if you would like to call him. I am not familiar with all the details.

Mr. THOMPSON. If there is such a man, as there probably is, you are not referring to that kind?

Col. BLETHEN. No; not at all. I am referring to the fellow that goes from town to town and agitates.

Mr. THOMPSON. I see. Well, give us more in detail where you draw the line, Colonel, as between the walking delegate who represents the union and who gives his entire time to it, and who is the right kind of a man, and the walking delegate who does not give his entire time to the union and is the wrong kind of a man.

' Col. BLETHEN. If we have a representative of the union who lives in Seattle, he will have plenty of work to do and be a part and parcel of us, and be regarded as one of our workmen. If he be a man who travels over the country, what is generally denominated as a walking delegate, he has no other interest than to disturb the present situation.

Mr. THOMPSON. Assuming, Colonel, that a radical organization—I won't name any—but assuming that there is a radical organization and that that organization has a representative who is permanently located in Seattle, who makes his home here—his wife and children live here—would he be the kind of a man who would be safe?

Col. BLETHEN. We would regard him as a part of the union located here, and who is interested here. Take the secretary of the Typographical Union, Mr. McCullough. He is that very kind of a man you speak of, one of the best fellows we have got.

Mr. THOMPSON. Assume the secretary of the Industrial Workers of the World or some representative was located here permanently, had his home here, his family here——

Col. BLETHEN. I do not see any reason why there should be any distinction.

Mr. THOMPSON. No distinction?

Col. BLETHEN. No.

Mr. THOMPSON. Are you acquainted with the Industrial Workers of the World, Colonel?

Col. BLETHEN. Not favorably. [Laughter.] I know something about them, Mr. Thompson. We have had trouble only with them all the time.

Mr. THOMPSON. What are your views of that organization?

Col. BLETHEN. I think if the rest of the unions would get together and put them out of business, we would be getting good results.

Mr. THOMPSON. They are an organization existing all over the country?

Col. BLETHEN. They are revolutionary in their movements, in their propaganda, and in their action. Revolutionists I have no use for.

Mr. THOMPSON. When you use the term "revolutionist," Colonel, what do you mean by the term "revolutionist"?

Col. BLETHEN. I mean to say that when the I. W. W. determine that a body of men, no matter who they are—take the typographical union, for example, in this city—and the I. W. W. think these men are not getting the wages they ought to have, if they can disturb it or interfere, they will proceed to do so for the purpose of breaking them up—not bettering them, but to destroy them— their purpose being to disorganize and destroy, not to organize and build up, the exact opposite of the typographical union, for example.

Mr. THOMPSON. Well, if the purpose of the Industrial Workers of the World was to organize rather than to disorganize, to build up rather than to tear down, to increase the wages of the men, better their condition, shorten their hours, then you have no objection to the organization?

Col. BLETHEN. No, sir.

Mr. THOMPSON. Is that it?

Col. BLETHEN. That is precisely it, Mr. Thompson.

Mr. THOMPSON. As you conceive the idea, it is an organization which is the antithesis of these things?

Col. BLETHEN. The exact opposite.

Mr. THOMPSON. Is there any positive or specific information you would like to give the commission?

Col. BLETHEN. Incidentally, when you were speaking of organizations—I presume the commission is familiar with the fact that the organization of the typographical union and the others, although the typographical union was the main mover, that caused the publishers of the United States to organize the American Newspaper Publishers' Association—there are now 800 or possibly 1,000 of them. By reason of this organization and the work which has been accomplished through the officers of that organization and the international officers of the typographical union, the pressmen's union, and the stereotypers' union conciliation and arbitration have been accomplished almost completely. in the United States.

Mr. THOMPSON. Col. Blethen, have you any opinion as to the wisdom of permitting or restraining what is ordinarily called soap-box street gatherings?

Col. BLETHEN. I would restrain them to this extent, Mr. Thompson: I would not allow them to speak in the public streets where they become a nuisance by reason of gatherings, loud talk, and filling the streets. There is no objection to their speaking, so far as I am concerned, in the public parks or open places where the people can congregate and hear them if they desire; but to get under the windows of a business office like ours, for example, and proceed to "orate" for an hour and a half, telling the 280 employees in that building what a son-of-a-gun I am [laughter and applause]—what an outrage it is to permit The Times to be published, and all that sort of a thing—I won't have them doing that if I can prevent it, and I have succeeded in preventing it so far. But I haven't the slightest objection to their going out upon Times Square, for example—we are putting up a building there—and "orating" all day or all night.

Mr. THOMPSON. The Times Building is down here on Second Street?

Col. BLETHEN. The present building, where we now operate, is at the corner of Union and Second. We are constructing a new building on Times Square.

Mr. THOMPSON. You have some war bulletins in the window there?

Col. BLETHEN. Yes, sir.

Mr. THOMPSON. Do the people gather around there and read them?

Col. BLETHEN. Yes. Oh, well, I don't know as they read them, but I think the war [laughter]—I think the war has been fought over about 40 times since The Times put up those bulletins. Sometimes the English are winning, sometimes the Russians, sometimes the Germans. The boys have a good time, anyway. They stay there until way into the night, when they can't read a bulletin in the window to save their lives, still " cussing " and discussing the whole problem, with prejudice, of course, according to their nationality.

Mr. THOMPSON. Would your views as to street-corner gatherings include an objection to department stores or any stores that have window displays—any store that has a window display which causes men to gather around and impede and obstruct travel in the highway?

Col. BLETHEN. Not the slightest. The I. W. W. might fill our square full if they just talked among themselves. It is the shouting—it is the disturbance of the employees on the four stories of our building—that disturbs. For example, the 67 men on the top floor hear the I. W. W. outside " cussing " me; they all go and look out the window [laughter and applause]. That would be true of the newsroom, where there are 55 to 60 more people. It would be true of the business and circulating departments; and it is that—the disturbance of the operation of this work in the gathering of the people—that annoys.

Mr. THOMPSON. You wouldn't want it to be understood that the objection on your part is personal to those gatherings?

Col. BLETHEN. No.

Mr. THOMPSON. Because they speak of you?

Col. BLETHEN. Not at all. If they want to talk about me and wouldn't disturb the work of my employees it would be all right.

Mr. THOMPSON. Well, then, your objection to what is called open-air speech-making——

Col. BLETHEN. Street speaking.

Mr. THOMPSON. Is purely local?

Col. BLETHEN. Purely local.

Mr. THOMPSON. Col. Blethen, in regard to the question of industrial unrest and any cures there are for it, have you anything to add to what you have said, in the way of remedy or suggestion to this commission?

Col. BLETHEN. I have studied that problem all my life. I do not know but one thing, and that is, to give men and women enough to do and keep them employed. That is the whole of it.

Mr. THOMPSON. That is all, Mr. Chairman.

Commissioner GARRETSON. Colonel, if you gave that a logical, practical interpretation, would the man who works five hours a day be three times as dangerous as the man who works 15?

Col. BLETHEN. Well, I think you have got the maximum too high, and your minimum too low.

Commissioner GARRETSON. Make it 8 and 16, and put it twice, or make it 8 and 12, and make it one ond one-half times as bad.

Col. BLETHEN. The man who is engaged in any legitimate business a reasonable number of hours at fair wages is a contented man.

Commissioner GARRETSON. The man who is not employed at all, take the day laborer, is the man who works the long day more contented than the one who works the short day?

Col. BLETHEN. Certainly not. The man who works 8 hours a day, the laboring man, is more contented than the man who works 12.

Commissioner GARRETSON. Then there is a point where your theory works down and then starts up, is that it? Just a sliding scale?

Col. BLETHEN. No; not a sliding scale, except you apply it to skilled and common labor. I think skilled labor should have fewer hours than common labor. I do not believe the common laborer ought to be compelled to work beyond the ordinary eight hours.

Commissioner GARRETSON. Does brain fag more easily than brawn?

Col. BLETHEN. Well, I don't know. I have been operating my brain for 67 years, and it has never got tired yet. I also do a great deal of physical work about the building and take much exercise, and I haven't become tired yet.

Commissioner GARRETSON. A man once charged that I didn't have brain enough to get tired.

Col. BLETHEN. What was that?

Commissioner GARRETSON. I say a man once charged me that I didn't have brain enough to get tired.

Col. BLETHEN. He evidently hadn't seen you. ·

Commissioner GARRETSON. If the idle poor are a dangerous element on account of idleness, what about the idle rich?

Col. BLETHEN. Pretty nearly as bad, except you can get rid of the idle rich, and you can't get rid of the idle poor. The poor can't go away. The idle rich can go to Europe where a hundred thousand of them are now stranded on account of the war.

Commissioner GARRETSON. In the bonus system that is maintained in the typographical union, what is your minimum, 35,000?

..Col. BLETHEN. I think it is—my impression is 38,000.

Commissioner GARRETSON. If a man sets 42,000, is he paid for each of those 4,000 excess over 38,000?

Col. BLETHEN. No, sir; not over the minimum. He is paid for half.

Commissioner GARRETSON. In other words, is he paid for each succeeding thousand half as much as he is paid for the original 38?

Col. BLETHEN. That is it.

Commissioner GARRETSON. Who gets the bonus, the employer or the employee?

Col. BLETHEN. Both. In other words, the man or woman who just as easily, with the same nerve, energy, and activity, sets 42,000 while the other man or woman sets 38,000, and has worked just as hard to set the 38,000, is entitled to a consideration on account of his superior natural ability, and that is the main reason we divide it with them. We don't work the man extra to do it. He works naturally.

Commissioner GARRETSON. He works naturally, but is there any greater expenditure of energy?

Col. BLETHEN. Not a bit.

Commissioner GARRETSON. Although more easily expended than in the other case.

Col. BLETHEN. No; I don't think so. You take two men and let them walk 10 blocks in this city, and one will get there about 50 per cent quicker than the other, and both men be in the same breath and same condition when they get there.

Commissioner GARRETSON. But would that be any sign that either his voltage or his amperage had not been reduced thereby?

Col. BLETHEN. No; but it would be a sign that applying that same example to his work, that he is entitled to his superior natural ability, and should be paid for it. ·

Commissioner GARRETSON. Because he has consumed more of his reserve force? ·

Col. BLETHEN. No, not by any means.

Commissioner GARRETSON. No?

Col. BLETHEN. The man that walks the 10 blocks 50 per cent quicker than the other fellow, who hasn't lost any more energy than the other fellow who has tried to keep up——

Commissioner GARRETSON. How about an electric car running up and down here upon a storage battery. If one does it one-half quicker than the other, what will be the relative record of the ammeter on that machine?

Col. BLETHEN. Well, you will have to ask an electrician. I am talking about natural ability.

Commissioner GARRETSON. You don't believe there is any analogy between nervous force and natural power?

Col. BLETHEN. Well, artificial power—natural force is one thing and artificial power is another.

Commissioner GARRETSON. On your statement in regard to agitators, I am a little interested in that. I am inside the list in this. I live in one part of the country and I am often in another. Have you any knowledge that a man. of that type, a nonresident, is often, in fact, regularly summoned by large employers to exercise a restraining influence over their own employees.

Col. BLETHEN. I have no personal acquaintance with any condition of that kind.

Commissioner GARRETSON. You have never heard of that?

Col. BLETHEN. I never had the experience myself and I have never had any personal acquaintance with anything of that kind.

Commissioner GARRETSON. You would be perfectly willing to verify the fact that such conditions do exist if they were cited to you?

Col. BLETHEN. If they were authoritative, certainly.

Commissioner GARRETSON. I say, to determine whether or not they were authentic. I don't know whether you have heard some of the testimony that has been given here.

Col. BLETHEN. I have only been here since 2 o'clock this afternoon.

Commissioner GARRETSON. Only since 2. It has been asserted here and elsewhere that employers as a class, through associations and otherwise, oppose the class of legislation that betters the condition of the workers, that is embraced in the class covering sanitation, hours of service, in some localities the minimum wage, and kindred legislation presumably as legitimate as that. Do you believe it is a consistent position to take for employers, or do you not?

Col. BLETHEN. I believe in being consistent; yes. But I can say so far as the publishers are concerned that they don't have to wait for any legislation touching sanitation. They enter into a cooperative understanding with the executive committee, who work almost entirely in that identical room, or at least one of them always does, and whenever any complaint is presented we have an examination by a health officer, for example, and immediately comply with whatever conditions or orders may be made for the improvement of those conditions without going to the legislature or the city council, or anywhere else.

Commissioner GARRETSON. Well, isn't the newspaper publishing fraternity in this fix—it is so busy throwing stones that it don't care to live in a glass house?

Col. BLETHEN. Well, we are putting up a building over here that is going to be all glass.

Commissioner GARRETSON. Well, you will keep it inside so nobody will want to get stones in there, probably.

Col. BLETHEN. I don't know. We may have to keep stones in there to keep the other fellow out, but we haven't arrived at that point yet.

Commissioner GARRETSON. If you have already conformed to these sanitary requirements without the enactment of law, do you consider that men. who have refused to conform to them are justified in contending against law?

Col. BLETHEN. That would be a natural thing for them to do, but I think we ought to have laws to compel them to do it.

Commissioner GARRETSON. And do you belive it would be legitimate to clog the enforcement of the law or interfere therewith?

Col. BLETHEN. No, sir; I don't.

Commissioner GARRETSON. Then you would hold that the methods of employers who did those things—well, how much better would they be than the methods that you seem to think obtain in the industrial world?

Col. BLETHEN. Well, it is pretty hard to answer that question.

Commissioner GARRETSON. That is a question of degree, is it?

Col. BLETHEN. It is pretty hard to answer that question.

Commissioner GARRETSON. I will waive it. That is all, Mr. Chairman.

Acting Chairman COMMONS. The agreements you have in the printing industry, are they what are known as closed-shop agreements?

Col. BLETHEN. Yes, sir; all union organizations are closed shop.

Acting Chairman COMMONS. And you find that this is the proper kind of contract, and that is the reason you make it. What are your reasons for making a closed-shop contract?

Col. BLETHEN. Simply because it controls the men under one organization, whereas if in the open shop you have no control. You control it yourself, but it keeps you mighty busy. The quarrels that come up between the nonunion men and the union men must be settled. Often the results are very adverse, whereas the union guarantees to give you good workmen, to control them, and see that all the conditions of the contract are carried out. We have never had more than two or three complaints against the union in 18 years.

I had an experience of four and a half years in Kansas City in running a nonunion office, and I compared the two, and comparatively speaking I prefer that which we have here to what I had there.

Acting Chairman COMMONS. You make separate agreements with the different unions?

Col. BLETHEN. Yes, sir; entirely separate.

Acting Chairman COMMONS. And they come to you at the same time or different times?

Col. BLETHEN. No, sir; the contracts all expire at different times, just as a matter of convenience. We could not take them all up at the same time. The conditions of work and other conditions are wholly different. To illustrate: The pressmen insist on a certain number of men running a quad press, being based on the 8-page paper. The double press has 16 pages; the triple, 24; the quad, 32; the sextuple, 48; the septuple, 56; and the octuple, the largest they make, 64, and contains 8 units. In our agreements with the pressmen they demand that a certain number of men shall be employed, according to the size of the press you run. If it be an 8-page paper, it is two men, for example. If a quad, four men; and if a sex, six men; and if an octuple, eight men. But when you get to the stereotypers you have no conditions of that kind whatever. The foreman employs the number of men necessary to do the work and works the number of hours that is agreed and at the wages agreed.

Acting Chairman COMMONS. Is the number of men on the press agreed to jointly?

Col. BLETHEN. Oh, yes; that is in the contract. That is after the conciliator has settled all details.

Acting Chairman COMMONS. That is part of the agreement?

Col. BLETHEN. We write it in the agreement and sign it up, and they are sent to the international offices for approval before they are put into operation.

Acting Chairman COMMONS. Do you have the agreement that is customary in many towns, in typographical unions, of requiring that a "mat", that is set up, or matrix that is set up, shall not be loaned or exchanged among newspaper offices?

Col. BLETHEN. We don't permit that. It is very irregular, however, among the publishers. Perhaps the majority use matrices, as we call them, but in our union where there is a certain kind of matrix, where the page, for example, is largely literature, largely printed matter, that has to be reset and destroyed. That is one thing we always fight over, but we always yield. The boys always win out on that. It does not amount to anything very serious, but I think the principle is wrong, provided from their standpoint the original type is set up by union men. They ought to accept that, but that is a thing we don't quarrel about in the end.

Acting Chairman COMMONS. Is their reason for insisting on that simply to make more work?

Col. BLETHEN. To make more work. The union will not permit a matrix set by the Post Intelligencer, for example, to be used by the Times. The type will have to be set up again. We don't complain about that. We think perhaps that would be all right; when it comes from abroad and we enlarge a paper that would not be enlarged, and it is done by union labor, we have a feeling we ought not to pay for the setting twice. But here the boys win out every time; but they don't in many other places.

Acting Chairman COMMONS. Have you ever figured out how much that cost you?

Col. BLETHEN. Yes; our foreman has gone through that a good many times. It will run, according to the month of the year, from $40 to $60 a week.

Acting Chairman COMMONS. In excess of——

Col. BLETHEN. That is just set up and thrown away.

Acting Chairman COMMONS. What per cent would that be of the total pay roll?

Col. BLETHEN. I would have to figure that out. Our total pay roll for printers runs about $2,300 a week.

Acting Chairman COMMONS. This would be an increase of forty to sixty dollars on twenty-three hundred?

Col. BLETHEN. Yes; along there; perhaps an average of $50.

Acting Chairman COMMONS. About 2 per cent increase?

Col. BLETHEN. Yes, sir.

Acting Chairman COMMONS. Two per cent difference in the wage cost?

Col. BLETHEN. Not to exceed 2 per cent.

Acting Chairman COMMONS. Not to exceed 2 per cent. Do these unions join in sympathetic strikes in the printing business?

Col. BLETHEN. We never have had one since I have been here.

Acting Chairman COMMONS. You have had no experience in that?

Col. BLETHEN. No, sir.

Acting Chairman COMMONS. Have you had any experience with the boycott?

Col. BLETHEN. Only among a lot of old women and crazy people, but never with the unions.

Acting Chairman COMMONS. Never any labor-union or trade-union boycott?

Col. BLETHEN. No, sir.

Commissioner O'CONNELL. What do women boycott for?

Col. BLETHEN. Some of our crazy women get on a moral reform, and if they can't use you they boycott you.

Commissioner O'CONNELL. Boycott your paper because you don't advocate the theory that they stand for?

Col. BLETHEN. Because they can't control it, showing they are insane, of course. [Applause.]

Commissioner LENNON. We are going to have order, or I will insist that the audience be cleared from the room. I am interested in this subject; I have been all my life. I have attended all kinds of meetings and I never disturbed one. It disturbs me, and if any more applause or laughing takes place I shall insist on secret sessions.

Acting Chairman COMMONS. Have you, Colonel, any opinion regarding the kind of legislation which should be recommended respecting the boycott?

Col. BLETHEN. I have very decided opinions about the strike and boycott and lockout. I think they ought to be written into the criminal law, every one of them.

Acting Chairman COMMONS. All of them prohibited?

Col. BLETHEN. Yes, sir. The day has arrived when employer and employee ought to be compelled to get together through a legislative enforcement—to conciliate and arbitrate, if it comes to that.

Acting Chairman COMMONS. Which means what is known as compulsory arbitration?

Col. BLETHEN. It amounts to that. It is a great deal better than strikes or lockouts, I think. I had the pleasure of saying that to our Secretary of Labor when he was here and attended the convention last year. I was one at the Press Club to help entertain him a little while. We had 40 or 50 visitors, and I made that point very plain. I have printed it a thousand times, perhaps. I have printed it and spoken it a thousand times, and he got up on his "hind legs" and just roasted the life out of me, to the satisfaction of the boys present. I said to the boys, "I am almighty glad I said what I did, because you would not have gotten this beautiful speech from a member of the Cabinet if I hadn't said it," and then I had the laugh on him.

Commissioner GARRETSON. There are a number of people who hold the same opinion with regard to war.

Col. BLETHEN. I don't know. I never went to war.

Commissioner GARRETSON. So far one has been about as successful as the other.

Col. BLETHEN. No, sir; you are off. Strikes have been reduced to that extent now that I don't believe one would be thought of in Seattle; I mean in our profession.

Commissioner GARRETSON. Have they been reduced by legislation ever?

Col. BLETHEN. No, sir; that is why I want them to try it.

Commissioner GARRETSON. If they have been reduced the per cent you claim without legislation, why not follow the same course?

Col. BLETHEN. Because the reduction has occurred among the intelligent classes of unions, while the other is the lower classes. You don't require as much law to take care of the respectable citizen who has property and a family as to take care of the hoodlum on the street.

Commissioner GARRETSON. Well, I don't know.

Col. BLETHEN. That is my opinion—you asked for it.

Commissioner GARRETSON. That is all.

Acting Chairman COMMONS. Any questions, Mr. Thompson?

Mr. THOMPSON. Just one question: You think that a national law, or law passed by the State limiting the hours of a man's work to 8 hours a day, would help on the question of unemployment?

Col. BLETHEN. Possibly it might. I would have a national law and not a State law.

Mr. THOMPSON. Do you believe the law should deal with such questions or should it leave that to the unions?

Col. BLETHEN. Well, the workers have brought it out in fine shape, but we are going into a good deal of law. Take our industrial insurance, that would never have been brought around except through big efforts, and I think that is a case where perhaps the employers did more than the employees to have it legislated and enacted. With us it does not amount to much because we try so faithfully to take care of our boys and girls that when we have an accident now and have to go to the industrial insurance they only get about half of what they got from us, and I take their check and keep them on the pay roll. They like it.

Mr. THOMPSON. That is all.

Acting Chairman COMMONS. That is all; much obliged. Call your next.

Mr. THOMPSON. Mr. Thompson.

TESTIMONY OF MR. JAMES P. THOMPSON.

Mr. THOMPSON. Will you please give us your name?

Mr. J. P. THOMPSON. James P. Thompson.

Mr. THOMPSON. And your business address?

Mr. J. P. THOMPSON. 208 Second Avenue.

Mr. THOMPSON. And your occupation?

Mr. J. P. THOMPSON. Organizer of the Industrial Workers of the World.

Mr. THOMPSON. That is the organization with headquarters in Chicago?

Mr. J. P. THOMPSON. Chicago.

Mr. THOMPSON. Of which Mr. Vincent St. John is general secretary?

Mr. J. P. THOMPSON. Yes, sir.

Mr. THOMPSON. How long have you been an organizer of the Industrial Workers of the World?

Mr. J. P. THOMPSON. I have been an organizer for the Industrial Workers of the World; that is, drawing a salary from them as an organizer, about since 1906. I was one of those who worked for it before it was born; I mean I helped organize it.

Mr. THOMPSON. You say you helped work for it before it was born; you mean as a similar organization?

Mr. J. P. THOMPSON. I mean I was one of those who worked to have it formed and took steps in starting it.

Mr. THOMPSON. How long have you been engaged in the work of propagation or agitation, or whatever you want to call it, along that line, Mr. Thompson?

Mr. J. P. THOMPSON. Well, let me see—I think I got to be a sort of agitator when I was a fireman on the Great Lakes, when I was about 15 or 16 years old.

Mr. THOMPSON. As you look over the labor field and look into the condition of the workers and look at the organization then in existence, what was in your mind that gave you the idea that a new organization should be formed? What was the reason that led you to that conclusion?

Mr. J. P. THOMPSON. Why, I saw the one big union of employers forming; I saw that in case of a strike in a shop that one craft would strike and the other crafts in that shop would remain at work and help the company to break the strike. From that I got the idea that every one in the shop should be organized together, from the man who scrubs the floor to the man who starts the engine. Then I saw that when we even succeeded in tying up a shop in that manner that they would sometimes be able to get scabs, what we call strike breakers. I saw then an organization must be formed in such a way as to cut off the raw material from one end of such a mill where strike breakers were working and refuse to handle the scab products brought out at the other end. Then we saw as we studied that one big union of bosses, employers' associations, and so on, that they met even those tactics by transferring orders to other shops—to other members of the employers' association; and so we got the idea that every one in a craft should stand together in the shop, and every shop in the industry should stand together, and then we saw, like in the case of the strike of the coal miners, we saw the railroad men haul scabs in on one train and haul scab coal away on another, and from that the idea formed that not only should every craft in an industry stand together, but the workers of one industry should back up the workers of another industry, and that we should all combine into one big union having for our motto an injury to one is an injury to all.

Mr. THOMPSON. Looking at the standpoint of the older organizations, wherein would you claim that there is a difference between yours and theirs, so far as the question of organization is concerned?

Mr. J. P. THOMPSON. The former, as I have just pointed out, is chiefly organized by crafts. They teach every one in a craft to stand together. Now, we say for the same reason that every one in a craft should stand together, for that same reason every craft in an industry should stand together, and every industry should stand together, the workers of one industry with another. And fundamentally the difference is vital; the craft union is founded upon the attempt to simply better the condition of the wageworker under present conditions. The I. W. W. is founded upon a recognition of the class struggle and that a revolution is rapidly approaching, and that the thing most vital for any workingman to do is to organize, not only for the everyday struggle with the capitalist but also to carry on production when capitalism shall have been overthrown. Now, your civil government has broken down in three States, I think I heard you say. It will break down in every State. There will be a general strike and revolt that will be too big for anyone to handle, only the organized workers. Now, by the way, I am the author of the I. W. W. preamble, and I would like to have you read, if you want to figure on our principles, the last paragraph, which says: "The army of production must be organized, not only for the everyday struggle with the capitalists, but also to carry on production when capitalism shall have been overthrown." I look to the time when the organization known as the Industrial Workers of the World, or a revolutionary organization formed on the same lines, will be the class who will save civilization from going back to barbarism. I see a time when our speakers can influence when no one else can.

Mr. THOMPSON. Well, Mr. Thompson, getting more to specifics on that proposition, how would you figure, for instance, that the old organizations, the craft unions, would fall down in the matter of production in case the capitalistic system went to pieces?

Mr. J. P. THOMPSON. The craft union to-day is a result, you understand. Of course, you understand that when any organization is first formed it is supposed to conform to the conditions of the time. And when those conditions change, if the organization does not change to meet the changed conditions, then we have what we call an out-of-date organization. Now, there are ideas that go along with out-of-date organizations, and the American Federation of Labor is out of date in form. It is out of date in spirit. It is a representative of the past, as far as organized labor is concerned. It is dying of dry rot. The I. W. W. has got the red-blooded part of the working class. And we are not organizing on craft lines but on class lines. And the I. W. W. is aiming not only to better our condition now but to prepare for the revolution.

Mr. THOMPSON. Just coming down to specifics, Mr. Thompson, what can you state to this commission, what facts or data of any kind can you give to them from which they can draw the same conclusions that you are drawing?

Mr. J. P. THOMPSON. Well, I would say to the commission, I understand that the law that created you says that you should investigate the underlying cause of social unrest. I think it foolish to ask the man who is satisfied with the system the cause of unrest. He would not tell you if he knew; many of them would not, anyway. You have had quite a lot of hypocrites; you have had men who were afraid of losing their jobs if they told the truth. But I would advise that if you really want to know the underlying cause of the social unrest that you should ask the revolutionist. Now, I claim to be a revolutionist——

Mr. THOMPSON. Well——

Mr. J. P. THOMPSON. And I claim to be able to answer that question—the cause of social unrest.

Mr. THOMPSON. Well, I will get to that, Mr. Thompson; but before getting to that the commission is commanded by Congress to examine into organizations of labor.

Mr. J. P. THOMPSON. Yes, sir.

Mr. THOMPSON. We are examining now through you, as we have done through others, into the Industrial Workers of the World.

You have made a statement that the older unions were organized under a condition which has passed away; that they carry with them a philosophy of action which does not fit present needs.

Mr. J. P. THOMPSON. Practically what I said.

Mr. THOMPSON. And that they are on the wane, but you are on the come.

Mr. J. P. THOMPSON. Yes.

Mr. THOMPSON. Now, what I ask is, it is clear—of course, it must be to you—that these are conclusions. They may be correct. It is not for me to question them here as counsel.

Mr. J. P. THOMPSON. I understand that.

Mr. THOMPSON. I simply want to get from you the facts, so that the commission itself, when it reads your testimony, may say that, "Well, from what he states, which appear to be the correct facts, his conclusions are correct or they are incorrect." Now, what I would like you to give the commission is some data with reference to the old organization which will prove the statements you make, or tend to prove them.

Mr. J. P. THOMPSON. Why, you want documentary proof?

Mr. THOMPSON. No; we don't limit you. You can take your own way of stating it. You can state what you hear or what you have seen yourself, or what you believe; but I simply ask you for facts rather than for conclusions.

Mr. J. P. THOMPSON. Well, since one of the printing industry was represented here a moment ago in the form of one of the employers, I will call attention to the fact that in San Francisco last winter the pressmen went on strike in the job-printing shops, and the union—so-called union—printers remained at work; the union bookbinders, and so on, remained at work; and by remaining at work they helped the company to fill their orders and helped the company to break the strike of the pressmen. And I also will take the testimony, while it is warm, from Col. Blethen that these people sign contracts running out at different times. That is sufficient proof of what I said about them breaking one another's strikes; it is a fact, not a dream or anything like that.

Mr. THOMPSON. That objection would go to the question of sympathetic strikes; that is to say, that the old organization does not indulge sufficiently in sympathetic—what are commonly called sympathetic strikes.

Mr. J. P. THOMPSON. No; I don't like the word "sympathetic" strikes.

Mr. THOMPSON. But I am talking about the word as the general public uses it.

Mr. J. P. THOMPSON. Well, the general public don't use the word in that sense; that is sympathetic. Now, here is the idea: If there is a strike in a restaurant, and a harness maker up on some street somewhere would go on strike in sympathy, you know—you might say it was sympathy, but we can get that in the dictionary; sympathy, that is the way we look at it. We say that the ice-wagon driver and the bread-wagon driver and the driver who delivers meat or ice or supplies of any kind to that scab restaurant are strike breakers, and it is a question of whether they want to be union men or scabs, not a question of whether they want to strike in sympathy, but a question of whether they want to help break the strike or win the strike, and if they do those things we call that union strike breakers.

Mr. THOMPSON. Well, now, in what other respects is the old organization unable to meet the new conditions?

Mr. J. P. THOMPSON. The old organization is not based on a recognition of the class struggle, and an organization that is not revolutionary—a labor organization that is not revolutionary can not rally to its support any red-blooded members of the working class. I will add further that I believe that the red-blooded part of the American Federation of Labor, when it comes to a show-down, will back up the I. W. W. better than they will the A. F. of L.

Mr. THOMPSON. What do you mean by the class struggle, as you have stated it?

Mr. J. P. THOMPSON. Well, whenever you get ready to ask me that question of the cause of social unrest, I think I could probably lay the foundation of the whole thing right there in a nutshell.

Mr. THOMPSON. Well, I said you might follow your own method, Mr. Thompson.

Mr. J. P. THOMPSON. Well, I understood you said later you would ask about that.

Mr. THOMPSON. Yes.

Mr. J. P. THOMPSON. The reason I say this, I would like to answer the whole thing at once in one way.

Mr. THOMPSON. You may go on and answer it; take up the question of indus. trial unrest, its cause——   •

Mr. J. P. THOMPSON. The class struggle all comes under that.

Mr. THOMPSON. And your cure. I want to get from you your opinion.

Mr. J. P. THOMPSON. Certainly; that is the idea; and it is worth whatever it weighs; that is the idea.

Mr. THOMPSON. Go right ahead.

Mr. J. P. THOMPSON. Now, the real cause of all social changes and revolutions are to be sought, not in men's brains, not in their more or less confused ideas of right and wrong or of truth and justice, not in the philosophy, but in the economics of each particular epoch. That is one of our sayings. We say that in order to understand the social problem it must be looked at as a process of natural history, governed not only by laws independent of the human will, consciousness, and intelligence, but, on the contrary, determining that very will, consciousness, and intelligence. Now, when we speak of the world, of the working class, we mean the workers of the world. We are as broad as the world. We claim that in studying economics we must consider it from the standpoint of the world. You never hear us talk about immigration being a bad thing; we believe it is a good thing, and so on. And so you might question me on that, if you wish, later. But here is the point, that I will just take, for example, this country, since I am an American for many generations, and naturally quite familiar with the history of this country. In the day of what we call petty industry in this country the tool of production was of a kind that could be used by the individual. The man who used the tool owned the tool. In the early days of our forefathers all they had to do was to kill some Indians and get the land, and then they could settle down on that land and make a living. They didn't have any railroads. The only railroad they had then was in the form of an ox team, and they took their own commodities to market. They didn't have shoe factories. The worker who made shoes made them by hand and carried his tools under his arm. When the farmer in those days wanted any clothing, he didn't go to the factory for it. The women folks used to be the textile mill in the home. They used to make the homespuns, knit the socks and the mittens, and make the clothing, the homespuns.

Now, if a man was up against it, as we put it to-day, why they would say: "Go out and take up a piece of land and settle down and make your own living." Well, now, there has a change come. There is an unrest here; look for the cause in a change in the economics, in the mode of production. The tool of production is not now a thing that can be used by an individual. The labor process has taken the cooperative form. You can not if you own a textile mill, you can not weave woolen cloth without the sheepshearer, or cotton cloth without the cotton picker. You can't weave cloth, then, even if you have wool or cotton without the ironworker to make the looms, and you can't have the building without the labor of the building worker. The tool of production to-day is not an individual tool, not a thing that one man can use. The cooperative plan or form has entered into the labor process. Now, here is what is the matter in the world: We have social production but we have private ownership of the means of production, and this divides the human race into two classes, the class who own the means of production and don't operate them, the class who operate them and don't own them. You never saw a railroad operated by the class that owns it, nor you never saw a railroad built by the owners of it. You will find one class own the means of production and another class operate them. The interests of these two classes are diametrically opposed. The interest of the employing class demands that we work hard for small pay. Our interest demands that we put the other class to work. To-day we not only have to feed ourselves, but we have to feed an idle, worthless class who have no more function in society than a bedbug. Now, in order that you may fully understand this, you have asked me in this letter to me, or in subpœnaing me, to mention the lumber industry. And I will explain the psychology of the lumber worker. I think, although I am a longshoreman, I am one of those undesirables who travel everywhere, not simply to stir up people, but to tell people what we believe can be done to make this a better world. Now, the logger, he walks out in the woods and he looks around at a wilderness of trees. He works hard in there. And what does he get? He gets wages that are below the dead line, I say dead line in wages means below the line necessary to keep him alive. They are being murdered on the installment plan. Now, they breathe bad air in the camps. That ruins their lungs. They

eat bad food. That ruins their stomachs. The foul conditions shorten their lives and make their short lives miserable.
When they ask for more, like the I. W. W. did—we asked for dry rooms, so we could have a place to dry our clothes. If we don't dry our clothes—I have got a bad cold, it bothers my throat—if we don't have—that is all right, I don't want any water, thank you. You know it rains very much. Now, speaking of this particular part of the country, which I always like to apologize for doing, as this is a world question—I am only using this as an example—in this part of the country, for example, it rains a great deal, and they work in the rain. If they didn't work in the rain they wouldn't work at all. When they come in from the camps they are wet, their feet are wet. They go into a dark barn, not as good as where the horses are, and the only place to dry their clothes is around the hot stove, made hot to dry the clothes. Those in the top bunk suffer from the heat; those far away, from the cold. Well, if they don't dry their clothes they put them on wet the next morning. Then they would have rheumatism. And when we asked for dry rooms in which to dry our clothes, a man like Weyerhaueser, who owns all this land here as far as your eye can reach—or a mind's eye can reach, almost. Oh, no, he can't afford to put in dry rooms. No. Why not? Well, business is business; And so the logger, he finds that he is nothing but a living machine, not even treated as well as a horse. When the horse is out of work he is glad of it. When the wageworker is out of work he is up against it; they turn the hose on him in Sacramento. All right. Now, to show you just how we look at this: We say that in the early days a man came into this western country—this is only an example of the western country—when land was cheap, and when politicians could be bought for two for a nickel—that is the way we put it in our own language, understand—they got possession of this land—like Morgan and those fellows of the so-called better class, you know, that bribe legislators, as in the New Haven Railroad proposition you know about. They got out here and by bribing and grafting and gunning and one thing and another they got possession of this land, this forest out here. And then they say to us: "You came too late. We own this land." "Where did you get it?" We know where they got it, they stole it. But they say: "We have a legal right," and all that stuff, a law they made themselves. Now, just to show you how we look at it, because that is the vital point, you know—you are talking now with a revolutionist. I believe I have the psychology of a revolutionist. And we look at that as just as ridiculous as it would be if we would go out into the forest, and we would see a lot of squirrels out there working, working hard gathering nuts.
Then in the winter we would go out there and we would see the nuts piled high and these same working squirrels in misery. We would say to them, "What is the matter?" "Why," they would say, "don't you know what is the matter? Why, those fat squirrels over there, they never worked, and they own all this forest here, and when we produce the nuts we turn all the nuts over to those fat squirrels. And then they have a lot of little clerks to sort out the wormy nuts, and on pay day they give us our snuff and our overalls and our hobnailed boots." The way the worker puts it the squirrel would get the wormy nuts. We claim that no man has any more right to own this earth than he has to own the air we breathe, that John D. Rockefeller has no more right to say, "I own that coal mine; I own the coal down in the earth as far down as hell"—you don't have to go very far in a coal mine to get to hell. You are in hell if you are in a coal mine, especially if it is Rockefeller's coal mine, because he murders more in proportion to the number than any other in the country.
We say they have no right to own this. Right is a relative term. They will own it just as long as they have the power to own it. And just the minute that we get the power we will do away with this thing of some human beings owning the things that other human beings must use in order to live. And now I will become a real American again. Abraham Lincoln said "the government of the people, by the people, for the people." Well, that is tame compared to the I. W. W., and our idea will prevail when those who are opposing it are forgotten. I believe that as much as that I am sitting here. We are the modern abolitionists fighting against wage slavery. Here is one of our sayings: "The industries must be owned by the people, operated by the people for the people, instead of being owned by the few, operated by the many for the few." And that in regard to social unrest, it is not the degree of exploitation so much as it is the fact of exploitation. If we remained in this room for many days here we would learn more about the room as we remained.

We would know that it was warmer in one corner and more cool in another. And so with any society—the longer we live in this capitalist society the more we learn about it. We have learned that the capitalist papers, as we call them, will lie, that they will lie—well, they will lie about the I. W. W.—see? And so, as the result of the lying and suggestions and misrepresentations on the part of the press, the workers are losing confidence. You know we used to say in this country that a thing was true, and prove it was by saying we saw it in black and white. Well, a man would try to prove a thing by saying he saw it in black and white in some of the papers in this country now would be a candidate for the insane asylum. And so with the courts. Now, we are losing confidence in the law. We have but very little confidence. I am speaking frankly of the working class all over the country and to those of the world; this applies to a more or less extent. The country most developed industrially will furnish to the more backward countries the image of their own future. Now, we are gradually losing respect for the law, because it is universally expressed in this way—there is one law for the rich and another law for the poor. Everyone, generally speaking, will admit that if you steal a loaf of bread you go to jail; if you steal a railroad, you go to Congress. Now, that is the way they express that idea. Now, the other class attempts to hold our class down by their high-handed methods, like the hop pickers' case. When you go to California you will hear about the hop pickers' case. Two men are in jail, sentenced to life imprisonment. They didn't kill anybody. Everybody admits they didn't kill anybody. They were telling the workers in that hop ranch what they thought ought to be done. There was no drinking water there. Every way the conditions were unspeakable. I won't take up your time with that. I expect you will get all of that in California. But these two men are in jail.

Now, it doesn't matter what you think or what I think, in a way; what I mean is this, that going from one end of this country to the other, any working man who knows anything about it believes those men are innocent, and every day they are in jail—every day they are in jail, just like rust eats iron, so confidence in the capitalist courts is dying in the hearts of the workers. Now, they can be highhanded, like in Ludlow. They can fire the tents there, and they did. And you have heard that old saying, the shot is heard around the world. When they fired the tents of Ludlow they lighted fires in the hearts of the workers they never can put out. We are not patriotic like we used to be in the sense that we will fight for the other class to get markets. We do not take any stock in this foreign-market business at all. The world's market for steel, the workers of the world produce the steel—and no matter whether the railroad is built in China or in England, it matters not to us as a class. We do the work, and all we get is what? As the wealth piles up on the one hand, misery piles up on the other, and the working class see this. They know that labor produces all the wealth. Now this puts it so any child can understand it. You know we form habits of thought. Now we workers know that if our class wasn't here on earth at all the other class would have to go to work. We know that well enough. If our class weren't here on earth and the other class wanted shoes, for instance, they would have to go ahead and make them; and if they didn't know how to make them they would have to learn how or go barefoot. Now, the difference between what we produce and what we get is the amount of which we are robbed. All capital is unpaid labor. Now, there are two armies in the world, the army of production and the army of destruction. The army of destruction is the military army; that is one of them. Now, the army of production feeds everybody. They produce it all; and what we want is for the army of destruction to disband and join the army of production, and then we who do the work—won't have to work so long. We will have the world's work to do, but we will have more help to do it, and then we won't have the capitalist class—that class who say: "We own the earth and the machinery of production." We want to put them to work and make them do their share. In other words, we want to do away with the wage system and establish the cooperative system in its place.

The labor process has taken the cooperative form, and the things that are used collectively must be owned collectively. And this class struggle will never end until the workers of the world organize as a class and take possession of the earth and the machinery of production and abolish the wage system.

Mr. THOMPSON. Now, Mr. Thompson, assuming that we were all in accord with your ideas, your philosophy of industry, taking society as it is to-day, formed of people with various views, with the majority not perhaps agreeing with your theories of production, what would you say to this commission that it could do, either by recommendation to Congress, to the various State governments, or to the workers—the people of the country—that would probably be accepted ånd would lead toward this newer society that you are speaking of?

Mr. J. P. THOMPSON. Well, since you put it so broadly, that you recommend to all the different ones what to do: Now, I would, to the Government, for instance, to put it that way, I look upon them as a committee of the capitalist class. But the government, political government, not the real ruling Government of the country; I don't mean that—I mean the political government. I mean that I would recommend to this commission that they say to the representatives: To all whom it may concern: That the cause of social unrest is to be found in the mode of production; that a revolution is inevitable; that we may delay that revolution a little; we may hurry it a little, but we can't stop it; and that everyone who is big enough to rise above local interests and see the inevitable should do all they can to lessen the birth pangs of the new society being born from the womb of the old. And to the capitalist class, I would say to them: "You are doomed. The best thing you can do is to look for a soft place to fall."

Mr. THOMPSON. That, Mr. Thompson, then, would be your practical suggestions to this commission?

Mr. J. P. THOMPSON. I would absolutely think that that would save—if the ruling class of·to-day were big enough to do that—I believe it would save much misery i■ the world.

Mr. THOMPSON. I don't mean that, Mr. Thompson.

Mr. J. P. THOMPSON. I don't know——

Mr. THOMPSON. I mean your idea of what can be accomplished.

Mr. J. P. THOMPSON. I lost one point. You asked me what I would recommend to the working people?

Mr. THOMPSON. Yes.

Mr. J. P. THOMPSON. You said all classes; it includes them. Generally, everybody leaves them out except us.

Mr. THOMPSON. It would include them, of course?

Mr. J. P. THOMPSON. All right; we would recommend to the working class that they organize as a class and depend for their labor laws, not upon the politician, but that they should organize and pass the labor laws in the union and enforce them on the job. Unlike the editor of the Seattle Record of the A. F. of L.—he says they, the A. F. of L., issue a paper. You asked them what the purpose of that union paper was, and he said—if I remember rightly, he said it was to teach the workers their rights under the law and to get them to work for the passage of better laws. Now, our idea of a labor paper is that it should teach the foolishness of going to these politicians to get these laws and that they should pass the law in the union and enforce it on the job. If you wanted to do away with child labor, organize and refuse to work with children.

Mr. THOMPSON. Any other practical suggestions, Mr. Thompson?

Mr. J. P. THOMPSON. I believe that the way to do away with the unemployed is this: Now, I mentioned a moment ago that there are two armies, the army of production and the army of destruction. I included the capitalists in that because when they eat it is destruction of property. When the workingman eats, it is, in a sense, productive consumption, like a locomotive eating coal. So, I say this: That—I don't mean that literally; that it is real production consumption when I say the workman eats. I don't mean that in the literal sense, but I mean it in one sense; but in regard to this army of production and the army of destruction, I want to use an illustration that I think will make clear the cause and cure for unemployment. Now, we will take the army of destruction in an enemy's country. Suppose that there is only a certain amount of food to eat, and it is all in the form of bread; suppose that when we come to see that that army of soldiers, the army of destruction, we see that they have nothing to eat but bread. But that one part of the army got eight or ten loaves every day and the other part of the army had no bread at all. We would think they were crazy. We would say: " Put that army on rations; give each five loaves, or whatever is necessary so it will go around." Now, we walk away from them, and we see the army of production, they do not live on bread—they do and they don't—they must have labor in order to live. Well, we see that some of that army get 8, 10, or 12 hours labor, and the others have none at all. Well, what would we do?

The same as with the bread. Now, we divide the bread among the soldiers, and so we should divide—now, notice—we should divide the work of the world among the workers of the world. Then, when we do that there will be no unemployment. If there is not work enough for all of us all the time, there must be work enough for all of us part of the time. This idea of some working 10 hours and others doing no work at all, that is out of date, ridiculous. This idea of little children being worked to death while strong men are out of work, no one but a savage will support that in our opinion. So we believe that we ought to shorten the workday, divide the work of the world among the workers of the world, and then there would be no unemployed. Then the other class in their struggle with us would find it hard to get scabs; they would have a hard time to get men to eat food that we had refused to eat, as there wouldn't be any unemployed to draw from. Well, when we got the unemployed out of the hands of the other class, the main club would be out of their hands, and then we would make the boss—we would force the boss—to pay us more wages for five or six hours than he does now for eight or ten. That is not all. When we have divided the work among the workers of the world, then we have gotten the bosses around on the slippery end of the stick. Then we will put them to work, and this system will be over, and we will·establish the cooperative system. That is revolutionary, but that is what we are after.

Mr. THOMPSON. That is all, Mr. Chairman.

Commissioner O'CONNELL. I want to ask you a few questions. In one of your direct answers to Mr. Thompson—how long has the I. W. W, that branch that you represent, been in existence as an organization?

Mr. J. P. THOMPSON. The I. W. W. was formed in 1905.

Commissioner O'CONNELL. There is another organization of the I. W. W., is there not?

Mr. J. P. THOMPSON. There is a small group of men with headquarters in Detroit, Mich. They are quite different from the I. W. W. They stole our name. They have a political idea instead of the union idea.

Commissioner O'CONNELL. They were originally connected with the I. W. W., were they not?

Mr. J. P. THOMPSON. No. One or two—I will tell you, the editor of their paper, the Socialist Labor Party paper in New York, came to the convention of the I. W. W. in 1908. We contested his credentials on very good grounds and he was refused a seat—just a moment and I will finish shortly; you asked me to be brief. After the 1908 convention when the politicians of the Socialist Labor Party found themselves outside of the I. W. W. they held a conference in Paterson, N. J., and they decided they would form an organization of their own with a political clause, and when they came to decide on a name there was much debate. They said, "Let us "—one of them, I believe, said this: "Socialist Labor Party"; "Socialist Labor Union." S. L. P.—S. L. U. But another motion prevailed, and they stole the name of the I. W. W. and called themselves the Industrial Workers of the World, although they don't amount to much.

Commissioner O'CONNELL. Are you a Socialist Mr. Thompson?

Mr. J. P. THOMPSON. I am not a parliamentary Socialist. I take no stock·in the ballot, the capitalistic ballot. I believe in the ballot in the union.

Commissioner O'CONNELL. Do you believe in the cooperative commonwealth?

Mr. J. P. THOMPSON. I believe in the cooperative commonwealth. I am really a revolutionary Socialist.

Commissioner O'CONNELL. The Socialist organization stands for that·clear through?

Mr. J. P. THOMPSON. The Socialist Party, they do stand for the cooperative commonwealth, at the same time they devote their energies chiefly to the patching up of capitalism.

Commissioner O'CONNELL. Do you believe in sabotage?

Mr. J. P. THOMPSON. Yes; I believe in some forms of sabotage.

Commissioner O'CONNELL. What forms?

Mr. J. P. THOMPSON. Whatever form will win. Now, that is a question of judgment. In order that I may be perfectly clear on that, I believe in eating, but I don't believe in eating poison. I believe in talking, but I don't believe in saying anything that I do not believe, for instance. So in the same·way·I believe in sabotage.

Commissioner O'CONNELL. Taking poison, for instance?

Mr. J. P. THOMPSON. No; of course I believe in talking, but that does not mean that I believe in saying everything; and because I believe in sabotage does not mean I believe in all forms of sabotage.

Θ Commissioner O'CONNELL. You mean destruction of property to obtain your ends?

Mr. J. P. THOMPSON. Well, to the point of destruction of property, you know that is such a question that you want me to answer it right off the bat, so I will go a little further: I believe that if there is a man behind you who is going to kill you now, I would kill him to save you. So I not only believe in destruction of property, but I believe in the destruction of human life if it will save human life. You understand? And so on. Now, it is all a relative term. So when you ask me do I believe in destruction of property, I don't as a general principle believe in the destruction of property, but as between the destruction of property and the destruction of human life, let the property go. I believe like the old abolitionists used to say: "One drop of blood shed by a master's lash outweighs a nation's gold."

Commissioner O'CONNELL. If your organization was involved in a strike in which great numbers, a small or large number of your members were engaged in battling for what you consider increased opportunities of life——

Mr. J. P. THOMPSON. Yes.

Commissioner O'CONNELL. And it came to a question of where in order to win that it would be necessary to destroy property, in an event of that kind, what would you do?

Mr. J. P. THOMPSON. Well, I wouldn't like to see a strike won, and have it go out through the country that it was won because we destroyed property. I will tell you why. I do not want to be misunderstood on that.

The I. W. W. teaches that the greatest weapon in the hands of the working class is economic power. Now, what I mean by that is we are the living parts of industry. All we have to do is to fold our arms and industry is paralyzed. If there was a street car strike and the motorman was a scab, I would much prefer to see them stop that car by use of their economic power than with a brickbat or club. In other words, I would much prefer as a lesson to the other workers who are fighting, instead of destroying the street car in times of a street car strike that they should stop that car by shutting off the juice at the power house. That would be a lesson.

Commissioner O'CONNELL. What is the total membership of the I. W. W.?

Mr. J. P. THOMPSON. The total membership of the I. W. W., I don't know, but I say this——

Commissioner O'CONNELL. I am taking Mr. St. John's word for it.

Mr. J. P. THOMPSON. I will say St. John doesn't know either.

Commissioner O'CONNELL. He is secretary.

Mr. J. P. THOMPSON. I know he is; but just like the A. F. L., they don't know how many members they have got. The A. F. L., for instance——

Commissioner O'CONNELL. I am not talking about the A. F. of L.

Mr. J. P. THOMPSON. I am only using that as an illustration; they don't know how many members they have got, because they have one man that belongs to four or five unions, and they call him five when he is only one. I know a man who is a member of a carpenter's union, and he is a machinist; yet he is one and the same man. What I mean when I say members of the I. W. W. is the actual paid up members. I don't know. St. John knows more about that, because he has got the books.

Commissioner O'CONNELL. He said about 13,000.

Mr. J. P. THOMPSON. Yes; I expect that is quite a big number, 13,000.

Commissioner O'CONNELL. The reason I was asking——

Mr. J. P. THOMPSON. What I want to say is, the membership of the I. W. W. is not to be reckoned by the absolute paid-up members.

Commissioner O'CONNELL. The reason I ask is because the statement made by you that the red blood——

Mr. J. P. THOMPSON. That is what I said.

Commissioner O'CONNELL (continuing). Is made up in this membership in the I. W. W.

Mr. J. P. THOMPSON. No; you misunderstand me. I said that an organization that stood for the present system and did not have a revolutionary goal, could not rally to its support any red-blooded members of the working class; that the red-blooded members of the working class believe this system is only a passing stage, in the economic development of mankind. No one who has any intelligence, I mean, and red blood at the same time—and anybody—of course, if you believe in slavery, because I have no use for anyone who believes in slavery, I despise a man, or I despise nothing more than I do a contented slave.

Commissioner O'CONNELL. Am I to understand you compare the 3,000,000 organized workers in the trade-union——

Mr. J. P. THOMPSON. Yes.

Commissioner O'CONNELL. About 3,000,000, including the labor organizations which are members—these 3,000,000 are entirely ignorant of the situation?

Mr. J. P. THOMPSON. No. I say that—if you will remember, I said—my memory is better than yours—I said I believe the red-blooded members of the American Federation of Labor would support the I. W. W. better than they would their own program.

Commissioner O'CONNELL. Then, as I take it, as compared to the members having the red blood it is indicated by their membership in your organization?

Mr. J. P. THOMPSON. What I have in mind when I say that they are red blooded is that—I was in the Lawrence strike. I was general organizer in the Lawrence strike, and I had occasion to see that the miners, the coal miners, you know, and so on—the money poured in, and they supported us in this country, enthusiastically, and their letters show, " You have got the only dope, go to it."

Commissioner O'CONNELL. That is all.

Acting Chairman COMMONS. Have you anything more? [After a pause.] That will be sufficient. You are excused.

Mr. Thompson, call your next witness.

Mr. THOMPSON. Mr. Pauly.

TESTIMONY OF MR. HENRY PAULY.

Mr. THOMPSON. Will you give us your name?

Mr. PAULY. Henry Pauly.

Mr. THOMPSON. And your address?

Mr. PAULY. 813 Eighth Avenue.

Mr. THOMPSON. And your present position?

Mr. PAULY. Clearing lands at Du Pont, Wash.

Mr. THOMPSON. Is there such an organization as the Itinerant Workers' Union?

Mr. PAULY. There is an international order of itinerant workers; this is Local 22.

Mr. THOMPSON. Have you any connection with that?

Mr. PAULY. I am chairman of the union.

Mr. THOMPSON. In the work you say you are doing, clearing land, is that in connection woth your union, or this matter?

Mr. PAULY. In connection with it, part of it.

Mr. THOMPSON. What kind of organization is the Itinerant Workers' Union?

Mr. PAULY. The Itinerant Workers' Union is composed of men following construction work, following the harvest fields, bridge builders, men doing all seasonal work, men following timbering, lumbering, most all seasonal work.

Mr. THOMPSON. Is it affiliated with any other labor organization?

Mr. PAULY. Fraternally, yes, sir; with the A. F. of L.

Mr. THOMPSON. Where are most of the members located in your union, the international organization as a whole?

Mr. PAULY. The international organization is at Cincinnati, Ohio; Jeff Davis is president of the international order, and Harry Shriber is secretary-treasurer.

Mr. THOMPSON. Where is the principal membership, in the East or Middle States, or the West here?

Mr. PAULY. In the East, the order is new in the West.

Mr. THOMPSON. What is the purpose of your union?

Mr. PAULY. The purpose of this union is to keep the itinerant workers from going and taking strikers' places, to get the men to organize, to better their conditions, to help their conditions during the winter months when there is 'no work.

Mr. THOMPSON. Are you engaged in work of that kind here in Seattle?

Mr. PAULY. Yes; I have been engaged in that work since the 26th of December.

Mr. THOMPSON. Now, in your own way, tell us what you are doing in that work, when you started, where you have worked, and how you work.

Mr. PAULY. Last November I finished up with the Government work. I was out of employment, and I shipped from Spokane to Lewiston, Mont. I paid two dollars and a half for the shipment to Lewiston. They were paying two dollars and a quarter a day for workers. I left Spokane, and I met a train that was going to Harlow with a bunch of men shipped from Seattle here. I forget the name of the little station on the Milwaukee where we met them. Anyway, when the Spokane shipment met the train from Seattle, we were all crowded so that there was not standing room for the men in there. They crowded us from Spokane into the car there, and we were in there from 9.30 that morning until away along the next afternoon without water or any place to lay down; some of them could not even stand up, the way they crowded us in there, and when we got to Lewiston there was about four or five hundred men laying around the prairie there, and they didn't know where the next bite to eat was to come from, and there was no work—the majority of the camps were closing down.

It was Sunday afternoon when I got to Lewiston. Monday morning there was a sign on the board—the Milwaukee road had a man catcher there, what they call a man catcher. When they needed any men up on the line, they would post it on the blackboard and load up the men and ship them up the line. They wanted 150 men at Amhurst, material yard men, Monday morning, and I landed there Sunday. I went down to the depot Monday morning, and I was one of the 150 men they picked for Amhurst. I went up there, and when I got there there was 150 men at Amhurst on a grub strike. The men demanded another cook or they wouldn't go out until they got another cook. They were paying five dollars and a half board, and they demanded something to eat. So they wouldn't furnish them another cook, and the men that didn't go out that morning to go to work, they fired them. So they ran 150 men of us that was idle and had shipped to Lewiston to Amhurst. The men were compelled to go to work, a lot of them hadn't eaten for a number of days. We were forced to go to work. I went out with the men after dinner, and I guess I looked pretty good to the foreman, and he put me to bucking ties, what they call bucking ties. The rest of the men were put in different gangs, steel gangs, and so on. I was taken down to a pile of logs, about 35 feet away from the dock. That was a cross-pile or bunch of ties left there, and I was told I was to get a cent and a half a tie. I started to buck some green railroad ties there. They were fir ties, green, that had been piled there, and I had about 45 feet to carry these ties up on a branch on a flat car and pile them. I noticed other fellows that had been there, and some of the ties were piled so that they were pulling these ties down from a pile that was piled along parallel with the railroad track. They used a pick or roll. I spoke to the timekeeper, and he said, "Your turn will come next, you will get a good pile, we divide that up." I finished a couple of cars bucking these piles of ties, carrying them. The next car I got I want a car where I could pull them off of the pile with a pick or roll. Well, I didn't get that car. They gave me another car to carry up. So I left the car there, and I told him it was pay day, if he could not give me a car the same as the others, I was taking equal chances. He told me he had no other work for me, if I didn't want to buck ties I would have to go and get my time.

I went to work and got my time and they charged me a dollar hospital fee for the hospital, and then I had to go back to Lewiston to get my money. The men had quite a time getting their money. After the men quit work there they had to go down to Lewiston to get their pay. I didn't have a whole lot coming, and I had to go back up the line to get what they call a traveling stake. I went to the gang there and went to work for the McGrath Service Co. They had a bunch of Americans and a bunch of Bulgarians. The white men were boarded with the Western Commissary Co. and the Bulgarians had a camp of their own and were buying the raw material from the Western Commissary Co., and the Western Commissary Co. was supplying them a cook free gratis. The food that they furnished there was in such condition that the men possibly could not stay. There was dysentery the same as we had in the Army in 1898 at Jacksonville, Fla. I worked there as long as I could. I went back to Lewiston and went to work. The frost had come and they could not work the servicing gang; they could not lay the rails. When I got to Lewiston there was about four or five hundred men laying around the prairie and more men coming down from the camps and still shipping in from St. Louis, Spokane, St. Paul, Minneapolis, and St. Louis, and things were getting pretty desperate there. We could get nothing to eat and the men could not get their time. They had trouble getting their money from the railroad company, and I tried to organize the men, and we tried to get the city attorney at Lewiston to collect our time, so that we could get away from Lewiston.

We could not organize the men, so I went to the city officials at Lewiston to force or have the railroad company give us a pass back to where they shipped us from. They called a special council meeting there on Monday, and I explained conditions as they were, and they took it up with the railroad company, and the railroad company started to ship us wherever we were shipped from—west; any way—we wanted to go to Spokane or Seattle, but they wouldn't ship the eastern shipment farther east than Mowbridge, N. Dak., so that the majority of men coming down from the work shipped to Seattle. That brought quite an influx of men into Seattle here. At that time Jeff Davis, the international president of the International Itinerant Workers or Hoboes of America, was trying to organize here in the city all unemployed to get some means of feeding and housing the men there were in the city, and there were men coming in from Montana, and they would make quite an army of unemployed. I got in the order or joined the union, the hobos' union, and with the assistance of the citizens here we managed to get a hotel here, the old Provident Hospital on Sixth and Madison.

The Itinerant Workers' Union elected me as their chairman. The central labor council here in the city that was paying rent for the building placed me in the building there as superintendent of the building. During the time I was in the hotel we registered some 2,200 men. We took care of the men; the men got two meals a day here; those that worked got three meals—the men that would saw wood or carry wood got three meals a day and the others got two, and then we would place out men as the work came in. We placed a lot of men out among the ranchers here; they got $10 a month, and some $15 a month, from these small ranches and board. In February the Itinerant Workers' Union took up land clearing. I took one contract to clear an acre out at Green Lake. We cleared an acre of ground in a day. Fifty of the men went out and cleared up the acre in a day. With that 50 men we had $50 left on the first contract that we paid part payment on a stump puller, and we bought a stump puller and bought other tools, and we started to contract clearing land out of the city, clearing city property.

We done some wrecking here. The hoboes' union went to anybody to make it a self-supporting institution from the 17th of February up to the present time; but our men, the majority are out in the harvest fields now. They have the trouble that most of the jobs they can't stay at long enough, as there are generally three crews to the job that the men are working on, seasonal work, which is only work that only lasts a certain period. The men have got to move, and every time a man makes a move it costs him money, and when the winter months come the man is here stranded in the city and no work here. All the work here is seasonal work; there is nothing permanent, and we have made all the efforts we can to make permanent work for the seasonal workers here, and the only solution that we can see at this time is to put the—give, the itinerant workers a chance to work on idle lands. We have made all the efforts that we can, but we wasn't very successful in getting work.

Mr. THOMPSON. Is there any place now where you are working on idle land?

Mr. PAULY. We have a few men that are staying here keeping up the organization with me. There are 17 of us that are clearing 80 acres at Du Pont, Wash., which we are finishing, and we will finish next Tuesday.

Mr. THOMPSON. What is it your intention to do with that land?

Mr. PAULY. We are clearing that for the Roy & Roy Milling Co.

Mr. THOMPSON. You are not clearing it for the purpose of putting it into agriculture for yourselves, but for another company?

Mr. PAULY. Clearing it for the Roy & Roy Milling Co. at so much an acre.

Mr. THOMPSON. What other kind of work have you got here for the workers, in order to take care of those who are out of work because of seasonal employment?

Mr. PAULY. Well we have placed men—we have placed about 2000 men in different lines of work as the work came up. We have averaged 500 men in one night at the Hotel de Gink last winter here. Some days we have fed over 900 meals a day to men that were out of employment.

Mr. THOMPSON. Where do you get the money to pay for these meals? From the work of the men, or how?

Mr. PAULY. The men have a fund that they call the kitty. After a man has earned a little money he would put some money in the general fund. Then we divide the men into what we call flying squads; we put one man on the bread detail, and another man on the milk, and so on, and one man would go to work cleaning out a dairy for the milk that comes back, and we would have a man, sorting spuds at the commission houses on Western Avenue. That is where we got our food supply here last winter for the unemployed.

Mr. THOMPSON. Have you carried on any agricultural effort other than what you have named?

Mr. PAULY. We have placed men, but as far as the union itself is concerned we have not. We have placed a considerable number of men throughout the country in agricultural pursuits.

Mr. THOMPSON. What is the scale of wages paid in this territory for farm work and ranch work and clearing land, and so on, the different kinds of work you people do?

Mr. PAULY. The wages are very poor. Lots of the small ranches pay from $15 to $20 a month and board. Some of the big dairy ranches pay from $35 to $45 a month.

Mr. THOMPSON. With board and room?

Mr. PAULY. With board and room. For the common labor the wages run from a dollar and a half to two and a quarter.

Mr. THOMPSON. Does he feed himself, then?

Mr. PAULY. He feeds himself and pays his board and hospital fee.

Mr. THOMPSON. That is, working generally for a company?

Mr. PAULY. That is working for a company.

Mr. THOMPSON. That is all, Mr. Chairman.

Acting Chairman COMMONS. Do you do any work for lumber companies?

Mr. PAULY. Yes, sir; I have worked for lumber companies the biggest part of my life.

Acting Chairman COMMONS. In what part of the State?

Mr. PAULY. I have worked in Wisconsin, Michigan, Arizona, and have worked around this State for a number of years.

Acting Chairman COMMONS. Has your Itinerant Workers Union placed men with lumber companies?

Mr. PAULY. The men place themselves generally with the lumber companies; we had no call from any lumber company for men since we organized.

Acting Chairman COMMONS. How do you find these 2,000 jobs—place the men?

Mr. PAULY. They come in over the telephone. We created an employment office while we were at the hotel, and advertised in the want column. People came there asking for help at the employment office.

Acting Chairman COMMONS. How many of your men went into the lumber business, logging and so on?

Mr. PAULY. The men as they left didn't leave word where they were going. They were going and coming.

Acting Chairman COMMONS. You don't know how many went into that. What report have you from those that came back comparing their positions in the lumber and logging camps and in the lumber mills with other work that you have. How does it compare?

Mr. PAULY. Well, all the conditions are different. Some camps work different hours. The sanitary conditions of the camps are different. Some camps change crews frequently, and others have a pretty steady crew. Some camps are different. Some make a practice of having three gangs.

Acting Chairman COMMONS. What do you mean by three gangs?

Mr. PAULY. One gang working, one gang coming, and another gang going.

Commissioner LENNON. How do you expect to effect any permanent relief for these people unless you work out some plan whereby you can locate them on land—or have you any idea in view as that?

Mr. PAULY. Why that was about all we could see at the time of depression, was idle land, clearing the land. There was no other work here, there was nothing permanent in the line of work.

Commissioner LENNON. Have you ever tried to cooperate with the governor of the State, or the legislature?

Mr. PAULY. That is what we were agitating to do, to get some State land to work in the winter time when we have nothing to do—to clear it.

Commissioner. LENNON. Yes; but I mean, have some of these idle workers cured of that habit of being itinerant workers and make permanent citizens of them, and give them land and have them and their families work it.

Mr. PAULY. The majority of the itinerant workers if they were given a chance to take a permanent job would gladly take it, but they usually keep us going.

Acting Chairman COMMONS. Have you taken this up at all with any organization of employers engaged in seasonal work, like lumber people or others?

Mr. PAULY. We have been to many of them looking for contracts to cut cordwood and cut cedar posts. We have gotten work wherever we could get it. We have solicited work and had men going around to different office buildings and soliciting work and advertised for work throughout the country here.

Acting Chairman COMMONS. When you take contracts, what terms do you make, by the day or job—or how?

Mr. PAULY. We take it by the acre or cord, or any way we can't get work.

Acting Chairman COMMONS. Then, how do you divide up among the members?

Mr. PAULY. It is according to how the men work. They may divide equally among those that are working together.

Acting Chairman COMMONS. On the clearing of the land?

Mr. PAULY. They share the expenses and have an equal division. They cooperatively work the land that we are working on now.

Acting Chairman COMMONS. Where does the title lie—who owns the stump puller?

Mr. PAULY. It belongs to the union, the men that have paid for it. Different men put in different time at clearing, and have paid for it.

Acting Chairman COMMONS. You keep account of the work and divide it according to the number of hours?

Mr. PAULY. The men that work on the job equally divide it among themselves.

Acting Chairman COMMONS. How much are you making by that method?

Mr. PAULY. That varies. Sometimes we make wages and other times we don't make wages.

Acting Chairman COMMONS. What do you call wages?

Mr. PAULY. Two dollars and a half a day is what we call wages here for labor.

Acting Chairman COMMONS. Do you get that in the lumber camps and sawmills?

Mr. PAULY. Yes, sir; on some work; and on others you don't.

Acting Chairman COMMONS. On railroad construction work?

Mr. PAULY. On railroad construction work they pay from $2 to $2.25 in these railroad camps. Most construction work is $1.75.

Acting Chairman COMMONS. Does that include board?

Mr. PAULY. No, sir; you pay your own board out of that and the hospital fee.

Acting Chairman COMMONS. Is it quite general, paying hospital fees throughout this country?

Mr. PAULY. You pay hospital fees most every job you go to, and if you change camps with the same company you pay twice a month.

Commissioner LENNON. Does everybody in the State of Washington pay hospital fees?

Mr. PAULY. Wherever you go all these employees pay hospital fees.

Commissioner LENNON. We have heard a great deal about it here.

Mr. PAULY. That is legal here, to charge you a hospital fee two or three times a month if you happen to change camps.

Acting Chairman COMMONS. How many, or did you ever guess, how many itinerant workers there are?

Mr. PAULY. Most of them are itinerant workers; there are no permanent factories here. It is most all timber work and seasonal work, harvest and so forth. The majority of the men in this State follow that line of work, outside of the few lucky ones that have something permanent.

Acting Chairman COMMONS. Do many of them have families?

Mr. PAULY. Some have. We had quite a few men shipped out here by the railroad companies that had families in the East last winter.

Acting Chairman COMMONS. In the East?

Mr. PAULY. Yes; that is where you have your majority of itinerant workers. Those here in the West are shipped out from the East by the railroad companies.

Acting Chairman COMMONS. That is the way they got here?

Mr. PAULY. That is the way they got here; shipped here by the railroad companies for railroad work—different construction work.

Acting Chairman COMMONS. Where do they get the jobs in the East—the employment offices?

Mr. PAULY. That is where the employment offices generally send these itinerant workers from, is the East; the majority of them. The majority of them that were stranded last winter were fellows from the East, sent out here by the different employment firms, St. Louis, St. Paul, Minneapolis, and Chicago. I expect after the construction work closed down they were up against it and they came to the coast because the railroad companies would not transport them back east farther than North Dakota.

ι. Acting Chairman COMMONS. Did you maintain these headquarters this summer?

Mr. PAULY. We have a home at 813 Eighth Avenue, which is closed. We have one man taking care of our quarters. We have our bedding and tools stored in the place.

Acting Chairman COMMONS. Any more questions?

Mr. THOMPSON. One more question. In this work you do around here in organizing the men is there any attitude that they take with reference to joining in sympathy strikes or otherwise?

Mr. PAULY. The men that join the hoboes union must take an oath that he will never act as a strike breaker.

Mr. THOMPSON. Do the men that join pretty generally observe that pledge?

Mr. PAULY. They have observed it here last winter when they tried to get strike breakers for Tacoma. The first place they came to was the Hotel de Gink to get a crew of men, and they were hooted out of the building. They were not very successful in getting a crew to open up the smelter.

Mr. THOMPSON. That is all.

Acting Chairman COMMONS. Anything further you wish to add as to what recommendations we ought to make, for instance, to the Federal Government or the State government as to what they should do?

Mr. PAULY. Yes, sir.

Acting Chairman COMMONS. What would you suggest?

Mr. PAULY. I wish to state that the majority of the men on the road are not there of their own free will. They are placed there through false-representations by the employment office that ships them out to the different work. The men get out there and don't get enough money to get back to where they came from. They get shabby in their clothes and get down and out.

· It is not the man's fault. There ought to be restrictions in regard to shipping men from one State to the other. They load the men down there into cars; the men are not given water for days at a time; they will not even get fresh water. They have to water hogs and cattle when they transport them over the country. They don't do that for the men when they ship them to the country.

Acting Chairman COMMONS. What kind of cars are they generally shipped in?

Mr. PAULY. Generally old passenger coaches. They put them on the back of the train and haul them through the country. ·

Acting Chairman COMMONS. Who pays the fare?

Mr. PAULY. The railroad company that uses them.

Acting Chairman COMMONS. They are shipped out for railroad purposes?

Mr. PAULY. The railroad company generally furnishes free transportation for the railroad contractors that are doing railroad work.

Acting Chaiman COMMONS. You say most of them start out in the East doing railroad construction work. Don't they come out and work in the harvest?

Mr. PAULY. They will find work if they can, and I have talked to the men, and most of them generally start their western trip in that way, ship out to work in the West.

Acting Chairman COMMONS. Don't they come to work on ranches or farms or in the harvest?

Mr. PAULY. Some of them come for the harvest, but the harvest is generally only as far as North Dakota. Generally the men shipped into Montana and Idaho and those places have been shipped there to do railroad construction work.

Acting Chairman COMMONS. Are they all English speaking?

Mr. PAULY. Some are and some are not.

Acting Chairman COMMONS. In your union, I mean.

Mr. PAULY. Ours are all English-speaking men. The foreigners are all organized, generally.

Acting Chairman COMMONS. What?

Mr. PAULY. All the foreigners that are on these construction works are generally organized and are contracted for by the season.

Acting Chairman COMMONS. They are not organized into any union?

Mr. PAULY. Not in our union. They are all English-speaking people in our union.

Acting Chairman Commons. The others are under contráct?

Mr. Pauly. The majority of the Bulgarians are generally organized among themselves. :

Commissioner O'Connell. Who owns the Hotel de Gink?

Mr. Pauly. Why, the hotel was owned by the Sisters. That is, the old hos: pital that was used temporarily to place the unemployed men here last winter during the time of depression.

Commissioner O'Connell. Have you rented it?

Mr. Pauly. We have rented the place, and the central labor council organization is paying our rent.

Commissioner O'Connell. Are they paying the rent now? ⌐

Mr. Pauly. It is out of existence. That existed up until the 27th of April. After things opened up and we got most of the men, the unemployed, to.work and we closed up the hotel.

Commissioner O'Connell. What rent was paid for it?

Mr. Pauly. Fifty-five dollars a month, which organized labor paid; organized labor paid the rent for the unemployed here in the city last winter.

Commissioner O'Connell. Do you have members employed around the city taking up various jobs of work? For instance, you say you wrecked some buildings?

Mr. Pauly. Yes; we wrecked buildings here last winter for fuel.

Commissioner O'Connell. Do your members demand the standard rate of wage and hours of work throughout the city?

Mr. Pauly. We haven't the chance to demand anything. We were lucky to get work last winter. There was no chance to demand anything. We went to work wherever we could get work. We had 25 men that worked at Bellevue, clearing land, that did not have no cover nowhere, no shelter of any kind there for over a month; was working out in the rain, and never had a chance to change clothes or anything, in a continuous rain.

Commissioner O'Connell. Do you think that the employers or those securing work for them took advantage of the fact that your members were in that condition who needed work, regardless of wages?

Mr. Pauly. They certainly took advantage of us here last winter, because we was down and out, no money, no work, and they took advantage in giving us work, and as far as wages were concerned, lots of times after we earned the money, in getting the money. We have right at this time a number of cases in court for work that was done by the men that we could not.get no money for after the work was done, because the condition we was in, lots of people took advantage of us, for this reason, that we had no way of protecting ourselves.

Commissioner Lennon. Did you take work that union men would otherwise have done?

Mr. Pauly. We tried to get work that did not interfere with any organized labor.

Commissioner Lennon. Your story seems to indicate that you built up what we might call—perhaps, in other countries they have names—cooperative employment agencies?

Mr. Pauly. We had a cooperative employment agency while we had the hotel; yes, sir.

Commissioner Lennon. I mean your whole scheme is a cooperative employment agency?

Mr. Pauly. It is one help the other cooperatively. That is the way we existed last winter—by cooperation.

Commissioner Lennon. I would suggest to you that you study the question of getting on the land permanently.

Mr. Pauly. We have studied it, and we know what we can clear.it for.in different ways. We have——

Commissioner O'Connell. That is, to clear the land and let the other fellow work on?

Commissioner Lennon. I mean clear it for yourself.

Mr. Pauly. I think we would have a pretty hard job in getting anything around this country. We are very lucky to get the work without getting land of our own.

Acting Chairman Commons. That is sufficient.

The commission will now stand adjourned. We will meet to-morrow morning at 9.30 instead of 10 o'clock. The witnesses will please be here at 9.30.

(Whereupon, at 4.45 o'clock p. m. of this Wednesday, August 12, 1914, the commission adjourned to meet to-morrow, August 13, 1914, at 9.30 o'clock a. m.)

SEATTLE, WASH., *Thursday, August 13, 1914—9.30 a. m.*
··Present: Commissioners Commons·(acting chairman), Garretson, O'Connell, and Lennon; also W. O .Thompson, Esq., counsel.
Acting Chairman COMMONS. The commission will be in order. Mr. Thompson, call your next witness.
·Mr. THOMPSON. Mr. Page.

TESTIMONY OF MR. PAUL E. PAGE.

Mr. THOMPSON. Will you give us your name?
Mr. PAGE. Paul E., Page.
Mr. THOMPSON. Your business address?
Mr. PAGE. Buckley, Wash.
Mr. THOMPSON. And your business?
Mr. PAGE. I am president of the Page Lumber Co.; in the lumber business.
Mr. THOMPSON. What branch of the lumber business are you in?
Mr. PAGE. In the manufacture of lumber and logging.
Mr. THOMPSON. That is the manufacture of the. raw material; are you making shingles?
Mr. PAGE. We don't make shingles, and we are not what is called a finishing mill. We try to get our lumber on the cars as near the log as possible—do as little ·finishing as possible.
Mr. THOMPSON. How long have you been engaged in the lumber business?
Mr. PAGE. Nineteen years.
Mr. THOMPSON. In this country?
Mr. PAGE. In this State.
Mr. THOMPSON. About how large an establishment have you got?
·Mr. PAGE. Our mill capacity is 90,000 feet a day.
Mr. THOMPSON. About how many men during the height of the season would you employ?
Mr. PAGE. Our force to-day is 138 men.
Mr. THOMPSON. Is this the season now for the work?
Mr. PAGE. That is our regular working force. We keep that force the year around.
· Mr. THOMPSON. What wages, as far as you know, are generally paid for the different classes of work in this State in the lumber industry?
Mr. PAGE. In our sawmill—this is sawmill work, does not include the yard—the minimum wage is $2.50, and the maximum is $6, and the average wage is $3.62.
Mr. THOMPSON. What would be the wage in the yard, as you have it?
Mr. PAGE. The wage in the yard has a minimum of $2.25, and a maximum of $2.25, and the average is $2.25.
Mr. THOMPSON. What would we understand by the yards; do you do any logging?
Mr. PAGE. The yard is where the lumber is handled after it is manufactured. In the logging camp the minimum is $2.50, and the maximum is $5.75,·and the average is $3.48; that is, for the loggers. The railroad has a minimum of $2.25, and a maximum of $2.25, and an average of $2.25 a day.
Mr. THOMPSON. Then, according to that statement, Mr. Page, the lowest wage you pay to any of the labor is $2.25 a day?
Mr. PAGE. This statement is made up on the last six months' operations. At that time the lowest wage we paid was $2.25. That was on the logging, and on the railroad, and in the mill yard. We are now paying $2 on the logging railroad; that is, railroad work—the laying of the ties and work of that kind, $2 now.
· Mr. THOMPSON. What, so far as your ꞏobservꞏ-ation has gone, Mr. Page, is the condition of labor in the lumbering industry in this State?
Mr. PAGE. Well, I′ have not noticed any more uneasiness in the labor in the woods and in the mills of late than there has been at all times since I have been in the business for 19 years, with the exception of the hard times in 1895, 1896, and 1897. At that time there was not so much unrest. And at that time we paid in the yard 90 cents a day, and we did not pay it in money.
Mr. THOMPSON. Have you had any conflicts with labor, what is ordinarily called strikes?
· Mr. PAGE. None whatever.
Mr. THOMPSON. Has the Page Lumber Co. had any?

Mr PAGE. Never.

Mr. THOMPSON. Do you know whether or not the men working for you are organized at all?

Mr. PAGE. I have never seen any organization. It has never come to me. I do not believe they are.

Mr. THOMPSON. With reference to the wages you pay, you mean to say that is the ordinary wage that the workers get in the industry in this State?

Mr. PAGE. Yes, sir.

Mr. THOMPSON. What would you say—were you here yesterday?

Mr. PAGE. Yes.

Mr. THOMPSON. Did you hear the testimony regarding the mill down at Centralia, I think it was?

Mr. PAGE. Yes, sir.

Mr. THOMPSON. If those facts were true they would be exceptional, would they not?

Mr. PAGE. Yes. But I do not think they are true. I have not seen that time statement, but I think the face of that time statement will show the wage was paid to a boy, not to a man. You can not hire men in the State of Washington to work anywhere for $1.35 a day. The employment offices here are posted. Anybody can read them on the outside, on the bulletin boards, $2.25, $2 a day. I do not know why a man would work for $1.35 when he can step into the employment office and get a job for $2.25 a day, and hire if he is a skilled lumberman, if he can get that.

Mr. THOMPSON. Have the lumbermen got an association?

Mr. PAGE. Yes, sir.

Mr. THOMPSON. Are you an officer of that association?

Mr. PAGE. Yes, sir.

Mr. THOMPSON. Do they keep pretty well in touch with the general conditions of the trade throughout the State through their association?

Mr. PAGE. Yes; that is the object of the association.

Mr. THOMPSON. Do they through this association know in a general way of the wages paid all over the State for the labor?

Mr. PAGE. No, sir; the association as an association has nothing to do with that.

Mr. THOMPSON. I mean through that would the men keep pretty well informed with the labor market?

Mr. PAGE. Yes; you would in talking with members of the association as you meet them at the association meetings.

Mr. THOMPSON. What kind of men usually work in the logging camps and in and around the mills?

Mr. PAGE. In the logging camps; that is, the logging camps proper that get out the logs, that is skilled labor, and it is composed largely of young men and mostly of unmarried men. They are a high-strung class of fellows and reckless; they are in a reckless business, a risky business, and they throw their money away; they are men of that kind.

Mr. THOMPSON. Well, take the men that work in these lumber camps generally, how long a year do they have—how much work do they have in the camp?

Mr. PAGE. Why most of the logging camps run the season through. Here in the Sound country as the winter approaches and as the timber is cut off on the lower levels we are going back into the mountains, and conditions are changing here somewhat now. A good many of the camps are up in the mountains where the snow compels them to stop logging in the wintertime, but as a general thing the camps run the year around.

Mr. THOMPSON. Could you make an estimate as to about how much work— take the lumber camps as a whole—the men would have during the year? It has been stated here it is seasonal work.

Mr. PAGE. No, sir; it is not seasonal work in this State. Last year we did not lose a day; we worked during the whole winter.

Mr. THOMPSON. That seems to be a pretty fair consensus of opinion of all the witnesses so far who have come on, that the men come down to Seattle during the off months in the lumber season. Where would these men come from?

Mr. PAGE. No, sir; that is not true. The men come to Seattle in this way: Take our best men in the logging business, take the best men in the logging camps of all the lumber industry and they work, say, 30 to 60 days, and

INDUSTRIAL RELATIONS AND REMEDIES, SEATTLE, WASH. 4251

then they stop work and draw their pay and come to Seattle, and a good deal of that money—a great deal of that money is simply thrown away, and then that man gets work in another camp and works there 30 to 60 days and repeats the operation and comes back to us. They are rovers, they. are restless; they want to travel from camp to camp; those are the best men; those are the skilled men. We have them and they keeping. coming back to us. Men that have worked for us for 17 or 18 years, they keep repeating that—going from one camp to another, and coming back to us.

Mr. THOMPSON. Well, would that be true of the average man?

· Mr. PAGE. That is true of practically all of them; 90 per cent of them.

Mr. THOMPSON. Ninety per cent. What are the conditions.surrounding the lumber camps? Are they such that a man could establish himself and have a family, or is it necessarily the work of single men?

Mr. PAGE. Well, some of the lumber camps are so situated that family men could work in them, but most of them are off at a distance. While they all have families, I don't suppose there is a camp in the State that has not more or less families in the camp, but as a general thing the loggers are single men.

Mr. THOMPSON. Well, in your opinion, looking at family life as you live it probably, and as you know it, and as you believe it ought to be, do you think the men in the lumbering industry in this State could carry on that kind of life and be engaged in that work under present conditions?

Mr. PAGE. Why, it would be pretty hard for the logger to do that. I don't think he has any inclination of that kind. I think it is the high-strung, reckless man that gets into the logging business. They are all the same.

Mr. THOMPSON. You mean that includes the common laborer, as you call them.

Mr. PAGE. Well, you must segregate the logging end of the business from the mill end. It is entirely different; the mill end is entirely different from the logging. Different class of men entirely.

Mr. THOMPSON. Well, take the mill end, are the conditions around mills and mill towns such that married men could work in the mills?

Mr. PAGE. Oh, yes; married men could work in the mills.

Mr. THOMPSON. And in the yards?

Mr. PAGE. Not so much in the yards, though. The yardman is a rover—he is worse than the logger.

Mr. THOMPSON. Is there anything in the conditions around the yard or in the work there that would prevent a man from carrying on family life?

Mr. PAGE. Yes. Well, now, let me explain this rover. We have a vast number of men in this State, swarms of them, as I suppose there is in other States, who work at a low wage. They are men who work at the construction of logging railroads, and they are the men who do the work in the yards of the lumber mills. Now, these men as a class won't work more than three or four days a week. That is all they want to work; and they are the rovers. They keep coming and going all the time. Now, let me illustrate that to you just a minute while we are on that.

Mr. THOMPSON. Yes.

Mr. PAGE. To show you how that, what that roving propensity is. Now, in working a crew of 138 men in January we worked 186 men, in February 222, in March 224, in April 229, May 234, and June 170. Now, those figures mean a little bit more than that. Now, the month of January 186 men were on the payroll to work 138. That means that their means had been exhaused for the Christmas holidays, and they went to work for a stake. In February they commenced to rove; March, April, and May, and June, before the 4th of July, in order to accumulate a stake for the 4th of July, we worked 170 as against 234 in May. That is the——

Acting Chairman COMMONS. Mr. Page, does that mean so many men hired, new men hired?

Mr. PAGE. Yes; our crew is 138 men. Now, in order to work that 138 men constantly we have on the pay roll 234 men; you understand?

Acting Chairman COMMONS. Constituting how many men that you have to hire during the year to keep up the force?

Mr. PAGE. That is what I am telling you. We use 138 men. But in order to work 138 men every day there are 234 men coming and going to take these places. One man works to-day and he drops out; another man takes his place to-morrow.

Mr. THOMPSON. Let me illustrate. If you have 138 men working steadily you hire 238 men during the month or have 238 on the pay roll, which means you hire 100 extra men during that month to keep up your regular force? ⸙ ⸗ 𝟫𝟪𝟥

Mr. PAGE. That is it exactly.   ⸗ ⸳ ⸲

Mr. THOMPSON. Now, referring to the matter which has been stated here, Mr. Page, that the most of the work on the Pacific coast in this neighborhood is seasonal work—fruit picking is seasonal work. It has been stated also that the lumber business is more or less seasonal; that the railroad work is sea-. sonal. What do you know about that? What would you say; would you say that is true?

Mr. PAGE. There is a good deal of seasonal work in these industries; a good deal of it.

Mr. THOMPSON. Well, have you ever studied the effect on the man's economic nature where he engages in seasonal work, as to whether it breaks down that steadiness, that continuous working habit that we see formed among other. workers?

Mr. PAGE. Why, to my mind that seasonal work don't enter into the propo-: sition of the idle man at all.

Mr. THOMPSON. No; but would it enter into the proposition of the habits of the man—some men who work steadily in factories down east, and work there year in and year out, they have the habit of going to work every day—of staying at work. Now, men who necessarily go into the fruit industry, they work for three or four weeks, and their work is done, and they have a business that calls them to search elsewhere for work. Now, what would that have in the way of an effect of giving a man the roving habit? Do you think it would?

Mr. PAGE. Yes.

Mr. THOMPSON. Whether they wanted it or not?

Mr. PAGE. Yes. I think the more a man roves the more he wants to rove. And I do not think it is the seasonal work that causes the roving.

Mr. THOMPSON. You do not think that is the cause?

Mr. PAGE. No; I do not.

Mr. THOMPSON. Have you given any study, Mr. Page, to that matter?   ⸱ ⸳ ⸱

Mr. PAGE. I am not a theorist, I don't believe. But I don't, believe that is the cause.

Acting Chairman COMMONS. What would be the cause?

Mr. PAGE. I think the cause is that you have got 15 jobs and 16 men. That is the only way I can look at it at all times.

Commissioner LENNON. What has the liquor habit to do with this condition of roving?

Mr. PAGE. I do not think the liquor habit is the cause of it. I think it is the result. I think men get to roving and then get into these liquor habits. That is my idea of it.

Mr. THOMPSON. Mr. Page, we have had some evidence here of a compensa- tion act in this State?

Mr. PAGE. Yes, sir.

Mr. THOMPSON. As a lumberman here, have you had anything to do with that?

Mr. PAGE. Yes, sir. The lumbermen were the people who started the first move toward passing a compensation act in this State.

Mr. THOMPSON. Now tell what you did when it was started, and in your own way tell us the story of the compensation act as you see it.

Mr. PAGE. In 1910 at the annual meeting of the West Coast Lumber Manu- facturers' Association, the association adopted the legislative committee's report, and that report condemned the conditions that were at that time exist- ing. There was a great deal of money paid by the employers to the liability insurance people. The man that got hurt got nothing, or got a small amount, and there were—there was a feeling in regard to the courts; they were un- satisfactory—and they asked for a mass meeting to see if we could not get the employers of labor and the laborers together and devise some means of remedying that evil. And that was followed by a mass meeting in Tacoma. And at that meeting there were representatives of labor, representatives of the employers. The governor of the State presided, and after a .two days', session he appointed a commission to see what could be done to draft a com- pensation act. And in that connection I would like to say right here, con- tradicting some of the testimony that appeared here—and I am not saying this in any malice at all—but the Federation of Labor of this State refused at that time to meet with the employers, on the ground that it was impossible for; the employer and the employee to get together on that proposition, and that the employer was not acting in good faith, but was trying to put one over on the lumberman. That commission was appointed and the bill was drafted and presented to the governor, and in turn presented to the legislature and passed with practically no amendments except the elimination of the first aid. That is the history of the compensation act of this State.

Mr. THOMPSON. Well, were there any objections by labor raised to the provisions of the bill that you wanted passed?

Mr. PAGE. The lumbermen indorsed the bill, and the State Federation of Labor of the State indorsed the bill without a dissent, I think.

Mr. THOMPSON. The same bill?

Mr. PAGE. The same bill. There was a controversy in the house when it came up before the house in regard to the first aid, and everything that was in the original draft of the bill that referred to first aid was taken out of the bill.

Mr. THOMPSON. Is there a bill pending relating to the first-aid proposition now?

Mr. PAGE. Yes; there is an initiative bill.

Mr. THOMPSON. What is the attitude of the lumbering interests toward that bill?

Mr. PAGE. We are opposed to the bill.

Mr. THOMPSON. What are the grounds?

Mr. PAGE. Personally, I am opposed myself to the bill on the principle of an initiative bill; I don't believe in it at all. Again, it is a loosely drawn bill. One of the provisions in the bill—the main provision of the bill—is that in case of an accident an employer is to pay $100, or whatever part of $100 is required, to give the injured employee service in the hospital. If it takes more than $100, the balance of that is to be paid from the accident fund, and the accident fund is secured by contributions from the employees. It seems to me it leaves an opening for a great deal of collusion between an unprincipled physician and the injured person, and there would be no end to the expense. It would be a great tax on the industry and really get nothing out of it, any more than they get now.

Commissioner GARRETSON. Mr. Page, you state that you are opposed to that, first because it is an initiative bill, and you oppose the initiative.

Mr. PAGE. Yes, sir; I do.

Commissioner GARRETSON. Is it the law in this State that the initiative is permissible?

Mr. PAGE. Yes, sir.

Commissioner GARRETSON. Do you take the position that even though a law is in effect, if it don't suit you, you refuse to be bound by it?

Mr. PAGE. Oh, no; oh, no. I am not a lawbreaker; but there are a great many laws that I don't agree with.

Commissioner GARRETSON. Oh, there are laws?

Mr. PAGE. What?

Commissioner GARRETSON. There are laws.

Mr. PAGE. Oh, they are laws; yes.

Mr. THOMPSON. Now, Mr. Page, referring to some testimony that has been given with reference to the influence on legislation which both sides bring to bear in this State, what have you to say about that, if anything?

Mr. PAGE. Well, there has been a great deal said here of how the employer in this State rules the legislation of the State. I can give you one example of what the employers of this State went after before the last legislature and what they got, and that is in relation to the compensation act.

We have got a lot of theorists in this State—a swarm of them—and we are raising them every day in our educational institutions. They never hired a man in their lives, and they never worked as laborers. They have got a solution for all of these difficulties that come up between capital—or the employer and the employee. They know all about the compensation question. What they don't know about compensation acts has never been written. Each and every one of them has got a pet amendment that he thinks, or she thinks, should be tacked onto our compensation act and if that amendment was put on the compensation act it would be a perfect act. Well, if we would turn that bunch loose at our compensation act, before they got through with it it would look like a crazy quilt. We would have no act. The lumbermen as an association decided that the only way to find out whether we did have a compensation act or whether we did not was to let the compensation act work out its own salvation,· and the only way to do that was to leave it alone; and we tried to devise some means of doing that.

I was instrumental in organizing what was called the general·legislative ·committee. I was made chairman of it, and I have been chairman·of the legislative committee for the lumbermen's manufacturers' association of this' State for the last eight years, and nothing that the lumbermen have done as an association in politics in this State—every particle of it has gone through my hands. I know all about it. This is not hearsay I am giving you;·I·know what I am talking about. This general legislative committee was organized. It consisted of representatives from every body of organized employers in this State, and we formed a plan and agreed upon what we wanted to have done with our compensation act, and that was to have it left alone—nobody· to bother with it at all; make no amendments; let it work out its ·own salvation. As chairman of that committee I went to the governor and· I presented the proposition to him and asked him to appoint a commission to investigate the compensation act and to meet with the industrial insurance commission, and if that commission decided that there were any amendments, to draw up the amendments and present them to the legislature—that is, this coming legis¹ lature—for passage.

The governor didn't seem to warm up to that proposition; sort of noncommittal. And I went to the industrial insurance committee. That was·a committee appointed by the house to handle all bills that were introduced that·had to do with the compensation act. I talked to the members of that committee as members, as individuals, and I talked before the committee as a committee, and stated what I wanted. They seemed to think that that was a business proposition, but the question was raised as to whether that really was the wish of the employers. And we thought we could demonstrate the fact that it was. And we called our people to Olympia, and we had a meeting before that committee which was·the largest gathering of business men asking for anything before the Legislature of the State of Washington that had ever been in Olympia for. any purpose. And all we asked was that the compensation act be left alone until it could work out its own salvation. The industrial insurance committee turned in that report, and the minute it was turned in there were 20 men on the floor each ·with an amendment to the committee's report and each .man with an amendment to the other fellow's amendment, and the friends of the bill got it off from the floor, and it was sidetracked.

Now, there was the representative employers of this State. This iniquitous sawdust ring that controls the policies of the State of Washington in politics— we were down there asking for as simple a thing as that, and we could not get it. .I don't think we control the politics of the State of Washington. .

Mr. THOMPSON. How do you view the industrial conditions? *I mean by that the relations in employment between the employer and the employee in this State.

Mr. PAGE. In what way?

Mr. THOMPSON. I mean as far as things go in this world. Is it satisfactory to you?

Mr. PAGE. Why, we have had no trouble with our men whatever.

Mr. THOMPSON. You think that the workers in this locality have any reasonable cause of complaint?

Mr. PAGE. I will tell you what I think. I think the earnest workingman who wants to get ahead and wants to be somebody and is looking for work and when he finds it works with his employer instead of working for him, I think that man is contented—reasonably contented and reasonably prosperous. While he don't have all the good things that there are in the world, there are a whole·lot of the employers that don't have all the good things. On the other hand, I think the fellow that is a rover and going from place to place and looking for a job and who has a grouch and who is listening to these agitators and reading all this stuff about the downtrodden laboring man and thinks that because there are idle rich in the world that never work, that society is all wrong, and he is abused because he has to work, I think that man is discontented and down and out the most of the time, and my private opinion· is that he gets just what is coming to him. The man that can't take pleasure out of an honest day's work, I don't think ·he fits in anywhere, and I think the man that wants to do that kind of work, while there are cases where he can't get it, I think in the majority ·of cases he can get it if he is looking for. it. .

Mr. THOMPSON. Then in your opinion, Mr. Page, the discontent which exists is mostly caused by agitators and by the rover, who really does not wish to be satisfied; is that it?

• Mr. PAGE. I think there is a great deal of it. As I said before, I think the main cause is there are not enough jobs to go around. I think that is making some of the discontent.

• Mr. THOMPSON. That cause would be a really serious cause of discontent?

Mr. PAGE. Yes; I think so.

Mr. THOMPSON. Take the country as a whole, take the industrial situation as you read about it in the papers and as you hear generally discussed, there is a really legitimate cause for discontent on the part of the workers?

• Mr. PAGE. No, sir; I don't think so.

Mr. THOMPSON. Now, for instance, this commission is appointed by the Government to look into the industrial situation, the relations between employer and employee; to look into the cause of discontent and unrest, if any exists. Do you think that this commission has any work to do. I don't mean to say— of course it must look into the question, but is there any legitimate cause for any recommendation to be made?

Mr. PAGE. Why, of course I have my ideas of what is wrong. I don't think I have a cure-all; I don't claim to.

Mr. THOMPSON. What are your ideas—what is your idea—of what is wrong, different or more than what you said? What would you say could be done?

Mr. PAGE. Well, I think, in the first place, this rover who wants to work three days out of the week and loaf the other four, I don't think there is any law—I don't think there is anything—that will ever touch him. I don't think that there is anything that will ever eliminate him, unless it is an education that starts in the family when he is a baby. I think he is here, and here to stay.

• Mr. THOMPSON. You think that vocational training of the young would be apt to change that, or have you any idea how that might be changed? You don't have to start with a man when he is grown up; we can start with him as a baby.

Mr. PAGE. The only way I can see is right at the mother's knee. That is where the training comes in.

Mr. THOMPSON. Train the mother?

• • Mr. PAGE. Some of them need training.

Mr. THOMPSON. What would you do with reference to the situation where there are only 15 jobs and 16 workers? What recommendation would you make to the commission?

Mr. PAGE. I think the only solution to that is to get the sixteenth man on the land and make a producer out of him.

• Mr. THOMPSON. How would you do that?

Mr. PAGE. In the first place, the only way to do it is to get the inclination to go onto the land into that man's mind. You can't force him on the land; you can't hire him to go on the land.

Mr. THOMPSON. Would you try and make land free. It has been stated most of the land is held by speculators and other people. Would you pass any Government regulation declaring, like single tax, saying people must pay a tax on land and can't hold it for speculation, and thereby let this sixteenth man get on the land free? What is your method of getting onto the land?

• Mr. PAGE. He wouldn't go. The only way to get him on is to get the inclination to go on the land. Let me give you an illustration here.

Right here at the back door of Seattle we have the valley of the Puyallup, the White, the Black, and the Green Rivers. That is probably as rich land as anywhere in the world. For all practical purposes for years this land has lain idle. Some has been used, but there was a great deal idle. There is a great deal idle now. We have had these unemployed men walking the railroad tracks back and forth through this land for years, and they haven't done anything with it. In the last few years the little Jap man came in. He paid thirty to fifty dollars cash rent for that land in advance, and he farmed it and farmed it for a few years and takes the proceeds and goes back to Japan an independent man; and the Japanese cousin or brother or uncle comes and steps on the rented land and does the same thing, and repeats it. The inclination to go on the land is there and he takes the land, and the fellow that is walking the railroad tracks with the bundle of blankets on his back has the same opportunity, but he hasn't got the inclination.

Mr. THOMPSON. What has taken that inclination from the man? I take it that it is generally conceded that all of our ancestors were agricultural people.

Mr. PAGE. Let me cite you one case. I don't know of a blacksmith in the

United States who is an efficient workman who wishes to have his son a black-smith, or I don't know a blacksmith's son in the United States who wishes .to be a better blacksmith than his dad. There is the point.

Mr. THOMPSON. I can illustrate better. I know very few lawyers who want their sons to be lawyers.

Mr. PAGE. Well, I don't blame them.

Commissioner O'CONNELL. They might want them to be better lawyers.

Mr. THOMPSON. The father wouldn't think that.

Commissioner LENNON. How about professors—do they want their sons to be professors?

Mr. THOMPSON. I don't know; I can't speak for them. What can you say in general as to conditions in the lumber industry which might have an effect on wages?

Mr. PAGE. Let me give you another illustration. Now, last year we had—last winter there was an estimate that there were 15,000 idle men in the State of Washington. I don't know whether there were 15,000 or 1,500. There were idle men here; no question about that. Last year this State imported into the State, according to the State reports, dairy products to the amount of $30,000,000, of butter, cheese, sheep, hogs, and cattle. Now, we had to bring in here, to feed these men that we have in the State, because we did not raise it ourselves, that amount; and there were 15,000 idle men in the State. That $30,000,000 is enough to pay that 15,000 idle men $2 a day for three years. Isn't there something wrong there, that those idle men weren't on the farm producing that stuff?

Mr. THOMPSON. Do you know anything about the work of Mr. Pauly, Henry Pauly, the head of the Itinerate Workers' Union?

Mr. PAGE. No; very little. I heard him yesterday.

Mr. THOMPSON. In the carrying on of your business have you met with any action by union labor which you consider detrimental?

Mr. PAGE. Oh, that is a matter of opinion.

Mr. THOMPSON. Have you been subject to any boycotts anywhere in your product?

Mr. PAGE. We have the California boycott, yes; we have always had that. That is——

Mr. THOMPSON. How does it affect the lumber industry here?

Mr. PAGE. Well, that is detrimental to the lumber worker here. You see, in the city of San Francisco we can not ship any finished lumber into that city, with the exception of flooring. Now, we take that lumber, take a .2 by 4, or a 2 by 6—we can ship into San Francisco rough, but we can't surface it. The lumber unions won't accept it, won't allow it to come in there, And as 'the result the surfacing of the lumber cost a great deal more in San Francisco than it would here in the mill. It is that much extra work that the San Francisco laborer gets and the Washington laborer don't get.

Mr. THOMPSON. How do you view that action, from your standpoint as a business man; what view do you take of it?

Mr. PAGE. Well, I think that resolves itself down to the same question that you have got 15 jobs and you have got 16 men. The fellows that have got the 15 jobs are going to hold them and let the other fellow look for himself, hustle for his own. That is the attitude of the San Francisco union as far as I can see. I can not see any other motive for stopping this surfacing of lumber here and coming into San Francisco unsurfaced other than the unions down there want that work for their men regardless of what the fellow up here in Washington gets.

Mr. THOMPSON. Well, would that bear any comparison with what is termed the tariff against products of other nations?

Mr. PAGE. Oh, I can't talk tariff; I don't know anything about the tariff.

Mr. THOMPSON. And I don't want to ask anything about the tariff. I mean just as an illustration, the tariff is more or less of a boycott on outside goods, is it not?

Mr. PAGE. You can lay any iniquity or any virtue on the tariff.

Mr. THOMPSON. I am not speaking about either evil or good.

Mr. PAGE. I don't know. I can't answer that question.

Mr. THOMPSON. That is all you have to say about that, your views on that?

Mr. PAGE. I believe so.

Mr. THOMPSON. Did you hear the testimony of Mr. Brown yesterday in regard to the conditions in the lumber camps?

Mr. PAGE. Yes, sir.

Mr. THOMPSON. Have you anything you would like to add to what he said?
Mr. PAGE. Oh, nothing more than he naturally would pick out the poorest conditions possible he could find and the poorest illustrations, and the most illy conducted camp.

Mr. THOMPSON. How are the housing arrangements in the best camp? What is the arrangement in your camp, for instance? What kind of bunk houses have you? How are their beds arranged? What is the bedding that they have? How often is it changed? Who takes care of it? What are the toilet arrangements? What kind of food do they get?

Mr. PAGE. We have bunk houses. We have what we call bunk houses. They are large houses with a hall through the center and a room at each end, and on both sides of this hall are rooms with doors and windows, locks and keys on the doors so that a man can have privacy in those rooms. The bunks are supplied with a mattress and springs, and the employees furnish their own bedding. We have a man that is called the bull cook. Every camp has a bull cook.

Mr. THOMPSON. You will have to repeat that name. I didn't get that name.

Mr. PAGE. That is a good name, bull cook.

Mr. THOMPSON. Bull cook?

Mr. PAGE. That is one of the names. He is the flunkey that takes care of the bunk house. He goes in there and fills the lamps and sweeps the building and keeps it clean, and in cold weather he has the fires started and the house warmed for the men when they come in from work.

Mr. THOMPSON. Is there any special place provided for the drying of clothing?

Mr. PAGE. These two rooms at the end of the building, they use those for drying.

Commissioner GARRETSON. The same room they sleep in?

Mr. PAGE. No, sir; it is in the same building; there is a hall running down through the building the same as if you would run a hall down through here, and there is a room on each side.

Commissioner GARRETSON. Do they have any bunks in?

Mr. PAGE. No; no bunks.

Mr. THOMPSON. What is the condition of the lumber industry in this State with regard to the business situation?

Mr. PAGE. Very bad.

Mr. THOMPSON. Well, is it temporary or has it been coming on for some time, or what?

Mr. PAGE. It is chronic.

Mr. THOMPSON. Chronic?

Mr. PAGE. Yes, sir; all the time. We have had some good spots, but the most of the time it is a depressed business.

Mr. THOMPSON. What are the causes for that, if you know?

Mr. PAGE. Overproduction is one cause; keen competition, high freight rates to meet that competition, substitutes, lack of organization, high taxes.

Mr. THOMPSON. What influence does that condition have on the wages that are paid in the industry?

Mr. PAGE. They fluctuate. The wages fluctuate up and down.

Mr. THOMPSON. With this condition?

Mr. PAGE. Yes, sir, to illustrate: In 1906 and 1907, while San Francisco was recovering, rebuilding from the fire and earthquake, previous to that time we were paying a dollar seventy-five for our cheap labor; that is, the labor we are paying $2 for to-day, the man who works on the logging railroad and the man who works in the yard. During those years we paid $2.75 for the same work. The price of labor goes up with the price of lumber, and it goes down with the price of lumber. I think that it goes up faster than it goes down.

Mr. THOMPSON. That is all, Mr. Chairman.

Acting Chairman COMMONS. Any questions?

Commissioner O'CONNELL. Yes.

Acting Chairman COMMONS. Mr. Page, Mr. O'Connell would like to ask you some questions.

Commissioner O'CONNELL. Mr. Page, will you explain to us this hospital system that is conducted by the lumber companies or by your company?

Mr. PAGE. Yes, sir; I will give you our individual arrangement, and it is the same as the other mills. There is a doctor by the name of Dr. Taylor at Kent, Wash., who has a hospital, and we arrange with him to take care of the men—sickness, accidents, everything but venereal diseases, for a dollar per head per month. When a man comes to work for us we charge him this dollar. If he works four days, he is charged 25 cents. If he works over four days, he pays the dollar. When he quits working for us, if he has been charged the dollar, and goes to some other camp, we give him a hospital ticket,, if he asks for it. It is there for him if he wants it, and that hospital ticket will be honored by any mill in the State of Washington. He goes to another mill and presents that ticket and says, "I want work." If he is put to work, he won't be charged by that other mill for hospital service until the expiration of the time of that hospital ticket; that is, for one month. We honor other mill hospital tickets, and our hospital tickets are honored by other mills. I will say there is an indifference on the part of the employee in asking for those tickets. I have paid off men myself, where I have written the check and made out the time check, and given them a hospital ticket, and they would look at it and tear it up and throw it on the floor and go off

Commissioner O'CONNELL. If a man worked four days for your company the latter part of the month, he is supposed to pay that dollar?

Mr. PAGE. No; if he works four days he is charged 25 cents. If he works five days he is charged a dollar. We have to establish a point somewhere in which to charge.

Commissioner O'CONNELL. Well, your number of employees you say is about 138?

Mr. PAGE. One hundred and thirty-eight.

Commissioner O'CONNELL. What number of accidents have you had—what number of your people have been sent to the hospital during, say, the past 12 months?

Mr. PAGE. Oh, we have quite a—I can't tell you the exact number, but we have had a good many.

Commissioner O'CONNELL. Twenty-five or fifty or a hundred?

Mr. PAGE. I should say not to exceed 50 in the last year.

Commissioner O'CONNELL. Well, then, if you had sent 50 people to the hospital and they had a dollar a month, wouldn't it appear they were paying a very high percentage for that hospital insurance?

Mr. PAGE. No; it don't seem so to me; no.

Commissioner O'CONNELL. This commission in its investigations at various places has come against various methods of corporations collecting hospital fees from their employees. In some instances we have found exceptional liberality in the things that may be enjoyed by the employees for that dollar; in others rather restricted. As, for instance, one concern we came in contact with within a few weeks, the employees pay a dollar a month into this hospital association. This hospital association is kept exclusively for their use. Six physicians are provided. Nurses are provided. A man not only gets care for himself, but he gets care for his wife and his children in all cases of sickness. He is paid a dollar a day if he is off sick, and he is paid a thousand dollars if he dies—out of this $1. And they have accumulated in addition $35,000 in this fund as a reserve fund.

Now, it would seem that if men only get just the bare hospital treatment for themselves in cases of accident, there is a great disparity as to what the cost is.

Mr. PAGE. No; but they get—you understand, Mr. Commissioner, they get hospital service for accidents and hospital service for illness together. I do not know what the institution is to which you refer, but there may not be the hazard in that institution, of accidents, that there is in the lumber business.

Commissioner O'CONNELL. Well, it is a mining industry. That is quite hazardous.

Mr. PAGE. Yes, sir. I will tell you where you can get that and get it complete, if you will ask that of Mr. Wallace, who comes here later.

Commissioner O'CONNELL. Comes on here?

Mr. PAGE. He is the gentleman who is on our industrial-insurance commission, and he is a mine worker, and mines in this State have a hospital of their own to which the miners contribute. They run the whole thing.

Commissioner O'CONNELL. Do the camps work Sundays?

Mr. PAGE. No; not as a rule.

Commissioner O'CONNELL. Not as a rule; but they do at times, do they?

Mr. PAGE. No; I don't know of any logging camp that works on Sundays. I don't know of any mill that runs on Sundays at all unless it is some special—for some special occasion, some special thing.

. Commissioner O'CONNELL. Then there is a recognition of one day in seven for rest?

. . Mr. PAGE. Oh, yes; yes.

Commissioner O'CONNELL. Does your company run a company store in connection with its business?

Mr. PAGE. Yes, sir.

Commissioner O'CONNELL. Are the men supposed to buy all of their supplies in this store?

Mr. PAGE. No; we don't care where they buy their supplies. We would rather not run the store. It is an expense to us.

. Commissioner O'CONNELL. All the commissaries are kept in that store for the feeding, and your cooking establishments are kept there?

Mr. PAGE. No, no; we have that somewhat divided. We keep the commissary for the benefit of the men and for the benefit of the families that we have there. We have quite a number of families at our place, although we are what you might call an outpost away up in the mountains, away from civilization—there is not a town within 20 miles of us.

Commissioner O'CONNELL. How do your prices compare where you are located with the prices in Seattle?

Mr. PAGE. They are the same. We can't ask any higher prices.

Commissioner O'CONNELL. You board all of your people?

Mr. PAGE. All but the married people; yes.

Commissioner O'CONNELL. What do they pay for board a month?

Mr. PAGE. Five dollars and a half a week.

Commissioner O'CONNELL. What are they fed generally?

Mr. PAGE. They are fed the best that money can buy. We don't believe that a logger can do the work that he has to do unless he has the very best of food; and he can't do it; that is all there is to it.

Commissioner O'CONNELL. Given meat three times a day?

Mr. PAGE. Do they eat three times?

Commissioner O'CONNELL. Meat?

Mr. PAGE. Yes; always—three times a day—and it isn't cow beef, it is beef—steer beef—the best we can buy.

Commissioner O'CONNELL. I suppose the proverbial bean is there occasionally?

Mr. PAGE. Bushels of them. That is a business proposition, to feed your men well, even if we didn't want to.

Commissioner O'CONNELL. Well, is that same care taken in connection with their housing, their sleeping and resting opportunities?

Mr. PAGE. Why, I think so. You have got a funny class of men to deal with in these loggers. Now, lots of times we will get loggers that will go in and throw the mattress out of the window and go up to the barn and get hay and put it in that bunk. That is what he wants.

Commissioner O'CONNELL. Are they furnished their hay and straw free?

Mr. PAGE. Yes, sir.

Commissioner O'CONNELL. But they furnish their own mattress if they want one?

Mr. PAGE. No, no; they furnish their bedding. They furnish their blanket, we furnish the mattress.

Commissioner O'CONNELL. They buy the blankets in your stores?

Mr. PAGE. Why, sometimes; not very many. Most of them have their blankets with them when they come.

Commissioner O'CONNELL. That is considered part of their trade, I suppose, when they are seeking employment?

Mr. PAGE. That is the badge of the trade.

Commissioner O'CONNELL. Part of their tools, as it were?

Mr. PAGE. Yes, sir.

Commissioner O'CONNELL. That is all.

Acting Chairman COMMONS. Mr. Garretson.

Commissioner GARRETSON. Mr. Page, when this man throws the mattress out of the window, is it ever because he has the idea that somebody else—something else has taken possession of it before he was there?

Mr. PAGE. Possibly.

Commissioner GARRETSON. How many other camps are under the supervision of this same doctor?

Mr. PAGE. I don't believe there is any more.

Commissioner GARRETSON. Just yours?

Mr. PAGE. I believe so; yes, sir.

Commissioner GARRETSON. How many hospitals serve your entire membership in your association, or in the lumber trade?

Mr. PAGE. Oh, I don't know. A great many.

Commissioner GARRETSON. Are there hospitals available in this territory contiguous to Seattle?

Mr. PAGE. Yes; a great many.

Commissioner GARRETSON. There were three named here yesterday.

Mr. PAGE. Oh, there are hospitals all over; they have to have the hospitals. These men have to be taken care of.

Commissioner GARRETSON. Are any of them built on the profits from this dollar?

Mr. PAGE. I don't know what built them.

Commissioner GARRETSON. How far is your camp from the hospital and the surgeon?

Mr. PAGE. About 45 miles.

Commissioner GARRETSON. Forty-five. Have you ever given any thought or investigation, or has your association, to the cost in other pursuits that are somewhat, at least slightly hazardous?

Mr. PAGE. The cost of the hospital service?

Commissioner GARRETSON. Yes, sir; to the men.

Mr. PAGE. No; I don't believe any——

Commissioner GARRETSON. Are you familiar with the railroad form of assessment for hospital service?

Mr. PAGE. No; I know that the railroad people have a very complete hospital at Tacoma.

Commissioner GARRETSON. Almost universal over the continent, and the charge universal. Do you know what that charge is?

Mr. PAGE. No; I don't.

Commissioner GARRETSON. A man that earns $50 or over is assessed 50 cents a month for all service for himself in illness or injury, and for medicines for his family, and trettment either in the hospital or at home for himself. If he earns less than $50, twenty-five cents a month. On that, many companies—are you aware of the fact that they build complete hospitals with a heavy overhead cost, and have amassed large amounts of reserve?

Mr. PAGE. Large amounts of reserve?

Commissioner GARRETSON. Yes; money.

Mr. PAGE. No.

Commissioner GARRETSON. You will admit, I suppose, that railroading is as hazardous as lumbering? Do you know anything of the figures or railroad injuries?

Mr. PAGE. I do not; no.

Commissioner GARRETSON. You have not seen the last report of the Interstate Commerce Commission to the effect that from 1890 to 1912, 1,675,854 were killed and injured?

Mr. PAGE. No; I don't know anything about that. I can't carry those figures in my head. But if you want to know how the lumber industry cripples up men, what proportion they have to the railroads, or to any other business, we have a complete report of that in the State here, and I would be glad to give it to you.

Commissioner GARRETSON. Well, wouldn't it look like any business that slaughtered that amount of men, if 50 cents or 25 cents will show a balance in favor of taking care of them exclusively, that a dollar is a good deal of 'a pudding for somebody?

Mr. PAGE. Oh, I don't know. That is the same old story. You can twist figures. You can take two hens and a scratch pad and make a million dollars in 24 hours.

Commissioner GARRETSON. You are a believer in the old adage that figures won't lie, but liars will figure?

Mr. PAGE. Yes; liars will figure and they will try to force a point by using part of the figures. I do not know any of those hospitals—I don't know of any doctor here in this State who has made a million dollars out of crippled men in the hospital service. They may have had that here, but I don't know.

Commissioner GARRETSON. Is there anything less than a million dollars worth stealing?

Mr. PAGE. Oh, well, now, what advantage is that to this commission?

Commissioner GARRETSON. It is worth this to this commission to know whether the workers as a class in any industry are exploited or not.

Mr. PAGE. That a million dollars is worth stealing?

Commissioner GARRETSON. Whether 25 cents is worth stealing from an employee—that is what is involved in it.

Mr. PAGE. I didn't come down here to argue or to get into any acrimonious discussion; if you want any information I am here to give it.

Commissioner GARRETSON. That is just the information I am after.

Mr. PAGE. I don't know anything about whether a million dollars is worth stealing or whether it is not.

Commissioner GARRETSON. If a man is charged unreasonably for a certain thing that is of interest to this commission. That is all there is in it. You spoke of lack of organization as being one of the causes leading to the chronic depression of the lumber trade. That is, organization on the part of the manufacturers; is that your understanding?

Mr. PAGE. Yes, sir.

Commissioner GARRETSON. Has it ever occurred to you that the depression in wages may be on account of lack of organization of those who are interested in getting the wages?

Mr. PAGE. No, sir; I don't think so. You get right back to that proposition again; you have 15 jobs and 16 men. If the 15 men organize how is that going to help the sixteenth man. If you take the sixteenth man in, how is it going to help the 15?

Commissioner GARRETSON. If there are 16 manufacturers operating in the field where there is only a market for the products of 15, wouldn't the logical outcome of organization be that they would distribute the market between the 16 or curtail the production?

Mr. PAGE. I don't know anything about that, but I can't figure out how you are going to do anything with the sixteenth man by organizing the 15.

Commissioner GARRETSON. Then what contributes to this depression on account of lack of organization of the manufacturers?

Mr. PAGE. Well, there is a lack of organization in this way, lack of knowing the conditions; lack of knowing the market; lack of confidence in each other to the giving of this inside information as to where is the best place to market, what is the best place and how is the best way to manufacture lumber.

Commissioner GARRETSON. Organization won't make the market any greater?

Mr. PAGE. Well, under the Sherman Act it won't.

Commissioner GARRETSON. It will just utilize what market there is to the best advantage, is that your idea?

Mr. PAGE. Now, let's see a minute.

Commissioner GARRETSON. Then wouldn't the organization on the part of the employees utilize the 15 jobs to the best advantage of the 16 men?

Mr. PAGE. No, sir; it wouldn't.

Commissioner GARRETSON. Then it is good for the employer or manufacturer, but not good for the employee?

Mr. PAGE. No, sir; you have a concrete illustration of that. I have just given it to you at Frisco, where the union wants all the surfacing of this lumber. They don't care whether the surfacers up in Washington are out of a job or not. If we would let the surfacing go to Frisco these men up here would not be working.

Commissioner GARRETSON. Haven't you lost sight of the real reason for that? That is because the Washington man is paid less than the union scale, while in Frisco he is paid the union scale?

Mr. PAGE. That is not so.

Commissioner GARRETSON. You think that Washington pays as much for the men as at Frisco. If that is so, what is your statement based on that you could do it lots cheaper here than you could do it there?

Mr. PAGE. Well, you can take a piece of lumber that comes off of the chains at a mill where a man reaches for it over here and puts it through this machine, and it is surfaced, you certainly can do it cheaper.

Commissioner GARRETSON. How long does it take to handle it——

Mr. PAGE. Wait a minute. You can do that cheaper than you can take and unload it from the ship onto the lighter and unload it from the lighter onto the dock, and from the dock into a wagon, and from the wagon to the planing mill, and onto the machine. You can certainly do it cheaper.

Commissioner GARRETSON. There is just one more operation?

Mr. PAGE. There is 40 more.

Commissioner GARRETSON. You have to put it to the barge dock and to the place of delivery. You interrupt that by going to the mill, just one movement added.

Mr. PAGE. No, sir; we have all those movements.

Commissioner GARRETSON. You would have all those to get the dressed lumber, and you are perfectly aware of the fact.

Mr. PAGE. No, sir; you are getting your wires crossed.

Commissioner GARRETSON. The movements from here to Frisco are the same.

Mr. PAGE. You can't tell me anything about the sawmill business, because I know all about it.

Commissioner GARRETSON. You can't tell me anything about the sawmill business in transportation, because I know something about it.

Mr. PAGE. When you think you can load it on the truck and run it off to the sawmill and put it through the machines and handle it as cheaply as you could where you take it off the chains and run it through the machines you are talking through your hat.

Commissioner GARRETSON. You will never make a case on that basis. The pleasure that comes out of the honest day's work you cited as one of the greatest enjoyments of man. What constitutes an honest day's work, 8 or 16 hours?

Mr. PAGE. I don't know.

Commissioner GARRETSON. How is that?

Mr. PAGE. I don't know.

Commissioner GARRETSON. Well, I want to know the gauge for pleasure.

Mr. PAGE. Well, I tell you what I think about it. I enjoy my work, I like to gain my end. If the work forces me to work 8 hours, I have to do it. If I have to work 16 hours, I don't like it.

Commissioner GARRETSON. There are two of us.

Mr. PAGE. But I will work the 16 hours, and I do get some satisfaction out of the 16 hours, although I don't like the fatigue of it.

Commissioner GARRETSON. You get more out of the 8-hour day?

Mr. PAGE. I get more; yes, sir.

Commissioner GARRETSON. You spoke of the men being discontented because they listened to the agitators and read literature along those lines?

Mr. PAGE. Yes, sir.

Commissioner GARRETSON. You don't mean by that you desire the employee to take all his opinions secondhanded from the channels furnished him by his employer?

Mr. PAGE. I don't think the employer makes any attempt to furnish him that.

Commissioner GARRETSON. Well, I don't know whether he does or not, but if he was barred from all the others, wouldn't it become their duty to furnish him something of that kind?

Mr. PAGE. I dont' believe in restricting anybody, and I don't think anybody in this country is restricted. He can read what he pleases.

Commissioner GARRETSON. Well, you stated, as I understood you, that the man who listened to the agitator and read the literature was, in your opinion, getting just what was coming to him under present industrial conditions.

Mr. PAGE. No, sir; I think the man who is listening to that and is discontented because he is listening gets just what is coming to him.

Commissioner GARRETSON. Do you believe the present industrial condition is an equitable one?

Mr. PAGE. No, sir; I don't.

Commissioner GARRETSON. You said the attitude of the employers toward compensation was that you desired it to be left alone and let it work out its own salvation.

Mr. PAGE. Yes, sir.

Commissioner GARRETSON. Have you ever made any study or investigation of the attitude of employers toward measures of that character for, we will say, we won't go back very far, let us say 60 years?

Mr. PAGE. In what way?

Commissioner GARRETSON. As to letting them alone.

Mr. PAGE. I don't think there has ever a parallel case come up.

Commissioner GARRETSON. Isn't it a fact that the eternal attitude of the employer has always been toward this condition that that existed to let it alone. For instance, the slave owners wanted slavery left alone. Their legislative attitude in regard to all social legislation has been eternally to let it alone;

and if that had been conformed to, we would have still been in the dark ages, wouldn't we?

Mr. PAGE. That is all bunk.

Commissioner GARRETSON. It doesn't matter whether it is bunk or not.

Mr. PAGE. It hasn't anything to do with the question at all. Here is a piece of machinery, a patented machine, and set up to do a certain piece of work. You look at it and start it up, and here comes along a theorist and says we want another gear over here and another here, let's stop the machine and put those on. Is there any sense to that? Why not test the machine and let it run long enough to see whether it needs them or not.

Commissioner GARRETSON. It is very possible that the machine had been running somewhere else and that running had demonstrated the necessity for another gear, is it not? Is every man going to work out his own experience, or is he going to avail himself of the experience of others?

Mr. PAGE. Well, he might work out his own, and he might avail himself of the experience of others.

Commissioner GARRETSON. The rule is we avail ourselves of the experience of others, is it not?

Mr. PAGE. How about new patents?

Commissioner GARRETSON. About new patents?

Mr. PAGE. Nobody has ever thought of before, the solution——

Commissioner GARRETSON. I suppose the inventor works that out before he puts it on the market.

Mr. PAGE. From somebody else's experience?

Commissioner GARRETSON. In mechanics, yes; there are certain fixed laws that any mechanic has got to take advantage of, are there not?

Mr. PAGE. If that is the fact all these things work themselves out without anybody's initiative.

Commissioner GARRETSON. There have been a good many things taken care of with legislation. Was the atttitude of the average employer toward the fellow servant defense?

Mr. PAGE. Yes.

Commissioner GARRETSON. And assumption of risk.

Mr. PAGE. Yes.

Commissioner GARRETSON. And contributory negligence.

Mr. PAGE. Yes.

Commissioner GARRETSON. And still nearly all have been abolished.

Mr. PAGE. We didn't have any of that in our compensation act.

Commissioner GARRETSON. It is the eternal attitude of opposition, is it not, that prevails toward social legislation?

Mr. PAGE. Why, I don't think so. I have just told you where the lumberman and the employer go hand in hand with the laborers in trying to get something new in our compensation act. That is a concrete example that we have in this State.

Commissioner GARRETSON. There has been very considerable testimony here as to the attitude of the employing associations on the enactment of that very bill.

Mr. PAGE. Yes.

Commissioner GARRETSON. And it is not in accord with the fact that they were going hand in hand.

Mr. PAGE. They don't know what they are talking about, then.

Commissioner GARRETSON. I suppose it is a matter that could be really demonstrated. .

Mr. PAGE. It can not be demonstrated. I know what I am talking about. I was chairman of the commission that drew the compensation act, and I know all about it.

Commissioner GARRETSON. Did the individuals of your association work in accord?

Mr. PAGE. On that commission?

Commissioner GARRETSON. I mean favoring the legislation?

Mr. PAGE. You mean all the individuals in our association, the lumbermen's association? No. We had a great many of them opposed to it.

Commissioner GARRETSON. And they played their lone hand if they desired to?

Mr. PAGE. Oh, certainly.

Commissioner GARRETSON. Can you furnish to this commission, Mr. Page— you state what seems to be at variance with the general consensus of testimony from both sides of your industry. Can you furnish this commission with a copy· of your pay rolls of a single logging camp anywhere, any one of them, for 12· months?

Mr. PAGE. Yes.

Commissioner GARRETSON. And would you do so?

Mr. PAGE. I will give you our pay roll. You can get the pay rolls from all the camps. Wait a minute; let me tell you.

Commissioner GARRETSON. I was only speaking of your own.

Mr. PAGE. Now, just a minute, let me tell you something. You go to the industrial commission and ask them for a copy of the pay roll· of not only our camp, but some other camp, and every pay roll that you like in every camp in the State of Washington; they will give it to you, you can have that. ·

Commissioner GARRETSON. They are a matter of record?

Mr. PAGE. Yes; they are a matter of record.

Commissioner GARRETSON. I did not know that they were. ,

Mr. PAGE. They have got the whole thing.

Commissioner GARRETSON. That is all.

Acting Chairman COMMONS. What was the premium which your business paid for insurance, liability insurance, prior to the enactment of the compensation law, as compared with what it costs now, is what I mean?

Mr. PAGE. We paid $1.35. That was the minimum. Just previous to the time that the question of the compensation act came up, the employers' liability insurance companies raised the rates of insurance in Oregon and said that they were going to raise them here. In fact the last time that we insured in the employers' liability insurance we were given a certain time to get in under the $1.35 rate, or, if we did not get in by that time it would be $1.50. Now, we paid them, we might say, $1.50, because that was what was coming, or existed at that time. Now, in the commission——

Commissioner LENNON (interposing). You paid $1.50 on $100 of the pay roll?

Mr. PAGE. Yes; I can give you that exactly. I have got here exactly what goes to make the cost of 1,000 feet of lumber, what labor gets out of it, and the whole thing. The industrial insurance was one and eight-tenths per cent of the pay roll.

Commissioner GARRETSON. Mr. Page, did that liability company quote you a higher rate at first than they did later on, under your local rate?

Mr. PAGE. No; they said they were going to raise the rate. ·.

Commissioner GARRETSON. They did not endeavor to hold you up in that direction?

Mr. PAGE. In the price?

Commissioner GARRETSON. Oh, yes.

Mr. PAGE. Oh, yes; that was the reason; they were going to. raise the price from $1.35 minimum, to $1.50.

Acting Chairman COMMONS. And the premium under the State plan is $1.80, isn't it?

Mr. PAGE. That is the way it worked out. From the last report the cost on the pay roll in the lumber industry was $1.77, if I remember correctly.

Acting Chairman COMMONS. On each $100?

Mr. PAGE. On each $100. But you can get that from Mr. Daggett. · He has got it all at his fingers' ends; he knows all about it.

Acting Chairman COMMONS. It costs something like 27 or 30 cents more than the older system?   •

Mr. PAGE. Yes; but I would say that under this system we are insured completely. Under the old system we were only insured for $5,000, and if we hurt a man or if we killed a man and a judgment was rendered against us for the death or injury of that man, if it was in excess of $5,000, we had to pay that excess; the insurance company paid up to $5,000. Under our compensation act we are protected entirely. There is no controversy between the employee and the employer under this act—no chance for a lawsuit. ;

Acting Chairman COMMONS. I don't quite understand why it should be that you had a first aid—I presume by first aid you mean medical service?·

Mr. PAGE. Yes, sir.

Acting Chairman COMMONS. With medical service? ·

Mr. PAGE. Yes.

Acting Chairman COMMONS. I do not understand why you had that in· the first draft of the bill and what occurred in the law—that was stricken. out in the legislature, I understand?

Mr. PAGE. Yes, sir.

Acting Chairman Commons. And now why do you object to it going back to the original plan that you approved when the commission made it?

Mr. Page. Oh, no; you didn't understand me. I am not opposed to first aid. I was in favor of that in the original draft of the bill; but I am opposed to this first-aid bill that is now to be initiated, not because it is an initiative measure, but opposed to the bill itself. I do not think it is——

Acting Chairman Commons. What would be your idea of a proper hospital and medical provision in a compensation law?

Mr. Page. I think the original first aid, as drawn in the commission's report, was about as near as we can get to a solution of the first-aid question.

Commissioner Garretson. That is, of dividing the expense?

Mr. Page. Yes; that is dividing the expense.

Acting Chairman Commons. What was that provision?

Mr. Page. It was a tax of so much a day upon the employer and so much a day upon the employee.

Acting Chairman Commons. During the period of sickness?

Mr. Page. No; every day. The objection to that was that there was no statistics in this State at all as to the number of accidents. There was the opportunity of piling up a great amount of money, and the politicians were afraid that if the Democrats were in power they would have a lot of money and a lot of power with the having of this money; and the Republicans were the same, they were fighting each other, they decided that it was wrong in putting it in, and they cut it out entirely.

Acting Chairman Commons. So there has no fund accumulated?

Mr. Page. No; it is not in the bill at all.

Acting Chairman Commons. It is paid out as it comes in?

Mr. Page. It was cut out of the bill. There is no first aid in the bill.

Acting Chairman Commons. Then the compensation proper that is to be paid by the employer solely—there were two provisions in the first bill, in the first draft, one covering hospital and medical services.

Mr. Page. That was first aid.

Acting Chairman Commons. That is what you call first aid?

Mr. Page. That was first aid. That was cut out of the bill. Now, all the expense, with the exception of the administration, is paid by the employer. The administration of the bill is paid for by an appropriation. The State pays for that. But all the costs come from the employer. Just for illustration: One of our men fell last spring and sprained his ankle. About the same time I fell and sprained mine. He was back in his work while I was still hobbling around with a cane. He got his compensation from the State. It cost him nothing at all. I got mine from the Iowa State Traveling Men's Association, which cost me considerable. He got more than I did.

Acting Chairman Commons. That is, compensation for being out of work?

Mr. Page. Being out of work.

Acting Chairman Commons. Not for the first aid?

Mr. Page. Not first aid.

Acting Chairman Commons. In addition to that, his insurance—his dollar a month—entitled him to medical treatment, did it?

Mr. Page. Yes; the insurance entitled him to medical treatment; that is, the dollar we charged him—his hospital fee; that has nothing to do with the compensation act at all.

Acting Chairman Commons. It did have in the first draft?

Mr. Page. Yes; the first draft. But that was eliminated; never was passed. That act never provided—the act as passed never provided for any first aid.

Commissioner Lennon. If the first-aid provision had been adopted as proposed, would it have done away with this dollar that has been paid now?

Mr. Page. Yes.

Commissioner Lennon. It eliminated all that?

Mr. Page. Yes; it is done away with.

Commissioner Garretson. They followed the Federal act in making that provision or the arrangement of that character in the present bill?

Mr. Page. Yes.

Acting Chairman Commons. Have you figured out how much additional expense it is to the builder in San Francisco, on account of this regulation of the unions there requiring surfacing to be done there, over what it would cost here?

Mr. Page. Yes; it is a great deal more expensive. I think we have in our association, the lumbermen's association—I think we have what is charged by the planing mills in San Francisco for surfacing lumber, and I will ask the manager to furnish you with a copy of that scale.

Acting Chairman COMMONS. But that wouldn't give the total difference, because you mentioned these other items—the double shipment, the double haul-ing, and various other items. I should think in order to get the actual difference you would have to take figures of what the costs are here.

Mr. PAGE. You might get that if you get a lumberman on the stand here who is familiar with the San Francisco trade, who ships lumber down here—he might be able to give you that information. We never ship anything into Frisco.

Acting Chairman COMMONS. Is there one that you know of?

Mr. PAGE. I think Mr. Mack—I think perhaps Mr. Mack can give you that in-formation. I do not know, because we don't ship to Frisco.

Acting Chairman COMMONS. This reduction in wages recently from $2.25 to $2, was that owing to the condition of the work?

Mr. PAGE. That is owing to a drop in the price of lumber that took place in May. There was a flat drop out here of 50 cents a thousand on common lumber in May.

Acting Chairman COMMONS. Was the amount that was dropped on the mill or was it an all-around drop of 10 per cent?

Mr. PAGE. It went all the way through. We made a sweeping reduction.

Acting Chairman COMMONS. Ten per cent?

Mr. PAGE. Ten per cent.

Acting Chairman COMMONS. And that has been in effect since May?

Mr. PAGE. No; that has been in effect since the 15th of July.

Acting Chairman COMMONS. The drop occurred in May?

Mr. PAGE. In May.

Acting Chairman COMMONS. And as a result of that drop wages have been reduced?

Mr. PAGE. We reduced our wages when we started up after the 4th of July close-down—July 15.

Acting Chairman COMMONS. Have any of the mills been shut down in the State on account of this drop?

Mr. PAGE. Oh, I don't know. A great many of the mills are idle. To illus-trate the lumber business, we have been in the lumber business for 19 years. Out of the 19 years we have been closed down 9 on account of the price of lumber.

Acting Chairman COMMONS. Closed down 9?

Mr. PAGE. We have been running 19 years; closed down 9, and running 10.

Acting Chairman COMMONS. During the past 3 years how much have you been closed down?

Mr. PAGE. We closed down our mill in 1910, and we didn't start it up until—we rebuilt our mill—dismantled our Buckley mill, and we built the other mill and did not start up until the 15th of July, 1913. We have been running now a little over a year. Previous to that time we came through one of these two-year close-downs.

Acting Chairman COMMONS. Do you engage any of your men—hire your men through employment offices? Or do they report——

Mr. PAGE. No; we hire them through employment offices.

Acting Chairman COMMONS. All of this additional force that you mention that you require, the monthly force, you hire them all through employment offices?

Mr. PAGE. Yes; we hire the men through employment offices because it is very seldom that men come to our camp to apply for work, because we are 2 or 3 miles from the Northern Pacific Railway Co., and it is quite a trip up there and back again, and they don't come. While we were operating at Buckley we never got many from the employment offices. They were coming and going all the time.

Acting Chairman COMMONS. It is only for the remote camps, then, that you have to depend on the employment offices?

Mr. PAGE. I think so, as a general thing.

Acting Chairman COMMONS. Do you get the class of help that is suitable for the work? That is, are there offices that deal in particularly—specialize in that line?

Mr. PAGE. Yes; we have one office here we get all our loggers from.

Acting Chairman COMMONS. Do you know what the men have to pay for their job?

Mr. PAGE. A dollar.

Acting Chairman COMMONS. Then they pay the employment office a dollar?

Mr. PAGE. I think they pay a dollar; yes.

Acting Chairman COMMONS. It has been stated here, men changing during the month pay this hospital fee as much as two, three, or four times.

Mr. PAGE. Yes.

Acting Chairman COMMONS. What do you know about that statement?

Mr. PAGE. I think they do; but it is the man's fault. If a man takes his card, his hospital card, there is not a mill in the State of Washington that won't honor a hospital ticket. But many of them take their hospital ticket and tear it up when he gets it; he says he is a great big husky fellow and he don't need any hospital ticket.

Acting Chairman COMMONS. Then, all have that rule, have they, that they will honor the hospital ticket?

Mr. PAGE. I do not know a mill that would dishonor one. I would hate like anything to dishonor a man's hospital ticket. I think he would be into me in one jump.

Acting Chairman COMMONS. Do you pay these hospital people all of this money? In what way is it paid? What kind of a contract is made?

Mr. PAGE. We turn it over on pay day; we make up what is due the physician from our pay roll, and a check goes out with the pay-roll check.

Acting Chairman COMMONS. He gets the entire amount?

Mr. PAGE. He gets the whole thing.

Acting Chairman COMMONS. He gets everything?

Mr. PAGE. Yes; everything.

Acting Chairman COMMONS. Then, he would be the one who would have to honor the hospital ticket?

Mr. PAGE. Yes; he is the man.

Acting Chairman COMMONS. And your contract with him requires that he shall?

Mr. PAGE. Our contract with him requires that he must furnish hospital service for that man for illness and accident for 30 days for a dollar.

Acting Chairman COMMONS. I am speaking of a man who comes with a ticket from another camp. Would he have a claim on the same hospital?

Mr. PAGE. He would have a claim on the hospital that he came from—that the mill had a contract with that he came from. For instance, if we work a man up at our mill and he had a paid hospital ticket, and he came down here to Seattle and got hurt, he could go to the Kent hospital, Mr. Taylor's hospital.

Acting Chairman COMMONS. I don't see how that has any effect on what you call honoring the ticket. Suppose that the man has left one camp and has come to your camp. He has a hospital ticket which entitled him to service at the camp which he left. An accident occurs to him at your camp. Do you say the hospital will honor that ticket?

Mr. PAGE. No, no; the hospital he comes from. We don't charge that man anything when he comes with a hospital ticket. He is not under our contract at all. He is still under the contract of the other man.

Acting Chairman COMMONS. You mean you don't charge him?

Mr. PAGE. We don't charge him.

Acting Chairman COMMONS. You take charge of this ticket?

Mr. PAGE. His hospital ticket; he has a hospital ticket——

Acting Chairman COMMONS. His ticket is good with you?

Mr. PAGE. No; he is entitled to the hospital service at the hospital where he paid.

Acting Chairman COMMONS. Then his ticket would not be of much value to him; he didn't need to keep it.

Mr. PAGE. Why not?

Acting Chairman COMMONS. Because he would have to go to that other camp that he had left to get hospital treatment.

Mr. PAGE. No. He would have to go back to their hospital. Their hospital might be nearer our operations than our hospital would be.

Acting Chairman COMMONS. How far from your camp is your hospital?

Mr. PAGE. It is 45 miles, I think, Kent is, from Eagle Gorge.

Acting Chairman COMMONS. So that in any case the man has to go some distance for hospital service?

Mr. PAGE. That is true of most of the camps.

Acting Chairman COMMONS. For hospital treatment?

Mr. PAGE. It is true of the camps. Of course, these hospitals right immediately adjoining—there are mills right here near the city.

·Acting Chairman COMMONS. In the case of a mill outside of Seattle in·other places the hospitals are near by also, are they?

Mr. PAGE. Where there is a town or city there is a hospital. 'We had a hospital at Buckley.

Acting Chairman COMMONS. Would you think that any measures of a· national character regulating unemployment might ·be adopted? Is there a' large immigration into this State from other States regarding the labor ·market here that could be remedied in some way?

Mr. PAGE. I think that is the whole trouble. Now, let·me illustrate: Now, here in the last 10 years we have had virtually all of the Alaska business that has developed. That has taken hundreds and thousands of men from the employed and unemployed; nobody knows where they came from; and we have had the automobile business that has come in in the last 10 years, and the ramifications of that business relative to labor are something that· nobody knows where they do extend. That has taken hundreds and hundreds of thousands of men. The same is true with the motorcycle business;.that put thousands of men into employment that were not in that employment 10 years ago. And, then, another thing is the moving pictures. The development· of that has taken thousands and thousands of men. But the trades have not absorbed this surplus of men that are in the country. I believe the reason that you have not is because you have in the eastern ports a constant stream of men·coming in here, and as soon as we make the job for the sixteenth man here comes the seventeenth. I think that if we could pass an immigration law that would not allow anybody to come into this country unless he came in to go on· a farm— if that were done, I think that would relieve the·situation to a great extent.

Acting Chairman COMMONS. So far as you know, does the State of Washington and the vicinity—is that true of the Pacific coast also?

Mr. PAGE. Oh, I don't think so. I think that condition is general.

Acting Chairman COMMONS. General throughout the country?

Mr. PAGE. I think so.

Acting Chairman COMMONS. Mr. Thompson, do you have·any other questions?

Mr. THOMPSON. Yes. ˙ ˙

Mr. Page, I understand the purpose of this commission is we want to get at such facts as you may have as bear on the industrial situation,· and then we want to get your views as to remedies that might be applied.! Now, in regard to the hospital service for which you charge a dollar a month, some questions have been asked you with reference to the amount or the proposition as to the surplus funds that have accumulated in other cases where hospital and medical service have been given where even less amounts have been charged. Do you know the facts under which these other funds are collected and the methods and ways in which they are paid out?

Mr. PAGE. No; I don't. I don't know anything about those hospitals.

Mr. THOMPSON. Now, you are a business man and you are· acquainted, of course, with the business law that you can repeat an operation, if you·have to repeat it hundreds and thousands of times, cheaper than you can perform a new operation each time. Isn't that correct?

Mr. PAGE. Yes, sir.

Mr. THOMPSON. It is probably, or it is as a matter of fact, we all 'know under that system of production that the National Biscuit Co., for instance, taking that as an illustration, is able to produce 'a package of biscuit· for 5 cents that any small manufacturer producing in very small amounts would be unable to place on the market?

Mr. PAGE. Yes, sir.

Mr. THOMPSON. Isn't that correct?

Mr. PAGE. That is correct.

Mr. THOMPSON. Now, might it be true that the same law of business, with the division of the overhead expenses into a very large amount of business, might be accountable for the handling of the hospital service and medical· attention?

Mr. PAGE. I don't think there is any question but what that is the fact.

Mr. THOMPSON. At least that law might apply there.

Mr. PAGE. It might apply there, probably does.

Mr. THOMPSON. You are not acquainted with the facts?

. · Mr. PAGE. Probably does.

Mr. THOMPSON. Now, in regard to the hospital and medical service which is supplied in the lumber camps here, how near are these camps 'together, how large are they, and what is the method of furnishing the service to the men?

Mr. PAGE. Well, I think the universal charge in the logging camps is the same charge of a dollar; I don't think any charge any more or any charge any less. The hospitals are private institutions. I don't know of any hospital that is run by any logging camp or by any mill. I think they all have the same methods.

Mr. THOMPSON. There seems to be, Mr. Page, a good deal of feeling about the hospital proposition. Do you think it would be possible that the various mills might join together and form an association by which this service could be rendered perhaps just as effectively, perhaps even more effectively, and serve for a less sum to the men? Do you think anything could be worked out of that kind that might help?

Mr. PAGE. Yes; I think perhaps something could be done.

Mr. THOMPSON. Now, in regard to the hospital ticket, what time does that run for—30 days from date of issue?

Mr. PAGE. Thirty days.

Mr. THOMPSON. Of the current month?

Mr. PAGE. Thirty days, the current month.

Mr. THOMPSON. You spoke of having the items that enter in the cost of producing a thousand feet of lumber.

Mr. PAGE. Yes, sir.

Mr. THOMPSON. Could you give those to the commission?

Mr. PAGE. Yes.

Mr. THOMPSON. Would you be willing to?

Mr. PAGE. Yes, sir. This is worked out on 10,000,000 feet of lumber, taken on the selling price of 10,000,000 feet of lumber. The fire insurance was nine-tenths of 1 per cent. Taxes, 1.4 per cent. Interest—that is, interest on timber contracts—4.3 per cent. General expense, 11.3 per cent. That general expense includes selling expense and new construction, oil, and belts, and things of that kind. Stumpage, 25 per cent. Labor, 55.3 per cent. That makes up the 100 per cent.

Mr. THOMPSON. I believe you had something to say as to how these figures were made up and what period of time they covered.

Mr. PAGE. They are made up from the operations that cover 10,000,000 feet, six months.

Mr. THOMPSON. That is, of your mill?

Mr. PAGE. That is, of our mill; yes, sir; the last six months of our operation.

Mr. THOMPSON. Would that be generally true of other producers of timber?

Mr. PAGE. It would with like mills. We haven't got a finishing mill; we don't finish the lumber. We try to get our lumber on the car as near the log as possible.

Mr. THOMPSON. Are such figures as yours kept by other mills?

Mr. PAGE. Yes, sir.

Mr. THOMPSON. Do you suppose the commission could ascertain the general cost in that way?

Mr. PAGE. If you could get this cost—this is a general example of a mill which is not a finishing mill. You probably can get the cost from complete finishing mills where they finish everything.

But the relative charge cost between a rough mill and a finishing mill—the change would only be in the labor, the amount that labor got out of it.

Commissioner GARRETSON. The proportion of the labor cost would be much higher in the finishing mill?

Mr. PAGE. Yes, sir; naturally.

Mr. THOMPSON. Referring to the hospital proposition again, do you know whether the section hands on the railroad receive hospital services or not?

Mr. PAGE. Oh, yes; they all get the same services of our men.

Mr. THOMPSON. I believe you answered that the company made no profit in the hospital services?

Mr. PAGE. No, sir; we make no profit.

Mr. THOMPSON. You pay it all over to the doctors?

Mr. PAGE. Nobody makes any profit on the hospital services.

Mr. THOMPSON. Is the compensation which is to be paid under the act in existence in this State in case of accident, in any way superseded or affected by the hospital services?

Mr. PAGE. No, sir; that has nothing to do with it at all.

Mr. THOMPSON. Is there any waiting period under your compensation act before compensation begins?

Mr. PAGE. No, sir.

Mr. THOMPSON. Do you know what is the case in other States?

Mr. PAGE. Yes, sir; there is a waiting period in various compensation acts. Mr. Daggett, who is going to appear here later, will give you all of that.

Mr. THOMPSON. Is Howard Taylor, speaker of the house, a partner of yours in business?

Mr. PAGE. Yes, sir.

Mr. THOMPSON. Was he at the time that this insurance act was passed?

Mr. PAGE. Yes, sir.

Mr. THOMPSON. Did he take any part in the fight being made on the first aid?

Mr. PAGE. Yes, sir.

Mr. THOMPSON. Was it an open fight?

Mr. PAGE. Yes, sir; an open fight. He was opposed to it, opposed to first aid, and I was in favor of it. There was dissension in the family.

Commissioner GARRETSON. A house divided against itself?

Mr. PAGE. A house divided.

Mr. THOMPSON. Did his vote have anything to do with defeating a reconsideration?

Mr. PAGE. Did what?

Mr. THOMPSON. Do you know what action he took during that time?

Mr. PAGE. Yes; the first aid was defeated.

Mr. THOMPSON. Well, did he defeat it on a reconsideration vote?

Mr. PAGE. Now, let's see how that did come. No, sir; I think he made an argument against it. In fact, I know he did, but just exactly how it was defeated I don't know.

Mr. THOMPSON. That is all, Mr. Chairman.

Commissioner GARRETSON. Just one more question, Mr. Page, on the hypothetical question that was put to you there. In regard to the distribution of the overhead charges—hospital charge against a large number of men—it probably amounts to cheapening in per capita instances.

Mr. PAGE. Yes, sir.

Commissioner GARRETSON. In the event an institution employing only 150 men—I am putting it near your own force——

Mr. PAGE. Yes, sir.

Commissioner GARRETSON. Suppose in a community where there were three hospitals and each one competed to perform the services and they were all notified of the small amount that was referred to here, 50 cents or 25 cents, and each of the three wanted the business, and would even pay a bonus to get it, wouldn't it be proof there was money in it, even at that figure?

Mr. PAGE. I think it would prove there was money in it, certainly.

Commissioner GARRETSON. Even at the lower rate?

Mr. PAGE. Yes, sir.

Commissioner GARRETSON. And without the large number to operate on?

Mr. PAGE. Yes, sir.

Commissioner LENNON. Mr. Page, I want to ask one question, I don't know whether I understood you correctly or not. Did you say out of 19 years in the lumber business you had only been able to operate 10 years?

Mr. PAGE. Yes, sir.

Commissioner LENNON. And the other nine years shut down?

Mr. PAGE. Yes, sir; shut down.

Commissioner LENNON. Well, if that is the case generally in the lumber business, isn't that the cause, or one of the great causes, in making men hobos, the falling off in their work and going from one place to another?

Mr. PAGE. No, sir; that is not general in the lumber business. The mills have worked here—most of the mills have worked here all the time. Some of the mills have closed down. Some of the mills thought that was the proper way to do when lumber was very low. We did, but we have changed our mind; we are going to run continuously now.

Commissioner LENNON. I think if you will run continuously 10 years you will find the stability of your force will be materially improved.

Mr. PAGE. Well, possibly.

Commissioner LENNON. That is all.

Acting Chairman COMMONS. You heard the testimony of others that has been given here. Is there anything that you care to say about any of their statements?

Mr. PAGE. Well, there is one thing I would like to say that I think there was an injustice, and I would like to correct it, and that is the letting out of Jack

Wallace on the industrial insurance board and the appointment of Clarence Parker. I think they called him.the weak member or weak brother. I served with Mr. Parker on the commission for months and months, and I didn't see he was a weak brother. There were three men that represented labor that were fitted to fill that position, who were interested in the bill and knew all about the bill. They were Jack Wallace and Clarence Parker and Mr. Henrietta. When Wallace was let out I think the governor used good judgment when he went and got.another of those men who was familiar with the bill and helped draft the bill and appointed him in Wallace's place, and I don't think Parker is the weak member. ·

. Commissioner O'CONNELL. Have you some reference to the statement made by Dr. McMahon the other day?

Mr. PAGE. Yes, sir.

Commissioner ·O'CONNELL. That is what was referred to in the weak-member part of the subject? · ,

Mr. PAGE. Yes, sir.

Mr. O'CONNELL. The change of officials in that department?

Mr. PAGE. Yes, sir.

Commissioner O'CONNELL. But there are some personal differences there between the doctor——

Mr. PAGE. Oh, I don't know anything about that; that is not testimony. I don't want to go into that thing at all. I don't know anything about that.

Commissioner O'CONNELL. Just a minute,· Mr. Page; don't get impatient.

Mr. PAGE. I am not impatient.

Commissioner O'CONNELL. Well, you are not very calm.

Mr. PAGE. All right; I will calm myself, then.

Commissioner O'CONNELL. I am not trying to inquire into any personal matters. If I ask·you a question that does not appeal to you, you simply don't need to answer.

. Mr. PAGE. Yes.

. Commissioner O'CONNELL. No differences on that at all. I wanted to get at what was meant by this testimony the other day if you know.

Mr. PAGE. I.don't know. I don't know why you bring out such testimony. It seemed to me it was malicious; that is all. I don't know whether there is any foundation for it or any reason.

Commissioner O'CONNELL. You think it is malicious. Now, what is the reason for its maliciousness?

Mr. PAGE. I don't know anything about the maliciousness, but when a man calls another man a liar I think he is doing it for maliciousness; I don't think Mr. Parker—— · ,

Commissioner GARRETSON. You mean unless he is a liar?

Mr. PAGE. I don't believe in Mr. Parker being called a weak member. He is not a weak member.

Commissioner GARRETSON. Bear in mind that statement was not made in response to any inquiry.

Mr. PAGE. I don't know why it was made, but the statement was made.

Acting Chairman COMMONS. Is there any other statement, Mr. Page, that you think should be made or anything that should be corrected?

Mr. PAGE. I don't know that I have given you anything of value. If there is anything I can——

Acting Chairman COMMONS. Well, we are very much obliged.

Mr. PAGE. All right, sir.

. Acting Chairman COMMONS. Mr. Thompson, call the next witness.

Mr. THOMPSON. Mr. Cooney.

TESTIMONY OF MR. NEIL. COONEY.

Mr. THOMPSON. Mr. Cooney, will you give us your name, please?

·   Mr. COONEY. Neil Cooney.

Mr. THOMPSON. And your business address?

Mr. COONEY. Cosmopolis, Wash.

Mr. THOMPSON. And your business, Mr. Cooney?

,   Mr. COONEY. Manager of the Grays Harbor Commercial Co., lumber business, logging, and so on.   . .

. Mr. THOMPSON. In what kind of business is this company engaged, Mr. Cooney?

Mr. COONEY. Principally lumber and logging.

Mr. THOMPSON. Principally what? I didn't hear.
Mr. COONEY. Principally lumber and logging.
Mr. THOMPSON. Lumber and logging?
Mr. COONEY. Yes.
Mr. THOMPSON. Well, now, that is about the same work that Mr. Page's company is engaged in?
Mr. COONEY. No; we——
Mr. THOMPSON. Well, give us a little more in detail; a brief statement of what you mean by lumber and what you mean by logging.
Mr. COONEY. Logging would be the same; sawmill would be the same. We also operate a box factory, tank factory, pump factory, and make pumps and go into several details with the lumber.
Mr. THOMPSON. Well, is it all connected with the lumber business?
Mr. COONEY. Well, hardly. We do specialty work more than any other mill probably on this coast; we get out more detailed stock than any other mill on the coast.
Mr. THOMPSON. You will have to speak a little louder, Mr. Cooney, because I don't think the commission can hear you. How long has your company been engaged in that work at Grays Harbor?
Mr. COONEY. Over 25 years.
Mr. THOMPSON. How long have you been connected with the company, Mr. Cooney?
Mr. COONEY. About 25 years.
Mr. THOMPSON. You have been superintendent a good many years?
Mr. COONEY. Well, I was foreman and superintendent; I am now manager.
Mr. THOMPSON. Now manager. Well, you have been manager a good many years?
Mr. COONEY. Well, four years I have been the active, the real manager. Before that I was assistant manager for about four years; prior to that I was superintendent.
Mr. THOMPSON. In other words, you are thoroughly acquainted with the business of the company?
Mr. COONEY. Yes, sir.
Mr. THOMPSON. About how many men do you employ in all your work there?
Mr. COONEY. Over 700 at the present time; about 600 men in the mill in the lumber business, and 100 in the camps.
Mr. THOMPSON. Is that the normal amount, or is that more or less?
Mr. COONEY. That is probably a little more at this time. We operate the year around, run steady, and we operate every working day in the year—that is, practically speaking—and employ from four to eight hundred men.
Commissioner LENNON. Operate Sundays?
Mr. COONEY. I say, practically speaking.
Mr. THOMPSON. You don't operate Sundays?
Mr. COONEY. No, sir.
Mr. THOMPSON. Now, with regard to the wages that you pay at your plant, what do you pay? What is the lowest wage you pay for ordinary labor per day?
Mr. COONEY. Twenty-six dollars a month and board—that is, $1 a day and board for a 10-hour day.
Mr. THOMPSON. One dollar a day and board?
Mr. COONEY. At the present time.
Mr. THOMPSON. Yes. What does your board consist of?
Mr. COONEY. Well, we get a boarding house that furnishes the regular board.
Mr. THOMPSON. Well, in the first place, it is three meals a day, I take it?
Mr. COONEY. Yes. sir.
Mr. THOMPSON. And what do you furnish them for meals; do you know?
Mr. COONEY. Why, no; I can't go into that detail, but I, as manager, don't get a complaint on the board probably once in two months.
Mr. THOMPSON. Would all complaints on the board come to you? You are a pretty busy man, aren't you, as manager of this big plant?
Mr. COONEY. Well, I grew up with the men and the foremen and complaints would come to me right quick.
Mr. THOMPSON. Now, to what number of the help does this $26 a month and board apply, of the four to eight hundred that you have?
Mr. COONEY. I have got the figures [producing papers]. On the last day of June we employed 675 men in the manufacture of lumber, and 223 were getting $26.

Mr. Thompson. What was the scale of wages paid to the next highest class of help?

Mr. Cooney. Thirty dollars.

Mr. Thompson. What is that?

Mr. Cooney. Thirty dollars.

Mr. Thompson. Thirty dollars a month?

Mr. Cooney. Yes, sir.

Mr. Thompson. And board?

Mr. Cooney. Yes, sir.

Mr. Thompson. Now, this board includes lodging, doesn't it?

Mr. Cooney. No, sir.

Mr. Thompson. It does not?

Mr. Cooney. No, sir.

Mr. Thompson. Just the meals?

Mr. Cooney. Just the meals.

Mr. Thompson. How many do you have of those?

Mr. Cooney. Seventy.

Mr. Thompson. Seventy. What is the next highest class of help?

Mr. Cooney. Thirty-five dollars.

Mr. Thompson. That you are paying.

Mr. Cooney. Thirty-five dollars.

Mr. Thompson. And board?

Mr. Cooney. Yes.

Mr. Thompson. How many have you of those?

Mr. Cooney. Sixty-four.

Mr. Thompson. What is the next highest class of help you have?

Mr. Cooney. Forty dollars.

Mr. Thompson. How many have you of those?

Mr. Cooney. Seventeen.

Mr. Thompson. Go on through the scale, Mr. Cooney, will you please?

Mr. Cooney. Ten, $45; nine, $50; fourteen, $55; eight, $60; one, $70; two, $80, making a total of 493. Now, we have got 183 that board themselves; they were hired for so much per day, and we pay them so much per day and they board themselves.

Mr. Thompson. How much do you pay them additional where they board themselves a month?

Mr. Cooney. We hire them for so much per day.

Mr. Thompson. Well, I mean how much do you calculate in your own business affairs that the man should get who boards himself?

Mr. Cooney. Our board costs us about 50 cents a day. We allow $15 for any of those men that are going to board themselves.

Mr. Thompson. Did you hear the testimony of Mr. Brown here?

Mr. Cooney. Yes, sir.

Mr. Thompson. Does his testimony with regard to $10 a month being allowed to the men, refer to your mill?

Mr. Cooney. That is incorrect. Mr. Brown is basing that testimony on 10 years ago. He worked for us at one time.

Mr. Thompson. But that is not true to-day, in your opinion?

Mr. Cooney. No, sir; I know it is not true.

Mr. Thompson. How do the men live, what kind of houses do they have, and where do they get them from? You say you don't lodge them.

Mr. Cooney. No; there are lodging houses—men that go into that business, that follow that business.

Mr. Thompson. Yes. Well, what kind of houses do they have; do you know?

Mr. Cooney. Yes, sir; they usually room in lodging houses, two-story.

Mr. Thompson. Yes.

Mr. Cooney. That will room from 20 to 40 men.

Mr. Thompson. Well, how are the men? Does each man have an individual room at night?

Mr. Cooney. In some cases.

Mr. Thompson. I mean as a rule.

Mr. Cooney. No.

Mr. Thompson. Of course, I presume in some cases they do.

Mr. Cooney. I should say that as a class it would be about two men to a room.

Mr. Thompson. About two men to a room? What kind of beds do they have?

Mr. COONEY. I think fair beds. ·

Mr. THOMPSON. Well, I mean—that is not very descriptive, Mr. Cooney.

Mr. COONEY. Well, I don't know.

Mr. THOMPSON. You don't know?

Mr. COONEY. No.

Mr. THOMPSON. Do you know how many? What is the basis of your in-formation that they only sleep two men in a room?

Mr. COONEY. From the fact that there is two or three of the lodging houses that we own.

Mr. THOMPSON. I see.

Mr. COONEY. And I would know from that.

Mr. THOMPSON. Well, now take the lodging houses that you own. Take one of them, for instance. Do you have names for them? · ·

Mr. COONEY. We own the building and rent it.

Mr. THOMPSON. Oh, you own the building and rent it. Then, you do not operate the house?

Mr. COONEY. None at all.

Mr. THOMPSON. And therefore your owning of the building would not help you—would not give you any information as to how many men sleep in a room, would it?

Mr. COONEY. No.

Mr. THOMPSON. Well, what other sources of information have you that only two men sleep in a room?

Mr. COONEY. Not any other.

Mr. THOMPSON. Not any other?

Mr. COONEY. No.

Mr. THOMPSON. So you really have no source of information outside of that?

Mr. COONEY. Well, I have got that source of them buildings that we own. ·

Mr. THOMPSON. But you say that you don't run them and you don't know.

Mr. COONEY. Well, I know about the rooms that they would not put any more than two men in a room.

Mr. THOMPSON. Well, how large are the rooms?

Mr. COONEY. Well, the rooms, I should judge, would be about 10 by 12, probably.

Mr. THOMPSON. Ten by twelve?

Mr. COONEY. Then there is many of the families in town takes roomers. ·

Mr. THOMPSON. Takes roomers. What rent do these men pay to the land-lords of those houses that your company owns?·

Mr. COONEY. I don't know that.

Mr. THOMPSON. You don't know what they have to pay for their rooms?

Mr. COONEY. No; I know about the rent of rooms—that is, from $3 to $6 a month.

Mr. THOMPSON. To the men?

Mr. COONEY. Yes, sir; 50 or 75 cents a week would be the most per man, or a dollar and a half for the room.

Mr. THOMPSON. Are many of the men that work for your firm married? ·

Mr. COONEY. We have got about a hundred men that is married or sons of married people that live at their home.

Mr. THOMPSON. Will you let me have that list or pay roll, Mr. Cooney? · ·

Mr. COONEY. Yes.

Mr. THOMPSON. This one here [indicating].

Mr. COONEY. I have got three different ones.

Mr. THOMPSON. I want the one you read these people off from—the number of people employed and the different rates of wages.

Mr. COONEY. Yes, sir [handing papers to Mr. Thompson].

Mr. THOMPSON. This is not very decipherable to me, Mr. Cooney, and I won't take the time. But, as I understood the figures that you gave here and read off the pay roll, and which our reporter has, the vast—the larger—propor-tion of your men work for $35 a month and under?

Mr. COONEY. You better give me that sheet and I will return it to you. [Ex-amining paper referred to.] Less than $35, yes; the larger proportion. ·

Mr. THOMPSON. The larger proportion?

Mr. COONEY. Yes.

Mr. THOMPSON. I probably haven't got the figures correctly, but probably three-quarters of them work for $40 a month and under.

Mr. COONEY. Yes; probably there would be that proportion. · ·

Mr. THOMPSON. Now, I would like to ask you, Mr. Cooney, whether—this is no criticism of your company at all, I simply want to get the facts, that is all.

Mr. COONEY. I want you to have them.

·Mr. THOMPSON. Whether under these conditions you think that men could live the family life, could have wives and children, at that rate of pay?

·Mr. COONEY. No, sir.

Mr. THOMPSON. In justice to you, I want to ask you this further question in·that connection, whether or not your company is making money in this business or not?

Mr. COONEY. No, sir.

Mr. THOMPSON. What was the result of that last month's business, if you know?

Mr. COONEY. The result of last month's business, which includes our stores and different things, was a loss of $515. We sold $104,000 worth of lumber.

Mr. THOMPSON.· Well, what was that, a normal amount of business for the month or not?·

Mr. COONEY. No; that was over normal.

Mr. THOMPSON. What?

Mr. COONEY. Over normal. Our average business would be about $90,000.

Mr. THOMPSON. You sold more and still you sold at a loss?

Mr. COONEY. Yes.

Mr. THOMPSON. Now, Mr. Cooney, I would like you to tell the commission why it is that if the lumbering industry of this State is to be judged by what your company does, why it is that this big industry—what has been stated to be the most prominent industry on this coast—isn't able to support its workers in an American way, provide for a man and wife and children. What is the reason for that?

Mr. COONEY. I don't know. We manufacture in the United States about 40,000,000,000 feet of lumber yearly.

Mr. THOMPSON. Don't you think that, say, like on the Pacific coast here, that is looked upon as being a great part of the country, with the principal industry not being able to keep the men the way men believe they ought to live, is a great cause of industrial unrest, bound to be?

Mr. COONEY. Yes, sir. The employers and the men have got to get together closer. Every employee should know the condition of his employer's business.

Mr. THOMPSON. My questions, Mr. Cooney, and I want all witnesses to understand the same, are not aimed to criticise you or to criticise your company. I want to simply get, as I told Mr. Thompson, who was on the stand yesterday, the facts that he has and his views.

Mr. COONEY. Put your question again, will you, please.

Mr. THOMPSON. Whether or not that fact in itself, no matter who is to blame for it, no matter if nobody is personally·to blame for it, the question of the fact that men can not live in an American manner—isn't that bound to cause a great deal of unrest?

Mr. COONEY. In our plant, Mr. Thompson, we work more laborers or low-grade help than any other concern on the Pacific coast.. Our company are large timber holders, and built the plant to utilize everything that is in the tree. We put in a large box factory. About half of our output goes into boxes, We are working at the present time 167 men in the box factory. We are working up a very low-grade stock that is usually burned up in other mills, or a lot of it, and making a cannery box which we have to sell at competing prices—we are a long distance from the market—for these boxes, and transportation is high. ·

Mr. THOMPSON. I understand, Mr. Cooney, that there are probably very urgent business reasons from a commercial standpoint why you probably have to make a low rate on the product which you sell. I am not entering into that question now. I am not criticizing your company nor you, but I just want your view of an industry where human beings are employed at a rate of wage which won't permit them to live according to the way a man must naturally feel he wants to live. What remedy would you suggest for that?

Mr. COONEY. Well, publicity would help.

Mr. THOMPSON. What?

Mr. COONEY. Well, publicity would help it.

Mr. THOMPSON. You think some regulation of competition might help?

Mr. COONEY. Well, I say if the men understood the exact conditions—just what our company is doing, what every company was earning, they would give more efficient help, would be more contented, would hold their jobs better, and would save their money.

Mr. THOMPSON. Well, if the condition of business was such, if competition caused you to make such low prices as you have stated, which does not permit you, no matter how much you might want to, still it does not permit you to pay a living wage as we understand it, how would the publicity of that fact help the men in being contented?

Mr. COONEY. The men are of the opinion that the employers are getting wealthy, that they are making a lot of money off of their earnings.

Mr. THOMPSON. Yes; but from my standpoint I am leaving that question out, of whether people make wealth or not. What I am assuming is that the wage you pay is the wage that competition forces you to pay, and I am simply asking you the question if that is the wage which the industry will pay—discontent is normal and natural—and what remedies would you have for it?

Mr. COONEY. I don't think there is any. Now, I might explain in regard to our business—that these dollar-a-day men, we develop them all we possibly can. We never go out for high-skilled help for our skilled help. We take them all from the ranks; we take these men if they show an inclination to work—if they are willing to work, do a fair day's work—we will advance them as fast as we possibly can.

Mr. THOMPSON. But your pay roll there, Mr. Cooney, doesn't show many high-paid men?

Mr. COONEY. Well, you haven't seen it all. This whole pay roll averages $2.40 a day.

Mr. THOMPSON. Well, I don't know; I doubt that it would show those figures.

Mr. COONEY. I will give you the pay roll to figure.

Mr. THOMPSON. I would like to have the pay roll turned in to the commission.

(See Cooney Exhibit No. 1.)

Mr. THOMPSON. What view do you take, Mr. Cooney, of the question of industrial unrest?

Mr. COONEY. I know it exists.

Mr. THOMPSON. Well, what is its cause and what suggestions have you to make with regard to it?

Mr. COONEY. Well, that one thing, publicity, would do more than anything else that I know of.

Mr. THOMPSON. Now, Mr. Cooney, have you ever had any strikes at your plants?

Mr. COONEY. Only in the shingle mill.

Mr. THOMPSON. In the shingle mill?

Mr. COONEY. Yes; we have had some small strikes in the shingle mill.

Mr. THOMPSON. Are the men in your shingle mill organized?

Mr. COONEY. I have an idea there are some union men there.

Mr. THOMPSON. What was the cause of the strike?

Mr. COONEY. More wages.

Mr. THOMPSON. When was it and how was it terminated?

Mr. COONEY. More wages—an increase of wages.

Mr. THOMPSON. What were the wages they got?

Mr. COONEY. Well, we haven't had a strike for five or six years, and I don't remember the details of it.

Mr. THOMPSON. You don't remember the details?

Mr. COONEY. No; but in all instances——

Mr. THOMPSON. Were the men organized at that time, if you know?

Mr. COONEY. I don't think so. We never aimed to have them organized. We have opposed it.

Mr. THOMPSON. Did you hear the testimony of Mr. Brown?

Mr. COONEY. Yes, sir.

Mr. THOMPSON. What have you to add to what he said?

Mr. COONEY. In what regard?

Mr. THOMPSON. Well, in regard to strikes?

Mr. COONEY. Well, he said so much that I don't remember. Mr. Brown worked for us one time, and I think he pulled off one of the strikes, but I didn't have any difficulty in settling with them.

Mr. THOMPSON. Well, was that the last strike?

Mr. COONEY. Oh, no; that must be 15 or 18 years ago.

Mr. THOMPSON. Well, how about the last strike? Who led that, do you know?

Mr. COONEY. I don't know.

Mr. THOMPSON. Do you know whether he had anything to do with it or not?

Mr. COONEY. I don't think so. As the head of the organization he would, probably:

Mr. THOMPSON. Well, he stated that the shingle weavers, as I understood it, were fairly well organized. You don't know about that?

Mr. COONEY. Yes; I know they are.

Mr. THOMPSON. They are a skilled class of help?

Mr. COONEY. Yes.

Mr. THOMPSON. But you don't know about the organization in your company?

Mr. COONEY. Well, I don't think they are organized, although I believe we have got some that are union men. My candid opinion is that the union has let us go; they are willing that union men shall work there with the non-union men.

Mr. THOMPSON. What wages do you pay the shingle weavers?

Mr. COONEY. We pay nearly the union scale, I think.

Mr. THOMPSON. What do you mean by nearly, Mr. Cooney?

Mr. COONEY. Well, for instance, 9 cents for packing and 16 cents for sawing.

Mr. THOMPSON. What is the union scale?

Mr. COONEY. I believe that is the union scale.

Mr. THOMPSON. Then you pay the union scale?

Mr. COONEY. Yes. I am not sure, but it is very close to the union scale.

Mr. THOMPSON. It is the piece-rate system?

Mr. COONEY. That is on the sawing and packing.

Mr. THOMPSON. Is there anything further you would like to say to this commission as to how the industrial unrest might be helped?

Mr. COONEY. I don't know.

Mr. THOMPSON. What wages do you pay in your logging camps?

Mr. COONEY. I can give you a list of what each position gets, as it is termed in a logging camp.

Mr. THOMPSON. Well, you might do that.

Mr. COONEY. Blacksmith, $3.75; helper, 2.75; buckers, $3.25; wood buckers, $2.50; chunk buckers, $2.75; chaser, for yarder, $3.25; for a hook-on, $2.75; choker men, $3.25; head cook, $90 and board; bull cook, $40 and board; flunkey, $35 and board; common labor, $2.50; engineer, chief, $3.75; swing donkey, $3.25; yarder, $3.50; roader, $3.25; hook tender, $6; knotters, $2.75; pump men, $3; rigging slinger, $3.75; swamper, $2.75; skidders, head skidder, $5.25; skid roadmen, $2.50; superintendent, $200 a month and board; timekeeper, $80 a month and board; faller—head faller $3.50; second faller, $3.25; filer, $3.75; flagman, $2.75; fireman, $2.50, and engineer, skid road, $2.75.

Mr. THOMPSON. With reference to the kind of houses that the men live in that are in the logging camps?

Mr. COONEY. They have the regular kind of bunk houses. I think they are a little above the average.

Mr. THOMPSON. You say they have the regular kind of bunk houses. Do you mean they have a house with bunks around the walls; two tiers of bunks?

Mr. COONEY. No, sir; one tier. They are separate bunks.

Mr. THOMPSON. I mean, is one bunk above the other?

Mr. COONEY. No, sir.

Mr. THOMPSON. Just one tier around the room?

Mr. COONEY. Just one tier around the room, and they are not connected; they are made separate.

Mr. THOMPSON. Separate beds. What kind of bedding do you furnish?

Mr. COONEY. We just furnish a mattress.

Mr. THOMPSON. Who takes care of the house?

Mr. COONEY. The bull cook; his business is to have the house swept out and the fires lit when the men come in, and take care of them generally.

Mr. THOMPSON. How about drying clothes?

Mr. COONEY. They will dry their clothes around the stove.

Mr. THOMPSON. Do you think that a good feature?

Mr. COONEY. In order to get this plain, our superintendent is a practical woodsman developed from the work and has studied it all his life. He is a man of family, has his men around him, and they are men of families, and they are all crowded around together, and I tell them to build the houses to suit themselves, and I don't interfere very much. The fact is they build to suit themselves, and as far as I know the men are entirely satisfied with their conditions, food, etc.

Mr. THOMPSON. What is the attitude that the company has toward union labor?

Mr. Cooney. We don't employ union labor.

Mr. Thompson. You don't? You have discharged men because they belonged to the union?

Mr. Cooney. No, sir; not that I know of.

Mr. Thompson. But you don't object to employing them?

Mr. Cooney. No, sir; we make no difference until the trouble comes up. I am satisfied we have several union men working for us—machinists, etc.

Mr. Thompson. But if you wanted a man for a certain kind of work and there were two men to choose from you would choose the nonunion man?

Mr. Cooney. If they were both equal, I would take the nonunion man in every respect, but I would make very little difference.

Mr. Thompson. You say you never discharged a man because he belonged to the union?

Mr. Cooney. I don't remember. There may have been several in the shingle mill and in the shingle business.

Mr. Thompson. Have you any trade agreement with your men either in the shingle business or elsewhere?

Mr. Cooney. None at all.

Mr. Thompson. Have the men ever approached you to get together with you on an agreement of any kind either verbal or written?

Mr. Cooney. They have years ago from the shingle mill.

Mr. Thompson. Did your company there make any agreement?

Mr. Cooney. No, sir; we agreed to be open shop.

Mr. Thompson. The only question they asked you was whether it would be open shop or closed shop. I simply want to get your views, Mr. Cooney, and your attitude toward organized labor. That is part of the work of this commission to investigate.

Mr. Cooney. We don't think it is practical, and we don't believe we can operate our plant with organized labor, and therefore we have made up our minds not to have organized labor.

Mr. Thompson. Will you give us the reasons that caused you to come to that conclusion that you can't operate successfully with union labor?

Mr. Cooney. My personal experience comes from operating the shingle mill.

Mr. Thompson. What was that?

Mr. Cooney. We would have a continuous run of a lot of fellows raised right in town—our town has about 1,200 people—they were good men and making money; all at once they would send in petitions for an advance in wages or a union or something of the kind.

Mr. Thompson. There was more than that experience, wasn't there, that caused you to reach that conclusion?

Mr. Cooney. Yes; Grays Harbor is a very large lumber district, and we are manufacturing within a radius of 6 miles along the river from two and a half up to three million feet of lumber a day. Every year or so or every two or three years there is a breaking out among the men. They will close down the mill and blow the whistle and go in a mob and take the crews all out. They have attempted to get our crew several times, but never got them.

Mr. Thompson. If you were a workingman, what view, then, would you have on the question of organization? Would that probably change your views?

Mr. Cooney. I can take my own experience. I came to this country from Canada right off the farm 34 years ago a common laborer, built myself up to the position I have, and had no education.

Mr. Thompson. Do you think every man has the same capacity to do that and the same opportunity that you have?

Mr. Cooney. They haven't the same capacity, but they have the opportunity more and more every day.

Mr. Thompson. Of course we will all admit and all know that there are some places at the top, but looking at the industry from a standpoint of the multitude every man can't be a superintendent or manager, can he?

Mr. Cooney. No, sir; but there is room.

Mr. Thompson. You say your industry needs 600 people to work there. There will be one of those 600 manager.

Mr. Cooney. Yes, sir.

Mr. Thompson. And one assistant, and so on down the line, and there must be a great many of what is ordinarily called hewers of wood and drawers of water to carry the work out. Looking at it from the standpoint of the man who works in the ranks, would you say from their standpoint organization is a good thing or not?

Mr. COONEY. From the men that are working in the lumberyards?

Mr. THOMPSON. For the workers generally?

Mr. COONEY. If they would organize right——

Mr. THOMPSON. I just want your view, that is all.

Mr. COONEY. This handling of lumber—no man should work at it without the idea of advancement. No man doing common work around the mill or logging camp that is willing to do a fair day's work that is not picked up and advanced quickly and promptly. Therefore no man that wants to get ahead stays in that class; they are continually shifting.

Mr. THOMPSON. To test your views, Mr. Cooney, suppose every man wanted to get ahead and work, you could not supply such jobs for everybody?

Mr. COONEY. No, sir; but it continues to come up. We are always short of high-classed men, with a surplus of low class.

Mr. THOMPSON. But the proposition which confronts the average worker is that nine-tenths of the workers must be in the ranks. That is true of industry generally everywhere the world over. Now, from the standpoint of those nine-tenths in the ranks, do you think organization is a good thing for them or not?

Mr. COONEY. Under certain conditions they could be organized.

Mr. THOMPSON. Well, assuming under certain conditions it is a good thing for the mass of the workers to be organized, what would you say as to what should be the attitude of capital or employers toward the desire for organization of this mass of people; how should it be approached?

Mr. COONEY. Well, you take the average man, they can't guarantee anything to the capital. They could not guarantee they would fulfill the bill. Let me give you an instance. We have a surplus of men that work for a dollar a day. We used to use them in piling lumber in the lumber yards. In the last year we have contracted that at 22 cents a thousand. The men are making from seventy-five to eighty or a hundred dollars a month. We can't put in a dollar a day man in there and do it as cheap. Now, if those men would organize and you could get them to agree to do the work as cheaply as we are doing it now, or cheaper, we would be ahead.

Mr. THOMPSON. Did you hear the testimony of Mr. Page here this morning?

Mr. COONEY. Yes; I could not hear it very well.

Mr. THOMPSON. He said there was a surplus of unskilled labor in this market; is that true?

Mr. COONEY. Yes, sir.

Mr. THOMPSON. How is it with the skilled market?

Mr. COONEY. In our class we can't get men to fill the positions.

Mr. THOMPSON. Would you think the fact there was a surplus would have something to do with the economic conditions?

Mr. COONEY. Well, I don't know; men come out here from the East in droves to the harvest fields, and make a little money, and then come to the coast and spend it.

Mr. THOMPSON. Of course, the harvest field—that is seasonal work?

Mr. COONEY. Yes, sir.

Mr. THOMPSON. They have to come here, probably, or go some place else, probably, to seek work.

Mr. COONEY. When jobs are scarce and men plentiful the men will hold their jobs and work every day, and do probably 25 per cent more work—I am speaking about labor when men are scarce and there are plenty of jobs. Therefore in dull times take it—we will say, for instance, in times like these—if lumber would go up and the war was over and everything all right, there would be work for everybody, simply because the men wouldn't work over two or three days in the week. When times are hard and the mills shutting down the men will work every day and will save their money.

Mr. THOMPSON. In your position as manager of this mill what thought do you give to the condition of the worker, and from what angle do you approach it? Do you approach it from the standpoint that you need so many workers and it will cost you so much money?

Mr. COONEY. The men will come and work, and the first thing I would do when superintendent would be to ask him where he came from and what work he had done, get a brief history of him, and put him to work. I would watch him, and if he was doing just a fair day's work would have him in mind for the job which he was best fitted for in the plant, and whenever there was a vacancy would pick him up and put him there. We aim to follow that up now.

Mr. THOMPSON. Do you pay any of your help anywhere as low as $10 a month and board?

Mr. COONEY. Probably some boys during school vacation.· Our planer. foreman has two boys working at the factory, one about 15 years of age and the other under age. He wanted them to work, and·so he went to ·the court and got an order. I don't know what he is getting; I expect .he gets $10.. . .r ˜

Mr. THOMPSON. Are you paying any people, say, 18 years and over as low as $10?

Mr. COONEY. We seem to have 10 men working for $20 a month ahd board. ᴐ

Mr. THOMPSON. How·about $10 a month?

Mr. COONEY. I don't see any, but I have an idea there is some working right now, some·boys. They would not be boarding, though; we would probably㏄pay them $20 a month, and the boys would board at home.   .; . ꞏ i. .

Mr. THOMPSON. Do you know whether or not it is true that·in one of the lodging houses owned by your company there is as many as nine beds .in ꞏone room and five in another?

Mr. COONEY. There is one of the lodging houses that has a front room and'a big ward in the back. I presume that is so.   .. ꞏ

Mr. THOMPSON. How many stores do you·operate in Cosmopolis?

Mr. COONEY. We operate a general merchandise store and꞉a cash˙grocery ˙store, as wᵉ call it, and a toggery.

Mr. THOMPSON. What is the theory of operating several stores?

Mr. COONEY. The business moved to a street other than the one we were using, and we wanted some place where the men could get what they wanted quickly.

Mr. THOMPSON. That is all, Mr. Chairman.

Commissioner LENNON. Do you sell any liquor?

Mr. COONEY. No, sir.

Commissioner LENNON. Is your company a corporation?

Mr. COONEY. Yes, sir.·

Commissioner LENNON. How much land do you own in that section of .the country?

Mr. COONEY. Timberland?

Commissioner LENNON. Yes; that is, all kinds of land. ᴸ ꞌ ᴐ,

Mr. COONEY. We own probably four or five thousand .acres. ꞇ .

Commissioner LENNON.·˙How early a date did you begin accumulating this land—how long ago?

Mr. COONEY. Twenty-five years ago.

Commissioner LENNON. What did land cost in those ꞌdays?

Mr. COONEY. Well, now, you will have to define the land. We don't buy land, but timber.·

Commissioner LENNON. After the timber is taken off, don't you own the surface?

Mr.· COONEY. Yes, sir.

Commissioner LENNON. Then, you buy the timber and·the land?

Mr. COONEY. But when we buy the timber, we buy the timber and don't· regard the land as of any value.

Commissioner LENNON. Of being of any advantage?

Mr. COONEY. That is, practically speaking.

Commissioner LENNON. What did you pay for timber 25 years ago?

Mr. COONEY. I don't remember buying any 25.years ago. ꞌ . ᴬ ˜

Commissioner LENNON. Well, the last ꞏtime when you· did.˙ ꞇWhen did you first begin to buy?

Mr. COONEY. The big body of timber wᵉ bought ꞌwe paid about꞉$2 a thousand for the stumpage.

Commissioner LENNON. How many thousand would there be on the acre?

Mr. COONEY. Well, a section, 640 acres, will have about 35,000,000.   ꞏꞏ ꞏ.ꞏ

Commissioner LENNON. Are there any opportunities now of that kind in that section of the country for the poor man?

Mr. COONEY. No, sir; not in that section. There is, though, in Oregon.·   : ꞏ

Commissioner LENNON. Are they near to transportation and the facilities for manufacture .as it is at Grays Harbor?

Mr. COONEY. No, sir.

Commissioner LENNON. Well, I have asked these questions to see how it was that you hád reached the conclusion that the man of to-day has·as good opportunity as the man when you started.

Mr. COONEY. Well, in other concerns. If he goes to a mill and works he·can work up to any position.

Commissioner LENNON. You think he could do that now?

{ Mr. Cooney. I know it.

Commissioner Lennon. Then, you don't know corporate power if you think so, because you could not do it.

Mr. Cooney. You could in the lumber and logging business; that is all I know.

Commissioner Lennon. If there is anywhere a business that is handled by corporations where the opportunity of the workingman is as great as it was under individual employment, I am going to study that industry very carefully and see if I can't recommend it to others. I know of nothing of the kind. If the lumber industry is an exception to the rule that it shuts off opportunities, I didn't know it.

Mr. Cooney. On the contrary, there is the finest chance in the country for a young man to come here and develop; I don't know of a concern on the coast where there is a better opportunity than with the Grays Harbor Commercial Co.

Commissioner Lennon. Do you believe that an industry that pays less than a living wage has a right to exist?

Mr. Cooney. I don't know; that is, less than a living wage, you would have to define that.

Commissioner Lennon. I mean by, living wage that kind of wage that will enable a man to live decently, to raise a family, to give them a proper education and have a dollar to spare for the emergencies of old age or sickness.

Mr. Cooney. Not if the man wants to get ahead. If the man wants to help himself he should have the opportunity.

Commissioner Lennon. That is, you believe—then would you reply that the business should not exist that pays less than a living wage?

Mr. Cooney. No, sir; that business has got a perfect right to live.

Commissioner Lennon. It has?

Mr. Cooney. That is, if the men refuse to help themselves.

Commissioner Lennon. What would become of society if all businesses paid less than a living wage, where would the people be supported from?

Mr. Cooney. Well, I can't answer that question.

Commissioner Lennon. Suppose there was in this city a business that paid less than a living wage that employed a thousand people. Those people have to live, and consequently they must live off of the production of other industries, isn't that so?

Mr. Cooney. Well, a living wage, what do you mean by that? We will take a man that goes down to us and goes to work for a dollar day, he can accumulate ten to twelve dollars a month.

Commissioner Lennon. He can?

Mr. Cooney. Yes; fifteen to twenty dollars a month.

Commissioner Lennon. And live as a man ought to live?

Mr. Cooney. Well, he will get good board, just as good board as he wants.

Commissioner Lennon. That is, he will have the opportunity to eat and something to cover his nakedness.

Mr. Cooney. That is it. And he will have the money, and if he wants to go ahead he will not be working in that job two weeks.

Commissioner Lennon. That is all I desire to ask.

Acting Chairman Commons. Any questions, Mr. O'Connell?

Commissioner O'Connell. No.

Acting Chairman Commons. Mr. Garretson?

Commissioner Garretson. Yes. You stated a moment ago, Mr. Cooney, you knew of no better opportunity for men to get forward than in your organization, your company.

Mr. Cooney. Well, I know that; I know he can get ahead there.

Commissioner Garretson. If there is so great an opportunity to get ahead in this country, what positions are open for a man to get forward to? On your pay roll you have one man who draws $200 a month, that is the highest gift.

Mr. Cooney. You are speaking about the logging camp now. I referred particularly to the sawmill.

Commissioner Garretson. All I know is the roll you gave. You had one man drawing $200 a month.

Mr. Cooney. That is our logging camp.

Commissioner Garretson. How many better positions have you with the mill?

Mr. Cooney. We haven't got many. But I regard anything over a hundred dollars a month as fair wages for a man that has nothing.

Commissioner GARRETSON. Would you regard a hundred-dollar position as an adult man's, or a strong man's ambition? ·

Mr. COONEY. No, sir.

Commissioner GARRETSON. He would not have gone very far forward, then, if he had the best you have to offer?

Mr. COONEY. No; he would have to go further than that to suit me.

Commissioner GARRETSON. Then, in general, you could only offer him a stepping stone on the road to advancement?

Mr. COONEY. We haven't got any employee slated to take my position. He can go down and have that in a few years.

Commissioner GARRETSON. If you are losing $815 a month——

Mr. COONEY. I didn't say $815, I said $515.

Commissioner GARRETSON. If you are losing $515 a month in the business you are conducting, how long is that position going to be in existence?

Mr. COONEY. We hope not long.

Commissioiner GARRETSON. You mean, you hope the loss won't continue long?

Mr. COONEY. Yes.

Commissioner GARRETSON. But it would absorb the position after awhile?

Mr. COONEY. Yes; if I can't manipulate it I will be out of a job.

Commissioner GARRETSON. There are three-fourths of your men whom you, in your answer to a question, stated wouldn't earn money enough to permit them to live and assume the family obligations.

Mr. COONEY. Not in their present position.

Commissioner GARRETSON. Certainly; but the positions are going to stay there, are they not?

Mr. COONEY. Possibly; no, sir. Now, a year ago we were paying for those positions, thirty to thirty-five dollars a month.

Commissioner GARRETSON. Now you are paying less?

Mr. COONEY. Yes, sir.

Commissioner GARRETSON. If your business continues in the condition it is, I suppose your idea is to pay still less?

Mr. COONEY. I will certainly do it before I will close ·down, if the men want it. I will put it up to them.

Commissioner GARRETSON. You stated, though, the present average .wage is $2.40.

Mr. COONEY. At the present time.

Commissioner GARRETSON. Then, the man who isn't earning the wage that will permit him to live humanly, is he able to pay his grocery bill with the average wage? If he is getting a dollar a day and the average wage is $2.40, can he use that $1.40 for any purpose?

Mr. COONEY. I don't get that.

Commissioner GARRETSON. What?

Mr. COONEY. I don't catch you on that.

Commissioner GARRETSON. You stated the average wage paid was $2.40?

Mr. COONEY. Yes, sir.

Commissioner GARRETSON. And you have a larger number of men that draw a dollar a day?

Mr. COONEY. Yes, sir.

Commissioner GARRETSON. Is the average you pay in your establishment of any value to the man who is only drawing a dollar a day? Can he buy anything with the knowledge that the average wage paid here where he is employed is $2.40?

Mr. COONEY. I don't catch that yet. You will have to make it clearer.

Commissioner GARRETSON. The doctrine of averages isn't worth anything to the man who is hungry and hasn't anything to buy a meal. He can't eat the average, can he?

Mr. COONEY. No, sir.

Commissioner GARRETSON. Then, the fact is that the average wage paid cuts no figure whatever in determining what are the wages of the largest number of individuals?

Mr. COONEY. I can't understand what you are getting at. Do you mean to ask me if the average wage we pay will support a family?

Commissioner GARRETSON. Oh, no. You stated that $2.40 is the ·average wage paid to all of your employees.

Mr. COONEY. That is it; yes, sir.

Commissioner GARRETSON. What I asked you was, If that average is any value whatever to the man who is·drawing less than the average? Does·that mean anything to him? Does he get it because it is your average wage?

Mr. COONEY. No, sir; he don't get any benefit out of that; not a cent.

Commissioner GARRETSON. Then, the average wage in itself is misleading, isn't it, as being stated as an average wage in an establishment?

Mr. COONEY. Yes, sir; it is misleading.

Commissioner GARRETSON. The law of average in itself is a device—well, it is like a fog; it obscures things. You run a number of stores?

Mr. COONEY. Yes, sir; we run some stores.

Commissioner GARRETSON. Do they all sell the same quality?

Mr. COONEY. No, sir.

Commissioner GARRETSON. Or do some of them sell all the things that are sold in any of them?

Mr. COONEY. I believe not. There may be some little difference; I don't know.

Commissioner GARRETSON. The one you referred to as a cash grocery——

Mr. COONEY. Yes, sir.

Commissioner GARRETSON. Is that patronized by——

Mr. COONEY. Everybody.

Commissioner GARRETSON. Regardless of whether employees or not?

Mr. COONEY. Yes, sir.

Commissioner GARRETSON. Are the prices charged at that store the same as where the employees deal on time tickets?

Mr. COONEY. Yes, sir. A man gets his money from us any time he wants it.

Commissioner GARRETSON. There is no difference in the charge whether it is against a time ticket or he is paying the coin down?

Mr. COONEY. No, sir. Somebody may tell you we run a coupon system. We do that to reduce bookkeeping. A man comes in that has a family and wants to get goods during the month; will take a coupon; and if he don't use it up, he will come in at the end of the month and get the cash.

Commissioner GARRETSON. He can cash it if he wants to?

Mr. COONEY. Yes, sir.

Acting Chairman COMMONS. Mr. Cooney, about these men that get a dollar a day; I don't know that I understand that correctly. Do, they get $26 a month, that is, the pay?

Mr. COONEY. Yes, sir.

Acting Chairman COMMONS. And board?

Mr. COONEY. Yes, sir.

Acting Chairman COMMONS. And the board is figured at how much a month, $15?

Mr. COONEY. Yes; that is what it costs us.

Acting Chairman COMMONS. So actually they are getting $1.50 a day?

Mr. COONEY. Yes; and the hospital dues out. We charge our men 50 cents a month hospital dues.

Acting Chairman COMMONS. You charge 50 cents a month hospital dues?

Mr. COONEY. We charge our men 50 cents a month hospital dues.

Acting Chairman COMMONS. The men get $1.50 a day. When did you reduce the scale of wages to this $26 level?

Mr. COONEY. Probably last fall, I think we cut it down from $30 to $26.

Acting Chairman COMMONS. What had it been? It had been $30?

Mr. COONEY. Prior to that time.

Acting Chairman COMMONS. What was it previously, before the $30 level was reached?

Mr. COONEY. Well, there is just one or two months in the year when we can not secure men, and we probably use more $35 and $40 men at that time.

Acting Chairman COMMONS. That is only just during the year?

Mr. COONEY. Yes.

Acting Chairman COMMONS. But you had a force there of how many to bring that up to 283?

Mr. COONEY. Two hundred and something, yes; this was the last month.

Acting Chairman COMMONS. How many men do you hire during the month; how many men are on your pay roll during the month?

Mr. COONEY. I haven't got the figures. They average about 10 a day probably, I think about that.

Acting Chairman COMMONS. That would be how many for the month?

Mr. COONEY. That would be about 260 a month; probably about 1,000 men, 800 or 900 men.

Acting Chairman COMMONS. Eight or nine hundred men?

Mr. COONEY. I would think so; yes.

Acting Chairman COMMONS. Do you keep that average force for the $26 men or for the entire force?

Mr. COONEY. For the entire force.

Acting Chairman COMMONS. That 600, your entire force, I thought you said was 600?

Mr. COONEY. Six hundred, yes; I said 600.

Acting Chairman COMMONS. How many men will you hire during the year to keep that up to a force of 600?

Mr. COONEY. Oh, keep it up, probably hire 2,500 to 3,000 men.

Acting Chairman COMMONS. About 3,000 men you would hire? -

Mr. COONEY. I would say so.

Acting Chairman COMMONS. Would there be that number, or a smaller proportion, of these shingle men there? Are they more steady or not?

Mr. COONEY. Yes; the shingle men are more steady.

Acting Chairman COMMONS. That would put these figures then that you hire five men to keep one man, to keep one job filled?

Mr. COONEY. Yes; according to those figures. Of course the shingle men are a very small part; we are only working about 20 men.

Acting Chairman COMMONS. Is labor more fluctuating in these lower-paid positions?

Mr. COONEY. Yes.

Acting Chairman COMMONS. Is your average of hiring five men to keep one position filled—you would have to hire many more men to keep up these?

Mr. COONEY. Yes.

Acting Chairman COMMONS. You stated, I think, your wages were lower than what is usually paid, this lower level, than what is usually paid in the lumber business in this State?

Mr. COONEY. Yes, sir. That is on account of our box factory and other factories in which we use a lot of men.

Acting Chairman COMMONS. You heard Mr. Page's statement as to the wages that they paid. I think the lowest was $2 now.

Mr. COONEY. Two dollars now.

Acting Chairman COMMONS. Does that correspond with the same class of labor that you pay $1.50 for?

Mr. COONEY. That is the sawmill and planing mill, we would probably not have but very few men at less than $2 in those departments.

Acting Chairman COMMONS. Your men working in the sawmill and the planing mill——

Mr. COONEY. Sawmill and planing would get probably the same wages—we work the cheaper class men in our box factory, in handling lumber for the box factory, ripping up lumber for betterment, etc.

Acting Chairman COMMONS. So that is the same class of employee that he described—you are paying substantially the same for that class?

Mr. COONEY. I think so. Now we aim to take a log and get all the money out of it we possibly can. We put a value on the labor of—I don't remember what Mr. Page's was—did he give the cost, or did he state it?

Acting Chairman COMMONS. He gave the percentage of the total cost.

Mr. COONEY. We put about from $7 to $8 a thousand labor on our lumber; and the average mill will put about $4.

Acting Chairman COMMONS. Then you carry it through the planing mill, which they don't have, and through the box factory?

Mr. COONEY. We aim to send our lumber out finished, ready for nailing up in position, finished lumber. Our principal busines is the finished product for retail around in the Middle West.

Acting Chairman COMMONS. Does that mean lumber that has been planed?

Mr. COONEY. Planed all ready for use.

Acting Chairman COMMONS. For example, do you ship into the San Francisco market?

Mr. COONEY. Very little.

Acting Chairman COMMONS. You do that planing work here that they do there?

Mr. COONEY. Yes; we finish our lumber. Our principal market is the Middle West. We go to the Atlantic.

Acting Chairman COMMONS. What men working on this planing work, ou this finished work—are they the men that get this dollar and a half?

Mr. COONEY. Yes; principally. A few of them in different places. I have the list here and I could read it off.

Acting Chairman COMMONS. The finished work and the box factory, then, is where the lowest wages are paid?

Mr. COONEY. Yes.

Acting Chairman COMMONS. You say the reason for that is because in that line of work, in finishing the boxes you are in competition with other places?

Mr. COONEY. Competition with mills and factories that are close to the market. We have another competition springing up now, which is the fiber box. We have to contend with the fiber box taking the place of the sawed box we had in the past.

Acting Chairman COMMONS. How long since you started to build up this planing and finishing and box industry?

Mr. COONEY. We have had it for 20 years.

Acting Chairman COMMONS. Have the conditions in that branch of industry been similar during the 20 years—that is, have you been compelled to pay lower wages there than you have in the rough work?

Mr. COONEY. We have to take the business as a whole. Take this class of labor, for instance, a young man will come out here from the East, generally shipped out to the wheat fields of Canada or eastern Washington where he will work a little while and from there he drifts down to our mill—a nice looking fellow with a trunk and a lot of clothes, and he will work for a little while and go away; and in two years or so he will come back with a roll of blankets and say, " I want something to do, give me work."

Acting Chairman COMMONS. Then you expect to maintain this finishing and box-factory work by that very transient labor?

Mr. COONEY. Yes; if we would have to pay $2, increase the rate, we would close down. We could not operate.

Acting Chairman COMMONS. And the advantage which comes to the workman is that there is always a large supply of transient labor in this district, passing through all the time?

Mr. COONEY. Passing through. We aim to run that the year around, prepare our boxes, this year; during the winter season we will stock up our supply of apple, pear, and prune boxes for next season.

Acting Chairman COMMONS. You stock up?

Mr. COONEY. We stock up.

Acting Chairman COMMONS. So that you keep running steadily?

Mr. COONEY. Yes, sir; keep it running all the time; yes, sir.

Acting Chairman COMMONS. You do not expect to keep the force steady at all?

Mr. COONEY. We will, if they will stay. We would be very glad if they would not change. We don't want them to change. Every time a new man comes in, we have got to educate that man.

Acting Chairman COMMONS. Would you think you could keep a more steady force if you could afford, in that branch, to pay $2.50 or $2?

Mr. COONEY. Yes.

Acting Chairman COMMONS. So that one of the reasons for that——

Mr. COONEY. It would be so much easier to operate the plant. One of our chief troubles is during this time of the year to keep help enough.

Acting Chairman COMMONS. They are·attracted by higher wages elsewhere?

Mr. COONEY. Yes; there are two seasons of the year in which the men move; in April they go to Alaska, and then July and August they go to the wheat fields.

Acting Chairman COMMONS. For this work do you get men through employment offices?

Mr. COONEY. Yes.

Acting Chairman COMMONS. That is for the box factory and finishing?

Mr. COONEY. Yes, sir.

Acting Chairman COMMONS. Do most of these men come to you?

Mr. COONEY. Whenever we are real short of men, we send to the employment offices for them.

Acting Chairman COMMONS. But you find that ordinarily outside of these two seasons that you mention—the two months of the year—that you can get plenty of men to come at that rate of pay?

Mr. COONEY. In the winter time; yes. This winter we will have an awful job to handle the men that will come begging for work. There will probably be 50 men around there all winter begging for something to do.

Acting Chairman COMMONS. In that case, of course, you do not appeal to the employment offices?

Mr. COONEY. No. Then an old man will come there, one who has worked for us, and he will say: " I have got to have something to do." I will take him out and say to the foreman " This is a man that worked for us two years ago, and we have got to take care of him."

Acting Chairman COMMONS. What class of work is there for these $1.50 men—is it feeding planing mills?

Mr. COONEY. Taking away—in a box factory; they would not feed planers; they will tie up lumber, take away, and work at different things.

Acting Chairman COMMONS. So it does not require any instruction at all?

Mr. COONEY. Some. But then we have a foreman that will educate them.

Acting Chairman COMMONS. A man can start in and in a day learn it the first day?

Mr. COONEY. Yes—he can do pretty well, if he wants to. In addition, in the country where we are it rains from 80 to 120 inches per year. That is the rainfall per year. We take those men that come to the plant, the strong, hardy men, and put them out in the yard, and work the men of that kind on the outside. The others we try to get in the box factory and planing mill and lumber sheds, trying to take care of them.

Acting Chairman COMMONS. Are there other factories, box factories and planing mills in the State?

Mr. COONEY. Yes; in Hoquaim there are two. The manager of one testified in a tax case there that he put over a million dollars in the plant, and that it was for sale at $250,000. He operated for a year and shut down the other day indefinitely. He reported that he lost $18,000 that year.

Acting Chairman COMMONS. What other factories are there, box and finishing?

Mr. COONEY. There is one more, the Northwestern; they are still operating.

Acting Chairman COMMONS. That business, then, is a losing business, that end of the business?

Mr. COONEY. Without you understand it and handle it right; it has not been successful on this coast.

Acting Chairman COMMONS. It has not been successful; but you think it can be made a success?

Mr. COONEY. In the way we handle it, we can manage to pull it along.

Acting Chairman COMMONS. If you had to pay $2 or $2.50 a day——

Mr. COONEY. I wouldn't attempt to operate it one minute.

Acting Chairman COMMONS. On your other work, your rough work, you make a profit?

Mr. COONEY. Well, we organize to take hold of this; if we were to shut down on this other work we would reduce our overhead expense all we could; we would have to change our organization. But we could take our other mill and do the same, run it, operate it the same.

Acting Chairman COMMONS. When you speak of the timber, do you own your own timber land, or do you buy such as is needed?

Mr. COONEY. We buy about two-thirds of our logs.

Acting Chairman COMMONS. Who are the owners of the timberlands that you buy from?

Mr. COONEY. Well, there are independent loggers down there that buy timber and own timber and put in logs for the market and sell them.

Acting Chairman COMMONS. You buy about two-thirds?

Mr. COONEY. We buy about two-thirds of our logs.

Acting Chairman COMMONS. And you own about a third, you say, yourself?

Mr. COONEY. Yes.

Acting Chairman COMMONS. How much timber land have you of your own?

Mr. COONEY. We have about 200,000,000 feet of timber.

Acting Chairman COMMONS. Would that be considered a small lot?

Mr. COONEY. That is very small considering the capacity of our plant.

Acting Chairman COMMONS. So practically you are not an owner of timberland to any degree?

Mr. COONEY. No; we aim to buy logs on the market.

Acting Chairman COMMONS. What do you pay for stumpage now?

Mr. COONEY. Stumpage on Grays Harbor now would not be less than $3.

Acting Chairman COMMONS. Has that increased?

Mr. COONEY. Yes. When we started at Grays Harbor stumpage could be bought for about 30 to 50 cents a thousand.

Acting Chairman COMMONS. Twenty years ago?

Mr. COONEY. Twenty-five years ago.

Acting Chairman COMMONS. So your profits do not come from any increase in the value of the timber that you own?

Mr. COONEY. No.

Acting Chairman COMMONS. You simply have to make your profit out——

Mr. COONEY. Out of the logs.

Acting Chairman COMMONS. And the state of the market and the competition squeeze you between the timber owner on the one hand and the box manufacturer on the other?

Mr. COONEY. Yes; and the competing markets of the country, you know. The price of lumber has reduced in the last 18 months. Anything that comes out of fir, which constituted practiclaly 90 per cent of the forests of the State of Washington—everything that a mill manufactures in fir has dropped in value from $2 to $7 a thousand, probably an average of $4 within the last 18 months.

Acting Chairman COMMONS. You know about the San Francisco cost of planing?

Mr. COONEY. No; I do not know.

Acting Chairman COMMONS. The cost of planing there as compared with yours?

Mr. COONEY. No; I don't know.

Acting Chairman COMMONS. What is your cost of planing?

Mr. COONEY. I think about a dollar and a half a thousand—everything.

Acting Chairman COMMONS. That includes labor and everything?

Mr. COONEY. And when you say planing——

Acting Chairman COMMONS. I don't know that I define it correctly, but we are trying to draw a line between this rough work and this finished work, which goes into the San Francisco market—the finishing end of the work.

Mr. COONEY. That would be anything that would feed through the planer from flooring and ceiling to dimension stock.

Acting Chairman COMMONS. Take the smallest class of work, is it about a dollar and a half?

Mr. COONEY. No; you take sized lumber, sized studding for wooden buildings which they use most of, is run through—dressing one side and one edge—that can possibly be done for 25 cents a thousand, easy.

Acting Chairman COMMONS. And, as I understand your situation, then, these low wages that you pay are simply in the finishing end which—where you are trying to do something which ordinarily would be done in the cities at cheaper labor?

Mr. COONEY. That is it.

Acting Chairman COMMONS. And so far as the rough work is concerned, your situation, and the wages you pay are about the same as those paid by Mr. Page?

Mr. COONEY. I think we pay a little higher, probably, for our skilled help than he does.

Acting Chairman COMMONS. Would you submit your pay roll, and classify it in such a way as I have suggested, your rough work and your finished work and so on? So that we can compare it with the other mills in the State?

Mr. COONEY. I could send the cost of operation—we can send the cost of operation of any of our departments.

Acting Chairman COMMONS. I don't mean the cost; I mean the pay roll.

Mr. COONEY. The pay roll?

Acting Chairman COMMONS. Yes; the pay roll by the classes.

Mr. COONEY. The wages we pay in the different departments?

Acting Chairman COMMONS. Designate the department by the class of work—rough work, box work, etc.

Mr. COONEY. Take the list I have here, it would give that; that would be sawmill, planing mill, box factory, handling, machine shop, etc.

Acting Chairman COMMONS. Yes; all of the employees in those several departments; the occupations.

Mr. COONEY. Naming the occupations?

Acting Chairman COMMONS. Yes.

Mr. COONEY. In the different departments?

Acting Chairman COMMONS. You have that there?

Mr. COONEY. No; I haven't, but I will make one and send it, if you will tell me where to send it.

Mr. THOMPSON. When can you get it?

Mr. COONEY. I might have that made by Saturday.

Mr. THOMPSON. You could forward to the Transportation Building at Chicago, when you get it done.

Mr. COONEY. Will you put the address down for me?

(See Cooney Exhibit No. 2.)

Acting Chairman COMMONS. Any other questions?

Mr. THOMPSON. Just a question or two.

Acting Chairman COMMONS. We will adjourn at the present time, and meet again at 2 o'clock. Will you return at 2 o'clock?

Mr. COONEY. Yes, sir.

(Whereupon, at 12.30 p. m. of this, Thursday, an adjournment was taken until 2 o'clock p. m. of the same day, August 13, 1914.)

AFTER RECESS—2 P. M.

The commission met pursuant to adjournment. Present as before. And thereupon the following proceedings were had:

Acting Chairman COMMONS. Come to order.

TESTIMONY OF MR. NEIL COONEY—Continued.

Acting Chairman COMMONS. Mr. O'Connell has some questions to ask.

Commissioner O'CONNELL. Mr. Cooney, I understand your firm to be a corporation—incorporated?

Mr. COONEY. Yes, sir.

Commissioner O'CONNELL. Under the laws of the State of Washington?

Mr. COONEY. No; the laws of the State of California?

Commissioner O'CONNELL. California?

Mr. COONEY. Yes.

Commissioner O'CONNELL. What was the capitalization of your company when it was incorporated?

Mr. COONEY. They incorporated two companies, and then joined them. I should think about $250,000—I don't remember.

Commissioner O'CONNELL. Has that capitalization been increased or decreased since then?

Mr. COONEY. It has been increased.

Commissioner O'CONNELL. How much?

Mr. COONEY. To five hundred thousand.

Commissioner O'CONNELL. It is now five hundred thousand?

Mr. COONEY. Yes, sir.

Commissioner O'CONNELL. How did the increase come to take place?

Mr. COONEY. When they combined the two companies.

Commissioner O'CONNELL. There were two separate companies?

Mr. COONEY. Two companies—two separate companies—the Grays Harbor Mill Co. and the Grays Harbor Commercial Co.

Commissioner O'CONNELL. What were those individual companies capitalized for before they were combined?

Mr. COONEY. I don't know—I estimated $250,000.

Commissioner O'CONNELL. Two hundred and fifty each?

Mr. COONEY. No; about $250,000.

Commissioner O'CONNELL. Then, when they were combined the capitalization was made $500,000?

Mr. COONEY. Yes, sir.

Commissioner O'CONNELL. Why was that increase of $250,000?

Mr. COONEY. I don't know.

Commissioner O'CONNELL. Had the business increased in some way?

Mr. COONEY. The business has continually increased.

Commissioner O'CONNELL. How is the stock held of the company?

Mr. COONEY. The stock of the company is held by individuals.

Commissioner O'CONNELL. Is it closely held?

Mr. COONEY. Fairly so.

Commissioner O'CONNELL. Who are the large stockholders?

Mr. COONEY. Pope & Talbot, of San Francisco.

Commissioner O'CONNELL. What per cent of the stock does he own?

Mr. COONEY. I don't know.

Commissioner O'CONNELL. Does the company pay dividends?

Mr. COONEY. Yes, sir.

Commissioner O'CONNELL. What dividends have they been paying?

Mr. COONEY. They have been paying 6 per cent on the capital.
- Commissioner O'CONNELL. Six per cent on $500,000?
Mr. COONEY. Yes, sir.
Commissioner O'CONNELL. Did the two companies before they were merged pay dividends?
Mr. COONEY. No, sir.
Commissioner O'CONNELL. After the combination took place the capital was increased from $250,000 to $500,000, and they began paying dividends?
Mr. COONEY. Possibly not then. They paid 6 per cent dividends—I have some stock in the company, and, as I remember, I have been getting dividends for about eight years. Previous to that they didn't pay anything.
Commissioner O'CONNELL. What is the total business of the company per year?
Mr. COONEY. We will sell close to a million dollars' worth of lumber per year. We do a merchandise business of about $150,000 a year.
Commissioner O'CONNELL. What is the net earnings of the company per year?
Mr. COONEY. Last year I think we earned about $25,000.
Commissioner O'CONNELL. That would be an average earning?
Mr. COONEY. No, sir; it has earned up to $60,000 a year.
Commissioner O'CONNELL. How does the company pay 6 per cent on half a million dollars from that earning?
Mr. COONEY. Six per cent is $30,000 a year. If they earned $60,000, they could ▮ay thirty.
Commissioner O'CONNELL. And if they earned twenty-five thousand?
Mr. COONEY. Pay it out of the surplus.
Commissioner O'CONNELL. What is the surplus of the company?
Mr. COONEY. About half a million dollars.
Commissioner O'CONNELL. About half a million dollars?
Mr. COONEY. With the value placed on the plant as it is. It is all in the plant. We owe now about $200,000.
Commissioner O'CONNELL. Well, this increase of capital from two hundred and fifty thousand to five hundred thousand, is that in real value or is it in what is known as water.
Mr. COONEY. That is in plant—real value in plant—if the plant is worth anything at the present time. If we were to say to a man, to any man, take this plant and operate it and we will pay the taxes, you wouldn't get a man in the State of Washington that would take it. If this eight-hour law goes into effect the plant will be worth nothing only for junk.
Commissioner O'CONNELL. Under normal conditions what would you say the plant was worth?
Mr. COONEY. Well, we have a plant down there that cost $1,060,000 that is for sale at $250,000, and they are offering a commission for the man who will sell it.
Commissioner O'CONNELL. How many salaried officers are there in the company?
Mr. COONEY. We have a president and a secretary. The president of the company I don't think is getting very much of a salary. Our secretary—I don't know what salary he is getting, but I think both would draw not to exceed $500.
Commissioner O'CONNELL. What is the salary of the general manager?
Mr. COONEY. Five hundred dollars.
Commissioner O'CONNELL. A month?
Mr. COONEY. And in addition to that I am the general manager—they furnish a house and keep it up.
Commissioner O'CONNELL. Does the general manager, or any other officer, receive a bonus of any kind at the end of the year for the business done?
. Mr. COONEY. Not a cent.
Commissioner O'CONNELL. Are bonuses of any kind paid to either officials or employees of the company?
Mr. COONEY. Previous to three years ago they made a habit of sending up a small bonus to the office help. When I became general manager and had control of it, I advised that they discontinue it simply because I felt if they were to pay a bonus the men working in the plant were as much entitled to it as the office men. Therefore it was discontinued.
Commissioner O'CONNELL. You make annual reports, I suppose, to the proper officials of the State, of the business done?

Mr. COONEY. Yes, sir.

Commissioner O'CONNELL. Is that in form that it can be filed with this commission?

Mr. COONEY. Now, I don't know as to that. I am not well up on bookkeeping. I suppose we make a report.

Commissioner O'CONNELL. You print an annual form, I suppose, for the directors or your shareholders—stockholders?

Mr. COONEY. The property books, the stock books, are held in San Francisco. San Francisco is the head office. I don't think we make a report to the Government, do we? We are not obliged to do that.

Commissioner O'CONNELL. Under the new law of paying on your earnings?

Mr. COONEY. Oh, on the income? Yes; that is made from our San Francisco office.

Commissioner O'CONNELL. What was the face value of the stock when issued, $100 shares or $50 shares?

Mr. COONEY. One hundred dollar shares.

Commissioner O'CONNELL. One hundred dollar shares?

Mr. COONEY. Yes, sir.

Commissioner O'CONNELL. Are they sold in the open market. Are they listed on any of the markets?

Mr. COONEY. No, sir.

Commissioner O'CONNELL. Not listed in any city?

Mr. COONEY. No; but last year there was about 900 shares on the market. The man I succeeded as manager had 900 shares; his health failed and he sold it.

Commissioner O'CONNELL. What is the market value of the stock now?

Mr. COONEY. That stock was sold at that time for, I think, $130 a share.

Commissioner O'CONNELL. If I wanted to buy some shares now, what could I purchased them for?

Mr. COONEY. I don't know. I will sell you mine.

Commissioner O'CONNELL. For what price?

Mr. COONEY. Are you ready to buy?

Commissioner O'CONNELL. Yes; I am a business man.

Mr. COONEY. All right, you can have them for a dollar and a half—one fifty.

Commissioner O'CONNELL. A dollar and a half a share?

Mr. COONEY. At one fifty a share.

Commissioner O'CONNELL. How many shares do you hold?

Mr. COONEY. I hold, I think, 312.

Commissioner O'CONNELL. Well, for a firm that is losing money—you say on your last month's business you lost money—$50 a share seems to be a 'pretty good price—I don't think we will trade.

Mr. COONEY. We have been building that business for 25 years. I have been working there as hard as I knew how to build up the business for 25 years and I am entitled to some profit on my work.

Commissioner O'CONNELL. Has your salary increased during that time?

Mr. COONEY. Yes, sir.

Commissioner O'CONNELL. What did you originally start with the company for?

Mr. COONEY. I think $100. I went there as a mechanic.

Commissioner O'CONNELL. Your salary has increased 400 per cent?

Mr. COONEY. Yes, sir.

Commissioner O'CONNELL. That is a pretty fair dividend?

Mr. COONEY. Yes; that helps.

Commissioner O'CONNELL. That is all I care to ask.

Commissioner GARRETSON. What did you pay for common labor, Mr. Cooney, at the time that the consolidation took place?

Mr. COONEY. I can't remember that.

Commissioner GARRETSON. About, approximately.

Mr. COONEY. Common labor, probably $30.

Commissioner GARRETSON. The same you are now paying twenty for?

Mr. COONEY. No; twenty-six.

Commissioner GARRETSON. Twenty-six?

Mr. COONEY. Yes.

Commissioner GARRETSON. Then, regardless of the fact that it is a losing corporation, the stock has advanced 50 per cent in value in that time on the quotation you make, while the shares of the men who are working have decreased $4 per share.

Mr. Cooney. It is not a losing proposition.

Commissioner Garretson. Well, the testimony was that within a given period——

Mr. Cooney. Last month.

Commissioner Garretson. You lost money.

Mr. Cooney. Last month; yes.

Commissioner Garretson. Was that testimony given with the idea of conveying the impression that it was a losing proposition and therefore you had to pay low wages?

Mr. Cooney. Yes, sir.

Commissioner Garretson. Then that testimony is not a fair exposition of the financial condition of the company?

Mr. Cooney. I don't——

Commissioner Garretson. I mean in regard to the losing of money.

Mr. Cooney. Why not? We have property that is worth $750,000. Are we not entitled to some interest on that?

Commissioner Garretson. Interest and book value are two entirely different things, aren't they?

Mr. Cooney. Well, take the book value of it, then.

Commissioner Garretson. Book value.

Mr. Cooney. Take 500,000.

Commissioner Garretson. What is your book value?

Mr. Cooney. Oh, the book value——

Commissioner Garretson. Yes.

Mr. Cooney. I think the book value would be about a million dollars.

Commissioner Garretson. Oh, the book value per share.

Mr. Cooney. Well, the book value is $100—$500,000.

Commissioner Garretson. How is that?

Mr. Cooney. Five hundred thousand.

Commissioner Garretson. The par value is five hundred thousand?

Mr. Cooney. Well, the book value would be the value of the stock and surplus, which I say is about a million dollars.

Commissioner Garretson. Then your book value is $200,000?

Mr. Cooney. The book value?

Commissioner Garretson. Your book value is $200 per share?

Mr. Cooney. Yes, sir.

Commissioner Garretson. And still it is such a losing proposition——

Mr. Cooney. We——

Commissioner Garretson (continuing). That you only pay $4 per month less wage than you did originally.

Mr. Cooney. The books of the company are open. We would be glad to show you all the facts in it, all the conditions, and the best way to get that would be for your experts to come down and see.

Commissioner Garretson. Well, your own statement now, as to the amount of surplus, your estimated value of the stock that you own and the relation of former wages and present wages gets strongly at cross purposes with each other, do they not?

Mr. Cooney. We are not making anything on the investment now. We are not making anything this year. We have an investment we put in, say originally, of $500,000. Instead of paying the earnings out of that we have increased the investment.

Commissioner O'Connell. You have piled up this surplus of $500,000 while wages have gone down?

Mr. Cooney. In 25 years. Wages haven't gone down all that time. You are taking this unusually low wage of $26 a month. The majority of them are not able to go out and get any work with the railroads or do laboring work. They are doing work where they could not do a laborer's work; that is my opinion.

Commissioner Garretson. When you send to these employment agencies that furnish you with this constant stream of changing men, do you arrange with them that they will hire you the flotsam and jetsam of industrial life that can't go anywhere else?

Mr. Cooney. No, sir; we will tell him we want so many for the box factory, or want so many men from some other place, and want good men, and he will go and send these down.

Commissioner GARRETSON. You have heard the testimony given to the effect that there are some places that keep ·three gangs, one gang coming and one going and one at work.

Mr. COONEY. That is our place.

Commissioner GARRETSON. You must have five gangs, on the testimony given this morning that you hired five men each year for every job.

Mr. COONEY. That is for the year.

Commissioner GARRETSON. Well, what are you doing with the other two; are you gathering them up ready to start? Is it a fact that the employment agency that does your business keeps a standing advertisement in the papers at Portland, Tacoma, and Seattle to supply the demand for labor of that class in your place?

Mr. COONEY. We haven't had a man from Portland for perhaps a year or six months or so. We only go to Portland when we are practically. boycotted in Seattle and Tacoma, when a notice is put up ," Don't go to Cosmopolis."

Commissioner GARRETSON. The place has a reputation, then?

Mr. COONEY. It has during strike trouble. It is one of the places that has never been taken.

Commissioner GARRETSON. How is that?

Mr. COONEY. All the time I have been there I have run the place.

Commissioner GARRETSON. And you have run it so that a boycott does exist?

Mr. COONEY. Boycott don't exist.

Commissioner GARRETSON. You said when you were boycotted you went to Portland.

Mr. COONEY. When we are boycotted from getting men.

Commissioner GARRETSON. That is what I mean.

Mr. COONEY. Yes, sir.

Commissioner GARRETSON. That is all.

Acting Chairman COMMONS. That is all, Mr. Cooney. Call your next witness, Mr. Thompson.

Mr. THOMPSON. Mr. Mack.

TESTIMONY OF MR. WILLIAM B. MACK.

Mr. THOMPSON. Will you give us your name?

Mr. MACK. William B. Mack.

Mr. THOMPSON. And your business address?

Mr. MACK. Aberdeen, Wash.

Mr. THOMPSON. And your business?

Mr. MACK. I am manager of the S. E. Slade Lumber Co., the Slade-Wells Logging Co., and the Hump-Tulips Logging Co.

Mr. THOMPSON. Tell us the kind of business, and where?

Mr. MACK. Logging and lumbering at Aberdeen; vessel interests along the coast.

Mr. THOMPSON. How many men are employed in the various branches of the business, giving the branches separately?

Mr. MACK. When the camps are running at full force we employ at the Hump-Tulips logging camp about 250 men; at the Slade-Wells, about 150; and at the mill about 160 men. At the present time the Hump-Tulips camps are closed, and the Slade-Wells camps are closed, because we can buy logs in the open market cheaper than we can put them in. Our mill is running, but we fear that the present war trouble is going to force us to close down the mill because we sell a great deal of our lumber to the foreign markets, principally on the west coast of South America and Mexico, and generally we get our pay from those countries in bills of exchange on London and Hamburg, and embargoes having been declared on the South American ports there is no prospect of our getting pay for the lumber, so that while we have vessels at the wharf and lumber ready to load we do not deem it advisable to take chances to load and ship the stuff. We fear we will be obliged to close down.

Mr. THOMPSON. What wages do you pay the various classes of people that you employ?

Mr. MACK. Well, in the mill, take band-saw filers, for instance, we pay $9 per day, and helpers $3.50. Our sawyers get $6 per day each, both our head sawyer and our second sawyer. We pay them both the same and insist upon equal ability. Our edger men get $4.25; our automatic trimmer men, $4.25; and the wages run down to $2.25—the minimum wage is $2.25 per day. We have very few men at that wage. The common laborer in the yard—we insist upon certain efficiency and pay about $2.50 a day for the major portion of our common labôr.

Mr. THOMPSON. That includes both the common labor you use in the mills and in the yards and in the logging camps?

Mr. MACK. Not in the logging camps. The logging camps are separate and distinct and should be treated altogether different. In the logging camps we pay our superintendent $250 per month, our logging foreman $175 per month. Both instances include board. Our cooks are paid from $125 to $150 per month and board; flunkeys, $45 and board; bull cook, $45 and board. The hood tender we used to pay $5.50 and board. We changed that to $6 and they pay their own board—that is, during this year. Our head loaders get $4.50 and $5; second loader, $3.50 and $4, and so on through the regular run.

Mr. THOMPSON. What do you pay for the ordinary laborer?

Mr. MACK. Ordinary labor—there is very little of it used in the lumber woods. We use it on the logging road—I mean logging railroad—and there the lowest we pay is $2.50 per day. Our locomotive engineer, we pay him $4.50 a day; firemen, $3.

Mr. THOMPSON. What kind of accommodations have you got for the men in the logging camps?

Mr. MACK. Why——

Mr. THOMPSON. Give the conditions generally.

Mr. MACK. Our camps, well, the Slade-Wells, for instance, is on a railroad, and we build houses there on cars. The bunk cars, I presume that you want to know more about, are built 40 feet long and 14 feet wide, 8-foot walls, and the maximum capacity of one of those cars is 16 men, or 8 single bunks in each end of the car, leaving a space in the center for a stove and for a kind of gathering place or social hall, theoretically, but practically it is used by the men for hanging up the wet clothes and drying them, although we have accommodations there for drying clothes. We have a room set apart in the camp for that purpose, but it is hardly ever used. The men will go in and take a bath, a shower generally, and change clothes, go to the camp first on their way from work and grab a change and go over and take this shower, put on their good clothes, and bring away the clothes that they worked in during the day and perspired in, and hang them up in the room that they live in. And to pass any edict or attempt to do that, you would lose your crew, who would say that you are trying to mollycoddle them. And you have got to understand the peculiar nature of your logger to understand that. He won't stand babying, he won't be dictated to, and he won't be interfered with.

Mr. THOMPSON. What other conditions have you in your camp—take sanitary conditions?

Mr. MACK. We have good toilet arrangements off at a distance from the camp, generally on running water. Often we have to pump the water in order to create a flow. Board walks are laid, and every convenience imaginable to make them as sanitary as we can. They are crude and rough.

Mr. THOMPSON. How about bedding?

Mr. MACK. The bedding we have embraced—we have, first, wire springs and on top of that a mattress. We charge for that 25 cents per month. Those springs and mattresses both are changed about once a year to keep them up. They are what we call three-quarter beds, simply for one man, and in a climate in the woods where it is damp and all the wires rust and they become saggy. The mattress gets hard. And we make a practice of renewing them once a year, and this $3 that we get from the men if they are working continuously, pays about one-fourth of the cost of the mattress and the spring.

Mr. THOMPSON. What do you do to take care of it, who has that work about keeping the camp clean, who does the work, the chambermaid work?

Mr. MACK. Well, we have what we call the bull cook. Then we have constant overseeing by the superintendent, by the foreman, and largely by the men themselves. Because the men take—rather take a pride in enforcing cleanliness. If a man comes in there, a "buggy," as they call him, why he is ostracized and kicked out of the camp. You will find that in nearly all well-regulated camps that the men regulate that themselves. But it is looked after closely, first by the superintendent and foreman, and by the bull cook under instructions from his superiors.

Mr. THOMPSON. To what extent do you use the employment agencies, I mean the private agencies, in the employment of help of any kind?

Mr. MACK. Very little in the camps. We have in Aberdeen an employment agent there that is hired by a number of the camps, a number of the logging companies that are constantly keeping the office open and answering telephone calls from the camp. No charge is made to the men, it is kept up by each logging company paying in a certain amount per month to this man for wages and office rent.

Mr. THOMPSON. Is any part of your establishment organized?

Mr. MACK. You mean labor?

Mr. THOMPSON. I mean labor.

Mr. MACK. No, sir; not that I know of. We probably have quite a number of union men working. We never ask a man his religion, his politics, nor any of his beliefs.

Mr. THOMPSON. How do you personally view organized labor?

Mr. MACK. I am naturally opposed to it.

Mr. THOMPSON. What forms the basis of your opposition?

Mr. MACK. Oh, it destroys individualism. Now, you take what I have particularly in mind, the testimony here relating to the logging camps. Now, there is not an American industry to-day that is as well individualized as the logging business. You hire a superintendent, a logging superintendent, and he has got a following in the way of foremen. Now, if you fire that superintendent or if he leaves you for any reason, universally the foreman will leave with him. Now, in turn, if a superintendent has a row with one of his foremen, nearly always his best men will go with the foreman—that is, there is a close companionship or comradeship, or whatever you may term it, they are close to one another. I don't know of any business in the United States that there is as much individuality about as there is in the logging business in the State of Washington as it is conducted to-day.

Mr. THOMPSON. Well, looking at it more particularly from the standpoint of the employer, what is your objection, or rather, how do you view unionism?

Mr. MACK. Well, I fear that in losing your individuality—that individual touch, that personal touch, if you please, that you get back, so that you run it about the way that our ships are being run—that is, that instead of your having a good feeling and a get-together and working for the best interests, that you will find that your men are not working with you, they are simply working for you. That term was used here to-day, and I think it is a very good one, and it is the curse of business in the United States to-day, that we are not working enough with our men or our men with us; we are out of sympathy with one another.

Mr. THOMPSON. From the standpoint of the worker, Mr. Mack, taking the field of industry as a whole here and elsewhere, how do you view unionism from his standpoint?

Mr. MACK. Well, if he is of less than ordinary ability, I think that perhaps unionism might perhaps assist him. But if he is of ordinary ability or above it I think that it is a handicap to him.

Mr. THOMPSON. Well, you think on the whole that the organization of men into unions has not helped the condition of labor?

Mr. MACK. I don't. I think that when they started that certain classes, in having the start were able perhaps to shoot up their particular product a little, and now that we are extending that we are just simply completing the cycle, and that they are no better off in any place than they were in the first instance. I believe that it retards the individual and as a dead-leveling process is nationally wrong and is not good for the country or for the men.

Mr. THOMPSON. Looking at the condition of the workers generally throughout the country, irrespective of whether they are unionized or not unionized.

Mr. MACK. Yes, sir.

Mr. THOMPSON. How do you view the condition, is it one that needs help or attention at all?

Mr. MACK. No, I think that—well, I believe that there is less discontent and less unrest to-day than usual in the world—well, in the United States. I think that it is simply more in evidence, discontent is more in evidence. You hear more of it. It is exploited more. There are more cures, more panaceas for it—like a bunch of fellows can go to work and talk to any individual, if he is not wise to the fact, they can talk him sick. That is, they can go to work and half a dozen men call on that fellow and tell him how poor he is looking, and he goes to bed before 6 o'clock violently ill, with his mind overmastered, if you please. I think, if you will pardon the expression, we are largely going nutty on the subject here in the United States.

. Mr. THOMPSON. Your opinion, then, would be that if we would put it out of our minds completely, it would be better?

Mr. MACK. I don't think that is possible, Mr. Thompson. But, as I view it, the people are better housed and better clothed and better nourished than I have ever seen them, and I have handled men practically all my life, and I am no young man, and that the country is better, the people are more contended, and they are saving more money, and yet you hear a wail going up that is greater and greater from them.

Mr. THOMPSON. Well, to what do you ascribe the improvement in the condition of the workingman that you speak of?

Mr. MACK. Natural betterment of conditions and their striving—that they are discontented, they always have been discontented, and we owe our natural greatness to our discontent.

Mr. THOMPSON. Would you give any credit for that improvement to the organization of the men into unions?

Mr. MACK. No; I think not. I think that you will find more discontent outside of the union than you will in the union. In other words, that you find in the union a lot of self-satisfied men that are looking to their leaders to be a Moses to lead them, while the other fellows are discontended and are striving themselves. And, as I say, their discontent, we don't want to discourage in this country, because it has made this country, and we need more of it to make our people struggle and get ahead. Discontent is not to be discouraged, in my judgment.

Mr. THOMPSON. Now, Mr. Mack, this commission has been appointed by the United States Government to look into this industrial question.

Mr. MACK. Yes.

Mr. THOMPSON. Now, what would you say to the commission that it should do, suppose you were on the commission, and you are here now as an adviser to the commission, one of the witnesses before it—now what would you say to them?

Mr. MACK. I don't believe I could advise it.

Mr. THOMPSON. Well, you have given them some advice already.

Mr. MACK. Well, that is as far as I go. I don't believe I could go any further.

Mr. THOMPSON. I don't want to keep on the one question too much, but you would not think, then, that the conditions in the country would call for any remedial recommendations by this commission to Congress?   .

Mr. MACK. I don't think so. I think we have had too many regulations, too many investigations, and too many—too much of turmoil, making the patient sicker.

Mr. THOMPSON. Well, then, that would be your recommendation to Congress, if you were on the commission, say?

Mr. MACK. Yes.

Mr. THOMPSON. That you would recommend that the doctrine of laissez faire should continue, the thing should be left alone for awhile?

Mr. MACK. I think our civilization must grow sympathetic, the Civil War made us more sympathetic. I believe this world war will make the world more sympathetic. I believe it is going to bring relief, and you will see a great expansion in the United States as soon as things have adjusted themselves, and you won't hear any more of this until the next hard times. The next time we have a panic, everybody for the storm cellar.

Mr. THOMPSON. Is there anything else you would like to add to what you have stated?   .

Mr. MACK. No, sir.

Mr. THOMPSON. That is all.

Commissioner GARRETSON. Mr. Mack, you referred to the logging industry as one that largely tended toward individualism, and you cited as an illustration thereof that if you discharged a superintendent, he was very apt to take all the foremen with him; that if the superintendent got into a row with one foreman and that the foreman should be discharged, he would be very apt to take all the best men with him—that was the way you cited it, was it not?

Mr. MACK. Yes, sir.

Commissioner GARRETSON. Is that an evidence of individualism or of tacit organization?

Mr. MACK. Of what?

Commissioner GARRETSON. Of tacit organization?

Mr. MACK. You are getting too deep for me. That word is not in my vocabulary.

Commissioner GARRETSON. I will bring it down—or shall I put it up? Is it evidence, of an understanding between the superintendent and the foreman that they will stand or fall together?

Mr. MACK. No.

Commissioner GARRETSON. It is not? What causes them to leave, then?

Mr. MACK. Loyalty.

Commissioner GARRETSON. Loyalty. What is organization between men but loyalty to each other?

Mr. MACK. Search me.

Commissioner GARRETSON. You rather conveyed the idea, or I misunderstood you, that organization had never bettered—labor organization had never bettered—the condition of men. Is that right?

Mr. MACK. You heard my testimony, Mr. Garretson.

Commissioner GARRETSON. You are familiar, I suppose, with railways—you are at least a passenger occasionally. Are you a believer in safety appliances for the benefit of all concerned, passenger trains and freight trains?

Mr. MACK. Am I examining you or you examining me?

Commissioner GARRETSON. I am examining you.

Mr. MACK. All right, sir.

Commissioner GARRETSON. You are?

Mr. MACK. Yes, sir.

Commissioner GARRETSON. Are you aware of what influence enacted all the Federal safety appliance laws on this continent? Do you know what agency had them drawn and enacted?

Mr. MACK. No, sir; I really don't.

Commissioner GARRETSON. If a labor organization had been solely responsible for the drawing and enactment of those laws, would they have been performing a good service to humanity at large as well as themselves?.

Mr. MACK. I think it was a desirable thing. I think it was the thinkers that helped that along, and your organization probably got behind it.

Commissioner GARRETSON. If the influence was able to enact it, was it a good purpose?

Mr. MACK. If you create a crying need and it is enacted, if some vociferous individual gets up and shouts for it, they can't claim all the credit for it.

Commissioner GARRETSON. If the organization stood all the expense of all the preparatory work——

Mr. MACK. I hope you don't mean they were insidious lobbyists.

Commissioner GARRETSON. They were not insidious lobbyists, they were open lobbyists. We very frankly accept the name. Would that matter if it went through be a desirable influence?

Mr. MACK. I will admit all that line of argument you are going to present. Time is short, and I will admit all you are going to bring out.

Commissioner GARRETSON. Good. Just one other. I don't know whether you will admit that or not. I want to say in a prefatory way that we sometimes criticize a man for his religious belief. Are you a Christian Scientist?

Mr. MACK. No, sir.

Commissioner GARRETSON. I thought you were from the remedy you gave for discontent. All you would have to do under that system is just to think there was no discontent and there would not be any. Is that your belief in the theory?

Mr. MACK. No, sir; psychological.

Commissioner GARRETSON. Psychological, pure and simple. That is all.

Acting Chairman COMMONS. It has been stated by one of the preceding witnesses that you might be able to explain to us this so-called San Francisco boycott. At least, tell us the difference in cost of thè finished lumber if it were finished directly from the Washington mills, and the expense there is in San Francisco on the basis of the regulations at that place. Do you have a planing or finishing mill?

Mr. MACK. I haven't got it for San Francisco.

Acting Chairman COMMONS. You have one in your own mill?

Mr. MACK. Yes, sir.

Acting Chairman COMMONS. Could you give us the cost of that work here in Washington as you have taken it from the rough or sawmill through the planing or finishing mill? I think that is the next stage, is it not?

Mr. MACK. Yes, sir.

Acting Chairman Commons. What is the added cost?

Mr. Mack. It will run from a dollar per thousand to as high as $8 per thousand, depending on the size and length and amount that has to be done.

Acting Chairman Commons. Now, is that purely labor cost that you are thinking of?

Mr. Mack. No, sir; that is everything; that includes labor cost, machinery, depreciation, etc.

Acting Chairman Commons. Suppose you put the cost in thousand feet up to the rough lumber you are going to finish.

Mr. Mack. Up to the rough——

Acting Chairman Commons. How many dollars per thousand feet would the different grades of lumber up to the time it was ready in the planing or finishing mill cost?

Mr. Mack. You would have to know the size and length.

Acting Chairman Commons. Take something that is the largest standard— which has the largest output.

Mr. Mack. Now, the largest items coming through the mills are 2 inches up to 12 inches in width. They are 2 by 4's and 2 by 6's, that means pieces 2 inches wide or 4 inches or 6 inches wide, that are commonly used for rafters and general construction.

Acting Chairman Commons. Do those have to be finished?

Mr. Mack. They have to be sized. It has to run through the planing mill and one side is dressed, and one edge is dressed so that they make a uniform width and thickness.

Acting Chairman Commons. That is the kind of operation, you say, that has to be done in San Francisco?

Mr. Mack. Yes. The charge, as I understand that, for that small stuff is a dollar per thousand, while we can do it in the mill for about 25 cents.

Chairman Commons. That is including labor and everything?

Mr. Mack. Yes, sir; including everything, because it can go right through the machinery just the same as any of our other material. It can go through with the minimum amount of labor and handling.

Acting Chairman Commons. That cost of $1 a thousand; if it would cost 25 cents a thousand, what would be the total cost of that class?

Mr. Mack. Offhand I would say it would be about 75 cents. When they take that lumber down into the yard it will probably cost them $2 per thousand to put that into a pile, if they take it from the vessel to the yard to be piled. Now, as your order comes in, then you have to move it from the pile to the planing mill and dress it, and then it goes out on the job. It would probably cost them $2, as I say, to put it through the yard; probably 50 cents a thousand more to get it from the pile to the planer.

Now, down there it costs a full dollar a thousand more to dress it, on account of working under certain regulations that slows up the operation. For instance, in the lot here, we will say, we will dress anything up to 2 by 8's—2 by 4's, 2 by 6's, or 2 by 8's. We have a planer with a divided roll and we can shove through two pieces at one time. It goes through quickly and is piled on the truck. Down below, under union regulations as I have seen them, one piece must be fed in at a time. They must have an extra man at the mill as a steward and an extra man at each machine with a rubber stamp putting the union label on each piece of lumber that goes through; so that it runs up the cost to the manufacturer, and ultimately the consumer, of about—well, I should say the average cost of at least $2.50 a thousand.

Acting Chairman Commons. Against 25 cents a thousand here?

Mr. Mack. Yes, sir.

Acting Chairman Commons. Now, take the selling price of that lumber—that class of stuff. What is the selling price of that class?

Mr. Mack. The selling price here of that stock to-day is not to exceed $7.

Acting Chairman Commons. Seven dollars?

Mr. Mack. Yes, sir.

Acting Chairman Commons. The shipping to San Francisco?

Mr. Mack. The shipping to San Francisco is about $3.

Acting Chairman Commons. Now, the cost, then, delivered is $10?

Mr. Mack. Ten dollars.

Acting Chairman Commons. Ten dollars delivered?

Mr. Mack. Now, as to the market there at this time I am unable to tell you.

Acting Chairman Commons. I am getting at the cost.

Mr. Mack. About $10.

Acting Chairman COMMONS. After you finish ·it, then you could deliver ·at ten twenty-five?

Mr. MACK. Yes, sir.

Acting Chairman COMMONS. At present it is costing them, based solely on cost figures, $12.50; that is the difference?

Mr. MACK. That would be about the difference; yes, sir.

Acting Chairman COMMONS. That is $2 more on the thousand?

Mr. MACK. About two dollars and a quarter more, is it not?

Acting Chairman COMMONS. Two dollars and a quarter more on $10; that is about 22 per cent more.

Mr. MACK. Yes, sir; I would say from 20 to 25 per cent more.

Acting Chairman COMMONS. That is, it is costing the builder in San Francisco about 20 to 25 per cent more?

Mr. MACK. Yes, sir.

Acting Chairman COMMONS. On account of this regulation, then?

Mr. MACK. That is something that the mills themselves in the North are divided on. It is economic loss there that we don't feel ·vitally .interested in; that is, San Francisco—incidentally, of course, the men that work in the mills—but as manufacturers we feel that it is not such a burning question.

Commissioner O'CONNELL. Take the difference between the rate here and the mills in San Francisco or the hours of work.

Mr. MACK. No; there is not.

Commissioner O'CONNELL. Do you know whether the millowners in San Francisco are not at the bottom of this arrangement to prevent what they .might consider lumber coming from cheaper conditions competing with them?

Mr. MACK. No; that is not true.

Commissioner O'CONNELL. No combination on the part of owners?

Mr. MACK. No; it is the labor.

Commissioner ·O'CONNELL. Purely labor?

Mr. MACK. A compromise. That was fought out in San Francisco at the end of the strike. It was a compromise.

Commissioner O'CONNELL. Do you suppose the fact is that their wages may be, instead of this difference of percentage, the figures here of 20 per cent, the difference of the wages may be 50 per cent?

Mr. MACK. I do not know what the difference is.

Commissioner O'CONNELL. And the difference in hours may be 20 per cent?

Mr. MACK. I say it is no part of ours. It is an economic loss we are not interested in.

Acting Chairman COMMONS. Can you furnish those figures, so that when we get to San Francisco we can carry out this comparison?

Mr. MACK. I think so.

Acting Chairman COMMONS. Will you do so?

Mr. MACK. Let me understand what figures you want.

Acting Chairman COMMONS. I wanted it for the class of lumber, the largest usage in building; that is what I want.

Mr. MACK. I will get that for you.

Commissioner GARRETSON. How large dimension stuff do you. speak of at the same price?

Mr. MACK. I would in the price I am taking include 2 by 4's, 2 by 6's, and 2 by 8's.

Commissioner GARRETSON. Three of those classes are all one price?

Mr. MACK. Practically one price.

Commissioner GARRETSON. That is a large part of your output?

Mr. MACK. Yes, sir. And I take it from 8 foot to 16. I will send you those figures.

Acting Chairman COMMONS. You may address them here.

Mr. MACK. All right.

Acting Chairman COMMONS. You had how many employees? I have forgotten the number.

·Mr. MACK. In our camps, in one 250 and the other about 150; in our mill, about 160.

Acting Chairman COMMONS. Now, taking the question that ·has been asked other witnesses, how many men do you have to employ in the month or during the year to keep up that force of about 500?

Mr. MACK. I didn't catch the question.

Acting Chairman COMMONS. You have 500 employees altogether, or a·little over?

Mr. MACK. Well, yes.

Acting Chairman COMMONS. How many men do you have to hire during the year to keep up that number?

Mr. MACK. I do not believe I can answer that. Our crews are pretty steady. In our woods—woods operations—there is a large shifting of what you would call the common labor.

Acting Chairman COMMONS. That is the $2.50 man?

Mr. MACK. That is the $2.50 man; and from that up to $2.75 they are large shifters. But, then, the skilled men, the so-called skilled men—snipers, knotters, buckers, and fallers—they are as a rule pretty steady.

Acting Chairman COMMONS. Have they families?

Mr. MACK. Many of them have in our district. We pay more wages in Grays Harbor district than are paid on the average on Grays Harbor, and we attract down in there more steady men; although we have a lot of the trash and some of the hobos, yet we get a pretty good class of men down there.

Acting Chairman COMMONS. Then take your mill. How about your mill—could you tell?

Mr. MACK. Yes. Now, we have the men shifting there. Our men would not shift in our mill; on the basis of 160 they would not shift over 4 a week. That is all in the men, such as men driving truck horses; we seem to have more shifting there than anywhere—men that are getting $2.50 a day for driving a single horse. And some of our men in the yards, they are getting $2.25 and $2.50. We find they are paid that wage because they are speedy men. In my judgment, every time you lose one of your employees there is an economic loss there; that it costs you something to break in somebody else.

Acting Chairman COMMONS. You state in the course of the year you would only have about 50 out of 150?

Mr. MACK. That is hardly fair to put it that way. I am talking now—there are times there, in harvest and fishing seasons, perhaps—in the fishing season we will probably lose half our yard crew. They follow fishing, a good many of them, in the yard. We have a great many Swedes, and they go fishing. Well, we have a temporary crew in there, and when they return the fishing season is over. That has been going on there for a number of years. And so we probably have more changes than 50 a year. I really could not give you the exact figures.

Acting Chairman COMMONS. You say 4 a month?

Mr. MACK. Yes; 4 a month, 50 a year.

Acting Chairman COMMONS. In the other branch?

Mr. MACK. In the logging?

Acting Chairman COMMONS. You mentioned logging and the mill. What was the other?

Mr. MACK. It is the mill I was talking about. The changes in the camps, I don't know. In the first place we have two absolute clearances in the logging camp. One is before the 4th of July, and the other is just before Christmas. Every man in your employ, your superintendent, your foreman, your cooks, everybody else clears at that time. It is an absolute clearance. It is not a foreman or a superintendent who goes back. You have got to hire him. It is an absolute clearance. If you have anything against him that you don't want to hire him again there is no ill feeling, you simply hire another superintendent, another foreman, and go on. It is a new clean slate. So that we have a complete change twice every year that way. And then during the other times—oh, there are a lot of them that are the most improvident class—there are a lot of them that just as soon as they get a stake, if it was hot—when it gets hot as it is in this room now—probably 25 per cent of your crew would go down; will say, "I am going to where there is cool beer." And you won't see some of the men in the morning, until they get all the cool beer they want, and then they will come back to you, but you have to hire other men to take their places. They are itinerants to a certain extent, independent, devil-may-care chaps, independent as a hog on ice. You can't talk to them; you can't order them around or anything. If a man undertakes to swear at one of them it is just as much as his job would be worth, his life would be worth. You have got to understand the fellow before you can appreciate his kind.

Acting Chairman COMMONS. Then the trouble is the same in the mills as in the camps, or is it more fluctuating in the mill?

Mr. MACK. Well, you have a different class of men in your mill. As your logger grows older, he marries and settles down, and then he generally becomes a mill man. There are quite a number of them, and they go along and they go into business in the town. They want to be near their families, because, you understand, those camps are away out in the woods, naturally. You start in a mill say to-day right in the wilderness, and in two years your camps are 4 or 5 miles from you; go on 10 years and they are off 40 or 50 miles. So that many of the camps are located at long distances from—well, from civilization. Out on the frontier, pioneers in the truest sense of the word. You are working under the crudest conditions and as near nature as it is possible for a man to get and get along. Now, the conditions, we hear some of them depict here, they undoubtedly exist. But you find universally, I think, that the largest concerns are running clean, very sanitary, as sanitary as they can get it, and well regulated camps. But the fellow that is small, that starts in with a shoe string, goes out here and gets a piece of timber—anybody can get it—you can start logging here that way. But whenever they do, just start in with the small way just the essentials—the stuff that is absolutely necessary to get along with, and they go out there. Some of the conditions are pretty crude. But they are bettered, and bettered as lively as possible. So that even when they draw a horrible pen picture, or horrible word picture, of the deplorable conditions in the camp, it is some poor chap that has no foothold; but as soon as they get bigger they get in better shape, and the bigger camps are in better shape.

Acting Chairman COMMONS. The difference in the rate of wages, does not make much difference, then, apparently, in the stability of the force. If you increase your rates of pay, make higher wages, do you leave the other more constant?

Mr. MACK. If your wages are general then it acts the other way. The quicker the man can get a stake the more it bothers them.

Acting Chairman COMMONS. If one gets higher than the other, are they pretty steady, is that your idea?

Mr. MACK. Just as I say, they are largely an improvident, unthrifty class. They want to keep the money in circulation.

Acting Chairman COMMONS. Is there any reason in your business for having a steady force?

Mr. MACK. Well, you have got to get along with that class of men. You have got to get good, strong, husky fellows that take kindly to that kind of work just the same as you have men on your skyscrapers putting your steel together, and all that kind of work, men on your surveying parties, railroads—you have got to get the young red-blooded husky that goes with that work.

Acting Chairman COMMONS. Do you work through employment offices?

Mr. MACK. No; the employment offices I spoke to you about that we had.

Acting Chairman COMMONS. Only your own?

Mr. MACK. Only our own.

Acting Chairman COMMONS. You do not get them through private offices?

Mr. MACK. No. We don't hire practically any through any of them. At times we will perhaps run shy of common labor, there are railroad men—sometimes we will have our agent in the employment office phone up and have the agent there send them. Generally that is the way it is done. We phone up here and ask if they can't send down such and such men. He probably sends 25 or 30 men, and they will be scattered between 8 or 10 different camps, you understand. This, Seattle, you understand, is the clearing house, this is the commercial center, and the labor is scattered over a large territory. The city of Seattle is one and Portland is another clearing house, the same way, for a good portion of Washington and all of Oregon. Aberdeen and Hoquiam are big lumber centers. There are over 2,000,000 feet per day of lumber manufactured, and some of the largest and best mills in the State there. There is quite a demand for labor. But often when a man gets out of work he wants to have a high old time, and he comes to Seattle, and when he strikes the streets here you will find more unrest and more discontent in the labor district in Seattle than anywhere else in the State. It has become so flagrant that we almost hesitate to send for men here to the city of Seattle. You are liable to get out a lot of fellows like that that are more uneasy, discontented, and real trouble breeders.

Acting Chairman COMMONS. Mr. Thompson, have you any questions?

Mr. THOMPSON. Just one more question: Do you know anything about the plant that Mr. Cooney is manager of?

Mr. MACK. Yes, sir.

Mr. THOMPSON. How do the wages there paid compare with the wages you pay?

Mr. MACK. They are altogether different. I run a sawmill, and we ship our lumber all over the world, largely offshore, but it is in a very crude or unfinished condition; but the commercial company have got a different business, altogether. They take the rough lumber, when I get through with it, and they go ahead and they spend more money on labor on that product there than I have up to the time that I quit on it. They finish their lumber, and they ship all over—you might say, all over the United States. They do but very little foreign order business. Now, their biggest business is in box making. I presume that their largest competitors are found in the city of Seattle or in Portland. You go down into one of those box factories, and you will find a lot of boys and a lot of girls working there. They are doing the work that those people here—men—ought to do. The commercial company are off from civilization, and when they start they just naturally go out after the misfits. They bring in everybody and anybody and pour them into the hopper to do the work.

Commissioner GARRETSON. Mostly culls?

Mr. MACK. No; they are not. I just want to say here that the majority are good men, and they are public benefactors. You take the man that strikes Seattle down and out, absolutely at the end of his resources, he can go along there and there is not a job open for him. He has got to either be an object of charity or get out, that is all. Here is the employment agency down here that has got a standing sign up there, "Men wanted," and it don't matter whether the man has got ability to earn a salary of a hundred dollars a minute or $1 a week, he can get a job there at $26, and he comes down. For instance, I have had two assistant managers—one succeeded the other—that are bright, brainy fellows; one is manager of the mill now, and the other is a manager of one of the largest independent logging companies. They both started in at $26 a month in that plant.

Commissioner GARRETSON. They were physical culls, just the same, from the description you give.

Mr. MACK. No. They were down and out financially. They were not physical culls. Both of them were pretty husky fellows. But they were both down and out, and they started in down there, and just as soon as they could do so they got into something better. My head accountant to-day is a man who started in there years ago. They are really recruiting stations for Grays Harbor. They are public benefactors. There is always a job open, and you will find them ready to take them. You go out in the streets of Seattle to-day, and there are two men—I think you will find there are two men here for every job that there is in the city of Seattle; that you must go outside of the city to secure work.

Commissioner GARRETSON. That is what is open for men in that plant?

Mr. MACK. You can call it what you please.

Commissioner GARRETSON. I did not name it.

Mr. MACK. Do not get sarcastic about it, because it is a fact, and we need more of those plants there, more in the State. There is not a place in the State of Washington but what ought to have more people to work up our lumbermen. If we did, we would have more men to work, and we would have a larger pay roll. It costs us about $3 for pay roll to men, and they may pay eight; who does the greatest good for the community? The money is brought out. You asked the question if I thought any industry that did not pay a living wage had a right to exist. I don't know.

Commissioner GARRETSON. No; it was that gentleman over there.

Mr. MACK. I don't know.

Commissioner GARRETSON. I asked it yesterday.

Mr. MACK. Now, you are insisting here in the United States on free, open competition. You go to work, you in the United States insisting on absolute open competition, but when you see the fruits of it you get sarcastic and find fault with it.

Commissioner GARRETSON. Who is insisting on open competition?

Mr. MACK. Show me. We have had investigating committees, and they all look alike to us. We have had investigating committees out here trying to put that in for the last five years.

Commissioner GARRETSON. What did they do to the railroad companies for open competition?

Mr. MACK. They are putting them on the blink, that is all. What are they doing? They are going into the hands of receivers. If this war hadn't started in, in six months half of your railroads in the United States would be in the hands of receivers.

Commissioner GARRETSON. They started things on the other side, all right. I want to ask you one question: I assume you are perfectly familiar with the movement of lumber from the stump to the consuming point?

Mr. MACK. Yes, sir.

Commissioner GARRETSON. Take the run of dimension stuff, the largest run of it from your mill; I want to follow that for a moment: You turn it out rough. You move it. I do not know what your movement is, possibly, from the mill to the dock, or from the dock to the next dock; I don't know—do you use lighterage?

Mr. MACK. No.

Commissioner GARRETSON. What?

Mr. MACK. Onto a vessel.

Commissioner GARRETSON. From the dock to the yard that you spoke of a little while ago there it was piled. That would be the ordinary movement?

Mr. MACK. You are talking about the mill end of it, are you?

Commissioner GARRETSON. No; I am talking about the San Francisco end.

Mr. MACK. Oh.

Commissioner GARRETSON. From the saw to your own pile, or to the car, do you market from that?

Mr. MACK. Well, of course we market it here.

Commissioner GARRETSON. You market it here?

Mr. MACK. Yes; down there; but that is a separate transaction we have no voice in whatever. We don't really know what they do at San Francisco.

Commissioner GARRETSON. Do you deliver in the pile or on the car?

Mr. MACK. We deliver at the side of the vessel at our dock.

Commissioner GARRETSON. How is that?

Mr. MACK. Deliver alongside the vessel at our dock.

Commissioner GARRETSON. You have a dock of your own?

Mr. MACK. Yes.

Commissioner GARRETSON. You deliver at your dock?

Mr. MACK. At our dock, and at the mill. That is one part. There are others that quote a price delivered on the dock at San Francisco.

Commissioner GARRETSON. Where you deliver on the dock at San Francisco, the movement from the saw, it was near enough to the dock that you could take it right from the dock, or do you have to transfer in a car?

Mr. MACK. You talking now again about San Francisco?

Commissioner GARRETSON. No. Your own dock.

Mr. MACK. No; our dock. Our mill is right on the edge.

Commissioner GARRETSON. So it is taken right from the saw and it goes on the carrier and it moves out, and the only interruption of that movement would be that you finish it; for instance, you size it when it goes on a carriage and is moved out?

Mr. MACK. I told you when it gets to San Francisco, now, then, it goes into the yard; that is universally the practice. It goes from the vessel. We will discharge it on the dock, we will say, and the yardman picks it up and moves it into the yard and piles it in a pile.

Commissioner GARRETSON. He does?

Mr. MACK. And when the order comes in they size it.

Commissioner GARRETSON. The movements that would put that in the pile in the San Francisco yards are exactly the same whether you size it or whether you do not, except that when it goes from the saw you have an automatic carrier to take it right to the planer?

Mr. MACK. No; just shove and pull them right off.

Commissioner GARRETSON. The movement is continuous?

Mr. MACK. Yes; practically so.

Commissioner GARRETSON. Consequently the only thing it adds here is the movement from the saw to the planer?

Mr. MACK. That is all.

Commissioner GARRETSON. And then it goes to the dock just the same as if it was rough?

Mr. MACK. Just the same.

Commissioner GARRETSON. And when it gets into San Francisco rough it is piled in the yard. The cost up to that point is just exactly the same whether it is smooth or rough, as far as transportation and handling are concerned, except if you plane they add 25 cents a thousand on the estimate you gave a little while ago; and when it moves from the yard in San Francisco to the builder the only difference is not only the difference in the handling—I am speaking now of handling the stuff—that if it is sized it will go direct from the pile in the yard to the builder, wherever he wants it; and if it is going to be sized there will be one movement added, namely, to the mill, because the movement either to the builder or to the mill is exactly the same and would be chargeable against the product anyhow. Is that correct?

Mr. MACK. I take it, now, the commission wants facts, and that is what you are going to get.

Commissioner GARRETSON. Is there anything involved but that one movement?

Mr. MACK. I don't know. Ask San Francisco.

Commissioner GARRETSON. I thought you knew.

Mr. MACK. I do.

Commissioner GARRETSON. The movement of lumber from the saw to the consumer.

Mr. MACK. I do. I told you, but you are trying to get me to say something else.

Commissioner GARRETSON. Well, we will find out.

Mr. MACK. Well, you can find out in San Francisco.

Commissioner O'CONNELL. I want to ask you a few questions. I asked Mr. Cooney the same question when he was on the stand: Is your company incorporated?

Mr. MACK. Yes, sir.

Commissioner O'CONNELL. What is its capital stock?

Mr. MACK. The capital stock, I think, is a million dollars—that is, the Slade Co.; the Slade Lumber Co.

Commissioner O'CONNELL. Shares of the par value of what?

Mr. MACK. I don't really know.

Commissioner O'CONNELL. How many shares were issued?

Mr. MACK. I would say, Mr. O'Connell, that our home office is in San Francisco and the accounts are all kept there, and that the mill—that I represent the mill end of it; simply the manufacturing end.

Commissioner O'CONNELL. Do you publish an annual statement?

Mr. MACK. They do in San Francisco. I don't publish them.

Commissioner O'CONNELL. Now, you could not give us any exact figures as to the earnings of the business or the corporation, only in your management?

Mr. MACK. I have seen the figures.

Commissioner O'CONNELL. Do you know whether they have paid any dividends?

Mr. MACK. No, sir; they have not paid any dividends for seven years.

Commissioner O'CONNELL. What dividends were paid before that?

Mr. MACK. They have paid as high as 15 or 16 per cent.

Commissioner O'CONNELL. Has the capital been increased or decreased during the organization?

Mr. MACK. I don't remember; I think not. I think the surplus was accumulated as a surplus in years past and that still stands. It has been diminished a little, but not much. The business has been unprofitable for several years.

Commissioner O'CONNELL. You mean by that that you have not been able to pay dividends in seven years?

Mr. MACK. No, sir; I mean we haven't hardly paid expenses.

Commissioner O'CONNELL. Haven't paid expenses?

Mr. MACK. No, sir; it may sound silly for a man to say he is running at a loss and losing money, but we have quite a plant there, and we estimate it costs us about $5,000 a month to shut down. That is, our insurance has to be kept up, and taxes have to be met——

Commissioner O'CONNELL. Your overhead charges.

Mr. MACK. Our overheard charges are going along, and if we can run and have a loss under operation below $5,000 we have saved money.

Commissioner O'CONNELL. We can get at San Francisco the other details?

Mr. MACK. Yes, sir.

Acting Chairman COMMONS. You own your timberland?

Mr. MACK. Yes, sir; we own considerable.

Acting Chairman COMMONS. Did you buy considerable?

Mr. MACK. Yes, sir; we buy a great deal.

Acting Chairman COMMONS. What has been the increase in this period in the cost of stumpage?

Mr. MACK. Well, the stumpage has more than doubled.

Acting Chairman Commons. What would be the quotation?

Mr. Mack. For instance, we bought stumpage—we bought stumpage about 10 years ago, about 600.000,000 at a dollar and a half, and that stands on our books to-day at about three dollars. That is, that the yearly cost is added to that, not declaring any dividends on it or any paper profits, but the carrying cost.

Acting Chairman Commons. The carrying cost?

Mr. Mack. Yes, sir. We wrote a very low rate of interest, and I don't care to go into that. You can get that, as I say.

Acting Chairman Commons. The market value of stumpage——

Mr. Mack. Has about doubled in the last 10 years. I would say it hasn't advanced any in seven years. We had a boom on the river, thanks to bountiful crops in the East during 1905, 1906, and 1907, and the San Francisco fire, and timber shot up. Logs here went from $7.50 and $8 per thousand to $12 per thousand in the log, and stumpage went up, stumpage followed. And it stayed up.. While the man that owns stumpage, if you wanted to buy, it was at this level, and it hasn't receded any, but it has not advanced any. So that stumpage has not increased since 1907 and could not be sold to-day for a price that was offered then.

Acting Chairman Commons. The man who has held stumpage during this period has made money?

Mr. Mack. No, sir; he has not. When we bought timber in the early days we bought timber as low as 25 cents a thousand. Then the carrying cost was small; the country was new and taxes were light, and it didn't cost so much to carry it, and it took longer for it to double. But once that stumpage got over a dollar, then the cost commenced to pyramid, and now one of the curses of the times is everybody is trying to unload, they are trying to liquidate. You take, say, $3 stumpage cost to-day; now, 6 per cent on that is reasonable interest—that is 18 cents per thousand per year. Now, your taxes will run up—it is averaging over 6 cents. Now, you have to spend something in fire patrol and looking after it, so that you can call that 1 cent per thousand; that is reasonable; you are not doing a great deal at that. Now, there is 18 cents, and 6 cents, and 1 cent; that is 25 cents per thousand per year. You take and pyramid that and compound it, as you would naturally do if you were loaning your money out, and see the way it is going up. The natural development of the country is not going to raise stumpage, I think, to a point that timber holding is going to be profitable. I don't believe it will ever be profitable again to hold timber.

Acting Chairman Commons. Any questions, Mr. Thompson?

Mr. Thompson. That is all, Mr. Chairman.

Acting Chairman Commons. That is all, Mr. Mack. Call your next, Mr. Thompson.

Mr. Thompson. Mr. Rucker.

TESTIMONY OF MR. W. J. RUCKER.

Mr. Thompson. Will you give us your name?

Mr. Rucker. W. J. Rucker.

Mr. Thompson. And your address?

Mr. Rucker. Everett, Wash.

Mr. Thompson. And your business?

Mr. Rucker. Lumbering.

Mr. Thompson. What company are you with?

Mr. Rucker. Rucker Bros. (Inc.) and Cavanaugh Timber Co.

Mr. Thompson. What kind of lumber business are you engaged in?

Mr. Rucker. We log and manufacture.

Mr. Thompson. How many men do you employ on the average?

Mr. Rucker. Well, I should say in the vicinity of 400.

Mr. Thompson. Mostly in manufacturing, or are they equally divided?

Mr. Rucker. Well, we manufacture probably—we have 250 men manufacturing, the balance in logging, and some road building outside of our logging operations.

Mr. Thompson. You have been here the last couple of days?

Mr. Rucker. Yes, sir; I have been here for two days; you promised to put me on two days ago, and to let me get away.

Acting Chairman Commons. We are very sorry we didn't do that, and we hope to be forgiven.

Mr. RUCKER. I see lots of people that were here. I have been around .here waiting, and I have other things to do.

Mr. THOMPSON. I haven't established much of a reputation as a promiser, have I?

Mr. RUCKER. I haven't as much confidence in you as I would have had.

Acting Chairman COMMONS. I take the blame, Mr. Rucker.

Mr. THOMPSON. You heard the testimony of the men who have been on the stand?

Mr. RUCKER. Yes, sir.·

Mr. THOMPSON. What have you to add either to what Mr. Brown said, representing labor, or the other men, speaking for labor in the lumbering field, or what have you got to add to what has been said to-day by the men representing the employers in the lumber field?

Mr. RUCKER. Well, I don't know that I have anything to add. I believe in the employment of labor that it is important that you treat them right, and that you keep a good sanitary condition about your camps.

Mr. THOMPSON. What view do you take of the conditions of labor in the lumber industry in this vicinity?

Mr. RUCKER. Well, I think it is very good. I don't believe there is labor in any part of the United States that compares with the labor in the logging camps and sawmills of Puget Sound. I believe they are possibly more intelligent, better informed, and, by being a little careful in selecting, just as honorable.

Mr. THOMPSON. What are the lowest wages that you pay for ordinary labor?

Mr. RUCKER. I think the lowest wages that we pay is $2.50.

Mr. THOMPSON. What percentage of the men in the lumber industry are married, if you know, and are they generally a married class of men or are they single?·

Mr. RUCKER. I could not tell you that. We have a system, a card system, that we take from our men, that we could make you up a report from.

Mr. THOMPSON. What proportion of work or how much work does a lumberman have during the year, if you know?

Mr. RUCKER. Well, we have not lost, I don't believe on account of weather conditions, to exceed 10 days in the last two years.

Mr. THOMPSON. Then, the men working for your company have had pretty steady work?

Mr. RUCKER. Yes, sir.

Mr. THOMPSON. If they wished to.

Mr. RUCKER. We want to keep going all the time if we can.

Mr. THOMPSON. Do you keep fairly well in touch with the labor conditions around this country?

Mr. RUCKER. Well, I don't know that I do, excepting our employment system. We have a card system that we take from our men, and then keep their addresses and try to do our own employing of men.

Mr. THOMPSON. Looking at the conditions of labor, as a citizen of the country, do you feel that it calls for any remedial measures of any kind, or how do you view it?

Mr. RUCKER. Oh, I don't think so. I think if a man wants to get out and succeed that he can do it. Certainly there are opportunities in this country.

Mr. THOMPSON. Then, as you view the conditions in the labor field here, if you were a member of this commission you would be compelled to say, in accordance with your views, that there was nothing that you saw that needed attention, and, therefore, you had nothing to recommend, we will say?

Mr. RUCKER. Well, I think that this commission will have to let labor hoe its own row. You go to taking care of labor—put a man in the shade and fan him, and he will never develop, he will never create. I don't believe the time will ever come when another man can look after the interests of his pastneighbor . He is liable to make pretty short grazing in the other fellow's pasture

Mr. THOMPSON. Well, is there anything that you would say about the industrial situation? Would you say that apparently, as you view it, that it seemed that the field is fairly good, that the men are fairly contented, that they had reason to be contented, or, if they are discontented, that they have no real justice back of their discontent?

Mr. RUCKER. Well, fioin my experience and our own operations, I would, say that they have not. Now, our average wage that we pay in the woods is at least $3.50. The average in the mill is more than $3, and I know that when I was starting out that I worked for $1 a day, and I know we had the same labor troubles at that time. I was mayor of a little town in Ohio, and I remember our militia went down to Cincinnati, where they had a bad strike, and was stoned and maimed up, and we have always had those conditions. I don't see that there is any way, excepting the individuals to work it out for themselves.

Mr. THOMPSON. Well, that brings me to part of your testimony that you gave, Mr. Rucker. You say that we have always had these same labor troubles?

Mr. RUCKER. Well, we have always had labor troubles and always have had them.

Mr. THOMPSON. I rather gathered from what you said that the condition was good?

Mr. RUCKER. Well, it is as good as it has ever been possibly—that is, for an average of a long period.

Mr. THOMPSON. Well, assuming that to be true, you believe there are labor troubles?

Mr. RUCKER. Oh, there has been for centuries.

Mr. THOMPSON. Well, now, do you believe that the Government and society as a whole should not study them, should not try to find out what is at the bottom of them, and should not attempt to take care of them; would you think that that would require some attention?

Mr. RUCKER. I don't know but that it is a good thing. I think that if I— I don't object to labor organizations. We employ men just as freely if they belong, and I would not object to joining a labor organization myself if I was working by the day. But just as soon as that organization undertook to impose upon an employer some man that had been discharged for destroying or wasting property, why, then, I would break with them right there. They have got to be fair, and the majority of the men in the logging and mill operations are just and right.

Mr. THOMPSON. Well, take labor as a whole.

Mr. RUCKER. Well, I could not tell you about it, except ours.

Mr. THOMPSON. The good with the bad, do you believe that organization is a good thing for the workingman?

Mr. RUCKER. I would be inclined to think it was.

Mr. THOMPSON. Well, what do you think should be the attitude of the employer if that is so; what would be the way to handle the problem involved in labor to-day?

Mr. RUCKER. Well, I don't believe my judgment in the matter would be of any value. I believe in every individual working out his own salvation. That is where it finally fetches up. Of course, if the Government has a commission, it may be of assistance. I don't think I would want a commission to dictate to me, though, how I shall run my business, if I have got to pay the bills.

Mr. THOMPSON. That would be your recommendation to the commission?

Mr. RUCKER. Well, I would want to have a good deal to say about my business if I was paying the bills.

Mr. THOMPSON. Well, as this commission is commanded by Congress to look into the condition of labor, into the organizations of labor, into the organizations of employers, into any unrest, if it exists, and if it does exist, the causes, and to suggest remedies—some questions have been sent to you in writing for you to give your views in the matter. What would you say to this commission about it now?

Mr. RUCKER. Well, I think that the thing they should do is to endeavor to discover that remedy. I am afraid they won't do it. I don't believe that this commission can aid very materially the man that won't aid himself or do for himself.

Mr. THOMPSON. Is there anything further you would like to say, Mr. Rucker, in any respect?

Mr. RUCKER. Well, there are a few things about taxes that worry me a good deal more than labor, but I don't know that it would be of any interest to the commission.

Mr. THOMPSON. That is all, Mr. Chairman.

Acting Chairman COMMONS. Mr. Rucker, you spoke about having an employment system of your own.

Mr. RUCKER. Yes, sir.

Acting Chairman COMMONS. Will you describe that system; does it take the place of the private employment office?

Mr. RUCKER. Well, I have a card here that we ask the men to sign, and they generally sign it. I think they sign it in all cases.

Acting Chairman COMMONS. That is filed and constitutes an address and mailing list, does it?

Mr. RUCKER. Yes. Now this card, we have it in blank:

"State particulars of your suspenison or discharge from any employment. Give the date of your employment and the kind of employment, the companies, and addresses."

Then on the other side we have this card numbered, and we want:

"Full name of applicant, employment desired, age, nationality, married or single, name and address of wife, father or mother, and self. Do you use intoxicating liquors? Date and character of past employment by Rucker Bros. Physical ailments or defects, if any, and state when, where, and nature of any physical injuries suffered."

Then we have a card that we address to their references, with a return card asking:

"Did he work for you as stated? Why did he leave your employ? Were his services satisfactory? Do you consider him intelligent, reliable, and industrious? Is he inclined to be careful or reckless? Do you believe him honest? Has he any distinct traits of character not mentioned above? State, if possible, for whom he worked before and after leaving your employ. Do you fully recommend him for the position of ———? "

This is addressed to the parties——

Acting Chairman COMMONS. Now, do all of the employees who apply for work sign and fill out this first card?

Mr. RUCKER. Yes; we haven't had any trouble about that.

Acting Chairman COMMONS. You ask them to fill that out?

Mr. RUCKER. Yes.

Acting Chairman COMMONS. Then you send out this inquiry to other employers in all cases?

Mr. RUCKER. Yes, sir.

Acting Chairman COMMONS. Then you keep a record?

Mr. RUCKER. Then we have a case that we file these in, and keep them all in there in regular order, so that when we have a place open we can reach them.

Acting Chairman COMMONS. Now, is the object of that—you apparently go into this matter of their qualifications more than others who have been before us—is it the object to secure a permanent force?

Mr. RUCKER. The best labor we can get.

Acting Chairman COMMONS. And keep them permanently?

Mr. RUCKER. And keep them permanently.

Acting Chairman COMMONS. You have heard the questions that have been asked about the transient character of this labor?

Mr. RUCKER. Yes.

Acting Chairman COMMONS. Can you state in any way to what extent you have a permanent and stable force?

Mr. RUCKER. Well, at our mill I would say that we have created homes and that enough have homes they have paid for, that in case every man would walk out of the mill that they would step right in and operate the mill. I think that in the last 15 years we have been instrumental in assisting, oh, possibly hundreds of people to comfortable homes. And in our camp—now I have heard a lot of testimony here about people furnishing all kinds of places for people to sleep in. Of course, now that is ridiculous, the working of some child or man and injuring them physically. Why, any man that does that is foolish. He injures himself when he does it. Now, with our camp, we have three buildings that are 140 feet long. Those buildings are divided into apartments of about 12 or 14. We have steam heat, electric light, hot and cold water. We furnish bedding, blankets, and linen sheets. We have our own washing outfit, electric washers and electric irons, and steam driers. We have a 60 by 16 boiler that heats these buildings and furnishes the hot water. We have a water system that cost a large amount of money, bringing it in possibly for a mile, spring water, 8-inch main, with 300-foot head that runs the turbine that generates the light. We have a sewer system that is laid probably 15 feet under the ground in places and 800 feet long that carries the sewage away from the building—got a toilet system, and everything, which is very expensive. This idea that people are not properly housed—I think in all of the larger camps that they are take care of. We furnish a janitor and he makes their beds and sweeps their rooms. We have a trained nurse, one of the best in the country, that stays right there to look after the men if they are injured. Of course we have the same hospital or doctor's service that the other camps have. And we believe it makes us money. We buy the best provisions we can. We charge these men $5.50 for board per week.

Commissioner O'CONNELL. I just want to interrupt just a moment, if you please. As I understand it, your wage rates are higher, from your, statements here, than has been stated to us by any witness we have had, isn't it?

Mr. RUCKER. I think so.

Commissioner O'CONNELL. The conditions under which they are housed, and their sanitary arrangements and those arrangements under which they live far exceed those that have been spoken of before. Some concerns tell us, and one concern only ran 10 years out of 19, and another is losing money—does your concern find it profitable to operate its business under the basis you tell us now?

Mr. RUCKER. Well, for a period of years we have done—we are satisfied. Under this administration we are not doing so well.

Commissioner O'CONNELL. You mean the Democratic administration?

Mr. RUCKER. Yes. But we hope to get through.

Commissioner O'CONNELL. Well, there may be a change some time, you never can tell.

Mr. RUCKER. Yes; I hope so.

Commissioner O'CONNELL. What I want to get at is, do you find it profitable as a business proposition to operate your business under the basis you speak of?

Mr. RUCKER. Yes; I believe it is more profitable than not, to give your men good treatment, give them wholesome food, and give them a good sanitary place to live.

Commissioner O'CONNELL. Then instead of sleeping on ordinary straw and hay, you furnish them a sheet to sleep on, on top of that, as I understand it?

Mr. RUCKER. Well, we furnish them sheets.

Commissioner O'CONNELL. I take it in some of these other camps they would scarcely know what a sheet was.

Mr. RUCKER. Well, I don't know, I have been in some camps that are very well kept. Now, this industrial insurance. We operated for 10 years prior to the passage of that act. We never paid a dollar insurance. We never paid a dollar damages. And now all at once we are dumped into an industrial insurance—last year, I think, we paid insurance amounting to—well, I will say between $7,000 and $10,000. Still we are paying this wage. Now, I would rather pay it to the men. During the period that we were operating prior to the passage of the act, we had an understanding with our men. We said, "Now, here you are taking a hazardous place here. You are going to get in front of a head saw. We are going to pay you a wage, not so much for your skill, but the risk. Now, we don't want you to hold us responsible for any accident that might happen here. We are going to furnish every safety device that we can think of. But you must assume the risk, we can't. We may be wound up here right off the reel if we have got to pay damages." Well, now, we had during that period probably, I should say, 12 or 15 men that were killed, and many men wounded. We never had a damage suit. We had one or two actions commenced, but were never brought to suit, and we never had to do anything in the matter of compromising them.

Commissioner O'CONNELL. Do you mean to say that you never paid anything to the heirs of these people, of men who were killed?

Mr. RUCKER. No, sir; we never did. We had a positive understanding, and these heirs had an understanding.

Commissioner O'CONNELL. Did they sign away their rights when they went to work there?

Mr. RUCKER. No, sir; it would not be of any value. No, sir; it was a matter of honor in selecting men, and men being honorable. There was an understanding, a positive understanding that they must not take that position.

Commissioner O'CONNELL. Do I understand you would prefer that condition to the conditions now prevailing?

Mr. RUCKER. Yes, sir; I certainly would. Now, we are compelled to pay here—in 10 years we are compelled to pay $75,000 or $100,000. I would rather give it to the men and let them insure themselves.

Commissioner O'CONNELL. Well, but as I understand, you didn't give it to the men.

Mr. RUCKER. No. Well, we give it in the wages and we are now compelled to insure the men under the law, but we don't do that voluntarily. I don't like it.

Commissioner O'CONNELL. Doesn't that appear to you as a humane matter?

Mr. RUCKER. Why, humane; quite humane. But I would rather pay it to the men and let them insure themselves.

Commissioner O'CONNELL. What became of the families, the wives and children of those who were married, who were killed?

Mr. RUCKER. Well, now, the sympathetic part of it; that is all good, we are looking at that.

Commissioner O'CONNELL. I am not looking at the matter of sympathy, but the actual living; these people have to live.

Mr. RUCKER. Yes; that is good. That is good. But we propose to pay the men this money and let them take care of themselves. Then we will know where we are getting off. Here is some fellow in the shingle mill that has got his finger scratched. He comes here to the commission and the commission gives him $300. I have ridden on the train when the boys were telling about that; the slickest lot of fellows in the country are these shingle weavers, and they know how to take care of themselves. They would be comparing and one would say, "I got $200 for that. Your finger there was scratched, you ought to get two or three hundred dollars."

Commissioner O'CONNELL. He couldn't very well keep that up, you know, and cut a little piece off of his finger every day or two?

Mr. RUCKER. No.

Commissioner O'CONNELL. He might get his arm up to the shoulder after a while.

Mr. RUCKER. Well, that is true. Those things are bad, and should be taken care of.

Commissioner O'CONNELL. Well, it seems that at least the trend of human activity now is that this sort of legislation is going on. It is coming; there is not any question about that. The question is to bring it about in the most reasonable and businesslike way, so that all in the industries and business will be taxed; that some won't escape and others have to pay it all; that all may be taxed somewhat.

Mr. RUCKER. Well, I will tell you, this tax system is all wrong. We pay, my brother and I—we ain't got a whole lot, either—I guess in 18 months we have paid $40,000 taxes in various ways, and I think that in the town of Everett there are about 6,000 people paying taxes; in Seattle here possibly 30,000 people paying taxes. You ask a Seattle citizen and he will tell you then there were 300,000 more that weren't paying. Now, what I would like to say is that every man that has a voting franchise should be taxed. Then we would have a Government, and we would have a different tax.

Commissioner O'CONNELL. Mr. Rucker, don't you suppose that with this taxation that is now being levied in your State for care of accidents, that that is going to have the effect of lessening accidents; it is going to have the effect of employers taking greater precautions around their factories and their workshops; that it is going to be a cry of safety first, and as accidents reduce, and as employers provide to prevent accidents, that then your taxes and your cost of carrying that insurance is going to drop, and drop constantly?

Mr. RUCKER. I think that labor ought to assist in carrying that burden. I don't think that industry should be confiscated.

Commissioner O'CONNELL. Well, from what I have heard this morning, there is some of the industry that has not been confiscated.

Mr. RUCKER. Well, I will tell you now, of course, we all have our hard places, I guess.

Commissioner O'CONNELL. Well, that is true. Is your company an incorporated association?

Mr. RUCKER. Well, Rucker Bros. (Inc.), is an incorporated association, and the Cavanaugh Timber Co. Rucker Bros., is private ownership; my brother and I own all the stock.

Commissioner O'CONNELL. You are a limited company, then, are you?

Mr. RUCKER. Yes. Now, we make a full report of our operations to the——

Commissioner O'CONNELL. What is your limit of capital?

Mr. RUCKER. Well it is a hundred thousand. But we make a report to the revenue department, so that——

Commissioner O'CONNELL. That is available?

Mr. RUCKER. That is all made in detail; yes.

Commissioner O'CONNELL. Yes. That is all.

Acting Chairman COMMONS. Would you be willing to file with the reporter those cards of identification?

Mr. RUCKER. Yes, sir.

(The papers referred to were submitted in printed form.)

Mr. RUCKER. We have another system at the bank or at the mill. We don't pay our men in money, we give them a deposit slip.

Commissioner O'CONNELL. Well, are you interested in the bank in any way?

Mr. RUCKER. Yes; we own the bank.

Commissioner O'CONNELL. You own the bank?

Mr. RUCKER. Yes.

Commissioner O'CONNELL. You don't want the money to get away at all, do you? Now we are getting acquainted.

Mr. RUCKER. Yes. I thought I had a deposit slip.

Acting Chairman COMMONS. It is all in the family, anyhow?

Mr. RUCKER. Well, anyhow, we make up a deposit slip instead of a check:

HARTFORD, WASH., _____, 191__.

Mr. _____:

We have placed to your credit in the bank of Rucker Bros. & Co. this day _____ dollars, as shown by the statement of your _____ wages below, which is subject to your check at any time.

RUCKER BROS. (INC.).

Then we give their time and hospital and board and store account and ledger account.

Commissioner O'CONNELL. It is simply a deposit credit you give them in lieu?

Mr. RUCKER. Yes; and then they have a check and check it out as they please.

Acting Chairman COMMONS. Would you just turn that in to the reporter?

Mr. RUCKER. Yes.

(The paper so presented was marked "Document Serial No. 440, August 13, 1914, Witness Rucker."

The paper referred to was submitted in printed form.)

Commissioner O'CONNELL. Do you pay them interest on their deposits?

Mr. RUCKER. We do if they leave it there for a number of months, and we encourage them to make investments, and we endeavor to get them securities if they save their money—warrants or any securities that they want. We want to see the men become prosperous and become taxpayers, we need help.

Commissioner O'CONNELL. Are your employees fairly good depositors?

Mr. RUCKER. Yes; very good, most of them.

Commissioner O'CONNELL. What is the capitalization of your bank?

Mr. RUCKER. There ain't no capital.

Commissioner O'CONNELL. A private bank?

Mr. RUCKER. Just a private bank—my brother and I.

Commissioner O'CONNELL. What is the last statement published by your bank?

Mr. RUCKER. We don't publish a statement.

Commissioner O'CONNELL. If you didn't do anything of that kind, you ought to make money.

Mr. RUCKER. What's the use?

Commissioner O'CONNELL. Well, what are the resources of the bank?

Mr. RUCKER. Well, the resources of the bank are whatever Rucker Bros. have; it is a private partnership.

Acting Chairman COMMONS. Unlimited liability as far as the bank in concerned?

Mr. RUCKER. Yes.

Commissioner GARRETSON. Any system of State bank examination in this State?

Mr. RUCKER. Oh, yes; there is under incorporated banks.

Commissioner GARRETSON. Private banks?

Mr. RUCKER. This bank doesn't come under that.

Commissioner GARRETSON. A private bank can be run here without any inspection?

Mr. RUCKER. Yes, sir. I think now there is a law that possibly next year that private banks will come under the provision of the State bank examiner, but that has not gone into effect yet. That law was passed, I think, some two or three years ago.

Acting Chairman COMMONS. To what extent is labor organized in your plant?

Mr. RUCKER. Well, I don't know; I never pay much attention to that.

Acting Chairman COMMONS. Do the organizers ever call on you—agitators?

Mr. RUCKER. Well, I know some of the men at the head of the labor organizations.

Acting Chairman COMMONS. Do they ever ask you to make any agreements—any trade agreements?

Mr. RUCKER. I don't think so.

Acting Chairman COMMONS. Have they ever presented a scale—a union scale—to you?

Mr. RUCKER. I don't know that they ever have. I think that we pay more than the union scale. I think they would be foolish to.

Acting Chairman COMMONS. You don't know what their scale is?

Mr. RUCKER. No; I don't. But I think, now, for instance, in the matter of shingles, that possibly 9 and 18 cents—9 cents for packing and 18 for sawing—is possibly their union scale.

Acting Chairman COMMONS. Is that what you pay?

Mr. RUCKER. Well, we may pay a little more than that. We make a little better shingles than our neighbors. We don't try so many. We saw them vertically, and we don't want them to saw over 30,000 to the machine, and we try to make them a little better, and we get a little better price for them.

Commissioner GARRETSON. You would rather have quality than quantity?

Mr. RUCKER. That is the idea.

Acting Chairman COMMONS. What is your total pay roll here?

Mr. RUCKER. Our total pay roll here, I think it is about—I think it runs right about $30,000 a month.

Acting Chairman COMMONS. Would you furnish us a table that would show the married men and the single men in all of your force?

Mr. RUCKER. Yes, sir; I will do that.

Acting Chairman COMMONS. Will you show on a given date the length of time that these men have been employed in your service?

Mr. RUCKER. Yes, sir.

Acting Chairman COMMONS. For each one, so that we could group them. The period of time they have been employed.

Mr. RUCKER. Yes; that is, we can get you the average.

Acting Chairman COMMONS. We don't want the average; we want it classified. I want to be able to say so many men have been in the service six months, so many have been in the service nine months, so many a year, so many five years. Could you do it in that form?

Mr. RUCKER. Yes; you want that for all the men employed; that is, in the sawmills and in the woods?

Acting Chairman COMMONS. Yes; I don't want to ask too much of you.

Mr. RUCKER. Oh, that is all right.

Acting Chairman COMMONS. Could you give also the number of men you have hired during the present year; that is, new men taken on in order to keep up this force?

Mr. RUCKER. Yes, sir; we can do that.

(See Rucker exhibit.)

Acting Chairman COMMONS. Will you mail that to us at our headquarters at Washington?

Mr. RUCKER. I don't know whether I have your address.

Mr. THOMPSON. At Chicago.

Acting Chairman COMMONS. At Chicago. Much obliged to you, Mr. Rucker, unless you have anything further to suggest.

Mr. RUCKER. I haven't anything to suggest.

Acting Chairman COMMONS. Much obliged to you. Call your next.

Mr. THOMPSON. Mr. Paterson.

TESTIMONY OF MR. J. V. PATERSON.

Mr. THOMPSON. Will you give us your name?

Mr. PATERSON. J. V. Paterson.

Mr. THOMPSON. And your address?

Mr. PATERSON. Seattle.
Mr. THOMPSON. And your business?
Mr. PATERSON. Shipbuilder.
Mr. THOMPSON. Are you connected with the company or for yourself? .*
Mr. PATERSON. I am the president of the Seattle Construction & Dry Dock Co.
Mr. THOMPSON. How long have you been connected with that company? .
Mr. PATERSON. Since the start of the company.
Mr. THOMPSON. About how many years is that, Mr. Patterson?
Mr. PATERSON. Two years.
Mr. THOMPSON. Are you interested in the ownership of the company?
Mr. PATERSON. I am.
Mr. THOMPSON. What business were you engaged in here prior to two years ago?
Mr. PATERSON. The same business.
Mr. THOMPSON. Then that is a firm, then?
Mr. PATERSON. The old company that the present company purchased.
Mr. THOMPSON. Your company is the company that built these two sub-marines?
Mr. PATERSON. Yes; and sold them.
Mr. THOMPSON. How many years have you been engaged in shipbuilding in Seattle?
Mr. PATERSON. Eight years, I think.
Mr. THOMPSON. Have you any connection with the metal trades' association?
Mr. PATERSON. I have.
Mr. THOMPSON. What is your connection?
Mr. PATERSON. Just as a member.
Mr. THOMPSON. Have you been president at any time of that association?
Mr. PATERSON. No, sir; I have never had the honor.
Mr. THOMPSON. Do you know what the purpose of that association is?
Mr. PATERSON. Yes, sir.
Mr. THOMPSON. Would you mind telling us?
Mr. PATERSON. To regulate the action of the employers.
Mr. THOMPSON. About how many firms or individuals are members of your association, and what territory does it take in?
Mr. PATERSON. Oh, I could not tell you the total number. It takes in the State here, and Oregon.
Mr. THOMPSON. Do you know whether or not it has—do you know about what per cent of the people engaged in the metal trades it has in its member-ship?
Mr. PATERSON. I don't know, but I should think practically all.
Mr. THOMPSON. More particularly for the purpose of the record, will you tell us what branches of the business the metal trades association includes?
Mr. PATERSON. The foundries, the ironworks of all kinds—all kinds of iron-works.
Mr. THOMPSON. Could you give some of the more important branches of it so that we could be sure to have a record of it?
Mr. PATERSON. The shipbuilding, logging engines, boiler making, and found-ries, the iron foundries and brass foundries.
Mr. THOMPSON. It includes all foundries and machine shops?
Mr. PATERSON. Yes, sir.
Mr. THOMPSON. No matter what the metal may be?
Mr. PATERSON. Yes, sir.
Mr. THOMPSON. Would you want to add to the statement of the purpose which you very laconically just compressed into a phrase?
Mr. PATERSON. Well, I think the most important object of it is to provide an exchange for labor.
Mr. THOMPSON. When you say to provide an exchange for labor, will you say what you mean by that?
Mr. PATERSON. Say a man coming here, he can go to the office and obtain employment, and if our company had to discharge a man who had been faith-ful to us he would go to the office and get help either here or Oregon or any-where else.
Mr. THOMPSON. When you say you maintain an office, do you keep a record of your employees?
Mr. PATERSON. Oh, yes; a very careful record.
Mr. THOMPSON. At this general office?

Mr. PATERSON. Well, I don't know about that; however, it keeps a record, and I keep a record, also.

Mr. THOMPSON. First, the association office. If a man is discharged from your plant, do you send a memorandum of that discharge to the association office?

Mr. PATERSON. We ought to, but I dont' know that we always do it.

Mr. THOMPSON. That is the theory of the association?

Mr. PATERSON. That is the theory. Anyhow, he has been there before, and he is told to go there.

Mr. THOMPSON. And if you employ a man and you didnt' know all about him, would you send to the association office to ask for his record?

Mr. PATERSON. Yes, sir.

Mr. THOMPSON. And they would send it to you?

Mr. PATERSON. Yes, sir.

Mr. THOMPSON. Do you know what kind of record they keep of the employes—what the record contains?

Mr. PATERSON. Just the particulars with regard to the man's ability, his honesty and character, and general record.

Mr. THOMPSON. Is your association affiliated with any other employers' association?

Mr. PATERSON. Yes, sir.

Mr. THOMPSON. What other employers' association?

Mr. PATERSON. Well, affiliated—they work together.

Mr. THOMPSON. Cooperate?

Mr. PATERSON. Yes, sir.

Mr. THOMPSON. What other associations do you cooperate with?

Mr. PATERSON. The National.

Mr. THOMPSON. The National Manufacturers' Association?

Mr. PATERSON. Yes; and metal trades, erectors, and Pacific Coast.

Mr. THOMPSON. National Foundrymen's Association?

Mr. PATERSON. Excuse me?

Mr. THOMPSON. National Foundrymen's Association?

Mr. PATERSON. Well, occasionally, not very often.

Mr. THOMPSON. What attitude or position does your association take with reference to general labor matters?

Mr. PATERSON. What attitude?

Mr. THOMPSON. Yes; or position.

Mr. PATERSON. Well, its principles, as stated, are to promote fair dealing.

Mr. THOMPSON. Have you any—in the first place, have you a constitution and by-laws printed?

Mr. PATERSON. Yes, sir.

Mr. THOMPSON. Could you furnish the commission with a copy of them?

Mr. PATERSON. I suppose I can. I can get one from the secretary.

Mr. THOMPSON. I would be pleased to have you do so. With reference to hours, is there any understanding generally in your association what the hours in trade shall be?

(Booklet entitled "Constitution and By-Laws of the United Metal Trades Association of the Pacific Coast," was subsequently submitted in printed form.)

Mr. PATERSON. Well, nine hours is the idea.

Mr. THOMPSON. Will one manufacturer or one metal tradesman aid another and expect those hours to be kept or not?

Mr. PATERSON. Yes, sir.

Mr. THOMPSON. And how about shop conditions? Is there any general—does your association take any notice of that?

Mr. PATERSON. Yes, sir; and insist upon decent treatment.

Mr. THOMPSON. Would you call your association a defensive association?

Mr. PATERSON. It has been, and offensive also.

Mr. THOMPSON. In case of labor troubles that one of your members had, would your association participate in that?

Mr. PATERSON. With extreme activity.

Mr. THOMPSON. What would be the form of your extreme activity?

Mr. PATERSON. Well, what we might call advice to our elected and paid employees in the city and State to carry out their oaths of office. That would be one thing.

Mr. THOMPSON. That is to say, the municipal authorities?

Mr. PATERSON. Yes, sir.

Mr. THOMPSON. You would be quick to tell them that they must maintain the law?

Mr. PATERSON. Yes, sir.

Mr. THOMPSON. What other activity would you carry out?

Mr. PATERSON. We might help them do it.

Mr. THOMPSON. What form would your help take?

Mr. PATERSON. Anything that was asked.

Mr. THOMPSON. That is pretty broad. It must run in certain defined fields or channels.

Mr. PATERSON. Occasionally, owing to the brutality of the union officers, men have been attacked on going home. We would help them to get home.

Mr. THOMPSON. I don't want to cross examine you on these things. What I would like for you to do is to tell us in your own way what you would do, whether you would employ armed guards or private agencies or private detectives, and how far you would go with it; whether you would assist the members of your association by money, or how?

Mr. PATERSON. No, sir; we never had occasion to. We find the union people, the unions are cowardly enough when it comes to the point. We have never had occasion at all to do that. Of course, if the city or State fails to carry out their duty we, of course, have the right to protect ourselves. On a celebrated occasion I told the chief of police here that I expected him to stop the occurrences, and he promised to do so. Failing that, I said, "I will do it."

Mr. THOMPSON. Did he fail, and did you do it?

Mr. PATERSON. He didn't fail.

Mr. THOMPSON. He didn't fail?

Mr. PATERSON. No, sir; they never fail when it comes to that.

Mr. THOMPSON. How do you personally—that is, apart from your association, how do you personally view the employment of private guards by employers in times of trouble?

Mr. PATTERSON. As a disgrace to the community.

Mr. THOMPSON. That is, you think it should not be necessary?

Mr. PATTERSON. Yes, sir.

Mr. THOMPSON. Do you think it is necessary generally?

Mr. PATERSON. It isn't necessary if the city authorities act.

Mr. THOMPSON. Some people say that that is an institution peculiar to this country; that in the other countries of western civilized lands that that is not done.

Mr. PATERSON. I am sorry to say that that is true.

Mr. THOMPSON. What is your reason for that? What is the cause of that difference?

Mr. PATERSON. Well, I have personally given this matter some attention, and every person who gets into office here—I don't say every person, there may be an occasional exception—has hopes of a further office, an office a little higher, and he has been taught by the noise that the union creates, that the unions have a tremendous power in the elections, and accordingly he plays to the unions. We have some examples here in town.

Mr. THOMPSON. Do you think to give any of these examples?

Mr. PATERSON. Our mayor. On a former occasion I heard him express his opinion of the unions in a language that—well, I wouldn't care to use it here.

Mr. THOMPSON. What are your views individually of the unions?

Mr. PATERSON. I think they are an absolute abomination.

Mr. THOMPSON. What is the view of the Metal Trades Association?

Mr. PATERSON. I am not responsible for their views.

Mr. THOMPSON. I know that, but does your association take a stand on the question of organization?

Mr. PATERSON. I think there is a divided opinion because some people have never clearly thought on that line, and they balance around and see what the newspaper opinion is and the prevailing opinion, and go with the tide.

Mr. THOMPSON. There is a association of your character in Chicago. I think that their attitude is that they don't want to see more than 40 per cent of the members in any shop organized, and when it threatens to get above that figure they take means to prevent it. Have you any such rule or understanding here in regard to that matter?

Mr. PATERSON. No, sir. Well, put it like this: Supposing that you had an institution of any kind, which was happy, and out of charity you took in the waifs or strays to a point that they began to control you. You would be apt to say that isn't the right thing, wouldn't you?

Mr. THOMPSON. Well, I probably would if I undersood what you mean,· but I·don't.

Mr. PATERSON. Our position is this: We don't employ unions. The business calls for special talent, and special talent is rarely found in the unions. The fact is that men of character will not remain in the unions; they won't be dictated to as to how their special talent shall be disposed of; and we find that that is the idea of the American Constitution—as it was special talent that created this great Government, which is rapidly being ruined—and, exercising our right to employ those people who are in sympathy with us, we exclude the agitators. The fact is, we are a haven of refuge for the abused union man.

Mr. THOMPSON. This country is?

Mr. PATERSON. No, sir; our plant is. Oh, this country is not. We have in our employment at the present time notorious agitators—perhaps not agitators, but partakers in disturbances in the East who have come here to· get rid of the unions and everything connected with them.

Mr. THOMPSON. You mean they were formerly union men and now they are not?

Mr. PATERSON. Yes, sir.

Acting Chairman COMMONS. I hardly hear what you are saying. I missed most of that sentence. Could you speak a little louder?

Mr. PATERSON. I will try.

Acting Chairman COMMONS. If you please.

Mr. THOMPSON. Your last answer, if I understood it correctly, is that your plant here is a haven of refuge.

Mr. PATERSON. Yes, sir.

Mr. THOMPSON. For agitators and union men who operated as such down East and have come here to get some peace and quit the union?

Mr. PATERSON. Yes, sir; well, not agitators—I wouldn't go to that extent. We don't want anyone here who is an agitator. There are plenty of agitators at home.

Mr. THOMPSON. Taking the fact, unless you dispute it, that people are generally of average ability——

Mr. PATERSON. They are not.

Mr. THOMPSON. While here and there men are deficient, and while here and· there men are more than of usual capacity, isn't it your opinion, taking the world over, there is a certain average of ability that men come close to, leaving· out the exceptional men?

Mr. PATERSON. I think that is a result merely because there is hardly any man developed—hardly any man develops.

Mr. THOMPSON. But taking history——

Mr. PATERSON. Oh, he has the ability, but he is tied down by organizations of all kind and idols of his creation and of the community's creation.

Mr. THOMPSON. Look over the industries and look over the history of the world before we had this thing we call unionism; don't it show a sort of average of the people? There were a few inventors and a few poets, a few writers, and there are comparatively few deficients. The above normal and subnormal are a small per cent of the population.

Mr. PATERSON. I don't want to be obtuse, but if you will go on, I will tell you if I agree with you.

Mr. THOMPSON. What I wanted to say is this: If you were an average man of the average ability, would you consider, the way you view it, that to join a union would be a good thing or a bad thing?

Mr. PATERSON. A very bad thing.

Mr. THOMPSON. Then, your opinion must be that the unions in the United States and other countries have not helped the conditions of the workers?

Mr. PATERSON. They have hurt it. I think in this country the average man is all you have got to be, the average, as defined by you there.

Mr. THOMPSON. Do you know of any union that puts a maximum wage on industry?

Mr. PATERSON. I never heard of one.

Mr. THOMPSON. Well, how would the establishment of a minimum wage necessarily hurt a more than extraordinarily capable man?

Mr. PATERSON. It wouldn't hurt him at all.

Mr. THOMPSON. Then, as far as the establishment of the wage is concerned, the unions haven't hurt the able man?

Mr. PATERSON. They haven't established the wage.

Mr. THOMPSON. Well, some places they have a minimum wage.

Mr. PATERSON. The extraordinary man is a very rare man—I mean a high-class man, who is original—you can't buy him at all. It is impossible to buy him. In the place he is he will be kept.   . ˡ . ᶠ·

Mr. THOMPSON. As you see it, what are the other objections to organization?

Mr. PATERSON. Paralysis of the individual.

Mr. THOMPSON. Let me get some concrete case. Restriction of output—is that one?

Mr. PATERSON. That is one.

Mr. THOMPSON. And limitations of the individual's right to work?

Mr. PATERSON. To choose. He is held down.

Mr. THOMPSON. What I would like to get—you seem to have pretty clear-cut, positive views on this subject——

Mr. PATERSON. Yes sir; I have.

Mr. THOMPSON. And I would like to get them before the commission, so that they can read this record over—those who are. not here—and those who are here can read it again and be able to form a conclusion from your testimony.

Mr. PATERSON. Yes, sir.

Mr. THOMPSON. Will you go ahead in your own way and tell your attitude and your position?

Mr. PATERSON. I am, first of all, a radical; I believe in going down to the root of the thing; and I first of all ask myself—I can tell you I have had great experience with the unions in England and Antwerp. Antwerp is one of the hottest of the hot. The unions there are absolutely different from anything here; that is, the leaders in Europe, as I have had to do with them personally, are entirely devoted to their cause. There is no personal question; there is no holding a job in it; it is not a money-making scheme, as it is here; there is no graft in it; there is no buying off the strike, as I have been offered here to have it bought off; there is nothing like that. There is not any exaction from the workingman. The unions here love him so long as he can pay, but the minute that he fails to pay, that minute the union drops him, registers a fine against him, and so on. And do you think the union will help the eastern union man here to get a job. Don't be deceived. No such thing. It is a closed cor-poration. Not only are the eastern American trade-union men bound up there with all other evidences of their slavery but they won't allow any boy to learn a trade here, if the employers are weak enough; that is to say, in the midst of our community we have a cancer which is eating the vitals out of this American people. And I hate it!

Mr. THOMPSON. Then it would follow, Mr. Paterson, that you can not, of course, believe in collective bargaining?

Mr. PATERSON. I have done collective bargaining in England with the Iron Boilermakers' Association. It was headed by men, who were business men, with business brains, and it was an advantage to the employer and a great advantage. I had a ship in dry dock. I told the men this, " You have got to go into those tanks. You will be paid extra. as usual." And they said, "What is usual?" I said, " Being a stranger here, I don't know. But being acquainted with Mr. Knight, I will inquire. But whatever it is, you will be paid." Well, we were in the dry dock and we were on the schedule and had to get out on our date. But the men came to me and said, " If you don't pay us a pound a hundred, we won't go on." I said, " Won't you? You wait and see, and I will tell you after." I telegraphed Newcastle, and ' Newcastle tele-graphed Cardiff, and that evening the head man from Cardiff came along and ordered those men right back. And I asked him, " What right have you to do that," and he said, " They are under agreement. They agreed if they de-part from the orders of this society they will be liable." The men were ordered back and told not to dare to break their agreement or to endanger the good name of the boilermakers' society.

Mr. THOMPSON. I would gather from what you now have stated that you believe in organization and collective bargaining, but not under the conditions you find out here.

Mr. PATERSON. No. I believe in freedom—that is, if the men want to organize they can do it, but they must not compel every man to come into that.

Mr. THOMPSON. But isn't that generally the attitude of the English trades unions? Haven't they got all the principles of American trades unionism with this exception, that perhaps they may not have as much of business in the trades union?

Mr. PATERSON. The new unionism, I have not been acquainted with that for a long while, and I don't know but at that time it was an advantage to every man to belong there.

Mr. THOMPSON. Isn't that true that the charge is made by the English manufacturers that there is a restriction of output?

Mr. PATERSON. I think that is so. They are becoming that way now. I don't know personally, but what I am telling you I know of my own observation.

Mr. THOMPSON. Of course, you don't question the right of the people to form an association?

Mr. PATERSON. Absolutely not.

Mr. THOMPSON. You have your own association?

Mr. PATERSON. Absolutely no. All I object to is any military action on the part of civilians.

Mr. THOMPSON. Now, assuming, Mr. Paterson, that as far as your attitude is concerned that it was the attitude of the employers in this part of the country or all over the country, that you had a strong association of your own, so that practically everybody that is in the metal trades in both the States of Oregon and Washington are in your association; assume that all the employers have strong associations; that they are associated for the purpose of giving active assistance to any member in case of labor trouble, and that as a result these ssociations of workers were nonassociated, the unions were disrupted, they were simply individuals that they had to deal with, do you think that under that condition that the worker would be as well off both as to his hours, to his pay, and to his working conditions as he would be with his own organization to assist and help him?

Mr. PATERSON. Exactly, or better.

Mr. THOMPSON. I think the deductions from that answer will cover a lot of other questions I wish to put to you. What wages do you pay, Mr. Paterson, here?

Mr. PATERSON. All kinds of wages. To every man according to his ability.

Mr. THOMPSON. Mr. Drew would like to have you state the different rates of wges that you pay.

Mr. PATERSON. Well, we pay as high as 55 cents an hour in the iron trade. The apprentices get 20 cents.

Acting Chairman COMMONS. Twenty cents for apprentices, did you say?

Mr. PATERSON. And the carpenters are paid as high as 50 cents; joiners are paid as high as 48; pattern makers, from 40 to 48 and 50; we have got a man at 50. Machinists and press men, 35 up to 50, 55 to 60. Riveters are paid on piecework, and we are trying to introduce piecework into everything.

Mr. THOMPSON. Mr. Paterson, you have stated your attitude, and if I may say so, perhaps your opposition to the ordinary trade union, as in the metal trades union. Are you acquainted with the methods and principles of the Industrial Workers of the World? What is your attitude toward them, and do you approve of their methods and principles?

Mr. PATERSON. When they first of all began I admired these people. They had ideas something above the common; something that could be developed. But at any rate, even if they are in error, I believe in the utility of error. I think that the man who is honestly and openly wrong is doing a very good work. And the contrast between the I. W. W. and the unions is tremendous to me. The I. W. W. appreciates the individual. He has got something to offer above the sordid, rotten existence. He has got ideals. And he is nearer to Almighty God than many other political propagandists that I know of.

Mr. THOMPSON. Do you hold a card in the I. W. W.?

Mr. PATERSON. No; I am not open to one. I like the name. That is a good name.

Mr. THOMPSON. How do your wages compare with the union scale, if you know?

Mr. PATERSON. Oh, they don't compare at all. A union man would not earn anything in our place.

Mr. THOMPSON. He would not?

Mr. PATERSON. He is outclassed entirely; absolutely outclassed; because you see the union man has been trained first of all as a union apprentice. He was put in the shop because the union allowed him—that is, he was allowed to earn his bread because the gang of miscreants who have no right to be in office at all or anywhere but in jail deny him the right to his American freedom. Of course a man who submits to that or a boy who submits to that is not worth anything. He could never become an I. W. W. That is one thing, gentlemen—I don't think this is a joke at all; no joke about it.

Commissioner O'CONNELL. How about sabotage?

Mr. PATERSON. I don't know anything about it.

Commissioner O'CONNELL. What do you think about that subject?

Mr. PATERSON. I have told you all I know. I just mean what I said, and if it is not clear enough I will make it a little sharper.

Commissioner O'CONNELL. Go to it.

Mr. PATERSON. Just you wait a bit and you will hear.

Mr. THOMPSON. You say that your scale does not compare with the union scale. Is it higher or lower?

Mr. PATERSON. Their scale is away below ours.

Mr. THOMPSON. That is why you pay higher wages?

Mr. PATERSON. They have been coming up to our scale all the time; trying to get up to it. It is impossible; economically impossible.

Mr. THOMPSON. What do you mean when you say it is economically impossible?

Mr. PATERSON. Any employer who pays that to the union people can't earn any money.

Mr. THOMPSON. Have you had dealings with the unions here?

Mr. PATERSON. No; they have had dealings with me.

Mr. THOMPSON. Well, now, what do you mean by that?

Mr. PATERSON. I mean that I had not been here a day when the distinguished member with a red nose came in smelling of drink to tell me that the local something or other—I haven't the honor to remember—had determined that we were to work eight hours a day. So this being quite new to me and unexpected I said, "Is that so; you tell me, sir, how it is going to be done." He said, "Why, what do you mean? Just simply do it; eight hours a day." I said, "Tell me what about our competitors, what about the railroad freight which we are paying against our 10 hour a day competitors in the East?" And he said, "It will right itself." "Well," I said, "yes; it will right itself by wronging everybody and putting an end to the business." Which, of course, was true. ."Well," he said, "think it over," and I said, "How is this going to be paid; have you found out?" "Oh," he said, "charge it up to the customer." That is union economics. They are just taking it from the other man; he will in turn take it, simply take it, and nobody knows where it ends. They simply don't know; ignorant men; don't want to know. All they want is graft. That is all—money- it is a money-making business.

Acting Chairman COMMONS. Could you be here to-morrow morning at the opening of the session or are you going to leave town?

Mr. PATERSON. No; I don't think I will be here. I have been here all day, and I am thoroughly tired. I can give you an hour to-morrow morning if you will take me first when I come here, but I dont' want to come here and hang around this place.

Acting Chairman COMMONS. Will you be here in the morning at half past 9 and we will hear you for a couple of hours in the morning.

Commissioner O'CONNELL. I think it will be very interesting.

Acting Chairman COMMONS. The commission will now stand adjourned until 9.30 o'clock to-morrow morning.

(Whereupon, at 4.35 o'clock p. m., on this Thursday, August 13, 1914, the commission took an adjournment until the following day, Friday, August 14, 1914, at the hour of 9.30 a. m.)

SEATTLE, WASH., *Friday, August 14, 1914—9.30 a. m.*

Present: Chairman Walsh, Commissioners Garretson, O'Connell, Commons, and Lennon; also, W. O. Thompson, Esq., counsel.

Chairman WALSH. You may proceed now, Mr. Thompson.

Mr. THOMPSON. Well, the examination in direct is finished, Mr. Chairman. Mr. Paterson.

TESTIMONY OF MR. J. V. PATERSON—Continued.

Mr. PATERSON. Will you excuse me a bit. I would not have come back here were it not to conclude the testimony I had only begun.

Mr. Thompson. I mean; Mr. Paterson, my examination had been finished.
Mr. Paterson. I had not completed that part of it.
Mr. Thompson. Oh.
Chairman Walsh. Well, if there is any other statement, Mr. Paterson, you may proceed.
Mr. Paterson. Yes; I was asked if I had anything to propose in the way of legislation, or anything to suggest as a cure for the undoubted unrest, as it is called. Well, I believe in going to the root of the matter, as I told you before. The cause of the unrest is, of course, primarily in the constitution of the man. There is a great deal that can only be gone into thoroughly in discourse. And if I become irritatingly discursive, you stop me.
Chairman Walsh. I didn't hear that, please.
Mr. Paterson. I say, if I become irritatingly discursive to stop me.
Chairman Walsh. All right.
Mr. Paterson. I understand that I am here asked to tell what I know and help you. That is what Prof. Commons told me, and that is what I have come here to do, and what I did yesterday was merely to clear away any cobwebs that might be in the minds of people with reference to the opinion I have about the utility of the unions. The right of the people to organize is limited only by their interference with the liberty of others. That is the foundation principle of government, of all possible government. Anything else is anarchy, will end in anarchy, and, as I said, I preferred the propaganda of the I. W. W. to the present drifting into anarchy which this Government is enduring. The class legislation which is being enacted is an outrage on the name of freedom. That will never cure the trouble; it will create more. I want to explain that I have no hatred of the union as a principle; what I hate is the use of a self-constituted power to enforce the will of a few men on any one man, because they are thereby taking away the man's elemental right as a citizen of this country. The trouble is that we have at the present time men in power, in the Cabinet, in the law courts, on the bench, in the legislature, in the offices of the city, whose one aim and object is self, self, and nothing else. And, gentlemen, self is the cause of all the unrest to-day. Each man is thinking of self and nothing else. Now, that is the real cause. And the only cure of it is in a departure from materialism and materialistic prepossession of any kind whatever. The denial of the spiritual principle in mankind is the cause of all this thing, and there is no doubt about it; it is tacit.
Chairman Walsh. It is what?
Mr. Paterson. It is tacit. We are thinking of nothing else than how much I can take from you and you from me. This is becoming a very long discourse, and I have not very much time; but I want to say this, that legislation is necessary to undo what has been done and to regulate and control self-constituted power. The federation of labor, the federations of employers, have no rights in this country at all more than the right of the private citizen. And if they usurp the right or suggest the usurpation of it they should be destroyed, absolutely annihilated as enemies of freedom. If this country does not stand for freedom it stands for nothing, and as a citizen I should help to destroy it.
If all we are caring for is our mutton, let us perish. That is what I say, for it is not worth living. Now, the movement of the I. W. W. is merely the cry of the oppressed; there is no getting away from it, you have got to be decent. You have got to be honest with yourself. It is misery become articulate. The union, on the other hand, is a cancer. The disease is in the body, to pass to the biological analogy again, or the pathological—the disease is in the body. The I. W. W. and other organizations, or disorganizations, of that kind are the symptoms only. That is all. The union is the independent cancer living on the disease. If the body were healthy the cancer could not be there, but the disease comes in, and the cancer starts in. And there it is living independently, gaining force and strength—to pass from the figure again—noisily distracting attention from the real troubles which are the cause of it all, and are the foundation of its existence. The origin of unionism was a similar condition to the origin of the I. W. W. movement and others. There was trouble; there was oppression, and the unions, which in the early days were merely the continuation of the guilds, overcame it by their sacrifice of themselves. But we don't see any sacrifice of the self in the unionism of to-day. We see the plunder of the workmen for a principle which will never help him—never help him; merely keep trouble stirred up.
Now, I say let's get down to the root of the whole matter; let's find out what is the cause. I don't hate you gentlemen because you are trade-unionists; I

don't care a button about you. If you are wrong, that is your affair; but I will not allow you to use the power which you have usurped, if I can, to intimidate me or any man that I feel myself responsible to as a trustee. Now, the cause of unrest is the success of selfishness. First of all, the amassing of a huge amount of wealth in the hands of a few people, that is an evil; that is a very great evil. The amassing of power or the means of it in the hands of any one man or body of men is a crime in the present age. We are having a horrible example of it in Europe. But there is nothing to prevent tyranny worse than the tyranny of the Kaiser or the Czar being right here. It is here now; it is here now. I know of cases right here in this town where union men coming·from the East were not allowed to obtain employment. They had their cards and everything else. They were starving, and I employed them. Well, that is merely a trifle. The power to force money, which is of course an easy thing to do, out of the workingman, out of the oppressed—because they are oppressed because they are weak; therefore they can be robbed—makes the union a vast fraud on mankind. There is no doubt about that now. There is no question it can't effect anything but disturbance; it is not doing any good; it is creating a feeling of war. It is a self-constituted authority. It exercises the power of life and death. It organizes destructive forces; it uses them. Therefore it is going to be abolished. The people take a long time to rise, but they are going to rise; they are·going to annihilate unionism. It is not doing any good; it never will.

Now, there are lots of good union men. Here and there we will hear, "I know a union man, and he is a good man." I know hundreds of them. I know hundreds of them, and I know what they are, the best of them, the good workmen, the married men; and they say, "We won't belong to the union, but we are forced to. We are afraid." Think of an American citizen having to say that. Think of the blood that has been shed for freedom, gentlemen, and this is freedom. In this country, in this West, the land of the free, men can come to an employer and say, "We have no quarrel with you; we know that you want to do what you can, but we are forced to this; we are forced. We don't want to go out. We have got children. It will be ruin to them. It will be starving and suffering, but we have got to go because we are forced." And the men are dogged to their homes. You have heard of it; it has been published often enough. But it does not hit your business man at all; he does not feel it; he is too busy. He is too busy to pay any attention even to the character of the legislator. The result is the legislator hears nothing but the howl of the blatant unionist, and he thinks—that is the idea—and he believes it, although the union never did and never will deliver the union vote. But the ability of the unions is immense. They have very able people. They are bound to have, or it would be impossible to do so much with so little real power. They have got absolutely no power at all, gentlemen, absolutely none, if you and I do our duty.

Well, now, accumulation of wealth is a good thing. Without it we could not live; and distribution of it is essential. I am not going to tell you how it ought to be accumulated and how it should be distributed or anything of the kind.

Chairman WALSH. I can't hear you. You pitch your voice away from us, Mr. Paterson.

Mr. PATERSON. I say, I can't pretend to tell you how it ought to be accumulated or distributed.

Chairman WALSH. Well, I don't follow you. How what ought to be accumulated?

Mr. PATERSON. Wealth in the hands of a few is wrong because it is power, that is all. It is quite possible—is possible—is a fact to-day that wealth is in the hands of a few, of some few who use it as a trust, as it is and must be. But the majority of people abuse power. That is the reason for democracy and representative government. We require, first of all, the·education of the individual because until each individual takes himself·by the throat he had better leave other people's throats alone. And there is ·the anxiety of each of us to control everybody else and not to control ourselves, that is another cause of the present trouble.

Now, here we have prohibition advocated. We want to prevent another·man doing something. We want to interfere with freedom, that is all. We·don't want that man to become a really free man. by gaining power over his inclination to get drunk. It is just as necessary, gentlemen, to inculcate the desire to overcome the agony to get rich. And it is more important,still ·to educate the people to the fact that the. best thing in the world is work, though I heard yesterday some of our friends here sneer at the fact that a man could enjoy his work. We are all trying to escape work, and that means we are trying to get into trouble, and we are going to be in it always. The educative powers that we are talking about. The school, for instance: The modern school is a curse. That is not education at all. Why, we are having the children and the young people here taught the veriest·rubbish, the veriest rubbish.

·We have even had professors of our university come down here and make propositions, if the papers can be depended upon, propositions to seize private property. This is what we are teaching the young, then we wonder about this unrest. You can't put a plaster over this, gentlemen, this is a sore; this is rotten; right down rotten. Now, we have at the head of the Nation a pro-. fessor who is so ignorant of his profession even that he tolerates, evidently from cowardice, for it can't be from ignorance, the horror of class legislation, the beginning of the end, in fact—the beginning of the end because if the unions and farmers have the right to special legislation, then the I. W. W., who outnumber them, have certainly got the right, and we have some rights ourselves, we poor workers—the real workers. Until you control the educative powers, you are going to have unrest all the time, because they are pushing out among the people men who are actively corrupting badly instructed people with all the elements of misery and idleness. They are taught that. And against all this power the unions are nothing; the I. W. W. propaganda, though there is a little of the higher·lift about it, that won't do·it. That won't do it. Therefore, each of us has· got to take hold of himself; get himself right first; ask himself what are you going to give up—not what are you going to get—but what are you going to give up for the good of all; and then we must elect honest men to Congress, and the half-made utter failures of lawyers will not be in the offices at all.

· Chairman WALSH. Ladies and gentlemen, we must have perfect order. I know you will assist us. We must have no exclamation or laughter, or anything of that sort. Now, proceed, Mr. Paterson.

Mr. PATERSON. Now, I think we require another law to control the self-constituted authorities—to make it impossible for any trade-union or any employers' association to perpetrate a crime on the community, and we want a strong public opinion at the back of that law, inspired by people who are real patriots, which means they want to give up something for their country; a public opinion so strong that the law will not be necessary.

We want business men who will leave their business, who will make a little less money and give·a little more time to the amelioration of conditions by their giving up something, giving up something. Then the I. W. W. will probably come to see that you can't jump into the millenium; that there never will be a millenium; that those things that they are seeking are mere appearances; that the realities which are urging them on are behind appearauces—it is the great spiritual principle which·makes it possible for this planet to exist, whatever it is. And it is because you do not invoke, gentlemen, the foundation of all things, the thing that you rest·on, the spiritual principle in nature. It·does not matter how crude our conception of it is, it is there. Here is your trouble. You are trying to use a man who is, if he is a man at all, if he has not fallen back, if he has not degenerated—if he has ascended on a biological plan, you are trying to use him as if he were a mere engine, a mechanism and nothing else.

Now, it is all necessary, this fighting and tumbling and war and everything else, is necessary to the education of you and me. And we had better recognize the fact and not hate each other, but hate each other's opinions heartily, if we are wrong.

I never got together with any group of people on any important question upon which I did not ultimately agree with them, or they agreed with me occasionally. And unless we are able to understand—if we want ·to, it is easy for us to understand—that only by sacrifice can this unrest be allayed, we are not going to do anything, and we will probably be in anarchy and war here, right here. There is no doubt of it. All the forces are here, the hatreds more·bitter than the hatreds of the French toward the Germans— far more so. All that is wanting is the means, the means. That is all that is wanting.

, Now, why should it be? Socialism is our dream. It may be·accomplished. · It.might be a very good thing, no doubt. But it can't be accomplished on the jump without losing the possibility of accomplishing it at all. That is going backwards.

No economic or political amelioration can be made by force. Force must be applied only as police to prevent the aggression of self-constituted authority.·

If we elect rotten people, which we have done, to Congress—our ·Congress is absolutely rotten, absolutely rotten—we have got to stand for that, you' and me. We have got to stand for it until we are wise enough to elect a Congress of the right kind. ·· · .·

We must not go and try to kill these men or destroy them or ruin their business or· starve their children or hurt somebody. It is our fault. Let ·us vote the right men into office.

Why, these infernal cowards, they won't come out and even tell you their real feelings. They will tell you one thing, gentlemen of the unions;.they will come to me behind your back and will say, "That is all ·right; of course we have to do that." I ask them, "What is that thing that I call a ·bedbug on their card? What is that? What necessary part of this campaign literature is this hideous thing here?" And they say, "Oh, you know we·have got to do that, have the union label—you know, the label." These are the facts, gentlemen, and you must know that.

Commissioner O.'CONNELL. What do you refer to by the bug? .

Chairman WALSH. Let him proceed.

Mr. PATERSON. That little union label. I wish you would let me design one for you.

Chairman WALSH. You mean the union label?

Mr. PATERSON. I mean the union label. Let me design one for you.

Chairman WALSH. Proceed.

Mr. PATERSON. And that is their answer, insincerity right throughout, from the President in the highest office right down through; from the mayor right down through all. Insincerity, that is what is the matter with us. And why is it? Because we don't begin by being honest with ourselves. I don't see the good in passing Clayton bills or any other kind ·of bills. That won't help us a bit, because, gentlemen, you will force us, the people,· to the point where we will fight you. We will rise with a counter revolution. We will fight you. We have a right to do it. We have got the power. We certainly have the power. We will destroy you if it comes to that. And·that is the end. That is what it is coming to. It is coming to a civil war, gentlemen, and we will fight. Don't ·be the least surprised about that. We ·will fight. That is what it is coming to. I am ready.

Now, I say, gentlemen, that unless you are prepared, each of you, to sacrifice your life for a principle, you should not be a voter at all. You have no right to vote. You have got no right to vote. Do you people· of the unions believe for one instant that all the claptrap that you hear is sincere? · .

The ·men.who are giving you the power are giving you the power because they·think you are paying them for it. They are buying your help; they are trying to buy mine. Now, how are you going to overcome·that? What law—what law is going to alter that? None, none; absolutely none, gentlemen. And the facts·are that if this community can not—I mean the whole ·country—if it ·can not adopt, readopt, the principles of the ·great revolution; what is going to become of us? We are going to pieces. I say that the only ·right use of force is police duty, and police duty not administered as ·a method of buying an election,· which it ·has been here, but police duty to prevent ·any action at all by self-constituted power. If there is any justification for the guillotine, it is the existence of self-constituted power. · It will come. Turn your backs on the past; don't read history; read the vaporings of the rotten professors that you have in your universities; read that trash and you will soon read—you will soon read of a worse revolution than that ·of France, far worse. ; · .·

To get right back. Read the history of the human race. Do not despise what has been gained by the experience of your ancestors, if you had any. We Americans are all proud of our ancestors, but it is only the·fact that we have ancestors—we don't know what ancestry means. These men suffered and fought and worked for us. And what are we doing? With levity·frittering away what we have received. The wealthy man who accumulates wealth, what is he doing? He raises his children to be disgraces. That is·all, until the name of wealthy Americans is a mocking in the world. The great·trouble is that the only ·thing we are thinking about is the accumulation of· money; And it turns to· ashes and rots in our hands, and it is poisoning our children.· ·

···Now, I tell you that until you find some law to overcome that you are going to have a pretty hard time. You won't find a law at all to do it except the law that is in every one of you, if you are honest and decent.

Gentlemen, I want to see the Clayton bill dishonored by Congress. The President who allowed it to pass, on any miserable plea, is forever disgraced in the history of this country as the worst enemy of the country ever had, the worst enemy of the workingman, the worst enemy of the union man—the worst enemy it ever had. And I want the Republican Party, if it must come in power, to be told before it comes into power what it has got to do. So before the next election comes along let us get right men—men who come right out in public and say, "We won't put the label on anything; we are free men; if you don't want to elect us for our principles, don't elect us at all."

Therefore, gentlemen, to prevent the aggression of the unions—I think we have laws now, but we are not content with our old laws; we have got to have new ones. So let us make new ones, but let us make one first of all to prevent the aggressions of any self-constituted authority, and let us make it to cover the employers just as much and no more and no less than unions. But let us have real, equal opportunity in the country. Let us have no talk about Government handling all the utilities, because that means graft—unfortunately it is true, gentlemen, it means graft. We are not educated yet. We have not been trained yet to be decent in our public affairs. Therefore leave it to the private corporations, the individuals; control them absolutely, as you like, or leave them free; control them so far as their encroachments on liberty are possible.

··And for the rest, how are you going to handle the unemployment? Now, there is a thing a real union could do to reduce this evil; the union whose officers don't make money at all. If in every community the machinist, the logger, or whoever had a union, or call it anything you please, an amalgamation of each craft with the object of improving the individual, making it an honor to belong to a union, there would be a means all through this country, facilitated hy the post office perhaps, whereby the surplus of labor might be placed where required back and forth. There is a practical, possible activity for a real union. A thing of that kind would help. But the union managers of the present—that is the whole trouble of it—they are paid officers whose interests are to create and continue disturbances, who can't live unless there is disturbance. Now, if there is no disturbance and the object of the union is the amelioration of the workingman, why can't we encourage the workingmen to become members of real unions, the real union that helps each member and does not rob the weak. The union began all right, but it is like everything else, like the church even, it has become rotten because of power—simply that thing that makes men drunk, this power over others. Sacrifice that, you gentlemen, dissolve your federation and say for the benefit of the workingmen this federation is dissolved; we want nothing for ourselves. Then every union in every town for every trade would have its own president, elected for one year or one month, who would be unpaid; the secretary also for the same time unpaid. I would deal with that union. I would deal with it. It would become an honor to a man to belong to a union because he could not obtain the grade in the union until he had proved by his work or his brain what he could do, and the union would be the means of taking the American boy, and instead of allowing him to spend his time in lust, teach him to work with the despised labor of his hands, which I am glad to say I did, and gradually, bit by bit, rise in the union knighthood, if you have got to borrow a name. And, gentlemen, your union unrest would be fixed right off.

A public opinion would be created instantaneously that no employers' federation in the world could stand against for one minute, not for one minute. You would restore the name of America as a land of good workmen, which it is not now.

There are very few good workmen here now. All our good workmen are importations. It would give to work a dignity which it only has, and men would be honored, not for their loud mouths, but for what they have done.

If I were the president of the federation of labor I would not lose a month in arranging my affairs. I would call together my lieutenants and tell them, "The time has come, gentlemen, when we have pushed this union business as far as we can push it. As patriots we are now called upon to sacrifice maybe our comfort, perhaps our lives, but we have got to do it. As patriots we will abolish the federation through what we are going to leave behind as our monument."

And I know—I know the men—that there is enough ability in the federation, in the trades-unions, to do that without any help at all. I know it; to create this plan of a union in every town and hamlet in this land, abolishing this permanent office proposition, all possibilities of grasping power, so that the young boys would feel it was an honor to belong to it, that the badge of the union of whatever grade meant a real worker and could be absolutely depended on. And then I would agree, if the men wished it, to collective bargaining, to this extent, a rate of pay for every grade. That rate would be arrived at in the discussion with the employers who would point out the basis of the possibility of paying anything at all, and the possibility of getting the work.

And then we would have real competition. We would have every man right, from ourselves downward or upward, working his best, doing his utmost. The more that is produced of real wealth the more the people will get. The more that is produced of nonwealth the less the people will get. Unemployment will result, starvation, and so on. But there is no such thing as overproduction of wealth, and wealth is the necessary part of the accumulation of what you have got to live on, what is possible to lay out to create more.

If you employ your people in shifting the scenes in your photo-play houses, or in polishing diamonds, or in anything of that kind, you destroy possible wealth. The people won't get it. The people will starve. Look at the broad acres that are waiting. Look at the men wandering around aimlessly, and the union meeting—nothing doing. But if there was a fight on you are there. And it is in your power not only to work it out but any man who has thought about it knows it is possible, and all that is necessary is the will and faith in mankind.

I noticed that you union men, the richest of you, the men who are exploiting the workingman most, the man that has the greatest power to grind down the workmen, who starves the apprentices, who prevents the apprentice getting his employment—I do not believe you are hopeless at all. I have got absolute faith in the spiritual principle in this world. I believe you have only got to see it once to turn right around. Mr. Gompers and the whole lot of you will earn a real name in history as constructive statesmen if you do what I suggest now. And you will get your men, the real men, taught the greatest thing of all—that the most valuable possession he can have is character. And you will have a nation of workingmen, and that is the greatest kind of aristocracy that I know of.

Now, one thing before I am done. We have educators of all kinds. We have got to clean house. We have got to clean out these professors; we have got to clean out the clergy who are creating conditions which are even impossible for themselves. The church—and when I say that I say all the churches; I am not talking about any particular church, but I am talking about the men who, instead of following the advice of the Great Apostle in his warning to think of everything that is pure and of good report, and any virtue and any praise—what do you think we have here? Don't imagine that we have any such thing here. To listen to the pulpit here you would believe that this was hell, this was hell; that there was nothing pure or clean or decent or possibly decent in the whole country. We hear nothing but denunciation, cursing, and blasphemy of the most shocking kind from the pulpits of this town.

Now, what sort of effect is that going to have on the people, if the alleged ministers of God spend their time in low vituperation, in self-seeking competition for money? That is all it is. It has become a business like everything else. It has become a business, a money-making proposition. The man who talks loudest, abuses people the most, and denies God, in fact—that is what it amounts to—he is the accepted man. His congregation is very, very prosperous. And the others who present what is pure and clean and decent—there is nothing doing there; they are going down.

Now, we have heard a great deal from the clergy with regard to the recent strike that happened here. I will ask any one of those gentlemen to come with me privately and let us talk over this teamsters' strike that occurred here, and I want to be convinced. What did the clergy do? The clergy said, "Why, nobody has any right to be anything else than a union man; anything else is un-American."

Well, it ought not to need, it ought not to need, any remarks at all. If it does, we are hopeless. But the possibility of a man attracting people who can talk like that, who denounces capital as if capital was a living creature with attributes belonging to a man. The men are so insincere, so rotten to the core, that they can't think straight. They can't see the facts. And these are the people that are teaching our I. W. W.'s and our unrest people the tenets of the Prince of Peace. It is just—in plain language, the pulpit of this town is disgusting. There is nothing more immoral, nothing. That is another of the causes of the trouble—that is, it is one of those things which are keeping things stirred up, preventing us analyzing this cauldron of rottenness. When they find they have got to get together, well, they get together, and a fine mess they certainly do make of it.

That is the situation, gentlemen. Now, I don't know whether I am tiring the commission or not, but I am tired myself.

Chairman WALSH. Proceed with anything more you have to say.

Mr. PATERSON. Constructively, that is up to the men that are elected. Let us have no more class legislation, or we will have it repealed by bayonets. We ought to; that is our duty to do that; and we will do it, no doubt about that. Let us have real legislation, reaffirm—solemnly reaffirm the Constitution of the United States, that is all, and we will use the Sherman Act or whatever act we ought to use, and we will really apply it, we don't need to make any other. We will prevent any destructive competition, and we will help all proper cooperation. Cooperation should be the principle of our organism; if it is not, we are going to die. The Government, or rather the Cabinet, provokes, however, attacks on wealth, or attacks the machine created to produce wealth, imagines that that is a service. They should say, here is the Standard Oil Co., a vast power in the hands of a few; abused, yes; but is there no good in it; has it done no good? It has done good. What has it done? It has cut the price of oil to a mere nothing; it pays the highest wages in the world; it has abolished the explosion that used to wreck homes and kill people; it is a splendid organization. Has it no good use? Why, certainly it has. The Harvester Trust, any trust that produces a thing cheaply, is a good thing, because all those trusts pay the highest wages, they learn how to produce cheaply, how to pay the highest wages, and distribute the most goods. If in doing that they have also done some wrong, why should we think of the wrong only? Why not see the right? Can't we legislate on this subject without looking on the Standard Oil Co. as if it were an inhuman being or devil, and applying to this company attributes which don't belong to any company, and can't? And all your reason is vitiated by this asinine illusion, just as the reasoning of Europe is distorted by this illusion of Germany as a devil or something of that kind, and that France is another, and so on, forgetful that that is merely a name that covers your limitations—your limitations of conception of a large number of human beings just like yourself, and probably a great deal better—probably a great deal better. And that applies to those gentlemen of the Standard Oil Co. and all those oil companies. By following the laws of economics, by discovering them in practice, they have amassed wealth that has amazed themselves, and it was a vast power that they didn't know how to use entirely properly. But in a measure they did use it properly, and for that plus, that something gained from the wilderness, let us be thankful and use it.

A BYSTANDER. Well, well.

Chairman WALSH. One minute, sir. You must not make any remarks, please.

Mr. PATERSON. And therefore let us have legislation, whatever is wise, to control the use of that vast wealth which is to become congested in the hands of a few and therefore abused, to control the operations of it or the destructive operations of it. And the right men to deal with that subject are the professors, the men—not because they are professors—but the men who have professed economics as a business and honestly have become instructed therein. And then we will have the millenium so far as we can have it. We won't have it, however, right off. There is an awful lot to be done. But until we have got the will to do it, gentlemen, it is all futile, and we are going to fight, because we will hold onto what we have got; and we know one thing, we know that freedom is essential. And the Clayton bill and all such legislation is going in the opposite direction. And the initiative and referendum and all this turning back on the experience of mankind is wrong. It is wrong. It is going to cost a fearful lot of comfort and effort to direct or else it is going to create trouble. You can't get anything that way. That is all I have got to say.

Mr. THOMPSON. That is all.

Chairman WALSH. That is all. Thank you, Mr. Paterson.

Chairman WALSH. Call the next, Mr. Thompson.

Mr. THOMPSON. Mr. Gibson.

TESTIMONY OF MR. J. BRUCE GIBSON.

Chairman WALSH. Please be in perfect order, ladies and gentlemen. 'We must catch up with our program, and I know you will assist us. Please be in perfect order. Silence must be maintained. We will proceed now.

Mr. THOMPSON. Mr. Chairman——

Chairman WALSH. Mr. Sergeant at Arms, the confusion must be allayed at the door there. Mr. Thompson.

Mr. THOMPSON. Mr. Gibson, will you give us your name?

Mr. GIBSON. J. Bruce Gibson.

Mr. THOMPSON. Give your business and address.

Mr. GIBSON. Everett.

Mr. THOMPSON. And your business?

Mr. GIBSON. Manufacturer of machinery.

Mr. THOMPSON. What is the name of the company you are with, Mr. Gibson?

Mr. GIBSON. The Sumner Iron Works.

Mr. THOMPSON. What kind of business is that engaged in?

Mr. GIBSON. Making sawmill machinery; engines, boilers, and so on.

Mr. THOMPSON. How long has it been engaged in that business?

Mr. GIBSON. Twenty-two years.

Mr. THOMPSON. And how long have you been connected with it?

Mr. GIBSON. Eight.

Mr. THOMPSON. How many people do you employ in that business?

Mr. GIBSON. Approximately 200 average.

Mr. THOMPSON. Are you also president of the Federation of Employers' Associations of the Pacific coast?

Mr. GIBSON. I am.

Mr. THOMPSON. How long have you been such president?

Mr. GIBSON. A year, practically.

Mr. THOMPSON. What is that association composed of?

Mr. GIBSON. Of different other associations; it is not an association, it is a federation.

Mr. THOMPSON. Yes; I know.

Mr. GIBSON. Of which the different associations of the cities of the coast are members.

Mr. THOMPSON. Could you give us that list, or have you got a printed copy of the list?

Mr. GIBSON. No, I haven't; but I have got a list of them given me by the secretary that has the correct names. Shall I read it to you?

Mr. THOMPSON. If you will, please.

Mr. GIBSON. The Employers' Association of Vancouver, British Columbia; Employers' Association of Washington, with headquarters at Seattle, which includes as well Aberdeen, Hoquiam, and the Grays Harbor district; the Employers' Association of the Inland Empire, Spokane; the Builders and Employers' Association of Tacoma; Employers' Association of Oregon, with headquarters at Portland, takes in the State; the Merchants and Manufacturers' Association of San Francisco; Merchants and Manufacturers' Association of Oakland; Employers' Association of Fresno; Merchants, Manufacturers and Employers' Association of Stockton; the Founders and Employers' Association of Los Angeles; and Merchants and Builders' Association of Los Angeles.

Mr. THOMPSON. Have you got a printed copy of the by-laws?

Mr. GIBSON. Yes.

Mr. THOMPSON. Of your association?

Mr. GIBSON. Yes.

Mr. THOMPSON. Will you give us that?

Mr. GIBSON. Yes; do you mean to turn it over?

Mr. THOMPSON. Yes; to the commission.

Mr. GIBSON. And not read?

Mr. THOMPSON. No; I do not care for it to be read.

(See Gibson Exhibit No. 1.)

Mr. THOMPSON. Briefly, tell what the purpose of this organization is.

Mr. GIBSON. The declaration of principles which heads those by-laws, the constitution and by-laws, states it very clearly. Would you like me to read it? It would not take but an instant?

Chairman WALSH. You may read it.

Mr. GIBSON (reading:)

" The name of this federation shall be the Federation of Employers' Associations of the Pacific Coast.

· " This federation is formed to foster and protect the industrial interests of the Pacific coast and adjoining territory; to unify the actions of its members upon matters where united and concerted action and a determined, fixed policy may seem wise and necessary; to secure for employers and employees the freedom of individual contract in the matter of employment; to oppose restriction of output, sympathetic strikes, lockouts and boycotts, and illegal persecution of individuals, all of which are a menace to the industrial progress of our Government and tend to the undermining of constitutional rights; to prevent any interference with persons seeking through honest effort to work and earn a living; to prevent or avert industrial disturbances, to harmonize differences between employers and employees, with justice to all concerned and to assist in the enforcement of the laws of the land; the investigation and adjustment, by the proper officers of the federation, of any question arising between members and their employees which may be referred to and come within the jurisdiction of the federation; the cooperation with other kindred organizations in the United States and Canada in the accomplishment of the objects hereinabove stated, upon such terms and conditions as may be determined by the several associations."

Mr. THOMPSON. From your reading of the objects and principles of the federation, do you deal mostly with the labor problem?

Mr. GIBSON. No. The labor problem is one of the problems of the federation; we have paid more attention to, in our federation, educational work among the different associations as to their conduct of business.

Mr. THOMPSON. Well, now, would you tell us briefly, Mr. Gibson, how you cooperate with the different associations? Take particularly in the case of industrial conflicts, such as strikes, what would you do in such a case? ·

Mr. GIBSON. We have not as yet found it necessary to have any conferences particularly on labor disturbances—that is, as a sole matter of a conference— for the reason that each association has been able to take care of their own affairs. But we hold meetings at intervals. Meetings will be held shortly in San Francisco. We feel now that we should take more active interest—that is, mobilizing our strength to oppose unreasonable demands on the part of labor · or unreasonable attitude 'of politicians in matters affecting us, and following this meeting we will have a very much stronger organization than we have now, covering a larger latitude and a larger and different variety of associations.

Mr. THOMPSON. Has your federation got anything to do with keeping lists of employees?

Mr. GIBSON. None at all. ·

Mr. THOMPSON. If that is done, it is done by the association? ·

Mr. GIBSON. The federation has nothing to do with it at all.

Mr. THOMPSON. Now, Mr. Gibson, a list of questions has been submitted to you, and in order to save time you can speak to those questions. I would like you to go ahead and make your statement.

Mr. GIBSON. To these questions here, you say?

Mr. THOMPSON. Or such statement as you wish to make to those.

Chairman WALSH. Are they the same we have here, Mr. Thompson?

Mr. THOMPSON. Yes.

Chairman WALSH. Give the number as you refer to them.

Mr. GIBSON. I will make a brief statement. Some of these I won't touch on, because I am not familiar with the subject.

Chairman WALSH. Those you are not familiar with, just indicate.

Mr. GIBSON. I will tell what it is. " Brief account of activities in connection with labor matters." I have already done that. Our labor connection has not been very determined, more advisory. " General causes of industrial dissatisfaction." It starts off with methods employed by " union shops and factories." I have made some memoranda on that. The two subjects, really, A and B, " methods employed by union shops and factories and restriction on output, difference between open and closed shops are practically one." The restriction of output is one of the bad features of union organization, and is illustrated in manufacturing costs. I have here a copy of some items in our plant, showing the difference in cost of operation during closed shop seven years ago, or eight years ago, when we had a union foundry and an open shop as at present. This is on standard machinery, of which we have a number of recurrences, and also as taken from our records.

Shingle machine, 26-inch saw collars, 6 as union; as open shop, 12. I will say to illustrate this that when the molder was on this work and tried to make 7, the steward in the shop stopped him. Shingle-mill gears, 4 to 10; friction pulleys, 3 to 8; main frames, 1 to 2; track, 1 as union shop and 2 and some small work as open shop; carriages, 1 to 2, and some small work as open shop; pulleys, 24 by 12, 1 to 2, and some small work.

In making pulleys we make them as the orders come in. During closed shop 1 man and a helper set up 36 by 10 and 24 by 10—that is, as closed shop. As open shop the same men or the same class of labor set up five 24 by 10, two 18 by 11, and two 16 by 11, a total of 9 pulleys with practically the same labor, as against 2 under the closed shop.

Spur-iron frictions, 36 by 8, 1 under closed shop and 3 under open shop. ·

Those are the records as we have them in our works.   .

As to the methods employed by unions, another method, that of picketing, has in our own case been very aggressive. Some seven years ago we had a union strike at the foundry, which we had very little trouble with, because most of the men came back and signed an agreement with us and tore up their union cards, the men we wanted. They have been working since on that same agreement for seven years. Four years ago we had a machinists' strike. Before the machinists' strike came on we were advised they were going to ask for an eight-hour day. We called the men together and had a conference; told them it would be absolutely impossible for us to grant the eight-hour day for the reason our competition was principally with the Allis-Chalmers Co., of Milwaukee; we were building the same line of machinery and competing for it in this territory. They were working on a 10-hour day, and we 9 hours; and our wages were 42½ cents an hour and theirs 37½; we were required to carry from four to six months' of raw material in order to have it on hand; they can go to the telephone and get any single order; we have to buy in carload lots in order to get the freight rate on the carload west. It makes our burden as heavy as we can possibly stand, and we told them all the conditions, and they thoroughly understood it, but the union had told them that they had to go out, and that was all there was to it. Twenty-seven of our mechanics walked out.

Following those matters—prior to this we had treated our men as well as anybody could possibly do it; there was a very friendly feeling between us. Following those matters they started picketing. We had a good many cases of men being beaten up by these pickets. They eventually built a house right at the approach of the bridge that we had to cross to go to our work, and stayed there continually on duty, calling the men scabs, following the men to their homes and threatening them, and going into the restaurants where they ate and calling them scabs, and trying to get the restaurant people to keep them out, and even went to the homes of the workingmen who were renters and saw they were forced out by threatening the men who owned the buildings.   ·

We had to rent a big building and put the men with families in there until they could get homes where they would not be molested. They went to the wives and kept after them and kept after them until the wives would try to get the men out of our shop because they were tired of the everlasting nagging that they got.

I was going to cut out some of this because your time is short. .

Chairman WALSH. We don't want to limit you, Mr. Gibson. We don't intend to cut you off. You are getting right down to the facts. Just proceed. Don't cut out anything for lack of time; we will not sacrifice anything that is important. Give us anything that you have.

Mr. GIBSON. The methods of doing business and the way it affects the community as well as the individual, those who have to work for a living. I will illustrate that: Some 14 years ago I bought a plant in San Francisco, a plant to sample gold and silver ores in. At the time I bought it there was ore laying on the floor of the plant worth $50,000 that had not been moved on account of the teamsters' strike in San Francisco. I think most of us who are here will remember the strike because it was a very aggressive one, and very serious. It lay there three months after I got the plant because I was not able to get it moved. In Frisco they had no rails on the wharf because the union had said such things were out of the question. They still have difficulty in getting tracks. They still had to haul it by teams at a cost of 50 cents a ton for a haul of about three blocks, which was an almost prohibitive price in the first instance, but it was impossible on account of the fact that I could not move it. ·

At the end of three months I lost patience, and with eight days and nine policemen I got the ore down to the wharf and also moved the plant to Oakland. I had open-shop conditions and got to the wharf with rails, and did business there for three or four years afterwards until the Smelter Trust bought me out.

That shows the injustice of arbitrary regulation of primary transportation which drives a man away from a community, and the community suffers by it.

"Limitation of apprentices." In our shop we give every son of every employee that we have that has been with us any length of time an opportunity to become an apprentice with us, and that is limited only by our ability to teach. We don't take an apprentice into our shop to learn by himself and learn incorrect methods of doing the business, but we have the foreman or some delegated assistant to him to teach those boys how to properly do the work, and how properly to fit his tool up, and what cut to make on the different articles he is machining up until he becomes at the end of the fourth year a skilled mechanic. He is really a skilled mechanic before then. We apprentice them four years. The rate of pay is small, but we don't take boys unless they are living with their families. It ranges from 8 cents—in the case of molder apprentices from 11 cents an hour to 28 cents an hour with a bonus at the end of the fourth year of $100. We give them that in cash. We had two that went out last month, and we gave them $100 each.

Machinists begin at 8 cents an hour and increase to 25 cents an hour with the same bonus. There is a good deal of injury done in the shop by machinists in the waste of material and the breaking of tools, so that necessarily we have to start them in at a low rate of pay; still the very lowest is 72 cents per day with the $100 bonus.

The limitation of these apprentices by unions is one of the most un-American things I can possibly imagine. Any class of foreigner that carries a union card can come into the country, and 15 minutes after he arrives he can get work as a mechanic. I presume that is a fact, I am not quite sure as to that, but I know it won't take him long to affiliate with some union or join it. A man that has any ambition and has become a skilled blacksmith or mechanic of any description would naturally wish to see his son follow in his footsteps, and if possible, make him more skillful than themselves, but on account of the limitation, why, he is barred from that, and all he can do is go in as a common laborer, as he can't apprentice himself to the shop if the limit has been reached; and as I say, it is the most un-American proceeding to limit our American sons to unskilled work.

Boycott on material. A cowardly weapon. The boycott is identical with the blacklist, and we never have practiced it so that I am really not clear in my mind; but I understand the blacklist is illegal, illegal by law, isn't it?

Chairman WALSH. In many States.

Mr. GIBSON. In our State?

Chairman WALSH. Yes.

Mr. GIBSON. Well, if the blacklist is illegal, why is it that to boycott or blacklist a merchant is legal? That is what I want to get into my head, especially as the boycott is so obnoxious in its way of doing business. There have been others who have talked on this boycott before me, so that it is not necessary for me to dwell on it. But my opinion, and my firm opinion is, that any judge that allows it in his district is not capable to hold the bench. It is a most disgraceful procedure on the part of the unions or anybody else that practices it. There are several questions here that I will read: "Relative advantages of piecework and day-wage system." "Attitude of workmen toward piecework system, premium or bonus system." None of these are we able to practice for the reason that our business is miscellaneous, and we can't divide up the work.

Chairman WALSH. You would not care to speak on that?

Mr. GIBSON. No; so I will just pass that.

"Effect of automatic machinery on opportunities of employment in metal trades." That, as an abstract theory with me, is that the more automatic machinery becomes the more we are able to produce at a low rate of cost per article, the more we are in competition not with ourselves but with the country, the world at large. We can not look entirely to a local territory in order to develop the country and you can't get employment unless the country is developed. We must do that first. But with the applicaion of modern methods of manufacture through modern machinery we necessarily must make more employment from the fact that we have broadened our ability to market our goods by lowering costs.

The matters that follow now have been touched on; that is, welfare work, the workmen's compensation laws, by those that already have had a great deal to do with it; pension systems, accident insurance, sickness insurance—they all follow in the same class. I am not prepared to speak particularly of them. I have views, but it has all been handled. Methods of conciliation and arbitration——.

Chairman WALSH. Do you have any views differing from what has been suggested by any other employer of labor? You might give them.

Mr. GIBSON. The only views I have is that the laws are good as passed in Wisconsin—I think it is. I have just been talking with one gentleman. These laws are very excellent and should be followed here in some way—that we should have laws that are a little more equitable than they are now to cover the compensation. And that the whole thing depends largely, in my mind, on the administration of the law and on the class of men that have to do with the actual workings of the law after it is put in force.

Chairman WALSH. Generally speaking, would you or would you not say the proper policy of this Government should be some sort of pensioning system and accident insurance and sickness insurance?

Mr. GIBSON. No; not generally speaking, for the reason that I think every man should have foresight enough and enough ambition to take care of himself by saving from his wages. He is not a good citizen otherwise; that is, if he has the ability to do it, I mean by that. Some people are poor because they can't help themselves.

Chairman WALSH. Methods of conciliation.

Mr. GIBSON. Methods of conciliation and arbitration. I haven't discussed that because we haven't any trade agreements. I haven't yet been able to see where we as a firm could ever arbitrate or conciliate or agree with a union in any way whatsover.

Seven years ago the union—the founders' or the molders' union—from Seattle came to Everett and said, "You are going to have trouble here and we would like to have the opportunity of unionizing your plant." "Well," we said, "We don't care to have that done, for the reason that we never have agreed with the union principles and never have been a union shop." "Well," they said, "You are practically all union, and there is only one man that is not, a man by the name of Mr. Billings, that came out with the Sumners from the East 22 years ago."

And after talking it over—we had two conferences with them, and they made their argument; and it eventually came to us that possibly there was some good in it, and we would try it anyway for a year. So we signed an agreement with them. It was signed by ourselves as officers. It was signed by themselves as officers, sent to Seattle and the seal put on it, and returned to us.

The understanding was this: That for one year we were not to have any demand for increased wages or decrease in hours in the foundry; that we were to have Mr. Billings put in an application for membership in the union, which he did. He became a union member, and we started in with our agreement.

Six weeks after that the molders walked out for an eight-hour day. That broke our faith in any agreements or arbitration, because until the unions—until, for instance, the American Federation of Labor, which I uderstand has an income of $24,000,000 a year, something like that; that has been given me in particular terms—until the unions can back their agreements up by the responsibility that is back of them the same as we are responsible for any agreement with them, until they do that, until the unions are able to get rid of men who might hamstring the horse—until they are responsible for that act, or whatever they might do which might come about through strikes, and that money could be attached for restitution, so long do I believe it is impossible to have trade agreements, conciliations, boards of arbitration, because they won't agree to anything that is not distinctly favorable to them.

Employers' associations, desirability of strong associations, field of activity of such associations, methods used by associations, maintenance of individual records of employees; do such records constitute a black list? Maintenance of employment bureaus. Maintenance of special squads of employees for use in strikes.

There is no question as to the desirability of employers' associations; because without them we are unable to properly develop our field of activities in marketing our products. We are not able to compare notes as to new devices for cheapening costs. We go into competition—unless we have associations we go into competition, one not talking to the other, and knifing each other.

Through associations we are able to get a more and better understanding of other people's motives.

The black list is a thing that is not practiced. I haven't anything to do with that and know nothing of it.

The maintenance of employment bureaus is necessary, most of all that we must have them for the reason that we will go down the street here this afternoon and we will see hundreds of men looking the boards over to see where they can get work. Without that they would be scattered; they would not know where to go.

The maintenance of special squads for use in strikes is only retaliatory. We have to do that in order to protect ourselves. We don't use special squads, but we tell the men that in case they are attacked to fight back; they will be protected by us to the full extent of our business, every dollar we have got; if they are injured in any way or injury ateempted, we will put it all in the pot until it is all gone.

"Justice in labor matters, inadequate, obsolete, and unfair laws." There are several things to say regarding justice. I know nothing about it at all. I am not a lawyer, but a business man.

Chairman WALSH. Speaking as a manufacturer, have you observed anything with respect to the law which you might think was unfair to either side, regarding the operation of laws that have become obsolete, on account of the growth in your association and such things?

Mr. GIBSON. No; there things that I was going to touch on later in the matter of suggestions as to what I had to say about the betterment of conditions.

Chairman WALSH. All right.

Mr. GIBSON. The only thing is, if the law is based on, if we get equity, if we get law administered as it is intended, right distinguished from wrong, that is all there is to it.

Chairman WALSH. Have you found the attitude of the judges to be fair or unfair?

Mr. GIBSON. Personally, no.

Chairman WALSH. Personally, no?

Mr. GIBSON. No, I never had. The only time that I ever appeared before a court of any description—twice I have appeared—was after our men got beat up, and I appeared then before the court to try to get the man who was responsible for it in each case put into jail. I was unable to do anything at all.

Chairman WALSH. Was it a lower court?

Mr. GIBSON. A lower court.

Chairman WALSH. You have only one instance in mind?

Mr. GIBSON. Two in mind.

Chairman WALSH. Two in mind?

Mr. GIBSON. That is the only time.

Chairman WALSH. Is there any responsibility that you could place on the prosecuting officers or the administrative officers?

Mr. GIBSON. No; it was wishywashy; it was just the fear of the labor unions as organized.

Chairman WALSH. Go ahead.

Mr. GIBSON. "The policing of industry, causes and effect of the policy of employment of private police and detectives—the causes and effect and extent." I don't know anything as to the extent. We have had to have our men deputized. We have been able to do that from time to time where the fight got so bad that they could not close their eyes to the fact that we needed protection. We have also had the patrol come to us at our call on other occasions where the mob was so great that we had to protect our men to get through them.

Chairman WALSH. In your observation, to what extent were they so made officers, and what sort of officers were they made?

Mr. GIBSON. They were deputized by the chief of police of the city.

Chairman WALSH. To what extent—what numbers?

Mr. GIBSON. I think we had six.

Chairman WALSH. Were they employees?

Mr. GIBSON. They were employees who had been threatened.

Chairman WALSH. Working at some craft at the same time?

Mr. GIBSON. Yes; they were mechanics in our shop working during the strike, and they had their lives threatened.

Chairman WALSH. They continued their work?

Mr. GIBSON. They continued their work; and it was very despicable; the way it was done; the threatening of their lives was passed to their wives by the wives of the union men—a very, very low-down trick.

Chairman WALSH. In your experience there were six instances of that kind in your industry?

Mr. GIBSON. Yes.

Chairman WALSH. Now, what have you observed as to the attitude of police and other civil authorities in labor matters where there were industrial disturbances?

Mr. GIBSON. What is that? I didn't understand you.

Chairman WALSH. Do you find anything to criticize or commend, or what has been your experience as to the attitude of police and other civil authorities in similar matters—when you called upon them to deputize men, were you satisfied with what they did?

Mr. GIBSON. In that instance, yes. My general observation is, however, that it is pretty hard to get a police judge or other judge to do what you want, for the reason that they are always playing to the galleries. So long as the judges of our United States are in politics, just so long will we get poorly administered laws. And the fear of the vote, the fear of organized labor is strong within then, although—as I think Mr. Paterson said, or somebody said—they never have won in it but once—delivered the goods. This last week we, have an illustration of the power of the labor organizations in our city. They are claimed to be 50 per cent organized by Mr. Brown. I presume that is a fact now for the reason that we have been able in this last week to elect a Socialist commissioner, a thing which would have been impossible under any condition, but there is where once they have delivered the goods.

Chairman WALSH. Have you had any experience with the use of the militia?

Mr. GIBSON. None.

Chairman WALSH. You said, I believe, you had some observations and some suggestions to make?

Mr. GIBSON. Yes; constructive proposals.

Mr. THOMPSON. Just one question.

Mr. GIBSON. Yes.

Mr. THOMPSON. Mr. Gibson, do you know the union scale of wages in the different lines of work you carry on?

Mr. GIBSON. No; I don't. I have here a statement of the wages we pay in our own plant, and I think they will compare more than favorably with any union scale of wages in the United States.

Mr. THOMPSON. Well, I have this question, how your wages compare with the union scale?

Mr. GIBSON. Well, I really am not informed as to the union scale of wages. We haven't regulated it by that at all. I have a long list here of the different classes; the machinists get from $3.60 to $4.05 per day, and work nine hours.

Mr. GIBSON. Molders, $3 to $4.25 per day, and so on.

The highest rate of pay we pay is for pattern makers, $4.05 to $4.50. The lowest rate of pay is $2.25, which is $25 cents an hour for common labor, and we only have one or two men on that basis; the balance are $2.50 a day for nine hours.

I would like to file this, because it is the rate of wages, shows the rate of wages, and what we always have aimed to do.

(See Gibson Exhibit.)

Mr. GIBSON. We think it will bring on the very highest class of mechanic, and we have better business, and think it is poor business to pay a low wage. As a matter of suggestion, I think one of the greatest causes of our social unrest is due to the allowance of yellow journalism, cartoonists that send out these bloody things depicting capital, and all that sort of thing, in the most abhorrent way. Let me suggest, I would like to read to you here from the Washington Socialist of July 16. I would like to read it.

Chairman WALSH. How long is it?

Mr. GIBSON. It is very short, if you would care to listen to it.

Chairman WALSH. Our policy is to take any documentary evidence.

Mr. GIBSON. It is in line with the argument I wish to make.

Chairman WALSH. About how long is it?

Mr. GIBSON. Just that [indicating].

Chairman WALSH. Very well. Go ahead.

Mr. GIBSON (reading):

"DEAR COMRADES: The article in the Washington Socialist of June 18, 1914, 'The Armed Citizen,' is a timely topic. It is very evident that capital, drunk with power and control, intends to exterminate those who have begun to think and deplore the misery, poverty, and ill treatment of the masses at the hands of the money lords, and therefore another civil war is certainly threatening. It is to be hoped that it can be averted, but, if not, I also hope that the proletariat will not allow itself and families to be slaughtered like sheep. It will he certainly necessary, as Victor Berger suggests, to procure arms and ammunition. Shoverling, Daly & Gales, New York City, sell the Mauser repeater, 18-inch barrel, high power, 7 and 9 millimeter, a shot, steel jacketed, or mushroom ball, range 2,000 yards, for $13.50. This is handy and perfectly sighted, clip-loading, and breechblock can be removed in an instant for cleaning. A long heavy rifle is not desirable. If we of the rabble make these preparations now, the money powers and their hired assassins may pause and consider."

It is articles such as that, allowed by the Government to be printed and circulated through our press, is one of the reasons for the unrest in labor conditions. That is one only, and it is mild compared with "The Armed Citizen" as it is edited, and it is treason. There is no other name for it—absolute treason.

Another suggestion—the business men must work, awaken to the fact more generally; we must send business men to the legislature instead of lawyers who have been unable to make the success in their own profession, and who go into it for money reasons. Practically no principles; they know nothing about business; they are just skilled to repeat something to a professor when they are in school, pass an examination, call themselves lawyers, and have the gift of gab, and they go to Congress or they go to our State body.

Through them we get all sorts of vicious, unnecessary laws. If we have business men that go in there who are honest and will make laws that will be properly administered by judges who are in some way—that we can put judges into office so that there won't be any interest, business interest, ahead of them, and a little of this unrest, a good deal of it, I think, will be a thing of the past.

I do not know that I have any further suggestions. As I felt the necessity of briefness in this matter it somewhat bothered me to clearly express myself. I think that is all.

Chairman WALSH. Any questions?

Commissioner LENNON. Yes.

Chairman WALSH. Commissioner Lennon wishes to ask you some questions.

Commissioner LENNON. In order that your impressions shall be corrected as to the income of the federation, I want to say this—and it is unusual for us to make this statement—that I have been treasurer of the federation for 25 years and am now treasurer. The income has averaged $10,000 a month; at the present time it averages $20,000 a month. That is the income of the federation.

Chairman WALSH. Any questions?

Commissioner GARRETSON. Yes.

Chairman WALSH. Mr. Garretson would like to ask some questions.

Mr. GIBSON. May I ask a question? I would like to be informed—is that the regular income, or does that include special assessments?

Commissioner LENNON. That includes the entire income. I handle all the money.

Mr. GIBSON. All the money?

Commissioner GARRETSON. In regard to apprentices—limiting apprentices—are you aware that there are organizations who use two apprentices to every mechanic, and eternally insist on more than the employer will furnish?

Mr. GIBSON. Well, that would be extreme.

Commissioner GARRETSON. No; not considering the business it would not.

Mr. GIBSON. If you will tell me what the business is possibly I can——

Commissioner GARRETSON. The railway service. The brakeman is apprenticed to the conductor in the railway.

Mr. GIBSON. Is he articled?

Commissioner GARRETSON. Individual articles have virtually ceased—never existed in that business—but it is the apprentice, and he stands in line for promotion whenever a vacancy occurs.

Mr. GIBSON. He is a helper, in other words?

Commissioner GARRETSON. He is in the form of helper apprentice.

Mr. GIBSON. We have helpers in our shop, what we called them, men; no boy——

Commissioner GARRETSON. That is not in our business, you know; no boy can get into our business, because it is an adult service. But that is the relation they stand in in that business.

Mr. GIBSON. I see.

Commissioner GARRETSON. You spoke of the obnoxiousness of the lawyer. What is the difference between the labor man refusing to buy goods that do not bear the union label—I will just put it on that because it is the commonest ground——

Mr. GIBSON. Yes.

Commissioner GARRETSON. And the employer refusing to employ union men?

Mr. GIBSON. The employer that refuses to employ union men under conditions is the exception.

Commissioner GARRETSON. But it has been declared repeatedly here within the last few days that they do refuse if they know it.

Mr. GIBSON. Where they are declared unfair and are really fighting against the union, how can they do otherwise?

Commissioner GARRETSON. I think not in many instances, but bear in mind——

Mr. GIBSON. We do not employ union men for the simple reason they boycott us, call us unfair to union labor, and they so class it. We do not care anything about that personally.

Commissioner GARRETSON. But if there be unfairness, how then?

Mr. GIBSON. It is a matter then largely of individual opinion as to what they wish to do in that matter. But my idea is, as I have them expressed, that the open shop does not discriminate against any man, whether he belongs to the union or whether he does not belong to the union, or whether he belongs to any other organization, or church, or whatever it is; and so long as we have that principle just so long is the boycott an absolute wrong, picketing, and all that sort of thing.

Chairman WALSH. Let me put the question and see if I get the point. The question was: Do you make any distinction between the employee, the worker, who boycotts your product, and the man, the manufacturer, who refuses to hire a man simply because he belongs to a labor union? That is the question.

Commissioner GARRETSON. I am only asking for your opinion personally. If the employer boycotts the union man, is it as great an offense as if the union man boycotts the product?

Mr. GIBSON. I have not seen any boycotting of union men, except where they brought it on themselves. There is no such thing as boycotting union men. If somebody fights you you must retaliate, you must fight back with the only weapons you have.

Commissioner GARRETSON. Is one equally iniquitous with the other, from your standpoint?

Mr. GIBSON. I don't understand the question.

Commissioner GARRETSON. If it should exist?

Mr. GIBSON. I have tried to explain to you that I don't think such a thing as a boycott against the union is possible.

Commissioner GARRETSON. If an employer refuses to employ a union man under any circumstances, if he knows it, is that a boycott?

Mr. GIBSON. There is no such thing in my estimation.

Commissioner GARRETSON. If he knows, if that is the case?

Mr. GIBSON. It is only when you have to fight back that you employ the weapon that is employed against you—you have to fight with the same weapons that are given you—retaliation; I do not think it originates with him—we do not originate that thing. There is a condition, but we never do originate that.

Commissioner GARRETSON. Are there unions that keep all their agreements?

Mr. GIBSON. Repeat that question, please.

Commissioner GARRETSON. Are there unions who never break agreements? As illustrated from your own plant?

Mr. GIBSON. Yes.

Commissioner GARRETSON. Do you know of any union that generally observes agreements and has never been charged with violating them?

Mr. GIBSON. The Brotherhood of Locomotive Engineers are a union which do not, I think, because they stand by their word, and they have never made any unnecessary trouble.

Commissioner GARRETSON. Is that the only one?

Mr. GIBSON. That is the only one I know of.

·Commissioner GARRETSON. Have you heard of the other railway brotherhoods violating agreements?

Mr. GIBSON. I included them in that one.

. Commissioner GARRETSON. They are not included; they are an independent organization.

Mr. GIBSON. I am not familiar with the organization of the railroad people, but I have heard this particular brotherhood spoken of in very high terms.

· Commissioner GARRETSON. Have you heard of an instance where their agreement has been violated?

Mr. GIBSON. No; I have not. ·

Commissioner GARRETSON. You read an article from the Washington Socialist.

Mr. GIBSON. Yes.

Commissioner GARRETSON. Just a moment ago—from a Socialist paper, I did not know just what it was. Were you here this morning at the opening?

Mr. GIBSON. Yes.

Commissioner GARRETSON. Would you consider that article any more incendiary than the testimony that you heard given before you came on the stand?

Mr. GIBSON. Mr. Paterson clearly expressed his views and gave the reason for them from beginning. to end.

Commissioner GARRETSON. Would you consider one article more incendiary than the other?

Mr. GIBSON. Mr. Paterson's remarks were explanatory as they went along. This is merely an invitation to go out and shoot—speaking of the Washington Socialist.

Commissioner .GARRETSON. And the other was a declaration of intent to shoot in a certain case. Now, what is the difference, Mr. Gibson, except the channel that is used as a form of expression?

Mr. GIBSON. Personally, I would not have used the language Mr. Paterson did, because I am more moderate in my ideas. But on the principle he is working on, that the man must protect himself against a force, that is in his idea and in mine obnoxious, when unrest threatens life and property. and everything there is, and it is fire, and it is everything that goes with it, I. think his attitude is properly taken. But he expressed it a little differently than I would. .I think he has the same opinion as mine, in saying that we have to fight back, and that we are going to fight to the last ditch.

Commissioner GARRETSON. Now, we suppose that the man who wrote the article that is published there had less ground for considering the force he assailed as obnoxious?

Mr. GIBSON. There is a difference between Mr. Paterson and. the editor of. that paper, or the editor of the other paper. He was asked the direct question as to his opinion; he does not go out proselyting or preaching this doctrine he might have expressed. He was asked and he is giving it as far as he thinks, and that is as far as it will go. It will end with Mr. Paterson as far as the inflammatory remarks, as you are pleased to call them, are concerned.

Commissioner GARRETSON. You expressed the opinion that the article was treasonable?

Mr. GIBSON. Yes, sir; it is treasonable.

Commissioner GARRETSON. Was the other? ·

Mr. GIBSON. No, sir; it was not.

Commissioner GARRETSON. That is all.

Chairman WALSH. Mr. O'Connell wants to ask a question.

Commissioner O'CONNELL. I just want to carry that a little bit further, Mr. Gibson:. Did Mr. Paterson, in his indictment of society generally, including our legislature, the church, the college, organizations of labor, express the general opinion held by the members of your organization?

Mr. GIBSON. No, sir; he does not. I am a believer and our organization is a believer in moderation in all affairs. Aiming to protect ourselves against the encroachment on our rights wherever it is necessary, but they always attempt to be moderate and· fair in all matters. I am not criticizing Mr. Paterson, · because he has his ideas and he is entitled to them. He has expressed them fully.

Commissioner O'CONNELL. I have no desire to criticize him.

Mr. GIBSON. Further than that, our organization is doing this; it will as quickly attempt to chastise, if chastisement is needed, an employer who stands out· for greed or anything that is wrong toward the laboring man or the community at large, as it will the organization locally of the Federation of Labor when they try to encroach on our rights. We have that feeling in this work. ·*

Commissioner O'CONNELL. That is all.

Chairman WALSH. That is all, thank you. Call your next.

Mr. THOMPSON. Mr. Taylor, take the stand.

TESTIMONY OF MR. J. A. TAYLOR.

Mr. THOMPSON. Will you give us your name, please?

Mr. TAYLOR. J. A. Taylor.

Mr. THOMPSON. And your business address?

Mr. TAYLOR. 317 Labor Temple.

Mr. THOMPSON. And your occupation?

Mr. TAYLOR. I am representing the machinists of District 26, Northwest.··

Mr. THOMPSON. What does District 26 mean in the machinists' organization?

Mr. TAYLOR. District 26 comprises Oregon, Washington, and British Columbia, in the contract shops.

Mr. THOMPSON. You say you are representing them, are you their agent?·

Mr. TAYLOR. Their agent; yes, sir.

Mr. THOMPSON. Representing the International Union?

Mr. TAYLOR. Representing the International Union.

Mr. THOMPSON. How long have you been such representative?

Mr. TAYLOR. Five years.·

Mr. THOMPSON. You might tell us more specifically, but still briefly, what kind of work you do as such representative.

Mr. TAYLOR. I take care of the business of the district so as to keep the organization in the three different States apprised of conditions of work, and where it is located, and otherwise keep the organization informed as to anything of that kind. If there is any grievances come up between employer and employee where we have an organization, before there is any action taken, as a general rule, I am sent to that part of the district to investigate the trouble, and if the men are wrong, see that they live up to their agreement, if they have one.

Mr. THOMPSON. Now some questions have been given you. In order to save time, will you just follow down those questions and make answer to such as you care to answer?

Mr. TAYLOR. All right. In regard to the general condition in the metal trades of Washington and the Northwest, I might say that the conditions here in the Northwest, regardless of what has been said, don't compare with the conditions in San Francisco. You have heard one of the men who has been on the stand here tell about how the Frisco people are being put out of business and have gone out of business on account of the union. As a matter of fact, the machinists and metal industries in Frisco work eight hours per day and receive $4 per day in wages. The wages up here run from, I should say, 30 to 35 cents an hour for machinists, to 45 cents in the nonunion shops. Regardless of what Mr. Gibson or Mr. Paterson say about the high rate of wages they have paid and are paying, I believe they must have a rate for the commission and a rate for other times when they come before such institutions as the wage board at Bremerton. The wage board at the navy yard every year goes out and tries to find out the rates of wages paid to all the trades in that locality, and every year they set the wages at the navy yard according to the basis of the wages paid in that locality surrounding it, in the mechanical line. This metal trades' association gave the wage board a list last year, stating that their mechanics were getting 30 to 35 cents as a minimum, I have forgotten which just now, and 45 cents.

That was the highest, I believe, that was given in, which would have a tendency to have the wages at Bremerton lowered, perhaps. We went out and got the rate of wages paid to the machinists—this was just the machinists alone, and brought in 115 affidavits, showing that the wages were from $4 to $5 a day in the union shop. I myself then went to the statehouse at Olympia—that was about the only way I could find out what wages were really being paid at the nonunion shops. You have all noticed the attitude of Mr. Paterson, and it would not be very healthy, I suppose, for a business agent to try to get into the Seattle Construction & Dry Dock Co. to investigate anything in the iron business. I might say, perhaps, he is one of the causes of industrial unrest in this part of the country. So I went to the statehouse at Olympia and looked through the files that are filed by the employers when a man is hurt under the

.compensation act, and investigated four shops where machinists were hurt, and in each case they had another rate. They had a rate there because, I believe, under the compensation act you are paid a rate according to the wages you have received. At least I understood that previous to that time, and in each case I found there they paid no machinist less than 45 to 50 cents an hour, which would lead me to believe that they had a rate for the compensation act and a rate for the Industrial Commission and a rate for the wage board at Bremerton. However, we held our wages at Bremerton and, I believe, got an 8-cent raise for the highest mechanics, and the rate over there is $4.17.

There has been a great deal said about competition that we are up against in this line of business and, I would say, that the manufacturers in Frisco, when they made their agreement for eight hours a day in the metal trades, made it with the understanding that the condition would be brought to eight hours a day in this part of the country as soon as possible, which would lead one to believe there was a very little competition from the eastern part of the country, or it would have been necessary to try and get the entire country on the eight-hour basis, and on a wage scale the same as theirs. So I don't believe that the question of competition in business enters into the conditions in this part of the country, as far as the mechanics are concerned, to any great extent. There is not so very much manufacturing in this part of the country, and I would say, if I haven't already said it, that although they claim that the business is being driven out, and that the unions have put the mechanics out of business in Frisco, that there are more mechanics employed in Frisco and Oakland than there are in the States of Oregon and Washington. I believe that statement is correct.

In regard to the fact that we can't be trusted in keeping our agreements, I want to point out the fact that the machinists have an agreement, this same organization, with the Milwaukee Railway, the Northern Pacific Railroad, and the Great Northern. We have had agreements with those roads since 1902, I believe, or 1901. The agreement is signed up or renewed every year. It covers wages, shop conditions, apprenticeship questions, and everything in that respect. The first year I was working at Missoula, Mont., when one of the schedules was signed for district 32 and helped get that schedule and was in St. Paul with the committee, and after we signed up the contract and went back the company broke the agreement, and we have a regular system by which we can bring that before the company and have the matter adjusted without having a strike or lockout or walkout or anything of that kind. When the agreement was broken I, as the representative, went back to St. Paul and took the matter up with Mr. Mitchell, who at that time was superintendent of motive power, and the matter was adjusted. At that time Mr. Mitchell told us he considered that from a financial basis that was one of the best things that the company had done; that by signing up the agreement with the men he kept better mechanics and they wouldn't move around so much, perhaps, on account of knowing that the wages and conditions would be uniform. We also made agreements with him that we were to work five days a week and eight hours a day in case of a reduction, so as to keep everybody employed, and the relations between this same organization that has been stated as causing so much trouble in the Northwest country in the contract shops for the last 10 years has been of the very best on those roads. If there was any little trouble come up in a local shop, the business agent that you have heard so much talk about is sent out to investigate, and there has never been a case on any of those roads where the men were found to be in the wrong or where they didn't take the matter up according to schedule and the constitution of the organization but what they have been forced to return to work. And the international organization, located at Washington, D. C., insists upon agreements being lived up to in that manner. Which would also show, I believe, that we have been responsible in agreements we have made.

When it comes to trying to enforce an agreement in shops like Mr. Paterson's, that has never had an agreement in it or where a union man has never been allowed to work, it is impossible for anyone to enforce a matter of that kind if the men in there take voluntary action.

Now, in regard to the next question, which, I believe, is existing conditions between the metal workers' union and the metal trades association in Seattle and vincinity, one of the objections we have to the employers in this part of the country, especially in the metal trades, is the fact that they take unto themselves the right to organize and set rates of wages and go out and preach the doctrine of organization to the man that owns the shops; say it is a good thing for him to control his market; it is a good thing for him to have an employment agency and to know all about the conditions in that district; it is a good thing for him to control the metal-trade industry in this part of the country as a business man, but turn around, on the other hand, and tell his employees in the shop this is a good thing for me, but it is a bad thing for you; you are an individual American citizen, you can bargain individually, and they get some individual bargaining.

That attitude is one that I think is very inconsistent. I myself believe that the employers in the metal industry ought to have an organization, or in any other industry, and I believe that the employees should be given the same right; that they have a right to organize and get together and draw up their agreement and schedule, so that they know they are going to go through for a year or whatever time it is, and that they will have peace; that they will have peace at all times. But when one or the other takes the stand that one has the right to do that and the other hasn't a right to do the same, why, the outcome generally is that there is trouble in some manner.

I believe Mr. Constantine the other day said that the metal-trades association was a branch of his organization, the employers' association, and stated that they didn't keep an employment agency. They have an employment agent at 222 Lyons Building. I have a card here which I will present from their employment agency. If a man goes to a shop and asks for a job that belongs to the metal trades' association here in this city, instead of employing him direct, they send him to Mr. Garrison, at 222 Lyons Building, and this form of card is made out.

Commissioner GARRETSON. How is the name spelled?
Mr. TAYLOR. I didn't notice that, but I notice they are very much alike.
Commissioner GARRETSON. I-s-o-n?
Mr. TAYLOR. I think so.
Commissioner GARRETSON. Good.
(See Taylor Exhibit No. 1.)
Mr. TAYLOR. They are asked the question when they go there if they belong to the union. We know, because we have sent men there to find out, and in some cases they have come back and said where they said they belonged to the union they told them they didn't want union men. They were running an open shop, and still they didn't want union men. Now, they have said right along here, I believe, that they were running an open shop, and that the metal trades association stood for the open shop. I have a letter here, which I will also present, of the proceedings of a meeting of the metal trades association which will show the open-shop attitude of the employers' association. It is very short and will show the open-shop question as the metal trades association views it. You asked the question in regard to how much of an organization they would be in favor of having in their shops, and I believe that this would answer the question. This is the United Metal Trades Association of the Pacific Coast:

SEATTLE, WASH., June 16, 1910.
To the members of the Washington district:
GENTLEMEN: At the regular monthly meeting held last night in this office, the following resolution was unanimously adopted:

"*Resolved,* That this association forthwith adopt the absolute nonunion shop." And the inclosed notice was ordered sent to all members of the association, with the request that they post in their shops on receipt of same. For the benefit of members of the association who were not present last night we will say that the association has taken this stand after giving the open shop a good trial and has found that the minute union men get into the shop they immediately start to organize and interfere with the nonunion men and create discord, and the meeting was unanimous in its declaration for an absolutely nonunion condition in their shops hereafter."

Yours, very truly,
UNITED METAL TRADES ASSOCIATION,
A. H. GARRISON, *Secretary.*

That is the open shop as the metal trades association views it, and that is one thing that caused trouble so far as the mechanics are concerned in this part of the country.

Now, in regard to their boycotting, I have two letters here. They take the stand that organized labor should not be given the right to boycott, and, I want to read just one sketch in here that would seem to show that the metal trades association use the boycott themselves.

" This is the United Metal Trades Association of the Pacific Coast, and there is one part that relates to cooperation:
" We wish to commend each member of the association for the cooperation he has given the other members. Since this strike has been declared, the members are working together more than ever, but we might help each other much more than we do without any inconvenience in the least. If you have work done outside, let one of the members do it. Generally this is done, but sometimes it is not, and it only encourages the firms that sign up with the unions to continue as they are if you give them your work. They are trying to tear down what you are trying to build up, and work given them helps them to do it. Don't forget this when you let work out."
It gives a list of the pattern shops at Portland, Seattle, and Tacoma on the open-shop plan.
There is another clause which I will read——
Mr. THOMPSON. Has that letter got a date?
Mr. TAYLOR. June 25, 1910.
(See Taylor Exhibit No. 2.)
Mr. TAYLOR. Here is a letter sent out from Portland, Oreg., dated March 11, 1911, a weekly letter, and I will just read one part of it on this boycott proposition:

" OPEN-SHOP CONTRACTS.

" We recently received a communication from Walter Drew, commissioner, National Erectors' Association, requesting a list of open-shop, steel-erecting concerns in this city. Mr. Drew advises us that it is the intention of the members of their association to let their work to open-shop contractors as far as possible all over the country. The Seattle office has supplied Mr. Drew with the names of open-shop contractors in Seattle, Tacoma, and Spokane. The members of this association will appreciate the efforts that are being made by the eastern associations in our behalf."
(See Taylor Exhibit No. 3.)
Mr. TAYLOR. Now, in regard to the 1910 strike, I want to say that as far as the 1910 strike was concerned, it was not a strike, it was a lockout. We sent out a letter and communicated with the metal trades association, asking that they meet with a committee from the organization of the machinists' district, to try and bring about a shorter working-day and better conditions in this part of the country along the same lines as those enjoyed by the mechanics in Frisco. They took no notice of this communication, and, as a matter of fact, in one of the largest shops in Tacoma, they immediately began locking out our men. I went to the Phoenix Engineering Co., in Tacoma, and met the two owners of that shop, and was in there talking to them for at least an hour and a half or two hours, trying to get them to be reasonable as far as letting men out was concerned; that perhaps there would not be a strike; that we might get together in some manner and adjust matters and prevent a strike. And in reply to that he said, " No; I am going to discharge all the union men and get all the good men on the market now, and get the best of the other shops."
We took it up with the international union and tried in every way to overcome the necessity of striking in that shop, but they made their statement plain that they intended to discharge the men, and the steel works over there started to do the same thing, and it was necessary to start the strike at Tacoma, I think, about 10 days before the strike was even voted on in Seattle.
I have a letter somewhere, I don't know just where it is at the present time, but I will furnish it—a letter from Portland, which is evidence that this is a fact. That states that Tacoma locked their men out. That was the first place that the trouble started. After the strike started, I think June 1 or 2, 1910, after we had written to the secretary of the metal trades' association, recognizing their association, although they wouldn't recognize ours, we sent individual letters to the employers asking for a conference, and we were willing even to allow a conference of the men in the shops. It didn't matter whether they met the men in the shops or met a representative of the organization, as far as I am individually concerned. There was not a reply to that.
Then we called up in Seattle here before going out—we called up every individual shop owner and asked him if he would meet a committee of his employees, and that was refused. Therefore the strike was declared.
When the machinists came out on strike the employers shipped in or brought men in from Chicago. I think there was 17 men shipped out here from Chicago. They were furnished with everything that money could buy, even to

whisky and other things on the way out, and arriving here they found there was a strike on. They were shipped out not knowing there was a strike on in this part of the country, and they had sent their baggage shipped in-care of Mr. Garrison, to the metal trades' association; and then, after they found out there was a strike on—and I want to say here that is why we do picketing, to let the men know that come in, not knowing about the trouble, that there is a strike, to walk along beside him and talk to him, and that was the instruction of every man when he went out on the picket line. We catch him on the picket line and tell him there is a strike, and they would refuse to go to work. There was quite a few union men came out on the train that brought some of the rest out. There was a few men that went to work. They would hold the men in the shops and hold them for the wages—hold their wages until they had paid for their transportation coming out here; so that it was necessary in one case where a man had worked some time in there to sue for the amount. There is a letter and some affidavits here in that respect. These are the affidavits here, I believe, of the men in regard to having been shipped out from Chicago. There is quite a bunch of them.

Mr. THOMPSON. Are you offering those in evidence?

Mr. TAYLOR. Yes, sir.

(See Taylor Exhibit No. 4.)

Mr. THOMPSON. Will you read just the names of those who are there?

Mr. TAYLOR. Affidavit, State of Washington, county of King——

Mr. THOMPSON. Just read the names of the people who made the affidavits.

Mr. TAYLOR. Herman Kottenbach, Robert Feja, Emil Krohn, Frank C. Parker, Henry W. Biggs, John Tomilgas, Adam Crocus.

Mr. THOMPSON. About what dates are those? About the same dates? I don't care for the individual dates, but just about the same, are they?

Mr. TAYLOR. August, 1910. They would hold the baggage checks and refuse to turn their baggage over to them, and would hold their baggage if possible. We never had to go to court in regard to that, I don't believe, but we would get the baggage in some manner—either lost our baggage checks or something else, and the baggage was received, at least in some cases.

Now, in regard to the pickets causing all the trouble in the strikes. I want to say that there was a good deal of trouble caused by the other side.

At the Washington Iron Works, there was just two or three of our men on the picket line down there, and the employees and, I believe, one of the foremen went to the top of the building and turned the fire hose on them, and also—I am not sure, but I think threw rotten eggs at them. Knowing that it would be repeated perhaps, the two pickets went down to that same place with one of the city officials, either the water or hydrant inspector, and they turned it on him and the two pickets from the same place.

I have something here on that. The Washington Iron Works' attachés had appeared on the roof of the office and turned the fire hose on them, drenching them to the skin. Again the police were appealed to, but could not do anything because the offenders could not be identified. But knowing that they had appeared on a former occasion and would probably appear again, which they did, they went down, and this time witnesses were taken, who identified them. It took a month and a half to get the men into court, and after the usual delay they were found guilty, in spite of the carefully concocted story which they gave to the court, aided by Attorney France, who is now, I believe, president of the Municipal League.

Other cases of violence, by police officer No. 65, who arrested one of our members, who by the way is a very small man, and at the behest of Mr. James, attorney for the metal trades association. We asked for the reason of making the arrest, and the police officer replied by smashing the man in the face and knocking him down and applying all the violent epithets that ever passed the lips of a human being. There was violence caused by the employers in that instance.

And at the Sumner Iron Works, in Everett, that Mr. Gibson spoke of, they did have a house there where the pickets remained in out of the wet in wintertime, and used to meet the men coming across the bridge, which crosses the river there, and talk to them with reference to coming out to assist to better their condition.

One case of violence that I know was committed up there, the son of one of the employers came out and declared himself, that he could whip anybody in the crowd singlehanded, and there happened to be a man in that crowd that thought perhaps he couldn't do it. So they just formed a ring and went at it. As a result of it, the picket got the best of the fight, and then the wagon was called. And as a matter of fact, quite a good deal of the trouble that is caused is caused by the men working in the shop—every man that is appointed as a deputy inside the shop is working as a mechanic, and they come out and cause the trouble.

In Portland, where I was located at that time, in one case one of the men that worked in the shop stated that the employer came in to him and asked him to go out and cause trouble on the picket line, and he refused. This same employer, when they would arrest our men for hardly nothing, went to the man who would go on his bail and tried to get him to take his name off so that the man would be kept in jail. That is about the tactics that they pursued in so far as trying to have peace theirselves was concerned.

The attitude of the court at that place was very partial to the employer. A man would be arrested for some offense where the maximum fine could not possibly be over $15 or $20 if he was found guilty, and they would place the bail at $500 cash bail to get him out. They would arrest him on Saturday afternoon when the banks were closed so that it would be necessary to go and get the cash. As a matter of fact there never was any of them ever got behind the bars, because we always had somebody telephone to us, and we would get them bail before they got in jail.

As a matter of fact, all that trouble in Portland was caused by the company wanting to get an injunction. The city passed an ordinance, antipicket ordinance, and they have the referendum in that city, and if they get enough signers they can refer the ordinance or law to the voters. It was referred to the voters at the next election, which held it up for a year, and at the regular election it was defeated, so that the employers tried to get an injunction to keep the men from standing out and letting people know that there was trouble in that place. And to do that we believe that there was quite a good deal of manipulation from inside the shop to cause the trouble when the men came out.

As a matter of fact we know—any union man knows—that we are always getting the worst of it in causing trouble on the picket line. That would be the last place where he would start it, if he was using good judgment, and the most of them used good judgment, and the most of them are under direct control of their organizations. And in all the cases, every case where any of our men has been arrested in the entire time of the strike, there never has been one found with a concealed weapon, and as much can not be said for the other side, for they carried both blackjacks and guns.

We can show a picture here, taken when these men came out from Chicago and started to go into work in one of these shops here. I believe one of the pickets was out there and talked to them, and let them know what the trouble was, and that was one reason they didn't go to work.

The secretary of the metal trades association, Mr. Garrison, was with the four of them to take them in, I believe, to the Moran plant, now the Seattle Construction & Dry Dock Co. And one of the pickets had a kodak and was taking a picture of the men as they went in. This angered Mr. Garrison to such an extent that he tried to kick the camera over. He succeeded in that, but he didn't succeed in stopping the picture. He is shown there in the attitude of one foot in the air, both fists clenched, an attitude which was not very peaceable, I imagine.

(The picture was submitted by the witness; it is not printed.)

Mr. TAYLOR. We have heard something, I believe, here, in regard to the union entering into politics. And I believe that that is the place for them. But we also can show here by a letter sent out by the metal trades industry, that the metal trades association also enters into politics.

Here is a letter which I will file, dated Portland, Oreg., May 4, 1911. This is the city election in Portland. This is a United Metal Trades Association paper:

"*Political situation.*—At a special meeting of the Oregon district held Tuesday evening, May 2, the following candidates were decided upon as being those who would work to our interests."

Then it goes on and gives a list of the mayor and the city auditor and all those people, which I will file. At the end it says:

"From what information we have at hand, the candidates named above are the best men in the field.

".We trust that H. E. Rushlight, Ed D. Williams, William H. Daly, and Ralph C. Clyde will be snowed under so deep that they can not get out for several years. These people do not hesitate to state their preference for organ-ized labor."

(See Taylor Exhibit No. 5.)

They used ·every means in their power to get the men in their shops ·to vote against these men mentioned. I will say, however, that they were elected; that is, three of them were elected, I believe.

Here is another instance of political action, so far as the employers' asso-ciation in the State of Washington is concerned. It is a newspaper clipping. It says:

" Stop-Look-Listen League asks 50-cent contribution for every employee in State.

" Waves eight-hour initiative bill as red flag in face of State industries."

This is taken from the Seattle Star.

" In an effort to obtain more money, the Stop-Look-Listen League is attempt-ing to inflame a class war between employers and ·employees, in its campaign against the ' Seven Sisters ' and other initiative bills, one of which· asks ·a universal eight-hour day.

"A ' jing ' letter has been addressed by the Stop-Look-Listeners to employers in Washington asking them to contribute 50 cents for every man and woman in their employ.

. " Show how to dodge law.

" Instructions are given foreign corporations doing business in Washington how to contribute and still avoid prosecution.

" In Chehalis County, R. A. Archer, one of the notorious Ed Benn gang of politicians, is sending out these secret letters:

" ' If the arrangement is satisfactory to you, kindly forward me a check for the amount of your assessment at as early a date as possible, making the same payable to the Stop-Look-Listen League.

" ' In the case of foreign or other corporations, their residence or principal office outside the State, or a corporation having a majority of its stockholders nonresidents of the State, its resident manager can be a subscriber to the fun, but must send his personal check for his subscription, as the law makes it a misdemeanor punishable by a fine to do otherwise.' "

(The paper referred to, an·extract from the Seattle Star of June 13, 1914, was submitted in printed form.)

In regard to the competition· between the different trades, between the metal trades industry in this country and the eastern metal trades industry—I have no specific thing to offer here in that respect, only in a general·manner.

We heard yesterday about the competition in the lumber business, and the lumber industry. Here is a clipping from the P. I., " Portland, Oreg., June 29," which will be of interest, perhaps, to the lumber interests, which will show that the competition coming from the East is not so keen on some· things as they would have us believe.

Chairman WALSH. Mr. Taylor, we have adopted a rule,· I don't know whether it has been adhered to strictly in these hearings, that all documentary evidence be simply handed in, with a description of what it is. That would apply to a clipping.

Mr. TAYLOR. I did not know that, Mr. Chairman, because the fact is witnesses· have been given plenty of latitude in the way of reading anything that was wished.

Chairman WALSH. We are going to try to get back to the rule.

Mr. TAYLOR. I will file that, and it just covers——

Chairman WALSH (interrupting). Describe the clipping, saying what it is.

Mr. TAYLOR. It covers the proposition of where the manufacturers of sash and doors in the South are asking for higher railroad rates so as to over-·come the competition of those people in the West. We would imagine that the employer, when·a law is passed, would live up to·at least that part of'it without an agreement with an organization. But as a matter of fact, we have a Government eight-hour law which says that all work shall·be done under eight-hour conditions. Labor organizations have worked, since previous to'1892,· to ·have such a law placed on the statute books. We ·passed the law in 1892, and an Attorney General of the United States ruled, although·it mentioned contractors, that it meant work done on Government property only, and did, not· consider battleships Government property; but if it was ·work done· on·· a private dock ·they could work as many hours as they wished; if the work was done in a Government yard, it had to be eight hours.

˙ If this building was built on this corner, all the work on the lot would have · ·
to ·be done under eight-hour conditions.· But the man who dressed the 'stone
although it was around here, could take it over across the street and work 24
hours if he wished. After this decision we worked several years to get the eight-
hour law established in Government work and for contractors and subcontractors working for the Government—we found plenty of opposition from this
National· Manufacturers' Association, and this employers' association affiliated
with it, but we got the law passed, I believe, in 1911, which we thought would
certainly stop this violation of the law as we saw it.

Now,· that law is in effect which states that either the contractor or subcontractor must work eight hours a day on Government work. 'We have no
organization in some of the machine shops and shipbuilding plants in · this
part of the country, and have no way of knowing whether that law·is violated
cr not. I have sent men to work in this place, and I have an affidavit here to
show the violation by one of the employers in this State of the eight-hour law. ·
This covers three or four days' work on the U. S. S. *General Mifflin* and the ·
U. S. S. *Dix*, which I will file.

Chairman WALSH. What is the name of the factory? .

Mr. TAYLOR. William C. Gates and the Seattle Machine Works, 8th day of
October, 1913. He made the statement that one man worked 36 hours continuously at one· of the machine shops on the Government boat although · the
eight-hour law is supposed to be in effect.

Chairman WALSH. This seems to be a good point to stop, and we will now
adjourn until 2 o'clock.

(The clipping referred to was submitted in printed form. For affidavit, see
Taylor Exhibit No. 6.)

(Whereupon an adjournment was taken at 12.10 o'clock p. m. of· this,
Friday, to 2 o'clock p. m. of the same day, Friday, Aug. 14, 1914.)

AFTER RECESS—2 P. M.

Chairman WALSH. You may resume the stand now, Mr. Taylor.

TESTIMONY OF MR. J. A.; TAYLOR—Continued.

Mr. THOMPSON. All right, Mr. Taylor. Proceed with your testimony.

Mr. TAYLOR. I have a notice of judgment in regard to the Chicago cases and
one affidavit extra in regard to the· shipping of men from Chicago, which ·I
wish to present.

·(See Taylor Exhibit No. 7.)

Mr. TAYLOR. Also——

Chairman WALSH. The affidavit of whom? Just give the name and date
please.

Mr. TAYLOR. This is Krohn—no; not Krohn, what a minute. · Of Walter
Leuzinger.

˙Chairman WALSH. And the date?

Mr. TAYLOR. Tenth day of July, 1910. I also have two affidavits to show the
attitude of the police in this city.

Chairman WALSH. The names.

Mr. TAYLOR. One of J. E. Hendricksen, and the other one of M. F. Krowl,
30th day of July, 1910.

(See Taylor Exhibit No. 8.)

Mr. THOMPSON. Briefly stated, what was that attitude that the affidavits
show?

Mr. TAYLOR. Well, it was against pickets and against the unions; that is,
they took a stand——

Chairman WALSH. What was it that Mr. Thompson spoke of?

Mr. THOMPSON. The attitude of the police at that time.

Mr. TAYLOR. The attitude of the police in those two instances was against
the organization, against the union.

I also have a copy of the letter, which I shall file, which was sent to the em-
·ployers' association and to the individual members at that time. The date was ˙
May, 1910.

(See Taylor Exhibit No. 9.)

I will also ·file a copy of the agreement which we asked for, which will show ·
we did not ask for the closed shop.

⁎(See Taylor Exhibit No. 10.) ˙

. I wish to file another paper of the American Anti-Boycott Association. · Just one paragraph of this I wish to bring out, the ruling of the supreme court of· Connecticut, which has ruled " that manufacturers may bind themselves together by penal bonds to adhere to the open-shop policy, and that such agreements are enforceable.   That manufacturers in any industry may make agreements with· each other to maintain the open shop, and it becomes unlawful for any labor union having knowledge of that agreement to use even lawful means to unionize that shop."

(The paper referred, entitled " July Bulletin," published by the American Anti-Boycott Association, 27 William Street, N. Y., was submitted in printed form.)

Mr. THOMPSON. Are you quoting from the paper?

Mr. TAYLOR. From this letter I have just filed.

In regard to the business agents and the representatives of organized labor that is such a detriment to the organized-labor movement, as spoken of this morning by Mr. Paterson, I wish to say that the business agent exists, and his position is held because of the attitude of the employers; when a committeee working in the employer's shop, in a great many cases, goes in in front of the management to ask for better conditions, unless he is subservient to the wishes of the employer to a certain extent, a great many times he is discharged, which makes it necessary for the organization to have a man whom the employer can not reach—so that the man working for him has nothing to do but get the man that is representing him, so that he does not get in bad ·with the man that is inclined to be unfair—I am speaking now of the unscrupulous employer. But for myself, I wish to say this at this time, that if the employers would· meet all of the machinists as machinists in this community that I represent, and would meet a committee from the shops and treat with them impartially as organized men and not discriminate against them, my resignation will be in his hands at any time.

I say that because I think I can make a living as a machinist; I have done it previously as master mechanic and in other occupations.

The next thing I want to take up is the strike of the machinists in 1907. That strike was called May 1, 1907, for the purpose of establishing the 40-cent minimum rate of wages—and by minimum rate of wages we don't cut off or curtail individual ability. We set a minimum scale that we think any mechanic that is worthy of shop room ought to be able to earn. That would be $3.60 a day for nine hours for a man who works to the one-thousandth part of an inch in a great many instances, and if the employers want to take the rest or any of the men in the shop as individuals because they are better able to earn more money than 40 cents, the sky is the limit. He can raise it just as high as he wishes. There is nothing in the organization that keeps him from going the limit and giving him the maximum rate and that will be satisfactory at any time with us.

A very respectful letter was sent to the employers' association asking for a conference, and no reply was ever received. A little later a letter was sent to the employers individually, to which only a few replied. As a last resort a committee was sent to the individual employers and the strike called on such as could not be persuaded to concede the reasonable demands. A very large per cent in the machine shops responded to the strike call; pickets were put on and the work was very effective, so much so that the employers were driven to hard straits to obtain men. Finding themselves losing out and growing desperate the employers sought to influence the police department to restrain the pickets and make their work ineffective. The mayor of the city after a thorough investigation of the pickets refused to give additional police protection as requested by the employers. I believe Mr. Moore was mayor at that time. Not being able to use the police department to prevent the pickets telling the truth to the prospective employees, they resorted to the court and sought and obtained an injunction which was the most drastic ever granted in this State. The hearing of the case in which it was sought to make the injunction permanent was from time to time postponed until about a year later when and after the object of the picketing had been defeated and the shops filled with men, and in addition . to that the strike being practically called off, the case was called and the plaintiff asked that it be dismissed.

It was granted by the court. The result was that that judge who issued the injunction and who had been elected by the largest majority· was, through force of public sentiment, dropped to the bottom at the following election. · ᴵ

I wish to present a copy of this injunction. I don't want to read it, but I · want to state that this injunction enjoins any of the men herein mentioned. I was working for the Willamette Iron Works at that time in Portland, Oreg., as one of their outside men, and I was vice president of this district. I am enjoined in this, and never knew that the injunction was issued until later. They enjoin any of the men that went on strike, or that even did not go on strike, Jon Doe and Richard Roe, and all the rest of them, from talking to any of the men, visiting at their homes and peacefully asking them to go out on strike, and refusing them the rights of the public highways leading to any of the machine shops that were on strike. And I place it here on file.

(See Taylor Exhibit No. 11.)

Mr. Taylor. Further, in regard to the administration of labor law, I wish to say that we have an eight-hour law in the city here. I believe that legislation is a good thing. I believe in the worker taking advantage of every opportunity to get better results for all the workers, not only the union workers, but anybody that works for a living, whether it is by legislation or whether it is by organization.

But I have found through actual experience that when we pass a law, unless we have an organization of some kind in the shop to see that the law is lived up to, to see that it is enforced, it is practically impossible to have it done.

Just last week one of those large concerns that we have heard mentioned this morning as being in competition with the metal trades' association in this country came out here to erect steam turbines and generators in the new city light plant.

The employers here must have known that these people were bidding in competition with them with the intention of breaking this law that other contractors, if they are honest, expect to live up to. And we did not hear of any employers' association taking up the question and seeing to it that the eastern concern lived up to that ordinance. But one of us business agents—we find the law is broken and take the matter up, with the result that they were instructed to live up to the ordinance or their contract would be annulled. We also got the decision that the inspector on the job hereafter should be held responsible. Heretofore the inspector on the job, while a man might work 15 hours and break the ordinance as often as he pleased—I don't know whether he shut his eyes or what happened to him, but he never was able to at least bring it before the board of public works. So that it is necessary to have an organization, even though you have a political organization. The two together work fine. Singly they don't get the results that we think we should have.

Any proposals for improvement in those labor laws is the next question. Especially the eight-hour law and another one where the minimum-wage question was involved, where a girl went before the minimum-wage board and her testimony did not particularly suit the man that runs the Troy Laundry, and where he discharged her for it and was fined by the lower court $100. Since that time it has been appealed to the supreme court.

I don't think that a fine is adequate to see that an employer or anyone else lives up to the law. If we go out here and break a law it is not always just a fine we get. Sometimes we get sent to jail. And I believe on the first offense when an employer breaks any of these laws that he should have the option of paying a fine; but when he breaks the law again on the second offense that you should give him a jail sentence the same as the English law.

In regard to the unemployment and extent and causes and possible remedies: I would take it not so much of an overproduction as an underconsumption. We can all use more goods. I could have better clothes than what I have got, I am sure, and everybody here perhaps could live a little bit better. We all are in a position that we could live better if we were able to do it. And if everybody was employed and employed so that they would remain employed, I think that you would reach a very good result in that respect.

I believe that some legislation some time in the future—I don't know how far removed that will be—will make it so that we will have conditions in this country where every man or every worker will be able to work when they are willing, and be able to feed their children and will be able to raise a family instead of having no children, or in some cases but one, as in this country. And government would find it a very good economic proposition to see that those conditions are brought about.

I believe that by reducing hours of labor and keeping everybody employed that you will have less dissatisfaction.

I believe that if the workers had more confidence in the people that are enforcing the law that we would have less dissatisfaction. We figure that we send a man to Congress, or we send him here or there or somewhere else politically, and he does not represent us sometimes when he says that he will.ᶠ We feel—perhaps we just feel it, but we know just the same—that we do' not always get the same consideration from a judge, even though he is elected, · as has been brought out here· this morning, when we are broke, down and out, that we get if we have got the kale—the money. I do not say by that that the courts could be bought, but I would leave the impression that an influence can be used.

In one case we find the secretary of state insisting upon interpreting some' laws to suit himself, where men that are elected to office of State, as the secretary, should apply the law as it reads. The people pass a law—a referendum law—that they can go out and get so many signatures to any law that they wish to put to referendum; they get 10 per cent of the signatures of the voters of the State; and they are checked over in the city where they come from, by the regular man—a clerk or whoever he is who has charge of it; the signatures are checked, and we find that there is enough signatures to some of those bills that the Stop-Look-Listen League do not wish to go on the ballot even to give the public a chance to say whether it was a good thing or a bad thing—we find our secretary of state, according to reports that I have from men that have been down there and have watched the counting and will substantiate by affidavits if necessary, that he has been very partial, and· he has been serving his master to the best of his ability.

I believe that is all the statement I have to make at this time.

Chairman WALSH. Any questions?

Cmmissioner GARRETSON. One question.

Chairman WALSH. Mr. Garretson would like to ask you a question.

Commissioner GARRETSON. Is it your experience as a machinist and representing that organization, as I assume, or having knowledge of it, that· the organization has, in the years gone by, maintained its contracts in precisely the same way as you heard it admitted this morning that the railway organization did?

Mr. TAYLOR. I would say to the extent we are organized. If we have a very poor organization—that is, weak——

Commissioner GARRETSON. Where you control the situation?·

Mr. TAYLOR. Where we control the situation we live up to our agreement positively.

Commissioner GARRETSON. That is all.

Chairman WALSH. Any other questions?

Commissioner O'CONNELL. You heard Mr. Paterson's testimony?

Mr. TAYLOR. Yes, sir.

Commissioner O'CONNELL. Now, Mr. Paterson stated that the ·rate of wages that was being obtained in the shipyard of which he was president was as high, if not higher, than the rates of wages being paid in this territory or this section of the country. In fact, they were so high it was economically impossible for other concerns to pay as high wages.

I take it from that he meant that if they paid those wages they could not succeed in business. I understand that the Seattle Construction & Dry Dock Co. is doing a regular marine work, building ships and repairing ships and· that sort of work?

Mr. TAYLOR. Yes, sir.

Commissioner O'CONNELL. They are operating their plant under the nine-·hour basis?

Mr. TAYLOR. Yes, sir.

Commissioner O'CONNELL. He stated a number of ·his machinists were be-· ing paid 37 cents an hour on a nine-hour basis.

Mr. TAYLOR. Well, he made the statement that they paid several different rates; 35 cents was the lowest.

Commissioner O'CONNELL. From that up to 50 cents.

Mr. TAYLOR. Sixty, he said, also.

Commissioner O'CONNELL. I think he said in one or two instances they paid 60 cents to some men. The Union Iron. Works, at San Francisco, is· a shipbuilding concern, is it not?

Mr. TAYLOR. Yes, sir.

Commissioner O'CONNELL. Of a considerable capacity, a large employer of labor?

Mr. TAYLOR. Yes, sir ; even larger than this one, I believe.

Commissioner O'CONNELL. The Union Iron Works has been operating· on the eight-hour basis for some years, has it not?

Mr. TAYLOR. On the eight'hour basis?

Commissioner O'CONNELL. Yes, sir.

Mr. TAYLOR. Yes, sir.

Commissioner O'CONNELL. And the minimum rate of wages paid in 'San Francisco for eight hours is $4, or 50 cents an hour?

Mr. TAYLOR. As I understand it.

Commissioner O'CONNELL. Are they competing with the shipbuilding concern in this city?

Mr. TAYLOR. Yes, sir.

Commissioner O'CONNELL. Do you know whether the shipyards in the East— for instance, the New York Shipbuilding Co., at Camden, N. J., which is one of the largest in the country—that concern has been operating on the eight-hour basis for some years?

Mr. TAYLOR. Yes, sir; it has.

Commissioner O'CONNELL. Do you know whether the Fore River Shipbuilding Co., at Quincy, Mass., has been operating on the eight-hour basis?

Mr. TAYLOR. It has.

Commissioner O'CONNELL. The Newport Shipbuilding Co., at Newport, Va., has been operating a great portion of its employees on the eight-hour basis?

Mr. TAYLOR. At least for the last year or two years.

Commissioner O'CONNELL. That the rates of wages paid by these concerns will compare favorably, if not to a greater degree, with the rate paid by the shipyard company in Seattle?

Mr. TAYLOR. I think they will. I think they would be a little better in regard to living conditions. Perhaps they live cheaper back there.

Commissioner O'CONNELL. And that the shipyard company meet their employees for the purpose of settling rates of wages, hours, and conditions of employment, and enter into contractual relations with them?

Mr. TAYLOR. I think that is a fact.

Commissioner O'CONNELL. That is true in so far at least as the Union Iron Works at San Francisco is concerned?

Mr. TAYLOR. Yes, sir. I was going to say I have no way of knowing how many 35-cent men there are in the Seattle Dry Dock Co. or how many 50-cent men, but I have never met a man out of there yet that got 50 or 60 cents.

Commissioner O'CONNELL. Do you know whether the metal trades association of this district, comprising the States of Washington and Nevada, I understand—is it those two States?

Mr. TAYLOR. The metal trades?

Commissioner O'CONNELL. Yes, sir.

Mr. TAYLOR. Comprising Washington and Oregon.

Commissioner O'CONNELL. Do you know whether a circular has been issued to the members of that association by the general secretary of this district to the effect that discontinuance of the open shop would be preferable and the organization of absolute nonunion shop lines?

Mr. TAYLOR. Yes, sir.

Commissioner O'CONNELL. Have you ever seen such a circular?

Mr. TAYLOR. I have seen it and placed it on file.

Commissioner O'CONNELL. Do you know whether that association has recently issued a circular advising its members to appear before this commission and in other words giving them permission to appear before the commission?

Mr. TAYLOR. I saw that letter yesterday, where it was stated that all union men would be here and that there would be union men on the commission, and advising all employers to be present at this meeting.

Commissioner O'CONNELL. Would that imply, if such circular had not been issued or such request had not been issued, that they might not appear before this commission?

Mr. TAYLOR. Well, I would take it that way.

Commissioner O'CONNELL. That is all.

Chairman WALSH. That is all; thank you. Call your next.

Mr. THOMPSON. There are some other questions that have been handed to me.

Chairman WALSH. All right. Proceed.

Mr. THOMPSON. Mr. Taylor, I hand you what purports to be a copy of the letter sent by Mr. Garrison to the commander of the naval yard; accompanying that is also a list of the people employed in the metal trades and the wages per hour that they receive. Will you kindly look at that and see whether that is in accordance with the information you found?

Mr. TAYLOR. Just a minute. I want' to take time with this. This gives a list of 55-cent machinists—12 machinists, at 55 cents; 27 machinists, at 50 cents; and 60 at 40 cents. I will say I never saw this list, but I am speaking from the information given this morning, given me by the machinists of the Bremerton yard, who are organized, that they had been led to believe, at least by some one in authority, that it was going to be necessary for them to go out and get affidavits to keep the machinists, the first-class machinists in Bremerton, from having a reduction in wages.

Mr. THOMPSON. What do they get?

Mr. TAYLOR. $4.08, I believe, at that time, or $4.07. I think they got a cent raise afterwards.

Mr. THOMPSON. From that list you have there—would that——

Mr. TAYLOR. I would like to finish—that they were led to believe in that respect, and were told by some one over there that the employers over here had stated that they could get all the machinists they wanted for 35 and 40 cents an hour, that that was practically their standard rate of wages. So far as getting a statement like this was concerned, it would be impossible for me to get it, perhaps. I never saw a statement like this at all.

(See Taylor Exhibit No. 12.)

Commissioner COMMONS. What is that paper?

Mr. THOMPSON. It is a copy of a letter Mr. Garrison sent to the commander of the navy yard at Bremerton, giving the wages of mechanics.

Mr. TAYLOR. But I will state that the machinists' scale would be even higher than that, so far as the union scale is concerned here. I have a list here, so far as the union wages are concerned here in this city and vicinity, or this city, and they run from 45 cents to 60 cents.

Mr. THOMPSON. That is all I wish to know about that anyway, because it will have to be established by other people before it can go in the evidence. How many men does the Union Iron Works employ, if you know?

Mr. TAYLOR. Well, I couldn't say as to that, not having been in Frisco but once in my life.

Mr. THOMPSON. Do you know whether or not they employ more now than they did six years ago, or less?

Mr. TAYLOR. I believe, perhaps six years ago—that would bring it along about—I don't know just what year that would be, 1908, or 1907. They were very busy just previous to the panic in 1907. And I believe it is the policy of the Steel Trust, and I think the Union Iron Works are a subsidiary company or belongs to them to do their shipbuilding in the East as much as they can.

Mr. THOMPSON. Do you know whether there have been more ships built in the Union Yards, or less, in the last five years, than previously?

Mr. TAYLOR. Well I know that the Union Iron Works has received three or four Government contracts for building Government boats. I know that in 1911 or 1912 that the shops in this district, especially in Portland, refused to compete on those contracts on account of having the eight-hour clause in them, and there was an editorial written regarding the matter in the Oregonian, I believe, in Portland, telling the employers of labor there that if they expected this to be an up-to-date community they would have to adjust themselves to the conditions that existed.

Mr. THOMPSON. Do you know how many ships have been built in union shops in the last five years?

Mr. TAYLOR. Union Iron Works?

Mr. THOMPSON. Is that what you mean; Union Iron Works?

(This question was asked Mr. Drew.)

Mr. TAYLOR. No; I couldn't say.

Mr. THOMPSON. Do you know how many machinists there are in Oakland, and how many in San Francisco, in round numbers?

Mr. TAYLOR. Well, I believe there is about 3,000 machinists.

Mr. THOMPSON. In Oakland? Where?

Mr. TAYLOR. In Oakland and San Francisco.

Mr. THOMPSON. Do you know how it is divided as between the two cities?

Mr. TAYLOR. Well, I judge that there is about two-thirds of them in San Francisco, or very close to it.

Mr. THOMPSON. But you have no accurate figures?

Mr. TAYLOR. Not accurately, no; but almost accurately. It is within, I would judge, a few hundred, a hundred or so of that.

Mr. THOMPSON. Is Oakland an open or closed shop town?

Mr. TAYLOR. So far as the machinists' agreement is concerned, we have never asked for the closed shop.

Mr. THOMPSON. Never have?

Mr. TAYLOR. Not in Oakland or San Francisco, either.

Mr. THOMPSON. Do you know whether there are as many machinists in San Francisco now as there were five or six or seven years ago? If not, what is the reason for it?

Mr. TAYLOR. I know there are more machinists in the union down there in Frisco than there was at that time.

Mr. THOMPSON. In relation to the——

Chairman WALSH. Do you know whether or not there are more machinists, in and out?

Mr. TAYLOR. In and out of Frisco?

Chairman WALSH. In and out of the union.

Mr. TAYLOR. Well, I have no positive way of knowing; only judging, as it were, from the increase in the union, that I can average it up in that respect—but I believe there is at least as many, if not more.

Mr. THOMPSON. In regard to the violations which you claim were made of the eight-hour law, have you called the attention of the authorities to it, do you?

Mr. TAYLOR. I got this affidavit and was instructed by a member of the executive board of the machinists, whose advice I took, to take it up with Washington, D. C., and not the district attorney here. That has been several months ago, and I have never heard anything about any action taken, or I have never received any letter in regard to it. I will say that I took it up with our business agent in Washington, D. C., and he wrote a letter stating that they were so busy that they would have quite a few other things to take up first.

Mr. THOMPSON. In regard to the Stop-Look-and-Listen League, what is that league; do you know?

Mr. TAYLOR. The Stop-Look-and-Listen League, as I understand it, is an organization that was organized a few months ago, I believe, to fight some of the bills that were presented for referendum vote; and I believe, as all of us believe, that it was organized by the employers' association—at least their attitude would show that.

Mr. THOMPSON. In the case where you said the hose was turned on the men, in the trial of that case, was it shown that the employer had notice of the fact that the hose was used?

Mr. TAYLOR. Yes, sir; I think it was.

Mr. THOMPSON. That is all, Mr. Chairman.

Chairman WALSH. That is all, Mr. Taylor; thank you. Call your next.

Mr. THOMPSON. Mr. Daggett.

TESTIMONY OF MR. FLOYD L. DAGGETT.

Mr. THOMPSON. Mr. Daggett, please give us your name.

Mr. DAGGETT. Floyd L. Daggett.

Mr. THOMPSON. And your business address?

Mr. DAGGETT. At the present time it is Olympia, Wash.

Mr. THOMPSON. And your position, Mr. Daggett?

Mr. DAGGETT. Chairman of the industrial insurance commission.

Mr. THOMPSON. How long have you been chairman of that commission?

Mr. DAGGETT. Since April 1, 1913.

Mr. THOMPSON. How long has that commission been in existence?

Mr. DAGGETT. The law went into active effect October 1, 1911, but the commission was in existence, I think, from July, 1911.

Mr. THOMPSON. Now, Mr. Daggett, you received some—I will ask you what you were previous to being chairman of that commission?

Mr. DAGGETT. My business has been the insurance business for a number of years.

Mr. THOMPSON. In this city?

Mr. DAGGETT. In the State of Washington.

Mr. THOMPSON. State of Washington. Fire insurance or life?

Mr. DAGGETT. Both. Well, fire and liability and accident insurance.

Mr. THOMPSON. I see. Now, you have gotten some questions in regard to the work of your commission that were sent to you?

Mr. DAGGETT. No, sir; I did not. I didn't even get the intimation of what line of testimony you wanted.

Mr. THOMPSON. It was sent to you, but I don't believe it reached you.

Mr. DAGGETT. I don't think so. I got my mail yesterday from the office.

Mr. THOMPSON. You might tell us as briefly as you can the scope and purpose of the commission, and the purpose of the law under which this commission was appointed.

Mr. DAGGETT. Well, the scope of the commission is the administration of the workmen's compensation act. The workmen's compensation act was passed by the legislature and went into effect October 1, 1911. The purpose of the act is the compensation of workmen injured in the several industries that are classed as extra hazardous by the said act, and the creation of a fund for that purpose.

Mr. THOMPSON. Now, Mr. Daggett, how is your commission organized; what kind of a force has it got, and how is the force divided?

Mr. DAGGETT. Well, you mean——

Mr. THOMPSON. Just state in your own way about your organization.

Mr. DAGGETT. Our departments, and so forth?

Mr. THOMPSON. Yes.

Mr. DAGGETT. There are three commissioners appointed by the governor, and the commissioners have joint powers and equal powers, the three.

Our departmental work: Our office force at Olympia is divided into our auditing department and claim-adjusting department. We have branch offices at Seattle, Spokane, Vancouver, and Bellingham for the convenience of our field work. The auditing department is for the purpose of visiting the employers and getting the amount of their pay rolls, because the fund out of which these accidents are paid is recruited by assessments upon the pay rolls of the employers in the several classes into which the industries are divided. That is a general description of our department.

Mr. THOMPSON. Well, in the carrying on of the work of the commission, do you find that your force, as you have it, is sufficient to cover the State properly?

Mr. DAGGETT. I think so.

Mr. THOMPSON. Can you tell us in a way what industries are covered by the act?

Mr. DAGGETT. The largest industry—or, that is, employing the largest number of workmen, and they have perhaps the largest pay rolls—is the lumber industry. Then the next would be the coal mines. Then we have other lines, the carpenter work, general construction work of buildings, everything pertaining to the general construction work, such as railroad work, street work, sewer work, and that character of work. In fact, nearly every line of work that is at all hazardous. We do not—the law does not contemplate covering such business as clerical work in retail stores or employments of that character.

Mr. THOMPSON. Is this automatic, or do these various firms register with you, or do you compel them to do it?

Mr. DAGGETT. Our law is compulsory.

Mr. THOMPSON. It is compulsory?

Mr. DAGGETT. All the employees comprehended in the act must come under the law, and all the workmen in these industries must come under the provisions of the law.

Mr. THOMPSON. And in the act, are the industries named, or do you determine whether or not an industry comes within the terms of the act?

Mr. DAGGETT. They are named in the act, although if any new employment should arise that was not then named in the act, that the commission thought was hazardous, or would naturally come within the provisions, they have the power to place it within the scope of the law.

Mr. THOMPSON. What is your opinion as to the relative merits of compulsory and optional insurance of this kind?

Mr. DAGGETT. Why, I think there is only one way to carry on this workmen's compensation proposition, and that is through a compulsory act.

Mr. THOMPSON. What is your reason for that?

Mr. DAGGETT. In the first place I think that every workman employed in the State in the same line of industry, and every employer in that same line of industry, should be upon an equal basis.

I think a workman has a right to the same conditions in one firm that he would have in another firm, and I think an employer as to cost and general conditions should be upon the same basis as his fellow employer. I also feel that under the optional law you don't have all the employers, you don't have the funds as well recruited for this purpose, and I don't think that the administration of the department is nearly so efficient.

Mr. THOMPSON. How are the funds recruited now?

. Mr. DAGGETT. The law names a basis rate for the industry. For instance, to use an illustration, in the lumber industry of two and a half per cent—two and a half dollars per hundred dollars pay roll. We make what we term "calls," .which are in effect assessments upon the pay roll of the employers listed in that industry, at such times as it is necessary to meet the requirements of the fund for the payment of accidents insured in that industry. We usually make them in quarterly calls, and for instance so far this year we have made one quarterly call in the lumber industries. What we term the adjustment call which I will explain in a moment, at the first of this year was sufficient to care for the accidents in that industry, up to say the 1st of April. The one, two, three call, which would be a three months' call, that was sent out then, has been sufficient up to the present time.

The employers paying into this fund, at the end of the calendar year if there is a surplus in the fund or if there is a deficiency in the fund, we make what we term an adjustment call. For instance, I will have to go a little into detail, I presume, on that.

Mr. THOMPSON. You may do that.

Mr. DAGGETT. We take from time to time the audits of their pay rolls. Now, at the end of the year we take their actual pay roll for the preceding year. That may vary, and generally does from the pay rolls that have been taken at different times during the year, and the call that is necessary on their actual pay roll to provide sufficient funds to meet the .previous demands,: or. the demands of the calendar year—that amount is levied upon this call, and that is called an assessment.

For 1913 our assessment—our adjustment call in the lumber industry was two-twelfths, or for two months.

Mr. THOMPSON. How is the rate determined, that the different industries should pay?

. Mr. DAGGETT. That is set down by the law itself in the original law.

Mr. THOMPSON. Well, in case of the adding on of a new industry, do you have power to do that?

Mr. DAGGETT. Well, the commission would have power to name what they consider an equitable rate.

Mr. THOMPSON. You haven't had occasion to do that?

Mr. DAGGETT. Not yet; no, sir.

Mr. THOMPSON. What does the injured man have to do in order to receive compensation for an injury?. Tell the process he goes through.

Mr. DAGGETT. The employers are provided with blanks. We have three blanks that are necessary to placing a claim before our department. One is the workman's application for compensation in which is recited also the circumstances of the accident and some other information. Then the employer's report of the same proposition, and then the attending physician's report. Those three are assembled in our department. Then if there is anything more we want, we get that from whatever source is necessary.

Mr. THOMPSON. How is the schedule of compensation arranged? Upon what basis?.

Mr. DAGGETT. It is provided in the law. For instance, we pay temporary disability, which we call time loss. Then we pay permanent partial disability, permanent total disability, and temporary loss of earning power. The time loss, or temporary disability, is the time that a man is disabled in the event that he does not have what we term a permanent partial disability. For instance, if a man would cut his hand or get it bruised so he could not work, and that should recover so there was no loss to that hand, he would be paid time loss. If a portion of that hand was severed, he would receive what we call permanent partial disability. And if both hands, or in any other way he was totally incapacitated permanently, why he would be put on the pension basis.

Mr. THOMPSON. Is the basis of judging these different industries left to the commission, or is that put in the act, too?

Mr. DAGGETT. The act defines what these various disabilities are, but there is, of course, a wide range of judgment on the part of the commission as to the extent of these injuries. For instance, on permanent or partial disability the law provides that the maximum shall be the loss of the major arm at or above the elbow at $1,500. All other partial or permanent disabilities are rated in proportion thereto. The commission in the early stages worked out a schedule which has been in effect ever since that time on these various disabilities.

Mr. Thompson. When the commission determines what the disability is, then the amount that is to be paid automatically, works automatically under the act?

Mr. Daggett. Yes, sir.

Mr. Thompson. Is the injured party permitted to get any other compensation. Can he sue, for instance, the party that caused the injury?

Mr. Daggett. Well, I will explain one point there. The law is based on the theory that in consideration of all of the accident being paid for, no matter as to the character of the accident—all defenses of the employer under the former liability system are taken away, and the right is taken away from the workingman to sue his employer. There are two points where the workman can sue his employer. For instance, if the employer has not paid his assessment, then the workman has the right to elect whether he will accept the compensation provided by the act or sue his employer. Again, if there is a third party injury to the employee away from the plant of his employer, he has the right of election as to whether he shall sue his employer or take under the act.

Mr. Thompson. Those are the only exceptions?

Mr. Daggett. Those are the only exceptions.

Mr. Thompson. What is your opinion—what opinion have you as to whether or not the awards under the act are compensatory or just?

Mr. Daggett. You mean sufficiently so?

Mr. Thompson. Yes, sir.

Mr. Daggett. Of course, I think that all of us feel that an injured workman can not be reasonably compensated on a money basis, and in individual cases I think our awards are much lower than they would get if they obtained an award through the court under the old system; but I think that it is a fair statement that under this system the workingmen will receive as a whole over the State at least three times as much as they ever did receive under the old liability system, except where the employer stepped in himself and voluntarily paid it. I am speaking of it as a legal proposition.

Mr. Thompson. What is the feeling, if you know, of the workmen and employers toward the law, so far as you have met them?

Mr. Daggett. So far as those we have come in contact with, I think it is very satisfactory.

Mr. Thompson. How does the cost of this insurance compare with the old rates?

Mr. Daggett. In some instances it is less and in some a little more, but I do not know that it is any more in any industry considering the complete protection that this act gives the employer, whereas under the liability system, he did not have complete protection.

Mr. Thompson. When you say did not have complete protection, you mean beyond a certain amount?

Mr. Daggett. Beyond a certain amount.

Mr. Thompson. How is this money held? Is it subject to confiscation?

Mr. Daggett. It is in the hands of the State treasurer, and when our awards are made the memoranda of that is sent to the State auditor, who draws a State warrant, and that State warrant is sent to the party to whom it is due. And the law provides that a claim can not be assigned in any way.

Mr. Thompson. Well, does the law also prevent its being attached?

Mr. Daggett. Yes, sir; it can not be attached by anyone, or paid, except to the man to whom it is due.

Mr. Thompson. Or garnisheed?

Mr. Daggett. It could not be garnisheed.

Mr. Thompson. Are there any exceptions to that, in case of doctors, or otherwise?

Mr. Daggett. No; there are no exceptions; and he can not even assign it voluntarily.

Mr. Thompson. Does your commission, or does the law, provide for any adjustment of doctor's fees in case of injury?

Mr. Daggett. The present law does not provide any hospital or medical attendance, and we have no supervision or jurisdiction whatsoever over that part.

Mr. Thompson. You do, however, make an allowance for burial fees?

Mr. Daggett. Yes; the law provides $75 for burial.

Mr. Thompson. Do you know why the law did not provide for the taking care of the doctor?

Mr. DAGGETT. I had no connection with the commission at the time that the law was prepared, and I have no knowledge of it in that respect, except hearsay.

Mr. THOMPSON. What is the general attitude of the doctors toward the injured? Is it influenced by this act one way or the other, so far as you know?

Mr. DAGGETT. Toward treating the injured, you mean?

Mr. THOMPSON. Yes.

Mr. DAGGETT. Why, where there is no contract system, I think the doctors feel that they are losing many of their fees that otherwise, under the old form or system, the employer paid. The man ofttimes is injured, and when he is ready for settlement with our department he is somewhere else, and the doctor does not come in touch with him so that he can get his fee. Again, it is quite often the case that the amount of the award is not sufficient to pay the doctor's bill. But to quite a large extent the men coming under this act are under the contract hospital system in one form or another, over the State.

Mr. THOMPSON. Do you have any medical service on the commission?

Mr. DAGGETT. Sir?

Mr. THOMPSON. Do you furnish any medical service?

Mr. DAGGETT. To the injured man?

Mr. THOMPSON. Yes, sir.

Mr. DAGGETT. No, sir.

Mr. THOMPSON. Of any kind?

Mr. DAGGETT. No, sir.

Mr. THOMPSON. Have no medical organization for any purpose?

Mr. DAGGETT. We have a medical organization for the purpose of adjusting claims.

Mr. THOMPSON. Adjusting claims?

Mr. DAGGETT. Yes, but not to furnish medical attendance to the injured man.

Mr. THOMPSON. What kind of an organization is that? How does it work?

Mr. DAGGETT. Why, we have a chief medical adviser, who devotes his time to inspecting these files of claims; and then we have appointed physicians at various centers, that we use to examine the claimants wherever necessary.

Mr. THOMPSON. In regard to that feature of the matter, does the medical fraternity, or does the hospital, take any attitude one way or the other?

Mr. DAGGETT. I don't think so; nothing unfriendly, so far as I know.

Mr. THOMPSON. What are the difficulties in the way of carrying out the administration of the act, so far as you have noticed?

Mr. DAGGETT. Well, the administration of the present law is working very smoothly and satisfactorily.

Mr. THOMPSON. Have you any suggestions that you would care to make as to how the law might be improved?

Mr. DAGGETT. There are only minor amendments that the commission are considering proposing to the incoming legislature—nothing of any particular moment, except that they did have in mind were preparing a so-called first aid or medical attendance feature. But there is an initiated bill, which, of course, if it is passed by the voters at the coming election, will take the place of the amendment that the commission were proposing or were about to propose.

Mr. THOMPSON. With regard to the first-aid proposition, what is your opinion on that? Do you think it is a desirable thing or not?

Mr. DAGGETT. I think medical attendance is desirable under proper supervision.

Mr. THOMPSON. Well, what do you mean by proper supervision? How would that be arranged?

Mr. DAGGETT. I think the supervision should be absolutely within the department, both as to the character of attendance, to see that a man does get the attendance that he needs, and also as to the fees, both as to hospitals and doctors.

Mr. THOMPSON. Does the compensation which is paid for injuries not only bear a relation to the kind of injury but also as to the salary the man gets?

Mr. DAGGETT. Yes. A man is paid on time-lost basis. A single man is paid $20 a month. Five dollars is added if there is a wife; $5 for each child under 16 years of age, up to a total of $35 a month. That is increased 50 per cent during the first six months, which makes the maximum time loss that can be paid $52.50 per month. That can not exceed 60 per cent of the man's wage. You take, for instance, a man earning $2 a day; that would be $52 a month; and he might have a wife and two children, enough to entitle him to $52.50, if it were not for the wage; but he will be put upon a 60 per cent wage basis, which will be $31.20, as I carry it in my head, in place of $52.50.

Mr. THOMPSON. Do you think that is a just feature of the law or not?

Mr. DAGGETT. I think, really, a wage percentage is better, perhaps, than a fixed scale.

Mr. THOMPSON. Where is the justice to that man who only gets $31.25 or $31.50, instead of $52.50?

Mr. DAGGETT. That is the theory that the law is now based on—that the low-wage man is entitled to a certain amount. I would fix a minimum.

Mr. THOMPSON. The chances are that the low-wage man is in need of assistance more than the high-wage man.

Mr. DAGGETT. That is possibly true. I would fix a minimum, so that the low-wage man would not be discriminated against.

Mr. THOMPSON. What do you think about the idea of having sickness and unemployment insurance; or have you given that any thought?

Mr. DAGGETT. I haven't given sufficient study to it.

Mr. THOMPSON. I see. How much more, in your judgment, would the proposed first-aid law increase the cost of the act?

Mr. DAGGETT. There are no statistics available in the State of Washington at the present time. The commission has not kept sufficient statistics upon which to base a fair judgment of that; but we are now endeavoring to compile statistics to have ready for the benefit of the incoming legislature.

Mr. THOMPSON. What would you say about Federal cooperation; have you any views on that?

Mr. DAGGETT. As to a general Federal law, you mean?

Mr. THOMPSON. Yes; cooperating with the State law.

Mr. DAGGETT. We are now placed in this peculiar position: Any man engaged in work of an interstate nature does not come within the scope of the act. For instance, there is a railway shop here in the city that part of their employees are engaged in interstate, which does not come under the act, and some of them are engaged in intrastate, which does come under the act. We sometimes have very difficult questions to decide as to just where the line is to be drawn. Take the case of a logging road; that comes under the act. But now just where does that logging road stop when it gets onto the interstate line? Take the case of longshoring. The law has been now interpreted to mean that if a man gets injured on the vessel he is not under our act, but until he gets to the vessel he is. Of course, it is quite common practice in loading a vessel for this same man to go clear into the hold of the vessel.

Mr. THOMPSON. There ought to be Federal cooperation, then, you think?

Mr. DAGGETT. I think so; yes, sir.

Mr. THOMPSON. Is there anything more you care to say to the commission?

Mr. DAGGETT. Nothing especially without you have some particular question.

Mr. THOMPSON. That is all, Mr. Chairman.

Commissioner LENNON. Mr. Daggett, if a man in the lumber industry; if two men in the lumber industry received exactly the same injuries and are receiving the same salary, have the same family responsibility, do they at all times receive the same amount of benefit?

Mr. DAGGETT. Well, there would be the same basis; the amount of benefit, for instance, if they had permanent or partial disability of equal character, they would receive the same amount. One man might get an injury and might recover more quickly than the other, and he would have less time lost, but he would be paid on the same monthly basis of time loss while his injury still existed.

Commissioner LENNON. Suppose he lost an arm or both legs?

Mr. DAGGETT. They would receive the same amount.

Commissioner LENNON. Always receive the same amount?

Mr. DAGGETT. Yes, sir.

Commissioner LENNON. There will be no discrimination?

Mr. DAGGETT. The wage scale does not affect that at all as to permanent partial disability—just on the time lost.

Commissioner LENNON. What authority has your auditing department to pass upon the amount of compensation to be paid for any specific injury?

Mr. DAGGETT. Well, you mean the claim department, I presume?

Commissioner LENNON. Yes; the claim department.

Mr. DAGGETT. Well, the general proposition is laid down in the law, and then the commission has authority to carry out that law wherever the specific amounts are not therein named.

Commissioner LENNON. Now, how do you satisfy yourself as to the accuracy of the pay rolls that are furnished by the employers?

Mr. DAGGETT. Our auditors are supposed to go to the original, and are so directed, and we presume they do.

Commissioner LENNON. Is there any other department of the State to which the employers have to furnish pay rolls to which you would have access?

Mr. DAGGETT. No, sir.

Commissioner LENNON. What is your view as to the lessening of industrial accidents by the establishment of this law in Washington?

Mr. DAGGETT. So far there has been practically no appreciable lessening due to the compensation act, but I think as the matter gets under way there necessarily will be, owing to the advantage to the employer of placing safety provisions around the employee in order to lessen the accident cost.

Commissioner LENNON. Under the law there must be a report of all accidents, no matter how minor?

Mr. DAGGETT. Yes, sir.

Commissioner LENNON. Was that the case before the law existed?

Mr. DAGGETT. No, sir.

Commissioner LENNON. Then there is a possibility that they may have been lessened and still the commission not know it?

Mr. DAGGETT. We haven't any statistics upon which to base any close conclusion.

Commissioner LENNON. It is a matter of opinion?

Mr. DAGGETT. Yes, sir.

Commissioner LENNON. Insofar as the blanks that are furnished for the application for benefits and on the part of the employer to make a statement of the injury, are they separate blanks, or do the two parties make returns on the same blank?

Mr. DAGGETT. We have both. Workmen that wish to make a separate statement on a separate blank has access to that at any time. The usual blank is a double blank.

Commissioner LENNON. A double blank; that is, the employer uses it and the employee also?

Mr. DAGGETT. Yes, sir.

Commissioner LENNON. What effect do you believe this law has had upon mitigation of industrial unrest among the people of this State?

Mr. DAGGETT. Oh, I don't know; I can't quite see that it has had any particular effect.

Commissioner LENNON. Well, was your business prior to going on this commission of such a character that would have brought you in contact with the wageworkers, so that you would know whether there was serious complaint as to lack of compensation when they were injured?

Mr. DAGGETT. My business was in, of course, a more limited territory than it is now, and I would not have come in contact with it so generally.

Commissioner LENNON. Were you a representative of a company that furnished surety for companies against liability?

Mr. DAGGETT. Yes, sir; several years ago. I have not been connected with that for the last 10 years.

Commissioner LENNON. That is all.

Chairman WALSH. Mr. Garretson has some questions.

Commissioner GARRETSON. The basis of compensation for the injury is on a per cent basis of the wage?

Mr. DAGGETT. No, sir; we have a fixed scale, but it shall not exceed 60 per cent of the wage.

Commissioner GARRETSON. You give a certain amount, regardless of what the wage may be, for a certain injury?

Mr. DAGGETT. For permanent disability. The time loss——

Commissioner GARRETSON. The time loss is based on the wage?

Mr. DAGGETT. It is not to exceed 60 per cent of the wage. For instance, a man getting three dollars and a quarter a day would get as much time loss as a man getting $6 a day.

Commissioner GARRETSON. A man earning $100 a month would get $60 for time loss?

Mr. DAGGETT. He would get—his maximum would be fifty-two dollars and a half.

Commissioner GARRETSON. No matter what he was earning, he could not get above fifty-two dollars and a half?

Mr. DAGGETT. That is the maximum, and that must not exceed 60 per cent of the wage.

Commissioner GARRETSON. Your rate, then, is really lower than New York or the Ohio scale?

Mr. DAGGETT. Yes, sir.

Commissioner GARRETSON. How do you pay—in the lump sum or weekly or monthly payments?

Mr. DAGGETT. Time loss is paid monthly.

Commissioner GARRETSON. Total disability?

Mr. DAGGETT. Total permanent disability is a monthly pension.

Commissioner GARRETSON. A monthly pension?

Mr. DAGGETT. Yes, sir.

Commissioner GARRETSON. What form is paid in the lump sum?

Mr. DAGGETT. The permanent partial disability, like loss of a hand or arm.

Commissioner GARRETSON. That is paid down at once?

Mr. DAGGETT. Yes, sir.

Commissioner GARRETSON. In those that are distributed over a series of weekly or monthly payments is the employer allowed to compound by the payment of a lump sum?

Mr. DAGGETT. The employer has no jurisdiction over this.

Commissioner GARRETSON. Over its administration in any way whatever?

Mr. DAGGETT. Not at all.

Commissioner GARRETSON. Are employers permitted or required to reinsure the risk?

Mr. DAGGETT. Why, they are required to come under this act.

Commissioner GARRETSON. I know; but in outside liability companies to reinsure them?

Mr. DAGGETT. No, sir; no provision.

Commissioner GARRETSON. They can do so if they desire?

Mr. DAGGETT. Yes, sir; we have no jurisdiction over that.

Commissioner GARRETSON. What guarantee exists in the event of the failure of the institution that has incurred obligations of this monthly pension character? Does the industry in which that belongs underwrite that risk?

Mr. DAGGETT. Yes, sir; in a sense they do, because the class must—an industrial class must pay the accidents incurred in that industry. Take the case of pensions for either total disability or for a deceased workman and his dependents, that pension is figured on the expectation of life, and not to exceed $4,000. That is immediately set aside in the hands of the State treasurer and invested as all State funds are.

Commissioner GARRETSON. The assessment don't cover that; there is an immediate levy made for the entire amount necessary to meet the demand?

Mr. DAGGETT. It is taken out of the current fund of the class and set aside.

Commissioner GARRETSON. It is taken from the current fund of the class and not from the individual employer?

Mr. DAGGETT. Yes, sir.

Commissioner GARRETSON. Oh, I see.

Mr. DAGGETT. Our law contemplated the class standing by itself, and not the employer.

Commissioner GARRETSON. In other words, if a man has been in business as an employer or manufacturer and has incurred liability of that character, virtually $4,000 is your limit?

Mr. DAGGETT. Yes, sir.

Commissioner GARRETSON. If he fails a month after that, his class has to take up and pay that?

Mr. DAGGETT. Yes, sir.

Commissioner GARRETSON. Are the so-called voluntary release schemes permitted to be organized by employers, or does your law abolish them?

Mr. DAGGETT. We have nothing whatever to do with any arrangement that the employer and employee make between themselves outside of the act.

Commissioner GARRETSON. They are not barred under the act as they were under the proposed Federal act?

Mr. DAGGETT. No, sir; they are not barred.

Commissioner GARRETSON. If an employee of a factory which is contiguous to a railroad track—I am giving you a question and an illustration at once—is injured by the railroad company, can that employee take his choice of choosing compensation or bringing action against the railroad company as a citizen?

Mr. DAGGETT. You speak of the railroad being right alongside of the plant, or in the plant, where the man works in his ordinary duties.

Commissioner GARRETSON. A wharf, probably, of the industry connecting with railroad tracks.

Mr. DAGGETT. If in the regular duties in the plant of his employer and injured by any cause, third party or otherwise, he must accept compensation under the act.

Commissioner GARRETSON. He must take the compensation?

Mr. DAGGETT. Yes, sir.

Commissioner GARRETSON. In that event does the right to recover from the railroad company revert to the employer?

Mr. DAGGETT. No, sir. The only right for recovery on a third-party injury comes where the employer is in default; that is, hasn't paid his assessment when due or when the man is injured away from the plant of his employer by a third party. He may be in the course of his duty and be away from the plant **of his employer.**

Commissioner GARRETSON. Then, in that instance, it would absolutely relieve the railroad company from liability for the killing of a citizen?

Mr. DAGGETT. Yes, sir, in that sense.

Commissioner GARRETSON. Are you familiar with the proposed Federal act in that respect?

Mr. DAGGETT. No, sir; I am not.

Commissioner GARRETSON. It passed the right of recovery to the employer if the employee was not allowed to exercise it?

Mr. DAGGETT. I would like to say there that the provisions of our law have never been squarely before the Supreme Court, and there is quite a contention by different ones as to just what the language of the law means in that respect, but I am giving you the way the law is being interpreted.

Commissioner GARRETSON. There has been no decision as to whether the right of recovery is wholly extinguished or not?

Mr. DAGGETT. There has been no decision to that effect.

Commissioner GARRETSON. Have you any data—did you have a commission here that formulated the compensation act?

Mr. DAGGETT. Yes, sir.

Commissioner GARRETSON. What was the conclusion of that commission under the liability process of what proportion of every dollar paid by the employer reached the injured man under the old liability system?

Mr. DAGGETT. I think their conclusions were that the employers of the State were paying about $1,300,000 in liability premiums. There was, of course, a number of employers in the State that were not carrying insurance, that was variously estimated at from a quarter to half a million of dollars, and I am informed that they concluded that out of the awards made by the courts on personal-injury cases but only about a quarter of a million dollars reached the injured workmen.

Commissioner GARRETSON. What proportion was that; I didn't follow it.

Mr. DAGGETT. It would be about a quarter of a million to a million and a half dollars.

Commissioner GARRETSON. That is a little lower than the average?

Mr. DAGGETT. Under the present act—under the 34 months' experience there has been about two and a half million dollars paid direct to the workmen, and a little over a million dollars set aside for pensions, and about a hundred and fifty payments on those pensions. The total amount that has been handled by the department in 34 months is just a little over $4,000,000.

Commissioner GARRETSON. Then what do you call your cost of administration in per cent?

Mr. DAGGETT. Of course, it varies under the different classes.

Commissioner GARRETSON. As a general average?

Mr. DAGGETT. As a whole it makes about a dollar eighty-three cents on all the classes. It will average that.

Commissioner GARRETSON. A dollar eighty-three cents?

Mr. DAGGETT. I think that is it; I have the figures here.

Commissioner GARRETSON. You mean one eight-hundredth per cent as cost of administration?

Mr. DAGGETT. No. Just a moment and I will give you the exact figures. The total pay roll for 1913—this is on the firms listed—is $91,973,771.64. The total claims paid that year was $1,686,176.87. The average cost per hundred of pay roll for the year 1913 is $1.83.

Commissioner GARRETSON. That is a cost of administration of one and eight-tenths?

Mr. DAGGETT. No, sir; that is not administration, that is claims paid. The administration is paid from a fund created by the legislature; it is not paid out of the contributions of the employers. Our administration expense for 34 months is seven and twenty-seven hundredths per cent on the amount contributed by the employers.

Commissioner GARRETSON. Then you would run about 9 per cent?

Mr. DAGGETT. A little less than 7½ per cent?

Commissioner GARRETSON. You are making a favorable showing according to the German standard.

Mr. DAGGETT. Yes, sir.

Commissioner GARRETSON. Although you don't administer as many features of the act as they do.

Mr. DAGGETT. No, sir.

Commissioner GARRETSON. You spoke of the question that arises as between interstate and intrastate. Have any of the tribunals of your State ever rendered a decision as to what employees, for instance, of the railroads were interstate and intrastate?

Mr. DAGGETT. That has only come before us in the case of longshoremen injured and the Federal circuit court—that is, as far as it has gone—has given a decision that I mentioned. That when the workman reaches the vessel he is under the admiralty jurisdiction or under interstate commerce, and he had a right of action against his employer or against the vessel.

Commissioner GARRETSON. Under the Federal act?

Mr. DAGGETT. Under the Federal act.

Commissioner GARRETSON. Federal liability act?

Mr. DAGGETT. Yes, sir.

Commissioner GARRETSON. You know of no decision that has ever been made of railroad employees themselves going further than those actually engaged in train and engine movements, do you?

Mr. DAGGETT. No, sir; we would have no way of getting any trainmen before our circuit court or supreme court under this act, except logging roads belonging to the different logging companies, and we include them in the act.

Commissioner GARRETSON. And lying wholly within the limits of your own State?

Mr. DAGGETT. Yes, sir.

Commissioner GARRETSON. That is all.

Chairman WALSH. That is all.

Call your next.

Mr. THOMPSON. Mr. Wallace.

TESTIMONY OF MR. JOHN H. WALLACE.

Mr. THOMPSON. Give us your name.

Mr. WALLACE. J. H. Wallace.

Mr. THOMPSON. And your business address.

Mr. WALLACE. Ravensdale, Wash.

Mr. THOMPSON. And your business.

Mr. WALLACE. Engineer.

Mr. THOMPSON. What kind of engineer?

Mr. WALLACE. Hoisting engineer at the mines.

Mr. THOMPSON. What kind of a mine was there?

Mr. WALLACE. A coal mine.

Mr. THOMPSON. How long have you been acting as hoisting engineer there?

Mr. WALLACE. As hoisting engineer two years previous to my acting as State secretary for the mine workers, which consumed three years. Three years that I was engaged as industrial insurance commissioner representing the employees, and since being relieved of my duties there I have returned to the same engine.

Mr. THOMPSON. I see. The industrial commission you speak of is the one that Mr. Daggett just spoke about?

Mr. WALLACE. Yes, sir.

Mr. THOMPSON. Of which he is chairman?

Mr. WALLACE. Yes, sir.

Mr. THOMPSON. You served, you say, for three years on that commission?

Mr. WALLACE. Practically three years; yes, sir.

Mr. THOMPSON. Well, what is your opinion of the act as it is administered, and of its benefit to the injured workmen?

Mr. WALLACE. Well, you have asked me a number of questions in one.

Mr. THOMPSON. Well, you may divide it up as you choose.

Mr. WALLACE. I think as a piece of humane' social legislation, it is a grand 'thing. ·I think that the intent and purposes of the act are correct. I think the basic principles of the law are just and 'fair. I question sometimes the ability or the honesty of those who are administering the law.

Mr. THOMPSON. Now, Mr. Wallace, will you give us briefly and more in detail what you mean by that?

Mr. WALLACE. In the first place, it may be necessary for me to state that I am a labor agitator, if you will use that term. I believe that I am as fair as the average employer of labor, probably a little more so. I have worked in the mines since I was 11 years old. I have carted men out, unrecognizable masses of humanity. I have seen their families ordered out of the company houses when father had been taken away from them, mother not knowing what to do with her offspring. The usual coroner's inquest was held and the usual verdict returned, of nobody to blame.

Under such conditions where the common law failed to provide a remedy for mother and the babies, I believed that some kind of social insurance, such as is enjoyed by Germany, England, and all of the European countries, should be enacted in the United States. As one of the leaders of my mining boys in this State, we took up the question in our convention several years ago, and in conference with our employers discussed the matter. Whether that had anything to do with the final outcome of a meeting that was called in Tacoma, while we were in session in the year 1910, or not, I can not say at this time. However, there was such a meeting called, our convention notified to send delegates, which we did, I being present in person to represent the mine workers of the State. We found upon our arrival at the meeting in Tacoma that part of the plan of campaign had been worked out, which provided for the selection of one labor candidate on a commission of five men, I believe, to draft some kind of an insurance act.

Our representative, who was then president of the State federation of labor, Brother Charles Case, refused to act upon such a commission, claiming that labor was not getting fair representation. The outcome of the resignation of Brother Case was the appointment of a commission by the governor, consisting of 10 men, 5 representing labor and 5 representing the employers of labor. These 10 men gathered statistics, prepared a bill, and submitted it to the legislature, embodying this first-aid clause that you have heard so much discussed during these sessions. We have heard that labor is ever ready to violate its agreements; that it will never stand pledged to the things that it says it will carry out. In good faith we expected that employer and workman would stand behind the bill in the legislature and see it enacted into law. Imagine our surprise then when without warning a relay force of employers served notice upon the legislature that they would not stand for the bill in its present form, that the first-aid clause must be eliminated, when they would permit the bill to be passed.

You have heard discussed the activity of the speaker of the house, who is a brother-in-law of Mr. Page, who left his chair, got out on the floor of the house, and made an eloquent appeal to the members to defeat the first-aid clause after it had either carried or the vote had been tied in the morning session. A reconsideration was taken and later defeated. These men have constantly ever since that time said just what they say here to these commissioners, " We are in favor of some kind of a first-aid clause." Since that time I have submitted a bill similar to the one embodied in the original bill, because our friends the employers said they were willing we should have a first-aid clause. I had the privilege of addressing the committee on labor and labor statistics when we presented that bill for the State federation of labor during the last session, and had the usual spectacle of the lumber interests of the State sitting around the table elbowing with the legislators and laughing me to scorn because they would not give me a hearing; told me that it would not be passed and could not be passed, and it was not.

They say now they are willing we shall have a first-aid bill. They don't mean what they say. They are fighting a bill now that is up on initiative by the people of the State. They have spent as much money as a first-aid bill would cost them, or the cost on first aid to the injured, already. And I dare say it will cost them a good deal more before we are done with them. We were in favor of social insurance, because we paid the bill anyway. The cost of casualty insurance in the State of Washington to the employers who were carrying casualty insurance was increasing rapidly.   In 1909 they paid over $600,000 for protection that guaranteed them protection up to $5,000, as you heard Mr. Page say yesterday.   It had increased to $900,000 in 1910. Just what it was for 1911 we can't tell.   But the experience of the United States was the experience of the State of Washington; and I have some figures here which give the premiums for the Aetna Life Insurance Co., the American Fidelity Co., the Casualty Co. of America, the Employers' Liability Assurance Corporation, Fidelity & Casualty Co., Frankfurt Marine Accident & Plate Glass Insurance Co., General Accident, Fire & Life Insurance Corporation, and several others.

Their premiums for 1910 were $27,815,046; their net losses $11,569,882. The percentage of loss paid, 41.6 per cent.   The commission expense, $16,-245,156.   Percentage of commission expense and profit to premiums, 58.4 per cent.

Out of the $600,000 collected in the State, the employers made the statement themselves that less than $200,000 found its way to injured workmen or the families of the deceased; in 1910 about the same proportion.   Sometimes without litigation, sometimes after men had been blacklisted because they dared to take action in the courts.   And altogether we wanted to eliminate another cause of friction between capital and labor.   We lent every energy to the passage of the bill, even though they left us with a one-legged law.   We were satisfied to take it for the experience we could glean from it as laboring people; we wanted to find out if this country was really as energetic and eager for conservation along the lines of human life as it is over its material things, such as minerals, timber, water power, and so on.   We wanted to find out if men amounted to more than money.

And I am sorry to say that ever since I have sat in this meeting I have heard discussed dollars and cents.   Men have been thrown in the discard, and we have been told gladly that we were paid $26 a month wages.   We have said that they could not raise a family on it under American conditions— give them an American living, an American education, and American opportunities that they speak so much about.   And yet we are worth $26 a month as against the millions that we are interested in—the forest, the mine, and mill in every place.   Men don't count; money does.

You asked a question awhile ago, Did the insurance prevent accidents? Had the experience in the State tended to lessen the maiming of men and the killing of men?   No; not by any means.   Under the first year's operation of the workmen's compensation act we killed 279 men.   Under the second year's operation of the act we killed 371 men, or 92 men more than we did during the first year.

We injured eleven thousand and some hundreds in 1911 and 1912, sixteen thousand in 1913.

Mr. THOMPSON. Mr. Wallace, you say you have some objections to the administration of the law.   What are those objections?   What remedies do you propose, or amendments to the law?

Mr. WALLACE. One of the men sitting here this morning said that legislation affecting labor can not be given vitalizing force and effect unless labor has a hand or at least some part of the enforcement of the law.   I believe in equity and right, in justice, in fair play.   And for the first two years that I was on that commission I believe that the men with whom I worked sought to give a square deal to every man.   An ex-commissioner is in this room now that I worked with, not a labor man.   Never belonged to a labor organization. A man who is a professional man.   Probably has no use for labor unions, or naturally would not have if he hadn't got a heart as big as all outdoors and was a real man.   I was associated with him for a long time, and as a lawyer, as a man that wanted to do what was right, give the workingman the benefit of the doubt, I have never met his peer among men.

It made little difference whether the labor representative on the commission was present when claims were passed or not, the labor member knew that men would get a square deal.   With the change of administration, however—and I may say this is true of the employers' representative on the original commission—with the change of administration, however, we began to get what we feared we would get when the law was enacted—that was politics.

We are getting plenty of politics in the administration of the industrial insurance law now.

You asked me why that I didn't think the law was being fairly administered. About the first thing that called my attention to an unfair attitude on the part of the present commission was the joint blank spoken of by the chairman, and which I took an exception to. I pointed out to the two commissioners serving with me that the joint blank was not fair to the laboring man; that the employer had those blanks in his charge; that the large percentage of laboring men in the State were unorganized, and, as a result, without a voice; that where the employer handed out the blanks to the workmen to fill in, if he answered the questions asked by the commission as he should answer them, and in all probability would answer them, he would do so without coercion or intimidation, sending in his own report, allowing the employer to do likewise. This was denied him under the joint-blank system and tended to intimidate him into keeping silence were the employers to blame for injury. I wanted to get statistics that were worth while and would be of educational value. For my pains I was informed that I was afraid of a too close relationship between employer and workmen, that I held the views of the labor agitator. The joint-blank intimidated the men against giving the information asked by the commission.

I notified the president of the State federation of labor, who is in the building now, as to what was going on, and had about decided it was about time for me to quit the commission. However, I had been told that if I did not cease my first-aid activities and stop preaching it—it was all right for me to have those views as long as I did not express them, give publicity to them—but as long as I continued to do that I was warned that some day my head would come off; that the governor had nearly got tired of hearing me talk first aid. Well, I have lived before I saw governors; in fact, I don't know that he is made out of any better mud than I am. And I continued to talk my first aid, and am doing it yet. However, I bearded him in his den one day and asked him if he would kindly inform me as to the statements that were emanating from his office, and which I was getting second and third handed, because I like to have my information direct. But I walked out as I went in, without any satisfaction.

I again notified my friend of the labor movement. Just about that time I was informed that an order has been given to the claim department—this also without my knowledge or consent—that hereafter where an employer's blank was received, and the physician's blank showing a probable time loss of two weeks or less, that no follow-up would be sent to the workman; that rather the employer's blanks—that the follow-up letter would not be sent up to the workman as had been the case heretofore, but that the workman failing to file his blank, the other blanks would be placed in the claim file and put in the no-claim file. The reason for this is obvious. The law provides that when a man's wages are reduced 5 per cent, or he has lost 5 per cent, he can claim compensation. That permits of a day and a half's time loss before he can file his report and receive compensation under the law. The scheme was to discourage the payment of claims for the first two weeks, thus making cheap insurance for the employers.

I was somewhat surprised when I learned of this, and I called in one of the men working in the office. I said, "When did you get an order to this effect?" He said, "The 22d day of June." This was late in October. "Who gave the order?" "The chairman of the commission." "What for?" "He said he had had a conference with the employers, and the employers did not like the idea of paying these small trivial claims." "But," I said, "the law does not give the commissioner the right to say what shall be paid or how they shall be paid. The law is specific." I said, "I shall take this matter up with the chairman upon his return to the office," which I did. I was informed by the chairman that he did not know anything about such an order. I said, "You what?" He said, "I don't know anything about such an order." And he suddenly brightened up and said, "I believe I do." But he said the other commissioner gave it. "Let him rescind it."

The law also provides that the action of two commissioners shall be the action of the board. Now, I had an equal say with the other commissioner, which the chairman stated here a while ago. I had as much power as either one of the other commissioners, yet I found myself in the position of having the chairman tell me that since the other commissioner had given the order, "Let him rescind it." He was the whole commission so far as the order was concerned. It was so palpably unfair that any man would have been glad to undo the wrong and the injustice done the workmen. I could get no redress.

At a later date I spoke to the other commissioner about it. He said he didn't give the order, didn't know anything about it. Then I demanded that the order be rescinded. There were fireworks in the office for a while. I did not get any redress that day; the next day I did. Copies of the original order, together with my order rescinding their order, and then their own order rescinding their first order are in the hands of the president of the State federation of labor in this meeting. I informed the president that I was not going to participate in such conduct any longer. I demanded a hearing at the hands of the governor, and I made my statement there, I think, as clearly and concisely as I am making it here, if not more so. The double blank was still being used, is yet. The conditions I have outlined are still being indulged in; men are receiving compensation according to the views of sometimes one commissioner and sometimes the subordinates; and the poor men in many instances being ignorant as to their rights under the law, accept their compensation in gratitude, and go their way.

This condition became so flagrant that at the meeting of the State federation of labor in Raymond last January I brought to the attention of the convention the conditions that existed in the industrial insurance department. Upon my return to Olympia I received a letter from the governor requesting me as to why I had criticized the other members of the board. This is my reply to the governor. (See Wallace Exhibit No. 2.) I should like to read it to you, but I know I am denied that privilege by reason of the ruling of the chairman this morning. But I shall try to convince you that what I said was true when I said the law was not being administered properly. After replying at length as to the spirit of the act as understood by the original commission that drafted it, by the men who were first charged with its administration, and by the large majority of people in the State who were its direct beneficiaries, I went into detail and specifically pointed out case after case for the governor's benefit where men were denied their just dues under the workmen's compensation law. In company with the man that preceded me in this chair I walked in to interview a man with a broken back. He had a wife and two children. He was entitled to the limit of the law, setting aside $4,000, out of which should be paid $20 a month to himself, $5 to his wife, and $5 to each of his two children, making a maximum of $35. The chairman of the commission, in my presence, offered that man and his wife $500 to settle the case. That is recorded in this document to the governor.

Another case was that of a man who had lost part of his vision at the concrete quarries. He was paid $525. And in accordance with the custom prevalent in the office, we had sent the employer a notice to the effect that we were to pay the man a lump sum of $525 for permanent partial disability, the man having returned to his former employment and getting the same wage. The employer objected, calling our attention to the fact that the man was able to earn the same money that he did before, and that his disability did not count. In order that we might not err, we had the man reexamined by another specialist, holding up the warrant for $525 in the meantime. The examination showed a more marked disability than the first. Whereupon I pointed out to the commissioners that since the second examination showed a greater disability than the first, the man was entitled to the increased award. They agreed with me. But some time later the original check for $525 was released. Two months afterwards I thought I would go through the files and see if that man had been paid his additional $225 to which he was entitled. He had not. I again took the matter up with the commission, and they paid the other $225. That man does not know to-day why he got it. Other cases which I have pointed out were those where men suffered permanent partial disabilities, and under the rating of our chief surgeon were allowed so much compensation.

But there crept into the business of the department a method of bargaining with men. And it does not take men long to find out when you bargain with them. Consequently there is an ever-increasing number of men now who will not accept what the commission gives or offers them; they want a little more. They are growing in numbers, so they tell me.

Another man at Everett had to sue for what was coming to him. The commission, without any special examination as to the merits of the award made, offered him an arbitrary amount, which he declined to accept, and entered suit in the courts for what he thought was right, according to the law. His judgment was better than the commissioners'. He received exactly what he asked for. However, he did not need to go through the court process to get it after an examination was ordered.

Numbers of these cases have been brought, as I said, to the attention of the governor. He has them in his office. They are a matter of record. This is not all.

I said I was working at the engine again, in spite of Mr. Paterson's statement to the contrary that union men sell out; I am working out. The law provides where a man returns to work at a less wage than he formerly earned, or at a wage which he earned prior to his accident, because of the accident his earning capacity is reduced, then he shall receive compensation in proportion to the lessened earning ability. One of the boys at the pit that I pull coal from came to the engine house the other evening to see me, and he said, "I wish you would help me get my money." He handed me this [exhibiting paper], showing that the department acknowledged that he had returned to work for $2.60 a day, where formerly he had earned $3.63. The man is a foreigner, and does not know the method of procedure whereby he can secure his compensation. They paid him up until May 11, I believe—yes—they know that he is working for a less wage than formerly. But on July 30 they sent him a letter saying: "This is to advise that compensation having been awarded you for time lost on account of said injury up to and including the 11th of May, your compensation ceases on said date, and the commission is considering your case as closed."

In the first place, they acknowledge by their blank that the man is not able to earn his former wage. The law gives him, and entitles him, to the difference between his former earning capacity and his present. That has been brought to the attention of the commission. Yet he gets a letter that he has nothing coming to him.

I say that I can not agree with the administration of the law in that manner. I, indeed, like to be honest. I like to be square. I want men to get what is coming to them. If we are wrong, let us right ourselves. But for heaven's sake let us give each other a square deal before we start accusing each other. All I want to do is to get what is right. Labor tried to be fair on that commission. Labor wanted what was coming to it. No more. Not any less. It stood for what it thought was right—at least this individual member of labor did. I have never voiced this sentiment before any public gathering relative to my dismissal from the industrial insurance commission. I care less about the job than I do about the principles involved in the administration of this law in simple, social justice to the workers of the State. But I do think it is high time that something was done to set the machinery in motion that will equitably compensate men according to the law, as poor as it is. That law will be of value, of social value, to the people of the State if you will render the assistance possible to make this insurance as cheap as it can possibly be made, not by depriving the man of the pittance that is his due under the law but by stopping this willful waste of life and limb. Let us have safety. Let us have accident prevention. The workmen of this State don't want the employers' money. We are willing to work for our living, and we ask for nothing.

Mr. THOMPSON. Are there some papers you would like to file with the commission later on with regard to other matters?

Mr. WALLACE. Yes. You may have this.

Hr. THOMPSON. Are there any other documents?

Mr. WALLACE. I have just another thing I wish to bring before the commission.

Mr. THOMPSON. What does that relate to?

Mr. WALLACE. This relates to the proportion of burden carried by the individual and the employer. You have asked what proportion of loss is borne by the individual, and what proportion by the employer. The history of the law would place the proportion of loss at about 66 per cent upon the workman, and at about 33 per cent upon the employer.

Mr. THOMPSON. What do you mean by "loss," Mr. Wallace, there?

Mr. WALLACE. Their loss of wages and hospital treatment as against the amounts that they receive in compensation.

Mr. THOMPSON. Have you got statistics on that, there?

Mr. WALLACE. I have some here. I am not clear as to one of these, but I have one for the month of January, 1914. I have some more, but unfortunately they are packed up with my goods in Olympia in the process of moving. This is a monthly report taken from the files where men pay for their own doctor and hospital treatment and shows this condition: The number of work days lost is about 5,000, and the amount of wages lost——

Mr. THOMPSON. Could that be filed with the commission?

Mr. WALLACE. Yes, sir.

Mr. THOMPSON. That statement?

Mr. WALLACE. This shows a total amount of——

Commissioner O.CONNELL. Gives those totals.

Mr. WALLACE. It shows a total wage loss and treatment cost of $26,699.80; the awards, $8,827.98.

Mr. THOMPSON. Just file that, if you care to, and file any other informa-- tion of that character. You may do that later on, if you wish, if you have anything else.

That is all.

(The papers so presented were marked "Wallace Exhibit No. 1" and "Wallace Exhibit No. 2," and are printed among the exhibits at the end of this subject.

Mr. Wallace also submitted Claim No. 28758, which is printed as "Wallace Exhibit No. 3.")

Commissioner LENNON. Mr. Wallace, in your position as commissioner, did you have any means of ascertaining how many workmen in the State come under the compensation law?

Mr. WALLACE. How many workmen?

Commissioner LENNON. Yes; in the State, men and women.

Mr. WALLACE. As nearly as we could estimate it we had about 160,000 men.

Commissioner LENNON. Had you any means at the same time of ascertain-. ing how many employees in the State are paying the $1 hospital fee under private arrangement?

Mr. WALLACE. From 55 to 60 per cent.

Commissioner LENNON. From 55 to 60 per cent?

Mr. WALLACE. Yes, sir.

Commissioner LENNON. Has the passage of the compensation law relieved to any considerable extent from the payment of the $1 rate?

Mr. WALLACE. Not at all.

Commissioner LENNON. That is all.

Commissioner O'CONNELL. Mr. Wallace, in the formation of this act, the preparation of it, rather, you say that there was a public meeting called of some kind to which employers and laboring men were called together.

Mr. WALLACE. Yes, sir.

Commissioner O'CONNELL. Do you understand, Mr. Wallace, that in that gathering the bill as originally drafted with the first aid clause was agreed to?

Mr. WALLACE. As a result of that gathering, the governor, who was chairman of the meeting, appointed a commission, at the request of the meeting, to draft the bill. The bill was unanimously reported by the five employers and the five workmen that were chosen from that meeting, who gave months of effort and study to the drafting of the bill.

Commissioner O'CONNELL. To whom the bill reported back, to the governor as the unanimous opinion of this commission?

Mr. WALLACE. Yes. It became his measure in the legislature.

Commissioner O'CONNELL. It would be fair to conclude, then, that the ap-- pointment of this commission, and the unanimous agreement upon a bill, would mean the carrying with it the support both of the employer and the employee?

Mr. WALLACE. The employer was responsible for calling the original meeting inviting the workmen.

Commissioner O'CONNELL. Did any of those who were prominent at that meeting at which this result occurred appear prominently as against the passage of the bill with the first aid provision in, before the legislature?

Mr. WALLACE. I was in Columbus, Ohio, during the debate upon the bill, attending a miners' convention that year, and did not return until the bill had' been disposed of, leaving one of the other boys to take care of the legislative work in my absence.

Commissioner O'CONNELL. What I am trying to get at is the position you stated that the employers took that they had not promised their support—that they had not affirmed their agreement?

Mr. WALLACE. They did.

Commissioner O'CONNELL. In this matter I was trying to ascertain just what their agreement was.

Mr. WALLACE. Well, their agreement was in asking us to go in with them and formulate a bill. It was their proposal.

Commissioner O'CONNELL. Was Mr. Page interested in it?

Mr. WALLACE. Mr. Page was chairman of the commission.

Commissioner O'CONNELL. Did Mr. Page stand on his original agreement?

Mr. WALLACE. The only one that did. Mr. Page sent 50 telegrams to lumbermen to come and assist in passing the bill; and I think he got one answer.

Commissioner GARRETSON. Under the law, Mr. Wallace, are the commissioners—or is the commission—authorized to compound with men for any claim that they may have under the law for a less sum than named therein?

.· Mr. WALLACE. Absolutely no.

·· Commissioner GARRETSON. The statement was made by the chairman of the commission, in response to an inquiry as to the amount of each dollar that reached the industry under the old liability system, that the cost was a million five hundred thousand, and of that about a quarter of a million reached the injured men—that is, 16⅔ cents out of every dollar. Was that in accord with the developments?

Mr. WALLACE. It was a little better than that.

Commissioner GARRETSON. What was it—around 33 or 34?

Mr. WALLACE. Something around 30 per cent.

Commissioner GARRETSON. It was in accordance with the findings of other commissions?

Mr. WALLACE. I think so.

Commissioner GARRETSON. That have investigated the subject?

Mr. WALLACE. Yes, sir.

Commissioner GARRETSON. That is all.

Chairman WALSH. Call your next witness.

Mr. THOMPSON. Mr. Lowman.

TESTIMONY OF MR. WILL A. LOWMAN.

Mr. THOMPSON. Mr. Lowman, will you give us your name?

Mr. LOWMAN. Will A. Lowman.

Mr. THOMPSON. And your business address?

Mr. LOWMAN. Anacortes, Wash.

Mr. THOMPSON. And your business?

Mr. LOWMAN. Salmon packer, and president of the Puget Sound Salmon Canneries Association.

Mr. THOMPSON. How long have you been president of that association?

Mr. LOWMAN. Several times. At the present time, since last March.

Mr. THOMPSON. What is the association for?

Mr. LOWMAN. The association is for the benefit of its members and the industry, largely in the promotion and introduction of the sale of canned salmon as a food product; for the purpose of conserving and perpetuating the supply of salmon; and such other benefits as may accrue by such association other than fixing any prices for the sale of purchase of the raw material or the finished product. Those two things are barred.

Mr. THOMPSON. Some evidence was given here with reference to conditions in the salmon industry. Are you aware of that evidence?

Mr. LOWMAN. Through our public press I became aware that highly sensational statements had been made here in such a way that isolated and individual cases were made to appear as the general rule.

Mr. THOMPSON. Have you read the evidence?

Mr. LOWMAN. I have read considerable of the evidence, and have it here, having secured it from this commission, or rather from the reporters for the commission.

Mr. THOMPSON. Will you tell us what you wish to say to this commission in regard to the conditions in the salmon-canning industry?

Mr. LOWMAN. Under ordinary circumstances such as this would have been passed over, but coming from an authority such as one high in the councils of the State Socialist headquarters, alias the University of Washington, we thought it would be wise to correct the impression that they would leave on the public.

Chairman WALSH. If you will, please take up those specific points in which you want to contradict the lady and state them, will you?

Mr. LOWMAN. The point is this, she stated in this evidence—by the way, I want to say she gave me a clean bill of health, for which I thank her.

Chairman WALSH. Please confine yourself to this matter.

Mr. LOWMAN. She has made statements of insanitary conditions; immoral conditions; minimum wage; exploiting of child labor; and of oriental labor being deprived of its right as a human being to work when in condition to work or not to work. A few possibly isolated cases of the kind, and in no event to exceed a fraction of 1 per cent of the total, should not be given as a reason for the confiscation of an industry by the State. It would be just as well to say that we are a State of thieves, murderers, and rape fiends because now and then an isolated crime of that kind is committed.

The salmon industry as a whole gets along in the very best of an understanding with its employees. The State labor commissioner will bear us out that we pay the highest wage to them. The industry is of a peculiar character in that it does all of its business in a very limited length of time; handles a very perishable product, and in the handling of this product sometimes finds it necessary that the facotry operate more than some given length of time, because if we did not there would be a loss of raw material, which loss is directly against the State law and is prohibited. In other words, the destruction of food fish is a prohibited thing and is an offense against the law of the State. When by reason of an overplus of raw material or the breaking down of machinery or the stoppage and slowness of production; it becomes necessary to work longer hours, this has been done, with the exception that it is not done in the case of women, so far as I know, as it is prohibited by law.

Women work eight hours in the industries of this State except in those of the canning of meats, fish, and fruits, where they are permitted to work 10 hours. Cases have been brought where women worked more than 8 hours on some part of the canning industry, other than mere handling and incasing in tin of the raw material, and a conviction was had, showing that the State labor department is active in seeing that even technical violations are prohibited and punished. The law was new and was not thoroughly understood, or even this case would not have been necessary.

To state that the conditions are immoral is a base slander on my neighbors' wives and children. It is considered a sort of a picnic by a good many to whom it is unnecessary, not at all necessary, in fact, that they work for a living. They want to work in the canneries for a limited length of time, attracted by the high wage.

This little slip of paper gives the daily earnings of an average woman hand filler in my own cannery for the last 25 workdays. At no time did she work over eight hours, and very little of the time over five or six, because the quantity of fish necessary to keep that line of machinery operating was limited, and the number of employees was practically unlimited. She made an average of 70 cents per hour, a total of $90—excuse me, I will have to put on my glasses before I can refer to any written statement.

Chairman WALSH. Just give the totals.

Mr. LOWMAN. Ninety dollars and eighty-nine cents in the 25 days, earning from $6.12 down to $1.85—it being piecework. In no case is any child paid less than an elderly person. The work by piecework is at a fixed rate per piece. The hours are at a fixed rate per hour, and it is the job we pay and not the employee. Therefore, we are not exploiting child labor. And I have recently been able to hear a judge say in our district that permits would not be granted except where it was shown that the minor's work was necessary to the support of the family. For which I am very thankful.

It has been stated that Chinamen were made what amounts to slaves. A slave who receives an average of $70 per month absolutely net of even the transportation of his baggage from his boarding house to the train and back again, regardless of whether that is San Francisco, Portland, or Seattle, is a slave to be envied by the man whom the gentleman just preceding me said worked for $26 a month.

I have here a list in no case of which a Chinaman received less than $285 and up to $410 and more, which wages were net from the 15th day of July to the 31st day of December. The company furnished all transportation, board, tools, and clothing necessary other than ordinary clothing, and in addition to these figures they were paid for every hour of overtime, Sundays, and holidays. This cannery is a fair sample of every cannery on Puget Sound.

It has been stated that boarding houses were fire traps and the bunk house an immoral place and an insanitary place, and that the food consisted solely, of bread. This is untrue. It was not stated that a passenger boat stopped at that cannery every day and that there was not a single employee there that was not able to step on that boat and leave any time he wanted to. And at that particular cannery—I must guess at what it is, but the description, covering as it does only one possible case that I can imagine of, I take it for granted that I am speaking of the right place—a woman was employed. This woman was a mother and a grandmother. She was employed as matron at this place.

She' was formerly in my employ, and left for the better wage she would get here; and she had carte blanche as to the commissary.

I am defending now another cannery. I know what I say to be true, because she has stated so to me before she went to take the job, while she was working on the job, and since she has quit the job. I believe every word she says.' I have known her for nearly 20 years.

As' to Chinamen crying because they had to get up in the morning, I am not prepared to say that one or more of them did not, nor am I prepared to say that they did. It is entirely possible that a Chinaman would be not unlike any other human being and would do anything that he happened to see fit at that time. But it was not because he had not had any sleep and was forced to go to work, because it is not true that a Chinaman can be made a slave of, because, when you want to talk unions, let me tell you that there is but one real, ironclad, bullet-proof, nonscratchable-with-a-diamond union in the salmon industry—that is the Chinese. They are a little the best business men and best organized labor there is anywhere, and your sympathy is wasted whenever you undertake to sympathize with them. They are practically all old men on account of the exclusion law, and their place can not be filled. Many years ago, when the salmon-canning industry was established, Chinese were practically the only labor available, and to-day they are the expert producers of canned salmon in the packing department.

A Chinaman of 25 or 30 years' experience knows all of those little things that you and I would have to devote as long an apprenticeship as he did in order to learn it, because his intelligence from that point of view is equal to ours, and I am not ashamed to say it.

As to toilet conditions, it is true that plain board places of this kind have been provided in some cases, but in every case where such is the case that has come to my attention—there are but a few of them—it is directly over the ebb and flow of the tide, and you could not produce a more sanitary condition, I am sure. I know in my particular case I do not have to answer that question, but those who do have to answer it are justified in saying that the condition there existing is not and can not be more sanitary—excuse me, I am just a little bit rattled. I have got about two hours and a half to say, and I am trying to say it in fifteen minutes—that is, the conditions, the sanitary conditions, in those places need no apology from that particular point of view.

Some canneries, as was stated in the evidence, give a hot meal at noon without any charge or reduction of wages. That is true in one case I can speak of, and the reason of it is every employee in that cannery is a neighbor, and I believe I can make money by doing it for this reason: If a woman had to walk a mile and get a cold lunch and walk back again, I believe I would lose more that afternoon in her efficiency than it cost me to give her a bowl of soup, two kinds of meat, two kinds of vegetables, bread and butter, cake, pie, or pudding, because it is a square meal, with coffee, tea, or milk. That is the reason I do it, and I believe it is wisdom, and I believe that the conditions existing between canners and their employees is evidenced by the fact that, as far as I know, I never heard anywhere of a fish strike.

Now, we pick up a heterogenous mass of laborers. We are rushed; to-day we had 2,000 fish and to-morrow 50,000. It is nature's method of providing this raw material, and no man can foresee the result of the day's harvest. The fish are invisible—they are in the water—and you can not tell until they are taken out; and when they are taken out by any other means than traps they are killed in the taking. In order to do this we pick up any kind of labor we can get, and you would consider that under those circumstances, and it is the opinion of all of you that if there was a ground, the faintest ground, for trouble we would have it.

Now, I have here a letter handed me by a gentleman who had to leave, a State official and head of one of the departments. This letter states:

" *To whom it may concern:*

" This is to certify that between the dates of June 15 and July 15, 1914, I personally visited the following salmon canneries: Anacortes, Lummi Bay, Everett, Neah Bay. The sanitary conditions of these establishments was found to be in a satisfactory condition.

" Yours, very truly,

" H. T. GRAVES,
"Acting Commissioner of Agriculture."

He is what might be called our pure-food man. I wish to file that, if you please, and this and this.

(The papers so presented, were marked "Lowman Exhibit No. 1" and "Lowman Exhibit No. 2," and are printed among exhibits at end of this subject.)

Mr. LOWMAN. It has been suggested that the State take over the salmon canneries. Up at Anacortes the State owns a stone quarry. We have to the west of it a privately owned stone quarry; to the south of it a privately owned gravel or stone quarry. And at Anacortes six active salmon canneries. The privately-owned stone quarry is operating night and day at a profit and paying regular wages. The gravel pit is doing the same thing, and so are the six canneries, while the State-owned stone quarry operated—when it .was operated—with convict labor, which cost nothing but the food and maintenance and guards, is to-day an abandoned proposition because it could not. be operated at a profit under those conditions. But if the State does want to take over the salmon canneries, I beg it take mine first at its invoice value. As to the statement that the State could take these over and that the State does own the fish, nothing could be more far from the facts. The State of Washington owns every foot of ground under the water whether .it is dry none of the time or part of the time, and under our law it may sell that part of the overflowed lands of the sea which are bare at low tide, but it can not sell but may give license or lease to those lands which are overflowed all the time. Therefore, the State of Washington has a perfect right to say that before you can put in a fish trap, or do this, that, and the other which uses the bottom of the sea, you must obtain from us a permit or license or call it what you will; but the State of Washington can not, nor could it by any stretch of the imagination give me a right and say to me you can not put in such a thing until I have first obtained a permit from the United States of America through its Engineering and War Department to obstruct the waters which belong to the United States Government and in which all the fish float.

Coming as they do from outside the 3-mile limit of the international waters of the world, large quantities of them coming through our waters merely as migratory to foreign waters, the claim that the State of Washington has absolute ownership has been made, but claims do not constitute facts; if they did, there would always be two facts to every cause, because there are always two claims. But nothing could be of less value than a fish in the water until after it is taken.

Dr. Pennington, head of the bureau of food research, stated to me last summer while my guest that it was absolutely necessary to the welfare of the United States that the entire food supply from every source be increased, because we are approaching that point where it would be necessary to look to greater efficiency in the production of all classes of food, and that we would have to look more and more to the sea—and she made the statement that the salmon canneries bore such a favorable comparison to the vegetable and fruit canneries of the United States that there was really no comparison.

Now, it would not have mattered about these statements if it had not been that salmon canning in Alaska and the United States is very largely centered in the State of Washington, and the injury being done by a false impression being spread broadcast by the report of such an august commission as this could not but attract the attention of the world. And such a statement going out was bound to be detrimental to the financial interests of the packer, the laboring interest of the employees, and the ability to make a living of the 5,000 independent fishermen of the State of Washington of all kinds and character. Those people, every one of them, are laboring men. Every one of them would feel any injustice or injury to the industry.

Just at this time, when the United States Government has gone to the extent of issuing a unique document and stating the comparative food value of salmon, and making it unique in that it gives a number of receipts for the serving of it, in order to introduce it into those countries through the Consular Service, where it has been barred by excessive duties—such a statement leaving such impression as it would is bound to be injurious to both labor and capital and the well-being of the State, and should not be permitted to go unchallenged.

I want to say there is a gentleman in the room, and I hope the commission will give him five minutes—that will be enough—who made a request at Washington of Secretary Redfield personally that he would have a national investigation of the canneries, and as a producer of Puget Sound and the president ,of the Puget Sound Canneries I want to ask you—and if I had the right I would demand it of you—that you do anything you can to secure a complete and thorough national investigation of the entire salmon canning industry in Puget Sound. With that, if you have no questions, I will thank you. Will you permit Mr. T. J. Gorman to take the next two minutes of my time?

Chairman WALSH. We are going to adjourn now until 9.30 to-morrow morning.

Mr. LOWMAN. Then let me finish the statement.

Chairman WALSH. All right.

Mr. LOWMAN. I will make the statement for him. Mr. Gorman, the head of Gorman & Co., made the request in Secretary Redfield's office in Washington, and I seconded that request to Secretary Redfield personally in my own office in Seattle, that we desired to have an investigation, a national investigation, of the entire salmon industry of Puget Sound and the State of Washington, and I sincerely hope that such an investigation will be made and that there will be such a complete refutation to such acts of legislation, for instance, as the recent initiative bill, which secured out of 400,000 votes, after raking this State with a fine-toothed comb, a measly total of 32,100 signatures, and some of them have sworn they didn't know what they were signing when they signed it.

Thank you.

Chairman WALSH. The commission will stand adjourned until 9.30 o'clock to-morrow morning.

(Whereupon, at 4.30 o'clock p. m., Friday, Aug. 14, 1914, an adjournment was taken until the following day, Saturday, Aug. 15, 1914, at 9.30 o'clock a. m.)

SEATTLE, WASH., *Saturday, August 15, 1914—9.30 a. m.*

Present: Frank P. Walsh (chairman), Commissioners Garretson, O'Connell, Commons, and Lennon. W. O. Thompson, counsel.

Chairman WALSH. The commission will please be in order. Call your witness, Mr. Thompson.

Mr. THOMPSON. Mr. Ernst.

TESTIMONY OF MR. A. B. ERNST.

Mr. THOMPSON. Give us your name.

Mr. ERNST. A. B. Ernst.

Mr. THOMPSON. And your business address?

Mr. ERNST. Olympia.

Mr. THOMPSON. And your business?

Mr. ERNST. Member industrial insurance commission of this State.

Mr. THOMPSON. How long have you been a member of the commission?

Mr. ERNST. Since the 1st of May, 1913.

Mr. THOMPSON. What business were you in prior to that time?

Mr. ERNST. Engaged in the mining business.

Mr. THOMPSON. I didn't catch that.

Mr. ERNST. Engaged in the mining business, and shortly before that in the newspaper and printing business.

Mr. THOMPSON. I understand you have a statement that you wish to make to the commission. Will you please make it.

Mr. ERNST. Why, the question was raised yesterday when Mr. Wallace was on the stand as to the single blank, you know, an objection to it from the laboring standpoint. After assuming the duties of commissioner I was assigned more especially the office work in Olympia, and in going over the details of the office and trying to figure out, because the law was new in its operation here, and trying to see where things could be improved, and talking the matter over with the chief of the claim department and the secretary, I found we had a great deal of trouble in getting in blanks from workmen that were injured. They didn't seem to understand the law, that they had to make a report. They seemed to think if they reported to their employer and sometimes to the doctor that that was their report, and in talking it over we came to the conclusion if the employee's report was on the back of the employer's that the timekeeper or foreman who would make the report would probably say to the man, " See here, you have to sign a report, and it is right here," and you can get them that way. Sometimes they don't understand the language and don't read very well, and you can have them made out in that manner, as two reports are necessary for the claim. That was the only reason that the blank was adopted. But across the top of it was printed in red ink, if the workman desired he could call for this Form 22, as it is called, answer these questions, and return direct to the commission. The company had these blanks (the employee's) and would pass them out to the men if they were asked for. There was no intention in any way, shape, or form to coerce the man from making a statement he didn't want to make.

We simply figured in the office that it really helped the workman, and the aim in the office was to expedite the payment of money as much as possible; for instance, a claimant makes a claim, and he is sick and injured, he needs the money, and all our aim was that he would get that money, the compensation he would be entitled to, just as quickly as possible. And this was simply one of the methods that we thought would expedite getting the injured man his pay.

Further, the statement was made that the workman was not being treated as fairly as he had been formerly. I can hardly understand that, for the reason that our annual report shows that the average number of work days the second year, under the administration of the new commission, had increased the days of disability and increased the amount of money per accident, so that rather than cutting men short it seemed that we were more lenient with them and were rather going the other way.

And as regards workingmen not getting what is coming to them, we reopen hundreds of claims. Sometimes a disability does not show at the time the claimant is paid for his time loss. And if we were to go into it and take up individual claims, we could find several hundred of them that the new commission opened that were closed by the former commission. I don't mean to say in that at all that they were closed intentionally to cut the workman's pay, but that they were simply closed because the accident or disability did not show. The new commission, whenever a man comes and makes that kind of a showing, reopens it gives him what, under the law, we figure he is entitled to. I can only cite this with regard to the treatment of the employees. During the last year we probably made final settlement in more than 1,000 claims per month. The average accident reports run from eleven to fifteen hundred a month. Now, we make final settlements in about—oh, over a thousand per month. Under the law, each injured workman who is not satisfied with the award made, has a right to appeal to the superior court of the county where he is.

I want to say that in checking our records not long ago, in ten months where we had made final settlement in eleven thousand four hundred and sixty and odd claims there had been ten appeals taken; one dissatisfied workman in a thousand.

Now, when a commission deals between the employer and the laborer and can make these awards so that there will not be more than one appeal in a thousand, it does seem to me that they are meeting and trying to meet the workmen and give them satisfaction under the law.

And that was the reason I would like to make this statement so the impression would not get out that the commission is not dealing fairly with the laboring man. The fact of it is the commission travels over a great part of the State and meets the men wherever they are, meets them just as they can, and gives them personal attention. I want to say here that there is not in all these claims that we have handled where Mr. Wallace was still on that commission where he asked to have the award increased, that the other commissioners turned it down. I want to say, too, that in that time that he made examinations like the other commissioners, and there was never any recommendation made by Mr. Wallace that was turned down.

There is nothing to show that there was any feeling, or any ill feeling, in the handling of claims. There was at times disputes on this in theory, but in actual practice, paying the men, giving the claimants what was due, I do not believe there is a record in our office, which is open to anyone who wishes to see, where a recommendation made by Mr. Wallace was not carried out.

The only time, I think, that Mr. Wallace and I had a real dispute on a claim was that, in his absence, I made an award of a pension to a mother in eastern Washington of $12.50 a month. Her son, 26 years of age, had been killed. The record showed that he had been contributing $25 a month toward the mother's support and toward paying for some land, State land, that she was living on. Mr. Wallace raised the technical objection that she had a husband living, step-father to the boy that was killed, although he was worthless, was not doing anything toward that mother's support—that we should not allow anything to the mother. He wrote a letter to the attorney general, and the attorney general held that technically she had a man that ought to support her, but that it was entirely up to the commissioners whether or not under the rules she was entitled to this award. I made the award of $12.50 a month; and the award is still being paid. That is really the only dispute that we have ever carried to a final conclusion where Mr. Wallace was overruled. That was in giving a pension to a mother who was depending on her son.

Now we are paying out monthly just about $100,000 to these injured workmen. The last six months' average is ninety-nine thousand and six or seven hundred dollars. So you might call it a hundred thousand dollars. And as I am saying, the records show that the injured workmen, the men that we come in touch with, that we settle their claims, they universally are satisfied with the action of the commission and with the operation of the law. Many times they think they are not getting the amount that they ought to have, many times we feel we are not giving the men all that they should have, but the law lays down certain rules and amounts that we try to follow out, and as near as we can we always give them what we can. It has been the rule with this commission and the former commission, I believe, to give the laboring man the benefit of the doubt, if there is any doubt, with regard to the amount that he ought to receive.

Mr. THOMPSON. Have you ever compounded any claims, Mr. Ernst?

Mr. ERNST. Beg pardon?

Mr. THOMPSON. Have you ever compromised any claims?

Mr. ERNST. I do not know what you call a compromise. For instance, a man is injured, and he has what you would call a permanent partial disability. For instance, he had a broken leg, and that leg after healing is not normal. We have the doctor make an examination of that, and he will say, "Well, that is 10 per cent injured, or 20 per cent injured," as the case may be. Now, then, the rating for the loss of a leg is $1,500; 10 per cent of that would be a rating of $150, and so on. I will say to the man, "The doctor rates you at a 10 per cent loss on that." The man will say, "Look here, now, it is more than that." And he talks that way, and the man feels that way, naturally. I will say, "I don't know. There is the doctor's rating. He is a medical man." Probably we have an X-ray picture showing what the result is. The commission has one of the best X-ray machines in the State, and makes the X ray free to the employee. I will say, "That is the rating, but I will make that $200." If you call that compounding, when we talk over with the man his injury, and we try to judge how much he has been injured, based on the loss of the arm at $1,500 or the loss of the leg at $1,500. Everything is rated in proportion to that.

Mr. THOMPSON. You changed from the individual form to the joint blank?

Mr. ERNST. Yes; I made the change. The individual blank is still in existence. We have it yet to send to the employee, if they wish it.

Mr. THOMPSON. When you made that change from the individual to the joint blank, did you change some of the questions from one blank to the other; I mean, did you give certain questions to be answered by the employer that formerly were answered by the employee?

Mr. ERNST. In this way: There were some of the questions that were hardly ever answered. The employer can answer some questions best, and we changed them, but left them on the one form blank and changed them only on the other. But in addition to that the commission got out a separate blank covering all the questions that the labor boys wanted to ask the man, and this blank is sent to the man now when the final payment is made to him. Formerly some of those questions were answered on the blank application for injury. I can just state that when a man has been injured and is suffering pain a great many of these questions are simply not answered at all, and our records show that on the former blank probably 10 per cent of the men answered certain questions, and under the way we are sending them now the same questions are answered by 90 per cent of the injured.

Mr. THOMPSON. Let me put it more concretely. When you made the change in the form of the blank did you take the question relating to the nature of the accident, cause, and treatment from the employee's form and place it on the employer's form?

Mr. ERNST. I didn't get that.

Mr. THOMPSON. Questions relating to the nature of the accident, causes of the accident, and treatment.

Mr. ERNST. Well, the wording of the question may have been changed, but the statement was right there; and the employees answered how they were injured, you know, and what statement they wanted to make. The form of the; question may have been changed.

Mr. THOMPSON. What were the reasons for any change, if you know?

Mr. ERNST. They were simply combining and shortening up to do away with some of the questions that were not answered. This was all done after: consulting with the claim department and the secretary and the workers in the office and going over the claims themselves and seeing how the questions, were answered. We changed the wording of some of them so as to make it, probably more clear to answer, and some were changed in order to make the questions come later when he (the workman) was more clear.

One of the questions in the blank was medical attendance. When the man. was first injured he had absolutely no knowledge of medical attendance. Now when we send the question out he is cured and ready to return to work, and all those questions are answered and we get that data much better than we did before. It was simply changing the system of getting the same result.

Mr. THOMPSON. That is all, Mr. Chairman.

Chairman WALSH. Any questions?   Mr. Garretson would like to ask a question.

Commissioner GARRETSON. Is it not true that any system that requires an employee to sign a statement prepared by or prepare one in the presence of the master or his representative, that the man, especially in minor injuries, is subjected to a form of duress?

Mr. ERNST. No, sir; I don't think so.

Commissioner GARRETSON. If he expects to retain his position in the case of minor injuries, isn't he unconsciously influenced by the presence of the master in making up the statement?

Mr. ERNST. Well, I might explain that in this way: You seem to go on the assumption that the employer does not want to pay the man for the injury. It is just the other way—we have more trouble with employers wanting to pay their individual employees higher than they are entitled to, because all employers are putting into the fund.

Commissioner GARRETSON. I am not going on the assumption—the question is based on knowledge of dealings between master and man.

Mr. ERNST. Well, the employee does not have to make out the blank there.

Commissioner GARRETSON. How is that?

Mr. ERNST. The employee does not have to make out any blank with the employer if he does not want to. He is furnished his blank. It says right there in red printing across the top——

Commissioner GARRETSON. Wouldn't it be a better practice to furnish them separately, absolutely separately?

Mr. ERNST. Well, they usually call on the employer for the blank. No workman carries a blank in his pocket, expecting to be injured.

Commissioner GARRETSON. Let it be through other channels he should get it.

Mr. ERNST. Every union organization in the State that asks for these blanks have them on file, and we have them on file at every suboffice as well as every doctor. I think every doctor that treats men—these contract doctors in the, camps all have these blanks on file, and they can get the blanks if they ask for them.

Commissioner GARRETSON. Why not make it absolutely separate; no connection between the two?

Mr. ERNST. It was simply done because there are a great many foreigners here that don't understand they have to make out a blank. We would have to write and write to them and they would say they have made it out, meaning that they told the doctor.

Commissioner GARRETSON. Well, for men of that class shouldn't the employer be absolutely barred from making it out, because it is subject to abuse—a man that is not familiar with the language?

Mr. ERNST. Well, we were figuring that we simply want to get the report quicker and get him his money.

Commissioner GARRETSON. Even though it costs him the money?

Mr. ERNST. Well, of course, if you look at it that way I have simply given. you the practice to give every injured workman the money he was entitled to and trying to get it to him as quickly as possible. I want to say we have improved the methods of the office in that way.

Commissioner GARRETSON. Couldn't it be made the subject of abuse?

Mr. Ernst. I suppose it could, but we find that the man that usually makes it out is the timekeeper or the foreman on the job, that works side by side with the man that is injured.

Commissioner Garretson. Sure; and isn't the timekeeper the man that is ordinarily charged with keeping the pay roll down?

Mr. Ernst. Well, but he has nothing to do with that.

Commissioner Garretson. I know the pay roll doesn't enter into this, but it is the habit of action of this man.

Mr. Ernst. Well, how could anything that the timekeeper would put on there influence the man's injury?

Commissioner. Garretson. It might not influence his injury, but it would prejudice his case by a statement that it was less than it was actually.

Mr. Ernst. There isn't anything under this law about whether it is the man's fault or the employer's fault or a mechanical fault. He is still paid his money.

Commissioner Garretson. I beg your pardon. I got a cross current here and a short circuit. Will you repeat that?

Mr. Ernst. Why, I say under the law here it does not matter whether it is the employee's fault or the employer's fault or a mechanical fault.

Commissioner Garretson. I know.

Mr. Ernst. If the accident occurred they are all paid, if it was during the working time.

Commissioner Garretson. But in the event that the man is dissatisfied with his award to the degree that he would like to go into the courts——

Mr. Ernst. Yes, sir.

Commissioner Garretson (continuing)——wouldn't he be prejudiced by the original statement he had signed or his case would be prejudiced?

Mr. Ernst. No.

Commissioner Garretson. What kind of courts have you?

Mr. Ernst. Well, I don't see how it could. That award is a matter between the commission and the man, and it is not based on the injury at the time it happened and the way it happened. It is based on the result of the injury.

Commissioner Garretson. Wouldn't the entire record of the case go into court?

Mr. Ernst. Usually does, but you see it is based on this: It is the result of the accident that the commission has to deal with.

Commissioner Garretson. But still his case might be prejudiced by statements that he made?

Mr. Ernst. No, no; because——

Commissioner Garretson. It could not?

Mr. Ernst. Well, as am just saying to you, the employee, no matter how the accident happens, is paid.

Commissioner Garretson. Is it a fact that the commission compounds with the man?

Mr. Ernst. No; not except the way I explained. We try to deal with them. A man comes up here with a bad foot. I sat in the office yesterday down here in the Alaska Building. He came in with a bad foot. "Well," I say, "the doctor gave you a rating of the loss of one-half of that foot." He would say, "Well, I don't know; I don't think that is it." "Well," I say, "here is what it is, and there is the foot." And so on. That is what we are allowed to pay. We talk these matters over. And I don't find any compounding in that. We aim to agree with the man and satisfy him. And, as I have said, we give him the benefit of the doubt. If we think the doctor's rating is too close, why we would rather add $50 or $100 than have him believe he didn't get what he was entitled to. No compounding.

Commissioner Garretson. Do you ever give less than the doctor's rating?

Mr. Ernst. Never have.

Commissioner Garretson. What is this dickering over?

Mr. Ernst. I want to say——

Commissioner Garretson. A question of law or a question of fact?

Mr. Ernst. What is that?

Commissioner Garretson. I say what is this compounding done on—on the basis of a question of law or a question of fact?

Mr. Ernst. Well, it is rather a question of fact, of what the amount of the injury is. And you naturally would expect the man who is injured and who has a bad arm or a bad leg to rather feel that he has more of a disability probably than the other man that has not the injury. I think that is human nature.

Commissioner GARRETSON. Under the terms of the law, do you believe or do you hold that the commission has the power, the legitimate power, to bargain· with that man?

Mr. ERNST. To what?

Commissioner GARRETSON. To bargain with him—negotiate.

Mr. ERNST. Well, I don't know what you would call bargaining. We are supposed to pay him for his disability.

Commissioner GARRETSON. Yes.

Mr. ERNST. Now, we say to him, "Here is what you are disabled, what we are figuring on."

Commissioner GARRETSON. Well, then, if he holds that under the law he is entitled to more——

Mr. ERNST. Yes.

Commissioner GARRETSON. Is it then your province by personal bargaining with him to pay him the amount you have named, or the amount that he demands, or an intermediate sum between?

Mr. ERNST. I think it is entirely up to the commission to pay the amount it believes ought to be paid to the man.

Commissioner GARRETSON. Well, then, should it not always be fixed by the commission and not subject to negotiation?

Mr. ERNST. It is usually fixed by the commission. Now, sometimes when we get an injured man, correspondence will ensue. The man was not seen; he was rated strictly on the doctor's rating; the commission may see him afterwards and believe the doctor's rating was too close and raise the doctor's rating. I have done that several times. I have never lowered it.

Commissioner GARRETSON. Have you ever placed the commission in the position by this compounding or bargaining that it could be charged with more or less justice that you were attempting to make a good showing for an economic administration and thereby invading the right or interest of the injured man?

Mr. ERNST. No; I think if any charge could be made, it would be made that we were rather paying more than less, because if you don't lower the doctor's rating, and rather raise it, you are certainly not doing the man an injustice.

Commissioner GARRETSON. You have absolute faith in the doctor's examination?

Mr. ERNST. Well, we have to judge according to the professional man to a certain extent. We have the·X-ray machine and get plates made and we see the conditions. We have the same medical adviser that was with the commission since the beginning of the law. He is still the medical adviser of the commission.

Commissioner GARRETSON. How wide has your experience been with physicians' examinations?

Mr. ERNST. Well——

Commissioner GARRETSON. How many years and in what numbers?

Mr. ERNST. Oh, mostly during this last year in connection with this work, and of course as we have to deal with doctors more or less during our lives.

Commissioner GARRETSON. Then you would not count it a matter of surprise that a man that had dealt with them as an official of an insurance company for 30 years might be somewhat skeptical of the infallibility of their findings?

Mr. ERNST. I don't think there is anyone infallible. I think we are all subject to making mistakes.

Commissioner GARRETSON. That is all.

Chairman WALSH. Anything else?

Mr. ERNST. Here is the blank.

(The paper so presented, entitled "Form 22. The Industrial Insurance Commission of the State of Washington—Workman's Claim for Compensation," was submitted in printed form.)

TESTIMONY OF MR. WARREN D. LANE.

Mr. THOMPSON. Your name, please?

Mr. LANE. Warren D. Lane.

Mr. THOMPSON. Your address and your business?

Mr. LANE. No. 711 White Building, attorney.

Mr. THOMPSON. You are on what commission; the State commission of unemployment?

Mr. LANE. No, sir; it is a city committee.

Mr. THOMPSON. You are on that committee?

Mr. LANE. Yes, sir.

Mr. THOMPSON. What is the purpose and scope of that committee?

Mr. LANE. That was a committee appointed by the Central Council of Social Agencies at the suggestion of the chief of police, during the last winter, to look into the conditions of unemployment and to help to alleviate those conditions if it was possible, and to make any recommendations we thought that would help to alleviate them.

Mr. THOMPSON. Did you make any recommendations?

Mr. LANE. We made our report to the Central Council.

Mr. THOMPSON. Have you a copy of that report here?

Mr. LANE. I have not.

Mr. THOMPSON. Would you be willing to furnish the commission with that report?

Mr. LANE. I would.

Mr. THOMPSON. Pleased to have you do that.

Mr. LANE. I was not chairman of the committee, but I prepared the written report.

Mr. THOMPSON. I will suspend my examination here, and Prof. Commons will take it up.

Commissioner COMMONS. What were the main points in your report?

Mr. LANE. We reported the conditions as we found them here, and then made some suggestions as to what we thought might be done to alleviate the local conditions not only for this year but for the coming years.

Commissioner COMMONS. What was the condition as to the number of unemployed?

Mr. LANE. There were no satisfactory statistics that could be obtained on that question. It would be largely a matter of estimate to say how many unemployed men there were. Of course we found definitely a certain number of unemployed men at the Hotel de Gink and also at the Brotherhood League, but that was, of course, a per cent of the whole of the unemployed. We also were waited upon by a committee representing the unemployed Seattle citizens. There was a committee of 30 or 40 waited upon us and said they represented 125 family men in Seattle who were out of employment. We investigated the Hotel de Gink to see its plan of operation.

Commissioner COMMONS. What did your investigation of this Hotel de Gink show as to its financial support and the use of its funds?

Mr. LANE. The investigation showed that the hotel had cared for about twenty-two hundred men at different times. Of course they were not all there at the time. There were perhaps three or four hundred there at a time. That the rent of the building had been paid by the Central Labor Council, $55 a month; that otherwise the institution was self-supporting; that they had furnished 70,000 meals; that they had earned their money by clearing lands and doing such work as they could pick up around town, especially on Western Avenue, where they would sort vegetables and get " seconds " for their work; they would carry their fuel from buildings which were being torn down, and so they managed to support themselves. We looked over the books, and I don't think there was a dollar or a cent that was misappropriated. Nobody in connection with it was allowed to have a cent's salary. Mr. Pauly donated his services. We found that the discipline in the institution was excellent; the men had to be in at 10.30 at night, and any man that was out—the books showed whether he was in or out. The question was raised some time when there were some burglaries in town and some holdups whether or not the men at this institution might not be responsible for those. Of course if anything occurred after 10.30 at night their books would show whether a certain man was in. But Sergt. Ryan, of the police force, was stationed there, and in conversation with him he told me that all the time he was there he had never found it necessary to interfere in the interest of discipline; that he considered the discipline perfect; and that at one time, to satisfy themselves, without any notice whatever they made a search of the whole building, and said they didn't find so much as a penknife that didn't belong there. The sanitary conditions were good; everything was kept scrupulously clean. The men's clothes were dry steamed when they came in, and altogether it impressed me as a very interesting and instructive social experiment.

Commissioner COMMONS. Have you any idea what proportion of the unemployed they took care of?

Mr. LANE. Well, they took care of more men than the Brotherhood League did; those were the only two places where large numbers were taken care of. If I were to make an estimate, including not only homeless men but all others in the city, I would say that there were probably fifteen hundred to two thousand unemployed in the city at one time.

Commissioner COMMONS. Fifteen hundred to two thousand altogether?

Mr. LANE. Yes; and they would take care of three or four or five hundred at a time, so that perhaps they might have taken care of one-fourth of the unemployed. If a man came into their institution that was not found worthy, he would be put out. If he was not ready to respond to work when it was offered, they would not have him there.

Commissioner COMMONS. What agency took care of that class?

Mr. LANE. They would generally drift down to the Brotherhood League or Salvation Army or the Volunteers.

Commissioner COMMONS. Did the police department take care of any?

Mr. LANE. Well, not that I know of. The police, of course, were interested in the matter; the chief was particularly interested in the matter, and it was at his suggestion that our committee was formed.

Commissioner COMMONS. Did you make any recommendation regarding the continuance of this kind of organization like this Hotel de Gink?

Mr. LANE. The report of the subcommittee which made the investigation was that it was worthy of our support; that is, our moral support. That is all, as I understand it, that they wanted. Mr. Pauly says if the people of this city will lend this institution their moral support they will make it absolutely self-supporting.

Commissioner COMMONS. Did you make any recommendation toward a municipal lodging house?

Mr. LANE. I don't think we recommended a municipal lodging house?

Commissioner COMMONS. On what grounds?

Mr. LANE. Well, it is somewhat of a question how good a thing a municipal lodging house is. I have no objection to one if properly conducted. I believe, however, in dealing with the unemployed that the very first thing that is necessary is to classify the unemployed. When you undertake to put all them, as you might say, "all cats in the same sack," and deal with them all in the same way, injustice is sure to result, and if a man is honest and willing to work and just simply unfortunate, to treat him in the same way you would a bum or a tramp would be unjust and would be demoralizing to him. So I would think that a municipal lodging house or a labor colony would be a desirable thing for certain classes of the unemployed. Those that are able and willing to work ought to have a chance to work. The first thing to do for them, the right thing to do for them, is to give them a job and not send them to any municipal lodging house or farm colony. Those who are unable to work ought to be treated as unfortunates, cared for, and that taken into account. Those who can work and won't work, there is another class of treatment for them. I can not see how you can deal fairly with the unemployed at all until you are able to face every man with a job.

For instance, if a man comes to you on the street and asks you for something to get a meal, of course there might be the presumption that that man is not worthy from the fact that he is begging on the street. But then perhaps after you have talked with him you do not feel sure but what he is worthy after all. He may be an exception. If you are in a position to say, now, "Here, you can get work at a certain place," you have got him classified. If he wants it, he will take it. If he doesn't want to work, it will show he is not worthy. So I would say the first thing in caring for the unemployed is to classify them and to treat each class in the way that his particular class calls for.

Commissioner COMMONS. Have you investigated private agencies, private employment agencies?

Mr. LANE. No; I have not. All I know about that is hearsay. I know it has been a very common source of serious complaint, about the employment agencies, and it has come to me from so many different sources, so frequently and so directly, that I have believed that there was just cause of complaint.

Commissioner COMMONS. Have you investigated the public employment agencies?

Mr. LANE. Yes; to some extent.

Commissioner COMMONS. What were your findings there?

Mr. LANE. We did not make any findings in the matter. The public employment office, as has been shown here before in testimony that has been given here, under present conditions is perhaps not in a position to compete with private agencies; that is, it is perhaps not used by the employer like the private agency.

Commissioner COMMONS. Did you go into the question of the reasons for that at all, why that should be?

Mr. LANE. No; I did not.

Commissioner COMMONS. That is all.

Chairman WALSH. Mr. Garretson would like to ask you a few questions.

Commissioner GARRETSON. I assume that you have taken considerable interest in this question, being connected with this committee?

Mr. LANE. I have taken interest in it long before I was connected with that committee.

Commissioner GARRETSON. I took that as an evidence that you were interested.

Mr. LANE. Yes.

Commissioner GARRETSON. Have you given any thought or made any investigation of the establishment of industrial farms and colonies for the class who refuse to work?

Mr. LANE. I know of such farms in Germany. I have studied those.

Commissioner GARRETSON. New York has established one of them, although it has not passed the primary stage yet. Have you an opinion as to the results, how that would work out?

Mr. LANE. I believe good results work out, but in the operating of that I should say that precautions should be taken all the time not to send a man to those colonies who is able and willing to work. I think the facts show that in the German labor colonies, for instance, there is a large percentage of criminals—I think something like 60 per cent. Now, to send an honest worthy man there to mingle with the criminals, the down-and-out class, I do not think that is logical.

Commissioner GARRETSON. It goes without saying that the willing man should not be sent there.

Mr. LANE. Yes.

Commissioner GARRETSON. But many men of necessity go there who were able and unwilling.

Mr. LANE. Yes; that is the place to treat them.

Commissioner GARRETSON. That is your idea?

Mr. LANE. Yes.

Chairman WALSH. Call your next witness.

Mr. THOMPSON. Mr. Distler.

TESTIMONY OF MR. RUDOLPH DISTLER.

Mr. THOMPSON. Give your name and your business address, please.

Mr. DISTLER. Rudolph Distler; Cosmopolis, Wash.

Mr. THOMPSON. What business are you in?

Mr. DISTLER. Why, I have retired from business there; I attend to my own affairs privately.

Mr. THOMPSON. Now, Mr. Distler, you have heard the testimony given here in regard to the conditions at Cosmopolis in the lumber industry?

Mr. DISTLER. Yes.

Mr. THOMPSON. Will you please briefly tell us, in your own way, the conditions which exist there, what you have to add further to what has already been testified to by Mr. Brown and by the others?

Mr. DISTLER. I know you are short on time, and I will make my remarks as short as possible, and will touch on the important matters. There are some very important matters——

Chairman WALSH. Refer to those important ones, Mr. Distler.

Mr. DISTLER. I think I will. The statement was made here that men were allowed $15 a month for board. There have been little changes made lately. I think it was on account of the fact that this investigation was coming. The fact is that last month the men were only allowed $10 a month for board, only those who received $35 and over had $15 a month. They made a distinction there. The idea is this: Why should a man pay tribute to a mess house——

Chairman WALSH. Let us try to get to the facts. Tell su what the facts are, and we will draw the conclusion as to why it should be so, or why it should not be so. The time is short. Just give us the facts now. Somebody has testified to something here that you think is not in strict accordance with the facts. Just give us those facts, then, as you understand them, minus the argument.

Mr. DISTLER. The men of family who board at home have to pay tribute to the mess house of $10 a month. Board costs $20 a month in the other place, and he can't board himself; that is, for less than that. So when they only allow $10 he has to pay a tribute of $10 for the privilege of boarding at home.

Now, in regard to pay day: The pay day is supposed to be on the first Saturday after the 10th, but in many instances often it happens that it is the second Saturday after the 10th. In between those times no cash has been paid. In fact, notice appears on the cashier's windows reading something like this: "Pay day the 22d; no cash will be paid until then. For coupons call next window."

This [indicating] is one of the coupons. They are issued from $1 to $20. This is made to compel those people to buy their groceries in those stores.

(The coupon book referred to, reading "The coupons in this book are good only for merchandise at the store of Grays Harbor Commercial Co. $1.00. Not transferable," was submitted in printed form.)

The statement was made that the company had three stores. The fact is they have got five stores. In a little town from twelve to fourteen hundred inhabitants, why is this done? Why five stores in a town of twelve hundred inhabitants? They have a general merchandise store; they have a furnishing goods store; they have a cash grocery store; they have an extra meat store; any they have another store, furniture and stuff, such things as that. But this furniture store has no special attention to it.

Chairman WALSH. Could you file that with the commission?

Mr. DISTLER. Yes, sir. Now, in regard to the coupon book, one more interesting point: When a man wants cash in between times, they take these coupon books and go to the saloons, and the saloons discount them for 20 cents on the dollar. The saloon occupies—the buildings are owned by the Commercial Co., three out of four saloons. Generally they are old, poor buildings, but they pay a high rent, and by getting this discount on the poor laboring man, for 80 cents on the dollar, and then turning it over to the company for a dollar, of course, it reduces their rent. Then, too, the fact that they are renting from the Commercial Co. makes them subservient to the company, and they will do what the company asks them in cases of election, etc.

Now, in the last two months that has been remedied to this effect, that a man is allowed to draw once in between pay day, but his cash is limited; he must bring the timekeeper's statement that he has a certain amount of money coming; then he is allowed to draw some of his cash money.

Now, about hospital fees: They only charge 50 cents hospital fees, but there is nothing, as was stated here the other day in regard to these hospital tickets, a man pays—if he goes to work on the last few days of any month, he is charged 50 cents, and he is charged 50 cents again if he works several days in the next new month. That makes it a dollar if he works the 10 days. He pays a dollar to the hospital fund for medical aid, and this won't amount to much, either. But their own timekeeper has made statements that there was as many as 3,000 men on the pay roll in one month. Labor leaders have investigated that years ago, and they found as many as 2,500 on the pay roll in one month. So every position is filled so often; if it is filled five times, the hospital fee amounts to $2.50 instead of 50 cents. In other words, they contract for the hospital, doctor and hospital—and I will say the hospital doctors are very good; I have no complaint to make of them at all—but I do not believe that the hospital or the doctor gets all the money that they collect from these laboring men.

When those men are sent by employment agencies—that is the greatest injustice ever practiced on labor; I know there has been much testimony, and we have gotten affidavits many different times sent to officials, but no relief. These men have been sent out for a certain job. Last Sunday I met a man who said he had been sent down there to get a position as machinist at $40 or $50 a month. When he got there there was no such position. They asked him to work in the mill for $26 a month and board. At first he went to work—he didn't know that he was not going to get $40 a month. Then he found he was only going to get $26, and he went to the time office and asked about it, and they said, "Yes; that is all you get." So he went away.

I want to call attention to another interesting point: The former prosecuting attorney, W. E. Campbell, of Hoquiam, Wash., told me last Saturday that he had all the information that there was collusion between the Grays Harbor Commercial Co. and the employment offices, and there was also collusion between the Grays Harbor Commercial Co. and the railroads, but he wouldn't give that testimony to me. He would give it to this commission if he was subpœnaed to do so.

Now, the fact is these men are sent down and the baggage is held. The railroad company keeps the baggage in their baggage room. If a man wants to take out his working clothes, he must leave his other clothes he wears in that baggage room. It is taken out and put in under supervision of some of the officials there. That is what the railroad companies do.

The prosecuting attorney further told me—I was aware of the fact—that a great many boys are sent down to work at $10 a month and board; if they don't board, they get $20. We have some in our neighborhood getting $20 a month, but that proves again they only allow $10 a month for board. Last month one of these boys was sent down for a certain job. When he came down he was put on machinery. He had never worked on machinery before, and they are crippled up; they are not experienced with this machinery,—they get their fingers cut off and cripple to a great extent. The worst part of it is that after working a couple of days they send them off again. This prosecuting attorney said that while some of these boys have bad reputations, yet some of them were honest boys and never had done anything wrong; but they had been discharged without any money and for no particular cause.

A boy walking across the bridge had some money in his pocket. One of these boys came along, had had nothing to eat, and he jumped on this fellow and held him up. He made a confession; he had never done anything like that before. This condition makes criminals. There is lots of other information you might get from prosecuting attorneys there. This commission would send a special agent down there, unbeknown to the company, and get information where they could get it, not from the company, but from the men around in town.

Now, when a man gets down there he is met at the depot by a rooming-house boss. The company owns the rooming house. I don't want to go into that matter; we have mentioned that before. But this man has to sign an order for one week's lodging. If he stays long enough, the lodging order is paid to the rooming-house boss. One of those bosses told me that he had lost not less than $50 from the men who did not stay long enough to pay off their rooming order that they had given him; that the company would always deduct their own expenses, railroad fare, and so on, from the money before they would pay these rooming-house charges.

Another point is that hardly anybody can get a job without a slip from an employment agency. This same man told me he had five men laying there in his rooming house for three weeks. They could not get a job on account of the fact they had not come from the employment agency. The company was hiring men every day, men coming in every day, and they were giving them jobs. These men had no slips and could not get a job. The marshal told me the same thing. He said the men were there, and they were hiring men all the time, but they wouldn't give these men a job on account of the fact they did not come from the employment agencies. He was keeping the men in jail overnight, and had the restaurant furnish the meals so they would not starve.

Now, this baggage is held. A man will redeem his baggage if he has a possible chance; he will work long enough to redeem it. I have seen photographs at Grays Harbor where wagonloads of 200 pieces of baggage was hauled from Cosmopolis to the railroad station in another town and shipped away. Second-hand dealers had bought it. Since then they have sold them more secretly. At the present day the Grays Harbor Commercial Co. has a pile of stuff set up which belongs to them poor fellows, that they had taken away from those poor fellows illegally. And this is done in the United States.

There are other things that are bad, that are real important about this mess-house condition. For instance, in the wintertime it often happens that a man only works nine hours a day, on account it gets dark too early and they can not see in the yards. So if after a man works 10 days, nine hours each day, he has practically lost one day, and he gets paid according to that. But they charge him that one day's board extra. On the other hand, they are making a practice of working a man what they call five-quarters time; that is, $12\frac{1}{2}$ hours a day. So after a man works four days five-quarter time he has put in five days' time, and they do not allow him for any extra board. That is another point. In other words, the company gains one day's board in four, on account of the man gets a dollar a day and board, and he has worked five days and only gets four days' board. In fact, a man gets less for overtime than he does for actual time.

And the living conditions—I won't say anything about the rooming houses and other things. The company has a good many cabins. I have measured ɪ them, and they measure on the outside 12½ by 6½.

'They have a good many of them around town, but in one particular place ɪ there are 15 cabins on a plot of ground 50 by 120. It is the back part of·some lot; there is a dwelling house owned by the Commercial Co. in .the front, and the pack part of the lot toward the alley is where these two rows of cabins are on a piece of ground 50 by 120. The cabins are cheaply constructed; they have · a partition, but without a door in the center, which divides it into two rooms, and there are two windows, one in the front and one in the back. These cabins are rented to men for $3 a month in these particular places. The cabins are divided by a sidewalk, 14 feet wide, and the whole is surrounded by a tight board fence 8 feet high, with an opening to the street, a 4-foot opening. These 15 cabins have one toilet together with two seats. They have one hydrant with a half-inch supply pipe. The condition of these cabins is extremely filthy. The odor and what you can see with your eyes is very bad. It has already been admitted in one place they have nine beds in one room, and in the other five, but I won't go into that.

Chairman WALSH. Now, your report, it appears, is full of details, and we have our investigator right here on the ground, and suppose you just submit that report and we will make a detailed investigation of that now, before we leave this country. It is not that I want to hurry you, but I think it can be covered more scientifically and with better satisfaction of your self and the commission.

Mr. DISTLER. All right. There is just one proposition I want to state.

Chairman WALSH. Go ahead and state your other proposition, or anything you wish to state for that matter, but I think we can do this in that way and it will be more satisfactory.

Mr. DISTLER. I want to file with the commission an open letter, a circular, which we sent to the governor and State representatives of the State of Washington. It was sent by the Citizens Progressive Club, of Cosmopolis. This letter is signed by O. A. Bergland, H. W. Stengel, and Christopher Schock, executive committee.

Chairman WALSH. What date?

Mr. DISTLER. This was in 1912, when the legislature was in session last.

(The letter referred to was submitted in printed form.)

Mr. DISTLER. We asked these men to relieve these conditions. I want to state that Gov. Hays promised the labor organization to do all he could, and to make a recommendation to the legislature for relief. When the time of the legislature meeting came he had changed his mind. Now, we have this before these State officers, and so far nothing has been done, but I would like to file it· with the commission.

Chairman WALSH. Very good.

Mr. DISTLER. I want to read just one more report to show the conditions and the result of this affair at Cosmopolis.

Chairman WALSH. Mr. Distler, we have a rule that all documentary evidence must be filed. We have applied it ever since yesterday morning to the witnesses. I don't want to limit you, but if it is a document you will have to describe it, not read it.

Mr. DISTLER. Well, it is pretty hard to understand. Of the 650 men employed in 1913—I will get the date.

Chairman WALSH. You may get the date out of there for any statement; that is all right.

Mr. DISTLER. The company has only 18 men with families which own their home in Cosmopolis.

Chairman WALSH. How is that; ·I didn't catch it? Eighteen men with families out of how many employees?

Mr. DISTLER. Six hundred and fifty. The United States census report shows the condition—that is, from 1900 to 1910 the town of Cosmopolis increased 120 · in population. At the same time the last United States census was made there were three railroad camps temporarily located in Cosmopolis, so the actual effect was we didn't have any increase at all, although Hoquiam, under the same ' conditions and not as favorably located as Cosmopolis, has had a tremendous increase of population.

Now, in the same period of time, 1900 to 1910, the Grays Harbor Commercial Co. more than doubled their plant, and still there was no increase in population· That shows the effect it has on our Government.

Chairman WALSH. Does that give those figures in there?

·Mr. DISTLER. Yes, sir; they are in there. I don't go behind these men. I believe these men are responsible and not the Commercial Co. I have written an open letter to W. H. Talbot, Fred Talbot, and A. W. Jackson, and others, officers of the Grays Harbor Commercial Co., of San Francisco and Cosmopolis, dated May 15, 1911, in which I appeal to them. I say: "Why continue to undermine the Government with the mess house? Why don't you as honest men make your money out of the lumber business as the other mills do?" This is the only mill that does that.

Chairman WALSH. I didn't catch that, and probably some of the other commissioners did not. You live at Cosmopolis, do you?

ⓐ Mr. DISTLER. Yes, sir.

˙ Chairman WALSH. What is your business, Mr. Distler?

Mr. DISTLER. Well, I attend to my own real estate just now. I have worked in lumber camps and worked in sawmills since I first came here. I worked 11½ hours per day in a sawmill.

· Chairman WALSH. You are a former workman yourself?

· Mr. DISTLER. Yes.

Chairman WALSH. And have made some accumulations?

· Mr. DISTLER. I have cleared more land than the next man. When a man speaks of going on land, I know it costs $250 an acre to clear the land. That is what it costs.· The land has got to clear itself. It has got to lie there for years and years after it has been logged off and burned over. Then it has got to clear itself. But talk about clearing a piece of green land, it costs $250 an acre.

⌐ Mr. THOMPSON. Mr. Distler, have you had any personal dealings with this company?

Mr. DISTLER. Yes; for instance, I deal with them now. If I can't buy my things from the other grocery store, I deal with them..

Mr. THOMPSON.· Just answer it briefly. There are some facts I am anxious to get at. You do deal with them?

Mr. DISTLER. Yes, sir.

Mr. THOMPSON. Have you had any personal controversies about your own personal matters with the company at any time?

Mr. DISTLER. I have not.

Chairman WALSH. Say, I don't think we care for that, Mr. Thompson. I suppose that is admitted, but we don't care for that, because we only investigate the facts regardless; it don't make any difference.

Mr. DISTLER. I want to say the present manager has relieved—has moderated some of the evils. The former manager was a good deal worse than this one is.

Mr. THOMPSON. The chairman says you need not answer that anyway, so that is all.

Chairman WALSH. Mr. Garretson wants to ask a question.

···Commissioner GARRETSON. Mr. Distler, when men apply there at Cosmopolis for employment and they are refused employment, while a regular supply of men is coming in from employment agencies, what is your opinion as to why these men are refused employment?

Mr. DISTLER. On account of not coming from the employment agency.

· Commissioner GARRETSON. Well, what underlies that?

Mr. DISTLER. ·Why, that is a strong indication that there is a collusion between the employment agencies and this Commercial Co. I have seen as many as 50 men laid off to make room for others coming in.

.Commissioner GARRETSON. That is all.

Chairman WALSH. That is all, thank you, Mr. Distler.

·Mr. DISTLER. This is my report.

(The papers so presented were marked "Distler exhibit." They consist of a printed paper entitled "An Open Letter," dated Cosmopolis, Wash., May 15, 1911, and two papers which are printed among the exhibits at the end of this subject.)

Mr. THOMPSON. Mr. McGill.

TESTIMONY OF REV. OSCAR H. McGILL.

Mr. THOMPSON. You may give us your name.

Rev. McGILL. Oscar H. McGill. I live in Seattle.. I am social-service secretary of the Methodist Church.

Chairman WALSH. I didn't catch you.

·Rev. McGill. I am under the home mission board as social-service · secre. tary. I visit the camps, and I am familiar with and put in all my time in log. ging and mining camps.

Mr.·Thompson. Now, Mr. McGill, will you tell us what you have. to say to this commission in regard to industrial conditions in these camps?

Rev. McGill. Yes, sir.

Mr. Thompson. If you please.

Rev. McGill. I would say that there has been considerable discussion in. dulged in as to the peculiarities of the logging man, and. that sort of thing, which is entirely beside the question.

I notice several of the men who have spoken of it here—Mr. Rucker made the statement that the men in Washington, the employees of the logging camps and mills of ·Washington were the highest-grade workingmen· in the world.·. Mr. Rucker, as is well known, conducts one of the cleanest and best-conducted camps in the State of Washington or anywhere. He; has no trouble with his men. I have been to his camp different times. His men live in .nice homes around there. He employs married men. He doesn't discharge them. Positions are at a premium. And when other camps are shut down and other mills have difficulty in getting men, he has no difficulty. The fact is, these men are susceptible to kindness and to treatment just like other human beings. , I be-. lieve the cause of discontent very largely—there is much discontent—I believe it is because these workingmen have been exploited in a way that is simply. indescribable, sir. I believe that the treatment they have had has made them independent, very independent, because their rights have been utterly ignored..

What is needed is more democracy. When a man will own, as the owner of these logging camps does, a whole community, a whole town, and refuses to allow discussion, refuses to allow his men to organize, to meet together ;.refuses to allow men to come in and address them, and if men come to address them they must go out on the public road or go off somewhere—meet out, as they do, in almost all those logging camps—he is wrong. ·In.many of them there is absolutely no allowance for the men to organize. I was in a place·just a short time ago where they would not allow a union man to walk across· the dock.

·Chairman Walsh. Where was that?

Rev. McGill. Port Angelus.

Chairman Walsh. Who was it?

Rev. McGill. The mill company. None of the longshoremen. ·That is nothing new. Why, Mr. Paterson right here, refused a man with a .union button to receive freight during a strike, or for some time, or union ·men to· work or go across his premises. And that is not anything new.

The fact of the matter is the men of this country—the workmen—are intelligent men. They have read. They do read. They think. And·the employment office, private employment office, and the graft of the doctors which amounts to an enormous amount, and the treatment these men receive in the bunk .houses, and the fact that at the end of the year they come out without money, embitters them.

These are seasonal trades. These men come out knowing that they have. worked and have worked hard. They work long hours, 10 or .12 hours a day. They climb these mountains before daylight in time to get·.up there; in the rain—and it rains here out in those mountains; they climb the mountains and get up there ·in time for daylight to go to work—a long day until dark, and then they come down at night.

And then they stay in these bunk houses. .I have seen bunk houses quartering 16 to 20 men without a single window in it. They build these bunk houses with the bunks built in as part of the house; build them right down against the floor, in a row—and here is a bunk, and here, and here. There are eight—four here and four above, and across the end the same, and across the sides, and not much room to go up and down. Often down in the middle of the house there is a double row of bunks. These men live in them; and there are no chairs, often no table. Up on the Milwaukee they have seven or eight bunk houses that are made large enough to hold 100 men, and the bunks are built into the wall. There· is no way of scrubbing the floor or cleaning it. Those bunk houses are 5 or 6 years old. I don't know just how old, but it is a num-ber of years since they started to work.

Commissioner Commons. Are those construction camps or lumber camps? ,

Rev. McGill. Those are construction camps, it just occurred to me.· This is a series of large bunk houses, some of them containing from 60 to 80 or 90 men.

Acting Chairman COMMONS. This is on construction work on the railroad?

Rev. McGILL. Yes; but it is the same thing, Professor, it is the same thing. The point that strikes me is that of the constant injustice to these men. May I give you an instance in this case up here? It is construction work. The men are sent out from the employment office here and put on railroad cars, and they can't ride when they go out; they can't ride on the ordinary cars. I rode up with them a short time ago and there was twice as many men in the baggage car as there should have been in there. They had their beds and stuff piled in the seats, and there was not room to sit down or scarcely to stand up. There was twice as many men in there as there should have been.

In the car I was in there were seven or eight people. Some of those men wanted to go back and sit in there with us, but they were not allowed to do so. A number of them came back and they were forced forward. A number refused to go, and the conductor and brakemen forced them out and one man they just dragged through and used language that was unprintable, in handling them. The men were given to understand that they were not to ride with the ordinary people, they were to ride in the baggage car. It is such treatment as this that makes these men bitter. In the camps there is more or less of what is known as welfare work, Y. M. C. A. work, and that sort of thing. There is one camp at Bellingham that has a large building built——

Commissioner O'CONNELL. What does the Y. M. C. A. do?

Rev. McGILL. They have a general secretary, Mr. Goodall, who has charge of four States, and he goes if he is sent for by the owner of the mill company or camps and establishes a camp Y. M. C. A. They build a building and then they pay the secretary $75 a month. They pay the secretary—Mr. Goodall furnishes the man—and the company pays the secretary, and he comes in and often he helps to work on clerical work or scaling logs or something like that.

Commissioner O'CONNELL. The secretary does?

Rev. McGILL. Yes, sir.

Commissioner O'CONNELL. Is that welfare work?

Rev. McGILL. Well, no; that is not welfare work, but I know some of them do that.

Commissioner O'CONNELL. What do they really do? What do they do for the people, the people that really do scale logs?

Rev. McGILL. They have phonographs and come to the city and from the public library get a lot of books and a big number of old magazines and put them in there, and this place is left open, and they have a pool room, and the men pay a dollar a month membership.

Commissioner O'CONNELL. For this welfare work?

Rev. McGILL. They pay this for welfare work.

Commissioner O'CONNELL. The men have to pay for everything?

Rev. McGILL. The company pays the secretary's salary, and the secretary is under the direction of the company.

Commissioner O'CONNELL. Where does this dollar a month go?

Rev. McGILL. To the payment of buying books and phonograph records and that sort of thing.

Commissioner O'CONNELL. That would buy a lot of phonograph records.

Rev. McGILL. I have here a letter that I will submit, if you please, Mr. Chairman, from a mill owner who writes a letter to the general secretary, stating why he is displeased and why he refuses to continue to pay for the services of the secretary. It would be very interesting to read that, if you care to have me.

Chairman WALSH. Just let it go into the record.

(The paper so presented was marked "McGill exhibit," and is printed at the end of this subject.)

Rev. McGILL. It is a letter in which he declares that the Y. M. C. A. secretary does not attend to his business because there was a strike there, and the Y. M. C. A. secretary had not been in touch with the men, and didn't inform the management that there was going to be a strike, and he didn't want the secretary any more.

Commissioner GARRETSON. He wanted to use him as a spy?

Rev. McGILL. Yes, sir; you will find it right there in the letter.

Commissioner O'CONNELL. As I understand this welfare work, in addition to the company paying the secretary, the men pay for the welfare work themselves by an assessment of $1 per month?

Rev. McGILL. Yes, sir.

Commissioner O'CONNELL. And, of course, the company gets the credit for having the system in existence?

Rev. McGILL. There is a lumber company up here that advertises that they have such a building. They have a pool room and card table and reading table in a large room. As a matter of fact, it is second-story room over the mess house downstairs, and the concessions that are sold—there is a man up there that runs a barber shop, and he pays a very high rate, a higher rate than he would pay in the city of Bellingham; and the man that sells soft drinks and that sort of thing; the concessions, I believe, rent for about $80 a month in that upstairs room. There are seats where the men can come and read and that sort of thing; but it is a very profitable investment, as I see it, $80 a month, for an upstairs room that is not even plastered or anything of that kind; but it goes along with that line of welfare work we hear considerably about at the camps that the employers are doing for the employees. The employees really pay that themselves. They know that; they are not fools. They know that they are being exploited to all this extent.

Commissioner GARRETSON. Do the men look on that as welfare work for the employer?

Rev. McGILL. Yes, sir; there is a severe bitterness on the part of these men all over everywhere, and it partly is because of this.

I might say this: That in these company stores the men are outfitted. A place like this Cosmopolis, for instance, where there are four times as many employees in the month as on the real pay roll, the men go down and buy from the company stores the clothing that they need; they buy it, and they pay there a much higher rate than they would pay in an ordinary store—a much higher rate. These men are charged higher for board than they ought to be. They pay no rent, everything is in the very crudest form, and it is a matter of extortion, and the men realize the fact. Every time he is gouged, whether five cents or a dollar, he realizes it, and he knows it.

Commissioner COMMONS. What about the construction camps of the railroad; what are the wages paid there?

Rev. McGILL. Well, I will tell you. In these special camps they are paying men $1.35 a day, and they board themselves. That is what they pay these Greeks and these in the special gangs, and they average about five days a week You may just stop and figure up what that amounts to. These men pay for the job and then are sent there to live in the cars and have to pay their board out of the $1.35 a day. They buy their shoes, and it is rainy, wet weather, and they have to buy slickers and oil coats. Then the men support families, or claim they support them. They often have families and they work at from $1.35 to $1.60 a day. The regular construction work runs $2 a day and under. I am speaking of the special gangs, and they work 9 to 10 hours a day.

Commissioner COMMONS. Where are these men recruited?

Rev. McGILL. They get them in the cities.

Commissioner COMMONS. Through the employment offices?

Rev. McGILL. Yes, sir.

Commissioner COMMONS. Or are they from contractors?

Rev. McGILL. I think largely of that nature, but all these people are from the employment offices. You can go down to the Wilms Employment Agency and find a sign that has been there, and you will find it in various offices, "Ten men wanted for box factory at Cosmopolis." A good many men go in and hire for the box factory. He is just as likely to be sent to the yards or the mill or somewhere else. He advertises that he wants 10 men for the box factory, and they may be sent to the yard or the mill. I saw the advertisement yesterday or the day before, and you can go down and see that sign.

Now, up here at this Milwaukee Tunnel, where about a thousand men, I think, perhaps six hundred to a thousand men are employed during the ordinary season of the year, the timekeeper told me that they change the ordinary men—that the average stay of the men was five days, about five days. The day I was there there were 90 men quit. He showed me a bundle that he said contained 90 certificates.

Commissioner LENNON. Time checks?

Rev. McGILL. Time checks; yes, sir; for the men. They pay those men in two checks, and they won't pay them until late in the afternoon, just before the train departs. They pay them in one check, the amount of their fare to Seattle; and if there is anything left to come to them, they give them another check. There were 90 men either discharged or quit that day, out of about 300 men at that end of the tunnel.

Commissioner GARRETSON. Are they employees—do you know—of the railroad company or the contractor?

Rev. McGILL. They are employees of the railroad company.

Commissioner GARRETSON. The company does the work itself?

Rev. McGILL. Yes, sir. I heard a man say that the entire night shift had been discharged that day. Now, as a matter of fact, the man in charge, and who has been in charge of that job, is a brother-in-law to one of the worst employment sharks in the city. He is a brother-in-law and employs all his men through this office, the Wilms Employment Agency. I am speaking plainly, but everybody knows the situation exactly.

Commissioner O'CONNELL. Do you mean to imply by that that there is collusion between the brother-in-law and the agency to employ and discharge the men and make fees—split the fees?

Rev. McGILL. Yes, sir; that is the impression among the men. The average time is five days, and they must pay their railroad fare. The first thing is 75 cent for a candlestick. He gets a little piece of iron that ought to sell for 5 cents, and he is charged 75 cents. That is simply a form of graft.

He is charged a dollar for doctor's fee. There are four or five times as many men employed each month as the pay roll would indicate. Then he is charged for whatever he wants at the company store. Of course he is charged—well, these various charges that come in there, they are put in together.

Now, then, these men work in this way; they work in different shifts in this camp, for instance. There are three or four or five shifts—they work variously. For instance, at midnight one shift would come in, and here are men trying to sleep, and here these men come in all wet, and they make their fire in the bunk house, say there are 60 or 80 men in the bunk house, and they light a fire and smoke and dry their clothes and talk. These other men are trying to sleep; they have worked hard, and they are trying to get a little sleep. The same thing happens in the daytime. The men, of course, are changing all the time, and it makes it very difficult for them to live in that way. The bunks are built right down on the floor. An 8 or a 10 or 12 inch board is run on the floor, and right around and over here again. There is no way of cleaning those. I suppose those bunk houses have not been cleaned since the bunk houses were built. A man said they often threw the mattresses out of the window. If you could see the mattress, you wouldn't wonder why they did. In this particular bunk house, where I talked the most, the men fight every night to see who will sleep on the table. There is just one table in the bunk house. They have reason to get just as far away from the bunks as they can. It is up in the mountains, and they can't sleep out of doors.

The toilet conditions are terrible—simply inexcusable. The toilet is behind the building up on the hill in very close proximity. The urinals are right between the buildings. Very many of the men have the impression that conditions are made in the camps just as bad as they can be so that the men will quit. The men do quit; they don't stay. They quit for various reasons. One reason that has not been given is this: A great many of them are out of work—they don't save any money; nobody could save money on the wages that they get; they live on coffee and "sinkers," as they call them, and they are physically not strong.

One reason the company is glad to have them quit at the end of four or five days is that they have squeezed about all out of them that there is in them. This logging camp and millwork is hard work, heavy work, and these men are exhausted.

Many of these men can't work more than 4 or 5 or 6 or 10 days until they must lay off. A great many of them are old men, and their physical condition is such that they can't stand it long. Many of them are not men adapted to it; they are men from every walk of life, and they drift into this seasonal employment. They are professional men and men of other classes, and they are not strong enough to do the work or stand it, and that is the reason they break down.

Commissioner GARRETSON. You mean also they are insufficiently nourished between jobs?

Rev. McGILL. Yes, sir.

Commissioner O'CONNELL. Has there been any study made of this matter and these conditions to ascertain what the real earnings of the men are, what real money they get out of the job and the real cost of living, and what the real charges are and whether they are fair or unfair, and how they compare with the charges in the city; what these insurance charges are; how much money the company really collects in the month from the number of men employed. If they employ 300 regularly and have 600 to make up the 300, they must collect $600, instead of $300.

Rev. McGILL. Yes, sir.

Commissioner O'CONNELL. Has there been any investigation made in the State by anybody authorized or unauthorized that have any figures and facts' getting at the real situation?

Rev. McGILL. Yes, sir; there has been a good deal of study. ·

Commissioner O'CONNELL. There has been study, I imagine; but I mean are there any facts gathered in?

Rev. McGILL. At the last session of the legislature the matter was quite fully presented, and there was a bitter fight made on the employment agencies. As a matter of fact, this first-aid clause that was defeated by the employers carried with it the question of employment, very largely of private employment agencies, and has to do with the doctor's fee, and these things are all linked together in that they form a part of the money that comes to the company' here from the men.

Commissioner COMMONS. The question was asked by Mr. O'Connell as to whether any figures of their earnings had been collected.

Rev. McGILL. You have heard these men say that they work their mills 6 months in the year, or work 6 years out of 13, and that sort of thing.

Commissioner O'CONNELL. What I wanted to get at is this: If they agree to pay the men $26 a month, whatever the case may be——

Rev. McGILL. Yes, sir.

Commissioner O'CONNELL (continuing)——and his board?

Rev. McGILL. Yes, sir.

Commissioner O'CONNELL. Now, there would be reason to suppose at the end of the month he would get $26, but from what I ascertain from the testimony given, there is a little charge here and a little thing there taken out, and a little deduction here and another thing there, and all that sort of thing, and really he would not get anything at the end of the month?

Rev. McGILL. You heard Mr. Mack say they charged 25 cents for beds, and all those things are taken out.

Commissioner O'CONNELL. And the change of straw and hay, do they have an extra charge for that?

Rev. McGILL. I suppose so; ·

Commissioner O'CONNELL. There has been no investigation made to see' whether a man really, for that matter, gets an existence?

Rev. McGILL. That is all they do get.

Commissioner COMMONS. You spoke about the Rucker camp. Do any of these criticisms of yours apply to that camp?

Rev. McGILL. Well, the worst features are eliminated. 'In the first place, you must know that a man who goes around with a bundle on his shoulder, in the first place, loses his self-respect to a large extent, because—well, just because he does. The men go around with bundles on their shoulders, and they are not like other men.

Commissioner LENNON. He is a nomad?

Rev. McGILL. All right; he is also a menace to society for this reason: He is likely to carry disease. It is a wonder if he does not. Every one of them is a menace to society.

Chairman WALSH. The question is whether it applies to Mr. Rucker's camp, any of those conditions you mentioned.

Rev. McGILL. I don't think anything I have mentioned does.

Commissioner COMMONS. You have visited how many camps in this State?

Rev. McGILL. Oh, I have visited a lot—most of them.

Commissioner COMMONS. How many would you say there were you visited?

Rev. McGILL. I don't know of any other camps like Mr. Rucker's.

Commissioner COMMONS. I mean the total number of all kinds of camps in this State that you have visited—a hundred?

Rev. McGILL. Yes, sir; more.

Commissioner COMMONS. One hundred and fifty?

Rev. McGILL. Yes, sir; I think so.

Commissioner COMMONS. Two hundred?

Rev. McGILL. No, sir; probably not.

Commissioner COMMONS. Now, what number would be like Mr. Rucker's?

Rev. McGILL. I don't know of any other camps like Mr. Rucker's.

Commissioner COMMONS. He is the only one of that type you speak of?

Rev. McGILL. I would not say just that type, because there are better and worse.

· Commissioner COMMONS. His is the best?

··Rev. McGILL. His is the best that I know of.

·.Commissioner COMMONS. Then these points you make, these criticisms apply to others in different degrees?

Rev. McGILL. Yes, sir.

· Commissioner COMMONS. How many would you say are of the lowest type that you have described, including having all of these worst features, out of the 150?

· Rev. McGILL. Well, may I answer the question differently?

· Commissioner COMMONS. Well.

Rev. McGILL. The question of the attitude of the men, as I understand it, is largely the question before this commission, and the fact that the doctor's fee and the employment fee and these different fees are taken advantage of, is one of the reasons and one of the causes that there is such a large amount of unemployment all the time—such a large number of men that are unemployed. It is the prinicipal, as I understand it, the principal reason. This discontent applies generally to the whole situation, that of the camps and everything pertaining to the camp life. The fact that one camp is worse than another does not make so much difference. These men, however, are taken advantage of everywhere. When they come to the cities——

Commissioner COMMONS. Are they taken advantage of in this financial way by these deductions in Mr. Rucker's camp, that you speak of?

Rev. McGILL. I heard him say he employed the employment agency some.

Commissioner COMMONS. You are pointing out in his camp all the sanitary and physical conditions are all right?

Rev. McGILL. Yes, sir.

Commissioner COMMONS. The other things, these deductions and fees, and that class of deductions or payments, do they occur there the same as in the others?

Rev. McGILL. I am not prepared to state. I hadn't thought of that particularly. I don't know definitely now.

Commissioner COMMONS. Now, these 150 camps you have mentioned, what proportion of them are construction camps of railroads. How many of them are there in the State you have visited?

Rev. McGILL. There are not as many now as there have been, and yet there are still quite a good many of them.

· Commissioner COMMONS. How do they compare with the lumber and logging camps?

Rev. McGILL. They are worse, a good deal worse. The men sleep in the hay, they just simply have hay, they don't undertake to have mattresses or springs, they generally just have hay to sleep in.

Commissioner COMMONS. When you speak of the logging camps and the mills in the lumber industry, what is the difference between the logging camps and in the mills?

Rev. McGILL. The men generally sleep in their homes at the mills.

Commissioner COMMONS. Has it been altogether logging camps you are talking about?

Rev. McGILL. Very largely.

Commissioner COMMONS. And not the mill camps?

Rev. McGILL. Not so much.·

Commissioner COMMONS. You have visited them also?

Rev. McGILL. Yes, sir.

Commissioner COMMONS. How do they compare with the logging camps?

Rev. McGILL. Well, when they are camps they are much the same. I mean where they run eating houses, some of the mills don't have eating houses, some of the mills don't run boarding houses at all.

Commissioner COMMONS. What is your recommendation for relieving the conditions. What do you think ought to be done?

Rev. McGILL. I believe there ought to be a right for men to do more as they please. I believe there ought to be democracy everywhere. If the men want to form an organization, they ought to have the right to form an organization, in the first place. I don't think any man has a right to tell another man he shall not associate with his fellow men ·on any plan he chooses to. That is one of the worst features, it seems to me.

Then, I believe there must be a larger, that we must more nearly come to a proper division of the products of industry. These men see these other men getting rich, and exploiting our natural resources. As Mr. Mack said, anybody could go out on a shoestring and start a logging camp, and if he could get enough men to work with him and postpone their pay until he sells his logs, he can do well. These men see the other man getting rich and making large amounts of money, and they themselves in utter poverty, and as long as that condition exists there will be discontent.

Commissioner COMMONS. More specifically, what would be your next ground?

Rev. McGILL. Well, I have to mention those two things, that is all I have to mention.

Commissioner COMMONS. Your second thing involves a great many things. What would be your idea about employment offices?

Rev. McGILL. There is absolutely no excuse for the employment office. The fight was made for the employment office, not by the employment agents themselves, as was stated on the stand, but by the employers. The city of Seattle stands ready to furnish every man a job and every employer a man, but these employers won't patronize the city office at all, and the city has an office here that goes begging. A few women telephone saying that they want a man for a couple of hours to wash windows, and the city employment office gets that kind of a job, but when they want a large number of men, they don't go to the city office, and they don't in Tacoma or Spokane.

Commissioner COMMONS. Would the remedy be to abolish private offices altogether?

Rev. McGILL. Yes, sir; absolutely.

Commissioner COMMONS. How would you do that?

Rev. McGILL. Take the fee away from them, that would abolish it very quickly.

Commissioner COMMONS. What other remedy would you employ. How about the deductions from pay. Would you have any legislation on that subject regulating that?

Rev. McGILL. Why, yes, sir; I would do that and I would make it illegal for any man to employ a man without giving him a place to live. It is utterly ridiculous to think that these men should have to outfit at these places as they do, from the company's store, and they often go off, as is stated, and leave their things. Some men have too much pride to carry a bundle of old blankets and comforts around town with them, and they leave them in one place and have to buy them again in the next place. They hope to get something better, but they don't. I would make it incumbent upon every employer of labor to furnish a place for the men to live decently and respectably.

Commissioner GARRETSON. If such things were not available where the employment was?

Rev. McGILL. Well, but they are available.

Commissioner GARRETSON. At the logging camps?

Rev. McGILL. They could be made available.

Commissioner GARRETSON. I mean if he could not reasonably procure them for himself. You wouldn't make the employer in the city of Seattle, for instance, house his employees?

Rev. McGILL. Oh, no, sir; not in that instance, because that would not be necessary.

Commissioner GARRETSON. That is the point I want to get clear.

Rev. McGILL. Oh, yes; I see.

Commissioner COMMONS. Any other line of legislation or particular thing that you think woud remedy or help to remedy the situation you describe?

Rev. McGILL. It has occurred to me that the employment office—the employment business, could be conducted through our post offices. I don't know whether that is practical or not, but it has occurred to me that in our post office, organized as it is in all places, it would be a very small matter to have a place something like we have for money orders or something of that kind, that would give the facts relative to employment at every place that the Government has a post office. To look after employing the men and filling out application blanks, and men wanting work, all they would have to do in the way of looking after the business could be carried on easily. It could change this whole situation very largely.

Commissioner COMMONS. Do you think employment could be made more steady and the men would stay longer than these number of days?

Rev. McGILL. Yes, sir.

Commissioner COMMONS. By these methods you speak of?

Rev. McGILL. Yes, sir.

.' Commissioner COMMONS. Do you think it possible to have men with families employed?

Rev. McGILL. No, sir; you will find it right down here.

Commissioner COMMONS. By your remedies, I mean—by your remedies that you suggest do you think that there would be an increased proportion in the number of families?

Rev. McGILL. Yes, sir; I would just like to say, if you please, that there is a less willingness on the part of men to assume the family relations, and it has come to be really in a shocking condition here, because largely of such institutions as that at Grays Harbor that has just been described here. Now, you will find it a very common thing to see a statement that no married men are wanted where there are hundreds of employees, such, for instance, as up here at the tunnel. Now, a married man finds that there is a premium on being an unmarried man, and there is a good many men that either stay or get unmarried because it is more convenient, I suppose.

Commissioner LENNON. Mr. McGill, have you ever considered the necessity of State inspections for these camps and mills and construction camps, similar perhaps in character to that which is applied to the mines? Do you think that would be helpful?

Rev. McGILL. Why, I don't think so, because we have such inspections.

Commissioner LENNON. You do have such inspection?

Rev. McGILL. Yes; and I think that the inspection is made honestly, as far as it can be. As was stated here, the State labor commissioner has no funds at his disposal. He has no way of finding out anything except as it is volunteered to him, practically, I should say, at least to a very large extent.

Commissioner LENNON. Well, of course, if the State won't provide for a real inspection it is valueless. That is self-evident.

Do you want to ask any questions, Mr. Garretson?

Commissioner GARRETSON. Yes. Mr. McGill, if other employers in the lumber business would follow the same method of treatment with their men as is evidenced in the case of the Rucker Lumber Co., do you believe that they would discover, as Mr. Rucker states, that there is plenty of the best men on earth available?

Rev. McGILL. Yes; I think so.

Commissioner GARRETSON. Does the treatment—from your experience and investigation do you believe that the treatment that is received in the average camp of that character would make barbarians of men?

Rev. McGILL. No.

Commissioner GARRETSON. What?

Rev. McGILL. Such as the Rucker camp, you mean?

Commissioner GARRETSON. No, no; in the average camp.

Rev. McGILL. Yes, sir. It has done so with our men here.

Commissioner GARRETSON. It reduces every standard of the man who is so treated. In your opinion, is it the duty of an employer to safeguard his men against exploitation by others?

Rev. McGILL. Yes, sir.

Commissioner GARRETSON. Even though he has no connection in that exploitation himself?

Rev. McGILL. It is.

Commissioner GARRETSON. And has your experience and investigation led you to believe that somebody in the control of hiring and discharge of men is in collusion for profit?

Rev. McGILL. Yes, sir.

Commissioner GARRETSON. With those on the outside?

Rev. McGILL. Yes, sir.

Commissioner GARRETSON. You have expressed some opinions here founded on a statement of the facts as you have presented them. Is the knowledge of those facts, as you have recited them, the opinions founded upon that knowledge, and the open expression of those opinions one of the things that constitute the charge against the clergy of Seattle that you have heard made here, in your opinion?

Rev. McGILL. I am not real sure that I understand your question, Mr. Garretson.

Commissioner GARRETSON. We have heard it said that the clergy of this city are utterly undesirable from the standpoint of the man expressing the opinion. Is it on account of opinions like you have expressed here, and the expression

of them, as to the attitude of employers toward employees in many instances, that that opinion is held?
Rev. McGILL. I think so.
Commissioner GARRETSON. You think it is?
Rev. McGILL. Yes, sir.
Commissioner GARRETSON. I suppose you could accept philosophically, then, the denunciation?
Rev. McGILL. Yes, sir.
Commissioner GARRETSON. What has the church been able to do, or tried to do, in the amelioration of these conditions?
Rev. McGILL. Well, the church——
Commissioner GARRETSON. Remember, I mean by the use of the phrase " church," every phase.
Rev. McGILL. The church is placed in a peculiar position. These men themselves are mostly churchmen.
Commissioner GARRETSON. You mean the master or the man?
Rev. McGILL. The men that own the industries.
Commissioner O'CONNELL. They are churchmen, you say?
Rev. McGILL. Yes, sir; largely. Quite largely. They largely subscribe to and pay to the support of the church.
Commissioner O'CONNELL. Would you imply by that that they are religious men?
Rev. McGILL. Yes, sir.
Commissioner GARRETSON. Do you mean religious men or claim to be?
Rev. McGILL. Well, they are; I think they are religious. I think Mr. Paterson is a very religious man.
Commissioner GARRETSON. That is all, Mr. Chairman.
Chairman WALSH. That is all. Call your next.
Let us have perfect order, please.
Mr. THOMPSON. Mr. Marsh.

TESTIMONY OF MR. E. P. MARSH.

Mr. THOMPSON. Mr. Marsh, will you give your name, your business address, and your position?
Mr. MARSH. E. P. Marsh; address, Labor Temple, Everett; president of the Washington State Federation of Labor.
Mr. THOMPSON. Now, Mr. Marsh, certain questions have been sent to you. Will you answer them in your own way?
Mr. MARSH. Yes, sir.
Mr. THOMPSON. Without any further questioning.
Mr. MARSH. I have been asked the organization and purposes of the State Federation of Labor. The State Federation of Labor, as its name implies, is a federation of labor organizations of this State, comprising 252 local unions and trades bodies, central bodies, with an approximate membership of 20,000. I should judge this is about 50 per cent of the organizations, or rather the organized membership of the State within the federation.
I might briefly outline its purposes by saying they would come; possibly under three heads: For purposes of organization, for purposes of legislation, and for the dissemination among people of all classes of industrial education.
The activities of the federation since its formation in 1902 have possibly covered the field of legislation more than any other field. At every session of the legislature the federation is represented there either by its president of some other man in official connection, looking after the passage, aiding in the passage, of labor lgislation; also of social legislation proposed by ther bdies r by individuals in which organized labor may have an interest.
I might say that—well, I might enumerate very briefly some of the more important measures in which the federation has been instrumental in securing their passage. There has been no measure of labor legislation proposed either by the federation directly or by affiliated bodies or by the railroad brotherhoods that the federation has not taken an active hand in assisting its passage.
I think the pieces of legislation which stand out are, perhaps, the women's eight-hour law, the workmen's compensation act, the minimum wage for women and minors, the creation of a female deputy labor commissionership under the direction of the department of labor, the full train crew bill, the electric headlight bill, and, possibly more important than all of these, the passage of the constitutional amendment providing direct legislation.

I might say in passing that the federation of labor is the first body in this State that went into the legislature itself and actively began the fight within that body for direct legislation; that we followed it up from the time the fight was first commenced about eight years ago until two years ago, when the constitutional amendment was submitted to the people and passed and became part of the organic law of the State.

I have been asked to describe the general industrial conditions. ·I think, Mr. Chairman, that they have been quite thoroughly described. I think it would be a waste of the time of the commission for me to go into that any further.

Chairman WALSH. If you would just strike those things that appear significant to you.

Mr. MARSH. I will do that.

Chairman WALSH. You understand, that have not been covered.

Mr. MARSH. I will do that.

Commissioner LENNON. We have about 12 people to hear in less than an hour.

Mr. MARSH. I will pass the question of industrial dissatisfaction, inasmuch as it has been quite fully covered.

" Constructive proposals within the scope of the commission." It appears to me, Mr. Chairman, that one thing that we need very much is Federal legislation which will clearly define labor's rights, organized labor's rights. Every one concedes the right of labor to organize, but we want to know exactly what our status is under the law. What may we or what may we not do? May we peaceably picket? May we peaceably boycott? In short, may we do collectively what the law allows us to do individually, holding ourselves the same as individuals are held, amenable to the law for any attempt upon the life of people or upon property itself. It seems to me also—I am very much struck with a line of testimony that has been brought out at this hearing advocating some Federal laws in the matter of distribution of labor and distributing authentic information as to industrial conditions that obtain throughout the country. It seems to me that is quite necessary.

Also some gentlemen on the stand yesterday spoke of publicity being the remedy. I rather agree with them. For instance, if you will allow me to cite briefly, I believe that if a corporation is paying less than a living wage or only a living wage, giving as a reason that it is running at a loss, and we find that 50 per cent of its capital stock is water, and it is attempting to pay 6 or 7 or 8 per cent dividend upon the actual valuation of its property and upon that water as well, it seems to me that the people should know that. It seems to me that that is one of the causes of our unrest.

It strikes me also that we need some Federal aid in the matter of land development, the matter of placing people upon the land. The land question is too great for me to go into at any length. But let me tell you and assure you, Mr. Chairman, that in this city, and I think it is typical all over the State, that the longing for a piece of land is in the hearts of the people. They want a piece of land, but it is held by speculators out of their reach. The time was when a man could come West, as he was displaced in the East, and settle down on a piece of land. You can not do it to-day.

Now, on uncleared land a conservative estimate costs $125 to $150 to clear ready for cultivation. Your land ready for cultivation will cost from $250 up, according to the character of the soil, its closeness to transportation facilities, and so on. Your people are absolutely debarred from going on the land. And it seems to me, if some system—I haven't this worked out—but if some system of Federal farm credits might be taken up and worked out by Congress to assist the people upon the land and assist immigrants upon the land it would go a long ways toward solving that problem.

A great many of these questions you have asked have been answered by other witnesses.

Chairman WALSH. Wherever you think they have been fairly answered by other witnesses you may omit those.

Mr. MARSH. The workmen's compensation law has been covered. I have been asked what I consider a proper basis of trade agreement. In the first place, let me say I am a firm believer in trade agreements, in that relation between employer and employee. I believe, in the first place, that the conditions under which the men agree to work, and the employers agree to employ them, should be so plainly and definitely stated in that agreement that it will be difficult to misconstrue them on either side.

My experience has been that in many of our trade agreements provisions have been vague, have been liable to misinterpretation upon both sides, and that has brought a great deal of the trouble. The basis, of course, of the trade agree-, ment is arbitration. I have had some experience there; and I have found that the odd member 'of an arbitration board—this is possibly a theory of mine; it has been my experience—has been a very prolific source of trouble. I have an occasion in mind where in a certain mill in this State they are still fighting after a period of 10 days in an attempt to get together—they are still fighting over the selection of the third man of that board, the odd man. .·

It seems to me that it has been argued that were there an even number upon the board a deadlock would likewise result. I think that that chance would be very much more than offset by the feeling in the minds of both parties to a dispute that there was no use jockeying for position in the matter of the third man, that there was not any—that the disposition would be to settle down and grapple with the problems involved in the disputes. That is my opinion upon the trade agreement.

Now, just one word about the character of organization, administration, and the degree of democratic control. You have heard throughout these hearings a great deal about the arbitrary, dictatorial methods of what have been termed "labor leaders." I want to say that I do not believe there exists to-day an organization anywhere as democratic in its make-up, in its opportunities, as the trade-labor movement. It may be possible that upon occasions labor officials do abuse their power. I think you will find that in every case where this happens it has been because of apathy and inattention upon the part of the membership itself that allowed that condition to come. As a general rule it has been my experience that your labor officials have been but carrying out the policies determined upon by the membership itself.

I am acquainted to a degree with the constitution, laws, and internal workings of a great many organizations, and many of them use the initiative, referendum, and recall in the transaction of their own business, election of officers, and so on. And I want to repeat the statement that there is no organization that I know of that has the opportunity for democratic control and management nor that is so managed, as the trades-union movement to-day.

Just a word, and I think that will finish the line of questions that I care to take up your time with:

I have been asked the effect of immigration upon industrial conditions. There is no question in my mind but what that has a large and a very bad effect. We have coming into this country something over a million a year—coming faster than we can by any possibility assimilate. As a consequence we have had a glutted labor market—the labor market centered in your industrial cities. I believe the reports made to Congress during the debate upon the Burnett measure showed that less than 2 per cent to-day of immigrants arriving were going upon the soil. They were going to your cities.

I just briefly wish to call your attention to a few conditions that touch us directly here at home—that have a direct bearing probably upon our conditions of employment in this State.

We are on the border between Washington and Canada. We have several hundred miles of practically unprotected, unpatrolled border. I lived upon that border for four years, at one of your ports of entry. I know that it is the easiest thing in the world for people to simply step across from the Canadian side to the American side. No question but that they do it in large numbers.

Let me say—let me make this explanation, Mr. Chairman and Mr. Thompson, that the facts that I am giving you now I am not at liberty to give their source. However, this is true: The Grand Trunk Pacific Railway, which has been doing construction work for many months in Canada, in one day last spring discharged 2,700 men, all of them southern Europeans, of those nationalities, and the last heard of them there they were striking for the line.

Let me cite you another instance which is authentic, which happened during the year 1913. Upon a ship arriving direct from Italy were 85 Italians, who came in a body to Chicago. Upon arrival there they were met by one of their countrymen. Thirteen of them were brought by this Italian to St. Paul, there given transportation by the Northern Pacific to Puget Sound, taken in a body, the 13, to the Sumas division of the Northern Pacific, placed at work upon construction work. One of these 13 was later found in the reformatory and deported. The man who brought them through from Chicago; was a section foreman in the employ of the Northern Pacific. I cite that case to you. Our waters are scarcely patrolled, probably for want of money and men. There is no question but that men are entering this country illegally, although it is, probably hard for a layman like myself to produce the absolute proof to that effect.

Commissioner LENNON. Does this apply to Chinese as well as others?

‹ Mr. MARSH. To a lesser degree, I think, than it does to the Russians, southern Italians, and people of those nationalities, although there is no question but that Chinese are still coming across.

I want to give just one more illustration. Our facilities for handling immigration on Puget Sound are of the very worst. We have a wooden rattletrap which we call a detention station at Interbay, a station which was condemned in the most vigorous terms by Immigration Commissioner Caminetti in his report to Secretary Wilson of the department. Despite the fact that the Panama Canal is completed and the first ship, I believe, one of the first ships, goes through to-day, despite the fact that heavy immigration may be expected, there has not been one dollar appropriated up to this time by Congress for the erection of a detention station, for its equipment, and for its manning; nor, apparently, has there been any disposition to make such appropriation. It seems to me that must be remedied. Admitting, for the sake of argument, that the canal opening does not increase the total flow of immigration, yet it is true that some of the immigration now arriving at Ellis Island and Boston will be diverted to Pacific coast ports rather than to Atlantic coast ports. Testimony has been given many times, once by former Commissioner Williams at Ellis Island, that upon certain days at Ellis Island it is necessary to physically examine and pass 150 immigrants every five minutes to keep the entrance way clear. Now, all of you know that is physically impossible. We don't want those conditions upon this western coast, and we do need Federal aid in the matter of strengthening and preparing for the immigration service on the Pacific coast to cope with the immigration which may be expected.

I might state, as a bearing upon our industrial conditions of this tide of immigration, there is a little town north of us, about 5 miles this side of Everett, called Mukilteo. There is a large sawmill in that place erected some 10 years ago. This mill employs 105 Japanese, 73 Greeks, and 109 whites. It would employ, did they employ whites rather than the Japs and the Greeks, 100 more men, all probably married men, bringing the population of that town—increasing it from 250, its present population, to 750, giving these 100 men the average family of five. I just cite that as one direct condition that we are confronted with in this State because of that labor.

· Mr. THOMPSON. That is all, Mr. Chairman.

· Commissioner GARRETSON. Mr. Marsh, I should assume from the position you hold that you are reasonably familiar with the general conditions that exist governing employment as well as other features of the labor questions?

- Mr. MARSH. I try to be.

Commissioner GARRETSON. Has it ever appeared to you, or has any investigation led you to reach the conclusion that many employers give the preference to single men on account of the fact that the compensation act gives more money to the man of family in case of injury?

Mr. MARSH. That may be true, offset possibly by the law recently passed allowing the dependents of a single man to sue in case of death or injury.

Commissioner GARRETSON. Is that a modification of the compensation act?

Mr. MARSH. No; that is entirely aside from the compensation act.

- Commissioner GARRETSON. It gives the right of recovery in accord with the old liability law in case of the death of a single man?

· Mr. MARSH. I think, however, that the compensation act now knocks that out, except as applied to railroad men or men who do not come under the provisions of the act. This bill I speak of was passed before the compensation act.

Commissioner GARRETSON. That is all.

Chairman WALSH. That is all; thank you. Call your next witness.

⁶Mr. THOMPSON. Mr. Gilbert. [No response.] Dr. Berglund.

TESTIMONY OF DR. ABRAHAM BERGLUND.

Mr. THOMPSON. Will you give us your name, address, and profession?

. Dr. BERGLUND. My name is Abraham Berglund. I am assistant professor of economics, University of Washington. My residence, Seattle.

Mr. THOMPSON. You may answer the questions that have been submitted to you.

Dr. BERGLUND. I have not received any list of questions.

Mr. THOMPSON. Doctor, how long have you been here in that position? ˙

Dr. BERGLUND. I have been here about one year.

Mr. THOMPSON. I will just ask you one broad question which will include what you probably have to say to this commission. Have you given any consideration to the question of industrial unrest?

Dr. BERGLUND. Yes; I have given some attention to it.

Mr. THOMPSON. Will you give us your views as to its cause, if it exists, and the remedies you suggest to this commission?

Dr. BERGLUND. There are some things I should like to call the attention of the commission to.

Chairman WALSH. Will you please pick out those things in particular that are on your mind that have not been touched upon?

Dr. BERGLUND. That have not been touched upon. For four years I was special agent of the Bureau of Corporations at Washington, D. C., and there were certain things in connection with the work of the bureau that I think are not frequently considered in the matter of wage conditions. Now, we have organizations of employers, and organizations of employees.

For a part of the time that I was in the bureau we made some study of the lumber industry, and I did some work on the organization known as the Yellow Pine Manufacturers' Association. That organization was an organization of lumber manufacturers largely for the purpose of bringing about increased prices. At any rate the indications point to that purpose in view. Now, that organization was not friendly to organized labor. If any labor organization was developed in any part of the district covered by the yellow-pine district, information was immediately sent to the different members of that organization. You have this organization, used for the purpose of increasing prices. You have here an organization that favors increase in prices, but is opposed to organization for increase of wages or the maintenance of wages.

Now, coupled with that you have, in order to maintain prices, restriction of output. Now, this restriction of output did not mean reduction in the hours of labor; not at all. Now, in such a time as 1904, when there was restriction of something like 30 per cent in the lumber manufactures, it did not mean that the hours of labor were reduced; men were thrown off, and we have what is called a stiffening in prices. Prices are maintained and not only maintained, but raised. On the other hand, wages remain the same; the hours of labor remain the same. We have organizations of this character, not only in the lumber industry but in other industries—organizations for increase of prices and curtailment of output. If men are seeking work, they are told that there are not enough jobs to go around. As one witness stated before this commission, you have 16 men for 15 jobs. Now, it seems to me that we have a relationship between the curtailment of output and number of jobs. That is one point that I wish to call the attention of the commission to.

Commissioner GARRETSON. With that, Doctor, while wage was maintained earnings were largely decreased?

Dr. BERGLUND. Earnings were largely increased; yes, sir.

Chairman WALSH. Go ahead, Doctor. Is there something else you wish to say?

Dr. BERGLUND. There is nothing particular. I do wish to say that the unemployment committee, of which Mr. Lane was a member—I wish to say in connection with the number of the unemployed in Seattle there were estimates ranging all the way from five to ten thousand. There were some estimates more than double that.

Chairman WALSH. Any definite figures at all?

Dr. BERGLUND. No definite figures.

Chairman WALSH. Anything else you wish to suggest?

Dr. BERGLUND. There is one thing that was touched upon by one of the members of the insurance department. I have here some figures in regard to the burden of—this is taken from the second annual report of the insurance department for the 12 months ending September 30, 1913. Something was said by one of the witnesses to the effect that the employers are compelled to pay all this compensation. But when you consider the matter of burden you have got to consider not simply the amount paid in for insurance, but also the wages lost. Now, in this report you have the burden resting something like this: In the case of award from both temporary disability and permanent partial disability, the percentage of loss borne by employers, 28.3 per cent; the percentage of loss borne by employees, 71.7 per cent.

, Commissioner GARRETSON. And that does not take into consideration suffering and the social loss of the men in any degree whatever—the injured men?

Dr. BERGLUND. No.

Commissioner GARRETSON. That is only the actual financial statement?

Dr. BERGLUND. Yes.

.·.Chairman WALSH. That is all, Doctor; thank you. Call your next witness.

. Mr. THOMPSON. Is Dr. Strong here?

TESTIMONY OF DR. SYDNEY STRONG.

Mr. THOMPSON. Give your name and address, and your profession.

. Dr. STRONG. Sydney Strong; my residence, 508 Garfield Street; I am a minister.

Mr. THOMPSON. Doctor, in order to save time, as our time is brief, you have a list of questions, have you not?

Dr. STRONG. Yes, sir.

Mr. THOMPSON. Will you answer those in your own way?

Chairman WALSH. Those, Doctor, that you think have not been answered, and a statement of anything that you think is significant or that may be of information to us.

Dr. STRONG. Mr. Chairman and Mr. Thompson, I have been a listener all through the hearings, and I will try to speak simply of a few things that may have been omitted.

I happen to be the president of the Central Council of Social Agencies. I mention this because it suggests a form of organization that has been of a little help here in Seattle, not primarily, but secondarily, in industrial matters.

. The committee on unemployment referred to was appointed by our executive committee, and the chief of police turned to us to make the appointment. That is one little side product. We also held a conference on immigration for three days during the past year. Our organization is made up of agencies—over 50—with delegates from one to three from each one, and these agencies being as wide apart as commercial club, chamber of commerce, Central Labor Council, and various charity organizations, Municipal League, etc., the purpose being to bring about a better understanding through fellowship, through acquaintance, through a common program, and through trying to bring to the minds of all the fact that the interests of all the citizens are fundamentally one and that there is no room for division. I think perhaps that is all I wish to say about that. If I may be permitted, I will file this statement.

(See Strong Exhibit No. 1.)

Dr. STRONG. The second thing I should like to present, if I may, is some statistics which I have gathered in regard to Japanese as bearing on the industrial situation here in-Washington. I will not take the time, perhaps, to read them, but simply to say that in my judgment, after quite a long study, not as an expert, but as a student in Japan and here for eight years, the Japanese is by many of our citizens, I think, wrongly judged.

(See Strong Exhibit No. 2.)

Dr. STRONG. He comes to our shores and is an economic asset, to say nothing of other things. I bring out here the number of Japanese that are here in Seattle and in Washington.

. Commissioner O'CONNELL. Have you those figures in mind, the number that are here?

Dr. STRONG. Yes.

Commissioner O'CONNELL. What are they?

Dr. STRONG. You mean in Washington?

Commissioner O'CONNELL. Yes.

.· Dr. STRONG. The number of Japanese in the State of Washington in 1912 was 10,551, about half of these being in Seattle.

Commissioner LENNON. Do you indicate as to the comparison of their wages with the wages of white people?

Dr. STRONG. The comparison as far as I can learn at the beginning is lower, but that on the whole the Japanese is not a cheap man at all, and that he responds very quickly to our living.

. Commissioner O'CONNELL. Did you ascertain what number of these were working in houses, doing work that should be done by females?

Dr. STRONG. The number given here is laborers, farmers and gardeners, students, professional and business men, and miscellaneous. No, I did not.

Commissioner O'CONNELL. Would you think the miscellaneous would include house workers?

Dr. STRONG. House workers, I suppose, miscellaneous, 870.

Commissioner O'CONNELL. That would not cover it, then.

Dr. STRONG. I presume not. Now, the only other things I should like to speak of is in the way of general observation. My knowledge is general, not specific. I may say that by way of preparation I have been a fraternal delegate to the Central Labor Council here and in another city; so have kept in touch, I think, possibly a little above the average of my ministerial brethren, with labor organizations and labor conditions. I think I may say that the relationship in Seattle between the citizens generally and the labor people is unusually good.

I should like to mention one element that ought to be brought in: The cultivation of a better spirit of approach on both sides. I know that this is not very tangible, but in my judgment it is quite important. I may speak of it as an economic asset. If the approach on the part of employers and of the employees to one another could be changed the result that we are all hoping for would be gained.

Now, to be practical: Two things I should like to favor have been referred to by the commission. One of these things is to have in Washington, possibly, a duplication of the national bureau. A bureau that might be used for the collection of statistics, for bringing men together, for arbitration or anything of that kind, would be of the utmost benefit.

I should lay the responsibility of the introduction of a better spirit into the labor controversy—I should lay it upon the employer. I think the employer should as a rule take the initiative.

I should be willing to guarantee in our own city, for instance, that if the directors of the employers' association and the officers of the Central Labor Council would be willing to sit down twice a month around the table and eat together and talk over frankly and freely their differences, I think it would reduce 50 per cent the difficulties we have existing between them. It is the unwillingness on the part of men to come together frankly and fairly and talk over their differences in a spirit of friendship without suspicion—that has been, I think, a part of our difficulty.

I should place it upon the employer as a rule to take the initiative. There are fewer of them, and public opinion has led him to take the lead in years and ages past, and my judgment is that as a rule the labor people have been more ready to conciliate than the employer. The employer should then take the initiative and welcome approaches—although there has been fault on both sides.

My only contribution, apart from other things that have been said, would be that any method by the Government or by local societies that would introduce a spirit of conciliation between the parties, recognizing that their interests are fundamental, would be a very great contribution to our problem.

That is all, Mr. Chairman.

Chairman WALSH. Any questions? That is all; thank you, Doctor.

At this point the public hearings at Seattle will now finally adjourn. There will be hearings here on the question of the smuggling of Asiatics, if any, into this part of the country upon Monday and Tuesday, but those hearings are necessarily executive.

The commission is very sorry that it has not been able to hear even all of the witnesses who have been summoned, on account of the length that is necessarily given to those who have testified, so that those who have been summoned but have not testified, if they will call upon the clerk here, they will be paid their witness fees.

Mr. THOMPSON. I might suggest, Mr. Chairman, that if some of the witnesses have their statements here, they can be filed with the commission and form a part of the record.

Chairman WALSH. Yes; any persons who have any suggestions that they had intended to elaborate on the witness stand we will be very thankful if they will turn them over to Mr. Dower, the secretary, or send in to the commission at Transportation Building, Chicago.

Mr. THOMPSON. Yes; send them in to the commission at the Transportation Building, Chicago.

Chairman WALSH. Or send them to the headquarters of the commission at the Transportation Building, Chicago.

I want to thank the witnesses and the citizens of Seattle for the very kindly cooperation which the commission has received.

(Whereupon, at 12.15 o'clock p. m. of this Saturday, Aug. 15, 1914, the public hearings of the commission were adjourned to Portland, Oreg., and an adjournment for executive sessions was taken until Monday, Aug. 17, 1914, at Seattle, Wash.)

STATEMENT OF HAMILTON HIGDAY.

: The following statement was submitted in writing by Mr. Hamilton Higday, assistant secretary, Seattle Port Commission:

· I presume my name is among those in the printed list of witnesses, because for about two years I was industrial insurance commissioner for the State of Washington, and because of my advocacy of what is called in this State "first-aid" legislation. The term "first aid," as used in this State, means the cost of medical treatment required by an injured workman, and is not furnished by employers or the State at the present time, but such costs must be paid by the workmen themselves. Our workmen's compensation or industrial insurance act thus needs supplemental legislation.

In the second place, I have persistently pointed out that the largest social result of the workmen's compensation ought to be a development to a high degree of safety in industrial processes.

First aid and safety represent my contribution to the aroused social conscience in this State. Based on an economic need, they are now becoming political demand. My bringing those ideas prominently to public attention undoubtedly cost me my position as a State official. My study of compensation systems in Europe and the enactments of other American States, coupled with my day-by-day experience administering the new Washington work-accident system, led me to the profound conviction that ours is a one-legged law. The working people of this State so regard it. As conceived, it was a fine piece of social legislation; but as passed by the legislature under the whip of the big lumber interests, it is only a half loaf.

The working people want safety first. They only dimly perceive that it can be achieved. Compensation for a preventable injury is more than an insult—it is a social crime. I have persistently pointed out that over 50 per cent of industrial accidents are preventable. The statistics of great corporations like the Illinois Steel Co. and the International Harvester Co., which have carried on safety campaigns, prove this incontrovertibly, as does the notable work of the Minnesota Labor Department and the Wisconsin Industrial Commission.

Because of these ideas, I am regarded as an agitator, or at least an upstart or theorist, by organized employers. However, the ideas go marching on. They have become a well-defined demand of the people of our State.

In August, 1912, with the cordial support of the governor, the majority of the three members of our Industrial Insurance Commission (that is, John H. Wallace and myself) issued Bulletin No. 1, a safety bulletin, and ordered our traveling auditors to post it in mills and factories throughout the State. It was a fair and appropriate placard. But the manufacture member refused to allow his name to go on it, and the name was stricken from the proof after it came from the printer. His objection was that it would stir up the laborers; that the lumber crowd would not want any "agitation.' So Wallace, representing labor on our board, myself appointed to represent the public, or lawyers, perhaps, issued the bulletin anyway. The opening paragraph, signed by Gov. Hay, read as follows:

"Preventing of work accidents is of vital importance to every employer, every workman, and every other citizen of Washington. Reports have been received by the industrial insurance commission of 9,912 men and women killed, maimed, and wounded in our State in 10 months, October 1, 1911, to August 1, 1912, out of an industrial army of only 100,000 to 125,000—eight or ten men out of each hundred employed. One-half of the suffering and the human and economic loss due to accidents is preventable. A systematic study of accident prevention—guards, speed, spacing—by workmen's committee, safety engineers, and private investigators, can not fail to yield beneficial results, stopping a needless drain on the industries of the Commonwealth in compulsory compensation, saving to workmen hundreds of thousands of dollars in wage-loss and medical costs, and returning safe and sound to the wives and children and mothers the breadwinners, whose worth can not be computed in human symbols of value. Cooperation with the industrial insurance commission and the State bureau of labor to this end is earnestly urged."

You will find a complete copy of this bulletin at page 94 of the first annual report of our department, 1912. You will also find that meetings called to consider safety in industries and suggestions of cooperative action among employers were absolutely ignored. At about the same time we sent out the safety bulletin we also issued and mailed to the large employers, secretaries of labor unions, and the State press, a circular giving a clear-cut article written by Prof. John R. Commons on the working of the Wisconsin safety system, where manufacturers, workmen, and safety experts work together to standardize machinery and shop practices and the prevention of injuries. Laboring men in this State heartily approved the idea, but employers to a man, so far as I know, utterly ignored it. In September we issued a 16-page pamphlet on "The Treatment Cost of Work Accidents," an address of mine before the State Medical Society, delivered in April. These three things constituted what the organized employers considered "propaganda" by a State official.

In September, 1912, I was selected by my associates, Pratt and Wallace, to prepare the yearly report required by our law. The first annual report, a volume of 516 pages, is the result. On November 19, while the book was still in the press, a delegation of six representatives of organized employers came down to the State capitol at Olympia, and as Gov. Hay told me, demanded my summary removal—asked for my head "with all the assurance in the world" and insisted that two chapters in that report be suppressed. These were the chapter on safety, at page 87, and the portion upon first aid and medical attention, at page 208. Mind you, they never came near the commission to argue the matter; they never attempted to meet the economic problems discussed. They simply ordered the governor to swing the ax. Among the six were E. G. Ames, of the Puget Mill Co.; Charles Patten, of the Atlas Lumber Co.; the president of the Metal Trades Association; and the secretary of the State Medical Association, whose office is next door to Ames. Ames is a son-in-law of Walker, the San Francisco lumber baron, and the Puget Mill Co. owns hundreds of thousands of acres of timber and logged-off lands in Washington. They operate the great export mills at Port Gamble and Port Ludlow. They are notoriously opposed to selling land, opening up roads, or paying on such land taxes which smaller men would be compelled to pay if they owned it. They do not want a country to settle up because settlers increase the fire hazard to their timber holdings. The metal trades men you have heard through their spokesman, J. V. Paterson, of the Seattle Construction and Dry Dock Co. I want to say that small employers objected strenuously to being put in the same class under the compensation act as Paterson's company, because of its wide reputation for heavy percentage of accidents.

The State Medical Society is a close corporation, which the secretary boasts that he runs to suit himself. He opposed first aid in fear that its trend would be toward State doctors on salary, as in Austria, or a State fee bill, as under the Lloyd George Act in England.

Well, we had a hot time in the governor's office from 2 p. m. until sundown—not argument, but collision. I was a nonpartisan efficiency appointee from my first position as district auditor in Seattle, and I told big business in plain terms when it lied and where it got off. The governor did not remove me, and the report was printed. It speaks for itself.

Now, it seems to me significant and of interest to this Federal Commission on Industrial Relations that representatives of organized labor are willing to meet officers administering laws affecting labor and discuss fully their merits and defects, while employers, as a class, are not; that labor men treat State officers with respect and even deference; that at public gatherings—men and women—the ordinary citizens in cities are glad to learn from public servants of the problems that confront them, but organized employers persist in regarding any official who is not a known representative of their class as an enemy, to be branded "agitator" or at least "politician" and quite likely "socialist," to be ignored at all times except on occasions of necessary business contact and thwarted whenever possible.

As a clear statement of the Washington compensation system for injured workmen I desire to file with the commission a copy of an address delivered by me at Wenatchee in December, 1912.[1] I call your attention to the analysis showing that workmen are carrying two-thirds of the cost of work accidents in Washington and the employer only one-third. To bring the statement right

---

[1] An article entitled "Industrial insurance act, Washington State," by Hamilton Higday, from the Pacific Builder and Engineer, Aug. 30, 1913, was submitted in printed form.

up to date, I refer you to the second annual report, issued by the present State commission for the year ending October 1, 1913, at page 101, dealing with 1,503 cases, where the data on medical treatment was complete:

Wages lost	$107, 296. 67
Cost of medical treatment	36, 206. 80

Total loss to workmen	143, 503. 47
State awards (total loss to employers)	47,164. 20

Now, employers know mighty well that is not an equitable distribution of the burden. In fact, small employers all over this State who work by the side of their helpers think injured workmen's doctor bills should be paid. The big business representative merely gets mad if the subject is raised. I remember meeting three of the leading men of the Cement Trust of the coast at the Tacoma Commercial Club. They asked me how the new compensation law was progressing. When I told them workmen chafed when confronted with doctor bills as big or bigger than the State awards they immediately congealed—ignored my presence, not even politely. The fact that workmen find their awards about equal their doctor bills, unless they are under the coercive hospital-ticket system, makes them feel that the law is framed against them. An old engineer at Tenino told me it was "another corporation skin deal." The courts are denied to the workman who wishes to sue his employer; he feels he is ch■ted by due process of law. He sees the law, in which his award about equals his doctor bill, as a measure of absolute protection to employers, but not fair compensation to him; he regards it as an employers' insurance act rather than a workmen's compensation act.

Employers who object to medical treatment being furnished a man, in addition to a compensation award for maiming, suffering, and loss of time, either contend that our workmen are getting more on the average than they could under the old common-law system in operation before 1911, which is true, or that it would raise the cost to industries of Washington much higher than such action has cost in States in competition with Washington, which is not true.

In fact, Washington stands pretty nearly alone among the 22 or 25 American States having some form of compensation in its failure to furnish medical attendance. The National Civic Federation sent an able commission over the country to examine the workings of such laws. Their findings are published as Senate Document No. 419, Sixty-third Congress, second session, and show, according to the Federation Review:

"With a few exceptions, the States require that the employer, in addition to the compensation, shall pay the medical bills of the injured workmen, with certain restrictions. Outside of the State of Washington the commission found no sentiment opposed to this requirement, it being generally conceded that the workman is not only entitled to medical treatment in addition to his compensation, but that it is to the interest of the employer and society to see that he receives it, thereby to minimize the extent of the disability."

Our first Washington report, at pages 18, 261, 277, shows how favorably employers in our State fare as compared with others. So when the special committee of big business tried to suppress discussions of safety and medical treatment, they did a stupid thing. They tried the method of domination, which seems to be their reliance, instead of cooperation. The average employer refuses to resort to cooperation except for joining hands against the consumer in fixing prices. The attempt to dominate embitters young men of this generation. It is akin to the smoldering fires kept alive by militarism in Europe. So, when I was waited on last winter by a committee of the State grange and the State federation of labor and asked to draft an initiative bill on first aid for submission to the people at the general election this fall, I willingly prepared it. I desire to file a copy of that bill[1] and a copy of the argument also prepared to accompany it in the State pamphlet that is mailed to each and every voter in the State.

(See Higday exhibit.)

Every obstruction has been put in the way of this and six other bills, called "The seven sisters," initiated by labor and the grange, and the attorney general has been, to put it mildly, conservative about them. The "Stop! Look! Listen!

---

[1] An act entitled "Initiative measure No. 9" was submitted in printed form.

League," an employers' press bureau with a $500-a-month secretary, has filled the metropolitan dailies and the weekly press with advertisements and mailed pamphlets broadcast just to keep the people from expressing their opinion on these measures at the ballot box. And the " joker " in the initiative law prohibits me or a union secretary from paying a man $3 for a day's work in circulating a petition among workmen or office people or in the fields. Labor has to fight to be heard. No wonder the demagogue gets a following. I want to file with this commission a copy of one of the " Stop! Look! Listen!" pamphlets. It deals with first aid at page 14.[1]

I also want to file a pamphlet against the workmen's compensation law, prepared by J. V. Paterson;[2] also a copy of my reply to it, published in the Survey June 21, 1913;[2] also a published criticism of the present commission by Robin Adair, connected with the Seattle street department.[2]

Now, a word about the effect of compensation system on safety. I think the law makes for safety. The laboring people think that since the workman can not sue his employer, that employer grows indifferent and the accidents are increasing. I do not concur. We have never before had the machinery for gathering information and could not know the astounding number of accidents occurring in our industries. Workmen were unfamiliar with our law when it first went into effect. Many accidents were never reported. The increase of from 11,896 the first year to 16,336 the second year means two things: First, that more men have been employed under the law; second, that accidents occurring are more nearly all reported and tabulated. Employers will come to see that it pays to study prevention and will try to keep down the premium drain on their business that now goes into the State accident fund.

I think our safety campaign and the publicity has stimulated the State labor commissioner to develop the shop committee idea which we recommended, a first step to appreciation and adoption of the Wisconsin idea of cooperation for safety. Big employers in the Pacific Northwest have heretofore been fighting safety agitation. They have gotten rich quick in appropriating natural resources; a lumber plant at Everett with $200,000 invested cleaned up $40,000 last year and complained of poor business. They strenuously object to the rules of the game of business being changed. A public official or university investigator who opposes them is branded as an undesirable citizen. You have heard the State university called a breeding place for Socialists, but I am informed in the economics department of that university there is not a single Socialist. Will Lowman, the Anacortes fish canner, sat before you with red face and gritted teeth to condemn the whole State institution, but I want to tell you that the employees of Ed. Sims, Port Townsend canner, boss of our last legislature, and head of the " Stop! Look! Listen! League," and about whom Prof. McMahon testified, are bitter against him and his type; and Will Lowman practically ordered Commissioner Wallace off his premises when he called to examine his pay rolls and explain the compensation act. That is his fundamental respect for law.

The lumbermen, I was told by Mr. Pratt, my associate on the commission, who took pride in being their representative on the board, contributed $15,000 to Ernest Lister's campaign for the governorship in 1912. Mr. Pratt told me in November, after Lister's election by the accident of 700 votes out of 350,000 cast, that he had been a contractor and would " listen " to employers; that he had gone broke with liabilities of $62,000 and assigned for the benefit of creditors, and thus needed the job. When Lister was inaugurated, notwithstanding the many pressing labor problems in this State, he never mentioned one in his message to the legislature, and I was removed four days prior to the date I had set in my resignation, in the endeavor to discredit the first-aid movement. The official reason for that removal, filed by Lister with the secretary of state, was that he had consulted with my associates and found inharmony existed. Wallace and I worked as a unit; the only inharmony was that felt by the lumbermen's man. Furthermore, the governor had never consulted Wallace, and the State paper filed was a deliberate lie. The reason was not political; it was industrial.

---

[1] Pamphlet entitled " Plain Talk to You " was submitted in printed form.
[2] Submitted in printed form.

STATEMENT OF MISS ADELLA M. PARKER.

˙˙The following statement was submitted in writing by Miss Adella M. Parker:

A PLAN TO INAUGURATE THE SINGLE TAX WITHOUT INJUSTICE.

ˉ In order to inaugurate the single tax without injustice to any of the present owners it is necessary to accomplish only two things:
1. To compensate the present owners only, not their heirs.
ˉˉˉ 2. To compensate the present owners to the amount of their investments only, ˙ not the unearned increment since investment, nor any future expectancy.

As to the first contention, heirs have no title to property other than that which is vested in them by the inheritance laws. These differ in different States and may be changed at any time, and are in fact frequently changed. And from the social standpoint, the man who could leave his heir a world of free opportunity would be leaving him a far greater heritage than any fortune.

As to the second contention, no man can claim a vested right in a future increment, inasmuch as a change in the laws of his period may at any time divest him of this property, nor does society guarantee to him the unearned increment which has already accumulated. Witness the ruthless squeezing out of the " water " in the express stock, the falling prices of land in England, " prohibition," and the abolition of slavery.

Adjustment on the basis of the first principle would be technically simple. All that would be necessary would be to deny to corporations the privilege of owning land and to refuse to heirs the right to inherit any interest in land other than perhaps a preferred right of occupancy.

Adjustment according to the second principle would be more difficult on account of the possibility of fictitious sales, yet many conditions of land ownership would yield to taxation at full rental value with no injustice whatever.

For instance, the following owners could raise no cry of injustice were the State to-morrow to begin to take all the rental value of their lands:
1. Heirs to land.
2. Persons who have received land as a gift.
3. Persons holding lands who have already collected in net rentals the full value of the purchase price.

The above-named classes of landowners stand in the position of one who has been the recipient of generous favors which have finally been withdrawn.

There remains only the case of the purchaser who has not yet realized on his investment. Let him keep his rentals until he does. Where this can be determined, determine it; where it can not (through fictitious sales or " padded " record price), let him keep his rentals until the present value has been recovered in rentals, basing this value on the capitalization of the rental to the highest bidder for the year following the adoption of this act, and in any case limiting the privilege to 20 years.

While this compensation may be regarded as reasonable means of making the transition from an unjust to a just system of taxation in the case of land which is in use, no such generosity would be necessary in the case of land which continued to be held out of use. Therefore, the law should provide that the full rental value of land remaining unimproved should be taken at the end of a much shorter period, say 10 years.

While this plan is intended to avoid injustice to certain owners of land who have purchased in good faith, and especially to such as are dependent upon land rentals for their livelihood, the fact must be overlooked that the real compensation in a just system would, in fact, be to those who have in all ages been shut out from the resources of nature. Such apparent advantages as these, the dispossessed, receive from the enactment of so moderate a reform as is herein set forth, can but slightly offset the tremendous handicap which they and theirs have had in the past.

Two general plans may be suggested in accordance with the principles laid down above.

Plan No. 1.—Individuals and partnerships only shall own land, and the full rental value of any interest in land shall be taken into the Public Treasury upon the death of that owner who had the title of record on the date that this law goes into effect.

Plan No. 2.—Estimating the present value of land at 20 times its rental value in the year following the enactment of this law, let the owner of any interest in land, whether individual, partnership, or corporation, retain the rentals until these (net) equal this estimated value, but in any case no longer than 20 years; and in the case of land still unimproved at the end of 10 years, let the full rental value be collected from that time.

These plans have the advantage of compensation to actual owners only, in the first instance by not disturbing the owner's right at all, but by reasserting the community right in the land at his death, and in the second instance by giving to the owner merely the value of his land, not confirming to his heirs nor even to him any unearned increment whatever.

Observe that these plans contemplate changes in the laws of inheritance, corporations, and taxation, which are matters of State control.

Some additional details would need to be worked out.

Taxation.—As the present system of taxation would be changed gradually if the first plans were adopted, let all changes in the rate of taxation cr in the increase in the assessment fall on land only. As rapidly as the full rental value of lands come into the tax fund, let this be used to lower the rate of taxation on property other than land until this disappears. And later abolish all licenses and fees in the same way.

Fixtures.—Provide that improvements upon real estate shall no longer attach to the land, but may be removable or shall be compensated for at their appraised value by those who get the right of occupation, at the option of the owner of the improvements.

Rights of occupant.—All land shall be subject to rental to the highest bidder, the occupant at the time the law goes into effect, and any occupant of one year thereafter shall receive the first year a rebate of 5 per cent, which shall diminish by 1 per cent yearly until a rebate of 1 per cent is reached, which the occupant at all times retains.

Heirs.—The rights of occupation may be inherited.

Exemptions.—Whenever any land pays the full rental value to the State, the improvements thereon shall be exempt.

Homesteads.—Land not to exceed 60 by 120 feet in cities and 1 acre outside cities shall be deemed a homestead when it is a dwelling place of the owner and no more than five persons other than relatives and dependents dwell thereon, and when no business is carried on therein which employs more than five persons. Owners of homesteads may receive a rebate of 2 per cent below the highest bidder.

Mortgages.—Interest of mortgages is an interest in land to the amount of investment, and is to be treated as any other interest in land. Mortgages on land and improvements to be separate.

Transition pensions.—Persons above 50 years of age whose land becomes taxable at the full rental value may, upon application, retain for the remainder of their lives such a portion of their rentals as would equal $1,200 per year. All persons above the age of 60 years not in the above-mentioned class may receive $600 per year.

Training.—As a part of the program of a change in taxation, let the State provide four years' training to any applicant with support meantime.

This support may be merely the "cost of subsistence," for, incidentally, it may be noted that the true standard of income is what one can produce in free competition or in voluntary cooperation in a free society, but during the years of training the standard of living may reasonably be limited to the cost of living if it is furnished by another.

Inequalities in compensation resulting from the adoption of the above-stated plans need not disturb us, inasmuch as no inequalities based on these principles could possibly be as unjust as the present system.

SUGGESTED QUESTIONAIRE TO BE SENT OUT BY THE DEPARTMENT OF LABOR TO ALL SCHOOLS AND CIVIC BODIES.

[By Adella M. Parker, Seattle, Wash.]

The following questions are raised for the purpose of arriving at sound conclusions with reference to the problems which will arise from the influx of immigration to the Pacific States through the opening of the Panama Canal:

1. Will the expected increase in the stream of immigration to the Western States lower the standard of living of the American workingman if there is no social adjustment either through changes in the laws or changes in the industrial relations?

2. What do you think would be the logical effect of this immigration if no such social adjustment be made?

3. If no such social adjustment be made is any special class likely to reap benefits from this immigration?

4. According to the Secretary of Agriculture, only 16 per cent of the arable land of the State of Washington is in use. What is the most feasible plan of getting this into use?

5. There are less than 7,000,000 people in the Pacific Coast States. How many more people can these States support without lowering the present standard of living of the laborer?

6. Is any social adjustment possible that would make it unnecessary for the laboring man to seek to reduce the hours and to get increase of pay for less work?

7. Will a minimum-wage law, if accepted and carried out, raise the standard of living?

8. Is there any way by law to promote an increase of wealth by diminishing unemployment and developing resources?

9. What measures can be taken to prevent transportation companies from charging all the traffic will bear?

10. Are there any changes in methods of taxation which would tend to promote industry, destroy special privilege, and raise the standard of living?

11. Can the standard of living be raised with increasing wages and lowering prices at the same time?

12. Can prices be lowered and wages be raised at the same time?

13. What system of credits would render the invention of money more advantageous to the people?

    (1) State issue of warrants, as in Pennsylvania and Georgia a century ago?

    (2) Municipal warrants, as in St. Louis, Mo.?

    (3) City banking, as in Dusseldorf, Germany?

    (4) Rural credit, as in Holland?

    (5) Cooperative banking?

14. If, as some students insist, it is only monopoly which prevents the raise in the standard of living, can these monopolies all be included in the following five:

    (1) Patents?

    (2) Credit?

    (3) Franchise?

    (4) Trade?

    (5) Land?

15. Which of these monopolies can be destroyed by State authority?

16. Is there any way whereby the evils of patent and trade monopoly can be reached by State law? Or by industrial action, or by community action?

17. Will raising wages alone, or lowering prices alone, raise the standard of living?

18. What is the cause of unemployment?

19. Will the shortening of the workday raise the standard of living?

20. Would there be any harm in the labor of foreigners in this country if every one got the full product of his labor?

21. Is the cash girl as efficient in her position as any adult would be and even more efficient; and, if so, why are her wages below subsistence?

22. What fixes wages?

23. How much wages ought a worker to receive? All he produces? Why does he not get all he produces?

24. Can the fact of how much a man produces be determined in modern production? How?

25. Has an employer the moral right to make all he can out of his business? Has an employee an equal right to make all he has the power to make?

26. What determines the share which the landlord, the capitalist, the business man, and the laborer each receive out of the total product?

27. Would child labor be used if the child got all he produced?

28. What economic interpretation can be put upon a business which does not or can not support all the persons engaged in it?.

29. If the employees are working for less than they can live upon, who is subsidizing the business?

30. Under what circumstances should children go to work when they are unable to produce enough to live upon?

31. Upon whom should rest the responsibility of training children until they are able to earn enough to live upon?

32. Should a business subsidize its own apprentices?

33. How much wealth is society capable of producing at the present time? ɪ

34. What are the main wastes which are preventing the increase of wealth in this State?

35. When is unemployment a natural and logical condition?

36. Should there be a midweek holiday?

37. Is unearned wealth a demoralizing influence on the individual?

38. Why did we build the Panama Canal if it is going to lower the standard of living?

39. Could the Panama Canal be made the means of raising the general standard of living? How?

40. Why have not the invention of refrigerator cars and of labor-saving machinery generally raised the general standard of living more rapidly?

41. Why is it that when a country gets settled up—that is, more workers come in—poverty increases?

42. How does a man earn?

43. How much wages ought a man to earn?

44. What is meant by finding a solution of the economic problem?

45. If all immigration into the United States were stopped, would that alone solve the economic problem? Why?

46. Will that nation outstrip the others which first solves the economic problem?

47. When the question of immigration and the alien ownership of land are represented to be the economic problems, is not the true meaning that these will lower the standard of living; the real economic problem, then, is how to raise the standard of living. Should not the question be stated in this way: If immigration and alien ownership of land can be shown to lower the standard of living, should these not be prevented? If it can be shown that these could actually raise the standard of living for both the American and the foreigner, should they not be encouraged? If it can be shown that immigration with adjustment of our land question would in fact produce better conditions for all the workers, should this be encouraged?

48. Is the real economic problem the question of immigration or the question of the alien ownership of land; is it not really the question of raising the standard of living?

49. Would the American standard of living be safer if it were universal?

50. Can foreign immigration be made a means of raising the American standard of living, and, on the other hand, can it be made a means of lowering the American standard, depending entirely upon other conditions than the laborers?

51. Should the community furnish to every man a means of earning a living?

52. Is the Ford plan of bettering conditions a sound one?

53. Are the "business interests" of a workingman as important to him as are the "business interests" of a capitalist to him?

54. What is the program of the Socialist, the Single Taxer, the Anarchist, the Industrial Unionist, the Progressive, the Wilson Democrat, the Taft Republican?

55. What wealth is unearned?

56. Will cost rates for light, heat, transportation, water, and telephones raise the standard of living with no other adjustment?

57. Is charity sound economics?

58. Would frugality raise wages?

59. Effect of free land on the price of labor?

60. If all unoccupied land were accessible, would the lack of tools be an insuperable obstacle to production?

61. If risk in business were eliminated either by insurance or by State capitalism, would profit naturally disappear?

62. Does production for sale instead of production for use introduce "risk" into enterprise?

63. Does production for sale and its incidental risks produce waste?

64. Who are the producers of wealth?

65. What incomes are earned and what are unearned?

66. Is there a "double standard" in incomes—one standard for the manual worker and another standard for others?

67. If a man produces wealth on free land and gets it all and produces the same amount of wealth on owned land and gets a mere subsistence, which did he earn?

68. Would socialism destroy any other ambition except the ambition for special privilege?

69. Under what conditions would greater efficiency on the part of the workers raise wages and under what conditions would this greater efficiency lower wages?

70. In condemning a coal mine would the State be morally obliged to pay for more than the investment?

71. In condemning a railroad would the State be morally obliged to pay for the franchise as well as for the physical valuation (investment)?

72. Would the fixing of the rewards of labor under State socialism necessarily be arbitrary?

73. Is it possible to determine how much each one produces in modern industry unless we eliminate the privileges?

ADDITIONAL STATEMENT OF MR. HENRY PAULY.

I was taking care of the unemployed here (in the city of Seattle) last winter and I went to see the secretary of the chamber of commerce to get some assistance in securing employment for the men, and the secretary of the Seattle Chamber of Commerce told me at that time that the chamber of commerce did not want the working classes in the city of Seattle at all—that they had no business here—and refused to help me in any way in securing employment for the men.

.The International Itinerant Workers' Union last winter took care of the unemployed in the city of Seattle. We gave lodging to 33,954. We gave 73,046 meals to the unemployed here, and tided these men over until they secured work or were able to go elsewhere.

(This I omitted in my testimony of to-day.)

HENRY PAULY.

Dated at Seattle, Wash., this 12th day of August, 1914.

ADDITIONAL STATEMENT OF MR. FLOYD L. DAGGETT.

INDUSTRIAL INSURANCE COMMISSION,
Olympia, Wash., August 19, 1914.

Mr. LEWIS K. BROWN,
Secretary United States Commission on Industrial Relations,
Chicago, Ill.

DEAR SIR: After the testimony given by Mr. Daggett, chairman of our commission, at the hearing in Seattle, August 14, followed by testimony of Mr. J. H. Wallace, ex-member of this commission, in which Mr. Wallace took occasion to make allegations of maladministration against the present members of the commission, I requested from Mr. Thompson, your counsel, permission to file additional statement with your commission as part of the records, which permission was granted.

We do not believe that your commission is interested at all in any personal matters pertaining to either Mr. Wallace or the present members of this commission, and are interested only in the question of the administration of the workmen's compensation department and whether, in your opinion, it is being administered fairly to the claimants. Mr. Wallace was allowed to file a copy of his letter to Gov. Lister, under date of February 28, 1914. We are filing herewith copy of letter of Commissioners Ernst and Daggett to the governor upon the same subject. These letters were induced by a communication from the governor asking us to state our views of the workings of the department and as to what reason, if any, existed for the disturbance of the previous harmonious action between the commissioners. We, as you will note, submitted our letter 19 days previous to Mr. Wallace, so we had no means of knowing the contents of his communication, and I am quite sure that he did not know the contents of ours when he wrote his, therefore, they are not in a sense, a reply to each other.

I wish to add, and I do not think it was brought out in the testimony of myself or Mr. Ernst, that practically all of our settlements are based upon a doctor's certificate, and when there is any complication in the injury, or doubt as to the result, we usually have more than one doctor examine. We wish to disclaim vigorously the assumption or insinuation on the part of any one that this commission is biased against the claimants, or are not giving them all that is possible under the present act. We have refrained from injecting politics into the administration of the department, either in its administrative or claim-adjusting features, and statements to the contrary are from political motives.

The writer was present at practically the entire hearing at Seattle and can readily understand how difficult it is for your commission to segregate real information from that which is biased. It is natural that one looks at a question from a biased standpoint, but we heard so much testimony given with an evident view to prejudice the conclusions of your commission, and this was not confined to any particular set of witnesses.

In connection with the statement herewith filed, wish to direct your particular attention to the testimony of our Mr. Ernst, in which he more fully went into some of the matters under discussion by Mr. Wallace.

Thanking you for your kindness, and adding that we are ready at all times to give your commission any further information that you may desire, I beg to remain,

Very truly, yours,

FLOYD L. DAGGETT, *Chairman.*

_____

OLYMPIA, WASH., *February 9, 1914.*

Hon. ERNEST LISTER, *Olympia, Wash.*

MY DEAR GOVERNOR: We have your recent favor requesting statement from us as to the condition of the industrial insurance department, especially as regards statements contained in the newspaper reports of an address given by Commissioner Wallace at Raymond recently, it being the meeting of the State federation of labor.

One of the statements therein was that the present commission had emasculated the workmen's compensation act. We do not quite know what he means by that statement, but a few days later in conversation with us in the office here, he made specific statements that we were not giving the claimants due consideration.

(2) That we were bargaining with the claimants instead of awarding them what were their just dues.

(3) That our sympathies were always with the employers and the workman did not get his just rights; and that the burden of proof in every instance would be thrown upon the workman, who was not in financial position to make such proof.

(4) That he was being ignored in the business of the department by the other commissioners.

Heretofore he has objected to the one-signature system that we are now using in handling claims through the office; to the single blank furnished for employers' and employees' reports, and also to the discontinuance of the follow-up letter, No. 22, or employees' reports in trivial injuries. We will take these up in the above order and submit the following for your consideration:

When we became members of the commission, it had been customary for the commissioners to sit around the executive table, and one of the commissioners would examine the claim files to see if the claim properly came within the scope of the law; it would then be signed and passed to another commissioner, who would append his signature and then passed on around the table, occupying the time of the commission for two or three days a week; then at the latter end of the week, the commissioners would take two or three claims and go to Seattle or Tacoma and spend Sunday, and come back Monday morning and be ready for business about Monday noon.

At that time, when the commissioners were considering these claims en banc, they had before them the findings of the claim and medical departments, and no other information upon which to base their conclusions. It resolved itself into a perfunctory performance as witnessed by the present chairman during the month of April while Mr. Pratt was still on the commission. At the present time, unless some extraordinary matter calls us all away, one commissioner is in the office all the time, and such commissioner, whoever he may be, appends his signature to the findings of the claim and medical departments, after he has examined the claim to see if it is complete and that the facts warrant the conclusion of the two departments; then, in executive session, each week, with the full commission present, these claims are formally approved, but in the meantime the work of the department has been facilitated and expedited, so that at no time is the work in any of the departments congested, and the time of delivering the warrants to the claimants has been reduced from 8 to 12 days in each case.

As long as the above plan meets with the legal requirements and so greatly facilitates the work of the office, and the time of getting the money to the claimants, and at the same time has allowed two commissioners the balance of the time for work in the field, it has occurred to us that it was not only business, but is also a considerable money saver in the operating expenses. The claims that have been handled by the one-signature method are what we determine routine claims; that is, they require no special investigation, the reports of the employer, employee, and doctor agree as to time loss and injury. All claims that present special features requiring special investigation are held up for consideration by the full commission, or are passed to one of the commissioners for personal investigation; or a special examination is ordered before one of the special medical examiners in the field. We can not see where any claimant has received any injustice from this method.

Mr. Wallace's contention is that he knows of cases where offers of settlement have been made for less than the amount awarded as recommended by the examining physician, or our medical department, and that different amounts would be offered from time to time until a settlement was reached; in other words, the accusation would mean that we endeavor to settle with a man as cheaply as possible without going into the merits of the case. If there has been any case of that kind, it has not come to our knowledge, and frankly, we do not believe that any authentic cases can be shown. In clearing from 1,000 to 1,200 claims per month, it would be extremely improbable that no error of judgment would occur, but to say that anything of this sort is intentional on our part we are quite free to say to you, sir, is not in accordance with the facts.

The large amount of claims passing through this department, and in many instances the small compensation that is awarded by the law not being sufficient to pay a man's doctor and other expenses, claimants become disgruntled, and are apt to make statements that, through ignorance or otherwise, are not in accordance with the facts. For instance, claimants will sometimes go from one commissioner to another endeavoring to quote what has been said to him, expecting to get a better settlement. However, it is the intent to award a man the amount his injuries merit under the schedules and compensation provided by law, and in nearly every instance this amount is determined by competent medical authority, and not by any individual judgment of some layman, even including the commissioners.

A perusal of our second annual report will show that the amount of days awarded per claim has increased, and the amount paid per claim has increased, and the appended table will show that the amounts paid during the past year is in excess of the amount paid the preceding year by the former commission. It would seem to us that this would be competent testimony to show the inaccuracy of that accusation, and while it is a difficult matter to reply definitely to such a general statement, we wish to say that your commissioners are not conscious of that fact, and while we endeavor to adjust the claims strictly upon their merits, whenever there is a question of doubt we always give the claimant the benefit, believing that through his unfamiliarity with legal and industrial conditions he is less liable to make his case clear than the employer.

Further evidence is that when the present commissioners came in charge of this department there were a large number of appeals and cases set for court trial which have almost entirely disappeared. Attorneys sometimes come with their clients before the commission, and quite as often send their clients to the commission without appearing personally, believing, seemingly, that they will receive the attention merited by their claim.

Mr. Wallace has not been ignored in the workings of this department, except that upon his own request, made when the other two commissioners were appointed, that he, being the political minority member of the board, did not desire to have any part in any changes or appointments to the personnel of the staff. In every other instance that we can now recall, when Mr. Wallace was here where he could be advised, he has had a full say in matters coming up before the commission, but in this instance we beg to call your attention to the fact that owing to his operation and succeeding disability he took no part in the deliberations of this commission from some time in July to the latter part of September, 1913, and since that time has been devoting the majority.of his time in preparing and making addresses before various bodies.

In addition to other duties, a perusal of the files will show that from May, 1913, to January, 1914, Mr. Ernst and Mr. Daggett have personally investigated and adjusted 654 claims, and Mr. Wallace 98. These adjustments have all beeñ made on outside trips, meeting the claimants personally.

We have endeavored to acquaint ourselves with the various phases of the operation of this department and familiarize ourselves with both the office and field work, and feel that we have done so. We think you will find that has not been the case with the other member of the commission. We believe that to-day there is a better understanding and more harmonious feeling between the employers, employees, and claimants than existed in April, when the present members were appointed by yourselves. The fact of the scarcity of appeals and the small amount of correspondence regarding adjustments will serve to indicate that this is a fact, in addition to what is said to us personally.

Referring again to the number of claims personally adjusted by the commissioners, we wish to say that these are the claims set aside for personal investigation and the list was as available to Mr. Wallace as to the other commissioners.

We are inclosing herewith statement of the secretary which goes into the various methods employed to expedite the work of the office, such as the single-blank proposition, the change in pay.roll, etc. We think you will remember. the discussion on the single blank when the executive board of the State Federation of Labor met last December in your office. As stated by the secretary, we are now using in addition to the single blank a separate workman's report which is available at the plant of the employer or at suboffices of the commission to any claimant who desires to make his claim that way.

The discontinuance of the follow-up for the No. 22 blank was also discussed in your office at this same meeting, and Mr. Wallace requested that we return again to the follow-up system. A perusal of the secretary's report will show you that there has been nothing gained by this, and by the continuance of the follow-up system the correspondence of the office has been materially increased. However, rather than do any injustice to any claimant we are now following up and asking for the workman's report in case it has not been previously filed.

To the complaint that the burden of proof is always put upon the workman, who is in no position to stand the financial or other expenses and inconvenience in substantiating his claim, wish to say that when a claim is presented it comes before the claim department, then to the medical department, and then to the commission, going through several hands in each department, where the facts are carefully weighed before reaching the commission. Now, when a claim is before the commission it must either be paid, specially investigated, or rejected. We do not believe it is the intent of the law that we take the position that Mr. Wallace has taken the last few days (which we never heard him take before that time), that where there was doubt about the legality of the claim or that the claim came within the scope of the compensation act it was the duty, of the commission to pay the claim and let the employer protest and appeal, throwing any expense incidental thereto to the employer. We interpret 'the law to mean to decide these claims without reference to the individuals in the case, and where we believe a claim does not come within the act it should be rejected, irrespective upon whom the burden of appeal would rest. We do not knowingly construe the law to the benefit of either employer or employee against the interest of the other, nor do we shirk the responsibility of a decision imposed upon us by the law.

In conclusion we wish to reiterate that we do not believe that any authentic cases can be produced to substantiate the purported accusations of Mr. Wallace in his Raymond speech or that he made to the other members of the commission one day last week. Further, we desire to say that we never knew of these contentions until just prior to the meeting of the Federation of Labor which convened in the city of Seattle in last December. Up to that time Mr. Wallace had seemingly acquiesced in the methods adopted by this department, and to that date had never made a suggestion to us concerning any of these matters of which he has just recently complained.

Therefore, as we have not changed our attitude toward the workingman, we can scarcely understand why the difference in the attitude of Commissioner Wallace has taken place. We believe that it is due to outside influences inci-' dent to the opening of this year's political campaign. The commissioners signing this statement have no political or other ambitions which they intend to further through the operations of this department, and have only the one aim in view—to give their very best services for the benefit of the people of the State of Washington, and are absolutely free from ulterior motives. In this statement we have endeavored to discuss every objection or complaint that is now known to us. If anything further is alleged, we would be very glad to have the opportunity to make a statement thereon. We have no personal feelings against Mr. Wallace nor against anyone else, and if he can work with the other commissioners as he did prior to December, 1913, we can still continue as harmoniously as could be desired.

There has been absolutely no friction between the two members signing this statement. We do not always agree as to our views regarding matters, but can freely and frankly discuss them with each other and arrive at a harmonious conclusion, and are working with full confidence in each other and with the utmost frankness. We believe that this condition should prevail among all the members of the department as it does exist among the employees. When we became members of this commission we found it more or less disorganized; there was friction between the secretary, chief of the claim department, and chief auditor—practically three separate institutions running under one department—more or less friction with the auditors in the field, and also with the field members and the office. Many changes had to be made in order to straighten these matters out, but we believe to-day that our department compares favorably in harmony, efficiency, and enthusiasm with any mercantile or corporate establishment in the State, public or private.

Respectfully submitted.

FLOYD L. DAGGETT, *Commissioner.*
A. B. ERNST, *Commissioner.*

ADDITIONAL STATEMENT OF COL. ALDEN J. BLETHEN.

The following supplemental statement was submitted in writing by Col. Alden J. Blethen, editor of the Seattle Daily and Sunday Times:

Answering the comprehensive question put to me by Examiner Thompson at yesterday's hearing, to wit, " What, in your judgment, is the cause of the great unrest now prevailing and what are the remedies? " I beg to submit the following statements in answer to the dual question and will segregate the same into two parts:

First. " What, in your judgment, is the cause of the great unrest now prevailing? "

Responsive to this question, I desire to say that in my judgment there are three most prominent and prevailing causes, to wit:

(1) The persistent and insistent enforcement of the antitrust law (Sherman) during the last decade.

(2) The enactment of the Underwood tariff law, whereby an entirely new schedule was created covering imports.

(3) The refusal of the Interstate Commerce Commission for a long period to grant to railway companies the right to increase their tolls in order to meet existing conditions.

Discussing these propositions in order, permit me to call attention to the following facts, which I believe are universally admitted:

(a) It is almost a truism that capital is timid, fearing to venture into new fields or take any action that carries risks of any kind.

(b) The persistent hammering which has been carried on against alleged trusts, in which enormous capital has been invested, and so done by several administrations, so that it is not a political proposition, has caused capital not only to halt but to retire—go into hiding and refuse to be active.

(c) Since activity of capital is absolutely necessary to the employment of labor, it follows as a sequence that when capital is halted labor must suffer.

When the enforcement of the Sherman antitrust law was put into operation, there was invested in the United States in various combines thousands of millions of dollars—and the holdings of these combines were widely scattered throughout the world—reaching out not only to the man of large means but to the ordinary ·investor—the man or woman seeking a better dividend than the savings banks or the municipal bonds paid—with the opportunity of an increase in value of the stock held, thereby gratifying that disposition residing in almost every human heart " to take a chance "—a desire to speculate—to have one's capital increased through the activities of a great number of people rather than through the activity of the individual owner.

The first successful dissolution of a trust or a combine at once caused fear and trembling to the holder of the stock of that organization and caused a consideration of the outcome of the investment when the law declared it to be illegal.

The continued activities of the legal department of the Government in putting all of these alleged trusts and combines out of business or segregating them into individual corporations and relegating them to various localities in different States has all the while had the effect of intimidating the investors and making them fearful that schemes of that character would ultimately cause loss, if not complete destruction of the investment, and hence the creation of a fear against all kinds of corporate activities.

The consequence has been that capital has halted; money has sought investments in gilt-edged securities and low-rate interest as a substitute for stock in corporations of an industrial character.

The result necessarily has been a curtailment of extension by all large corporations—a withholding of the increasing opportunity for fear it may find itself in the clutches of the law.

In other words, great business has been hampered and almost throttled by the continued enforcement of a law which was ambiguous in its terms and because of its nonenforcement for years after its enactment led many men to take steps that afterwards put them in the position of being violators of that law.

All this, of course, has curtailed industrial growth everywhere and caused reductions little by little, until a very large amount of capital has become inactive in the industrial world, with the result that thousands upon thousands of laborers have suffered by loss of work.

THE EFFECTS OF THE UNDERWOOD TARIFF LAW.

This statute has been in active operation now for a period of nine months, and within that time we are told by the Bureau of Commerce and Labor that exportations of American products have decreased $212,000,000, the segregation being as follows:

Exports of partially manufactured materials	$30, 000, 000
Exports of raw materials	32, 000, 000
Exports of finished manufactured products	51, 000, 000
Exports of foodstuffs	99, 000, 000
Total	212, 000, 000

It may yet be said that the exportation of foodstuffs has not been affected by the tariff to any considerable extent, and therefore the net loss by reason of the tariff may be reduced to $111,000,000.

Another statement furnished by the same authorities shows that in the months of April, May, and June—the last three of the fiscal year—the imports increased almost $83,000,000 while the exports decreased over $76,000,000, making a grand total of almost $160,000,000 in both imports and exports during a period of only one-third of the time since the law went into effect.

Of course, it follows without argument that when the United States permits either one hundred millions or one hundred and sixty millions worth of products to be imported from foreign countries instead of being manufactured in the United States, it deprives the laboring man of this counttry of just that amount of wages which enter into the production of these goods as labor.

Continue to extend this for a series of years, and this country will be substituting the product of other nations, where men and women are paid a less wage, for the product of this Nation; and every time a dollar is expended in Europe for that which we wear or consume in America, every time a dollar will be taken from the American laborer.

INTERSTATE COMMERCE COMMISSION DELAYS.

Without any desire to criticize a great national commission which has undoubtedly produced a great deal of good to the country, it is apparent now and was prospectively apparent for a good while that the long delays of the Interstate Commerce Commission in permitting railroads to raise their tolls for freight especially has caused tremendous stagnation in the railway business.

The decision rendered by that body within a week, whereby on the same amount of freight carried last year an increased income will be received exceeding $47,000,000 is positive evidence that the railroad officials were right in making their demands and that the commission has put thousands upon thousands of men out of work because they have so long withheld this now granted privilege.

One has only to observe that these railways, during this interim, have made practically no extensions of lines, have not added to their rolling stock, have not kept up their proper repairs, but have just lived from hand to mouth waiting the action of the Interstate Commerce Commission in behalf of increased toll.

If this opinion had been rendered one year ago, then at least $40,000,000 would have been expended in improvements, which would have gone almost entirely into industrial lines and kept in employment thousands upon thousands of men who have been laid off because the railroads did not dare to undertake this additional expenditure without the right to earn the money with which to liquidate the same.

Observe that this position of the Interstate Commerce Commission relates to a very small portion of the United States in territory, though it may comprehend one-half of its railway system. Therefore, if similar treatment be accorded to the rest of the railroads in the United States, and done so speedily, there is no reason in the world why the railway companies of this country will not expend one hundred millions of money within the next 12 months following their right so to do.

While I have no exact statistics from which to quote, it is commonly reported that throughout the United States more than a quarter of a million of railway employees of every character have been laid off, thereby being deprived of their ordinary earnings, and almost entirely because of the refusal of the Interstate Commerce Commission to grant to the railroads the right to earn money enough with which to make the necessary improvements, extensions, and repairs which their business requires.

WHAT ARE THE REMEDIES?

Coming to the second part of Examiner Thompson's question—"What are the remedies?"—I have repeatedly expressed the following opinion editorially in The Times:

The enactment by Congress of an affirmative or positive law touching the subject of great business, so that every body of men who desire to enter into industrial activities may know affirmatively what they can do without jeopardizing their liberty and involving their property in litigation.

Because of the continued prosecution of capital by the legal department of the Government, business men are in great doubt as to what they can legally do with their money, and especially that class of business men who always desire to live within the law.

If Congress is willing that a dozen men living in as many States shall put together an aggregated capital of $1,000,000 and enter into an industrial undertaking that promises to pay more than the ordinary interest received from bonds of first-class character, and yet by reason of that aggregated capital will be able to manufacture larger products than a single individual can do with $100,000 capital, then let the law say that they can do it in plain language.

Taking this as an example, let the law affirmatively tell all kinds of business what it can do and still live within the law, so that every man who is competent to enter business may thoroughly understand his rights from the plain reading of the law.

Then, as a sequence to this, let the Government of the United States call off this legal warfare against capital and say to the world that it is going to rest on the victories it has won and see if the examples which it has made will not be sufficient to prevent other men violating even the Sherman antitrust law.

The instant that capital is invited by a national law to come out of hiding and undertake great activities under a law that will protect it from being constantly attacked and ultimately destroyed, then capital will once more seek investment in this country, existing industries will be increased, new ones will be built up, and the great mass of the unemployed of the United States to-day will resume employment as they had it for so many years prior to the active enforcement of the Sherman antitrust law.

Respectfully submitted.

ADDITIONAL STATEMENT OF DR. ABRAHAM BERGLUND.

UNIVERSITY OF WASHINGTON,
Seattle, August 25, 1914.
UNITED STATES COMMISSION ON INDUSTRIAL RELATIONS,
Transportation Building, Chicago, Ill.

GENTLEMEN: With your permission, I should like to substitute the inclosed written statement for the testimony which I gave at your hearings in Seattle. The transcript of my testimony does not bring out the meaning which I intended to convey. On account of the pressure of time and the confusion which prevailed in the room when I testified, I did not express myself as I should have done under ordinary circumstances. The written statement covers only those points which I intended to bring out in my testimony.

Respectfully,

ABRAHAM BERGLUND.

For four years I was a special agent of the Bureau of Corporations at Washington, D. C. In connection with my work in this bureau I came across certain things which, it seems to me, have a bearing on wage conditions, and possibly on unemployment. In the lumber industry, of which I made some study, we have associations of manufacturers formed largely for the purpose of maintaining or increasing prices. This purpose is usually denied by the members of such associations, but the evidence secured by the bureau was practically conclusive that this aim was in view when many of those associations were formed, and that they were effective in increasing prices far beyond what the natural conditions of supply and demand in the lumber industry would warrant. This evidence has recently been published in Part IV of the Commissioner of Corporations' Report on the Lumber Industry.

While these associations were putting forth their efforts to augment prices there was often evinced in their correspondence a tone of deep hostility toward trade-unions. In the case of at least one association, when any labor organization was formed in any part of the district in which its members conducted their operations word was promptly sent to all members directing them to watch their employees. Thus while we had organized efforts to increase prices and profits on the part of the manufacturers—and that in violation of law—similar efforts on the part of employees to raise wages or in other ways better their economic condition—though perfectly legal—were frowned upon, if not positively resisted. In the report of the commissioner of corporations just alluded to, the commissioner in his letter of submittal states that between 1897 and 1907 the prices of lumber increased from 80 to 200 per cent. Any such increase in the prices of commodities in general without a corresponding increase in wages must mean a decided lowering of our boasted American standard of living.

In order to increase prices output was often limited. Restriction of output in the lumber industry did not mean reduction in the hours of labor. The hours of labor remained as usual, but numbers of men were thrown out of employment. It was stated before this commission that one difficulty in the labor situation is that there are not enough jobs to go around. As one witness put it, there are 16 men for 15 jobs. When there is such organized effort to limit output in order to increase prices there must be at least some curtailment in the number of jobs to go around. Of course, it is difficult to draw very definite conclusions on this point, but I think it is not amiss to say that the problem of monopoly— the artificial restriction of output in order to secure abnormally high prices—is to some extent related to the problem of unemployment. In 1904 in the yellow-pine region the lumber manufacturers by general agreement reduced their output some 30 per cent. The percentage of workmen discharged during this period of curtailment was probably not less than 30 per cent. While this reduced output was in part necessitated by the industrial depression of that year the upward tendency of prices which immediately resulted and which went far beyond the prices prevailing before this curtailment was agreed upon showed that this restriction in production was much greater than necessary. While the manufacturer profited by higher prices the workman got no corresponding increase in wages, and his field of possible employment was restricted.

Another matter of which I should like to speak is the relative burdens borne by employers and employees on account of the workmen's compensation law of this State. The burdens of industrial accidents are not borne entirely by the party who pays the insurance. There is the loss of wages sustained by the worker during his period of disability. There is also the medical expense which the injured employee must meet in this State, as there is no "first aid" paid under our law. When the loss of wages and the expense of medical treatment are taken into consideration the employee bears a larger proportion of the burden of industrial accidents than does the employer. The following figures taken from the Second Annual Report of the Industrial Insurance Department for the 12 months ending September 10, 1913, pages 101 and 102, will illustrate this fact.

During the year commencing October 1, 1912, and closing September 30, 1913, 12,380 claims under the workmen's compensation act were settled by the Industrial Insurance Department of Washington State. Of 1,722 cases, of which estimates of the cost of medical treatment and loss of wages were made, the results were as follows:

TABLE No. 1.—*Awards resulting in temporary disability only.*

Number of cases reported	1, 503
Number of work days lost	35, 102
Total amount of wages lost	$107, 296. 67
Total cost of medical treatment	$36, 206. 80
Awards for temporary total disability	$47, 164. 20
Total loss on account of disabilities (wages lost plus cost of medical treatment)	$143, 503. 47
Amount of loss borne by employers (awards for temporary total disability)	$47, 164. 20
Amount of loss borne by employees (total loss minus awards)	$96, 339. 27
Percentage of loss borne by employers	32. 9
Percentage of loss borne by employees	67. 1

TABLE No. 2.—*Awards resulting in both temporary disabilities and permanent partial disabilities.*

Number of cases reported	219
Number of work days lost	9, 737. 5
Total amount of wages lost	$32, 651. 05
Total cost of medical treatment	$14, 432. 15
Awards for temporary total disability	$13, 340. 19
Awards for permanent partial disability	$51, 435. 50
Total loss on account of disabilities (wages lost plus cost of medical treatment)	$47, 083. 20
Amount of immediate loss borne by employers (awards for temporary total disability)	$13, 340. 19
Amount of immediate loss borne by employees (total loss minus awards for temporary total disability)	$33, 743. 01
Percentage of loss borne by employers	28. 3
Percentage of loss borne by employees	71. 7

NOTE.—The awards for permanent partial disabilities are excluded from the above comparisons for the reason that these awards are made in payment for future reduced earning power, and hence ought not to be compared with the immediate loss of wages and cost of medical treatment.

The figures in these two tables are given as they are in the report referred to. It will be observed that in stating the toal losses on account of disabilities in Table No. 2 no account is taken of the $51,435.50 paid in awards for permanent partial disability. This figure would materially increase the proportion of burden brone by employers. Even making all due allowance for this, however, it will be seen that while the workmen's compensation law of this State has been a material aid to the wage earner the burden of industrial accidents seems to rest more heavily upon the employee than upon the employer. I may also add that a former worker in the industrial insurance department states that about 25 per cent of all men injured in Washington and coming within the scope of the law pay more in doctor's bills and hospital fees than they receive in compensation.

Respectfully submitted.

ABRAHAM BERGLUND.

EXHIBITS.

OLSON EXHIBIT NO. 1.

MERCANTILE CONFERENCE, SENATE CHAMBER, CAPITOL BUILDING, OLYMPIA, WASH.,
MARCH 31 AND APRIL 1, 1914.

Meeting called to order at 9 a. m. by Mr. E. W. Olson, chairman of the industrial welfare commission. The entire commission, composed of Mr. Olson, Mr. Marvin, Mrs. Silbaugh, Mrs. Swanson, and Mrs. Udall, were present. This commission and the following representatives composed the conference: Mr. E. W. Olson, 'chairman; Mr. J. L. Paine, Mr. W. N. Cuddy, and Mr. George J. Wolff, representing the employers; Mrs. Elizabeth Muir, Mrs. Florence Locke, and Miss Mayme Smith, representing the employees; Mrs. Frances C. Axtell, Prof. W. G. Beach, and Mr. J. D. Fletcher, representing the public.

Prayer by Rev. Marvin.

Roll call by secretary. All members of the conference and all·members of the industrial welfare commission answered to the roll call.

The CHAIRMAN (reading):

To members of the mercantile conference:

After due investigation of the mercantile industry of the State of Washington, this commission has found that the wages paid to female employees in said industry are inadequate to supply them necessary cost of living and to maintain the workers in health, and this commission has further found that in said industry conditions of labor exist that are prejudicial to the health or morals of the women employed in said· industry.

Therefore, by virtue of the authority vested in it by section 174, Laws of 1913, State of Washington, this commission has called a conference composed of an equal number of representatives of employers, employees, and the public, which after due consideration is to recommend to this commission the amount of an adequate wage in said mercantile industry to permit a self-supporting woman to maintain herself in decency and comfort, and to also recommend other conditions of work hereinafter specified. Said conference so selected is composed of the following members:

Mr. J. L. Paine, W. N. Cuddy, and George J. Wolff, representing the employers; Mrs. Elizabeth Muir, Mrs. Florence Locke, and Miss. Mayme Smith, representing the employees; Mrs. Frances C. Axtell, W. G. Beach, and J. D. Fletcher, representing the public.

Therefore in accordance with the foregoing, the Industrial Welfare Commission of the State of Washington herewith submits to the conference the following questions:

What is the sum required per week to maintain in decent conditions of living a self-supporting woman employed in a mercantile establishment in the State of Washington?

The requisites for such decent conditions of living are itemized in the list below:

Meals, room, shoes and rubbers, repairing shoes, stockings, underwear, petticoats, suit, coat, dresses and aprons, incidentals, shirt waists, handkerchiefs, corsets, corset waists, gloves, neckwear, hats, umbrella, repair of clothing, church and other contributions, medicine and dentistry, street car fare, newspapers and magazines, stationery and postage, association dues, insurance, vacation expenses, amusements, and laundry.

What length of lunch period is demanded for maintenance of health of mercantile employees?

What provisions should be required in each mercantile establishment for (*a*) toilet for women workers? (*b*) Rest room? (*c*) Ventilation?

INDUSTRIAL WELFARE COMMISSION.

4414

I wish to state that Roberts's Rules of Order will govern, and wish to refer you to section 5 of the "Regulations of Commission Governing Procedure of Conferences," which reads as follows:

"When the conference is called to order by the chairman, it shall deliberate under parliamentary law and no question shall be discussed that is not germane to the conditions of labor or cost of living of working women or minors as applied to that particular trade or industry. Roberts's Rules of Order shall govern."

We are here for the purpose of discussing the minimum wage for the women workers in the mercantile industry only.

Mr. PAINE. Does that include office employees?

The CHAIRMAN. It does not include office employees, except in the mercantile establishments—all women employed in the mercantile establishment would be included.

I wish you would all turn to page 99, section 10, which says: "The secretary of the commission or a shorthand reporter shall be present at each conference and shall record the minutes of the meetings and shall be ex officio secretary of said conference." Also section 8, which says:

"The Chair shall not permit the discussion of the question as a whole until after each item of the cost of living has been taken up in the order given in the estimate blanks prepared by the commission, unless otherwise directed by a majority vote of the conference. After proper deliberation and discussion of questions that have been presented to the conference by the commission, the conference shall then, upon request of the commission, proceed to make recommendations upon such questions as the commission may designate."

Also section 9:

"The members of the conference so selected shall be paid their actual traveling and hotel expenses while attending said conference (out of the regular appropriation set aside by the legislature), provided that evidence of such expense be filed with the commission and sworn to in the manner provided by law, and it is further provided that before being allowed said expenses are to be approved by the commission."

I wish to say in this connection that we would like to have you make out your vouchers as soon as you return home and send them in so that warrant may be sent you. Itemize everything under 50 cents and furnish receipts for everything over 50 cents. I again wish to draw your attention to section 8, which reads:

"The Chair shall not permit the discussion of the question as a whole until after each item of the cost of living has been taken up in the order given in the estimate blanks prepared by the commission, unless otherwise directed by a majority vote of the conference."

Referring to section 1, we see that—

"A conference shall consist of nine persons and a member of the commission, who shall be chairman of said conference, three to represent the employers, three to represent the employees, and three to represent the public. One of the members representing the public shall be appointed by the chairman as chief interrogator. A member of the commission shall act as chairman of the conference."

The commission, at its meeting yesterday afternoon, decided that it would be best to have a chief interrogator chosen from the three representing the public, the other two members of conference, representing the public, to be associated in the work of interrogating; therefore, we have appointed Mr. Fletcher as chief interrogator to be associated with Mrs. Axtell and Prof. Beach.

We will now discuss the cost of living—meals.

Mr. FLETCHER. Is it the desire that we take up these questions item by item?

The CHAIRMAN. That is the desire.

Mr. FLETCHER. Those who know more about the expense of women's meals should speak. I have little knowledge along this line.

Mrs. AXTELL. Section 7 says that we shall establish a minimum wage for both women and minors. Are we to consider the minor question?

The CHAIRMAN. Not the minors.

Mr. FLETCHER. What is the desire of the Chair as to the method we should pursue? I would suggest that we hear from the employees as to their views, then from the employers, and then the public, so as to get the views of all.

The CHAIRMAN. I think that would be a good idea.

Mrs. LOCKE. No girl can retain her health for less than 15 cents for breakfast (consisting of coffee and rolls); for dinner she needs more substantial food—I would suggest 20 cents; and for supper she should have meats or something to that effect, and you can't get a meal for less than 25 cents, making the total for the week $3.90, including seven days. I am putting that at a very low price.

Mr. FLETCHER. Your figures would show $4.20 for the week, Mrs. Locke.

Mrs. LOCKE. I was just estimating that in my mind.

Mr. FLETCHER. I would ask the other representatives of the employees if that would meet with their ideas.

Mrs. MUIR. I have on my list, for breakfast, 15 cents; lunch, 20 cents; and dinner, 35 cents. We work hard all day and are very hungry at night, and I consider that a very small amount for our meals.

Mr. FLETCHER. Miss Smith, how does your list compare with these two?

Miss SMITH. I had thought in my mind that 75 cents a day would be correct, but that would be, perhaps, a little high, and allowing 35 cents for dinner would make the total 70 cents per day.

Mr. FLETCHER. I would like to hear from the representatives of the employers as to their ideas.

Mr. PAINE. Mr. Chairman, in the matter of the first two items, meals and room, they are very often considered together, as a great many take their meals at the same place where they room, or they have a fixed sum for both. I would consider the first two items under one head. If we take our meals around from place to place it would cost us more than a fixed boarding house would charge. They have, in that way, a sort of a home. I have made some investigations as to what board can be secured for in Spokane, and find that at the present time conditions are more favorable than when this report was given out. Recently there has been established in Spokane a woman's hotel, which accommodates 100 girls, and their rates there, for three meals a day and a room and accommodations of the home, are from $3 to $7 per week; this includes lunch (if they wish to take it to a place of business or at home), no deductions being made if they eat down town. The room at $3 is the dormitory style; for $4 they have rooms where two girls room together; for $5 separate rooms. This is one place where girls can economize in board. A great many girls prefer to rent a room and there cook their meals, but to go to the restaurants is very extravagant, I think. Of course, if the employee gets a good salary I believe in them having a room alone or a suits of rooms, but we are discussing to-day the minimum wage that one can support herself on. I think they should be able to get board and room, a little distant from center of city, at $4.50 or $5 per week.

Mrs. LOCKE. Is that including lunch?

Mr. PAINE. I think it is.

Mrs. LOCKE. In Seattle it is impossible to get board for $4 and get your lunch in the same place. In some places they will give you lunch for $5. If you go away from the center of the city, you can get it for $4.50 and pay car fare.

Mr. PAINE. This establishment I was speaking of is in walking distance.

Mrs. MUIR. Mr. Chairman, we haven't these establishments in all places. I know it is a saving to cook yourself, but many women can not stand this after working eight hours a day. If you go out very far you can't get a desirable room for less. If you want to get a real cheap room, you can get that right down in the heart of the city, but in a place that is not fit to live.

Mrs. AXTELL. On page 54, do you agree with the item under Spokane, that you can live on $20 per month, Mr. Paine?

Mr. PAINE. It may not be the universal rule, but I think they would allow them to take their lunch if they wish to. Most stores have lunch rooms, and I think $20 might include lunch that could be taken if they wished.

Mrs. LOCKE. Mr. Chairman, I would like to hear from the merchants what the price of a meal should be. What they would like to have a girl eat.

Mr. FLETCHER. Will you gentlemen give us your ideas on that?

Mr. WOLFF. We want to do what is fair to the employees, and everyone present is perfectly willing to aid this conference in bringing about this condition. I have figured meals and room together, and I find that, the figures I have are sufficient to keep a girl in fairly well standing. I made it a point to talk with a good many girls who have been earning their own living on a small salary. On this basis I have estimated my figures, but the first item may be not very high, and other items are perhaps a little high. I observe that some people like to eat better than others, others like to spend more on clothes;

In other words, women are not all constituted the same way. I have practically cut out my lunch, and I find I can work better if I do not eat much for lunch. When out of the city I often eat a 10-cent breakfast, as I can do better work and eat a larger meal when I get home after 6 o'clock, so perhaps for that reason I have estimated my first item on a small scale. I figure that $5 is sufficient for a minimum room and meal. A little later on I intend to make the suggestion that this conference might issue a pamphlet on how a person can get along with so much a week; there are a good many young people who do not know how to spend their money. They spend it in an easy way, and at the end of the week find out they have spent more than they should. We all need education in that line. We overreach our bounds, and I think this should be one of the important features of this conference to teach and educate people how to live right and not extravagantly. I think cooking one's own meals is more extravagant and takes more energy.

Mr. FLETCHER. Mr. Wolff, I would suggest that you go right down the list and give your items.

Mr. WOLFF. The shoes and rubbers I figure at $7.50; that is, allowing two pairs of shoes at $3 per pair and two pairs of rubbers at $0.75 per pair; reparing of shoes, $1.50 per year; hosiery, 12 pairs at $2.50 per dozen or $2.50 for hose per year; I figured on two suits of $1 underwear for summer, or $2 for summer underwear; and two suits of fall underwear, at $1.50 a pair, making a total of $5 for underwear; two petticoats at $1 each, mercerized petticoats; one good suit, at $20 (the employees get 20 per cent discount on suits, in other words, a suit sold to the public for $25 would be $20 to an employee).

Mrs. LOCKE. Does every merchant give 20 per cent—is it universal?

Mr. PAINE. I think it is the custom to give 20 per cent.

Mrs. LOCKE. I have always got but 10 per cent on suits—I am speaking of Seattle.

Mr. WOLFF. My employees get 20 per cent. I have figured on $15 for a coat; $17.50 for the dresses (one serge dress at $10 and a simple evening dress or some other kind, at $7.50). Many girls get material and make a new dress. They sometimes get the material for $1.50 and make the dress. I have allowed $1 for aprons, four aprons per year, at 25 cents each; four shirt waists, at $1 each; $1.50 for hankerchiefs; two corsets, at $1 each, making $2; corset waists, $1; I figure two pair kid gloves, at $1 each; two pair fabric gloves, at 25 cents each, would be $2.50 for gloves; neckwear, at $1; I figure two hats, at $3.50, would be $7; one umbrella, at $1; I estimated the laundry at $15 per year.

A girl can repair her own clothing, I think. For medicine and dentistry, I think, $20 is sufficient; for car fare, $35; for newspapers and reading matter, $5; postage, $3; lodges, $3; vacation, $10; amusements, $10; church and other contributions, $5; incidentals, $5; making the total for the year, $467.30.

I have only one employee that would come under the minimum wage and, in fact, the records would show that I am far above the average of a minimum wage, but in considering the different employers, I feel that I should be fair to the employers even if I don't know them and also fair to the employees. Some employers might have a number of employees that they would have to pay small wages to, but I don't know of any progressive merchant who don't recognize efficiency. I find that a person that don't earn any more than a minimum price, they don't care to keep them. I think if a girl is where she only gets a minimum price and she is worth more, she can get a position elsewhere.

Last week a young lady moved away from Aberdeen who received $15 per week. I have a young lady filling that position at $10 a week, but I would rather have the $15 a week girl than the one for $10. The price is kept down to the minimum for a girl who is not worth more. All employers are looking for the efficient clerk and there is a good deal of rivalry between employers in getting the most efficient clerks.

Mr. FLETCHER. Your figures come to about $9 a week.

Mr. WOLFF. Those are the figures I have estimated to the best of my judgment.

Mr. FLETCHER. Did you figure these yourself or did you talk to the other gentlemen?

Mr. WOLFF. We each had a sort of list of our own, but last night we got together and compared figures so that this is practically the opinion of all of us.

Mrs. MUIR. You say the gentlemen have worked together and have come to these conclusions. We girls haven't had time to get together, haven't even had time to think, so our ideas will be rather crude. Mr. Wolff speaks of caring more for clothes than eating; perhaps he cares more for clothes than food, or perhaps he eats a 75-cent dinner in the evening which does away with that lunch that he missed at noon. If a girl is not fed right she can not look right and can not sell the goods.

Mr. FLETCHER. Mrs. Muir, could you give us your idea in regard to Mr. Wolff's list?

Mrs. MUIR. I'm not quite prepared for that.

Mr. FLETCHER. Mrs. Locke, can you tell us your ideas?

Mrs. LOCKE. I will do my best. In regard to going home and sewing, a girl can't work eight hours a day and then go home and sew. She can't stand it. She should go home and rest, read, or something of that sort, but keep her mind off of work. She can mend her clothes or do some little thing, but as far as making a dress and making it look right, she can't do it. In regard to a suit, I think a $25 suit is none too good for a girl to work in. A suit bought this year is for best and next year she can wear the old suit to work and get a new one again.

Mr. FLETCHER. Have you figured board and room?

Mrs. LOCKE. For a week I have figured for board, $4; for lunch, $1.40; and for lodging, $2.50; for clothes and shoes, a week, $1; $1.15 to have shoes half-soled during three months. Repairing of clothing, 25 cents; laundry, 50 cents. The laundry I have figured extremely low, as a girl usually wears white shirt waists and needs at least three shirt waists a week, sometimes the fourth one, and they cost from 25 to 35 cents to be laundered. For medicine and dentistry, 50 cents per week; speaking for myself I have needed very little in the dentistry line. Street car fare, 60 cents for six days; newspapers and magazines, 50 cents per week; stationery and postals, 15 cents; association dues, 10 cents; insurance, 10 cents; vacation, 25 cents; church and other contributions, 15 cents; gifts, 10 cents; making the total for the week $12.

Mr. FLETCHER. Mrs. Muir, will you read us your list?

Mrs. MUIR. For board I have $4; luncheon, $1.40; lodging, $2.50; shoes and rubbers, $1; repairing shoes, 25 cents; laundry, 75 cents; medicine and dentistry, $1; street-carfare, 70 cents; newspapers and magazines, 50 cents; stationery and postage, 20 cents; association dues, 10 cents; insurance, 10 cents; vacation expenses, 25 cents; amusements, 25 cents; church contributions, 10 cents; gifts, 10 cents—you see I havent' allowed anything for incidentals. Why, I couldn't begin to, for that is such a big item; for instance, I might break one of the lenses in my glasses and that would mean several dollars, or one might have to go to the dentist and pay $50 out in one week, so you see I couldn't allow for incidentals, as I have no idea how high they might come.

Mr. FLETCHER. What was your total for the week?

Mrs. MUIR. I haven't summed it up.

Mr. FLETCHER. I believe your figures would come to $13.20 for the week.

Mrs. UDALL. Mr. Chairman, we haven't heard from Mr. Cuddy.

Mr. CUDDY. I have been waiting to hear from all the employees.

Mr. FLETCHER. Miss Smith, will you give us your items?

Miss SMITH. I have figured mine up by the year. For a room, $6 per week; lunches, $1.20 per week; shoes, two pairs at $4, or $8 for year; rubbers, $1.50 per year; hosiery, at $3.50 per dozen, or $3.50 per year; underwear, $6; petticoats, $4; suit, $25 (with, perhaps, an extra skirt); coat for $15; dresses and aprons, $20 (this would include one summer dress and some other light dress); shirt waists, $10; handkerchiefs, $1; corsets (two pairs, at $2 a pair), $4; corset waists, $1.50; gloves, $3.50; neckwear, $1; hats, $15; umbrella, $2.50; repair of clothing (cleaning of suits, etc.), $2; laundry, 50 cents per week, or $31.20 for the year; dentistry and medicine, 50 cents per week, or about $26 per year; car fare, 70 cents per week, or $36.40 per year; newspapers, $4 per year; stationery, $4 per year; association dues, 10 cents per week, or $5 per year; vacation, about $12 per year; amusements, about 20 cents a week, or $10 a year; church, $5 per year; and incidentals, $5 per year.

Mr. MARVIN. You make no allowance for insurance.

Miss SMITH. No; I make no allowance for insurance, as I have never looked into that matter.

Mr. MARVIN. None of you ladies make any allowance for insurance.

Mrs. LOCKE. I made 50 cents per month allowance for insurance, as I am carrying $1,000 insurance. I also have to pay $1 extra every three months, making about $12 per year.

Mr. PAINE. Mr. Chairman, is not this a new feature for employees to be insured? What is the idea in regard to insurance—life insurance?

The CHAIRMAN. Life insurance, I suppose.

Mr. MARVIN. I had the thought of accident insurance, not life insurance, but sickness.

Mr. FLETCHER. I think it should be sickness insurance or accident insurance.

Mrs. LOCKE. Not long ago there was a paper distributed around the store by some doctors, explaining how we could pay 10 cents a week to a certain association and that would take care of us in case of sickness—that is, we could go to the association hospital and get free medical treatment. The only charges were 10 cents a week, but I would not join it, as I belonged to a similar association in the East, and when I was sick I got very poor treatment at their hands. In fact, it was not satisfactory at all, and for that reason I did not care to be stung again.

Mrs. AXTELL. Mr. Chairman, is there any movement for insurance for women in the State similar to the industrial insurance for men?

The CHAIRMAN. I haven't heard of any movement like that—most of the girls, I think, carry insurance in old line companies or Ladies and Knights of Security, etc. They carry more life insurance than accident or sick insurance, I think.

Mrs. SWANSON. Isn't there a law against a health insurance for women?

Mr. FLETCHER. I do not know; there are so many laws passed I can't keep track of them; but I can't imagine why such a law should be passed by the legislature.

Mrs. SWANSON. I was told there was no insurance company carrying insurance for women in this State.

Mr. PAINE. In the matter of life insurance, I think it should be ruled out of this, as it is something for survivors. I think insurance is not carried to any large degree by employees. I think at least 75 per cent do not carry insurance. Some establishments have the custom of allowing a certain time during the year for sickness, their salary goes on just the same. Other firms allow the vacation of a week at full pay. We should try to get at this from the standpoint of the average employee. What would naturally and necessarily be required? We should not let our fancies flow on to all the clothes we want, but just those that are needed.

Mrs. MUIR. You speak of the vacation and of saleswomen being given a week's vacation. In some establishments you have to work a year before you get a vacation. In speaking of clothing, a saleswoman, in order to stand before the public, has to look neat and clean—they wear their garments every day and every day, and still the employer expects them to look well. If we buy real cheap clothing, in a little while you have no clothing or no money. If you buy a real good suit, it will last so much longer. In some of the department stores they demand that a girl dress quite up to date. We all express our views the way we look at them. In regard to sickness, I find that if an employee is really good and gets sick once in a while, the merchant does not take any out of her wages; her salary goes on just the same.

Mr. WOLFF. Two weeks ago in my store I had one of my employees sick. She worked Monday and was sick the rest of the week, returning the following week. This employee gets $18 a week. When she came to the store Monday she got her check just the same as if she had been there. She got it because she deserved it. For that reason I feel that as this woman was sick she ought to be compensated. We want to be charitable, but fair in every way. The mother can spoil the child by being too good to the child. She might do everything possible for it while it is small, but she might not look far enough to see that she is doing the child harm. In the same way we can spoil our employees. If we adopt a law giving in to the ladies to keep from arguing with them, we could do them harm in the same way. We want to educate them more than anything else. Mrs. Locke's speaking of repairing clothes. I realize every girl is not adapted to make clothes, but I think the person should be brought up to do these things as far as possible. If we get things too easy they go easy, and the money is spent too easy. A person may be in the habit of doing a certain amount of work. They don't try to do more. President Wilson shaves himself, and yet many men go to the barber shop who are not nearly as busy as President Wilson; but he makes that his business, although he has a great deal to occupy his time. I think I work longer than any of my employees. After supper I take care of the horse, clean the stable, and I feel better, as it is a different kind of work; I feel it is a pleasure. If we take all the work away from the younger generation and make it too easy for them in a few years they won't want to do any work at all. We are here to do something that means a great deal of good for the saleswoman. I think we have a fair-minded conference here, and I think we can do a great deal of good. This is very important work, and if we pile up a lot of expense to business interests, who will pay for it in the long run?

If it cost the State a certain amount to run the offices and if the taxes are not sufficient to pay for the expense the taxes are going to be raised. If you raise our expenses to a higher standard than they can stand, then we will have to mark the goods higher. We have to go slow or the merchant will go to the wall. I pay the very best, and only one of my clerks would come under the minimum wage, as I am considered one of the best wage payers in the State. If we pay too much for the minimum we decrease efficiency. We have to make them feel that they earn their money, and if they do earn it they figure a few times before they spend it.

Mr. FLETCHER. We are all very glad to hear Mr. Wolff's opinion on this matter, but I think we should get down to business now and compare the figures we have. Miss Smith, what was your average for the week?

Miss SMITH. I figured it up at $11.98 for the week.

Mr. FLETCHER. What was your average, Mrs. Muir?

Mrs. MUIR. My average was $13.20 for the week, with no incidentals. Mr. Wolff spoke of employees being sick. I was speaking of the vacation. Some employers do pay girls if they are good workers and are sick one or two days. May I ask in what department they pay $18 per week?

Mr. WOLFF. In the alteration department.

Mrs. MUIR. When you pay a girl real small wages they are not willing to do more than they have to. You ask them why they do not do this or that, and they answer, "Why should I? I am not going to do more than I have to. I only get 'so much' per week." Mr. Wolff also spoke of taking care of his horse in the evening. That is a diversion for him, and then he is outside; it is a different kind of work than he has been doing all day, and it is not as hard as having your head bent down and using your eyes all evening sewing on a dress. Most of the girls do some sewing, but to try and make a dress it is too much to do in the evenings.

Mr. CUDDY. Mr. Chairman, there would have to be an entire revolution in business if we passed a law such as our friends would like. The women on this board, I think, do not send all their clothes to the laundry. In my store I have given a very liberal discount—more than 10 and 15 per cent, but usually 20 and 25 per cent, which makes the clothing almost at cost. The Stone-Fisher Co. give 25 per cent in their ready-to-wear apparel; the discount is usually more than 10 per cent. In reference to the work, I do not think that selling is such hard work as we are led to think. Most of the large stores have rest rooms for their employees to rest a few minutes a day, and their work is not so terribly exhausting. It is hard, but not so nerve-racking as you would think. Again, another question that we must consider in a minimum wage around $12, there are lots of girls who are not worth that. Their efficiency is not up to that standard. In numbers of stores, especially in our large department stores, if a minimum wage were put to effect there would be numbers that would be dismissed; they are not worth that much.

Prof. BEACH. Are you speaking of minors?

Mr. CUDDY. No; I was speaking of those who are over age.

Prof. BEACH. Do you think the law would take into consideration whether she earns it or not, but rather what is the minimum for existence? Is she worth this much? That is not our question.

Mrs. AXTELL. I would like to know if you dismiss these girls from the notion and pattern departments if you have any other girls you could put in their places. Could the merchant fill the place in every instance with another girl?

Mr. CUDDY. We certainly could. I feel that board and room could be found for around $5 per week. It would be plain but wholesome. My suit item is away under $25—is from $15 to $22.50—don't you think so, Mr. Paine?

Mr. PAINE. Yes; I think so. The average is from $15 to $22.50. A gentleman brought me an item that he said one of his young ladies brought him voluntarily. She said that was all she had to live on; she and another lady room together; they get part of their meals and live on $6 a week, also lay up a little money by using the strictest kind of economy. She does her own washing and buys the plainest of things. I have a young lady in my store getting $10 a·week and I know she saves money, but I think $6 is too small, but it is being, done. . The average girl would have a very difficult time living on $6 a week.

◦ Mr. MARVIN. Did you have what the other folks are supplying us with—did you have an average for the week?

Mr..CUDDY. 'I have about the same as Mr. Wolff and Mr. Paine—about $9 per week.

◦ Mr. WOLFF. I had a letter from Seattle a few days ago, from a young lady who attends the university, and she told me that she notices in the paper that I was appointed to the conference, and also that Prof. Beach was to be a member. She said you will find him a very pleasant gentleman. This girl started to work for me on.Saturdays during the time she went to school. After school she worked for me, starting in at a dollar per day. She could adapt herself to clerking very well and was worth more than a dollar a day. She was taking shorthand and went to business college. Within two and one-half years her salary with me was $85 per month. She worked for $1 a day because she had no experience in store work. She later attended to the cash and made herself, in my estimation, very valuable and I paid her $85 a month, and whenever she comes back for Christmas vacation she comes to the store and works for a few days. I think it is a good plan to start them in on a low basis and as efficiency improves raise them just as much as·they are worth.

One point about vacation and sickness. I had the experience in my store, when I first started in business, that some of the girls would only come to work at noon and would not even telephone to me. They would complain of having a headache, but upon investigation I would often find that they had been out in the evening (to a dance, for instance), and would stay at home until noon perhaps to sleep. I noticed this was worked so often that I said no money will be paid unless they are here, but if they are out their time will be deducted. I haven't these same people in my employ now. I have a fine crowd; it is just like a big family, and I know these girls won't stay away from work unless it is necessary and then they will call me up. If employers are taken advantage of they will shut up like a clam.

· Mr. FLETCHER. Mr. Chairman, I think Mr. Wolff's ideas are not the ones we have to take into consideration here. It is rather a question of the minimum wage. Can you tell us what States have minimum-wage laws in force?

The CHAIRMAN. In Oregon they have a minimum wage of $9.25, and in Utah, $7.50. These are the only two States that have to this date established a minimum wage, as far as I know.

Mrs. AXTELL. If they have this law in operation in Oregon we would like any data as to how they act.

The CHAIRMAN. The rulings of the commission were suspended until the case could be heard before the supreme court. The law provides that they must hold a conference for each industry. Our law is patterned after their law in a great many ways.

Mr. MARVIN. The attorney general of the State of Oregon ruled that they might make one rate for the State and one for the city of Portland. The commission in Oregon has not made two rates, but they may do so.

Mr. CUDDY. Nine dollars and twenty-five cents is the rate for women wage earners in the city of Portland and $8.25 in the State of Oregon, I believe.

Mr. MARVIN. No; I believe the conference made certain recommendations, but I do not think the committee passed upon them.

· The CHAIRMAN. Here are the rulings of the Oregon commission:

" No person, firm, or corporation shall employ any experienced adult woman in any industry in the State of Oregon, paid by time rate of payment, at a weekly wage rate of less than $8.25 a week, any lesser amount being hereby declared inadequate to supply the necessary cost of living to such women workers and to maintain them in health.

¯ " Nor shall any such person, firm, or corporation employ women in any industry in the State of Oregon for more than 54 hours a week.

" No person, firm, or corporation owning or conducting any mercantile establishment in the city of Portland, Oreg., shall pay to any experienced adult woman worker a wage less than $9.25 a week."

· Prof. BEACH. The prime things we have to go upon are the estimates that are made upon the investigation of the commission as to the cost of living in the State of Washington. We seem to have our estimates that range from $9 to $13. No one seems to think it possible for a woman to live on less than $9. Our problem will be to determine between the difference of $9 and $12. I question whether the situation in Oregon affects us very much. Our problem is a somewhat different one as it stands now. We ought to determine somewhere between the maximum and minimum shown by the representatives here. I might add that the investigations of your commission show an amount that lies between $9 and $12. The figures shown here are a minimum approaching or above $10. The total shows an estimate close to $10 and this evidently seems to be that they are not exaggerating the needs. At the university it is very difficult for any of the students to find board and room for less than $6 per week unless several board at one place.

Washing, especially a certain amount, I think, should not be done by employees after working eight hours. This is the limit of work that a woman ought to do so we ought not to expect her to do work after her eight hours of work is done. Sewing, too, I think should not be done in the evening.

Mr. WOLFF. How about fancywork?

Prof. BEACH. A little fancywork is all right if they do not use their eyes too long. There is a big difference between the work of the employer who is interested in it because he is manager and the employee who does the same work day after day, and we can't expect her to take an interest in doing work in the evenings—of course, something like fancywork is all right.

Mrs. AXTELL. In looking over the figures of the employers and employees and the welfare commission we have a minimum wage of $8.98 and from the employees, Mrs. Locke $12, Mrs. Muir $13.20, and Miss Smith $11.98. From your book we have a minimum wage of $10. To get the matter before the commission in motion form I move that the sum of $10.75 be designated as the proper amount to maintain a working woman in decency and comfort in the mercantile establishments in the State of Washington.

Prof. BEACH. I second the motion.

The CHAIRMAN. It has been moved and seconded that the sum of $10.75 be designated as the proper amount to maintain a working woman in decency and comfort in the mercantile establishments in the State of Washington. Are you ready for the question?

Mr. FLETCHER. Question.

Mrs. MUIR. A girl will do her work better if she can lay a little aside for a "rainy day." I think that is a somewhat reasonable amount.

Mr. CUDDY. I would like to say, in reply to that, that if such a law would become effective a great many department stores in our State would have to change their lines of business. The department stores could not operate under such a law.

Mr. FLETCHER. What is the average that they pay in the department stores such as Rhodes Bros.?

Mr. CUDDY. I would say that the average city department store pays right around $8.

The CHAIRMAN. It is just 12 o'clock, and I think we should adjourn for lunch. Motion is in order for adjournment.

Mrs. AXTELL. I move we adjourn.

Mr. FLETCHER. I second the motion.

The CHAIRMAN. It has been moved and seconded we adjourn for lunch. All in favor signify by saying "aye"—"no"—the "ayes" have it. We will adjourn until 1.30.

AFTER RECESS—1.30 P. M.

The CHAIRMAN. Meeting will please come to order. The motion before the house is the question of making the minimum wage $10.75 per week for women in mercantile establishments in the State of Washington.

Mr. PAINE. Before we proceed with that discussion I would like to know in regard to the minor help. I would like to have information as to whether this body is to take up the minor question or not?

The CHAIRMAN. We haven't asked the conference to take up that point, but would like to hear anything there is to be said on it.

Mr. PAINE. Minor and also apprentice help. Do I understand you to say, however, that it is not a matter that the conference is supposed to consider?

The CHAIRMAN. We have a ruling from the attorney general on the question of apprenticeship, that it need not be submitted to the conference, and in regard to minors that the commission, the law states, may be empowered to issue an obligatory order fixing the minimum wage without submitting it to the conference.

Mrs. AXTELL. Do I understand that your commission decides what the wage for minors should be, and also in regard to apprentices?

The CHAIRMAN. We have come to no definite decision, but would like to hear any point discussed. The attitude of the commission on that question is that we want to receive all the enlightenment that we can and want to hear both sides of that question. .

Mr. PAINE. It seems to me that the two things are very closely connected in the matter of consideration from an employer's standpoint. Under the present system of education it now falls upon the employer of labor to educate a saleswoman. There is no regulation in this State that provides this instruction through the public schools. Wisconsin and some other States have such a law. They educate them in salesmanship, how to handle and make a sale, and to handle a customer—all these are vital points. The young girl leaves the grade school or high school, comes to the employer, makes application, and asks that the merchant take her and teach her something useful, as she may have to be self-supporting at some time. The burden of education falls upon the employer, and it costs a great deal to educate people in our line of business. If we have to take them and educate them, it seems to me that the employer should be entitled to pay a wage that would enable him to spend the extra pains and time in bringing them to a state of efficiency in order to compete with those who are experienced. I think a good idea would be to pay $6 per week to the apprentice for the first six months, at the end of the first six months advance them one dollar, at the end of the second six months advance them another dollar, at the end of the third six months advance them the third dollar, and at the end of this year and one-half period they should get the minimum wage that may be decided upon here to-day. If this is not the case, there are a great many who feel that they must help their parents in taking care of the family; and if they could not get into the stores at a wage of this kind and as an apprentice they would not be able to get in at all, and consequently would not be able to help the family at home. This gives them a chance to earn while they learn. A great many places—employers have schools of their own where they put them through a regular course, but this is very expensive and not practicable for a large percentage.

The CHAIRMAN. In reference to the question of apprentices, I desire to read section 13 of the law:

" For any occupation in which a minimum rate has been established, the commission, through its secretary, may issue to a woman physically defective or crippled by age or otherwise, or to an apprentice in such class of employment or occupation as usually requires to be learned by apprentices, a special license authorizing the employment of such licensee for a wage less than the legal minimum wage * * *." .

No flat ruling could be made in regard to apprenticeship. It's my individual opinion that a flat ruling is not feasible under this section of the law for the reason that a flat ruling would make it possible for a girl to be employed in a position where no period of apprenticeship exists.

Mr. PAINE. Mr. Chairman, what do you consider apprenticeship? .

The CHAIRMAN. An apprenticeship is a period of learning in some trade that is skilled.

Mr. PAINE. Do you consider salesmanship such a trade?

The CHAIRMAN. It would depend entirely upon the nature of the work. There are certain employments in factories that do not need a period of apprenticeship, while there are others where a short term of apprenticeship is needed and still others where a longer term is needed. It was the intention of the legislature to determine the period of apprenticeship as well as the rate of pay— that is my conception of that section of the law. .

Mr. PAINE. In that respect our law would differ from the Oregon law?

The CHAIRMAN. They have no such provision. .

Mr. FLETCHER. How about the minor situation, would you consider that you could fix one scale for the minors regardless of age or qualifications?

The CHAIRMAN. I believe that while we haven't had an opinion from the attorney general on that question, it seems clear to us that the question of minors is entirely separate from the question of apprentices. We would have authority to make a general ruling covering the minors.

Mr. PAINE. You would not think of having a graduated scale to pay them?

The CHAIRMAN. I think it would be possible if you think it practicable. That would only include boys and girls under the age of 18 years.

Mrs. LOCKE. In regard to $6 for six months, that is a long time to get but $6. She is a pretty good saleslady at the end of six months if she is ever going to be a saleslady, and $6 a week won't pay expenses. Mr. Paine, where do you usually place your apprentices?

Mr. PAINE. I put her at a little job of wrapping packages, etc., which is not hard.

Mr. WOLFF. There has been apprentices since the beginning of business. We can't expect one to start out in business and be a business man or woman with-out starting down at the bottom and learning step by step. We are starting on a new adventure here, we do not understand it ourselves yet, we are just feeling our way. In time, next year perhaps, and our services to the com-munity will be more valuable. We are trying our best, and we think our serv-ices next year will be worth more money. An apprentice should be taught the business. Many young girls do not care to go to school but want to learn some business. A woman came to my store the other day, and she said, "I wish you would find a place for my daughter, she does not care to go to school." I started the girl in at $7.50 per week, but she had had no experience what-soever. She worked two months and learning showed no ability to work, she was not useful or reliable. For instance, this girl sold a lady a piece of embroidery at $1.59 per yard. This customer had bought the same kind of embroidery at 59 cents per yard just the week before. This lady gave the girl the money, got her package, and went out. After she got home she found the mistake in the price of the embroidery and called me up. I looked into the matter and found it should have been 59 cents instead of $1.59. She had also made a mis-take in the multiplication and in her addition.

I tell you it is no pleasure to call up a customer and try to explain how these things sometimes happen, but it makes a merchant feel very uncomfortable to try to apologize for such mistakes. Wouldn't you rather go to a girl who has the experience and not to the apprentice to who makes mistakes? After 6, 12, or 18 months they are useful, but during that time the merchant is losing more than he is gaining. I learned the mercantile business in Germany, and had to work three years for nothing. I came to Olympia 26 years ago and worked for $2.50 per month and board, sending $1 each month home to Germany. If a person goes through this kind of experience they learn something. If they work without the proper effort on their part they don't get the right training, and they don't know anything about merchandise, with the exception of a few. If a girl has to work 18 months and gets a raise every six months they make better saleswomen. Some boys get $1 a day for delivering packages, but they leave at the end of the week because they can get 50 cents more somewhere else, delivering meat, for instance.. They don't consider if it will do them any good or mean more to them later on. These same boys are often delivering meat at $12 or $15 per week or working in a grocery store at $65 per month, when they might have stayed with the mercantile business and advanced and became one of the head clerks or a window dresser at a wage of $25 per week.

Prof. BEACH. Is there not only a few positions where a boy or girl can raise themselves? Is it not a fact that most of them can go just as high and then have to stop?

Mr. WOLFE. We always look for good men; we take some one who can do the work.

Prof. BEACH. In what way can the saleslady educate herself along the mer-cantile lines? What have you to give the saleslady a knowledge of furs—as to where the furs came from and the relative costs of furs; have you a definite way of teaching her those things?

Mr. WOLFE. If a person takes enough interest in those things, we take them in to a confidential position, and show them the difference of the furs.

Prof. BEACH. If a girl wanted to find out you would give her considerable instruction in the fur selling?

Mr. WOLFE. We have trade journals, and if they feel inclined to read some of our journals they can. We figure that if they are capable they are of more value to the store. I am a great believer in an apprentice. You have to ad-vance the same as in school, when a pupil passes from one grade to another in order to advance. You have to understand your business, you have to be up to date, for that reason I favor strongly the apprenticeship question, not only for the benefit of the employer, but for the employee as well. There are not many boys who have the patience to stay in one department long enough to learn much about it. They want to be moving every few months and will leave one store for a very little higher wage and go to another store. It reflects upon the store when a clerk makes a bad mistake in waiting upon a customer. They do not wish to misrepresent the store, but it is just ignorance on their part. The clerk did not mean to measure anything short; he thought he was doing the right thing, but he often makes mistakes, and for that reason I think this commission should allow for an apprenticeship period of some kind.

, Mrs. AXTELL. Having made this motion as to a minimum wage, I would like to hear from Mrs. Preston as to what the public schools have decided to do in regard to training girls for occupations. It is a question as to whether the employer can give the better training or whether the schools can give the better training.

; Mrs. PRESTON. I feel unprepared to come before this commission to-day, and I can only, in speaking to you, go back to the legislature of the State of Washington—it is responsible for some action, through its schools, in vocational training. We have had manual training in all the large schools for some time, but it has only been recently that we have been getting it started in the smaller districts, along practical lines. Last session of the legislature I came here a new superintendent, and I felt somewhat confused with the conflicting bills; but I said at once, this State wants vocational training, but the people who introduced the bills, many of them, were not educators. They would say I am introducing this bill because some one wanted me to. I am very much in favor of vocational training in our schools. When the next session of the legislature comes we will be ready to give something definite to the State of Washington. I wish, Mrs. Axtell, that you could ask me questions, as I have not quite gotten into the spirit of the meeting.

Mrs. AXTELL. These merchants are affected very much by taking away the apprenticeship—the minimum wage would be the least wage they could use in their employment.

Mrs. PRESTON. The continuation school, I think, is what is needed for the employers and employees alike. We have, down at Auburn, a plant being worked out on that line. This is being given very careful consideration in this State at this time. The public school, through this plan, shall give to the State of Washington more than it has ever given before.

Mrs. AXTELL. Will every boy and girl be trained so that they can earn their living when they come out of the public school?

Mrs. PRESTON. That is held to be true in Massachusetts, where the matter is being worked out very satisfactorily. It will take some time to be perfected, but I believe it is possible.

Mr. CUDDY. Is the State of Washington planning to teach girls and boys textiles?

Mrs. PRESTON. The schools are planning to teach the scholars textiles. The University of Washington and the State college are making a very careful study of the home economics, and you will find that textiles are going to be taught in the high schools.

Mr. CUDDY. That would just affect those who are just entering the public schools?

, Mrs. Preston. The time has come when the girls are not going out without knowing textiles.

Mr. CUDDY. It will be two years yet that the merchant will have to teach the girls.

Mrs. PRESTON. Have you anyone in your establishment who could teach textiles as they will be taught in school?

Mr. CUDDY. Yes; I think I have.

Mrs PRESTON. Where did they get their training, may I ask?

Mr. CUDDY. Some were educated in schools and some through the hard knocks of experience. I did not know before that it was being taken up in the schools to any great extent.

Mrs. PRESTON. The schools are taking up this matter and have been for some time. Miss Craig has been in every part of the State this year, and is teaching vocations.

Mrs. MUIR. In what department, Mr. Cuddy, do you commence your apprentices?

. Mr. CUDDY. In any department. After they have worked six months I might advance them to some other department. Will this commission take up the minimum wage and also the apprenticeship question? Are the inexperienced people to come up before this commission—will that apply to all?

The CHAIRMAN. All over 18 years.

Mr. CUDDY. A young lady might finish high school and then go into the millinery department to pack boxes, but she would not be worth the minimum wage.

The CHAIRMAN. The fact of the matter is you would not employ her.

Mr. CUDDY. We haven't brought up very thoroughly the idea of small-town expenses. The town of Sumner or Buckley, the expense of living is far below what it would be in the large city. A small store would almost be prohibited to run. A woman running a notion store could not afford to pay $500 or $575 per year for wages. If you will look up the Oregon law you will see there are two minimums fixed. I think we should economize and make a minimum wage of $9.50, and if we see this is not sufficient we will make it larger. I, therefore, offer an amendment to the motion substituting the sum of $9.50 for $10.75.

The CHAIRMAN. Will you kindly withhold your amendment for a few moments, Mr. Cuddy, while we hear a little more about the vocational schools in other States?

Mr. CUDDY. That is all right.

The CHAIRMAN. I would like to ask Mrs. Preston about the vocational law in the State of Wisconsin. Does it do away with the apprenticeship system in the State of Wisconsin? I believe the employer under the law is required to enter into a contract with the industrial commission, and it is mandatory that he allow his apprentices to go to this school one-half day in each week, but it does not do away with the apprenticeship system. Am I right about this?

Mrs. PRESTON. I believe Prof. Beach can answer that better than I.

Prof. BEACH. The continuation school operates with the apprenticeship system in Wisconsin. The employee must get instruction about five hours a week at this continuation school. The Wisconsin law insists that the contract shall be taken up through the employer and certain wage be given to employees.

Mrs. AXTELL. The employer must make them competent for their department of work. An apprenticeship of selling goods does not mean in any one department.

Prof. BEACH. Would you give an apprentice a training that would last over two years? The Wisconsin idea is to say that he must learn the business pretty thoroughly under a definite system of instructions.

The CHAIRMAN. I am under the impression that the law in the State of Wisconsin does not include the tuition of its pupils along the lines of apprentices. During the last session of the legislature a bill was introduced which provided for continuation schools in connection with our public-school system throughout the State. This bill was drawn up by a committee of which I was a member, and at that time I was quite conversant with the Wisconsin law; however, my mind is somewhat hazy at this time, yet, if I recollect correctly, I believe the Wisconsin employer, under the law, is required to enter into a contract with the industrial commission, and it is made mandatory, that he allow his apprentices to go to school one-half day each week, but this does not do away with the apprenticeship system.

Last winter I heard Mrs. Raymond Robbins deliver a lecture in Seattle on the minimum-wage law, in the course of which she referred to the apprenticeship system in effect under the industrial commission in Wisconsin. Mrs. Robbins made the statement that the commission in Wisconsin entered into a contract with the employer that he must retain the apprentices in his employ at the minimum wage after the apprenticeship period had been served. She stated that this information had come to her from the outside, and she was not certain that it was correct. At that time I was in no position to correct her in the matter, but later on I wrote to the industrial commission of Wisconsin concerning it, and got a reply to the effect that no such ruling had been made. I realize that the apprenticeship question enters into the question of the minimum wage very materially.

Mrs. UDALL. Mrs. Preston, is there anything definite being done along this line in the night schools?

Mrs. PRESTON. All of our larger high schools are giving considerable training to the millinery department.

Mrs. SWANSON. What percentage of the girls take this vocational training?

Mrs. PRESTON. I am unable to tell this, but I do know that there are a great many more than one would think; for instance, the Tacoma High School won in the vocational training, and there were about 900 in that department, I believe, although I am not sure I have the number just right. In the high schools in Seattle and Spokane and in the University of Washington and the State college there are a great many taking vocational training.

Mrs. SWANSON. Does the girl taking the classical course have time to take this vocational training?

Mrs. PRESTON. The girl taking the classical course does not need the vocational training and does not take it as a rule.

Mrs. MUIR. The saleswoman is born and not made. If she does not show her ability within a week or two she has to get out. Speaking of furs, the employer oftentimes does not know the name of the furs himself. We deal with the public directly, and we have to know a great deal about what we are handling. We have to make everyone feel good, and keep smiling even though we don't feel like it. You speak of the girls not feeling tired or looking tired when they leave the stores at night; we are probably smiling, but it is because we have so got in the habit of smiling. I am talking for those who are worse off than I am. The law demands that we have a living wage, and I know you want to do the right thing. We had better pay a little more and keep our girls who are Christians as Christians. I have to talk a great deal or I wouldn't make a good saleswoman. Mr. Wolff spoke of hiring a girl and keeping her two months and then discharging her because she made a mistake. Do you think, Mr. Wolff, you were giving her a fair chance?

Mr. WOLFE. I would like to correct your statement; I said that this young lady who worked in the store about two months made a great many mistakes. I did not discharge her; I told the friend of the family to tell the mother of the girl that I did not think she would ever make a good saleswoman. She was not suitable for store life. I also have in mind a very fine young lady who worked for me for a number of years and then went to Portland. She came back to Aberdeen and I gave her a position in the same department at a salary of $15 per week. It's the character of the person concerned that we consider, and what they desire to do. That is what makes the difference in salary. In regard to making a contract—I don't think this contract idea is a very good one. I learned the business in a two-year contract in Germany. If I had left before the contract was up, I would have had to start in all new at some other store. A girl who works in one store for two months could go to another store as an apprentice and get credit for the two months she had worked in the first store. A contract for one and one-half years would not be good, for I don't think the employee should be bound to stay in one store. The question of minors is far more important than the question of apprenticeship. An apprentice may start in the millinery department. The proprietor has the expense of teaching the girl the trade.

The CHAIRMAN. Mrs. Locke, how long does it take a girl to learn a department?

Mrs. LOCKE. To be a clerk you don't have to know every thread in the lace. Even the employer does not know a great deal about lace ofttimes, and a customer does not know lace very thoroughly either. It takes about six months for a girl to learn a certain department, as lace. A saleswoman is not made, as has been stated before; she is born a saleswoman. In Kansas City, Mo., I started in to learn the trade at 12 years of age. At 16 I was a stock girl and I knew the business thoroughly. I have advanced in salary because I have a stronger mind and demand larger wages.

Mr. MARVIN. Would it not be a good thing to fully discuss the question of apprenticeship and have you tell us what you think about these things?

Mr. CUDDY. The store of Marshall Field & Co. take a girl in, but she does not go into the store; she is kept out of sight; she has imaginary people for customers to whom she sells things, and in this way she gets her training before she goes into the store as a saleswoman. She is taught how lace is made and the value of articles, but she is not allowed to go down into the department.

Mrs. LOCKE. A party in Seattle, when he found out that I was coming up to this convention, came to me and said, "Mrs. Locke, I am trying out a plan in my store, I have taken five inexperienced girls into my store, two in the domestic department, one in the suit department, one in the laces, and one in the handkerchief. I have been watching these girls very closely and the books of three of these five are averaging more than the books of some of the girls I have had behind the counter for a number of years. Why is it?"

Mr. CUDDY. In a year they will probably be worth a great deal more than they are now.

Mrs. LOCKE. Not unless they get higher wages and are encouraged.

Mr. FLETCHER. I think we should get back to the motion and the reason why we are here to-day.

Mr. MARVIN. In regard to this question of minors and apprentices, I want to get just as much out of you as possible without you deciding it. All these questions must be considered in connection with the minimum wage—we can't get any away from it. I think I am here because I know a good many thousands of women and girls in the State of Washington and I am going to say that I wanted information on the subject. I want you all to speak freely. These subjects are so interwoven that you can't evade the questions. We would like to know what you would recommend before we do certain things that are in our power. It doesn't seem possible to submit any of these subordinate questions, but it will be very nice to escape responsibility. We want all the light that we can possibly have on the subject. We think the highest type of employers have been chosen, the highest type of employees and the loftiest type of disinterested parties. Between the period when Mrs. Preston's vocational education is in use and the work of this commission, you have some desperately pressing questions in the State of Washington to-day that need attention in regard to the girls. The reason you were chosen was because we believed you could get together.

We are remembering in whose interests the bill was framed, but we should remember also that the employer himself is just as much to be considered. What we want to do is to approximate the thing. I have learned a good deal on the minor and apprenticeship question, but I think we should get down to business as soon as possible.

Mr. PAINE. I arise to second the amendment offered by Mr. Cuddy. We do not think it is practical, at this time, to name a wage as high as was first made, inasmuch as the State of Washington is a new State and this is a new idea and we must go at it slowly. I, therefore, second the amendment of Mr. Cuddy.

Mr. CUDDY. I simply made the amendment of $9.50 for $10.75, as formerly suggested.

The CHAIRMAN. An amendment was offered to the motion that the sum of $9.50 be substituted for $10.75.

Mrs. MUIR. Do you hire people because you want to help them? No. There are people working in the stores who don't need the money. They have hausbands who make a big salary. Why do you employ them? We must bring out every phase of this for the benefit of these people. The people expect a great deal from the sales girl, they expect them to dress stylishly, a little bit up to date, and they can not do it on such small wages.

Mr. WOLFF. I give these ladies credit for the stand that they take but at the same time I would like to have them consider that we shouldn't be too hasty. If we take any extra measure it would be very much criticized everywhere. If the conditions are such that the business men are taxed more than they can stand, the person would rather go to some other State where they can do business for less money or a smaller per cent. I ask you all to use a little caution in taking a vote. We sometimes go too fast and then see our mistake when it is too late. We ought to use caution at all times.

Mrs. LOCKE. I think a motion has been made by one of the disinterested party that the minimum wage be $10.75; one of the employers has made a motion that it be $9.50—and I hereby make an amendment to the effect that the minimum wage be $10.25; that would make it 50 cents off. Therefore, my amendment is that the sum of $10.25 be substituted for the sum of $9.50 in the amendment of the original motion.

Mr. FLETCHER. I second the motion.

The CHAIRMAN. An amendment has been offered by Mrs. Locke that the sum of $10.25 be substituted for the sum of $9.50 in the amendment of the original motion, and seconded by Mr. Fletcher. Are you ready for the question?

Mr. WOLFE. When the time comes for this body to adjourn, I want to see a smile on everybody's face. I want it to be satisfactory to the employers of the State of Washington and also to the people of the State of Washington. If we go beyond what we feel the merchants can stand it will cause dissatisfaction. We must consider the notion stores or the stores who do business on a cheaper scale than we do, so I think that $10.25 would be more than some of the employers could stand.

Mrs. MUIR. If the employers think they can not stand this what are the girls going to do?

Mrs. LOCKE. Just imagine 25 cents for amusements.

Mrs. MUIR. Mr. Wolff, you speak of being cautious. That is the trouble, we have crept for years; we have been cautious or we wouldn't be here to-day. Your business will pay better if you pay the $10.75, for you will get better services. The stores in Los Angeles close their doors at 1 o'clock on Saturday and the merchants say themselves that they get better results. You speak of going to church—why we are too tired to go to church on Sunday— we have too much to do and besides we do not dare to spend the money for car fare and church contributions, but we must stay home and mend our clothes. Why, many girls even wash and iron on Sunday; what do you think of that?

Mr. FLETCHER. I would like to call attention to the ruling of this commission that "no member of the conference shall be entitled to speak more than twice on any subject, or more than five minutes at a time, except by unanimous consent of the conference." This conference has been brought together to find out on what a woman can live decently and healthfully. It seems to me that this last amendment is a very good one, although I would like very much to see the $10.75 carried, but, as has been suggested, we will have to go slow. These men do come in competition with mail-order houses in Oregon, Idaho, and other neighboring States; but there is a question in my mind if the matter in hand can be raised or lowered; $10.75 will mean about $1.46 or $1.47 per day. That is about as low as a man or woman can live decently or in good health.

Mr. PAINE. The point we are trying to get at is, What is the amount that a girl can live decently and in good health? We are trying to arrive at that. I have a little statement here that I wish to make. The girls do not seem to be shabbily dressed or look as if they were not well fed or well taken care of that we see in the department stores. We have had, out of about 200 employees, 108 girls who are now and have been getting from $6.50 to $10 per week. They have no other resources; some live at home. Above the $10 schedule we have 94 that are getting $11 and over, some getting $15, $25, and $35 per week. Out of 108 their present salary is $918 per week, or an average of a little less than $8.50. This is a good deal under what any of these are speaking of at the present time. Girls in this establishment are well fed, well taken care of, and well dressed. A wage of $9.50 would take care of them better than they are now.

Mrs. LOCKE. How many of them are living at home?

Mr. PAINE. I can not tell. We don't try to get girls who are working and living at home, especially.

Mrs. LOCKE. No girl that is self-supporting can live on $6.50, $7.50, or $8.50 and retain health and decency.

Mrs. PAINE. This State is young and must be taken care of. We are dependent upon the development of this State and we have a great deal to do. It would be positively a mistake for us to put this so high it would defer the developments of manufacturing. That is what our chamber of commerce is trying to do—to get industries in the State.

Mr. MUIR. I think there should be rest rooms, free lunches for girls in the mercantile establishments. Are not bookkeepers included?

The CHAIRMAN. Yes; bookkeepers are included in mercantile establishments.

Mr. MUIR. That was my understanding.

The CHAIRMAN. I have probably experienced considerable laxity in not holding the members of this conference down to the rules that govern; but I have done so with the feeling that every freedom should be given to each member to present his or her views to the utmost degree possible that we may come to an agreement and reach an unanimous decision as to the amount of a minimum wage. I feel that it is for the best interests of both the employers and employees, as well as for the people of the State of Washington, to have a little more light on this subject than we have thus far obtained. I would like to see this matter come to the point where there will be an absolute agreement on all sides. If this could be done, it will mean much toward helping the commission in enforcing the rulings when they become effective. If this conference can render a unanimous decision, it will tend to create a favorable sentiment throughout the State. A divided house on this question will also mean a divided State, and I am sure that every member of this conference will agree with me that if we can reach a unanimous agreement there will be little chance for a protest, both sides having thereby conceded that it is a fair minimum wage.

This is a very important matter that we have before us, because it involves not only the welfare and happiness of the working girls of this State, but it involves also the industry which we have under consideration and which will have to bear the increase that must be paid to these girls, and which they are entitled to.

I can not help but feel that I am warranted in making an appeal to each and every member of this conference to persevere toward reaching a unanimous decision. It appears to me that I would not be just in ending the debate so long as anyone has anything to say on the subject that will enlighten us. I believe that this conference can come to a direct agreement in this matter—that spirit is manifest on both sides.

Prof. BEACH. The question as to whether we have any right to consider·. the effect on the business or actual employing conditions has been brought be-· fore us. In one sense I question if we have any right to consider it, as ·our· original reason for meeting here was to determiñe the minimum wage of living. for women. It isn't the question of whether the minimum wage will help· the business; it is the question of whether the business will have a right to survive; so in one sense we have no right to consider whether the minimum· wage will drive out certain firms of business. Higher wages ·have, wherever they have been tried, tended to make better business. Some mercantile estab-· lishments are directly harmful to the people of Washington. We are not con-· sidering whether there are businesses which will not in the end be improved or some of them which will not cease to exist. On the other hand, I think we ought to recognize that the representatives of the employees speak with a good· deal of feeling, and there's a reason. I can't help but recognize the fact that far more is seen of the actual coñdition of living by those who represent the employees than by any other persons present. They speak because they face conditions as they really exist. We ought to recognize that the price of goods within the last 10 years has gone up so much that it has made it harder for the employee to live—the cost is 50 per cent more to-day for the ordinary retail prices. Six dollars to-day does not mean what it did six years ago. It is the person receiving the really minimum wage, the low wage, who first feels the pressure.

Then we face the fact that if a real living wage is not paid to the employee, if $6 is paid, and one can't live on $6, some one else is paying the actual living wage. I am 'inclined to believe that we should meet the wage that is suggested—$10.25. I believe that there is no danger of our going too fast. I believe personally with the statement made by one of the members, that we have gone desperately slow.·

I think that a wage of as low an amount as the Oregon wage will mean little to the employee. On the other hand, if it were possible to state to the people of Washington that we had reached a unanimous opinion, it would mean a great deal more. I would like to know if it would be possible for you to agree·upon $10. I say it only as a suggestion. Would it be possible for you to come to an agreement on $10?

Mr. CUDDY. Many men in· mills are getting $1.75 and $2 per day and are· supporting families. Even at $9.50 it would ·mean a 20 per cent jump in some of the stores.

Mrs. AXTELL. ·If it takes $10 for the average woman to live decently on, and if she is only getting $6, then the father or brother is paying the difference between the $6 and the $10. I went into one of our most fashionable dressmaking establishments in our city the other day and asked the owner what she was paying her girls. She said from $1.25 to $8 per week. She·is now charging as high as $100 for a gown, and I asked her why she did not pay them more. She said she would only have to charge more for the making of her gowns if· she did. In· the same way, if the wages are raised to the saleswoman, it will come upon the people who purchase the goods, but they are willing to pay it. It will be a great help and much value to the people of the State of Washington if we can come to a unanimous vote.

Mr. FLETCHER. It is true that all laws practically have to depend upon the public for their enforcement. If our representatives of the employers and the employees can get together, it will tend largely to solve the enforcement of this law. I think $10.25 is small; yet if, as Prof. Beach has suggested, the two interested parties could agree on $10 a week, I suggest $10 a week, for the reason that the commission has largely in its recommendations suggested $10 as the minimum wage. Our report says that the commission found that present conditions are not as they should be. They found that in mercantile industries the wages paid to employees are inadequate to supply them necessary cost of living and to maintain the workers therein in health, and that the conditions of labor therein are prejudicial to the health and morals of the workers. I would ask the representatives of the employers and the employees if they won't agree on a $10 basis. I would not vote for $10 per week, nothing less than $10.25, unless I thought that $10 would bring a unanimous vote.

Mrs. LOCKE. If we girls would decide on $10, would you gentlemen come up·to it?

Mr. MARVIN. I believe that there is such a splendid spirit in this conference that it would be a· great pity to let anything come in that would widen the gulf, but rather that everything be introduced that would bring us together. It seems to me that it would be better to have an effective minimum wage that was unanimously decided upon by all the representatives here so that the people throughout the State would not raise any questions. I think we have reason to be proud of the splendid spirit of the three men who represent the employers. I never saw three men, in a meeting of this kind, who have so little of the class consciousness. If the chair would make a motion that three, at least, of the representatives here meet a few hours later and talk this matter over (one from those representing the employers, one from the representatives of the employees, and one from the disinterested party), I think they could find a common basis on this matter.

· Mr. FLETCHER. I would suggest that Mr. Wolff, Mrs. Locke, and Prof. Beach get together and hold a conference, not deciding anything definite, but just talk the matter over, and we could meet again at 7.30.

The CHAIRMAN. It is moved and seconded that we adjourn until the hour of 7.30 and the chairman be instructed to.appoint a committee to meet and report at 7.30. All in favor signify by saying " aye." [All vote " aye."] I appoint Mrs. Locke, Prof. Beach, and Mr. Wolff as a committee to get together and talk this matter over. We will now adjourn until 7.30 to-night.

AFTER RECESS—8 P. M.

The CHAIRMAN. Meeting is called to order. Secretary will please call the roll.

Mr. FLETCHER. I move that the secretary be instructed to dispense with the calling of the roll, but simply note that all are present.

Prof. BEACH. The committee is in rather a dubious state. I think it would be possible for the commission to recommend a definite wage between the three, if it were possible for all the representatives present to agree upon it, or if some feeling of certainty in regard to the apprenticeship question could be obtained. The employers present have expressed the feeling of their right to use apprentices at a lower wage. If they could feel sure that some such plan as the Oregon plan would become the plan of this State, they would probably agree on a wage of $10. The representatives of the employers think they might come to a wage of $10 if it were unanimously decided upon. In regard to the apprenticeship question, the commission and not the conference has the right to decide about the apprenticeship system. The commission is not yet ready to say what it will do along that line. We are still therefore in a position that it would seem that, other things being satisfactorily settled, the employers might come up to $10 and the employees come down to $10 and that we could agree on a definite amount. We are not ready to report on an absolute· agreement, because of the possibility of employing a definite number of apprentices at a lower wage. I wish it were possible for us to reach that point. The vital thing is for both sides to reach an agreement.

Mr. FLETCHER. Is the commission in a position to give their idea along the line of minors?

The CHAIRMAN. After hearing Prof. Beach's report, I think it would be well for the commission to have a meeting and consider it. If this conference desires to know something about the apprenticeship question, I think it would be well for the commission to consider it and to see what could be done. We have done considerable investigating and I believe we could do no less than to have a meeting of the commission and discuss the matter. In the meantime it might be well for the committee to get together again and further discuss their end of the problem. What kind of an apprenticeship system would this conference like to have us consider? Along what lines?

Mr. WOLFF. The Oregon conference has an apprenticeship clause of 12 months at $6 per week for the first six months and $7.50 per week for the second six months. I think we could consider the apprenticeship at, say, $6 for the first six months, $7 for the second six months, and $8 for the third six months. If the apprenticeship clause were not in force in this State, I would just like to show how it would effect the girl who was just starting in and who worked· alongside of the girl with experience. She wouldn't have a chance with the girl who has had experience.

Mr. FLETCHER. Mr. Wolff, is there any system in stores of increasing wages? Do you have any system or do you just increase as you think they should be?

Mr. WOLFE. There is a report kept of the saleswomen by number, the amount paid per week or per month is mentioned, and the amount of their sales. If a girl gets $10 a week and don't sell $10 worth of goods a week, she is not advanced as fast as the girl whose sales are good.

Mr. FLETCHER. How long is it ordinarily that a girl has to work at low wages, say, $6 per week?

Mr. WOLFF. It all depends on circumstances.

Mr. FLETCHER. How long would they continue at those wages?

Mr. WOLFF. A girl started at $6, if in two weeks she shows she has ability, she is advanced to $7.50.

Mr. PAINE. It is sometimes from six months to a year before she is advanced.

Mrs. AXTELL. I would like to ask if the merchant would consider if girls come in as apprentices, through the commission, if the term of apprenticeship would be lengthened or determined by the commission?

Mr. WOLFE. I think it is not a good plan. There are too many apprentices in the State.

Mrs. AXTELL. You don't think their plan is feasible? If a girl were to leave your employment at the end of six months, she would have to have a recommendation from you. An apprentice would get her card from this commission. She would start in at a store and work five months, and when she left she would show on her card that she worked five months.

The CHAIRMAN. There are a few establishments in the States who have no girls who have worked 18 months.

Mr. WOLFF. If a girl worked during vacation, that would be applied on her apprenticeship.

Mr. CUDDY. A girl may come to me and state that she had worked a certain number of months and all we have is her word, but by this card system she would have to make affidavit saying she had worked a certain number of months.

Mr. PAINE. That would be very simple. I think this card system is a very important thing.

Mrs. UDALL. The Oregon law says "the length of term or apprenticeship shall be 18 months." I wish to say that the commission has not any intention of doing so and has told the mercantile men in private conference that they probably could not obtain the extension of the one year's apprenticeship period even if it were put up to the public conference, which action would have to be taken if the ruling were changed at all. The opportunity of putting this matter up to a conference is left with the mercantile men, however, and if they desire to submit the question to such a hearing the commission can not refuse them.

The CHAIRMAN. Wouldn't the 10-cent stores be inclined to take advantage of a ruling of that kind and take the inexperienced apprentices for the first six months and then discharge them and take a new relay and then discharge them, and so on?

Mr. PAINE. That would not last very long, the supply would soon stop.

The CHAIRMAN. Would the employers be willing to do this—this is clearly a suggestion—would the employers be willing to limit the number of apprentices employed in each establishment to a certain percentage?

Mr. PAINE. I think they would.

Mr. CUDDY. I can't see why they wouldn't. I can't see how a store could keep getting new apprentices.

Mrs. MUIR. Mr. Chairman, some one said there would be so many apprentices. A girl applies at a store for work and she has a letter from the last firm where she worked, but it is not the letter that does the work, it is the capabilities of the girl.

Mrs. LOCKE. Mr. Chairman, I think that each and every one of us have to start at the bottom and climb the ladder step by step. You take a girl who is left alone, her clothes are good, she applies for a position and she says she has had no experience; she goes to work at $6 per week and the second six months she gets $7 per week. She pays $2.50 for her room and 15 cents for each meal, which makes $3.45 a week; 60 cents for car fare; adding up that amount, it comes to $6.25. The next month after the six at $6, she gets $7. At the end of the year's time she should get the minimum wage, for she is in debt and her clothes are worn out, as she has not been able to get any during the year, and she needs the minimum wage to live on.

The CHAIRMAN. Would you apply that to all occupations in the mercantile establishments?

Mrs. LOCKE. I think $6.50 is the very smallest that should be given.

Mrs. SWANSON. Do you think the average girl goes into the department store with clothes enough to last a year?

Mrs. LOCKE. No; I was speaking of an exceptional girl. The average girl would not have clothes to last six months. The minimum wage that we are trying to get at now is not what we should have. We should get $8 for the inexperienced help.

Mr. MARVIN. I would like to ask these three ladies whether, in their judgment, after 12 months, a girl over 18 years of age would be capable of earning the minimum wage. Whether they think that 12 months is long enough to demonstrate.

Mr. PAINE. We can't say that all girls will be worth a certain amount. We have girls who start in at $6 and are getting $15 at the end of the year. Others never get more than $7 or $8.

Mr. MARVIN. I have put these same propositions up to the labor leaders of this State, yet the women of this State have looked the matter over and they do not want a long term of apprenticeship.

Mrs. PAINE. The only use we make of apprentices is to wrap packages and do little odd jobs.

Mrs. LOCKE. Are bundle wrappers to get the minimum wage at the end of the year? When are they to learn the business?

The CHAIRMAN. I will read the section of the law covering the point of apprenticeship.

"For any occupation in which a minimum rate has been established the commission, through its secretary, may issue to a women physically defective or crippled by age or otherwise, or to an apprentice in such class of employment or occupation as usually requires to be learned by apprentices, a special license authorizing the employment of such licensee for a wage less than the legal minimum wage; and the commission shall fix the minimum wage for such person, such special license to be issued only in such cases as the commission may decide the same is applied for in good faith and that such license for apprentices shall be in force for such length of time as the commission shall decide and determine is proper."

I do not think there should be apprenticeship needed in all departments of a mercantile establishment.

Mr. CUDDY. In what department do you mean would not need apprentices?

The CHAIRMAN. I would go to your books in order to determine that. I would consider such occupations which show on your books that a girl had never advanced in them above the wage at which she started are not apprenticeship occupations. I don't think there is an apprenticeship in the 10-cent store. I think the average girl can hand out goods over a 10-cent counter after a week's experience.

Mrs. SILBAUGH. The 10-cent store merchants say the girls do not have to sell the goods; the goods sell themselves. Some departments in a mercantile store would come under the same heading.

Mr. FLETCHER. I doubt very seriously if any of the employments Mr. Paine has in mind would come under the apprenticeship head. Can't you employers leave the minor and apprenticeship propositions to this commission?

Mr. CUDDY. I hardly think there are as many girls under 18 years of age employed as you are led to believe. The average girl is 16 or 17 before she finishes school.

Prof. BEACH. I think this report says that about one-half of the girls are minors throughout the State.

Mrs. LOCKE. This minimum wage is going to give better salesmanship throughout the store in every way.

Prof. BEACH. You will find a statement on page 90 that between 11 and 12 per cent of the workers are minors.

Mr. MARVIN. As I figured it up, there are a little over one-twelfth of them minors, as you will see from the table on page 18; about 25 per cent of the whole.

Mr. WOLFF. The minimum wage for the city of Portland is $9.25; the minimum wage for the minors is $6.25. Now, I think the people of the Oregon Industrial Welfare Commission are all fair-minded people. It is the fair stand of the commission that has won the good will of everyone, but I think they must realize that we must look at this from all sides and be cautious.

Mrs. AXTELL. You don't think the Oregon commission could beat ours, do you, Mr. Wolff?

Mr. WOLFF. No; I think we have a fine commission.

Mr. FLETCHER. Miss Gleason says $10 is the minimum wage upon which a girl can live.

Mr. WOLFF. There is not a State in the Union that has a minimum wage as high as our friends here would like to have us consider.

Mr. MARVIN. I think it should be remembered that there are only three States in the Union who have passed any minimum wage at all, and the rest haven't passed any laws.

Prof. BEACH. I believe, since the apprenticeship idea can not be considered by this conference—that is, they can do nothing definite about it, and the employer can not get a very large proportion of people who would be considered apprentices; the law is also pretty definite in regard to minors—as this conference can do nothing with these things, I feel very much like proposing to the conference that we substitute for the motions that we have had before us the $10 wage as a minimum wage, with the general understanding that we have had on the problems regarding apprentices, that we agree on a $10 minimum wage. I will make this in the form of a motion—that is, that the sum of $10 be an adequate minimum wage.

Mr. FLETCHER. I will second that substitute, with the understanding that it be voted for unanimously, but if we can not get all to agree to that, it will be my right to withdraw this second.

Mr. CUDDY. I would like to say that after the meeting this afternoon, Mr. Paine and I thought that we would like to get in communication with some of the other people in the State, so we called up Seattle and Tacoma and talked to the various merchants' associations. They were extremely opposed to the $10 minimum, stating that it was $1.50 higher than throughout the State of Oregon, and they considered it altogether too high. They thought that for a start it was entirely too high, and that we ought not to jump at this in too sudden a manner, but that $9 would be about right. They stated that they couldn't even stand $9.50.

Mrs. AXTELL. When this law was made, it was made that we establish a minimum wage for women workers whereby they might live decently and healthfully. If conditions had been right, this law would never have been made. Conditions were wrong, and the law was made. If we wanted to at this time we could have communications pouring in to us, too, but we did not try to get into communication with anyone.

The CHAIRMAN. Getting back to our motion again. It was moved by Prof. Beach, as a substitute motion, that the sum of $10 be an adequate minimum wage for women in the mercantile establishments. Seconded by Mr. Fletcher, reserving the right to withdraw his second if the vote was not unanimous. Are you ready for the question?

Prof. BEACH. Question.

Upon roll call the following vote was recorded:

Ayes: Mrs. Locke, Mrs. Muir, Miss Smith, Mrs. Axtell, Mr. Fletcher, and Prof. Beach.

Noes: Mr. Paine, Mr. Wolff, and Mr. Cuddy.

Mr. FLETCHER. Having reserved the right to do so. I withdraw my second to the motion just voted upon, and as it is now 9 o'clock I move that we now adjourn for to-night.

Prof. BEACH. I second the motion.

The CHAIRMAN. Mr. Fletcher, having reserved the right to withdraw his second to the motion just voted upon if a unanimous vote was not forthcoming, takes advantage of that privilege, and the motion does not prevail. It has been moved and seconded that we adjourn until 9 o'clock in the morning. All in favor of this motion will signify their assent by saying " aye."

(All voted "aye.")

We now adjourn until 9 o'clock to-morrow morning.

WEDNESDAY—9 A. M.

The CHAIRMAN. Meeting will please come to order and secretary be instructed to call the roll.

(Roll call by secretary; all present.)

The motion that was voted upon before we adjourned last night was offered by Prof. Beach as a substitute motion, that the sum of $10 be recommended as an adequate minimum wage, and same was seconded by Mr. Fletcher, who reserved the right to withdraw his second if the vote on said motion was not unanimous. The motion was 6 to 3, so Mr. Fletcher had the right to withdraw his motion, which he did.

Mr. FLETCHER. I withdrew that second to the motion. I understood last evening that the commission might be able to report along the line of the apprenticeship question. Some of the employees have suggested that if the commission would suggest their intention as to allowing apprentices—for a period of a year—the first six months at $6 and the second six months at $7. Have the commission held their meeting, and have they anything to suggest? It was suggested that the number of apprentices be limited—that is, 1 apprentice to every 6 experienced employees, or 2 to every 12 employees. That was merely suggested by Mr. Cuddy.

The employers would be willing, it is thought, if the commission would give them that assurance, to perhaps vote on the $10 minimum wage. The major fraction would allow them two appentices, 1 apprentice for 6 employees up to 9 employees; out of 10 employees they would be entitled to 2 apprentices. In other words, 17 apprentices to every 100 employees.

The CHAIRMAN. Does the Chair understand that there is practically an agreement between all the members of the conference to the effect that if the commission would adopt a ruling to that effect that they would vote on the $10 wages?

Mr. FLETCHER. I haven't talked to all the gentlemen, but Mr. Cuddy just told me that they had practically come to that agreement.

Mr. PAINE. I think the matter of apprentices should best be left to the commission. Is a motion in order or an amendment to an amendment? I think that the employers have the desire to treat fairly this question and that they are inclined to recommend a fair minimum wage and that we feel it quite important that the ■nference shall unite on some wage that they can recommend unanimously. The matter between the employee and employers seems to be a little at variance. I would make this motion, that the conference recommend the minimum wage of $10 with the understanding that the commission set an apprenticeship period of one year, six months at $6 and six months at $7; but that they allow 17 per cent of the total number of females employed as apprentices and leave the minor question to the commission.

Mr. CUDDY. I second that motion.

The CHAIRMAN. It is moved and seconded, as a substitute motion, that a minimum wage of $10 be allowed, with an apprenticeship period of one year, the first six months at $6 and the second six months at $7, and to limit the apprenticeship period in the different establishments to 17 per cent of the total employees.

Mrs. AXTELL. I move as an amendment to this substitute motion that we give $2 per day, or $12 per week, as the minimum wage straight, and that the matter of apprenticeship be left to the commission entirely. I am making this motion because all the concession seems to be on one side, that of the employees, and I do not think it fair to them.

Mr. FLETCHER. What do you think as to the legality of our making a recommendation such as Mr. Paine has suggested? We are here to decide upon a fair minimum wage for the employees in the mercantile establishments, and I do not believe we can have any string attached to it. The recommendation as proposed is to fix the amount of $10 as conditional. I do not know if that is permissible. I think that we ought to propose a straight minimum wage and not recommend anything on condition that something else be done.

The CHAIRMAN. I think the conference should not recommend anything. The commission has not asked them to recommend.

Mr. FLETCHER. I doubt if Mr. Paine's motion is in order. I doubt if we have a right to say an employee in a mercantile establishment shall live on a certain amount, providing the apprenticeship is fixed at a certain period and amount of wages by the commission.

Prof. BEACH. I, too, think it is not permissible.

The CHAIRMAN. Since that point has been raised the Chair hadn't thought of that phase of the question, and I think the Chair is justified in ruling that motion out of order.

Mr. FLETCHER. I think the Chair is certainly right.

Mr. PAINE. It is quite a vital thing, as the two come so closely together, and it was my idea that we should have some idea as to what the commission expected to do along this line. Can we get at this in some other way?

The CHAIRMAN. I feel that it would be a concession on the part of the commission to offer any compromise, and it might be possible to do so in the event that we could get a unanimous vote on the $10 minimum; unless the commission is assured of that we can not suggest anything.

Mr. MARVIN. I sometimes wonder whether the highest point of all freedom is not the yielding or giving up. I wonder whether that doesn't lie at the base of all legislation. I wonder whether we ought to entertain the idea that we can't get together. I wouldn't like to come within a thousand miles of preaching, but I would like to suggest to the ladies that it is not a step down but a step up from an abominable position. If we think of it as coming up from what has been, I think we shall see in it a vast improvement. I do believe that we are coming to a place where it would be a great pity not to get together. My own personal views of the matter are these: If this commission, after bringing you nine good folks together, should fail in getting a unanimous vote on anything, there is very little hope that it could bring nine other good folks in this State together who could agree.

Mrs. AXTELL. Do you think the concession should all be made on one side?

Mr. MARVIN. I don't like to answer that question, but it seems to me that back of that there lies an actual condition, out of which we are going to take a vast number of the women of the State of Washington, and I know Mrs. Axtell's mind is so much more acute than mine; still I wonder if Mrs. Axtell is not somewhat of an idealist, and is this not a practical condition and that concessions should be made on both sides.

Mr. WOLFF. After hearing Mrs. Axtell, I can realize the views she takes. From her point of view she thinks it should be fair that both sides should meet on half basis. I would like to explain to this conference how and why we came to the conclusion of offering a minimum of $9. I might say the minimum should be $8 or $8.50, and then it would have brought the figures nearer to what they should be, but we suggested $9, and I want to show you the fair stand that the employers take, and I think there is not a person in this room who will not agree with me. Before coming here I inserted a communication in every paper—daily, weekly, and semiweekly—on Grays Harbor, and asked the employers to express their ideas on the subject. In investigating the costs of living I have talked to women who work for more and some who work for less than $10. I wasn't selfish and narrow minded, not picking the people that I knew would agree with me, but I have talked with women who would not be affected by a low wage rate, and I have talked with women who would be affected, and they told me if they could only get $9 they would be satisfied. I based my minimum on the judgment of women who have to live on $9 or less. For that reason I do not see how we could take any fairer stand than we did. We thought $9 would be fair, as our figures came to $8.98. For that reason I would like to say to Mrs. Axtell that $9 by the workers is considered a very fair wage, so you can see the employers are not selfish; they want to take a very reasonable stand, but they must protect the interests of the other employers of the State.

Mrs. AXTELL. Do I understand that we can get a unanimous vote on the $10 minimum?

Mr. WOLFF. Yes; if we can be assured that we can get an apprenticeship period as was suggested.

Mr. FLETCHER. I think the $10 basis that we have figured on is fair; it is not as much as I would like to see, but, as suggested by Mr. Marvin, we are somewhat in the nature of a revolution in the business of the State. All of the business houses will have to readjust themselves even on the rate of $10. I think $6 or $7 is low for apprentices, but the old idea of apprentices was that they work for two, three, or four months at no wage. At the end of that time she is properly entitled to a great deal more money. This is a great step forward, and we have to step along slowly and feel our way and get this law into perfect effect. Experience will always show us improvements that I believe will easily be made as the law is applied and works out. The thing that I would like to see is to get all the people back of this law to get it started. I believe all the people will see where it must be improved. This that we are doing to-day will only last for one year, then it can be changed. In regard to the $5 or $7 for apprentices, women all over this State have been working for years at $6 and $7 or less. Now, the girl will start at a better wage than a great many of the women have been working for. I would ask these women if they are willing to vote for $10 as a minimum wage in the mercantile establishments if the apprentices wage shall be fixed at $6 for the first six months and $7 for the second six months. If this first motion is carried for $10, do you ladies feel that you, as representatives of the women of this State, could vote for such a recommendation to the commission? That don't necessarily have to be the wage decided upon, but if it should be it would be a step in the right direction and it only has to last for one year. No one can get everything they want, but all life is made up of compromises and I would like to know if the ladies don't think they can join in a recommendation of this kind.

Mrs. MUIR. I understand that this commission was appointed because they had investigated and found that these girls were working for $6 and $7 per week and could not live respectfully and healthfully on this amount. What do you gentlemen consider a good length of time for a girl to become an experienced worker?

Mr. FLETCHER. At the end of the year a girl will get $10 per week or whatever is decided upon by the commission.

Mrs. MUIR. Don't you think they will keep bringing girls as apprentices into the store? You see there is a great army of people always wanting work.

Mr. FLETCHER. I don't think a store would prosper by always hiring new clerks. Mrs. Muir, would you suggest no apprentices at all?

Mrs. MUIR. I should suggest two months at $6 per week for an apprentice. At the end of the two months she is entitled to the minimum wage of $10. Some of them at the end of two months are first-class saleswomen.

Mrs. LOCKE. You are allowed 17 girls out of 100 girls for apprentices. Mr. Paine contends that he employs about 800 girls.

Mr. PAINE. No; not all girls.

Mrs. LOCKE. Well, we will take a store that hires 800 girls, for instance, that would be 136 inexperienced girls—where would they all work?

Mr. PAINE. In my particular line of work there is plenty for all of them to do.

Mrs. LOCKE. I do not think a girl can live on $6 per week. The very least she can live on is $7 per week, and I think a year is too long for a girl to work as an apprentice. It didn't take me that long to learn the business.

Mr. FLETCHER. How would you think six months at $7 and six months at $8 would be?

Mrs. LOCKE. That would be a little better but it would make it very hard for the girl to live on even that.

Mr. CUDDY. How are they getting along now?

Mrs. LOCKE. They are not getting along on it alone—they are selling their souls, sir.

Mr. CUDDY. This is what one of the girls in Tacoma, who is getting $6 a week, says, " I always buy the best of food but I use it economically and get along very well on $6 per week." But we will let that drop and try to get down to business. We are here to try to get together on some agreement.

Mrs. MUIR. Our lists were ridiculously low but you gentlemen's were much lower. Why is it, gentlemen, that you don't want to give this $10 minimum? Can't you afford it?

The CHAIRMAN. I would like to call your attention to page 18 of the report of the commission. You will find there that out of 5,155 employees in the State of Washington 2,777 are getting $10 or over per week and 2,267 are getting under $10. Therefore a wage of $10 would be a benefit to over half of the women workers in the State. The proposition has been made here that 17 per cent of these women be classified as apprentices. We find here that 25 are getting less than $4; 43 from $4 to $4.95; 99 from $5 to $5.95; 332 from $6 to $6.95; 488 from $7 to $7.95; 660 from $8 to $8.95; 620 from $9 to $9.95; 2,267 being the total number of employees receiving under $10 and 2,277 receiving $10 and over.

Mr. WOLFF. If these girls who are getting $4 and $5 per week had worked one year they would get the minimum of $10 if this was the wage fixed, also all the apprentices receiving $4 and $5 would be raised to the $6 minimum for the apprentices, if this is the amount decided upon by the commission.

Mrs. SILBAUGH. In regard to this report, I wish to say that it is perfect, so far as it goes, but there are a great many we didn't hear from, so it would also lift a great many more girls from a lower to a higher wage than we are now figuring on.

The CHAIRMAN. I want to say in regard to apprentices, I assume that to be a maximum amount of six months at $6 and six months at $7. That would not preclude the commission from issuing a permit saying the girl could work for two months only and then get the maximum. Is that the idea you have?

Mr. FLETCHER. Yes; that was my idea.

The CHAIRMAN. If we would make a ruling that if a girl was an apprentice and should work 6 months at $6 and 6 months at $7, then supposing she had already served 9 months as an apprentice, wouldn't it be the duty of the commission to issue her a permit to receive $7. The law would permit the com_mission to extend the time of the girl.

Mr. FLETCHER. I think the conference should consider as to whether or not we should agree on a minimum wage of $10. I would like to make a recommen_dation like this: "I would recommend that the commission allow a period of apprenticeship in mercantile establishments for such period and at such wages and under such rules and regulations as the commission may prescribe. In this connection, would further recommend that the apprentice period do not extend more than one year and the wages be not less than $6.50 a week and the per_centage of apprenticeship of total employees do not exceed 17 per cent."

Mrs. LOCKE. If you would compromise by making the period of apprentice_ship 6 months and bringing the wage up 50 cents, that would be fine.

Mr. PAINE. I want to ask if Mr. Fletcher had in mind the percentage.

Mr. FLETCHER. I did add that I further recommended that the apprentice_ship do not extend over a certain length of time.

Mrs. LOCKE. I think that percentage is rather high. I want to do my very best to help conditions while I am here at the conference, and I know there are lots of girls who have been down to the grindstone for so long that I think $7 a week would be like a mountain, but they can not live on $6.

Mr. MARGIN. Mrs. Locke, I am glad to hear you say that. Doesn't it seem right to do something that is within reach of everyone. To take 18,000 girls in the State of Washington and lift them from under the $10 wage to the $10 and then lift a considerable number of others who are at the present time under the $6.50 up to the $6.50—does that seem to be worth while? Does it seem to be worth while to lift these 18,000 girls out of this "under ten" to the "ten"?

Mrs. UDALL. I am wondering if you all realize that unless this conference does not come to some definite understanding that we will have to call another meeting, but none of you will probably be on the next conference. Some one else will have to decide these questions.

Mrs. AXTELL. When Mrs. Udall spoke of the apprenticeship period and if this conference did not come to some definite understanding, it made me think of the time when the law was before the House and how long it took us to decide this thing. The legislature thought that this commission could get together so much better and could make so much more just wages than the legislature, that for that reason the commission was appointed. Now, we come together and I think there is a spirit of compromise, and I think we could come together on the $10-a-week wage and leave this apprentice period to the commission. I think they are perfectly capable and willing to be fair about it. I think they will give you gentlemen a fair apprenticeship period and will give you a fair minor wage.

The CHAIRMAN. I would like to say that we have representatives from the public that are practically taking the same position that the commission are— a position of neutrality. Would it be well for the three members representing the disinterested public to meet with the commission and talk this apprenticeship period over? I believe they are perfectly fair in this matter and something might be done if we can get together and talk this over without any interference from other parties. If that will be allowable we might be able to accomplish something.

Prof. BEACH. It seems to me that this conference must eventually pass some motion on the question of minimum wage. It must not be entangled with any question of apprenticeship. The best we can do in regard to apprentices is to talk it over and we have talked it over very thoroughly, so we will now have to leave it to the commission for its final decision, and we have great faith in their ability. The law distinctly gives you the positon of doing the deciding. You must not take from us anything that looks like dictation, so I think we must try now to decide on the problem of wage. I think the employers can reach the point of $10, but they would like to feel assured that the apprenticeship period will be as they wish it. The ladies think the apprenticeship period should be short. If the employers can pay $10 on the basis of the idea that that is not an exorbitant minimum, then I would feel that we have pretty nearly reached the point, if you can agree that that is reasonable, with a rational commission to work out other matters, and there are one or two other matters of vital importance which this commission will have to take up. But if you can reach the conclusion that $10 is not too high and you can make it, then you ought to be able to pass a measure of this kind. I wish we might proceed with the motion.

I will move that you substitute for the motions that you have before us a motion recommending to your commission that the conference approve of $10 as a minimum wage.

Mr. FLETCHER. I second the motion.

Mrs. AXTELL. I withdraw my motion.

Mrs. LOCKE. I would suggest that if they would take six months for an apprentice at $7 a week and at the end of the six months they are to get a minimum wage, I think that would be doing justice to all.

The CHAIRMAN. It has been moved by Prof. Beach, and seconded by Mr. Fletcher, as a substitute for previous motions, that the sum of $10 be recommended to the Industrial Welfare Commission as an adequate minimum wage for experienced adult women employed in the mercantile establishments in this State. I would ask Prof. Beach if I have put this motion correctly.

Prof. BEACH. Yes; that is correct.

Mr. PAINE. I believe that the employers would like, realizing that this matter is up to the commission to decide, you to understand that you have no recommendations coming from us, but would like to embody in the second resolution the facts that we have outlined heretofore, understanding, however, that it is up to the commission to reject or adopt this resolution. We would like to go on record as attempting to do what is for the best interests of the employers and employee. We want to go on record as having attempted to assist the commission in arriving at what is fair and right. In giving a short period of apprenticeship I feel that we would not be doing right by the employee.

Mrs. AXTELL. Mr. Paine, would you also be willing that the others make their recommendations?

Mr. PAINE. I think it would be fair.

Mrs. AXTELL. Mrs. Locke, then you can put your recommendation up to the commission.

Mr. MARVIN. Then, Mrs. Axtell, would you be willing to put up a recommendation to the commission also?

Prof. BEACH. I think there would be nothing unlawful in doing that. The three different parties will only present their views to the commission for their consideration.

The CHAIRMAN. We will have a moment's recess to get these resolutions in shape for the commission.

AFTER RECESS.

The CHAIRMAN. The meeting will now please come to order. The motion before the house, which was read a moment ago, is to the effect that the sum of $10 be recommended by this conference to the commission as a minimum wage for experienced adult women employed in mercantile establishments. The secretary will please call the roll.

(Upon roll call the following vote was recorded:)

Ayes: Mrs. Locke, Mrs. Muir, Miss Smith, Mrs. Axtel, Mr. Fletcher, Prof. Beach, Mr. Paine, Mr. Wolff, and Mr. Cuddy.

Noes: None.

The CHAIRMAN. The motion for a $10 minimum wage for women workers in mercantile establishments has been carried unanimously.

Mr. FLETCHER. I think we might as well go on in regard to a recommendation as to minors and apprentices. I think we ought to leave this matter entirely to the judgment of the commission. I move that we take up the provisions that should be required.

The CHAIRMAN. The question before the house is what length of lunch period is required for the women in the mercantile establishments.

Mr. FLETCHER. Mrs. Locke how long do you think a clerk should have for the lunch period?

Mrs. LOCKE. I think they should have at least one hour, and I believe this is given in most of the stores; it is in our store, with 15 minutes for rest in the morning and afternoon.

Mr. FLETCHER. How about in Tacoma, Mrs. Muir?

Mrs. MUIR. Tacoma merchants give one hour.

Mr. FLETCHER. Miss Smith, how long in Spokane?

Miss SMITH. I think one hour is the usual time given.

Mr. FLETCHER. I move that the conference recommend to the commission that the period of one hour be required in all the mercantile establishments for lunch.

Mr. PAINE. I second the motion.

The CHAIRMAN. It is moved and seconded that one hour be given as the period for noon luncheon. All in favor signify by saying " aye." [All voted " aye."] Now we will consider what provisions should be required in each mercantile establishment for (a) toilet for women workers, (b) rest room, (c) ventilation.

I haven't made much of a survey of the mercantile establishments, but I have found in many of the factories that women have to go into a toilet next to a gentlemen's or used by the gentlemen, so I know these conditions do exist.

Mrs. LOCKE. At one time I worked on a power machine in a factory in the East, and the toilet conditions were very bad there; I have also heard that they were not good in the factories in Seattle. The women employees sometimes have to go downstairs and into another building, and when busy at work it takes a lot of time, and conditions should be changed.

Mr. FLETCHER. How about the mercantile establishments, Mrs. Locke?

Mrs. LOCKE. In large department stores they are much better than in factories—at least, all I know about.

Prof. BEACH. In the 10-cent stores, Miss Gleason says the condition is very bad.

Mrs. LOCKE. The conditions in the 10-cent stores are very bad, and I think it ought to be looked into. The ventilation is also bad; oftentimes the windows open into an alley which is covered over, and thus they get practically no fresh air.

Mrs. SILBAUGH. I was with Miss Gleason when she made investigation of some of the 10-cent stores. The girls in some places had to go down dark stairways, where the ventilation was bad, and into another building to reach the toilet.

The CHAIRMAN. If the conference so desires, it may debate on the other two questions—rest rooms and ventilation.

Mrs. LOCKE. I think in every store there should be two or three couches in a rest room, so the girls could go and lie down when they are not feeling well. I think they should have a comfortable lunch room, where it is nice and clean, where the girls can go and eat their lunches if they are bringing them to the store in order to be economical. In many of the stores they have a lunch room, but it is not very clean, and the rest room has only stiff-backed chairs and no rockers to rest in. I think they should have couches to lie on, even if just for 15 minutes.

Mrs. MUIR. I never thought much about a rest room. I don't have much time for rest. I am busy from 9 to 12 and from 1 until 6. If I have to buy a pair of shoes or a new hat or anything of the sort, I have to get them at noon and run and do my errands after I eat my lunch. Unless I have something to do that takes up my hour, I go straight back to the store, so I don't have time to lie down. I need it, I will confess, but I am interested in my work and neglect myself.

Mr. MARVIN. I would suggest that you appoint a committee consisting of Mr. Paine, Mrs. Axtell, and Miss Smith to draw up resolutions on these matters and bring them before the commission.

The CHAIRMAN. I think that would be a good idea ; then the conference would be able to consider them.

Mrs. LOCKE. Another thing I would like to bring up—there is not a store in Seattle that gives proper heat to the girl. There is not a girl in our store that did not go home two, three, or four days last winter on account of colds. I myself have lost more than that. We have to wear sweaters, which is very bad, as we take them off when we go out, and then catch cold. I wear woolen underwear, and pay a little more than a dollar and a half per pair for them. The ventilation in the 10-cent stores is very bad.

I also think there should be vestibules or storm doors to keep the draft out, as the girl in the drug department or any department up near the door gets so much draft. Its to maintain health we are speaking of, and to help the girls. Many of the girls are out of work a great deal on account of colds.

Mrs. SILBAUGH. On my investigations I have found in Seattle that one or two of the stores have storm doors, but in some instances it has been very noticeable where they needed them.

Mr. WOLFF. I favor all Mrs. Locke has said, and I think most of the employers in the State would also favor these suggestions. In regard to conditions, I would like to say in the larger department stores the women employees and men employees should use a different clock. Before they leave the store they have to punch the same clock, and my idea is that they stand in line too close togther. So I think there should be two clocks—one for the women and one for the men.

Mrs. MUIR. That would be an awful expense.

Mr. WOLFF. The employer will have to buy the clocks and stand the expense.

Mrs. MUIR. But the little apprentices will have to pay for the clocks, as they do all the other expenses. Let the women work on their honor, as the little children do in the schools.

Prof. BEACH. It is nearly 12 o'clock, and I think Mr. Marvin's suggestion of a committee is a very good one; the committee being suggested is also a good one, and I should like to make the suggestion that the committee made up of the three persons proposed—Miss Smith, Mrs. Axtell, and Mr. Paine—get together and draw up their resolutions.

Mr. FLETCHER. This matter of these rules and regulations, I think this should be left to the commission, and I make a motion that the conference recommend to the commission that it issue such obligatory orders as in its judgment may be necessary to provide proper toilet facilities, rest rooms, and ventilation for women workers in mercantile establishments of the State.

Mr. PAINE. I second that motion.

Mrs. MUIR. It is necessary that your stores be open about 20 minutes before the girls come in so that the fresh air can circulate and get the foul air of the day before out of the building.

The CHAIRMAN. It has been moved by Mr. Fletcher and seconded by Mr. Paine that the conference recommend to the commission that it issue such obligatory orders as in its judgment may be necessary to provide proper toilet facilities, rest rooms, and ventilation for women workers in the mercantile establishments of the State. All in favor signify by saying "aye." [All vote "aye."] I am glad to see you all leaving in a good spirit, and if we can keep the people of the State in as good a frame of mind I think we will be able to enforce this law properly. I want to thank you all for the confidence shown and for the feeling of good will expressed by all. Motion is now in order for adjournment.

Mr. FLETCHER. I move we adjourn.

Mr. PAINE. I second the motion.

The CHAIRMAN. It has been moved and seconded that we adjourn. All in favor signify by saying "aye." Carried.

PEARL E. MOTZER, Secretary.

OLSON EXHIBIT NO. 2.

MANUFACTURING CONFERENCE, SENATE CHAMBER, CAPITOL BUILDING, OLYMPIA, WASH., MAY 12 AND 13, 1914.

Meeting called to order at 9 a. m. by Mr. E. W. Olson, chairman of the industrial welfare commission. The entire commission, composed of Mr. Olson, Mr. Marvin, Mrs. Silbaugh Mrs. Swanson, and Mrs. Udall, were present. This commission and the following representatives composed the conference: Mr. E. W. Olson, chairman; Mr. Fred Krause, Mr. O. B. Dagg. and Mrs. O. C. Fenlason, representing the employers; Miss Emma Foisie, Mrs. Belle Robair, and Mrs. F. H. Lawton (née Miss Margaret McInnes), representing the employees; Mrs. W. C. Mills, Mr. Edgar C. Snyder, and Prof. W. M. Kern, representing the public.

Roll call by secretary. All members of the conference and all members of the industrial welfare commission answered to the roll call.

The CHAIRMAN (reading):

To members of the factory conference:

After due investigation of the manufacturing industry of the State of Washington, the industrial welfare commission has found that the wages paid the female employees in said industry are inadequate to supply them necessary cost of living and to maintain the workers in health, and this commission has further found that in said industry conditions of labor exist that are prejudicial to the health or morals of the women employed in said industry.

Therefore, by virtue of the authority in it vested by section 174, Laws of 1913, State of Washington, this commission has called a conference composed of an equal number of representatives of employers, employees, and the public, which, after due consideration, is to recommend to this commission the amount of an adequate wage in said manufacturing industry to permit of a self-supporting woman to maintain herself in decency and comfort, and to also

recommend other conditions of work hereinafter specified. Said conference so selected is composed of the following members:
Fred Krause, O. B. Dagg, and O. C. Fenlason, representing the employers; Mrs. Belle Robair, Miss Emma Foisie, and Mrs. F. H. Lawton, (née Miss Margaret McInnes), representing the employees; Mrs. W. C. Mills, Edgar C. Snyder, and Prof. W. M. Kern, representing the public.

Therefore, in accordance with the foregoing, the Industrial Welfare Commission of the State of Washington herewith submits to the conference the following questions:

What is the sum required per week to maintain in decent conditions of living a self-supporting woman employed in a manufacturing establishment in the State of Washington? The requisites for such decent conditions of living are itemized in the list below:

Meals, room, shoes and rubbers, repairing shoes, stockings, underwear, petticoats, suit, coat, dresses and aprons, shirt waists, handkerchiefs, corsets, corset waists, gloves, neckwear, hats, umbrella, repair of clothing, laundry, medicine and dentistry, street car fare, newspapers and magazines, stationery and postage, association dues, insurance, vacation expenses, amusements, church and other contributions, and incidentals.

What length of lunch period is demanded for maintenance of health of factory employees?

What provisions should be required in each manufacturing establishment for (a) toilet for women workers, (b) rest room, (c) ventilation?

INDUSTRIAL WELFARE COMMISSION.

According to the rules and regulations and in accordance with the law we are required to have a secretary for this conference, and the Chair will entertain a motion for the election of a secretary. The commission presents the name of Miss Pearl E. Motzer.

Prof. KERN. I move that Miss Pearl E. Motzer be elected our secretary.

Mr. SNYDER. I second the motion.

The CHAIRMAN. It is moved and seconded that Miss Pearl E. Motzer be elected secretary; all in favor signify their assent by saying "aye."

(The motion was carried.)

Before we go any further, I wish to speak with regard to your traveling and hotel expenses. The State auditor requires that you furnish vouchers covering all your expenses, and I wish you would make them out as soon as you return home and send them in at once, so that we can pass on them at the next meeting of the commission. If there is anything you wish explained you may stop in at the labor commissioner's office and the young lady will explain to you anything that you do not understand.

If you will turn to page 103 of our report, I wish to read to you section 10 of the law in order to impress it upon your minds:

"If, after investigation, the commission shall find that in any occupation, trade, or industry, the wages paid to female employees are inadequate to supply them necessary cost of living and to maintain the workers in health ,or that the conditions of labor are prejudicial to the health or morals of the workers, the commission is empowered to call a conference composed of an equal number of representatives of employers and employees in the occupation or industry in question, together with one or more disinterested persons representing the public; but the representatives of the public shall not exceed the number of representatives of either of the other parties; and a member of the commission shall be a member of such conference and chairman thereof."

I might say in this regard that the commission has designated me to be chairman of this conference.

" The commission shall make rules and regulations governing the selection of representatives and the mode of procedure of said conference, and shall exercise exclusive jurisdiction over all questions arising as to the validity of the procedure and of the recommendations of said conference. . On request of the commission it shall be the duty of the conference to recommend to the commission an estimate of the minimum wage adequate in the occupation or industry in question to supply the necessary cost of living, and maintain the workers in health, and to recommend standards of conditions or labor demanded for the health and morals of the employees. The findings and recommendations, of the conference shall be made a matter of record for the use of the commission."

If you will turn to page 99, I wish to read section 5:
"When the conference is called to order by the chairman it shall deliberate under parliamentary law and no question shall be discussed that is not germane to the conditions of labor or cost of living of working women or minors as applied to that particular trade or industry. Roberts's Rules or Order shall govern."

Now section 8:
"The Chair shall not permit the discussion of the question as a whole until after each item of the cost of living has been taken up in the order given in the estimate blanks prepared by the commission, unless otherwise directed by a majority vote of the conference. After proper deliberation and discussion of questions that have been presented to the conference by the commission the conference shall then, upon request of the commission, proceed to make recommendations upon such questions as the commission may designate."

We are confronted with a condition in this conference to-day that we did not have in our mercantile conference. The welfare commission has been requested by quite a number of factory men whose particular lines of business are not represented by any of the members of this conference, that they be granted the privilege of appearing before the conference to speak on the effect the minimum wage will have on each of their particular lines of industry. This privilege has been granted to them by the commission prompted by a desire to have the situation presented from as many angles as possible. Under these circumstances the Chair would suggest that the conference rules be temporarily suspended and the floor given to these visitors that they may be heard. Many of them are present now, and Mrs. Silbaugh advises me more will arrive on the 3 o'clock train this afternoon.

(Mr. George L. Sawyer, from Spokane.)
Mr. SAWYER. I would like to speak about the new industries.
The CHAIRMAN. About how long would you like to speak?
Mr. SAWYER. About 15 minutes, I think.
The CHAIRMAN. All right, Mr. Sawyer, we would be glad to hear you.
Mr. KRAUSE. I move that the rules and regulations governing this conference be suspended, and that the factory owners present be permitted to speak before this conference.
Mr. DAGG. I second the motion.
The CHAIRMAN. It is moved and seconded that the rules and regulations governing this conference be suspended, and that the factory owners present be permitted to speak before this conference. All in favor signify their assent by saying "aye." [All voted "aye."] The ayes have it.

Before we proceed with our regular order of business permit me to impress upon your minds that under the minimum-wage law we are confronted with a problem that is entitled to the deepest consideration by this conference. The law says that this conference must determine and recommend to the industrial welfare commission the amount of a wage upon which a self-supporting woman can maintain herself in decency and comfort. In order to arrive at a logical conclusion in this regard we have here at my right three ladies, who represent the employees in the factory industry. These ladies are here to tell us as near as they can what the average self-supporting woman needs to maintain herself in health, decency, and comfort. At my right we have three gentlemen, representing the employers in the industry, and I predict that they will endeavor to prove that the industry in which they are concerned will not be able to bear the impost of a wage such as the law contemplates; that their establishments are in competition with sweatshop and prison labor in the East and will be stifled by an increased wage scale. Of preeminent importance to this situation is the part that society will play in settling this wage dispute. Centered between the two contending sides of this controversy we have three representatives of the public, and let me say to you that in the final analysis of this question these three members representing the public will cast the deciding vote.

The responsibility of a fair and reasonable wage, considered from every standpoint, is placed upon these three members. They are here to tell us what the public will do if the necessary wage places the manufacturer in this State at a disadvantage in competing with the sweated industry in the East. After all the real employer of the wage earner is the public, and if the public will do its duty in purchasing the product of the well-paid girl then the gulf that now exists between the manufacturer and the wage earner will rapidly disappear. I hope that every member of the conference will try to do their best to reason out this problem, not only from a standpoint of the women who are working in the industry but from the standpoint of the employer who has his capital invested in the industry. If it is necessary for the public to bear a greater burden than they now bear they should be willing to bear it.

We will now be glad to hear from Mr. Sawyer at this time if he is ready.

Mr. SAWYER. I would like to have the notes that are in your office.

The CHAIRMAN. All right, if you prefer we will call upon some one else. Anyone may have the floor now who so desires. Mr. Krause, can't we get you to open the discussion?

Mr. KRAUSE. I would like to sit back and hear the conference start this, but I want to say that I am interested in this question, as I have talked with each one of the conference and with a large number of our business men in the city. In starting this discussion, Mr. Chairman, Mr. Sawyer, who is going to speak, is a member of our chamber of commerce. They have put up a campaign to do something for the city of Spokane. We must make eastern Washington a better place for all classes of people. We appealed to the business people to such an extent that they feel that something must be done to rebuild and re-create new industries. That is the work that they started last week, and I would be glad to do all I can to get this conference to arrive at a just wage for everybody.

Mr. FENLASON. Mr. Chairman and colleagues, I have not had much time to study this matter, but am deeply interested in this from several standpoints—from the standpoint of the manufacturer, from the standpoint of our employees, from the standpoint of the State of Washington—the public in general. The question, as I understand it, is: We are to determine what is the amount per week that a woman can live comfortably and decently on, and I want to say this, so far as a member of this commission, my influence and acts will be based on what that one great man said—Abraham Lincoln—" Labor is prior to and the invention of capital. Capital never could have succeeded unless labor made it, therefore labor is much superior to capital and is entitled to much the higher consideration." We first should consider the laborer.

I had your request sent me a few months ago to fill out this blank and I didn't have any idea, at that time, that I would have to get into the " jack pot." I gave this proposition careful consideration and I compiled these figures along this line. I said, now, if my daughter had to work for a living what do you think she ought to get. You will find my answer on page 67, paragraph 5:

" In reply to your request the writer has made an estimate based on the theory that the girl or woman employed was not living at home, or with friends, but was compelled to pay her way the same as a man would among strangers. There is one important item of expense not enumerated in the schedule, viz, lost time on account of sickness or the want of a job. Therefore, the writer believes his estimate of $633.70 is a conservative one."

Now I have no reason to change my mind; not at all. I want to say to you that it is my opinion, and I believe it is the opinion of every man, that a girl or woman living an independent life away from home can not live on much less than $10 or $12 per week.

There is an ethical side as well as a practical side to this question. I stand here to say that a girl should receive $10 or $12, only it is my contention that those who are not efficient should have a term of apprenticeship. Can we do that in justice to the employer and can we do it in justice to the girls and women? It is just as essential that our women have employment, even though the standard may not be as high as I have stated in my estimate.

I manufacture berry boxes—a folding berry box is our principal business. I will just show you; I have a sample here. I hope some of these shirt men have brought along their clean collars. This is a plain box and it is collapsible. The minimum wage in our industry, if it was $10 or $12 per week, wouldn't cut much figure because we would simply raise the price of the product. In Michigan the girls are working 9 hours and receive less pay than our girls are getting for 8. It is only a question of whether you want the girls to make the berry boxes here or let them be manufactured in some other locality. What we are going to do on our eastern trade is to ship our raw material to our houses in the East and let them staple our boxes there. In our particular line, if they should put a minimum wage at $12, or perhaps $10, men would be employed instead of girls. Suppose we establish $7.50 per week, we couldn't employ any girls for less than $7.50 per week—if we should establish a $7.50 per week minimum then we should establish a certain apprenticeship period, at which there are no fixed wage, say three or four months for apprenticeship.

When you first put a girl on to work who don't understand the line of business it takes a higher priced employee first to educate her. I would be in favor myself of no fixed wage, but I would spread that out over a long period or a reasonable length of time so she could get adapted to the business. If you establish $7.50 then I think the apprenticeship period should be short. Suppose you establish a higher minimum, $10 or $12, then you should have a longer apprenticeship period, say, based on six months or a year. I would submit two things to the employee—a low minimum wage, about $7.50, with very short apprenticeship period or a higher minimum wage with a longer apprenticeship period. I wish that some of my gentlemen friends would give us their opinion about this question. Their businesses are considerably different from mine. In my business three months or four months and a girl would develop so that she is an efficient worker. Some girls who earn $1 per day set down and don't try to earn more, but say, "Well, papa don't want me to work." I would provide for just that class of people. I recognize, however, that God has made men and women as we find them; you have to use the material that God has given you, as nature has provided it.

I think the thing for us to find out is what the different industries could stand. I think the best plan is to give them what they earn for the first few months, and if they don't earn what they get "can" them.

I appreciate what Mr. Olsen said. He thought the employees would stand off against us and that the public will decide our scrap. That is not my viewpoint at all. I am going to give labor the first consideration, and I am going to stand for just as high a minimum wage as we can pay and not vote the girls out of a job. I thank you.

Mr. SNYDER. Mr. Chairman, the spirit shown by the member of the conference who has just spoken seems to be for the success of the conference. It is undoubtedly true, as the Chair has shown, we are divided into three distinct groups; we are grouped like some of the parliamentary groups—right, left, and center. I recognize the responsibility in this instance resting upon the center. I am very much gratified by the attitude shown by the member on the left. I want to simply enter in behalf of the center a plea, an earnest plea, that none of us may take that attitude that is taken by the typical trader who enters into a transaction—that his asking price is always somewhat higher than his taking price. It appears to me that we will get farther and arrive there sooner if we would all frankly endeavor at the outset to come as nearly as possible to a fair basis, not to have the representatives of the workers demand something unreasonable at the very beginning in the hope thereby they may get a better concession, not to have the employers to demand an unreasonably low wage and then keep raising it, but I would like therefore to urgently ask that that be our attitude throughout this conference.

Mr. FENLASON. I think having this minimum wage is going to increase the efficiency of the employees. The class of girls that I spoke of who said, "I only want to earn $1," when they know they must earn more than $1, will try to become more efficient. I think the principle of the minimum wage will help the manufacturer along that line. The girls will soon find out that they have to get a move on them to hold their jobs.

Mr. SNYDER. It is undoubtedly true that in all factory lines you will find girls who after a fair trial can never be efficient in your particular line of work. They should not be considered in the minimum wage for the average worker.

The CHAIRMAN. Mr. Sawyer may now have the floor.

Mr. SAWYER. Mr. Chairman, ladies, and gentlemen, I am here to-day in behalf of those industries that are not yet born. I am here representing one section of the State, but the same applies to all sections of the State. Our industries are before us, not behind us. There are at this time interests in the larger sections of the State devoting a great deal of time and a great deal of money to take care of and to bring in new industries into our State. It is true of Spokane, Seattle, Tacoma, Bellingham, Everett, and many other smaller places. It is due to conditions in the Eastern States that this movement of minimum wage has been started in the West and in our State. We have not gone far enough with our industries to settle a question of this kind. If you will make a survey through the records of the courts as regards receiverships, bankruptcies, etc., you will be surprised to find the number of our industrial institutions that have in the last five years gone to the wall. Those who are here in this conference have been a little more fortunate. The real question before the manufacturer to-day is his ability to compete with the East. Do we all realize what percentage of industries are successes in the first case? It is necessary to put up 10 factories; in other words, it fails ten times before it succeeds once.

The western manufacturer has to depend upon the East almost entirely for raw materials. Our manufacturers out here have to depend on from 7 to 10 days in which to get the raw material. They consequently have to carry a larger stock than the eastern manufacturer, and this makes an added burden for the western manufacturer to bear. In other words, our markets are restricted. Our labor is one of the most difficult questions which we have to meet. Our western labor costs more, our girls receive higher wages here than they do in the East, there is no skilled labor in our lines in the West. The freight rates are a great deal higher in the West on account of it being a new country, and, generally speaking, for the same transportation cost in the East the factory can reach 90,000,000 consumers, where for the same freight rate they could only reach 4,300,000 here in the West. The western people are not educated to put money in industries. The result is that it costs more for the money; it makes a difference in costs of operation of 3 and 4 per cent. In fact, there is no one to go to for financial help. Then there are numerous added costs to the western manufacturer. He was perhaps successful in business in the East, but he comes out here to the West, and he is slow to grasp the western conditions. It is hard to get the right kind of help and to secure the right management, so these things all go to make it harder for the new employer.

I am not going to tell you what the conditions are in Spokane, for they are not the conditions that should be published. Unless we put a minimum here that is within reason—unless we put a minimum wage here that will keep the eastern manufacturer out—some of the girls will be out of work. I know of one establishment where they employed 30 girls; that man would prefer to use girls; but on account of the legislation in this State regarding girls he is putting men in.

Back of all this legislation is the desire to better the girl. Let us be sure that in attempting to better the girl we do not cripple the employer, but let us look at it from the employer's viewpoint as well as from the employees'.

Mr. FENLASON. What industry do you refer to where they would rather have girls than men?

Mr. SAWYER. The manufacture of woolen goods. Please understand that I have been looking for the man who is in trouble and needs help—not the successful one.

Mrs. MILLS. Do you think the failure is due to the wage that has been paid the girl?

Mr. SAWYER. It has in some industries. It is due to the 30 or 40 reasons that I have just mentioned.

Miss FOISIE. Can you cite in one instance where it was the wages paid to the girls?

Mr. SAWYER. I can say this: That it was due to the lack of money—that the man ran out of money. It is all these things taken into consideration that make the business a failure.

Prof. KERN. As a matter of fact is it not true that the men who are starting up these new industries, they are really experimenting?

Mr. SAWYER. Yes; in many instances. They have to experiment in order to get started. It is all an experiment. In one instance a man came here with a large amount of capital, but couldn't get the skilled labor they wanted. Tried to stock up with raw material and then it laid on the shelf. It is all an experiment here in this western country. If those eastern men can not make a success of it, who can?

Prof. KERN. Is there much competition among the employers to get the experienced help?

Mr. SAWYER. Yes, sir; there is. It is hard to get good experienced help here. The man I am considering is not the ordinary man who succeeds, it is the exceptional man. In the first place, it is hard to get these eastern manufacturers to come out here, but if they come they are likely to fail.

Mr. SNYDER. You spoke, Mr. Sawyer, of girls receiving a small wage and said there were very few who received $3 per week. Is it not true that over half of those employed receive less than $10 per week?

Mr. SAWYER. Yes; I think it is.

Mr. SNYDER. A really efficient girl makes over $10, does she not?

Mr. SAWYER. A girl of overefficient average would get over $10. I am speaking of the man who is starting. The man who is in the back end of some shack or third floor of some building.

Mr. SNYDER. The employer would rather have a girl who is capable of earning $10 per week or over; she is really worth more to him, is she not? · ·

Mr. SAWYER. He wants to get the most efficient girl he can get. I am simply saying this on account of all these conditions a man has to meet; you can very easily put them out of business. The little fellow has no momentum to carry on over these conditions.

Mr. SNYDER. Does it matter anything to him whether he pays $3, $4, or $8 per week or pays considerably over $10 per week, providing he gets the returns.

Mr. SAWYER. It matters to this extent: That if he can pay $10 and operate, it is all right. The girl shared in her employer's success or failure. We don't want to shut him up so she can't work for him.

Mr. SNYDER. If we should decide on a certain minimum wage which, we will assume, will drive out of employment a considerable number of girls, will that minimum wage thereby have any undesirable effect upon the employer, assuming that he will still be able to have a sufficient supply of labor?

Mr. SAWYER. I don't understand your question, Mr. Snyder.

Mr. SNYDER. Suppose a minimum wage of $10 is fixed, which will drive out of employment the girl whom the employer finds can not earn $10 per week; he will discharge them, but the other girls that remain in his employ will be able to earn more than $10. How is the employer affected?

Mr. SAWYER. If be can get enough girls to fill the factory, if he can get sufficient girls who can earn $10 per week, he will be satisfied. If he can see that he can run on it and can get a sufficient quantity to fill his demand, he is satisfied.

Mr. FENLASON. Do we want in this State many more of those industries like the kinds you have mentioned here? You said you were here on behalf of industries not yet born. I hope they never will be born. Do we want those classes of industries? No; we don't want those industries. The going concern is more competent to pay the wage than one that is starting. We don't want to bear down the wages of our women. I am opposed to that "shack proposition."

Mr. SAWYER. I am not making any plea for anything of that kind. It isn't a one-sided proposition. Let us make sure that she receives a small wage rather than no wage at all.

Mr. FENLASON. I was only taking your own words. Are you in favor of a wage in order to protect the class of people who work in shacks?

Mr. SAWYER. The manufacturer of to-morrow is the one back somewhere in some shack learning the business.

Mrs. ROBAIR. Has that employer got to learn his business at the expense of his employees?

Mr. SAWYER. No; but we all have lots to learn, and the new employer has to learn by experience. If he gets skilled labor, he will pay what he should.

Miss FOISIE. The people who come out here should know their business before they come.

Mr. SAWYER. There is no eastern man who can come out here and know all the business; even with years of experience men will sometimes turn right around and fail.

Mr. DAGG. I move that we have a recess, say, for 10 or 15 minutes.

Mr. SAWYER. Before we do I want to thank the conference and commission for allowing me to state in my feeble way my views on this question.

The CHAIRMAN. You have heard the motion made by Mr. Dagg that we go into recess for 10 or 15 minutes. Does anyone second that motion?

Mr. KRAUSE. I second the motion.

The CHAIRMAN. It is moved and seconded that we go into recess for 10 or 15 minutes. All in favor of this motion signify their assent by saying "aye." The "ayes" have it.

AFTER RECESS.

The CHAIRMAN. The meeting will please come to order. There is no particular question before the house; merely a general discussion of the factory-wage problem.

Mr. FENLASON. In your opening remarks you stated that the lady employees of the State would tell us about the necessary cost of living, and I move that they tell us some things along that line.

The CHAIRMAN. I rather think it would be best to postpone that until we hear from the other men. Are there any gentlemen here from the outside that would like to speak on the factory problem and the wages paid? Would Mr. Williams like to be heard? I understand he came here for that purpose. (Mr. Williams of Seattle.)

Mr. WILLIAMS. Yes; I would like to speak. I am in the factory business. We manufacture wash dresses for women and children and children's play suits. Things along those lines.

If there is any question that you could ask that would lead up to the line that you wish me to take up it would help to get me started. I have not been here long enough to get the drift of the meeting.

The CHAIRMAN. The matter that this conference has mainly been called for is to establish a minimum wage for workers in the manufacturing industry. The question has been raised by the manufacturers of the State that the industries of the State can't bear a high minimum wage. That the different manufacturing concerns, the industry as a whole, can not bear a higher wage than they are now paying.

Mr. WILLIAMS. I would like to be understood as confining myself entirely to the garment manufacturing. We pay by the piece. There are very few paid by the week. We are bound to base our work upon the piece and maybe a girl this week would earn $8 and next week more or less. She has a bundle of work and on Saturday afternoon when she checks in her work, if she has that bundle completed and it is accepted by the inspector, she is paid for that bundle. We couldn't in the piecework say she would earn this much this week and so much next week. Now, of course, there has been a certain feeling of just what the effect would be if the minimum wage is fixed in comparison with Oregon. On a great many garments we do perhaps not make over 50 cents per dozen, so we would have to bring up the price of the garment if the minimum wage was fixed above a certain amount. I was talking with one of the manufacturers from Harrisburg, Pa., and he said, "We work 10 hours per day and our girls are satisfied to earn $1 per week."

We will try to make our factories well ventilated like they should be and just as comfortable as possible for the girls, but the girls don't have to wear as many shirt waists a week as the girls selling goods to a customer as in a mercantile establishment and they are not obliged to dress the same while at work, so that would be some saving to them. We think everyone on this commission wants to be just, and that is what the manufacturer wants—justice. We want it considered from our standpoint as well as from the standpoint of the employee and the lines we are engaged in, also the competition we have to meet. If you will allow me to go further, we have had in our employ a few elderly ladies that could not get employment in other lines of work. Those people are satisfied to work for $6.50 and $7 per week. They have been able to maintain themselves on that with a little help from other sources. It wouldn't hurt us as much as it would them if the minimum wage was high. What is to become of the ones who can't meet the requirements to get a high minimum wage? I think if the wage was put reasonably high the factory would be allowed to exist and it would not work a hardship on the women. In our factory if a girl is quick and gets hold of the work quickly, she gets $3 the first week on piecework and an increase the second week if she has improved. It sometimes happens in cases of this kind that the work done by people beginning we have to sell for one-half price. We never complain, but are willing to keep these people if they show signs of improvement after the first week or two. The second week the girl earns about 50 cents more.

Not having been in your session this morning I don't know just what you have discussed, but I will be very glad to answer your questions honestly. If it were possible for a different regulation for the garment manufacturers and if there could be some way of averaging it to cover each individual class of work, it seems to me that it would be more nearly just to each line of business. I am not prepared just at this time to go into what we would like to have as an apprenticeship period, but further on, if you care to ask me any questions, I will be glad to truthfully answer to the best of my knowledge.

The CHAIRMAN. Do you mean it would be best to separate the pieceworkers from the time-workers?

Mr. WILLIAMS. I mean the different occupations. I believe the paper-box makers work mostly by the week. One girl will start at $3 and will work up to $8.50 or $9. Another girl will start in at the same price and will never get more.

The CHAIRMAN. Is there anybody who wishes to ask Mr. Williams any questions?

Mrs. ROBAIR. What is the highest wages that you pay your girls?

Mr. WILLIAMS. We have girls who get from $13 to $16 a week.

Mrs. ROBAIR. In our factory some of the girls get as much as $20.

Mr. WILLIAMS. We have been told that we pay more than the union scale for our line of work. We allow the girls to go into the union, however, if they wish.

Mrs. MILLS. Does this gentleman allow any of the work to be taken to the homes? We have some factories where part of the work is taken to the homes.

Mr. WILLIAMS. Sometimes we have done that. We have allowed some to take work home but it has inconvenienced us a great deal. We prefer to have everything made under our own inspection.

Mr. FENLASON. What is the average wage of your employees?

Mr. WILLIAMS. It would be pretty hard to tell you that. Some of them get from $13 to $16, some less.

Mr. FENLASON. Would 50 per cent of your employees be under $7 per week?

Mr. WILLIAMS. Perhaps not.

Mr. SNYDER. Mr. Williams, why do you suggest a segregation of piece-workers from the time-workers.

Mr. WILLIAMS. Perhaps the girl would earn $2 more this week than next week, because she hasn't finished her work. The girl who lacks $2.50 of making the minimum wage some weeks—we don't want to have to pay that. Is there anything further?

Prof. KERN. Mr. Williams, I would like to ask if there are a good many minors in your factory?

Mr. WILLIAMS. We sometimes have a few who come to work as soon as they are 16. One girl from England—a very small girl—came to me for work and I told her she would have to have a permit, but she was past 16 I found upon investigation. She never gets but $7 or $7.50, but she seems entirely satisfied with that. She is not as rapid as some of the others.

Mr. SNYDER. You stated the store girls were under considerable greater expense than the factory girls. I would like you to indicate, if you can, what this expense is.

Mr. WILLIAMS. Our girls come to work and change and put on a work dress. The girl in the store would have to wear more shirt waists and would wear out her skirts quicker.

Mr. SNYDER. Can you estimate what that expense would be?

Mr. WILLIAMS. No; not exactly. The stores, however, are not in competition with the other States, while we are directly in competition. Some of the stores require a uniform clothing, they must maintain the same uniform that the other girls have; they have the expense of getting this dress when they first start in. We don't require this uniform dress.

Mrs. ROBAIR. If a girl changes her dress, she has to have the wear and tear on her best clothes going back and forth to the factory, and she also has the extra expense of a work dress that she wears in the factory. If she has a work dress she has to send it to the laundry and has this added expense.

Mr. WILLIAMS. A girl does not need to wear the same suit to the factory that she would wear to the store to clerk all day.

Mr. SNYDER. To what extent is that situation met by the fact previously referred to that the factory girl is at a disadvantage with the girl in the store, as the girl in the store is able to get a discount and is more able to take advantage of the sales in the stores?

Mr. WILLIAMS. Our girls can take advantage of what we make. Our girls get out at 4 o'clock and have from then until 6 to shop. I think our girls have just as much advantage of the sales as the store girls. The store girls are not allowed to take advantage of the sales more than anyone else.

Miss FOISIE. The girls in the stores are excused from the stores during the morning hours and can do their shopping. They are also allowed 25 per cent discount on their suits and 15 per cent discount on other goods. A girl going shopping at 4.30 or 5 is tired or in a hurry and she hasn't the energy or vitality to buy her clothes that she would have in the morning.

Mr. WILLIAMS. The girl who buys one of those dresses and gets a 10 per cent discount has to pay more than if she got them from us. If Oregon has a certain schedule of price regardless of how much it takes to live in this State, if the industries are going to grow and this State is going to call for new industries, we must consider competition.

Mr. KRAUSE. The young lady there, Mrs. Lawton, knows nearly every girl in Spokane, I believe, and has been employed in Spokane. You have employed girls yourself, have you not, and your basis for employing girls is efficiency, is it not? You have had a good deal of trouble in getting girls who were efficient, didn't you?

Mrs. LAWTON. As a general rule I did not have much trouble.

Mr. KRAUSE. I claim that our business is built upon a competitive basis. Our business is divided into two industries—candy and crackers. Our commodity must be put on the market at a competitive price. Are any of you ladies loyal enough to pay more for a package of biscuits made here than for one made in Chicago that sells for less?

Mrs. SILBAUGH. We are not educated up to that yet.

Mr. KRAUSE. The price established in this commodity is a standard price, and under the pure-food laws each package must contain so many ounces or so many pieces. We men are each representing a certain company, and we each think we are making a very nice line of goods. We are only allowed to hire our girls eight hours a day; the same kind of industries in the East can work the girls 10 hours. Our rate of wages is from 20 per cent to 30 per cent higher than our competitors, so I believe, Mr. Chairman, that these points are pertinent to the establishment of the business. We are not all as fortunate as our friend here, Mr. Fenlason. He can say to the girls, " We have no competition ; we don't need to keep you ; we can put in men." The average girl comes into our factory for work—she wants to become a chocolate dipper. I start her in at wrapping packages. The greatest trouble we have is to get a girl to know how to use her hands. It takes a lot of our patience in order to get the girls to know how to use their hands. I will be very glad to answer any questions that I can in regard to this matter.

(Mr. F. Stevenson, of Tacoma.)

Mr. STEVENSON. May I have the floor a minute?

The CHAIRMAN. Yes ; indeed. What business are you in, Mr. Stevenson?

Mr. STEVENSON. I am a garment manufacturer. Suppose a girl takes a bundle of say two dozen garments on Friday morning. Suppose this bundle amounts to $4.16. At the present time we are allowing them to hand these bundles in on Friday evening. Perhaps, she will have the bundle done before she gets her pay for it or the reverse would be that the girl, instead of handing in that bundle she may have to hold it over and, if we have a minimum wage, we have to pay her $2 or $3 more for the week than she has earned. The commission should take this into consideration on this piecework basis.

The CHAIRMAN. Would that be remedied by averaging for the month?

Mr. STEVENSON. Yes ; it would be remedied that way.

Mr. MARVIN. Would the monthly plan be better than taking an estimate as to what is done?

Mr. STEVENSON. I think it would.

Mr. WILLIAMS. A girl should just get what she earns while she is an apprentice, I think. Then she would be learning the business and at the same time earning just what she produces. There are so many inefficient ones starting in all the time that we need some sort of apprenticeship.

Prof. KERN. You say you have a great many people who come to you to begin work that are inefficient. Do you have a good many minors that come to you for work? Do you think it is possible for the public schools to cooperate with the factory in training the girls from 15, 16, and 17 years?

Mr. WILLIAMS. We have students from the economical department of the University of Washington come to our factory to investigate. We would be glad to pay for the time they are in the schools, if the schools could cooperate in training them.

Prof. KERN. At the present time there is a commission in this State to make a State-wide study of the question of vocational training. Do you think it is possible for the schools to cooperate with the factories successfully? The plan is that the child shall be in school during one day in the week. If there is any reason why that sort of a scheme couldn't be made in the State, I would be glad to know of it.

Mr. BLACK. I would like to say that we can teach a girl in a week the things we would want her to do. Then it is a matter of practice until she knows the business well. They come to our factories, and they have to work up to speed on our particular line of work. We can only educate them in our factory in our particular line of business. The thing that I am interested in, and it is only natural, is the inefficient girl—the competent girl don't need any legislation to make her living. I want to ask these young ladies if this commission would fix a minimum wage of $1 per week would it affect the girl making garments in the State?

Mrs. ROBAIR. I don't know as that would affect any girl in the State. I know it wouldn't affect any girl in the factory I work in now, but will it affect the girl in the factories that come is as a new beginner at anything? She is very discouraged if the minimum wage is fixed at $5 per week. There would be some encouragement for the girl if the minimum wage was fixed at a reasonable price. The majority of the girls are industrious and ambitious and want to make the most that they can. If a girl finds that the girl working next to her is averaging $7 per week, if she was only making $5 per week she wouldn't be contented with $5; she would want to make $7. If the minimum wage was $5 they would sit down and would not try to ever make more than $5, but the manufacturer would soon weed them out. They couldn't keep them. I think that if the girl had a wage to start on that was encouraging, I think it would encourage her to make more.

Mr. BLACK. What effect would it have on the girls if the minimum was $10 per week?

Mrs. ROBAIR. I think the majority would come up to that.

Mr. BLACK. Don't you think a high minimum would work a hardship on the competent girl and help the incompetent girl? For instance, the girl who puts pockets down on the trousers legs of the overalls?

Mrs. ROBAIR. Where was your floor lady at that time?

Mr. BLACK. A girl who worked 10 months is supposed to know where the pockets should go. We have away above the average lot of factory girls—in fact, we have very intelligent girls, but still these things sometimes happen. We are willing to pay the girls all they earn, but these mistakes are sometimes inexcusible.

Not long ago I had a man come to me and try to sell me some overalls. I said, " No ; I am in the overall business myself." He said, " I can sell overalls to you and you can't make them and sell them as cheap as if you buy them from me and sell them to the merchants." He asked me a price that was ridiculously low. I asked him how he could do it and he said, " What is your overhead expense for a pair of overalls." I told him. He then said, " Well, I get free rent, free power, and have no taxes to pay but have 250 convicts to work each day. That makes my expenses about 37½ cents as against your $2.50—can you beat it? " He said, " We sold $7,000,000 worth of overalls in the United States last year."

The State of Washington should pass a law that when you ship " convict-made " goods into this State you should be compelled to put a label on it saying it is " convict made." These convicts are put to work making aprons, dresses, children's dresses, and overalls, and when they come out of prison they are as helpless as babies. That is the most vital thing—we do need a minimum wage for a competent girl, but we also need laws against the man who will go around and put a pocketbook on the back of a desk and get the person to vote for him.

We are not pleading for anything except that you don't put the girls out of work completely by a high minimum wage. I know that no legislation that you will make will benefit anyone in my employ. You can't make any legislation that will help my 250 girls, but you can hurt them with a high minimum wage. I have one in my employ that her maximum is $23.80 and her minimum is around $18. When she first came to me she wasn't quite old enough to work and had to wait for a few days, but she has proven herself to be a good worker. I would like to speak on apprentices. We certainly want an apprenticeship period.

The CHAIRMAN. Mr. Black, I would like to interrupt you, as it is now 12.15, and I think we should adjourn for lunch.

Mr. SNYDER. I move we adjourn for lunch until 1.30.

Prof. KERN. I second the motion.

The CHAIRMAN. It has been moved and seconded that we adjourn until 1.30. All in favor signify their assent by saying " aye." [All voted " aye."] The ayes have it; we will adjourn until 1.30.

AFTER RECESS—1.30 P. M.

The CHAIRMAN: The meeting will please come to order. The secretary has informed me that she has quite a bit of difficulty in hearing the speakers. I would ask each one to speak a little louder and more plainly.

I think Mr. Black has the floor, and he may resume his address to the conference if he wishes to do so.

Mr. BLACK. I thank you for the opportunity to finish. I don't just remember where I left off. I think the manufacturers of Seattle that I know are disposed to be fair and just to their employees. It is the one who makes the good wages that is profitable to us. I conduct a cafeteria in my establishment, not as a matter of charity, because the girls are able to pay for what they get. It is a selfish business with me. If a girl gets a good lunch at noon, she feels better and does better work in the afternoon. Miss Foisie asked if the employees should be responsible for the manufacturer who comes here without experience from the East. I say "no." If the manufacturer isn't able to run his business, the employee shouldn't have to suffer. Neither should the employer be responsible for the inefficiency of the employee. The best way I can explain this matter of apprenticeship is this: You are a business man and you want a stenographer. You send uptown and you advertise. The girl makes her application, and you ask her if she can run a machine. She says no—would you hire a teacher, furnish the girl with a machine, and then pay her a salary? No; that would be ridiculous. That is exactly what we are doing in the factories, we are teaching the girls a trade that will put them beyond want if they will apply themselves.

We should not be put in a position where we have to pay them while we are teaching them. You ladies and gentlemen are here to determine a minimum wage for a girl that will keep them in health and comfort. You are not here to fix the wages of women. You are here to establish a wage that will protect the girl from taking $3 per week. When you give her a reasonable minimum wage she won't stay in that class very long. I hope you will give me the credit of being honest when I say that I am interested in the girls. I am here for the girls as much as I am here for the manufacturer. We want a reasonably fair condition, and we don't want to put the factories out of business. We want a minimum wage that will meet her wants until she can do better. We have tried paying a girl an apprenticeship wage while she is learning. We found it a failure because it destroys the individuality of the woman. Some just want a job for one or two weeks until their husbands, perhaps, are able to work. No matter what girl comes to our place to work it costs us from $25 to $50 to teach her until she earns something. That is all I have to say. If you want to ask me any questions, I will be very glad to answer them.

Mr. SNYDER. What is the minimum amount, in your opinion, upon which a girl can live decently and comfortably on.

Mr. BLACK. I don't want to discuss that, because I am sorry for the girl who has to live on $12 or even $15 a week. We must not lose sight of the fact that these figures have been compiled by girls who are making good wages. This wage is to protect the inefficient girl. The girl we want to protect is the girl who might go wrong. When a girl gets a reasonable amount of money in her pocket every Saturday night she is safe. The responsibility is not as great—I am saying this honestly. We are the pioneers in the State and we have had a hard pull. We have not lost five years since we started. We have to take every man and every girl and teach them the business. Those two women are as independent as any two women in the State of Washington as long as they keep their health, because they have a trade.

Mr. SNYDER. We must not lose sight of the fact that we are dealing with a condition in another sphere. A law has been passed which makes it unlawful to pay an inadequate amount to women workers.

Mr. BLACK. But some of our factory girls pay $35 for hats in a year and $15 for corsets. This law is not protecting that girl.

Mrs. UDALL. Can't you give an estimate of the amount an average girl should get? Not the one who spends the most or the one who spends the least, but the average girl.

Mr. BLACK. I haven't asked any of our girls. I can tell you what I lived on when I first went to work. The first week after I went to work I got $5 per week, and that lasted for the first year; $6 per week for the second year, and $7 per week for the third year.

Mr. SNYDER. There have been changes since that time.

Mr. BLACK. I understand that. If I can't pay my help a living wage I don't want them.

Mr. MARVIN. This conference and this commission are supposed to find out from all available sources what is required to enable a woman in the State of Washington to live decently and healthfully on, and presently I would like to know what you think, and if you have not made up your mind I would like to have you take it under consideration.

Mr. BLACK. Understand that it is not my idea to try and get a low minimum.

Mrs. ROBAIR. Don't these people who work in those different branches—don't they have to live?

Mr. BLACK. Don't place the minimum so high that it will work a hardship on the girls.

Mrs. ROBAIR. I don't think it is going to. You said it took three weeks to learn this trade. The manufacturer would know whether a girl would be an operator in four weeks, at the most, and I think the apprenticeship period would not have to be over four weeks.

Mr. BLACK. You could tell in four weeks whether she would be an operator.

Mr. KRAUSE. I should say that the girl who comes to Mr. Black for a position for a short time comes from the solicitation of the mother and gets help from the family, but at the end of six months she is a help to the family herself. The heads of families sometimes come to me seeking employment for their daughters, saying they are not able to earn enough money to support the family, and appeal to me to find something for the daughter to do. She is one of the family unit, and after a few months is able to contribute something toward the support of the family.

Mrs. ROBAIR. If her father is giving her her board she is no help to the family.

Mr. KRAUSE. She is a help as long as she brings $5 home to the father.

Mr. ■LACK. A girl should not be paid any more than she earns. I would like to have not less than three months in which a girl should get just what she earns. I think a reasonable wage for the beginner would be $6 for the first week, $5 and what she earns for the second week, $4 and what she earns for the third week. The next three months she should get $1 per day and what she earns, and after that she should receive the minimum.

Mrs. ROBAIR. I think myself that would be a good plan.

Mr. BLACK. You know that with the competition we have with the outside world we can't raise our piecework.

Mr. SNYDER. I think we need a reasonable minimum wage during the period of apprenticeship, and do you think it would work all right on this sliding scale?

Mr. BLACK. I am sure that would work to advantage for over 50 per cent of them at least.

Mr. MARVIN. I think from what you say, Mr. Black, that you are rather opposed to Prof. Kern's proposition. I would just like to ask you whether you do not think there is some compensation if the new manufacturer would get the girls at the best period of their lives. That might compensate them for the shortness of time they would have them. Suppose you take them at 15 or 16 years of age. If you take them after they have passed 18 years of age the period of adaptation is surely passed.

Mr. BLACK. I think taking them at the period of age you speak of would be an advantage. We find the girls learn more readily at 16 than at 20 years of age. We want the girls who have never earned anything. We never hire a laundry girl to work in our factories, as it is a different kind of work altogether. I can't see where this part-time school would work to advantage.

Prof. KERN. I believe that your difficulty is that you don't understand the situation. I don't think you want a girl at 18 who has been drifting around instead of a girl at 14 or 15 who is just out of school and who has to continue to go to school one day out of each week. You are going to know at the end of one or two years whether the girl is going to become especially good. The girl may decide during this time that this industry is not the thing she wants to do.

Mr. BLACK. I can't agree with you, Professor.

Prof. KERN. There is a part-time cooperation between the industry and the school.

Mr. BLACK. The first thing a girl comes in we teach her to thread the machine. Then to run the machine. She knows the whole thing in two or three days. Then, as I said before, it is just a matter of practice to get up speed. I do not think those things can be taught in the schools.

Prof. KERN. Nobody is going to teach those things to her but you. We are simply increasing her general intelligence.

Mr. SNYDER. It is a fact that in any degree that we can increase our mental intelligence, just to that extent she is able to speed up her machine. You were speaking of this girl you employ at $18 per week to teach efficiency to the girls— is it not self-interest on your part?

Mr. BLACK. It is purely selfishness.

Mr. SNYDER. The more efficient the girl is the more profitable for you.

Mrs. ROBAIR. Did you say that you furnished free lunches for the girls?

Mr. BLACK. No; they pay for them. It is a cooperative plan.

Mrs. ROBAIR. Don't you charge enough for the meals so you get enough to pay the cook?

Mr. BLACK. We just charge enough to pay expenses.

Mr. SNYDER. You are not yet prepared to give this conference the amount necessary to maintain one of your girls decently and healthfully? That is what we are here for.

Mr. BLACK. I know it is. I don't like to fix that for this reason: Suppose a girl is experienced in candy making. The minimum wage is $7.50, but business is dull. The small place can not take that girl and she must therefore be without work altogether.

Mr. SNYDER. We are compelled to consider the question of the amount. Can she live on $7.50 per week?

Mr. BLACK. She can live for a while.

Mr. SNYDER. Let me ask you if it is fair to lay much stress on the " $35-hat girl." She may be willing to scrimp helfself on underwear in order to get her hats.

Mr. MARVIN. In making up our report there were extremely high estimates and extremely low estimates which were thrown out. For instance, anything under $300 was not representative and some were as high as $800 and $900, which were not representative.

Mr. BLACK. All I ask for you to do is to be fair to the women employed and to the employers.

Mr. FENLASON. I would like to get a little information. There is no necessity of us going outside the scope of this act. I would like to read on page 101, paragraph 2, which says:

" It shall be unlawful to employ women or minors in any industry or occupation within the State of Washington under conditions of labor detrimental to their health or morals; and it shall be unlawful to employ women workers in any industry within the State of Washington at wages which are not adequate for their maintenance."

Has this commission got any authority or right to fix a wage for apprentices less than is provided by that paragraph? If this commission has no right under the law to consider an apprenticeship wage, let's then pass on to what the law says we shall consider. We are to consider a wage that will be necessary to support a girl in a decent and healthful way.

The CHAIRMAN. I wish to direct you to section 13, page 105, which reads:

" For any occupation in which a minimum rate has been established the commission, through its secretary, may issue to a woman physically defective or crippled by age or otherwise, or to an apprentice in such class of employment or occupation as usually requires to be learned by apprentices, a special license authorizing the employment of such licensee for a wage less than the legal minimum wage; and the commission shall fix the minimum wage for said person, such special license to be issued only in such cases as the commission may decide the same is applied for in good faith and that such license for apprentices shall be in force for such length of time as the said commission shall decide and determine is proper."

We have already made a ruling with reference to apprentices in mercantile establishments. While that ruling states that it will be the policy of the commission to issue apprentices' licenses, if it is necessary we have the authority to extend the period of apprenticeship. If we find it necessary to make a special investigation of a particular case, we have that privilege.

Mr. KRAUSE. We are not here to discuss the apprenticeship question, are we?

The CHAIRMAN. No; but we would like to be enlightened on that question.

Mr. SNYDER. I would say that undoubtedly sections 2 and 13 must be construed together.

Mr. FENLASON. I want to speak from the point of compensation that an employee should receive during the apprenticeship period that this commission might fix. Now, I want to bring out this point a little clearer, that Mr. Black touched on. In Mr. Sawyer's address this morning before he finished the lady in the center asked this question: Should the employees, the girls, be compelled to stand the burden of the inexperienced employer. In other words, if the employer starts out in a small way should the employee be compelled to work for a low wage in order that the employer might do business in that way. Mr. Sawyer didn't seem willing to answer that. I want to say "no." I want to take the other side, the side of the inefficient employee. Here is a girl or boy that the professor is going to send out from the school to work in those industries. The boy or girl has had no experience; they know nothing. I submit that it would not be fair to compel the manufacturer to pay that inexperienced employee a wage equivalent to the minimum wage that you propose to establish. Under a piece-work proposition I believe it would be fair and just that there should be no wage established for the apprentices, we will say, for a period of 60 days. The apprentice should then get what he earns. Then, after that I think there should be a reasonable minimum wage. We will say at the end of four months they should receive the minimum wage, and at the end of the first sixty days should get $1 per day.

Mr. SNYDER. Is there not this difference between the two propositions that have been brought up, namely, Mrs. Robair has been answered by you that the employee should not have to bear the failure of the employer, but that it would be all right for her to share in the responsibility if she had a share in the results that would come with success that might come later on?

Mr. FENLASON. Have you ever employed any men or girls?

Mr. SNYDER. Yes, sir.

Mr. FENLASON. Well, then, you know what these gentlemen say to be true. Here is the head of a family—the husband lost his job or is sick. The wife comes down and makes application for a job; perhaps just wants to stay long enough to make expenses until her husband is well or back to work. Or perhaps a girl yill come and just want to earn enough to buy a new dress or hat. After working two or three weeks she leaves. In order to protect the employers from just such people I think that for the first 60 days at least there should be no minimum set for the apprentice to receive. After that time there should be a wage, because the girl or woman who would come down and stick it out that long, she deserved a position.

The CHAIRMAN. You are speaking of pieceworkers only, are you not?

Mr. FENLASON. We start in at $1.25 and all at least at $1 a day, but they all want to do piecework right away, because they can make more. I think for a day proposition the first 60 days would be a resonable time for an apprentice.

Mr. CONSTANTINE. Mr. Chairman, may I have the floor?

The CHAIRMAN. Yes; you may.

Mr. CONSTANTINE. I want to say that there is nothing but honest desire on the part of the employers to cooperate with the employees. This morning the conversation was almost entirely on the question of competition, and particularly to call the attention of the members of the commission to this fact. You will find more interest in the competition question at this conference, perhaps, than will be shown at any of the other conferences. Our closest competition is with the State of Oregon. Directly east of us we have little competition until we reach the Twin Cities. South of us we strike the manufacturers of Portland. There they have fixed the minimum at $8.64 for the State of Oregon. That allows them to work the girls 54 hours as against 48 hours in the State of Washington. At the same ratio of nine hours as against eight in this State, the rate of wages in the State of Washington as compared with Oregon ought to be $7.68. I have one point I would like to bring to your attention. Suppose you do fix a minimum wage in the State of $7.68 as against $8.64 in Oregon, even at that the State of Oregon's manufacturers will have a degree of advantage over the State of Washington. While his maximum hours per week may not exceed 54, he is allowed to work the girl as much as 10 hours per day, providing, however, that the hours per week do not exceed 54. It means that the manufacturer may take and fluctuate his hours. It means he may work the girl 8, 9, or 10 hours for three succeeding days, or he may work them 10, 9, or 8 hours for three days. He can start at a low point and work to the peak point, or he can work his force a little heavier in order to get out his orders. In Washington we are limited to eight hours per day.

I think that is all I have to say, and I want to thank you for the privilege of the floor. While I am not an employer of labor to any large extent, I am constantly thrown with them, as I am their secretary. When the minimum-wage bill was brought before the legislature no effort was made to defeat the passage of the minimum-wage law for women. It is to the credit of the employers of the State that they were broad-minded enough to not try to defeat it. I wish you would bear the competition question in your minds and the effect that a high minimum wage would have upon the girls. All big moves of progress must necessarily damage someone, but we want to take care of the girls. I thank you.

Mrs. YOUNG. Mr. Chairman, may I have the floor?

The CHAIRMAN. Yes, Mrs. Young.

Mrs. YOUNG. Having been in touch with the public-school work for the last 30 years, I have looked into this matter quite thoroughly. I heartily approve of the cooperation of the manufacturer and the educators.

You agree on a certain minimum wage that is all right for the time being, but the men are going to pick out the girl who is the most efficient. The girl that can not come up to the standard must go to some other occupation..

I say vocational training is going to come to our schools in the next year. You have to take into consideration efficiency. You must segregate the girls and get them started right; the manufacturer is not going to.

Mrs. MUIR. I would like to know if this woman is a manufacturer or an employee?

Mrs. YOUNG. I am neither. I am a woman. Give us cooperation; that is all we ask. I thank you.

(Mr. Moore, of the Spokane Dry Goods Co.)

Mr. MOORE. The lady who just spoke has given you my sentiments exactly, although I may not be able to express myself as clearly. There are about 400 employed in our particular line in the State of Washington. Most of the points that I had expected to discuss have been covered by the manufacturers present. I heartily believe in fair justice to the girls, but I think we will be doing her an injustice by placing the wage too high. If she can not come up to the minimum, the employer will not keep her. Has the State provided a way to protect this girl? I have had girls come to me for employment who have been failures elsewhere and have been able to give them employment at a low wage. We also have a number of old ladies who are earning $6 and $7 per week. It is merely an act of charity for us to keep these old ladies, and if this minimum is set too high, what is to become of these inefficient girls and old women? I have compared the price of some of our lines of work with others in the same business. In some cases they are lower, but, as a general rule, on an average, they are about equal. The Spokane Dry Goods Co. do not pay wages such as some girls think they need, but, let me ask, how could a business as large as the Spokane Dry Goods Co. ever reach this point of success in life if they did not treat their employees fair? I do not say it in any boasting manner, but the Spokane Dry Goods Co. and its affiliations are the largest mercantile establishment on the Pacific Coast.

Mrs. ROBAIR. I would like to ask you if most of your employees are not married women?.

Mr. MOORE. I could not answer that question intelligently. I don't know whether they have husbands or not. While it may not be fair to the married women, we try to give work to the girl that is self-supporting. Sometimes conditions will influence us otherwise. Suppose a woman comes to us for work, and she has had a lot of experience; she is married; a girl comes to us at the same time as an inexperienced clerk. We hire the married woman in that case.

Mrs. ROBAIR. If a girl came to you that was self-supporting and didn't have experience, and a woman came to you at the same time who didn't have to support herself, but who had experience, would you give preference to the self-supporting women?

Mr. MOORE. If we were in no hurry to get out a big lot of work, we would hire the inexperienced self-supporting woman.

Mr. KRAUSE. If you knew the experience was equal, you would give the single girl the job?

Mr. FENLASON. What is your reason for giving the self-supporting girl the preference?

Mr. MOORE. For the reason that she has a harder time to get along in life.

Mrs. ROBAIR. What is the reason that you can't get experienced help in your line of work?

Mr. MOORE. I don't know as I can answer that question. The experienced help does not seem to come to Spokane. A person don't think of getting off the train there when coming out from the East. They don't know what a city we have..

Mrs. ROBAIR. You have advertised for girls in Tacoma, have you not?

Mr. MOORE. Yes; but I don't know of any we ever got from there. The main and vital point that I hope you will consider is the competition. I don't think this conference is going to fix a rate that is going to hurt the Spokane Dry Goods Co., but if a high minimum wage is fixed it certainly means that we manufacturers are going to work to get the most efficient girls we can get. In view of the fact of the minimum wage that is going into effect, one department store in Seattle has laid off 15 girls. I can not go on record as to that, but I heard it.

Mr. FENLASON. Do you know what the average wage is that the Spokane Dry Goods Co. pays?

Mr. MOORE. I wouldn't like to go on record as to that, but I think the prices paid are about the same as Mr. Black's, as our business is somewhat similar. I would like to ask this conference what is going to determine the experienced help. We have had girls come to us that have had three or four years' experience in other places and we have had to break them in in our business. What is going to determine experienced help?

Mr. SNYDER. Are you prepared now to give us an estimate of the amount that would be adequate for a girl to live decently and healthfully on, Mr. Moore?

Mr. MOORE. I am not, as there have been no blanks reached my hands from the commission. In our establishment about 5 girls out of 65 filled out the blanks and turned in the estimates. They said they were satisfied and didn't want to mix up with the law. It is true that we were paying one girl $10 per week and she turned in her weekly earnings to this commission at $7.50. Another girl had been getting for the past four months $10.68 per week, and she also turned in her average earning at $7.50.

Miss FOISIE. Do you know if these girls live at home?

Mr. MOORE. I think one lived at home, but I don't know about the other.

Miss FOISIE. Perhaps they were living at home and did not handle their own money. What do you think a girl should have to live decently and in comfort?

Mr. MOORE. I am not prepared to say that.

The CHAIRMAN. I believe these gentlemen will be able to give us some opinion in regard to that question when we take it up item by item.

Mrs. ROBAIR. Couldn't the gentleman tell us what he thinks his sister ought to get in order to live decently and healthfully?

Mr. MOORE. I am sorry to say I have no sister.

Mrs. ROBAIR. I beg your pardon. Did you say you only employ 65 employees?

Mr. MOORE. Sometimes we run up to about 90.

Mr. DAGG. It don't seem as if we get anywhere by this sort of conversation, and I believe that these people ought to get down to business.

Mr. WILLIAMS. I would like to have a little more to say.

The CHAIRMAN. We are waiting for these gentlemen who are coming on the 3.30 train; in the meantime you may proceed if you wish to.

Mr. WILLIAMS. I feel that we are going to be justly dealt with; that the thing that ought to be considered, as far as we are concerned, is the sum that has been fixed in Oregon, $8.64; also that they have a nine-hour law. I believe that if a girl is careful she can maintain herself on $7.68 per week.

Mr. SNYDER. Will you be willing to take one of these form blanks, No. 4, and indicate what you think it would cost a girl to live on?

Mr. WILLIAMS. I have not looked into the different items of cost.

Mrs. ROBAIR. In Tacoma there is no girl who can get a furnished room for less than $8 per month.

Mr. WILLIAMS. If the commission want to make a high minimum wage they should provide some way for the girls who will be thrown out of employment.

Mrs. ROBAIR. I understand that the minimum wage is a wage that a girl can live decently and healthfully on.

Mr. BLACK. It is a wage that will protect them until they can make more money. She has no business living down town in a steam-heated hotel.

Mrs. ROBAIR. What is a girl going to do that has no home?

Mrs. LAWTON. In Spokane it is not very easy for a girl to get into families. I have had about five years' experience, and the least a girl can live on is $9 or $10 per week. We have to deprive ourselves of lots of things even then. Whatever amusements you get you have to get from your friends.

Mr. BLACK. What does a girl expect from a minimum wage. This is just a wage to protect the girl until she can make more money.

Miss FOISIE. Do you know of any place in Seattle where a girl can get a room under $2?

Mrs. ROBAIR. There is not a boarding house that you would want any of your girls to live in, Mr. Black. Would such a boarding house help a girl morally and physically?

Mr. BLACK. I think there are some respectable places where a girl can room for less than $2 per week. There is a place out near Ballard where they would be very glad to get girls. I know of a place where they would take a number of girls; they have, in fact, a number of university girls there who help with the work to pay for part of their board.

Mr. MARVIN. Is there not a difference between the girl from the university, who is using her mind all day and then doing physical work in the evening, and the girl who works eight hours in a factory?

Mr. KRAUSE. Yes; that is true. Last Friday a lady said to me, "I have a friend coming from Chicago who is an experienced chocolate dipper; can you give her employment?" I said, "You bet I can." There is no question about the experienced help getting work; it is the inexperienced that we must look after.

Mrs. UDALL. Do you make an object of hiring a girl that lives at home?

Mr. KRAUSE. We make a practice of it.

Mrs. UDALL. Why?

Mr. KRAUSE. On account of the moral side of it.

Mrs. UDALL. Is the parent contributing partly to the support of the child?

Mr. KRAUSE. No; I don't think so. Perhaps the girl has never worked before, but her father is not able to support all of the family of five or six. The minute this girl helps to support herself or buys her clothes she is a distinct benefit to her family.

Mrs. ROBAIR. She doesn't support herself unless she pays her board. If she paid her board, $4 per week, and then her room, how could she clothe herself?

Mr. KRAUSE. I said that the minute she is buying her clothes she is a help to the family. Perhaps at the end of the year she is self-supporting.

The CHAIRMAN. Are you speaking of the minor?

Mr. KRAUSE. I am speaking of the average girl that comes to us.

Miss FOISIE. May I ask the proportion of time-workers that you have?

Mr. KRAUSE. We have possibly 85 per cent pieceworkers. We start the girls in now at $6 per week. I take it that you are one of the best operators in the State in your line of business. At least I have heard that.

Miss FOISIE. That was simply a compliment.

Mr. FENLASON. Two years ago I was in New York City. I had heard so much about the tenement district that I went down into the new Bowery district, and this is what I saw: I saw thousands and thousands of little children sitting out in the sidewalks, and of all the degredation I ever saw it was there. If we have to have industries that will bring that class of people, I hope to God that we don't get them. There is one thing about the cost of living—the board for girls. We are trying to combine two things in one. We have to meet a condition we are afraid to come out and say what it costs a girl to live on—to live away from home. You talk about the girl boarding for $4 per week; it has been my experience that the average family don't want girls to board. I put my board about $7 per week. I don't think it possible to get board for less than $6 per week. I don't think it can be done. Of course, you have to consider efficiency, but a girl can't live decently on less than $12 per week. If the girl is going to live independently it will cost her at least $10 per week. But the question is, Will the industries of the State stand a minimum of $10 per week. That is really what they ought to have.

Mr. SNYDER. I would like to suggest that we possibly may save time if all those from whom we expect to receive, estimates of the amount upon which a girl can live will fill these blanks.

Mr. FENLASON. I would like to hear from the ladies on the other side of the house. We are the employers; you are the employees, and you are asking for something. Maybe we can meet your request without any trouble.

Mrs. LAWTON. I would like to say that I kept house for about five years; my sister and I lived together. We had a room which cost us $10 per month, and we found that we couldn't live on less than $10 per week.

Mr. KRAUSE. Your wages were more than $10 per week?

Mrs. LAWTON. I started in at $4 and worked for six months at that. We did our own washing and cooking, and we found that we couldn't live on less than $10 per week. We also did our own sewing.

Mr. KRAUSE. If a factory were given to you what would you start the girls in at?

Mrs. LAWTON. Knowing the business as I do, I would start them in at $10 and give the other girls more, as I know the profit that they make.

Mr. KRAUSE. What do you know about the profits of the business where you worked?

Mrs. LAWTON. I know what he paid for the business; what he made in six months, and the whole thing was told me in a conversation I had with him.

Mr. KRAUSE. Do you know why the Riley Candy Co. failed?

Mrs. LAWTON. The Riley Candy Co. failed because the owner was a cigar maker and the candy maker was a Greek, and didn't know his business.

Mr. SNYDER. Did any of these concerns fail because of the high wages they paid their help?

Mrs. LAWTON. Riley's were paying $10 per week when they failed.

The CHAIRMAN. That is a retail business?

Mrs. LAWTON. Yes; but they did wholesaling, too.

Mr. WILLIAMS. Suppose that minimum wage should be placed at $10 and I employ 50 girls and they earn only $7 per week.

Mrs. LAWTON. You would be very foolish to keep them.

Mr. WILLIAMS. I am glad the commission has the question of apprentices to settle. I believe that this commission with the facts that you have before you are wise enough and just enought to give justice in your decision. Not long ago a woman came to my factory, she said she had two little children and asked to come and learn the trade. We didn't have a place for a woman of that kind then, but I have been giving that woman little lengths so that she can go home and make dust caps and sell them to her friends and thus make a little money. If you are going to base a minimum wage on what you believe is necessary for a woman's maintenance you will be doing her harm, because businesses are not going to hire women that they will lose money on. You are going to do an injury that can't be undone to the woman who can't earn a high minimum wage.

Mr. DAGG. Arn't those cases liable to come in too fast for the commission?

Mr. WILLIAMS. The point I am trying to make is that this commission is going to be just.

Mr. SYNDER. I believe this commission is going to be just and also that this conference is going to be just and that is why I would like to respectfully insist that before Mr. Williams leaves us he would be good enought to leave with us an estimate to show us his ideas of the cost of living.

The CHAIRMAN. Before we complete this general discussion and go on to the cost of living, we have two gentlemen withus who just came in on the train, and I will now call on Mr. H. B. Fisher, of Seattle, who would like to be heard.

Mr. FISHER. I understand that this meeting is for the benefit of the female wage earners of the State. I am in the millinery business, and after our girls serve their apprenticeship they earn from $10 to $30 per week. We take these girls in and for about four weeks we actually lose money on everything they touch. All they can do is line hats. As you all well know, no two hats are alike. Each one is individual. We take them in and train them so that afterwards they make trimmers for our customers. Each season the experienced ones drop out and we have new girls all the time. It is entirely different from factory work. Another thing I would like to say is that most of the girls live at home. The millinery schools charge $25 to teach a girl for six weeks. After the girls have served their apprenticeship and if they make trimmers they can then earn from $15 to $30 per week. There are any number of trimmers in this State getting $25 per week. When a girl is competent, and I guess a great many of your ladies know, it is a question of price to get her, for our millinery work is not like ordinary factory work. You have to combine colors and have to know how to form these shapes together. It is individual work. Each hat is an individual thing. If a girl is a good trimmer she soon knows it and can get a good wage. The girls also have to develop speed. A girl can not learn to be a trimmer in less than three seasons. If the minimum wage is placed too high we can't take these girls in.

The CHAIRMAN. What is the minimum wage that you pay now for these girls?

Mr. FISHER. From about $2 to $6 for the first three seasons. The first season the wage is about $2, the second season, $4.50, and the third season, $6 per week for apprentices.

The CHAIRMAN. What is a seasonal period?

Mr. FISHER. About 16 weeks. The first 16 weeks we pay about $3, the second 16 weeks, $4.50, and the third 16 weeks, $6.

Miss FOISIE. If a girl isn't a born milliner can you make one of her?

Mr. FISHER. No; a trimmer is an artist, just like a sculpturer.

Miss FOISIE. The wages you spoke of would mean very little to the girl as the seasons are so short.

Mr. FISHER. I know lots of girls that are milliners that go to department stores during our quiet seasons. Others go out and pick berries, and in that way get outdoor exercise and also earn a little money. They also get the Christmas work after our fall season. You will all grant that millinery is high as it is. If you had to pay more money for your hat you wouldn't like it. I understand there is a percentage of apprentices allowed in each factory.

The CHAIRMAN. That is to be decided by the commission.

Mr. FISHER. Mr. Stadaker and I thought if we could get 25 per cent for apprentices as millinery is something that has to be learned.

The CHAIRMAN. What does the apprentice do in the interim between these seasons?

Mr. FISHER. She will go to the stores and be a clerk. Our dull season is now while it is quite busy in the stores.

Mr. MARVIN. How many of the girls stop with making bandos.

Mr. FISHER. We buy them. They put in the linings and learn to handle the materials.

Miss FOISIE. Do you teach differently than they teach in the millinery stores?

Mr. FISHER. For a retail store we have to sell the hats there very cheap.

The CHAIRMAN. When do these girls become proficient in their work so that they can command a minimum wage?

Mr. FISHER. They should after the third season.

The CHAIRMAN. Does the average girl become proficient after the third season?

Mr. FISHER. Yes; I think as a general rule. Of course, you must understand that the hats change every season. Perhaps they have been working on a certain style of hats and then the next season the style is entirely different and they have to learn the new styles.

Mr. MARVIN. You are an artist yourself or you wouldn't be where you are. How soon do you discover whether the girl is going to make a proficient milliner?

Mr. FISHER. We ought to know in the third month.

Mr. MARVIN. Wouldn't it be a kindness to tell her as soon as you find out if she will not make a milliner?

Mr. FISHER. Yes, sir. She would be a loss to us also, and it would be an injustice to her to let her stay and be a loss.

The CHAIRMAN. You stated that these girls would be a loss to you in the beginning.

Mr. FISHER. At first they can not make a cent for us.

Mr. MARVIN. If she is a born genius do you discover it after the first season?

Mr. FISHER. Yes, sir. The girls usually know their values and we don't aim to keep them down. There are outside trimmers who don't really work for us. They just apply to us for work and we take them in. They have to know the styles for the coming season, so we take them in and pay them $6 per week. They are glad to work for nothing just to learn the new season. During the season they then earn $12, $15, $18, $20, or $25, but they ask to be taken in even if they have to pay for the opportunity of learning the new season. They are not our regular help. The girls are very well satisfied and glad to get $6 per week.

Mrs. SILBAUGH. Do you know the custom in the eastern houses?

Mr. FISHER. Some of the houses won't take them, as they are actual money losers. I think that at $6 per week we are not making any money on them, as they do not work.

Mrs. SILBAUGH. Where do they go after they leave your establishment?

Mr. FISHER. They go to Olympia, Tacoma, Everett, Bellingham, Spokane, and other cities.

Mr. SILBAUGH. Do many go outside of the State?

Mr. FISHER. Yes; some go to Montana and Idaho, but most of them stay in the State. The western styles are very different from the eastern styles. We have trimmers come out from the East who just want to see the West and make a little money while they are here. They ask me to take them in and say they are a trimmer. If we can't recommend them and say that their work is good, we take them in for a couple of weeks and then send them out when we have a chance to supply one of our trimmers. In that way we do the girls a good turn by taking them in. We are very glad to do this.

Mr. SNYDER. We men are touched by one end of this hat business. To what extent does your situation effect the general situation? How many girls are involved in this trimming school?

Mr. FISHER. We have sometimes as many as 50 transients.

Mrs. MUIR. What do you pay the people who make frames?

Mr. FISHER. An apprentice can't make a wire frame. One-sixteenth of an inch will spoil the whole hat. We have to take a first-class girl to teach an apprentice a certain thing.

Mrs. MUIR. How long does it take them before they can make a wire frame?

Mr. FISHER. It depends upon the girl's own ability. Some learn in two or three months; others can't do it.

Mr. STADAKER. These frames are made in a regular wire-frame factory. It takes them six months to learn to make these frames.

Mr. SNYDER. After a girl has gone there for three seasons at the wage rate of $3, $4.50, or $6, what would be the next payment?

Mr. FISHER. About $8. While we think the minimum wage in Oregon is not any too cheap for many girls, I think it should not be over $8 in order to give us a chance to compete.

The CHAIRMAN. Have you strong competition with Oregon?

Mr. FISHER. Yes, sir.

Mr. MARVIN. Do you understand the law in this State. It says: " It shall be unlawful to employ women or minors in any industry or occupation within the State of Washington under conditions of labor detrimental to their health or morals; and it shall be unlawful to employ women workers in any industry within the State of Washington at wages which are not adequate for their maintenance."

Do you think a woman can live on $8 per week?

Mr. FISHER. I don't think she could live very well on it. They all have to improve to be a trimmer and get the big wage.

The CHAIRMAN. I assume you are an expert in millinery values. I would like to ask your opinion as to what the hats that the representatives of employees here are wearing, which are extraordinary nice hats, are worth?

Mr. FISHER. It depends where they buy the hats. You can get good hats from $5 up.

Mrs. ROBAIR. When you just pay the girl $2.50, why do the hats cost so much?

Mr. FISHER. You understand that the stores must make some profit. Each hat is different and we have to keep getting new styles. We don't keep the girls lining hats all summer. They make flowers and fix ribbons.

Miss FOISIE. You run it very different than most places.

Mr. FISHER. We try to teach them to be thorough milliners. Our aim is to get good help.

Miss FOISIE. I would like to ask if the minimum wage that was fixed in the mercantile establishments covers the millinery department in the department stores.

The CHAIRMAN. Yes; in all mercantile establishments.

Mr. FISHER. I think I have stated everything I wished to say and thank you for your attention.

Mr. MARVIN. You gentlemen understand that you are here to recommend a minimum wage that you think a girl could live on. I think Mr. Fisher suggested $8.

Mr. FISHER. A minimum wage would not necessarily mean that a girl would have to work for that. If she knows she can get more money she will soon leave. A lady came to me once and said, " Can you give me a position?" I said, " I don't know. Who are you, and where did you work?" She said she came to the coast for her health and had been getting $50 per week in the East. She just wanted to work two weeks and would have come under the head of transients.

Mr. SNYDER. What do you regard as a minimum amount that will enable a girl to live decently and healthfully on? Do you regard $8 per week enough?

Mr. STADAKER. It would keep her for awhile. I think we have but one girl working for us that does not live at home. That one gets $10 per week.

Mr. MARVIN. May I ask how many of them are married women whose husbands could support them.

Mr. STADAKER. One.

Mr. FENLASON. Don't you think these manufacturers of hats are responsible for the high minimum wage?

Mr. SAWYER. I think we should investigate the word minimum. That means the very lowest that we can get. I think we are talking a little above the minimum. What we should find to-day is the absolute mimium that a girl can live on.

Miss FOISIE. Don't the law say decently and comfortably?

Mr. SAWYER. Yes; but don't get away from the idea that we are talking minimums. I have watched with considerable interest the statements of the different manufacturers. I find that they are employing a good many girls who are living at home. As I understand it this minimum wage is to be established for girls who are self-supporting. Now, the reports of manufacturers here, unless they are incorrect, show that a large percentage of the girls are living at home.

The CHAIRMAN. The law doesn't take into account the girl living at home. let me read what it says:

" It shall be unlawful to employ women or minors in any industry or oceupation within the State of Washington under conditions of labor detrimental to their health or morals; and it shall be unlawful to employ women workers in any industry within the State of Washington at wages which are not adequate for their maintenance."

Mr. SNYDER. Don't forget this, that there are girls in every walk of life who are decent working for less than $10 and are living comfortably.

The CHAIRMAN. Now, I don't believe the law contemplates that we should establish a minimum wage of such proportion that a girl can be satisfied in all of her desires. We know that some girls want a great deal more than other girls, and I believe it is the duty of this conference to establish a wage based on the cost of living as per items mentioned. I think we ought to go into these matters thoroughly, even if it takes a whole week. I think we ought to be positive in our conclusions.

Mr. SAWYER. There are people living on less than $10 per week. Some of you might say a girl is entitled to her own room, but I know that two girls rooming together can economize.

Mr. KRAUSE. I lived in an Eastern State on a great deal less than $10. I also lived in Montana, and it cost me a great deal more. I think the girl that is establishing herself for future earning power and is coming under this minimum wage must make sacrifices at some time. The employer must have averages and maximums or his business is a failure.

Prof. KERN. How could we arrive at a reasonable solution of this if we didn't analyze it?

Mr. SAWYER. There are places in Spokane where you can get board for $3 and help a little with the work. Don't forget that we are talking minimums. The very least that a girl can live for.

Mrs. LAWTON. Could you tell me any places in Spokane where a girl can get board for $3?

Mr. MOORE. The Ladies' Hotel.

Mrs. LAWTON. The girl who stays there is accepting charity.

Miss FOISIE. The Y. W. C. A. will take girls in, but that is charity.

Mr. BLACK. If we pay a girl $9, and she only earns $6, is not that charity?

Miss FOISIE. Yes; but you expect to get returns later on.

Mr. MARVIN. I am sure we all want to arrive at a conclusion in this matter. The Attorney General's Office has clearly told us that this minimum wage must be made in view of a self-supporting woman. The girl who has to keep herself. I do not believe it is up to this conference to interpret. The law has clearly stated that you must answer the questions as to what a self-supporting girl, in the State of Washington, needs to maintain herself in comfort. That question, it seems to me, has been settled for us.

Prof. KERN. As I understand it, there is an institution where girls can stay for $3, but that is a charity institution.

Mrs. LAWTON. The girls have to work after hours to help keep it up.

Mr. KRAUSE. It is purely a business proposition and no charity institution.

Mrs. LAWTON. Why are they running the home if it is not a business propositiou—still the girls are accepting charity by staying there. Why do they do it if it is not for profit?

Mr. KRAUSE. Don't you think some good ladies are interested in the girls?

Mr. SNYDER. I would like to ask the capacity of this Spokane house;

Mr. MOORE. It has about 200 rooms, I think, but I am not positive.

Mr. KRAUSE. Its purpose is to give these girls who have no homes a chance to get a nice home under nice conditions. Single rooms are so much per week and room for two girls cheaper.

Mrs. ROBAIR. When you come to get a single room, don't you have to pay as much as in any hotel?

Mr. KRAUSE. I believe you pay about $4 or $5.

Mr. FENLASON. I would like to ask Mr. Marvin this question: I understand the attorney general has said the minimum wage shall be sufficient to support a woman in decency and comfort. If we establish a minimum wage so high that it would be shown that the women would lose their jobs, would we be doing our duty under this law? If we should establish a wage of $12 or $10, if it could be shown that in many of our industries men would take the place of women, would we be doing our duty?

Mr. MARVIN. Not having any written opinion as to that from the attorney general's office, your duty is to determine what a minimum wage for a self-supporting woman in the State of Washington should be. Just as it was in the mercantile conference, so it is here; you men and women have been chosen after so much care, and so much thought and you understand that you men were chosen after some of us have known you for 20 years; you women were chosen under the big conviction that we could get together and that concessions would have to be made on both sides; and the other three, the unbiased public, is also chosen with as much care. I am sure we can get together. None of us are responsible for the framing of this law. Mr. Snyder's interpretation of this law has been very clear and I think correct. I think that is the way the minimum wage must be fixed, and I profoundly hope that we will get together. I sincerely hope we can get together. I don't think anyone will have all their own way.

The CHAIRMAN. It is now a quarter after 5, and I think we ought to get down to real business.

Mr. FENLASON. I would like to know what assurity we are going to have that this law is going to be enforced. I wish each and every one of you would give me your opinion as to the enforcement of this law.

The CHAIRMAN. Why not carry that over until to-night and give them a chance to think it over.

Mrs. ROBAIR. I am self-supporting and also have another to support. Taking into consideration the board a girl has to pay in Tacoma, her lunches she has to get, and the prices she must pay for them, I don't see how she can get along on less than $10 per week. In Tacoma or in places that I have lived it would cost me on an average of $12 per month for my room and I would then have to furnish my own wood. Another thing, I would not live in the average rooming house. I would have to do my washing and my ironing, and this is not permitted in many of the rooms. We have to buy the foodstuffs in such small quantities that it costs more than in large lots. I find it cheaper to furnish my own rooms and do my own cooking. You can exist on bread and water just as you can exist on $5 or $6 per week; there are girls doing it, but you can not live and live right.

They are girls who go without necessary things to eat; they don't carry anything for their lunch but bread and butter; but do those girls live or just exist? There are places in Tacoma where you can get board, where they will not put up your lunch, for $4. Then the girl must get her lunch down town or go without. To get a living and not just exist I think the working girl should have $10. I hope this commission won't make class distinction between two sets of working girls. Why shouldn't the girl who works in the factory be as clean as the girl in the mercantile establishment? You take a candy factory or cracker factory—why shouldn't they be as clean, keep their clothes just as clean, as in a store. We want our candy to be clean and we want the girl who makes it to be clean. You take a laundry girl and they have to work harder than any other girl, and should be paid as much as the girl in the mercantile establishment.

Mr. Black states that it took three weeks for his employees to be operators. He brought up the question about prison-made goods. Why do the manufacturers buy these prison-made goods? They put their operators out of a job by doing so. Why don't the manufacturers get together and make a good big stand against it? They would soon help rid the State of Washington of prison-made goods. They would soon help the State to be rid of it completely. Another thing, Mr. Black stated that in prison when those people who learn that trade are let out they are just like babies and have no trade. A girl who learns the overall trade in his factory is a skilled workman. What is the difference?

Mr. BLACK. Because you girls wouldn't work with a man who comes from prison. I know that a girl can live and live decently on less than $10. I know from actual experience that the cost of living is a great deal higher than it was 10 years ago, but I still contend that she can live on less. than $10 per week.

Miss FOISIE. I think this thing has been thoroughly covered, and I certainly agree with Mrs. Robair that a girl can not live decently on less than $10. I myself for a good many years haven't lived on $10 per week; and I don't thing anyone can comfortably live on $10 per week.

Mr. SNYDER. I move that we adjourn until 8 o'clock this evening.

Prof. KERN. I second that motion.

The CHAIRMAN. I has been moved and seconded that we adjourn until 8 o'clock this evening. All in favor signify by saying "aye." [All voted aye.] The ayes have it.

AFTER RECESS—8 O'CLOCK.

The CHAIRMAN. The meeting will please come to order. It appears to the Chair that we have just about exhausted our general debate, and if it is the pleasure of the conference we will now take up the question of the cost of living. According to the rules and regulations of the conference we will take this up item by item. Our first item on the list is meals and room. We can either discuss them separately or together. We will not discuss the total amount until after we have gone over every item, one by one.

Mr. KRAUSE. The minimum wage, as I understand it, is the rock bottom or the very least that a girl can possibly get—the very lowest point to be reached. It is not the standard of wages but the very lowest amount that is accepted. If the minimum is accepted as an earning power, then the party that is in the condition of accepting the minimum wage, they haven't established themselves of an earning power. The person who hasn't any earning power and is only a minimum-wage earner can not expect to partake of the good things that are due the minimum-wage earner. A girl that is the minimum is no asset to the producer, consequently, would be an expense to the company—the minimum wage which in all cases is a charitable proposition, for until they pass that low minimum they are no good to the producer. I submit as a fair basis for the two items—the girl that is a minimum-wage earner is no producer. Girls do live on $4 per week and get nice surroundings.

Miss FOISIE. Do you personally know of any places where you can get such board?

Mr. KRAUSE. I can give you one-half dozen places where a girl can get room and board in Spokane for $4.

Mrs. ROBAIR. You stated that you take the girls that were home girls—now will these same families that will take your girls in, will they take the self-supporting girls?

Mr. KRAUSE. Yes; there are families that will take them in. I know of one place in particular—a traveling salesman, who travels out of Spokane, whose wife would take a girl for a companion.

Mrs. LAWTON. There are not enough of those cases to accommodate all the girls. I have found it very difficult to find room and board at $4.

Mr. KRAUSE. Then, how did you get along when you were only receiving $4?

Mrs. LAWTON. I wore clothes I was not very proud of.

Mr. KRAUSE. If you had to, couldn't you get places for girls at that rate, Mr. Moore?

Mr. MOORE. I could get room for two girls together for $3.

Mr. KRAUSE. I know this is true. I don't submit this as a general rule, I submit it, as the minimum, as the extreme cases in all instances in the State of Washington. It is not the general rule.

Mrs. ROBAIR. I think that we ought to take these two items separate—room and meals.

The CHAIRMAN. I think that we ought to take the items both ways and find a happy medium.

Mrs. SILBAUGH. Unless the girls are not in walking distance, meals and room can not be obtained at the same place.

Mr. DAGG. Most of them take their lunches with them.

Mr. KRAUSE. These girls who bring their lunches, our company has supplied an annex for these girls where they can eat their lunches. Each girl has a locker and there are chairs and a table and a. heater if they care to make coffee. There is not 1 girl out of 50 that leaves the establishment for her lunch. Some of the girls come from Hillyard, 5 miles out of Spokane, and bring their lunches.

Mrs. UDALL. Do most of them live at home? Of course, they naturally bring their lunch from home.

Mr. DAGG. In our particular case we have a dining room; coffee can be made on the gas stove; takes one-half hour to get coffee ready, and each one takes a turn at making it.

Mr. KRAUSE. Mr. Roberts, of the Imperial Candy Co., has a cafeteria, and sells things very cheap. That plan is followed by the largest firms in Boston and other large cities.

The CHAIRMAN. Most of the factories of any size at all have a lunch room.

Mr. STEVENSON. In Tacoma at the factory the girls bring bread and butter and get meat, potatoes, and coffee at the lunch room. All of the girls but five or six in the factory do that and they live within three or four blocks of the factory. Do you find that condition, Mrs. Robair?

Mrs. ROBAIR. We have a very nice cafeteria in connection with our factory where we can get meat, potatoes, and a cup of coffee for 10 cents. Then it is 5 cents extra for bread, pie, or cake.

Mr. STEVENSON. In our overall, pants, and jacket department those employees have to go to the other building for lunch.

Mrs. ROBAIR. I do not think that Mr. Day's factory, that Mr. Stevenson represents, is the average factory, as everything is very convenient there for the girl. We mustn't base the minimum wage upon the home girl, but take the self-supporting girl, the girl who has to support herself. We have to take the girl who has no father or mother to support her. It doesn't seem quite right for the father and mother to give her her board and room free of charge. The minimum, as I take it, is what a girl must have to live on, waht is really necessary for a girl to live upon. If the home girl receives her board at home, her father and mother are paying part of her expenses and she is giving it to the manufacturer, because she is not receiving enough to live on.

Mr. KRAUSE. She is not giving the manufacturer anything, because she is not producing anything for the manufacturer. I claim that a minimum-wage worker is not producing anything for the manufacturer. The home girl is just that much more fortunate in having her parents to help her. She is just establishing herself, laying a foundation for her future. She is not giving the manufacturer anything, because she does not produce anything yet.

Miss FOISIE. Are you not referring to the apprentice and not the minimum-wage worker?

Mr. KRAUSE. Not necessarily. The apprentice clause takes under the minor age of 18.

Mr. MARVIN. No; you are mistaken.

Mrs. UDALL. Did you understand that you were to start the girl with the minimum wage?

Mr. KRAUSE. We start ours at $6 per week, that is the minimum.

Mrs. ROBAIR. You just said a girl that is not a producer is the minimum-wage earner.

Mr. KRAUSE. We now have the privilege of making our own arrangements about the apprenticeship period and the wages paid. We are not under obligations to pay any more than we see fit. We take them and give them a try-out period. If at the end of two or three weeks they show any aptitude we keep them, and they can earn much more than $6 doing piecework.

Mrs. ROBAIR. I would say, taking these two items of meals and room together, that it would be only fair to put it at $5 per week for room and board for a woman.

Mr. SNYDER. I think it would be a good idea to go through with Mr. Krause's list and find out what he gets for his total.

Mrs. MILLS. I think our record gives us some very different information as to meals and room.

Mrs. SILBAUGH. On page 13 you will find the list of questions complete.

Mr. FENLASON. Supposing that each and every one of us fill out this list, and then we will take our list from our own viewpoint. I would like to present some real figures and facts. I was surprised to find out what we are giving our girls to live on and what they figure it costs to live on. Fifty-eight of our girls I asked to come to my office and answer these questions: Are you living at home, where do you board and room, do you pay room rent, are you married, single, or widow, are you satisfied with your wages? What wage do you suggest as a minimum wage for girls? The average age of these 58 girls is 22; 41 are living at home; 22 are not paying anything for board and room. The average wage for these 58 girls for month of April was $9.38;

36 were single. In answer to the question: Are you satisfied with your wages, 25 said yes, 20 said no, and the balance didn't answer. Then, when I asked what do you think a fair minimum wage, some didn't answer, others said we don't know, we want all we can get. One little girl I asked if she was satisfied with her wages, and she said, "I should say not." I said, "What wages do you think you ought to have" and she said, "$11." Some I asked, "What do you pay for board" and they answered, "Papa says I can have all I earn." I think that $4 per week or $208 per year for table board is sufficient, and $8 per month for room.

Mr. MARVIN. What is your average?

Mr. FENLASON. $9.38 for the week.

Mrs. ROBAIR. I figure that meals taken outside would be $208. There are 52 weeks in a year, so we have to pay over some months.

Mr. FENLASON. We all seem to take the position that the girl that lives at home that her folks are giving her board and she isn't paying her way. This matter depends entirely on where a girl lives. The average wage of a people is always equal to the average cost of living.

Miss FOISIE. I think the cost of living keeps on going up, and the wages do not go up.

Mr. KRAUSE. We are out of the game so far as shipping the manufactured product back to the Eastern States. The Eastern manufacturers think a minimum wage of $10 would hit us awfully hard.

Mr. DAGG. There is a good percentage who make less than that, and they will have to be discharged.

Mrs. ROBAIR. There are only seven that get below $10 of the pieceworkers in our factory and only four day workers that get below $8 per week. We have sanitary conditions. I am not appealing for the girls in the factory where I work, but for the women throughout the State of Washington who need the protection of this commission.

Miss FOISIE. I would like to ask Mr. Dagg if he don't think the women in his factory would come up to the minimum wage if there was one to work for.

Mr. DAGG. I don't think they could do it. There are women who have been there for a long time—possibly 50 or 55 years of age—and I don't think they could come up to a high minimum.

Miss FOISIE. Wouldn't they in most cases come under that special clause?

Mr. DAGG. I don't know about that part of it.

The CHAIRMAN. I want to say that this commission will have to have absolute proof that the worker is disabled and entitled for the permit. We can't issue a permit to any woman unless she is defective in health or physically disabled.

Mrs. ROBAIR. In our factory I find that we have four that are really inefficient—two from old age, one has the rheumatism, and the other is slow and aged. There are also two others that will never average much. They never will make garment workers.

The CHAIRMAN. I should say that the commission would have to abide by the intent of the law; and if these women are not speedy enough to produce a sufficient amount of goods to earn a minimum wage, we would not be authorized to issue licenses. They would have to leave that industry and place of employment and go elsewhere. That is going to be the result of the minimum-wage law. It was so in New Zealand, and it has been everywhere it has been tried out. It means a higher standard of efficiency.

We are not getting very far with the room and meals. I think we had better hear from somebody else on this matter. What do the members of the public think?

Mr. DAGG. How is living in Walla Walla; very high?

Prof. KERN. The particular place I know of I am led to believe that we can get good table board for less than some of the figures that have been given. I had perhaps figured the room a little high; that it would cost probably $3 per week, including heat and light.

Miss FOISIE. Aren't there factories throughout this State where a girl can never get over $9 per week?

Mr. KRAUSE. What percentage of the factories in Seattle are in that condition? Don't you find the average factory willing to pay the employees what they deserve?

Miss FOISIE. I don't think the time workers ever reach a very high wage.

Mr. KRAUSE. I suppose you know that the factories in the State of Washington must be inspected. If there is an elevator in the building, it must be inspected. The health officers demand that the conditions in that factory must be up to a certain standard. There must be a certain standard established in these certain things. You owe it to your fellow workers to see that a factory that is not up to the standard is inspected.

Mr. FENLASON. Women have the right to vote; I am glad of it. But in asking for a $10 minimum do you think it fair to ask more for women than for men? A $10 minimum for eight hours is 25 cents per hour, or $2 per day, or $2.50 per 10 hours. I am just giving you these things to consider. You are asking more pay for the women and girls than the men are getting in the mills in lots of places. You suppose you are making it $10 because you know the profit in the business. You said you get $10, and you also said that the cheapest employee where you are working gets $6. If you have to increase the $6 to two-thirds, you yourself should be entitled to the same rate of increase; that 'would be giving you $20 per week.

Mrs. LAWTON. That would not be any more than I would be earning for the employer.

Mr. FENLASON. Don't you think you would be taking advantage of the poor man?

Mrs. LAWTON. I know the expense of the business and I know what the business ought to get. I don't see why the owner should get all the profits.

Mr. KRAUSE. Do you know the cost of running the business?

Mrs. LAWTON. I think I do.

The CHAIRMAN. We will have to get back to the cost of board and room.

Mr. SNYDER. I want to say that I have endeavored to get a little information from Seattle, and I haven't been able to find, in Seattle, board for less than $4 per week. The least I can find for single room was $1.50.

The CHAIRMAN. We have our table of the investigation made by the Industrial Welfare Commission. We classified ads in all the leading newspapers in the State. This ad was signed " A working girl." We received 344 replies. Part of these were investigated by members of the commission, but we did not have the time to investigate all of them. We have here a list of 344 rooms. Some of them including board. There are rooms at $1.25, $1.50, $1.75, and $4 per week.

Mr. KRAUSE. Are there many offers of board and room at $4?

The CHAIRMAN. Not very many at $4. I will read you a list of replies we received from Seattle, Tacoma, and Spokane.)

(Chairman read from report of commission.)

Mr. KRAUSE. Was that an advertisement by the commission?

The CHAIRMAN. Yes, sir. Here is the way the ads were worded : " Wanted board and room by working girl; state price per week." " Young lady employed in downtown district desires room and board; state price."

Mr. KRAUS. I still maintain that under the new conditions, pertaining to working girls, including our " women's hotels," these are factors in our question of girls away from home. I happen to know Mrs. Cunningham, who is stationed at the Northern Pacific depot in Spokane with the view of locating girls. Mrs. Cunningham is paid by the women's clubs and the associations of women's clubs are sponsor for the Woman's Hotel. She is a writer of some note and a very bright woman. She is depot matron, and looks after the girls.

Mrs. ROBAIR. I do not think the discussion of the women's hotels and these homes for girls should be allowed. Please lets rule that out. We are talking about a girl that is going to support herself. The club women and business men help to support these homes and the girls who stay there are therefore accepting charity. Besides, it costs as much for a girl to live at the Y. W. C. A. as at a good hotel.

Mr. MOORE. I know women in Spokane who are living at this home, and I know it is not a charity institution.

Mr. SNYDER. I gather that it is self-supporting, except for the original investment.

Mr. KRAUSE. It is considered an ideal place for girls to live.

Mr. MARVIN. Is it subject to taxation?

Mr. SNYDER. If it is not subject to taxation, that classifies it. It is then a charity institution.

Mrs. MUIR. I am not an employer or an employee at present, but I was talking with one of the ladies who has something to do with conducting a woman's inn in Tacoma, for which the girls can get board and room for $3 per week. She said we have found that some of the girls can not live on the wages they receive, so we have established the home for their benefit. It is away out from the business district and the girls have to tramp away out there in the dark at night.

Mr. KRAUSE. This place in Spokane is established so that the girl who can not afford to pay high board can stay there and be thrown with the better class of girls who do pay high board.

Miss FOISIE. The Y. W. C. A. will bear me out that they carry part of the burden of the girl. They have a certain number who are positively on charity. They live on $2 and $3 or whatever they can afford to pay.

Mr. DAGG. I should think we ought to get back to our list.

Mr. MARVIN. I would like to ask if any of you have completed the whole list.

Mrs. MILLS. Yes; I have.

Mr. FENLASON. I move that each member of the conference fill out his own list for discussion.

Mr. DAGG. I second the motion.

The CHAIRMAN. It is moved and seconded that each member of the conference fill out his own list for discussion. All in favor signify their assent by saying "aye." [All voted aye.] The ayes have it. Miss Foisie, what have you?

Miss FOISIE. Six hundred and seventy-one dollars and seventy-five cents.

The CHAIRMAN. Mrs. Robair?

Mrs. ROBAIR. Five hundred and ninety-nine dollars and fifty cents.

The CHAIRMAN. Mrs. Lawton?

Mrs. LAWTON. Five hundred and sixty dollars.

The CHAIRMAN. Mrs. Mills?

Mrs. MILLS. Five hundred and fifty dollars and ten cents.

The CHAIRMAN. Prof. Kern?

Prof. KERN. Four hundred and eighty-two dollars and fifty cents.

The CHAIRMAN. Mr. Snyder?

Mr. SNYDER. I would rather you pass me by for the present.

The CHAIRMAN. Mr. Krause?

Mr. KRAUSE. Three hundred and seventy-four dollars and five cents.

The CHAIRMAN. Mr. Dagg?

Mr. DAGG. Four hundred and eighteen dollars.

The CHAIRMAN. Mr. Fenlason?

Mr. FENLASON. Six hundred and thirty-five dollars.

The CHAIRMAN. The average, then, would be $536.35. It is getting quite late, and do you not think we had better adjourn until to-morrow and take it up item by item?

Mr. KRAUSE. I move we adjourn.

Mr. SNYDER. I second the motion.

The CHAIRMAN. It is moved and seconded that we adjourn until 9 o'clock in the morning. All in favor signify their assent by saying "aye." [All voted aye.] The ayes have it—we will adjourn.

WEDNESDAY, MAY 13.

The CHAIRMAN. The meeting will please come to order. The secretary will call the roll.

(The roll was called; every member present.)

Mr. SNYDER. I asked the conference last night to pass me by, but on careful consideration I have been able to arrive at figures which total $493.

Prof. KERN. I figured it over somewhat more carefully afterwards, and I would change my figure from $482.50 to $510.

Mrs. LAWTON. I had my figures at $560 and I find that they should be $565.

Mr. FENLASON. Mr. Chairman, I would suggest that we take it up along the same line as we did yesterday; I would suggest that we only act on one's estimate at a time. I think that would be fair.

The CHAIRMAN. Do you think we should take it up item by item?

Mr. MARVIN. We could hear from each one of the conferees as to their figures.

The CHAIRMAN. Miss Foisie, what are your figures?

Miss FOISIE. I have revised mine and am just making them out. I am not quite ready yet to give a total. Yes; I have $601.25 now.

The CHAIRMAN. Mrs. Robair?

Mrs. ROBAIR. Mine is $599.50.

The CHAIRMAN. Mrs. Lawton?

Mrs. LAWTON. I have $565.

The CHAIRMAN. Yours, Mrs. Mills?

Mrs. MILLS. Five hundred and twenty-six dollars and ten cents.

Prof. KERN. I have $510.

The CHAIRMAN. Mr. Snyder's is $493. Yours, Mr. Krause?

Mr. KRAUSE. Three hundred and ninety-nine dollars and five cents.

The CHAIRMAN. Mr. Dagg?

Mr. DAGG. Four hundred and eighteen dollars.

The CHAIRMAN. Mr. Fenlason?

Mr. FENLASON. I want to say at this time that I have no reason to change my figures of $635, unless you may eliminate some of the items. I want to say what possibly might be eliminated in order to make the figures less.

The CHAIRMAN. My suggestion is to have the member of the employees' side who has the highest figure debate the question with the member of the employers' side who has the lowest.

Mr. FENLASON. I think it is right and just that we hear from our lawyer friend first and then I would suggest that we hear from the professor, because he is supposed to be wise, and then from the lady who is the friend of the girls.

Mr. SNYDER. I think Mr. Fenlason is entirely correct except as to his time. The time has not yet arrived for me to speak, but will more properly come after we have heard what the employers and employees have to say. They have given us totals, we want to know what makes up these complete lists. We should first know what we are to reconcile and have the basis upon which to bring about that reconciliation.

Mr. FENLASON. Will you permit me to answer that question. I think my colleague is absolutely wrong. I want to call your attention to my particular position. I am a manufacturer and employer of girls. I have been unable to agree with my two colleagues. My estimate of this thing is the highest of all. I wish to reserve the right to correct my figures by a system of elimination to which the ladies must agree. I am thinking of what a woman can live decently on. I am not thinking how it is going to affect the industries. If this conference is willing to eliminate certain things, if the ladies are willing to eliminate them, then I am willing. I being an employer and being the highest man on the list I want to meet you halfway on a compromise. I said I absolutely would not vote with them on the minimum they are going to ask for. I think it is right and just that we hear from the other side of the house first.

The CHAIRMAN. I regret to' say that I can not see it in the light that Mr. Fenlason 'does. We haven't gone into the matter item by item yet, therefore we .do not know if their proposition is tenable, neither do we know if the proposition of. the employers is tenable. However, if the commission desires to override the ruling of the Chair, it may do so.

Mr. FENLASON. Then, I suggest, Mr. Chairman, that we start out and let the two lowest on the employers' side speak and then the lowest on the employees' side—well, anyway, I want to be left out of this.

The CHAIRMAN. Do you make that as a motion?

Mr. FENLASON. Yes; I move that the lowest on the employer's side and the highest on the employees' side and in that routine discuss the cost of living.

Mrs. ROBAIR. I second the motion.

The CHAIRMAN. It has been moved and seconded that the member representing the employers having the lowest estimate and the member having the highest estimate on the employees' side present their list to the conference for discussion. All in favor signify their assent by saying " Aye." [All voted aye.] The ayes have it.

Mr. KRAUSE. I have changed one figure and that is the figure of board and room. I have put it at $4.50 per week, that brings my total up to $400.05, or an average of $7.68 per week. I will be glad to take each item up separately .and show how she can live decently and honestly upon this scale. Please understand, though, that I am speaking of the minimum girl. My contention is this, that the minimum should be $7.50. I am basing my argument upon that fact, but I know that the average girl who works in the factories in the State of Washington earns a great deal more than $7.50.

Miss FOISIE. After anyone has passed their term of apprenticeship,· I do not think they are a nonproducer.

Mrs. ROBAIR. Mr. Chairman, how is the apprenticeship period in the mercantile establishments?

The CHAIRMAN. We allow a period of apprenticeship of one year to anyone who has had no experience.

Mrs. ROBAIR. Our minimum wage begins after she has served her apprenticeship.

Mr. SNYDER. The law clearly provides that we are to provide a minimum to maintain a woman in decency and comfort. Therefore, I think we are basing our estimate on the wrong ideas.

The CHAIRMAN. The chair will have to sustain the objection made by Mr. Snyder.

Mr. FENLASON. Do I understand the ruling of the Chair to mean that in defining what a self-supporting woman is, that it is not to be taken into consideration whether, when she is working for her employer, that she is producing enough for her employer. If she has the full profit of what she produces, if that wouldn't support her, is she self-supporting?

The CHAIRMAN. It appears to me that we must not lose sight of the question of the standard of efficiency in this matter. The standard of efficiency and the minimum wage whatever that may be, are related to one another. If the minimum wage is established so high that the average girl will not earn a profit for her employer over the standard wage, it will throw the girl out of employment, therefore, it would be well to determine, for our guidance, what is the standard of efficiency of a girl that can earn this proposed wage, yet we must base it upon the cost of living as nearly as possible.

Mr. KRAUSE. I would say that the average I have in mind is above $10. The point I was trying to illustrate was the minimum. I conclude that this commission will take care of the apprenticeship period, and after she has served this period she becomes a minimum-wage earner.

The CHAIRMAN. Yes; that is correct.

Miss FOISIE. For board and room you have $4.50, Mr. Krause?

Mr. KRAUSE. Yes; that is right. I claim we can live under these conditions. I don't think that a girl can ever afford to pay more than $4.50 for a room; but I think she can start out on that and as her wages advance she can get a better room.

Mrs. ROBAIR. If she can live in a $4.50 room at one time there is no reason why she should raise it or live in a more expensive room just because she is making a couple of dollars more.

Miss FOISIE. For board and room I have $6.

Mr. MARVIN. I think Mr. Krause should go through his list.

Mr. SNYDER. I move that Mr. Krause be instructed to proceed with his entire list, and that thereafter Miss Foisie give us her list.

Mr. FENLASON. I second the motion.

The CHAIRMAN. Have you heard the motion made by Mr. Snyder, and seconded by Mr. Fenlason, to the effect that Mr. Krause read his list and discuss it item by item. All in favor signify their assent by saying "aye." [All voted aye.]

The ayes have it. The first understanding was that the two members were to debate each item.

Mr. FENLASON. Mr. Chairman, I believe the records will show that we moved that the lowest estimate on this side and the highest on that side debate their propositions. I think none of the rest of us has anything to say until they get through. I think the motion that was made and carried covers the point.

The CHAIRMAN. I think Mr. Fenlason's point is well taken. Proceed with the debate. Have we reached anything definite about board and room?

Mrs. ROBAIR. I thought we came to the conclusion that the board and room was $5.

The CHAIRMAN. There was no conclusion made. We ought to arrive at some general understanding.

Mr. MARVIN. Mr. Chairman, I understand that no one is to talk except these two who are giving their items.

The CHAIRMAN. I think the two parties debating should have the floor; but any member has a right to ask any question in order to bring out any point that they want discussed.

Mr. MARVIN. It seems to me that those who are interested have the parallel items at the conclusion of the list. We could each discuss the items.

The CHAIRMAN. The Chair takes the position in this matter that these figures are undoubtedly based on reason. The reason should be brought out. When I submit a figure of any kind I usually have some reason for it, and I believe these two members are fully qualified to say why they have estimated these figures. I think we should give them an opportunity to state their reasons.

Mrs. MILLS. I think it wise for us to keep in mind that one of these parties lives in Spokane and one in Seattle.

The CHAIRMAN. These investigations didn't show that the cost of living was very much different between Spokane and Seattle.

Mr. KRAUSE. I have not investigated the cost of these items. I haven't any authentic figures for these estimates. I haven't gone to the stores and priced these different articles of dress. I submitted my figures. What is your yearly basis on those figures?

Miss FOISIE. I have $182 for meals and $130 for room.

The CHAIRMAN. Does the conference wish to ask any questions relative to meals and room?

Mr. DAGG. I would like to say that for a young lady to room and board in two separate places is more expensive. As long as we are figuring on what is the minimum, we ought to take that into consideration. I figured $25 per year for car fare, and some of these places are within walking distance. Some of those out of walking distance are as low as $3.50.

The CHAIRMAN. The next will be shoes and rubbers.

Mr. KRAUSE. I have $7.

Miss FOISIE. I have $11.

The CHAIRMAN. Miss Foisie, how many pairs of shoes do you think a girl needs in a year?

. Miss FOISIE. In a great many of the factories the floors are very uneven, and the average girl would need two pairs of shoes, one pair of low shoes, and one pair rubbers.

Mr. KRAUSE. I think the girl will need them all right, but I don't know of any factory where the floors are as you speak. The floors are a very important matter, and in most of the factories the girls change their shoes and uniforms before starting work.

Miss FOISIE. In a great many of the factories I know of they don't change their shoes or have uniforms to wear; and where a girl treadles all day she breaks her shoes down. I contend that two pairs of high shoes and one pair of low shoes is not any too many.

The CHAIRMAN. We have made quite a thorough investigation in the factories of the State, and we find that a great many of the girls change their shoes when they come into the factories. We recommended lockers in some of the factories where the girls could keep their shoes and where they could not be stolen. I believe that the girl in the mercantile establishment is required to wear a higher-priced shoe and is not able to change them for a cheaper shoe during working hours.

Miss FOISIE. In the candy factories and those places they don't change their shoes; they could if they wanted to, but a great many do not, and the candy drops on their shoes and wears the leather out.

The CHAIRMAN. Before we pass up the question of shoes and rubbers, what is the price of a pair of rubbers?

Miss FOISIE. Fifty, sixty, and seventy-five cents. Sixty-five is the medium.

The CHAIRMAN. We haven't heard of the average price of the shoes.

Mrs. ROBAIR. I think it is more reasonable to pay $4 for a pair of shoes than $2. One $4 pair lasts longer than two $2 pairs.

Mr. DAGG. You don't need to use the minimum in buying things, you can pay $4 or $5 for shoes if you want to, but you must remember that we are discussing the minimum girl now.

Mrs. ROBAIR. I have worked in the shoe factory myself—I know what kind of leather is put into these $2 shoes.

The CHAIRMAN. Would $3.50 be a fair price for a shoe? Two pair at $3.50 would be $7.

Mrs. LAWTON. I don't think any girl can work with just two pairs of shoes. The candy gets on the shoes and rots the leather.

The CHAIRMAN. We will now pass to repairing of shoes.

Mr. KRAUSE. For repairing of shoes I have allowed $2.

Miss FOISIE. It costs 75 cents to have a pair resoled. I have allowed $1.50 for repairing of shoes.

The CHAIRMAN. What have you for stockings?

Miss FOISIE. Six pair of 25-cent hosiery will last for six months.

Mr. KRAUSE. I have estimated this at eight pairs of 25-cent stockings, or $2.

The CHAIRMAN. We will pass that up and go to underwear.

Mr. KRAUSE. I have no facts, but put an estimate of those who seem to know more about it. I have $3.25 for underwear.

Miss FOISIE. A great many are obliged to get suits with a mixture of wool on account of the cold weather. I have my figures at $6 per year.

Mr. KRAUSE. I will be glad to accept your figures as I have no argument. For petticoats I have allowed $3.

Miss FOISIE. I have allowed $5.

The CHAIRMAN. We might ask what is the price of petticoats worn by those in the commission.

Mrs. UDALL. Mr. Krause is constantly being annoyed by some one interrupting him.

The CHAIRMAN. Yes; that is right. It will not be allowed hereafter.

Mr. SNYDER. The chair made a suggestion that the ladies on the commission give us an estimate of this item.

Mrs. SILBAUGH. I pay from $1 to $1.50 for my petticoats. I never wear out more than two in a year.

Mr. KRAUSE. A girl can get along on $2 for petticoats. I will change my estimate to $2 on petticoats.

The CHAIRMAN. We will hear from Mrs. Swanson.

Mrs. SWANSON. I buy material, good material, and make four petticoats every year. I should say $3 would be more than enough to cover the cost every year. I buy material that will stand washing and buy edging so you can make them yourselves very reasonable.

Mrs. ROBAIR. I must ask these women if they will take into consideration the fact that these girls have to change their petticoats more often than the woman at home. She has to change every two or three days and she must have more than two.

Mrs. SWANSON. I think that is a matter of personal weakness. I have always found that if I go into the kitchen I must put on a big apron.

The CHAIRMAN. We will now pass on to suits.

Mr. KRAUSE. The girl that I have in mind, the minimum girl, don't go to the first showing of a spring style to get a suit. I am frank to say that speaking from my own experience the average price is about $25. I will submit $15 as a fair price for a minimum girl for a suit.

Mrs. SILBAUGH. I think $20 is very reasonable.

The CHAIRMAN. How about coats?

Miss FOISIE. I had $12.50 for a coat and $20 for a suit.

Mr. KRAUSE. I have $10 for a coat.

The CHAIRMAN. Dresses and aprons?

Mr. KRAUSE. I consider that a girl under these conditions would not buy party or lace dresses. Our girls do not buy aprons, we furnish the aprons for them to wear in the factory. They have no expense as far as the factory is concerned for their uniform.

Miss FOISIE. Not many of the factories furnish the uniforms.

Mr. MARVIN. I wish you to bear in mind what this lady says. I think your factory is an exception. Isn't there a saving of 50 cents a week in your factory.

Miss FOISIE. I think there should be four aprons at 75 cents per week.

Mr. KRAUSE. It adds to the appearance of the factory to have the girls wear uniforms.

Mr. SNYDER. The commission does not feel that they can ask all the factories to furnish uniforms.

The CHAIRMAN. I might say that whenever we suggest a thing like that the average employer seems inclined to comply, especially the larger ones. We will now pass to shirt waists.

Mr. KRAUSE. I have allowed $5.

Miss FOISIE. I have $8 for shirt waists.

The CHAIRMAN. Miss Foisie, I would like to ask you this, is it necessary for one working in a factory to have as many shirt waists as one working in a store?

Miss FOISIE. The constant use of our arms makes our shirt waists wear out very quickly, and we have to get a good many shirt waists.

The CHAIRMAN. Isn't it true that a girl working in a mercantile establishment is required to buy a finer class of waists?

Miss FOISIE. It is not necessary for them to pay more for their waists, for they are right there when the sales open and can take advantage and get better values; besides, they have better judgment in regard to materials.

Mr. KRAUSE. I should say that for the average girl $8 is all right; but take the minimum girl, I think it is too high. Five shirt waists at $1 each is enough for the minimum girl.

Mr. DAGG. Would that girl, under those conditions, save anything by buying the material and making those shirt waists?

Mr. SNYDER. The noon hour is getting close, and I would suggest that we speed up a little.

The CHAIRMAN. Yes; I think we had better.

Mr. FENLASON. There seems to be a tendency to have the girl do her washing, her sewing, and those things in the evenings after she has worked eight hours. We don't ask a man to do his washing after working eight hours.

The CHAIRMAN. Suppose we pass on to corsets. What is the usual amount paid for a corset?

Mrs. LAWTON. I would like to suggest that it all depends upon the size of the girl. I pay $3.50 for my corsets.

Miss FOISIE. I have allowed $5 for corsets and $1.50 for corset waists.

Mr. KRAUSE. I have allowed $3 for corsets and $1.50 for corset waists.

The CHAIRMAN. How about gloves?

Miss FOISIE. I have $3.75 for gloves. A girl ought to have four or five pairs a year.

Mr. KRAUSE. I have $2.

The CHAIRMAN. Out of 138 estimates received from employees and 162 from employers, we find that the average estimate for gloves is $4.23 for employees and $3 for the employers. We will pass to neckwear.

Mr. KRAUSE. I am not in a position to argue neckwear, as I don't know what it covers, but I have allowed $1.

Miss FOISIE. It covers collars, jabots, etc. I have $2.50.

The CHAIRMAN. We will pass to the next item—hats.

Miss FOISIE. I know some minimum girls that would go without something to eat in order to have a hat.

Mr. KRAUSE. I think $5 is plenty for hats.

Mr. FENLASON. Would you want to have a girl wear a hat in the summer time and the same one in the winter?

The CHAIRMAN. Let us hear from the ladies in regard to this, Miss Foisie?

Miss FOISIE. A girl can't fix up a last year's hat for less than $1, and I don't think she can get a new one under $4. Often a minimum girl would wear a retrimmed one to work, but she needs a new one for best.

Mr. KRAUSE. I am not going to argue the question with you.

The CHAIRMAN. Can a woman use a hat for two seasons?

Miss FOISIE. Yes; it can be done. I have allowed $10 for hats.

The CHAIRMAN. How about umbrellas?

Miss FOISIE. I have allowed $2.

Mr. KRAUSE. I have $1.

Mr. MARVIN. I think $1 for Spokane and $2 for Seattle is all right.

Mr. KRAUSE. The next item is repairing of clothing. I have not allowed anything for this, as the girl would repair her own clothing.

Miss FOISIE. I have allowed $7 for repairing of clothes.

The CHAIRMAN. From the lists we have 162 from employees giving an average of $5.19 for repair of clothing and 138 from employers giving an average of $4.18 for repair of clothing.

Mr. KRAUSE. I have figured $3 for laundry for the year, because, as I said, this minimum girl would do part of her own washing at home.

Miss FOISIE. Would this private family that you speak of, taking in a girl at $4.50, be willing to let her do her laundry in the kitchen and use the electric iron?

Mrs. UDALL. That is one of the strong reasons why they don't want a woman roomer and boarder.

The CHAIRMAN. How about dentistry and medicine?

Miss FOISIE. If a girl joins a hospital association she pays $12 per year to belong to it. I have allowed $25 per year for medicine and dentistry.

Mr. KRAUSE. I have $10, and for street-car fare $30.

Miss FOISIE. We agree there; I also have $30. For newspapers and magazines I have $5

Mr. KRAUSE. I have $3. The average girl who is working has to establish herself. She comes to the factory without any training or trade and no vocation, so she must necessarily share part of the sacrifice in establishing herself.

Miss FOISIE. The fact that you want her to become intelligent, she should have one magazine a year at least.

Mr. DAGG. When a girl is striving to hold her expenses down, can't she use the magazines of her associates?

Miss FOISIE. That is often done. One girl will subscribe to a magazine, and then will exchange with other girls, and in that way they get to read several magazines.

Mr. KRAUSE. Don't overlook the public library, for they use it a good·deal.
Miss FOISIE. A girl has to pay 5 cents to get a new book. It is hard to get'the current magazines at the library.
The CHAIRMAN. Does the average working girl subscribe for a magazine?
Miss FOISIE. Yes; they do, to a large extent. If she gets a magazine at all, she wants one of the best.
The CHAIRMAN. The girl we are trying to provide for can not agree to have all of her desires provided for. This list of yours is vastly high, and is far in excess of any minimum that will probably be allowed. We will now consider stationery and postage.
Mr. KRAUSE. I have allowed $1.
Miss FOISIE. She don't send any packages back home on that.'
Mr. KRAUSE. No; my minimum girl is not at that stage yet. She is rather receiving packages from home.
Mrs. ROBAIR. Do you mean that she is receiving help from home in packages?
Mr. KRAUSE. What is in those packages I do not know.
Miss FOISIE. I have $8 for the next item; any girl would pay $8 per year·for unions.
Mr. KRAUSE. Our girls pay 70 cents per year. Doesn't that have a sick benefit with it?
Miss FOISIE. Yes; for $7. We are figuring sickness in that, $7. Everybody pays some dues. The different unions vary as to what the assessment fee is. In the stores they usually have associations among themselves and pay dues of some kind.
Mr. KRAUSE. I have nothing for insurance.
Miss FOISIE. I have $12. Supposing that this girl is sensible; she will take out an endowment when she is young and the rates are cheaper.
Mr. KRAUSE. I believe that, but this girl, until she gets past the minimum-wage period, does not need insurance.
Mr. DAGG. Do you carry insurance?
Miss FOISIE. I do not.
Mrs. ROBAIR. I am insured, and I also have my child insured.
The CHAIRMAN. How about vacation?
Mr. KRAUSE. This girl has no vacation period yet; she will get one next year. However, I have allowed $10 for vacation expenses.
Miss FOISIE. I have waited all my life for vacation, and I have given this minimum girl $20 for vacation.
The CHAIRMAN. Any remarks on that? If not, we will pass on to amusements.
Miss FOISIE. I have $12.50 for amusements.
The CHAIRMAN. How about church and other contributions?
Miss FOISIE. No girl would want to go to any church and be on the charity list. If she can not dó a little, she does not want to go. The girls ought to be encouraged to go to the churches. Often at $6 per week a girl can be made to feel that she is helping some one else.
Mr. MARVIN. I think when any church gets into the place where it is sup-ported with a few rich men it has lost its purpose. You raise a barrier imme-diately between the church and the people. A girl can't preserve her self-respect and go to church without contributing her little bit.
Miss FOISIE. The church can not help her by taking away her self-respect.
Mrs. ROBAIR. There are lots of girls who won't go to church unless they can take part in the church work and pay their little contribution. Girls are dropping away completely from church just for that very reason.
The CHAIRMAN. We have records from 112 girls, nearly all receiving a very good wage. The average amount contributed toward the church is $1 per month for mercantile employees and $1.35 for factory employees.
Mr. MARVIN. I think $10 is high. This law is to take away the thought that the girl is on the charity list. Some provision should be made for that, not for the sake of the church but for the sake of the girl. I think $6 would be a fair estimate.
Mr. FENLASON. When I gave that $6 to the church I looked at that as purely a gift. Under amusements I was pretty high. Under the head of incidentals I allowed $15.
Mr. SNYDER. I move that we now adjourn until 1.30.
Prof. KERN. I second the motion.
The CHAIRMAN. It is moved and seconded that we now adjourn until 1.30. All in favor signify their assent by saying "aye." [All voted aye.] The ayes have it.

AFTER RECESS—1.30 P. M.

The CHAIRMAN. The meeting will please come to order. The secretary will please call the roll.

. (The roll was called; all members were present.)

. Mr. SNYDER. I think it has not yet been definitely decided upon by Mr. Krause and Miss Foisie just what concessions will be made.

. Miss FOISIE. Why should not the other members of the conference say what their, opinion is on these same items? .

· Mr. DAGG. It took us all morning to hear these two lists, so I think we should try to settle it. .

The CHAIRMAN. It seems to me that in order to expedite matters we should have a motion of some kind before the house.

Mr. DAGG. In our factory on week work we pay $8.; for an apprentice we pay $6. This law has nothing to do with an apprentice, but the regular wage for a minimum worker. Since we have taken the highest figure from the employees and the lowest figure from the employers, I would like to suggest that we strike an average. I would like, in order to settle the minimum wage, to make the suggestion, or it could be put to a vote, that we take $8 for the minimum wage. That is a motion, if it is in order.

Mrs. ROBAIR. I don't think that is really high enough. She can exist on that, but this commission is to find a minimum wage for a self-supporting woman.

Mr. FENLASON. Mr. Chairman, I wish to make a motion relative to minimum wage. My colleague here moved that it be $8; no one seconded it. I am going to move that the minimum wage, based on 48 hours per week, is $9. There is no second to that. Is it in order to speak on that motion before it is seconded?

The CHAIRMAN. You may speak on it.

Mr. FENLASON. If the ladies on the other side will accept that, if in their judgment they deem it fit, I am willing to vote on it. I am told by my colleagues that they will fold their tents and go home before they will submit to a minimum wage that is somewhat less than the motion I have made. I want to call your attention to this fact, that this law has been passed, and it is a great advantage to the women workers of this State to be able to have such a law. We have the principle of the minimum wage established. Now, if we can get together on this first conference so that the employers, employees, and disinterested public can agree, I think it will mean much toward enforcing the law.

I want to call your attention to a remark that my friend here made: " It is the duty of the parent to provide for these girls who are going to work." I submit it is also the duty of society to provide conditions so that the fathers and mothers of the country can provide for these girls. I think we are laying too much stress on the minimum or lowest wage these girls can live on. It says on the blank, " Below is given a statement which I believe to be a fair estimate of the amount required yearly by a prudent, self-supporting woman employed in a mercantile, mechanical, or other industrial establishment in order to maintain herself in reasonable comfort." When I was asked for my estimate it included all classes of women, and I want to say to you that I believe all classes of women on equal basis. I see no reason why a girl in a store should receive more than a girl working in a factory. I want to call your attention to the law itself. Those questions have nothing to do with the minimum. They do not ask us for the minimum. They ask us for the average wage on which a woman can live decently and respectfully. I find from my investigations that $4 per week is about as low as any girl can get 21 meals for and $8 per month for a room. I think boarding and rooming at different places is an expensive way to live. The very lowest price that a girl can get board and room for is $5 per week, or $260 per year. I wouldn't even want to say $5 per week unless the ladies would agree to that. For shoes and rubbers I have $9—two pair of shoes per year at $3.50 per pair, two pair rubbers at $1 per pair. One fifty for repairing of shoes. Twelve pair of stockings per year, at 50 cents per pair, or $6. Underwear I have put at $7. I have therefore made the motion that the minimum wage be $9, as I think the ladies will be able to compromise on that.

Perhaps I am a little high on suits. I have $30. I do not think one suit a year is enough for a girl. Do you want these girls for 365 days to wear the same suit? She can buy one costing $20 and one costing $10, for instance. I provide $20 for coats. Nothing is said about raincoats. I figure a girl should have two coats a year—one costing $12 and one costing $8. For shirt waists I have one at $3, one at $2.50, and one for $2. A girl, to live decently, wants to have a change of clothes. I want them to feel that they are supporting themselves in a decent way. You can't buy a reasonably good corset for less than $2. I figure that is very cheap. For corset waists I have figured that the average girl should be able to make them. I want to see my wife have a nice corset waist, don't you? We are working on the wrong principle. We are trying to rectify something that the foundation is absolutely wrong. We don't need gloves, but we have come to that stage where we have to consider these things, whether we absolutely need them or not.

Seventy-five per cent of human energy is exerted to satisfy the eye. We asked these girls to dress so that they are fit to look at. I have allowed $10 for hats; $1 is good enough for an umbrella. I eliminated repair of clothing because the girl ought to do her own repairing. For laundry I allowed $26 per year, which is only 50 cents per week. I don't see anything wrong with that. Our employees pay $1 a month for medicine. We have an arrangement with the hospital and the employees pay $12 per year. They get medical attendance and surgical attention. I allowed $20, and it would be optional with the girl if she had hospital services. I have estimated $36 per year for street car fare. That is twice a day, going to and from work for 360 days. For newspapers and magazines I have allowed $5. If there is any one thing I would like to have my employees do it is to read and keep in touch with the current events of the day. I think $5 isn't very strong for newspapers and magazines. For stationery and postage I have $7. One letter per week would be $1.56—I think $7 per year is fairly conservative. I have allowed $8 for association dues. Now, that might be eliminated, but we men belong to lodges and if the girls want to belong to these institutions they have the right. Insurance, well, now, that is a proposition that is not essential. If this woman is never going to be married and is going to work in this industry year after year, she ought to be insured. I thought a woman ought to have a little something, pay a little premium on a policy, so I have allowed $18 for insurance.

I don't think we should squeeze these girls down to the last point; the men and women who are going to make the laws for our Nation. The trouble is we are trying to fit in an ethical proposition to an unjust economical proposition. A man who has a heart can't argue them both from the same viewpoint. There is no mention of the time a girl loses from sickness or looking for a job. These are items of cost, to the women and girls. I think a girl ought to have two weeks' wages for vacation. I figure $6 for church. Then, too, if a girl goes to church and Sunday school 52 Sundays in a year, that is 5 cents car fare each time. Shall we want her to wear her old suit and hat that she wears every day? Under incidentals there is a dozen things that a woman has to have, but I have just allowed $15. After going over these figures I find that I have $614.50, and after eliminating everything I possibly could I still have $487.50. I couldn't advocate any wage that would produce less than $487.50. It is altogether too low to support a girl right. I think it is up to the people on the other side. To get this in shape I have made a motion of $9, providing the ladies are willing to compromise.

Mr. DAGG. I have made a motion that the chair take a vote on the $8 minimum wage.

Mr. SNYDER. In order that our record may be kept straight I desire now, without committing myself, to second the motion of Mr. Fenlason, reserving my privilege to withdraw my second if the vote is not unanimous.

The CHAIRMAN. It is moved and seconded that the sum of $9 be designated as a minimum wage. The motion is seconded by Mr. Snyder, reserving his right to withdraw the second if the vote is not unanimous.

Mr. FENLASON. Mr. Chairman, the motion was not put in that way, and I, as mover of the motion, want a square deal and honesty. I had much rather that he eliminate the proposition that he withdraw his second if the vote is not unanimous. I would much prefer, if it were possible, for the ladies to second that motion, if you can see your way clear. Am I out of order? Here is the proposition I want to put up to you: If you ladies can second that motion that puts me on record that you are willing to stand for a mimimum of $9. I recognize that this commission says it takes $10 to support a girl that is working in a mercantile pursuit.

Mr. SNYDER. Mr. Chairman, I want to say that I agree with nearly all that Mr. Fenlason has said, but the only reason—the very reason why I made my second in that way is to facilitate just what he is after. I want it put in the right order and we can still find out from the ladies present here what their attitude is; that is why I made the second in that manner and not to bar the ladies in any way. It is important, of course, that we arrive at a unanimity, and for that reason I don't want a vote that will be carried and still leave us here as two factions.

The CHAIRMAN. The Chair can not refuse to accept the second made by Mr. Snyder to the motion. Mr. Fenlason, you have said that the motion has not been put properly, so, in order to have this motion worded in our record in the proper manner I have written it down. I will put it as follows:.

"It has been moved and seconded that no person, firm, association, or corporation shall employ any female over the age of 18 years in any factory establishment at a weekly wage rate of less than $9, such wage being the estimate of said conference of the minimum wage adequate in such occupation and industry to supply the necessary cost of living of such employees and to maintain them in health."

The majority rule holds, and Mr. Snyder has reserved the right to withdraw his second in case the vote is not unanimous.

Mr. KRAUSE. The motion before the house is to vote on $9 as a minimum wage.

The CHAIRMAN. Are you ready for the question? You have heard the motion as read.

Mr. SNYDER. Question.

The CHAIRMAN. The secretary will please call the role.

(Upon roll call the following vote was recorded:)

Ayes: Mrs. W. C. Mills, Mr. Edgar C. Snyder, and Mr. O. C. Fenlason.

Noes: Miss Emma Foisie, Mrs. Belle Robair, Mrs. F. H. Lawton, Prof. W. M. Kern, Mr. Fred Krause, and Mr. O. F. Dagg.

The SECRETARY. The roll call stands 6 noes and 3 ayes.

The CHAIRMAN. The motion is lost.

Mr. SNYDER. I reserve my right to withdraw my second.

Mrs. ROBAIR. Mr. Chairman, we have gone over these items carefully, but I would like to give you a few of my figures. If a girl does not dress decently she is looked down upon—the average school girl is looked down upon if she does not dress like the other girls. For dresses and aprons I have two street dresses and two house dresses. I think she needs two aprons for the factory when she is at work and four for the house. She ought to have a waist for her suit and four for the house. She needs two pairs of corsets at $4 each, for the year, one pair of winter gloves, one good pair for summer and two pairs of cheap gloves to wear to work. For neckwear I have allowed $2. One umbrella at $2. I have also allowed $6.50 for repair of clothing. I am going to ask if these gentlemen have really considered what a girl's laundry consists of. She has to have all her clothes laundered and if she is boarding she has no place to do it in her room. She has to pay 25 cents to get shirt waists laundered and house dresses 25 cents. For medicine and dentistry I have allowed $40. Street car fare, $36.40; newspapers and magazines, $3.85; stationery and stamps, $10; insurance, $15; vacation expenses, $25; amusements, $10; incidentals, $30; and my average is $599.50. We have taken these all into consideration and we find that a self-supporting girl can not live on less than this amount. We must allow for the girl who has to pay her board and room and who has to pay two car fares each day. The girl is not any more sure of her health and strength than anyone else and for that reason she should carry insurance. Therefore, I have come to the conclusion that it really takes $10 for a woman to be self-supporting. I am considering a girl who has served her time. I move that the minimum wage in the State of Washington be $10.

Miss FOISIE. I second that motion.

The CHAIRMAN. Is that subject to the wording of the motion we have put before?

Mrs. ROBAIR. Yes, sir.

Mr. MARVIN. What does your total come to?

Mrs. ROBAIR. Five hundred and ninety-nine dollars and fifty cents for the year.

Mr. MARVIN. Then it is $11.92 for the week.

The CHAIRMAN. It has been moved by Mrs. Robair, and seconded by Miss Foisie, that no person, firm, association, or corporation shall employ any female over the age of 18 years in any factory establishment at a weekly wage rate of less than $10, such wage being the estimate of said conference of the minimum wage adequate in such occupation and industry to supply the necessary cost of living of such employees and to maintain them in health.

Are you ready for the question?

Miss FOISIE. Question?

Mr. FENLASON. I want to know if anyone could not vote on this question if they wished? I could conscientiously vote for $10, but in view of what I have said to my colleagues I would like to pass and not vote this time.

Mr. SNYDER. I am prepared to vote on this proposition, but, as Mr. Marvin has said, what we most want is unanimity, and I therefore want to protest against excusing anyone from voting. We can reconsider upon proper motion any decision that may be taken.

The CHAIRMAN. There is no provision in our rules and regulations for excusing a person from voting and I think therefore it would be better for you all to vote one way or the other. Are you ready for the question?

Mr. FENLASON. I want to ask who seconded this motion? .

The CHAIRMAN. Miss Foisie. If there are no further remarks on the question we will have a roll call. The secretary will please call the roll.

(Roll call by secretary upon which the following vote was recorded:)

Ayes: Miss Emma Foisie, Mrs. Belle Robair, Mrs. F. H. Lawton, Mr. Edgar C. Snyder, and Prof. W. M. Kern.

Noes: Mrs. W. C. Mills, Mr. Fred Krause, Mr. O. B. Dagg, and Mr. O. C. Fenlason.

The SECRETARY. The vote stands 5 ayes and 4 noes.

The CHAIRMAN. The motion is carried.

Mr. SNYDER. Mr. Chairman, I am of the opinion that we have not accomplished much. I move that we reconsider the motion.

Prof. KERN. I second the motion that we reconsider the previous motion.

The CHAIRMAN. It is moved and seconded that we reconsider the motion. All in favor signify by saying "aye." [All voted aye.] The ayes have it.

Mr. MARVIN. I ask you whether, at this stage, it would not be advisable to ask the chairman of the conference to select a committee of three—one from each of the parties—to confer on this matter. Does that sound feasible to you?

Mr. SNYDER. I think, Mr. Chairman, that that suggestion is entirely appropriate and that plan is entirely feasible, and I therefore move that we now take a recess until 4.30—the chairman, before the recess, to appoint a committee of three, consisting of one of the representatives of the employers, one of the employees, and one of the public, to consider the question of a resolution to be presented to the conference.

Mr. DAGG. I second the motion.

The CHAIRMAN. It is moved and seconded that we take a recess until 4.30, and that the Chair appoint a committee of three to confer during the recess.

Mr. MARVIN. I wish to suggest that you take Mr. Olson into consideration.

Mr. SNYDER. I would like to include that in my motion.

The CHAIRMAN. Is that subject to the second?

Mr. DAGG. Yes, sir.

The CHAIRMAN. You have heard the motion stated; all in favor signify their assent by saying "aye." [All voted aye.] The ayes have it. I will appoint Miss Foisie, Prof. Kern, and Mr. Dagg to make up the committee. We will adjourn until 4.30.

AFTER RECESS.

The CHAIRMAN. The meeting will please come to order. We will now hear a report from Miss Foisie, who is chairman of the committee.

Miss FOISIE. Well, we have been out some little time but have failed to arrive at anything that is positively an agreement. We have spoken to the other employees and have heard from the employers yesterday and to-day, and knowing that they are trying to be fair we have decided that we would accept a $9 minimum and do the best we can and hope for something better in the future.

Prof. KERN. I move that we adjourn now until 8 o'clock.

Mr. DAGG. I second the motion.

The CHAIRMAN. It is moved and seconded that we adjourn until 8 o'clock, but before we do it has been suggested that we hear from the manufacturers' side and see what they have to say on this question. We would like to have a report from Mr. Dagg.

Mr. DAGG. It seems that the manufacturers can't come together on anything higher for a minimum wage than $8.50. The representatives of the employees seem to think that they ought to have $9 and we can't see it.

Mr. SNYDER. I am still of the opinion that no resource should be overlooked which may bring about a reconciliation of these figures and a unanimous agreement. In the hope that there may be a further effort to bring about such an end, I renew the motion that we adjourn until 8 o'clock.

..The CHAIRMAN. It is moved and seconded that we adjourn until 8 .o'clock; all in favor signify by saying " aye." [All voted aye.] The ayes have it. · ·

AFTER RECESS—8 P. M.

The CHAIRMAN. The meeting will please come to order. When we adjourned we had before us the resolution to reconsider the adoption of a $10 wage. What is your pleasure?

Mr. SNYDER. I think the proper course is either for us to vote upon this re-adoption, or reject, or else that someone else make a motion to amend the $10 motion.

Mr. FENLASON. I move as a substitute for the $10 minimum a wage of $8.75.

Mr. KRAUSE. I second that motion, and with your permission would like to give my reasons for seconding that motion. I have presented to the conference here the last two days figures that I thought correct for working girls to live upon in the State of Washington. We have discussed the matter and my figures have not been adopted. The conference does not agree with my proposition. I put myself on record with some of the members that my opinion, for the good of the working girls, was along certain lines. . I said I would just go so far, and after this conference was in session one of the members asked me if I would appear before this extra session and discuss it. After I left here Mr. Dagg came to me and said, " Mr. Krause, it seems an awful pity that we can't arrive at some agreement, and we should get some sort of a concession from you." I have given you folks the benefit of my honest opinion of the things I thought was the fair matter pertaining to this girl question. You don't agree with me and that is your privilege. If you think I have been on the wrong side I will withdraw what I said was my ultimatum. I will be very glad to take your suggestion, and it is on that ground that I now second this motion and will support an $8.75 minimum wage.

The CHAIRMAN. Shall I read the motion as we have it drafted?

Mr. FENLASON. Yes, please.

The CHAIRMAN. It is moved by Mr. Fenlason and seconded by Mr. Krause " That no person, firm, association, or corporation shall employ any female over the age of 18 years in any factory establishment at a weekly wage rate of less than $8.75, such wage being the estimate of said conference of the minimum wage adequate in such occupation and industry to supply the necessary cost of living of such employees and to maintain them in health." Are you ready for the question?

Mr. SNYDER. Mr. Chairman, I am ready to vote upon this motion, but I would like very briefly to explain my vote as it shall be given. I haven't said anything in this conference by way of elaboration of the figures at which I have arrived after very careful consideration. The figure of $493, which I gave you, was the absolute minimum upon which a girl can decently and comfortably live in this State for one year. I think, furthermore, that in arriving at a weekly minimum that we should recommend to this commission it is not proper for us to divide the actual total by 52 as has been assumed by these gentlemen. We must find, I am convinced, a lower divisor for these reasons. In the first place, the girl that we are discussing here, like all other normal persons, is conceded to require at least a week of vacation. That week must be deducted from the 52, as her expenses are as great as during the rest of the year. Again, in most of the factories there will come periods when there will be a shutdown, there will be breaks in the machinery, etc., and changes of various kinds which all involve the throwing out of employment of the girl. That period may not be, in some of the factories, more than a few days, or it may be a month or more, but it must all be considered. Again, we know that the girl, more than the man, must be conceded the right to stay away from work because of necessary illness at times. There can be no fixed period for that, but she will have to be away part of the time, and during that time her expenses will be at a greater degree than during the rest of the year. I can not say how many weeks that will take off from the 52, but I know it will take some off. Therefore I can not feel that while I am voting for a minimum wage I am voting for a wage that she will get 52 times during the year. We are just as much bound to ascertain as nearly as we may what is the smallest sum upon which a self-supporting woman working in factories in the State of Washington can healthfully and decently maintain herself, as a juror is to decide a case. I say, therefore, there is a limit to the point to which we can go in deciding what is a reasonable requirement in the case, but I am also led to concede that there is a little'leeway allowed,· so I believe I stretched that leeway to the fullest extent when I voted for a minimum wage of $9 per week. I believe we have reached that point where every reasonable concession has been made. I have tried to be fair, to consider honestly and fairly the views presented by all sides, and to try to bring about a unanimous decision. I want to plead with my friend from Spokane that $1 under the minimum already fixed for girls in the mercantile establishments is surely low enough.

I am satisfied they are under no really greater cost of living, at any rate, are not under a cost of living that is greater by $1 per week than the girls who work in the factories. Much as I regret to vote against the motion I must say that I shall have to vote on this motion "no."

Mr. FENLASON. I certainly agree with everything my colleague has said,· but it is too late. You all well remember that I tried to persuade the disinterested ones to talk long before this so we could know where they stood, not leaving it to the last here when a motion has been made and is ready to be voted upon. It isn't a question of arguments now but we have all fully made up our minds what we will do. My friend says his conscience will not permit him to deviate from this. I think that sometimes it is right to do wrong that good may come of it. What is conscience, anyway? How do you define that thing? The only line of demarcation between a human being and a brute is conscience. Your conscience or my conscience never told us what is right or what is wrong. Our conscience does not tell us but our conscience gives us the desires to do right. Your conscience is just as good as mine but we have different intellects. This man's intellect is telling him that this is the right thing to do and that man's intellect is teling him that that is the right thing to do. My conscience is telling me that I am doing the right thing myself, although I have put to you a proposition that I am perfectly willing to admit is wrong, but I put it to you on the basis that it is sometimes right to do wrong that good may come of it. I am only talking to these three ladies because when they take their vote these three manufacturers will agree with you, and I submit that if the employees and the manufacturers are able to agree, unless it is very unreasonable, the disinterested public should agree with us. I am going to vote for this substitution just on this principle that it is right to do wrong because good will come of it. You will get more by getting together than you may think.

Mr. DAGG. As a suggestion I would like to hear from the other two members representing the public.

Mrs. MILLS. For months—for years—this problem has been before me and I have studied it very closely. My figures are based on actual experience and I have not been able to reduce it below $10 per week. I think that conscientiously no girl could continue, after her apprenticeship, longer than a year on that basis. Rather than to go away from here after this lengthy session, without coming to some distinct understanding, I have conceded the one fact that it is best to come to a $9 wage, but I would not for one single moment say that if I thought a girl could be kept on $9 for more than one year.

Prof. KEEN. Every individual is to a greater or less degree his brother's keeper. What would affect one is going to affect all of us. We are all living here together. What is good for one man is good for anther man. I have been led to believe that the public, as a rule, is not very much concerned about what is going to happen to one or two industries. The general public is not very much concerned as to what is going to happen to the manufacturer but they are concerned over what is to become of the girl. They are infinitely concerned about the girls 14, 15, 16, and 17 years of age that are dropping out of public schools and going into our industries. I spent considerable of my life in the city of New York and I know something of the condition that exists on the east side. If we have to have a slum district in any city in the State of Washington—if we have to transport New York's east side to the State of Washington, it is infinitely better that we have no industries in the State of Washington.

I am not quite sure I know just how much a girl ought to have to support herself decently and comfortably. I have tried to arrive at some figures, and it does appear to me from the figures that I have been able to get that this amount for a self-supporting woman ought to hinge somewhere around $9. Feeling this, I think it would be best if this delegation could agree upon this amount as a minimum wage. It seems to me that it would be a perfectly splendid thing that the State of Washington has fixed the highest minimum wage in the mercantile establishments of any State in the United States; that we believe in protecting our mothers and our daughters and the girls who are working in the industries, and we believe that $9 is the minimum amount upon which a woman can support herself in decency and comfort.

The CHAIRMAN. Are you ready for the question?

Mr. FENLASON. Mr. Chairman, I certainly hate to see a vote taken on this. Can not we split the difference with the ladies?

Mrs. ROBAIR. I will split, then, for $8.99.

Mrs. LAWTON. It seems to me that the least we can live on is $10, and I don't see how we can come down 25 cents.

Mrs. ROBAIR. It has been proven here in these last two days that a minimum wage for a girl should be $10, and we have said we wanted $10. We have come half way and we have all on the conference but one. Do you think it will enlarge your business to let this go into the newspapers with you the only one holding back?

Mr. KRAUSE. If you don't agree with me, you record your vote the way you believe you should.

Mr. SNYDER. We give you credit for taking the stand you have as long as you feel that you are doing right, and we have no desire to have any one of us go away from here with any feeling of dissatisfaction. I therefore, in order to proceed in what I believe to be now the proper order, I wish, Mr. Chairman, to move an amendment to the substitute motion, substituting $9 for $8.75.

Mrs. ROBAIR. Don't you think a girl should have $9 to live on?

Mr. FENLASON. May I answer that question for my friends? It has come to a point where it don't enter into what it costs. This gentleman tells us that he has gone the limit. This other gentleman tells us that he will go a little further if we can get together. Is this the proper way for this thing to break up? I move that we proceed with this vote as it stands, and if we vote it down I will move that we adjourn until to-morrow.

Mr. MARVIN. I want to say to you, my friends, that there is no possibility for a number of years to come in the State of Washington in which you will reach an ideal condition. It is not a question as to whether we shall reach an ideal condition, but whether we shall reach something a little lower than the ideal. We are coming out of a condition that is extremely deplorable in some factories into something that is infinitely better. I had thought perhaps this difference might be split and make the amount, say, $8.90. I do not believe a thing is lost until it is lost, yet a unanimous vote is so infinitely better that I take it upon myself to suggest this thing.

Miss FOISIE. I would like to second Mr. Snyder's motion.

The CHAIRMAN. It has been moved by Mr. Snyder and seconded by Miss Foisie that the sum of $9 be substituted for the sum of $8.75 in the previous motion.

Mr. FENLASON. Let us vote on our amendment as it now stands and then we can move to reconsider it and put the other one. When this convention breaks up and we are not together it must go out to the citizens of the State that we couldn't split 25 cents.

The CHAIRMAN. The only way we can get things straightened out would be for you to withdraw your motion substituting $9 for $8.75 and the second.

Miss FOISIE. I am perfectly willing to withdraw my second.

Mr. SNYDER. I will, with the consent of Miss Foisie, who seconded the motion, withdraw my amendment.

The CHAIRMAN. Are you ready for the question? Do you want me to read the previous motion again?

Mr. SNYDER. Please.

The CHAIRMAN. Be it resolved that this factory conference does hereby make the following recommendation: "That no person, firm, association, or corporation shall employ any female over the age of 18 years in any factory establishment at a weekly wage of less than $8.75, such wage being the estimate of said conference of the minimum wage adequate in such occupation and industry to supply the necessary cost of living of such employees and to maintain them in health."

The secretary will please call the roll.

(Upon roll call the following vote was recorded:)

Ayes: Mr. Fred Krause, Mr. O. B. Dagg, and Mr. O. C. Fenlason.

Noes: Miss Emma Foisie, Mrs. Belle Robair, Mrs. F. H. Lawton, Mrs. W. G. Mills, Prof. W. M. Kern, and Mr. E. C. Snyder.

The SECRETARY. The vote stands 6 noes and 3 ayes.

The CHAIRMAN. The motion is lost.

Mr. SNYDER. I wish to renew the motion now for $9, unless the Chair rules a that we must proceed to vote upon the original motion.

The CHAIRMAN. It seems to me that that is what would be required. We should vote on the original motion of $10. Do you wish it read?

Mr. FENLASON. Please.

Mrs. ROBAIR. I am willing to withdraw my motion for $10.

Miss FOISIE. I withdraw my second to that motion.

Mr. FENLASON. I would like to ask what is before the house?

The CHAIRMAN. While the motion for reconsideration has been withdrawn, the original motion is still before the house.

Mr. SNYDER. I think the record will show that the motion to reconsider was voted upon and carried.

The CHAIRMAN. I desire to say that the motion that was up for a $10 wage is before the house.

Mr. FENALSON. I move that we indefinitely postpone the motion for a $10 minimum wage.

Mr. SNYDER. I second the motion.

The CHAIRMAN. It is moved and seconded that the motion for $10 be indefinitely postponed. All in favor signify their assent by saying aye. I think we had better have a roll call. The secretary will please call the roll.

(Upon roll call by the secretary all voted aye.)

The motion is carried.

Prof. KERN. Mr. Chairman, I have felt all the time that these girls ought to have $9 per week. I have tried to stand for that, but I would rather sacrifice 10 cents a week on it than to have it go out over the State that we couldn't split 10 or 15 cents. If Mr. Krause will join me in this, I will move you that the minimum wage be set at $8.90.

Mrs. MILLS. I second the motion.

Mr. KRAUSE. I will be very glad to join you in that.

The CHAIRMAN. Upon motion, duly made by W. M. Kern and seconded by Mrs. W. C. Mills, the following resolution was introduced:

" Be it resolved, That this factory conference does hereby make the following recommendation to the industrial welfare commission in reference to the minimum wage in the factory occupation and industry:

" That no person, firm, association, or corporation shall employ any female over the age of 18 years in any factory establishment at a weekly wage rate of less than $8.90, such wage being the estimate of said conference of the minimum wage adequate in such occupation and industry to supply the necessary cost of living to such employees and to maintain them in health."

Are you ready for the question?

Mr. SNYDER. Question.

The CHAIRMAN. The secretary will please call the roll.

(Upon roll call the following vote was recorded:)

Ayes: Miss Emma Foisie, Mrs. Belle Robair, Mrs. F. H. Lawton, Mrs. W. C. Mills, Prof. W. M. Kern, Mr. Edgar C. Snyder, Mr. Fred Krause, Mr. O. B. Dagg, and Mr. O. C. Fenalson.

The SECRETARY. All voted " aye."

The CHAIRMAN. The resolution is carried unanimously.

Mr. FENALSON. I understand that there remain before us two other questions propounded by the commission, first, the question as to the length of the lunch period; second, the question regarding toilet, rest rooms, and ventilation. I move that we endeavor to proceed to answer those questions.

The CHAIRMAN. The commission wants the conference to make a recommendation as to what length of lunch period is demanded for health of factory employees.

Miss FOISIE. I would like to make the motion that each factory should decide that for their own people, knowing the location of their factory and the different arrangements in the factory. Some places where they have a cafeteria in the factory the noon hour is not really necessary. I think that most employers have proven themselves more than kind and considerate on that question. I would like to make the motion that it be left to the individual factory.

Mr. DAGG. I would like to second that motion.

The CHAIRMAN. The chair would suggest that no recommendation be made in the matter. The commission could hardly issue an obligatory order to that effect.

Mr. SNYDER. I move you, as a substitute motion, that in answer to the second question propounded by the commission to the conference that, as the conditions in the various factories are so different, that we are of the opinion that we can not properly make a recommendation applicable to all cases.

Prof. KERN. I second the motion.

The CHAIRMAN. Are you ready for the question? All in favor signify their assent by saying " aye.'

(All voted aye.)

The ayes have it. The next question before the house is what provisions should be required in each manufacturing establishment for, first, toilet for women workers; second, rest room; and third, ventilation. I desire to read to you what the mercantile conference adopted in that regard:

" Every mercantile establishment where females are employed shall be properly heated and ventilated, and shall provide and maintain adequate facilities and arrangements, so that such employees may obtain rest when in a state of fatigue or in case of illness, such requirements being demanded, in the opinion of said conference, for the health and morals of such employees."

Miss FOISIE. The only question that occurs to me is whether the recommendations are needed in all the factories. It is entirely proper that there should be some rest facilities, but I know of some factories where it would be an imposition to insist upon special rest rooms.

Mr. KRAUSE. The small manufacturer who only employs one, two, or three girls can not afford a lunch or rest room, but the girls go into the office to eat their lunches. I believe that the commission will be fair in their ruling on that.

Mrs. LAWTON. I think there should be separate toilets for ladies and gentlemen. The ventilation, too, should be looked after. In some places it is very poor and there is no place to hang the wraps in some factories.

Prof. KERN. Would a recommendation passed here and accepted by the commission be authority?

The CHAIRMAN. Yes, sir; in regard to toilets, ventilation, and rest rooms.

Mr. KRAUSE. Wouldn't it be all right to make a recommendation similar to the one made by the mercantile conference?

The CHAIRMAN. That would be all right.

Mr. KRAUSE. I move that we adopt the same resolution to apply to the factories.

Prof. KERN. I second the motion.

The CHAIRMAN. Upon motion duly made by Mr. Krause and seconded by Prof. Kern the following resolution was introduced:

"Be it resolved, That the factory conference does hereby make the following recommendation to the industrial welfare commission in reference to standards of conditions and labor demanded by the health and morals of employees in such factory occupation and industry:

" Every manufacturing establishment where females are employed shall be properly heated and ventilated, and shall provide and maintain adequate facilities and arrangements, so that such employees may obtain rest when in state of fatigue or in case of illness, such requirements being demanded in the opinion of said conference for the health and morals of such employees."

Are you ready for the question?

Prof. KERN. Question.

The CHAIRMAN. The secretary will please call the roll.

(Upon roll call the following vote was recorded:)

Ayes: Miss Emma Foisie, Mrs. Belle Robair, Mrs. F. H. Lawton, Mrs. W. C. Mills, Prof. W. M. Kern, Mr. Edgar C. Snyder, Mr. Fred Krause, Mr. O. B. Dagg, and Mr. O. C. Fenlason.

The SECRETARY. All voted " aye.'

The CHAIRMAN. The resolution carried unanimously.

Prof. KERN. I am going to make a motion regarding the apprenticeship question:

" Be it resolved, That it is the sense of this conference that the solution of the apprenticeship problem must be found in the part-time continuation school in which the public school and industry cooperate to train the worker from 15 to 18 years of age in general knowledge, technical knowledge and skill, and we respectfully urge the industrial welfare commission to take immediate steps to secure such legislation as will serve to inaugurate the vocational education in the State of Washington."

; Mrs. Mills. I second the motion.

The Chairman. You have heard the motion read. All in favor signify their assent by saying "aye." [All voted aye.] The motion is carried. , •·ll ι.ι

As it is getting rather late, and I think we should bring our meeting to a close, on behalf of the welfare commission I want to thank you all for coming here and giving us your cooperation in this matter. I wish you would .all come to the office and we will have these resolutions written for you to sign.. Motion is now in order for adjournment.

Mr. Snyder. I move we adjourn.

Mrs. Mills. I second the motion.

The Chairman. It is moved and seconded that we do now adjourn sine die. All in favor signify their assent by saying "aye." [All voted aye.] The ayes have it, and we do now adjourn.

Pearl E. Motzer, Secretary.

OLSON EXHIBIT NO. 3.

Laundry Conference, Senate Chamber, Capitol Building, Olympia, Wash., May 14 and 15, 1914.

Meeting called to order at 9 o'clock a. m. by Mr. E. W. Olson, chairman of the industrial welfare commission. The entire commission, composed of Mr. Olson, Mr. Marvin, Mrs. Silbaugh, Mrs. Swanson, and Mrs. Udall, were present. This commission, and the following representatives, composed the conference: Mr. E. W. Olson (chairman), Mr. A. Jacobson, Mr. Frank Nixon, and Mr. W. J. Doust, representing the employers; Mrs. Julia A. Wilson, Mrs. Hilda O'Connor, and Miss Johanna Hilts, representing the employees; Mrs. R. C. McCredie, Rev. R. H. McGinnis, and Judge E. M. Day, representing the public.

Roll call by the secretary: All members of the conference and all members of the industrial welfare commission answered to the roll call.

The Chairman (reading):

To members of the laundry and dye-works conference:

After due investigation of the laundry and dye-works industry of the State of Washington, this commission has found that the wages paid to female employees in said industry are inadequate to supply them the necessary cost of living and to maintain the workers in health, and this commission has further found that in said industry conditions of labor exist that are prejudicial to the health or morals of the women employed in said industry..

Therefore, by virtue of the authority in it vested by section 174, laws of 1913, State of Washington, this commission has called a conference, composed of an equal number of representatives of employers, employees, and the public, which, after due consideration, is to recommend to this commission the amount of an adequate wage in said laundry and dye-works industry to permit a self-supporting woman to maintain herself in decency and comfort, and to also recommend other conditions of work hereinafter specified. Said conference so selected is composed of the following members:

A. Jacobson, Frank Nixon, and W. J. Doust, representing the employers; Mrs. Julia A. Wilson, Mrs. Hilda O'Connor, and Miss Johanna Hilts, representing the employees; and Mrs. R. C. McCredie, Rev. R. H. McGinnis, and Judge E. M. Day, representing the public.

Therefore, in accordance with the foregoing, the Industrial Welfare Commission of the State of Washington herewith submits to the conference the following questions:

What is the sum required per week to maintain in decent conditions of living a self-supporting woman employed in a laundry and dye-works establishment in the State of Washington? The requisites for such decent conditions of living are itemized in the list below:

Meals, room, shoes and rubbers, repairing shoes, stockings, underwear, petticoats, suit, coat, dresses and aprons, shirt waists, handkerchiefs, corsets, corset-waists, gloves, neckwear, hats, umbrella, repair of clothing, laundry, medicine and dentistry, street car fare, newspapers and magazines, stationery and postage, association dues, insurance, vacation expenses, amusements, church and other contributions, and incidentals.

What length of lunch period is demanded for maintentnce of health of laun-dry-and dye-works employees? ·

: What provisions should be required in each laundry and dye-works estab-lishment for (*a*) toilet for women workers, (*b*) rest rooms, (*c*) ventilation?

INDUSTRIAL WELFARE COMMISSION.

If you will turn to page 103 of the report of the commission, I would like to refer you to section 10, which I will read so you may have a thorough under-standing of the reason for which you are called here.

" If, after investigation, the commission shall find that in any occupation, trade, or industry, the wages paid to female employees are inadequate to supply them necessary cost of living and to maintain the workers in health, or that the conditions of labor are prejudicial to the health or morals of the workers, the commission is empowered to call a conference composed of an equal number of representatives of employers and employees in the occupation or industry in question, together with one or more disinterested persons representing the public; but the representatives of the public shall not exceed the number of representatives of either of the other parties; and a member of the commission shall be a member of such conference and chairman thereof. The commission shall make rules and regulations governing the selection of representatives and the mode of procedure of said conference, and shall exercise exclusive jurisdic-tion over all questions arising as to the validity of the procedure and of the recommendations of said conference. On request of the commission, it shall be the dut■ of the conference to recommend to the commission an estimate of the minimum wage adequate in the occupation or industry in question to supply the necessary cost of living, and maintain the workers in health, and to recom-mend standards of conditions or labor demanded for the health and morals of the employees. The findings and recommendations of the conference shall be made a matter, of record for the use of the commission."

I will now ask you to turn back to page 99, where I will read section 8. I would like to read section 5, on that page, first.

" When the conference is called to order by the chairman, it shall deliberate under. parliamentary law, and no question shall be discussed that is not ger-mane to the conditions of labor or cost of living of working women or minors as applied to that particular trade or industry. Roberts's Rules of Order shall govern."

Now section 8:

" The Chair shall not permit the discussion of the question as a whole until after each item of the cost of living has been taken up in the order given in the estimate blanks prepared by the commission, unless otherwise directed by a majority vote of the conference. After proper deliberation and discussion of questions that have been presented to the conference by the commission, the conference shall then, upon request of the commission, proceed to make recom-mendations upon such questions as the commission may designate."

With reference to section 9, I wish to say with regard to your traveling and hotel expenses that the State auditor requires that you furnish vouchers cover-ing all your expenses, and I wish you would make them out as soon as you return home and send them in at once so that we can pass on them. If there is anything you wish explained, you may stop in at the labor commissioner's office and the young lady will explain to you anything that you do not under-stand.

I desire to say that yesterday, in our factory conference, owing to the fact that there were so many divers interests, we permitted a free discussion by all persons present. The commission, however, feels at this time that the repre-sentatives of the employers in the laundry conference are thoroughly con-versant with all conditions, and it is the desire and ruling of this commission that no discussion be carried on on the outside. However, that does not pro-hibit.the conference from asking for information.

According to the rules and regulations, and in accordance with the law, we are required to have a secretary for this conference, and the Chair will enter-tain a motion for the election of a secretary. The commission presents the name of Miss Pearl E. Motzer.

Rev. McGINNIS. I move that Miss Pearl E. Motzer be elected secretary.

Judge DAY. I second the motion.

The CHAIRMAN. It is moved and seconded that Miss Pearl E. Motzer be elected secretary. All in favor signify their assent by saying " aye." [All voted aye.] The motion is carried.

The Chair is not decided, in his own mind, which is the best way to open the conference and I feel that it is no more than right that this matter be left to the conference; of course, as you all understand, a minimum wage will be based, according to law, on the cost of living of a self-supporting woman There is no question but what other conditions should enter into our discussion and we shall not bar any question that is pertinent to the matter of establishing a minimum wage; therefore, I would like to have suggestions from any members of the conference.

Mr. JACOBSON. In view of the fact that the question has been so thoroughly aired in the preceding conferences and the further fact that we are here for the specific purpose of ascertaining what it costs a girl to live on, I would suggest that the best way and the simpliest way to get at this is to get right down to figures now.

The CHAIRMAN. If that is acceptable to the conference we will then commence the discussion of the cost of living. In accordance with the rules formulated by this commission, in reference to the cost of living, it states that each item shall be taken up separately before the question as a whole is discussed; therefore, we have first on the list meals.

Mr. DOUST. Wouldn't it be better to fill out these forms rather than to write them on a pad?

The CHAIRMAN. I think so.

Mr. JACOBSON. Mr. Chairman, may I be permitted to ask a question or offer a suggestion?

The CHAIRMAN. Certainly.

Mr. JACOBSON. It developed in one of the former conferences that there was a tendency on the part of one side to make out an extremely high estimate of this cost of living; also, on the other side possibly to make out a much lower one. Now, I want to know if that is going to be the policy in this conference and I think a suggestion at this time would be timely. My suggestion is to get right down to the point where the least concessions will have to be made, and I think we can eliminate a great deal of discussion.

The CHAIRMAN. If you all have your schedules complete I would like to hear from somebody in reference to the first item—meals. Has anyone any remarks to make?

Mrs. O'CONNOR. Mr. Chairman, I have it figured this way—meals at 75 cents per day for 365 days would be $273.75.

The CHAIRMAN. Would you care at this time to submit your figures on room?

Mrs. O'CONNOR. I have that figured at $150 per year. I would like to hear from the other members what they think we ought to live on.

Miss HILTS. That equals $2.88 per week for room. I think anyone will agree with me that we can't get a decent room for less.

The CHAIRMAN. In order to open this discussion I would like to ask the members representing the employees whether, within their knowledge, they have ascertained what percentage of laundry employees get their room and board at the same place. Many of the laundries in the different cities lie away from the business center of town where restaurant services are not adequate. It may be that a large percentage live with families. I think that is a very important point to bring out.

Miss HILTS. A majority of the girls, owing to the present salaries, can not afford to live with families, but are living in rented rooms. These figures that we are giving you are for the cost of living from that standpoint. We are giving you Seattle figures as we have investigated there.

Mr. JACOBSON. Would it not be wise to go right on through with this proposition of board and room? I should think that the policy would be to have the other members make up their list.

The CHAIRMAN. That is a very good suggestion as far as I am concerned, Mr. Jacobson, and I would call upon you for your figures and then we will go down the list.

Mr. JACOBSON. I haven't compiled any figures for separate rooms and meals for the reason that my experience teaches me that I never could find myself able to live in that way. I always found it cost me a great deal more to live that way than to find a boarding house where I could get my meals and room together. I have arrived at this list from experience on the basis of board and room together. My figures for board and room together for a girl, based on this minimum wage, is $4 per week. The other side will probable say that is impossible. I want to say that it is possible, and we are able to show that it is possible, and that girls are living to-day, in the city of Seattle, on $4 per week for room and board.

Mr. MARVIN. That would make it $208 for the year?

Mr. JACOBSON. Yes; $208.

Mr. NIXON. In the town where I am doing business I can find a limited number of places where I can get board and room for $3.50 a week and would guarantee to find a great many more places where it could be got for $4. A great many of my employees are boarding there at that rate. I have allowed $208 for the year.

The CHAIRMAN. What have you, Miss Hilts, for board and room?

Miss HILTS. We have figured this thing down, as I said before, on the basis of living in light-housekeeping rooms. We have this figured down at the rate of 60 cents per day; that makes a total of $219 per year.

The CHAIRMAN. Mr. Doust, will you submit your figures?

Mr. DOUST. My figures are based on $4 per week, and I based those figures on actual experience. I had two telephone calls recently asking if I had any girls who wished board and room at $4, so I am positive it can be found at that price.

The CHAIRMAN. We would like to hear from Mrs. Wilson. Will you kindly submit your figures?

Mrs. WILSON. I count on a room—a good one—at $2 per week. As Mr. Doust says, there is a place where you can get fairly good meals, but a person don't want to confine themselves to that one place. One can not get board and room at the same price now that they could a few years ago. As commodities raise and the price of things go up, wages must go with them. I want to say right here that we don't want to crush any establishment, but we do want a wage upon which we can live decently and comfortably. The laundry girl earns all the money she gets, and she is entitled to a pretty fair wage for the work is hard. I have walked back and forth from the laundry six days a week just to save car fare. Let us build up humanity instead of tearing it down, and in helping the working girl you will be building up humanity.

Mr. MARVIN. You didn't give us your figures.

Mrs. WILSON. I figured meals at 60 cents per day and room at $2 per week.

The CHAIRMAN. That totals $323 for room and board together.

Mrs. WILSON. If we have to buy our own fuel we have to count on that, too.

Miss HILTS. In our figures we estimated a heated room.

Mrs. WILSON. We have to add the cost of fuel to this room rent—I think about 75 cents would be about right.

The CHAIRMAN. Seventy-five cents per week?

Mrs. WILSON. Well, perhaps 50 cents; that would make the room $2.50 per week.

Mrs. O'CONNOR. I would like to have it understood that she is speaking of Spokane and we are speaking of Seattle.

The CHAIRMAN. It is right and proper that we should know the part of the country which one is speaking of.

Mrs. O'CONNOR. It is much harder for a girl to get a room than a man. You can't get room and board for less than $5.50 per week.

Mr. JACOBSON. Mr. Chairman, I move that we hear what the public has to say on this.

The CHAIRMAN. I was just debating, within my own mind, inasmuch as the representatives of the public are occupying the position of mediators, it seems to me that we ought to thrash it out just as far as possible before we hear from them.

Judge DAY. I think we ought to hear more about this question from the employers and employees.

The CHAIRMAN. I rather think it would be a good plan to go right down the list and hear all the items discussed. According to the rules and regulations the Chair is permitted to appoint one of the members representing the public as chief interrogator. I take pleasure in designating Rev. McGinnis as interrogator. I will appoint the other two members representing the public as associated with him. I am informed that the average of those figures that have been presented amounts to $285.66. You can verify this by your own figures. Unless there are further remarks on this question of board and room, we will proceed to take up the next item—shoes and rubbers.

Mr. DOUST. Can we go back and consider these things later if we pass over them?

The CHAIRMAN. Yes, indeed. Has anyone got any figures to present on the next item?

Mrs. O'CONNOR. Mr. Chairman, I think that a girl needs three pairs of shoes at $3 per pair, and she also needs one pair of oxfords at $3 per pair. I have worn $2.50 shoes, but have ruined my feet in so doing. I have a total of $12 for shoes per year.

Judge DAY. Does that include rubbers?

Mrs. O'CONNOR. No; I have never worn rubbers in Seattle, but have always lived close to the car line.

The CHAIRMAN. Miss Hilts, what have you for shoes and rubbers?

Miss HILTS. I have figured three pairs of shoes at $3, equaling $9; one pair of dress shoes at $3, and one pair of rubbers at 50 cents per pair, making a total of $12.50 for the year.

The CHAIRMAN. I presume I had better call on you next, Mrs. Wilson, if you have your list prepared.

Mrs. WILSON. I am a little hard on shoes and the floors in the laundries are also hard on them. I wear out about four pairs of shoes each year, and I pay $2.50 for them. That would be $10 per year for shoes. I usually get cloth rubbers. I think they are 60 cents; that would be $1.80 for three pairs. I never can get shoes soled for less than 50 cents.

The CHAIRMAN. I would like to hear from the employers' side on this question.

Mr. JACOBSON. For shoes and rubbers I have $7.75; that is one pair of shoes at $3, two pairs at $2, rubbers 75 cents, making a total of $7.75.

The CHAIRMAN. Do you think you can buy a lady's shoe at $2?

Mr. JACOBSON. My wife has been able to buy $2 shoes. We are trying to get at the average or minimum cost, not what a girl may want to have, but what she can live on.

Miss HILTS. If I were to have the shoes I would like, I would have to pay a great deal more. I can buy a shoe in Seattle for $2.50 that will last me, probably, for one month and then they look far from dressy. I find that $3 is the cheapest shoe that I can get in the city of Seattle.

Mr. DOUST. The lady who buys four pair of shoes this year, would she have to buy four pair of shoes next year—that is, couldn't she wear this year's old shoes to work next year?

The CHAIRMAN. Mr. Nixon, what have you?

Mr. NIXON. I have $6.75; two pairs of shoes, one at $3.50, one at $2.50; and one pair of rubbers at 75 cents.

The CHAIRMAN. Mr. Doust.

Mr. DOUST. I have figured two pairs at $4, and one pair of rubbers at 75 cents, making a total of $8.75.

The CHAIRMAN. I would like to hear from the ladies as to how much longer the average $4 shoe would last than the $2 shoe?

Miss HILTS. You can have the $4 shoe resoled twice; but when the sole of the $2 shoe is worn, the shoe has completely lost its shape.

Mr. DOUST. I have found, in speaking with our girls, that they prefer to get a $4 shoe and to have them resoled three times than to get a cheaper shoe. The third time the shoe is resoled it makes a good shoe to wear in the laundry.

Rev. McGINNIS. How long do you wear a $4 pair of shoes before you have to have them resold?

Mrs. O'CONNOR. I am sorry to say that I never have had a pair of $4 shoes.

Rev. McGINNIS. Can you tell, Miss Hilts?

Miss HILTS. I put a new pair of shoes on, wear them to the laundry, and in six weeks they have to be repaired; then they last about four weeks longer.

Mr. JACOBSON. I have noticed that our girls wear a sort of sandal—broad heels, heavy sole—when in the laundry. I don't know what they cost; but I should think they would be very economical.

Miss HILTS. I wish to state that that is the style of shoes I wear in the laundry, and I pay $3 per pair for them.

The CHAIRMAN. We will now take up the question of repairing shoes. What have you ladies for that?

Mr. JACOBSON. I have $1.50 for the repair of shoes.

Mr. NIXON. I have a like amount.

Mrs. O'CONNOR. I want you to realize that leather has gone up in price. It costs $1 for a pair of half soles. If you want rubber heels that is extra. My estimate is $2.40 for the year.

Miss HILTS. I have estimated it at $2.50: that allows two pair of half soles during the year, and one pair of rubber heels.

The CHAIRMAN. What are your figures, Mrs. Wilson?

Mrs. WILSON. I always have to get my shoes half-soled quite often. I pay 25 cents to have the heels lowered and rubber heels put on.

Rev. McGINNIS. Four pairs of shoes half-soled would be $4.

Mrs. WILSON. One can get it done for 50 cents; that makes it $2 for the year.

The CHAIRMAN. The next item is stockings. Mrs. Wilson, will you give us your figures?

Mrs. WILSON. I really couldn't give you a figure on that, for I haven't bought any stockings for so long I really don't know the prices any more.

The CHAIRMAN. What is your estimate, Miss Hilts?

Miss HILTS. I have two dozen stockings at $3 per dozen, that would be $6, and one pair of silk stockings at $1.50, making a total of $7.50. I made my estimate at $4.50, however, and wish to state that I eliminated that pair of silk stockings.

The CHAIRMAN. Mrs. O'Connor.

Mrs. O'CONNOR. I have figured eight pairs of stockings at 25 cents a pair, or $2; two pair at 50 cents, $1; making a total of $3 for stockings for the year.

Mr. JACOBSON. I have stockings at $1.20, eight pairs at 15 cents.

Mr. NIXON. I have eight pairs at 20 cents, making $1.60.

Mr. DOUST. I have 10 pair at 15 cents, making $1.50.

The CHAIRMAN. It is 5 minutes to 12 o'clock, and the Chair will entertain a motion to adjourn until 1.30, or whatever is your pleasure.

Mr. DOUST. I move we adjourn until 1.30.

Mr. JACOBSON. I second the motion.

The CHAIRMAN. It is moved and seconded that we adjourn until 1.30, all in favor signify their assent by saying " aye." [All voted aye.] The ayes have it. We will adjourn until 1.30.

AFTER RECESS—1.30 P. M.

The CHAIRMAN. The meeting will please come to order. I think, there is too much of a difference in the figures given so far. The three members representing the public are evidently going to settle this proposition, if you people give figures that are unreasonable you are not doing justice to them, therefore, I think it would be well for you to get closer together. It would be best to do this in the beginning rather than to have so many concessions to make later on, I am not speaking any more to the employers than to the employees. The last item we had under discussion was stockings. The next is underwear. Will the ladies submit their figure on that item?

Miss HILTS. Mr. Chairman, I have this estimated at $6 per year. That allows for three union suits at the rate of 75 cents for winter, three for summer at 75 cents, and $1.50 for other muslins. Total, $6.

Mr. JACOBSON. I have $5 for underwear. Two suits at $2 and two suits at 50 cents each.

Mrs. O'CONNOR. I have $1.50 for three union suits for winter, and three at 25 cents for summer.

Mrs. WILSON. I have allowed for two suits woolen underwear at $2, four suits at 50 cents, $2, making a total of $4.

Mr. DOUST. I also have $4.

The CHAIRMAN. Is there any discussion on this item?

Rev. McGINNIS. Mr. Chairman, we seem to be pretty close together on this, in fact, almost a unanimity.

The CHAIRMAN. The next is petticoats. I will have to call upon the ladies again. Miss Hilts have you your figures prepared?

Miss HILTS. I have that at $4, that allows for three petticoats for work at 50 cents, $1.50, one white petticoat at $1, and one silk petticoat at $1.50.

Mrs. O'CONNOR. I have one silk petticoat at $2.50, one white petticoat at $1.50, and two for work at $1, makes $5 for total.

Mr. JACOBSON. I have two petticoats at $1 each, $2.

The CHAIRMAN. Mr. Doust knows about the cold weather in Spokane. We can probably get a pretty good idea from him as to how many petticoats are needed.

Mr. DOUST. I don't know much about petticoats though: I move that we hear from some of the ladies on the conference or from the public.

The CHAIRMAN. I think they would be glad to give their opinions.

Mrs. SWANSON. I believe this minimum girl ought to be able to make a petticoat for $1. I have a petticoat that I got for 87 cents on sale, and it is real good. I think four at $1 apiece would be sufficient for a year.

Mrs. SILBAUGH. Considering the line of work that they are doing I think that $4 is quite reasonable; of course, I know that laundries are quite hard on clothes.

The CHAIRMAN. We will now pass to the next item—suits. We would like to hear from the ladies on that item.

Mrs. O'CONNOR. In the estimate in this report the girl is allowed two suits per year. I would rather take the money that is allowed for two suits and put it into one good suit. I consider I can get a good suit for $40.

Rev. McGINNIS. Mrs. O'Conner, may I just ask if you are still bearing in mind that this is a minimum wage that we are working on?

Mrs. O'CONNOR. I have found that one is economizing by buying one good suit rather than two cheaper ones and I do not think one can get a good suit for less than $40.

The CHAIRMAN. How long would a suit of that kind last—how long would it be in style?

Mrs. O'CONNOR. A working girl don't expect to dress in style. I don't try to follow the styles.

The CHAIRMAN. How long do you estimate that a suit of this kind will last?

Mrs. O'CONNOR. It will really last two years.

The CHAIRMAN. That would mean it would be $20 per year for suits?

Mrs. O'CONNOR. No; I mean that the suit I get this year would be for best wear and next year it would do for work.

Mr. DOUST. I have tried to be fair in making up this list and tried to get down to the necessities of a girl making a minimum wage. But I want to say that my wife don't get a $40 suit; if she gets a $25 suit, she is doing well. She would not think of paying $40 for a suit any more than I would.

Mrs. McCREDIE. I think the young lady is somewhat justified in taking the stand she does. It is true that a $40 suit will last longer and look better than two $20 suits. However, I believe I would recommend a $30 or $35 suit; I think I could get a good suit for that price.

The CHAIRMAN. I would like to ask Miss Hilts what her estimate is.

Miss HILTS. I have that estimated at $35, and I would expect to get one new suit each year.

The CHAIRMAN. Mrs. Wilson.

Mrs. WILSON. I have two suits a year—one at $20 and one at $10.

The CHAIRMAN. I think the law contemplated that we should try to determine what the self-supporting girl should live on decently and not extravagantly. It is merely a question of which is the most economical. Mr. Doust, what is your opinion.

Mr. DOUST. I have one suit at $20.

The CHAIRMAN. Mr. Jacobson.

Mr. JACOBSON. I have a little different idea about this and have grouped the next few articles. My idea is worked out like this: Two dress skirts, one at $3 and one at $5, making a total of $8. Then, two coats, one at $10 and one at $20, making a total of $28 for skirts and coats; this would take the place of suits.

Rev. McGINNIS. I think we might be able to get together on that suggestion.

The CHAIRMAN. If it is so desired, we might consider that question.

Mr. JACOBSON. As I said, I have two dress skirts, total $8; two coats, total $30; then three dresses at $2.50 each, $7.50; and four aprons at 50 cents, or $2. I have allowed for four shirt waists at $1 and two at $2, or $8. This makes my total for all, $55.50.

Mr. MARVIN. Mr. Chairman, I would like to hear from one of these ladies on those four items.

Miss HILTS. In the last three articles—dresses and aprons and shirt waists— I think he is very reasonable. His coats are a little higher than we have. In averaging all of them it is pretty close to our estimate.

Mr. MARVIN. What have you for the estimate of the four articles, Miss Hilts?

Miss HILTS. I had it at $60.

The CHAIRMAN. Mrs. O'Connor; what do you think about these figures.

Mrs. O'CONNOR. It would be satisfactory to me at $55.50

Mr. DOUST. My estimate was $52 for the total, but it was guesswork.

Mr. NIXON. Mine is $56.

Miss Hilts. I will withdraw my former statement and accept $55.50, if it is agreeable to everyone.

Mr. Marvin. May I ask whether in many laundries of this State there is provision for an outer garment while at work?

Miss Hilts. I don't know of any; we furnish everything ourselves.

Mr. Doust. I never heard of any laundry doing it.

The Chairman. There is none that do to my knowledge. We will now pass to the next item, which is handkerchiefs.

Miss Hilts. I have allowed $1 for handkerchiefs.

The Chairman. I am not going to call on the employers for this because I know they will agree to this. We want you to start out with corsets, Mrs. Wilson.

Mrs. Wilson. I have allowed $10 for the year, and I buy a cheap corset but get a good many during the year.

Mrs. O'Connor. I find that in a laundry a girl can't get along with less than three corsets during the year. I have allowed for three at $3.50 apiece, or $10.50 for the year.

Miss Hilts. My figures are the same as Mrs. O'Connor's on that—$10.50.

Mr. Jacobson. I am not going to ruin my girl's health by putting her in corsets; she is going to wear two pair at $2 each.

Mr. Nixon. I have two pair, amounting to $3.75.

Mr. Doust. I have two pair at $2, or $4.

Mr. Marvin. My wife insists that a $3.50 corset is a cheaper corset. That is quite an item, isn't it, girls? We are trying to avoid too much discussion, but I think that in this case the higher-priced corset would be the most economical.

Mrs. Swanson. I have averaged the figures; they are $7.04.

Mr. Jacobson. May I ask if you think the figures available here that the employers sent in?

(Mr. Olson read list sent in by employers.)

The Chairman. The next is corset waists. What have you, Mrs. O'Connor?

Mrs. O'Connor. I have it figured at four corset waists at 75 cents, which would be $3.

The Chairman. Miss Hilts?

Miss Hilts. I have allowed four at 50 cents and one at $1, making a total of $3.

Mrs. Wilson. I have four at 25 cents each, or $1.

Mr. Jacobson. I have three at 50 cents each, $1.50.

Mrs. Nixon. I have a total of $1.

Mr. Doust. I have three at 50 cents, or $1.50.

The Chairman. The next item is gloves. I would like to hear from the employers this time in the matter of gloves.

Mr. Doust. I have two pair of gloves at $1 each, $2.

Mr. Jacobson. I have three pair at 50 cents each, $1.50

Mr. Nixon. One dollar and fifty cents for gloves; three pair at 50 cents.

The Chairman. Mrs. O'Connor, what is your estimate?

Mrs. O'Connor. I allowed $1 for work gloves and $2 for a good pair, making a total of $3 for the year.

The Chairman. Miss Hilts?

Mrs. Wilson. I have four pair at 50 cents each, $2

Miss Hilts. I have allowed $1 for work gloves and $1.50 for good gloves.

The Chairman. Neckwear. You girls ought to be able to tell us something about this. Miss Hilts, will you start this?

Miss Hilts. I have neckwear estimated at $1.

Mr. Jacobson. We won't fight on that. I have the same.

Mrs. Wilson. I will allow $1, too.

Mrs. O'Connor. I think $1 will cover neckwear.

The Chairman. The next is a very grave question. Hats. I believe we will call on the laundrymen and see what they think should be expended for hats.

Mr. Jacobson. I have allowed for two hats, one at $2 and one at $5; total, $7.

Mr. Doust. I have two hats at $5, $10.

Mr. Nixon. I have one at $3 and one at $5, making a total of $8.

Mrs. Wilson. I have two hats at $5 each, making $10.

Miss Hilts. I was just going to suggest that we agree on $10 for hats. We have decided to come down to that if the employers will all agree to it.

Mr. Jacobson. We will meet you.

The Chairman. The next item to be considered is umbrellas.

Mr. Doust. I think we ought to allow one umbrella each year.

Mrs. WILSON. I think we ought to have one umbrella a year at $1.

Miss HILTS. My figures are $3.50 for an umbrella which will last two years.

The CHAIRMAN. We will pass to repairing of clothing.· Does the average laundry girl repair a good deal of her own clothing?

Mrs. O'CONNOR. Yes, sir. About the only thing she sends out to be repaired is her suit coat. That would be about $2.50.

Miss HILTS. I have that at $2.

Mrs. WILSON. I have placed mine at $5 because I never do any sewing.

The CHAIRMAN. The next item is laundry. About how much do you find that you have to expend per week or per year for your laundry, Mrs. O'Connor?

Mrs. O'CONNOR. I have allowed $20 for one year. I figured it at 40 cents per week, which makes $20.80, but have made it $20.

The CHAIRMAN. Do you get any advantages from the laundry?

Mrs. O'CONNOR. Yes; we get 50 per cent off.

Miss HILTS. I have the laundry at $15 per year. In case we get our laundry in to go over in the " hold over " we get it done for one-half price. Some laundries will not allow their work to be done for half price unless you bring it yourself.

Mr. DOUST. We give 20 per cent. Most of our girls have their work rough dried.

Mrs. WILSON. I pay about $5 per year for laundry, and I usually do my own washing.

Mr. DOUST. As a matter of fact, they don't bring their clothes to the laundry as a general rule. Girls are permitted to use our irons during the noon period.

Miss HILTS. The mangle girls do not have time to do this. The girls in the department where I am get off early on Friday and Saturday, and they do it then.

Mr. JACOBSON. I put the figures for the laundry at $6.

Mr. NIXON. Mine are $5 for laundry.

The CHAIRMAN. Medicine and dentistry is the next item.

Mr. DOUST. I have $10.

Mr. JACOBSON. That is a hard thing to estimate, because some people require a great deal in this line and others very little. I have estimated that at $8 for the year.

Miss HILTS. Ten dollars is agreeable to the girls if the employers will agree on it.

Mr. NIXON. I have $5 per year for this.

Mrs. WILSON. Ten dollars is my estimate, too.

The CHAIRMAN. The next is street car fare.

Mrs. O'CONNOR. I have street car fare at $36 per year.

Miss HILTS. I have $36 per year.

Mrs. WILSON. My estimate is $36 for street car fare.

Mr. DOUST. I have $30 for street car fare.

Miss HILTS. We have found in our investigation in Seattle that 75 per cent of the girls pay street car fare.

The CHAIRMAN. If a girl pays street car fare and comes quite a distance to the laundry, the price of her room is usually cheaper; for that reason the board and room should be taken into consideration with the street car fare. Here is another thing we found, through our investigations of the laundries and mercantile stores: A great many of the laundries are located close to the residence district, while the stores are a great deal farther away. We have to consider price of board and room in connection with street car fare.

Mr. JACOBSON. What is the average for street car fare in the reports sent in?

(Chairman read from reports.)

The CHAIRMAN. The average is $27.58 for the year. A majority of these figures come from the larger cities. We had a great deal of difficulty getting the laundries in the small towns to send in their figures.

Mr. DOUST. Considering the fact that girls are continually traveling 365 days in the year, they certainly would take advantage of the rates. I think the $30 proposition is fair or even a lot higher than the average girl would need.

The CHAIRMAN. What are your figures, Mr. Jacobson?

Mr. JACOBSON. I have mine at $25.

Mr. NIXON. Mine are $25 also.

Mrs. O'CONNOR. I would recommend that we accept Mr. Doust's figures of $30 on the street car fare.

The CHAIRMAN. I think in this matter we ought to keep in mind the entire State. We are legislating for girls not only from Seattle, Tacoma, and Spokane, but from all sections of the State. There are small laundries that have to be considered, and I think the figures offered by the employers are more than reasonable.

Judge DAY. I find that a large number of the people live at home and not far away from the laundries, but very few come from a long distance in Bellingham.

The CHAIRMAN. I didn't get your figures, Mr. Nixon.

Mr. NIXON. Twenty dollars.

The CHAIRMAN. The next is newspapers and magazines.

Mr. JACOBSON. I put down here $3.

Mr. DOUST. I have $3.

Mr. NIXON. I have $2.50 for newspapers and magazines.

Mrs. O'CONNOR. I have $3.

Miss HILTS. I have $3.

Mrs. WILSON. I also have $3.

The CHAIRMAN. The next is stationery and postage. How much do you think the average girl expends for paper and postage? I mean the average laundry girl, Miss Hilts.

Miss HILTS. I have $2.50.

Mrs. O'CONNOR. I also have $2.50 for postage and stationery.

Mrs. WILSON. I gave $2.50.

Mr. DOUST. Two dollars.

Mr. JACOBSON. One dollar.

Mr. NIXON. Two dollars.

The CHAIRMAN. The next on the list is association dues.

Mrs. O'CONNOR. My association dues are $7 per year.

Rev. McGINNIS. Is that the average amount paid by most of the girls?

Mrs. O'CONNOR. Most of the girls belong to some association or lodge.

Miss HILTS. My figures are $7.

Mrs. WILSON. Mine are $5.

Mr. JACOBSON. I have allowed $2. I would just like to know what the average girl asks for. I would like to know, from your records there, what the average figures are on this question.

(Chairman read from report.)

Mr. DOUST. I have $1.50 on that. I do not think we should place this figure very high, because so many of the girls don't pay anything. I know a great many girls in our laundry do not pay anything for association dues. It seems to me that these ladies are just giving what they pay. I don't think they base their figure on what the average girl pays.

Mrs. O'CONNOR. We have based our figures on what other girls pay. I pay $12 myself. I haven't considered myself in this average. The girls do not all belong to unions, but they like to belong to some lodge, as the I. O. G. T., Knights and Ladies of Security, or the Rebeccas.

Judge DAY. Would many of those associations include these girls?

Miss HILTS. Why, yes; our laundry girls belong to something of the kind.

Rev. McGINNIS. In the laundry in which you work, what per cent of the girls belong to the Rebeccas?'

Miss HILTS. I couldn't say, as I don't know the exact number.

The CHAIRMAN. What are your figures, Mr. Nixon?

Mr. NIXON. I have $2.

The CHAIRMAN. The next is insurance. Are there many girls working in the laundries that carry insurance?

Miss HILTS. There are a number of them who carry insurance. Usually those who have some one dependent upon them.

Mr. DOUST. I don't think we can take those into consideration.

The CHAIRMAN. What is your estimate, Miss Hilts?

Miss HILTS. Five dollars per year.

Mrs. O'CONNOR. Five dollars for the year.

Mrs. WILSON. Mine is $5 per year.

Mr. DOUST. I have $3.

Mr. JACOBSON. I didn't allow anything for insurance.

Mr. NIXON. I have allowed $5 for insurance.

The CHAIRMAN. Vacation expenses.

Mr. JACOBSON. I have allowed $8 for vacation expenses.

Mr. DOUST. I have allowed $10.

Mr. NIXON. Ten dollars.

Miss HILTS. I have that at $15.

Mrs. O'CONNOR. Fifteen dollars.

Mrs. WILSON. I have allowed $12.

The CHAIRMAN. We will pass to the next item, amusements. Mrs. O'Connor, will you tell us what you think a girl ought to have for amusements for the year?

Mrs. O'CONNOR. I have it figured at $10 per year.

Miss HILTS. I have $10.

Mrs. WILSON. Ten dollars.

Mr. JACOBSON. Ten dollars.

Mr. NIXON. Five dollars.

Mr. DOUST. Eight dollars.

The CHAIRMAN. Church and other contributions.

Mr. JACOBSON. Six dollars.

Mr. DOUST. Five dollars.

Mr. NIXON. Six dollars.

Miss HILTS. The girls are willing to meet the gentlemen at $5.

The CHAIRMAN. The last item is incidentals.

Mr. JACOBSON. I have allowed for incidentals $12.

Mrs. O'CONNOR. I am allowing $10.

Miss HILTS. Ten dollars.

Mrs. WILSON. Ten dollars.

Mr. DOUST. Ten dollars.

Mr. NIXON. Ten dollars.

Mr. MARVIN. Would you care to know what each one has estimated? I have it all summed up. Mrs. O'Connor, $608; Miss Hilts, $604.25; Mrs. Wilson, $569.80; Mr. Doust, $493.25; Mr. Jacobson, $480.95; Mr. Nixon, $472.60.

Mrs. SWANSON. I have averaged all of your items and divided the sum by 52; the result is an average of $9.12 per week.

Mr. MARVIN. I wish to say that I have made a mistake of $100 on each total. Please take $100 from each total.

Mr. JACOBSON. I move that we adjourn for 15 minutes.

Mr. NIXON. I second the motion.

The CHAIRMAN. It is moved and seconded that we adjourn for 15 minutes, but I wish to say that it is now about 5 o'clock, and if there is nothing special to come before the meeting the Chair will entertain a motion to adjourn until to-morrow morning. Our secretary has been at work night and day, and I think she needs a rest.

Mr. JACOBSON. I move that we adjourn until 9 o'clock to-morrow morning.

Rev. McGINNIS. I second the motion.

The CHAIRMAN. It is moved and seconded that we adjourn until 9 o'clock to-morrow morning. All in favor signify their assent by saying "aye." [All voted aye.] The ayes have it; we will adjourn.

FRIDAY, MAY 16—9 A. M.

The CHAIRMAN. The meeting will please come to order and the secretary will please call the roll.

(Upon roll call by the secretary all answered "present.")

Before we proceed any further with our deliberations I would like to have you turn to page 101 of the report. I want to read to you section 2 of the law:

"It shall be unlawful to employ women or minors in any industry or occupation within the State of Washington under conditions of labor detrimental to their health or morals; and it shall be unlawful to employ women workers in any industry within the State of Washington at wages which are not adequate for their maintenance."

Also section 3, which says:

"There is hereby created a commission to be known as the Industrial Welfare Commission for the State of Washington, to establish such standards of wages and conditions of labor for women and minors employed within the State of Washington as shall be held hereunder to be reasonable and not detrimental to health and morals, and which shall be sufficient for the decent maintenance of women."

I believe that the legislature, when it passed this law, had the purpose in mind that no woman in the State of Washington employed in any of its industries should be paid less wage than is required to support her in decency and comfort. They did not take into consideration the one who lives at home nor the women who receive support from the outside. They took into consideration just the woman who is self-supporting. That being the case, I want to impress upon your minds this morning that we must follow that law in order to be within the spirit of it.

There was quite a diversified opinion here relative to the matter of the cost of board and room yesterday. I was somewhat astounded at the remarkably low figures of some in regard to board .and room. I do not think that some of the lowest figures that were given were based upon the best judgment, but I am of the opinion that some of the figures that were given were rather high, which was because of these extremely low figures. Now, I appeal to the members of the conference to get right down to business—to find out what is required in the way of board and room. That, I think, is one of the things that ought to be given just and honest consideration. As one of the members of the employees' side said yesterday, if a woman is not properly fed she can't do her work right.

I don't expect any extravagance, but I don't think the minimum-wage woman should, be placed on the starvation basis. We have, I think, here to-day with us a conference that is willing to be fair in this matter. We must consider this woman who toils. We have these figures here that range from $208 up to $369 for board and room. There is no reason why this great difference should exist. This commission has made quite a thorough investigation of this matter and have formed quite a fair idea as to what board and room should cost a woman. Our investigations have shown, as you will find on page 48 of the report, the average annual cost of board and room as $273 within walking distance and $267 outside of walking distance. As I said yesterday, I think we should consider street car fare in regard to board and room. I think that is fair. Where a room is located down town, in the business district, board and room is probably higher. Let us consider these matters and do justice to our-selves, to the girls, and to the employers. I assure you that the Industrial Welfare Commission of the State of Washington, who have been given this matter to handle, must abide by the spirit of the law, which is that a self-supporting woman must have an adequate wage based upon the cost of living. I do not think it would be proper of me to accept a motion determining what a minimum wage should be until we have come to some fair estimate of the cost of board and room. We do not want it to go out to the State that this board has cut down on a woman's board; therefore I think we should thor-oughly discuss this matter and come to some tentative conclusion.

Mr. JACOBSON. Mr. Chairman, would it be permissible at this time to let me make some explanation of my position in this matter? I want the ladies on the other side to know that my personal likes and desires are not being taken into consideration in this. I am chosen to come here and represent an industry, the same as a man is supposed to represent his colleagues when he goes to Congress. This is on the same principle. You girls are sent up here to repre-sent the working girls—that is, the girl who is to receive the minimum wage. You girls understand the meaning of the word "minimum." You understand we are not endeavoring to fix a schedule of wages in the same manner that a trade organization does; we are endeavoring to establish the least wage that a girl can consistently live on in decency and comfort. I am not here to repre-sent the Rainier Laundry Co., of Seattle, nor the city of Seattle. I am here to represent the laundry industry and am attempting to stay within the bounds of reason. I am sure that everyone present will say that any girl can live respectfully and healthfully on what I am going to lay before this commission. This is not an altruistic business I am sorry to say; there are some problems in our business that have to be looked into. I will just simply state, with ref-erence to this board and room, I am absolutely conscientious in presenting this case. I believe there are a great many self-supporting women that are living on $4 per week for board and room. It is not my purpose to state that the girls shall live on $4 per week, but it is a question of whether she can do so. The rest of the items, I want to say at this time, vary so little on this sheet of mine, with the exception of the item of board and room, that I think it would be possible to come together.

Mrs. UDALL. Do you know anything about these places where a girl can get board and room for $3.50?

Mr. JACOBSON. I really do not know, but that information can be obtained.

Mrs. UDALL. The Y. M. C. A., Women's Inn, and such places are charitable institutions. That is the reason I have asked you this.

Miss HILTS. Mr. Jacobson says he is very confident that a girl can obtain board and room for $4 per week. I don't think he has investigated very thoroughly or he would know that a girl can not live on the board and room that they receive. They give a little coffee and toast for breakfast. For lunch a little meat, potatoes, and coffee and bread and butter, and for dinner coffee, bread, and butter, with perhaps a piece of pie or cake.

Mr. JACOBSON. Have you ever boarded at any of those places, Miss Hilts?

Miss HILTS. No; I never have, and I don't think Mr. Jacobson has, either.

Judge DAY. Miss Hilts, let us try to get down to something. Have you actually talked to these girls who board at the cheaper boarding houses? Are you speaking merely from what you think or can you give us the names of girls who are now living in those places?

Mr. DOUST. Mr. Chairman, I believe that I would ordinarily be as liberal as anyone in granting the demands of the girls over there. I have investigated this board proposition pretty thoroughly before I came here, and what I said about this board for $4 per week is true. There is a place right next to my plant with board for $4 per week. The girls from the laundry used to go over and get their dinner and bring it over and eat it in the laundry. The high wage did not cut so much figure with the mercantile conference, for they said they would raise the price of their goods if the wage were placed high, but that is something we can not do. We are in competition with two outlawed firms. There are the Chinese laundries and the House of the Good Shepherd in Spokane to compete with. They go out and solicit business in competition with us. The Japanese laundry in Spokane runs night and day. Their price list is 30 per cent lower than ours. How are we going to raise our wages and still do business. We can't do it; that is all there is to it. It seems to me that when the legislature makes laws to protect these people they ought to also protect the people who own these businesses. On this particular question I am satisfied that a girl in Spokane can get good board and room, and board on which she can do all kinds of work in a laundry, for $4. When our girls leave the laundry they don't go out as if they were worked to death.

Mrs. UDALL. May I ask you the same question I asked Mr. Jacobson—have you investigated any of those places?

Mrs. SWANSON. Mr. Krause was quite sure the Women's Hotel was self-supporting. Have you investigated it?

Mr. DOUST. The owner of the Women's Hotel sent out posters to our laundry. This hotel is absolutely self-supporting. It has been in operation in Spokane for a good many years, and I am sure it is not a charity institution.

Mr. MARVIN. I think they expect to make no returns on it.

Mr. DOUST. The women's clubs are behind this, but there is no charity about it.

Miss HILTS. Mr. Doust, can you give us about the number of laundry girls there are in the city of Spokane? Could you give us an estimate?

Mr. DOUST. We have 80 girls in our laundry.

Miss HILTS. That would nearly fill up the hotel alone.

Mr. DOUST. There are just about 13 girls in our laundry who do not live at home.

Mrs. UDALL. I still maintain that if the women maintain this home that it is a charity institution.

The CHAIRMAN. The advertisement says: "Rooms for 100 boarders for prices ranging from $3 to $8 per week." We have no means of knowing if the minimum price is going to give the girl proper accommodations.

Mr. MARVIN. I wish to say that, even if it could be proven that this institution was self-supporting, if it is not a business proposition, that to that extent it partakes of the nature of charity, and against any such thing I should have to enter my protest.

Miss HILTS. That would make an average of $5.50 per week if the rooms run from $3 to $8 per week.

The CHAIRMAN. What I contend is that these rooms in Spokane are not going to settle the question. I want to read to you what our investigations have shown with reference to rooms in Bellingham.

(Chairman read from report.)

Mrs. O'CONNOR. I should think we could easily come to some agreement on this thing. I think we should come to some definite decision. I don't think it is necessary to argue any longer on that.

Rev. McGINNIS. Mr. Chairman, I think we have come to a place in our discussion where we are neither going forward nor backward; we are standing still. In order that we may get together I would suggest that you appoint a representative from each of the three parties here, who will retire and take this matter up and see if we can not arrive at some definite understanding.

The CHAIRMAN. Do you make that as a motion?

Rev. McGINNIS. I do.

Mr. DOUST. I second the motion.

..The CHAIRMAN. It has been moved and seconded that I appoint a committee of three to get together and try to come to some definite understanding on this matter.

Mr. DOUST. I would like to amend that and include Mr. Olson on that committee.

Rev. McGINNIS. I would be very glad to include Mr. Olson on that.

The CHAIRMAN. All in favor signify by saying "aye." [All voted aye.] The ayes have it. I would request the conference to remain here until we return. I will appoint Mrs. O'Connor, Mrs. McCredie, and Mr. Doust on the committee.

Mr. DOUST. I would rather you appoint one of the other men. I would rather not serve on that committee.

The CHAIRMAN. I would rather not change my decision. I think you would be a very fair representative on that.

Mr. MARVIN. While this may not seem to cut any figure with you, I think it was a good plan to choose you three, as Mrs. O'Connor belongs to the west side, Mrs. McCredie to the center, and you belong to the east side of the State.

The CHAIRMAN. That is the reason I appointed you on this committee.

AFTER RECESS.

The CHAIRMAN. The meeting will please come to order. We have been unable to arrive at any conclusion whatever, and I would ask that we adjourn until 1.30 p. m.

Mr. JACOBSON. I make a motion that we now adjourn until 1.30 o'clock.

Rev. McGINNIS. I second the motion.

The CHAIRMAN. It has been moved and seconded that we adjourn until 1.30 o'clock. All in favor signify their assent by saying "aye." [All voted aye.] The ayes have it. We will now adjourn.

AFTER RECESS—1.30 P. M.

The CHAIRMAN. The meeting will please come to order. As reported just before the noon hour, the committee which had been appointed was unable to bring in any decision at all, and the Chair would suggest that another committee be appointed to bring in their decision.

Judge DAY. Mr. Chairman, I don't want to take too much out of the hands of the Chair by motion, but I would like to move that another conference committee be appointed, composed of one from each one of these branches, and I would name Mrs. Jacobson, Rev. McGinnis, and any one of the ladies from the employees. I make that a motion.

Mrs. O'CONNOR. Mr. Chairman, I served on the other one, so I think it would be up to those two.

The CHAIRMAN. It is moved and seconded that a committee composed of Mr. Jacobson, Rev. McGinnis, and a member from the ladies (selected by the conference) be appointed on a new committee.

Judge DAY. The Chair should select one.

The CHAIRMAN. Would Miss Hilts be satisfactory?

Judge DAY. Yes, sir.

The CHAIRMAN. It is moved and seconded that a committee, composed of Mr. Jacobson, Rev. McGinnis, and Miss Hilts be selected to confer on this matter and bring in a decision in 30 minutes. All in favor signify by saying "aye." [All voted aye.] The ayes have it.

AFTER RECESS.

The CHAIRMAN. The meeting will please come to order. I desire to say that the committee which was appointed was unable to reach any conclusion, and the question is now before the house in the same manner as before the committee was appointed. As you probably know, it is necessary to obtain a vote on this question before this conference can adjourn.

Mr. DOUST. I move that a committee of the balance of the conferees get together.

The CHAIRMAN. I doubt very much if we could get together. I would suggest that some kind of a motion be made.

Mrs. McCredie. I move that we fix the minimum wage at $9 per week. I might say here that this is not as large an amount as I think they should have, but under the conditions I make this motion in the hope that we can get something better later on.

Miss Hilts. I second the motion.

The Chairman. It is moved by Mrs. McCredie and seconded by Miss Hilts "that no person, firm, association, or corporation shall employ any female over the age of 18 years in any laundry and dye-works establishment at a weekly wage rate of less than $9, such wage being the estimate of said conference of the minimum wage adequate in such occupation and industry to supply the necessary cost of living to such employees and to maintain them in health and comfort." Are you ready for the question?

Mr. Jacobson. Do I understand that if this motion is carried it is to stand?

The Chairman. There is nothing said about that. I presume it is merely to get a test vote on the question.

Mr. Doust. It seems to me that it doesn't cost any more to maintain a girl in the State of Washington than in the State of Oregon. I can't see where the consistency of the thing is.

The Chairman. Are there any further remarks?

Rev. McGinnis. Do I understand clearly that this rate of wages is to be paid when the 48 hours have been completed in the week—if a fewer number of hours, then the rate is pro rata? Is that right?

The Chairman. Yes, sir. It is pro rata. I would think that would be right. It would be based according to the 48 hours.

Judge Day. A week would be 48 hours. If it was pro rata it would be based upon the hour.

The Chairman. It is computed on the hour basis.

Rev. McGinnis. I would move to amend that resolution and make it read $8.90 instead of $9.

The Chairman. An amendment is offered to this resolution. I don't hear any second.

Judge Day. I second the motion.

The Chairman. It has been moved by Rev. McGinnis and seconded by Judge Day, "that no person, firm, association, or corporation shall employ any female over the age of 18 years in any laundry and dye-works establishment at a weekly wage rate of less than $8.90, such wage being the estimate of said conference of the minimum wage adequate in such occupation and industry to supply the necessary cost of living of such employees and to maintain them in health and comfort." Are you ready for the question?

Judge Day. Question.

The Chairman. The secretary will please call the roll.

(Upon roll call the following vote was recorded:)

Ayes: Miss Johanna Hilts, Mrs. Julia A. Wilson, Mrs. R. C. McCredie, Rev. R. H. McGinnis, Judge E. M. Day, and Mr. Frank Nixon.

Noes: Mrs. Hilda O'Connor, Mr. W. J. Doust, and Mr. A. Jacobson.

The Secretary. The motion stands, 6 ayes and 3 noes.

The Chairman. The motion is carried, the question, however, can be ratified.

Mr. Jacobson. Do I understand that if the amendment is carried it will establish a precedent?

The Chairman. No; we are to ratify that by another motion.

Judge Day. It would be proper now to vote for the question as amended.

The Chairman. I might explain that this was moved to get a test vote. If some one wants to make a motion for the regular resolution so that our minutes will show a motion has been passed in its regular form, the Chair will entertain such a motion. It is not necessary to have this voted on again, as it was merely a test vote. That was the intention of it, was it not, Mrs. McCredie?

Mrs. McCredie. Yes, sir.

The Chairman. In order to lay aside any doubts on this matter we will put this original motion: "It is moved that it is the sense of this conference that the sum of $8.90 per week is the amount sufficient to maintain a woman engaged in the laundry industries. This amount is subject to ratification by proper resolution of this conference." Are you ready for the question?

Mrs. McCredie. I will repeat this motion in the wording that you have been using:

"Be it resolved, That this laundry and dye-works conference does hereby make the following recommendation to the industrial welfare commission in reference to the minimum wage in the laundry and dye-works occupation and industry:

"That no person, firm, association, or corporation shall employ any female over the age of 18 years in any laundry and dye-works establishment at a weekly wage rate of less than $8.90, such wage being the estimate of said conference of the minimum wage adequate in such occupation and industry to supply the necessary cost of living of such employees and to maintain them in health and comfort."

Miss Hilts. I second the motion.

The Chairman. You have heard the resolution just read, all in favor signify their assent by saying "aye"; contrary, "no." The secretary will please call the roll.

(Upon roll call the following vote was recorded:)

Ayes: Miss Johanna Hilts, Mrs. R. C. McCredie, Rev. R. H. McGinnis, and Judge E. M. Day.

Noes: Mrs. Hilda O'Connor, Mrs. Julia A. Wilson, Mr. W. J. Doust, Mr. Frank Nixon, and Mr. A. Jacobson.

The Secretary. The motion stands—5 noes and 4 ayes.

The Chairman. The motion is lost.

Mr. Doust. I move that $8.50 be adopted as the minimum wage.

Mr. Jacobson. I second the motion.

The Chairman. Upon motion duly made by Mr. W. J. Doust and seconded by Mr. A. Jacobson, the following resolution was recommended:

"Be it resolved, That this laundry and dye-works conference does hereby make the following recommendations to the industrial welfare commission in reference to the minimum wage in the laundry and dye-works occupation and industry:

"That no person, firm, association, or corporation shall employ any female over the age of 18 years in any laundry and dye-works establishment at a weekly wage rate of less than $8.50, such wage being the estimate of said conference of the minimum wage adequate in such occupation and industry to supply the necessary cost of living of such employees and to maintain them in health and comfort."

If this motion carries, it stands. Are you ready for the question?

Mr. Nixon. Question.

The Chairman. The secretary will please call the roll.

(Upon roll call the following vote was recorded:)

Ayes: Rev. B. H. McGinnis, Judge E. M. Day, Mr. W. J. Doust, Mr. Frank Nixon, and Mr. A. Jacobson.

Noes: Mrs. Hilda O'Connor, Miss Johanna Hilts, Mrs. Julia A. Wilson, and Mrs. R. C. McCredie.

The Secretary. The motion stands—5 ayes and 4 noes.

The Chairman. The motion is carried.

The Chairman. The next question before the house is what length of lunch period is demanded for maintenance of health of laundry and dye-works employees.

Mrs. O'Connor. I move that not less than one hour shall be allowed for noonday luncheon to any female employee in any laundry and dye-works establishment in the State of Wisconsin.

Mrs. McCredie. I second the motion.

The Chairman. Upon motion made by Mrs. Hilda O'Connor and seconded by Mrs. R. C. McCredie, the following resolution was recommended:

"Be it resolved, That the laundry and dye works conference does hereby make the following recommendation to the industrial welfare commission in reference to standards of conditions and labor demanded for the health and morals of employees in such laundry and dye works occupation and industry:

"That not less than one (1) hour shall be allowed for noonday luncheon to any female employee in any laundry and dye works establishment, such requirement being demanded for the health of such employees."

Are you ready for the question?

Miss Hilts. Question.

The Chairman. The secretary will please call the roll.

(Upon roll call the following vote was recorded:)

Ayes: Miss Hilda O'Connor, Miss Johanna Hilts, Mrs. Julia A. Wilson, Mrs. R. C. McCredie, Rev. R. H. McGinnis, Judge E. M. Day, Mr. W. J. Doust, Mr. Frank Nixon, and Mr. A. Jacobson.

The Secretary. All voted aye.

The CHAIRMAN. The motion is carried.

The next question is what provisions should be required in each laundry and dye works establishment for (*a*) toilet for women workers, (*b*) rest rooms, (*c*) ventilation?

Mrs. McCREDIE. I make the following as a motion:

"Every person, firm, or corporation engaged in the laundry business and employing males and females in the same establishment shall provide for such employees suitable and proper wash and dressing rooms and water-closets for males and females, and shall provide not less than 250 cubic feet of air space for each and every person in every workroom in said establishment; and the water-closets, wash and dressing rooms used by females shall not adjoin those used by males, but shall be built entirely away from those and shall be properly screened and ventilated; and all water-closets shall be at all times kept in a clean and sanitary condition.

"No person, firm, or corporation engaged in the laundry business and employing males and females in the same establishment shall require or permit both males and females to labor together in sorting soiled garments, but this labor shall be performed by either males or females alone and at a time when the opposite sex is not present."

Miss HILTS. I second the motion.

The CHAIRMAN. You have heard the reading of this resolution; it has been moved and seconded. Are you ready for the question?

Mr. DOUST. I want to say that if this motion is carried it would put some of the girls out of work. We have, at the present time, men and women marking clothes, two working at one end of a table and one at the other end, and if such a motion were carried and put into effect the girls would be thrown out of employment and men put in their places.

Rev. McGINNIS. I would like to have an expression from the girls. There seems to be two resolutions in this one we have read. If one of these were left out it might perhaps be carried. With the two together it might fail.

Mrs. McCREDIE. If we might dispose of this more easily I will withdraw the last part of the motion in regard to the soiled clothes. It would then read like this:

"Every person, firm, or corporation engaged in the laundry business and employing males and females in the same establishment shall provide for such employees suitable and proper washrooms and provide them with chairs, soap, and towels, and dressing rooms and water-closets for males and females, and the water-closets, wash and dressing rooms used by females shall not adjoin those used by males, but shall be built entirely away from those and shall be properly screened and ventilated; and all water-closets shall at all times be kept in a clean and sanitary condition."

Mr. JACOBSON. It might be a good idea to embody in this resolution that the factory laws do not cover this phase of the resolution. I would also say that this would work a hardship on the small laundry. In my particular plant it wouldn't make any difference.

Mrs. McCREDIE. I wish to withdraw my resolution until we have something drafted along this line.

The CHAIRMAN. Was that motion withdrawn with the consent of your second?

Miss HILTS. Yes, sir.

Mrs. McCREDIE. Mr. Chairman, I wish my motion to read like this:

"Every person, firm, or corporation engaged in the laundry and dye-works business and employing males and females in the same establishment shall provide for such employees suitable and proper wash and dressing rooms and water-closets for males and females; and the water-closets, wash and dressing rooms used by females shall not adjoin those used by males, but shall be built entirely away from those and shall be properly screened and ventilated; and all water-closets shall at all times be kept in a clean and sanitary condition."

Miss HILTS. I second the motion.

The CHAIRMAN. You hve heard the resolution read and seconded; are you ready for the question? If there is no remarks we will put it to a vote. The secretary will please call the roll.

Upon roll call the following vote was recorded:

Ayes: Mrs. Hilda O'Connor, Miss Johanna Hilts, Mrs. Julia A. Wilson, Mrs. R. C. McCredie, Rev. R. H. McGinnis, Judge E. M. Day, Mr. W. J. Doust, Mr. Frank Nixon, and Mr. A. Jacobson.

The SECRETARY. All voted aye.

INDUSTRIAL RELATIONS AND REMEDIES, SEATTLE, WASH. 4501

The CHAIRMAN. The motion is carried.

As there is nothing further before the house, I want to thank each and every one of you for acting on this conference, and before you go away I would like to have you sign these recommendations that have been made to the commission so that we may have them in shape. Motion is now in order for adjournment.

Rev. McGINNIS. I move we adjourn.

Mrs. McCREDIE. I second the motion.

The CHAIRMAN. It is moved and seconded that we adjourn sine die—all in favor signify their assent by saying "aye." [All voted aye.] ˙ The ayes have it—and we do now adjourn.

PEARL E. MOTZER,
Secretary Laundry Conference.

CONSTANTINE EXHIBIT NO. 1.

CONSTITUTION AND BY-LAWS OF THE EMPLOYERS' ASSOCIATION OF WASHINGTON.

[Organized February 9, 1911.]

DECLARATION OF PRINCIPLE.

We believe in harmonious industrial relations between employer and employee, and that the latter shall receive adequate compensation and timely advancement for his services, measured by his individual efforts. We shall not countenance any employer who does not pay a fair day's wages for a fair day's work. Nor any employee who shirks a fair day's work for a fair day's pay.

We are unalterably opposed to the principle of the closed shop. It is un-American and illegal and unfair to the independent workman who does not desire to join a union, to the employer who prefers to operate an open shop, and to the public. Therefore, we shall defend the right of every workman to be free to dispose of his time and skill advantageously, and we shall maintain the right of every employer to conduct an open shop.

We are strenuously opposed to lockouts, strikes, sympathetic strikes, boycotts, and kindred evils. We will resist those selfish interests which through coercion, false statements, and violence disrupt the relations of peace and unity existing between the just employer and his employees.

Law and order are essential to the commercial progress and development of the communities of our State. We pledge our support to the properly constituted authorities for the impartial enforcement of law and the strict maintenance of order at all times and in all places, so that the communities of our State may enjoy their constitutional and inalienable rights to peace, liberty, and security for life and property.

BY-LAWS.

ARTICLE I.

NAME.

The name of this organization shall be The Employers' Association of Washington.

ARTICLE II.

MEMBERSHIP.

SECTION 1. The membership shall consist of individuals, corporations, partnerships, and employers' associations employing labor in any branch of industry. Any such individual, corporation, partnership, or employers' association may acquire membership in this association and have representation as provided by Article V after signing the membership roll and payment of dues.

SEC. 2. Members shall be elected by the board of directors in such manner as the board may prescribe.

SEC. 3. Each individual, corporation, partnership, or employers' association holding membership in the association, and entitled to vote, shall designate one person to represent him or it in the association; the person so designated may be represented by proxy, provided such proxy is presented by a partner in a firm or an officer or director in any corporation which may be a member of the association, by consent of a majority of the members of the board of directors present at any meeting.

ARTICLE III.

OFFICERS AND DIRECTORS.

SECTION 1. The government of this association shall be exercised by a board of directors of —— members who shall be elected at the first meeting of the association, one-third of whom shall serve one year, one-third two years, and one-third three years, the length of service of each class to be determined by lot.

The annual meeting of the association shall be held on the second Thursday in February of each year, at 2.30 p. m., at the rooms of the association in Seattle, at which annual meeting —— members to replace the outgoing class shall be elected by ballot as members of the board of directors, whose terms of office shall be three years. Any vacancies in the other classes shall also be filled at the annual meeting by ballot, and a majority of the votes cast shall be necessary to elect.

Special meetings of the association shall be called by the president upon written request of nine members. Notice of special meetings shall be mailed to each member at least three days prior to the date of holding such meetings.

SEC. 2. The board of directors shall meet within one week following the annual meeting, and shall elect from its members a president, vice president, and treasurer, who shall hold office until the next annual meeting or until their successors are elected and qualified. The board of directors shall also appoint a secretary and manager; one person may hold both offices.

SEC. 3. The board of directors shall hold regular meetings on the second Tuesday of each month, unless otherwise ordered. Special meetings may be called at any time by order of the president, and shall also be called at the request in writing of three members of the board. Seven members of the board shall constitute a quorum. The board of directors may fill any vacancy in its body by election by ballot from the members of the association, to hold office until the next annual meeting.

SEC. 4. The board of directors shall attend to all matters referred to it by the association; shall govern, manage, and act for the association in all emergencies; shall reject or approve applications for membership and resignations; shall suspend or expel members for cause. It may appoint employees and agents of the association, prescribe their duties, fix their compensation, and appropriate such sums from the treasury of this association for such purposes as it may deem necessary.

SEC. 5. The president, or in his absence, the vice president, shall preside at all meetings of the association and board of directors. In the event of their absence, a meeting of the association or board of directors may elect its presiding officer. The president shall, with the manager, sign all written contracts and obligations of the association. He shall appoint all committees for the current fiscal year, and shall have power at all times to fill vacancies in such committees. He shall perform such other duties as the board of directors may assign to him.

SEC. 6. The president shall appoint the following standing committees: An executive committee of five members, a finance committee of five members, and a membership committee of five members.

The executive committee may be appointed every three months and shall serve until their successors are appointed and qualified. It shall be the duty of the committee to visit the office of the manager from 1.30 to 3 p. m., at least once each week to confer with the manager and direct the work of the association, and shall have full power to conduct the affairs of the association, subject to the approval of the board of directors.

The finance committee shall finance the association, supervise expenditures, and do any and all things to maintain the association on a sound financial basis, subject to the approval of the board of directors.

The membership committee shall devise plans for securing membership and pass upon all applications for membership, subject to the approval of the board of directors.

SEC. 7. The secretary shall keep correct minutes of all meetings, both of the board of directors and the association; shall have the custody of all books and papers, excepting those belonging to the department of the treasurer; shall collect the fees and dues of the members and all other moneys due or coming to the association, and shall pay .the same over to the treasurer, taking his receipt therefor, or the receipt of such bank as the treasurer may designate. He shall keep the records and conduct the general correspondence of the association; he shall notify each person elected to membership of his election, and that upon signing the by-laws he will be a member of the association.

SEC. 8. The treasurer shall receive from the secretary all moneys belonging to the association and shall receipt for and keep a correct account of the same. He shall pay out such moneys only upon written order of the manager, countersigned by the president. He shall make a detailed financial report to the association at each annual meeting, and at such other times as the board of directors may require.

SEC. 9. The officers and employees of the association shall, if so requested by the board of directors, give surety bonds for the faithful discharge of their duties in such sums as the board of directors may from time to time require. At the expiration of their several terms all officers shall turn over to their successors all moneys, property, books, and papers of the association in their possession. All bonds shall be for the benefit of and payable to the association; the surety companies issuing such bonds shall be selected by the board of directors, and the premiums therefor shall be paid for by the association.

SEC. 10. Fifteen members of the association shall be a quorum at any meeting for the transaction of business.

SEC. 11. A committee, to consist of five members of the association, to nominate directors for the ensuing year, shall be elected by ballot by the board of directors at a regular meeting of the board one month preceding the annual meeting of the association.' The duty of such committee shall be to nominate members who have consented to serve for the term of three years, and as many other as may be required to fill any vacancy in the board which may have occurred during the year. Said committee shall make and sign such recommendation, and report to the board of directors the names of the parties recommended by them, at least 10 days prior to the date of the annual meeting.

`ARTICLE IV.

SECTION 1. The monthly dues of the members of this association shall be—

	Per month in advance.
Less than 5 employees	$1. 00
Over 5 less than 10 employees	1. 50
Over 10 less than 15 employees	2. 00
Over 15 less than 20 employees	2. 50
Over 20 less than 30 employees	3. 00
Over 30 less than 35 employees	3. 50
Over 35 less than 40 employees	5. 00
Over 40 less than 50 employees	7. 50
Over 50 less than 75 employees	10. 00
Over 75 less than 100 employees	12. 50
Over 100 less than 150 employees	15. 00
Over 150 less than 200 employees	20. 00
Over 200 less than 250 employees	25. 00
Over 250 less than 300 employees	30. 00
Over 300 less than 350 employees	35. 00
Over 350 less than 400 employees	40. 00
Over 400 less than 500 employees	50. 00

CONTRIBUTING MEMBERS.

This membership is confined to individuals, partnerships, and corporations not especially employing men, but interested in the work of the association.

Dues from $1 to $50 per month.

SEC. 2. Additional funds may be provided for by special assessments, the amount of which shall be determined by the board of directors.

SEC. 3. Any member three months in arrears in payment or assessments of dues may be suspended or expelled by a two-thirds vote of the board of directors.

SEC. 4. Any member who is in arrears for a period of 90 days in the payment of any sum due the association shall not be entitled to the benefits of member-·ship in the association in the settlement of any difficulty arising between himself and his employees: *Provided, however,* That the board of directors may after careful consideration and by a majority vote grant to any such member. the privilege of participating in all of the benefits of membership.

ARTICLE V.

VOTING POWER OF MEMBERS.

·Each member in good standing shall be entitled to one vote: *Provided,* That when assessments paid by a member exceed $100 per annum, he shall be entitled to one additional vote for each $100 so paid. No member shall, however, be entitled to more than three votes at any association meeting.

ARTICLE VI.

SECTION 1. These by-laws may be amended at any meeting of· the association by a two-third vote of the members present. Notice and copies of proposed amendments shall be furnished to the secretary at least 20 days before the date of the meeting at which it is proposed to consider them. The secretary shall cause notice of such meeting to be printed, together with such proposed amendments, and sent to each member at least 10 days prior to the date thereof.

ARTICLE VII.

Roberts's Rules of Order shall be recognized as the standard authority · of this association.

ARTICLE VIII.

The order of business of any meeting of this association shall be:
1. Call to order.
2. Reading the minutes of previous meeting.
3. Reports of officers.
4. Reports of committees.
5. Unfinished business.
6. New business.
7. Election of officers.

CONSTANTINE EXHIBIT NO. 2.

(This pledge was urged upon all candidates to the legislature of 1913 by the labor unions and allies. An agent of the unions in both senate and house recorded the votes of the members and these later were so informed. The method has coercive effect on the legislator.)

JOINT LEGISLATIVE COMMITTEE OF DIRECT LEGISLATION LEAGUE OF WASHINGTON.

[State Federation of Labor, Farmers' Union, State Grange.]

DEAR SIR: The joint legislative committee are anxious to inform their membership and the many other voters of the State who look to them for guidance as to your attitude, if elected to the legislature, on the following issues, upon which these organizations have mutually agreed to support one another in securing the enactment of the legislation thereon.

Your signature in the blank space below each measure outlined signifies that you approve of such legislation and will use your best endeavors to enact same into law in such form as will effectually guard the interests of the masses of the people whom the measure is aimed to benefit.

1. A constitutional amendment granting to the people the right to amend their constitution by the initiative. The accompanying bill (see next page) passed the house (1911 session) by a vote of 77 for, 15 against, and 4 absent. Your signature on the blank line below pledges your support of this bill as

printed, with only such amendments as may be acceptable to the joint legis-**lative committee.**

Signed_____.

2. A law permitting cooperative associations to form corporations' for the **transaction** of any lawful business on the cooperative plan; providing for the payment of interest on paid-up capital stock, setting aside a percentage of the net profits for a reserve fund and the distribution of the remainder of said profits by uniform dividends upon the amount of purchases of shareholders and upon wages and salaries of employees.

Signed_____.

3. A law making it a misdemeanor for any person to demand or receive, either directly or indirectly, from any person seeking employment, or from any person on his behalf, and remuneration whatever for providing him with employment. Also providing free State employment agencies in such number as to facilitate the prompt distribution of labor in response to demands.

Signed_____.

4. A change in the rules of the house and senate which will eliminate the power of the rules committee over legislation by substituting a system whereby each senator and representative will by a vote express his preference as to what bills shall be considered daily those measures having the highest vote to have preference on the calendar.

Signed_____.

5. A law providing for the regulation and supervision by the State of investment companies or other corporations organized to sell stocks or bonds to the public, in a manner similar to the present system of bank examination, the purpose being to prevent the fleecing of innocent people by wild-cat companies organized for such purposes.

Signed_____.

Address_____

Legislative district_____.

NOTE.—Read carefully the explanatory notes and references on next page, showing the needs of the above legislation. Failure to sign and return to the undersigned within 10 days will be construed as a negative answer. Your reply will be given the fullest possible publicity in order that those interested may know your attitude toward these measures.

Explanatory remarks may be written on the back thereof.

Sign and return to_____.

Very truly, yours,

Address_____.

EXPLANATORY NOTES.

1. Proposed amendment to our State constitution giving the people the right to initiate amendments to our constitution. The following is the bill referred to in the preceding pledge:

AN ACT To amend section 1 of Article XXIII of the constitution of the State of Washington, relating to amendments, and providing for the amendment of the constitution by the initiative.

Be it enacted by the Legislature of the State of Washington,
SECTION 1. That at the general election to be held in this State on the Tuesday next succeeding the first Monday in November, 1914, there shall be submitted to the qualified electors of the State of Washington for their adoption or rejection an amendment of section 1 of Article XXIII of the constitution of the State of Washington, relating to amendments and providing for the amendment of the constitution by the initiative, so that the same shall read as follows:

ARTICLE XXIII.

SECTION 1. Any amendment or amendments to this constitution may be proposed in either branch of the legislature, or by the people, as hereinafter specified; and if the same shall be proposed by the legislature and agreed to by two-thirds of the members elected to each of the two houses, such proposed amendment or amendments shall be entered on their journals, with the ayes and noes thereon, and be submitted to the qualified electors of the State for their approval at the next general election: *Provided, however,* That the people reserve to themselves the power to propose, independent of the legisla_ture, any amendment or amendments to this constitution by petition setting fourth the full text of such proposed amendments, signed by not less than 10 per cent, nor in any case more than 50,000 of the legal voters of this State, the percentage required to be determined from the whole number of electors who voted for governor at the regular gubernatorial election last preceding the filing of any petition, and filed with the secretary of state at least four months prior to the next regular election, who shall submit the same to the people for their approval or rejection at the next regular general election; and if the people approve and ratify such amendments or amendment by a majority of the electors voting thereon, the same shall become a part of this constitution, and proclamation thereof shall be made by the governor: *Provided,* That if more than one amendment be submitted, they shall be submitted in such a manner that the people may vote for or against each amendment separately.

The style of all bills for constitutional amendment proposed by initiative petition shall be: *"Be it enacted by the people of the State of Washington."*

SEC. 2. The secretary of state shall cause the amendment proposed in sec_tion 1 of this act to be published for three months next preceding the said election therein described in some weekly newspaper in every county where a newspaper is published throughout the State.

SEC. 3. There shall be printed on all ballots provided for the said election the words:

"For the proposed amendment of section 1 of Article XXIII of the constitu_tion, relating to amendments, and providing for the amendment of the con_stitution by the initiative."

"Against the proposed amendment to section 1 of Article XXIII of the con_stitution, relating to amendment, and providing for the amendment of the con_stitution by the initiative."

SEC. 4. If it shall appear from the ballots cast at the said election that a majority of the qualified electors voting upon the question of the adoption of the said amendment have voted in favor of the same, the governor shall make proc_lamation of the same in the manner provided by law, and the said amendment shall be held to have been adopted and to have been a part of the constitution from the time of such proclamation.

(Read Review of Legislative Proceedings by Joint Legislative Committee under heading "To amend the constitution by the initiative" (H. B.), No. 60.)

2. The growing tendency of to-day toward cooperative institutions in the fruit, grain, dairy, and other farm products, cooperative factories, workshops, banks, and stores makes it imperative that legislation be enacted in the interests of those who participate in such cooperative corporations, to the end that uni_formity of organization and methods of conducting such institutions in the inter_ests of the great number of shareholders will be adhered to. Wisconsin has such a law, which commends itself to our people.

3. Private employment agencies, in their endeavor to bring the man and the job together, have to a large degree become systematic machines to exploit workmen for the financial gain of themselves and the employers or foremen with whom they frequently divide the profits of the business. Ex-Mayor Pratt, of the city of Spokane, cites as an illustration of the evils of the present system the case of a laborer that was sent 14 times upon one job of work by the same employment agency, paying a $2 fee each time, earning $120 and paying out $28 in employment-agency fees.

Efforts of other States to regulate paid employment agencies have in a large degree failed. The Federal Government, which enacts legislation in behalf of the sailors, has succeeded by striking directly at the heart of the evil and mak_ing it a misdemeanor to withhold any fees from a seaman's wages for having secured him employment. This does not eliminate paid employment agencies, but shifts the costs of fees, if any, from the employee to the employer. Such a law, together with State free employment agencies, will most effectually solve the question of prompt, economic, and successful distribution of labor in response to honest demands.

4. *Power of the rules or calendar committee.*—Read Review of Legislative Proceedings by Joint Legislative Committee, under heading "Organization of legislature and committee on rules and order," and you will immediately see the need of the change to a majority-rule system.

· ·5. The necessity of regulation and supervision of all companies selling stock or bonds to the public, so that assurance may be given that the company is not a ·fake, but a legitimate investment, is apparent ·to all. · Under such a law (blue-sky law)·Kansas has driven from the State all fake·investment companies. With its adoption an innocent·public would be protected from being fleeced by United Wireless and similar companies organized for no other purpose.

Inquiries for further information addressed to any of the undersigned will be promptly replied to.

Trusting that you will carefully consider these matters and make your reply on the inclosed pledge blank, we remain,

FRED J. CHAMBERLAIN,
Chairman, Puyallup, Wash.,
ALMER MCCURTAIN,
Davenport, Wash.,
CHAS. R. CASE,
Secretary-Treasurer, 1518 Sixteenth Avenue North, Seattle,
Joint Legislative Committee.

CONSTANTINE EXHIBIT NO. 3.

STOP! LOOK! LISTEN!

INTERNATIONAL BROTHERHOOD OF ELECTRICAL WORKERS,
. LOCAL UNION No. 77,
Seattle, Wash.

DEAR SIR: Very recently a business man in Seattle who has more than $10,000 invested in an enterprise signed a contract for two years with "The Electric Co.," legally known as the Puget Sound Traction, Light & Power. Co. This company some two years ago was declared unfair to organized labor in Seattle and vicinity. This man claimed he did not know this fact. His receipts dropped to such an extent that in a short time he would have been compelled to go, out of business. He investigated and found the cause. He thereupon applied to the Central Labor Council of Seattle and vicinity and an investigation was made by a committee of said council. He claimed he did not know the facts, and the committee, believing him, relieved him of further loss by a report the gist of which was published in the Union Record and Seattle Herald of recent date. He will in the future stop, look, and listen.

Do you wish to be placed in the same predicament without the excuse· he gave? You can not say you did not know—this informs you of the fact that the Puget Sound Traction, Light & Power Co. is unfair to organized labor. If you are using this unfair product of this unfair company and your receipts are not coming up to your expectations, you will know the cause of at least a part of the lack of income.

If you are contemplating using electric light and power it would be advisable to sign a contract with the city of Seattle—your own company—for light and power. Every user of city light in any business is known to Local Union No. 77, International Brotherhood of Electrical Workers. They send communications to the other 105 affiliated unions, representing about 60,000 population in this city and vicinity, and they are always on the job. A word to the wise is sufficient. Don't afterwards say "I did not know" (it was loaded).

Stop! Look! Listen! For city light—your own plant and property—call Main 8500, Local 56, and a solicitor will be sent you.

Yours, truly,

LOCAL UNION No. 77, I. B. E. W.

(This· letter was sent out by the above union to a large number of retail establishments during the summer of 1914. It is typical of their methods of intimidation.—*Earl Constantine, Manager.*)

CENTRAL LABOR COUNCIL OF SEATTLE AND VICINITY,
Seattle, Wash., May 30, 1914.

DEAR SIR: A letter was read at the last regular meeting of this council again calling our attention to the fact that you are still employing Japanese help in your kitchen, and I was instructed to notify you that as·long as an American citizen continues such practice while there are thousands of people, citizens of·

REPORT OF COMMISSION ON INDUSTRIAL RELATIONS.

this country, out of work, we condemn such practice and will warn every one
from patronizing such eating places. We hope and trust that some day the very.
Japanese which you are employing will open up a place next door to you and
take all trade away from you and send your good American dollars to Japan. ·
.You can not afford to ruin your business, but you can build it up; and I trust
that you will give this matter a little better than passing attention and turn
your eating place into that kind in which every American citizen would like to
eat, and eliminate that yellow streak that at this time mars your concern.
Very truly, yours,

R. LOEWE, *Secretary.*

(This letter was sent to several delicatessen restaurants, and illustrates one
of the coercive methods commonly employed by. unions in attempting to
unionize retail shops.—*Earl Constantine, Manager.*)

McMAHON EXHIBIT.

CONTRACT FOR FISHING SEASON 191__.

Whereas _____, hereinafter designated as the party of the first part,
is engaged in the business of hiring men for the purpose of working in the
canneries of the Pacific coast; and whereas the undersigned, _____,
hereinafter designated as the party of the second part, is desirous of being
employed by the party of the first part:

Now, therefore, for and in consideration of the party of the first part securing employment by the party of the second part, and for certain other good
and valuable considerations passing to the party of the second part from the
party of the first part, and for the further consideration of the covenants and
agreements hereinafter set forth, it is agreed herein by and between the said
party of the first part and the party of the second part, as follows:

· 1. The said party of the second part is hereby employed to work for the said
party of the first part for the entire season of 1914 at _____ and in and
about and around such cannery, or in, around, and about such other cannery
as may be hereafter designated by the party of the first part. ·

2. It is expressly agreed and understood by and between the party of the first
part and the party of the second part that the fishing season for 191__ shall
commence at such time as is designated by the party of the first part, and shall
end at such time as is designated by the party of the first part, and shall commence when the party of the first part has secured transportation for the
party of the second part, and when the sailing ship or steamboat is ready to
leave any port in the State of Washington, or any port, for such cannery or
canneries as may be designated by the party of the first part, and shall not
end until after the full fishing season at such cannery or canneries so designated by the party of the first part shall have ceased, and until all the fish
canned at said cannery shall have been canned, the cans lacquered, labeled, and
cased, and the casings fully stenciled and ready to be loaded upon the steamer
or boat to be transported from said place of shipment. ·

3. That during the fishing season of 1914, each day's work by the party of
the second part shall be 11 hours, from 6 o'clock a. m. until 6 o'clock p. m. ' ·

4. That no extra time shall be allowed in any manner whatsoever for time
prior to the run of fish, during which time the party of the second part, or other
employees, are preparing and making cans.

5. The party of the first part agrees to pay to the party of the second part for
said full season's work the following-named sum, to wit, the sum of $200
(usually $150), and in addition thereto agrees to pay to the party of the second
part 15 cents per hour as overtime for all work done by the party of the second
part between the hours of 6 o'clock p. m. and 6 o'clock a. m., but no overtime or
Sunday work shall be allowed for making cans.

6. The party of the second part shall be paid $1.65 per day for Sunday work
during the run of fish and 15 cents per hour as overtime between the hours
of 6 o'clock p. m. and 6 a. m., when it is necessary that the party of the second
part shall work to take care of the run of fish.

7. If requested to work on Sunday or overtime, the party of the second part
shall do so at any time, under the direction of the Chinese foreman, the Japanese
foreman, or the agent or person in charge of the cannery, and if the second party

shall refuse to work on Sunday or overtime, then the party of the first part shall have the right to deduct from all wages due the party of the second the sum of 25 cents per hour for each hour that the said second party shall refuse to work on Sunday or overtime, and the same shall be deducted from the wages of the party of the second part at the end of the season.

8. It is further agreed that should the party of the second part strike, refuse to work, cease work, or demand higher wages, the party of the first part shall have the right to employ a third person or persons to take the place of said person who may strike, refuse to work, or demand higher wages, or additional board or food, and in that event all amounts earned by the said person so employed to take the place of the party of the second part who shall cease to work, strike, or demand higher wages, additional board, or food shall be deducted by the party of the first part from the amount due to the party of the second part at the end of the season.

It is further agreed that if the cannery at which the party of the second part has hereby agreed to work should burn down or be destroyed, or if the work at said cannery should close before the end of the fishing season for said year, the party of the first part shall have the right to remove the party of the second part from such cannery to any other cannery or canneries in order to complete a full season's work as herein agreed, and should the cannery at which the party of the second part is employed burn or be blown down or cease to work before the end of the fishing season and should the said party of the second part refuse to be transferred to such other cannery or canneries as the party of the first part may designate, he shall collect under this agreement in such amount as the time which he worked before the destruction or shutting down of said cannery actually bears to a full season's work, and no more, and should said cannery at which the party of the second part has herein agreed to work be blown down or destroyed before the end of the fishing season, and should the party of the first part not being able to transfer the party of the second part to some other cannery or canneries, then the amount which the party of the first part shall pay under this agreement is such sum only as the time actually worked by the party of the second part bears to a full season's work.

9. The party of the first part shall pay the transportation of the party of the second part both ways from Seattle to the cannery and return, provided the party of the second remains and works the full season as herein agreed; but if the said party of the second part does not remain and work for the full season then there shall be charged up to the party of the second part and deducted from his wages his transportation both ways.

10. It is agreed and understood by and between the party of the first part and the party of the second part that board shall be furnished to the party of the second part by the Chinese contractor, the same as is usually furnished to Chinese laborers, and that the owner or owners of the cannery shall furnish to the party of the second part a place to sleep in some building or tent provided for that purpose.

11. The party of the second part agrees to remain at the same class of work during the whole of the season; but the foreman of the cannery, or the person in authority, may change the party of the second part to any other work he desires in and about the cannery or canneries; and there shall be no increase or decrease of wages by reason of the change of work.

12. If the party of the second part does not do the work that he is directed to do by any foreman in the manner designated, or if the party of the second part is incapacitated by sickness or any injury he may receive by reason of his own fault, or on account of any person whomsoever, the party of the second part shall be charged 25 cents per hour for each hour that he does not work and 25 cents for each meal that he may receive while not working, and the said amount or amounts shall be deducted from his wages at the end of the season.

13. It is further agreed that as soon as the fish begin to run the party of the second part must be in bed not later than the hour of 10 o'clock at night, and no gambling, carousing, brawling, shouting, or loud noises shall be indulged in, in, around, or about the cannery or sleeping places of the party of the second part, or of any other laborer after the said hour of 10 o'clock p. m., and should the party of the second part not obey this provision, then and in that event the foreman in charge of the cannery, the Chinese foreman, or the Japanese foremen, shall have the right to deduct the sum of $5 for each time the party of the second part shall be guilty of any such prohibited conduct,

said sum to be deducted from the wages of the party of the second part at the end of the season.

14. The party of the second part further agrees that he will not sell, give, or furnish any liquor to any Indian or Indians or to any person employed in, around, or about the said cannery in which he may be working during the continuance of this contract, and if he fails to keep this provision, then and in that event he shall work a forfeiture to the party of the first part of any and all wages and claims due to the party of the second part under and by virtue of this contract.

15. Should the party of the second part engage in brawls or fights, or become intoxicated, or shout or make loud noises after the hour of 10 o'clock p. m. during any of the said fishing season, the party of the first part shall have the right to forfeit this contract and to retain as liquidated damages to the party of the first part 25 cents for each hour of work from the time said contract is forfeited until the end of the fishing season, and shall have the right to discharge the party of the second part for any such conduct.

16. It is further agreed that the party of the second part shall pay to the party of the first part the sum of $3.50 per season as part of the consideration for obtaining said employment and in consideration of the party of the first storing any personal property which may be left with the party of the first part by the party of the second part, and for forwarding any and all mail that may come into possession of the party of the first part for the party of the second part to such cannery as the party of the second part may be employed, said sum to be deducted from the wages of the party of the second part at the end of the season.

17. All wages for the season shall be paid at the end of the season, at the office of the party of the first part, in the city of Seattle, King County, Wash., within seven days after the return of the party of the second part to Seattle.

18. It is further agreed by and between the parties hereto that any money that may be loaned or advanced by the party of the first part to the party of the second part before the beginning of the fishing season may be deducted from the wages of the party of the second part at the end of the season.

19. If the party of the second part shall willfully destroy any property owned by the person or company owning any cannery at which the party of the second part may be employed, or any property belonging to the Chinese contractor at said cannery or the foreman of the party of the first part, the value of all such property so destroyed shall be deducted from the wages of the party of the second part at the end of the fishing season's work.

20. The party of the second part has been fully informed and knows that neither the Japanese foreman in charge of the Japanese laborers, the Chinese foreman, or any person whomsoever other than the party of the first part has any authority to alter, change, or modify any of the terms or conditions of this agreement or to contract any bill or to incur any liability or indebtedness for any purpose whatever and that any such alteration or attempted alteration if made by any person other than the party of the first part shall be absolutely void, and that the parties to this agreement shall be held and firmly bound by this contract as originally signed and entered into between the parties hereto and not by any change or modification thereof.

21. The party of the first part shall deduct from the earnings of the party of the second part under this contract, at or before final payment is made, all charges for any and all goods or merchandise which the party of the second part shall procure from the owner of the cannery, the Chinese contractor, the Japanese foreman, or the Chinese foreman at the said cannery.

22. The party of the second part and the party of the third part hereto fully understand this agreement and all the covenants set forth and contained herein, and they and each of them agree to be bound thereby; they and each of them both understand that the party of the first part has heretofore made and entered into a binding contract with the Chinese contractor at the cannery, or canneries to which the said party of the second part may be sent to perform labor, binding contracts to furnish healthy, sober, industrious, and competent Japanese laborers to perform the work and labor which the party of the second part has agreed to perform; that the canneries to which the party of the second part has hereby agreed to be sent are remote from places where laborers may be conveniently obtained and that the party of the first part will sustain damages in an amount equal to or greater than any amounts provided herein should the party of the second part fail to faithfully keep and perform each and all of the covenants and conditions of this agreement. The

said parties hereto understand that if the party of the second part shall go upon a strike or cease to work, or become intoxicated, or engage in brawls, or furnish liquor to the Indians or any laborer at said cannery or canneries, the Chinese contractor and his foreman have the right to demand that the party of the first part shall, or his foreman shall, discharge the party of the second part and remove the party of the second part from said cannery, and that the party of the second part, in such event, will be charged for all meals thereafter consumed at said cannery by the party of the second part after being discharged, and that the said Chinese contractor has the right to charge against the party of the first part the sum of 25 cents per hour for all time which the party of the second part shall refuse to faithfully work, as provided in this agreement, and that this is the reason why this contract is made as it is made, and in order that the party of the second part shall faithfully perform said contract and perform the full season's work as herein agreed, not only during the time the fish are actually being caught and canned, but until all the fish are caught and canned, the cans tested, lacquered, labeled, and cased, and the cases nailed and fully stenciled ready for shipment.

In witness whereof the parties to this agreement have hereunto set their hands and seals this_____day of____:_____, A. D. 191__.

_____ _____ [SEAL.]
_____ _____ [SEAL.]
.   _____ _____ [SEAL.]

BROWN EXHIBIT.

No. 92.

EASTERN RAILWAY & LUMBER CO.

CENTRALIA, WASH., *July 31, 1914.*

Pay-roll statement.

Name: Kessler, A.

Wages: 4.5 hours, at $1.50 _____ $6.75
Less 10 per cent_____ .67

                                                                    6.08

Balance due, per check herewith_____ 6.08

No. 83.

EASTERN RAILWAY & LUMBER CO.

CENTRALIA, WASH., *July 31, 1914.*

Pay-roll statement.

Name: Bristow, L. B.

Wages: 22.4 hours, at $1.75_____ $39.20
Less 10 per cent_____ 3.92

                                                                    35.28
Total deductions_____ 1.00

Balance due, per check herewith_____ 34.28
                                                                    1.58

                                                                    35.86

No. 46.

EASTERN RAILWAY & LUMBER Co.

CENTRALIA, WASH., *July 31, 1914.*

Pay-roll statement.

Name : Ogden, M.

```
Wages: 4.5 hours, at $1.75_____ $7.87
Less 10 per cent_____   .78
                                                                      ─────
                                                                      7.09
                                                                      ═════
     Balance due, per check herewith_____ 7.09
                                                                      1.58
                                                                      ─────
                                                                      8.67
```

No. 28.

EASTERN RAILWAY & LUMBER Co.

CENTRALIA, WASH., *June 30, 1914.*

Pay-roll statement.

Name : Sage, S. A.   Month : June.

```
Wages: 26.2 hours, at $1.75_____ $45.85
Less 10 per cent_____   4.58
                                                                      ─────
                                                                      41.27
Deductions:
     Cash_____ $6.00
     Rent_____  7.00
                                                            ─────
     Total deductions_____ 13.00
                                                                      ─────
     Balance due, per check herewith_____ 28.27
```

No. 34.

EASTERN RAILWAY & LUMBER Co.

CENTRALIA, WASH., *June 30, 1914.*

Pay-roll statement.

Name : Sage, W. H.   Month : June.

```
Wages: 20.2 hours, at $1.75_____ $35.35
Less 10 per cent_____   3.53
                                                                      ─────
                                                                      31.82
Deductions:
     Cash_____ $10.00
     Hospital _____   1.00
                                                            ──────
     Total deductions_____ 11.00
                                                                      ─────
     Balance due, per check herewith_____ 20.82
```

EASTERN RAILWAY & LUMBER CO.

CENTRALIA, WASH., *July 31, 1914.*

Pay-roll statement.

Name: Sage, W. H.

24.4 hours, at $1.75	$42. 70
per cent	4. 27
	38. 43
ductions	1. 00
ɪlance due, per check herewith	37. 43
	1. 58
	39. 01

COONEY EXHIBIT NO. 1.

Wages.	Sawmill.	Planing mill.	Box factory.	Handling.	Tank and pump factory.	Dry kiln.	Machine shop.	Carpenter and blacksmith shop.	Mess hall.	Power.	Shingle mill.	Total.
onth, including												
			10									10
									15			15
	20	13	88	114	2	20	2	1		11	2	273
	15	8	17	16		5	1	1	2	4	1	70
	9	10	14	17	1	2		1	1	6	3	64
	6	3	2	4	1		1					17
	2		1		1				1		5	10
	1	1	2				1		2	1	1	9
	1						7	6			1	14
							6	1				8
									1			1
									2			2
ay, not includ-:												
		5	9	2	3		1			1		21
	1	1	4	2			2					10
		1	3	3						1	1	9
	2	1	3	9								15
			1		1						4	6
	1	2	4	3		1				1		12
	1										1	2
	2	2	2	1			1			1		9
								1				1
	4	2	2	7	2		2			2	3	24
	1		1	2			2	3				9
	1	2		2				1			4	10
	1		1	1		1	3	3				10
	4	2		1				1			2	10
	1											1
	2		1	1			1			1	4	10
	2	1		1	1							5
											1	1
				1								1
	3		1					2				6
	2						1					2
	1											1
	1											1
		1										1
			1									1
	1											1
	1										1	1
	1											1
	87	55	167	187	12	30	30	21	24	30	33	676

$2.40.
ɪs, $19 to $22 per week.
16 and 25 cents per thousand.
) and 12 cents per thousand.
914.

Clerical force and various foremen, June, 1914 :			Clerical force and various foremen, June, 1914—Continued :		
1 at $250		$250	1 at $100		$100
4 at $200		800	1 at $85		85
1 at $175		175	1 at $80		80
1 at $165		165	2 at $55		110
2 at $150		300			
2 at $125		250	18		2, 635
2 at $110		220			

COONEY EXHIBIT NO. 2.

Log boom.—Scaler, $7.70 per day, no board; first boom man, $3.50 per day, no board; second boom man, $3 per day, no board; third boom man, $2.50 per day, no board.

Sawmill filing room.—Head filer, $7 per day, no board; second filer, $4.50 per day, no board; first helper, $3 per day, no board; second helper, $50 per month and board.

Sawmill.—Foreman, $4.25 per day, no board; pond man, $2.25 per day, no board; deck man, head rig, $35 per month and board; sawyer, head rig, $6.50 per day, no board; setter, head rig, $2.75 per day, no board; doggers, head rig, $2.40 per day, no board; off-bearers, head rig, $35 per month and board; sawmill oilers, $2.90 per day, no board; second sawmill oiler, $2.50 per day, no board.

Side rig: Deck man, $35 per month and board; sawyer, $4.25 per day, no board; setter, $2.30 per day, no board; doggers, $35 per month and board; off-bearers, $35 per month and board.

Edger: Edger man, $4.25 per day, no board; edger man's helper, $35 per month and board; off-bearer from edger, $30 per month and board; lever man for live rolls, $40 per month and board; slasher man, $35 per month and board.

Trimmers: Trimmer man, $3.50 per day, no board; trimmer feeder, head end, $40 per month and board; trimmer feeder, tail end, $2.30 per day, no board; trimmer, deck, $35 per month and board.

Sorting chains: Foreman, $3 per day, no board; marker, $3 per day, no board; laborers, $26 to $35 per month and board; resawyer, $3.25 per day, no board.

Lath mill.—Foreman, $3.25 per day, no board; bolter man, $35 per month and board; feeder, $35 per month and board; lath puller, $35 per month and board; lath tier, $30 per month and board; laborers, $26 to $30 per month and board.

Machine shop.—Shovelers, $30 to $35 per month and board; master mechanic, $6.75 per day, no board; shop foreman, $4.50 per day, no board; assistant to shop foreman, $3.25 per day, no board; machinists, $55 to $60 per month and board; engineer, $2.70 per day, no board; electrician, $2.70 per day, no board; sprinkler man, $2.50 per day, no board; pipe fitter, $2.50 per day, no board; steam fitter, $2.90 per day, no board; apprentices, $30 to $40 per month and board; head fireman, $2.50 per day, no board.

Blacksmith and carpenter shop.—Head blacksmith $4 per day, no board; horseshoer, $3 per day, no board; apprentices, $35 per month and board; head millwright, $4 per day, no board; carpenters, $2.50 per day, no board; millwrights, $50 to $60 per month and board.

Handling.—Fir-yard foreman, $3.50 per day, no board; spruce-yard foreman, $2.70 per day, no board; stacker foreman, $2.50 per day, no board; dry-kiln foreman, $3 per day; shipping foreman, $3.85 per day, no board; car checker, $3.25 per day, no board; tallymen, $40 to $50 per month and board, finish grader, $2.65 per day, no board; laborers, $26 to $35 per month and board.

Tank mill.—Foreman, $3.50 per day, no board; helper, $45 per month and board; cut-off men, $2.50 per day, no board; laborers, $26 to $30 per month and board.

Mess house.—Steward, $175 per month, board and room; assistant steward, $80 per month, board and room; head cook, $80 per month, board and room; second cook, $45 per month, board and room; baker, $70 per month, board and room; butcher, $50 per month, board and room, flunkeys, $25 to $35 per month, board and room; laborers, $26 per month, board and room.

Shingle mill.—Foreman, $5.75 per day, no board; filer, $4 per day, no board; cut-off man, $3.25 per day, no board; power bolter man, $3.25 per day, no board;

knee bolter, $3.75 per day, no board; deck man, $2.75 per day, no board; pond man, $2.75 per day, no board; sawyers, 16 and 25 cents per M, no board; packers, 9 and 12 cents per M, no board; tallyman, mill, $3.25 per day, no board; tallyman, car, $2.75 per day, no board; engineer, $3 per day, no board; fireman, $2.50 per day, no board; millwright, $3.25 per day, no board; block piler, $2.50 per day, no board; laborers, $2.50 per day, no board; sprinkler man, $3 per day, no board; watchman, $2 per day, no board.

Planing mill.—Foreman, $5.20 yer day, no board; machinists, $3.50 per day, no board; filer, $2.75 per day, no board; feeders, $35 per month and board; graders, $40 to $50 per month and board; tiers, $30 per month and board; head grader, $3 per day, no board; ripsaw feeders, $35 per month and board; resawer, $40 per month and board; laborers, $26 to $30 per month and board.

Box factory.—Foreman, $6.25 per day, no board; assistant foreman, $4 per day, no board; floorwalkers, $2.30 per day, no board; tallyman, $3.25 per day, no board; resawers, $2.10 per day, no board; nailers, $30 to $35 per month and board; printing, $30 to $35 per month and board; tiers, $30 to $35 per month and board; head tier, $40 per month and board; planer man, $50 per month and board; feeders, $35 per month and board; cut-off men, $30 to $35 per month and board; ripsawyers, $30 to $35 per month and board; offbearers rip and cut-off saws, $26 to $30 per month and board; oiler, $35 per month and board; first fireman, $2.75 per day, no board; fireman's helpers, $39 per month and board, head filer, $5.25 per day, no board; filer's helper, $2 per day, no board; laborers, $26 to $30 per month and board.

RUCKER EXHIBIT.

Statement covering married and single men employed by Rucker Bros. and period of their employment at their mills and camps; Aug. 1, 1916.

SAW AND SHINGLE MILL.

	Married.	Single.		Married.	Single.
Length of service:			Length of service—Contd.		
1 month	4	5	3 years 5 months	1	2
2 months	1	4	3 years 6 months		3
3 months	6	11	3 years 7 months	4	1
4 months	10	10	4 years	12	3
5 months	2	2			
7 months	5	1	Total 4 years	20	11
8 months	1				
9 months	1		4 years 4 months	2	1
10 months	1	1	4 years 5 months	2	1
11 months		2	4 years 6 months	1	
1 year	6	9	4 years 7 months	1	1
			4 years 8 months	1	
Total 1 year	37	45	4 years 10 months	1	
			5 years	4	1
1 year 1 month	1	1			
1 year 3 months	3	2	Total 5 years	12	4
1 year 4 months	2	1			
1 year 5 months	1	1	5 years 3 months	2	1
1 year 6 months		2	5 years 5 months		2
1 year 7 months			5 years 6 months	1	
1 year 8 months	2	2	5 years 7 months	1	
1 year 9 months	1		6 years	1	
1 year 11 months		1			
2 years	3	8	Total 6 years	5	3
Total 2 years	16	18	6 years 6 months	2	
			6 years 8 months	1	
2 years 2 months			7 years	7	1
2 years 3 months	2				
2 years 4 months	4	3	Total 7 years	10	1
2 years 5 months	3	3			
2 years 6 months	1		7 years 3 months	1	
2 years 7 months	1	2	7 years 4 months	4	
2 years 8 months	1	1	7 years 6 months	7	2
3 years	11	2			
			Total 8 years	12	2
Total 3 years	23	11			
			10 years		1
3 years 2 months		1			
3 years 3 months	1		Total 10 years	135	96
3 years 4 months	2	1			

Statement covering married and single men employed by Rucker Bros. and period of their employment at their mills and camps; Aug. 1, 1916—Contd.

LOGGING CAMP.

Length of service:	Married.	Single.	Length of service—Contd.	Married.	Single.
1 month	4	10	1 year, 5 months		6
2 months	2	2	1 year, 6 months	2	
3 months	3	2	1 year, 7 months		3
4 months	2	5	1 year, 8 months	2	6
5 months		4	1 year, 9 months	5	3
6 months		2	1 year, 10 months	2	7
7 months		3	1 year, 11 months		1
8 months	3	1	2 years	1	2
9 months		1	2 years, 3 months		1
10 months	1	3	2 years, 4 months	1	
11 months	2	3	3 years, 10 months	1	
1 year		10	4 years	1	1
1 year, 1 month		3			
1 year, 3 months	2	2	Total	36	81
1 year, 4 months	2				

Number of new men employed Aug. 1, 1913, to Aug. 1, 1914, to keep up force at Hartford mills.

1913:		1914:	
August	8	January	4
September	14	February	1
October	13	March	15
November	1	April	20
December	None.	May	17
		June	2
		July	8

Number of new men employed Aug. 1, 1913, to Aug. 1, 1914, to keep up force at Camp Cavano.

1913:		1914:	
August	11	January	7
September	16	February	4
October	13	March	4
November	7	April	13
December	6	May	14
		June	12
		July	15

Many of the married men own small farms and during the spring and fall months they lay off for the purpose of doing their farm work.

GIBSON EXHIBIT.

CONSTITUTION.

ARTICLE I.

NAME.

SECTION 1. The name of this federation shall be the Federation of Employers' Associations of the Pacific Coast.

ARTICLE II.

OBJECTS.

SECTION 1. This federation is formed to foster and protect the industrial interests of the Pacific coast and adjoining territory.

SEC. 2. To unify the actions of its members upon matters where united and concerted action and a determined, fixed policy may seem wise and necessary.

SEC. 3. To secure for employers and employees the freedom of individual contract in the matter of employment.

SEC. 4. To oppose restriction of output, sympathetic strikes, lockouts, and boycotts, and illegal persecution of individuals, all of which are a menace to the industrial progress of our country, and tend to the undermining of constitutional rights.

SEC. 5. To prevent any interference with persons seeking through honest effort to work and earn a living.

SEC. 6. To prevent or avert industrial disturbances, to harmonize differences between employers and employees, with justice to all concerned, and to assist in the enforcement of the laws of the land.

SEC. 7. The investigation and adjustment by the proper officers of the federation of any question arising between members and their employees which may be referred to and.come within the jurisdiction of the federation.

SEC. 8. The cooperation with other kindred organizations in the United States and Canada in accomplishment of the objects hereinabove stated, upon such terms and conditions as may be determined by the several associations.

ARTICLE III.

MEMBERSHIP.

SECTION 1. Membership in this federation shall embrace all Pacific coast associations and civic bodies directly or indirectly interested in the employment of labor in labor conditions; also corporations, firms, or individuals who are not affiliated with any association which has membership in the federation. All members must sign the roll by their authorized officers and comply with the constitution and by-laws.

ELECTION OF MEMBERS.

SEC. 2. Members will be elected by the executive council in such manner as the board may prescribe.

ARTICLE IV.

GOVERNMENT.

SECTION 1. The government of this federation shall be exercised by an executive council to be elected in the manner hereinafter set forth.

ANNUAL MEETING.

SEC. 2. In October of each year an annual meeting of the various members of this federation shall be held; place and date of meeting to be determined by the executive council.

Prior to the annual meeting each association shall, by ballot, select an elector, who shall be properly credited by them to represent them at the annual meeting, for the purpose of nomination and election of such officers as are provided by the constitution and by-laws.

ELECTORS.

SEC. 3. At the annual meeting of the board of electors to be held for the ensuing year shall be chosen as follows:

One elector from each association member of the federation, provided the total members of said association number less than 500; and one elector for each additional 500 or major part thereof: *Provided, however,* that each separate association shall have not less than one vote or more than three votes on the board of electors.

EXECUTIVE COUNCIL.

SEC. 4. Within 10 days after election the board of electors shall meet at some designated place and elect by ballot in such manner as they may prescribe seven members to be known as the executive council, who shall hold office until their successors shall have been elected and qualified.

OFFICERS.

SEC. 5. The executive council immediately after its election shall organize and elect from among its own members a president, vice president, and treasurer, who shall hold office for one year or until successors are elected and qualified. The executive council shall be the administrative body of this federation and it shall put into effect its rules and regulations and shall have full power to act in such manner as it may deem advisable in the fulfillment of the objects of this federation.

ARTICLE V.

DUTIES OF OFFICERS.

SECTION 1. The duties of the president, vice president, and treasurer shall be the duties that usually pertain to these positions.

BONDS.

· SEC. 2. Bonds shall be required from each officer as may be deemed necessary by the executive council.

EMPLOYEES.

SEC. 3. The executive council may engage such employees as it may deem necessary.

SECRETARY.

SEC. 4. The president shall have the authority to appoint · a secretary for the executive council.

REVENUE.

SEC. 5. The dues and assessments of this federation shall be levied as follows:

Individuals, firms, and corporations employing labor may be admitted as members in the federation with dues not less than $5 per month.

Associations or organizations composed of different employers, who have a membership of less than 50 firms, corporations, or others in their association shall pay $5 per month.

More than 50 members and less than 100 members, $10 per month.

More than 100 members and less than 200 members, $15 per month.

More than 200 members, $25 per month.

The minimum of dues shall be not less than $5 per month, for any individual or association, and all dues shall be paid monthly in advance.

ARTICLE VI.

SECTION 1. This constitution may be amended by a two-thirds vote of the members of the association, either by ballot or by letters, provided the proposed amendment has been mailed to all members of the association at least 10 days before the amendment shall be voted upon. Each organization to have the same voting power as for electors.

BY-LAWS.

ARTICLE I.

PRESIDENT—DUTIES.

SECTION 1. President to call the meetings of the board; in his absence the vice president. Upon petition of three members of the executive council the president must or the petitioners may call said meeting.

ARTICLE II.

SECRETARY—DUTIES.

SECTION 1. Secretary to keep a full and accurate record of the transactions of the federation and perform all the duties that may come to him.

ARTICLE III.

TREASURER—DUTIES.

SECRETARY 1. Treasurer is to have charge of the moneys; disburse same · by vouchers signed by the president and secretary.

To make annual report and to have books properly audited.

ARTICLE IV.

ORDER OF BUSINESS.

(1) Roll call, (2) reading of minutes, (3) report of officers, (4) report of committees, (5) appointment of committees, (6) unfinished business, (7) new business, and (8) election of officers and committees.

ARTICLE V.

AMENDMENTS.

SECTION 1. These by-laws may be amended in the same manner as prescribed for the amendment of articles of constitution.

RULES.

SEC. 2. Cushing's Manual shall be recognized as the standard authority by this federation.

SUPPLEMENTAL STATEMENT OF J. BRUCE GIBSON BEFORE THE UNITED STATES COMMISSION ON INDUSTRIAL RELATIONS, HELD IN SEATTLE AUGUST 14, 1914.

Working conditions and number of mechanics receiving certain wages in 33 of the largest firms in western Washington.

	Number of firms.
Work nine hours per day	33
Work one hour less on Saturdays	2
Work one-half day on Saturday during summer season	2
Work one-half day on Saturday whole year	5
Allow time and half overtime to 12 p. m., double time after 12 p. m., Sundays and holidays	29
Allow time and half overtime to 10 p. m., double time after 10 p. m., Sundays and holidays	4
Allow double time after 5 p. m., Saturdays	2

NUMBER OF MECHANICS.

Rate per hour.	Machinists.	Molders.	Boiler makers.	Black-smiths.	Pattern makers.	Electricians.	Joiners.	Steam fitters.
57½ cents						1		
55 cents	12	1		1	1			
53 cents		1			1			
50 cents	27	7	1	1	6			
48 cents					4			
47½ cents	2							
47 cents	2							
45 cents	69	36	8	4	17	5	9	
44½ cents	13	7		1	2			
44 cents		1						2
43 cents	30							
42½ cents	13							
42 cents	13		3	1	2	5	13	10
41 cents		1						
40 cents	60	4	3	3	3	4		3
39 cents		4						
38½ cents	1	1						
38 cents	6	5						
37 cents	1							6
36½ cents	1	2						
36 cents	2	5						
35 cents	2			1		2		
33½ cents	1							
33 cents	1	1						
30 cents							3	

FEDERATION OF EMPLOYERS ASSOCIATIONS OF THE PACIFIC COAST,
J. BRUCE GIBSON, *President.*

Attest:

UNITED METAL TRADES ASSOCIATION OF THE PACIFIC COAST,
A. H. GARRISON, *Secretary, Washington District.*

TAYLOR EXHIBIT NO. 1.

CARD OF INTRODUCTION.

PEARCE & HENDRICKS,
      816 First Street.

The bearer, Carl Swanson, wants position as lathe hand.
U. N.

UNITED METAL TRADES ASSOCIATION PACIFIC COAST,
A. H. GARRISON, Secretary.

TAYLOR EXHIBIT NO. 2.

WEEKLY LETTER No. 71.

UNITED METAL TRADES ASSOCIATION OF THE PACIFIC COAST,
Portland, Oreg., June 25, 1910.

Machinists' strike.—There has been practically no change in the situation since our. last weekly communication to you. Four men struck in the shop of the Sedro Woolley Iron Works, but several new men have been secured in other places so that, taken as a whole, we have gained more than we have lost during the past week.

In Seattle several new men have been put to work and some of the old men have returned to their jobs, so that they are now in better condition than at any time since the strike was called.

In Tacoma conditions remain about the same, with the balance in our favor.

In Portland we have gained a little on the situation. No more men have struck and a few new men have been secured; some of them are. proving themselves to be good mechanics. No more of the old men have returned.to work during the past week, but we have good reasons to believe that several of them will within a very short time, as we know some of them really want to come back, but are waiting for others to come with them and make a start.

We have no report of any change in any other locality:

The members all seem to be more determined than ever to fight this thing to a finish at the present time. There are several small shops outside the association affected by the strike, but they are fighting just as hard as any of the rest of us to maintain the open shop and the nine-hour day.

Los Angeles.—All reports from Los Angeles indicate that the employers are determined not to give in and that they are gradually gaining ground.

Cooperation.—We wish to commend each member of the association for the cooperation he has given the other members. Since this strike has been declared the members are working together more than ever, but we might help each other much more than we do without any inconvenience in the least. If you have work done outside, let one of the members do it. Generally this is done, but sometimes it is not, and it only encourages the firms that sign up with the unions to continue as they are if you give them your work. They are trying to tear down what you are trying to build up and work given them helps them to do it. Don't forget this when you let work out.

Pattern shops.—We now have two first-class, open-shop, pattern shops in Portland and one in Seattle. William Prehn Pattern Works and the Portland Pattern Works, of Portland, and the Puget Sound Pattern Works, of Seattle, belong to this association, and we believe you will get better and cheaper work by patronizing them than you will if you give your work to some union concern.

Teamsters' strike.—The teamsters' strike in Portland is rapidly drawing to a close. About half of the teams are now running and new men are being secured every day. We understand the teamsters of Seattle have about decided not to strike. No doubt the result of the strike here in Portland and the decided stand taken by some of the firms in Seattle has caused this change.

Liens on vessels for repairs.—We note the following from the bulletin of the New York and New Jersey branch of the National Metal Trades Association:

"The United States Senate and House of Representatives have passed the maritime lien bill, which makes uniform throughout the United States the laws relating to liens on vessels for repairs, supplies, and other necessaries, and supersedes the provisions of all State statutes conferring liens on vessels in so far as they purport to create the rights of actions against vessels for such repairs, etc. This bill was introduced in the Senate and House at the request of the New York and New Jersey branch and the New York and New Jersey Dry Dock Association and it not only makes uniform the laws on this subject, but corrects the confusion due to State statutes and conflicting decisions of the admiralty courts in construing such statutes.",

The members of this association will be interested to know that this bill has passed, and we wish to thank each of them for the assistance they have given in getting the bill through.

Respectfully submitted.

.   UNITED METAL TRADES ASSOCIATION.

TAYLOR EXHIBIT NO. 3.

WEEKLY LETTER No. 70.

UNITED METAL TRADES ASSOCIATION OF THE PACIFIC COAST,
Portland, Oreg., June 18, 1910.

Machinists' strike, Portland.—During the past week there has been but very little change in the condition of the strike here in Portland. A few of the strikers have applied for their places as nonunion men and have been given their old jobs. A few machinists have been picked up, so that the shops are in better condition just now than at any time since the strike was called. Every shop in Portland is running at the present time.

Seattle.—Since the last weekly letter the Washington Iron Works have lost 14 men. Four of these have already returned to work and some new men have been secured, so that at present they are not suffering at all for men. The other shops in Seattle are putting on new men every day, and at the present rate of hiring men it will be only a very short time until they will all have all the men they can use there.

Tacoma.—About the only change in Tacoma is that several new men have been put on, so that the shops are in a better position to turn out work than they have been since the strike was declared there, or probably we should say since the men were laid off, as the two largest shops in Tacoma discharged all their union men before the strike was called.

Everett.—The Sumner Iron Works of Everett are gradually filling the places of the men they laid off before the time they had set to strike had arrived. They have a number of men working.

Victoria, British Columbia.—The machinists are all out in Victoria. Our member there, the British Columbia Marine Railway Co., having lost about 10 men.

Other sections where members of the association are located remain as last week; no trouble, except in Astoria. The machinists have stated that they would call the men out in Spokane, but up to date it has not been done.

Regarding the shops that have signed up, wish to state that no member of the association has given in, and none of the outside shops have signed up during the past week.

As reported last week, no shop of any consequence in either Seattle, Tacoma, or Portland has signed the agreement. The following are the names of the shops in Portland that have signed agreements with the union: Willamette Gas Engine Works, Mr. Concoff; Portland Elevator Co., Mr. Cornfoot.

WEEKLY LETTER No. 105.   .

PORTLAND, OREG., *March 11, 1911.*

Annual convention.—The fifth annual convention of the United Metal Trades Association will be held at the Commercial Club, 937 South C Street, Tacoma, Wash., April 14 and 15. Mark this date on your calendar now and begin making arrangements to be in Tacoma at this meeting. It comes but once a year, and your presence is necessary. Further particulars will be given later.

Plant dynamited.—The new $1,000,000 plant of Iroquois Iron Co., of Chicago, was dynamited the night of February 24. Detectives working on the case have obtained evidence which shows that the explosion is the result of union-labor trouble, and suspicion falls upon a number of union agitators. This plant was constructed under open-shop conditions, and a number of nonunion men had been employed on the contracts. Fortunately no lives were lost, although one of the watchmen was within a short distance of some falling débris. It matters little to people who will do such work whether any lives are lost or not.' '

Typographical men strike.—Men belonging to the typographical union in Chicago struck recently for a different scale of pay than their agreement called for. The following telegram was sent out by J. M. Lynch, president typographical union: "Strike unauthorized, illegal, and without warrant. You are authorized to publish this dispatch." It is simply another case of a few hot-headed union men taking things into their own hands regardless of any previous agreements and going on strike. The union directed these men to return to work, which they did.

Columbus street car strike.—The March number of Hampton's Magazine contains a story of the street car strike in Columbus, Ohio, last fall. According to this article, Fred Fay, of the International Carmen's Union, came to Columbus and organized what men he could, the result of which was a strike later on. As the men were being organized 35 of them were discharged. The union demanded that they should be given their old places back. Rather than have a strike the company agreed to reinstate all of them, providing that the men who were promoted to fill the vacancies would consent to giving up their places. All of them were put back in their old places except four. These men were finally given city positions, and the strike was averted, at least for a time. The company had fulfilled its promise.

A strike was called to take effect on July 24 at 4 a. m., before the cars started from the barns. Out of the 1,225 men employed by the company only 325 men walked out, this being about 26 per cent of the number of men employed. This 26 per cent, with the agitators brought in from outside sources, caused many riots and wrecked 200 cars. On October 18, by a vote of 90 to 32, all that was left of the original 325, the strike was declared off.

This strike cost the State $200,000, the city $40,000, the company $250,000, and the unions $100,000, to say nothing of the loss of trade during that time. The men got exactly what the company agreed to give them before the strike, and many of them lost their positions. The result is about the same as the result of most strikes. Nobody is benefited except the walking delegates and the officials of the union.

Open-shop contracts.—We recently received a communication from Walter Drew, commissioner National Erectors' Association, requesting a list of open-shop steel-erecting concerns in this city. Mr. Drew advises us that it is the intention of the members of their association to let their work to open-shop contractors as far as possible all over the country. The Seattle office has supplied Mr. Drew with the names of open-shop contractors in Seattle, Tacoma, and Spokane. The members of this association will appreciate the efforts that are being made by the eastern associations in our behalf.

N. M. T. A. convention.—The National Metal Trades Association will hold its convention at the Hotel Astor, New York, April 12 and 13. This promises to be a very interesting convention, as important subjects will be discussed by able men. If any of our members are to be in the East at this time, we would urge you to attend this convention.

Yours, very truly,

F. C. PORTER, *Secretary.*

TAYLOR EXHIBIT NO. 4.

AFFIDAVIT.

STATE OF WASHINGTON,

County of King, ss:

Herman Kottenbach, being first duly sworn. says: That he is a machinist by trade; that he is 29 years' old, a native of Germany, a resident of the United States, and has taken out his first papers declaring his intention to become an American citizen; that affiant resided in Chicago, in the State of Illinois, until Monday, August 1, 1910; that affiant was informed by Walter Leuzinger, one of the affiants in another affidavit, that one Hastings, who maintains an employment bureau at 182 Dearborn Street, in said Chicago, would furnish the affiant work at his trade, and suggested that affiant apply for said work or employment; that affiant went to the said employment office or agency conducted by said Hastings and made application for the said employment; that the said Hastings then and there stated to the affiant that he had work he could furnish the affiant at Seattle, Wash.; said work or employment was that of a machinist's position, from 30 to 50 cents per hour, for a nine-hour day. Affiant then asked the said Hastings whether there was a strike on at Seattle or whether there was any other kind of labor trouble affecting the work, and affiant then and there told the said Hastings that he would not go as a strike breaker and did not want to work where there were any labor troubles; that said Hastings then and there told the affiant that there were no labor troubles of any kind or character at said Seattle and that the work offered was in all respects as represented theretofore by the said Hastings.

That affiant was then offered a paper to sign, and affiant then told the said Hastings that he would not work for less than 45 cents per hour, and thereupon the said Hastings told him that it would be all right and requested him to sign the said paper, and that affiant did then and there sign some unknown paper. That affiant is not well versed in the art of reading English print, and that said Hastings gave him no time to read the same, nor did he offer to read it to him, and the affiant signed the said paper hurriedly and without knowledge of the contents thereof. That if the said paper contains anything at a variance with the statement made herein the said statements in said paper are wrong and untrue. That on Monday, the 1st day of August, 1910, the said Hastings furnished the affiant with transportation to said Seattle, and the affiant then and there, on said day, journeyed from said Chicago to said Seattle, where he arrived upon the 4th day of said August. That upon arriving in said Seattle, in company with one Wheeler, an agent for the said Hastings, who accompanied the affiant and others on the said trip, affiant and others with him in like circumstances were met by one Garrison, who the affiant has since learned was the secretary of the National Metal Trades Association; that said Garrison took the affiant to the Arlington Hotel, in said Seattle, and on the following day the said Garrison accompanied the affiant and others to the Moran Co., a corporation engaged in boilermaking, engine and iron shipbuilding, said Seattle. That, affiant, upon arriving at the said place of business of said Moran Co., learned that there was a general strike on and that the labor union for the machinists at Seattle had placed the said company on the unfair list, and that no union machinists were employed at the said plant. That the affiant had told the said Hastings in Chicago that he would not work where there was a strike, and that upon learning that a strike was in progress affiant refused the said employment. That the said representation made by the said Hastings in Chicago that no strike existed were the ones which controlled the affiant and caused him to leave Chicago to procure the said employment in Seattle.

HERMAN KOTTENBACH.

Subscribed and sworn to before me this 10th day of August, 1910.

[SEAL.]   WINTER S. MARTIN,
A Notary Public in and for the State of Washington, Residing at Seattle.

AFFIDAVIT.

STATE OF WASHINGTON,
County of King:

Robert Feja, being first duly sworn, upon his oath deposes and says: That he is a native of Germany; that he is 24 years old, is a machinist by trade, and that he has resided in the United States four years and a half and has declared his intention to become a citizen of the United States; that he was in Chicago, Ill., on and before August 1, 1910; that affiant went to 182 Dearborn Street, in the city of Chicago, in company with one Adam Crocus, in response to an advertisement in a Chicago paper, and then and there, on the 30th day of July, 1910, applied for a position as a machinist in the city of Seattle; that affiant talked with one Hastings, who had charge of the office, and who the affiant learned was the secretary of the National Metal Trades Association for out-of-town shops; that the said Hastings told the affiant that he needed men for the machinist trade in Seattle, Wash.; that he offered the affiant 45 cents per hour and free transportation to the said Seattle; that said Hastings was asked by the affiant if there were any labor troubles of any kind at Seattle and if there was a strike there; and that said Hastings then and there told the affiant that no labor troubles of any kind existed there at this time, or the date of the said conversation; said that there had been a strike for eight hours, but that the matter had been settled and there was no trouble of any kind there now; that affiant then told the said Hastings that he would not work where there was a strike or where there were labor troubles.

That said Hastings furnished the affiant transportation to said Seattle, and the affiant journeyed to Seattle in company with said Crocus, Kottenbach, and upon arrival were taken to the plant of the Moran Co., and affiant then learned that there was a general strike in progress and that said strike had existed since the 1st day of July; that affiant was induced to leave Chicago and journey to Seattle solely on the representation that no strike existed at the Seattle place of employment, and that he would not have left the said city of Chicago·if he had been informed as to conditions in Seattle.

That affiant has read the affidavits of his companions who came to Seattle with him and the things therein stated are true.

ROBERT FEJA.

Subscribed and sworn to before me on this 10th day of August, 1910.

[SEAL.]   WINTER S. MARTIN,
   A Notary Public in and for the State of Washington, Residing at Seattle.

AFFIDAVIT.

STATE OF WASHINGTON,
   County of King, ss:

Emil Krohn, being sworn, says:

That he is 50 years of age, a citizen of the United States, and a resident and elector of the State of Illinois for more than 17 years last past.

That on the 1st day of August, A. D. 1910, in the city of Chicago, affiant, in response to an advertisement in a newspaper, called upon one Hastings at 182 Dearborn Street; that said Hastings employed affiant to go to Seattle and work as a machinist for Moran Bros.; that affiant asked Hastings three or four. times whether there was any strike or labor trouble among the machinists at Seattle or in Moran's shop, and each time Hastings declared to affiant that there was no strike or any other kind of labor trouble at Moran's or at Seattle; that affiant informed Hastings that if there was a strike or other labor trouble at Seattle or at Moran's he would not accept the employment, and he was assured most emphatically by Hastings that there was neither strike nor labor trouble of any kind either at Moran's shop or anywhere else in Seattle.

Hastings stated to affiant that the wages to be paid at Seattle ranged from 35 cents to 50 cents per hour, and that affiant would be paid 48 cents per hour and given permanent employment.

Hastings stated to affiant that it would cost him, Hastings, and the people he represented between $54 and $56 to transport affiant to Seattle, but did not inform affiant that it would not cost affiant a single penny for his transportation between Chicago and Seattle.

Affiant left Chicago August 1 and arrived in Seattle August 4, 1910.

Affiant was met at station in Seattle by one Garrison, agent and secretary for Metal Trades Association; six other men accompanied affiant from Chicago to Seattle, one of them holding the tickets for all seven and being given charge of the party by said Hastings.

Said Garrison took affiant and the other men to a hotel on arrival.

Affiant asked said Garrison three times whether there was any strike on in Seattle or at Moran's, and he was informed most positively by Garrison that there was no strike at Moran's or in Seattle.

Affiant learned after he commenced work at Moran's that there was a strike on there among the machinists, and that there had been a strike at said Moran's shop every day since the 2d day of June, 1910.

Garrison took affiant to Moran's shop on the 8th day of August, and affiant worked there as a machinist for 81 hours, or until the 18th day of August, 1910, and on leaving the employment of Moran's he was refused the wages due him and he was obliged to commence an action against the Moran Co. for the recovery of his wages.

EMIL KROHN.

Subscribed and sworn to before me this 20th day of August, 1910.:

[SEAL.]   THOMAS B. MACMAHON,
      Notary Public for the State of Washington, Residing at Seattle.

AFFIDAVIT.

STATE OF WASHINGTON,
    County of King, ss:

Frank C. Parker, being first duly sworn, says:

That he is a native American, 23 years of age, and is a machinist by trade and occupation. That he resided in Chicago, Ill., until the 30th day of July, 1910, when he left for Seattle to engage in work as a machinist. That affiant answered an advertisement in one of the Chicago papers, which advertised the statement that skilled machinists were wanted in Seattle, Wash. That affiant went to 182 Dearborn Street, in said Chicago, and talked with one Hastings. That said Hastings told the affiant that men who were first-class skilled machinists could find employment through him at Seattle, Wash., and that he would give him free transportation to said Seattle. That said Hastings told the affiant that the job would pay from 36 to 50 cents per hour. That affiant came to Seattle and found a general strike prevailing.

                                                    F. C. PARKER.

Subscribed and sworn to before me this 10th day of August, 1910.

[SEAL.]   WINTER S. MARTIN,
               Notary Public in and for the State of Washington,
                                    Residing at Seattle.

AFFIDAVIT.

STATE OF WASHINGTON, *County of King, ss:*

Henry W. Biggs, being sworn, says:

That he is a citizen of the United States, an elector of the State of Illinois, and for 20 years last past has resided with his family in the city of Chicago.

That for 28 years last past affiant has been and has worked as a machinist of the first class.

That on July 6, 1898, affiant entered United States Navy as a machinist aboard the U. S. S. *Richmond*, and on the 2d day of February, 1899, was appointed chief machinist aboard U. S. S. *Olympia* at Manila, Admiral Dewey, commander.

That on the 6th day of July, 1899, affiant was appointed by President McKinley as warrant machinist on first-class U. S. cruiser *Baltimore*, and continued in said capacity of warrant machinist until the 26th day of November, 1904, since which time he has followed his said trade in said city of Chicago.

That on the 2d day of August, 1910, affiant read an advertisement in Chicago Daily News stating " Wanted—Machinists—35 cents to 50 cents per hour. Must be competent for jobbing on the Pacific coast. Apply room 30, 182 Dearborn Street."

Affiant called at said address at 4 p. m. on said day and inquired what the job was on Pacific coast and was referred to a rear office, where a man named Hastings, a crippled person, received affiant and asked him how long he had been a machinist, and affiant told him as above related and exhibited to him all of his official papers; Hastings said to affiant he must be pretty well up in marine work and he was just the kind of a man he wanted in Seattle; that it was a marine shop he wanted him to work in; it is Moran Bros.' shop. Hastings informed affiant his transportation and all expenses would be paid, and if affiant remained with Morans six months they would consider and make the transportation a bonus, and it would cost him nothing and not be deducted from his wages; that he should get his baggage together and start at once, and that he could bring his family out to Seattle, too, in a very short time. Hastings further told affiant he would probably be paid 50 cents per hour right at the start.

Affiant asked Hastings if these was any trouble or strike on at Morans, and Hastings replied that there had been no trouble or strike at Morans in four or five years.

Hastings told affiant that they had both union and nonunion men working together in Moran's shop; that it was strictly an open shop and union men were employed there as readily as nonunion men, and that the only reason for offering men a bonus of their transportation was because it was hard to get men to go to the Pacific coast and not because there was any strike or other trouble there.

Hastings insisted on taking charge of and checking affiant's tools and stayed away from affiant until train had commenced to pull out of the station the day he left Chicago, August 3, at 10.15 p. m. Hastings kept check for affiant's tools and rushed up to him after the bell rang for train to start, thrust a paper into affiant's face, and asked him to sign it; that Hastings kept the paper folded so affiant could neither read its contents nor see what was written upon it, but, trusting to the representations of Hastings, affiant signed the paper while train was in motion, and Hastings kept it and put it in his pocket, giving affiant two single dollar bills to purchase food en route between Chicago and Seattle, which was all the money affiant had, and affiant went hungry most of the trip, leaving his wife and six children behind him in Chicago waiting for him to send for them.

Hastings gave affiant a card with the name of Hastings and Independent Foundry Co., Portland, Oreg., printed thereon and told affiant to present card to man who was to meet him at train in Seattle, and if you don't meet anybody go to an address he mentioned in an office building in Seattle and men there would look after him.

Affiant arrived at Seattle 8.15 p. m. Saturday, August 6, 1910, but no one met him at the train. Sunday, 7th, affiant went to Morans. Watchman there requested affiant to wait for the timekeeper to come, and when he came he telephoned a man named Garrison and told him affiant was there, and then telephoned clerk at Grand Union Hotel to fix up a machinist he was sending over to the hotel.

Timekeeper, whose name affiant learned is Tweady, asked affiant for his Navy commission and said he would take care of it for affiant; affiant asked for his tools and was told that Garrison would attend to it.

Affiant called at Moran's yard Monday morning, August 8, was met by said Tweady, to whom he told that he had been brought to Seattle on misrepresentations; that Tweady then told affiant there had been no strike or labor trouble at Morans in over five years.

Affiant demanded his warrant he had received in Navy, which Tweady took away from him the previous day, and his tools. Tweady told affiant to go and see Garrison about his tools, and he would find there was no strike and no labor trouble at Morans.

Affiant declares that labor conditions in Seattle and at Moran's shipyard were misrepresented to him and that he was told there was no trouble of any kind with the machinists in Seattle or at Morans.

That affiant never would have left his job and his family in Chicago if the truth had been told to him by aforementioned Hastings when he called at his office in Chicago in response to the advertisement printed in the Chicago Daily News.

HENRY W. BIGGS.

Subscribed and sworn to before me this 8th day of August, 1910.

[SEAL.] THOMAS B. MACMAHON,
Notary Public for the State of Washington, residing at Seattle.

AFFIDAVIT.

STATE OF WASHINGTON,
County of King, ss:

John Tomilgas, being sworn, says:

That he has resided in Chicago for six months last past.

That during the last week of July, 1910, affiant read an advertisement in Chicago Daily News stating machinists were wanted for Pacific coast, wages to be paid 30 cents to 50 cents per hour.

Affiant went to the address given in newspaper, room 30, at 182 Dearborn Street; affiant was met at said address by the agent who published said notice, and was told by said agent he wanted him to go to Seattle and work on steam engines, and that he would pay affiant 45 cents per hour permanently, and if he was a good machinist he would be paid 50 cents per hour.

Affiant asked said agent if there was a strike or any trouble at the machine shop where affiant was going, and he was told by the agent that there was no trouble and no strike on among the machinists in Seattle, that it was an open shop where affiant was going.

Affiant told agent he was no strike breaker and that if there was a strike in progress at Seattle he would not go there to work, but he was assured by the agent that there was no strike and he was urged to go to Seattle forthwith.

Affiant left Chicago Monday night, August 1, 1910, arrived in Seattle Thursday, August 4, and was met at station by another agent and taken to a hotel. Affiant was taken to Morans' shop on Friday morning, August 5.

Affiant told Seattle representative of Morans that he would not go to work if there was a strike in progress, and that he had been assured by Morans' agent in Chicago that there was no machinists' strike in Seattle, and particularly was there no strike on at Morans; that Morans' agent in Seattle, whose name affiant has since learned was Garrison, informed affiant that there was no strike at Morans and to come along with him to work.

That on going to work affiant learned there was a strike at Morans and had been for a long time.

That affiant was induced to come to Seattle and to go to work at Morans under a misrepresentation, and affiant would not have come to Seattle if the truth concerning the labor situation had been told him.

JOHN TOMILGAS.

Subscribed and sworn to before me this 8th day of August, 1910.

[SEAL.]   THOMAS B. MACMAHON,
       Notary Public for the State of Washington, residing at Seattle.

AFFIDAVIT.

STATE OF WASHINGTON,
     County of King, ss:

Adam Crocus, being sworn, says:

That he has resided in Beverly, Mass., two and one-half years; that he has resided and worked as a machinist in Chicago, Ill., for four months last past and until the 1st day of August, 1910.

That on Thursday, the 28th day of July, 1910, affiant read an advertisement printed, published, and circulated in the Daily News of Chicago, stating that machinists were wanted, all around machinists, apply to 182 Dearborn Street, Chicago, at room 30.

That on Saturday, July 30, 1910, affiant went to the above address with his friend, also a general machinist, and were met by a Mr. Hastings, secretary of National Metal Trades Association for out-of-town shops; Hastings told affiant that he needed 17 first-class all around machinists to go to Seattle, and he exhibited a telegram to affiant containing the above declaration; that said telegram was signed by one Garretson, and purported to be sent from Seattle to National Metal Trades Association at Chicago.

Hastings promised to pay affiant 50 cents per hour at Seattle in the Moran shop, and that affiant would be provided with work as a machinist eleswhere in Seattle at the same wage of 50 cents per hour if he did not like to work at Moran shop; that affiant was further told by Hastings that National Metal Trades Association was paying the fare of machinists to Seattle and affiant would be supposed to work at least six months for the association at Seattle, but not at Morans unless he liked the work there.

Hastings told affiant and other machinists present at the time that there was no trouble or any strike at Morans.

That affiant, with five other men, left Chicago, in charge of a man representing and acting as agent for Hastings and National Metal Trades Association, and arrived in Seattle Thursday, August 4, and were met at the train by Garretson, who took affiant and others to hotel. That affiant told Hastings in Chicago that if there was a strike on at Seattle he would not go there, and Hastings assured him there was no strike at Seattle and particularly at Morans. That Hastings asked affiant not to tell anyone that he promised to pay affiant 50 cents per hour at Morans.

ADAM CROCUS.

Subscribed and sworn to before me this 8th day of August, 1910.

[SEAL.]   THOMAS B. MACMAHON,.
      Notary Public for the State of Washington, residing at Seattle.

TAYLOR EXHIBIT NO. 5.

WEEKLY LETTER No. 111.

UNITED METAL TRADES ASSOCIATION OF THE PACIFIC COAST,
Portland, Oreg., May 4, 1911.

Machinists' strike.—The figures given below show the amount of money taken in by the machinists' union of this coast for the month of January, 1910, and January, 1911:

	January, 1910.		January, 1911.	
	Amount.	Days' pay assessment.	Amount.	Days' pay assessment.
Los Angeles	$228.57	$56.28	$212.15	$5.00
San Francisco, No. 69	792.54	107.51	494.52	16.88
San Francisco, No. 715	34.60	6.88	30.40	3.13
Sacramento	84.45	27.50	87.12	
Oakland	262.85	60.00	226.65	10.00
Portland	87.40	13.75	61.10	
Astoria	15.25		15.70	
Tacoma	51.10	5.00	32.35	3.75
Seattle	88.26	18.76	60.70	2.50
Everett	50.20	7.50	58.55	5.00
Bellingham	7.45	7.50	7.15	7.50
Aberdeen	4.25			
Victoria, British Columbia	22.85	30.00	19.50	2.50
Vancouver, British Columbia	108.75	15.10	22.00	1.25
Spokane	78.90	12.50	50.05	2.50
Total	1,917.32	368.28	1,377.94	60.01

These figures show a difference of $539.38 in one month's assessments. In January, 1910, the machinists' union, No. 68, of San Francisco paid in the total of $792.54. In January, 1911, this same union paid in only $494.54, which is only 62 per cent. This means that 38 per cent of the members of the union No. 68 have either left San Francisco or dropped the union during the last year. Inasmuch as practically all machinists working in San Francisco are union men, it would appear that business has fallen off there between January, 1910, and January, 1911.

The figures for Portland show a total of $87.40 for January, 1910, and $61.10 for January, 1911. Deducting the $13.75, the days paid assessment, from $87.40, the total gives us an assessment of $73.65, against $61.10 in January, 1911. Where are the machinists who have been paying this difference of $12.55? The unions claim that all their men are holding out. Several of them have either withdrawn from the union or left this lodge.

The figures in reference to Tacoma and Seattle will show a greater reduction in the number of members in the lodges there than it does in Portland.

The union is not only losing the strike but in trying to secure an eight-hour day they are gradually losing their members, which, if they continue for a few years with the same results as the past year, will deplete their organization entirely.

Political situation.—At a special meeting of the Oregon district held Tuesday evening, May 2, the following candidates were decided upon as being those who would work to our interests:

Mayor, Gay Lombard.

A. G. Rushlight made certain promises to the unions; among others, that he would appoint a union man as chief of police.

City auditor, Edward M. Lance.

City treasurer, J. H. Richmond.

City attorney, Frank S. Grant.

Municipal judge, Albert E. Gebhardt.

Councilman at large, George B. Cellars, J. J. Jennings, and E. L. Mills.

Councilman to fill two-year unexpired term of Thomas C. Devlin, John H. Burgard.

Councilman to fill two-year unexpired term of Gay Lombard, H. J. McInnis.

From what information we have at hand, the candidates named above are the best men in the field. We trust that A. G. Rushlight, Ed. D. Williams, William H. Daly, and Ralph C. Clyde will be snowed under so deep that they can not get out for several years. These people do not hesitate to state their preference for organized labor.

Los Angeles.—Some of the papers recently reported that there were 30,000 men in line in the labor-union parade which took place a short time ago in Los Angeles. As a matter of fact, there were, by actual count, 7,800 men, and in that number was included a large delegation from the cities of Bakersfield, Fresno, Riverside, San Bernardino, Pasadena, and other surrounding towns.

Thirty-five pickets, arrested about three weeks ago charged with conspiring to violate the picketing ordinance, are awaiting trial. After the examination of several hundred men, a jury was selected, but one of the jurymen was taken sick, which made a vacancy and delayed the trial.

We are very much interested to know how.this case comes out, and will notify you the results. Very little picketing has been done since the arrest.

Yours, very truly,

F. C. PORTER, Secretary.

TAYLOR EXHIBIT NO. 6.

AFFIDAVIT OF WILLIAM C. GATES.

STATE OF WASHINGTON,
County of King, ss:

William C. Gates, being sworn, says:
That he is a citizen of the United States of America and a resident of the State of Washington; that he is a general machinist by trade and has worked and followed said trade since 1903.

That on the 8th day of October, 1913, at Seattle Machine Works, he worked nine hours on the U. S. transport Dix, repairing and overhauling main feed-pump gear, bushings, and pins.

That on October 9, 1913, at Seattle Machine Works, he worked nine hours on U. S. steamer General Mifflin and U. S. transport Dix, on feed pump, rigging, and oil feed pump.

That on the 10th day of October, 1913, he worked on the General Mifflin, taking out and overhauling oil pump, for a continuous period of 15 hours.

That on the 11th day of October, 1913, he worked nine hours, and on the 13th day of October, 1913, he worked nine hours, all on same boat, the General Mifflin, at said Seattle Machine Works, overhauling and taking out oil pump.

WILLIAM C. GATES.

Subscribed and sworn to before me this 21st day of October, 1913.

[SEAL.]   THOMAS B. MACMAHON,
              Notary Public for the State of Washington, residing at Seattle.

TAYLOR EXHIBIT NO.

SEATTLE, December 2, 1910.

MACHINISTS' UNION,
Labor Temple, Seattle.

, GENTLEMEN: The celebrated case which we brought in behalf of Emil Krohn against the Moran Co. last summer has dragged at slow length along in court until now.

, The.Moran Co. was compelled to pay, and finally did pay, the judgments secured against them yesterday. After deducting the cost of the suit, I inclose check for $15, and not knowing Krohn's whereabouts, I send his check to you.

THOMAS B. MACMAHON.

AFFIDAVIT.

STATE OF WASHINGTON, County of.King, ss:

Walter Leuzinger, being first duly sworn, says: That he is a native of Switzerland; that he has resided in the United States for three years last past; and that he has declared his intention to become a citizen of the United States, and that he is a machinist by trade; that he answered an advertisement in the Chicago Daily News, which said advertisement stated that first-class men as machinists were wanted at Seattle, Wash.; that affiant went to the place named in the said advertisement, namely, 182 Dearborn Street, room 30, in said Chicago, Ill., and then and there applied for a position as said machinist in Seattle, Wash.; that affiant has read the affidavit of Herman Kottenbach, and the facts therein stated are true; that said Hastings told the affiant that there was no strike on at Seattle, and that the affiant would be furnished labor and work at his trade of machinist in said city; that affiant journeyed to said Seattle with said Kottenbach, and then and there upon arrival learned that there was a general strike on at Seattle, and that the said Moran Co., to whom the said Garrison took the affiant and others for employment, was on the unfair list, and that a general strike has been on since July 1, 1910; that the representation made to affiant that there was no strike at Seattle was one of the material representations concerning the said prospective employment at Seattle, and that affiant would not have sought the employment nor would he have signed any agreement to work and labor as a machinist in Seattle, if he had learned that a general strike existed; that affiant acted upon the statements made to him by said Hastings and was deceived thereby, and upon learning that strike existed in Seattle, refused to so work and labor.

WALTER LEUZINGER.

Subscribed and sworn to before me this 10th days of July, 1910.
[SEAL.]   WINTER S. MARTIN,
A Notary Public in and for the State of Washington, residing at Scattle.

TAYLOR EXHIBIT NO. 8.

Hon. C. W. WAPPENSTEIN,
Chief of Police of the City of Seattle.

DEAR SIR: Pursuant to your request we hand you berewith the affidavits of J. E. Hendricksen and M. F. Kroll to the effect that your Officer Blount did, on the 30th day of July, 1910, use profane language in making an arrest of one of our members and, apparently, went out of his way to assist Moran's in their conduct of the strike now in progress at their yard.

On the trial of the member arrested by Officer Blount it developed that the case against Hendricksen was so weak that the city attorney asked to have it dismissed on the ground that there had been no violation of any ordinance or statute by said Hendricksen. (Stenographer's report of the proceedings before Judge Egan attached hereto.)

THOMAS B. MACMAHON.

CITY OF SEATTLE *v.* J. E. HENDRICKSEN.

Police Officer Blount, after being duly sworn, testified as follows:
At Saturday noon, this man is one of the machinists on strike and we followed the man from Moran's shipyards to a restaurant and followed him back again and the man here kept talking to him and I told him to go away and leave him alone, and he told me he would like to know where I was at, and I told him if he did not leave the man alone I would have to send him in, and I sent him in.

CITY ATTORNEY. I would not ask for a conviction in this case and I move that it be dismissed.
(Case dismissed.)
The above and foregoing report made by Stenographer Frank Herbert, of United States Commissioner Bowman's office on the 1st day of August, 1910.

THOMAS B. MACMAHON.

STATE OF WASHINGTON, *County of King, ss:*
M. F. Kroll, being sworn, says: That he is 35 years of age, a citizen of the United States, an elector of the State of Washington, and a resident of the city of Seattle for more than 10 years last past; that on Saturday, July 30, A. D.

1910,' between the hour of noon and 2.30 p. m., affiant was standing on Charles Street, at the corner of Railroad Avenue, in said city of Seattle, when he saw J. E. Hendricksen approaching and proceeding in a westerly direction on Charles Street; that when said Hendricksen reached a point about 10 feet distant from affiant one Tweedy, bookkeeper for Moran Shipyard, accosted Hendricksen, who was standing with his hands in his pockets; that almost immediately Officer Blount, a patrolman of said city, came up to Hendricksen and, without any cause or provocation, and without any word being spoken to him by Hendricksen, stated to Hendricksen in an exceedingly loud and angry tone, "God damn you; you are a lot of God damn kids trying to win a strike; damn you, I have a good mind to put you under arrest"; that thereupon said Officer Blount laid hands on said Hendricksen and took him to the patrol box on First Avenue between King Street and Seattle Hardware Co. store; that Hendricksen did not protest or resist arrest in any way.

M. F. KROLL.

Subscribed and sworn to before me this 1st day of August, 1910.

THOMAS B. MACMAHON,
Notary Public for the State of Washington, residing at Seattle.

STATE OF WASHINGTON, *County of King, ss:*

J. E. Hendricksen, being sworn, says: That he is 25 years of age, a citizen of the United States, an elector of the State of Washington, and a resident of the city of Seattle for more than eight years last past; that on Saturday, the 30th day of July, A. D. 1910, affiant was walking west on Charles Street, near Railroad Avenue, in said city, about 12.30 o'clock in the afternoon; that he had his hands in his pockets so no one might say that he put his hands on anyone to whom he might speak; that a man, apparently a machinist, was walking in the same direction with affiant; that affiant stated to the man, "The machinists are on strike at Moran's "; that affiant said nothing further to the man up to this time; that the man answered affiant by saying, "I am not working at Moran's "; that affiant then said, "Excuse me, I thought perhaps you were a machinist working for Moran's "; that affiant had then walked to within 10 or 12 feet of one M. F. Kroll, at which point a patrolman in uniform of the Seattle police, whose name affiant has since learned was Blount, yelled to and at affiant and said, "God damn you, I told you not to speak to them men that didn't want to talk to you." Affiant answered said Blount by saying, "I did not stop the man, I only told him the machinists were on strike at Moran's, and that is all he could be offended at if he is offended "; that Blount then said to affiant, "God damn you, I have a good mind to pull you into jail "; that Blount then came up behind affiant and took affiant by the shoulder and walked him to patrol box on First Avenue; that affiant made no resistance; that after affiant was placed under arrest Officer Blount said to him further, " God damn you, you send a lot of kids down here expecting to win a strike "; affiant told Blount he had no right to swear and use so much profane language, that affiant could prefer charges against him for it; that Blount then said to affiant, " I don't give a damn what charges you prefer against me; I have got you now and I will send you to jail, whether you stay there or they keep you or not, but I will put you there just the same."

J. E. HENDRICKSEN.

Subscribed and sworn to before me this 1st day of August, 1910.

THOMAS B. MACMAHON,
Notary Public for the State of Washington, residing at Seattle.

TAYLOR EXHIBIT NO. 9.

INTERNATIONAL ASSOCIATION OF MACHINISTS,
HOPE LODGE, No. 79.

GENTLEMEN: Letter sent to individual employers May, 1910.

We, the undersigned committee, representing Machinists' Hope Lodge, No. 79, of Seattle, are desirous of entering into a working agreement with your firm and have herein inclosed a copy of the proposed agreement which we have submitted to every employer in this city for their consideration.

Our purpose in wishing to enter into this agreement with you is to keep pace with the constant change in industrial conditions throughout the country. As workingmen we desire recognition and protection. We desire to increase our pay in accordance with the increased cost of living. We desire to give our employers as much of our time in the shops as justice to our family, and health will permit, keeping for ourselves a sufficient amount of time to travel to and from our work and for recreation and rest.

We trust that you appreciate the position that we are taking in this matter, and that you will not feel that we as workingmen are antagonistic to your rights and interests as employers, as it is our earnest desire to agree and cooperate with you, to give you the best service that we have, and to work to the end that both the employers and employees shall be mutually benefited.

This move perhaps is a new departure from the old system of doing business, but one which the changing in industrial conditions was bound to bring about sooner or later, and now that this time has arrived we sincerely hope that the employers will show the same kind of feeling and give us the same consideration that we have shown to them, in order that a settlement may be reached that will be agreeable and beneficial to both parties.

If there is any part of this proposed agreement that you would like to take up with us, we would only be too pleased to meet you and discuss it with you.

Please send your answer to the Secretary of Hope Lodge, No. 79, I. A. M., if possible or at least by June 1.

Thanking you in advance for whatever consideration you may show us, we remain,

Very respectfully, yours,

HOPE LODGE, No. 79, I. A. M.

[SEAL.]

TAYLOR EXHIBIT NO. 10.

AGREEMENT BETWEEN THE INTERNATIONAL ASSOCIATION OF MACHINISTS AND THE FIRM OF _____, BELLINGHAM, WASH.

Rule No. 1.—Eight hours shall constitute a day's work.

Rule No. 2.—The minimum rate of wages for machinists shall be $3.60 per day.

Rule No. 3.—All time worked over the regular eight-hour day up to 10 p. m. shall be paid at the rate of time and one-half, and all time worked after 10 p. m., including Sunday and legal holidays, shall be paid at the rate of double time.

Rule No. 4.—One apprentice may be employed for the shop and one additional apprentice for each five machinists employed.

This agreement shall go into effect ____ and remain in effect until_____ after which time either party desiring a change shall give 30 days' notice.

Signed for the International Machinists' Association.

This agreement is signed with the understanding that if, during the life of this agreement, the above-mentioned organization allows any of its members to work over eight hours per day or for less than the above-mentioned rate per day in any of the contract shops in the city of Bellingham, Wash., this agreement will be null and void.

Signed for the International Machinists' Association:

TAYLOR EXHIBIT NO. 11.

IN THE SUPERIOR COURT OF THE STATE OF WASHINGTON.   FOR KING COUNTY.

Order No. ——.

The Moran Co., plaintiff, v. Lodge No. 26 of International Association of Machinists, R. G. Cook, J. A. Taylor, W. Jordan, P. H. Stevens, H. F. Breckman, A. J. Pitch, J. B. Lamb, D. G. Morris, Victor Chreist, F. L. Buckman, Richard Roe, and John Doe, Iron Molders' Union, No. 158, J. M. Johnson, W. W. Marugg, William Stafford, Thomas Fife, William Legas, Frank Wacker, John Morris, John Doe, and Richard Roe. International Brotherhood of Boiler Makers and Iron Ship Builders, Lodge No. 104, John Long, Frank Downing, John Osborne, James McGill, Robert Molander, H. Todd, W. H. Clark, D. Cooper, W. Cooper, John Doe, and Richard Roe, defendants.

The above-entitled cause coming on for hearing in this court on Monday, May 27, 1907, and defendants having appeared by counsel in opposition to the application of the plaintiff for a temporary injunction herein and proof having been submitted to the court in behalf of both the plaintiff and the defendants and the court having been fully advised in the premises, adjudges that a case has been made by the plaintiff for a temporary injunction herein: Now, therefore, upon application of plaintiff and its counsel, it is hereby ordered that the defendants and each of them, as well as all persons aiding or abetting them, including the members of all defendant unions, are hereby restrained and enjoined from each and all the following acts:

1. From in any manner interfering with, hindering, or obstructing the business of the plaintiff, or its agents, servants, or employees in the maintenance, conduct, or management thereof.

2. From compelling or inducing, or attempting to compel or induce, by threats, force, violence, insults, or any species of intimidation, any of plaintiff's employees to quit the service of the plaintiff.

3. From preventing or attempting to prevent by means of threats, force, violence, insults, or intimidation any person or persons from freely entering into or continuing in the employ of the plaintiff.

4. From congregating about or near the premises of the plaintiff or in the streets, approaches, or places adjacent or directly leading to the premises of the plaintiff for the purpose of intimidating its employees or preventing or hindering them from fulfilling their duties as such employees, or for the purpose of inducing or coercing by threats, violence, or by intimidation, any of the plaintiff's employees to leave its service, or any person to refuse to enter its service.

5. From going singly or collectively to the place of residence of said employees for the purpose of attempting to induce any of them by means of threats or any kind of intimidation to quit the service of complainant.

6. From preventing or attempting to prevent, by threats or intimidation, any person from entering into contractual relations with the plaintiff.

7. From doing any act whatsoever in furtherance of any conspiracy or combination formed for the purpose of injuring plaintiff, or in any manner interfere with the plaintiff in the control of its business, and from directing, aiding, or abetting any scheme, design, or plan to interfere with the free and unhindered control of the plaintiff in its business and the free choice or will of any servant, agent, or employee of plaintiff.

8. From displaying any banners at or near the premises of the plaintiff for the purpose of intimidating any of the employees or customers of plaintiff, or deterring others from entering its employ.

9. From picketing said plaintiff's place of business or picketing the homes, boarding houses, or places of residence of any of the said employees.

10. From annoying, harassing, accosting, intercepting, ridiculing, hindering, insulting, or otherwise interfering with any of the employees of the plaintiff or with any person who may desire to enter the service of plaintiff, for the purpose of inducing such employees to quit said service, or preventing other persons from entering therein.

Done in open court this 3d day of June, A. D. 1907.

R. B. ALBERTSON, *Judge.*

TAYLOR EXHIBIT NO. 12.

DECEMBER 2, 1913.

Mr. JOHN RICHARD BRADY,
Commander Puget Sound Navy Yard, Bremerton, Wash.

DEAR SIR: We are inclosing you herewith tabulated list showing the working conditions and wages paid the mechanics in 33 of our western firms, hoping that this will be of some benefit to you.

We would appreciate very much if you would send us a copy of your new wage schedule, so that we can note any changes that have been made.

Thanking you in advance for the courtesy, I beg to remain,

Yours, very truly,

A. H. GARRISON, Secretary.

Working condition and number of mechanics who receive certain wage in 33 of the largest firms in western Washington October, 1913.

Number of firms.

Work 9 hours per day_____ 33
Work 1 hour less on Saturdays_____ 2
Work one-half day Saturday during summer season_____ 2
Work one-half day Saturday whole year_____ 5
Allow time and half overtime to 12 p. m., double time after 12 p. m., Sundays and holidays_____ 29
Allow time and half overtime to 10 p. m., double time after 10 p. m. Sundays and holidays_____ 4
Allow double time after 5 p. m. Saturdays_____ 2

Number of mechanics.

Rate per hour.	Machinists.	Molders.	Boiler makers.	Blacksmiths.	Pattern makers.	Electricians.	Joiners.	Steam fitters.
57½ cents					1			
55 cents	12	1		1	1			
53 cents		1			1			
50 cents	27	7	1	1	6			
48 cents					4			
47½ cents	2							
47 cents	2							
45 cents	69	36	8	4	17	5	9	
44½ cents	13	7		1	2			
44 cents		1						2
43 cents	30							
42½ cents	13			1				
42 cents	13		3	1	2	5	13	10
41 cents		1						
40 cents	60	4	3	3	3	4		3
39 cents		4						
38½ cents	1	1						
38 cents	6	5						
37 cents	1							6
36½ cents	1	2						
36 cents	2	5						
35 cents	2			1		2		
33½ cents	1							
33 cents	1	1						
30 cents							3	

TAYLOR EXHIBIT NO. 13.

	Output.	
	As union foundry.	As open shop.
Standard castings, 1 molder and 1 helper:		
Shingle machine—		
26-inch saw collars	6	12
Gears	4	10
Friction pulleys	3	8
Main frame	1	2
Track	1	¹ 2
Carriage	1	¹ 2
Arbor pulleys, 24 by 12 inches	1	¹ 2
Molding machine work, 1 molder and 1 helper:		
Pulleys—		
36 by 10 inches	1	
24 by 10 inches	1	
24 by 10 inches		5
18 by 11 inches		2
16 by 11 inches		2
Spur iron frictions, 36 by 8 inches	1	3

¹ And some small work.

WALLACE EXHIBIT NO. 1.

January 1, 1914.

Claim No.	Work-days lost.	Wages lost.	Cost of treatment.	Award for time lost.	Award for disability.
29259	24	$108.00	$19.50	$27.65	
29697	55	192.50	55.50	63.45	
30006	51	255.00	50.00	103.00	
30773	15	52.50	5.00	17.30	
32050	13	58.50	11.50	18.75	
29612	8	18.00	20.00	9.20	
32175	11	30.25	10.50	18.15	
31873	3½	7.00	2.00	4.05	
31341	25	56.25	10.00	33.75	
31987	20	50.00	2.50	23.05	
32336	11	33.00	15.00	12.70	
31543	13½	47.25	4.00	15.60	
30225	10	27.50	36.00	11.55	
29742	71	177.50	4.00	106.50	
31593	18	40.50	5.00	20.75	
31671	24	168.00	10.00	41.50	
31057	14	35.00	2.50	21.00	
30992	9	21.60	25.00	10.40	
30810	26	58.50	3.00	30.00	
30414	48	120.00	18.50	72.00	
29001	34	85.00	41.75	39.20	
31550	2	6.00		2.90	
31480	14	42.00	2.50	25.20	
31428	12	30.00	3.00	18.00	
26987	104	260.00	50.00	120.00	
32264	9	22.50	2.00	13.50	
32215	13	29.25	6.00	15.00	
31675	39	175.50	64.50	45.00	
32094	5	12.50	10.50	5.75	
32030	24	72.00	7.50	41.50	
31853	20	50.00	12.00	30.00	
31854	25	68.75	22.40	36.05	
31885	26	58.50	15.50	35.10	
32231	16	36.00	5.35	18.45	
31452	39	106.75	75.00	45.00	
30755	30	75.00	50.00	34.60	
29493	86	510.00	25.00	124.05	
31545	18	72.00	7.00	20.75	
31997	15	41.25	3.50	24.75	
31679	6	17.40	5.00	6.90	
31511	29	65.25	22.50	39.15	
31376	27	67.50	10.00	40.50	

January 1, 1914—Continued.

Claim No.	Work-days lost.	Wages lost.	Cost of treatment.	Award for time lost.	Award for disability.
31193	12	27.00	6.50	13.85	..:
30646	37	88.80	15.00	42.70	
30657	43	107.50	1.50	64.50	
19873	99	222.75	103.50	129.35	
32470	8	27.60	14.25	11.55	
32156	7	24.50	3.75	10.10	
32184	22	55.00	2.80	25.35	
32187	12	30.00	3.50	17.30	
31817	19	47.50	6.50	28.50	
31721	6½	22.75	6.00	7.50	
32625	6	16.20	5.00	9.70	
32075	4½	18.00	25.00	9.10	
31784	13	38.09	3.50	18.75	
31380	13	42.25	3.00	15.00	
30944	10	60.00	15.00	17.·30	
31011	51	102.00	10.00	76.50	
25115	12	42.00	10.00	40.10	
27819	16	80.00	6.00	32.30	
31610	18	45.00	5.00	25.95	
32024	26	52.00	14.50	31.20	
32323	22	132.00	16.25	38.05	
32310	21	129.15	60.00	30.30	
32274	10	40.00	13.15	20.20	
31709	14	42.00	5.00	20.20	
31347	10	27.00		11.55	
31321	3	7.80	5.00	3.45	
31295	8	22.00	2.00	9.20	
31218	40	140.00	8.00	57.70	
27751	99	356.40	25.00	139.90	
31802	5	16.25	7.00	5.75	
31177	10	27.50	9.50	16.50	
28227	14	38.50	3.25	16.15	
31196	17	38.25	12.00	19.60	
31825	12	42.00	10.00	24.25	
31856	6	10.02	15.00	6.00	
13149	8	24.00	20.00	11.55	
31374	27	135.00	20.00	46.75	
31587	13	26.00	6.50	15.00	
31609	20	60.00	10.00	28.85	
31355	1½	3.51	1.00	1.75	
30928	29	101.50	7.50	33.45	
31135	11	27.50	20.00	16.50	
31279	27	54.00	10.00	32.40	
28176	15	81.25	40.00	48.75	
31335	11	44.00	7.00	12.70	
30477	40	100.00	15.00	60.00	
30642	24	60.00	18.00	36.00	
31888	18	112.50	18.00	36.35	
31504	13	26.00	5.50	15.00	
31643	4	9.00	2.50	4.60	
31309	2	6.90	12.00	4.05	
30351	34	136.00	58.00	39.20	
31001	5	22.50	6.00	10.10	
31732	32½	81.25	24.00	37.50	
30850	23½	38.75	10.00	35.25	
31917	10	25.00	5.20	15.00	
31647	12	30.00	5.00	18.00	
31101	36	108.00	3.00	41.55	
29956	49	134.75	20.00	80.85	
31827	9½	19.00	20.00	10.95	
31127	2½	11.25	7.00	9.20	
32207	12	49.80	3.50	17.30	
31482	11	38.50	5.00	22.20	
30011	8	24.00	25.00	14.40	
28210	62	248.00	84.05	89.40	
31766	26	78.00	13.00	37.50	
29755	35	84.00	20.00	40.40	
31965	10	42.50	6.00	17.30	
31701	18	54.00	5.00	32.40	
31288	24½	55.10	30.00	28.25	
31603	7	14.00	12.00	8.40	
31875	15	33.75	8.00	20.25	
31081	12	24.00	4.00	13.85	
31830	3	7.65	3.00	3.45	
29041	68	187.00	20.00	78.45	
31795	14	70.00	28.00	20.20	
30894	22	55.00	17.00	33.00	
31978	14	35.00	10.00	20.20	
30894	22	55.00	17.00	33.00	
31978	14	35.00	10.00	20.20	
31502	25	78.75	31.00	41.25	

January 1, 1914—Continued.

m No.	Work-days lost.	Wages lost.	Cost of treatment.	Award for time lost.	Award for disability.
....	8	40.00	4.50	16.15	....
....	42	147.00	18.00	48.45	....
....	32	91.20	15.00	55.40	....
....	40	160.00	18.00	80.75	....
....	13	52.00	15.00	15.00	....
....	6	16.50	1.50	6.90	....
....	30	75.00	36.00·	45.00	....
....	25	90.00	....	43.25	....
....	9½	25.65	.50	10.95	....
....	6	24.00	.85	12.10	....
....	41	205.00	69.00	59.15	....
....	128	448.00	165.00	147.65	....
....	83	228.25	175.00	95.75	....
....	9	27.00	4.50	10.40	....
....	29	67.50	15.00	40.00	....
....	156	429.00	85.00	225.00	....
....	32	49.60	25.00	36.90	....
....	6	27.00	2.50	12.10	....
....	160	576.00	250.00	212.35	....
....	71	213.00	70.00	102.40	....
....	42	189.00	35.75	48.45	....
....	43	118.25	30.00	70.95	....
....	11	39.60	5.00	15.83	....
....	26	68.90	12.00	41.35	....
....	6	19.50.	5.00	6.90	....
....	12	36.00	12.00	21.60	....
....	9	37.44	....	13.00	....
....	10	25.00	5.00	11.55	....
....	3	7.50	3.00	3.45	....
....	12	30.00	5.00	13.85	....
....	9	31.50	5.00	18.15	....
....	12	30.00	....	18.00	....
....	18	72.00	10.00	36.35	....
....	6	24.00	4.00	6.90	....
....	18	72.00	37.50	25.95	....
....	17	46.75	6.00	25.50	....
....	24	60.00	1.50	36.00	....
....	7	26.95	22.00	8.05	....
....	34	130.90	54.00	39.20	....
....	6	13.50	....	6.90	....
....	28	98.00	10.00	32.30	....
....	21½	43.00	10.00	24.80	....
....	10	27.50	5.00	16.40	....
....	10½	26.25	5.00	12.10	....
....	19	42.75	23.50	25.65	....
....	5	13.75	3.00	8.25	....
....	10½	28.87	8.00	17.35	....
....	13	49.14	12.50	18.75	....
....	13	29.25	12.00	15.00	....
....	14½	34.80	10.00	16.70	....
....	12	54.00	1.40	17.30	....
....	18	40.50	12.00	24.30	....
....	6	15.00	14.00	9.00	....
....	9	22.50	30.00	13.50	....
....	6	16.20	10.00	6.90	....
....	23	69.00	20.00	41.40	....
....	6	13.50	3.50	6.90	....
....	10	28.00	5.50	11.55	....
....	39	136.50	15.00	56.25	....
....	13	65.00	26.15	26.25	....
....	2	5.00	7.00	2.30	....
....	8	20.00	15.00	12.00	....
....	11	30.25	15.00	12.70	....
....	3	7.50	....	3.45	....
....	26	78.00	8.00	46.80	....
....	5	11.25	5.50	5.75	....
....	14	59.50	6.00	28.25	....
....	13	44.20	17.00	26.25	....
....	32	96.00	12.85	36.90	....
....	10	30.00	3.00	18.00	....
....	44	110.00	10.20	50.75	....
....	15	41.25	10.00	24.75	....
....	5	30.00	20.00	10.10	....
....	8	16.00	2.00	9.60	....
....	16	48.00	8.50	18.45	....
....	18	54.00	2.00	20.75	....
....	12	36.00	10.00	13.85	....
....	8	16.00	3.00	9.20	....
....	17	85.00	3.50	34.30	....
....	49	122.50	25.00	56.50	....
....	208	686.40	232.00	275.00	....

January 1, 1914—Continued.

Claim No.	Work-days lost.	Wages lost.	Cost of treatment.	Award for time lost.	Award for disability.
28845	21	94.50	.35	24.20	
31727	12	48.00	10.00	13.85	
30695	32	128.00	25.00	36.90	
30663	18	24.00	10.00	14.45	
29454	9	10.44	10.00	6.30	
Total (207 claims)	4,807½	15,190.31	3,828.25	6,682.28	
28646	26	52.00	15.00	30.00	100.00
29263	31	186.00	15.00	44.70	100.00
29740	54	216.00	150.00	109.05	1,500.00
29366	23	115.00	20.00	39.80	25.00
28965	26	156.00	15.00	45.00	50.00
29874	30	105.00	63.00	34.60	87.50
26792	167	459.25	145.00	235.55	150.00
22985	180	630.00	258.00	198.45	100.00
28062	93	279.00	100.50	160.95	125.00
30609	30½	152.50	22.00	61.60	87.50
30251	30	90.00	65.00	34.60	25.00
26766	29	87.00	15.00	52.20	275.00
30802	29	87.00	25.00	33.45	275.00
26926	37	111.00	150.00	64.05	100.00
24481	44	132.00	300.00	50.75	400.00
29727	60	171.00	50.00	86.55	175.00
30303	42	210.00	12.00	60.55	25.00
23915	26	71.50	200.00	42.90	525.00
21911	12	12.00	3.65	7.20	87.50
31307	25	200.00	20.00	43.25	87.50
30822	46	126.50	17.00	66.35	50.00
30722	42	94.50	160.00	48.45	175.00
30876	38	114.00	20.60	43.85	112.50
25289	68	204.00	55.00	78.45	75.00
29151	78	261.30	140.00	90.00	225.00
31768	13½	438.75		26.35	50.00
28404	30	82.50	40.00	34.60	25.00
28602	12	42.00	60.00	62.25	400.00
26096	66	330.00	28.00	185.75	25.00
26616	33	49.50	150.00	28.55	100.00
31390	34	76.50	25.00	45.90	62.50
Total (31 cases)	1,455	5,341.80	2,339.75	2,145.70	5,550.00

WALLACE EXHIBIT NO. 2.

STATE OF WASHINGTON,
OFFICE OF GOVERNOR,
Olympia, February 5, 1914:

Hon. J. H. WALLACE,
Member Industrial Insurance Commission.

DEAR SIR: In going through the newspaper clippings received by me, I find one from the Raymond Herald containing a part of your address delivered to the State federation of labor at the meeting held in Raymond a few days ago. A copy of this clipping I am herewith inclosing, so that you may have an opportunity to see just exactly your statement as given by the press.

It would appear from this statement that in your address you criticised severely the other two members of the industrial insurance commission, indicating that they were making an effort to "emasculate the law and that many causes for complaint had occurred during the past few months which you were powerless to prevent."

It is my desire that the best possible results be obtained from the operation of the industrial-insurance law. There is no doubt in the minds of those who have given careful study to the matter but that the law is proving to be an excellent measure in the handling of this particular line of insurance. I have at all times endeavored to impress upon the commission the necessity of their becoming thoroughly acquainted with the law and putting forth every effort to properly administer it. Inasmuch as this article from the Raymond Herald indicates there is a marked difference of opinion between the members of the commission regarding the method of administering the law, I desire to have from you a statement concerning wherein these differences occur and giving to me such facts as will be of service in arriving at a proper conclusion regarding the actions of the members of the board. I hope that you will take sufficient time in the preparation of your answer to this request so that you may present the information called for in a clear and concise manner. I recognize that the work of the commission covers a large amount of detail; that this detail must be worked out carefully and correctly for the purpose of getting the proper results from its operation. I hope you will present such facts as you may have wherein you feel the other members of the board have not done their duty, so that I will be able to arrive at a fair and impartial conclusion from the facts submitted.

I have written to each member of the commission to-day. To the other two members of the commission I have forwarded a copy of the clipping, the same as is herewith inclosed, and have requested each of the other two members to submit to me a statement also in writing.

Awaiting your reply to this communication, I am,
Yours, truly,

ERNEST LISTER, *Governor.*

OLYMPIA, WASH., *February 28, 1914.*

Hon. ERNEST LISTER,
Governor of the State of Washington, Olympia, Wash.

MY DEAR GOVERNOR: Complying with your request of February 5, desiring a statement from me re the differences existing between the other members of the board and myself, your request being made as result of statements made by me at the federation of labor meeting in Raymond on Wednesday afternoon, January 22, 1914, I am indeed pleased that the privilege has been granted me to explain some of the administrative details of the workmen's compensation law, which, in my opinion, are not receiving the consideration they necessarily should, and because, in my opinion, legislation of this character can not possibly be successful without the hearty cooperation of all forces affected, to the end that it might be administered equitably, justly, without fear or favor, for the good of all parties concerned.

During the time I have been connected with this work I have endeavored to present my views in as nonpartisan, unbiased, and candid manner as it is possible for one man to deal with other men, and have felt free at all times to advance theories, which to me seemed practical and beneficial, in the hope that the most possible good would accrue to the people of our State as a result. I am also free to confess that, in my opinion, this is the only successful method of dealing with large humanitarian problems.

In studying the question of social insurance we are brought face to face with a great economic waste, which every class of people interested in great social problems admits existed under our old former common-law procedure. Moneys were being paid into channels diametrically opposed to the interests of those who should receive them. Expensive litigation was indulged in to defeat the ends of justice. Orphan homes, county poor farms, and charitable institutions were crowded to capacity because of the large number of destitute people, the direct outcome of industrial misfortune. It was to correct such conditions, to make brighter the dark day, to inspire hope where despair had come, to bring together into a closer unity of faith and action the man who performs and the man who plans our great industrial operations, that workmen's compensation laws came into being.

In the administration of our workmen's compensation law the first requisite for success must be found in the men charged with carrying out its provisions. This is vitally important, since they must necessarily be men of good judgment, capable of thinking justly, fearless in upholding its principles, bringing careful thought and study to the intricate problems confronting them, equitable and just in the payment of awards. This, with a careful analytical interest in the ultimate possibilities to be realized from such legislation, together with a knowledge of the laws of other countries and States, embodying the social significance attached thereto, should command the attention of every person directly affiliated with this great problem.

These principles comprise the greater significance of social insurance as outlined by and promulgated in the report of the original commission prior to the enactment of the law. Both the employer and employee saw in the spirit and letter of the act not alone the paying of moneys for injuries but the larger and more vital benefits that would accrue as a result of education and experience from such legislation.

With these things in mind, the commission first appointed to administer this law devoted itself religiously to its great humanitarian work. Problems of administration were taken up and decided not by any individual commissioner but by the commission; questions of moment affecting the interests of all parties were debated and conclusions arrived at; claims were disposed of in a spirit of fairness and equity under the law; employers and employees received the same courteous treatment, the commission embodying the idea that while compensation was necessary when workmen were injured, the prime factor was not compensation but accident prevention.

This spirit, these sentiments, have actuated the writer, since the day of his appointment, to assist in carrying out the legislative intent of this great law, and, as one of its advocates, I am still of the opinion that you will appreciate its greater virtues in a systematic effort to decrease the number of unnecessary accidents, to conserve, as far as possible, life and limb, and thus make unnecessary the enormous financial drain upon industry now demanded in apology for this great human waste.

In the creation of a department to administer this law provision was made for the appointment of three commissioners, upon whom should devolve the duties of successfully carrying into effect the provisions of the act. It was the intent that all questions arising under the law upon which decision should be rendered must be concurred in by a majority of the board. This also contemplates a thorough familiarity with all phases of the work on the part of each member of the commission, to the end that whatever action is taken upon any problem arising thereunder each commissioner would be fully advised thereon. This would also, in my opinion, prohibit the discussion and final settlement of any problem demanding a ruling by the board, the validity of which might be questioned, with less than the full board present, in order that every phase of the subject under discussion be brought out and action taken after a thorough painstaking effort to apply the law justly in accordance with the merits of the case.

This was the policy pursued prior to the appointment by you of the two commissioners now serving with me, and was, for some time, indulged in by them, but later, for reasons best known to themselves, dispensed with. Changes in the policy of administration have been made without my knowledge or consent, and actions taken in which I could not concur, either from a legal or honorable standpoint. Policies affecting the welfare of both employers and employees are being carried out which, in my opinion, are a menace to the interests of both. It is because of my inability to remedy these conditions, after using every honorable influence with the other members for their correction, that I was compelled in the interests of my own good name and character to make the statements I did at the Raymond convention.

Permit me to say that my disagreement as to the policies outlined by the other members of the board affords me no particular pleasure, as I have sought by every honorable means to render all the assistance possible to the end that we might work in harmony with each other, in order that the law be made a success. Furthermore, I willingly and frankly contributed the information gleaned from my experience in the work, since its inception. However, for some months past the other commissioners have seemingly studied how to avoid a fair, honorable, and impartial application of the law and its provisions, and for a number of months have arbitrarily carried into execution theories of their own without warrant under the law, in theory or in fact, and refuse even at this time, although having been notified by attorney general's office that such methods are illegal, to desist from their policy. I refer specifically to the payment of claims as carried on at this time: Claims are assembled in the assembling department, passed on by the claim agent, where the amounts due injured workmen or the dependents of those skilled are compiled; claims are then forwarded to the executive room, where it is the duty of the commission to inspect them carefully and, if found correct, attach their signatures for payment. Under the provisions of the law it is the duty of the department to pass upon the legitimacy of these claims, to see that they are figured correctly, that the amounts paid are in accordance with the act, and that all conditions necessary to their passage and payment have been complied with.

For some months past these claims have been figured as usual by the claim department, forwarded to the executive room to be passed on by the commission, but instead of having the careful, conscientious, and legitimate scrutiny of at least two members of the board, they are signed arbitrarily by one commissioner without any investigation on his part as to the legitimacy of the claims or the merits of the award made. This, in my opinion, and I have so stated to the other members of the board, is absolutely contrary to the spirit and letter of the law and has been the source of much injustice, in that some claimants have not received the consideration and awards to which they were justly entitled, while others have received more than the letter or spirit of the act entitled them to. The only excuse offered by the chairman of the commission for not following out the policy as contemplated by the law, of having two commissioners with the chief surgeon pass upon every claim, as was the case under the original or old commission, was that he was not going to have two men spending their time around the office.

Another cause for complaint, and one which in my opinion merits special attention, is the position taken by your appointees where men have been injured to the extent of being permanently totally disabled. This, I believe, to be one of the most unfair attitudes taken by any set of men intrusted with the man as well as the money side of this great humanely interesting problem. The viciousness of this attitude was first brought to my attention during the early months of their appointment, when a victim of industrial misfortune, totally blind, presented himself to the commission, in the hope of getting some relief by settlement, for a lump sum. Upon this particular day the attorney general, W. V. Tanner, was in the commission's office when Mr. Daggett suggested a lump-sum settlement on the basis of $1,500 in full and final payment for injuries received. The attorney general advised him, in the presence of the other members of the commission, that if settlements were made on this basis it was high time that some one took action to have the law repealed. It is unnecessary to state that the man was afterwards placed on the permanent pension roll.

This advice seemingly satisfied but for the moment, since repeated attempts have been made to make settlements on the basis of $1,500 where men were permanently totally disabled. One such attempted settlement caused a furore in the particular locality where the claimant lived, a resolution being sent out to all labor bodies of the State condemning the action of the commission, even though the man was afterwards placed on the permanent pension roll and is now receiving his payments each month.

Permit me to say that while $1,500 is the maximum which may be paid for a permanent partial disability, nowhere within the pages of the law is it either written or implied that the commission shall arbitrarily fix the amount for permanent total disability at $1,500, or any other amount, excepting that they may not, when converting into a lump sum, final payment in cases of permanent total disability, pay more than $4,000, which is specifically stated in section 7 of the act.

One of the administrative problems facing the original board, and one which gave food for serious thought, was the section just referred to. After carefully analyzing every feature of the act and studying it from various angles the commission became firmly convinced that since the protection afforded by this law was not primarily for the mother, who is in most cases capable of caring for herself, but rather for those who were defenseless and helpless in dealing with economic conditions, namely, the children, that no lump-sum payments would be made, but dependents placed on the pension list receiving monthly their stipends, according to section 5 of the law. If this theory is predicated upon sound judgment with thought only for the good of our future citizenship and a spirit that demonstrates an endeavor to do that which is best for those intrusted to our care, most uncanny is the thought that any man, claiming to serve the people on this board, can justify his position by offering lump-sum settlements of $1,500, in the hope that such will be accepted in lieu of any amount between $1,500 and $4,000, which the law justifies us in giving.

Among the specific cases coming under this head, and which I have in mind, having been brought face to face with them, either by protest from the parties affected or by discussion of them by their friends, is one No. 22723, showing that the injured man was blinded by premature blast, losing the sight of both eyes and suffering other injuries, which leave him permanently totally disabled for life. This man was injured on June 6, 1913, monthly payments being made as per schedule. On January 5, in a letter dictated to the commission by Mr. Daggett, who had evidently interviewed the man in person, he makes the following statement:

"INDUSTRIAL INSURANCE COMMISSION,
"Olympia, Wash.

" GENTLEMEN : I have this day, on behalf of the commission, tendered claimant a settlement for $1,500 as full and complete payment for injuries now existing, or that he be placed on a pension of $20 per month from this date, either settlement to include time loss to date, with a lump-sum settlement. I am convinced that by an operation upon the leg and removal of cataract from the left eye he will have reasonably good result to the leg and about one-third to one-half vision of the eyes. Without these operations he is entitled to a permanent total disability. He has elected to take the pension, and I recommend that same be allowed.

" FLOYD L. DAGGETT."

It will be seen from this letter that the thought seemingly uppermost in the mind of the commissioner was to close claim regardless of the condition of the claimant. I have never been able to conjure in my mind where the idea took root in the minds of the commissioners that they had any legal or moral right to offer settlements on this basis. This method, however, is entirely too prevalent, as the theory of law was not to bargain with claimants, but to make settlements, where such were legitimate, on the basis of right and justice under the law and not on a basis of economic necessity.

Another case, referred to earlier in this article, is claim No. 22800, where the man appeared before the commission and was accorded the same treatment and made the same offer as in the previous case. Claimant refused to accept the $1,500, and some time later I was dispatched to investigate this man's condition and placed him on the permanent pension roll. This is the case in which the people in the community in which he lived voiced their vigorous protest at the action of the commission in offering the claimant the sum of $1,500; wrote your honor a letter relative to the matter, suggesting that if a change in the commissioners were made they would greatly appreciate it. They have since circulated their protest throughout the State, calling the attention of laboring men to the business methods employed by this department.

Another claim, No. 4166, where the injured person received a fracture of the spine. Receiving monthly payments for some time, he was confronted by one of our adjusters and offered a lump sum of, firstly, $1,000, and then $1,250 in a final settlement of his claim. This he refused to accept. At a later period, in company with Mr. Daggett, we paid this man a visit, when Mr. Daggett offered him $500 in full and complete settlement of his claim. To this both the wife and husband protested, the man at that time being still on crutches. Upon leaving the house I informed Mr. Daggett that the man should be placed on the permanent pension list, as, in my opinion, he would never again be able to perform any gainful labor. A few days afterwards the claim was acted upon by the commission and the sum of $4,000 set aside, from which payments are being made.

Such arbitrary actions as these on the part of the commission are doing more to crystallize unfavorable sentiment than all the good it is doing in other directions. Why the commission should attempt to make settlements with men during the time their injuries are indeterminate is, in my opinion, but a relic of the old casualty insurance method of making settlements and entirely out of harmony with the trend of modern thought as embodied in workmen's compensation laws. But it is not only in permanent total disability cases that our actions are being criticized. Even more pernicious is this system of barter in blood for dollars and cents where the injuries result in permanent partial disabilties.

Under the system now prevalent in this department little attention is paid to the ratings made by the chief surgeon, since those who do the most protesting and threatening receive the most when the bargain is finally struck, only those accepting what they are offered by the commission feeling they are being dealt with honestly and in good faith getting the ratings made by the chief physician and awards in keeping with showing made by him on special examination reports.

To such an extent has this been carried that one man, whose claim number is 15150, received much more in compensation than he was legally entitled to. He sustained severe injuries, which caused a permanent partial disability, for which our chief surgeon made a rating of 8 degrees, or $200. Rather than accept this amount he appealed from the findings of the board, engaged a lawyer to defend him in the courts, but was finally settled with by Mr. Daggett in the sum of

$850. This is one of the most extraordinary examples of settlement bargaining that has come to my notice.

As a direct result of the settlement made in the case just referred to, and one which bears out my former statements relative to the ratings made by the chief surgeon, is the attitude taken by claimant No. 24405. This man was injured June 17, 1913, suffering a fracture of the femur; monthly payments have been made in accordance with the law, and on January 17 the claim was closed as to time loss, with a rating of 16 degrees, or $400, for permanent partial disability. This man has since engaged a lawyer, who, on February 17, appeared before the commission with his client, demanding $850, the sum total to be made up in additional time loss, or in any other manner, as long as the full amount paid totaled $850. As a result of the attorney's interview with the commission, the chief surgeon's rating has been raised from 16 to 22 degrees, with an additional time loss of two and one-half months, which would make $800. In a letter written to the attorney on February 21 by the claim department, under instructions from the other members of the board, is the following:

" Mr. ROGER MARCHETTI,
   " No. 217 Lyon Building, Seattle, Wash.
" DEAR SIR: Referring to the claim of Dominic Fazio, on account of injury sustained June 17, 1913.
" Will you kindly advise claimant that this commission, in addition to the compensation already allowed him, will make further award of $50 to cover two and one-half months' time loss, and $150 additional for the permanent partial disability. This, added to the payments already made, which amounted to $600, will give him a total of $800 for the accident.
" Kindly advise if your client will accept this amount. An early reply will be appreciated.
   " Yours, very truly,
                    " INDUSTRIAL INSURANCE COMMISSION."

In this case the chief surgeon made a special examination of the claimant on February 17, making two radiographs, neither of which show any injury to the bone. In his special report the chief surgeon makes this statement:
" His disability should be estimated at two-thirds loss of leg at knee, or 16 degrees. which seems to me is entirely reasonable."
Yet, in spite of this, the rating has been raised arbitrarily by the commissioners without warrant under the law and, in my opinion, in strict violation of it.
If the commission can rate permanent partial disabilities in a more competent and efficient manner than our chief surgeon, whose life work, it seems to me, has peculiarly fitted him for such a position, then why the necessity of having him make examinations, since the commissioners are more expert than he. On the other hand, if it is admitted that our chief surgeon does not understand his business and is not capable of determining fairly and with reasonable accuracy permanent partial disabilities, or other results accruing from injuries, it would seem the duty of the department to replace him with a man in whom they have absolute confidence. In my opinion, however, this is unnecessary, as our chief surgeon is eminently capable of filling the position he now holds, as I have found him to be honest, efficient, and equitable in dealing with injured workmen who have been ordered before him for special examinations.
Another peculiar condition with which I am confronted is to be found in claim No. 19451. In this case the claimant was injured by a log rolling on his leg and breaking it. The firm was in default at the time and the claimant so notified, being advised that he could either sue his employer, as provided in the law, or take under the workmen's compensation act and assign his claim to the State. After numerous letters had been written by the claimant and this department to each other claimant finally assigned his claim to the State and accepted compensation as per the law. This claim shows a time loss of 83 days, with payments on the basis of $37.50 per month, the maximum that can be received by man and his wife. By some peculiar rating, unknown to the writer, this man received in payment for time loss only $194.70; the sum total payment in this case to which the claimant was justly entitled was $119.70; he, therefore, received $75 to which he was not entitled under the law, because of negligence on the part of the commission in not carefully scrutinizing claims

4544 REPORT OF COMMISSION ON INDUSTRIAL RELATIONS.

before attaching their signature thereto. This is signed by Chairman F. L. Daggett.

In claim No. 23915 we find another exhibition of the utter disregard of equity and justice in dealing with claimants, since this particular case forced itself upon the commission's attention because of the different ratings for permanent partial disability by the two specialists who reported on this man's condition. He suffered a severe injury to the left eye on June 8, which caused a very bad central corneal ulcer. On November 8 an examination was made by a specialist to determine the loss of vision, if any, and report made to the commission accordingly. This report showed a probable loss of vision entitling the man to 21 degrees, or $525, for permanent partial disability. As is customary when such payments are awarded, the employer was notified as to the amount the man would receive for the disability sustained. The employer immediately voiced his protest in a letter addressed to the commission, whereupon the commission had the man reexamined in order to ascertain if a mistake had been made by the first examiner. Accordingly, one month later, another special examination was made by another specialist, who found the man's vision much more impaired than when the first examination was made. The examination made by the second specialist showed that the man had practically no industrial vision with the left eye, and considered it very doubtful if the man would ever obtain any useful vision. In accordance with this later report, the man was rated by our chief surgeon as having nine-tenths loss of vision in the left eye, which would entitle him, under a fair and impartial application of the law, to $750. Upon receipt of the second special examiner's report I took up with Commissioner Ernst, in the presence of Dr. Mowell, the difference in rating, and insisted that since the latest report showed an impairment greater than that received in the first report the claimant was entitled to the difference in rating, said difference being an additional amount of $225. I made this statement very clear, because, as pointed out by me to my brother commissioner at that time, if the rating by the specialist making the second report had been less than that estimated in the first report there would have been no hesitancy on the part of the commission in reducing the amount in proportion to the lessened disability. It was only fair, therefore, that since the second report showed an increased disability the award should be increased accordingly. To this Commissioner Ernst seemed to be agreed, yet on January 15, 1914, the warrant for $525, which had been held up awaiting the second examination, was released, and the additional $225, to which the man was justly entitled according to the second specialist's report, has not been paid.

Another case brought to my attention was that of claimant No. 22281. Injury was such as to necessitate the amputation of part of the right foot. This accident occurred on May 28, 1913. On June 3 another amputation was necessary, causing the entire loss of the foot at the ankle joint. On August 25 card was received, showing that second amputation had been made; card marked showing a disability of 30 degrees. No report, however, was attached showing that the rating was made as a result of a special examination, yet the claim was closed on this basis on September 28, 1913. The man refused to accept the $750, placing his case in the hands of an attorney, contending that he was entitled to $1,000 as a result of the permanent partial disability sustained. After the attorney had been brought into the case a special examination was made of the man on December 16 in the presence of Mr. Daggett, and an award of the amount contested for, i. e., $1,000, was paid the claimant. Now, it seems to me that if the man was entitled to $1,000 in the last instance he was entitled to the same amount when the claim was finally closed on September 28, without the necessity of being compelled to engage counsel to procure for him that to which he was justly entitled.

On November 18, while in the Seattle office assisting Commissioner Ernst in passing upon claims, there being present a number of claimants who were desirous of receiving their awards, there appeared two claimants, the claim number of the first being 24125, the other being claimant No. 21873, both complaining of the arbitrary method taken by Commissioner Ernst in attempting to make settlements with them for injuries received.

In the case of claimant No. 24125, claimant was injured on July 3, 1913, showing a severe injury to the shoulder. The man was still unable to work, but had been offered as final payment three months' additional time loss from October 3 in order to close out his claim. No special examination had been made upon this case by anyone, yet the dislocation of the shoulder had caused an atrophy of the muscles, which would imply that the man was suffering from some nerve involvement, which prohibited the use of the arm at any kind of work. Upon complaint of the claimant that he was not being fairly treated I advised him to come to Olympia to be examined by Dr. Mowell. In accordance with the results of the examination made at that time the claimant was awarded six months' time loss, and asked to return for another examination at the end of that period to definitely determine his condition at that time.

The other claim, No. 21873, was a much more aggravated case, since the man had suffered a fracture of the right arm on May 13, 1913, receiving monthly payments as per the law and closed out on time loss only. This claimant made the statement that he had taken his case up with Commissioner Ernst, claiming a permanent partial disability, which, upon examination by me, seemed to be very apparent. I accordingly ordered him before our special examiner in Olympia, who made two radiographs of this man's arm, which showed an overriding of the bone, with a displacement of the lower fragment down toward the ulna; this prevented complete supernation, which caused a permanent partial disability. He was accordingly awarded an additional $200, to which he was, under the act, rightfully entitled.

On the 19th of the present month I was handed a claim for investigation at Black Diamond, claim number being 32143. The peculiar feature in connection with this claim is shown on the summary sheet and demonstrates very forcibly the lack of attention given these claims by the members of the board. First monthly payment awarded was for $52.50, the maximum provided by law for temporary total disabilities to claimants having a wife and two or more children under the age of 16. The second payment, which was made in closing out the claim on a time loss of 23 days and which should have been rated in accordance with the act at $46.45, was computed on the basis of payment to a single man, at $30 per month, and an award of $26.25 made and voucher sent in final settlement thereof. This is a glaring example of the signing of claims without scrutiny on the part of the commission, the award for the first month being signed by Commissioner Ernst and the second by Chairman Floyd L. Daggett.

Another claim which shows the same lack of careful consideration is No. 29282. This claimant was severely injured on October 17, 1913, suffering a fracture of the neck of the femur; his report was made out by the nurse at the hospital, showing that he had received a wage of $2.50 per day; the employer's report, however, showed that the wage received by this man was $2.75 per day. Claimant having a wife, and two children under the age of 16, would have been entitled to $52.50 per month, had this amount been less than 60 per cent of his monthly earnings. Unfortunately, however, the smallness of the wage placed him within the 60 per cent rule and he was paid on the basis of 60 per cent of $2.50 per day, instead of $2.75, as shown on the report of the employer, his monthly award being $39 on that basis. He received three payments of $39, when, thinking his award was small and that some mistake had been made in its computation, he notified the commission, by letter, as to the wages he was paid prior to the accident; this increased his monthly award from $39 to $42.90, the additional amount for the three months previous being forwarded on the fourth payment made him. This discrepancy would no doubt have been discovered by the board before the first award was made had the claim been examined by the commission prior to its passage for the first monthly payment; however, neither the claim department nor the commission made this discovery until the claimant, himself, brought it to the attention of the department.

These are some of the concrete cases which have been brought to my attention, either by the claimants themselves, their friends, or from actual experience in the field and in the office, and are not the result of any investigation on my part to collect such evidence against my fellow commissioners. Numerous complaints have been made to me on my travels throughout the State, and if a careful inspection of the files were to be made, there is no doubt that other instances of a similar character would be discovered, which must, in my opinion, reflect everlasting discredit upon the men who are now intrusted with the administration of this law.

Instead of devoting themselves to the administrative problems confronting us, familiarizing themselves with the work, doing justice as between employer and workmen, the commission has degenerated into a claim-agency bureau, whose sole ambitions appear to be to make settlements as cheaply as possible and as quickly as possible, to the exclusion of any other thought of the intent and purposes of the act.

Details of administration are left to the heads of departments, one commissioner remaining in the office to sign claims arbitrarily, which in itself is illegal, without any perusal of the same whatever and with seemingly little care as to their validity, as long as the stamp of approval has been placed upon them by the claim agent. The other two commissioners have for months been acting ' as adjusters of claims, doing work which properly should be delegated to men in the field, whose duty should be to make reports to the commission, who, in turn, should have the most aggravated cases examined by specialists and X · rayed when necessary, reports being submitted to the commission, when final action should be taken and disposition of the claims made.

Under present conditions, two of the commissioners are supplied with a number of claims each week, or thereabouts, go their different ways, examine and have examined claimants in different parts of the State, and in a great many instances arbitrarily settle with them, having them sign final settlement vouchers in relinquishment of all further claims against the State. This is contrary to the spirit and letter of the act, since the law does not place within the province of any individual commissioner the right to arbitrarily judge as to the claimant's condition nor the awards that shall be paid him. Legally, this can only be done by a majority number of the board, and this policy was strictly adhered to until recently.

As a result of the adoption of this system, fewer examinations are being made of injured men in an effort to accurately establish the disabilities sustained, there having been a marked decrease in the number of examinations made in proportion to the number of claims settled, as between the first and second fiscal years of the operation of the law. In this connection, let me state that during the first fiscal year 843 special examinations were made by physicians other than Dr. Mowell, our own special examiner, in the settlement of 6,358 claims; during the second year, during which the present board has had charge most of the time, only 1,122 special examinations were made on 13,168 final settlements, and for the four months ending January 31, 1914, 292 special examinations have been made in the settlement of 4,524 claims. This falling off in the number of special examinations, the necessity for which is unquestioned, is directly traceable to the method now in vogue for making settlement without rhyme or reason, excepting that somehow they be made.

Every other department of administrative work has been sacrificed to this one fad, which, in my opinion, but demonstrates more clearly every day the mistaken idea that men, whose judgment has been warped, whose whole career has been spent in an atmosphere directly out of keeping with a work of this character, can hope to bring to it the qualities that would eminently fit them for carrying it out to a successful conclusion. The prevailing idea which is apparent to me, at least, is that the worth of a commissioner in this department must be based upon the number of claims he can close up, the right or wrong of the matter eliminated, as if he were making a dollar and cents record for himself as do men thus engaged for casualty insurance companies. Under such conditions, which have been imposed upon me until I can no longer refrain from voicing a vigorous protest, not only on behalf of myself but on behalf of the citizenship of the State, I charged that the law was being emasculated, robbed of its virile strength, warped, and dwarfed into anything but the thing it was intended to be, either in the minds of those who first drafted it or the great mass of people who are its direct beneficiaries.

The administration of this act should be imposed upon three commissioners, as provided for under the law, who shall be commissioners in fact as well as in theory, devoting their time to the administrative affairs of this great work, and even though the detail work intrusted to their care be enormous, they will still find time to attend to the necessary field work, employing adjusters to do the bulk of the work they now perform, for which the legislature made a generous appropriation. When these conditions have been met by the commission the intent and spirit of the act will in some measure at least have been complied with.

Desiring, as I believe you do, the greatest possible good to be accomplished for the people of the State by those intrusted with the handling of their affairs, I submit this report in the hope that after you have given it a fair and impartial investigation and have satisfied yourself as to the accuracy of the same, I shall be favored with a statement as to the conclusions arrived at.

Trusting that I have made myself clear, I am,

Very sincerely, yours,

J. H. WALLACE, *Commissioner.*

WALLACE EXHIBIT NO. 3.

CLAIM No. 28758.

SEPTEMBER 17, 1913.

I was injured while working for the city of Seattle by trying to stop a runaway team. Was trampled on by the horses and the dump wagon ran over the lower part of my limbs and the small of my back, causing a blood tumor to form the full size of my back and extending 6 or 8 inches down on the hips. Had the aspiration needle used twice, and afterwards had an incision of 2 inches made for a drain. Was discharged from the hospital October 9, 1913, but was under the doctor's care for some time after, as the incision had not healed. My family consisted at the time of a wife and three children, and expecting a fourth, which came April 27, 1914, the oldest being 6 years. Received the first State warrant October 27, 1913, which was for $42.90, then was called to the office of Commissioner Ernt, 501 Alaska Building, on November 22, 1913. He asked me how I felt, and what my doctor had said about my case, and when I told him that the doctor had told me that it might be six months, a year, or even two before I would be able to do my full capacity of work, and at that he could only guess at it, which he didn't care to do, he said that he would allow me two warrants for $42.90, and that I might go back to work the first of the year—understand, there was already one warrant past due me. When I refused to consider his proposition, knowing my condition, and the possible outcome, with my family dependent on me for support, he "raised his bid" to three warrants.

At that time I was only able to be about with the aid of a cane, and it was five months before I was able to work, but, of course, could not do my full capacity.

On March 21, 1914, I was called again to the office of Mr. Ernt, who had Dr. Mowell, State physician, examine me. He (the doctor) said he would like to have an X-ray plate made of my back, that he might be able to tell whether or not any bones were broken; and that, as it would cost the State $10 to have it taken in Seattle, and only 75 cents in Olympia, he suggested that I go to that place. As no provision was made by the State for my transportation to and from Seattle to Olympia, and as I had no money, one of the commissioners suggested that I borrow $5 from some friend, and that it "would be made all right for me" in my next State warrant, which I did, but when my check came, which was my seventh, I received only $35—$7.90 less than my regular check, and no additional money to cover that which I had borrowed for my expenses while on my trip.

When I made a further claim for compensation, and a claim for the promised money due me, and for the elastic band, which the doctor has ordered for my knee, I was told by one of the commissioners that if I would sign a final settlement voucher he would allow me another State warrant for $35, and said he was doing more for me than he ought, but was doing it at his own risk. Because of the fact the State allowed me so little for the maintenance of my family, the $42.90 or $35 per month needing to cover rent, provisions, fuel, clothing, hospital, and doctor bills for wife and two children, who were also ill, I was obliged to go to work before I was able, and now there are days when I can scarcely work at all, and days when I actually have to leave my work and come home. However, even missing days of work now and then I am better able to support my little family and pay occasionally on my debts which have accumulated during my disabled period. I wonder if one or all of those commissioners would, or could, place themselves in my place, how they would feel over my treatment. In seven months' time I received $292.40.

J. W. COULON,
816 Tenth Avenue, Seattle, Wash.

LOWMAN EXHIBIT NO. 1.

Mrs. Grace Pringle, Anacortes, Wash.: $2.17, $2.69; $1.85, $2.06, $1.99, $5.28, $3.32, $2.10, $2, $2.10, $5.25, $1.75, $5.25, $2.97, $6.12, $4.59, $3.78, $5.77, $1.23, $3.24, $4.02, $5.98. $5.49, $5.84, $4.05; total, 25 days, $90.89.

LOWMAN EXHIBIT NO. 2.

COAST FISH CO., CHINESE LABOR, 1913.

Name and wages of employees: Ju Yuen, $350; Go Mow, $400; Wong Hoy, $360; Ho Fook, $380; Seid Sing, $360; Go Wing Song, $350; Go Bow, $360; Go Su, $370; Wong Och Hong, $400; La Man, $370; Seid Woo, $410; Chin Lam, $285; Lvain Free, $360; Gong Yow, $400; Go Shung, $360; Yee How, $400; Go Jat, $390; K. Ishimitsu, $420; Jung Wy, $330; Lee Fook, $330; Yung Wah, $400; Wong Fuey, $400; Seid Sang, $400; Seid Sing, $410; .Seid Ju Lot, $410; Jayung Ming, $400; Mon Hung, $340; Jun Hang, $400; Luo Hung,· $400; Law Doon, $390; Wah Sam, $330.

These wages are net, as the company furnishes all transportation, board, tools, and clothing necessary, other than ordinary clothing, and in addition to these figures they were paid for every hour of overtime and Sundays and holidays.

DISTLER EXHIBIT.

Where there is a will there is a way.

"That it is the first law of self-preservation that any State or Nation may, and of right ought to, do all those things which are necessary to perpetuate its. own existence; and to abolish all those practices and to counteract all· those influences which are calculated to ruin the body politic and destroy society."— Declaration of Independence.

In the summer months from 10 to 40 men are brought in daily by false representation. Men are discharged or quit of their own accord fast enough to make room for the incoming horde. The baggage of the dupes is held by the company till employement fee, railroad fare, hospital fee, etc., is worked out. By far the greater portion of unfortunates will redeem their belongings, by submitting to this peonage system. All baggage not so redeemed is sold by this company to secondhand dealers. From 200 to over 400 pieces of baggage is sold at a time. Modernized highway robbery. The truth of the matter is if labor was treating capital as capital is treating labor in Cosmopolis, the militia would be camping in town to bring labor to time.

Our prosecuting attorney says we need additional legislation to stop the crime, which he fully admits is being committed; our legislator says there is law to reach these criminals. The late lamented grand jury (if I was correctly informed by Prosecuting Attorney Campbell) had several good friends of the Commercial Co. in their midst—and so the crime goes on undisturbed. Then up to date this corporation had power and influence enough to muzzle press, gag officials, and blindfold justice.

Since the above was written, the second serious robbery has taken place in Cosmopolis within the last few months. D. F. Spiegle's establishment was broken into and goods to the value of about $200 were taken. The alarm is given, every newspaper comes out in large headlines, the sheriff ·and police officials take a hand in the case to land and punish the robbers. At the same time, next store to Spiegle's, the contents of more than 180 pieces of baggage is being sold. This plunder represents only a very small percentage of baggage illegally obtained by the Grays Harbor Commercial Co. annually· from the most needy class of laboring men. The added value of this article was considerably greater to the owners, than the value of articles was taken from Spiegle's.

So the vital question after all is: Who are the robbers and who are the robbed?

Within the last four years new factory and mill located in South Aberdeen (which joins Cosmopolis to the west) ; this and the building of the O. & W. Railroad caused an increase in population and gave the town new life. No independent man who has the courage to stand by his convictions would stay long in the employ of the company, and he would not be wanted, either; those who are here and work for the company for years are subdued and are afraid at any time to express their opinion contrary to the company; and some of them have often betrayed the interest of the town, the best interest of their wives and children, at the request of the company.

The mess-house policy of the company is detrimental to our Government system and society, through its discrimination against the men of family; it is absolutely unnecessary. When men are hired they are given a nominal wage, which includes board in the mess house. Should a man not desire to board at the company mess house he is allowed but $10 a month, and as good board will cost approximately $20 per month the men are practically forced to accept the board at the mess house. About 500 men are now so compelled to board at this place... Such condition is not only a detriment to the men, but works a vital damage to the town in general, as it makes it impossible for a man with family to accept employment under such conditions. This state of affairs works directly against the rearing of families, which is the foundation of civilized government.

Another evil is the company stores. The town is incorporated and has now a population of about 1,400. In this small town the company conducts five stores. If not directly then indirectly a pressure is brought to bear to make the company employees deal in these stores.

The coupons are (within the last two years) issued at intervals; when so issued it is between pay days instead of cash. These coupons are good in any of the company stores, but of course do not give the employee the same opportunity to buy as in other stores.

I could show next how the company prevents the growth of the town. On different occasions it has tried to prevent the location of mills even in South Aberdeen. The former manager of this company dared and threatened Wm. Mack to build the Union Mill in South Aberdeen. Mr. Deming, who located in South Aberdeen, was also threatened, and so stated in the Aberdeen World. This indicates the absolute control of the public press by the company.

Another illustration: Some years ago John J. Carney, editor of the Aberdeen Herald, approached me with a proposition for me to put up $1,000 in cash, either in a bank or otherwise, but so he could collect the money when he had accomplished his part. He would guarantee that in less than one year's time he would make the Grays Harbor Commercial Co. abolish its mess-house system. As I did not have the sum of money required, I saw others of Cosmopolis, who told me to take him up, as we could get the money all right. In the meantime there appeared in the Herald an item something like this: "If conditions in Cosmopolis are such as reported—and by all appearance they are so and even worse—then a most thorough investigation is an urgent need." The day after these lines appeared I saw an official of the Commercial Co. enter the office of J. J. Carney. Later on I called on Mr. Carney and notified him that we were ready to enter into his proposition. He told me then that he had changed his mind, and it was all off. Since then J. J. Carney has championed the Grays Harbor Commercial Co. in all its doings.

I could show where the leading banker of Aberdeen was brought to time by this company. The company, threatening to start a bank in Cosmopolis, changed his attitude. Before this time he had put up money on different occasions to expose the wrongdoings of this company. For instance, we went in together and bought shares in the Grays Harbor Post, a labor paper, which for a considerable time did gallant work for bettering the conditions and denounced the methods practiced by the Grays Harbor Commercial Co. This same paper has since been disowned by the labor unions for its change of front.

I could show the active part taken by this company in elections. In one of the recent school elections we found 50 illegal votes cast by mill employees who were urged to vote by the straw bosses of the company. The company used to have absolute control of the town council and board of school directors.

WAGES AND DEDUCTIONS FROM WAGES.

Wages paid by the Grays Harbor Commercial Co. consist of cash, coupons, and board. The general wage is $26 per month and board. There are, however, many young men working for the company for $10 per month and board, or $10 per month and a bonus of $10 instead of board. The men are hired by the month, but paid by the day. The pay day is supposed to be the first Saturday after the 10th of each month, but it frequently happens that it is the second Saturday after the 10th. The wages are paid only to the last day of the preceding month. Between pay days, instead of cash, coupons have been paid, except where a man quits or is discharged, then the balance due him is paid in cash. I have been informed that within the last two or three months a limited amount of cash is paid once in between pay days. Coupons are cashed by the saloons, but discounted 20 cents on the dollar. The saloons in turn use the coupons to pay their rent to the Commercial Co. This is one reason why the saloon element holds with the Commercial Co. Another reason is that the saloon men of Cosmopolis rent from the Commercial Co., and in this way the·company controls this element, three of the four saloons in town being located on property owned by the Commercial Co.

Chief among the deductions is a charge of 50 cents per month, or any part thereof, for hospital fee. While this is not an unreasonable deduction where a man works straight through from month to month, but when a man has to pay 50 cents for the last days of one month and 50 cents for the first day of the next month it becomes a gross injustice. It has been claimed that the Commercial Co. has had as high as 2,500 different men on their pay roll during one month. Three thousand is the statement by their own timekeeper. From this it is apparent that each position has been filled approximately five times, making each position pay hospital fee of $2.50 for the month. The company engages the doctor and hospital by contract, and I believe the doctor and hospital are both good, but I do not believe they receive all of the money collected for this purpose.

Another deduction is made, as follows: When men arrive in Cosmopolis they are met at the depot by the lodging-house bosses, who take them to their lodging and who require them to sign an order on the company for a week's lodging. This order is then placed with the company, and the deduction is made from the wages accordingly. It is claimed by men coming to work for the Commercial Co. that this deduction is held out, even though the men do not remain at the lodging house for the full period of a week. On the other hand, a rooming-house boss told me yesterday morning that he lost more than $50 in the last year on men who stay only two or three days, as the company retains all of their own claims before they allow whatever may be due the rooming house.

In many instances a further deduction is made from the first month's wages, as follows: Frequently men without funds applying to certain of the employment agencies of Seattle or Portland will be given a slip entitling them to employment in the mill or camps of the Grays Harbor Commercial Co. and ticket entitling them to transportation to Cosmopolis. Under arrangement with the Commercial Co. the regular employment agency charge for securing employment. This, together with the regular railroad fare, is then deducted from the wages of the employee, and the baggage of the employee is held by the Commercial Co. as security for the repayment of these sums. In the event that the employee does not wish to remain with the company until his wages are sufficient to offset these various deductions the baggage will be retained and ultimately sold to pay the difference. The company now has a large amount of baggage on hand.

WORKING HOURS.

The ordinary working day of the employee of the Grays Harbor Commercial Co. is a 10-hour day, and it is on the basis of a 10-hour day that the company pays the wages of $26 a month and board. In the wintertime, however, it is frequently impossible to work more than nine hours during a day, and at such times a deduction is made from the wages of $26 per month accordingly. It will readily be seen that such a system works a reduction, at the same time requiring the employee to pay for 1 day's additional board in 10. In 10 days' time, each nine hours, the man is credited with nine days' labor, but is charged 60 cents extra for the one day's board. On the other hand, in the summer time during the long days employees of the company are frequently worked what is termed five-quarter time; that is, 12½ hours per day. During this season, although the actual cash wage is increased proportionately, no allowance is made for the matter of board. And here again we see that this failure to make allowance for board results in an advantage to the company, the company gaining the benefit of one day's board on each man for every four days of employment. The men receive less than for straight time.'

LIVING CONDITIONS—BOARD, ETC.

The company owns four large rooming houses, which are rented to individu-. als, who in turn rent out rooms to the employees of the company. In one of these rooming houses I have seen nine beds in one room and five in another, rent $1 to $2 a week. Otherwise the houses and rooms did not look bad, except the three old houses known as the Grays Harbor Lodging House, which have been run as one house. These should be condemned. The company also has a large number of cabins, the average size of which is 12½ by 16½ feet. They were cheaply constructed, with a partition wall dividing the cabin in two rooms, with two windows and one door. These cabins are rented at the rate of $3 per month, without furniture. At one place there are 15 of these cabins on a piece of ground 50 by 120 feet. This plat is the rear end of some lots the front of which are occupied by a dwelling house belonging to the company. The 15 cabins stand 8 and 7 in line, facing each other, and divided by plank walk 14 feet wide, the cabins being 2 feet apart. The whole is surrounded by an 8-foot high board fence, with a 4-foot opening to the street. There is but one toilet for the 15 cabins and one hydrant to supply water, this hydrant being connected to a one-half inch service pipe. The cabins and the surroundings are extremely filthy.

The company also conducts what is commonly known in this community as a mess house, where the employees of the company are boarded. So far as the food furnished in this mess house is concerned, I believe there is now comparatively little complaint. Under the former management very poor food was furnished, and Chinamen were employed as cooks, and the whole place was uncleanly. Under the present management conditions surrounding the mess house have improved, and there is little complaint upon the character of the board furnished. The objection of the people of Cosmopolis to the mess house is as an institution, and not because of the particular conditions surrounding this particular mess house. My objection to the mess house as an institution is based upon the facts as hereinafter set forth in my discussion under the head " Effect of conditions on the community."

CHARACTER OF EMPLOYEES.

All races are represented among the employees of the Commercial Co., but at the present the predominant element apparently is Croatian. At one time, a number of Hindus were employed but it was found that these men would not patronize the mess house of the company, and at the present time there are none of this nationality in the employ of the company. The large percentage of the employees of the company are single men, because it is impossible for a family man to keep his family on the wages received from the company. A great many of the employees of the company are young men, some of them mere boys. Comparatively few of the employees of the company are citizens of the United States. Of a population of about 1,400, Cosmopolis has a voting population of about 350.

TREATMENT OF EMPLOYEES BY FOREMEN.

I am not in position to furnish any information on this topic.

REGULARITY OF EMPLOYMENT AND LENGTH OF WORKING SEASON.

The company works regular hours and is very seldom shut down. The personnel, however, of the employees is continuously changing. It is generally understood that the Grays Harbor Commercial Co. keeps three crews in motion—one coming to work, to take the places of men actually engaged in work, the crew which is actually engaged in work, and the crew leaving the works whose places they have just taken.

METHOD OF EMPLOYING WORKMEN.

Nearly all employees secure their employment through employment agencies of Portland and Seattle. It is practically impossible for a man to secure work for this company unless he comes armed with a slip from an employment agency. The county officials are, and for a number of years have been, besieged by workmen who have been sent to the Grays Harbor Commercial Co. by employment agencies of Seattle or Portland with the promise of some particular position—as timekeeper, electrician, foreman, or the like—these men pay for the job which they are told by the employment agencies they will get upon arriving at Cosmopolis, when, in fact, their sealed ticket from the employment agency calls for and they are offered jobs as common laborers in the yards of the company. It has been impossible to directly connect up the Grays Harbor Commercial Co. with these employement agencies, and the railroad company which furnishes the transportation, but in a recent conversation with a former prosecuting attorney of Chehalis County, W. E. Campbell, I was advised by Mr. Campbell that he, from his own experience and investigation, is convinced that there is a combination existing between the Grays Harbor Commercial Co. and these employment agencies before referred to and the railroad company, and that he would so testify if subpœnaed before this commission, also in regard to other information in his possession. The fact is that the railroad company keeps the baggage and men must change their good clothes for working clothes in the baggage room of the railroad company and is not allowed to remove baggage.

AFFECT OF CONDITIONS ON THE COMMUNITY.

As to the effect of conditions on the community, I would first refer to the increase in population which has come to the towns of Grays Harbor as shown by the United States census for 1900 and 1910. During those 10 years Hoquiam's population increased from 2,608 to 8,171.. The population of Aberdeen increased from 3,747 to 13,660, while Cosmopolis, which is as favorably situated and should have shared in any prosperity coming to either of the other cities, shows an increase in population for that period of 10 years of 128, the population being 1,004 in 1900 and 1,132 in 1910. At the time when the 1910 census was taken three railroad camps were temporarily located within the city of Cosmopolis and these men were enumerated as inhabitants of this town, and during the same time—1900 to 1910—the Grays Harbor Commercial Co. more than doubled its plant. The following open letter, which was published in the Cosmopolis Times May 22, 1913, over the signature of Rudolph Distler, gives in concise form some statistics showing the effect of conditions on the community:

" The town of Cosmopolis, with a population between 1,300 and 1,400 souls, has only 200 families and householders. (Householders include bachelors and widows without family.)

" Eighty-eight heads of family own their home in Cosmopolis.

" The Grays Harbor Commercial Co.'s plant is practically the only industry in town and employs about 650 men. About 575 of these employees are boarding in the company's mess house.

" Only 60 heads of family are employed in or about the mills, planers, tank, box factory, offices, and stores of the Grays Harbor Commercial Co., and only 18 of these own their home in Cosmopolis.

" That the town of Cosmopolis offers a most desirable place for residence is proven by the fact that 48 families, besides many single men, live here who make their living in Aberdeen, this notwithstanding the highest street-car fare known of. Of these, 23 own their home here.

" The remaining 92 heads of family are engaged in fishing, railroading, logging, hotels, stores, etc. Forty-seven of these own their home in Cosmopolis.

" This condition is the result of discrimination against the man of family and the mess-house policy practiced by the Grays Harbor Commercial Co.

" These statistics are the result of a census taken during the first week of March, 1913, by the deputy assessor."

Another effect on the community was made apparent at the time the witness and writer of the foregoing letter attempted to have the same published. No newspaper on Grays Harbor, except the labor paper, would publish this communication. The editor of the Cosmopolis Times finally agreed to publish it under advertisement rates.

McGILL EXHIBIT NO. 1.

I quote here an excerpt from a letter written by the manager of an $18,000,000 corporation, in which he rebukes the local Y. M. C. A. secretary for failing to perform the duties of a spy and strike breaker, and illustrating what may be expected, and is expected, from any subsidized institution, religious or otherwise:

" I have been much dissatisfied," the letter reads, " with the Y. M. C. A. ever since 74 men walked out from camp No. 1, on the 5th day of June. This is the most men that have walked out of any other camp in the country. In our camp No. 2, where there is no Y. M. C. A., not a man went out. If the secretary had had the company's interests at heart and been onto his job he would have been close enough to the men to have prevented this walkout, or notified us of the existence of I. W. W. organizers. When the secretaries are at the camp and think they must simply toady to the men and let the company go to hell does not appeal to me, and I have about came to the decision that we can not make this thing satisfactory to the company the way it is running. Of course, if the company was not paying any of the bills it would be none of our business, but it is a business proposition with us to see that we get value received for the money we spend."

These and like experiences convince we that an evangelism to reach these men must be free from entangling alliances and independent as to support.

McGILL EXHIBIT NO. 2.

REPORT OF THE INVESTIGATION MADE ON MAY 8, 1914, OF THE SNOQUALME TUN-
NEL AT ROCKDALE OR WEST END.

I met Mr. Horrocks, the superintendent of the works, and he had one of the men go through the tunnel with me, and told me to talk with any of the men I wanted to. The tunnel at this end is in 8,521 feet. I went through the tunnel to the header on the high line and back on the low line. I found about 3 inches of water on the low line. The tunnel men tell me that they would rather have that amount of water than to have the floor dry, from a sanitary point of view, as the water helps to kill the gas and keeps the air cool, also helps the muck-ers. I found more gas in this end of the tunnel than the east end, on ac-count of a gasoline motor that hauls the cars on the low line. They have three fans running in the tunnel, but they don't keep the air pure by any means. I took this matter up with the superintendent, but as the time is so short now before the headers come together (then they will have plenty of ventilation) that it would not pay to install a new system at this time.

I went through the bunk houses. The company have just built eight new bunk houses. They have sanitary steel bunks and are in very fair condition. The four old bunk houses were in a very unsanitary condition; piles of dust and old socks, boots, and clothes under the bunks. I took Mr. Horrocks and showed him the dust and rubbish. He said I was justified in making a kick, and he called the two janitors in and showed them the dust and gave them strict orders to sweep the floors and under the bunks once a day and scrub the floors at least once a week. The timekeeper is to make at least two inspections a week of each bunk house and see that they are kept clean or lose his job. There are bedbugs in all the old bunk houses. The men tell me there are no lice around the camp. They are using disinfectants around the camp; also use chloride of lime in the closets; an incinerator in both camps, where they burn all the garbage, sweepings from the bunk houses, old clothes, and boots.

In talking with the men some of them said the lunches were no good that were sent into the tunnel. I picked out several as the waiter was taking them in to the men, and I found each one contained the following: Six sandwiches—three boiled beef, two ham, and one cheese—one piece pie, cookies, and doughnut, and hot coffee. I had three meals while I was at this place, and I think the food is above the average for railroad camps. Most of the men who complained of the food are the ones that work in the tunnel, where they have to breathe impure air and powder gas to some extent.

The company employs about 425 men in this camp. There is an average of 30 men leaving every day and about that many coming in. I might say that most of them are the type of men that travel on the road a great deal of the time, and as soon as they get a few dollars they want to move. The men pay from $1 to $2.50 to the Wilms Labor Agency for the jobs. They are given a pass to the tunnel. When they quit or get discharged they are given two checks. One is to pay railroad fare; the other covers balance due. Both checks are alike, except the amount. Nothing is deducted for the railroad fare from Seattle to the tunnel. I talked with a number of men who had quit, and they all told the same story. Some of the men beat their way to Seattle and save the fare.

The Chicago-Milwaukee Railroad are boring this tunnel by day work, and there is no contract work, except the commissary. The Sullivan Contract Co.;

of Seattle, have this contract on both ends of the tunnel. They charge $5.25 per week for board. All men work in the tunnel for $3 or less per day; get rubber boots furnished free. If you want to buy them they charge from $5.50 to $7.50. Overalls and jumpers, $1.25 each. Tobacco and soft drinks at Seattle prices. Socks, 20 per cent above Seattle prices. In fact, all clothing sold in the commissary will average 20 per cent above Seattle prices.

All the bunk houses have hot and cold water, steam heat, and plenty of windows, so the men can get fresh air if they so desire. I saw the men come in and lay down in their bunks all covered with mud, so you will see that it is a hard matter to keep them clean. A great deal depends on the men. There is plenty of water and two shower baths, if they want to use them.

I am under the impression that conditions have improved since Mr. McGill wrote them up, and I think my trip will do some good along the same line. Mr. Horrocks said he would welcome an investigation by the State or county officers any time they wanted to come, but not the Seattle bunch, as he did not think they were giving him a square deal. I recommended a few changes around the machinery for safety, and he put a man to work making the changes.

I inclose scale of wages. This applies to both ends of the tunnel; also explains bonus system.

I met two young men who were going to work at Rockdale as I went up on the train. I posted them what to look out for and keep a memorandum of facts as they found them and report when they come to Seattle.

C. H. YOUNGER,
State Factory Inspector.

REPORT OF INVESTIGATION MADE ON MAY 7, 1914, OF THE SNOQUALMIE TUNNEL, EAST PORTAL.

I went in the tunnel on the high line to the heading and back to the portal on the low line. I found from 4 to 10 inches of water on the low line. All the men have to wear gum boots and slickers who work back of the heading. There is quite a lot of water seeping through the top of the tunnel, and the work is very disagreeable in several places. I talked with a number of the men in the tunnel. Only two complained of the work and conditions in the tunnel. I next went through the bunk houses. There are three of them. One has all-steel sanitary bunks, the other two have wooden bunks, and they were very dirty. The janitor only sweeps the alleyways and the high places. I called the foreman's attention to the dirt under the bunks, and he called the janitor in and set him to work. I went through the kitchen. I found it in a sanitary condition, so far as I could see. I also went through the dining room while meals were being served. There was plenty of good and wholesome food. Although some of the men told me that it was above the average on the day I was there. I had dinner with the men, and I was unable to find any fault with the food. All the bunk houses have steam heat and hot and cold water. There are two shower baths in the power house for the use of the men if they desire to take a bath. They employ about 225 men in this camp. All the men are hired through the Wilms Labor Agency, 221 Occidental Avenue, Seattle, except what men they can pick up on the road. I talked with a number of men who had quit work and were going back to Seattle. The sentiment of the majority of them was that they wanted to get back to Seattle, and did not like the work in the tunnel. I think the trouble is two-thirds of the men who go up to work in the tunnel have never had any experience in tunnel work, and they don't stay any longer than they have to. There is very little trouble with gas in this end of the tunnel, for they are only in 3,512 feet.

C. H. YOUNGER,
State Factory Inspector.

SCALE OF WAGES, SNOQUALMIE TUNNEL, WEST END.

TUNNEL.

Heading: Shift bosses, 50 cents per hour plus bonus and a half; 12 hours per day. Machine runners, 45 cents per hour plus bonus; work 6 hours on, 12 hours off, or 24 hours in three days. Machine helpers, 35 cents per hour plus bonus; work 6 hours on, 12 hours off, or 24 hours in three days. Muckers, 30 cents per hour plus bonus; work 6 hours on. 12 hours off, or 24 hours in three days. Nippers, 30 cents per hour plus bonus; work 12 hours per day. Teamsters, $2.75 per 12-hour shift.

BENCH.

Shift bosses, 50 cents per hour; work 10 hours per day. Machine runners, 36 cents per hour; work 10 hours per day. Machine helpers, 28 cents per hour; work 10 hours per day. Muckers, 22½ cents per hour; work 10 hours per day. Nippers, 25 cents per hour; work 10 hours per day.
Motor men (gasoline locomotives), $4 per 12-hour shift. Donkey engineers, 30 cents per hour; work 12 hours. Brakemen, 25 cents per hour; work 12 hours. Dump men, 25 cents per hour; work 12 hours.

CONCRETE WORK.

Spaders, 27½ cents per hour; work 11 hours. Shovelers, 25 cents per hour; work 11 hours. Gripmen, 22½ cents per hour; work 11 hours. Cement men, outside, 25 cents per hour; work 11 hours. Gravel chute men, 25 cents per hour; work 11 hours. Hopper men, 25 cents per hour; work 11 hours. Carman, below mixer, 25 cents per hour; work 11 hours. Engineer, 30 cents per hour; work 11 hours. Laborers, inside, 22½ cents per hour; work 10 hours. Carpenter helpers, 25 cents per hour; work 10 hours. Laborers, outside, 20 cents per hour; work 10 hours. Carpenters, 35 cents per hour; work 10 hours.

GRADING, OUTSIDE.

Powder man, 25 cents per hour; work 10 hours. Laborers, 20 cents per hour; work 10 hours. Hammermen, 22½ cents per hour; work 10 hours.

BONUS (FOR DRIVING OF HEADING).

For each man working in the heading bonus is figured in 10-day periods from the date he hires. The number of feet over 100 driven in each period is paid to him as an extra allowance, 1 foot counting as one hour. For example, a mucker working 30 days, or through three 10-day periods, in which, say, 90, 140, and 160 feet of heading were driven, would get 30 cents×8×30=$72; +40+60=100 hours bonus, at 30 cents=$30, or a total of $102.

MEDICAL SERVICES.

A doctor is maintained at each end, with office near the portal. Have hospital arrangements with Pacific Hospital, Seattle, and in emergency with Dr. Kirby's Hospital at Cle Elum. Hospital deductions are made from men at the rate of 20 cents per day for the first five days that a man works in each month, or a maximum charge of $1 per month.

PAYMENT OF MEN.

For steady men, pay day is 20th of the month, covering previous month's wages. Men quitting or discharged are paid in full, with bank check on Metropolitan Bank, Seattle. For convenience of all, a check for $1.75 is issued to each man going away who has that amount due him, and another check for the balance due him. Also for the man's convenience in getting checks paid, on the back of each check issued the payee's signature is taken and this signature is certified by paymaster, and the bank honors checks on a repetition of the signature. Stamp used for this purpose is shown below.

AMOUNT EARNED PER MAN.

Taking pay rolls for month of April, 1914, about 1,040 different men were carried on these rolls. Seven hundred and thirty-eight time checks for April time have been issued, amounting to approximately $16,000, making an average " stake " of about $20 per man over and above his deduction. Besides the 783 men paid off, pay rolls show the names of about 100 men who started to work, but worked only an hour or so, and left without having any money due them.

————— —————,
Engineer and Superintendent.

ROCKDALE, WASH., *May 8, 1914.*

COPY OF STAMP USED ON CHECKS.

The undersigned signature of the payee is for identification, and not an indorsement of this check.

(Identification signature.)

I certify that the above is the signature of the payee of this check.

‾‾‾‾ ‾‾‾‾,

Agent.

STRONG EXHIBIT NO. 1.

STATEMENT OF SYDNEY STRONG, PRESIDENT CENTRAL COUNCIL OF SOCIAL AGENCIES, SEATTLE, FROM A MEMORANDUM OF QUESTIONS FURNISHED BY THE UNITED STATES COMMISSION ON INDUSTRIAL RELATIONS, AT THE SEATTLE HEARING, AUGUST 13, 1914.

The Seattle Council of Social Agencies was organized in 1912, Mayor George F. Cotterill having issued a call to 200 representative citizens to meet June 24, 1912. At the present time there are over 50 social agencies in the organization, each agency being represented by from one to three delegates, serving for one year.

The agencies included in the council are as representative, as far apart as the university, the school board, the library, the health department, the Commercial Club, the Central Labor Council, the Municipal League, the Ministers' Federation, and others of similar character along with 20 or so charity agencies.

The purposes of the council are: First, the promotion of fellowship among existing agencies, largely by means of a better understanding each of the other's work and of the city as a whole; second, the promotion of social intelligence by serving as a bureau for the dissemination of ideas and methods, by investigation, and by exhibits and surveys; by the working out of a social program for the whole city, in harmony with which various agencies may develop; and by acquainting the public mind with social problems; third, the promotion of social efficiency by the prevention of unnecessary duplication of efforts, or the creation of unnecessary new agencies; by acting on request in the capacity of adviser in matters pertaining to a single agency, or to several agencies in their relation to each other; by assisting the public authorities in adopting social measures that may be for the public good; by assisting in the initiation of new work as emergency may demand.

In general, the council proposes, in view of the rapid development of industries and the centralizing of populations that are imminent, to help work out that larger intelligence and efficiency both as to plans and as to details which will enable this city of the Northwest to meet its own problems in a broadly constructive and adequate way.

The theory of the council is that all wholesome agencies in the community have a point of social contact with each other; that this point of contact is the place to look for community prosperity, and that the final test of any agency is its social efficiency.

The work of the council has thus far been necessarily slow. It has, however, already done inestimable good in bringing together representatives of all sects and sections of the community. It has done two or three large pieces of social service, as for example, in the caring for the National Conference of Charities and Correction in 1913, and in carrying through a big child welfare exhibit in 1914, which was attended by 50.000 people. It has been used as the instrument for organizing a commission on unemployment, and in December, 1913, and January, 1914, is instituted a conference on immigration, while in January, 1913, it held a prelegislative institue for the purpose of discussion of proposed social legislation to come before the biennial State legislature.

The council constitutes a splendid instrument to be used for conciliation and arbitration in industrial strife—but as yet these waters have not been ventured upon.

STRONG EXHIBIT NO. 2.

: INDUSTRIAL SITUATION WITH REGARD TO THE JAPANESE.

umber of Japanese in the State of Washington.

```
-------------------------------------------------------------  8, 507
-------------------------------------------------------------  2, 044
                                                               --------
-------------------------------------------------------------  10, 551
```

Number of Japanese in the city of Seattle.

[The statistics made by the Japanese Association, Seattle.]

	Male.	Female.	Total.
....	1,020 3,030	800 170	} 5,020

```
(skilled and unskilled) _____ 1, 200
ind gardeners_____ 1, 000
_____   350
ial and business men_____  630
ious _____  870

males)_____ 4, 050
```

nnection: 3 Christian churches and 3 missions, 1 Buddhist tem-
in women homes.

JAPANESE IMMIGRATION.

CONSULATE GENERAL OF JAPAN,
San Francisco, Cal., January, 1911.

ng figures prepared by this consulate general from statistics
the foreign office of the Japanese Government show the tendency
ent of Japanese to and from the continent of the United States
endar years 1908, 1909, 1910, and 1911.

Year.	Departures from Japan for the United States.			Arrivals in Japan from the United States.		
	Non-laborers.	Laborers.	Total.	Non-laborers.	Laborers.	Total.
....	2,304	1,522	3,826	307	5,186	5,493
....	1,254	659	1,913	290	4,248	4,538
....	2,098	924	3,022	278	4,823	5,101
....	1,967	1,953	3,920	322	5,605	5,927
....	7,628	5,058	12,681	1,197	19,862	21,059

Year.	Laborers departed from Japan for the United States.	Laborers arrived in Japan from the United States.	Excess arrivals in Japan.
....	1,522	5,186	3,664
....	659	4,248	3,589
....	924	4,823	3,899
....	1,953	5,605	3,652
....	5,058	19,862	14,804

In other words, during the past four years there has been a decrease of 11,152 Japanese laborers in the population of the United States. The distinction between laborers and nonlaborers is made from data gathered in Japan at the time passports are issued. In the case of Japanese returning from abroad, an arbitrary distinction is based upon the passenger lists of vessels. Saloon passengers are classed as nonlaborers, all others as laborers. This method never far varies from the truth.

Concerning the accuracy of the foregoing figures, it may not be amiss to quote from the last annual report of the Commissioner of Immigration to the Secretary of Commerce and Labor of the United States for the fiscal year ended June 30, 1910. Under the head of Japanese Immigration, he says, page 125:

"It is both interesting and gratifying to observe how nearly the figures covering departures from Japan, kept by the Japanese officials, agree with those kept by the officials of the bureau, the difference being too slight to call for particular notice."

CONCLUSIONS ABOUT THE JAPANESE.

1. Must deal with them on the basis of equality.
2. Question of assimilability:
   Have shown capacity to absorb others' ideas and institutions.
   Open minded.
   Ownership of public utilities obtains in Japan.
   Seattle—do not tend to segregation.
   Democratic.
3. Labor problem:
   Japanese not cheap men; do displace, but make places.
   Do not, as rule, underbid American labor.
   Wages on coast have not been brought down.
   Wages advanced in those occupations in which Japanese engage—Sawmills, shingle mills, railroads.
4. As an immigrant:
   Purchase 89 per cent of material used in living requirements.
   About 80,000 in United States.
   Fewer than four years ago.
   Scattered over the country, although bulk in California, Washington, and Oregon.
   Majority farmers.
   Professional, large percentage, next to Germans.
   Amount of money, per capita, next to English and Germans.
   Ninety-seven per cent from 14 to 41.
   Educational test—smallest rate of illiteracy.

The Japanese of Seattle show distinct but courteous effort to enter into American life. Their merchants join the commercial bodies, subscribe to all civic affairs, and go wherever welcome. The Japanese Christian churches in Seattle are prompt to do their part and the pastors modestly but faithfully do their share. Indeed, the majority of the local Japanese would prefer not to build up distinctly Japanese Christian churches, but to scatter in the various American churches of the city, but they receive little encouragement.

The Japanese meet every overture looking toward friendly relations with promptness. Where there is a want of assimilation, it is usually not their fault. Their children are in the public schools; they "rally round" the Stars and Stripes; they adopt as many American ideas and customs as permitted; they learn English, study American history; are acquainted with Longfellow, Emerson, Washington, and Lincoln, and understand and appreciate the American spirit.

But can the Japanese be worked into our democracy? Assuming that they are a noble people, that in certain forms of art, in ability to organize to the point of minute details, in courtesy, cleanliness, and family discipline they are our superiors—after all, can they, being orientals, be worked into our scheme of life? Let me in answer mention a few things.

They reveal many democratic ideas; they have the open mind, which is fundamental to democracy. They stand for the "open door" in international politics quite as much as America. In their village and town life there is a good-natured fellowship between all classes. I was impressed on the steamers by the comradeship shown between officers and sailors. I am informed that the same is true in the army and navy. The students in the universities of Japan purposely dress in simple attire to show their disregard for external wealth. In fact, with the majority of the Japanese, money is a secondary consideration. Japan is socialistic in point of Government ownership of public utilities. Even Bernard Shaw is nearly satisfied with the extent to which Japan has carried Government ownership. Prof. A. B. Hart, of Harvard, says "socialism is realized in Japan." If the Japanese in America were allowed a voice and a vote they would be found almost solid in favor of our democratic movements, such as the governmental ownership of railways, of lighting and heating enterprises, of forests, of mines, of telegraphs, of telephones—for these things have been done in Japan for years. The Japanese Government is a kind of benevolent socialism.

It is in the labor world, however, that the greatest concern is felt by Americans. Can the Japanese be worked into our industrial scheme of things? It must be said at the outset that the labor world of Japan is quite different from ours. Wages are one-fifth what they are here; hours of work are longer; women are employed by the thousands; child labor is common. Labor is not organized as with us. Conditions, however, are rapidly changing, and for the better. There are many "model factories" in Japan.

When we turn to the Japanese in America, they do much work, for example, in farming that would be done by no one else; also, they are rather keen on securing good wages. Those Japanese I have known are good buyers, good livers, and not inclined to lower wages. If the Japanese were permitted to join the ranks of organized labor, I have the conviction that lowering of the standards of living or wages could not be charged against them. My advice to organized labor is to invite them to join their ranks, for among them would be found some of the ablest champions of the causes dear to the unions.

The solution of the "Japanese problem" will be found in our according to Japan full recognition; to treat with her on the basis of friendship and equality; to grant to her people who are in our borders the same privileges we grant to the people of the favored nations, as to the English and Germans. This is the way Japan treats Americans who come to her shores. If at any time it seems to our Nation that too many Japanese are coming, a "gentleman's agreement" will rectify the situation. But the Japanese who are here should be treated as are those from other favored lands. To do otherwise will be unfair to a noble people and a source of permanent irritation and danger.

HIGDAY EXHIBIT.

INITIATIVE MEASURE No. 9.

AN ACT To encourage industrial safety and relating to treatment of workers injured in extra hazardous employment, fixing pecuniary liability therefor, providing for arbitration of disputes, prohibiting certain deductions from wages, and imposing duties on the industrial insurance department.

[Submitted by State Federation of Labor, Farmers' Union, State Grange, and Direct Legislation League.]

ARGUMENT.

Initiative measure No. 9—the "first-aid" bill—deserves the approval of citizens of the State for the following reasons, among others:

1. General purpose: The bill was drafted to accomplish three primary objects: (1) Stimulate the prevention of work accidents, (2) assure injured men speedy and certain medical care, (3) abolish the coercive "hospital-fee" system and place employees' sickness funds under State supervision.

2. Limited to extrahazardous trades. The bill applies only to extrahazardous trades, and fills the gap left by the legislature of 1911, when the first-aid provision, so-called, was stricken from the workmen's-compensation act. That law as passed left the workman to pay his own medical bills. It also prohibited the injured workman from suing his employer, even where his medical care costs far more than he is awarded from the State accident fund. This is true even in cases where injury from inexcusable negligence of the employer or his agents would have resulted in jury verdicts of $5,000 or $10,000 under the

common law. Employers in dangerous trades are thus absolutely insured against litigation; the workman gets only what the State gives him.

Briefly the present bill imposes upon the employer the duty of paying for the doctering and medicines needed when the men whom he employs for his own profit get hurt in his service. Where the surgical or hospital expenses exceed $100 the State then steps in and pays the excess out of the collective accident fund.

3. "Safety first." The key idea of this bill is: An act to encourage industrial safety.

To achieve greater safety in dangerous occupations is progress; to pay compensation after a preventive injury is mere apology. Any act of organized society which measurably reduces the sum total of human agony from industrial accidents—with their waste of human working power and the driving from home of women and children unfitted for breadwinning—deserves the vigorous support of every citizen.

Fifty per cent of work accidents are preventable. "Safety first" has become a slogan throughout the Nation. Safeguards on dangerous machines are only a first step. Undue speeding of men, needless litter at the plant, bad light, unwarned green hands, defective apparatus, unconsiderate foremen—preventable accidents result largely from such causes which are wrongly classified as trade risks. It is in the power of the employer to stop injuries from such things; and generally at slight expense and with equal output. A half dozen State factory inspectors can not be held responsible for the safety of 160,000 men in our extrahazardous trades.

The boss who sees his accidents in his balance sheet, surely, automatically, will get his scientific management ideas to working and prevent accidents.

The small employer is not going to be put out of business by a $9 or a $90 doctor bill; the big business manager can't shift it onto his men as now and deceive his stockholders. Public opinion will know just where to put its thumb from reports required and published. And the thoughtful, humane employer will find that he is assessed fewer compulsory insurance premiums by the State to pay compensation for the maimings caused by his slave-driver competitor who regards men as merely something to exploit.

4. Remedies a cruel injustice. Men who work with their hands are now carrying two-thirds of the financial burden of work-accidents in Washington, and the employers only one-third. This is proven incontrovertably by cold statistics. See the 1913 report of the industrial insurance commission, page 101. And on top of this is the physical suffering and the want and worry passed on to the family where there are dependents.

Each year 15,000 serious industrial accidents occur in the State. In 1,503 cases, where the data was complete, the results were:

Total amount of wages lost_____ $107,296.67
Cost of medical treatment_____   36,206.80
                                                                   ─────────────
     Total financial loss to workmen_____ 143,508.47
State's awards (cost to employers)_____   47,164.20

5. Brings Washington up to standard. The spirit of the age insists that industry shall bear the cost of its accidents. Twenty-five American States have passed workmen's compensation acts and the employer is obliged to pay for medical attendance for injured men as well as the definite money damage laid down by law. Washington is almost alone in compelling the workmen to pay the treatment cost.

"With a few exceptions," reports a notable commission of the National Civic Federation, "the States require that the employer, in addition to the compensation, shall pay the medical bills of the injured workmen, with certain restrictions. Outside of the State of Washington, the commission found no sentiment opposed to this requirement, it being generally conceded that the workman is not only entitled to medical treatement in addition to his compensation, but that it is to the interest of the employer and society to see that he received it, thereby to minimize the extent of the disability."

What is right in California, Oregon, Illinois, Wisconsin, Michigan, Ohio, New Jersey, and Massachusetts, is also right in Washington.

6. Abolishes the vicious hospital ticket system. Certain organized employers, acting through the anonymous Stop-Look-Listen League, are bitterly opposing the standardizing of what humane hirers of men do as plain Christian duty. These men say, "We already take care of our injured men." But they mean

they have given some contract doctor the corporation's franchise of treating its men and are deducting the dollars every month from the pay envelope of each of their laborers as a " hospital fee " to pay him, notwithstanding the often poor quality of his slapdash services. This bill will compel the contract doctors to meet professional competition on their merits, to the benefit of suffer-ing workmen.

One hundred and sixty thousand workmen are covered by the compensation act. About 57.5 per cent, or 90,000 men, are under the benevolent compulsion of the deduction-from-wage, pay-in-advance installment system of putting up the medical cost of treating accidents. This means the workmen are putting up $1,000,000 a year for " hospital fees." This is collected by the companies, not the State—an unofficial, unaudited " accident fund." Thus they maintain the " hos-pitals " out of their own pockets—as the price of their jobs. The employers last year were assessed $1,600,000 by the State to pay the fixed damages for the kill-ings and injuries in the dangerous trades. Nearly 15,000 awards were made by the State accident board. The average cost of medical treatment was $25, a total of about $375,000. Will anyone be convinced that sickness of employees (family ills and chronic disorders are not treated on " hospital ticket ") ab-sorbed the $625,000 balance of the men's money?

7. Responsibility for immediate medical care. When a man is hurt outside of the big mills, logging camps, or construction gangs, where the " hospital fee " is held out, no one is legally responsible for his prompt and efficient treatment. If he is penniless, the hospital or capable doctor doesn't want the case. The State pays no surgical, nursing, or other bills. The boss doesn't enthuse over guaranteeing them. Charity is thus called upon. Initiative bill No. 9 will change this indefensible system.

The governor's commission of 1910-11 which framed the workmen's compen-sation act put a first-aid fund into the bill, but the lumber barons and other big business dictators killed the provision in the legislature, leaving a one-legged law. In 1912-13 the majority of the industrial insurance commission, in its first annual report, after operating the law a year and a half, recommended substantially this initiative bill. Gov. Hay, the Progressive Party platform, and organized labor all urged first aid, but the legislature again smothered it. The State federation of labor, the farmers' grange, and the Direct Legislation League now appeal direct to the people for the relief and justice long denied.

PAULY EXHIBIT.

COMMITTEE REPORT.

To the chairman and members of the citizens' unemployment committee:

Your committee, appointed on March 28, 1914, consisting of J. B. Powles, chairman; Dr. J. E. Crichton, Prof. A. Berglund, E. B. Ault, C. K. Bliss, and W. D. Lane for the purpose of investigating conditions of unemployment in this city and making recommendations, beg leave to report as follows:

Your committee first investigated the institution known as the " Hotel de Gink." This institution was first established by Mr. Jeff Davis, president of the International Itinerant Workers' Union, and is now under the management of Mr. Henry Pauly. " Itinerant workers " are commonly known as " hoboes." The " hobo " should not be confused with the " tramp " or " yegg." He is an itinerant workman, and plays a necessary part in our industrial system. These men occupy a portion of the building formerly occupied by the Providence Hos-pital. The rent, amounting to $55 a month, is paid by the central labor council; otherwise the institution is self-supporting. The men have taken several con-tracts for clearing land and have recommendations from those for whom they have worked. They have purchased a stump puller, at a cost of $300, and other machinery for the clearing of land, and are anxious to obtain contracts for that kind of work. Men doing this work have slept in the open while on the job. Vegetables for the " hotel " have been obtained by working at sorting and taking the seconds for pay. Certain restaurants have also donated food not suitable for their use. Fuel has been carried from razed buildings, where it could be obtained for taking away.

The institution has lodged and fed 2,250 men, at a cost of $765.20. Seventy thousand meals have been furnished. Each member who gets work is required to contribute to its support. An accurate set of books is kept showing all moneys received and disbursed. At the present time about 106 men are being cared for.

Strict sanitary rules have been established. A man on entering is required to have his clothing "dry steamed," and to take a bath. The building is kept . clean and habits of personal cleanliness enforced.

Strict discipline is maintained. A "court" has been established, before ꞌ whom offenders against the rules and good order of the institution are brought. If found guilty, they are disciplined or expelled. The men are nearly all American citizens. No incendiary or revolutionary progaganda is tolerated, and obedience to the law is inculcated. The building is decorated with the American flag. Cooperation and self-help are the basic principles of the institution.

We interviewed Sergt. Ryan, of the police force, who corroborated the foregoing statements. He stated that at the time he was stationed there he had never been called upon to interfere in the interest of good order. No stolen property was discovered in the building. Upon entering every man is given a number and a record kept of every night that he is in, which must be before 10.30 in the evening. We believe that the institution is conducted along right lines and is worthy of support. The owners of the building have given notice that no more rent will be accepted after April 25. The men have another building in view, which they hope to be able to obtain. They believe that their institution could be placed upon a completely self-supporting basis. They desire the moral support of the people in these efforts.

Your committee next visited the Brotherhood League, which is in charge of Mr. Martin. One hundred and fifty men were found there. The league furnishes cot beds in a fairly well-ventilated upstairs room for 10 cents for those who are able to pay; others sleep on the floor downstairs, where the ventilation is insufficient. We saw a number of men wrapping their feet and legs in newspapers, presumably to keep warm. It was the opinion of Mr. Martin that 75 per cent of these men would work if the opportunity were afforded. He thought that most of them would be out within a month, many having already left. This institution is maintained by private contributions.

Several cases of extreme necessity among our own citizens have come to your committee's knowledge. At one meeting we were visited by a committee of four, representing, as they said, 125 married men of the city who are out of work, some of whom are in great need. About 40 of these men were in waiting on the outside. They impressed your committee as being worthy and extremely anxious to find work. We also interviewed a millman, who gave us his experience in the employment of labor. He thought it unwise for the newspapers to publish that men would be furnished work here, for the reason that it creates a false impression as to the certainty of getting work and the wages to be paid, and so causes an influx of men to the city.

Scarcity of employment is not peculiar to Seattle. It is a local manifestation of a condition quite general. We are informed that conditions are worse here than in previous years. Some of the local men told us that they had never found it impossible to obtain work before.

Your committee recommends that the general committee be made permanent, at least until there shall be a board of public welfare or some public body which can can take charge of the work. We believe that such a body is necessary—one which will have the time and facilities for investigation and for securing work, which this committee does not possess. We recommend that an appeal be made to the citizens of Seattle to provide work for those worthy and most in need. We believe that many of our people, if they saw and understood the need as your committee has been brought to see it, would be willing to provide temporary employment. To do this it will be necessary that some place be provided to act as a clearing house, where applications for laborers might be made and where clothing might be sent for distribution. Itinerant workers are prepared to clear land if work of that kind can be procured for them. We believe that they should receive our moral support and such practical assistance as possible in their effort to establish a home for the itinerant worker.

Similar conditions in the future should be anticipated. If possible, a certain amount of public work should be reserved to be done during times of industrial depression. Care, however, should be taken in the kind of publicity given to our efforts to provide work for the unemployed. In our opinion, the general committee should do everything possible to relieve the present situation,- and particularly should give attention to the prevention of similar conditions in the future.

Respectfully submitted.

—— ——, *Chairman.*

LETTERS IN RE TESTIMONY OF DR. THERESA S. McMAHON.

The following letters were filed by the Association of Pacific Fisheries in regard to the testimony of Dr. Theresa S. McMahon, and were ordered to be made a part of the commission's record:

BLAINE, WASH., *August 15, 1914.*

ASSOCIATION OF PACIFIC FISHERIES,
Seattle, Wash.

GENTLEMEN: Our attention has been called during the past few days to articles in the daily press seriously reflecting upon the salmon canneries of this State, and purporting to be evidence of Dr. Theresa McMahon before the Federal Industrial Commission, which are so grossly unfair, unjust, false, and malicious that, if allowed to stand without protest, may be accepted as truth by the public and the commission.

Referring first to the Chinese contract, the old method of contracting for processing the pack at a fixed sum per case is no longer in vogue. A small force of orientals is employed during the entire season, and for this force a memorandum contract is made guaranteeing the wage, the length of time of employment, the hours of work, overtime, etc. Eleven hours is the extreme length of a day's work, and is only executed during a few days of the season when delay would be injurious to the pack. The usual hours for labor in our cannery is from 7 a. m. to 6 p. m., with an allowance of one hour at noon for dinner. All labor over 11 hours is paid overtime, but it is seldom extra hours are necessary.

During the rush season, rarely extending more than three or four weeks for the Sockeye pack, extra labor is employed, which is paid by hourly wage.

Sanitation.—The cannery operated by this company has one main longitudinal and 11 transverse sewers, which are daily flushed, and when the cannery is in active operation a stream of water is pumped through and continued all night. All machines in use are cleaned off by steam under 100 pounds pressure at noon and also at the end of the day's work, after which they are washed off by a stream of water from a steam pump and the whole cannery and fish house floor washed off and squeegeed down. Salt in abundance is then liberally sprinkled over the tables and floors, and the cannery is thus kept perfectly sweet and clean. We have sanitary drinking fountains at either end of the cannery, washing troughs and basins supplied with water from faucets for the employees, and in a separate and secluded building near the cannery, in a location not traversed by any male employees, is a rest room and toilet for the female employees. The toilets for the males are at a far distant point and entirely separated from the cannery.

Some women are employed at present during the packing season, a few at light work, such as attending the weighing machines, etc., who are paid 25 cents per hour, but the main body are employed in the packing. This work is paid for at a stipulated sum per case, and it is not unusual for a fast worker to earn $5 per day—indeed, on different occasions several of our girls made $5.80 a day.

Some of these girls live in the adjoining town and come and go morning and evening, bringing their lunch with them; others live in neighboring districts, and for these we have provided the following living accommodations: Situated on the Gulf of Georgia side of our property and bordering the high-water mark on the bathing beach, we have three cottages or bungalows and one mess house, all painted white. The cottages are divided into five rooms with a central room supplied with a kitchen range, table, shelves, etc., for those who desire to cook their own food. Each room has a doorway leading to the central space as well as a separate doorway leading outside. We supply good iron beds, mattresses, and chairs, five for each room, but there are never more than three, or at most four, persons in any one room. The cottages are all connected with wide platforms, and outside of each one is a suitable place for washing supplied with running water. All are electric lighted.

The mess house is a long building containing a mess room arranged with tables covered with white oilcloth, benches, etc., sufficiently large to accommodate 100 people if necessary; adjoining it is a large airy kitchen with a hotel range, extra-size hot-water boiler, sink, and other accessories for a well-appointed kitchen, and leading from it is a large pantry and a cook's room. Outside the kitchen is a covered porch having on one side a modern bathroom and separate from it stationary wash tubs, both with hot and cold water, and on the other side a modern toilet.

We supply a cook and helper, all kitchen and cooking utensils, all mess furniture, heat, and electric light.

The mess pays only for the actual food furnished which is ordered by the cook or one of the matrons who attend to the good order and wants of the female employees. Under this arrangement the cost has never been more than 10 cents per meal or 30 cents per day for board and room. Frequent inquiries as to whether the girls were obtaining plenty of wholesome food invariably received the reply from cook and matrons that not one singe complaint had been made during the season, and that all were fully satisfied with the conditions.

The writer was here during the entire season and on several occasions inspected the quarters for the purpose of ascertaining their condition and to learn if anything could be added that would improve them and add to the comfort and welfare of those living in them. He invariably found them neat and clean and never once heard one complaint.

The girls employed come from the best of families in this section of the country and are presided over by two experienced matrons. The writer has seen these girls daily at work and at play and can testify that nowhere amongst the high or low can girls be found who are neater, cleaner, or more orderly than those employed at this cannery. To reflect upon the morals of these girls is a malicious outrage which should receive the condemnation of every well-thinking person.

It is a difficult matter to set forth in a letter the conditions prevailing here, and it is only by actually seeing the work that a proper understanding can be had.

We would, therefore, ask that the commission visit us and inspect our cannery and surroundings at any time, nay more, we will pay for any reasonable expense incurred by this commission in making us a visit, in order that the members may ascertain for themselves the true conditions and know, if the press reports are correct, what malicious and false evidence has been presented.

Yours, very truly,

ALASKA PACKERS ASSOCIATION,
JEFFU F. MOSER,
General Superintendent.

APEX FISH CO.,
Anacortes, Wash., August 20, 1914.

ASSOCIATION OF PACIFIC FISHERMEN,
Seattle, Wash.

GENTLEMEN: Our attention has been called recently to a number of articles which have appeared in some of our daily papers, purporting to be the evidence of one Dr. Theresa McMahon before the Federal Industrial Commission.

After reading these articles over carefully we feel that it is our duty to ourselves, to the industry we represent, and to the consuming public to emphatically contradict the statements made by Dr. McMahon as being absolutely untrue, unjust, and of a most malicious character; so much so that we do not believe that the commission will give it very much credence. However, we wish to be placed on record in the matter.

As regards to hours of labor, there is not a semblance of truth in the statement made, and we are paying the highest wages of any industry on the coast, and our employees are from some of the finest families in the town. Our female employees are practically all hand fillers, who make as high as $6.50 to $7 per day of 10 hours, never working more than that time and usually only 7 or 8 hours per day.

We earnestly request that the commission, either as a whole or that they select some member, visit our plant and make an investigation for themselves. We have always endeavored to conduct our business in the most sanitary and up-to-date manner. We should like to have you insist that the commission visit us, as we invite inspection at all times.

Very truly, yours,

LEE H. WAKEFIELD, *President.*

F, C. BARNES Co.(INC.),
Portland, Oreg., August 24, 1914.

ASSOCIATION OF PACIFIC FISHERIES,
Seattle, Wash.

GENTLEMEN : I have just been reading a notice that was published in the **Seattle " P. I."** on August 12, which I would like to call your attention to, as I **consider it very unjust.** It does not speak the truth in regard to employees in any of the canneries that I have ever visited and especially in our plant, and if allowed to stand without protest may be accepted as truth by the public and the **commission.**

Referring to Chinese contracts, that is an old method that was adopted years ago and now is no longer in vogue. The small force of orientals employed during the season are guaranteed for a certain period of time, or a certain number of months' work. The hours for work covered by these contracts are 11, and all over 11 hours is considered overtime, and employees are paid an agreed price for overtime. This is only done during extreme rush times. The usual hours for labor in our cannery is from 7 a. m. to 6 p. m., with an allowance of one hour for dinner. The rush season does not generally exceed over three or four weeks.

All machinery in use is cleaned off with steam under 100 pounds pressure at last twice a day and the floors and entire workroom is cleaned up and washed down every night thoroughly. Salt in abundance is then liberally sprinkled over the tables and floor of the cannery, thus keeping them perfectly sweet and **clean.**

Some women are employed during the packing season at light work, such as **attending to the weighing** machine and salting cans, and are paid 25 cents per **hour.**

We furnish a mess house for our Chinese employees and sleeping quarters, paying them no less than $50 per month and making them an allowance of $8 per month in addition for board. Although they furnish the supplies for their mess house, we pay the cook who does the cooking for them and we also pay the freight on their supplies and furnish them with wood and water. Besides this we pay the transportation from wherever this help is hired to the cannery and return. The white help are women that are hired in the cannery. They are paid by the hour and board themselves at their houses.

These are the conditions at our plant in South Bend, Wash.

Yours, truly,

F. C. BARNES Co.
By F. C. B.

. CARLISLE PACKING Co. (INC.),
Bellingham, Wash., August 25, 1914.

ASSOCIATION OF PACIFIC FISHERIES,
Seattle, Wash.

GENTLEMEN : Our attention has been called recently to articles which have appeared in some of our daily papers purporting to be the evidence of one Dr. Theresa McMahon before the Federal Industrial Commission.

After reading these articles over we feel that it is a duty to ourselves, to the industry we represent, and to the consuming public to emphatically contradict and denounce the statements as being absolutely untrue, unfounded, and unjust, so much so that we are loathe to believe that the commission will give the testimony as made by Dr. McMahon any credence, and we wish to be placed on record in this matter as follows :

We are, I believe, paying the highest wage of any industry on the coast. Our employees are composed of members of some of the finest families in the towns tributary to our plant.

Our female employees are employed filling cans by hand, and make as high **as $5, $6, and $6.50** per day of 10 hours. The majority of them are comfortably **situated in tents** a short distance from the cannery, where sanitary conditions can not be anything but of the best.

We have always conducted our business at this cannery in the most sanitary methods possible, and we earnestly request your honorable body, or any **other investigating** committee, to pay us a visit at this or any other time in **the future ;** in fact, we will gladly welcome such an investigation to prove **the injustice** as reflected by the testimony as referred to in this letter.

Yours, truly,

FRANK WRIGHT, *President.*

EVERETT PACKING CO.,
Everett, Wash., August 24, 1914.
ASSOCIATION OF PACIFIC FISHERIES,
Seattle, Wash.

GENTLEMEN: The statements made by Dr. Theresa McMahon, in her testimony before the Commission of Industrial Relations, in the Federal building, on August 12, 1914, were so entirely unjust and so utterly unfair to the canning industry that it should not be allowed to pass unchallenged.

Speaking for the plant of the Everett Packing Co., of Everett, we desire to say that we employ white help entirely in every department, using men, women, girls, and boys. These employees are all residents of Everett, and a large per cent of the boys and girls are from the high schools of the city, who work during their summer vacation.

Seventy-five per cent of our men employed are paid 30 cents per hour, while the girls and women are paid almost altogther by piecework and earn from $2.50 to $5 per day of eight hours.

The old system of having the packs put up under contract at a stated price per case is no longer followed, and during the rush period of the canning season, when a certain number of the machines are operated overtime, the operators are paid well for such overtime, and we leave it largely to volunteers as to who will put in the overtime, some working overtime one day, while others do the same work the day following.

During the time the plant is in operation 10 hours a day, lunch is served, free of charge, at 9.30 a. m. and 3.30 p. m., and all work at the plant is stopped in each separate department while the employees are eating same.

Our girl employees dress neatly and in uniform; they are orderly and, as stated above, are residents and members of some of the best families of the city.

Were they not paid well and entirely satisfied with conditions at the plant they would certainly not remain in our employ.

As to cleanliness, general sanitation, etc., about the plant, we cheerfully invite inspection and investigation either day or night.

Yours, very truly,

J. O. MORRIS.

HOQUIAM, WASH., *August 21, 1914.*
ASSOCIATION OF PACIFIC FISHERIES,
Seattle, Wash.

DEAR SIRS: I have read an article in the Post-Intelligencer, of Seattle, under the date of August 12, 1914, headed "Minimum wage puts a premium on child labor—Attacks the canneries." This article was so entirely wrong and misleading that I can not let it pass without writing you this letter.

In the past with the old solder system we were compelled to use Chinese labor, and, owing to the system which the Chinese have of doing business, we were compelled to contract with Chinese labor contractors, who agreed to work their men 11 hours per day. In none of those contracts did those Chinese laborers agree to lose 25 cents per hour in case they refused to work overtime, nor was there at any time any such deduction made from their wages by myself. Since the sanitary system has been in operation with me, we have used all white labor. The lowest wages which we have paid to women was $1.75 per day. As soon as the women became used to their work they were put on piecework, where they could and did always earn more than $1.75 per day, some of them earning as high as $4 per day. The greater number of these women have homes in Moclips, a few of them, however, coming from outside towns during the canning season; some of them stopping at hotels and others with private families. I have never heard any complaint from these women as to any changes which they might desire in and around the cannery, and I do not believe that any such have ever been made, as they have always been at liberty to bring any complaints that they might wish to make to my attention. I am utterly at a loss to understand why Dr. McMahon should make such statements, unless through ignorance.

Yours, truly, W. W. KURTZ.

BROOKFIELD, WAHKIAKUM COUNTY, WASH.,
August 22, 1914.

Mr. J. J. REYNOLDS,
    Secretary Association of Pacific Fisheries, Seattle, Wash.

DEAR SIR: In reply to your circular letter of August 18 and the one previous, we wish to say that it is impossible to answer all the assertions made by a lot of agitators. All we can say is that our cannery is open for the inspection of the public or for inspection by any State officer.

We do not employ any women at present. We do employ two or three girls for about a month. They label cans at that time and they work eight hours a day.

Our cannery is built entirely over the water and does not need any sewers, etc.

    Yours, truly,

    J. G. MEGLER & Co.

———

PACIFIC AMERICAN FISHERIES,
    South Bellingham, Wash., August 20, 1914.

ASSOCIATION OF PACIFIC FISHERIES,
    Seattle, Wash.

GENTLEMEN: We have been requested by some of the packers to express our views on the criticisms made by Dr. Theresa McMahon before the Federal commission in Seattle. Mrs. McMahon's charges were very sweeping, but I don't think that she really meant all that she said. Speaking for our own plant, I can say that Mrs. McMahon went all through the plant last year, and after going through it complimented us upon the conditions existing. Mr. Olsen, the labor commissioner, went through at the same time, and we invited criticisms and suggestions, and we do not know of any suggestion that they had to make or any criticisms. None of the male or female employees in our plant are housed in such a manner as she describes, and they all live at home. The plant itself is all over the water, and the tide ebbs and flows twice a day, so that all dirt or anything that would be insanitary is carried out to sea. The offal from the fish is taken into conveyors and runs clear through the plant into scows, and from there is taken to our fertilizing plant five miles away.

I think it useless to try and go into details explaining what we have around our plant, but we invite inspection. This is the way for the commission to get at it, visit the plants, and make their comparisons, and not take the prejudiced testimony of various people, or if any of these witnesses specified any particular plants that are not right, go after them and see that they are put right. If we are among that number, which I don't believe we are, tell us where we can better conditions, and we will gladly do it.

    Yours, very truly,

    E. B. DENNING, *President.*

———

PILLAR ROCK, WASH., *August 21, 1914.*

ASSOCIATION OF PACIFIC FISHERIES,
    Seattle, Wash.

GENTLEMEN: Our attention has been called to the evidence of Dr. Theresa McMahon, purported to be given before the Federal Industrial Commission, in regard to salmon canneries.

We can not see how anyone with average intelligence could make such a report, if, as the doctor says, she had visited any salmon cannery. We always welcome visitors, and as a gentleman and lady who spent a week's vacation at our place this summer said, "Why, we were always led to believe that a person could hardly live at a salmon cannery, and that one would never eat canned salmon if he saw it put up. Now, after inspecting your cannery we want to order a case of salmon sent home for this winter." As regards hours of labor, all our canning help is oriental, as we are isolated. There is not a girl or boy working in our plant. Hours are from 6 to 12, with one hour for noon, and 1 to 6; all other time is paid for as overtime. Some of the work is piecework, where a fast man makes from $5 to $6 in 11 hours. As regards sanitation, all offal goes into the Columbia River; also all sewage. We have an abundant supply of good mountain water running from the faucets all day. The floors are washed down and salted well at the end of every day. The machines are cleaned

4568 REPORT OF COMMISSION ON INDUSTRIAL RELATIONS.

first with steam twice each day and washed with the hose once. All benches are washed, scrubbed with a broom, and salted; all trays the same, and put out in the sun to dry. And if anyone can show us how we can make our place more sanitary we will gladly adopt their suggestions.

Very truly,

PILLAR ROCK PACKING CO.
W. B. STARR, *Secretary*

SAN JUAN FISHING & PACKING CO. (INC.),
Seattle, Wash., August 22, 1914.

ASSOCIATION OF PACIFIC FISHERIES,
Seattle, Wash.

GENTLEMEN: In reference to working conditions in the canneries on Puget Sound we have little knowledge outside of our own plant. We are located in Seattle, where facilities for board and lodging are ample, hence maintain no boarding house of any description. We employ no female labor whatever, except the lady stenographers in the office. Our cannery operatives, outside of skilled labor, are Chinamen secured through a Chinese contractor, this contractor being also the foreman in charge of his Chinese crew.

We pay the Chinese laborers $60 per month each for a period of five months, in addition to which they receive an allowance of $9 per month for board. We also furnish and pay for their Chinese cook, furnish them good quarters, built according to the plan furnished by the Chinese contractor and under the regulations of the ordinances of the city of Seattle. They also receive free wood, free water, and free light, and pay no rent for their quarters.

Our white labor in the cannery department in the skilled branches is paid from $80 to $125 per month. These men all live at home. The unskilled white labor employed consists of a few boys at light work, handling empty cans, light machines, etc. These we pay 20 cents per hour. They also live at home, so far as we are informed.

During practically the entire season the hours have run from 7.30 a. m to 6 p. m., with an hour off at noon.

As far as sanitation is concerned there is no establishment of a manufacturing character in the State of Washington kept any cleaner or more sanitary than our plant. This is one of the first requirements of every employee, that he is to be clean himself and keep his machinery or tools, as the case may be, perfectly clean.

We have visitors every day from every part of the United States, who, not having seen a cannery in operation, are curious to see and observe the methods employed in putting up canned salmon, and we have yet to hear the first one make any statement that any of these operatives or any of the operations are not conducted in a thoroughly clean and sanitary manner. In fact, most of them express surprise at the very clean and net appearance of everything in connection with the work, as they have all read more or less of the same class of statements made by this Mrs. Dr. Theresa McMahon, and have been led to believe by these misstatements that the salmon canneries were a mass of filth. Such statements are a malicious libel and do the industry in this State incalculable harm.

We are glad you are taking this matter up in such a way as to demonstrate just what actual conditions are, and to refer such wild and untrue statements as were made before the Federal Industrial Commission.

Very respectfully,

F. A. TWICHELL.

J. L. SMILEY & CO.,
Blaine, Wash., August 21, 1914.

ASSOCIATION OF PACIFIC FISHERIES,
Seattle, Wash.

GENTLEMEN: We have noticed in the daily newspapers purported reports of Dr. Theresa McMahon's evidence before the Federal Industrial Commission, which are so unfounded in fact, and so grossly unjust and unfair to the salmon canners of this State and their employees, that we feel the public is entitled to an impartial and honest statement of the actual facts.

In the first place, with reference to contracts for oriental labor, we believe a copy of our contract will speak most plainly for itself, and you will therefore find a copy of this contract attached, the same being in the form of a letter addressed to the Japanese contractor. You will notice that there is no requirement as to the number of hours' work each day, but it is verbally understood that 10 hours during the greater portion of the season, and not to exceed 11 hours during the rush, shall constitute a day's work. All such labor is paid 20 cents per hour for overtime, but there is absolutely nothing in the contract which would compel any oriental laborer to work extra time unless he so desires, this being entirely optional with him.

With reference to sanitation, employment of women and girls, etc. All machines in use are thoroughly cleaned at the end of each day's work. The floors, tables, etc., are properly washed, scrubbed, and plentifully sprinkled with salt, so that the entire cannery is at all times clean and sanitary.

We have a women and girls' rest and toilet room, which is located in one corner of our building, away from the male employees. This is equipped with sanitary towels, toilet paper, sanitary drinking fountain, and flush closet. The women and girls are all of good moral character, and their surroundings are of the best; they themselves would be the first to condemn and refute any report to the contrary. We consider them ladies, and they are treated as such. A number of them have voluntarily branded the newspaper reports as a most malicious reflection upon themselves as well as upon the canneries.

Most of them are employed at piecework, and they earn from $3.50 to $7 per day of 10 hours. Some are employed at light work by the hour, for which they receive 20 to 25 cents per hour; children of 14 and 15, employed at labor which can not in any manner work harm to them, receive 15 cents per hour, and the opportunity to secure work of this kind during the summer season has proven itself to be of greatest benefit to those needing it.

Neither oriental nor white labor are compelled, or even requested, to work any excessive length of time. Our present employees consist principally of those who have worked for us in preceding seasons, and the mere fact of their return year after year would itself refute the above reports as contained in the newspapers.

Our cannery and all its operations are at all 'times open to investigation, and the employees may be freely questioned as to their treatment and surrounding. We can not understand the source or foundation of such reports and believe this matter should be presented to the commission for an investigation, which we believe is justly due us and our employees.

Very truly, yours,.

J. L. SMILEY, *President.*

J. L. SMILEY & CO.,
Blaine, Wash., May 4, 1914.

Mr. ROY NOMURA, *Seattle, Wash.*

DEAR SIR: Have your letter of 2d. Regarding the furnishing by you of Japanese labor for our cannery work here this season, we understand you will furnish us 10 men, from June 15 to December 1, at a price of $240 for 3 men and $225 for the other 7 for the entire time, we to furnish board and house for men to live in free of charge. In case any extra men are hired, we to pay them $45 per month, including board. We to pay a cook for the season the sum of $220, and to pay 20 cents per hour for overtime for work done at night or on Sundays to all cannery men. We to pay you for your services for the season $425; also pay transportation charges by boat for all men furnished to and from Seattle to Blaine. You are to board all men furnished, for which we are to pay you the sum of $9.50 per month for each man. We are to furnish the necessary rubber boots and oil aprons free. We are to advance the necessary money to pay for groceries as required. We believe the above covers everything. You will note we state the men are to be here ready for work on June 15; we think, however, July 1 will be soon enough.

If this meets with your approval, kindly acknowledge receipt, and oblige,

Yours, very truly,

J. L. SMILEY & Co.

ASSOCIATION OF PACIFIC FISHERIES,
Seattle, Wash.

GENTLEMAN: We have recently observed some unfavorable comment on conditions in salmon canneries situated in the State of Washington. We do not operate to any great extent in that State, having only a small cannery situated on the Chehalis River at Aberdeen. The help employed at that·point has been chiefly white girls and men, who for the most part have lived at their own homes or in lodgings of their own choosing. This cannery is ·not equipped with any particular rest room for either male or female help. The hours worked is usually from 9 to 10 hours, the 10-hour day being the máximum, and overtime paid after 6 p. m. We have, however, a cannery at Astoria, located within the corporate limits of said city, in which white labor is also employed, our filing being done by girls and women, as well as the labeling, and under a piecework system which permits of an experienced operator earning from $2.50 to $3.50 and $4 per day. This help furnishes its own board and lodging, either at their own homes or at near-by boarding houses. The cannery is not equipped with any particular rest room, but is equipped with sanitary drinking fountains and separate toilet rooms for male and female help. We aim to keep it scrupulously clean by cleansing each machine used for crimping with steam hose and flushing our floors with steam-driven pump, as well as using a liberal amount of salt throughout all departments, thereby making the whole cannery sweet and clean. For this plant the maximum hours of labor are 10; the usual amount worked runs to 9. The wages for the male help range from $45 to $75 per month. We may say that we feel our plant is kept in such state of affairs that an inspection of its premises by any Government officials would be invited and acceptable to us.

Yours, very truly,

T. NELSON.

WARREN PACKING CO. (INC.),
Portland, Oreg., August 20, 1914.
ASSOCIATION OF PACIFIC FISHERIES,
Seattle, Wash.

GENTLEMEN: In answer to a statement before the Commission on Industrial Relations by Dr. Theresa McMahon as to conditions in salmon canneries, we herewith are making an exact statement of facts as existing in our canneries at Cathlamet, Wash., and Warrendale, Oreg., on the Columbia River.

At both of these canneries only Chinese and Japanese labor is employed, as no other labor is available on account of the situation. The canneries operate from May 1 to about September 1, a period of four months. The heavy run of fish does not last for more than two or three weeks at a time, but in order to take care of them it is necessary for us to employ for the entire four months the maximum number of laborers so as to have them available for the short period of heavy runs. These men are paid from $250 to $350 each and are furnished with board and lodging in addition free of charge for the entire four months. This is equivalent to from $62.50 to $87.50 per month and board and lodging. They work 11 hours per day when there is work to be done, and are paid extra for overtime and for all Sunday work.

During the greater part of the season when the work is slack the laborers work only as long as is necessary to pack the fish received, and this amounts at times to not more than two or three hours a day. Consequently the average time of work per day over the four months does not amount to more than seven or eight hours for each day.

Our men are very well satisfied with conditions in our plants, as is evidenced by the fact that the same men come back voluntarily year after year and apply for their old positions.

Yours, very truly,

GEO. A. WARREN, *Secretary.*

WILLAPA HARBOR FISH CO.,
South Bend, Wash., August 12, 1914.
ASSOCIATION OF PACIFIC FISHERIES,
Seattle, Wash.

GENTLEMEN: Referring to the articles in the daily press relative to the salmon-canning industry of the State of Washington and purporting to be evidence of Dr. Theresa McMahon before the Federal Industrial Commission, the above company desires to be placed on record as stating that material matter as set forth in the articles of the press are wrong, unfair, false, and malicious, and must surely emanate from some one who is entirely ignorant of the up-to-date methods of operating a salmon cannery.

This company has no Chinese contract, with the exception of the agreement as to the wage for a regular days' labor of the different classes of such labor performed, a regular days' labor is from 7 a. m. to 6 p. m., with one hour off for noon, and should the rush season require overhours, then the laborer is paid for such overtime.

The sanitation of the cannery of this company is good, the machines of all kinds are steamed, cleaned, and the floors, tubs, and tables are cleaned in salt water and salt each day, the female toilets are far distant from the others, and the whites and Chinese have separate toilets.

During the packing season we have in the employ of this company several women and girls, who receive from $1.50 to $2 per day for 9 hours' work, commencing at 7 o'clock a. m. and quitting at 5 o'clock p. m., with one hour off for noon; nearly all of the females employed are over the age of 18 years.

It is far better for a body to visit the several canneries and observe for themselves than to take evidence from some person who is either ignorant of the true conditions existing, or is maliciously opposing the salmon-canning industry.

Very respectfully,

ELBERT PEDERSON, *Manager.*

STRIAL CONDITIONS AND
IN PORTLAND, OREG.

r this subject, see pages 4737 to 4770.)

COMMISSION ON INDUSTRIAL RELATIONS.

PORTLAND, OREG., *Thursday, August 20, 1914—10 a. m.*

Present: Chairman Walsh and Commissioners Commons, Lennon, O'Connell, and Garretson; W. O. Thompson, counsel.

Chairman WALSH. The commission will please be in order.

Mr. THOMPSON. Gov. West is unable to be present.

Chairman WALSH. And when may we expect him here?

Mr. THOMPSON. He sent word that he was prepared to testify yesterday, and made arrangements for it, but did not think he would be present, as his time was so occupied, but that he would make every effort to come if he could find time.

Dr. Young.

TESTIMONY OF DR. F. G. YOUNG.

Mr. THOMPSON. Will you please give us your name and your business address?

Dr. YOUNG. F. G. Young; Eugene, Oreg.; University of Oregon.

Mr. THOMPSON. What department are you connected with at the University of Oregon?

Dr. YOUNG. Economics and sociology.

Mr. THOMPSON. How long have you been connected with the university in that capacity, Doctor?

Dr. YOUNG. Nineteen years.

Mr. THOMPSON. Nineteen years?

Dr. YOUNG. Yes; not exactly the same chair, but virtually.

Mr. THOMPSON. And in the course of your 19 years that you have been connected with the university out here, Doctor, have you had occasion to look into and to study the industrial conditions which exist in this part of the country?

Dr. YOUNG. Only in a general way, as I would have occasion through being in charge of the work of economics and sociology. No special occasion arose for any close study or investigation.

Mr. THOMPSON. And in the course of that work, Doctor, have you made a survey of the general industrial conditions?

Dr. YOUNG. Not in any systematic way. I tried to keep in touch with things.

Mr. THOMPSON. Will you tell us, Doctor, what study you have made of these conditions, and how you view these conditions to-day?

Dr. YOUNG. In Oregon?

Mr. THOMPSON. In Oregon; and in that part of the State which you are located in.

Dr. YOUNG. Excepting in a few of the trades, the conditions are rather primitive—that is, there is no fully developed conditions into the classes of the employers and the employees. There is no marked class consciousness of distinct interest or how to handle their condition—antagonistic interests, if they are conscious of it; that is, Oregon in its industrial development is somewhat in the condition which the older countries in the eastern part of the Nation was in before the factory stage arrived. Of course, we have the lumber industry and others that have been somewhat developed—industrial development, the capitalistic system of organization—yet we are an undeveloped State. So that there is no close organization as between the capitalistic class and the laboring class.

Mr. THOMPSON. Doctor, the inquiries of the commission, of course, are not limited to simply a study of the organizations.

Dr. YOUNG. Yes.

Mr. THOMPSON. We are to study the relations that exist between the employer and the employee, whatever they may be. In such thought as you have given to the situation here, are there any facts bearing on that relationship that you could give to this commission?

4575

Dr. YOUNG. Well, it would seem that it would be highly advisable that both interests, the interests of labor and the interests of capital, were to become apprised of the need of organization, that they are not under a condition that is normal unless they do have organization or solidarity. And it would be well if there were any means of obtaining it, if the business interests in Oregon could come to realize that the trades-unions are an essential feature of the developed industrial system, and also that the employers in their respective lines could furnish their interests by uniting, and then developing the ideas of collective bargaining and of treating with each other under conditions which would tend to bring into systematic study their exact, their vital relations. That is, it seems to me, one thing that is necessary. Of course, probably I am not sure that it is advisable to hurry that, but that is one element.

Mr. THOMPSON. Doctor, into what classes does the bulk of the labor of this part of the country divide itself; what industries, rather?

Dr. YOUNG. Well, agricultural industry, and the lumber industry, the fishing industry, and the manufacturing generally of other lines than the lumbering. Of course, in agriculture we have divisions, into horticulture——

Mr. THOMPSON. Well, Doctor, taking those divisions of labor in the various industries in the State. Take the agricultural, what would you say of conditions of labor in that industry in this State?

Dr. YOUNG. Why, it is in a very chaotic condition, I think. It is seasonal employment that exists to a very large—very marked—degree, and the conditions that characterize individualism, every employee taking care of his own interests, and every employer looking out for his own particular interests.

Mr. THOMPSON. Well, in that branch of the trade it is more or less seasonal, isn't it, Doctor?

Dr. YOUNG. Yes, sir; it is.

Mr. THOMPSON. Well, what do the people who work in that industry do when that industry does not require their services? Where do they go; what becomes of them; do you know?

Dr. YOUNG. No, sir; there has been no survey made from the results of which to make any statement that has any basis of fact to warrant the statement. I suppose some of them go into the lumber camps, others are out of employment during a large part of the season.

Mr. THOMPSON. Take the lumber industry, now, Doctor, the fishing industry and the manufacturing; you might tell what you know about those.

Dr. YOUNG. I say I haven't definite enough information to make it worth while.

Mr. THOMPSON. Have you given any thought, Doctor, to the condition of the working people as a class as to whether there is a state of unrest or not existing among them, industrially? What are your views about that?

Dr. YOUNG. I think they are all conscious that conditions should be improved; that they deserve much better than they have, but they haven't that degree of clearness of ideas as to procedure or leadership, except, of course, in a few trades, to enable them to rise from their present quite unsatisfactory conditions, in so far as that condition is made unsatisfactory to their being the weaker party in the clash of interests.

Mr. THOMPSON. Well, what would you say as to the cause of this unrest on their part; how would you analyze it?

Dr. YOUNG. They are not getting their share of the profits of the industry.

Mr. THOMPSON. Well, in any specific industry is their more or less of a marked condition of that kind, or is that just a general feeling among all people who work?

Dr. YOUNG. I don't know of any particular trade or industry in which any peculiar degree of discontent exists.

Mr. THOMPSON. Well, do you think that the degree of discontent, if such exists as you have stated it in this part of the country, is such as to receive the attention and consideration of this commission?

Dr. YOUNG. Why, I should think so, because this commission will no doubt develop the conditions that obtain in the older parts of the country. with the development of our manufacturing interest, and this section should not be put under the necessity of traveling the long road of trial and experiment and going all the wrong ways without finding the right one. I think the commission could serve it in a very marked measure by pointing out what, in their opinion, are the features that characterize a satisfactory condition in the relations between employer and employee, and the procedure through which our community here in its primitive stage could short cut to this desirable condition.

Mr. THOMPSON. Now, what recommendation would you make to this commission to remedy in whole or in part. these conditions which you speak of, which are, of course, the practical scope and purpose of such commission as this?

. Dr. YOUNG. Well, I think the school should have in its curriculum a representation of this problem;. that is, the school should bring to the youth growing up a clearer outlined idea of the vital elements in industrial developments. And furthermore there should be, I think, recommended by this commission such surveys as will make as definite as possible to the different proposed industries in this community their prospects of succeeding; that is, their market problems and their problem, power and labor pertaining to other factors that determine whether the industries are normally located and developed in this region. I should say that the commission could be of great service in outlining the procedure or program that the authorities, the agencies, institutions responsible for those interests in the community to the people in this community, should outline to them, or that through their wider studies of the subject should be taken along.

Mr. THOMPSON. Have you any suggestions in that regard, any concrete suggestions to the commission?

Dr. YOUNG. Well, the University of Oregon is developing a system of commercial and industrial surveys that—we should be gratefully delighted. to have the cooperation of this commission in aiding us to advance that work as far as possible. And then, too, as a third feature that I think if, the whole matter of industrial organization should be made—I don't know just how, just what agency we should rely upon, but the whole problem that rests upon industrial organizations, the accomplishment of that should be promoted and cleared up as much as possible.

Mr. THOMPSON. Have you made ·a detailed study of the operation and the effect of the minimum wage law in this State?

Dr. YOUNG. The minimum wage law?

Mr. THOMPSON. Yes.

Dr. YOUNG. No. I have not made any specific inquiry into it.

Mr. THOMPSON. That is all, Mr. Chairman.

Chairman WALSH. Mr. Lennon, would like to ask you a few questions.

.Commissioner· LENNON. Doctor, what causes led to the people of Oregon being pioneers in welfare legislation, the law limiting the hours for women workers and to the establishment of wage boards? Was there industrial unrest that brought that to the people's attention, or what brought it?

Dr. YOUNG. Well, in a city like Portland the conditions approximate those of the older cities of the East. That fact together with the people of Oregon, I think you will acknowledge, have a quite complete emancipation from tradition, and are alert as to what is desired, and so cast about for remedies, even though the evils or the ills are not so severe as they might be elsewhere. That is, just as in Australia and New Zealand you find them very radical in their social legislation. while I do not believe that in either of those cases the ills reach anything like the degree that they have in the older countries like England.

Chairman WALSH. Any questions?

، Commissioner COMMONS. Yes.

Chairman WALSH. Prof. Commons.

· Commissioner COMMONS. Have you made a study that would enable you to tell about the proportions of the employees in these different industries, take the lumbering and logging.

Dr. YOUNG. No; my courses do not cover the labor problems. My assistant has those. I supposed he would be called as a witness here. And then those facts, so far as they are extant, are to be found in the report of our commissioner of labor and statistics.

Commissioner COMMONS. That gives the total laboring population?

Dr. YOUNG. I think so. I am quite sure.

Commissioner COMMONS. And distribution?

Dr. YOUNG. That is his responsibility to collate the statistics of labor.

. Commissioner COMMONS. Then you yourself would not be able to give us information regarding how labor is organized?

Dr. YOUNG. No. You better rely upon some others in your list.

Commissioner COMMONS. Who, for instance? ·

Dr. YOUNG. Mr. Stack would be one of them, and Mr. A. H. Harris, who is here.

Commissioner COMMONS. Have you followed the operation of the initiative and referendum in this State with reference to labor legislation?

Dr. YOUNG. In a general way.

Commissioner COMMONS. Well, what have been some of the laws that have been put upon the statute books through the initiative, and who inaugurated them, and how did they get up the petitions, and so on?

Dr. YOUNG. Well, now, I can't be sure of just which ones of our labor laws were secured through the initiative and which ones through the regular legislative assembly enactment.

Commissioner COMMONS. In general, what has been the experience of the State in your judgment with reference to the kind of laws enacted by the legislature and the kind enacted through the initiative and referendum—or the initiative particularly?

Dr. YOUNG. I should say that if there is any marked difference those enacted through the process of the initiative are somewhat more radical, more extreme probably. They have to be quite simple in order to be fully comprehended by the people, or at least to have an interest taken in them by the people. But they are generally more radical.

Commissioner COMMONS. Well, are they enacted in such form that they can be carried out without further action by the legislature?

Dr. YOUNG. Most of them are. Nearly all of them are.

Commissioner COMMONS. They create agencies?

Dr. YOUNG. They do.

Commissioner COMMONS. Administrative agencies and so on?

Dr. YOUNG. Yes; the legislature is not under the necessity of supplementing them.

Commissioner COMMONS. Now, what about the efficiency of that class of legislation, as to the agencies that have been created under the initiative? Have they been such that those agencies are competent and have had sufficient power to carry out the intent of the initiative law?

Dr. YOUNG. Just now I am not clear as to what particular labor law was enacted. Probably you know better than I.

Commissioner COMMONS. No; I don't know. I am asking you.

Dr. YOUNG. The secretary of state's report would answer that.

Commissioner COMMONS. You haven't followed that out—haven't inquired into that?

Dr. YOUNG. Not in regard to that; no. I should say though, as your question implies, that the initiative does not lend itself to the most efficiency in securing good, effective legislation for social reform purposes.

Commissioner COMMONS. Well, is that opinion of yours based upon any particular investigation of that question, or is it just a general summing up?

Dr. YOUNG. Why, the general trend of initiative legislation, and the way in which the measures are reveloped here in this State, indicate that it is a matter of common sense that you can not—that they can not be developed, that they can not be matured so as to be effective.

Commissioner COMMONS. I think that is all.

Chairman WALSH. Any other questions?

Commissioner GARRETSON. Yes.

Chairman WALSH. Mr. Garretson would like to ask you some questions. Commissioner Garretson.

Commissioner GARRETSON. Doctor, from your standpoint and information, can the individual laborer working by himself stand any chance of securing a reasonable degree of economic justice?

Dr. YOUNG. Not unless he is in close personal relation with his employer.

Commissioner GARRETSON. The personal equation is the only one that can make it possible?

Dr. YOUNG. I think so.

Commissioner GARRETSON. Then have you any opinion as to whether he can secure a greater degree of immediate corrective for what he believes are his disabilities—economic disabilities—by legislative action or by organization with others of his kind?

Dr. YOUNG. I should take it that it would be necessary, as a first step, to organize and get solidarity of opinion, class opinion—yes, class opinion—in order that they might be in position to develop legislation.

Commissioner GARRETSON. And would he, even if legislation were enacted that was reasonable, would he be able to secure its proper administration afterwards better if he was in a highly organized state than in a disorganized

Dr. YOUNG. No. Public opinion, of course, is a necessary basis both for intelligent legislation and for effective administration. And organization is necessary in order to give point and clearness.

Commissioner GARRETSON. To apply public opinion? ·

Dr. YOUNG. Yes.

Commissioner GARRETSON. That is all, Mr. Chairman.

Chairman WALSH. That is all; thank you.

Mr. THOMPSON. One more question I would like to ask: Doctor, do you know whether the supply of labor is greater than the needs here in this State?

Dr. YOUNG. It is greatly in excess in the winter months, the slack months. ·

Mr. THOMPSON. That is all.

Mr. Francis is compelled to go away, and he has left here a written statement containing the replies to the questions sent to him.

Chairman WALSH. Let it be filed.

(The papers so presented were marked " Francis Exhibits Nos. 1, 2, 3, and 4." The statement marked " Exhibit No. 1 " is printed on pages 4726–4736. Exhibits Nos. 2, 3, and 4, respectively, are " Constitution, By-Laws, and Trade Rules of the District Council of Carpenters of Portland, Oreg., and Vicinity," etc., adopted August, 1913; " Declaration of Principles and By-Laws of the Employers' Association of Oregon;" and " Constitution of the National Association of Stationary Engineers," revised and adopted by the national convention at Boston, Mass., September 2–5, 1902, and were submitted in printed form.)

TESTIMONY OF MR. E. J. STACK.

Mr. THOMPSON. Will you please give us your name and your business address?

Mr. STACK. E. J. Stack. My business address is 162½ Second Street. ·

Mr. THOMPSON. And your position?

Mr. STACK. Secretary of the State Federation of Labor of Oregon.

Mr. THOMPSON. How long have you been secretary of the federation?

Mr. STACK. This is the third term. A term is a little more than two and a half years.

Mr. THOMPSON. How long has the federation been in existence?

Mr. STACK. Well, it has been in existence twelve years and a half. ·

Mr. THOMPSON. Is the federation affiliated with any other bodies or body; and if so, what are they?

Mr. STACK. It is affiliated with the American Federation of Labor.

Mr. THOMPSON. Is it affiliated under the same rules and in the same way that other State federations of labor are affiliated?

Mr. STACK. Yes, sir.

Mr. THOMPSON. How many unions are affiliated with your organization, local unions, if you know, or international?

Mr. STACK. Why, approximately, I should say, including central bodies, unions would be about 56 now.

Mr. THOMPSON. Has your organization a constitution and by-laws?

Mr. STACK. It has.

Mr. THOMPSON. Are they printed?

Mr. STACK. Yes, sir.

Mr. THOMPSON. Would you be willing to furnish the commission with a copy?

Mr. STACK. Yes, sir; I haven't one with me; I didn't think to bring one with me.

Mr. THOMPSON. Will you send one to us?

Mr. STACK. Yes, sir.

Mr. THOMPSON. In lieu of that, you may state briefly the purposes of your organization.

Mr. STACK. The purpose of the State federation is to further remedial legislation. That is its chiefest purpose. It is composed of local unions throughout the State, and the head federation through its convention and the executive board in the interim of the convention looks after legislation and makes that its chiefest work. However, it also does what it can in organization work.

Mr. THOMPSON. Well, now, you might tell very briefly, if you will, what you do in furtherance of that work, whether you have agents at the capital, whether you circularize your members or the public or have campaigns or mass meetings, or what. Just tell us briefly.

Mr. STACK. Our plan briefly is to circularize the locals that are affiliated and also all unions that are not affiliated—there are some that are not—in Oregon, and to give what publicity we can through letters and circularization, and in measures particularly we maintain a legislative commission to attend sessions of the legislature and do what it can in the interests of legislation.

Mr. THOMPSON. And in the doing of that do you urge such legislation as you think ought to be passed and oppose such legislation as you think ought not be passed?

Mr. STACK. Yes, sir.

Mr. THOMPSON. And to what extent and in what manner do you seek to take part in elections, if any, or do you extend your activities to that extent? .

Mr. STACK. No, sir.

Mr. THOMPSON. Of seeking to elect members who are favorable to you or in opposing men who are not?

Mr. STACK. No, sir; we haven't done that as a body except in the last primary. In the last primary we endeavored to elect members to the legislature—three members of the organization of labor—and failed.

Mr. THOMPSON. In that regard, what did you do? Did you seek any pledges, or did you simply indorse generally those candidates whom you thought were proper ones and oppose those whom you thought were not proper?

Mr. STACK. Our method in this was through a convention committee at the last convention of the State federation. This committee was appointed, and the committee circularized all local unions affiliated with the State federation and asked them for legislative timber, and from the names submitted selected one or two and according to their political affiliations put them on the primary through the petition.

Mr. THOMPSON. Now, in regard to the passage of laws. There is the referendum in this State—the initiative and referendum?

Mr. STACK. Yes, sir.

Mr. THOMPSON. Has your organization taken any interest in either advocating or opposing laws through that means, too?

Mr. STACK. It has; yes, sir.

Mr. THOMPSON. What other statements would you care to make in regard to the activities of your organization from a legislative standpoint?

Mr. STACK. Well, in a general way that is the activity of the federation.

Mr. THOMPSON. How long have you been connected with organized labor?

Mr. STACK. Fourteen years last June.

Mr. THOMPSON. What is your particular union?

Mr. STACK. I am a cigar maker.

Mr. THOMPSON. How long have you been out on the west coast here?

Mr. STACK. All my life, nearly.

Mr. THOMPSON. All your life? Have you made a sort of survey in the way of industrial conditions in this vicinity?

Mr. STACK. No, sir; only those I have come in contact with. I haven't neither had the time or money to give the time to a survey.

Mr. THOMPSON. Tell us what you know, such facts as you know, that bear on the relations—that is, the conditions of labor in the particular branches of industry?

Chairman WALSH. What crafts are organized? Did he state that?

Mr. THOMPSON. No, sir.

State what crafts are organized?

Chairman WALSH. First, state what crafts are organized that you have definite information about.

Mr. STACK. There is an organization in nearly every craft except the lumbering industry and the packing industry, such as fruit-packing plants, and even in the lumber industry there is the shingle weavers who have now extended their jurisdiction to take in all the people working in the lumber industry, although they are not organized to any great extent yet.

Mr. THOMPSON. What would be the best organized union, or craft?

Mr. STACK. Among the best organized are the printers and cigar makers, They have what they call a 100 per cent organization.

Mr. THOMPSON. Any other lines you care to speak of?

Mr. STACK. I don't know of any others that are so thoroughly organized.

Chairman WALSH. There has been evidence that there were organizations in the lumber industry. What are they?

Mr. THOMPSON. The chairman would like to know what has been done in the timber industry. You mentioned the fact that the shingle weavers had no independent organization over the rest of the workers. What have they done generally in that line. Do you know?

Mr. STACK. They have offered membership to people working in the timber industries, and have attempted by themselves, but without any aid from the State federation, to organize the workers of the timber industry, and they have been gathering members regularly.

Chairman WALSH. Have you made any investigation or study of conditions in logging camps, in the timber industry, from the standpoint of the laborers that are not connected with your association?

Mr. STACK. Only that which we hear from persons; no personal organization.

Chairman WALSH. Has there been any organized effort on the part of the organized crafts to discover conditions in these logging camps?

Mr. STACK. Yes; they have made some effort to learn the conditions, and their method has been one of inquiry of the people who are working there.

Chairman WALSH. They never go out there? Do you have any organizer that goes into the camp?

Mr. STACK. Not from the State federation.

Chairman WALSH. Any investigator?

Mr. STACK. No; the State federation has none.

Mr. THOMPSON. Is that all, Mr. Chairman?

Chairman WALSH. Yes; that is all.

Mr. THOMPSON. Have you made any study of the condition of labor in the various industries here, as to whether there is dissatisfaction or not?

Mr. STACK. Yes.

Mr. THOMPSON. What is your opinion in regard to it?

Mr. STACK. Why, my personal opinion is that there is a considerable spirit of unrest in most of the industries that are not very well organized.

Mr. THOMPSON. What is the cause of that industrial unrest at this time, in your opinion?

Mr. STACK. Long hours, low wages, and bad working conditions.

Mr. THOMPSON. In what trade or industry would you say the unrest is the greatest in this locality?

Mr. STACK. In seasonal occupations, where migratory workers are working.

Mr. THOMPSON. Give us the names of those in the order in which those are the worst, from that standpoint.

Mr. STACK. Well, in the fruit-packing industries, and in—well, in the wheat fields, where men work in the fields, in the logging camps working short shifts, the men are sent out to camps and do not stay long. The conditions, they claim, are bad there. The men are charged a fee from the employmenut agent and a hospital fee, and then they are turned loose again in a short time. And during the season, say, where operations run over half the year a camp that would ordinarily require three or four hundred men probably there has been men by the thousand there.

Mr. THOMPSON. Do you think, Mr. Stack, that the men are let go and others hired? What is the reason for doing that, if you know?

Mr. STACK. Well, I do not know other than it would be a connivance on the part of the employment agent and the men who hire the men, to split fees. I know this, that there has been arrests made in the city of Portland and the license taken away from them for that very reason, within the last week.

Mr. THOMPSON. Do you think there would be any other purpose in that? Do you think the supply of labor would have anything to do with that proposition?

Mr. STACK. Yes; the supply would have something to do with it, and then, too, the fact the men are kept on the go keeps them from organizing.

Mr. THOMPSON. Have you any other matters to suggest to the commission in that connection? I mean, with the hiring and discharging of a large number of men, when to fill three or four hundred jobs they are hiring thousands?

Mr. STACK. The only suggestion I would have to offer would be if the commission is equipped to do so, to make the survey itself and give publicity to it.

Mr. THOMPSON. What other suggestion would you make to this commission that it could reasonably enforce to help the conditions of labor in this locality?

Mr. STACK. In a general way?

Mr. THOMPSON. Yes; generally, and that would help labor generally throughout the country?

Mr. STACK. Well, I don't know anything that would be more beneficial to labor in this part or in any other part of the country than to survey, and then the widest kind of publicity given to the findings.

Mr. THOMPSON. Have you any views as to whether or not there might be such a thing as national employment offices established?

Mr. STACK. We thought lots about employment offices.

Mr. THOMPSON. Did you make a tentative suggestion in a bill in that respect?

Mr. STACK. Yes; we have. The State federation had a bill in the legislature.

Mr. THOMPSON. I mean, did you get it from this commission, a tentative suggestion?

Mr. STACK. No. We had a bill in the legislature to provide for a State bureau; a national bureau might be better.

Mr. THOMPSON. Well, what would you say with reference to machinery for adjusting industrial disputes, such as a national council, or industrial council that could investigate labor conditions, that could give publicity to them? Either during the time of peace or in times of industrial trouble, that could mediate and conciliate the parties and also act as an arbitrator, or appoint arbitrators in case it was agreeable? What would you say as to that?

Mr. STACK. Well, I would say that would be good—arbitration, if it were agreeable; I would think that compulsory investigation would be one of the best things, conciliation wherever possible, and arbitration where it is agreeable, but by all means investigation.

Mr. THOMPSON. Is there any other suggestion you care to make to this commission, Mr. Stack?

Mr. STACK. It doesn't come to my mind now, any that I care to make just now.

Mr. THOMPSON. Is there some effort being made here to employ people who are out of work on account of seasonal work on the public work?

Mr. STACK. Some effort is being made to take care of unemployment?

Mr. THOMPSON. Yes; what do you think of it? What is your view if there is?

Mr. STACK. It is only a makeshift.

Chairman WALSH. Has there, or is there any effort being made to do away with seasonal employment by putting the workers upon public works?

Mr. STACK. Last winter there was an effort made. This year there has been several efforts looking to some relief measures, but in nearly all instances it is to provide a rock pile.

Mr. THOMPSON. That is all, Mr. Chairman.

Chairman WALSH. Well, now, has there been any definite move outside of an attempt to provide a rock pile in the city to take care of seasonal labor in this State, to your knowledge?

Mr. STACK. Yes; there has been.

Chairman WALSH. Please state what it is, Mr. Stack.

Mr. STACK. There has been an effort to provide a law that would permit the State to build roads in seasons of unemployment.

Chairman WALSH. Has that taken any other form except an attempted introduction, or the introduction of such a law in the legislature?

Mr. STACK. No other attempt.

Chairman WALSH. Is that as far as it has gone?

Mr. STACK. Yes.

Chairman WALSH. Prof. Commons would like to ask you some questions.

Commissioner COMMONS. Do you have records, or have you made inquiries, which would show the number of people unemployed in the lumber industry in the State?

Mr. STACK. We have not made any.

Commissioner COMMONS. About how many do you think there are unemployed in lumber and logging?

Mr. STACK. Lumber and logging?

Commissioner COMMONS. Yes.

Mr. STACK. The men that work in the industry, between 30.000 and 40,000.

Commissioner COMMONS. How many of them would be in the shingling—the shingle weavers?

Mr. STACK. I don't know.

Commissioner COMMONS. The seasonal labor that is employed in fruit packing and harvesting, and so on, have you any notion or idea as to whether there has been any investigation to show about the total number that are engaged?

Mr. STACK. No; I have not.

Commissioner COMMONS. In the height of the season?

Mr. STACK. There has not been by our federation.

Commissioner COMMONS. Have any been made?

Mr. STACK. Not to my knowledge.

Commissioner COMMONS. Are the building trades organized in Portland fully?

Mr. STACK. Yes; the building trades are organized.

Commissioner COMMONS. And in what other cities are they organized?

Mr. STACK. In Astoria and Salem, and in Eugene partially, and some organization in Baker.

Commissioner COMMONS. Are they represented? What bills has the State federation of labor or the labor element in the State initiated under the initiative law?

Mr. STACK. The employers' liability law and the eight hours for public works.

Commissioner COMMONS. Is that all?

Mr. STACK. That is all that they have initiated themselves. They have aided in other measures.

Commissioner COMMONS. What?

Mr. STACK. They have aided others, and those, as far as they have initiated themselves, the employers' liability and the eight hours for public works.

Commissioner COMMONS. Have they aided other organizations in promoting other bills?

Mr. STACK. Yes.

Commissioner COMMONS. What other organizations have you aided?

Mr. STACK. The Grangers, and the Farmers' Union, and the Farmers' Society of Equity, and the People's Power League.

Commissioner COMMONS. That makes three. What others?

Mr. STACK. The Grangers, Farmers' Union, Farmers' Society of Equity, and the People's Power League; four.

Commissioner COMMONS. Four of them. Is there an alliance between those various organizations to each promote initiative bills that others initiate?

Mr. STACK. Yes.

Commissioner COMMONS. They circulate petitions jointly, then?

Mr. STACK. Yes.

Commissioner COMMONS. Was this done in the case of the employers' liability?

Mr. STACK. No; not then. That was one of the first bills that the State federation initiated, and it did not have that machinery at that time.

Commissioner COMMONS. How about eight hours on public works?

Mr. STACK. The other organizations aided in giving publicity to it; we initiated it ourselves.

Commissioner COMMONS. Did they circulate a petition?

Mr. STACK. No; we circulated it ourselves.

Commissioner COMMONS. Has the employers' liability law been amended or legislated upon in any way by the legislature?

Mr. STACK. Yes—no; not by the legislature. It has been—the wording of it has been changed by the courts, constructions upon it changed by the courts.

Commissioner COMMONS. But the initiative bill proposed a complete scheme of employees' compensation?

Mr. STACK. Employers' liability.

Commissioner COMMONS. Is that what we know as the employees' compensation law? You have no compensation law?

Mr. STACK. Yes; we have a compensation law.

Commissioner COMMONS. What is that?

Mr. STACK. A compensation law.

Commissioner COMMONS. In case of accident, compensation?.

Mr. STACK. Passed at the last legislature, the compensation law that is now a statute provides regular compensation for employees.

A VOICE FROM THE AUDIENCE. Louder, please.

Mr. STACK. To provide compensation for the employees in hazardous occupations and provides means for others to have compensation under the act. It is optional with them—an optional compensation.

Commissioner COMMONS. You have a commission to demonstrate or administer?

Mr. STACK. Yes.

Commissioner COMMONS. What was the employers' liability law that you initiated—just what did that provide?

Mr. STACK. That was to fix the responsibility for accidents.

Commissioner COMMONS. Did that overlap the compensation law?

Mr. STACK. No; there was no compensation law at that time.

Commissioner COMMONS. Then this compensation law takes the place of that liability law?

Mr. STACK. It does whenever the employees come under it.

Commissioner COMMONS. Oh, I see; it is optional.

Mr. STACK. With the employer; it is not optional with the employee. It is supposed to be, but it is not.

Commissioner COMMONS. What proportion of the employees organized in this State are under the compensation law?

Mr. STACK. I haven't that information. The law just came into operation the 1st of July. They are just now making it effective.

Commissioner COMMONS. What would you estimate the total number of organized labor or members of organized labor in this State?

Mr. STACK. Well, I haven't any means of giving a correct idea of the total number.

Commissioner COMMONS. Just those that are represented in the State Federation of Labor. Your per capita would show that?

Mr. STACK. Yes, sir.

Commissioner COMMONS. What would that show?

Mr. STACK. That would show approximately 11,000. Of course, we have no railroad unions of the State. I should judge it would be between sixteen and seventeen thousand.

Commissioner COMMONS. The total number sixteen or seventeen thousand?

Mr. STACK. Yes, sir.

Commissioner COMMONS. What would be the number organized in Portland?

Mr. STACK. Why, about around 8,200 or over.

Commissioner COMMONS. About half of them are in Portland?

Mr. STACK. Yes, sir; the bulk of the union men are in Portland.

Chairman WALSH. Please speak a little louder.

Mr. STACK. The bulk of the union men are in Portland.

Commissioner COMMONS. That includes the railroad brotherhood as well. To what extent have measures been taken by your organization to organize the common or unskilled labor in the various industries of the State—that is, those which are not represented by the craft unions or labor helpers or common laborers working along with them? To what extent has there been any organization of that class of labor?

Mr. STACK. They are very hard to organize. The efforts that have been made are those that are usually made through public meetings at times and by sending literature to the workers themselves.

Commissioner COMMONS. Is there anybody whose business it is, either in any of the city central bodies or in the State federation, to organize the common unskilled labor?

Mr. STACK. Not particularly the unskilled common labor.

Commissioner COMMONS. Do you have Federal labor unions?

Mr. STACK. We have none here at the present time except the civil service workers' organization.

Chairman WALSH. I can't hear you, Mr. Stack, and I am sure Brother Garretson is having great trouble. Please pitch your voice a little higher.

Mr. STACK. This is a very hard room to hear in.

Chairman WALSH. Well, help us all you can by talking louder.

Commissioner COMMONS. What is this civil-service organization that you speak of?

Mr. STACK. Merely an organization of civil service workers who are chartered by the American Federation of Labor as a Federal union.

Commissioner COMMONS. What kind of work are they engaged in?

Mr. STACK. All classes.

Commissioner COMMONS. Work for the city?

Mr. STACK. City employment.

Commissioner COMMONS. Is that organization in the city of Portland?

Mr. STACK. Yes.

Commissioner COMMONS. How many members has it?

Mr. STACK. I don't know.

Commissioner COMMONS. Is it represented in the central body?

Mr. STACK. Yes.

Commissioner COMMONS. Does it include all the workers on the street?

Mr. STACK. Any of them; it is organized as a Federal union—anyone that chooses to join on the streets or——

Commissioner COMMONS (interposing). Have they a business agent?

Mr. STACK. No; they have no business agent.

Commissioner COMMONS. But aside from that there is no organization of a Federal labor union to take in the unskilled and the unorganized?

Mr. STACK. Not at the present time.

Commissioner COMMONS. What unions have separate organizations for helpers, or what might be called unskilled labor?

Mr. STACK. Why, you will learn that better from the building trades' representatives.

Commissioner COMMONS. Is there some one here from them?

Mr. STACK. Mr. Osborne and Mr. Sleeman will give you that information.

Commissioner COMMONS. Is your residence in Portland?

Mr. STACK. No; I live at Multnomah Station, just outside of Portland.

Commissioner COMMONS. Was this initiative for eight hours, was that adopted by the State?

Mr. STACK. Yes.

Commissioner COMMONS. Does that apply to all bodies, local, county, and town?

Mr. STACK. Yes; applies to all political subdivisions of the State.

Commissioner COMMONS. In your effort to elect candidates to the legislature, do you print the legislative records of candidates?

Mr. STACK. No.

Commissioner COMMONS. You don't?

Mr. STACK. No; we keep a legislative record of all candidates.

Commissioner COMMONS. But this record of the legislators is not published and distributed over the State?

Mr. STACK. Only to the local unions. It is a matter printed in the proceedings of the conventions, and, of course, anybody that wants it may have it. But it is sent only to the local unions and to the libraries that call for it. They are on the mailing list, and to the different federations of labor throughout the United States. That is our mailing list.

Commissioner COMMONS. Has organized labor any other initiative measures which they are pressing or circulating, to come before the voters?

Mr. STACK. Not any that it is circulating itself. It has interested itself in several measures that will come on the ballot in November. One of them particularly is the women's eight-hour bill, initiated, however, by the women's eight-hour league.

Commissioner COMMONS. Who on this list has been active in circulating that, any of the witnesses?

Mr. STACK. I don't believe there is any that are on your list.

Commissioner COMMONS. What other measures are you assisting in the initiative?

Mr. STACK. We are assisting in the $1,500 tax-exemption measure, particularly, the abolishment of the senate, and of the proportional representation plan for the legislature.

Commission COMMONS. When do these come up for voting, this fall?

Mr. STACK. November 3; yes, sir.

Commissioner COMMONS. I have no more.

Chairman WALSH. Mr. Garretson, have you some questions?

Commissioner GARRETSON. Mr. Stack, do you know of any other compulsory act in effect on this continent, except the Canadian act?

Mr. STACK. Compensation act?

Commissioner GARRETSON. No; compulsory investigation.

Mr. STACK. No; I don't.

Commissioner GARRETSON. Are you familiar with the workings of that act?

Mr. STACK. No; I am not.

Commissioner GARRETSON. Are you familiar with the attitude of the very trade-union men who originally favored it, toward it since that time?

Mr. STACK. I am not.

Commissioner GARRETSON. Then, you have no practical knowledge in regard to the working of compulsory investigation, and whether or not it is favorable to the laboring man?

Mr. STACK. No; but I think that any industrial situation that won't bear investigation ought to be known, and that on whatever side would fall the brunt of publicity ought to bear it.

Commissioner GARRETSON. But do you believe that there should be a legal restriction against protective action by laboring men while that investigation was taking place?

Mr. STACK. I do not.

Commissioner GARRETSON. You are aware of the fact that such a provision is inserted in the Canadian industrial-disputes act?

Mr. STACK. No; I am not familiar with it.

Commissioner GARRETSON. That is all.

Chairman WALSH. Mr. Lennon.

Commissioner LENNON. Mr. Stack, are there any women's organizations represented in the State federation of labor?

Mr. STACK. Yes, sir.

Commissioner LENNON. How are the women of this State who are wageworkers, how are they feeling toward the 10-hour law that was passed here some time ago, applying to women?

Mr. STACK. Well, you will find that information better given to you from Mrs. Gee, whom you have called, a member of the women's organization, who can tell you.

Commissioner LENNON. Well, doesn't the State federation of labor take up matters of that kind and make a study of them?

Mr. STACK. No——

Commissioner LENNON. The application of laws of that nature?

Mr. STACK. No, sir; it hasn't made any particular study; it has left the question of the application of the law to women workers—to the women's organizations that are affected thereby.

Commissioner LENNON. What has the State federation of labor done as to industrial or vocational education for the children of this State? Have you taken up that subject at all and given it any consideration?

Mr. STACK. It has given whatever consideration it could give to the subject. When the matter was presented—the matter was brought to our attention in the Oregon schools, taking up the question of vocational training, and the State federation approved of the plan for teaching practical things in the schools.

Commissioner LENNON. Have you ever considered the advisability of continuation schools or part-time schools, where the children go into the industries where they put them, and have an opportunity on the employer's time to continue their study in the schools?

Mr. STACK. We haven't considered that phase.

Commissioner LENNON. That is all.

Chairman WALSH. Anything else? One minute. Is there any strike or lockout in this community at present?

Mr. STACK. Strike or lockout?

Chairman WALSH. Yes, sir.

Mr. STACK. Well, there is the railroad federation strike—the men are still on strike; it has been going on two years in September.

Chairman WALSH. Any others?

Mr. STACK. No others.

Chairman WALSH. When was the last strike in this community?

Mr. STACK. The last strike was within a month or two back is all.

Chairman WALSH. What was the craft, or in what industry was the strike?

Mr. STACK. It was on the water front.

Chairman WALSH. The longshoremen?

Mr. STACK. Yes, sir.

Chairman WALSH. Is there any organization among the longshoremen?

Mr. STACK. Yes.

Chairman WALSH. Is it an affiliated union organization?

Mr. STACK. Yes.

Chairman WALSH. How large an organization is it? What per cent of the workers in the industry?

Mr. STACK. Well, it is nearly a complete organization, I should judge.

Chairman WALSH. How was the strike ended?

Mr. STACK. By mediation; it only lasted a day or two.

Chairman WALSH. Was it over the question of hours and wages, or what was it, briefly?

Mr. STACK. Briefly, it was the question of another organization.

Chairman WALSH. Jurisdictional disputes?

Mr. STACK. Well, there was hours and wages involved in it, too, by checkers. If you would like to get the information about the longshoremen particularly, I would refer you to Mr. Mattson, who is here now, and who was present at the hearing, and is, I believe, here now.

Chairman WALSH. What other industrial disturbances have there been prior to that one, prior to the longshoremen?

Mr. STACK. Why, there have not been very many industrial disturbances here, more dissatisfaction and unrest than real outbreaks. There was a bad one on the East Side in a little cannery over there.

Chairman WALSH. How many workers involved in it?

Mr. STACK. I should judge 35 or 40 people.

Chairman WALSH. How many?

Mr. STACK. Thirty-five or forty people working there, I guess; I don't know how many people there was. They were not affiliated, and when they went on strike they had street meetings and they immediately came in contact with the city officials.

Chairman WALSH. Has there been any effort on the part of your organization to organize those people in the canneries, and has there been any investigation made about the conditions of labor and hours by your organization?

Mr. STACK. Not at that time.

Chairman WALSH. Now, what other disturbances have there been within the past year aside from the longshoremen and this one cannery in which you say there were 35 or 40 people involved?

Mr. STACK. Disturbances?

Chairman WALSH. Yes; what other strikes or lockouts.

Mr. STACK. There have not been any.

Chairman WALSH. There have not been any?

Mr. STACK. There have not been any strikes or lockouts.

Chairman WALSH. Sir?

Mr. STACK. There have been occasionally little disturbances in the building trades line that didn't amount to anything, no prolonged strike.

Chairman WALSH. No prolonged strike or lockout in the building trades. How many men or workers were involved in the longshoremen difficulty?

Mr. STACK. I could not give you that information.

Chairman WALSH. Could you give it approximately? Was it hundreds or what?

Mr. STACK. No, sir; I could not give it with any degree of correctness.

Chairman WALSH. Any boycott now going on? Any declared boycott against any business house or manufacturing establishment in this city?

Mr. STACK. Yes, sir; there is quite a number being boycotted; boycotts being prosecuted to a greater or less degree.

Chairman WALSH. About how many?

Mr. STACK. Well, there is the list—the unfair list of the Central Labor Council that carries possibly a dozen or so.

Chairman WALSH. Have you the unfair list with you?

Mr. STACK. No, sir; I haven't.

Chairman WALSH. Could you furnish it to the commission this afternoon at 2 o'clock?

Mr. STACK. Mr. Harris, the editor of the Labor Press, could give it to you.

Chairman WALSH. Could you do it?

Mr. STACK. Yes, sir.

Chairman WALSH. I wish you would. What means are taken to give publicity to the 12 or more boycotts that are on at the present time?

Mr. STACK. The general distribution of this literature among the union men, giving a knowledge of those on the unfair list, and occasionally a banner is carried in front of the business house.

Chairman WALSH. How many places in the city now in which banners are being carried?

Mr. STACK. Well, to my knowledge there are two.

Chairman WALSH. Are there any other places being boycotted for any reason except those two?

Mr. STACK. Not to my knowledge.

Chairman WALSH. Is it legal in this community to make declarations by word of mouth in relation to boycott?

Mr. STACK. It is not illegal to make declarations. It is not illegal to carry banners.

Chairman WALSH. Why do they carry banners instead of making verbal statements in regard to the alleged unfairness?

Mr. STACK. Why, it is an easier method of letting people know. A banner is carried for the purpose of letting the union men and their friends know. It is a sort of publication.

Chairman WALSH. It is simply their way of publishing the alleged facts?

Mr. STACK. Yes, sir.

Chairman WALSH. They could also state it verbally in this community; is that correct?

Mr. STACK. I am not quite clear on that point as to the law, but I believe it is correct.

Chairman WALSH. Has there been any claim that any limitation has been placed on the right of free speech in this community?

Mr. STACK. Yes, sir; there have been claims to that effect.

Chairman WALSH. To your knowledge, are the claims well-grounded or do they have no basis—has the right of free speech been denied here to your knowledge?

Mr. STACK. Yes, sir.

Chairman WALSH. In what respect?

Mr. STACK. I will have to go back a little, if you will permit me, to make it clear.

Chairman WALSH. Very well; go back a little and make it clear, if you can.

Mr. STACK. There was initiated a bill to prohibit the gathering of citizens on the streets and prohibit the carrying of banners. These bills were initiated by interests and were defeated.

Chairman WALSH. Where?

Mr. STACK. At the polls by the initiative; and after that the people who gathered on the streets, their manner of using the streets and gathering crowds was objected to by the authorities, and they were dispersed by the police authorities.

Chairman WALSH. Were any of them arrested?

Mr. STACK. Yes, sir.

Chairman WALSH. About how many arrests were made?

Mr. STACK. I could not tell you. There were numerous arrests; some people arrested many times.

Chairman WALSH. Was there any organization gotten up on one side or the other for the purpose of vindicating the right or limiting it or questioning it?

Mr. STACK. Any organization?

Chairman WALSH. Any organization for the purpose of insisting upon speaking or insisting it should not be done that way?

Mr. STACK. Well, there was a number of people gathered together under what they called the Free Speech League, and their idea was to conserve that right— the right of free speech.

Chairman WALSH. Did your organization take any part in it one way or the other?

Mr. STACK. No, sir; it did not.

Chairman WALSH. Were any of your organizations involved in it? Was the direct legislation which was attempted directed against what you say is being done here now—carrying banners in front of places said to be unfair to your organization?

Mr. STACK. I don't quite get that clear.

Chairman WALSH. I say, was that proposed direct legislation forbidding that directed against the practices that you say are being indulged in at the present time?

Mr. STACK. Yes, sir.

Chairman WALSH. Did your organization take any part in attempting to defeat the legislation?

Mr. STACK. Yes, sir; it did.

Chairman WALSH. Have you any knowledge as to the attitude of the local courts toward offenders, alleged offenders, in the free-speech cases? Were the courts fair; did they treat them fairly or otherwise, to your knowledge?

Mr. STACK. To my personal knowledge, I could not say; but from the mouths of people who were there, the courts dealt rather harshly with them.

Chairman WALSH. What is the attitude of mind of those directly affected as to the conduct of the courts in those cases?

Mr. STACK. It is very bitter.

Chairman WALSH. It is very bitter?

Mr. STACK. Yes, sir.

Chairman WALSH. And how as to the administrative officials—the policemen, sheriffs, and the like?

Mr. STACK. Well, they are regarded possibly as the agencies, and come under that same feeling, perhaps.

Chairman WALSH. As the agencies of what—of advocating the right or suppressing it, or what?

Mr. STACK. For the suppression.

Chairman WALSH. Has it or has it not caused bitter feeling?

Mr. STACK. It has caused bitter feeling.

Chairman WALSH. That is all. Mr. O'Connell would like to ask you a question.

Commissioner O'CONNELL. Have we somebody on this list, or can you give us the name of some one who knows thoroughly the conditions of employment existing in the canneries, in the logging camps, and the fishing camps of the State?

Mr. STACK. I don't know whether you have the labor commissioner on there, but I should judge Mr. O. P. Hoff, labor commissioner, could give you that information.

Commissioner O'CONNELL. He does not seem to be on here.

Mr. STACK. He is present here but not on the list.

Commissioner O'CONNELL. He is here, is he?

Mr. STACK. Yes, sir.

Commissioner O'CONNELL. You will see he is subpœnaed?

Mr. THOMPSON. Yes, sir. He is not on the list to-day.

Commissioner O'CONNELL. That is all.

Commissioner LENNON. Before calling another witness, I want to ask that the witnesses talk as if they were shouting "fire." It is really a shame that men should take the stand and two witnesses be almost entirely unheard by the members of the commission itself. I could talk so that everybody in this room could hear, either from the witness box or anywhere else.

Chairman WALSH. Call your next.

Mr. THOMPSON. Mr. Averill.

TESTIMONY OF MR. A. H. AVERILL.

Chairman WALSH. Take that chair and we will see if we can inaugurate a new system.

Mr. THOMPSON. Give us your name and business address.

Mr. AVERILL. A. H. Averill, Portland, Oreg.

Mr. THOMPSON. And your business?

Mr. AVERILL. I am in the machinery business, and also president of the chamber of commerce.

Mr. THOMPSON. How long have you been in the machinery business in Portland?

Mr. AVERILL. About 25 years.

Mr. THOMPSON. How long have you been connected with the chamber of commerce?

Mr. AVERILL. I have been connected with the chamber of commerce for the last five years.

Mr. THOMPSON. During that time, of course, you have had the industrial question before your eyes?

Mr. AVERILL. Somewhat; yes, sir.

Mr. THOMPSON. I mean, the relations between employer and employee?

Mr. AVERILL. Yes, sir.

Mr. THOMPSON. What, in your opinion, is the condition of labor in the various industries in this locality. Generally, first, and then specifically.

Mr. AVERILL. Well, I think there is a feeling of unrest on the part of labor.

Mr. THOMPSON. Is it more particularly pronounced in one industry as contrasted with another, or is it general?

Mr. AVERILL. I think it is quite general.

Mr. THOMPSON. What, in your opinion, is the underlying cause of this unrest?

Mr. AVERILL. I think there are several causes; one of them is our seasonal occupations. Another is the agitator.

Chairman WALSH. Ladies and gentlemen, we must have complete order, in order to have a hearing. Everyone here will have an opportunity to be called, that is on the list, but please don't make any demonstration of any kind. I know that you will assist us to do that. We have found it to be absolutely necessary.

Mr. THOMPSON. If you could divide it into stronger causes and weaker causes, would the seasonal method of work be the major?

Mr. Averill. I think, perhaps, it is. There is a tendency on the part of the unemployed to flock to the city during the time they are not occupied in the work, and that is the time that they become restless and disturbances arise.

Mr. Thompson. In regard to the relationship of those workers who are engaged in seasonal work—allaying their unrest in part, at least, what would you suggest as to what can be done?

Mr. Averill. One thing that would help very materially would be to have more manufacturing industries here where we could work them more months during the year.

Mr. Thompson. You mean industries where when they were released from the seasonal work they could come and find employment?

Mr. Averill. That is my idea, that would be one relief.

Mr. Thompson. Have you any specific idea as to how that might be done?

Mr. Averill. No, sir; I have not.

Mr. Thompson. Have you made a sort of general survey of our industrial conditions here and what might be done by way of relieving it. Have you got a general statement you would like to make in answer to the questions that have been submitted to you by the commission?

Mr. Averill. I have had it prepared; yes, sir.

Mr. Thompson. Well, will you give it to the commission in your own way?

Mr. Averill. Well, I hardly know how to begin on this, because this is more statistics than anything else that has been prepared relative to the matter.

Mr. Thompson. Can you give the various divisions into which the statistics fall, and then, perhaps, you might file it with us, and then I might go on and ask some definite questions. Take first, what have you there to offer?

Mr. Averill. Well, the question of manufacturing, I touch on it, and I might say that as president of the chamber of commerce we have had numerous people come to us to look into the situation relative to establishing manufacturing plants here in Oregon, and particularly in and around Portland, and we have found in many instances that they have been frightened away and gone elsewhere on account of various conditions that exist here.

Mr. Thompson. What are those conditions?

Mr. Averill. One of the conditions was the uncertainty of the laws that might be passed; another condition was the labor condition.

Mr. Thompson. Well, in what regard did they consider the law uncertain, and in what angle did they view the labor situation as different from other States?

Mr. Averill. The principal thing relative to the law was prior to our present workmen's compensation law. We had an employer's liability law that manufacturers considered quite drastic, and they were afraid to come here and operate under that law, according to their reports to us.

Mr. Thompson. That objection has been now——

Mr. Averill. Quite largely removed, although not entirely.

Mr. Thompson. What other law did they fear?

Mr. Averill. That was the principal one.

Mr. Thompson. Was there any opposition to the initiative and referendum?

Mr. Averill. Yes, sir; there was at first on account of their not understanding it.

Mr. Thompson. As far as you know?

Mr. Averill. None of us understood the initiative and referendum at first, and we haven't got to understand it entirely yet.

Mr. Thompson. You are not quite as much afraid of it now as you were before?

Mr. Averill. I think not.

Mr. Thompson. Well, now, what would you say—is that all you wish to say about the effect of legislation?

Mr. Averill. I think so.

Mr. Thompson. What have you to say with reference to labor?

Mr. Averill. It was found by many manufacturers that labor was paid more here than elsewhere where the same class of goods was being built, that they must compete with. Particularly those coming from the far East found that they would have to tie up money in larger stocks here than in the East, where they were nearer headquarters, where they could procure the stocks on short notice.

Mr. Thompson. You mean raw material?

Mr. Averill. Raw material; yes, sir. And in addition to that they were obliged to pay greater wages than the eastern manufacturer paid in making the same goods; they were fearful that they could not compete successfully with other localities.

Mr. THOMPSON. What particular lines of industry have you in mind, Mr. Averill, when you speak of that?

Mr. AVERILL. I have a memorandum here, I think, of some who have—we have had glass industries, hat factories, pipe-casting plants, machine factories for woodworking construction, and numerous other smaller industries, that have applied here and have been lost to us. At least we did not gain the plants.

Mr. THOMPSON. Well, which of those will you say that the fact that labor received a higher wage, or expected a higher wage here, drove away?

Mr. AVERILL. Well, I don't believe that I would be able to point out any particular one.

Mr. THOMPSON. The fact that labor asked and received a higher wage, was simply one general factor?

Mr. AVERILL. General factor, yes.

Mr. THOMPSON. That mitigated against establishing a business here?

Mr. AVERILL. Yes, sir.

Mr. THOMPSON. Has any comparison been made of the wages paid here compared with the industries down East?

Mr. AVERILL. I think I have no information on that line. I have some information relative to wages paid here, in various lines.

Mr. THOMPSON. Is that in those statistics?

Mr. AVERILL. Yes, sir.

Mr. THOMPSON. Has any comparison been made as to the cost of living here and in cities far East?

Mr. AVERILL. No; there has been no comparison made that I know of. Although I am of the opinion that the cost of living is a little higher here than in some eastern localities.

Mr. THOMPSON. In your opinion would that account for the higher wage demanded?

Mr. AVERILL. It would account for part of it; yes, sir.

Mr. THOMPSON. Part of it? How do you view the higher wage demanded here? Do you think it is an obstacle to the growth of this part of the country?

Mr. AVERILL. I think it is to a degree; yes, sir.

Mr. THOMPSON. Well, how important would you place that?

Mr. AVERILL. Well, I can illustrate that possibly better by speaking of our shipping here. We are handicapped greatly on account of the wages paid longshoremen, demanded by them in loading and unloading our vessels, as compared with Puget Sound ports. As an illustration, I have had a comparison made, which I would like to read:

In the Puget Sound district they pay for handling general cargo, 45 cents per hour; overtime, 55 cents per hour. In Portland, general cargo, 55 cents per hour; overtime, $1 per hour. In handling wheat and grain in Puget Sound ports they pay 50-cents per hour straight time; 75 cents per hour overtime. Here we pay 55 cents straight time, and $1 overtime.

Mr. THOMPSON. When you speak of Puget Sound ports, Mr. Averill, do you mean that that wage appertains in Seattle, for instance?

Mr. AVERILL. Seattle and Tacoma.

Mr. THOMPSON. Seattle and Tacoma?

Mr. AVERILL. Particularly. In handling lumber in Puget Sound ports, straight time is 50 cents; overtime, 75 cents. In Portland it is the same on lumber. All other general cargoes, in Puget Sound, 50 cents straight time; overtime, 75 cents. Portland, 55 cents; and overtime, $1.

The foremen in Portland—I don't have it for Seattle—the foremen here get 65 cents straight time, and $1.10 overtime. Down the river, which would be below St. Johns and on the Columbia and Willamette Rivers—below that point the straight time is from 50 to 65 cents per hour, and the overtime 75 cents to $1 per hour. Of course, that territory is all tributary to Portland, and is controlled by the same rule.

Mr. THOMPSON. Are those differences in wages, Mr. Averill, sufficient, in your opinion, to drive business away from this city?

Mr. AVERILL. The shipowners claim that it is, and I am satisfied that it does hinder us here in our shipping.

Mr. THOMPSON. What other matters would you care to bring to the attention of this commission, Mr. Averill, along that line or others touching on the question of relations of employer and employee?

Mr. AVERILL. Well, I don't know that I have anything particularly to bring out. If questions were asked, I could probably give you information that would be more satisfactory.

Mr. THOMPSON. In regard to the organization of labor here, is the labor in connection with the longshoremen organized or not, do you know?

Mr. AVERILL. It is; yes, sir.

Mr. THOMPSON. What influence, if any, does that have on the price of wages?

Mr. AVERILL. Of course, that would be only an opinion; I think it has considerable influence.

Mr. THOMPSON. You think it would raise wages?

Mr. AVERILL. It think it would; yes, sir.

Mr. THOMPSON. What would be your suggestion as to how this situation might be brought about so that Portland would stand on an equality with Seattle and other places?

Mr. AVERILL. Well, I think the principal thing would be to determine wages by the merits of the laborer, his efficiency.

Mr. THOMPSON. Well, you think the general scale of wages is too high here, or too low, as compared elsewhere?

Mr. AVERILL. It is too high as compared with other ports, especially for overtime.

Mr. THOMPSON. Have you any views with reference to the organization of the employees into unions? Do you think that that is a good thing or not for industry and a good thing or not for the workingmen?

Mr. AVERILL. I think it is if the efficiency of the employee is taken into consideration.

Mr. THOMPSON. You are in the machinery business?

Mr. AVERILL. Yes, sir.

Mr. THOMPSON. What have you to say in regard to your own establishment with reference to those question?

Mr. AVERILL. We always consider efficiency in making our wages.

Mr. THOMPSON. Do you deal collectively with your men or not?

Mr. AVERILL. Yes, sir.

Mr. THOMPSON. And they are organized, are they?

Mr. AVERILL. I don't know that they are organized. It is a question that I have never asked. I misspoke; I wasn't paying attention to your question. We deal individually with our men instead of collectively. But the question of union or nonunion has never come up with us in any way.

Mr. THOMPSON. Have you any opinion as to the effect on industry, on production, of organization or nonorganization of the workers?

Mr. AVERILL. It would be merely a matter of opinion with me.

Mr. THOMPSON. I mean, taking either the quantity of goods produced, or the wages, or any other factor?

Mr. AVERILL. I haven't had experience that I could answer that intelligently.

Mr. THOMPSON. You belong to an employers' association, do you?

Mr. AVERILL. Yes, sir.

Mr. THOMPSON. You believe in organization?

Mr. AVERILL. Yes, sir.

Mr. THOMPSON. I take it, for both parties?

Mr. AVERILL. Yes, sir.

Mr. THOMPSON. I don't think of anything more, Mr. Chairman.

Chairman WALSH. Do you want to ask some questions, Mr. O'Connell?

Commissioner O'CONNELL. Yes.

Chairman WALSH. Mr. O'Connell would like to ask some questions.

Mr. THOMPSON. I want to say that we would like to have you file those papers, or any others.

Chairman WALSH. Yes; would you kindly submit those facts or documents, which you have?

Mr. AVERILL. Yes, sir.

(The paper so presented was marked "Averill exhibit," and is printed among the exhibits at the end of this subject.)

Commissioner O'CONNELL. Mr. Averill, what concerns have gone out of business or have moved from Portland in the last few years because of this high rate of wages and the conditions that you speak of?

Mr. AVERILL. Well, I don't have them in mind at the present time. I noticed by the paper this morning that a mohair manufacturing establishment had just gone out of business.

Commissioner O'CONNELL. A mohair; how large a concern was that?

, - Mr. AVERILL. Well, I believe they employed something like 150 men.

Commissioner O'CONNELL. Have they failed in business, or——.

Mr. AVERILL (interposing). I understand that they simply did not get markets for their products, and had to move elsewhere.

Commissioner O'CONNELL. What is the comparison of the rates and the wages in your business in Portland with San Francisco?

Mr. AVERILL. I don't know; I haven't that information at hand.

Commissioner O'CONNELL. You work, I suppose, nine hours here, do you, in your plant?

Mr. AVERILL. In our plant we work from 8 to 10 hours. During the summer season we work 10 hours, and during the winter season 8 hours. In explanation, I might say that we do not have a machine shop. We simply deal in machinery—it comes to us——

Commissioner O'CONNELL (interposing). Oh, you don't?

Mr. AVERILL. It comes to us very frequently in a knocked-down condition, and we have to have our men to set it up. We have a machine shop in which we have one machinist. We have blacksmiths and woodworking men.

Commissioner O'CONNELL. You would hardly dignify that by calling it a machine shop?

Mr. AVERILL. Not a machine shop; no.

Commissioner O'CONNELL. I thought you were in the manufacturing business.

Mr. AVERILL. No.

Commissioner O'CONNELL. Simply in the sales business?

Mr. AVERILL. Simply in the sales business. . .

Commmissioner O'CONNELL. That is all. I thought he was a manufacturer.

Commissioner COMMONS. Have you information with regard to port charges here as compared with Tacoma and Seattle?

Mr. AVERILL. I haven't it——

Commissioner COMMONS. And outside?

Mr. AVERILL. With me here.

Commissioner COMMONS. How do your port charges compare with the charges in this place—the tonnage charges?

Mr. AVERILL. I think they are about the same. I wouldn't be quite positive on that question, however. I could get that information for you, and file it with you this afternoon, if you should wish.

, Commissioner COMMONS. I wish you would.

Chairman WALSH. I wish you would please do that, and hand it to Mr. Thompson.

Commissioner O'CONNELL. Something as to this question of overtime that you spoke of being very high here. How much overtime work is there compared with Seattle and Tacoma, for instance?

Mr. AVERILL. I have an idea that there isn't any comparision in the overtime.

Commissioner COMMONS. You mentioned one line, longshore work, and said that there was the same condition, or seemed to be in the lumber, wasn't it?

Mr. AVERILL. I believe it was; yes, sir.

Commissioner COMMONS. How do you account for the fact that in that line, the lumber—I suppose that must be one of the largest items of shipping in this locality?

Mr. AVERILL. Among the largest shipping; yes, sir.

Commissioner COMMONS. About what proportion, would you say, of the longshore work was in lumber as compared with all of the others you have mentioned? Half of it? Is that half of all of your shipping in this port?

Mr. AVERILL. I don't know that I would have that information at hand. I haven't it with me.

Commissioner COMMONS. It is the largest single——

' Mr. AVERILL (interposing). The largest single item.

Commissioner COMMONS. How do you account for it being on the same scale with the Puget Sound in the lumber handling as far as longshoremen are concerned, as against the others? .

Mr. AVERILL. Possibly because the lumbermen are in a position to do the loading themselves to a very great degree. . Many of them own their own vessels and could load them with their own help.

Commissioner COMMONS. They do not rely on . the local longshoremen's organization?

Mr. AVERILL. I think they do, but they are in a position to load themselves if they should so desire.

Commissioner COMMONS. Are they able to keep wages down to the Puget Sound level?

Mr. AVERILL. I should presume that was one reason.

Commissioner COMMONS. That is all.

Commissioner GARRETSON. Mr. Averill, the morning paper described the closing of the mohair factory wholly and absolutely to the tariff, instead of the wage.

Mr. AVERILL. I think they mentioned the tariff.

Commissioner GARRETSON. Oh, yes. You make the statement that since the institution of that plan it has continually grown until it has reached its capacity, and now since the tariff has created an impossible condition that it closed down.

Mr. AVERILL. The question was not asked me as to whether the institution had closed on account of labor troubles. The question was asked as to why the institution had left here, and I spoke of it in that connection.

Commissioner GARRETSON. That is the ascribed cause in that instance.

Mr. AVERILL. In the paper that was mentioned.

Commissioner GARRETSON. And in the case of these other enterprises that you describe as to Portland, when the average enterprise is going to be started, especially if the originator of it, or the owner, the one who expects to move is coming from the East, doesn't he investigate, or send his proposition to all of these cities, or to a number of them?

Mr. AVERILL. I should presume that he would; yes, sir.

Commissioner GARRETSON. And it could only, under the most favorable conditions, go to one, any how?

Mr. AVERILL. I should suppose so.

Commissioner GARRETSON. Consequently it would be listed as lost by the three or four to whom the proposition was presented?

Mr. AVERILL. I should suppose so.

Commissioner GARRETSON. In this high overtime rate that you cite, is not the actual reason of a different proportion of overtime reached that it prohibits the payment of overtime altogether?

Mr. AVERILL. I know shipmasters have complained to us about the longshoremen lagging when they are on straight time in order to get an opportunity to put in overtime.

Commissioner GARRETSON. Well, is it not where you are oversupplied with labor, as seems to be the case here, a large portion of the year, on account of seasonal employment, doesn't it work the moment that the day is concluded that instead of paying overtime to those men a new gang starts?

Mr. AVERILL. I do not know what the working of the rule is.

Commissioner GARRETSON. That is ordinarily the result, is it not, where overtime is prohibited?

Mr. AVERILL. Well, those who are better informed can give you the information.

Chairman WALSH. He says he can not.

Commissioner GARRETSON. Yes. Now, with regard to the agitator being one of the causes of unrest, and I assume that you use the term as applied either to the street speaker, the publisher of—well, for want of a better term, the yellow journals, the writer of books, or any agency that declaims in regard to economic injustice; am I correct?

Mr. AVERILL. Well, to a certain degree; yes.

Commissioner GARRETSON. Bear in mind I am not overlooking the officers of labor unions, I am putting them in the list also.

Mr. AVERILL. Yes.

Commissioner GARRETSON. Is it not true in regard to the average agitator that his influence comes from the fact that from his auditors, or among his auditors, he strikes a responsive cord, he voices what they feel?

Mr. AVERILL. To a certain degree, I suppose; yes.

Commissioner GARRETSON. And that unless he dealt with a real condition he would be powerless to excite the people, or to get his crowd?

Mr. AVERILL. Probably so.

Commissioner GARRETSON. And in reality the agitator is an evidence instead of a cause, is he not, largely?

Mr. AVERILL. Well, I am not required to enter into an argument along that line.

Commissioner GARRETSON. It is not a question of argument. You have defined that as one of the causes of unrest.

' Mr. AVERILL. Yes.

' Commissioner GARRETSON. I do not desire to enter into the argument of the case, but to really determine whether the agitator himself is not the outgrowth of the unrest instead of the cause of it, an effect, in other words, instead of a cause?

Mr. AVERILL. Well, I don't know as to that.

Commissioner GARRETSON. If he did not have something real to talk to the people about, would he have any standing?

Mr. AVERILL. Well——

Commissioner GARRETSON. In your opinion.

Mr. AVERILL. Take the soap-box agitator here in Portland, when he will get up and damn the Government, damn the American flag, damn every one who has any property, and damn them for having property, I consider him a dangerous agitator.

Commissioner GARRETSON. Well, is not the dangerous effect the effect of certain underlying causes? Have you ever investigated one of those men, Mr. Averill?

Mr. AVERILL. No.

Commissioner GARRETSON. I mean to know why he did all this?

Mr. AVERILL. No.

Commissioner GARRETSON. That is all.

Chairman WALSH. Call your next witness.

Mr. THOMPSON. Mr. Swett.

TESTIMONY OF MR. ISAAC SWETT.

Mr. THOMPSON. Give us your name, please?

Mr. SWETT. Isaac Swett.

Mr. THOMPSON. And your address, your business address?

Mr. SWETT. 812 Yeon Building.

Mr. THOMPSON. And your occupation?

Mr. SWETT. Lawyer.

Mr. THOMPSON. How long have you been practicing here?

Mr. SWETT. About 18 years.

Mr. THOMPSON. Are you also executive secretary of the Oregon Civic League?

Mr. SWETT. I am.

Mr. THOMPSON. How long have been such secretary?

Mr. SWETT. Oh, I don't know; several months; six or eight months or so.

Mr. THOMPSON. How long has the Oregon Civic League been in existence?

Mr. SWETT. A year, roughly.

Mr. THOMPSON. What are the purposes and objects of the league?

Mr. SWETT. To examine matters that pertain to the public welfare, civic matters, matters economic, and any matters political, practically in all things that concern the welfare of the people, particularly of Portland and the State of Oregon, however, in general. Of course, we are——

Mr. THOMPSON. Has your league any written by-laws or constitution?

Mr. SWETT. We have.

Mr. THOMPSON. Would you be willing to furnish the commission with a copy?

Mr. SWETT. We only have one copy, and we do not like to part with it. However, we expect to have it printed shortly, and in such case I shall be very glad to furnish a copy.

Chairman WALSH. If you will furnish it to the stenographer we will have copies made, and also for you.

(The by-laws of the Oregon Civic League were submitted by Mr. Swett and are printed among the exhibits at the end of this subject.)

Mr. THOMPSON. You say your league is taking an interest in the questions generally affecting the welfare of the people?

Mr. SWETT. Yes.

Mr. THOMPSON. Economically, and you mean by that you look into questions affecting the relations of the employer and the employee?

Mr. SWETT. Incidentally, that is one of the matters; yes; and, in fact, we consider all matters that pertain to the welfare of the people, within the scope of our work, anything that is brought out in an important way prominently before the people, we feel it our duty to investigate.

Chairman WALSH. May I make the suggestion, Mr. Thompson, suppose you give us the general objects and plans of your organization, and follow that up by the activities you have engaged in?

Mr. SWETT. Our purposes really are educational. We propose to present, and do present, to the public the things that are of moment and pertain to the welfare of the people. We present it to the public from an educational standpoint, not for the purpose of partisanship, or partaking for the one or the other side, but to present the things to the public that pertain to their welfare. For instance, there are matters that are now before the people in the shape of the initiative petition for the abolishment of the senate. This matter, then, is presented to the public by those favoring it and those opposing it. Those best acquainted with the subject present it to the civic league at its meetings. We have again the matter of the proportionate representation that is being submitted to the people during this campaign. And we have had this matter discussed.

We have had the matter of prohibition discussed; all things that pertain, that are of moment and of importance we are merely discussing them. When, however, the matter leaves no other than one particular course that the people should take, we feel it our duty to participate in a remedy. For instance, we determine that in a remedy so far as our ability gives us—for instance, we have done that in the matter of unemployment during the last winter. It became a very serious matter in the city of Portland, and we devoted ourselves very much to this, and I believe that the main work in caring for the unemployed in the city of Portland was that that was done by the Oregon Civic League. They organized the whole of it. Whatever else was done was a consequence of it, as a consequence of our work and our request for assistance, because it was a public matter. It was merely a matter initiative and presented through proper channels to do this work.

Chairman WALSH. You may proceed with a description, a concise description of any other activities of your organization if you have any in mind.

Mr. SWETT. I think that the broad statement that we present every side of the things that are of public concern would be a proper answer to your question.

Chairman WALSH. Does that apply to things other than proposed laws?

Mr. SWETT. Yes. For instance, we have had the matter up of the jail in the city of Portland, the manner of their conduct. We have not had the matter of free speech. That was simply because this was the trouble before the league was fully organized—the Oregon Civic League—but this would have been a matter probably that we would have participated in if it appeared to be a matter that there should be but one side to, we would have simply taken the stand that it is proper that a certain course should be taken. On the other hand, if it is a matter subject to several different views, we would have probably had views on it.

Chairman WALSH. Who determines that question?

Mr. SWETT. How do you mean; what question?

Chairman WALSH. Who determines the question of whether or not a matter is debatable?

Mr. SWEET. Oh, it must be a matter all of us concede is not debatable.

Chairman WALSH. And if it is not one?

Mr. SWETT. I stated——

Commissioner O'CONNELL. Do you agree upon the proposed question?

Mr. SWETT. Not at all; not at all. Both sides are presented.

Commissioner O'CONNELL. Do you offer a conclusion to the public?

Mr. SWETT. No; merely that the matter of prohibition would be presented; that Mr. Some-one would debate, some one having a thorough knowledge of the question, a thorough knowledge of the question in favor of the proposition, and some one else who is opposed to prohibition will present his view or her view.

Chairman WALSH. How many members have you in your organization?

Mr. SWETT. Oh, some two hundred and odd members.

Chairman WALSH. And have you any officers who receive compensation?

Mr. SWETT. No; not now. At one time the Secretary was compensated. There was another secretary, but at the present time no one is compensated.

Chairman WALSH. How frequently do you have meetings?

Mr. SWETT. Outside of the summer months—we have now adjourned—we have met Saturdays, every Saturday noon at lunch, and the meeting was between 12 and 2, an opportunity being given to all people during that time to come that desired to do so. Outside of this there is an executive board that met twice a month, or rather every other Monday, every two weeks, who discussed the

matters that are of importance to present to go on with the work as the executive board laid it out.

Chairman WALSH. Do you pass upon the qualifications of candidates for public office, as municipal leagues do in some cities?

Mr. SWETT. We have presented the public officers, we have requested all of the important candidates for public office to come before us and present their views. We have usually had two at one meeting.

Chairman WALSH. Your league is nonpartisan from every standpoint?

Mr. SWETT. Entirely so.

Chairman WALSH. And it is open to workers as well as employers?

Mr. SWETT. Yes.

Chairman WALSH. Has it taken up the question of the organization of employers and employees in any respect?

Mr. SWETT. No.

Chairman WALSH. Has it taken up the question of the outside, or what is called the radical labor organization in their relation to the community?

Mr. SWETT. Only in so far as having, for instance, one extremist to present his views, John Devine, whom you no doubt have heard, and, indeed, let any prominent person having a very thorough knowledge of any particular ideas here in the city of Portland, we would consider it our function and place to present his views to the people.

Chairman WALSH. I gather, then, that your organization is purely educational, is it not?

Mr. SWETT. We are organized purely for that, but I say if, however, something occurs that we feel requires action, as I say, we did in the matter of unemployment.

Chairman WALSH. Would you consider it within the scope of the organization, for instance, to attempt to mediate a difference in a labor trouble?

Mr. SWETT. I believe if an extreme condition existed here in Portland that it would be within our sphere.

Chairman WALSH. Would you consider it within the sphere of your organization to interpose in a difference over the alleged right of free speech?

Mr. SWETT. Yes; I desire—by the way, personally, if you do not mind, I have had very much, come very much in contact with that, and I should desire very much a little later on, at the proper time, to touch upon that.

Chairman WALSH. Well, we will let you do it now.

Mr. SWETT. Well, all right, I will go into it, then. I have had——

Chairman WALSH. Before we get to that, I am going to ask how are you financed, how do you take care of the finances?

Mr. SWETT. We have dues that are paid by members, $2 a year or more; each member pays $2 or more per year. And this is sufficient for our expenses.

Commissioner O'CONNELL. What is the number of the membership?

Mr. SWETT. I say, something around 200 or over. There are some paid more, several a few hundred dollars.

Mr. THOMPSON. Just touching upon the industrial——

Chairman WALSH. Very good. Mr. Thompson desires to ask you something.

Mr. THOMPSON. Just touch upon the industrial problem. What if any investigation or work has the league done with regard to that matter, touching the matter of the employer and the employee?

Mr. SWETT. As between the employer and the employee, no; I can not say that the league as such has done anything between the employer and the employee. Our work last year was very large, I say, in the matter of the unemployed. We were confronted with a situation, a severe condition here where a large number of people were out of employment. We found they were not only out of employment, but utterly destitute. That there were probably thousands, we do not know the exact number, in fact we did not know the number and do not know the number of those to-day, the exact number, within several thousands, of the actual number that were destitute, or of the actual number that were unemployed. We have no statistics to that end at all. We have some statistics, though, covering only a very limited area. But the estimates range anywhere probably between 2,000 and 25,000, so wide is the range as to the cases, as it were, of the unemployed during last winter.

· However, we had made an investigation, we sent out committees to discover as to whether or not there was a large number of people that were utterly destitute, no shelter, and without food. This committee reported that it found a very large number of people that were sleeping, in one instance, in a store,

all over the floor, in the basement, without blankets, that those people were
eating one meal a day, many of them, and some one meal in two days, and that
many of the lodging houses were packed with people; that the hallways, the
stairways were littered with men sleeping there at night. A serious condition
was there, and it presented itself in a rather alarming way, and action was
immediately taken to find whether we could not place them in one house. We
found we had a building here in the city called the Gypsy Smith Tabernacle,
a very large building, that could hold very many people, probably all we needed;
that this, I say, was the city's property, it was leased by the city. Every effort
was made to induce the city authorities to open that. The city authorities were
very loath to do so. There was, I believe, pressure brought to bear upon them
by certain interests not to do so. But eventually the building was opened. The
city paid for the fuel necessary to keep the stoves going, and some nine hundred
men, upon an average, slept there between, roughly, the fore part of January
and the 15th of March. Before that we were assisting them by having meal
tickets. This by private subscription and some public subscriptions. I think
the city gave $100 to it. To feed them at this place a municipal kitchen was
opened, or rather the kitchen was opened that was conducted entirely by the
men and not by the municipality, and that the men themselves, they formed an
organization by themselves, and although the city had feared, the city authorities feared that they would be disorderly there, and had policemen placed to
quell any improper conduct, there was no difficulty at any time, no call at any
time for the police.

They were fed there nights and mornings, ranging from a small number of
some four or five hundred until eventually there were about 1,000. At times
there were 3,000 meals given there a day; over 3,000 on several days. The
money for the meals was, or the food, was gotten by these men forming committees among themselves, going about the city requesting subscriptions in the
shape of food stuffs. Sometimes there was a shortage and some of us had subscription of money from people, and we would fill out or buy the things that
they were unable to obtain for themselves. But the city, after the first payment I think of $100, and outside of supplying fuel and also the light and
taking away the garbage, and supplying the soap—outside of that gave nothing
to feed all these men. These men were fed two meals a day, a meal in the
morning and a meal at night. As I said, outside of that assistance that was
given by the city, all of that was done practically by the men themselves outside
of money tht came in through other means, was really paid to us or to the secretary or chairman of the committee.

I say that the rest of that was done by the men themselves. They had an
executive committee, and thorough order was kept at all times. I believe that
as a consequence of that—indeed the city authorities and anyone knowing
anything about it, admits that as a consequence of that—there was less crime
in the city or Portland than at any time during recent years, that these men
were the means of keeping absolute order there. Well, they had a barber shop,
for instance, of their own, had barbers of their own, to shave them all. They
had shoemakers to repair the shoes of the men. And then they had other floor
committees to keep the place clean. All this work was done by the men themselves, done by the men without remuneration at all. At one time very shortly
after the opening of the Gypsy Smith Tabernacle, the cry was raised that it was
liable to be a breeding place for disease, and we were informed that some one
was taken with some contagious disease. And consequently the place was
closed by the municipal authorities, and these men were thrown out upon one
of the stormiest nights that we had ever had here in the city of Portland.
Several hundred men were thrown upon the street, and there was absolutely
no place to go to, and nothing told them where they should go, simply that the
place was closed and that they could not come there. After very much effort,
we persuaded the city authorities to again reopen the place, and it was reopened
to stay open until somewhere between the 15th and 20th of March, I think it
was the 18th or 19th; somewhere about there.

I might say that there was very much data being taken by, particularly
the people of Reed College—the instructors and professors of Reed College had
taken very much interest in this themselves, perhaps more than any other
body of people here in the city of Portland who worked there, and had taken
very much data of very great importance, I think, to this work; and Mr. Wood,
who was subpœnaed here, will be able to give the data relative to that.

Mr. THOMPSON. Now, Mr. Swett, referring to this condition of unemployment which existed in the wintertime——
Commissioner CARBETSON. Let me ask one question in that connection.
Mr. THOMPSON. Yes. · · ·
Commissioner GARRETSON. Mr. Swett, it really developed among those men a communal system for the time being?
Mr. SWETT. Yes, sir; a very thorough one, a very laudable one; there is nothing but praise to be given for their work.
Mr. THOMPSON. Do you expect that condition to exist again this winter?
Mr. SWETT. We have——
Mr. THOMPSON. Well, do you?
Mr. SWETT. Yes, sir. We have had ccommittees at work, having in mind the possibility that there will be a recurrence of this, and are endeavoring to meet that condition. I might say that we have divided the work in this manner at the present time. We have committees working upon legislation relative to unemployment, a committee upon finding employment, and a committee upon relief, and we expect to be able through these committees to care for that situation.
Mr. THOMPSON. Through what avenue do you think that relief can be had—what kind of work can be given to men, what can be done for them?
Mr. SWETT. I should have said that the city did employ and the county did employ certain men during the past winter, particularly the city. The city spent some—well, I have heard the estimates, ranging anywhere from $18,000 to $20,000 perhaps, to give employment to the men. At first the effort was to employ merely the married men, and some $3 a day was paid to the men for work by the city—that the city was giving. Only I think—they were only employed there two or three days; I think two days a week. Eventually this was stopped, and work was given them upon the—for to crush rock, and they were paid 75 cents a yard, cubic yard, for crushing it, or breaking the rock up. And only a small amount of work was permitted to be done by them. I think they were only permitted to crush 75 cents' worth a day; not permitted to do any more work than that. And eventually this work was stopped. And we found that there was very little that we could do in the matter of obtaining employment for men. Every effort of ours, of course, at first was expended to find employment for the men. It appeared as though that was the thing for us to do. Upon an endeavor to that end, however, we found that it was impossible to do very much; that there was generally a large number of men out of employment everywhere, and that there must be a very large number of men that were in absolute need.
Mr. THOMPSON. Briefly, have you got any specific idea of what can be done now by the men this winter?
Mr. SWETT. Personally, I will say that I am working upon—as one of the committee, in endeavoring through these things to find employment, as well as the matter of relief. I am very much afraid that as a matter of finding employment we will be enabled to do but very little. I can't see that it will be possible for us to do much in that line at all, and that in the end our work must be in the matter of relief if conditions are to continue as they are.
Mr. THOMPSON. Do you know whether anybody else—the public authorities or other people—are contemplating public work to be done by the men now?
Mr. SWETT. We have taken this matter up with the public authorities. We have taken this matter up with both the municipal and county authorities, and are corresponding with the different counties in the State and as well as in an extent with the Federal authorities to find whether there iss not some way by which we may be enabled to defer work that should be done now, or perhaps to do work during the coming winter that should be done the summer following. But we are meeting with little success in that.
Mr. THOMPSON. Referring to work perhaps done by others, have you ever heard of anybody else making any effort, outside of your association or league?
Mr. SWETT. I have——
Mr. THOMPSON. I mean public work. Just briefly, Mr. Swett.
Mr. SWETT. Well, I should say generally, no. People have been studying upon the matter, and then the knowledge that these committees are taking up this work, they are leaving it to the committees. The committee on finding employment consists of a large number of people. For instance, the governor of the State is a member of it. One of the commissioners of the city is a member, and so on. It includes a very large number of representative people—

I won't say·a large number, but a number of representative people· of ail classes, pretty much all classes.

Mr. THOMPSON. Do you think that any system of employment agencies, public employment agencies—national, by which work might be found. else-where than in this community, would help that situation at all?

Mr. SWETT. I do. I do believe that employment agencies that are local can not be of very much service. I believe that the best employment agencies are the agencies—is to be the agency that is general and inclusive of· the whole country. The State employment agency, or the employment agency that is to be conducted by a State, and that should be one that would include 'the whole State, would be very, very far superior, in my opinion, to the agency that would be by the city. And, of course, in my opinion, too, an agency'of the Federal authorities, if it could be done by the Federal Government, would be far superior to that that could be done by the State. If you will permit me, I ·have had the questions presented to me by the committee, and have made a more or less concise statement of the answers that I wanted to give to them.· And if I will be permitted I would like to state them in that way. I believe probably I would give them better.

Mr. THOMPSON. Go ahead.

Chairman WALSH. Very good. Just refresh your memory from that and give it orally.

- Mr. SWETT. Well, to give it orally—this would only take 10 or 15 minutes, I think, and would cover the ground fairly.

Chairman WALSH. Very good. Just proceed.

Mr. SWETT. The question was asked as to the extent and causes of dissatisfaction and unrest in industry. And I answer, the extent of dissatisfaction and unrest in Oregon is utterly out of proportion to the ·natural conditions here. The undeveloped natural resources should have made a condition of · plenty. Prosperity should be the reward of every thrifty, industrious person.· The minerals and forests properly should be a means of plenty to the comparatively· small population of this State. The main wealth, the land, practically the whole of it, lies idle; this main means for material welfare stands largely unused while many people that need it are permitted, on account of improper system, to be unhappy, unsheltered, and starving. ·If the natural resources of this western· country were properly developed there should be no extreme want or poverty. And I answer as to the constructive proposals within the scope of the commission's authority for improvement of conditions and alleviating unrest: Opportunities ought to be provided that the moneyless be permitted to purchase land. Perhaps, small tracts would be best. Ten, twenty, or forty acres, depending upon quality. This to be paid for in small payments covering long periods, the first year or two, perhaps, without any payments. Assistance should be given by advancing some means to cultivate the land, and until crops are raised. There should be schools to each practical farming and the best means to contend with conditions. Experts should teach and. direct to proper farming. Few here know of the best that any particular locality may turn to. It will probably serve a better purpose to study· our soils for the best agricultural purposes than any other studies we now· turn to. Farming may and should be made attractive, paying as well as healthful. Our energies should be bent to these ends. The most wholesome attractions of the city may be within reach of the farmer. This knowledge and proper striving to that end is of immense importance. Public schools should not only turn to industrial training but to the study of industrial and economic problems. There should be proper educations to the ever-developing and swiftly changing conditions. There should be a thorough knowledge of the demands or call·to the professions or trades. Statistical knowledge of economic conditions are of greater practical importance than exact· knowledge of correct dates of historical events. I think insurance against ·unemployment a large means of solving the problem of unemployment. The essence is that the workman averages his earnings between good and bad ·times; that all workmen share the risk to which each is exposed.

In Europe certain unions insure against unemployment. In this country unions insure against unemployment during strikes. We insure against death and against illness, and a most beneficent end is thus served. · European investigators assure us that there is no insurmountable obstacle. against insurance· for unemployment. By insurance the right may be given to every employee to insure against unemployment. Insurance would save the workman humiliation and suffering and the community from the duty and burden to care for starving and homeless and from having to face a condition that makes unfit for a time at least large armies of unemployed. To be unemployed causes large numbers to become unemployable. I think the workmen's compensation act carries with it the salient features—I refer now to the workmen's compensation act of this State—carries with it the salient features of the scheme of insurance against unemployment. The State, employer, and employee are vitally interested that extreme want incident to unemployment be intelligently met. The State, employer and employee must discover to what degree each should contribute to the fund necessary to successful insurance. I am asked as to the extent, causes, and measures for the relief of unemployment and irregularity of unemployment, and I answer: We have no reliable data as to the extent of unemployment. So defective is this knowledge that we do not know to this day, as I have stated, within perhaps 5,000, of the number of unemployed in this State. I presume it is the purpose here to not dwell upon the casual employment, but rather on the unemployed that are in want or destitute circumstances. There are a large number of seasonal unemployed that either save enough to carry them over to further employment or that go back to farms or other vocations from which they temporarily turned to earn ready cash. The extent of destitute unemployed, of course, varies. In unusually severe conditions, as last winter, it was extreme. I believe that there were about 8,000 destitute, or near destitute, unemployed in Portland last winter. The causes are numerous. Seasonal unemployment refers, in this State, mainly to unemployment during winter months. Last winter this was made more severe on account of the closing of certain industries earlier in the season. Many mills were closed that would usually run during winter months. The depression in the East probably brought in unusual numbers to this coast that expected better conditions here. Depressions locally let out large numbers that otherwise would have been employed.

I may say that during this winter I am of the opinion that unless conditions change materially and present a different aspect than they do now, it is strongly probable that we will have a more severe condition this winter than that of last winter, because the men were enabled to earn less this year than they were last winter. There is less of a stake, as it were, by the men; less of ability to contend with the conditions than they were able to last year.

The necessity and methods of regulating private employment offices: Present methods of employment agencies work much injustice upon workmen. Men are exploited by manipulations of agencies; are often discharged after working a short time; are unable to save. There is a large waste of time and money. Power should be given to proper officials to investigate books and records of these agencies; to subpoena witnesses and compel them to testify relative to conduct of business. Power should be given to revoke licenses for flagrant abuses. There should be large powers for the strict regulation of employment agencies.

Desirability of public employment offices and principles that underlie their operation: I think public employment offices are very desirable, if properly conducted. These offices should be distributed in various parts of the State. I am decidedly of the opinion that they should be conducted by the State rather than by the cities. Indeed, if conducted by the United States Government throughout the entire country a much better end would be served.

As to State offices, these should be clearing houses of information, that labor be properly distributed throughout the State. Present deplorable conditions, where men from the southern part of the State come to the north to be employed, while those from the north go to the south or east and west, as the case may be, should not be tolerated. There is a great waste of time and money just where there should be a great conservation of both. The employees should have reliable information of labor conditions. The employer, likewise, should be acquainted with labor conditions. There should be cooperation of employer and employee in many lines, and particularly to the elimination to every degree possible of rush and slack seasons of employment.

Large contracts should be made to run longer periods. Proper and as com piete data as possible to every employee and to everyone seeking employment and to the employer of the demand and the supply of labor in the different occupations and in the various seasons should be given. This data should be constant and correct to the latest minute possible. Authority and means should be given to the State to gather this information, and the proper statistics and data be obtained in order that the employer and employee should have better knowledge of labor conditions; that the dovetailing of industries, both public and private, be effected, that work may be properly distributed during all seasons. This authority should include the power to investigate conditions of camps, shops, mills, factories, and all places of employment of men, women, and children everywhere to enforce proper conduct to employees. Power should be given to compel attendance of witnesses and production of records. All persons should be privileged to testify before these officers. The welfare of the laborer is of important concern to all people. It is a public matter,· and the public is as much entitled to the power here suggested as in the matter of public corporations.

I might say here it is my opinion that a public institution—public agency—conducted by the State should be conducted in this manner: It should be in charge of one person very well paid, and he should have the power to employ a clerical force with a moderate remuneration. But the system we have here in this city of paying a man a very small salary is one that must follow, in my opinion, with inadequate service.

Commissioner COMMONS. You have public free employment offices in this city?

Mr. SWETT. We do have.

Commissioner COMMONS. Also other cities?

Mr. SWETT. No, sir; Portland is the only place I know of in this State.

I think the community realizes interest of the community in industrial conditions and relations between employers and employees. I think the community realizes the importance of and the vital interest it has in the relations between employers and employees. This interest will become greater as the realization of its importance becomes more apparent. Most of us in the cities are in one class or the other, and the question strikes close to home.

Certainly it concerns a very large and vital part of the urban community. As the relations between employers and employees are better the community profits most.· The employee can not be treated successfully·as a machine or as on animal. To do so must mean dissatisfaction and discord.

Rights and powers of the community to interfere in industrial matters and most desirable organization for community action. It can scarce be denied that the community has both the right and the power to interfere in industrial matters. Industry is vital to progress and public good.

I think a closer union between employer and employee is extremely important. There should be a cooperation in industry between all concerned. The welfare of the employee is of as much importance to the community as that of the employer.

The welfare of the Nation is not dependent upon wealth, but much more upon the proper distribution of wealth.

Mr. Ford, of Ford auto fame, is a notable instance, a splendid example of the practical ability of the cooperation between employer and employee, and interesting the employee in his work. Not only has Mr. Ford made that system pay, but he has actually become famous on account of it. The employee here is paid better, is happier, and is feeling a personal interest in the business. There are many instances of the wisdom and practicability of the idea. Altogether, however, this phase of industrial affairs is scarce recognized anywhere. To the ordinary business man, capitalist, or large financial concern no attention is given this. To the present commission seeking means of improving industrial unrest this phase should be given deep study and seems to me of importance.

The viewpoint of the laborer necessarily becomes important.· A laborer can not be treated as a machine; each laborer is an independent entity. Capital can not well continue its independent aloofness and solidarity. Fundamentally capital is much more dependent than labor. Only conformance to law and order and voluntary submission has made labor dependent on capital. Labor can at any phase divorce itself from accumulated wealth and not only exist· but prosper. Wealth is utterly helpless without and wholly dependent upon labor.

It is the knowledge of these facts that causes strikes, that causes extreme views as those of the I. W. W.'s, and so-called radicals. It is the knowledge of these facts that causes industrial unrest. Accustomed means· of recognizing· the worth of wealth, of conforming to regulations of capital,· and of sacredly ·respecting rules and customs by which capital does business may not continue indefinitely without recognizing the worth of the laborer. It is only in recent times that·regulations of public or quasi public institutions was in some degree· effected. Now it is more or less a matter of course. Not long ago capital would have considered it an act of utter anarchy to question its business affairs, so long as it paid its debts; now, there is an ever-increasing tendency to subject even private institutions to close scrutiny where the public welfare is concerned. This tendency must develop as the place of the workman becomes better understood. Discord between labor and capital works a hardship upon both. A partnership or association between the two must work a beneficial end. A personal interest and part ownership in the business will lessen strife, if not largely destroy it. Were it not that a large percentage of the people expect to work into some degree of independence there would probably be much greater unrest. The prize ever before people to work into a state of wealth has been a large deterrent to more discord than we have had.

I think the development or closer relationship between the employer and the employee should be the large endeavor of people and government.

Chairman WALSH. At this point we will adjourn until 2 o'clock.

(Whereupon, at 12.30 o'clock p. m., Thursday, August 20, 1914, an adjournment was taken until 2 o'clock p. m., of the same day.)

AFTER RECESS—2 P. M.

Met pursuant to adjournment. Present as before.

TESTIMONY OF MR. ISAAC SWETT—Continued.

Chairman WALSH. Resume the stand, please, Mr. Swett.

Mr. SWETT. I think I have answered in so far as having perpared the written answer, answers to the questions. I come now to the note I have made concerning free speech, and I prefer, perhaps, to make some questions concerning that.

Chairman WALSH. You may proceed.

Mr. SWETT. There was very much trouble in Portland in the matter of speaking upon the streets. Perhaps the trouble began in a strike that was going on at the canneries in the city of Portland. At any rate, namely, on Sixth Street, between Washington and Alder, that may be said to be the busiest portion of the city, almost so, away from Washington Street. Washington Street is that part of the city, it can be said, that is right close to Washington on Sixth; that is the next cross street perhaps to Washington Street. And the men were presenting their views there, it had been claimed by the city, in too strong a manner, and they were refused permission to speak there. The men then endeavored to speak at other places, and the sheriff of Multomah County told them that they must stop; that they can not speak there. These men believed that they had the right to speak there, and I believe that the sheriff had no more authority to tell them not to do so than did any layman. That if any law—if there was any infraction of the law that infraction was upon the part of the sheriff in endeavoring to prohibit a person from doing that that he had a perfect right to do. I believe that only in case there was a riot—in case there was danger of riot, of inciting a riot, the danger of the crowd or mob doing that that was unlawful, unless there was such a case there was no more right or power upon the part of the sheriff to prohibit speaking than there was upon the part of any person; no power, no right there at all.

But the chief ordered them to stop speaking. These men endeavored to speak at several places, and were ordered everywhere to stop, and they were arrested, every one that attempted to speak. Men would get up and say merely two or three introductory words, as "Ladies and gentlemen," and immediately they would be pulled down and arrested. In order to make sure that such was the case, I sent a young man from my office to discover the exact facts, and to himself endeavor to speak and to see to it that he said nothing but what was proper. He got up on a box and said, "Ladies and gentlemen," and said no more. And he was pulled down and arrested. This continued until there was very bitter feeling, and the citizens of Portland believed that the procedure of the chief was entirely improper, wrong from every standpoint, and that it was an invasion of the personal rights and liberties of man. And eventually this matter was straightened out in the efforts of others. I might say further, that I myself had seen the chief and told him he had no right to stop this speaking, and that I would speak there at a certain place and a certain time, and I did, and I was not arrested, and from that time on there were no arrests made by the chief. Later this matter was taken up with the city authorities, who placed a certain ban, as it were, or a certain prohibition to speak anywhere except in certain places, and this was taken up by several citizens of the city of Portland, representing the working people. The matter was taken up with the mayor with a view of showing to him there was nothing improper to prohibit in this. I do not believe there was any power on the part of the mayor to stop speaking then. It may be a police power, but it would only be by that construction to be the right within the power of the police in case there was danger of public tranquility being disturbed.

There was nothing indicative to that end by the men that endeavored to speak. There was no danger to that end at all, as far as the matter appeared then.

None the less, the mayor, who is at the head of the police department—we have, as you know, a commission form of government, and it is divided into several departments, one of them the police, and that is under the head of the mayor, and therefore under his control—we had a committee, I say, to see the mayor, and eventually an arrangement was made by which men were permitted to speak in the city of Portland upon the streets of Portland, although even now that permission was only in a limited sense—at Alder Street, between Fourth and Sixth. And I believe if there was any condemnation for the action taken in the matter of speaking upon the streets, those condemned should be those in authority and that endeavored to stop speaking, to wit, the sheriff of this county and the mayor of this county—of the city.

Chairman WALSH. Any questions, Mr. Garretson?

Commissioner GARRETSON. Yes; I would like to ask one or two.

Chairman WALSH. Mr. Garretson.

Commissioner GARRETSON. Mr. Swett, you referred to the fact, or you used the language earlier in your statement, that when it was proposed to open the tabernacle for the lodgment of the unemployed, that certain interests opposed it. Were they individuals or organizations?

Mr. SWETT. Generally speaking, it may be said it was the business interests of the city of Portland, who were very much afraid of the consequence of having these people to be cared for in that manner. There seemed to be and there was at that time a feeling of financial unrest, and the business people seemed to be afraid that this would tend to exaggerate that condition, and that this matter must not be known throughout the State, that there was a condition in the city of Portland demanding assistance of the people in general; that there was starvation; that there was a large number that wanted shelter. They didn't want that phase of it to be distributed to the people throughout the country. They wanted the idea to be that this was a very prosperous ciy. I think that was the main reason. There are again a great many others that are generally opposed to matters of that kind entirely. They are of the opinion that this is merely the view of a few people who have exaggerated notions of conditions of that kind; that, as a matter of fact, there was no property, or very little of it.

Indeed, there were a considerable number of people during the very worst period that claimed very positively that there was no want in the city; that there was no starvation; that there was nobody who could not get work. I have personally phoned a good many people requesting their assistance in the shape of funds on account of the need at the tabernacle, and many of them answered me that there was no need of it, men could obtain employment; that we were entirely in error in that we were taking a place in the community that was harmful in this, that we were presenting a theory that could not be.

Commissioner GARRETSON. And those were the interests that opposed it?

Mr. SWETT. Generally speaking; yes, sir.

Commissioner GARRETSON. Have you ever in the course of your connection with these questions found anything that led you to believe that a considerable portion of the unemployment, or of the excess of men over positions at a great many portions of the year, were caused by—well, rose-colored advertising of the golden opportunities of the Northwest?

Mr. SWETT. Yes. Yes. I positively think so. I believe very, very many people were drawn in this country upon the theory that it was a land of honey and——

Commissioner GARRETSON. And milk.

Mr. SWETT. Milk and honey.

Commissioner GARRETSON. Flowing with milk and honey.

Mr. SWETT. And they, I say, came in because of the theory that an opportunity for earning a livelihood would be given to every one that would come here, either the opportunity to earn a living or the opportunity to earn a living without striving for it in the extreme degree that is necessary elsewhere.

Commissioner GARRETSON. They learned when they got here that they had to do their own milking, and there was no honey?

Mr. SWETT. Yes.

Commissioner GARRETSON. Have you found a tendency in some cases on the part of the authorities to permit public speaking, providing the speaker didn't say anything?

Mr. SWETT. Yes. Not only that, but at the same time public speaking was prohibited upon the streets of Portland to these men, there were men that were speaking upon religious subjects at the same time and at the same place——

Commissioner GARRETSON. In other words, they could talk if they would say what the authorities wanted them to say?

Mr. SWETT. Yes. And here in the city of Portland every time there has been an election, men were speaking upon almost every corner in the city of Portland, and there was no prohibition of any, not one prohibited from speaking.

Commissioner GARRETSON. No instance, then, where the city administration, for instance, prohibited anybody from advocating their reelection, the reelection of the present administration?

Mr. SWETT. Not at all; not at all. Upon the contrary, it is a common thing in Portland that the streets are crowded with men listening to men, candidates, or to those desiring the election of one or another candidate.

Commissioner GARRETSON. That is all, Mr. Chairman.

Chairman WALSH. Any questions. Is there anything that you have not stated that you wish to state?

Mr. SWETT. My attention is called to the fact just now that at the same time and at the same place where men were being prohibited from speaking there was a billboard giving the results of the national baseball game, and the streets, the streets at that place was absolutely blocked, blocked in full with men, and nothing was said; nothing was said to prohibit these people congregating there. They were permitted to do so.

My attention has been called to some matter by somebody before I took my seat in the stand here, by two people in the audience, that at the cannery—that there were people that were working—this particular cannery had been on a strike—that there had been people that had been working and earning from 10 to 50 cents a day. They stated that those people would be up here to-morrow if it would be the desire of the committee to learn whether such was the case here in the city of Portland; they had been earning and giving all of their time to the work that they had been employed at, earning from 10 to 50 cents. I do not know of those facts.

Chairman WALSH. Give the names to Mr. Thompson and he will take care of that.

That is all, thank you.

Call your next witness.

Mr. THOMPSON. Dr. Wood.

TESTIMONY OF DR. A. E. WOOD.

Mr. THOMPSON. Give us your name.

Dr. WOOD. A. E. Wood.

Mr. THOMPSON. Sit down, please. Your business address?

Dr. WOOD. Reed College, Portland.

Mr. THOMPSON. What is your profession?

Dr. WOOD. Teacher.

Mr. THOMPSON. What branch of knowledge?

Dr. WOOD. Instructor in social science at Reed College.

Mr. THOMPSON. How long have you acted as such?

Dr. WOOD. I have been here for three years.

Mr. THOMPSON. Prior to that time, where were you engaged?

Dr. WOOD. In Boston.

Mr. THOMPSON. The same work?

Dr. WOOD. No; I was a student in Harvard University, and also engaged in social work in the city of Boston.

Mr. THOMPSON. Dr. Wood, in your work here in Portland have you had occasion to look into the industrial problem as it relates to the relations between employers and employees in all its phases?

Dr. WOOD. In some phases, yes; in some degree.

Mr. THOMPSON. ·To what particular phases have you given more thought than to others?

Dr. WOOD. Well, I·was a member of the Portland Vice Commission, and I made some investigation for the economic aspect for the vice commission re-· port; I was a member of the commission that drew up the minimum-wage·law; the committee of the consumers' league that drew up the minimum-wage law; I was also interested in this matter of unemployment last winter, and made a survey of about 450 men who were in the tabernacle.

Mr. THOMPSON. Are you a member of the civic league?

Dr.· WOOD. Yes, sir.

Mr. THOMPSON. I omitted to ask one question of the prior· witness. From what sources are these funds drawn? Who contributes the money that goes to make up the organization?

Dr. WOOD. The funds of what—the civic league?

Mr. THOMPSON. Yes.

Dr. WOOD. It is at present supported entirely ·by the subscriptions of members, individual members; $2 a person.

Mr. THOMPSON. Are those from business men or labor unions or where?

Dr. WOOD. Well, pretty general. There have been some other subscriptions of large amounts, from different public-spirited citizens ·in this community, but most of the support of the organization is by individual contribution of yearly subscriptions.

Mr. THOMPSON. Now, taking up some of this work you have been doing, will you give us still more in detail, but still briefly, some account of this work you have done—for instance, under the minimum-wage law, what brought it about and ·what was the condition you sought to remedy by the law?

Dr. WOOD. Well, in the first place in regard to the details of the investigation for the minimum wage, the secretary of the minimum-wage commission will be here to-morrow, who herself made the detailed investigation, and I think she can give you more in detail the facts as to ·wages, etc., ·in regard to working women in Oregon than I can.

Mr. THOMPSON. Will that also be true with reference to the working out of the law?

Dr. WOOD. Well, yes, sir; possibly I can say somewhat in regard ·to that.

Mr. THOMPSON. I would like to have you.

Dr. WOOD. I attempted to find out whether there was any· great amount of un-employment caused by the operation of the minimum-wage·law, people being thrown out· of employment because they could not earn the legal minimum wage: So far as I have been able to ascertain there has not been any great amount of that. I have had one or two students working on the question and questioned somewhat the employers in regard to it. I haven't found any great amount of unemployment caused by the necessity of paying the minimum ·wage. There have been some statements made—unproved as far as I am concerned—· that employers might take advantage of the apprenticeship clause in the minimum-wage law and hire apprentices for the year during which they might pay them apprentices' wages, and then take on other apprentices. I haven't been able to ascertain how much that· has been done, and as far as I know· not ·a great amount of it has been done. I think it is a most important part of the work to be gone into, and if Miss Gleason can give you information on that, I think it would be a good thing.

Mr. THOMPSON. Are there any other phases of the working of the law that you have investigated and any conclusions you have arrived at which you. could state to the commission?

Dr. WOOD. Well, it seems to me that the minimum wage ·ought to in ,time standardize the industries in which women are employed and bring them· up to a higher standard, and if there are any persons who can not earn the minimum wage we ought to know who they are and take some action in regard to them. It seems to me that that is one of the advantages of the ·minimum wage, it will at least let us know who can't earn the minimum wage, and· let us make provision concerning them.

Mr. THOMPSON. How long has the minimum wage law been in force in this State?

Dr. ,WOOD. I think 'the first ruling went into effect last fall sometime,' last October or November sometime. I think the first ruling went. into effect· then. I think there have been five rulings ·by· the commission ·thus far, as· far, as I· know. A year, I think, a little less than a year ago, the first one was ·passed.

Mr. Thompson. We have other witnesses here subpœnaed on that subject, and they would have more detail than you would?

Dr. Wood. I think so.

Mr. Thompson. Now, then, going to other matters of legislation and progressive work here, Mr. Wood, what would you say with reference to them?

Dr. Wood. Well, there is a matter in which I am interested, and that is the question of industrial diseases. People who have been conversant with the industrial questions know that besides accidents there are a great many industrial diseases, and the visiting nurses' association two years ago petitioned the State board of health and aked them to require the reporting of industrial diseases. The board of health replied there were no industrial diseases in Oregon. A year passed, when I with some others sent to them considerable literature concerning industrial diseases, and still the reply was that there were none in Oregon.

Two students of mine made an investigation through questionnaires sent to physicians regarding industrial diseases that came under their observation, and in a very brief investigation of about a month several hundred cases were discovered that physicians had treated of industrial diseases, showing that even in Oregon, with a comparatively small number of manufactories they still do have plenty of industrial disease.

Mr. Thompson. What classes of manufactories would these come from, and what was the nature of the trouble?

Dr. Wood. Some cases of lead poisning, and some cases of so-called cement poisoning, the cement dust aggravating lung trouble, and there had been a considerable amount of liver trouble caused by men in employment where standing constantly is required, and then there have been a considerable number of cases of deafness due to construction work and the noise of it, and some cases of disease to the eye through irritant dust, and some shingle poisoning, which is a thing which is not so severe but is very prevalent in Oregon, I understand. There is a shingle poison that comes from the cedar. Sufficient, I think, to show that there is a cause of destitution there and a cause of trouble unless proper social effort is directed to prevent it.

Mr. Thompson. What, if any, remedial measures have been suggested, or what is being studied?

Dr. Wood. In that regard?

Mr. Thompson. Yes, sir.

Dr. Wood. I think the first thing is for the reporting of all industrial diseases, require them just as required to report in case of typhoid and scarlet fever, and so forth. Know what they are, and then require the installation of such drafts and other means in the various manufactories which will prevent as far as possible the occurrence of the disease and place the victims of the industrial disease on the list of recipients of compensation for industrial injury.

Mr. Thompson. How far have you progressed with the advocacy of that, or with the remedy? Have you done anything concretely?

Dr. Wood. Well, we are hoping this fall—the American Association for Labor Legislation has taken up—has drawn up a model bill for the reporting of diseases, and some people who are interested are presenting that bill to the legislature. Several States have that already in force, and it might be advisable in Oregon.

Mr. Thompson. That is the association with headquarters at New York?

Dr. Wood. Yes, sir.

Mr. Thompson. Now, Mr. Wood, coming to the question of industry, the specific economic relations between employer and employee, what would you say with reference to the conditions in this locality? Are they free from unrest or is there a great deal of unrest, and why so?

Dr. Wood. I think one of the leading causes of the unrest is the unemployment situation. I think that is the one outstanding cause, one of the leading causes.

Mr. Thompson. Briefly, what is the cause of that?

Dr. Wood. Well, most of it has been stated here this morning. I think the seasonal occupations that Oregon industry is subject to, perhaps the overrushing of industries at special times, and then also the fluctuation in demand for products, and moreover the number of men that come to Oregon under more or less misinformation or ignorance concerning conditions here.

Mr. Thompson. What remedy would you apply to such situation?

Dr. Wood. Well, I think one of the first things to do is to establish both State and national labor exchanges, and gradually supplant or standardize the private employment agencies. I have a questionnaire here, a study of about 500 men employed last winter, and one of the men in the hall present asked me to be sure to emphasize the fact that one of the leading causes of distrust and unrest is the alleged abuses of the private employment agencies. I haven't gone into this personally investigating them, but if half of them are true, such as are stated to be so, there certainly is a great cause of unrest right there and a cause of great injustice and great misfortune and destitution.

Mr. Thompson. Well, what other causes are there and what do you say with reference to them?

Dr. Wood. Well, I think that unless, as was shown this morning, unless more industries come to Portland, and if any great amount of immigration comes here to the northwest with the opening of the Panama Canal, I think there will be a still more serious situation here unless we have the industries to absorb the new population of workers who come.

Mr. Thompson. You haven't got any definite suggestions that the commission might carry out?

Dr. Wood. Well, I think with regard to the immigration phase of it, that there is very urgent need of accurate facts being known throughout this country and throughout Europe concerning conditions here in Oregon and more effort being expended upon the distribution of the immigrants who come here.

I think the present immigration commission does good work, so far as it goes, in telling what the agricultural opportunities are for immigrants coming here. But they wish to draw farmers of small capital who come here. As a matter of fact, the farmers with capital among the immigrants who come here constitute only 1 per cent of all the immigrants, according to the United States census, and as a result all the State money being expended upon immigration is being spent on that 1 per cent. Of the other immigrants who come here very little is done to get them to the lands, and if they continue to come we shall have slums and other conditions that have developed in the East to an even greater degree in Oregon.

Mr. Thompson. Have you given any thought to the general industrial question, not only as it relates to Oregon, but as it relates to the whole country—the relation between employer and employee? How do you view that?

Dr. Wood. Well, I think it is the gravest question we have to face. It is a pretty big order to answer, I think, about the general industrial situation. But personally I think that the education, public education by such a body as this is one of the first things to be done—to let people know generally. I don't think the middle classes generally know about the industrial conditions of the wage earner. I think a great deal more sympathy and more interest would be established among them if they really knew what the conditions are.

Mr. Thompson. What, in your opinion, could the workers do, or could this commission suggest to Congress or to the States or to other people that would help in the adjustment of the industrial problem?

Dr. Wood. Well, the suggestion that we have a national labor exchange established, with branches in every State, and coordinated with all the State and municipal bureaus will help to eliminate the evils unnecessarily associated with unemployment. I don't think they can do entirely away with unemployment, but they certainly can do away with a large part of it. And I think another feature of the question is the low wages of adult male workers. I haven't any survey in Oregon, except with regard to these 500 men of whom I speak of, but I think it is said that the average yearly wage of male wage earners in this part of the country is about $650 a year. That is not enough to support a family on. I think the sooner that we can standardize wages for adult males, and those that can not earn it, either because they are deficient in some way—adopt some policy of caring for them—I think the sooner we shall be on the road toward gradual amelioration.

Mr. Thompson. With regard to the question of industrial conflicts that exist in industry from time to time, have you any suggestions to make with reference to them as to how they might be helped?

Dr. Wood. Well, I have not had so much experience there, but merely from what one reads it is not enough to qualify me to state any conclusion. I think that the more investigation, the more discussion, and the more mutual understanding that can be brought about through investigation, compulsory investigation, so that public opinion may be roused to see the justice of the situation, I think that that will alleviate conditions.

Mr. THOMPSON. Mr. Wood, a list of questions was submitted to you for you to touch upon such as you felt you had some information to give to the commission upon. Is there anything further with regard to them or other matters that you wish to say to this commission now?

Mr. WOOD. Well, I think the question was asked this morning with regard to industrial education. I think, to begin with, the children of the community is one of the first requisites. And there is a great deal in contemporary education that is worthless. We spend nine years in grade work and three more years in high-school work. The high schools reach less than 9 per cent of the community, and the grade schools do not prepare people generally for earning their livelihood and child labor ensues. And I should think the establishment of continuation schools, such as they have in Wisconsin, such as was developed in Germany, would have a great deal to do in informing the young people and preparing them for wage earning in life, and preparing them for earning their own livelihood and to know the conditions, and to instruct them in hygiene and citizenship, and in the purpose of industry. I think one of the great things that causes trouble is that the wage earner does not see the purpose of it all. He sees nothing but the grind and does not know of the purpose in it at all. And I think the only way the public schools can be made practical is to make them more related to the real business of life, and we shall alleviate some of these conditions.

Mr. THOMPSON. Mr. Wood, did you make some study of the men in the tabernacle last winter?

Dr. WOOD. Yes; I have a questionnaire about 447 of these men I made in cooperation with my colleague, Prof. Ogburn, and also in connection with members of the unemployment league themselves.

Mr. THOMPSON. Could you briefly state the results of that investigation, and could you file a copy of that more detailed investigation with the commission?

Dr. WOOD. Yes.

Chairman WALSH. Has it been published?

Dr. WOOD. No, sir. It will probably be published by the college, but has not been so yet.

(At this point Dr. Wood submitted the report referred to, and the same is printed among the exhibits at the end of this subject.)

The questionnaire was submitted to the men, which was drawn up by members of the executive committee of the employment league and myself and others to submit it to the men. The questionnaire covered general names.

Dr. WOOD. The unemployment league was a league of the unemployed men themselves who, I believe, last December—at the opening of the tabernacle, December 29, they had on their roster some 3,500 men. After, as Mr. Swett said, the tabernacle was open it was they who organized and who directed that work in a very commendatory way, which, I think, draws upon them very great commendation for the order and general condition of the way the place was conducted. From the fact that crime in the city last winter was less than for years, according to the police commissioner's report, I think is evidence of the fact that the relief work that was given, whereas not solving the problem, yet solved it as far as last winter was concerned—this questionnaire was concerned.

Commissioner COMMONS. They handled and conducted that tabernacle themselves?

Dr. WOOD. They conducted it themselves. There was absolutely—they were cooperative with the civil league, and the city officials after a while cooperated with them. They spent—I believe the city spent $300 in medical service in various ways on the tabernacle. I don't know how much they had for fumigating the hall; at least some was spent upon the men. And then a policeman was there occasionally, I believe, at night; but for the most part the hall was run and the league was organized by the men themselves.

Commissioner COMMONS. Did they have their own officers; did they elect them?

Dr. WOOD. They had an executive committee of five chosen from their numbers, a subcommittee to regulate, and there were some disturbances there of men which did not reach the outside, but some discussion among the members. I think one significant fact about it is in that discussion that occurred among the members, whereas the so-called agitators tried to get control of it, the I. W. W. members, the other members of the unemployment league made them cease the disturbance or leave the hall. As a matter of fact, they did leave the hall and the thing ran smoothly after they left the hall.

Commissioner COMMONS. Were the officers that they elected members of the I. W. W.?

Dr. WOOD: I don't think they were last winter. I think some may have been members of the I. W. W., but I do not think they were last winter.

Commissioner COMMONS. Could you give us the names of those officers?

Dr. WOOD. One of them I know—Mr. Spicer. I am quite sure he was here this morning, but I don't know whether he is here this afternoon or not. I do not see Mr. Gilbert.

Commissioner COMMONS. How did they organize to maintain discipline?

Dr. WOOD. Well, they divided up into committees. There was a committee on rustling for grub, there was a committee on kitchen and cooking, there was a committee on order, and I think there was a committee on securing employment. Each committee made requisitions for the men under them to serve, and the rustling committee went about among the merchants of the community, and it must be said to the credit of the merchants that many of them helped out very generously in giving food. And the unemployment committee did all they could to find employment; went around and posted notices of jobs, and the food committee cooked the food and washed the dishes.

Commissioner COMMONS. That is, all the committee did this?

Dr. WOOD. Of the men themselves.

Commissioner COMMONS. Of the unemployed themselves?

Dr. WOOD. Yes; absolutely.

Commissioner COMMONS. Did they form any organization or union of any kind?

Dr. WOOD. No; so far as the unemployment league they did not. I think some of them had been members of the union or were members of the union; but for this relief of the situation last winter they were the unemployment league, and known as such and not affiliated with any other organization so far as I know.

Commissioner COMMONS. Did the Central Labor Union assist them?

Dr. WOOD. I don't know. If they did receive any assistance from the Central Labor Union I don't think it was very much. I think possibly individual members of the Central Labor Council may have helped them. I do not think they made any organized effort to do so. I have these facts here and I do not know how you want them—a record of the length of time the men were out of work, the amount they had, why they were out of work, and various other facts—I don't know how you want that.

Commissioner LENNON. Do you show there as to what efficiency had to do with unemployment; that is, men who had gone into blind alleys and never had an opportunity to acquire sufficient knowledge to earn a living; do you go into that?

Dr. WOOD. That, I think, does not come out directly in the survey, but I have, in talking with men, drawn unquestionably that that had—I think if our public school system, for example—if they could hold the youths until 18 years of age and educate them on broad lines, first industrially and then give them a detailed knowledge of one or two trades, it would facilitate the life of the man when he gets out in industry, and possibly make himself take care of himself, as any education that is worthy of the name should. I think that industrial education and what goes along with it is a very good thing—in our public school system I think the schools should hold longer. I had a young man here in the audience before I came up here bring out the fact that the night school had closed a month earlier this last year. He wanted to take in the night school and continue working, but they were closing down. No reason why the night school should close in April. I think the night school should continue more or less during the summer, and not continue only until April, as they have done this year; they ought to continue right through the year.

Commissioner LENNON. Did you hear the testimony of Mr. Swett regarding the free speech agitation here?

Dr. WOOD. I did, sir.

Commissioner LENNON. Do your conclusions differ from him in any degree, or do you corroborate what he said on the subject?

Dr. WOOD. I was away at the time, out of the city at the time—that summer time—I was out at the time of the agitation, and I have no evidence concerning it except there is just this fact: We have a great many investigations going on. Now, the investigation of the vice commission that took place the summer before this cannery trouble took place, and in that vice commission's report it is written that that cannery was—not naming by name—but that there were conditions inimical to human life and prosperity and general welfare in the. cannery conditions, the conditions of health, the condition of hours of employ- ment; violation of law, and so on, and that commissioner's report was paid for, and the city paid $4,000 to have that commission's report, and nothing was done about 'it until trouble comes out. I sometimes wonder as to what these com- missions' reports do, what good they do after they are published. They do not facilitate things any in getting things done. That could be avoided. That could have been avoided if the report had been read and action had been taken. Commissioner O'CONNELL. Do you have this commission in mind?

Dr. WOOD. No, I don't believe so; I don't think so.

Commissioner COMMONS. About these 400 or 500 men that are employed there, have you got anything showing the amount of money that they had when they came to town?

Dr. WOOD. I have that, sir; and in addition to that I have got a list of men who had over $200, the 39 of them that had over $200, and $341 who had under $200. I have the list of how the money was spent.

Commissioner COMMONS. What does that show? Does it show they were wasteful and extravagant in manner of living?

Dr. WOOD. I got 440 of the men; they all didn't answer the same questions and these may vary, but of the 440 men 341 spent the stake for living ex- penses, 12 for sickness, 17 for the support of others, 17 on drink, 2 men were robbed, and 2 miscellaneous expenses.

Commissioner COMMONS. What were the sums which they brought in?

Dr. WOOD. Well, they bring in—90 per cent of the men brought in under $200, and of the remaining 10 per cent 39 brought in sums over $200. Now, I have also the length of time out of employment for those men. Of the men 391 who had under $200 were unemployed; the average unemployment amongst the men under $200 was 2 months and 14 days. and that is their average stake per week they would have to spend would be $5.46, if you had it divided into weeks. The men who had over $200 were unemployed slightly longer time than these. It seems to me evidence of improvidence among the men having over $200, unless there were facts which the men did not mention; but the improvident cases, if there are any, I think will fall in the cases of dis- satisfaction, involuntary dissatisfaction, involuntary, brought upon them.

Commissioner COMMONS. Did you find what had been their employment, what industry they had been employed in?

Dr. WOOD. I have the detailed facts concerning the 39 men over—you mean the men with respect to their stakes?

Commissioner COMMONS. The 500.

Dr. WOOD. Yes; I have the list of the occupations.

Commissioner COMMONS. What industry contributes most to the unemploy- ment?

Dr. WOOD. I have the occupation list of the work here somewhere, and I think from the census data it would seem that the lumber industry is one of the great causes; that is one of the greatest seasonal industries in the State, the lumber industry; according to the State labor commission's report there are 21,000 men engaged in the lumber industry, which operates only 182 days of the year. And unless those men find other work it means they are out of work. That is according to the State labor commission's report. And it would seem that is the great difficulty with the leading industry, and that figures in the employment of the State.

Commissioner COMMONS. What was the next largest?

Dr. WOOD. Well, so far as manufacturing industries are concerned, the con- struction work, which does not figure in the State—in the report of the census; of the 447 men, 288 were unskilled laborers, either just laborers or railroad- construction men or teamsters, and doubtless do construction work, and it is hard to do construction work in the winter months here, and I think the men working in construction work are out of employment largely during the winter months, a large part of the year.

Commissioner COMMONS. Do you believe there were many skilled workmen among this list? What proportion are skilled?

Dr. WOOD. Out of the 447 men, 227, or a little over one-half of the men, gave occupations that were skilled occupations. That is, provided they were efficient in those occupations and had not been so long out of employment they had forgotten their art.

Commissioner LENNON. Was that analysis sufficient to reach a conclusion whether they were what is termed handy men or whether craftsmen?

Dr. Wood. It was not quite sufficient without more detailed investigation regarding the men at work. I have the facts as to why the men are out of work. The great proportion of them were asked the facts regarding the reasons why they left their last three jobs. Each man gave three reasons, and there were over 1,200 answers, and there were eight hundred and some of them gave the reason that they were laid off, naming the employment, naming the place where they were, and that they were laid off. I think that unquestionably that was the biggest cause of unemployment in the industry.

Commissioner Commons. That means that the industry shut down or——

Dr. Wood. That means, I think, either that the industry shut down or the weather—because of lack of funds or that the weather was bad; either one of those conditions, or that the job was finished—any of those three things.

Commissioner Commons. Speaking of these as to whether they were handy men or craftsmen, did you get anything about their union membership, as to whether they belonged in the union or not?

Dr. Wood. Yes, sir; I have something in regard to that. Three hundred and twenty-six men replied on the question of whether they were members of the union or not, and of the 326, 126 said they were not members of the union; 102 said they were members; 12 said they were former members of the union; 21 said they had union beliefs, possibly they may have been formerly union members; 5 said they were in one big union; 14 I. W. W.'s; and 46 made no reply to the question.

Commissioner Commons. When the hundred and two—was it?

Dr. Wood. Yes, sir.

Commissioner Commons. Said they were members of the union?

Dr. Wood. Yes, sir.

Commissioner Commons. Did that mean they were in good standing, paying their dues at the present time?

Dr. Wood. I don't suppose they were paying their dues last winter, but I presume it means they considered themselves as members of the union. Whether the union did or not, I didn't follow it up.

Commissioner O'Connell. I presume they would not be required to pay dues if they were not earning anything?

Dr. Wood. No, sir.

Mr. Thompson. I would like to ask you, Mr. Wood, if you remember whether the labor union, the Employers' Association of Oregon, or the Portland Chamber of Commerce contributed or assisted in raising funds for the support of the unemployed last winter?

Dr. Wood. The chamber of commerce gave $100.

Mr. Swett. Not as such, they gave it individually.

Dr. Wood. Individually, $100. I don't know about the employers' association.

Mr. Thompson. How about the labor unions?

Dr. Wood. I don't know whether they gave anything or not.

Commissioner Commons. Mr. Swett could answer that.

Mr. Swett. Yes, sir; I have an itemized statement of the money given. The unions did not give as such. There might have been some union members that gave individually.

Chairman Walsh. How about the employers' association?

Mr. Swett. None as such.

Chairman Walsh. How about the chamber of commerce?

Mr. Swett. Fifty dollars was given by the editor of the Journal, and 10 others gave $5 a piece, making $50. They were all members of the chamber of commerce and met at the chamber of commerce, and in response to the call for money they individually gave that money.

Chairman Walsh. Where did most of the money come from, if you know?

Mr. Swett. The money came from individuals, just individuals who gave money. There were requests for assistance, and in response to the request, they sent money or gave money.

Commissioner Commons. You spoke of an immigration commission, what is that commission?

Dr. Wood. That is the State immigration commission, appointed by the governor, I think, and consists of five or six members. I don't know the text of the law establishing them, but I think they got a sum from the State every two years, and I am quite sure that they spend most of it in publishing facts, which is a very good thing considering that a great many steamship companies are soliciting immigrants, that are said to be not giving the facts. It is a good thing to know the facts about Oregon, but I think more should be done than they are doing.

Commissioner COMMONS. Where are these circulated?

Dr. WOOD. I think they are circulated all throughout Europe. I think there are a great many through Europe, I know they are mailed to Europe.

Commissioner COMMONS. If a person comes to this State with $1,500 or $2,000 or $1,000, and wants to get into farming, what is the way? For example, I came across a man out of employment and he said he had lost $1,500. He claimed to have come here with that and that it was taken away from him in some way. Is he taken care of by the State commission?

Dr. WOOD. I think if such a man knew about the State commission, and would go to them, I think they would do their best to inform him in about the best place to go as a farmer. I think they would do their best in that respect. I don't know what the means are for his knowing where they are.

Commissioner COMMONS. There is no agency of that kind?

Dr. WOOD. I think they have an office in the Commercial Club Building in this city, they have an office in this city.

Commissioner COMMONS. Do the real estate dealers of this State have any organization to discipline their unscrupulous members?

Dr. WOOD. I don't know of any; I don't know that they do.

Commissioner COMMONS. Does your State commission work in connection with the real estate dealers?

Dr. WOOD. I think they do to some extent. I think they are at present engaged in making a map of Oregon, showing the available lands which are open for cultivation and which may be had for a small amount, and I think they would have to work with some of the real estate people.

Commissioner COMMONS. Do you know as a matter of fact or has your investigation shown that any of the unemployed here came originally with some sum of money with which they expected to buy a home, and then got left and lost the money. Do you find many of those?

Dr. WOOD. One man testified in this report I have as having had a $784 stake which he spent. In answer to the question how it was spent, he gave two replies, one was a Hillsboro land deal, and the other was an attempt to establish an automobile business.

Commissioner COMMONS. Would you consider that a very large appreciable element in the causes of unemployment here?

Dr. WOOD. No, sir; I don't think I should. My opinion is that not enough men come here with large enough stakes.

Commissioner COMMONS. It isn't a feature worth investigating then?

Dr. WOOD. I don't think so.

Commissioner O'CONNELL. Was there any estimate made as to the time these men were in Portland—this number of men here at this place?

Dr. WOOD. Thirty-four per cent of them had come to Portland since January 1.

Commissioner O'CONNELL. Last January?

Dr. WOOD. Yes, sir. The hall was open from January 1 to April 1, and this survey was made about the middle of February, and the middle of February 34 per cent of the men had come since January 1.

Commissioner O'CONNELL. How long had the other per cent been there?

Dr. WOOD. All the way from two to six months, and a few over a year—some 10 or 12 over a year.

Commissioner O'CONNELL. They might be considered as itinerant workers?

Dr. WOOD. Yes, sir; I think they are largely migratory workers.

Chairman WALSH. Mr. Garretson would like to ask you a question.

Commissioner GARRETSON. Doctor, you seem to have given considerable study to the question of employment agencies. Have you traveled far enough along the road to have definite ideas in regard to one or two matters I want to ask you about? That is, if a system of interlocking State and Federal agencies were established, to be thoroughly effective, they would have to reach every hamlet and crossroads virtually, wherever the mail went?

Dr. WOOD. Precisely.

Commissioner GARRETSON. To make them absolutely effective, telegraphic communication would be almost a necessity?

Dr. WOOD. Yes, sir.

Commissioner GARRETSON. And would not that carry out the necessity of public ownership of telegraph lines?

Dr. WOOD. I should think so.

Commissioner GARRETSON. Now, carrying it a step further, the eliciting of the information becomes valueless unless you can utilize it by connecting the men and the jobs?

Dr. WOOD. Yes, sir; I think so.

Commissioner GARRETSON. Must the carrying out of that, in your opinion, require a system of cheap industrial transportation for workers going to work or not?

Dr. WOOD. Precisely. I think so, particularly here in the Northwest where distances between industrial centers are so great. I have been camping up the line up on Columbia River this summer, and camping with the boys, and we fed an average of one man a day there going through from Portland out to the harvest fields, walking to the harvest fields, riding on the train until they got put off, and then getting off and walking. Those cases have come and have forced home on me that fact. A great expense among these men and how their stake was spent was in traveling. I think we need cheap transportation for laboring men.

Commissioner GARRETSON. Your investigation in other countries has developed the fact that wherever the railroads were not owned by the Government there was cheap industrial rates?

Dr. WOOD. Yes, sir.

Commissioner GARRETSON. And out of all proportion to the passenger rates?

Dr. WOOD. Yes, sir; I think there should be something of that sort established.

Commissioner GARRETSON. Do you believe there should be permitted to exist a system of employment agencies that depends for its maintenance and profit on the tribute levied upon the man out of work?

Dr. WOOD. Just the question put that way, I certainly do not. Nothing should exist which does not serve the public.

Commissioner GARRETSON. That is a question purely ethical?

Dr. WOOD. That is purely ethical, but as to allowing to exist the unregulated and unsystematized employment agency, I certainly do not. They should be standardized or put out of business.

Commissioner GARRETSON. The question is founded upon this state of affairs that might exist; if this national system was founded, should the other be allowed to flourish by the side of it if the other properly performs its function?

Dr. WOOD. If it properly performs its function—I think private effort might act as a check, and if the private agency could do the thing better than the public, then it ought to do the business.

Commissioner GARRETSON. Here is what prompted the question: It has been testified before this commission in former instances, not here, that employers as a whole, and especially organized employers, would not patronize the free agency established through municipal control.

Dr. WOOD. Yes, sir.

Commissioner GARRETSON. Reasons not always given; that they preferred to avail themselves of other agencies that did exist, which it was shown were not high class—to use a charitable term?

Dr. WOOD. Yes, sir.

Commissioner GARRETSON. If a State or municipal—if a State or Federal system is instituted, should it be exclusive?

Dr. WOOD. I think it should be, unless, as I say, you always allow room for any private individual, if he thinks he can do the job better, let him try it; but if it should appear that it is impossible to manage the State bureau unless the others are put out of business, I think the State bureau is what we want.

Commissioner GARRETSON. Would it be possible for those to be subsidized in this manner—it has been testified here that there exists places where there are three gangs of men, at least, in existence for every job, one coming and one working and the other leaving?

Dr. WOOD. Yes, sir.

Commissioner GARRETSON. Might it be to the interest of the employer who desired to avail himself of such a system, to make it profitable for the private employer even if he had no real mission to perform?

Dr. WOOD. I can't see how it is profitable to any employer to create discontent among his workmen.

Commissioner GARRETSON. He may think it is profitable.

Dr. WOOD. He may think it, but he is misinformed, and working in ignorance. It seems to me contentment is the basis of all things in industry, and it seems to me until we can get conditions where that prevails, I think we have to educate every body involved.

Commissioner GARRETSON. It was testified before this commission, I will say to you, that in an industry that has 600 positions, that the number of men hired during one year to fill those 600 positions was in excess of 2,500.

Dr. WOOD. Well, charge the fees to the employers and not to the men.

Commissioner GARRETSON. That would meet one side of it, would it?

Dr. WOOD. Possibly so.

Commissioner GARRETSON. That is all.

Commissioner COMMONS. Have you looked into that matter at all, to see whether there is a splitting of fees between the employers and private agencies?

Dr. WOOD. I have heard a good deal of that rumored, but I, myself, haven't investigated. Personally, I don't know.

Commissioner COMMONS. You would not know whether in the case of a corporation it would be the management of the corporation, or whether it would be the foreman or superintendent?

Dr. WOOD. I should think it would be the latter. I can't conceive of how any such unjust practice would be to the advantage of the corporation.

Commissioner COMMONS. You haven't investigated that?

Dr. WOOD. No; I haven't.

Commissioner COMMONS. Who has been investigating that?

Dr. WOOD. Well, I think that possibly Mr. Gilbert and Mr. Spencer might give you some information, the men whose names I gave you. I don't know. I have heard a good deal of it rumored. I think it has been investigated.

Commissioner O'CONNELL. How many employment agencies are there in the city?

Dr. WOOD. There are 18 in the city directory.

Commissioner LENNON. Does your table show the ages of these men?

Dr. WOOD. Yes, sir; it does.

Chairman WALSH. That is all. Call your next.

Mr. THOMPSON. Mr. Harris—A. H. Harris.

Chairman WALSH. Is he on the program?

Mr. THOMPSON. Yes.

TESTIMONY OF MR. A. H. HARRIS.

Mr. THOMPSON. Mr. Harris, will you please give us your name?

Mr. HARRIS. A. H. Harris.

Mr. THOMPSON. Your business address?

Mr. HARRIS. 219 Goodnow Building.

Mr. THOMPSON. Your occupation?

Mr. HARRIS. I am editor of the Labor Press at the present time.

Mr. THOMPSON. What is the Labor Press?

Mr. HARRIS. It is the official organ of the State federation of labor and of the Portland Central Labor Council.

Mr. THOMPSON. How long have you been editor of that paper?

Mr. HARRIS. Twenty-three months.

Mr. THOMPSON. How long has the paper been in existence?

Mr. HARRIS. Twelve years.

Mr. THOMPSON. How long have you been on the coast here?

Mr. HARRIS. Since 1891.

Mr. THOMPSON. Around Portland?

Mr. HARRIS. Well, I have been in Washington and Oregon since 1891.

Mr. THOMPSON. During that time what unions have you been connected with, if any?

Mr. HARRIS. Typographical.

Mr. THOMPSON. During that time?

Mr. HARRIS. Yes, sir.

Mr. THOMPSON. Now, as editor of that paper and in touch with labor conditions generally, have you had occasion to make a survey of the relations between employer and employee in this part of the world?

Mr. HARRIS. I hardly think I have had time to make a survey. I think I have a reasonably fair comprehension of the real conditions that exist.

Mr. THOMPSON. Well, you have given more or less attention to that, haven't you?

Mr. HARRIS. Yes, sir.

Mr. THOMPSON. What is the condition that exists here in that regard?

Mr. HARRIS. Well, there is a condition of unrest and dissatisfaction, I think, nearly equally divided between the two interests.

Mr. THOMPSON. What do you mean by the two interests?

Mr. HARRIS. I think that the men representing organized capital are dissatisfied with the conditions that exist as well as the men representing organized labor.

Mr. THOMPSON. Of course, what I am referring to now is the relation existing between the two.

Mr. HARRIS. Yes.

Mr. THOMPSON. Not the general economic conditions. Why do you say that—what are the grounds upon which you base your statement?

Mr. HARRIS. Well, I find the general condition of unrest among the men that I meet and deal with, and in dealing with the business men of the town I find the same general conditions expressed by them. They have in their minds grievances that make them as badly dissatisfied, perhaps, as the conditions that confront the other side of the question.

Mr. THOMPSON. Well, follow that out and tell us, from the standpoint of labor, the ground. What would you suggest as remedies, and tell us how labor views the dissatisfaction of the employer.

Mr. HARRIS. Well, the employer, in the first place, is working under a financial condition on this Pacific coast that makes his work perhaps more difficult than at first seems possible, and the general tendency of men is that when they are struggling financially they are irritable and are liable to feel that they are aggrieved when they are not. On the other hand, organized labor on this Pacific coast is working under peculiar conditions, largely on account of the unfortunate immigration to this coast and on account of the unemployment that largely follows that and which opens the gap between the two interests, with absolutely no well-grounded reason for it.

Mr. THOMPSON. What is your suggestion to bridge that gap, or at least make communication less straitened between the two ranks?

Mr. HARRIS. My theory of that is organization. I see no solution to that problem except in organization.

Mr. THOMPSON. You mean organization of both sides?

Mr. HARRIS. Both sides.

Mr. THOMPSON. How would you accomplish that, or how could it be suggested that it be accomplished?

Mr. HARRIS. Well, I think the effort on the part of labor organizations in this country is to get an effective organization among the workers of the country, and, as near as I can ascertain, the employers of the country are very nearly organized as a group now.

Mr. THOMPSON. Well, then, both sides are trying to be organized now?

Mr. HARRIS. Yes; I think so.

Mr. THOMPSON. Well, is there anything you can say with regard to that? If that is the remedy or the best remedy and they are trying to do it what can be done to help it?

Mr. HARRIS. The problem of organizing the unskilled worker is the biggest problem before this country to-day, in my judgment, and it is going to be a slow process. I don't know; I haven't the remedy for that. But the disorganized condition of the unskilled worker in this country is the biggest problem in my judgment of this whole economic unrest.

Mr. THOMPSON. Well, what is being done by organized labor along that line, if you know?

Mr. HARRIS. The American Federation of Labor, I think, is making efforts in practically all of the large centers to get the unskilled together in Federal unions. But a great many of them are working under conditions that make it almost impossible for them to affiliate with organized labor because of the danger of being dismissed or the fear of being dismissed from their positions. It is a sense of fear that exists in the mind of the unorganized worker, whether it should exist or not; it does exist in his mind and is very hard to remove.

Mr. THOMPSON. What other steps could be taken by labor? You say that the American Federation of Labor is making some effort. Are there any efforts to be made outside of the American Federation of Labor?

Mr. HARRIS. Well, the Industrial Workers of the World have been organizing among the unskilled for quite a long time. I don't know how far they have progressed. The last membership statement I saw was about 14,000 or 15,000, I think.

Mr. THOMPSON. Well, what do you consider is the best method by which these unorganized workers might be organized?

Mr. HARRIS. I think the successful organization of them is going to come through the American Federation of Labor.

Mr. THOMPSON. Have you any suggestions by which they might be accelerated in any way?

Mr. HARRIS. Perhaps.

The labor movement in this country for a number of years has crystallized largely with the skilled men, because they were really in control of industry until the labor saving machinery and the specialization made it easy for the unskilled man to hold such a large part of the jobs in the country. The skilled man has been largely weeded out through specialization and division of labor, and it is coming to a point where the unskilled man becomes the real power in the labor situation in this country. He being usually an extreme individualist has always been slow to accept organization, and likely will be slow to accept organization until his economic condition forces him to realize the real necessity for cooperative efforts.

Mr. THOMPSON. There is nothing that you could add specifically to what is being done by the A. F. of L. and other organizations to perfect the union among the unskilled workers?

Mr. HARRIS. No; I think it is going to be a slow, hard process and will require some little time, and I believe it will be done and within not so many years.

Mr. THOMPSON. Is the central body here in Portland or Oregon doing anything to help the American Federation of Labor organize these workers?

Mr. HARRIS. Yes; the Central Labor Council has helped organize a Federal union in town that has taken some part in the organization—in the gathering together of the unskilled workers. But it has not been able to get the membership that it perhaps should have gotten up to the present time.

Mr. THOMPSON. To what exent is the central body here helping the shingle weavers organize in the lumber industry, if you know?

Mr. HARRIS. I don't think the local central body has been expending very much effort in that way. The organizations have been contributing money directly to the international in Seattle, and the international has been handling the organization among the lumber workers.

Mr. THOMPSON. Do you know what kind of effort is being made by the A. F. of L. or the shingle weavers to organize those men?

Mr. HARRIS. Why, up to a few months ago a very well organized effort was being made in nothern California and Washington and Oregon to organize in the larger lumber camps. Whether it is being carried on at the present time or not I am not sure.

Mr. THOMPSON. What would you say about the canneries in that respect?

Mr. HARRIS. About the canneries?

Mr. THOMPSON. Yes.

Mr. HARRIS. The only canneries—the only cannery that I know anything about personally is the one in Portland. The canneries at Astoria—the fish canneries—I know nothing about personally. No effort has been made, so far as I know, to organize the cannery workers in this town recently.

Mr. THOMPSON. What is the condition of organized labor here in the crafts themselves? Do you know as to their organization and the percentage of organization?

Mr. HARRIS. That is rather difficult to say. I think that there are about three or four lines that are pretty well organized. The printing trade is well organized. The water front, or the longshoremen, are well organized. Perhaps nearly a hundred per cent in both cases. The cigar makers are, I think, a hundred per cent organized. In the brewery interests in town there are nearly a hundred per cent organized—I think a hundred per cent.

Mr. THOMPSON. What work is being done by either of these, or all of these, toward assisting unorganized workers to be organized?

Mr. HARRIS. With the exception of what you might call moral suasion, not very much at the present time.

Mr. THOMPSON. Now, with reference to the industrial unrest, what other suggestion have you to make as to the causes for the unrest and the remedies for it?

Mr. HARRIS. I think one of the conditions that confronts me in my work is the man who has been the victim of the blind-alley job. I think that that is the problem that we have to face in this country in the next few years. And I think that one of the problems that deserves more consideration than this is vocational guidance. I think that there are more men struggling along who have been the victims of the blind-alley job than; perhaps; any other one thing among the people I meet and the conditions that I have a chance to study.

Mr. THOMPSON. Exactly what do you mean by guidance as differentiated from vocational education?.

Mr. HARRIS. I think that guidance comes before education, or should come before education. If a man has proper guidance the education is simple. If he has improper guidance, or no guidance at all, the education may not do him as much good as harm.

Mr. THOMPSON. Well, will you carry that guidance back to boyhood days?.

Mr. HARRIS. Yes; I think——

Mr. THOMPSON. When would you begin with it?

Mr. HARRIS. I would begin about the formative period in a boy's life, and I would give the boy a chance to understand himself and his own faculties, and I would help guide him toward the line of work or the class of work in which he will meet the least resistance and have the best chance of success. Then I would base his education upon the individual qualifications or characteristics of the boy, not on any course of study.

Mr. THOMPSON. To put it to you practically, for a given city or town, would you have a survey made of the town vocationally—as to how, many bricklayers and plumbers and bookkeepers and stenographers, etc., might be needed, and then would you educate them accordingly?

Mr. HARRIS. I see no reason why the wheat exporter in this country should spend thousands of dollars to keep in touch with the wheat crop in this country for the sole purpose of manipulating the market when we have nobody who spends $2 to take care of the boy crop of this country, which is worth everything to us.

Mr. THOMPSON. I mean, I was trying to give some practical tendencey to your answer.

Mr. HARRIS. Yes, sir.

Mr. THOMPSON. What would you say about that, or what would be your suggestion?

Mr. HARRIS. I think society owes as much to the boy, to help him in his vocational selection, as the wheat man owes to his business in getting the information upon which to base his judgment and his speculation. In other words, there should be a method somewhere in this country of boys finding themselves before they go into a blind-alley job, and society should help them get together that material.

Commissioner LENNON. May I interrupt you?

Mr. THOMPSON. I am practically through.

Commissioner LENNON. I just want to ask him one question right on this phase: I would understand you to indicate your belief as being to treat the boy individually—not boys en masse—but give every boy a chance to grow on the means that he has for growing?

Mr. HARRIS. Absolutely so; each individual case by itself.

Mr. THOMPSON. Mr. Harris, now what other suggestions have you to make; I mean, what other causes of unrest? You have mentioned two now. What other causes are there, and what would be the remedies?

Mr. HARRIS. Well, on this Pacific coast the problem of immigration has been, in my judgment, one of the real causes of our present unrest. A great many men have come into this country who have been thrown back upon industry, discouraged, and having lost all the money they brought with them. A great many of those men have been men with families, who had limited means and who found land conditions, or land values, so out of reach on this coast that nothing but failure stared them in the face. They were forced out upon industry with nothing but a family on their hands, and the result has been that the labor market has been more or less crowded all the time, and is now.

Mr. THOMPSON. Will we understand by that that you think land is being held here in anticipation of a growing population?

Mr. HARRIS. There is no doubt but what land values have been raised in this country for the last 8 or 10 years, year by year, until it has reached an unconscionable speculative value.

Mr. THOMPSON. What would be your remedy for that?

Mr. HARRIS. I have no remedy for that. The men who own the land got it when it was very cheap, and I guess they can keep it.

Mr. THOMPSON. Well, what other causes of unrest here?

Mr. HARRIS. Well, there is one other contributing cause, perhaps, and that is the employment of women and children in a great many places where men óught to be. That is not confined to the Pacific coast any more than it is to any other part of the country. But there has been in the last few years a strong tendency to employ women and children because they were cheap, and let the men go idle or seek jobs beneath the ordinary job at which they should be employed. That has forced a condition of unemployment among middle-aged men and particularly among men past middle life, that I detect all up and down the coast.

Mr. THOMPSON. Did you hear what was said by Mr. Wood on the question of unemployment and employment exchanges and the question of unemployment?

Mr. HARRIS. Yes, sir.

Mr. THOMPSON. What have you to add to that?

Mr. HARRIS. Well, my theory of the unemployment—or of an employment exchange, is that with perfect organization we have no use for private employment agencies nor public employment agencies. The labor unions control their unemployment problem entirely without the assistance of either one of those methods.

Mr. THOMPSON. But until you reach perfect organization, which you have stated will be very slow, what would you say about public institutions?

Mr. HARRIS. I am in favor of public employment agencies operated—if they are operated as effectively as the post office we would not have any trouble with the employment problem in this country so far as the employment agent is concerned.

Mr. THOMPSON. Mr. Harris, other questions were submitted to you. Do you care to speak to the commission upon them, or are there any other suggestions you would like to make touching industrial problems?

Mr. HARRIS. One matter I would like to mention before I leave, and that is that I think the representation made to the commission this morning in regard to the charges along the water front here for labor by the longshoremen—I think the conclusions are hardly warranted by the facts. .

I think that as near as I can understand conditions on the coast, and I have given some thought to the water front, there is not a port on the coast that is as poorly equipped to handle cargo as Portland. I think the gear, the machinery, the equipment of the docks in Portland is about as poor as could be got anywhere. And I think the discrimination, if there is discrimination against shipping in Portland, comes from an entirely different angle than the wages of the men, or even the overtime of the men. I would like to ask the commission if it would be permissible that Mr. Madsen be called to give the facts in relation to that case. I am reasonably familiar with it, but not familiar with it enough to give the facts to the commission.

Chairman WALSH. Any questions?

Commissioner LENNON. Yes.

Chairman WALSH. Mr. Lennon.

Commissioner LENNON. Was it known to the members of the unions here last winter that there were this large number of men at the tabernacle unemployed, and that the unions gave no assistance to them?

Mr. HARRIS. The facts in the case are that very early in the season and before any action, I think, was taken by anybody, the Central Labor Council appointed a committee of three to take that matter up. And that committee went to the governor at Salem and had an interview with him and went to the county commissioners and to the city commissioners in Portland to arrange, if possible, for some public work to be started before the movement was made toward the tabernacle opening.

Commissioner LENNON. Were there any printers in this city last winter that were taken care of by public or private charity?

Mr. HARRIS. Printers?

Commissioner LENNON. Yes.

Mr. HARRIS. Not that I know of; no, sir.

Commissioner LENNON. Were there any union men that you know of?

Mr. HARRIS. During the period of the tabernacle, I presume that five or six men came to me at the office discussing unionism, and they were members of unions. But there was not, perhaps, one of them that was within, perhaps, six months of good standing.

Commissioner LENNON. I say I was surprised at the testimony—this has nothing to do with the examination—because in the eastern country we take care of the union men.

Mr. HARRIS. So far as I know there was not a union man in good standing in the tabernacle last winter.

Commissioner COMMONS. What would you say as to the probabilities. about that list of 102 names that Mr. Wood had? He said they were union members in good standing.

Mr. HARRIS. During the period of the tabernacle's existence, I think two or three or four men had interviews with me who had been members of railroad brotherhoods. Two or three of them were badly crippled. had been in accidents and were badly injured; that is, so that they had been put out of the service. And they had dropped from the brotherhoods and were what might be called scraps on industry, victims of misfortune who had got beyond their organizations entirely.

Commissioner COMMONS. And here were 102 men, who I take it represented quite a number of trades and crafts. Of course, they would still be in good standing, even though they didn't pay their dues, provided they were out of work, and yet they were among this large number of unskilled laborers and nonunion laborers who were not being taken care of by the unions. You have no knowledge of only these five or six cases that you mentioned?

Mr. HARRIS. Personal knowledge, no. My judgment is that a large number of the men in the Gypsy Smith Tabernacle have been the victims of promoted immigration to this coast. And quite a number of them had left their organizations and come out West here, and perhaps left their organizations permanently when they met reverses on this Pacific coast. And while they had been members of organizations, they did not so consider themselves at the time as members in good standing of any organizations. They had become backsliders a good deal like the average churchman does.

Commissioner COMMONS. I want to ask Mr. Wood about these men.

Dr. WOOD. I am here.

Commissioner COMMONS. You have a list there of 102 that said they were union men?

Dr. WOOD. Yes.

Commissioner COMMONS. You have a list also of some who said they had been in the unions?

Dr. WOOD. Yes; a number of them said they had been in the union.

Commissioner COMMONS. How many were they?

Dr. WOOD. Twenty-one said they had been in the union.

Commissioner COMMONS. Are you quite certain that those who said they were now members of the union were accurately stating the facts?

Dr. WOOD. Well, I think that they were telling the truth; yes. My judgment is that they were.

Commissioner GARRETSON. Isn't it a fact that many of the men who belong to labor unions, after they are suspended are given a period following the date of that suspension wherein they can again become members by the payment of their dues, and during that period the organization does not count them as members, but they are very apt to count themselves as such?

Mr. HARRIS. I think that is true of every organization I know anything about. The period will run from three months to nine months or a year. In some cases it will run a year.

Commissioner GARRETSON. They are stricken off the organization rolls, but because of their right to reinstate themselves by payment, they claim that they are union men?

Mr. HARRIS. Yes; and they really can be reinstated without question, by payment of their dues.

Commissioner COMMONS. But the question now is, Are they entitled to aid from the union during this period when they are out of work?

Mr. HARRIS. No.

Commissioner COMMONS. There is no provision by which they can be taken care of by the union?

Mr. HARRIS. Not after a man is once dropped for nonpayment of dues, he has no financial claim upon the organization.

Commissioner COMMONS. But suppose he had been dropped because of unemployment.

Mr. HARRIS. Well, if he let his organization know that he had been dropped through unemployment, that would be different. But very few men will do that.

Commissioner COMMONS. Well, then, it is probable that these 102 men who claimed to be members of the union in good standing, had simply failed to apply to the unions for assistance

Mr. HARRIS. I think so.

Commissioner Commons. When they might have had it if they had applied, is that your conclusion?

Mr. Harris. That might be true in most cases. A great many men when they get away from home and get stranded don't let the organization know that they are out of employment. They allow themselves to lapse for nonpayment of dues without any word of explanation at all.

Commissioner Garretson. Isn't it a fact that the average member of a labor union almost invariably if he gives notice to the local to which he belongs that on account of unemployment he is unable to pay his dues, that the local will pay it for him and keep him in good standing?

Mr. Harris. I never knew a case where they would not.

Commissioner Garretson. In regard to the men that you spoke of as being ex-members of the railroad brotherhoods, isn't it a fact that the railway brotherhoods have the most comprehensive system of insurance against injury, and relief systems, of any of the unions—as good as any unions in existence that you know of?

Mr. Harris. Yes, sir; that is true.

Commissioner Garretson. And isn't it a fact that any member of those organizations, injured under those circumstances, would receive large payments from those insurance funds therefor, and afterwards the relief funds, if he kept himself in good standing after getting his insurance?

Mr. Harris. I think that is true as I understand the organizations; yes.

Commissioner Commons. It was stated, I think, this morning, you could give us information in regard to some of these boycotts that were being declared. What are the principal boycotts that are now on?

Mr. Harris. Well, the principal boycott, I presume, amongst the group is the boycott against Lipman-Wolff Co.

Commissioner Commons. Will you give a history of that boycott, what was the grievance and how did it originate?

Mr. Harris. That is a long story and I am not as familiar with that as some other people, and if you will——

Commissioner Commons. Did that grow out of a strike?

Mr. Harris. No; it grew out of a dispute between the organizations after the construction of the building, the new building in which the Lipman-Wolff store exists and operates at the present time.

Commissioner Commons. What was the dispute about the building?

Mr. Harris. The building was built under unfair conditions. If you want to get the story of the building, you have on your list two members of the building trades who know those conditions, Mr. Sleeman and Mr. Osborne.

Commissioner Commons. Are there any other than those stated on the list that could give us information? Perhaps there are some others we haven't got on the list.

Mr. Harris. There are about 14 or 15 of them, perhaps, in some of them, against the ice companies; that is rather an effective boycott.

Commissioner Commons. What is the boycott on the ice companies?

Mr. Harris. They refused to operate on the 8-hour day. Under the arrangement the scale of the engineers here in town the shops must go onto an 8-hour day, and they refused to go under the 8-hour day, so they are operating with nonunion engineers.

Commissioner Commons. On two shifts, 12-hour day?

Mr. Harris. I don't know; I think they are working about 10 hours, but I don't know.

Commissioner Commons. Does that cover their teamsters, too?

Mr. Harris. No; it does not cover the teamsters.

Commissioner Commons. Are the teamsters organized?

Mr. Harris. The teamsters in the ice plants are not organized.

Commissioner Commons. What other boycotts have there been?

Mr. Harris. Well, there is a boycott on against the Portland Flouring Mills Co.; Theodore B. Wilcox and his products.

Commissioner Commons. What is his grievance?

Mr. Harris. That was because he constructed his building, the Wilcox building, with open shop, with nonunion.

Commissioner Commons. Did he construct that or did the contractor construct it?

Mr. Harris. It was constructed under contract, I guess.

Commissioner Commons. And you boycott the owner in that case, although the contractor was the man who employed nonunion men?

Mr. HARRIS. He knew thoroughly, and understood thoroughly before the contract was let, the conditions under which the contract was going, and we understand he instructed that the work go that way.

Commissioner COMMONS. Is he otherwise unfair, except as regards the construction of that building?

Mr. HARRIS. I think not. None of the other interests are organized except the longshoremen and grain handlers, who handle his products in the warehouse.

Commissioner COMMONS. He is fair toward them?

Mr. HARRIS. Yes.

Commissioner COMMONS. What other boycotts have they?

Mr. HARRIS. Well, there is a boycott against the Hazelwood Creamery, I think, because it refuses to operate with engineers on the 8-hour day.

Commissioner COMMONS. That is, the stationary engineers have declared that. What others?

Mr. HARRIS. Well, there are two or three minor boycotts against some electrical supply houses, because they refuse to employ union electricians, and one meat market because it has had trouble with the meat cutters.

Commissioner COMMONS. Is that a question of employing union men or a question of wages?

Mr. HARRIS. I think in that case it was a question of hours.

Commissioner COMMONS. Are most of these boycotts based on the employment of nonunion men, or are they based on—you mentioned some which were complaints as to the 8-hour question. Does the employment of nonunion men enter also into that question?

Mr. HARRIS. No. I think the principal boycott here in town, or the largest number of them, are based on the 8-hour day.

Commissioner COMMONS. And these that deal with the construction of buildings are based on the employment of union men?

Mr. HARRIS. Yes.

Commissioner COMMONS. I think that is all.

Commissioner LENNON. Just one question on this. When a union applies to the central body for approval of a boycott, is it approved. or what action is taken first by the central body?

Mr. HARRIS. Well, when a boycott is asked for it must go through the section of the central body to which the union properly belongs. The section having approved the boycott it is passed up to the Central Labor Council, and the Central Labor Council, I think, refers it to the executive committee, and the executive committee holds it over, and upon the report of the executive committee the boycott is usually either indorsed or rejected.

Commissioner LENNON. What has the executive committee had to do during the time they have hold of it, what do they do?

Mr. HARRIS. Well, the executive committee usually makes a reasonably full investigation of the facts of the case by seeing the people at interest—the unions that are affected, the men who own the plants, or the buildings—and make a reasonably full investigation of the facts in the case upon which to base their findings.

Commissioner LENNON. Do they undertake to settle it?

Mr. HARRIS. I think they do if there is a chance. They usually can ask for more time to assist in settling it, for instance, if they wish to make a settlement, I think, they usually take the time and make an effort to settle it.

Commissioner LENNON. That is all.

Commissioner COMMONS. Do you publish in your paper a list of these boy. cotts?

Mr. HARRIS. Yes, sir.

Commissioner COMMONS. Under the name " unfair," or what is the name?

Mr. HARRIS. Under the name " unfair list."

Commissioner COMMONS. Has that been before the courts in this State?

Mr. HARRIS. I don't know whether it has or not.

Commissioner COMMONS. Do you know of any cases at all?

Mr. HARRIS. No; I don't know. I would not want to say whether it had been or not, because I am not sure about that.

Commissioner O'CONNELL. In some cases does the manufacturers' association publish a paper, or any of the manufacturers?

Mr. HARRIS. The manufacturers' association, I think, last week or within the last two weeks, began the publication of an official publication. Heretofore the manufacturers' association has been represented by the American Manufacturer, published by a private enterprise.

· Commissioner O'Connell. Do they publish an unfair list of any kind?

Mr. Harris. I do not know as to that.

Commissioner O'Connell. Are there any boycotts, alleged boycotts on their part, in the city?

Mr. Harris. None that I know of.

Commissioner O'Connell. Or a black list?

Mr. Harris. I hear rumors of alleged blacklisting, but I don't know anything about it personally.

Commissioner O'Connell. Allege—charge that the manufacturers are driving out firms that are favorable to the unions in this city?

Mr. Harris. Well, I think quite a little correspondence has passed in the last—the manufacturers, no; not the manufacturers, the employers' association has issued——

Commissioner O'Connell. Well, in any form, I don't care whether it is the manufacturers' association or not.

Mr. Harris. There are two organizations; they are entirely separate. The employers' association and the manufacturers' association are entirely separate.

Commissioner O'Connell. Either one of them.

Mr. Harris. The employers' association issued a letter, a pretty strong letter, in relation to the Meier-Frank Building some time ago. I think the letter was published in the Labor Press, and the original copy of the one I had photographed, I think, is in existence.

Commissioner O'Connell. Can you get those and furnish them to the commission?

Mr. Harris. Yes; I think I can this afternoon.

Commissioner O'Connell. That is all.

Chairman Walsh. That is all.

Mr. Thompson. One moment. Do the unions here take an active part in politics?

Mr. Harris. As unions; no, sir.

Mr. Thompson. Do they seek to elect union men to positions in the city council and other municipal places?

Mr. Harris. The last meeting of the State federation, at Astoria, authorized a committee to take up the matter of assisting in electing members to the legislature, and that committee made an effort in the primary election to secure the nomination of three or four men on the various tickets, but failed.

Mr. Thompson. Have you got many union men in elective places in this city?

Mr. Harris. No; we have not, with the exception of one or two places.

Mr. Thompson. That is all.

Chairman Walsh. That is all. Thank you. Call your next witness.

TESTIMONY OF MR. T. H. BURCHARD.

Mr. Thompson. Will you please give us your name?

Mr. Burchard. T. H. Burchard.

Mr. Thompson. What is your business address?

Mr. Burchard. At my home, 829 East Eleventh Street north.

Mr. Thompson. And your business is what?

Mr. Burchard. I have got so many positions, I don't know which one you mean.

Mr. Thompson. Take all of them, then.

Mr. Burchard. I am a musician by occupation. And I hold office of president of the Oregon State Federation of Labor and president of the Central Labor Council of Portland and vicinity.

Mr. Thompson. What is the form and purpose of the State federation of labor? Is it affiliated with the American Federation of Labor; is it similar to other State federations?

Mr. Burchard. Yes, sir.

Chairman Walsh. Is this the same organization of which Mr. Stack was secretary?

Mr. Thompson. I was just going to ask. Mr. Stack is your secretary, is he not?

Mr. Burchard. Yes, sir.

Mr. Thompson. Did you hear his testimony this morning?

Mr. Burchard. Yes, sir.

Mr. Thompson. Is there anything you care to add to what he said with regard to the federation and its activities?

Mr. Burchard. Well, I think he covered the ground pretty thoroughly as far as the organization is concerned.

Mr. Thompson. Then we will go right to the question of the industrial situation here. How long have you been president of the State federation of labor?

Mr. Burchard. Well, this is my second year.

Mr. Thompson. And you are pretty well acquainted with conditions of labor here in this territory?

Mr. Burchard. Well, fairly well.

Mr. Thompson. What is your opinion of the condition of labor here in the various industries, or in your particular industry, if you are more particularly acquainted with one?

Mr. Burchard. Well, I don't consider them very good.

Mr. Thompson. What is the reason? What industry? Perhaps you would rather particularize. What industry have you more in mind?

Mr. Burchard. Well, to begin with, business is quiet in all industries. The fact of the matter is, there is no business. But the men keep flocking in just the same. And the more men comes, the less business there is. The country in my estimate is overflooded with Greeks, Slavonians, Italians, and things of that sort, people who have no idea of what they are brought here for, or anything of that kind. They are used like cattle after they get here.

Mr. Thompson. Do you think there is too much immigration, that that is one of the causes of unrest?

Mr. Burchard. Yes.

Mr. Thompson. Now, what is the cause of immigration, if you have any idea on that?

Mr. Burchard. Cutting wages, perhaps.

Mr. Thompson. I mean what causes people to come here?

Mr. Burchard. Why, I think they are brought here by alluring literature; I have an idea, from the reports that can be gathered, that that is what brought them here.

Mr. Thompson. Well, what remedy would you have for that situation?

Mr. Burchard. Well, there are several that could be used. One of them would be to at least have the immigrants that come here to this country to be informed to the rightful conditions that do exist here, and, in addition to that, to be able to read and write.

Mr. Thompson. Along the line of the immigration bill being introduced in Congress?

Mr. Burchard. Yes, sir; the Dillingham bill.

Mr. Thompson. What other causes of unrest, leaving now out of consideration the fact that business is slack and that immigration is large.

Mr. Burchard. Well, of course, there is a whole lot of things here that could be remedied, I suppose, if there was a way to get at them to remedy them, but it is pretty hard to get at some of these things. There is the unemployed. There is the problem that, I think, will be a great deal worse this winter than it was last, from the simple fact that there is about, in my judgment, of the unskilled, possibly 60 per cent of the men in this city ain't working right now. This is summer time. I would not dare to predict what it will be this winter.

Mr. Thompson. Did you hear Mr. Harris's testimony with reference to the organization of the unskilled workers?

Mr. Burchard. Yes.

Mr. Thompson. Is there anything you care to add to what he said about the organization of the unskilled workmen?

Mr. Burchard. Well, there are several things confront the man that is not a skilled laborer. There are a good many things that would hinder them from being organized. In the first place, he is afraid to be organized from the simple fact that he has seen other people organized and has seen them immediately thrown out of work for doing it. You can hardly blame the man not wanting to go right straight and do something that would lose him his job. You can't hardly expect him to do that.

Mr. Thompson. Is there any opportunity among the unorganized workers to help themselves by organization?

Mr. Burchard. By organization?

Mr. Thompson. Yes. I mean do they seek to organize themselves at all?

Mr. Burchard. Well, of course at times they do that; it is kind of spasmodic. They take a notion once in a while they ought to be organized, and about the time you get them ready to be organized some fellow from the other side throws a bomb in the camp and it is all off.

· Mr. THOMPSON. What do you mean by throwing a bomb and the other side?

Mr. BURCHARD. Tells them where they are at.

Commissioner COMMONS. What do you mean by other side?

Mr. BURCHARD. I mean the man who is employing them. They won't be organized then, because they are afraid of their job; they would lose it, that is all. You take, for instance, the men in the civil service here. If all those men would organize the chances are they would all lose their jobs; that is the only thing to it.

Mr. THOMPSON. What constructive proposition have you to make within the line of the commission's scope that would help the industrial situation?

Mr. BURCHARD. Well, the way we are hooked up here, with so many people that really can't talk the language of this country at all, it is a pretty hard problem to say what would be good to do. Of course, the people that can talk— can speak our language fluently—if we could get them organized and could get rid of them that can't speak our language, we might have a chance to do something.

Mr. THOMPSON. What about the question of unemployment? You have heard what has been said about public employment agencies. What have you to add to the testimony already given?

Mr. BURCHARD. Well, I will tell you. I haven't been in a position for the last three or four years to have a great deal to do with employment agencies, but prior to that I did have a little insight into the employment agencies here. About four or five years ago the Oregon Electric—that is, the Willamette Construction Co.—was building a piece of road from Gardner Home to Forest Grove. They employed about 250 Greeks out there, and I went out there to run one of their work trains for them. I am a kind of jack-of-all-trades; work at a little of everything. I began railroading when I was pretty young and worked part of the time in railroading until that got so tough I could not stand it, and then I went into the music business, and when it got so rotten I could not stand it I would go back to railroading; and that is the way I work it, back and forth, and I am still at it. This was one of the jobs I worked on. It was the Oregon road being built, but the Willamette Construction Co. was constructing the road, and they had on three work trains and had about 250 Greeks and Italians and Slavonics and Austrians out there, mostly Greeks.

I found out after I was out there a little while that they had really three gangs there—one coming, one going, and one working—and it worked fine. It went along all right until the contractor or general foreman and the employment agency had a falling out about something. There evidently wasn't something coming through, or something; I don't know just what the outcome of it was; but they had bookmen on the job—what they call bookmen—there could not any of these fellows talk at all—the bookman—it was hard to make him understand. You had to watch them all the time, or they would get out some place and kill themselves. A half dozen would get out and saw themselves off of a limb or something. You had to watch them all the time. You put four or five on a flat car to unload steel, and it would take about two white men at each end of the car to watch them from being thrown out under the rails or something. You had to stick there all the time and watch them. That was the way they were working. At any rate, the employment agents and apparently this general foreman got into some kind of a mix-up and the general foreman came around to the bookmen and says: "You boys come through with a man a week and 1 will keep you boys the rest of the season," and as long as I stayed there the rest of the boys were there. I don't know how the thing worked out, but before that there was three gangs all the time—one coming, one going, one working.

Mr. THOMPSON. Are there any other constructive suggestions you have to make to the commission, Mr. Burchard?

Mr. BURCHARD. Well, I don't know as there is. As I said before, there is a whole lot of organization work that could be done if a man could get at it, and it is my opinion that if the men could be organized, that there would be a whole lot more harmony between the men hiring men and the men themselves. There is a lot of times a man loses a job when it is not his fault; it is just a lack of understanding between the man he is working for and himself. For instance, if a man putting up a building some place hires a big bunch of men, and if he hires a bunch of men not organized, we will say, not a labor organization—it don't make any difference what trade it is, whether plasterers, bricklayers, or woodworkers, or steel men. Now, if he has organized men he has men that have worked together for several years, and he has a concrete organization to start his building from the ground up, and there is not going to be any time wasted or material wasted; but if he is hiring unskilled men, you might say, that is, men unorganized, he has all classes of men, even some tailors working on the job, and there is going to be some wood butchered there before they have the thing done, and there is going to be lots of different kinds of material wasted, and lots of time. That is where I think that organization, providing the employer would understand the situation and get right down to cold facts and hard tacks, and concede the fact that organization was the best for themselves as well as the men, there would be something done. You could do something. Either then the men could be held down, so that they would give a decent day's work for a decent day's pay, and they would have living conditions and living wages, and the other man would profit likewise, in my estimation.

Chairman WALSH. Any questions? That is all.

Mr. BURCHARD. I would like to say, though——

Chairman WALSH. If there is anything you could suggest—I didn't ask you before.

Mr. BURCHARD. In regard to some of the boycotting that is going on here. There is one on now that wasn't mentioned—well, there is two of them. There is one against the Home Telephone Co.—between the electricians and the Home Telephone Co.—that I think is a very just one, and there is another one on the Broadway Theater here. Everything absolutely that could be done was done to try to settle those two affairs before they were put on the unfair list, and there was no chance.

Chairman WALSH. Those are existing boycotts by your organization?

Mr. BURCHARD. Yes, sir.

Commissioner COMMONS. What is the issue in the Home Telephone Co.?

Mr. BURCHARD. They have refused to hire union men or treat with union men at all.

Commissioner COMMONS. It is a question of unionism?

Mr. BURCHARD. Just simply closed them out.

Commissioner COMMONS. And in the other case, what is the reason?

Mr. BURCHARD. The building was let to an unfair firm, Hurley & Mason, and they want to work an open shop, and where they could not get the men to do the work they were willing to hire union men, and where they could get these other butchers for 50 cents to a dollar cheaper, they wanted to do that.

Chairman COMMONS. The boycott in this case is on the owner of the building for letting a contract to a contractor who hired nonunion men?

Mr. BURCHARD. We feel whenever we negotiate with a man and tell him a certain contractor is unfair to us, and if the contract is let to him that he understands that that condition exists, that that man is unfair to us because he will hire nonunion labor; consequently if he goes ahead and lets the contract to that man, he knows what he is going to expect—that we won't work on the job. He knows that when he lets the job he lets that with that expectation, wanting to do that.

Commissioner COMMONS. And in this case he is fair in all other particulars, is he?

Mr. BURCHARD. Yes, sir.

Commissioner COMMONS. But he is unfair in this one?

Mr. BURCHARD. Yes, sir; he knew, though, what he was going into; he wasn't going into it blindly at all. The committee even went clear to Seattle to talk with him over the matter, and tried to adjust it before anything was done either to the building or otherwise by the contractor.

Commissioner LENNON. Are there union musicians playing in the Broadway Theater?

Mr. BURCHARD. Well, it is not done yet. The chances are that they will.

Commissioner LENNON. What are the conditions in your trade; how is your business?

Mr. BURCHARD. Well, you know music is a luxury, rather than a necessity, and that is the first thing they cut off. You can imagine how business is—pretty bad.

Commissioner LENNON. You can go out railroading, then?

Mr. BURCHARD. I am going out looking for some hand-car man's job pretty quick.

Commissioner LENNON. That is all.

Chairman WALSH. That is all, thank you. Call your next.

Mr. THOMPSON. Mr. Sleeman.

TESTIMONY OF MR. B. W. SLEEMAN.

Mr. THOMPSON. Give us your name.

Mr. SLEEMAN. B. W. Sleeman.

Mr. THOMPSON. Your business address?

Mr. SLEEMAN. 162½ Second Street.

Mr. THOMPSON. Are you business agent of the building trades council?

Mr. SLEEMAN. I was up until three months ago.

Mr. THOMPSON. What are you now?

Mr. SLEEMAN. I represent the carpenters.

Mr. THOMPSON. Business agent?

Mr. SLEEMAN. Yes, sir.

Mr. THOMPSON. How long have you been in the building trades in this city?

Mr. SLEEMAN. I have represented the building trades council about four years.

Mr. THOMPSON. Are you pretty well acquainted with conditions in the building trades?

Mr. SLEEMAN. Yes, sir.

Mr. THOMPSON. What are the relations now between the contractors and the building trades unions in Portland?

Mr. SLEEMAN. As far as the large responsible contractors are concerned, I will state that with the majority the relations are favorable.

Mr. THOMPSON. Well, you say with the big contractors. Is there any association of them?

Mr. SLEEMAN. No, sir.

Mr. THOMPSON. They have not. The masons, then, and the other contractors in the building lines are not associated here in any organization?

Mr. SLEEMAN. There is no organization of general contractors at all; we have to deal with them individually.

Mr. THOMPSON. When you say the conditions are favorable with the big contractors, what do you mean by the statement " conditions being favorable "?

Mr. SLEEMAN. I mean to state that the last two or three years we have been able to manage our conditions somewhat without any strike or lockout.

Mr. THOMPSON. Tell us what the conditions are. What are the hours and rates of pay in the different lines?

Mr. SLEEMAN. Why——

Mr. THOMPSON. With the big contractors.

Mr. SLEEMAN. Our hours are 8 hours a day, 44 hours a week, in most of the organizations.

Mr. THOMPSON. Most of the organizations?

Mr. SLEEMAN. Yes, sir.

Mr. THOMPSON. What are the rates of pay in most of the organizations?

Mr. SLEEMAN. Well, carpenters, $4; painters, $4; steel workers, $5 a day; plasterers, plumbers, and steam fitters and bricklayers, $6 a day; the electrical workers, $4.50 a day; and laborers, common laborers, from $2.50 to $4 a day.

Mr. THOMPSON. When you say that the conditions are favorable with the big contractors, do they pay higher wages and give shorter hours than other contractors?

Mr. SLEEMAN. Well, we have been able to maintain a better organization.

Mr. THOMPSON. I know, but I want specifically, Mr. Sleeman, to get at this point. Is it a matter of wages or hours that conditions are better with big contractors than the small ones?

Mr. SLEEMAN. Both.

Mr. THOMPSON. Or is it a matter of organization?

Mr. SLEEMAN. It is a matter of organization.

Mr. THOMPSON. In other words, the wages are paid pretty nearly the same by everybody?

Mr. SLEEMAN. No, sir; where the men are unorganized the wages are much less.

Mr. THOMPSON. I know; but I mean in dealing with the contractors here. Where the union deals with the small contractors, do you get the same wages you do with big contractors?

Mr. SLEEMAN. Yes, sir.

Mr. THOMPSON. Do you deal with small contractors?

Mr. SLEEMAN. Yes, sir.

Mr. THOMPSON. I would like to have you tell the commission wherein the conditions are better with the large contractors. In what respect, and what you mean by they are better in organization.

Mr. SLEEMAN. Well, through the organization in the building industry we have been in position to demand better conditions from the contractors hiring a large number of men, especially among the skilled mechanics, and inasmuch as the skilled mechanics have been organized we have been able to get better conditions for the laborers.

Mr. THOMPSON. What do you mean by better conditions? You mean where you deal with large contractors requiring a large number of skilled men you have union jobs?

Mr. SLEEMAN. Yes, sir.

Mr. THOMPSON. That is what you mean?

Mr. SLEEMAN. Yes, sir.

Mr. THOMPSON. In what other respects, if any, are conditions better?

Mr. SLEEMAN. Well, we have in the last three or four years in this city—about four years ago a majority of the work in the largest buildings in this city was in every line not less than 10 hours a day and several lines 7 days a week. At the present time the majority of the work is being done at 8 hours a day and 5½ days a week. We have made that much improvement by organization.

Mr. THOMPSON. That is due to what, in your opinion?

Mr. SLEEMAN. Organization of the building industry, of the building mechanics.

Commissioner COMMONS. Is that general through all the building trades?

Mr. SLEEMAN. Yes, sir.

Commissioner COMMONS. Bricklayers as well as others?

Mr. SLEEMAN. Well, not so particularly the bricklayers, because they have always been fairly well organized, but we have bettered the conditions of those other organizations that were not so well organized. For instance, you take the laborers, the concrete laborer at that time was working at any old price, from $2.50 down—not up, but down—and working any hours. It didn't matter what their hours was, the middle of the night or Sunday or any old time. At the present time we have got for them an organization where their wages at this time for pouring concrete are $3 a day and eight hours, and have over-time the same as mechanics.

Commissioner O'CONNELL. Which of the building laborers or organizations is it that works with the hod carriers?

Mr. SLEEMAN. The hod carriers are all organized. They have a fair organization.

Commissioner O'CONNELL. And all other laborers that work on the building?

Mr. SLEEMAN. As I said, we have organized the concrete men, but we haven't to any great extent organized the common laborers.

Commissioner O'CONNELL. Does not the building labor organization, the hod carriers, take in all building laborers?

Mr. SLEEMAN. Yes, sir.

Commissioner O'CONNELL. So that they are all in the building organization?

Mr. SLEEMAN. Yes, sir.

Commissioner O'CONNELL. They are being organized?

Mr. SLEEMAN. Yes, sir.

Commissioner COMMONS. You mean there is a union ready to take them in, but they are not all taken in yet?

Mr. SLEEMAN. The building laborers, namely, the men who help the plasterers and bricklayers, and pouring the concrete, that is what we have organized at the present time, and we are endeavoring at this time to organize all the common laborers in the building industry, and we have been successful to some extent with the common laborers, but the rest of the men are well organized.

Mr. THOMPSON. What per cent of the work done is done here under what you call favorable conditions or union conditions?

Mr. SLEEMAN. I should say in the large work, about 80 per cent of it.

Mr. THOMPSON. There has been something said about boycotting growing out of this building trades situation. Who are the contractors on the Lipman-Wolff Building and the Broadway Theater, two buildings that have been named?

Mr. SLEEMAN. A firm known as Hurley & Mason.

Mr. THOMPSON. What wages do they pay, and what hours do their men have, if you know, and how large is this firm?

Mr. SLEEMAN. The Hurley & Mason Co. three or four years ago had practically the bulk of the work, the large work. Their hours were 10 hours and no overtime, so that made it any time, 10 hours or any old time. But 10 hours was the regular day's work. In my own particular craft, that of carpenter, they paid any wages, 30 and 40 cents, and some men 50 cents an hour. Their conditions were much below that of the union conditions.

Mr. THOMPSON. Well, what are the conditions among them now? Do you know?

Mr. SLEEMAN. The conditions at the present time are somewhat better. They have reduced their hours to nine hours a day. They are about the only concern in the city of any magnitude, that is, building concern, working over eight hours.

Mr. THOMPSON. How do their wages compare with the union scale?

Mr. SLEEMAN. Not so good.

Mr. THOMPSON. Do you know what they are?

Mr. SLEEMAN. Well, I would not be positive, although I know they are better than they were. In my own particular line of carpentry, I believe that they are just a little below the union scale of wages, because we demand time and a half for overtime, and that is something that they don't get.

Mr. THOMPSON. Have you had a strike in the building trades in this city in the last two or three years?

Mr. SLEEMAN. Not of any magnitude.

Mr. THOMPSON. Not of any magnitude?

Mr. SLEEMAN. Let me see. We had a strike of the electrical workers; that was about three years ago.

Mr. THOMPSON. Were there any important principles involved in any of the strikes?

Mr. SLEEMAN. Just the rate of wages.

Mr. THOMPSON. Just the rate of wages. Nothing, then, in connection with the strike that would be of interest to the commission, as you look at it?

Mr. SLEEMAN. I don't think so; no, sir.

Mr. THOMPSON. Have you got any views as to the conditions of labor generally? In other words, with reference to the relations between employer and employee in this part of the country?

Mr. SLEEMAN. Beg pardon.

Mr. THOMPSON. Have you any views with reference to the relations which exist between employer and employee in this part of the country as to whether they are friendly or unfriendly, generally speaking?

Mr. SLEEMAN. Well, I believe that the conditions are different. There is no organization of employers other than there seems to be that of the employers' association, and as far as my experience has been with the employers' association, whenever we are in trouble or a little difficulty with any of our employers, why they are on the job to widen the breach instead of bringing us together. We at times have a little misunderstanding with some of our employers, and I found we always come out all right, but the employers' association haven't done anything, to my knowledge, to help us settle the difficulty other than to make the breach wider, because of the fact that we have to deal with the employers as individuals. Well, one employer thinks one way and the other the other, and there is no concrete foundation to work on.

Mr. THOMPSON. Then you believe it would be a good thing if there were employers' associations in the building trades?

Mr. SLEEMAN. Yes, sir; I believe if the employers in the building industry were in an organization and we could meet them as an organization it would be a whole lot better.

Mr. THOMPSON. Then, you would suggest unionization of the employers?

Mr. SLEEMAN. I believe in organization of the men, and I don't see any reason why the employers should not organize.

Mr. THOMPSON. Take conditions of labor outside of those crafts in the building trades, what is that here. You have been here all day?

Mr. SLEEMAN. Yes, sir.

Mr. THOMPSON. Have you heard what has been said by other witnesses in regard to that?

Mr. SLEEMAN. Yes, sir.

Mr. THOMPSON. What have you got to add to what has been said about unemployment and conditions of labor, etc.?

Mr. SLEEMAN. Well, here is what we have had—men in the building industry have had their time occupied so much by their own troubles, we haven't had so much time to give to the study of other difficulties. But I know that there is a great deal of unrest among all the laboring men in this city, due 'to the fact that the men are unemployed—that is largely the case. When men are not working—I know in my own particular organization' when the men are working there is no trouble; when they are not working, there is discontent. Another thing is, our wages have not been raised—not increased enough in proportion to the expense of living. It is making it a whole lot more difficult for a man to live on the same amount of money now than it was a few years ago.

Mr. THOMPSON. What have you to say with reference to the boycott that has been spoken of here. Have you anything to add to what has been said already?

Mr. SLEEMAN. Nothing other than I believe that whenever a building—speaking of one of our own institutions—has been constructed under un. favorable conditions or under conditions not recognized 'by those men that are organized, I think we should have the right to let the public know it.

Mr. THOMPSON. That is all you care to say about that now?

Mr. SLEEMAN. I think that is all.

Mr. THOMPSON. Have you anything else to say to the commission with reference to any subject that would come before it, or with reference to any of the questions submitted to you, that would be of value?

Mr. SLEEMAN. No, sir. I would answer any question you might like to ask me.

Chairman WALSH. Commissioner Lennon would like to ask some questions.

Commissioner LENNON. I understood in the beginning of your testimony you indicated there might be some difference between the large and small contractors. Now, suppose a union contractor worked on the largest building ever constructed in this city to-day, and to-morrow he worked on a $1,500 house, but they are both union jobs. Does he get the same wages in both places?

Mr. SLEEMAN. Absolutely.

Commissioner LENNON. I was afraid there would be some misunderstanding.

Mr. SLEEMAN. My reference there was that the large employers—the reason I made it the large employers, the responsible employers, is, we deal with them and have a whole lot more success with them than we have with the small employers. That is why I made the difference in that respect.

Commissioner LENNON. Last winter when unemployment was acute ·here, did the carpenters' union take care of the unemployed carpenters where it was necessary for them to have help?

Mr. SLEEMAN. Our organization takes care of all its men to its limit. Very few men that are not taken care of by our organization.

Commissioner LENNON. I want to ask a question that has not been asked here, and see if you have ever given it any consideration. In the ordinary arrests in this city that come before the police court for drunkenness, for abuse of their wives or children, or ordinary misdemeanors, have you any real knowledge—I don't mean guesswork, but knowledge as to whether the union men show up as well as the nonunion men of the community. Not simply guesswork, if you don't know anything about it, say so.

Mr. SLEEMAN. I can't say I have given it any study at all. I know a man goes out and gets into court—members of our organization, if they beat up their wives, it is not very good for them when they come back to the organization. But outside of that, we haven't made any particular study except there are very few of our men that I know of that ever get arrested. We haven't had any necessity of helping anybody out in cases of that description.

Commissioner LENNON. That is all.

Chairman WALSH. Any other questions?

Commissioner COMMONS. I have a question I would like to ask: This firm you speak of, I have forgotten the name.

Mr. SLEEMAN. Hurley & Mason.

Commissioner COMMONS. You say they have in case of carpenters, employed them nine hours?

Mr. SLEEMAN. Yes, sir.

Commissioner COMMONS. And at 30 to 50 cents an hour?

Mr. SLEEMAN. I don't know exactly; I think they have increased their wages. They pay them, as they rate it, what the men are worth. They were paying 30 to 40 and 50 cents an hour, but that was three or four years ago.

Commissioner COMMONS. What is the union minimum scale?

Mr. SLEEMAN. Fifty cents an hour.

Commissioner COMMONS. Do you know of any number employed by this other firm at less than 50 cents an hour—carpenters?

Mr. SLEEMAN. Well, I haven't individually at this time asked the men what they were getting. I know some of the men at this time are getting 50 cents an hour, nine hours a day. On the last job they have, I haven't gone into it myself.

Commissioner COMMONS. What do you get for overtime?

Mr. SLEEMAN. Time and a half and double time for Sundays and holidays.

Commissioner COMMONS.· So that if you work nine hours you would have——.

Mr. SLEEMAN. Four dollars and seventy-five cents.

Commissioner COMMONS. And what would they get for nine hours, $4.50?

Mr. SLEEMAN. Yes, sir.

Commissioner COMMONS. How many buildings have they constructed here that are now being boycotted?

Mr. SLEEMAN. Two, right now.

Commissioner COMMONS. What are they—Lipman-Wolff——

Mr. SLEEMAN. And Broadway Theater.

Commissioner COMMONS. Those two?

Mr. SLEEMAN. Yes, sir.

Commissioner COMMONS. And what is the actual ground of the boycott—that they are a nonunion establishment?

Mr. SLEEMAN. Yes, sir; that they will not employ union men and the conditions maintained by·the organization.

Commissioner COMMONS. Would you furnish us with figures—statistics that would show this increase in wages and the reduction of hours since the beginning of this period of organization which you said was about four or five years ago?

Mr. SLEEMAN. Yes, sir.

Commissioner COMMONS. Could you get that from your different organizations so that we could have it?

Mr. SLEEMAN. Yes, sir; I think we could.

Commissioner COMMONS. Will you do that?

Mr. SLEEMAN. Yes, sir.

Commissioner COMMONS. You understand what is wanted?

Mr. SLEEMAN. What is it you· want?

Commissioner COMMONS. You said four or five years ago there was not much organization in the building trades?

Mr. SLEEMAN. Yes, sir.

Commissioner· COMMONS. Take the wages and hours prior to that period, and also show them at the present time, both for the union establishment and for the nonunion éstablishment.

Mr. SLEEMAN. ·All right, sir.

Commissioner COMMONS. That is all.

Chairman WALSH. Anything else? That is all; thank you. Call your next.

Mr. THOMPSON. Mrs. Lizzie Gee.

TESTIMONY OF MRS. LIZZIE GEE.

Mr. THOMPSON. Give us your name.

Mrs. GEE. Mrs. Lizzie Gee.

Mr. THOMPSON. And your business address?

Mrs. GEE. My business address is 92 East Grand Avenue.

Mr. THOMPSON. What official position have you with the garment workers?

Mrs. GEE. I have no official position at the present time.

Mr. THOMPSON. Are you connected with the United Garment Workers' organization?

Mrs. GEE. Oh, yes.

Mr. THOMPSON. A member of it?

Mrs. GEE. I am a member of it.

Mr. THOMPSON. Did you have some official position with it?

Mrs. GEE. Not at the present time.

Mr. THOMPSON. How long have you been a member of the organization?

Mrs. GEE. Twelve years.

Mr. THOMPSON. In and around Portland?

Mrs. GEE. In Portland.

Mr. THOMPSON. What local do you belong to, or what craft?

Mrs. GEE. Two twenty-eight.

Mr. THOMPSON. Is that divided into pants makers and vest makers and coat makers?

Mrs. GEE. No, sir; it is mechanics. I am connected with the mechanics' clothing.

Commissioner COMMONS. What does that mean?

Mr. THOMPSON. What is that, overalls?

Mrs. GEE. Overalls; all kinds of mechanics' clothing—coats, and aprons and shirts and overalls.

Mr. THOMPSON. In your position as a union worker connected with the organization, have you some ideas with reference to the condition of labor in this locality?

Mrs. GEE. Well, do you mean particularly women, or to all?

Mr. THOMPSON. All labor, or such parts of the labor field that you are acquainted with. Have you some field that you are in touch with?

Mrs. GEE. Well, I have been very much interested in the labor field for the past 12 years.

Mr. THOMPSON. In your opinion is there a state of unrest, or not, in the labor world here?

Mrs. GEE. Well, at the present time I can say there is.

Mr. THOMPSON. What, in your opinion, is the cause of that unrest, if any exists?

Mrs. GEE. Well, it is the lack of sufficient employment.

Mr. THOMPSON. And what is that due to—too large a number of workers here, or what?

Mrs. GEE. A large number of workers; and a majority of them are working too long hours.

Mr. THOMPSON. What particular trade have you in mind now, or industry?

Mrs. GEE. Well, I have no partcular trade or industry in mind; in all.

Mr. THOMPSON. What would you say in reference to what could be done to help the matter in that regard? Would shortening the hours be a sufficient remedy?

Mrs. GEE. No; it would not be sufficient, but it would help.

Mr. THOMPSON. What other remedy would you advocate or would you suggest?

Mrs. GEE. Well, I don't know as I am in a position to take up the matter. There are a great many people taking up questions to-day, but it seems that they can not solve them.

Mr. THOMPSON. You were presented with a list of questions, were you not?

Mrs. GEE. No; I was not.

Mr. THOMPSON. Take your own field, for instance, the garment makers' field, what would you say in regard to that? What are the conditions there?

Mrs. GEE. Well, the conditions in the garment workers' field locally are not good.

Mr. THOMPSON. What is the cause for their condition?

Mrs. GEE. Lack of demand for wearing apparel.

Mr. THOMPSON. Of course, that could only be helped by more business.

Mrs. GEE. That could only be helped, I presume, by more business.

Mr. THOMPSON. Are there any statements or suggestions that you would like to make to this commission touching your own industry, or in your particular industrial field?

Mrs. GEE. Why, as far as my own industry is concerned locally, we are organized.

Chairman WALSH. How many members have you, madam?

Mrs. GEE. We have about 300 members.

Chairman WALSH. How many are engaged generally in the garment industry in Portland?

Mrs. GEE. All of them. There are only the one local in the State of Oregon.

Chairman WALSH. Have you a 100 per cent union, or are there a number of unorganized ones in the industry?

Mrs. GEE. Well, in that particular trade we have; in that one particular trade.

Chairman WALSH. Do you have any special knowledge of the garment industry generally, outside of this making of garments for mechanics?

Mrs. GEE. Well, no; because I have not been—I am only speaking from an experienced standpoint.

Chairman WALSH. What are the wages paid to the members of your own craft in Portland?

Mrs. GEE. In my craft it is principally piecework.

Chairman WALSH. What would you say were the average earnings of your workers? Classify them.

Mrs. GEE. Well, under the average earnings of the workers, that will take the poor and the best, the apprentice and all, I would say an average wage of $9.

Chairman WALSH. What is the highest paid worker in your particular craft?

Mrs. GEE. You mean—that don't apply to pieceworkers?

Chairman WALSH. It applies to the pieceworkers; what is the highest wage made by those in your craft?

Mrs. GEE. Oh, the highest wage made?

Chairman WALSH. Yes.

Mrs. GEE. Well, the highest wage made is made by the pieceworkers, and I would say the highest wage made is $25 a week.

Chairman WALSH. How many of this membership of yours makes $25 a week would you say, approximately?

Mrs. GEE. Well, there isn't a great many of them.

Chairman WALSH. Well, how many?

Mrs. GEE. Well——

Chairman WALSH. Can you give the percentage?

Mrs. GEE. Out of 300 I presume there would not be more than 50.

Chairman WALSH. Fifty that would get $25?

Mrs. GEE. That is pieceworkers.

Chairman WALSH. I understand. Now, then, what is the lowest wage made by those pieceworkers?

Mrs. GEE. Well, you understand piecework, when a pieceworker goes to work they make what they—they just receive what they make.

Chairman WALSH. Certainly.

Mrs. GEE. And an inexperienced pieceworker that has no idea of the system or the running of a power machine——

Chairman WALSH. I would not want one like that.

Mrs. GEE. You wouldn't want that one, you would want one, say, that had been there a year, then?

Chairman WALSH. Yes; an average paid worker in your craft.

Mrs. GEE. I would say, then, that would be $10.

Chairman WALSH. So that the pay for a maker of mechanic clothing, you would say, ranges from $10 to $25 per week.

Mrs. GEE. Yes.

Chairman WALSH. In this community how many would you say get approximately $10 a week?

Mrs. GEE. Well, I would say that more than two-thirds.

Chairman WALSH. More than two-thirds make $10 a week?

Mrs. GEE. Yes.

Chairman WALSH. And then the balance would range between that and $25?

Mrs. GEE. Yes. That is speaking—that is saying after a year's experience.

Chairman WALSH. How many hours a day do you work?

Mrs. GEE. Eight hours.

Chairman WALSH. And what are the rules of apprentices? How many apprentices are there in that particular craft?

Mrs. GEE. As far as the pieceworkers are concerned they are all apprentices until they qualify themselves, or until a certain period.

Chairman WALSH. Under any rule that you care to designate yourself, how many apprentices are there in your particular craft?

Mrs. GEE. Well, I couldn't answer that because I do not—now, then, I would say, that in our particular trade they are coming and going all the time.

Chairman WALSH. So that you could not tell how many there are at any particular time?

Commissioner O'CONNELL. You have no apprentice rules?

Mrs. GEE. No; we have no apprentice rules.

Commissioner GARRETSON. The operative who works the first day gets the same price for the garment that he makes as the one that has been there five years?

Mrs. GEE. Yes; but as a rule—now, I will say, I am speaking for the firm I am working for, I do not say all firms do that, but the firm I am working for has a rule if an operative comes in and they see that he is likely to make a good operator, it would pay to keep him, they will make their wages up if they don't make enough, say, for the first two or three weeks to enable them to get along.

Mr. THOMPSON. What has been the effect of the minimum wage law, if any, on your industry?

Mrs. GEE. There has been no effect on my particular industry, except our union scale for paid workers; we paid, the average was $8 a week, and the minimum wage raised it to eight sixty-four.

Mr. THOMPSON. The garment workers who are making mechanics' clothing are pretty well organized, are they not?

Mrs. GEE. Yes.

Mr. THOMPSON. How are the garment workers who are making ordinary clothing; are they well organized or not, do you know?

Mrs. GEE. Not organized.

Mr. THOMPSON. What effect has the eight-hour law had on your industry?

Mrs. GEE. What effect would it have?

Mr. THOMPSON. Did it have, or have you got it?

Mrs. GEE. We haven't got any eight-hour law. Our organization gave us our eight hours.

Mr. THOMPSON. That is all, Mr. Chairman.

Chairman WALSH. Anything else?

Commissioner LENNON. How many weeks' works are you able to make in any year, do you suppose?

Mrs. GEE. Well, we are able to put in a year's work.

Commissioner LENNON. Do you have steady employment?

Mrs. GEE. Have so far, for 12 years.

Commissioner LENNON. For your 300 people?

Mrs. GEE. For the 300 people. We are now on a vacation for a month.

Commissioner LENNON. One month?

Mrs. GEE. Usually they do not close the place I am in. They allow their operatives to go a certain length of time, and so on.

Commissioner LENNON. If they permit some of the operatives to go do they get the 52 weeks' work a year?

Mrs. GEE. Well, it is to their option. If they want to go they can go and take their vacation if they see fit, if they care to.

Chairman WALSH. That is all; thank you. The commission will now stand adjourned until to-morrow morning at 10 o'clock.

(Whereupon at 4.30 o'clock p. m. an adjournment was taken until 10 o'clock a. m. of the following day, August 21, 1914.)

PORTLAND, OREG., *Friday, August 21, 1914—10 a. m.*

Met pursuant to adjournment.

Present: Chairman Walsh, Commissioners O'Connell, Lennon, Garretson, and Commons; also W. O. Thompson, counsel.

Chairman WALSH. The commission will please come to order. You may proceed, now, Mr. Thompson.

Mr. THOMPSON. Mr. Lorntsen.

TESTIMONY OF MR. H. M. LORNTSEN.

Mr. THOMPSON. Please give us your name.

Mr. LORNTSEN. H. M. Lorntsen.

Mr. THOMPSON. And your address—business address?

Mr. LORNTSEN. Box 138, Astoria, Oreg.

Mr. THOMPSON. And your business?

Mr. LORNTSEN. I am secretary of the Columbia Fishermen's Union and secretary of the Columbia River Protection Union.

Mr. THOMPSON. How long have you been connected with that organization?

Mr. LORNTSEN. I have been a member of the Columbia River Protective Union since 1887. I have been secretary since 1899, in the spring.

Mr. THOMPSON. How large an organization is that, and with what other bodies, if any, is it affiliated?

Mr. LORNTSEN. In the United Fishermen's Union there are six locals on Puget Sound. There is one at Broderick, Sacramento; there is one at Unqua, Oreg.; one at Siskiyou, Oreg.; and one on the Columbia River.

Mr. THOMPSON. Have you a printed constitution and by-laws?

Mr. LORNTSEN. Yes, sir.

Mr. THOMPSON. Have you a copy of it with you?

Mr. LORNTSEN. No, sir.

Mr. THOMPSON. Would you be willing to furnish the commission with a copy?

Mr. 'LORNTSEN. Certainly.

Mr. THOMPSON. If you please.

(Booklet entitled " Constitution and By-Laws of the Columbia River Fishermen's Protective Union, Local No. 2, United Fishermen of the Pacific," was subsequently submitted in printed form.)

Mr. THOMPSON. Please tell us briefly the aims and purposes of your organization and the class of workers it takes into it.

Mr. LORNTSEN. The aim and object first when we started was to better the condition along the line of the prices of fish, because as unorganized fishermen we had absolutely no show with the packers. They paid whatever they pleased, and if you would not take it—well, get.

I got a little table here taken from the United States fisheries report, showing the price paid for raw materials, and what they obtained for canned goods before the organization started. I also have something after that.

In the year of 1866 they commenced to can salmon on the Columbia River. They paid then 15 cents apiece for salmon and got $16 a case. In 1867, 20 cents was paid; they got $13 a case. In 1868, 20 cents; $12 a case. In 1869, 20 cents; $10 a case. In 1870, 20 cents; $9 a case. In 1871, 20 cents; $9.50 a case. In 1872, it was 22½, and they got $8 a case. From 1873 to 1879 it was 25 cents apiece, and they got from $4.50 to $7 a case. In 1880 it was 50 cents, and they got $4.60 to $4.80. In 1881, 60 cents apiece, and $5 a case. In 1882 and 1883, 75 cents, and $5 a case. In 1884, 50; $4.70 a case. In 1885, 75 cents, and $4.70. In the year of 1886 they were going to pay the fishermen 45 to 55 cents apiece. That was the price set by the packers, and the fishermen refused to accept, and they formed the Columbia River Fishermen's Protective Union. They only demanded 10 cents more a pound, and they got it after a struggle, to the end of May. They organized on the 11th of April and they struck on the 15th of May, and then the packers was able to figure out that they could pay the price. Now that then brought to the fishermen approximately——

Mr. THOMPSON. Give us more definitely, but still present briefly, the classes of workers in the organization?

Mr. LORNTSEN. That is, the gill-net fishermen?

Mr. THOMPSON. The gill-net fishermen and the packers, and in the canneries, too.

Mr. LORNTSEN. No; they have nothing to do with that.

Mr. THOMPSON. They haven't anything?

Mr. LORNTSEN. No; it is only the fishermen that is in the organization. Now, that brought to the fishermen then about $134,000 more than they would have had without the organization. Before that time the fishermen used to come to Astoria in the spring, and when the season was over they went somewhere else; but with the establishment of the union Astoria commenced to build up, the fishermen realized that they had something to live for, to live there for; something that they could bank on, and they settled down.

Mr. THOMPSON. Just a moment. When you speak of the price that you pay you mean for a fish?

Mr. LORNTSEN. Yes.

Mr. THOMPSON. You said sometimes 75 cents a fish. Was that a single fish?

Mr. LORNTSEN. That was a single fish; that is, for the fish at that time.

Mr. THOMPSON. Paid to the fishermen?

Mr. LORNTSEN. Yes, to the fishermen.

Commissioner COMMONS. What is meant by a case?

Mr. LORNTSEN. Forty-eight cans of 1 pound.

Commissioner COMMONS. How many fish?

Mr. LORNTSEN. That is an average of three fish.

Mr. THOMPSON. When you say you paid $5 for a case, what do you mean? To whom did they pay that?

Mr. LORNTSEN. That was what the packers received for it.

Mr. THOMPSON. Oh, the packers received that?

Mr. LORNTSEN. I want to say here, gentlemen, that there is absolutely no relationship between the price paid for raw material and what they receive for the canned goods. They paid as little as possible and got all they could, that is all.

Mr. THOMPSON. Three normal fish, you say, would make a case of average size?

Mr. LORNTSEN. We figure an average of three fish to a case.

Mr. THOMPSON. Go ahead.

Mr. LORNTSEN. Then the following year they raised the price to 80. cents and 90 cents, and have no trouble in getting it. That brought again to the fishermen, then, something like $328,000 more than we would have had without an organization. The fourth year was a dollar, and then $1.25; $1.25 they are paying for fish caught by private rigs. Used to have cannery rigs and didn't get so much, because in that case the canneries charged up against it; but they got $1.25 the third year, and that brought over $500,000 to the fishermen. That is the difference between the—I wouldn't say the difference between 45 and 55, say, the first year, in 1886, but we said that probably the canneries would have paid 75 cents without an organization on the river; but still the difference between 75 and $1.25 gave them over $500,000 for the fish that year; and the following year was the same thing, he had the same price, but the pack was not so big, but they cleared anyhow over $400,000, and gave on the river the biggest amount they had. Then the fishermen had heard all around about it, and the packers tried to get men in here to fish as cheap as possible. We then struck in—let us see, that was the fourth year—the ninth year it was we had struck. We had a couple of strikes after that, but the last strike we had was in 1896.

Mr. THOMPSON. What is the condition of the fishermen now? Is the organization in healthy condition?

Mr. LORNTSEN. Not as they should be. They would be a whole lot better off if more of them had sense enough to get in.

Mr. THOMPSON. What proportion of the men engaged in salmon fishing on the Pacific coast are in your organization?

Mr. LORNTSEN. Well, on the Columbia River we have about 2,000 men, and the local sound, Puget Sound, I don't know exactly the number, but all the fishermen in the locality where locals are in existence, they are all in. But they are only small locals. Down on the Sound I think there is one that has 60 members in the organization, practically every man is down there.

Mr. THOMPSON. About what proportion are organized?

Mr. LORNTSEN. In Oregon and Washington?

Mr. THOMPSON. Yes.

Mr. LORNTSEN. Well, altogether that is about a half organization; sailors and trappers, they have got their own organization.

Mr. THOMPSON. Your organization does not include those?

Mr. LORNTSEN. No; we have nothing to do with them.

Mr. THOMPSON. What are the prices that you are getting for fish now?

Mr. LORNTSEN. This season we have been paid 6 and 7½ cents a pound.

Mr. THOMPSON. What will the average fish weigh?

Mr. LORNTSEN. Well, it is pretty hard to tell exactly, about 20 pounds, 22 pounds, 23 on an average; yet it goes approximately between 63 and 65 pounds to a case.

Mr. THOMPSON. How much do you figure you would get out of that—the fishermen?

Mr. LORNTSEN. We are getting 6 cents a pound for the small fish—that is, fish less than 25 pounds.

Mr. THOMPSON. You would get a little over $3.50 a case, the fisherman would to-day?

Mr. LORNTSEN. Yes, sir.

Mr. THOMPSON. What does a case sell for to-day?

Mr. LORNTSEN. The tall cans is sold at $1.95; the flats, $2.10; halves, $1.25; ovals, 1 pound, $2.65; and half pound ovals, $1.80 per dozen.

Mr. THOMPSON. How many dozen in a case?

Mr. LORNTSEN. Four.

Mr. THOMPSON. Well, you had all the figures figured out as to what the fishermen got and what the cases sold for as to the others, but you don't seem to have the later figures figured out in that way. Could you get those figures up and give them to the commission later on?

Mr. LORNTSEN. Like this?

Mr. THOMPSON. What is that?

Mr. LORNTSEN. Like I have it here?

Mr. THOMPSON. You had some figures that gave the price per pound and per case?

Mr. LORNTSEN. Yes, sir.

Mr. THOMPSON. You can give us those figures so that we can figure it out ourselves?

(See Lorntsen exhibit.)

Commissioner COMMONS. What is the present price per case?

Mr. LORNTSEN. It don't sell by the case any more, it goes by the pound.

Commissioner COMMONS. Formerly when you got a dollar and a quarter for fish, what would it work out now?

Mr. LORNTSEN. We get more.

Commissioner COMMONS. What would it work out now?

· Mr. LORNTSEN. I don't know exactly.

Commissioner COMMONS. A dollar and a half?

Mr. LORNTSEN. Probably.

Commissioner COMMONS. What does a case work out now?

Mr. LORNTSEN. That is what I just said. It is a dollar and ninety-five cents per dozen for talls, and two dollars and ten cents for flats.

Commissioner COMMONS. Take on the basis you started on.

Mr. Mr. LORNTSEN. Well, it would be about $8——

Commissioner COMMONS. Where they get $5 a case in 1880, what would they get now—in 1880?

Mr. LORNTSEN. They would get about seven dollars and some cents.

Commissioner GARRETSON. Eighty cents.

Commissioner LENNON. Seven dollars and eighty cents?

Mr. LORNTSEN. Yes.

· Commissioner COMMONS. About $7.80, and you are getting about $1.50 per fish; that is, three and a half a case you are getting, and they are getting seven eighty a case. That is about the way it is now?

.Mr. LORNTSEN. Yes.

· Commissioner O'CONNELL. How much money do you make, how much, for instance, a week, a day, or a month? Let us get at the real money you make.

Mr. LORNTSEN. Well, the real money is very poor picking when it comes really down to that.

Commissioner O'CONNELL. Let us see, how much money do you earn a month?

Mr. LORNTSEN. The average, you see, per boat on the Columbia River would not go over $600.

Commissioner O'CONNELL. Now, a boat—how many men in a boat?

Mr. LORNTSEN. That is two at the most.

Commissioner O'CONNELL. Six hundred dollars a month for two?

Mr. LORNTSEN. No, sir; for the season.

Commissioner O'CONNELL. Oh, the season.

Mr. LORNTSEN. About six hundred; they average $600.

· Commissioner O'CONNELL. Now, do you mean to say that a fisherman only earns $300 a year?

Mr. LORNTSEN. He has got to do something else or he would starve.

Commissioner O'CONNELL. At fishing.

Mr. LORNTSEN. He won't make that, even, at an average.

Commissioner O'CONNELL. Now listen, and see if we can't get it. How long is the season, how long does he work at fishing each year?

Mr. LORNTSEN. The season at present commences May 1 and ends at August 25.

Commissioner O'CONNELL. That is May, June, July, and August, four months.

Mr. LORNTSEN. Yes; practically four months.

Commissioner O'CONNELL. That is all the fishing he does in a year, is it?

Mr. LORNTSEN. Well, most of it, do a little fishing in the fall and in the winter, but it don't amount to much.

Commissioner O'CONNELL. In those four months, how much money would he make?

Mr. LORNTSEN. At an average, probably make $200.

Commissioner O'CONNELL. Two hundred dollars a season for fishing?

Mr. LORNTSEN. Yes.

Commissioner O'CONNELL. Now, what does he do during the balance of the season?

Mr. LORNTSEN. Does anything he can get hold of.

Commissioner O'CONNELL. What do they do as a general thing, do they hang around?

Mr. LORNTSEN. No, no; there is some of them got little farms of their own, some go into other work, some longshoremen, some work in the mills, some work on the road, strike out at anything else, anything they can do.

Commissioner O'CONNELL. The occupation which they follow, or profession, that of fisherman, they only make $200 a year at it?

Mr. LORNTSEN. At an average. There is men, of course, that makes probably as high as a couple of thousand dollars' worth of fish, but there is other boats that don't get hardly anything.

Commissioner COMMONS. How much do they have invested in their boats and equipment?

Mr. LORNTSEN. Well, a gasoline boat comes somewhere around $600, and a net—one net will be at least $400, you might say.

Commissioner COMMONS. A thousand dollars?

Mr. LORNTSEN. Yes, sir; $1,500; some of them got two nets.

Commissioner COMMONS. And you say that they get $600?

Mr. LORNTSEN. Well, that is an average.

Commissioner COMMONS. Does that cover interest on that boat, out of that six hundred?

Mr. LORNTSEN. They generally figure that one-third of a catch goes to cover the rig.

Commissioner COMMONS. Then this $600 is net after the one-third?

Mr. LORNTSEN. No, sir; nothing net about it.

Commissioner COMMONS. The gross——

Mr. LORNTSEN. Yes, sir.

Commissioner COMMONS (continuing). Revenue is $600, out of which they have to pay for their rig?

Mr. LORNTSEN. Yes, sir.

Commissioner COMMONS. And meet the depreciation, and so on?

Mr. LORNTSEN. Yes, sir.

Commissioner COMMONS. And get whatever is left for earnings?

Mr. LORNTSEN. Yes.

Comissioner LENNON. How long do they use these boats; how many years?

Mr. LORNTSEN. Oh, a boat, by taking good care of it, it will last a good many years, but the net can't be depended on more than two years.

Commissioner LENNON. Will a boat last 10 years?

Mr. LORNTSEN. Yes.

Commissioner O'CONNELL. You mean to say that a net that he pays $400 for will only last two years?

Mr. LORNTSEN. Not to be depended on. Some won't last that long.

Commissioner O'CONNELL. Then, if he only makes $200 a year, he is buying nets with all the money he gets?

Mr. LORNTSEN. Yes; some of the canning men got to suffer for that.

Commissioner O'CONNELL. You mean to say out of these earnings, this $200 on an average that you say they make each year, that every second year they buy a new net that costs $400?

Mr. LORNTSEN. Oh, no: I didn't say that. The $200—there is $600 average to the boat. That is divided into three. Two hundred dollars goes into the rig. If that don't cover it, why the man that owns the rig, he has got to stand it.

Commissioner LENNON (addressing Commissioner O'Connell). Go ahead, Jim, and find out how much these men make.

Commissioner O'CONNELL. I want to find out how much money, when you go home Saturday night or at the end of the year, how much money you have got left out of your job of fishing four months?

Mr. LORNTSEN. Some don't get any; haven't paid their bills.

Commissioner O'CONNELL. He is in debt?

Mr. LORNTSEN. Yes; and not even paid the boat puller.

Commissioner O'CONNELL. Getting worse.

Commissioner COMMONS. How much do the best ones make?

Mr. LORNTSEN. Oh, the best one—some of them will probably get up to as high as $2,500 worth of fish, but that is only exceptions—some few boats. I guess the high boat on the river to-day is about 13 or 14 ton.

Commissioner COMMONS. How much will they make?

Mr. LORNTSEN. That is an average of $130 a ton—a hundred and forty to one hundred and thirty dollars a ton.

Commissioner COMMONS. That makes about twenty-five hundred. How many would be making that?

Mr. LORNTSEN. That is not many.

Commissioner COMMONS. Is that irregular?

Mr. LORNTSEN. Some years they make a good deal.

Commissioner COMMONS. And some years not?

Mr. LORNTSEN. Well, it depends a great deal upon how the fish are running and what chances the men take.

Commissioner COMMONS. Does one man own the boat and the other man work for him?

Mr. LORNTSEN. As a rule.

Commissioner COMMONS. Are both in the union?

Mr. LORNTSEN. Sometime, and sometimes not. We want them in.

Commissioner COMMONS. Which one is in the union?

Mr. LORNTSEN. Sometimes one, and sometimes the other; just depends upon what sense a man has got.

Commissioner COMMONS. Well, the helper, is he paid wages by the other man?

Mr. LORNTSEN. He is paid so much per cent—one-third, as a rule.

Commissioner COMMONS. He gets one-third?

Mr. LORNTSEN. As a rule.

Commissioner COMMONS. And the other gets the other two-thirds for the boat and rig?

Mr. LORNTSEN. Yes, sir.

Mr. THOMPSON. Is that all?

Chairman WALSH. Yes.

Mr. THOMPSON. Mr. Lorntsen, have you any knowledge or information in regard to the cooperative canning factories in this State?

Mr. LORNTSEN. Yes; I ought to know something about it. I am the one that started it.

Mr. THOMPSON. I see. Well, how large an institution is that? How many people does it employ, where does it have its place of business, and what amount of fish does it handle in dollars and cents? Tell us briefly.

Mr. LORNTSEN. In the first place, probably the gentlemen want to know how we started up that cannery, what brought us to do it. I think that ought to be shown up in your report just as well as anything else.

Mr. THOMPSON. Will you please briefly state that?

Mr. LORNTSEN. Yes, sir; as I said, up to 1896 we had—that year we had four strikes. We had for years been receiving 3 to 5 cents a pound for fish; but the packers combined and was not going to pay 4 cents. They put up a cash bonus that would be forfeited if any of them paid more than 4 cents a pound. The market had nothing to do with it, that was simply a combine, and they were going to break the organization. A man came out from Chicago and he turned the packers topsy turvy. We had a strike, then, until the 26th of June. The leaders of the strike, of course, then, we had a compromise, and the leaders of the strike were informed that they would take the fish from the fishermen that year, but after that they would not be able to deliver to any packing company on the Columbia River. Of course, then, we said we would pack our own fish. We got together about $20,000. We got the ground on tick, lots more on tick, built a plant worth $32,000, did the work ourselves, and put up 44,000 cases of salmon. We had a great deal of opposition. Of course, the other packers didn't like to see us succeed, and they blocked us in the market and everywhere else, and it was asserted we were going to hell before the end of that year. He hasn't got us yet. We were also told we would never see 5 cents a pound for fish if we called the strike. We commenced with our packing in 1897; it was only 4 cents a pound on the river then, and the following year it was only 4 cents a pound; but bye and bye the packers could not stand it themselves, the other side, and they commenced to go to the wall; they had to loosen up a little bit, and when they loosened up that helped the two of us also. Since then we have had pretty fair sailing. Of course, there were tight pinches once in a while when we got a little too much salmon on hand, like it was last winter, but I think we have done fairly well. We have been able to pay the ruling price on the river and pay some dividends besides. That is to say, after the ruling price on the river has been paid, also the running expenses, such as interest on the capital stock, depreciation, a little money put into an emergency fund, and whatever is left is turned over to the fishermen regardless of whether shareholders or not. All the stockholders or shareholders has got in the company is 6 per cent interest for his money; that is actual cash; there is no water in the stock.

There was a good many fishermen come over to fish, and we have been able to pay dividends. In 1899 we paid $5 a ton dividends above the price paid, and in 1901 and in 1902 there was only $2.50 per ton paid, but since that time it has not been any less than $10, and it has been as high as $20 for the early fish, except last year when it was only $5 a ton. It has paid as high as $40 a ton on some fish as dividends. This is the money that went direct to the fishermen. In the other case it would have gone to the packers.

Commissioner O'CONNELL. Is the total from earnings—the earnings shown there?

Mr. LORNTSEN. No, sir; it is just a memorandum, I have jotted down. I didn't know what questions would come up. If I had known you wanted a paper, I would have made one.

Mr. THOMPSON. How many fish in dollars and cents did the cooperative proposition run the last year or the last fiscal year?

Mr. LORNTSEN. Probably around several hundred thousand dollars worth of business. In 1911 we did over a million dollar business.

Mr. THOMPSON. How many people does it employ?

Mr. LORNTSEN. There is probably 350 or 360 boats fishing, and we have an average of two men in the boat. A few boats have only one man in them on the river. There is quite a bunch in the cannery; I don't know exactly how many we have, but there is quite a bunch of people.

Mr. THOMPSON. Do these men receive separate wages—of course, they do?

Mr. LORNTSEN. Yes, sir.

Mr. THOMPSON. What are they paid?

Mr. LORNTSEN. Those working in the cannery are not getting anything as dividends or anything like that. They are paid according to the ruling price of wages paid in other places. They are paid probably a little more—probably 10 per cent more.

Mr. THOMPSON. Than the union scale?

Mr. LORNTSEN. Well, there is no union among them.

Mr. THOMPSON. No union?

Mr. LORNTSEN. No; the fact is, those that work in the canneries haven't got any organization.

Mr. THOMPSON. I mean the men who work for your cooperative enterprise?

Mr. LORNTSEN. They have no union among themselves; not those working in the cannery.

Mr. THOMPSON. Are they all stockholders in this cooperative proposition?

Mr. LORNTSEN. No.

Mr. THOMPSON. Have you sought to organize them at all?

Mr. LORNTSEN. We had them organized one year. We were endeavoring one year to have the packing done by white labor exclusively, but we found out it was impossible to do so and compete with them. It cost us about $6,000 or $7,000 more to put up the pack than if we had had the Chinese contract like the rest of them. Then, there was another company that tried the same thing, but they also discarded it. Of course, that was before the sanitary canning machinery came into use. Since the sanitary canning has come into use it is different. Out in the —— cannery there are nothing but while employees, except there are half a dozen old Chinks and Japs that are working there. They have been there a long time and they are doing the butchering. They are paid so much a day.

Mr. THOMPSON. What interest has your organization taken in the organization of the people working in the canning factories?

Mr. LORNTSEN. Well, we had no objection to them organizing. We would rather see them organize, because it is a whole lot better if they do organize than individually. We had an organization there some years ago, but it went by the board. But I think the time will come, however, when they will organize. They ought to be organized, anyway. It wouldn't hurt us any at all. It would be a whole lot better for the community if they all were organized in all lines of business—canneries and others.

Mr. THOMPSON. That is all, Mr. Chairman.

Chairman WALSH. Do you want to ask any questions?

Commissioner COMMONS. Is your union affiliated with any other union?

Mr. LORNTSEN. They are affiliated with the American Federation of Labor through the International Teamsters' Union of America and the United Fishermen of the Pacific.

Mr. THOMPSON. That is all.

, Chairman WALSH. That is all, Mr. Lorntsen, unless there is something you wish to add. I wish you would submit those documents you have here containing these figures, and also if there are any suggestions you would like to make, we would be glad to have them.

Mr. Lorntsen. Well, I think while I am in the chair I might as well take up the hindrances to the work of fishing on the Columbia River.

Chairman WALSH. Very good.

Mr. LORNTSEN. Now, in the first place there is the salmon industry that is taken off on account of the greed of those that fish above tidewater. I am going to use plain language.

Chairman WALSH. Do, sure.

Mr. LORNTSEN. It is a fact that the Columbia River is the only stream that the salmon protection is along the line of destruction. We have passed laws and laws time and time again for the protection of salmon. But there is never any protection at all. It is only protection for a few men so that they will be able to gobble up all the fish. That ought to be regulated.

I know the Federal Government has done that in Alaska or wherever they have any authority; they won't allow any fishing above tidewater. In fact, fishing above tidewater and stationary fishing appliances in the rivers has been abolished everywhere where they are doing anything for salmon protection. But not so on the Columbia River, because there is a few men up there, who are getting rich on the ruination of the industry, and are not going to give it up as long as they can make money, regardless of the rest. There is absolutely no reason why the Columbia River should not yield at least 600,000 cases of first-class salmon. They do not yield 300,000 now. It is an inferior grade, something that the canneries would not have looked at when I first came here on the river.

Then there is another thing the Federal Government has to do to help with the fisheries on the Columbia River. They are filling up the channels with all the barriers they can possibly put in, whether they are needed or not, and it would seem to me that they are looking out—they claim it is for navigation—but some of the obstructions there are put there, they haven't been a help to navigation, but they have destroyed thousands and thousands of dollars' worth for the fishermen. That is what it is doing. The Federal Government, or the War Department, went and planted three mines down in Pick Up Spit, the best fishing ground on the river. Then they could not get them up. It was just an experiment to see if they would stay. They stayed there so well that they couldn't get them up at all. And I am certain that $75,000 worth of damage has been done to the gill fishermen through the Government.

Then there is another rule that was placed to protect the gill-net fishermen. It is a part of the pilot laws that when they are trolling or fishing with any kind of a drag net they shall display certain lights. That ruling is good for such as mentioned in the law, but it is the worst thing that ever happened to the fishermen. You be out in a dark night in a little boat in the river and you have got two strong lights right up over your head and it blinds you. You can't see anything. And along comes a vessel and you can't tell whether you see the port light, you don't know whether that is the port light or whether it is a fisherman drifting there. And consequently the fisherman hasn't got time to get his net out of the way, and the vessel will run over it and destroy it. The law don't provide for it, it is a rule of the coastal department.

I have taken up the work, but they can't do anything. I took it up with Senator Lane and asked him to have it revised, a proviso inserted to exempt the gill-net boat from that, though the gill-net boat is not in the law, but it seems to me that they have got a move on foot to drive the individual fisherman from the river, so that the trappers and seiners can get the whole business. They are corporations. I do not think that is going to help solve the river problem in the State.

Then there is another thing that hampers us a whole lot. It is a lack of the enforcement of the law of the State. It says in Oregon that before you can fish you must have a license. Before you can get a license you must be a citizen, or declare your intention, and have lived in here a year in the State before you can get a license. But they don't care for that. All they want is the $5 license. That is all it seems they care for. Of course there is a whole lot, they have no legal right to fish, but they are there and taking away the bread and butter from the people that live in Oregon and Washington, the men that would help them to build up and keep the salmon industry. I think if the people of the State of Oregon and Washington would take a little. more interest in the fishery and see that it is carried on, we would be better off. But there are thousands and hundreds of thousands of dollars taken away. from the Columbia River to somewhere else. They have no right ·to·come here, those men have no right to come here.

I know this much, if we had the proper laws for the Columbia River, the protection of the Columbia River salmon, there would be no fishing above tide water; there would·be no stationary fishing appliances at all. If we got that it would be only five or six years until the Columbia River would yield double the amount of fish it is now. That is proven by the laws that was en: acted for the coast streams in 1901, and that shows conclusively what common sense laws and regulations will do.

In 1901 the law was enacted to take away the stationary fishing appliances and fishing above certain lines in the coast streams of Oregon, and the Columbia River was included in that. But during the juggling, and so on, the Columbia River was exempted after it was passed.

In 1901 the total catch of coast stream salmon was less than 700,000, and less than 3,000,000 pounds silver sides. The law was enacted in that session, and in February, in 1906, the salmon catch in the coast streams increased to 3,019,000 pounds silver sides. They couldn't say that this was the result of the hatcheries, although they are commencing the hatcheries too early to have the result. It was simply common-sense laws, and the salmons had an opportunity to go take care of themselves, and you can't beat nature. I know that they have some bastard breeds of salmon in the Columbia River now. They get in the hatchery and they mix them up regardless of whether good or what. That is one reason that we had such a poor salmon river last year, the poorest since I have been on the river.

Commissioner LENNON. Do you mean to say that the United States Fisheries Department breeds salmon that are not of the best quality?

Mr. LORNTSEN. Well——

Commissioner LENNON. You are a fisherman. I don't know. I want to understand what you say.

Mr. LORNTSEN. Certainly; if they take salmon in the early part of the season and mix them up it is going to be poor. What you want is to have the early salmon go up and take care of themselves. The late salmon don't go up very far up the river, and they spawn before they get up. Take the salmon in the Columbia River now, and they spawn, and they have never been used. Simply take last fall. I don't know how many hundred tons of fish was taken and just dumped overboard. They couldn't use them, but they had to kill them. If they had left that salmon alone it would have been different. But it was changed to so late, and they fished above the tidewater and with stationary appliances and traps and seines, because they catch that fish in clear water, and they cut down the fish in the spring when it is first class, and, of course, they have gill netters, when the fishing is best, they do that in muddy water. They cut that out for the protection of the salmon. That sounds very good. But you can't fish salmon in the Columbia River from March 1 to May ·1· And the result is that the salmon go up and that man gets them. Then they open the season to the 25th of August, when there should be no fish caught, the fish should be left alone. There should be no fishing on the Columbia River at· least after the 10th of August, there should be no fishing until in October. And then you would have some results.

I know this much, if you take the fishing and take good care of them like they have done in Alaska—where in 1907 they had a half pack. They went to Washington to lay the matter before Straus and Roosevelt, and when they found out the truth they closed up the fishing in that river entirely. Since that the fish have increased, but the packers was interested, somebody in Washington fighting it, and all they cared for ·was the present question, and never mind the future. But when the question was brought to Mr. Roosevelt, he said, "Gentlemen, are you the fishermen?" "Yes, sir." He says, "Do you want to protect the salmon for the coming generation, so that they can have salmon as well as yourselves?" "That is what we are after." He says, "I am with you," and he said it closed right there, and there never was any shortage of fish as long as they kept the Wood River and the other river closed: The Wood River is the principal place. Now, if the Government· hadn't closed up the Wood River to give the salmon a chance to get· to the spawning beds up the river, why shouldn't the Government close up the river heads and let the fish get up there to spawn and protect themselves. That is the thing the Columbia River Fishermen's Union are fighting for since they started in 1886, to protect the salmon, because we realized if there are no salmon to catch, we don't care if they are a dollar a pound, it wouldn't amount to anything to us. I guess that is about all.

Mr. THOMPSON. That is all.

Chairman WALSH. Any questions? That is all. This thing ought to be given very careful study by somebody on the commission idividually and then pass it up so that we can all consider it. If you could get a public sentiment behind your proposition, as it appears on its face, there should be no question about it.

Mr. LORNTSEN. In 1908 we had public opinion with us. We carried the measure to stop fishing by 26,000 majority, but from the governor down the whole line every official is against us. Even the attorney general had to go and ask the Federal court for an injunction to enforce the law in the State of Oregon. That is what we are up against. When the measure carried by 26,000 majority, and then the legislature went to work and repealed that law through the jugglery—well, next time—there is only one thing, if we can get the fishermen to see it and get the public to see it—they are getting educated along those lines in the State of Oregon—another time when we go before the people with the measure we are going to clean up if the legislature won't do it. It has to be done—either, one thing, they have to do that or we will have no more salmon, that is all.

Chairman WALSH. Thank you, Mr. Lorntsen.

Mr. LORNTSEN. You are welcome.

Chairman WALSH. Call your next.

Mr. THOMPSON. Mr. Banfield.

TESTIMONY OF MR. M. C. BANFIELD.

Mr. THOMPSON. Will you give us your name?

Mr. BANFIELD. M. C. Banfield.

Mr. THOMPSON. Your business address?

Mr. BANFIELD. 1401 Yam Building.

Mr. THOMPSON. And your business?

Mr. BANFIELD. Well, I am vice president of the employers' association. You know what business the vice president usually does—how much it amounts to. When they make a man vice president he is usually sidetracked, so that I guess I am out of work now really.

Mr. THOMPSON. Have you any other associations, Mr. Banfield?

Mr. BANFIELD. No, sir.

Mr. THOMPSON. Were you one of the organizers or the organizer of the Employers' Association of the Pacific Coast?

Mr. BANFIELD. I was.

Mr. THOMPSON. The employers' association——

Mr. BANFIELD. The Employers' Association of the Pacific Coast; I organized it.

Mr. THOMPSON. Will you tell us the inception of that organization, and the objects and purposes, and the reason it was formed?

Mr. BANFIELD. Yes, sir. It was organized for the protection of the industries of the Pacific coast—a clearing house, as it were, or a switchboard to notify quickly the industries along the coast of any one particular industry that might be attacked—any one or more that might be attacked by the enemies of labor and capital.

Mr. THOMPSON. Well, what was the attack that was expected and feared?

Mr. BANFIELD. How is that?

Mr. THOMPSON. Was there an attack that was expected?

Mr. BANFIELD. Well——

Mr. THOMPSON. Or was there any danger that caused you to make that organization—specific danger?

Mr. BANFIELD. Well, I will divide it in three classes: There is the employer, the employee, and the barnacle on the body public—constitutes all on earth. There is none left after you have the employer, the employee, and the barnacle on the body public—that is, the man who is a leech. Then, after you have those three there are none left. So that you can draw your own conclusions from where we expected the attack.

Commissioner O'CONNELL. I don't quite get that yet, Mr. Thompson. [Laughter.]

Chairman WALSH. Please be in perfect order.

Mr. THOMPSON. I say I rather assume the witness did not want to make it more specific. Do you wish to make that more specific, Mr. Banfield?

Mr. BANFIELD. It seems to me it is plain. I have divided it in three. There is the employer, there is the employee, there is the barnacle, the leech, the man who never works, who commonly is considered a bloodsucker. That is rather hard language; I didn't intend to use that, but you seem to insist on it. The Employers' Association of the Pacific Coast was organized for the protection of labor and capital. Now, you can draw your own conclusion from where we expected the attack.

Mr. THOMPSON. Well, I take it, it was from the bloodsucker.

Chairman WALSH. Please put that in plain terms, Mr. Banfield, if I may ask you to do it. Now, you say you did it, or it was designed to protect labor and capital.

Mr. BANFIELD. Labor and capital.

Chairman WALSH. The men who work in the industries and the men who own the industries. Now, just be plain; whom do you designate as "barnacles"? They are not the consuming public.

Mr. BANFIELD. I have named the two——

Chairman WALSH. Well, I know——

Mr. BANFIELD. The consuming public is the employee and the employer. Then, when you take two from three you must have what is left.

Chairman WALSH. Well, we might as well have it plain.

Mr. BANFIELD. That is as plain as I desire to make it. I have no names to call it. I would rather you gentlemen would call it.

Chairman WALSH. So far as I am concerned, it is impossible for me to do so. Is there a class of people—how do they earn their living?

Mr. BANFIELD. I think the question is unnecessary. I refuse to answer it, because every man that is here knows. It is superfluous.

Chairman WALSH. It is superfluous? Is there a class of people that live without working in any industry?

Mr. BANFIELD. I drew—I outlined three classes.

Chairman WALSH. Well now, then, do you put in that other class those people who have retired from business, perhaps, and have investments on which they live?

Mr. BANFIELD. Are they not the employers?

Chairman WALSH. Well, are they? I don't know. That is exactly it.

Mr. BANFIELD. Sometimes they are not.

Chairman WALSH. Well, are they?

Mr. BANFIELD. If they are not, they are in the class that I have just mentioned.

Chairman WALSH. Or are they the ones, that is, those that have been engaged in industry and have retired and are living upon investments, such as stocks and bonds and so on?

Mr. BANFIELD. I call those employers in the pure and simple sense of the word; they are employers.

Chairman WALSH. Whether they have inherited those investments or earned them?

Mr. BANFIELD. The man who has inherited those is pitiable. The man who earns them knows how he has got them.

Chairman WALSH. Is he a barnacle?

Mr. BANFIELD. Yes; I think the man who inherits those things becomes a barnacle.

Chairman WALSH. Of course, you would include in that all dishonest persons that live by dishonesty—thieves and pickpockets and burglars?

Mr. BANFIELD. I certainly would think they would come in that class.

Chairman WALSH. You would call them barnacles?

Mr. BANFIELD. Yes.

Chairman WALSH. Now, are there any other persons that live without industry except those that I have mentioned?

Mr. BANFIELD. There are some.

Chairman WALSH. Would you include doctors and lawyers?

Mr. BANFIELD. No; they are professional men.

Chairman WALSH. You would not include professional men?

Mr. BANFIELD. They are employees; they are always employed by some one.

Chairman WALSH. Now, then, I wish you would just designate right here any others than those which you have designated which might be included as barnacles.

Mr. BANFIELD. I don't aim to be on record as naming them. There are too many, in the first place, to enumerate to advantage.

Chairman WALSH. Well, could you classify such persons, outside of those that I have suggested to you?

Mr. BANFIELD. I am not classifying anybody. Everybody knows what this investigation is for and everybody knows what I have said—what it means.

Chairman WALSH. Well, I wish to assure you in all seriousness and honesty that I don't know what you mean, Mr. Banfield.

Mr. BANFIELD. You don't know who I mean when I speak of employers and employees and the barnacles on the body public?

Chairman WALSH. I don't, sir.

Mr. BANFIELD. Well, sir, that is a man who earns nothing, lives off of others, and tries to make his living by his jawbone, either in politics, either by working up schemes on somebody who works, making them believe that he can get more by following his cue—in a thousand ways; that is the barnacle on the body public.

Chairman WALSH. Then, you would include in your term "barnacles," the politician, the man who runs for office?

Mr. BANFIELD. Many of them. I will outline what I mean by politicians later on.

Chairman WALSH. Very good. Well, now, what else is there? You said politicians and——

Mr. BANFIELD. Grafters.

Commissioner COMMONS. Agitators?

Chairman WALSH. He didn't say that.

Mr. BANFIELD. No, sir; I didn't use the word " agitators."

Commissioner COMMONS. You didn't say agitators?

Mr. BANFIELD. No, sir; I didn't because when we come to that, we right here are agitators; we are agitating a question that should be left alone, interfering with individuality. I didn't use the word " agitators."

Chairman WALSH. Well, what else besides politicians would you like to use in the term " barnacle "?

Mr. BANFIELD. All those who get their living without energy.

Chairman WALSH. All those who get their living without energy?

Mr. BANFIELD. Yes, sir.

Chairman WALSH. Do you mean physical energy?

Mr. BANFIELD. Physical energy. And, as I said before, the employees include all professional men of every class, because they are always employed by somebody.

Chairman WALSH. Well, now, is there anyone left out of your designation as " barnacles," whatsoever?

Mr. BANFIELD. How do you mean?

Chairman WALSH. Any class of persons that are left out. I am trying to elicit now what you mean by " barnacles." You have added certain politicians which you say that you will describe later on.

Mr. BANFIELD. Yes; I will.

Chairman WALSH. Now, then, what other persons or classes of persons have you left out that you wish to include in the term " barnacle "?

Mr. BANFIELD. I don't wish to classify them. It seems to me that you are trying to make me say something, and I will tell you right now I am not going to say it.

Chairman WALSH. Well, I assure you——

Mr. BANFIELD. Because you know I am not going to tell you what you already know, because you know more about it than I do.

Chairman WALSH. Well, I assure you that I am not trying to make you say anything, Mr. Banfield, except to get your meaning of that term. Now, as I understood you, you say that the organization was begun to repel assaults on your industry.

Mr. BANFIELD. On labor and capital.

Chairman WALSH. Upon labor and capital by the enemy?

Mr. BANFIELD. Yes, sir.

Chairman WALSH. Now, you are asked to designate what you meant by that, and you have given it as the barnacle upon the body politic or body public?

Mr. BANFIELD. The body politic is all right.

Chairman WALSH. Yes. Now then, you have designated certain classes of people that you would term barnacles, and what I am trying to find out is if you include any person else in that class, and I wish to say that I don't know what you mean, and I haven't in mind any specific designation that I expect you to make.

Mr. BANFIELD. Well, Mr. Chairman, I am sorry that I do not or can not handle the English language better so that I could get you to understand what I mean.

Chairman WALSH. Have you expressed as well as you can now in the English language the classes that you mean to term "barnacles," or are there some that you do not wish to state?

Mr. BANFIELD. I do not wish to classify any, because I have made three classes, the employer, the employee, and the barnacle on the body public, that is the man who does not work. I don't class him. What I mean by that is the man who is trying to live without any energy—physical or mental—just getting a drag down, as it were, living off of the earnings of the man who is trying to make a living by the machine tool or any other line of life, the crowd that hangs onto him, instead of working themselves and making a living, hanging onto him on a percentage of his wages paid in for their keep.

Chairman WALSH. Would you include money lenders and interest——

Mr. BANFIELD. Of course, when you come to money lenders, they are necessary men in that line of business.

Chairman WALSH. You would not include those, then?

Mr. BANFIELD. I would not include bankers. They are all employers.

Chairman WALSH. None of the professions?

Mr. BANFIELD. None of the professions.

Chairman WALSH. Literature, poets, and the like?

Mr. BANFIELD. No, sir; they are all serving their place in the world. I am talking of the barnacle that lives off the earnings of others.

Chairman WALSH. Without physical or mental energy?

Mr. BANFIELD. Without physical or mental energy, only for graft; those are who I am talking about.

Chairman WALSH. You may proceed [addressing Mr. Thompson].

Mr. THOMPSON. Now, Mr. Banfield, will you kindly——

Chairman WALSH. Would you include dealers in real estate?

Mr. BANFIELD. Many times they pretty nearly fall into that list, though I do believe that they make some effort to live.

Chairman WALSH. Would you include holders of real estate for increasing values?

Mr. BANFIELD. I am not classifying. You might go into that until we never would get through. It seems to me what I have said should satisfy any man that wants the truth. Now, I can't give you any more than give you the whole truth. It is all a matter of opinion. Now, you can use yours and just use mine for what it is worth.

Chairman WALSH. One moment. I am trying to be specific, and I certainly would not say to you that I thought you were not trying to state this honestly, because I believe you are, Mr. Banfield.

Mr. BANFIELD. Yes.

Chairman WALSH. But when I say that this is a specific fact, as I understand it, that you created an organization to repel the enemy——

Mr. BANFIELD. Yes.

Chairman WALSH. A certain class; it is not going too far to ask you to specifically state who are included in that class.

Mr. BANFIELD. I did.

Chairman WALSH. What we are trying to do is to get at the facts. Are these organizations proper? Should they be made? Should the Government encourage them or discourage them? And to get at that fact we must certainly know the surroundings. That is not a matter of opinion.

Mr. BANFIELD. I stated that fact. I outlined in three classes——

Chairman WALSH. Will you excuse me just a minute? Prof. Commons says he would like to ask a question.

Mr. THOMPSON. Yes.

Commissioner COMMONS. I take it, Mr. Banfield, that what you mean is the officials of trade-unions?

Mr. BANFIELD. If you choose to name it so, sir, I think that you have come pretty close to it at the first guess.

Commissioner COMMONS. You mean business agents and those who receive salaries from trade-unions?

Mr. BANFIELD. I have said all on the matter I wish to say.

Commissioner COMMONS. Do you consider that they live by graft?

Mr. BANFIELD. I have said all on the matter I wish to say.

Commissioner Commons. Can you give us specific instances of where the officials of these unions have practiced graft?

Mr. Banfield. I never dealt with the agents of unions.

Commissioner Commons. Of your own knowledge, you don't know they have grafted?

Mr. Banfield. No, sir.

Commissioner Commons. Then, of your own knowledge you don't know that they are barnacles?

Mr. Banfield. I didn't call them barnacles.

Commissioner Commons. I thought you said that I guessed it right.

Mr. Banfield. No. [Laughter.]

Chairman Walsh. Ladies and gentlemen, let us have perfect order. Restrain your feelings.

Mr. Banfield. I said you made a pretty good guess. I didn't say you guessed it right. I said you made a pretty good guess. You got, probably, some of them.

Commissioner Commons. I am trying to get at the actual facts, in order to analyze and make up my mind upon the facts as you state them, as to whether they are barnacles and grafters.

Mr. Banfield. I think from the way you express yourself that you can make up your mind awfully quickly if you wish.

Commissioner Commons. Well, I will ask you this question: Do you feel that it is any advantage to labor in the different crafts to organize in order to raise wages and to shorten their hours?

Mr. Banfield. I think that organizations of all kinds, except for the investigation of possibly Government financial affairs and municipal, county, and State—I think commissions for that is sometimes good. But outside of that I think that all organizations, all commissions, and all interference with individual liberty is a failure.

Commissioner Commons. Then I take it that you think that the organization of labor is included under the head of the classes of organizations which are a failure?

Mr. Banfield. I mean to say this: That I came to this country when I was 19 years old—40 years ago. Wages to-day are not as good as they were then. At that time I went to work on the farm for $20 a month. The man who is a better man than me worked—with the name of Chris, who was a soldier in the Franco-Prussian War—he got $25 a month and his board and his horse kept. The man next better than he got $30 a month. And I will say right here that the average business man to-day, or the average banker to-day, is not as well off as the man who worked at that time for $30 a month—as that man saved his money—as that man would be had he done so—and if he does not save his money, the earning and the opportunities of earning can not help him.

But I mean to say that after all this carnage of blood and murder, or organizations one fighting the other, the conditions here to-day are not any better than they were 40 years ago, taking all things into consideration. The man who worked for the $30 a month and saved his money would be better off than the average banker, the average business man anywhere in the United States to-day. That is what I mean.

Commissioner Commons. Is this organization that you are vice president of and that you organized, is it created to destroy these organizations of labor?

Mr. Banfield. I am not vice president of any employers'——

Commissioner Commons. When you organized it, was that your intention?

Mr. Banfield. No, sir; never thought of organized labor—of destroying it—because organized labor I never had any quarrel with.

Commissioner Commons. Well, would you consider that any organization can get along without salaried officials?

Mr. Banfield. They had better.

Commissioner Commons. If you can drive out all the salaried officials out of the labor organizations, would you not destroy the organizations?

Mr. Banfield. I am not trying to drive them out. I have nothing to do with them—never have had.

Commissioner Commons. You are trying to abolish them, aren't you?

Mr. Banfield. No, sir; no, sir. I am trying to abolish nothing.

Commissioner Commons. Assuming that I am right and that these salaried officials are barnacles, you are trying to put the barnacles out of business?

Mr. BANFIELD. No, sir. That is impossible. They will always be with us, like poverty. But we are trying to do the best we can to live and get along without the interference of barnacles, as far as we can.

Commissioner COMMONS. Well, then, your idea is to regulate?

Mr. BANFIELD. No. We do not care anything about them. Just go along and tend to our business; but see when the time comes of an attack of the barnacles, do everything within our power to protect ourselves.

Commissioner COMMONS. That is all.

Chairman WALSH (addressing Commissioner Garretson). Do you want to ask him?

Commissioner GARRETSON. Yes; I would like to ask one question: You were an organizer for the employers' association?

Mr. BANFIELD. For the Employers' Association of the Pacific Coast.

Commissioner GARRETSON. For the Employers' Association of the Pacific Coast?

Mr. BANFIELD. Yes, sir.

Commissioner GARRETSON. Under salary?

Mr. BANFIELD. Yes, sir; employers' association.

Commissioner GARRETSON. Under salary?

Mr. BANFIELD. Never thought of it; and I think any man working for any organization that draws a salary is a coward.

Commissioner GARRETSON. If he is, does that make him hesitate to describe in general terms that which he attacks?

Mr. BANFIELD. How is that?

Commissioner GARRETSON. Oh, I was just wondering how that cowardice worked out, what is the difference. I want to ask you this: What is the difference between an organizer for an employers' association and an organizer for a labor union in their status?

Mr. BANFIELD. I don't catch your point.

Commissioner GARRETSON. If you were an organizer for an employers' association and I the organizer of a labor union, would we be in the same class?

Mr. BANFIELD. Didn't I tell you what the organization was organized for at the start?

Commissioner GARRETSON. You know what the labor union is organized for, I suppose?

Mr. BANFIELD. I have heard.

Commissioner GARRETSON. I have heard what employers' associations were for.

Mr. BANFIELD. It was heard along this coast with disastrous effect.

Commissioner GARRETSON. That isn't the question. What is the relative status of the two organizers?

Mr. BANFIELD. I told you when I started in what we were organized for, and that is all I wish to say about it. You can analyze it if you wish, I don't care. It has no effect on me.

Commissioner GARRETSON. I might be afraid to analyze it.

Mr. BANFIELD. I don't think you would be afraid.

Commissioner GARRETSON. You stated that your purpose was to protect labor and capital?

Mr. BANFIELD. Yes, sir.

Commissioner GARRETSON. Who did you hold your credentials from on behalf of labor?

Mr. BANFIELD. I made the statement of that in my first remark, and I will not discuss it or be drawn into argument over it. You know all about it, and anything I might say would not make it better or worse.

Commissioner GARRETSON. Then you are a self-elected representative of labor?

Mr. BANFIELD. Just as you feel about it.

Commissioner GARRETSON. Just as I would be a self-elected representative of the employers, if I claimed to represent them?

Mr. BANFIELD. Just as you wish to think about it.

Commissioner GARRETSON. That is all. Thank you.

Mr. THOMPSON. Mr. Banfield, will you kindly state, if you have anything further to state about the purposes of your organization, and if nothing, will you kindly state the activities carried on by the organization; what they have had to do with matters which are within the purview of your objects?

Mr. BANFIELD. Did everything in our power to keep labor employed; that covers it all.

Mr. THOMPSON. And in doing that did you encounter any strikes of employees, or boycotts of employees, or anything of that kind?

Mr. BANFIELD. No, sir; the federation of employers did not deal with those things.

Mr. THOMPSON. Is there anything you possibly, Mr. Banfield, would like to say in regard to those matters?

Mr. BANFIELD. No, sir; nothing whatever.

Mr. THOMPSON. Are there any opinions or constructive suggestions that you would like to make to this commission relating to or dealing with the relations of employer and employee?

Mr. BANFIELD. No, sir; I don't know that there is any opinion I might have that would do you any good. I have my own opinion as to those things. I don't believe that any man has a moral right to sign away to part of the public that which belongs to all the public, the right under him to make their living, under any circumstances, and I would not under any circumstances sign a contract to employ my labor through any channel unless a man held a gun over my head and compelled me to do it, and then I would sign it, but within 10 minutes I would get a gun and kill him and take it away from him before he got an opportunity to show it to anybody, because I would be so ashamed of it.

Mr. THOMPSON. Is there any other statement you would like to make to this commission?

Mr. BANFIELD. Well, there are some things here I thought I might speak of, but I don't know that it would do much good. You have here " General opinion regarding causes of industrial dissatisfaction." I might say something along that line.

Mr. THOMPSON. We would be pleased to have you, Mr. Banfield.

Mr. BANFIELD. Now, we don't have to go out of this room for one of the causes. I don't know how many people are here, but you can see the number as well as I can. Every one of us should be doing something instead of being here. This day and this hearing here caused the greatest disturbance, the greatest dissatisfaction in the city among certain classes, of anything that has happened. Every one of us here, if we were earning something to-day, it would be far better than this inquiry going back to the Government. If we could only get away and work and stop the agitation instead of having one organization bucking the other—in short, I will say that the old adage, " Prepare for war in time of peace," is a failure, an absolute failure, and has never been so exemplified before the world as it is to-day in the old country, and this organization of labor pitted against capital is brought about through the influence of those who don't care either for labor or capital. In many cases they are not taxpayers, and I maintain that all of this inquiry interferes with the individual liberties of men to get out and do their work as they please. It is all wrong—no good will come from it. In the first place, take the curbstone politician to-day; he gets out—I am speaking of our city and municipal affairs—he promises anything and everything before election, and after election he will deceive the men who voted for him; will turn his attention to those things which are wrong; he will rob the taxpayers that voted for him, and go into connivance for graft; sell his soul and body and birthright; we have them to-day. I met some walking on the streets of Portland in the last 30 years that I know were in politics when I came here, and are now down and out with one foot in the grave, but tottering along the streets—a sorry sight to look at. It is one of the things that is the cause of dissatisfaction here. The voter and workingman who votes for that fellow, he knows how he is treated and what becomes of his taxes—you can't keep him from it. He has to pay. He will sell what he has, but he knows. Then you take the higher-up politician, the man who keeps his ear to the ground for the number of votes regardless of the question at issue whether right or wrong. It is a serious matter. He is not figuring whether it is right or wrong. That fellow is causing a great deal of dissatisfaction—more than we think for. We expect something from those men when they go into the higher places of our political conditions, and we are deceived. That causes dissatisfaction.

Then you take the deck of cards that was stacked in Baltimore, with five aces and a joker, our worthy President being made the joker unknowingly and unwillingly. Those things cause a great deal of dissatisfaction. I spoke of the joker in the sundry civil bill. There was a clause put in that, wrapped up along with the appropriation which had to pass to run the Government, of which the President said when he signed it, " I can find no necessity for this either in theory or fact," but it was signed nevertheless. The Clayton bill is now pending; what he will do with that remains to be seen. But, gentlemen, I want to tell you when this game of cards is played out and those cards have to be thrown face up on the table, and the five aces and the joker turned up, there is going to be hell. Those things are causing dissatisfaction among the working people of this country. They all know it. I don't need to say what it was or what those clauses were; you all know—every one of us knows it was class legislation; dangerous to the country at large—everybody knows that. But that was the stack of cards—the deck of cards that was stacked up at Baltimore between that disreputable man Gompers and the man whom we have now——

Chairman WALSH. One minute. We have tried to conduct our investigation without allowing any person to characterize any other individual——

Mr. BANFIELD. I will withdraw that.

Chairman WALSH. This applies, of course, to everybody, you understand. I wouldn't allow Mr. Gompers to take the stand in New York and characterize you.

Mr. BANFIELD. His name was so publicly known I thought it wouldn't hurt him, but I will withdraw using Mr. Gompers's name.

Chairman WALSH. Any person's name.

Mr. BANFIELD. I will say those having charge of the affairs, of which he was managing at that time.

Mr. THOMPSON. I would just like to ask you one question.

Chairman WALSH. Maybe Mr. Banfield hadn't finished. Was there something else you wished to say?

Mr. BANFIELD. Well, I have gone along with that. I just want to say it seems to me what you are after is to find out the dissatisfaction with labor. Those are some of the things that are bringing it about, and my advice would be to cut it all out; give the men individual liberty, the same as I had when I was a boy myself. Don't tie him down to eight hours. If you want to make a law for women and children all right, God bless them, let them get along with as little work as possible. But keep the men at work; idle hands find mischief still for men who are out of work. I did not quote it exactly, but you know what I mean. The man who is out of work is in a bad way, and is liable to do things he should not do. That is what I wanted to get at.

Mr. THOMPSON. Just one question, Mr. Banfield: Viewing the breakdown of the civil government in the State of Michigan and the State of West Virginia, also viewing the breakdown of not only the civil government but the martial government in the State of Colorado and the United States had to go in and help keep the peace and order, and taking into consideration those things arose out of the conflict between employer and employee, in view of those things, would you say there was nothing for a commission like this to investigate in this relationship?

Mr. BANFIELD. I mean to say, as I said at first, organization was the cause of it, and they are all wrong. The employers' association is wrong; organizations of labor, so far as interfering with business, is wrong. And as I said before, prepare for war in time of peace, and you will have war sure, and that is what has brought that about in Colorado. Now, I worked in Colorado 35 years ago in the mines. We never heard anything about trouble there. Wages at that time were just the same as it is to-day. What good do you get out of it? What is it all for? But what is it that keeps up this organization? It is the politician who truckles to the man who says, "I can give you so many votes." I know a man to-day who is United States Senator and when he was sent for by an employer to come and see him on a matter, he did not have time and could not come—but a negro man, called Dollar Bill, wired him he had five votes he could get but it would cost something. He was down on the next train. That is what is the matter, and that is what brings up the fight between organized labor and capital.

Chairman WALSH. Did you communicate that crime you have just mentioned to the prosecuting attorney?

Mr. BANFIELD. I did not. I don't think it would have done any good, because the prosecuting authority at that time and the man who did it were very particular friends. In fact, that is one of so many things.

Chairman WALSH. Is that character of crime prevalent in the Northwest?

Mr. BANFIELD. All over the United States, but not as much as it used to be.

Chairman WALSH. Have you investigated this particular act you speak of between this negro and the United States Senator?

Mr. BANFIELD. It would not be necessary to investigate it. When you know a thing you can't find out by investigation.

Chairman WALSH. You absolutely have that fact within your knowledge?

Mr. BANFIELD. It was given to me by reliable authority. Just as though you, Mr. Walsh, were to say to me that so and so happened, I would believe it. Just so I can believe this.

Chairman WALSH. Anything else?

Mr. BANFIELD. I would like to speak along the lines, and I expect that is what you wanted me for, of labor troubles that was here in the teamsters' strike, and there has been——

Chairman WALSH. We would be very glad to have you speak of the local labor troubles.

Mr. BANFIELD. I happened to be for some reason selected to handle the draymen's strike here at that time. I believe I was selected for the simple reason—this happened in 1909—in 1901 I had a strike with my own teamsters on the east side of the river, and in fact on this side. We had at that time about 100 teams. A pamphlet was issued so worded—I am sorry to say I haven't got one I can give you, I would like to give you one—" This is not a strike or a question of wages or hours, but a question of principle, recognition of the union." They had formed a union, as I knew; I had met in the hall with them at different times, talked with them, smoked their cigars, had a glass of beer with them, and was glad they were organized. We had given them all the advice we could, and told them, I said, " Boys, stay with your organization for hours and wages, and you will conquer the world." That is the statement I made to them. I said, " The minute you try to interfere with a man's business there is where you are going wrong." Well, they started out with this strike, and we were all a happy family before the strike came about. I had men working for me for 10 or 15 years.

Chairman WALSH. Excuse me, Mr. Banfield, what is your line? I did not catch it.

Mr. BANFIELD. Fuel. The Banfield Fuel Co. at that time. I advanced him money, he and others who were working for me, to pay for their homes, and buy farms they were buying. When they made payments they would say, " Mr. Banfield, I am a little short this month, and I would like for you to advance me some now and take it out of next month's check." And I gave it to them. They were working for me at that time, and they had bought their homes and bought little farms, and they were paying it out. A little 10-acre tract up within a very few miles of Portland, and he had a farm that he bought at that time, and it has made him very well to do. I was glad to do those things. After this strike came about this man came into my office, his name was Miller, and I said, " Miller, are you going to leave me, too? " He was a Scandinavian, a fine fellow, and he broke down and cried. He said. " Mr. Banfield, I have to." I said, " Are you afraid, Miller, I will not treat you right? " I said, " Don't you know the number of horses that I have got and that you would be the last man that I would let out, that we have to have some one to take care of our horses even though we went out of business? " He said, " I know, Mr. Banfield, but I was held up last night until 2 o'clock in the morning, and they wouldn't let me go, and they told me if I didn't come and join them, that they would kill me."

Then I said, " Miller, you are going to leave? " He said, " Mr. Banfield, I have to." That man cried like a child. He was a man 40 years old. He knew all I had done for him, and that we would treat him all right if he had given it up, but he wasn't strong enough to stem the tide. He wasn't of my make-up, and possibly not the same as some of the rest of us here, because if he had, he wouldn't have been to see me that morning. He might have been somewhere else. That was one of the things. Well, the strike went on, and the depredations that were caused were numerous. They would take the back off the wagons, and cut the harness. We had a lot of night work at that time, and had about 40 teams working at night. And they would cut the harness, and then they would get out in front of the teams at night, on a dark night, and run a bed sheet on a pole in front of the horses, and whirl them around, turn them around, and snap off the tongue and all those things. In fact, the son of the chief of police here followed one team and wagon up the street and let the end gate out and let the load out onto the street, just couldn't help it. That was the spirit that was taught into the boy and pushed along. This wasn't the right thing to do. I finally got an injunction out, and we worked our way along until we had plenty of men to do our work without them. Then I wrote a letter and told him that I didn't want this agitation, that I could use more men, and I sent them a list of the names of the men that might come back to work; but all those that were causing depredations which I knew of I wouldn't employ any more. They settled the thing up and sent a dispatch to San Francisco that Banfield' had capitulated to the wishes of the union, and it came out in red lines.

We went along for a little while. Two months later, though, I met a man coming up on Sixth Street with one of our valuable teams. The team cost six or seven hundred dollars. He was driving down Sixth Street and on a heavy trot. They were too large horses to trot, and should not have been trotted. I whirled my buggy around and followed, for fear they might get away from him; went to the corner at the depot. I drove down and went around to the depot, and at one place I saw my team standing there without a driver and the lines without being tied, and I stood by the side of the team; they were all excited. Finally the driver came out and got on the wagon. I didn't say anything to him. I turned my buggy around and drove back to the office; phoned down to the yard, "When Jack comes in take his team from him and give him his time check"; that I didn't want him any more. So that was done. The next morning about 8 o'clock six of my teamsters came into the office. I said, "Well, boys, what's the matter?" They said, "We came to see you on a little matter." I said, "Where are your teams?" They said, "They are in the barn." I said, "What do you want to see me about?" "Well," he said, "we came up to see if you won't give Jack another chance—put him back to work again." I said, "Is it going to cost me $30?" which I figured my time worth— $5 apiece. I said, "Is it going to cost me $30 to know, or tell you whether I will put a man back or whether I have a right to discharge a man?" They said, "Well, this is orders from the union, Mr. Banfield—that we are to come to see you this morning to give Jack another chance." I said to my bookkeeper, "You give those men their time." I said, "Boys, I don't need you any more." I went into my private office and one came in and he said, "Mr. Banfield, this is all right with us, but I suppose you want what will happen in the morning?" I said, "I don't know." I said, "If I can't live without you, I can't live with you; that's a cinch." So I said, "I am ready, if needs be, to walk out of Portland on the ties along with you, barefooted, before I will ever, under any circumstances, deal with the labor organization again in any shape or form." This was only one or two of the conditions that came about. They drew the line while I was working under those union arrangements on making four loads of wood a day's work. Sometimes four loads would be a day's work. Some places we have to go 20 blocks with deliveries, and other places only 4. But they had made up their mind there in the union that four loads was a day's work, and that no more should be done. So one afternoon we found them out in the yard—four men sitting in a wagon playing cards—about half past 3 or 4 o'clock. We wanted to know what was the matter and they said they had done their day's work; that the union decided four loads a day was a day's work; that they had hauled their four loads. So I suppose you gentlemen know—any man who is in business would know—what happened to those fellows right then; that is, you can surmise what happened to the men, with a man of my temperament, can't you?

Chairman WALSH. Please, in a brief way, tell us what happened to the gentlemen.

Mr. BANFIELD. So that happened what you are thinking about.

Commissioner O'CONNELL. What was it?

Chairman WALSH. Just proceed. I really was thinking about something else.

Commissioner O'CONNELL. What did occur?

Mr. BANFIELD. They all got fired, naturally. I suppose that you who would handle men under the same circumstances, you wouldn't stand for men sitting in the wagon playing cards at half past 4 in the afternoon. And the only way to do was to let them go out and play cards. So those are many of the things. When you come down to the teamsters' strike here in 1909, the draymen came to the employers' association for assistance. I was president of the employers' association, and I called a meeting of the executive board and invited all of the draymen to lunch at the Commercial Club, to have this thing properly aired, and the questioning of the draymen was left almost to me. And I said, "Now, gentlemen, I want to know what your grievance is." He says, "We have been paying two seventy-five and they want $3, and we can't pay it." I said, "What else?" He said, "They have been sending us men, and we can't hire any men only through the union, and they will send us men who are hanging around

there, and sometimes they are no good ; and if we send them back we get a call over the phone that we have got to keep this fellow until we can get some one else who is better." And he said, " That condition has worn us out."
"Well, now," I said, "the employers' association will assist you in this strike just under these conditions: That you go out and hire your men, give them all they ask—$3 a day—and give them a week to come back. That is one of the conditions. And the other condition is this, that if you take it up and every one of you will relieve yourself from any responsibility from any conversation with anybody you have been dealing with, except the men involved, to me, I will not take the matter up or have anything to do with it where you interfere with that affair in any shape or form." And they were offered $3, and the men, many of them, phoned into the employers wishing to come back, and the employers told them that they were made guardians of their own safety, and they didn't want to come back under those conditions. There were many of them wanted to work, but couldn't come back on account of a fear, and we had a great deal of damage done at that time. Some of the union men were very active, and this strike proceeded because they were fearful of coming back, not because they didn't want to come back ; they were paid all they were asking, but there was a higher power somewhere that made them afraid to come back. So I immediately saw what we were up against, and I sent to get men to come in to take their places after I warned them and give them four days' notice that if they didn't take their teams at a certain hour, a certain day, others would take their places.

To make it short, their places were filled. Many of them were paid $3 a day, and I think the same wages are paid to-day. All the fight was over signing up for three years to employ all your men through our organization. That was the question at issue. The wages they asked they were paid. There was no question about hours. There was no question about overtime. All those things were agreed on. It came right down to having agreed to the right of recognition. The same thing as I was saying a while ago is all rot, one organization bucking the other. You are going to have trouble when you prepare for trouble. All this preparation because one or another is wrong. It is brought about by curbstone politicians, inquiries, higher-up politicians, that if our administrative government had a feeling of interest, that there was no class legislation, that it was all wrong and would not bend their knees to a promise that was made that never should have been made—now, those things, in my estimation, are what are disastrous and cause, as you say, this unrest, and, in fact, I don't believe the unrest, as far as——

Chairman WALSH. Say, please confine yourself to any other local disturbances locally. We were on that subject and we are trying to confine ourselves to it.

Mr. BANFIELD. The first strike, the draymen's strike——

Chairman WALSH. First, let me ask you, the draymen's strike came to an end by your employing outsiders, and you did not accede to the demands to recognize the union?

Mr. BANFIELD. There has never been a strike won in Portland by the union.

Chairman WALSH. So, as it was not won it is still going on?

Mr. BANFIELD. It is not going on.

Chairman WALSH. You said the men that were on a strike stopped ; the disturbance is at an end?

Mr. BANFIELD. Yes.

Chairman WALSH. Any other local disturbance you have in mind, Mr. Banfield?

Mr. BANFIELD. No local disturbance, I never paid much attention to. Of course, you will find the plumbers have some little trouble, but they settled it up among themselves and didn't call a strike. I mean a strike where the public——

Chairman WALSH. Yes. Have you detailed the only strikes that have existed here within the last year?

Mr. BANFIELD. Yes. There have not been any strikes here in the last year. The last strike was the teamsters', in 1909 ; none of my men went out. They all stayed at work. I had settled my affair in 1901. They went out and they never came back. And those that were working for me knew better than to try to get them.

Chairman WALSH. What was the date of the draymen's strike?

Mr. BANFIELD. 1909 ; mine was 1901.

Chairman WALSH. Anything else you wish to mention?

Mr. BANFIELD. I don't know that I could say any more.

Chairman WALSH. Very well; we thank you, Mr. Banfield. Call your next witness.

Mr. THOMPSON. Mr. Hunter.

TESTIMONY OF MR. L. D. HUNTER.

Mr. THOMPSON. Please give us your name.

Mr. HUNTER. L. D. Hunter.

Mr. THOMPSON. You need not stand up. You may sit down.

Mr. HUNTER. Oh.

Mr. THOMPSON. And your business address?

Mr. HUNTER. 107 Second Street. I am manager of the Pacific Stationery & Printing Co.

Mr. THOMPSON. Are you also secretary of the Portland Typothetæ?

Mr. HUNTER. Yes.

Mr. THOMPSON. How long have you been such secretary?

Mr. HUNTER. About a year.

Mr. THOMPSON. How long have you been engaged in the printing business here?

Mr. HUNTER. About 11 years—12 years.

Mr. THOMPSON. Can you tell us briefly, Mr. Hunter, the relations now existing between the printing and publishing companies and the printing trades unions?

Mr. HUNTER. Well, we are in harmony so far as I know. The typographical union, we have no trouble with the bookbinders' union, and the girls' bindery union, they have all been very peaceful. The only trouble we had was with the pressmen's union.

Mr. THOMPSON. Is there a strike on in that line of work now?

Mr. HUNTER. About nearly two years ago they were striking; they made an arbitrary demand which we could not accede to and run our business.

Mr. THOMPSON. What were the points of dispute?

Mr. HUNTER. Well, something along the line that Mr. Banfield explained; they demanded there should be a foreman to each two presses, and if there wasn't anything for the presses to do he could sit down and take it easy; along those lines, a very arbitrary rule.

Mr. THOMPSON. Can you recall them now specifically?

Mr. HUNTER. I had a copy of their rules they presented to us, I suppose about the size of this [indicating pamphlet] in small type, about 21 articles, I think it was, we were to follow.

Chairman WALSH. Excuse me, Mr. Hunter, what was the date of that?

Mr. HUNTER. Nearly two years ago, as near as I can remember. I haven't got the exact date.

Mr. THOMPSON. This is all, then, you can state specifically as to the points at issue?

Mr. HUNTER. They gave us until Monday morning to sign up with them, and go by these rules, what is called the pressmen's union. Now, the pressmen's union, what is called the pressmen's union, and the feeders' union, while they are separate they are allied in regard to strikes or anything of that kind. And of course the pressmen's union is the only thing we recognize as employing printers. But the feeders' union is made up of young boys and inexperienced help; that is, in a great sense. They went on a strike demanding an increase in wages, and also that we would accede to those rules, the shop rules is what they call them. And before they went on a strike they asked if we would not meet them, and we says, "No, we will not recognize you; we will meet the pressmen, but we will not meet the feeders." Finally we decided to meet them and confer with them. There was very little done at that meeting except we decided we could not run our shop and compete with outside work and accede to the demands. And we told them so. But they arbitrarily stated that next Monday morning—this was on Saturday—next Monday morning if we did not accede to their demands and rules they would go out on a strike. Knowing that they would we immediately wired Chicago and got all the men we wanted. We brought in two or three coaches of men and put them to work. And, of course, we had a great deal of trouble with the men. They were men picked up in Chicago, New York, and St. Louis, and we were very badly handicapped for competent help. We managed to get along. Business was very quiet, there was not very much work of any kind so far that is concerned, and we got along by exchanging men very nicely. But they done everything possible to interfere with our men. We had our men protected by guards. We had them collected in a hotel, and we fought the thing along for six months, and they done everything possible to get our men to quit. Finally they cooled down a little. Well, after they cooled down a little—some of the pressmen are nice fellows, we had nothing particular against them, and I believe some of them were employed—quite a number have been employed since at the same wages that they demanded.

And I might say that the label—the employing printers represented about 90 per cent of the output, and there was a demand that the union label be put on all their work. Of course, we can't have the label unless we employ union men in the pressroom. Some of these men have gone back to work—some of the old men—in fact, I think a majority of them are now employed—old union men are employed in the shop. Whether they are still members of the union I don't know. They claim they are not. But we don't raise that point; as long as they behave themselves and work we are satisfied.

Mr. THOMPSON. In picking up these men you needed to take the places of the strikers did you join or work with the National Typothetæ?

Mr. HUNTER. Yes; we did.

Mr. THOMPSON. You are the local branch of the national organization?

Mr. HUNTER. Yes.

Mr. THOMPSON. You have the same rules and same regulations governing you in the violations that they have?

Mr. HUNTER. No; we have no rules and regulations at all; just simply the employers' association, and we simply—we pay so much dues to have a fund to help one another out in case of trouble or anything, the same as anybody else would.

Mr. THOMPSON. Referring to the demand that you say the pressmen made of you——

Mr. HUNTER. Yes.

Mr. THOMPSON. Could you find those and file them with us, do you think?

Mr. HUNTER. Could I get them?

Mr. THOMPSON. Yes.

Mr. HUNTER. I doubt very much. You see, that happened nearly two years ago. I had a copy of them, but whether I have now or not I don't know.

Chairman WALSH. Were they published in the newspaper at the time?

Mr. HUNTER. I think it was—no; I don't believe it was, either. I don't think they were published in the paper.

Mr. THOMPSON. Has your association, or have you individually, as a printer, agreements and arrangements with the other organizations in the printing industry?

Mr. HUNTER. Well, we had with the typographical union. It is just simply verbal; it is an understanding. I don't think there is any written agreement with them.

Mr. THOMPSON. Well, are you speaking now of yourself or of the typothetæ?

Mr. HUNTER. The typothetæ has no agreement with any organization. It is just simply a little local organization.

Mr. THOMPSON. Speaking for the trades now, do you know whether there is among the printers—the master printers—generally arrangements and agreements, either written or verbal, with the printers, with the crafts in the printing industry?

Mr. HUNTER. No; we have not. We have not any written agreement or any understanding. It is just simply to this effect, that they specify what their wages shall be, and we consent to that and give them what wages they demand. I believe previous to that, about five years ago, they signed up agreements—the typographical union—but I don't think that is in effect any more.

Mr. THOMPSON. Do what might be called union wages and union hours exist in this city?

Mr. HUNTER. Absolutely. We work in our pressroom—we work just the same as we did before; we give them just the same wages. But the serious objection to what we had in the closed shop is we are only permitted to employ one apprentice. And I know in my shop when I employ an apprentice they would always put up a job on him so he would spoil some work or something, so as to get rid of him. So we could not get a young fellow that wanted to learn the trade from school. That was the serious objection to the unions, and also to the typographical union to-day.

Mr. THOMPSON. Have you got any comment that you would care to make on the question of the organization of employers and employees—as to whether, it is advisable or inadvisable?

Mr. HUNTER. I think if a union like the typographical union—we never had any trouble with them; they are always peaceful; they are always willing to meet us and talk things over and come to an agreement. The bookbinders' union is the same way; no trouble at all. We have no trouble. I believe now they have a strike in Tacoma with the typographical union. I don't know regarding what the causes are.

Chairman WALSH. Have you found your organization to be advantageous to the industry generally?

Mr. HUNTER. With the exception they don't allow only one apprentice to each four men. That is out of the question, to break in new men from out of school.

Chairman WALSH. Not the typothetæ; your organization.

Mr. HUNTER. Oh, beg pardon. I thought you said the other.

Chairman WALSH. Have you found it advantageous to your industry here locally to have a typothetæ.

Mr. HUNTER. Well, I can't say to that. I do not know what we could do against the union if we did not have.

Chairman WALSH. You believe you need an organization, and you find it advantageous to have one?

Mr. HUNTER. To that extent we do; yes.

Chairman WALSH. Have you found it likewise to be desirable to be affiliated with the National Typothetæ?

Mr. HUNTER. Of course, they are the controlling spirit, like any union.

Chairman WALSH. You find it well to be in touch with them?

Mr. HUNTER. We have not been in touch lately with the national organization, and I know very little with regard to that. We simply pay in dues, and that is about all it amounts to.

Chairman WALSH. Is there anything else you would like to say that might enlighten the commission on the general subject of having, if possible, more harmonious relations between employers and employees?

Mr. HUNTER. As far as we are concerned individually, I don't think it would be any more harmonious with regard to the employing printers with the typographical union and bookbinders.

Chairman WALSH. You find conditions at this time, then, in your industry satisfactory?

Mr. HUNTER. Satisfactory; we have no trouble with them.

Chairman WALSH. Mr. Garretson, would you like to ask a question?

Commissioner GARRETSON. You found the typothetæ useful to you in the strike by putting you in communication with people where you could reach these pressmen from Chicago, New York, and St. Louis?

Mr. HUNTER. We were not members at the time we had the first strike. We called on them, and we asked them if they would help us find men, and I think they did. We sent men back each to secure men.

Commissioner GARRETSON. They referred you to agents there in the different localities?

Mr. HUNTER. We hired through advertising in the papers.

Commissioner GARRETSON. That is all.

Chairman WALSH. That is all. Call your next witness.

Mr. THOMPSON. Mr. Howell. [No response.] Mr. Kroner.

TESTIMONY OF MR. ERNEST M. KRONER.

Mr. THOMPSON. Will you please give us your name?

Mr. KRONER. Ernest M. Kroner.

Mr. THOMPSON. And your business address?

Mr. KRONER. My business address is 623 Worcester Building, Portland.

Mr. THOMPSON. And your business?

Mr. KRONER. I am an architect.

Mr. THOMPSON. How long have you been engaged as an architect in Portland?

Mr. KRONER. I have had an independent office for perhaps 10 years.

Mr. THOMPSON. Are you acquainted with the relations existing between the building contractors in this city and the building trades unions?

Mr. KRONER. Fairly so; yes, sir.

Mr. THOMPSON. What is the status of that relationship?

, ‖ Mr. KRONER. At the present time and for some years immediately past the conditions of employment and the relations between the employers and employees have been very satisfactory. · There has been at times a small disagreement, and the building trade is hardly ever without some contention. But comparing the conditions at Portland with those in other port cities we might say we have been fairly free from any serious disagreements. We have had no strikes that led to any trouble, and we have had no disagreements that entailed in tying up of the entire industry—not in recent years.

Some 10 years ago I was engaged in construction work, not at that time running an architect's office, but I was at that time a member of the Master Builders' Association and carried on a considerable amount of construction work. And at that time we had a general strike of the carpenters, which, through the usual sympathetic strikes, involved practically the entire building industry. It also involved the sawmill employees and the planing mill employees. And yet, as long as I remember now, at that time, during the general disturbance of this trouble, there occurred comparatively few serious breaches of the peace.

Mr. THOMPSON. What would you say with reference to the condition in this city for the last two or three years?

Mr. KRONER. The city of Portland for the last several years, at least, has been fairly inactive, comparatively inactive in the building line. Of course it is the general tendency of labor organizations to withdraw those of their demands that are most objectionable during times of quiet seasons, and to increase and emphasize their demands through busier seasons; so that during the most recent years there has been comparatively little friction of any consequence.

Mr. THOMPSON. What were the main points involved in any troubles you have had here in the last two or three years?

Mr. KRONER. Well, I recall a disagreement between the stonecutters and the bricklayers concerning the setting of stone. The question was as to whether the bricklayers should be permitted to set stone in the wall after the stonecutter had dressed it, or whether the stonecutter should be entitled to do that. It involved, for a short time, the tying up of several buildings, if I remember correctly, and was finally settled between the unions.

Mr. THOMPSON. That was a jurisdictional trouble?

Mr. KRONER. That was a jurisdictional trouble, I think.

Mr. THOMPSON. How prevalent are such troubles in this city, if you know?

Mr. KRONER. Well, they form possibly a considerable percentage, maybe one-half of the things that come up to the surface. Many of those things are more or less unimportant and cause no general disturbance of the business, or I, personally, did not take any notice of them. We had an electricians' strike. We had a disturbance on some of the buildings here owing to the disagreements between the steel erecting firms and their employees. But they seemed to have, in the course of a little while, gradually played out. Of course we have on our streets placards boycotting different buildings here and there that are carrying on as a result of those disagreements, and we have them every day, but they don't affect the industry materially at the present time.

Mr. THOMPSON. As an architect, you are the agent of the owner, the building, contractor?

Mr. KRONER. The architect's position in connection with building erection is somewhat peculiar. The architect is certainly the agent of the owner, but he is also, to a certain extent, and must function in his capacity as an architect as an arbitrator between the contractor and the owner, and in that capacity he is supposed to help both; that is, I think, at least as far as his judgment in settling disputes is concerned.

Mr. THOMPSON. As an architect how do you view the proposition of the organization of building trades into unions?

Mr. KRONER. That enters, of course, into a very broad field of discussion. I view it, not only view it as an architect, but I view it as a citizen, and with your permission I will view it both ways, if my ideas are of any interest whatever. On the whole I will say that here in our city we find trades organizations have been moderately fair in their demands. As I stated before they accomplished, or have done, a considerable amount of detriment, but there has been no great deal of agitation to which employers and owners could reasonably object. Of course the object of every labor organization and every craftsmen's organization is to advance the compensation of the particular craft that they represent regardless of how that advancement, as a rule, regardless of how that advancement would affect the general public and even those who work with them, in and around them, other workmen in other classes, other crafts. And to the extent to which a labor organization is capable of control-. ling the entire field, to that extent, of course, their demands increase. ·

Now, where a labor organization has a fair percentage of its particular craft in its control and not all of it, it has tended, in my opinion, to establish the equilibrium between the disputes of the employer to ·get as much as possible for his work regardless of the expenditure for living, and it has. been generally the disposition of the workman to get all he could for his work. They have operated in. that particular condition to establish what you might call equitable conditions. When a labor organization completely controlled the field they did what might be expected of them, they overreached themselves, having completely monopolized their field, but in that case, as a rule, the condition has resolved itself into an effort, on the part of the employer, for the purpose of counteracting this result, and the final result, as a rule, was that the employer monopolized the field as much as he could, and the employee monopolized the field as much as he could against the public.

Mr. THOMPSON. What branch of the building industry is that in evidence in this city, if any?

Mr. KRONER. Well, right at the present time there is no labor union, as far as I know, that completely dominates the field, and if there were such a one employment is so scarce right now that this condition. wouldn't crop out, wouldn't come to the surface, but in the recent past——

Mr. THOMPSON. Go ahead.

Mr. KRONER. I was going to say in the recent past we have had an example, at least within the last 5 or 6 years we have had an example, of this final development, as I note it, of the organization of labor on one side and the complete organization and control of employers on the other side, in the case of the plumbing industry. The plumbers at that time practically controlled the plumbing labor market. That is to say, substantially every journeyman plumber was a member of the union, and at the time I speak of the building activities were quite brisk, so that they were in a position to enforce their demands, which came one upon the other and became quite burdensome. As a result of that the master plumbers' association, which was either then formed or came into more lively existence, was formed and the two combined under an agreement whereby the master plumbers' association agreed to employ none but union plumbers, and the journeymen plumbers' union agreed to work for no one but the master plumbers, and then they took the material men, the wholesalers, and agents of manufacturers into this combination, and they agreed to sell no merchandise in the plumbing line to anyone excepting this combination, and as a consequence of that they of course robbed the public—they outrageously overcharged the public; I will withdraw the term "robbed" and say they outrageously over-charged the public—and in order to keep this combination alive they had a system whereby every contracting plumber obligated himself when he took a contract to deposit with the treasurer of the master plumbers' association a certain fixed sum for every plumbing fixture which he installed, and this sum was accumulated and at certain intervals distributed between those of the master plumbers who did not have any contracts.

Mr. THOMPSON. What was that sum?

Mr. KRONER. It was related to me that at one time it was $5. and another time $2.50 per fixture, so that it would amount in the ordinary bathroom to about $25 under one plan and about half that much on the other plan. They set that amount aside, and that amount was given to the unsuccessful contracting master plumbers in order to prevent them from bucking the combination in the event that they didn't get any business. So that it appears to me. as an entirely disinterested person, not being associated either with the employers' association or a labor union or anyone else, and by my own appointment, somewhat representing the general public, that when a labor organization completely dominates the field and employers have banded themselves together and completely dominate their end of it, all those who are not inside of that combination are sufferers from this sort of thing. .

Mr. THOMPSON. Do you know whether this sum that was laid aside was added to the price of the contract?

Mr. KRONER. It was undoubtedly added to the price of the contract; it could come from nowhere else. In fact, my observation was that when· this combination finally went to pieces and finally dissolved under threat of prosecution by the Federal Government, or at least under fear of it, when it finally dissolved, the prices of plumbing goods and of plumbing installation and building material decreased instantly.

Mr. THOMPSON. Do you know whether or not the plumbers' union has anything to do with the granting of licenses in this city?

Mr. KRONER. To the extent to which they are able to influence the appointment of the plumbing inspector and officers in connection with the sanitary inspection of the city they seek to do so, and I from my knowledge and experience in a residence extending over 25 years, I don't think any man has ever been in the plumbing inspector's office or near it or any public office in the sanitary department of the city, as far as plumbing inspection is concerned, who has not been a member of the plumbers' union, and I think those who are in there now are, and I think that—I don't think there ever was an official in connection with that department who was not a member of that union, and I imagine when he is in there he is there as a member to a considerable extent, which is somewhat detrimental to public service.

Mr. THOMPSON. In what manner could he regulate or interfere with the granting of licenses? How would he operate?

Mr. KRONER. I have had complaints brought to me privately, conversationally, from men who undertook to establish themselves in business. That is not in the very recent past; that was some five or six years ago, perhaps about six years ago. They found it impossible to obtain a license because they were not members of the plumbers' union.

I have particularly one case in mind of a man who undertook for a considerable time to establish a business here and who was refused this license. It appears that there is a certain religious denomination, a certain church or sect, which has, or seems to have, an opposition or objection to its members belonging to a labor union, and this person was a member of this church and entirely opposed to joining a union, and he applied for a considerable time for a license to do business in Portland, and didn't get it. There were several others, and the charge was made by them to me in conversation that the reason why they were unable to obtain licenses to do business and pass the examination that was presented to them was because they were not members of the union.

Commissioner COMMONS. Are there both journeymen licenses and master's licenses?

Mr. KRONER. Yes, sir.

Mr. THOMPSON. Is there much work produced here in shops—building material, for instance?

Mr. KRONER. I beg pardon.

Mr. THOMPSON. Is there much building material of any kind or character produced in the shops here?

Mr. KRONER. No, sir—the plumbing line, you mean?

Mr. THOMPSON. Or any line. Carpenter work, for instance?

Mr. KRONER. In the building material, of course we have very large and extensive saw-mill industries that produce not only all the lumber that we require but also for export.

We have also important planing-mill industries that produce sash and doors and things of that kind, all that we use locally.

Mr. THOMPSON. What percentage of the material that is used here would you call open-shop material?

Mr. KRONER. So far as I know at the present time, the saw mills and the planing mills and these sand and gravel docks that form the material portion of the building material here, are operating under the open-shop principle without discriminating against any employees on account of their affiliation or otherwise with the unions.

Mr. THOMPSON. But the brickyards are different?

Mr. KRONER. The brickyards, I think, are practically operating on the same principle. I forgot to mention those; yes.

Mr. THOMPSON. Then, would you say that practically all of the building material here is open-shop material?

Mr. KRONER. I think so.

Mr. THOMPSON. In regard to the work of the union in the erection of buildings, has there been any effort to restrict the output, as far as you know?

Mr. KRONER. Well, you refer, I imagine, to the idea that a workman makes an effort to not exceed a certain amount of work in a given time.

Mr. THOMPSON. No. I refer more particularly to a general agreement. I am not talking about the individual, but a general understanding or intention on the part of the members of any of the building trades to limit output?

Mr. KRONER. At the present time conditions of labor in the building trades are such that anyone holding a position for a job on a building in the capacity of a mechanic is pretty apt to undertake to hold it by rendering a good day's work for his pay. I would say this, that that condition shifts as employment becomes more frequent, and there is a disposition on the part of building mechanics, as soon as they feel secure in their work, to not make themselves unpopular among their fellows by doing any more work than anyone else does. The general tendency of that would be to depress efficiency in the entire crew.

Mr. THOMPSON. Well, is that your feeling about it?

Mr. KRONER. That is my observation that extends over some years of personal knowledge of the subject.

Mr. THOMPSON. Are you acquainted with the wages that are paid in open shops? How do they compare with wages paid to the union workers, bricklayers and carpenters?

Mr. KRONER. There is at the present time practically no difference in erecting work, so far as wages are concerned, between the carpenter that works as a union man and one that works as a nonunion man. The fact is the question has not been disturbed very much, and the great majority of the men employed at erecting work in buildings, as I meet them, are union men. But in the very recent past they have not pressed the idea of refusing to work with a nonunion man, which they invariably do when work becomes abundant.

Mr. THOMPSON. Are there any firms, I mean contracting firms, that have a different scale of hours and a different wage from the union scale of hours and wages in this city?

Mr. KRONER. The smaller contractors, those that employ two or three or four men, a half a dozen or such a matter, and work in the lighter construction, possibly vary considerably in the wages that they pay at the present time. But it appears to me that the larger construction work is carried on almost exclusively on the scale that is known here and generally agreed upon as the union scale of wages.

Mr. THOMPSON. Were you here yesterday?

Mr. KRONER. I was not.

Mr. THOMPSON. Anything further you would like to say to the commission?

Mr. KRONER. Why, I thought that I would suggest to the gentlemen of this commission something on the subject that has been brought up here this morning, and that is the effort on the part of labor unions to prevent the employment of apprentices, and to practically destroy the apprentice system. I have felt for many years, and as I noticed the result of this system, I am becoming more confirmed that the trades-unions of the United States are committing a grave mistake and are working seriously to the detriment of this country in undertaking to prevent the youth of the country from learning a useful and gainful occupation. I place that as a charge against the trade-unions, perhaps the most aggravated and serious one that I can think of. There are many people that object to unions on other ground. But my principal objection to the trade-union, one that I think goes deeper to the prosperity and perhaps in a sense goes deeper to the unrest in this country, is the fact that we have lost for some years now entirely the system of apprenticeship that used to be in vogue, and that used to prepare the young men of this country for their life work.

That has not been the fault of the labor unions, because that has been the condition of the shifting of the methods of construction to some extent. But from their own selfish standpoint the crafts trade-union has invariably, so far as my observation goes, used every effort to prevent the employment of young men in the capacity of apprentices. And I hold and will suggest to you gentlemen that that is a grievous injustice to the young men that want to learn these trades. I remember——

Commissioner O'CONNELL. Would you have that absolute and unlimited; leave it entirely in the judgment of the employer how it should operate?

Mr. KRONER. I certainly believe that any young man in these United States is entitled, if he has the ambition to be so, to learn the trade of a shoemaker, or a plumber, or a plasterer, or a machinist without the interference of any man or any combination of men. I think when they undertake to do that they trespass upon a right that has never been denied to any man in any civilized country. And a denial of that right is a denial that is as barbarous as anything that is charged against the tyrranical Governments of Europe; that is as barbarous as anything that has been in the past years.

ʃ Commissioner LENNON. Do you know——

Commissioner O'CONNELL. Just a minute, Brother Lennon, excuse me. Would you have any protection thrown around the boy at all in the way of employer giving him proper opportunities and facilities to learn the trade?

Mr. KRONER. I certainly believe that the employer's duty should be to have certain supervision and to charge himself to some extent with the responsibility of turning out a mechanic if he took an apprentice.

Commissioner O'CONNELL. Who would be the judge of that sort of thing, supposing the employer entered purely into the running of an institution of apprentices, how would they be taught?

Mr. KRONER. I don't think the employer could operate any plant with apprentices. I don't see how he could.

Commissioner O'CONNELL. You may not think it, but it is being done.

Mr. KRONER. I know what every employer's experience has been, and my own has been, and I have employed a fairly good-sized number of men at times, as much as 30 or 40—that the most thoroughly trained man is the one that last leaves the job when work gets slack. I think you gentlemen will find that that has been generally the experience of men employing help.

Commissioner O'CONNELL. Don't you think that men, tradesmen, ought to be in a way capable of judging to some extent, at least in a small degree, as you can imagine, as to the number of people that ought to go into a trade, so that they may have an opporunity to support themselves after they learn the **trade?**

Mr. KRONER. They certainly should have the right to judge all they want to. But standing upon my own ground, if I was a boy 16 years of age, and I wanted to be a machinist, I should assert that right to be a machinist here in this country against any declaration of any labor union or anybody to keep me from it.

I can't see any moral ground upon which the union can take that stand. If the men who finally become the journeymen in that particular line are too numerous, they must certainly seek other fields of employment. They do now. But to prevent any person from acquiring a proficiency along such lines as he feels most qualified, is, in my opinion, nothing short of criminal.

When I first came to these United States something like 30 years ago, the people of this country were the admiration and the astonishment of the world, owing to the uncanny ingenuity that they possed in mechanical matters. All over Europe you heard of the Yankees being the most inventive and the most clever mechanics that had ever been produced. Every little device that was known in Europe was known as a Yankee trick. And I will tell you, gentlemen, the people of America have lost that leadership to-day.

Commissioner LENNON. Is that corroborated by the records of the patent offices in Germany and the United States and Great Britain?

Mr. KRONER. I don't think, sir, that the records of the patent offices would be any evidence as to whether or not the people are good mechanics or bad. They might keep on inventing, but they don't now hold the leadership in important inventions that they held 20 years ago.

Commissioner O'CONNELL. Were they indenting apprentices 30 years ago when you came to this country, as they are now?

Mr. KRONER. The apprentices 30 years ago had not been completely obliterated. There were 30 years ago shops in which apprentices were employed and regularly installed as apprentices with a regular term of service. I served such a term as that 25 years ago myself, and that was the common practice around that part of the United States.

Commissioner O'CONNELL. Have you any idea as to the number of apprentices that were employed 30 years ago, and the number of mechanics, as compared to now?

Mr. KRONER. I can only say to you that I learned the sheet metal worker's trade in a shop that had somewhere between—they were migratory birds at that time, and they came and went.

Commissioner O'CONNELL. They haven't got over it yet.

Mr. KRONER. But, striking an average. I would say they employed on an average possibly six journeymen workmen. They had two apprentices and one who might be called and was pretty well on as an apprentice—they had on an average probably two in that line of trade, two apprentices to four workmen. But they refused none an opportunity to learn the business. The journeymen did not, and the omployers did not refuse anyone an opportunity.

There was no effort at that time, so far as I know, to prevent any person from entering or from becoming either a blacksmith or a tinsmith——

Commissioner O'Connell. What I want to get is, have you any idea as to the time 30 years ago, comparing the number of apprentice boys that were learning the trades in the shops at that time as compared to the number now being taught, as, for instance, learning the machinist's trade. I learned the machinist's trade 30 years ago in a shop where there were more than 30 machinists, and I was the only apprentice boy in the shop. They would not have more than one or two boys. Can you show me a machine shop to-day with 50 machinists, that there are not at least 10 or 15?

Mr. Kroner. I don't think there are that many. I think that right here in Portland you will not find more than one apprentice to five or six machinists. The plasterers' union has confined apprentices to one to every six mechanics. And every labor-union in town has a schedule of apprentices that they will permit to work in connection with workmen. But I am not going to say to you gentlemen that these men should not use their influence to some extent in preventing any one trade from being overcrowded with mechanics. But I do say that they have no right to shut the gate of opportunity on the man that wants to learn that business. They might shut out the best mechanic.

Commissioner O'Connell. Do you believe there should be any investigation at all as to the method of putting the boy on probation, to ascertain whether he should be a machinist or a lawyer or something else?

Mr. Kroner. I think that would be the boy's and his parents' business to find out.

Commissioner O'Connell. It ought to be let run wild, as it were?

Mr. Kroner. I don't think that anyone at all under our present conditions, social and political, should undertake to dictate the career of any boy that has an ambition to learn a trade. If he is not fit for it, he will probably drop out in the end and will fill up the great gap of laborers that is constantly being recruited from the population. But I do say that we can't prevent the individual man from drifting where he belongs, and we should not shut the gate or shut the door to the man the believes he is fit and refuse him an opportunity.

Commissioner O'Connell. Have the architects got an association in this city, an organization of any character?

Mr. Kroner. Yes, sir.

Commissioner O'Connell. You are a member of it?

Mr. Kroner. No, sir.

Commissioner O'Connell. I might ask, why not?

Mr. Kroner. Why, I have never seen fit to associate myself with them. It is probably temperamental with me to go it alone. I do not particularly have any objection to their association, any more than I prefer to be entirely unhampered to carry out my ideas and do in my business and my office as I please.

Commissioner O'Connell. Do you find that the organization of the architects in any way interferes with your business?

Mr. Kroner. None at all. None in the least.

Commissioner O'Connell. Hampers you in any way?

Mr. Kroner. Not in the least. If anything, I think they are a help to me. If there was any occasion presented itself, I think they would assist me.

Commissioner O'Connell. Is there any effort on the part of the architects in Portland to prevent the architects from outside of Portland coming in and getting business here?

Mr. Kroner. There never was——

Commissioner O'Connell. Is there any jealousy about that?

Mr. Kroner. There is not the slightest feeling of that kind, so far as I am aware, among the architects. They not only help each other, as a rule, in professional matters, but they maintain at their expense a school for the teaching of young draftsmen right here at the present time in this city. And architects whose business is worth a great deal of money and whose time is very valuable, will be very often seen spending that time showing some young draftsman something that he ought to know, from the sheer feeling of good-fellowship and a desire to give the young man an opportunity to advance in that particular line of work. And that is the feeling, I think, that ought to prevail everywhere.

Commissioner O'Connell. There are a number of organizations of labor that are conducting most successful apprentice schools.

Mr. KRONER. I wish to give them full credit for that. I don't wish you gentlemen to understand that I have any antagonism against the labor unions on the whole, any more than there are certain things about which I am very decided, possibly, and I thought this was a good occasion to present my views.

Commissioner O'CONNELL. You mentioned the fact of the combination between the plumbers and the supply men, and so on, that it did keep prices up, but after the decision of the courts against that combination that prices were lower. Do you think that the plumbing supply people have entirely eliminated their efforts to maintain that restriction?

Mr. KRONER. At the present time there is no evidence that I can see of any combination among them.

Commissioner O'CONNELL. Could I, if I were a citizen of Portland, walk into any plumbing supply house in Portland and buy a complete set of plumbing supplies for my house?

Mr. KRONER. You could not buy anything unless you were a plumber.

Commissioner O'CONNELL. Isn't that restriction, then?

Mr. KRONER. Well, I suppose that it is fair to discriminate between a wholesale house refusing to sell its goods at retail. You will find the same condition if you go to some wholesale paper house or some wholesale shoe house. If you go in there in a wholesale shoe house and ask them for a pair of shoes, they will tell you they are not selling shoes at retail. You can buy anything you wish in any plumbing shop, or anything except a strictly wholesale house. And they have, all that I know about, the same regulations. And I haven't in my practice recently discovered any combination.

Commissioner GARRETSON. Do you believe that the prosecution of the Bath Tub Trust in Pittsburgh, and the Master Plumbers' Association of Sioux City, Iowa, has exercised any influence to make them suppress evidence of it elsewhere?

Mr. KRONER. That would undoubtedly have a tendency to make them very careful. The prosecution of the Furniture Trust here in Portland was the cause of the dissolution of this plumbing combination. That is how they came to quit. When they saw that, then they quit.

Commissioner GARRETSON. You are familiar with both cases I referred to?

Mr. KRONER. Somewhat, yes. Yes; in a general way.

Commissioner GARRETSON. In this limitation of apprentices, Mr. Kroner, bear in mind in my craft every journeyman has two apprentices and usually is fighting for three. So I am not under that ban. But isn't it true that the limitation of apprentices has been brought about more largely by the employer in the specialization of lines, which unfitted his shop for teaching a trade, than by any other influence?

Mr. KRONER. I would answer that this way: That what you mention has been a contributing cause; but just to what extent it has contributed would be largely a matter of opinion based upon the opportunities of observation.

Now, here in this western country many young men can't and won't enter employment of this character that I speak of as apprentices because they are afraid of being nagged. That is the truth. And it is also true that the labor unions look with considerable displeasure upon the efforts on the part of, for instance, the public schools to institute manual training and the Y. M. C. A. to teach trades. They are not in favor of those things. Their influence and very attitude toward it is hostile. Now, that is so, generally speaking, however much individuals may look upon the condition.

Commissioner GARRETSON. Isn't that a localism?

Mr. KRONER. I could only speak of that as being local, for I have no information as to how that thing is elsewhere.

Commissioner GARRETSON. Have you ever made any investigation to know what the attitude of the international is toward vocational schools?

Mr. KRONER. Which international?

Commissioner GARRETSON. The internationals of the various shop trades, the machinists, for instance.

Mr. KRONER. No; that I don't know.

Commissioner GARRETSON. Well——

Mr. KRONER. But, of course, what I say, I wish to add just one word. What I say in connection with these matters must be largely taken as relating to the building trades, as I don't have much but a very vague information in the others.

Commissioner GARRETSON. And your experience and knowledge of them here?

Mr. KRONER. Mostly the building trades. Well, I would say that I have years ago. Of course, what I speak of is confined, or should be confiend, largely to the building trades, but, then, I think these conditions as I state here will maintain pretty generally in the building trades. And going outside of the field of the building trades, I would want to be understood as having no special information that is valuable, perhaps, because I am not familiar enough. * .

Commissioner GARRETSON. I would like to ask you in regard to one other matter. Speaking of the tendency when work was plentiful of the man not to do more than his associate was doing, and this tendency to lower the day's output, have you ever noticed that tendency any more strongly with union men than with nonunion men under exactly the same conditions? »

Mr. KRONER. Under those conditions that you mention, those conditions that you mention are only noticeable in such times as when business is quite brisk.

Commissioner GARRETSON. Yes.

Mr. KRONER. And in those times the union man and the nonunion man do not usually mix. That is, the union makes it an invariable rule to not work on any building with a nonunion man, and it is difficult to gain any comparative idea as to how the two together work. However, where nonunion men will work on one building exclusively——

Commissioner GARRETSON. That is what I mean.

Mr. KRONER. And union men will work on another building exclusively, at the same time and under the same conditions, it is probably fair to say that the nonunion man will be less influenced by that feeling than the union man will.

Commissioner GARRETSON. Does that impulse come from humanism or from organization?

Mr. KRONER. The impulse, I imagine, comes from this fact: That the union men meet from time to time, they hold each other steadfast in what are considered their ideas and what is proper for the advance of their conditions, while the other men scatter around and have no meetings. I think to a certain extent there have been times, it must be, I think, evident to every person that there have been times when unions to a certain extent controlled their men by fear, and while a man might like to build up a few more brick in the wall than the others, he hates to do that for fear of being marked out as undesirable from the union standpoint, if you please. And I think that influence is largely noticeable when the times are good.

Chairman WALSH. The commission will now stand adjourned until 2 o'clock this afternoon. Is there something else you wish?

Mr. THOMPSON. Yes.

Chairman WALSH (addressing the witness). Please resume the stand at 2 o'clock.

(Whereupon, at 12.30 p. m., on this, Friday, the 21st day of August, 1914, an adjournment was taken until 2 o'clock p. m. of the same day.)

AFTER RECESS—2 P. M.

Met pursuant to adjournment. Present as before.

Chairman WALSH. You may proceed now, Mr. Thompson.

Mr. THOMPSON. Rev. Father O'Hara.

Chairman WALSH. One minute. We were not through quite with Mr. Kroner. Commissioner Lennon wants to ask you a few questions.

TESTIMONY OF MR. ERNEST KRONER—Continued.

Commissioner LENNON. Are you acquainted with the limitation of apprentices fixed by the general constitution of the building trades?

Mr. KRONER. You mean the constitution of——

Commissioner LENNON. The carpenters' brotherhood.

Mr. KRONER. Of the National Association?

Commissioner LENNON. Yes.

Mr. KRONER. I am not. .

Commissioner LENNON. Are you aware that in the building trades as well as others that the apprenticeship rules and limitations set by the unions is very rarely reached by the employers? ·

Mr. KRONER. You mean that the limitation that the building trades have set upon apprentices——

Commissioner LENNON. Yes, sir.

Mr. KRONER. Is not used up by the employer?

Commissioner LENNON. That is what I mean—not used up by the employer.

. Mr. KRONER. Well, yes, sir; that may be the case in some instances. It is because the union won't permit the apprentices around them.

. Commissioner LENNON. Oh, no; not where they allow it—not where their law permits it.

Mr. KRONER. My observation is that they won't have them around on the building; they won't take an interest in them and won't teach them; they won't have them around. They make it disagreeable for the young men that haven't fully learned the trade, and as a consequence of that the young man doesn't see any incentive to undertake to work around a building without any instruction. In other words, I have been some 20 years working around buildings as a mechanic, contractor, and architect; I don't remember of an instance where about the building the mechanics have taken it upon themselves to teach or foster or to make easy the work of the apprentice. That feeling is so universal I don't remember at the present time of a single instance where that rule did not maintain.

Commissioner LENNON. The evidence submitted to the commission at various times, while much of it is on the line of yours, at the same time the testimony as given very clearly indicates that the limitation permitted by the unions is not used up. Have you ever investigated as to whether it is true?

Mr. KRONER. I know this—I know that one plumbing contractor, a master plumbing contractor, told me that the union refused him the privilege of employing ■is own son as an apprentice in his own shop. I know that frequently in the past complaints in a conversational have been made to me that owing to the unfriendly attitude of the men it was impossible to keep the young men employed around the building.

Commissioner LENNON. Have you any sons?

Mr. KRONER. I have.

Commissioner LENNON. Are they going to be metal workers?

Mr. KRONER. No. I have one son—he is an engineer—and the other one is too little to know what he is going to do.

Commissioner LENNON. Your sons are like mine; they want to follow some other business besides that of their father. You mentioned regarding the Y. M. C. A. and its manual-training trade school work. As a mechanic, do you know of any Y. M. C. A. institutions in this country that efficiently teach a trade?

Mr. KRONER. I would say that the rudiments of carpentry and of several other branches are efficiently taught in the Portland trade school, and I would say that the preliminary instruction that the young men get in the Y. M. C. A. here and in some others is excellent as far as it goes. Necessarily that degree of perfection that a mechanic obtains after years of practice at his trade can not be expected from any school.

Commissioner LENNON. Well, in what capacity are such boys usually employed after leaving the Y. M. C. A., as handy men or mechanics, or what kind of employment?

Mr. KRONER. That would depend upon some conditions of the trade. If there was a lack of mechanics they are generally able to hold down a job as a mechanic. I have had young men working for me who came out of these schools who did men's work and got men's wages.

Commissioner LENNON. That is they could use a saw and hatchet?

Mr. KRONER. Well, they have very often a better understanding of the science of framing or of the science of trigonometry or geometry as applied to carpenter work and framing and joining than some more experienced workers who have not had the scientific principles. They have in a great measure, in a great majority of the cases, they are picked-up men; that is to say men who never had any apprenticeship. They have never learned the trade, but they have merely worked at it until they have achieved a certain degree of proficiency, the degree of proficiency depending upon the natural aptitude of picking up things from the men as they see them work.

Commissioner LENNON. Is that true of mechanics or to the better class that are on the building?

Mr. KRONER. That is true, I should say, of 60 per cent of the mechanics that do the framing and carpenter work in general construction. It is true of 90 per cent of the men that do the woodwork on reinforced concrete and on similar construction. It is true of 95 per cent of the painters. It is true of 60 or 70 per cent of the plasterers, and it is true of anywhere from 40 to 60 per cent of the bricklayers, according to the way I would size them up in my experience of handling these men.

Commissioner LENNON. Well, the apprentice system—that is, as it was originally known—having disappeared, is it not usually the case that mechanics are developed from working as helpers and assistants, as a kind of apprenticeship, and not bound for a number of years and all that kind of thing, but they get the experience through working with finished mechanics?

Mr. KRONER. Yes; that is the way the men learn their trade now, generally speaking. Through that system he lacks that training that he should have to qualify him to become a mechanic. In other words, he does not acquire the science of his business, but he learns the bad traits, the tricks of the trade, as well as the good ones. And he copies from the man he thinks is better than he is, and he copies his methods.

Commissioner LENNON. Do architects do that, too?

Mr. KRONER. Undoubtedly; I have no excuse for the architects. I think they ought to confess to them, if they do that sort of thing.

Commissioner LENNON. That is all.

Chairman WALSH. Any other questions?

Commissioner COMMONS. I want to ask a question. Is it not your idea that in the way in which a modern building is built it is not possible, in the way in which a modern building is rushed up, for a mechanic to give very much instruction or attention to apprentices?

Mr. KRONER. Well, I should say that if the attitude in a general way of the mechanics, all of them, about the building was friendly and helpful toward the men that come as apprentices I am sure that only in the rarest cases would an employer object to such an amount of time as might be taken up by the finished mechanic in pointing out things to one who is working as an apprentice. It is true that every system of training by workmen of apprentices would have to be done jointly by friendly cooperation of the employer and the employee.

Commissioner COMMONS. You don't know of any agreements where they have agreed jointly to train apprentices?

Mr. KRONER. In the building trades we have no such agreements. I don't happen to know of anything of that kind having been done.

Commissioner COMMONS. Nor any arrangement for instruction outside of the actual work on the building?

Mr. KRONER. Oh, yes. The employers have been taken here in this city, for instance, an interest in the trade schools, and as an association the employers as well as the architects and some other citizens in all walks of life who are interested in this question have promoted the interests of our State school, the Oregon Agricultural College, which teaches much of the preliminary scientific work that goes to make up a mechanic. But all these things here have been in a sort of unfinished way. The necessity for some work of that kind exists. No one has taken a firm hold of it, and I think the labor unions could do more, perhaps, with the present state of public sentiment, and the friendly state of public sentiment that exists here, generally speaking, to find a solution and assist in a solution of that question than any other one body of public men or any other one class of men.

Commissioner COMMONS. How is this local trade school that you speak of financed?

Mr. KRONER. It is a part of the public-school system. It is under the direction of the public-school board, and it is strictly a public school, a branch of the public education.

Commissioner COMMONS. They have practical instruction?

Mr. KRONER. They have practical instructors in their practical mechanics.

Commissioner COMMONS. How long a period does it cover?

Mr. KRONER. I am not familiar with their curriculum. I have had a draftsman from the public schools who had graduated there after the term of one year, which he had devoted partly to mechanical drawing and partly to instruction in carpentery, and he was probably more effective than the average. He was as effective as the average school graduate, I should say. He was an unusually bright boy. And I would say, from my experience with him, I think the instruction is successful.

Commissioner COMMONS. Is there any provision by which they can get that instruction while they are apprentices and going along with actual work?

Mr. KRONER. I feel there is no doubt that if the application was there for that kind of work that the public-school authorities would be ready to furnish the instruction, but I don't right now know whether they have any evening course for mechanics or not. I think not.

Commissioner Commons. Do you think the master workmen or employers in the building trades would be willing to permit these apprentices to go to these schools in the daytime on the employers' time?

Mr. Kroner. That would be a question everyone would have to answer for himself, after consulting his bank account.

Commissioner Commons. Has that ever been proposed?

Mr. Kroner. Nobody has proposed it to them.

Commissioner Commons. Instead of night schools, having it in the daytime on the employer's time?

Mr. Kroner. Nobody has proposed it, and I don't think it would be practical.

Commissioner Commons. Say, a half day a week?

Mr. Kroner. It might be accomplished by general agreement to assist in that way. But what the attitude of the employing contractor would be as to that, I don't know. They would likely be friendly to a thing of that kind if it didn't embarrass their bank account too much.

Commissioner Commons. It is simply the German system.

Mr. Kroner. Yes, sir.

Commissioner Commons. You have never proposed that?

Mr. Kroner. I have never been requested to furnish my views to the public authorities, and I have never furnished them.

Commissioner Garretson. Take the other side, where the mechanics in the shop are employed on the piecework system, as is common, and in some sections general, could the journeyman whose time allowance for the performance of a certain job, for which he is paid a certain amount of money and is determined by the stop watch under the efficiency system, could he be expected to give a minute to the instruction of an apprentice, legitimately?

Mr. Kroner. No, sir; he could not be expected to put his time in if he was working by the piece; but there is little of that sort.

Commissioner Garretson. You know how universal it is in the machine trade, or how common it is. Haven't those agencies been in existence and put in force and effect by employers been a large factor in the exclusion of the apprentice?

Mr. Kroner. I should think what you refer to and it would be more particularly true, of the factory production, shoe shops and machine shops.

Commissioner Garretson. That would apply more strongly than to the building trade?

Mr. Kroner. In the building trade the amount of work done by piece is negligible.

Commissioner Garretson. I know it is, but I am speaking of industries in general.

Mr. Kroner. I should judge in factories, manufacturing institutions such as you describe the teaching of apprentices would be more particularly the province of the employer.

Commissioner Garretson. In fact, wholly by men who were paid for the period and expected to perform that service?

Mr. Kroner. I think that your position is quite just if that is what you refer to.

Commissioner Garretson. Have you seen the tendency in trades of that character on the part of the employer to furnish such instruction?

Mr. Kroner. Well, now, we have in our northwestern country here—we have as far as I know very few, and those are undeveloped specimens of this species of industry you speak of. Our principal industries are the lumber business and possibly fruit and the development of fruit and fruit canning and work of that sort, and the question as you have it does not apply in any magnitude at all here.

Commissioner Garretson. But in the older countries where machine-shop practices exceed, then it becomes vital and is a factor?

Mr. Kroner. I should undoubtedly say in the factory like Fall River or in Connecticut where they manufacture mechanics' tools, where every bit is piecework and goes through a machine——

Commissioner Garretson. And the man is a machine tender and stays a machine tender.

Mr. Kroner. Yes, sir.

Commissioner Garretson. And specializes the work?

Mr. Kroner. He is not specially characterized as a mechanic.

Commissioner GARRETSON. That is all.
Chairman WALSH. That is all. Thank you. Call your next.
Mr. THOMPSON. Reverend Father O'Hara.

TESTIMONY OF REV. FATHER EDWIN V. O'HARA.

Mr. THOMPSON. Will you give us your name?
Rev. O'HARA. Edwin V. O'Hara.
Mr. THOMPSON. And give us your address?
Rev. O'HARA. 62 North Sixteenth Street, Portland.
Mr. THOMPSON. How long have you been located in this city?
Rev. O'HARA. Nine years.
Mr. THOMPSON. Are you the chairman of the Industrial Welfare Commission of Oregon?
Rev. O'HARA. Yes, sir.
Mr. THOMPSON. Father, will you kindly tell us the objects, aims, and purposes of your commission?
Rev. O'HARA. The commission was created by the legislature of 1913 to provide for the welfare of women and minor workers in the State, and the law as drawn up—the first sections are the sections outlining the duties of the commission—state that it shall extend to things that are defined by the law. The law says it shall be unlawful in the State of Oregon to employ women for unreasonably long hours, under conditions detrimental to their health and at wages that are inadequate to maintain them in health and decency; and that it shall be unlawful to employ minors in the State under conditions that are detrimental or hours that are unreasonable, or at wages that are unreasonable, and it is the business of the commission to determine in individual occupations at times just what precisely are these conditions. So that the law as laid down by the statute, the commission has a duty similar somewhat to the duty of a railroad commission, to determine matters of fact and consequently to say what hours are unreasonably long and what conditions are detrimental and what wages are inadequate.
Mr. THOMPSON. How many members has your commission?
Rev. O'HARA. There are three members of the commission.
Mr. THOMPSON. What so far has the commission done with reference to these questions?
Rev. O'HARA. The commission has after organizing in June, 1913, first called some informal conferences to see whether the employers would not voluntarily agree to conditions and wages and hours which would be reasnable, and then not require legal machinery. After a number of conferences it was found nothing could be done in that way, and we began the holding of legal conferences.

First, for the city of Portland we held a conference on the mercantile business in Portland, and the manufacturing business in Portland, and office work in Portland. And then, having these conferences and the rulings which came from them, we held a State-wide conference on all occupations throughout the State not already regulated. Now, the sum and substance of these rulings is as follows: In the mercantile business in Portland the minimum wage was fixed at $9.25 a week for experienced adult women workers. The number of hours a week was 50 or 51, I am not sure—50, I think. The women were prohibited to be employed in the mercantile business in Portland after 6 o'clock in the evening of any night of the week. Those are the rulings for the mercantile establishments in Portland. Then, in the office establishments, all office help, the same minimum wage was fixed—$9.25 a week—and the hours practically were fixed at 50, but not determining any number of hours a day. Of course, they all come under the provisions of the State law of 10 hours a day. Then, in the manufacturing establishments of Portland a ruling was made that the minimum wage should be $8.64 a week—that is 16 cents an hour for a 54-hour week was the explanation of that figure—and that 54 hours be the maximum hours. And this was the case where the commission was enjoined, or sought to be enjoined, by a paper-box manufacturer from carrying this provision into effect.

The case was taken to the courts, and the constitutionality of the law was upheld both in the lower court and in the Supreme Court of Oregon, and now the same case has been appealed to the United States Supreme Court, where it is pending. After these rulings were made a State-wide conference was called to consider all occupations not already dealt with. And the provisions of that State-wide conference—the recommendations which were finally adopted by the commission were that $8.25 a week should be the minimum in any occupation throughout the State for an experienced adult woman worker, an adult woman being one over 18. That not more than one year should be permitted in any occupation in the State of Oregon, in order that a woman should be qualified under what is meant by "experienced." We were not discussing apprenticeships in any trade term; we were discussing it for the purposes of this law, and we called it experienced, that after a woman had one year's experience in any occupation whatever she was entitled to be considered experienced in the sense of this law, and get the minimum wage for an adult woman worker. Then, a further provision of the State-wide conference was that in no mercantile or manufacturing or laundry establishment in Oregon should a woman be employed after 8.30 at night. These are substantially the rulings. Further, there is a ruling that an inexperienced woman, a normal worker, one who is not defective in any way, shall get at least a dollar a day in any occupation, and no woman may be in Oregon—no normal woman over 16 may be employed in Oregon at present for less than a dollar a day for the number of hours that are permitted. And no apprentice can be employed for less than a dollar. So those are substantially the rulings that have been made.

Mr. THOMPSON. How long have those rulings been in effect?

Rev. O'HARA. They have been in effect since last fall. Some of them went into effect in November and December and January, and I think the last one went into effect about the 1st of February, and the first some time in November. It took us a certain length of time for the commission to make these rulings. The provisions of the law are that a conference representing the employers, employees, and members of the public has to be called, and the commission submits to this conference of nine members, three representing each element— the commission submits questions concerning what are reasonable hours, what are wages sufficient for decent maintenance, and what are decent conditions. This conference recommends back to the commission, makes its recommendations to the commission. The commission, if it accepts the conference, must give a month's notice four times in the public press, four successive times in the public press, for the holding of a public hearing on these recommendations. And after the public hearing is held the commission may or may not, in its judgment, make the rulings mandatory.

The conferences have all recommended unanimously. All of the rulings of the commission up to date have come both, in the first place, from a unanimous recommendation of employers, employees, and the public, on the conference; and, secondly, a unanimous decision of the commission. There has been no question at any time of division of opinion as to the justice and reasonableness of these rulings. I may say that the law has had the support of public sentiment from the beginning, being passed by the legislature without reference to political parties, not being a political issue—unanimously passed by both houses of the legislature. And this was due, I think, in some degree, to the fact that the reason which was alleged by the committee that had the framing of the law—was one which must make this legislation permanently popular—and that is that emphasis was not placed—indeed, the question was not raised—of the relation of morality—of sex morality to low wages at all. That question was never raised by our committee that had the putting up of this law, for two reasons: In the first place, the committee doubted whether the relation was very close; and, secondly, it knew that any such suggestion was an insult to the women workers of the State whom we tried to help, because we don't believe that there is any large amount of immorality. That is just the important point. What we did find as the result of our investigation was that the girls were living on two meals a day, and living under conditions that they should not be permitted to live in—two or three rooming together in a dark, unlighted room. Some one else can tell you better—more about this—than I. But that is the argument on which this legislation was passed—that no woman worker in America should be compelled, after she goes through a whole day's work, to live on less than enough to maintain her under decent conditions. And that is the argument which will maintain popularity forever, because it is essentially just and the American people feel that that is a reasonable and just regulation of business.

So that the law has been popular and was supported by the commercial bodies as well as also by the labor unions. We were glad to report that we had the strongest recommendations both of the Central Labor Council of Portland and the State Federation, and also of the Commercial Club of Portland. And we have no reason to believe that anyone, employer or employee, who has taken the bother of investigating either the law, its purposes, or its method of administration has anything but support for it. Now, effects of the law, if I am not running——

Chairman WALSH. Yes; proceed.

Mr. THOMPSON. Go ahead.

Rev. O'HARA. In the first place, the prohibition of night work in the city of Portland in the mercantile establishments meant that about 3,000 girls would have an opportunity to have a Sunday to themselves, and it was an unmitigated good thing. It means that there is no employment of women in the mercantile establishments in Portland after 6 o'clock on any night of the year. Secondly, in regard to the limitation of hours, we had been working under a 10-hour law—a 10-hour law for the State. The States north and south of us are working under eight-hour laws for women. Now, the commission might have been able to secure a more stringent regulation than a nine-hour law, but it was the general feeling of everyone connected with the legislation and the conferences that it was better to secure a favorable minmum wage; and, besides, the question of an eight-hour law comes before the people at this coming election, and the people of Oregon will have an opportunity to say whether they favor the eight-hour law for women I am speaking of. And the commission felt that since the law was initiated it would be glad to leave that important matter to the decision of the people of the State, instead of trying to secure such legislation by commission, which might result in beating down the wage. Now, it was confidently predicted there would be a great many women lose their positions as a result of this legislation; and there are two things to be said: In the first place, the shortening of the hours has thrown a few women out of employment, as it has done in every State, though with the nine-hour day—the 54-hour week—in Oregon it naturally is not as stringent as the eight-hour day in California and Washington; but the fact that it prohibits the women from working as many hours as men work in factories beside them will naturally displace a few women. That has happened. There is one factor that I know of that had about 15 or 20 women working, who were displaced by men. It was, fortunately, as far as the humanity is concerned, a factory where women should not have to work anyhow, being of a nature that—noise and everything attached to it—was not what one would consider desirable work. There has been some tendency in certain places to use that and similar things as showing that the minimum wage regulation has thrown women out of employment.

Now, our office has yet to hear from half a dozen women in the State of Oregon who were thrown out of employment by the minimum-wage regulation. We have only had three applications for permission to work for less than the minimum on the part of experienced workers. There has been, as we will refer to later on, perhaps, some disturbance among the learners. But as far as experienced workers, and they are the only ones affected directly by the legislation, there have been only applications for three to work for less. Now, there are seasons which occure when the force in various large establishments is very much diminished; where, for example, a large concern will lay off a very large number of women at two seasons in the year; and they have attributed this, of course, to the wage legislation. But the same thing happened last year, and it happened this year, and it will happen next year, because of the fluctuation of the business. But it is not due to any legislation. There are just as many women employed. We have the pay rolls and are in power to get the pay rolls of all the establishments in Oregon employing women, and we had secured quite a number of pay rolls of last year, and we have them this year—a large number of establishments—there is not any evidence of any less women employed. Now, in a great many establishments there is no evidence of any less women employed now than there was a year ago. Of course the business depression that is on at the present might naturally explain a smaller force that is to be found in certain occupations. That is all to be said, I think, in reference to the results of the rulings of the commission.

There are certain other results. One is to stimulate the movement for trade schools—continuation schools. The commission has taken up with the larger stores the question of establishing the continuation schools in salesmanship, and we made a special inquiry this summer into the work of Mrs. Prince's school, in Boston, and are recommending to the local school board informally, not having it in our power to formally recommend it, that such instruction be given, given at a time during the week, not at night school, but day work; giving time where they may go and learn to be more efficient. And the idea is very well ·considered by the local ·large stores, and the question is· up to the local ·school board. There are a great many problems· that have come before the commission in the course of its two years' work, but I do not know whether you want any more.

Commissioner LENNON. Before leaving the subject I wish you would inform us as to the change in wage because of the action of this commission in any specific case, and also of the powers you have to reopen a finding. Suppose you had made a finding, what powers have you to reopen it;

. Rev. O'HARA.· In reference to the first, it may.be said there has been a very notable increase in wages among business girls in mercantile establishments in Portland. Where $30 and $35 was the common wage among these girls, those who have had a year's experience are now getting $40 as·a minimum. The same is true in the mercantile establishments. There has been a very considerable increase. The rulings of the Oregon commsision were very moderate; and just because of the thing you suggested secondly, that the commission is able to reopen these things at any time as a practical question, with these rulings both employees as well as employers felt that the purpose of the law would be better reached by having moderate rulings to begin with, and the rulings of $9.20 and $8.64 are considered to be very moderate.

In other States which have adopted the same law—in fact, the exact law we drew up—have made considerably more stringent regulations and 75 cents a week more in its minima throughout. So the rulings were moderate, with the understanding that the commission, as a continuing commission, could reopen these matters at any time. I will say, though, that there are certain occupations which have not yet been affected by the wage rulings. The wage rulings so far made affect only time payment. The question of piece-rate payment was such a complicated one that the commission is just now calling a conference to consider it and first settle the time-rate payments and get that matter cleared up and to take one thing at a time. And so the question of piece rate has not been affected, although the standard has been set and there may be some question as to whether the standard could be enforced, but the commission is about to open—call a conference to discuss that question.

There are other questions. There is one other question that might be opened, and that is the short week in the laundries. There is a question that is just now being discussed. Our secretary has just compiled a report of the laundries of Portland, and we are calling a conference shortly to consider that question of wages in the laundries. Whereas the hourly rate may be very satisfactory, the weekly rate is very bad, because 75 per cent of the girls are not working full weeks. They are working from 40 to 48 hours out of 54, and only a small number of them will work a full week; consequently, if paid by the hour, the pay check at the end of the week is not the minimum. But we have arranged our minima; they are all rates, not amounts. Consequently that matter is still to come up; and I would say that at the present time the laundries have not been notably affected by our ruling, owing to that fact. And that is the reason the special conference is being called, I think. There may have been a few girls—a score of girls—whose wages have been raised by the present regulation.

Commissioner GARRETSON. The wage is satisfactory, but the earnings are not?

Rev. O'HARA. The wage rate is satisfactory, but the length of the week is a short week. What can be done is still in the future.

Mr. THOMPSON. In determining the amount of the minimum wage, it apparently varies, of course, in the different lines of work. Generally, what did the conference and the commission take into consideration in arriving at the figures named?

Rev. O'HARA. It took into consideration the cost of room and board and clothes. Those were the large items, and it was figured that $25 a month was required for decent room and board in Portland, and that figure—around that amount; perhaps $22.50 instead of $25—that would scarcely include the noonday meal; that is, for very large numbers. A small number could get room and board for less than.that, but not very much less at the time these rulings were made. Then there was diversity of opinion as to the matter of women's dress, as might be expected; but a compromise or practical view was adopted, which brought the figure up to its present sum.

The matter of vacation and dental fees and medical fees and reading and recreatilon and all those things were discussed, but it would be hardly true to say that they were taken practically into account, because they were subjects that gave such a varied opportunity for opinion, and if each of them was added it would have sent the minimum very much higher than was felt would be practicable to start with. It was a matter of practical judgment, and I think everyone concerned felt that that was the best way to start.

Mr. THOMPSON. In regard to the variation of the figures of the minimum wage for the different industries, did that arise from a different view of these main items?

Rev. O'HARA. Yes, sir; the matter of clothes.

Mr. THOMPSON. Or the industry itself?

Rev. O'HARA. The matter of clothing. For example, between mercantile and manufacturing establishments in Portland the difference between $9.25 and $8.64 a week, it was supposed by the conference that the girls who had to meet the public as saleswomen or as office girls would have to dress more expensively, at least have more laundry and that sort of thing, than the girls working in factories. That was the supposition of the conference in making this difference.

Mr. THOMPSON. Is there anything further, Father, you would like to say with reference to this industrial welfare commission?

Rev. O'HARA. Perhaps I would say that one of the causes of uneasiness among women workers has been the secrecy of the wage scale—the fact that women working side by side don't know what each other are getting—and consequently there has been no standard of women's wages—absolutely no standard of women's wages, except what they could be gotten for. That is, it was not even the law of supply and demand, because there was a great factor of ignorance—ignorance of what their work was worth on the part of the employees that made it even worse for them than the law of supply and demand if that had been allowed to operate directly, and I feel personally that there is one of the greatest evils connected with the employment of women; that is, the lack of a standard—the lack of publicity as to what women were getting. I believe if the public knew generally what women were getting in many of the industries, that they would demand better conditions for them. All of these things others may discuss better than I.

Mr. THOMPSON. Have you given any consideration to the question of unemployment?

Commissioner GARRETSON. Let me ask one question before we leave this subject.

Chairman WALSH. All right, Commissioner Garretson.

Commissioner GARRETSON. Has there been any instances where women were disciplined or discharged for testimony given before the commission as to violations of the law or undesirability of conditions under which they worked?

Rev. O'HARA. No, sir; because the commission made careful investigation and inquiry as to how the employers would treat their employees before getting them to testify, and it was impossible to get women to testify from certain industries; that is, from certain occupations. There were certain stores, for example, where it was impossible to get the women to testify from.

Commissioner GARRETSON. They were convinced they would lose their jobs?

Rev. O'HARA. Yes, sir.

Commissioner GARRETSON. Your experience is the same in that as similar commissions in other States?

Rev. O'HARA. Yes, sir.

Commissioner GARRETSON. That is all, Mr. Chairman.

Commissioner COMMONS. I would just like to ask a question about the prosecutions under this law and the penalties. How are those carried on?

Rev. O'HARA. The prosecutions under the law are taken care of by the State labor commissioner, who has the enforcement of all labor legislation, although the commission has also authority to do it. The State labor commissioner has the machinery to do it and has prosecuted under this law, and I think that every provision of the rulings there have been prosecutions that have occurred and fines inflicted and wages given under every provision of the law. No prosecutions were undertaken until after the Supreme Court of Oregon upheld the law. It was felt it would be unwise to start prosecutions until that had been done. In reference to—what was the question you asked me?

Commissioner COMMONS. Is it the prosecuting attorney or the district attorney that prosecutes, or can the commissioner employ his own counsel and prosecute?

Rev. O'HARA. The State labor commissioner—the commission has to employ the district attorney or attorney general's office, and the State labor commissioner has, I presume, to employ—I am not fully familiar with the machinery of his office, but he is able to bring these prosecutions.

Commissioner COMMONS. Does he employ his own counsel if he can not get the district attorney to act?

. Rev. O'HARA. There has been no question like that that has arisen. It is the duty of the labor commissioner to enforce the labor laws of the State, and all the cases have been prosecuted by him without any question.

Commmissioner COMMONS. Do you know about any difficulty of getting evidence of violations of the law? Has that question come to your attention at all in any way, as to whether women and girls——

Rev. O'HARA. I could not cite any specific case of that, although I have heard—well, I know of cases like this, where complaints would be telephoned in to us by telephone or sent in with annonymous signatures, or no signatures, or where the name would be given, and we would be told we must not use their name, and of course that is quite common. That has happened in a number of cases. That, I think, is what you refer to.

Commissioner COMMONS. In such cases, of course——

Rev. O'HARA. We can't go ahead.

Commissioner COMMONS. You can't get evidence?

Rev. O'HARA. No, sir.

Commissioner COMMONS. You get a number of such letters, do you?

Rev. O'HARA. Yes, sir. I should say there are from week to week, there is a call of that sort—no great amount of them, but still we have them.

Commissioner COMMONS. How about the promptness of prosecution of the cases? Is there prompt action, or is there delay in getting decisions, getting action?

. Rev. O'HARA. No, sir; I think the matter has been done very promptly, very satisfactory by the labor commissioner. He has taken and handled the matter very well.

Commissioner COMMONS. That is all.

Chairman WASH. You may proceed now, Mr. Thompson.

Mr. THOMPSON. Along this same line, Father, I would like to ask you one question, whether in determining the wages the conference simply took into consideration the needs of the single individual, or whether they took into consideration—considered the individual as part of the family, or as one supporting others?

Rev. O'HARA. The conference had only one question put to them in reference to wages, and that is, What sum is necessary in Portland in this occupation to maintain a self-supporting woman in decent but frugal livelihood. The state of the business and the question of whether the woman was living at home or adrift don't enter at all into this question. The commission took no cognizance of those questions.

Mr. THOMPSON. Nor whether she is called upon to support others?

Rev. O'HARA. No, sir; not in fixing the minimum, because it is fixing it for a whole occupation.

Mr. THOMPSON. Referring to the question of unemployment, have you given that some thought and consideration?

Rev. O'HARA. Yes, sir; during the past two months. Two months ago I was asked by the American Association for Labor Legislation to organize in Oregon an Oregon section of the American Association on Unemployment, and we have organized such a committee, which has been making an investigation during the past two months. The American Association has sent on an investigator, who has spent the last two months in Oregon, and has written up a report, which is now ready for the press, and the report has shown a number of things in regard to unemployment in Oregon. In the first place, it has shown where a large amount of the unemployment comes from—that it is a question of seasonal unemployment; that there are some 30,000 men employed in Oregon in the summer, against—in all occupations except agriculture—against 23,000 in the winter. There are 7,000 who are left idle in the winter, due to the seasonality of occupations. Of these about one-half are employed in the lumber and timber industry. About 16,000—15,000 at the highest period in September and about 11,000 in the winter. So that leaves about 5,000 men whom the lumber and timber industry employs in the summer and does not employ in the winter.

Our investigation has gone further into the various trades, and has got some information which I haven't at hand just now, but indicates what are the months of highest and lowest employment in the various trades. Now, the purpose of our investigation was, first, to determine that fact—the fact that there is seasonality of employment. It is not a question of overpopulation, but it is a question of having a limited number of industries and the industries employing men, particularly at one season; and the work which the American Association for Labor Legislation has outlined was to make an inquiry into what could be done to remedy that situation: First, by shifting public employment and, second, by stimulating new occupations. And in reference to these matters we have been in communication with all the cities and counties of the State of Oregon and have received varying answers showing that in some places it would be possible to do the road work during the slack season; that the stonework especially could be done. There are certain irrigation projects that could be done. There is obviously a large amount of building which is done every winter—here in the valley especially.

Many of our public schools buildings have been constructed right through the winter, and that, with some thought on the part of the public authorities, it would be possible at least to shift the work so that the public employment would not come on at the time the private employment is at its highest. Whether it could be shifted clear to the period of worst unemployment is a practical question for engineers and others to settle, but there is a large amount of public work that could be done at times when the private employment is not at its highest, and that is the first recommendation of our committee to the public authorities of Oregon—that they look into the matter of shifting their work. Secondly, there is work which could be taken up that is specially suited to the winter season, and that is land clearing. There is a vast amount of logged-off land in Oregon which, if it were cleared, would be suitable for agriculture, but which, owing to many reasons, is not being cleared, with the result we are lacking in agricultural population, and it would be good economy to put people to work at clearing that land. Now, it will cost a good deal of money to clear land, to clear this logged-off land, and land is being held at a very high value—too high for farming purposes in many cases.

But there are two things to be done. One would be to interest the private owner—the owner of those in employing men during the winter and clearing off the land. That, doubtless, will be done; that is being done. There are plenty of private owners who are doing it. But, secondly, that method will probably not work until the experiment has been carried on on a fairly large scale, and there is no obvious reason why the county could not undertake to carry on some of this land-clearing operations during the winter and not lose any money at all; make it a straight business transaction and give employment to men during the winter in clearing land. There are many details of this to work out by both the owners of land and the public officers. But clearly there is opportunity here for giving work—for creating an industry that will really be economic and won't be charity in the least; that it will be socially useful and at the same time pay its way. Now, there are many other things besides land clearing. I mentioned rockwork and drainage. There are large parts of the valley that need drainage—tiling—and this work can be done in the winter. Then, a brief statement of what can be done in that line: Our further investigations have taken us into the field of employment agencies and the question of paying wages by cash instead of paying by check, which can only be cashed in the saloons.

And the question of unemployment insurance, and the question of part-time schools, the idea being to have the schools conduct classes—trade schools especially during the bad winter months, and have the boys under 21 go to school, instead of being competing with their elders at that time. This arrangement, of course, as everyone knows, is the arrangement in Chicago; and, as I learned from the school authorities there, is very successful and takes out of competition at that particular season of the year, when employment is very dull, boys who ought to be going to school and learning something to improve themselves at their trade.

In the matter of paying checks by cash, these are recommendations which our committee is making to public officials especially, to aid which it hopes to have organized this afternoon, or to start to organize this afternoon, later on in the afternoon, an official committee. We are asking the State officials and the county of Multnomah and the city of Portland officials to meet this afternoon and organize an official committee to do these things: First, to see that public work will be shifted as far as possible; second, to see what the State can do in providing public work, economic public work during the winter; and, thirdly, to see what the city can do in regard to getting a much more effective employment agency. Our idea is not that the city employment agency is the ideal, but that until the legislature meets the only practicable thing to do is to develop the efficiency of the Portland Free Employment Agency.

Now, these are a few of the features of the report which will be made by our committee.

Mr. THOMPSON. With reference to the question of the employment agencies, have you looked over the tentative suggestions to be incorporated into a bill, which the commission has?

Rev. O'HARA. I have just looked over them. I am not in a position to express any opinion on them further than to say that the general ideas are undoubtedly the ones on which progress will have to be made.

Mr. THOMPSON. Have you any idea with reference to that problem, as to whether a Federal employment bureau with agencies throughout the United States would be a good thing or not?

Rev. O'HARA. I think it would be undoubtedly a good thing, because sometimes when employment is at its height in one section of the United States it is very low in another, and an efficient Federal bureau would be able to get the information to the workers. I think that is true.

Mr. THOMPSON. Is there any other thing you would like to suggest ·to the commission in regard to the industrial problem, particularly things constructive that might come within the scope of the commission's work?

Rev. O'HARA. There is one other problem that I haven't much information concerning outside of these two lines of constructive work except as to a third, which is not directly industrial, and that is the housing question. And I believe that that is the source of a great deal of the·industrial unrest, it is the fact that the industrial population is not properly housed, and I believe that what is n██ded for them is good housing legislation that will especially provide for the distribution of the industrial population away from the center and not crowd them and hive them in unsanitary and unsatisfactory dwellings and tenements and unlighted rooms. That is another feature of this matter, but apart from, that is not directly industrial, but it has a very large bearing, in my mind, on the industrial matter.

There is one thing that I would like to call your attention to in regard to the law, the industrial commission law in Oregon, and that is that appeal from the rulings of the commission in matters of fact is denied. There is no appeal to the courts from the rulings of the commission in matters of fact.

Chairman WALSH. That has been upheld in this State?

Rev. O'HARA. That has been upheld by the supreme court.

Commissioner GARRETSON. Only on questions of law.

Rev. O'HARA. Only on questions of law, and that prevents endless litigation keeping these things tied up in the courts.

Chairman WALSH. Any other questions?

Commissioner GARRETSON. Yes.

Chairman WALSH. Mr. Garretson.

Commissioner GARRETSON. Has it been alleged, or has there been increase in the prices by laundries, it being alleged that it was made necessary by added costs of operation growing out of the application of this law.

Rev. O'HARA. What I have observed is that this law has not as yet affected the laundries to any notable extent. The laundries would come under that ruling which says that $8.25 is the minimum, but $8.25 a week for a 54-hour week, but when they only work them 46 hours or 48 hours, they are only paying them $6 or $7 as a minimum, and consequently there is a very small proportion of the laundry industry that has as yet been affected by the rulings.

Commissioner GARRETSON. But, do you know if they have raised the prices?

Rev. O'HARA. I am not informed on that subject.

Commissioner GARRETSON. It is not always necessary, is it, to have a reason in those things if you have a good excuse?

- Rev. O'HARA. No. That has been shown in more cases than one, because many things have been attributed to the law which on investigation are not due to it at all.

Commissioner GARRETSON. One other matter. You touched on employment agencies. Was there not a hearing held here the other day in regard to the granting of a license to an employment agency, or the withholding the license, which brought out certain facts with regard to the methods which were followed? Have you any knowledge of that hearing?

Rev. O'HARA. No; I have not, except through the ·papers. I saw the fact reported—as reported in the public press. I have knowledge of a hearing of the employment agencies themselves before our committee on unemployment where those charges were very emphatically·denied.

Commissioner GARRETSON. Yon don't know, then, whether those statements were made under oath before the city council, as to offers that were made by employment agencies to employers who would expediate the movement of men?

Rev. O'HARA. I don't know whether they were made under oath. I presume they were, if it was any testimony that was taken.

Commissioner GARRETSON. That is all, Mr. Chairman.

Chairman WALSH. Any other questions? That is all. Call your next.

Mr. THOMPSON. Mr. Wood.

TESTIMONY OF MR. C. E. S. WOOD.

Mr. THOMPSON. Sit down, Mr. Wood. Give us your name, please.

Mr. WOOD. C. E. S. Wood.

Mr. THOMPSON. And your business address?

Mr. WOOD. You want my full name? Those are my initials.

Mr. THOMPSON. Yes—I mean your business address.

Mr. WOOD. 616 Spaulding Building.

Mr. THOMPSON. And your profession, Mr. Wood?

Mr. WOOD. Lawyer.

Mr. THOMPSON. How long have been located in Portland?

Mr. WOOD. Before going any further, Mr. Thompson, I would like to correct an error. I have been summoned here as counsel for the labor unions. Now, so far as I know there is no such attorney in town. They have occasionally come to me individually, individual unions and individual members of the unions, in their legal difficulties. And I have appeared in a number of their cases, but I have no permanent legal relation with the unions as attorney and client.

Mr. THOMPSON. I see.

Mr. WOOD. There are some things that I probably would say here to-day that the unions would not agree to at all.

Mr. THOMPSON. Mr. Wood, how long have you been practicing law in this vicinity?

Mr. WOOD. Thirty years.

Mr. THOMPSON. Thirty years; and you are pretty well acquainted, couse-quently, with the industrial conditions here?

Mr. WOOD. Well, with the general aspect. I would not say with all the details from time to time.

Mr. THOMPSON. In your opinion, does industrial unrest exist here—by that I mean the unrest because of the relations between the employer and the employee particularly?

Mr. WOOD. Does it exist here particularly?

Mr. THOMPSON. Yes.

Mr. WOOD. No, sir; not in my opinion. There are not enough people need to live here yet; we are not crowded enough to have a really crucial and vital unrest.

Mr. THOMPSON. What would you say of the unrest that exists as to its kind and degree, and what in your opinion are the contributing causes to it?

Mr. WOOD. I think that the unrest is due to ignorance, as I may say all evil is due to ignorance. I do not think that the employer and the employee understand each other. I think, for example, on the employer's side they are perfectly sincere in their ideas that in battling for the open shop they are battling for the individual liberty of a man to sell his labor as and where he pleases. According to my view they fail to see that all they are battling for is the right for themselves to get the benefit of a relentless competition; that everybody that is born has to live, and everybody that is born becomes a competitor with every other body in the labor market.

And when these gentlemen contend for the God-given right of the individual to sell his labor as he pleases. though they are sincere in it, in my opinion, they are simply providing one more monopolistic privilege that they will get the benefit of the wolfish competition amongst labor and live. Now, that is one thing that the employers don't understand.

The employee, on the other hand, and the labor unions do not seem to me to understand that they themselves are an evil, only justified from the fact that they are battling a greater evil; that they are an evil, in my opinion, because they invade the liberty of the peaceable individual in his peaceful activities. They dictate how many hours he shall labor, what wages he shall get, and what amount of labor he shall perform; how many apprentices shall learn the trade, and invade the province of the employer, tell him what he must do, all of which invasions of personal liberty are, to my mind, theoretically wrong. But as long as the greater evil of the monopolies of the capitalistic class exist the labor union is a life preserver and may necessarily be self-preservation with all its evils.

Now, turn to the other side. The capitalistic employer again with perfect sincerity says, "Why, we can't submit to having the labor unions become a labor trust, a labor monopoly, and sell labor at their own terms." But they are none of them able to see that labor must form that trust, which I think is theoretically bad, and as long as the capital and the employer has the greater and more vital trust of the control of the land, the source of production, the control of money, the blood of commerce, and the control of the taxing power, which taxes by force money out of the pockets of the laborer. These are the greater monopolies, and with all due deference to this commission I do not think this or any other commission is doing anything but palliative work, and closing over the sores until they get down to the root of what makes these, what are the monopolies and privileges that make the conflict between labor and the employer. [Applause.]

Chairman WALSH. With all due respect to the enthusiam of the audience I must ask you, if you please, not to repeat that. I know it is human nature to do that, when a proposition that is popular is put in a well-phrased manner; but kindly assist us, because it makes for disorder, as we have discovered in other places. I know you will. Proceed.

Mr. ▮HOMPSON. Mr. Wood, looking at the proposition of palliatives which, apparently, is your opinion of what may be done, what constructives or palliatives will you suggest to this commission that it might recommend to Congress, or to the various States, or to the public at large, that would help in the evolution of the industrial problem, that is to say, between the employer and employee.

Mr. WOOD. Well, I am afraid I can not put forward anything, for the reason I am so grounded in the belief that the palliatives simply delay the time of fuller understanding, divert the attention to superficial things, and really prevent an understanding of the real subject.

For example, it is to me like this: That here is a hose filled with water, under pressure from the head at the back, which has been bursting for ever since the history of man in some spot or other, and we run to that particular spot and try to plug it up, but we never try to get back to the source and cut off the head. It seems to me that all these palliatives are but incidental, you can not change the economic force of gravity a bit more than you can change the physical force of gravity.

For example, you start an eight-hour law. Mind you, I have been battling for these eight-hour laws, and I have joined these forces advocating palliatives, because it was an expedient for the moment. But now you are asking me for my views as to what ought to be done. You take the eight-hour law; that is, a law cutting down the hours of labor and preserving the price of the longer day, the 10-hour. And that price was established in this open cutthroat market of labor competition. And it was in competition of trade also between each manufacturer or storekeeper with his neighbor. So that that price was the result of economic gravity. If you make the labor two hours less than inevitable, if the employer was paying all that the competition permitted him to pay and he does not get by two hours as much labor out of it, you have only shifted the economic burden to somebody to pay, and that is the consumer. That is all very well as long as the consumer can pay. But the higher price of consumption will diminish the demand. And so it goes. There is no economic freedom anywhere.

Mind you, I don't believe even in eight hours a day. I am like Steinmetz, of Cornell, when he said that nobody ought to work in drudgery in uncongenial labor more than four hours a day. I do not think that if I labor as an artist for 15 hours a day—I do not call that labor. That is self-expression. So many a mechanic has the same form of self-expression in his art, in his science. But no man ever wanted to go down in a mine for self-expression. I think four hours a day is enough.

Chairman WALSH. We have asked a number of people for constructive suggestions as to the present system of industry. Now, inasmuch as you have stated very forcefully that you do not believe much in palliatives, I wish you would just proceed and state to the commission what you consider the fundamental maladjustment of the economic situation.

Mr. Wood. I would be very glad to, as far as my opinion is worth anything.
Chairman Walsh. We would be glad to have your opinion.

Mr. Wood. Take Father O'Hara's statement about clearing the logs off the land. Before you can go in and clear it, by the State or county, you have got to buy it from the man that has already taken God's usufruct off of it, you have got to pay him for his title before you can get the right to go in and clear the logs off the land. It is laying there naked, useless, and unemployed.

Now, he will hold that title, as you know perfectly well, by the same feudal title that land was held years ago under the feudal barons' of Europe. He is holding it by a title which would allow him to call the sheriff and put you or me off this stumpy land, this loggy land, put us off as trespassers. He is holding it by title, the logic of which is that if his title should be placed in my hands for the whole earth I could tell all the rest of you to get off the earth. And you would either have to go to the sea and live off salt water and fish or commit suicide.

Now, there is something to begin with. This old antiquated feudal paper title to that land by the monarch or the successor, the Congress of the United States, hands out lands that neither of them ever saw, indifferent as to whether it is ever to be put to a beneficial use.

We have that in the placer mines, the title depending on you. If you did not use your placer and keep it up, you lost title to it. And the strain of that runs through the mining laws to-day here on the Pacific coast. We don't hold water by any such foolish title. No title on earth can theoretically give you use to water, give you right to water on the Pacific coast, except as you apply it to a beneficial use and only so far as you apply it to that use; and when you cease to apply it to that us it is then open and public water and the next man that will come along and put it to a beneficial use. And I think that should be the law for land. That is one thing.

I think that the next thing is that there should be freedom in banking. The panic of 1907 gave us a lesson which has been followed to a certain extent in the present currency bill. But neither of them touch the real theory of what banking should be as laid down by Proudhon in his book, translated originally by Dana, of the New York Sun, or by Creedon, the author of Mutual Banking, which in substance is this: That any body of men may form themselves into a banking establishment and issue their notes upon assets furnished with security, and that the interchange of exchange is to be a mutual understanding and a premium arranged among themselves out of necessity. And that would reduce money, the price of money, to the mere cost of doing the banking business, as it would in the grocery business. It is estimated by Green that 1 per cent per annum would be the use of money. There is another suggestion along the road of one of the most important needs of society and one of the most important ingredients between capital and labor which goes to make up wealth, the use of money.

Then I would suggest, which is already becoming to be a little better understood under the present administration, that no government with the force of its marshals and its sheriffs behind it has a right to take money out of the pockets of the consumer in taxes except for the absolute need of the general public use; not to give it in charity, not to give it in beautifying, not, certainly, to give it in bonuses and in tariffs. That tax should be regarded in the sense of a moral theft from the consumer and should be taken as lightly as possible.

In the early days we did not have property here; 40 years ago because the land was open, and the few people that dribbled in here found an easy place for home. You could not put the thumbscrew on them; you could not put any pressure upon it. But here is Oregon to-day, with its 33,000.000 acres east of the mountains alone—one-fourth of the timber of the United States—and you can not go and get an acre of timber. It has all been forcibly-taken, tied up with those paper titles. You can not in all those millions of acres go and locate a friend of yours on a single homestead that is ready and willing to support the family without drainage, irrigation, or the expenditure of capital.

I do not believe that you can find a homestead in Oregon which without further expenditure of capital, drainage, and irrigation—something of that kind—that stands ready and fertile to support the family. Everything that is desirable has been taken up on speculative forestalling. Not an acre of that land. I have got some of that land myself. I am a forestaller speculator. I have got some eastern land out in eastern Oregon. But what would be the use of my stepping down and out and saying that I would not hold it. Instead of being a mere change of name some man will step in, and, instead of Wood holding it, Jones would hold it. There would be no change in the legal institution by which it is held. So take these vast holdings of our timber, as I said, they are being held speculatively by people who are putting them to no use at the present time.

Take the iron. All the iron in the United States is held by James J. Hill·and his associates in the United States Steel Corporation. They are not using them, not using a tithe of them; but they can bar everybody else from using them.

Take the 120 square miles of anthracite coal in.the United States, all there is in the world, owned by four railroads. They are not even scratching it, small as it is. But they can keep everybody else off by this paper·title. There, I think, is your source of poverty and your unemployed. ᐧ.

Chairman WALSH. What would you suggest as to the change that should be made in the law with reference to land titles?

Mr. WOOD. As an anarchist—I am an anarchist myself. [Applause.]

Chairman WALSH. Kindly do not indulge in applause. If I must explain it further, sometimes very unfair things are said to which some people will applaud, and I am sure you want to help us, in order not to have disorder. This gentleman is expressing his views very well and.forcibly, and if you will kindly try·and control yourselves you will help us out.

Mr. WOOD. With the commission's permission, I would like to say these gentlemen here sitting are here on a great public duty, strangers amongst us, and I do not think any expression of opinion ought to be given on either side by the audience. I hope that you will not any more.

Chairman WALSH. Thank you. Now, go into it fully.

Mr. WOOD. Why, I would think—allow me, as I have said, that in that regard I would like to say this, and I say it with respect, but I think the most ignorant people I know are the business element, in the sense that I consider·it ignorant. They are very able ·in·the success for the acquisition of wealth. But.that is their specialty. Beyond that they don't know, and I consider it ignorance when you do not·know the struggle of life that is going on around, you do not know the problem of the future that is staring you in the face. I think the most ignorant man of his generation was perhaps Charles I of England; then Louis XVI.· They lost their heads. ᐧ ᐧ ᐧ ᐧ

Now, what I mean by this ignorance is, you will ask the best business men, the biggest of them, and the bankers, what is socialism, and they say that is a cranky notion of dividing up everything every so often and letting the unfit profit by the fit—and, of course, I am not going into what socialism is here; I am·telling you that is my judgment of my own friends, as much as they. know about it. You ask what is anarchism. It is throwing bombs and killing crowned heads. That is about as much as they know about that.

Now, my view of anarchism is that it is the ideal which we have conceived,· toward·which we will approach when instead of forcible cooperation of society we will arrive at such a conception of self-interest that we will cooperate peaceably and voluntarily without the force of government at our back. Every board of trade, every club is an anarchistic association. And when the merchants of Chicago got together and watered their streets by combination it was an anarchistic association, and so on.

Now, then, my view would be to make the title to land not the Henry George theory, though I am working with the single taxer, I. get into every wagon that is going my way, I think, but when you ask me for my idea, my theory, it is not the single Henry George theory, though he said that he left them the husk and the State took the kernel. My idea would be to have land held exactly as water is held, as I said those placer mines used to be in 1849. Make it determinative on the use, the beneficial use and occupation of the land. Let a man have his ownership in himself, but not an ownership in the land. That if he voluntarily abandons it, no matter what the improvements are, and he voluntarily abandons them, he abandons them to the person that will make the best use of them, and that this use must always, as in the case of water, be divided and created into superior and inferior uses. You can't have water out here— there is only just so much water—you can not ·have it for irrigation when a city is starving for water and has nothing to drink; you can not have it for mining when they need it for raising crops for food. And so it goes. There is a superior and an inferior use. ᐧ

ᐧ So there would be in land, and broadly speaking, I would make title to land depend on just so much as the man or men could beneficially put to use. For example, take those anthracite coal miners. They ought to be allowed within a demarcation that ᐧcould be given for their reasonable beneficial use for a certain term and beyond that extend it again and extend it again as they used it, leaving all outside to be taken up by miners themselves that would go in and mine it if it was free.

Commissioner COMMONS. Mr. Wood, have you tried your hand at drafting a bill along those lines?

Mr. WOOD. No, sir. It is absolutely useless to try to put a bill through until it is backed up by public sentiment. Neither this State nor the United States would accept my views.

Commissioner COMMONS. I do not see how we could know except we could have a bill which would show us how it would work in practice. If you could draw up a bill that could be——.

Mr. WOOD. I could draw a bill.

Commissioner COMMONS. Which would be definite, which would define the procedure, work it out, your superior use and your beneficial use, and so on. Define it so we could understand it, and then it might receive some consideration; but in its present form I do not see how it helps.

Mr. WOOD. I can dictate a bill right into the record here. Land shall only be held by the person making actual beneficial use of it, only so much as is needed for his purpose; and the superior use shall always control the inferior use. There is your bill.

Commissioner COMMONS. Now, would you have the commission investigate and ascertain these uses and make findings like the welfare commission does, or would you simply leave it to the courts to determine?

Mr. WOOD. The courts have already made it.

Commissioner COMMONS. How could they in a particular piece of land unless they go out and investigate?

Mr. WOOD. They have not made in regard to land; they have in regard to water.

Chairman WALSH. Make a suggestion, if I may interrupt you——

Commissioner COMMONS. That is what I wanted to know.

Chairman WALSH. As to what would be a definite superior and an inferior use.

Mr. WOOD. Well——

Chairman WALSH. That is, define it in law, in an administrative way, so that we could put such a suggestion in force.

Mr. WOOD. Well, I would say that city use for homes, for a home is superior, for an aggregation of homes the city was superior to them; for agriculture, raising of food was superior to grazing, if it were capable of both uses, if the land was capable of but one use. Grazing land only can be put to that use. Mining land is, as a rule, only capable of that use. It would settle itself. You do not have to strike out this way. You can take the Henry George doctrine, where he says he leaves you all your machinery, leaves your machinery, and he simply——

Chairman WALSH. Prof. Commons is trying to put your idea into form. Suppose a serious attempt was to be made by the Government to do this. Now, you have dictated what you say a law would be. Of course that would go if it was in a fundamental law. Now, then, how would you then get down to the actual operation of the question of superior and inferior use? That is, would those not be questions of fact in many instances, in a multiplicity of instances? How would you do that? Would you allow courts to declare it? Would you have a board declare it, or would you attempt to do it by the use of the lawmaking power?

Mr. WOOD. I don't think those details are material; but to answer your question, I think I would do it by a commission to find the facts, as our water commission does here, with an appeal from that commission to the courts to settle the law.

Chairman WALSH. Now, was there something you were going to say when I interrupted you? You started to say that you need not be left to this device.

Mr. WOOD. Yes; I was going to say that those familiar with the Henry George doctrine know that one reason he adopted was that he leaves all the machinery exactly as it is now. He simply levies a ground rent in the shape of a tax and abolishes all other taxes. Now, that is simple; that does not make any alteration in the present machinery. It has been up before the people a great many times in specific bills.

Commissioner COMMONS. Wouldn't that be better than your system?

Mr. WOOD. Well——

Commissioner COMMONS. And accomplish the same thing?

Mr. WOOD. No; I don't think it would, Professor, be better, because I want to abolish it; I want to attenuate atrophy, get down to the leanest lines of this thing we call the State with its power of interference with the individual, and therefore I prefer my own line. You see, the single tax still keeps alive a State to collect and expend these taxes. I would like it to be done by a voluntary association.

But I am not going to quarrel with that. If anybody will start the single tax in the United States, they will have my hearty support.

Chairman WALSH. Let me ask you, in your work as attorney at law here, in the following of your profession, I understand you to say that at times you have represented the unions?

Mr. WOOD. Yes, sir.

Chairman WALSH. Has that been in injunction cases or otherwise?

Mr. WOOD. No.

Chairman WALSH. Briefly, if you will state what your service has been.

Mr. WOOD. My services have been in drafting bills to go before the people by the initiative; regulating the hours of labor by State, county, and municipal employment, in drafting laws regulating the hours, in testing that same law in the supreme court, and in testing the female limitation of labor law. Such as that. I never have appeared in any of the court contests against the injunctions issued against labor. There have been very few of them here.

Chairman WALSH. Have you observed the conduct of the judicial and administrative officers with reference to the application of laws in the performance of their official duties in cases involving labor disputes, so that you could say whether in the main that it has been fair and impartial or otherwise?

Mr. WOOD. Yes; under the old system of the old primary and the old convention and the old boss rule, and the old war-horse politician, such questions as did then arise were adjudicated unfavorably to labor, but they were few. That is going back some years, and, as I say, the pressure has not reached us yet. We have got less than a million people in this State, although I say the lands are bottled up.

But latterly, under this new Oregon system, with the direct primary and the abolishment of the convention and the judges themselves becoming in feel and touch with the people, I think the inclination is to sympathize with and, so far as the law justly permits, to side with labor. I think, other things being equal and the scales hanging even, that labor would be apt to get the best of it.

Chairman WALSH. Are the grand and petit juries summoned democratically; do they represent all classes of the people in their make-up as a rule, in the city of Portland?

Mr. WOOD. Well——

Chairman WALSH. Have you the grand jury system here?

Mr. WOOD. Yes; we have the grand jury system.. I think fairly so, although perhaps there is not the usual proportion of the heavier business men. They either are not called or get out of it, and the jury therefore represents more the middle-and farmer—the middle and farmer class. The laboring and proletariat class are not so apt to get on there.

Chairman WALSH. Are there any other questions? I think that is all; thank you, Mr. Wood. Call your next.

Mr. THOMPSON. Mr. Smith.

TESTIMONY OF MR. AMADEE M. SMITH.

Mr. THOMPSON. Mr. Smith, will you give us your name, please?

Mr. SMITH. Amadee M. Smith.

Mr. THOMPSON. And your business address?

Mr. SMITH. 1401 Yeon Building.

Mr. THOMPSON. And your business?

Mr. SMITH. I am not active in business. I am interested in several.

Mr. THOMPSON. I don't get you.

Mr. SMITH. I say I am not active in business.

Mr. THOMPSON. You are not active in business?

Mr. SMITH. No.

Mr. THOMPSON. How long have you lived in Portland or in the neighborhood of Portland?

Mr. SMITH. Well, I have lived in Portland about thirty-two or three years. I am a native Oregonian.

Mr. THOMPSON. Are you a member of the industrial welfare commission?

Mr. SMITH. I am; yes.

Mr. THOMPSON. Did you hear the testimony of Father O'Hara?

Mr. SMITH. Yes.

Mr. THOMPSON. Is there anything that you would care to add to that testi-mony with reference to the commission?

Mr. SMITH. Well, there is—no. There is one or two impressions that I think he gave that I would like to correct, however.

Mr. THOMPSON. You may do that.

Mr. SMITH. I think unintentional, however, on his part.

Mr. THOMPSON. You may do that.

Mr. SMITH. He gave the impression, or rather I got the impression, sitting in the audience and listening to him, that the effort to get information was largely forestalled by the employer. I don't think he meant to give that. That has only been in a few cases where that has occurred. The employer as a rule has not in any way hindered us in our efforts to get information.

Mr. THOMPSON. I think he just stated that as an exception, if I remember correctly.

Mr. SMITH. Yes. It was only in a very few cases that that was done.

Mr. THOMPSON. Is there anything else that you care to add to his testimony?

Mr. SMITH. No; except that I think the employers, as a rule, have been ready to adopt our suggestions; that is, there has been no particular opposition, except in a few cases. As a rule, though, all employers have dropped into line and fulfilled our requests.

Mr. THOMPSON. Do you believe in such commissions as yours?

Mr. SMITH. Well, I am not ready to say that I am. I am not opposed to them, but I am not ready to say that they are going to solve the problem entirely. I don't know yet that they are. I think that they have done some benefit in this State.

Mr. THOMPSON. Are you a believer in a minimum-wage law—in the establishment of a minimum-wage law?

Mr. SMITH. I think it has a tendency to eliminate the unqualified. I don't know what is to be done with them yet. I am not able to determine. I think, though, that that is true, that the unqualified are to a great disadvantage with the minimum-wage law.

Mr. THOMPSON. But you have no suggestions?

Mr. SMITH. I have no remedy yet to suggest.

Mr. THOMPSON. You were given a list of questions here, were you not?

Mr. SMITH. No; I don't think I was.

Mr. THOMPSON. Well, with reference to the industrial unrest, which is said to exist in this part of the country, have you any suggestions constructively to make to the commission?

Mr. SMITH. Well, I don't know that I have. I don't know that it is any worse here than it is in any other section of the country, and the problem is a wide one. I think that a great deal of the unrest is caused by—I think a great deal of it is imaginary, and is probably fomented by the—well, what is called yellow journalism, and by the politician that desire to gain a few votes, and other similar reasons.

I think that there is more work to be had, if the men are candidly and honestly looking for it, than we really want to do. Now, it is my experience, I have not been an employer for a few years, but previous to that I was an employer; and during all the many years that I did employ men, I could always find plenty that were out of work and that were not looking for work. I think that is largely true to-day. Of course, I do know that there are many, very many deserving people, but I do not think it is local in its cause.

Mr. THOMPSON. To treat it as a general proposition, country wide, if you please, Mr. Smith, what would you say of the question of unemployment? Is there a serious problem there, and, if so, what would help it? Do you think that a Federal employment agency would do it, or bureau?

Mr. SMITH. Well, I would not be surprised but that it would help it some. That would enable those that were requiring labor to find it, and those that were hunting work would also be able to find work; yes.

Mr. THOMPSON. Are there any other suggestions that you would like to make to the commission, Mr. Smith?

Mr. SMITH. No; I have none. That is all.

Mr. THOMPSON. That is all.

Chairman WALSH. Prof. Commons would like to ask a question or two about this law.

I. Commissioner COMMONS. I would like to ask you about the getting of evidence and the prosecutions under this law, especially on the wage question.

Mr. SMITH. Yes, sir.

Commissioner COMMONS. Have you made any investigations of the complaints that have come in?

Mr. SMITH. Yes, sir; I have, as far as I can. A great many complaints come in over the telephone. Now, just the other day, I had a lady call me up over the phone, she said she had two daughters—I will just give you this as an illustration of it—that were her support.

Commissioner COMMONS. Yes.

Mr. SMITH. That they had been employed, but that they were both out of work. She began to complain about the minimum-wage law. She said that her daughters were discharged on account of that law. She said that that was the reason given. I asked her where they were employed, and she would not tell me where they had been employed. I asked her her name, so that I could investigate it and run it down to see whether there was anything to it, and she would not give that. Now, that is the type of complaints we get very largely. Very, very few complaints come in over a really genuine signature, so that we can run them down. Wherever they do, we do run them down to see whether there is anything to it.

Commissioner COMMONS. Do you get what may be considered a considerable number of complaints?

Mr. SMITH. No, no; few, not many.

Commissioner COMMONS. This was a complaint of being discharged because they were not competent to earn the wage?

Mr. SMITH. Yes.

Commissioner COMMONS. Do you get complaints that the minimum wage is not being actually paid or that there are some deductions or something of that kind?

Mr. SMITH. Well, I have no personal knowledge upon that. I believe you have Miss Gleason coming, and she has all those things, and she can tell you exactly.

Commissioner COMMONS. That is all.

Chairman WALSH. Mr. Garretson would like to ask you some questions.

Commissioner GARRETSON. Mr. Smith, what do you believe underlies this refusal to establish the identity or to sign the signature to these complaints or statements?

Mr. SMITH. Well, I have tried to get them. When they have done that I have tried to show them that any information that they gave us would be of a confidential nature and that they need not at any time fear our disclosing of them, even though we should find that they were trying to—but you can't overcome it.

Commissioner GARRETSON. You can't overcome it?

Mr. SMITH. No.

Commissioner GARRETSON. It is the belief that it would injure their future chances of employment, isn't it?

Mr. SMITH. No; I was going to explain as to that. I don't think so, altogether. I think that while they may feel that way, I think that that is largely imaginary with them.

Commissioner GARRETSON. Well, that may be.

Mr. SMITH. Yes, sir.

Commissioner GARRETSON. But I mean the belief is there.

Mr. SMITH. Oh, yes; I presume it is. I presume it is.

Commissioner GARRETSON. You spoke of the fact that you believed the minimum-wage law was an injury to the unqualified?

Mr. SMITH. Yes.

Commissioner GARRETSON. That is, those that don't measure up to the requirements?

Mr. SMITH. Yes, sir.

Commissioner GARRETSON. But it is an advantage, is it not, or is it, to the great body of workers who are qualified?

Mr. SMITH. Yes, sir; I believe that is true.

Commissioner GARRETSON. In the absence of a law, then—under the law it is only the unqualified or inefficient who are injured?

Mr. SMITH. Yes, sir; I believe that is correct.

Commissioner GARRETSON. In the absence of law, does not that same unqualification injure the whole body, by lowering the standard of pay?

. Mr. SMITH. Well, I don't know as to that. I don't believe that the standard of pay was materially increased in most industries in the city of Portland.·

Commissioner GARRETSON. Only of the lower paid?

Mr. SMITH. Yes, sir; that is all.

Commissioner GARRETSON. Those who have developed an extra high degree of efficiency were not helped?

Mr. SMITH. No, sir.

Commissioner GARRETSON. But the average probably were?

Mr. SMITH. Oh, yes; there was unquestionably a per cent who got more money.

Commissioner GARRETSON. Your conclusion would warrant this fact—that while the inefficient are injured by the law, all except the extra efficient were probably injured by the nonexistence of the law?

Mr. SMITH. Yes, sir.

Commissioner GARRETSON. Then really it is the lesser of two evils?

Mr. SMITH. Yes, sir; I think that is true.

Commissioner GARRETSON. That exists?

Mr. SMITH. Yes, sir.

Commissioner GARRETSON. What is the make-up of the commission?

Mr. SMITH. You mean how many?

Commissioner GARRETSON. I know how many, but I mean any qualification as to representation. What interests are represented?

Mr. SMITH. No, sir. I notice in your announcement of myself being on here that it is stated I represent the employers.

Commissioner GARRETSON. That is what made me ask the question.

Mr. SMITH. I never have employed women at all in any of my work. I never have been an employer of women. Not only that, I was asked by Gov. West to take the place on the commission without his asking me anything about it or telling me what he desired me to represent, so that I am really not a representative of any particular interest.

Commissioner GARRETSON. I didn't know but what the matter required representatives from three classes, as this commission.

Mr. SMITH. The law does say so, but I was not assigned to that.

Commissioner GARRETSON. Then you are the representative of the employing class regardless of the fact that you never employed women and children?

Mr. SMITH. Then there is another factor. I have never taken any direction or consulted the employing class in regard to it, except as we sat around the table in the commission.

Commissioner GARRETSON. Were you identified with the formation and passage of the bill?

Mr. SMITH. No, sir; I was not in this State when it was passed.

Commissioner GARRETSON. That is all, Mr. Chairman.

Chairman WALSH. That is all; thank you. Call your next.

Mr. THOMPSON. Mr. Woodward.

TESTIMONY OF MR. W. F. WOODWARD.

Mr. THOMPSON. Give us your name, please.

Mr. WOODWARD. W. F. Woodward.

Mr. THOMPSON. And your business address?

Mr. WOODWARD. Alder, at West Park.

Mr. THOMPSON. And your business?

Mr. WOODWARD. Druggist.

Mr. THOMPSON. What firm are you connected with, or is it a firm?

Mr. WOODWARD. Yes, sir.

Mr. THOMPSON. What firm?

Mr. WOODWARD. Woodward, Clark & Co. and Woodward-Clark Co. One is a retail and the other a jobbing concern.

Mr. THOMPSON. They are both located in Portland?

Mr. WOODWARD. Yes, sir.

Mr. THOMPSON. How long have you been in that business here?

Mr. WOODWARD. Thirty-two years past.

Mr. THOMPSON. In the conduct of your business have you had anything to do with the minimum wage?

Mr. WOODWARD. We have.

Mr. THOMPSON. And the establishment of hours for women and children?

Mr. WOODWARD. Yes, sir.

- Mr. THOMPSON. Now, will you tell us, Mr. Woodward, how that affected you
in your business and your views in regard to the commission and the standards
they have set?

Mr. WOODWARD. These questions were sent to me when Mr. Manly sent his
subpoena, and I attached answers thereto. May I read them off?

" Mr. THOMPSON. Yes, sir; you may read them off. .

Mr. WOODWARD. That simplifies them, perhaps.

Question No. 1. This relates purely to my own concern, my reply.

. Mr. THOMPSON. No; we are touching the whole broad industrial field.

Mr. WOODWARD. I replied first as to our own affairs.

Mr. THOMPSON. Well you may read your answers off as you have them.

Mr. WOODWARD. We had only 10 immediately affected by the minimum wage
ruling among the women, and the increase was slight, $6.50; the total number
of wage earners, 46; the total amount of normal weekly pay roll was $590.25.
The number of employees discharged because they were not worth—believed to
be worth the standard wage fixed by the minimum-wage law, there were none.
And a brief statement of the effects of the minimum-wage law on business and
on the relations between employers and employees. This is general, this reply,
inasmuch as our manufacturing is perhaps inconsequential, or, at any rate,
not large.

. In so far as the law has affected our own business, the consequences are negligible, our manufactured products requiring the employment of women being
largely of a noncompetitive character. Were we, however, manufacturers in
a large way, requiring the use of female help, the hours and wages demanded
under the laws of this State would bring us into direct and immediate competition with States where such a law is not in existence and where the wage
schedule for women is very much less; and, therefore, on all products where
the cost is largely determined by the amount of female labor required would
affect us injuriously, even to the extent of making it impossible for us to
compete.

Now they ask as to the relations. The relations between employer and employee in our own case have not been materially changed inasmuch as the
hours of labor previous to the passage of the law or the making of this ruling
had always met with the approval of our employees.

Question No. 7. If legislation affects competition with firms not covered by
the Oregon minimum-wage law, please state location of principal competitors.

This is general. Manufacturers and employers, that refers to States where
women and children are employed at a nominal wage, particularly principally
the New England States, New York, Pennsylvania, New Jersey, and the States
to the south.

It should be borne in mind that Oregon being a relatively sparsely settled
State and, in a large measure, remote from the trade centers of the country,
we labor at the present time under a number of disadvantages which the minimum law as to wages and hours will no doubt for a time accentuate, rendering
it increasingly difficult to establish industries on a profitable scale.

In a conference a few days ago with the heads of the larger department
stores—

Question No. 1. The number of employees whose wages were increased as a
result of the minimum-wage legislation approximated 22 per cent of the total
number of female employees. These were taken from their records and are
fairly exact.

The amount of such increase in relation to the total pay roll, both men and
women, approximated 2 per cent.

Question No. 2. The number of employees discharged because they were not
believed worth the standard wage fixed by the minimum-wage law? •

'As nearly as could be ascertained, none. The process of elimination going on
just as it ever had in the past. The increase in wages fixed by the commission
might possibly have accentuated or accelerated slightly the movement, but none
would admit it or could ascertain that fact.

Question No. 3. The general effect of the minimum-wage law on business?

Negligible, except for the loss of the Saturday night shopping hours.

. In addition to that, I might say we have always had, as far back as my experience, open hours on Saturday evening. It is still permissible, but, under the
ruling of the commission, women could not be employed in the evening hours,
and it automatically closes the larger stores. The question whether it was a
benefit to those affected or not raises an opportunity for argument. There
seems to be a well-defined sentiment that there is one evening in the week

when a class of the people who need the time, and who get it at no other time, ought to be permitted to transact their business, and that women working during those evening hours, if it did not increase the total number—if they came later in the morning and could serve during Saturday evening—it would be a help. It would not work a hardship. There are some indirect effects. The necessity of closing at 6 o'clock or 5.30 rendered it necessary at places to discharge some of the women and replace them with men, which, as I say, works a hardship.

Chairman WALSH. Do you know how great that was. To what extent it occurred? ·

Mr. WOODWARD. It arises, and its effect, Mr. Walsh, would be a very difficult matter. There are four large department stores here, and I think they were all open Saturday evenings, practically, until the time that this ruling was made, and they ceased at that time.

The smaller stores where men are employed, for instance, haberdasheries and the like, were not affected, necessarily. They had no women help. But where women entered into or were a large proportion of the amount of help, to stop them practically closed these stores.

In our own business we necessarily have to carry out the evening hours, and that necessitated that we were compelled in some cases to replace women with men. We had to have some one at the place and we could not have a woman. We must, therefore, get a man.

Question No. 4. The effect on the relations between employers and employees.

The law has not materially changed the relations heretofore existing. That is an indefinite question. I don't know whether it means friendliness or a disposition to employ or discharge. If that is the point, it has not affected it.

Question No. 5. The effect of the law upon the efficiency of the workers.

That was very fully discussed. The increase in wages was hardly large enough to work any radical change in the minds of those receiving it. They all seemed to arrive at the conclusion that it had not materially changed the nature of the individual.

Learners and apprentices. The present law provides for a minimum weekly wage of $6 for these classes, which is a reversal of the usages of previous years, when their teaching or calling was paid for by the learner, or, if not paid for, at any rate the mere matter of learning the business was regarded as some consideration. That has now been changed.

Question No. 2. The law has apparently not affected employees who work but fractional days, part of a day or part of the regular week.

Question No. 3. The effect of the minimum-wage legislation on the general level of wages.

There was none, apparently.

Question No. 4. The extent to which women are displaced by men as a result of the minimum-wage legislation.

None as to the larger establishments.

Question No. 5. The relation of industrial education to minimum-wage legislation.

The answer written here is none. We haven't here vocational institutions, so that the question would hardly enter into our State. We haven't a great number of large factories where the necessity arises for fitting growing boys and girls for that product. The public schools have taken that up, but it is still in its infancy.

Question No. 6. The problem of employees alleged to be too incompetent to be paid the standard wage.

This was discussed very fully. The public has been increasingly educated to demand a higher degree of efficiency and service on the part of those with whom they deal. The minimum-wage law has not materially affected this demand. The weeding out of the incompetent, inefficient, or inept from all those positions where they may be brought in contact with the public will continue in a greater degree without regard to the present law.

There is a notation here that the inhibition of working hours for saleswomen, after 6 o'clock p. m., has lessened the volume of business in the stores affected, and in the interest of fairness the closure should be made general without regard to sex.

Mr. THOMPSON. Have you any general observations you would like to make with reference to this law?

Mr. WOODWARD. Yes, sir. Gentlemen, our State law has been administered evidently with an effort toward fairness, and I do not believe, speaking for the merchants with whom I have come in contact, that there is any feeling of hostility toward that law. There is a feeling that in some of its phases—not the law, but in some of their phases—the rulings might be modified.

I have spoken of the Saturday evening question, and not in an absolute or fixed sense; but they all regard it as a step in the right direction, and should now be supplemented by such Federal legislation as would place our State on a parity with others. We have taken a step forward, there can be no question but we have done it at the expense of the merchants and the public, and also of the women themselves, and until we are fortified by nation-wide legislation in these matters we are traveling the road alone and unaided.

Mr. THOMPSON. Of course that would refer to such matters in which you come into competition with other States?

Mr. WOODWARD. Yes, but you see we do. There are, indeed, but very few industries in which we are not sooner or later brought into competition. Of course, we haven't constructed them all yet.

Mr. THOMPSON. Has this interstate competition had any effect on industries because of the minimum wage and fixing the hours of labor?

Mr. WOODWARD. I believe I am correct in stating that it has, and that it will grow in a greater degree. I would cite one concern.

One of the officers told me yesterday that his minimum wage scale represented about double that of, for instance, the Rowell Co., of New York, and Year, of Philadelphia, in the manufacture of certain classes of paper goods. They are able to hire help at practically half his wages. They take the ocean rate and deliver the goods here, so that he is practically cut out of the business, and until that is adjusted he must relinquish that particular field of activity. I merely cite that as an illustration, and it would apply to many classes of goods. We would find it in our own small laboratory here, where we put up various toilet articles, preparations, and the like, that we are brought directly in competition. Our wages, $9 a week, when we compete with concerns in New York paying three dollars and a half or four or five dollars. It is obvious we can never make very much progress, that our sales must be based largely upon the individual liking of our patrons.

Mr. THOMPSON. Any other suggestion you care to make?

Mr. WOODWARD. Not except to thank you.

Mr. THOMPSON. That is all, Mr. Chairman.

Chairman WALSH. Thank you, Mr. Woodward; that is all. Call your next.

Mr. THOMPSON. Miss Gleason.

TESTIMONY OF MISS CAROLINE J. GLEASON.

Mr. THOMPSON. Will you give us your name, please?

Miss GLEASON. Caroline J. Gleason.

Mr. THOMPSON. And your business address?

Miss GLEASON. 610 Commercial Block.

Mr. THOMPSON. You are secretary of the industrial welfare commission?

Miss GLEASON. Yes, sir.

Mr. THOMPSON. You have been so since its inception?

Miss GLEASON. Since the law went into effect a year ago in June.

Mr. THOMPSON. What work were you engaged in prior to that time?

Miss GLEASON. Prior to that time I had taught for two years, and for three years I had been engaged in social work; that is, so called.

Mr. THOMPSON. Have you made any study or are you acquainted definitely or generally with the conditions of the women workers in Oregon?

Miss GLEASON. Yes, sir; I made a study under the consumers' league prior to the passage of the law, and of course after the law came into effect my whole work has been to look after the condition of the women workers in the State.

Mr. THOMPSON. Generally speaking, what is the condition of the women in industry in this State?

Miss GLEASON. Compared with eastern conditions, it is very good; but taking individual industries in special spots, there are some conditions that were poor, perhaps very bad, I might say, prior to the passage of the law, and all have not been cured to date.

Mr. THOMPSON. What industry would you mention particularly where the conditions are poor, and what are the causes you assign for that?

Miss GLEASON. There are no industries which as a whole are poor. That is, I would not say that the manufacturing industry as a whole was in a poor condition or the department stores. We found individual establishments in different lines of work which were poor. Just generally speaking, I would say we found one telephone establishment which was in poor condition on sanitary grounds and also on the question of wages. I don't wish to insinuate that the whole telephone situation was. I would be more likely to mention something that wasn't than something that was now.

Mr. THOMPSON. What has been the general complaint or what has been the greater cause of complaint, the question of hours or wages or working conditions?

Miss GLEASON. The question of wages was of much greater complaint than the question of hours. We did have the 10-hour day and the 60-hour week, and that was generally lived up to, but the question of night work, regardless of the fact that the girls did not work more than 10 hours a day, was also a question that was more complained about, I might say, than the question of wages. The wages were bad enough. They were very bad. We found wages ranging from nothing—beginning wages, ranging from nothing to $5 a week, with the emphasis on the $3 class.

Mr. THOMPSON. What are the principal industries which employ women?

Miss GLEASON. The department stores of the city, I should say, average about 3,000. The manufacturing establishments, I should judge, between 2,500 and 3,000. The telephone industry, in round numbers, about 800. The laundry industry in this city between—well, exactly a month ago they had 768. Those are the principal ones, I think. The restaurants, perhaps about 400. Hotels, probably 300.

Mr. THOMPSON. How about the canning industry?

Miss GLEASON. The canning industry I have classified with the manufacturing. The canning industry in the two establishments in this city employ between three and four hundred girls. There are probably—well, there are probably 400—more than that, between five and six hundred women engaged in the State in the canning industry in the busy season. That is for about six weeks in the year.

Mr. THOMPSON. You say you did make a survey of the women in industries in this State for the consumers' league prior to the passage of the act?

Miss GLEASON. Yes, sir.

Mr. THOMPSON. Was that survey used as the basis for urging the legislation?

Miss GLEASON. Yes, sir; it was the chief basis. It was the only thing we had.

Mr. THOMPSON. Was that survey printed?

Miss GLEASON. Yes, sir; I have a copy of it here.

Mr. THOMPSON. Would you be willing to give the commission a copy of that?

Miss GLEASON. Yes, sir.

Mr. THOMPSON. Will you please do so?

(Document entitled "Report of the Social Survey Committee of the Consumers' League of Oregon," dated Portland, Oreg., January, 1913, was submitted in printed form.)

Mr. THOMPSON. In the first place, is there anything particularly you would like to call the attention of the commission to in this survey you made?

Miss GLEASON. Well, no, sir. The general conditions there stated. I have stated, as mentioned in that report, as to the matter of wages. We found some establishments taking women in and not paying them anything. Other establishments paying them a dollar and a half per week for what they considered a year's work. That is, two seasons of three months each. That is not a year's work, of course.

We found that the girls were living, as Father O'Hara stated, under anything but livable conditions. I investigated a number of houses personally, and had one or two of my assistants do so. We found them living in attic rooms which were not heated at all, or heated by stoves. The girls had to carry their own fuel up the three flights of stairs, and in addition to the cost of the room they had to furnish their fuel.

In some instances we had girls who were eating only two meals a day because they could not afford more, and in one particular line of work, where the work was very hard, one girl said it was a fortunate thing she did not have the time that she was entitled to—to eat—because if she had not been too tired she would not have had the money to buy the meal, anyway.

We found one girl who was an office employee at $20 a month. She was a girl 19 years old, whose money ran out on Friday, and a friend of mine happened to call on her Saturday to see how she was getting along and found the girl would have nothing to eat until Monday, when she would get her pay check.

Of course these cases I am mentioning are extreme, but they were not the only ones in existence; and the fact that there is even one representing each type was bad enough.

Mr. THOMPSON. In the establishment of the minimum wages in the different industries, did you carry on, as secretary of the commission, investigations?

Miss GLEASON. In the establishing of the wage?

Mr. THOMPSON. Yes.

Miss GLEASON. Yes.

Mr. THOMPSON. By the conferences?

Miss GLEASON. Yes.

Mr. THOMPSON. What generally was the nature of the work you did, and how did you carry it out?

Miss GLEASON. The investigation was finished in January of 1913, and the law went into effect six months afterwards, in June. The commission began the calling of conferences almost immediately, so that the facts which were printed in the report were used as a basis for the—were used partly as a basis. The employers·for the most part were not satisfied with the findings of the report and carried on their own investigations, but found that the facts were practically the same as stated in the report, so that not many new investigations were made to establish the wage. The experience of the employees in the conferences, however, was called upon in every case, and new lists of costs of room and board, and clothing, and dental work, and medicine, and so on, were made up.

Mr. THOMPSON. In the establishment of these standards, was a great deal of information gathered that was in a statistical form that was printed and used by this commission?

Miss GLEASON. No; just the minutes of the meetings were kept, which embodied the statistical information that was presented. There wasn't anything like the amount of statistics that is in the report that was presented. The meetings were generally very informal, and a great many of the compilations were destroyed by some of those who offered them, then and there.

Mr. THOMPSON. You have heard what Father O'Hara and Mr. Smith said with the method of arriving at these figures?

Miss GLEASON. Yes.

Mr. THOMPSON. Is there anything you care to add to what was said in that respect?

Miss GLEASON. No; I think they covered the ground completely.

Mr. THOMPSON. Is there anything further you would care to say about the conferences that were carried on, any information that would be of value to the commission, different from what they said?

Miss GLEASON. I think not, except that there was not any doubt at all as to what everyone felt about the passage of the law and the good it would do and the truth of the cost of living that it would bring out. I mean there was very little left unsaid. There was no reticence whatever on the part of either the employers or the employees in arriving at the wage decision. It was not a matter of doubtful reasoning; they are not the result of doubtful information.

Mr. THOMPSON. As secretary of this commission, have you had any complaints, first, from women who have not received the minimum, or who have complaints to make about the way it is administered by the firms?

Miss GLEASON. Who have received the minimum or who have not received the minimum?

Mr. THOMPSON. Who have not.

Miss GLEASON. Yes; I have complaints ever so often, not a great number. I have more, as Father O'Hara and Mr. Smith both said, unsigned complaints than I have signed. I have even had women in the office who have refused to give me their names because of that fear that they would lose their positions. That is probably one of the greatest obstacles that there is to the enforcement of the law.

Mr. THOMPSON. About how many would you say have come into your office and told you things, that didn't want to give their names?

Miss GLEASON. Well, I didn't count.

Mr. THOMPSON. Well, have there been many?

Miss GLEASON. I have made records, of course. I have had as many· as six in one delegation from one firm at a time, and three, and. sometimes, one. I suppose we have had between fifty and a hundred in person, and more over the telephone. A larger number over the telephone.

Mr. THOMPSON. When you get these complaints, do you investigate them?

Miss GLEASON. If I don't do it personally, I refer it to the deputy labor commissioner·of·this district, who does do it.

Mr. THOMPSON. Generally speaking, what is the method you follow in investigating a complaint about the wages or the hours?

Miss GLEASON. I go into the establishment. Well, it all depends. Of·course, there are different ways of doing it. Sometimes we have to do it secretly. Sometimes we send people in there to work and find out what the·real truth is. Sometimes we send for the pay rolls. And sometimes I go in person and tell them—first ask general questions about the conduct of the business and the wages that are paid and the experience of the employees, and· then tell them that I have had this complaint and give them a chance to deny it or show ·me that it is not true.

Of course, we have access to the pay rolls, and that is where it is possible—sometimes it is almost impossible to follow up a complaint like that without revealing the name of the employee. I mean that the employee would be so well known by the facts surrounding the complaint, that following it up in the open way would mean her dismissal. At least she thinks it would. And so it is not always an easy thing to do, and it is not a thing that we always do do, because of the employee's unwillingness to have us proceed.

Mr. THOMPSON. What generally has been the attitude of the employer toward these investigations, if you care to state?

Miss GLEASON. Well, that depends a great deal on the personality of the man or woman, I think. Only in two instances have I been refused access—and that was when the law was in the courts—to the books of the .firm or to the employees. It enabled me to go there and speak to the employees. They ask men to come to the front door, though, and of course I have never gone to the back door myself. They seem to think that I am perfectly open about it and show my hand, as the saying is, and they will not hesitate to show theirs. · · · ·

Mr. THOMPSON. Have you had to prosecute any of the employers under this law?

Miss GLEASON. Yes, sir. The labor commissioner has prosecuted. The law permits the collection of back wages. If a woman is employed for less than the ruling calls for, she may collect her back wages at any time. And back wages· have been collected in several instances. And then some employers have been prosecuted on the score of overtime, but not very many on the score of not paying the minimum to adult workers.

Mr. THOMPSON. Do you keep a record of the cases that are brought to enforce the law?

Miss GLEASON. I keep a record of everything that comes to my office. · Some of the violations go to the deputy labor commissioner first; but anything that comes to me, I have a record·of.

Mr. THOMPSON. What has been the general result, if you can state it, of those prosecutions?· Have they resulted in convictions or in dismissals of the cases?

Miss GLEASON. As far as I know, they have all resulted in convictions.⁻ In just one, in the dismissal, I believe, where the evidence was·not sufficient to convict. That was a case of overtime and was not a case of wage.

Mr. THOMPSON. About how many of those cases have been brought, if you· know, in round numbers?

Miss GLEASON. I think not more than 12.

Mr. THOMPSON. Not more than 12?

Miss GLEASON. Of course, in one case I might say that I think there were eight women involved in the demand for back wages. That was a· case of ap-·' prentices, where women were taken on as apprentices and ·paid $3 a week when they should have been paid $6.

Mr. THOMPSON. There were 12 distinct prosecutions?

Miss GLEASON. Well, that is just in round numbers.

Mr. THOMPSON. Yes. Did they appertain to any particular line of industry, or were they scattered among them all? · · · · ·

Miss GLEASON. They were varied; decidedly varied.

Mr. THOMPSON. That is to say, you didn't find in· the mercantile establishments more violations than in the· manufacturing?•

Miss GLEASON. No.

Mr. THOMPSON. Or anything else?

Miss GLEASON. Of course, we did have a number of complaints while the law· was in the courts, but as Father O'Hara said it was not the attitude of the commission then to prosecute because the employers doubted the possibility of.the prosecution,·or of a·conviction being given and preferred to wait. · ·

Mr. Thompson. Do you know whether or not the passage of this law and the establishment of minimum wages under it has affected any firm particularly in its business, or do you pay attention to that?

'▪ Miss Gleason. Yes, sir; I pay attention to everything that has any connection with the law. I have heard of none that it has affected. One firm that wished to keep open evenings, one of the mercantile stores, did not dismiss any of the women that I know of, but did put on young men for the evening work, dental students and others.

Mr. Thompson. Well, have you studied at all this question that is called interstate competition, as related to the hours of labor for women and the minimum wage?'

Miss Gleason. I knew something about the conditions in the East and from personal visitation there of the establishments and of the wages, and I worked with an organization in Chicago which was in the heart of the large factory district, so that was a study of it there, inasmuch as what I learned, I mean in connection with that, and then, of course, we always hear from the employers that they are suffering here on account of competition with the East.

Mr. Thompson. But you have seen no concrete evidence so far?

Miss Gleason. No; but my experience has been that the prices here are higher for the line of goods than they are for the same lines of goods in the East. It seemed to me that they are balanced up. But I am not authority on the prices and on the costs in the East.

Mr. Thompson. So far as you know, has the law been favorably received by the women and by employers generally?

Miss Gleason. Yes; generally it has. We have received a great deal of cooperation from the employers. We have had some complaints, of course, from women who have not understood it. But it seems to me that more often the complaint is made when there is some selfish interest attached to it. Then we have had complaints from women where we thought they didn't realize what was for their own good. For instance, we had a petition from one factory one time asking that the lunch hour be shortened to one-half hour, as it had been until the commission made a ruling that it should be 45 minutes. This was because they could get out 15 minutes earlier in the afternoon, and they didn't like to stay there that long. But our conference thought it was better for them to have 45 minutes at noon.

Mr. Thompson. Is there any additional suggestion that you would like to make to this commission with reference to the law as to any amendments that might be made, or any other statement in that regard?

Miss Gleason. No. I think we have about the best form of law here that there has been so far. It seems to me that the commission form of regulating wages is the best form, because with the commissioners the subject can be handled closer for each industry than it can by a flat wage. And it is possible, also, under our law, where it is not possible under other laws, to make regulations for localities. There is no doubt but that the smaller towns and rural sections of the State have a lower cost of living than a city does, and our law permits the regulation of wages for such localities. It also permits us to issue permits for the physically defective and the crippled, and we have done that in some instances.

There is a very great deal might be said on the question of learners and apprentices. And I am not in accord with some of the things that were said earlier here to-day. I am sure that the law is going to do a great deal more good. Our commission has said by its ruling that apprentices must be paid $1 per day, and that is going to do more good than harm, if it is going to force the opening of vocational schools. Our experience is, and this was the basis for that ruling, that learners and apprentices, so called, are not taught to-day. They are taken on as learners and apprentices, kept six months or a year, and paid perhaps nothing, or a dollar and a half a week, and at the end of that time they don't know the business as the employers say they will when they take them on. They are kept on the unskilled lines of work. In the dressmaking work they may do the overcasting of seams and the sewing on of hooks and eyes, and different little details like that, and the same thing in the millinery trade. So that the statement that the old system used to be that the learner would pay was true enough when the learner learned something, but nowadays they don't learn the business. They are not much further along at the end of the time.

Then, another thing, as to the fact that the incompetents are going to suffer from this law, it seems to me that a great many of the so-called incompetents.

nowadays are misfits, who have been allowed to come into a position and are willing to stay there because it pays them something. Young girls start' out without the faintest idea in the world of what they want to do or where they are going, and they may get something that is very- easy, and if · they' are dismissed they are often ignorant as to where to go to find the: next position. Our law requires that every beginner shall have a dollar a day,·and it ·comes out that only those beginners are going to be retained who are 'going to show that they will learn the business. Those who will not will be dismissed. ⋆And those who are dismissed will have to think of something else, and eventually find their right place.

Then, too, it is going to start, I am sure, good vocational schools. The employers say that our present trade school and our other classes that ·are· conducted by organizations do not train the girls. But I have seen schools in the East that did train them into very efficient workers. And there is no reason why we can't have them here.

At present they are not protesting very loud, but I think the dressmakers will a month hence, when the season opens, against the $1-a-day ruling for apprentices. And I think that will lead in one way to a solution of the apprenticeship question, and will bring us nearer to the vocational school than we are now.

 Mr. THOMPSON. Anything more you wish to say?

Miss GLEASON. Nothing more.

Chairman WALSH. At this point, we will adjourn until to-morrow morning at 10. [Addressing the witness:] Please come back in the morning at :10.

(Whereupon, at 4.30 o'clock p. m., an adjournment was taken until the following day, Saturday, August 22, 1914, at the hour of 10 o'clock a. m.) ·

PORTLAND, OREG., *Saturday, August 22, 1914—10 a. m.*

Present: Chairman Walsh, Commissioners Lennon, O'Connell, Garretson, and Commons; also W. O. Thompson, counsel.

Chairman WALSH. The commission will come to order. Miss Gleason, you may take the stand again now.

TESTIMONY OF MISS CAROLINE J. GLEASON—Continued.

Chairman WALSH. Prof. Commons wishes to ask a few questions.

Commissioner COMMONS. You spoke of the apprenticeship provision—apprentices and learners and possibly others.

Miss GLEASON. I did mention some others also.

Commissioner COMMONS. What proportion—how many apprentice or learner permits have you issued?

Miss GLEASON. We have no system of issuing permits. Anyone who has had less than a year's experience may be employed as an apprentice. There is a danger that a woman who wants work badly, who has had more than a year's experience, will say that she is an apprentice and will go on as such and be given the apprentice's wage. That is a matter that the commission is going to take up in the near future, the registration with the firms of those who say they are apprentices, who are taken on as apprentices partly to guard the firms as well as the girls, because the woman who is taken on as an apprentice, if she consents to work for a dollar a day and later it is proven she is experienced, she may collect the back wages for an experienced worker; so that unless there is some good system of registration the employers will be imposed upon; but it is a matter we have to handle in the future. ·   '

Commissioner COMMONS. Then, you have no record of the number of apprentices or learners?

Miss GLEASON. We have no record; no, sir; other than from—we have no record at all. I know in the laundry at present, because I have just finished an investigation of them, there were last April 768 women·employed in the laundries and 75 of those were apprentices. ·

Commissioner COMMONS. About 10 per cent.

Miss. GLEASON. Yes; about 10 per cent. ·   .

Commissioner COMMONS. Did you investigate those cases of apprentices· to find out whether they are actually inexperienced?

 Miss GLEASON. Yes; I investigated a great number of them personally and found out. And I am quite sure that they are in the laundries for the reason that that is an industry in which the workers shift frequently. And a number of these apprentices were girls under—not a great number, but probably a half were girls under 18 or very near 18.

Commissioner COMMONS. You are planning, then, a system of permits, are you, or registration? How do you propose to avoid evasion of the law?

Miss GLEASON. It is a question that we have never gone into thoroughly. It almost seems to me that the apprentice would have to register with us also at the same time that she registers with the firm.

The trouble in this section of the country is that a number of women will come from the East, and it will be very difficult to find out whether or not they have had experience. If a woman were applying who had worked only in Oregon, it would be easy enough to insist before she be given employment that she furnish evidence from her former employer as to whether or not she had been employed and how long. But it is a more difficult question where we have such numbers coming, as we do have, not only from the far Eastern States but from the States near here. And it is frankly a problem that we have not gone into yet.

Commissioner COMMONS. Well, you would not know, outside of the laundry business, whether the proportion was about the same as you have mentioned—about 10 per cent?

Miss GLEASON. No; I could not say definitely from my own knowledge, from my own—oh, yes; knowledge. Talking with the women and talking with the girls, and from past investigation, I think that it would be about the same. But I haven't any—I can't give you any definite information on that.

Commissioner COMMONS. I take it that there is only one organization or union of women employees here.

Miss GLEASON. There are two; the bookbinders organized as well as the garment makers.

Commissioner COMMONS. Well, now, in case of the garment workers, do they have agreements, trade agreements, with their employers?

Miss GLEASON. Yes; they have. The garment workers organized. The garment workers work almost entirely by piecework, of course. Even the first ones to come on, the girls who have never handled a power machine, are put on at a piece rate. A few are put on at labeling at a dollar a day. They may be kept at that for a year, and if they are, rather than raise them to the minimum the employers will put them on at piecework. It is possible——

Commissioner COMMONS. If they have a trade agreement with the employers, then your minimum-wage law comes along; does that modify the trade agreement? Suppose their trade agreement provides for less than that—less than your minimum of a dollar a day.

Miss GLEASON. Yes; our wage law——

Commissioner COMMONS. Your wage law will interfere with their trade agreements?

Miss GLEASON. Yes. For instance, if they receive a dollar a day—the bookbinders require that for the first six months the apprentice shall receive $6, the second six months $6.50, and at the end of a year $7. Now, under our law at the end of a year she must receive $8.64.

Commissioner COMMONS. Then you do not permit a union to make an agreement for a minimum less than——

Miss GLEASON. No.

Commissioner COMMONS. The State minimum?

Miss GLEASON. No.

Commissioner COMMONS. That is, you are really taking the place of organized labor?

Miss GLEASON. Well, in arranging the wage rates perhaps we are. We could hardly—I think we could hardly—make an exception in a case like that.

Commissioner COMMONS. I am getting at the effect on trade unionism. Is it better, then, for the women to give up their union than to accept the law?

Miss GLEASON. They don't have to give up their union. They are only too glad to get the extra.

Commissioner COMMONS. Then, from the standpoint of the employer who makes the agreement with the union, you come in with the State law and invalidate that agreement. Wouldn't that be the view from his standpoint? He is probably giving them higher wages at one point in consideration of the lower wage at another.

Miss GLEASON. No; he is not in the bookbinders' union, especially, because at the end of the first year they are earning six dollars and fifty cents, when they must be raised to seven; at the end of the second year they are earning seven; at the end of the third year they must be earning.eight. And then it, depends upon whether—what they call pamphlet girls—I believe the table girls, do less skilled work than the girls who bind the pamphlets. About the highest . wage that a girl who does not become a forelady reaches in the bookbinding trade, even though she works from 12 to 15 years, I have heard them tell me · that the highest they get is about ten or eleven dollars a week. I have had, girls who have had from 11 to 13 years' experience at the trade tell me that, they never earn more than ten or eleven dollars. The best of them earn fifteen, but no shop has more than one or two foreladies.

Commissioner COMMONS. That is in the bookbinding trade?

Miss GLEASON. In the bookbinding trade.

Commissioner COMMONS. How would it be in the garment workers?

Miss GLEASON. In the garment workers, as I said, they work almost entirely by piecework, so that a woman of a number of years' experience will earn $20 to $25 a week.

Commissioner COMMONS. The beginner, the apprentice, at the end of the first year would earn that?

Miss GLEASON. The apprentices on piecework rates start out and perhaps will not earn more than $4 a week for the first two or three months. They say at the end of three months if she is not earning a dollar a day she is not worth keeping and they will discharge her. Our laws up to the present have not applied to pieceworkers. A man who has had girls entirely on piecework is not compelled to pay over $8.64 a week.

Commissioner COMMONS. The beginner?

Miss GLEASON. Not if she is on piecework. The law so far only applies to the time-workers. The standard, of course, of minimum wages has been fixed, but the rulings say specifically they must apply only to time workers. The question. of piece rate is one the commission is going to take up this fall in conference.

Commissioner COMMONS. That question has really not come to an issue, then?

Miss GLEASON. No.

Commissioner COMMONS. As to whether the commission is going to take the place of the unions in the matter of apprentices.

Miss GLEASON. Well, some of the union women have discussed it with us, and at first I think they showed some alarm; but they realize that if our law could bring about a higher wage than they get that it would be a good thing. They did not think they would have to do away with their organization, they hadn't any intention of disbanding, but still they seemed to think it would be a good thing if we could get a higher wage than they could. Of course, they realize this, I think, too, that women are very hard to organize. They. are hard to make realize what they have a right to ask for and what they should not ask for. But this is—the minimum wage agitation probably is awakening some of them to a sense of what they may legitimately get, where they would never take any interest if it were put to them.

Commissioner COMMONS. Well, then, does the minimum wage have a tendency to induce them to organize and go into the union. Does it have a tendency to strengthen the union?

Miss GLEASON. Well, I don't know about that, we have so few unions here.

Commissioner COMMONS. Well, just take the two unions you know about.

Miss GLEASON. No, sir; I don't think that the wage has any effect on them. I think that the interest—that the union members are more interested in their own union than they are in the wage discussion. What I mean is that they will not leave the union because—the union will not be given up because of the wage legislation, I am sure, because the spirit is too strong.

Commissioner COMMONS. That is where they are already organized?

Miss GLEASON. That is where they are already organized, but I have seen no signs of further organization because of the wage. I don't believe that the women are going to organize, not in the present year. Maybe a few years, per-, haps five or six years from now, when they are accustomed to bargaining more closely, as men are, they may begin to think of it.

Commissioner COMMONS. Do these unions assist you in getting evidence of violations?

Miss GLEASON. Yes, sir; they do. They have come to us when there have been violations in their own plant, their own establishment, they have come to us for us to prosecute.

Commissioner COMMONS. Have they furnished witnesses who will testify?

Miss GLEASON. Yes, sir; they have. They offered to, the one case that I have in 'mind was last winter some time. Let me see, what. was that. I think it was the case of a woman who had—it was the case of a girl who had worked for a year at a dollar a day, and she was put on piecework at the end of the year and could not earn the dollar a day. Some of the other women came to us to know whether or not the man had a right to do that, and what we would do. And they were perfectly willing to furnish witnesses and everything. But, of course, he had a right to do that then under our present arrangement for time and piece workers.

Commissioner COMMONS. Well, are you more able to get witnesses to testify where they are organized than where they are not organized?

Miss GLEASON. Yes; I am sure of that. They have a certain—well, they depend upon each other for moral support where they don't depend upon each other when they are not organized.

Commissioner COMMONS. Well, in the case of unorganized women, have you had any of them that have testified to violations of the law?

Miss GLEASON. No; not any that I can recall since our law has been in effect.

Commissioner COMMONS. Well, in the case of organized women have you had any?

Miss GLEASON. Well, we didn't have that one case, too.

Commissioner COMMONS. You have had no actual prosecution?

Miss GLEASON. No; you see we have really had very few cases in court, because the constitutionality of the law was being tested for so long.

Commissioner COMMONS. Then, how do you base your conclusion that they are much more ready to testify?

Miss GLEASON. Because the members of the unions will come to me and give their names and their addresses and all the information that I want. offhand, without any solicitation, without any urging. And the other women will not do so. As I say, they will come and tell me their tale, but will refuse to give me their names. They will tell me cases of rank injustice, and sit in front of me and refuse to tell me even who they are. I have had other cases of women coming to make complaints, friends of the employee, who would give me their own names, but would not give me the employee's name, and sometimes not even the firm's name. Sometimes they will give me the firm's name, but I could not possibly locate the employee by just simply having the firm's name, where a great number of people are employed. And I have had other cases where I could locate everybody, but I was begged not to proceed, because it meant the loss of the girl's position.

Commissioner COMMONS. I think that is all.

Chairman WALSH. Anything else?

Commissioner GARRETSON. One question, Mr. Chairman.

Chairman WALSH. Mr. Garretson.

Commissioner GARRETSON. Miss Gleason, don't you find that the women workers regard the minimum-wage law in regard to unionism as male workers regard, for instance, eight-hour legislation, as supplemental to their trade agreements, and an aid instead of an obstacle?

Miss GLEASON. We did not find that so at first, but I am speaking now with the remembrance of the delegate of the union who was here to arrange the rates with the garment workers particularly. She was very much opposed to the minimum-wage law until we showed her where we thought it would be a good thing and would not harm the unions. And I think that the same thing may be said of the others. I spoke to the bookbinders, I believe, at the time that we were carrying on the investigation, and they were a little touchy until they understood exactly what it was going to do.

Commissioner GARRETSON. But when they learned its practical working out, that was all right?

Miss GLEASON. Yes; they believed it was supplemental, and they were glad to have it.

Commissioner GARRETSON. That is all, Mr. Chairman.

Chairman WALSH. That is all; thank you.

Mr. THOMPSON. Mr. Howell.

TESTIMONY OF MR. GEORGE H. HOWELL.

Mr. THOMPSON. Mr. Howell, will you please give us your name?

Mr. HOWELL. George H. Howell.

Mr. THOMPSON. Your address?

Mr. Howell. 163 East Fifteenth.
Mr. Thompson. And your business?
Mr. Howell. Printer.
Mr. Thompson. Are you connected with the typographical union here?
Mr. Howell. I am.
Mr. Thompson. In what capacity?
Mr. Howell. Just as a member.
Mr. Thompson. As a member?
Mr. Howell. Yes, sir. I have been an officer at various times in the local organization, and also an officer in the international.
Mr. Thompson. How long have you been located in Portland?,
Mr. Howell. Well, about 25 years.
Mr. Thompson. What have you to say with reference to the condition existing now in the printing trades in this city, particularly relating to the relations of employer and employee?
Mr. Howell. Well, in the newspaper branch of the business the conditions are good. They are better than they were under the old hand-set conditions, where men worked all the afternoon and threw in their type and then returned at 7 or 8 in the evening and worked until 2 or 3 in the morning setting their type. The introduction of the machines did away with that afternoon work. Now they work seven hours and a half. But in the commercial end of the trade the conditions have improved, but at the present there is a little difficulty between the commercial printers and one of the crafts represented in the printing industry.
Mr. Thompson. What craft is that, Mr. Howell?
Mr. Howell. That is the printing pressmen's international organization.
Mr. Thompson. Can you tell us the nature of that difficulty? Let me ask you, have you got a copy of the demands that were made by that craft?
Mr. Howell. No; I have not. I think it was the month of September, 1912, they sent a very curt communication to the employers saying that on and after such a date the following scale would go into effect. It is the absolute fact that no effort was made to interview the employers at that time. I will state now that I am secretary of the Allied Printing trades Council, and this is an organization composed of delegates from all the crafts in the printing industry. There are nine organizations in this city represented in that body. But, when this strike occurred, no member outside of the pressmen's organization knew anything of this.
Mr. Thompson. You haven't got a copy of the demands made by the pressmen on the employers?
Mr. Howell. I have not. It called for a very slight increase in wages.
Mr. Thompson. What is the present situation in that trouble to-day?
Mr. Howell. The employers claim they are working under the open shop in their pressrooms, and to all intents and purposes they are.
Mr. Thompson. When did this trouble begin?
Mr. Howell. About two years ago this coming September.
Mr. Thompson. This council you speak of, is it a regular organization, and has it been in existence for a long time?
Mr. Howell. Yes, sir; it has.
Mr. Thompson. Has it a constitution and by-laws?
Mr. Howell. Yes, sir.
Mr. Thompson. Have you got them with you?
Mr. Howell. No, sir; I have not.
Mr. Thompson. Would you be willing to furnish us a copy of them?
Mr. Howell. Yes, sir.
Mr. Thompson. Is your body affiliated with any other labor organization?
Mr. Howell. No, sir; it is not. Its primary purpose—in fact, its only purpose—is to boost the union label.
Mr. Thompson. But it is made up of men who belong to ,the international union?
Mr. Howell. Yes, sir; they have three delegates from the typographical union and three delegates from the web pressmen and three, delegates from the printing pressmen and three delegates from the printers' assistants and three delegates from the photo engravers and three delegates from the bookbinders and three delegates from the bindery women and three delegates from the electrotypers.
Mr. Thompson. Is there anything further you would care to say about the condition of labor in the printing industry here?

Mr. HOWELL. Well, at the present time there seems to be a disposition on the part of large employers of labor in this city, men like Mr. Banfield, who are determined to crush labor and wipe the labor unions out of existence. They are absolutely merciless in their methods; they think nothing of driving a man out of town, and in this last pressmen's strike it is a fact that one of the pressmen—now, Mr. Banfield is not affiliated with the printing industry, but he is an active member of the employers' association of this city—and it is a fact that one of these pressmen who was financially involved, was about to lose his home, he had to call on Mr. Banfield and intercede with Mr. Banfield to withdraw his objection, that he had an opportunity to go back to work in one of these struck shops.

Mr. THOMPSON. What was the answer?

Mr. HOWELL. I believe he finally gave his permission.

Mr. THOMPSON. Why was it necessary to go to Mr. Banfield? Do you know?

Mr. HOWELL. They are part of the manufacturers' association of this city, who stand for the open shop of the employers' association.

Mr. THOMPSON. Was he the only man this pressman could have gone to? I want to get what you intend the commission to understand by that.

Mr. HOWELL. Well, I don't know whether he was the only man, but he is the man who is a leader.

Commissioner LENNON. He was the man representing the employers in the **fight?**

Mr. HOWELL. Yes, sir.

Commissioner LENNON. And the employers insisted that anything of that kind had to go through his hands?

Mr. HOWELL. As I understand.

Mr. THOMPSON. Have you given any consideration to the industrial conditions which exist here; that is, as to whether there is unrest or not?

Mr. HOWELL. Well, of course, this is a sparsely settled community, and the conditions that exist here are not as bad as exist in the more thickly settled portions of our country. But the opening of the Panama Canal is fraught with danger to the working classes unless something is done to prevent the people from Europe coming in here and competing with labor.

There is one thing that I would like to say in reference to the testimony of—this may not be in order at this time, but it is in my mind—that Mr. C. E. S. Wood yesterday in testifying spoke of the ignorance displayed by the average business man in reference to these great industrial problems and even the trade-union movement, that they know little of it. and all that they do know is the accounts that they see in the papers from time to time regarding strikes and lockouts, and I would like to read at this time the preamble of our organization, **if it is in order.**

Mr. THOMPSON. You mean of your international organization?

Mr. HOWELL. Yes, sir.

Mr. THOMPSON. We have that already in evidence.

Mr. HOWELL. No; this is the local.

Chairman WALSH. Read it.

Mr. HOWELL (reading):

" Preamble: To establish and maintain an equitable scale of wages, to protect ourselves from sudden or unreasonable fluctuations in the rate of compensation for our labor, and also to protect just and honorable employers from the unfair competition of unscrupulous and unreliable rivals; to defend our rights and advance our interests as workingmen; to create an authority whose seal shall constitute a certificate of character, intelligence, and skill; to build up an organization where all worthy members of our craft can participate in the discussion of those practical problems upon the solution of which depend their welfare and prosperity as workers; to foster fellowship and brotherhood; to aid the destitute and unfortunate, and provide for the decent burial of deceased members; to develop and stimulate, by association and social converse, those kindly instincts of humanity that most highly adorn true manhood; to encourage the principle and practice of conciliation and arbitration in the settlement of differences between labor and capital; we, printers of the city of Portland, Oreg., do adopt and promulgate this constitution."

Mr. THOMPSON. I want to ask just one more question. In the newspaper field when a piece of work is set up and published in one of the papers and the matrix is taken to another paper, do they reset their type again and redistribute it?

Mr. HOWELL. Yes, sir; unless published in the same establishment and owned by the same firm.

Mr. THOMPSON. That is all..

Commissioner LENNON. Does the typographical union in -Portland work under an agreement, either written or· verbal, in the commercial part of the trade?

Mr. HOWELL. No, sir; not at present.

Commissioner LENNON. Are the printers employed by these firms union men largely, or entirely so?

Mr. HOWELL. With the exception of the pressroom all departments are union; the electrotypers are absolutely 100 per cent union, and the photo-engravers ·are union.

Commissioner LENNON. How has the scale been made under which you· work? Has it been made by joint committee of the employers and your union, or by the employers entirely or by yourselves entirely; how is it made?

Mr. HOWELL. The last scale—our scale was made by conferences. We had numerous conferences and, of course, the newspaper scale was·made——

Commissioner LENNON. I know about that.

Mr. HOWELL. You probably have heard so much about that you are familiar with it.

Commissioner LENNON. I have been dealing with it myself.· Then after you have these conferences wasn't a verbal agreement finally reached between the representatives of the union and the representatives of the commercial printers, establishing that scale?

Mr. HOWELL. Well, it was established in that way, but each union acts independent of every other union.

Commissioner LENNON. I mean just for the. printers, the members of the typographical union, not any of the other printing trades, but just those.

Mr. HOWELL. That was adopted after a conference that was mutually satisfactory to both sides.

Commissioner LENNON. Does it prevail in nearly all the printing offices of this city?

Mr. HOWELL. It does in 90 per cent—95 per cent. The wages at the present time are $25 a week for eight hours' work.

Commissioner LENNON. That is hand work or machine?

Mr. HOWELL. That is hand work.

Commissioner LENNON. What is the machine scale?

Mr. HOWELL. $31.10 for daywork; $34 for night.

Commissioner LENNON. That is all.

Chairman WALSH. Mr. Commons would like to ask a few questions.

Commissioner COMMONS. I thought you said at first that you had no agreements with the Typothetæ.

Mr. HOWELL. We have no agreements with the Typothetæ.

Commissioner COMMONS. Then you say you have agreements with the commercial printers?

Mr. HOWELL. No; not with the commercial printers; the newspaper printers.

Commissioner COMMONS. Take the book and job offices, that is what I understand is the commercial printing.

Mr. HOWELL. Yes.

Commissioner COMMONS. Which comes under the Typothetæ, does it not? ·

· Mr. HOWELL. Yes.

Commissioner COMMONS. How is the scale made with those offices?

Mr. HOWELL. Why, it is first taken up in our organization. There is·a committee appointed to draw up a scale of prices, and after we have drawn up· what we consider right and proper we submit that to the employers. Before they had their organization it was submitted to the individual firms. For instance, we would send a committee to one printer and the same committee would wait upon another; but since they have an organization, why, we have treated with that organization. That is the way we——

Commissioner COMMONS. You mean a committee of the Typothetæ.

Mr. HOWELL. Yes, sir.

Commissioner COMMONS. When you reach an agreement, is that put in writing?

Mr. HOWELL. Well, no; it was not.

Commissioner COMMONS. Is that true of all the other printing trades? Do they negotiate in the same way with the Typothetæ?

Mr. HOWELL. The commercial end; I think so.

Commissioner COMMONS. And there are no written agreements?
Mr. HOWELL. No; not now. There was at one time.
Commissioner COMMONS. That is, before the Typothetæ organized you had a written contract?
Mr. HOWELL. Yes.
Commissioner COMMONS. Signed by each individual?
Mr. HOWELL. Yes.
Commissioner COMMONS. Now you have no written contract signed by the organization; they are simply verbal understandings, are they?
Mr. HOWELL. Yes, sir.
Commissioner COMMONS. How about the question of the employment of union members? Was that taken up in the discussion with the Typothetæ?
Mr. HOWELL. Well, it is understood they are to be union labor.
Commissioner COMMONS. Well, what is meant by that understanding? As I understand it——
Mr. HOWELL. Well, it is an organization of union men and women treating with a firm.
Commissioner COMMONS. But you don't have any agreement; if you don't reach any agreement at all—don't put it down in writing. Does the Typothetæ consider their shops as open shops?
Mr. HOWELL. It considers their pressrooms open.
Commissioner COMMONS. Then I suppose the employee dealt individually with each establishment?
Mr. HOWELL. Yes, sir.
Commissioner COMMONS. So far as the Typothetæ is concerned as an organization, you do not bring up the question of closed shop or open shop?
Mr. HOWELL. Not as yet we haven't.
Commissioner COMMONS. But you do settle that individually with each firm?
Mr. HOWELL. Yes, sir.
Commissioner COMMONS. That is what you mean by saying it is understood that they should be union men? Has there been any case where the union has brought up the matter to an employer? I am not speaking of newspaper offices.
Mr. HOWELL. Of union labor, employing union labor?
Commissioner COMMONS. Yes, in the commercial end, do you mean have they brought up the question of the employment of union men?
Mr. HOWELL. No; they have not. They do not employ a man unless he is a member of the union. Whenever they want help they telephone to the secretary's office; they send to the office of our secretary, 207 Oregonian Building, for help. He has a list there of unemployed, and from that list he sends them down. They do not make any attempt to put on nonunion men.
Commissioner COMMONS. Does the Allied Printing Trades Council belong to the Central Labor Union?
Mr. HOWELL. No.
Commissioner COMMONS. It is just individual unions?
Mr. HOWELL. Has no affiliation, either delegate——
Commissioner COMMONS. Do you know whether the typothetæ belongs to the employers' association?
Mr. HOWELL. Why, some of the members do.
Commissioner COMMONS. But not as an association?
Mr. HOWELL. I couldn't say. It would be just my opinion.
Commissioner COMMONS. You spoke of the printing trades council as mainly organized to promote the label. Do you declare boycotts on firms that are not fair?
Mr. HOWELL. Well, we have not for a number of years. We appoint a committee, and this committee waits on the firm that is getting the printing done and asks them to use the union label, and we keep at it in that way. We send committee after committee. We have not placed any boycott on anybody.
Commissioner COMMONS. You spoke about 5 per cent that are not covered by these agreements. Do they employ any nonunion men?
Mr. HOWELL. Yes, sir; there are one or two firms employ nonunion men in this city.
Commissioner COMMONS. Have you any boycotts on those firms?
Mr. HOWELL. No more than what is in the Labor Press. We do not patronize——
Commissioner COMMONS. How do you get that authenticated or authorized in the Labor Press? Do you have to bring it up?

Mr. Howell. It is brought up to the central labor body that we have been unable to adjust differences between such and such a firm in our organization, and that we request that such a firm be placed on the unfair list, and we don't patronize——

Commissioner Commons. How is that handled in the Central Labor Union?

Mr. Howell. I believe they have a committee first who see if they can settle it.

Commissioner Commons. They endeavor to settle it?

Mr. Howell. Yes, sir.

Commissioner Commons. And then when it is finally placed on the unfair list must it be by the vote of the entire Central Labor Union?

Mr. Howell. Yes.

Commissioner Commons. So that they can veto your request?

Mr. Howell. Yes, sir.

Commissioner Commons. Now, there are two establishments you say that are on the unfair list?

Mr. Howell. Well, there are some—I am positive of one; I do not know as to two. Of course, there are a number of very small establishments that employ no help; they are just simply a part of the trade. A man with a little money can buy a press, but these people are not those who employ help. There is only one that I know of that is not a member of our organization that does not employ our members.

Commissioner Commons. Then do you go to the other business men of the town who are having printing done and ask them to patronize the label houses?

Mr. Howell. Yes, sir.

Commissioner Commons. Do you have a committee for that purpose?

Mr. Howell. Yes, sir.

Commissioner Commons. And do they visit most of the business men? .

Mr. Howell. Well, they are not making any campaign and have not for some time past.

Commissioner Commons. Is the city or State or county printing issued with the label?

Mr. Howell. Not now. Some of it once in a while is. It was for a long time, had the label; but since they have adopted the commission form of government and appointed a purchasing agent the work is let out to the lowest bidder; it goes to any shop.

Commissioner Commons. Does the Allied Printing Trades Council take that up with the city authorities?

Mr. Howell. They have not as yet.

Commissioner Commons. That is all.

Chairman Walsh. Anything else?

Commissioner Garretson. Yes. This pressman that you spoke of that had to get permission to return to work, he had been on strike, had he?

Mr. Howell. Yes, sir.

Commissioner Garretson. And did he go to Mr. Banfield to get him to withdraw his opposition, or to intercede for him?

Mr. Howell. To withdraw his opposition.

Commissioner Garretson. The attitude was virtually that if a man on a strike here loses out, he has to get a license from the employers' association before he can work here in any capacity?

Mr. Howell. He is practically a blacklisted man.

Commissioner Garretson. Would there have been any possibility of a settlement between the striking pressmen and the employing printers if these two agencies had been left to settle their trouble without outside interference?

Mr. Howell. Yes; I think it could have been settled.

Commissioner Garretson. Does the employers' association, as a rule, from the standpoint of labor men in the town, or from the standpoint of citizens, act as an agency to minimize trouble and effect settlements and understandings between employers and employees, or the opposite direction?

Mr. Howell. The opposite direction.

Commissioner Garretson. All classes of employers band to support one man who is having labor trouble?

Mr. Howell. Don't make any difference what that trouble is or how just the cause may be, they are " agin the Government."

Commissioner Garretson. I suppose they do not support the sympathetic strike on the part of labor, do they?

Mr. Howell. I suppose they do.

Commissioner GARRETSON. But still they follow what is the exact parallel of a sympathetic strike in their methods. Is the natural outgrowth, in your opinion, as a man conversant with the policy and practice of labor unions—will the natural outgrowth of the attitude of several manufacurers' associations, whether State or National, be that the labor unions will combine to act together if they follow the lines that are followed by the manufacturers' associations?

Mr. HOWELL. Yes. I believe in the crafts organizing. I would like to see every industry in the printing business in one organization. I think it is wrong for me as a printer——

Commissioner GARRETSON. As against the craft system?

Mr. HOWELL. Yes. I do not think it is right for me as a printer to enter into an agreement with my employer to tie up my labor for three years by contract, when the next man who comes after me in a year has to go up against that, and by means of my contract I am forced to work, if the man gets in trouble.

Commissioner GARRETSON. In other words, if you profit by the example of the employers' association and the manufacturers' association you are bound to do that in self-defense?

Mr. HOWELL. They are doing that very same thing that way.

Take the case in Stockton, when the employers determined to make that an open shop; when the controversy had been on several weeks they served notice on the newspaper publishers that unless they did away with the union label that they would withdraw their patronage. This was followed by the action of the typographical union, who sent a notice to these publishers of these newspapers that if that stand is taken by the employers of Stockton, we will set up your papers for nothing. And this was followed by a telegram from the international organization that that would be used in payment of wages of all these men. The same thing was done in the street car strike. They waited upon the publishers and forbid them to give a true account of the strikers' conference on the trouble. That thing is creeping more and more into the industrial situation of this country.

Commissioner GARRETSON. Do you know whether or not when a contract is let in this town under union conditions all the members of the employers' association belonging are notified of the man in giving the contract having union regulations entirely?

Mr. HOWELL. I believe that to be a fact.

Commissioner GARRETSON. Have you seen such a communication?

Mr. HOWELL. I have seen a communication in the Labor Press recently when Meier & Frank contemplated the erection of their new building, that they sent out a communication asking the employers to use their influence with the firm of Meier & Frank to prevent that building going up under open-shop conditions.

Commissioner GARRETSON. Under union-shop conditions.

Mr. HOWELL. I mean under union-shop conditions. And just a word about this courthouse in which we are now sitting. The east wing was constructed piecemeal, one contractor getting a certain portion of it and another another, and the work was delayed. But when they came to the erection of the west wing it was thought advisable by the county commissioners to call for bids for the completion of the west wing. And when those bids were opened the successful bidder was one of the most famous builders in this country, the firm of Thompson & Starrett, who erected the Yeon Building in this city and also the Annex—the building called the Annex of Meier & Frank's, under union conditions. Their bid was in the neighborhood of $50,000 lower than the nearest competitor. And notwithstanding that the employers' association, I am informed, got very busy, and by a connivance with the architects, the firm of Widener & Lewis, that bid was thrown out and new bids were called for, and Thompson-Starrett was practically driven from this State.

Commissioner GARRETSON. Then a boycott is in effect on the other side that is as effective as any boycott could be on the part of labor?

Mr. HOWELL. Yes; even more so, because they have all the power of massed capital.

Commissioner GARRETSON. That is all, Mr. Chairman.

Mr. HOWELL. I would just like to read one little article that I have here on the reason for labor organizations' existence at the present time more than ever. This is an editorial taken from one of the papers of this city at the time of the controversy between John D. Rockefeller and the gentleman who was sent by President Wilson to interview him [reading]:

"When John D. Rockefeller, jr., testified before the congressional committee he maintained that the mine owners were simply contending for the right of

REPORT OF COMMISSION ON INDUSTRIAL RELATIONS.

the individual miner to make his own terms and to join a union or not, as he pleased. He still maintained the obsolete theory that freedom of contract is possible between the great corporation, 40 per cent of the stock of which is held by his father, and an individual miner, whose sole capital is his physical strength and his skill. Merely to state the proposition is to prove its absurdity. Freedom of contract can only exist between parties that are equal. As against massed capital, labor can only exercise this freedom by a combination that it may act as a unit."

Chairman WALSH. Do you know of any other instance such as you mentioned about the pressman securing permission from Mr. Banfield to go back before he could go back?

Mr. HOWELL. No; I don't.

Chairman WALSH. That is the only instance you know. Do you know how many pressmen who went out upon the strike returned to the employment?

Mr. HOWELL. Well, nearly all.

Chairman WALSH. But in numbers, how many?

Mr. HOWELL. Well, I could not say.

Chairman WALSH. Could you approximate it?

Mr. HOWELL. Maybe 30 or 40.

Chairman WALSH. Anything else?

Commissioner COMMONS. I would like to ask on what grounds did the Allied Printing Trades Council decline to support the pressmen either in the matter of—I presume the label is still furnished to those firms that have the open shop?

Mr. HOWELL. No.

Commissioner COMMONS. With the pressmen?

Mr. HOWELL. No; they haven't. They haven't the label. We had about 50 shops that had the label. Now we only have about 12 or 14.

Commissioner COMMONS. The label is then only given to those that have union pressmen throughout, is that it?

Mr. HOWELL. Yes, sir.

Commissioner COMMONS. On what ground did the council withhold support, or a sympathetic strike, we will say? Why was no sympathetic strike called on behalf of the pressmen?

Mr. HOWELL. Because we had to obtain the sanction of our international officers, and the request for the strike had to come from the president of the International Printing Pressmen and Assistants' Union, Mr. Barry, before it could be considered by the then president of the international union, Mr. James M. Lynch. That request was never made by Mr. Barry.

Commissioner COMMONS. It was simply, then, that was the only reason, was it, because the pressmen hadn't asked for the sympathetic support of the other trades?

Mr. HOWELL. I believe that to be a fact.

Commissioner COMMONS. Would your contracts have tied you up so that you could not have supported them?

Mr. HOWELL. Yes, sir.

Commissioner COMMONS. Was that the reason why the request was not made?

Mr. HOWELL. That was the main reason.

Commissioner COMMONS. The reason why the request was not made?

Mr. HOWELL. Yes, sir.

There is just one other thing I would like to state on this same question of the boycott and how the law looks upon this question as affecting labor and as affecting property interests: At the time of the A. R. U. strike in 1894 the General Managers' Association——

Chairman WALSH. Say, I don't want to limit you, Mr. Howell, but we are trying to cut out pure argument, you understand. If there is any fact connected with the situation here or that has come under your observation elsewhere, why, of course, it is all right. But mere argument we are trying to cut out.

Mr. HOWELL. I am not making an argument; I am just making a statement.

Chairman WALSH. Well, a statement in the nature of an argument we also try to eliminate, if you call it that. You can state——

Mr. HOWELL. Well, here was the condition.

Chairman WALSH. Here is the idea. I don't want to cut you short, if there is anything that you think is significant here that you know about of your own knowledge, or indirectly through hearsay, why you may state it.

Then we will try to make a study of the decision in the A. R. U. case, and draw our own conclusions. You get the point.

Mr. HOWELL. I understand the nature of this commission is to investigate industrial conditions throughout the country and present a report and, perhaps, suggest a remedy.

Chairman WALSH. Yes.

Mr. HOWELL. To do away with some of the evils——

Chairman WALSH. Yes.

Mr. HOWELL (continuing). That we have to contend against.

Chairman WALSH. That is the purpose of the commission.

Mr. HOWELL. And the enforcement of the law is necessary, absolutely necessary; yes, sir.

Chairman WALSH. Well, I have made the statement. I don't want to hamper your statement. Exclude argument, and go ahead.

Mr. HOWELL. Well, I just wanted to state, at the time that that strike was called, or prior to it, the American Railway Union found this condition: That the 24 railroads entering the city of Chicago were controlled by the General Managers' Association. And all questions affecting hours and wages and other conditions were considered by that General Managers' Association. And in order to combat that great mass of capital Mr. Debs conceived the American Railway Union. But the power of the court and the power of Government was used to crush that union. And the late President, Taft, in rendering his decision, used these words: "The great conspiracy that existed." The American Railway Union—the Sherman law had just been passed, in 1890, and the great conspiracy that existed in violation of the Sherman antitrust law was the conspiracy of the General Managers' Association. And had he foreseen that at that time, or had he seen that at that time and invoked the power of that law——

Chairman WALSH. Had who seen it?

Mr. HOWELL. Taft.

Chairman WALSH. Well, do you have any personal knowledge as to whether he did see it or not?

Mr. HOWELL. I read his decision.

Chairman WALSH. Well, go ahead.

Mr. HOWELL. The great evils that exist in this country through massed capital, had the Sherman antitrust law been in force at that time, probably this commission would not now be in existence.

Chairman WALSH. Anything else?

Commissioner GARRETSON. No.

Chairman WALSH. That is all, Mr. Howell.

Mr. THOMPSON. Mr. Tait.

TESTIMONY OF MR. JOHN TAIT.

Mr. THOMPSON. Mr. Tait, you may sit down.

Mr. TAIT. Yes, sir.

Mr. THOMPSON. Please give your name.

Mr. TAIT. John Tait.

Mr. THOMPSON. And your business address?

Mr. TAIT. East Tenth and Pine Streets.

Mr. THOMPSON. Your business?

Mr. TAIT. I am president and manager of the Troy Laundry Co.

Mr. THOMPSON. That is a company engaged in the laundry business?

Mr. TAIT. Yes, sir.

Mr. THOMPSON. Not in the machinery business?

Mr. TAIT. Not in the machinery business.

Mr. THOMPSON. Now, how long has your company been in existence here?

Mr. TAIT. The company was first incorporated in 1894. Previous to that they have been known as the Troy Steam Laundry from 1899.

Mr. THOMPSON. How many people does your laundry now employ?

Mr. TAIT. About 120.

Mr. THOMPSON. About how many of these are women and minors?

Mr. TAIT. About 90.

Mr. THOMPSON. About 90?

Mr. TAIT. Yes, sir.

Chairman WALSH. He said women and minors.

Mr. TAIT. Well, there is no minors.

Mr. THOMPSON. No minors?

Mr. TAIT. No minors.

Mr. THOMPSON. Can you state to this commission what, if any, effect the establishment of a minimum wage in your industry has had on the industry itself and on the workers?

Mr. TAIT. I can give you some figures here.

Mr. THOMPSON. Have you a list of questions there in this regard?

Mr. TAIT. A list of which?

Mr. THOMPSON. Questions furnished to you.

Mr. TAIT. I have.

Mr. THOMPSON. You may answer those in their order.

Mr. TAIT. Yes; I will answer that list of questions; first read the questions and I will answer those.

The first question that is asked is that of the number of employees whose wages were increased as the result of the minimum-wage legislation. The answer is this: There are 687 increased by the shortening of hours; 115 increased in wages. The shortening of hours was this: That some of the plants in the city were working 9½ hours a day. Under the ruling of the minimum-wage scale 54 hours a week, or 9 hours a day, was the rule. The same wages were paid to those employees that were working the 9½ hours a day when they worked 9. There was no reduction in wages made in that. But there was an actual increase through the minimum-wage scale on 115. They received that.

Commissioner COMMONS. One hundred and fifteen employees?

Mr. TAIT. One hundred and fifteen employees increased in wages.

Commissioner COMMONS. One hundred and fifteen different employees had increases?

Mr. TAIT. Had increases, besides 687 who had received a benefit of the shortening of the hours, which of course was a natural increase in their hourly scale of wages.

Commissioner LENNON. That is based on the entire industry or simply on yours?

Mr. TAIT. It is based on the entire industry from the facts which I have received.

Commissioner LENNON. Oh, yes.

Mr. THOMPSON. Go right ahead.

Mr. TAIT. Second, the amount of increase in regular weekly pay roll as a result of the minimum wage scale. The amount was $400 on account of reduction of hours, and $107.50 increase on the weekly, what might be called on those who were benefited by the minimum-wage scale, directly benefited in the increased wages.

Commissioner GARRETSON. How many are engaged in the entire industry; how many persons?

Mr. TAIT. One thousand one hundred and fifty-seven.

Commissioner GARRETSON. Men and women?

Mr. TAIT. Men and women.

Commissioner GARRETSON. How many of those are women?

Commissioner COMMONS. Six hundred and eighty-seven.

Mr. TAIT. Not quite—more than that. Six hundred and eighty-seven were benefited by the changing of the hours, and probably those would be women to a great extent. There would be 687 and 115 out of that 1,157—I didn't get that number, I thinght I had it in mind, so that I could give you that answer. I think probably the number of women employed would be about 800.

Commissioner GARRETSON. Eight hundred?

Mr. TAIT. About that; I wouldn't want to be positive as to the number, but about that number.

Commissioner GARRETSON. All right, go ahead.

Mr. TAIT. The third question is: Total number of wage earners, which was 1.157.

The fourth question is total amount of normal weekly pay paid wage earners. Thirteen thousand two hundred and twelve dollars and thirty-eight cents per week, or $687,038.56 per year.

Commissioner GARRETSON. Is that men and women?

Mr. TAIT. Men and women.

Commissioner GARRETSON. Have you the women separately?

Mr. TAIT. No, sir. I say the amount per week is $13,212.38, and the total per year $687,038.56.

The fifth question is: Number of employees discharged because believed to be not worth standard wage fixed by minimum wage law.

There has been quite a number discharged during the past year, some through that cause and some through the falling off in business.

It is very hard to find out what the direct cause is of an employee being discharged under the present conditions, because the business has been reduced in volume very materially during the last 12 or 15 months, and it was impossible to get anything of that statement. There was possibly between 30 and 40 who were affected, and out of that number—were affected probably on account of inefficiency.

Question No. 6. Brief statement of effects of minimum-wage law on business and on relations between employers and employees.

The answer to that is on account of increased wages it has been necessary to increase the cost of our products, and in that way the public have in many instances refused to pay the increased price, causing a reduction in our volume of business.

To show the standing of the pay rolls June, 1913, and June, 1914, I have taken off those figures. The pay roll for the laundry business in June, 1913, which was a year ago, was $57,243. In June, 1914, $52,849. Practically a difference of $5,000 a month, or $60,000 a year. This is not chargeable to the minimum wage scale; it would not be just to charge it in that way, but due to the conditions of the business as it exists at the present time in Portland, and possibly all through the country the same conditions exist.

Commissioner GARRETSON. Affected all business?

Mr. TAIT. Affected all business that way.

Mr. THOMPSON. Now, Mr. Tait, you say that on account of the increase in wage cost it will be necessary to increase the charges to your patrons?

Mr. TAIT. Yes, sir.

Mr. THOMPSON. And they have, you believe, on account of that increase, reduced the amount of business they do with you?

Mr. TAIT. Yes, sir.

Mr. THOMPSON. If I remember correctly, you say about 115 of these 1,157 workers had their wages increased by the minimum wage?

Mr. TAIT. That is right.

Mr. THOMPSON. What per cent of the total pay roll, if you can state it, would the increase in wages amount to? You have stated the present pay roll amounts to six hundred and odd thousand dollars a year.

Mr. TAIT. I would have to figure that up to state positively. You must grant there was an increase in the pay roll to the employees when it reduced the number of hours, because this reduced the output, and it increased the cost of production.

Mr. THOMPSON. Has any study been made, if you know, as to whether the decrease of hours half an hour a day has resulted in the lessening of the output?

Mr. TAIT. It has.

Mr. THOMPSON. It has?

Mr. TAIT. It has.

Mr. THOMPSON. Would you mind stating upon what study that is based?

Mr. TAIT. The most careful study can be made in what is known as the mangle room. In the mangle room in keeping track of the number of pieces which go through the different mangles each day, it shows a decline in the volume of work going through that department. I haven't got the figures with me that I could give them to you, but I could get them for you.

Mr. THOMPSON. What other department would it operate in?

Mr. TAIT. It would operate in all departments where they are working on daily wages. It wouldn't affect so materially the piecework departments, because it does not affect the cost of production on that particular article.

Mr. THOMPSON. What proportion of the work and what kind of work is done on the daily wage, and what on the piecework, in the laundry business?

Mr. TAIT. It is not general. In some plants it is one department and some plants another. I can speak for the Troy Laundry Co. only. Our mangle room is on the hourly basis. Our shirt starching is on the piecework. Our shirt ironing is on the piecework. And our collar department is on the hourly basis. Our ironing basis—hand-ironing department—is on a per cent basis. They are paid a certain per cent on each garment handled by the employee, based on what is charged to the patron.

Mr. THOMPSON. Could it be said that the most skilled work is on the piece rate?

Mr. Tait. It is.

Mr. Thompson. On the basis of the piece-rate workers being the most skilled, of course they get the highest wages?

Mr. Tait. Yes, sir; they do.

Mr. Thompson. What proportion of the pay roll, offhand, if you could state, would be paid the skillful workers compared to the unskilled workers?

Mr. Tait. I could not tell you offhand. Those figures I have, but I wouldn't like to estimate it, because I might be entirely wrong in my estimate of those figures.

Mr. Thompson. How do the number of employees compare to the skilled line?

Mr. Tait. In our plant the greater number of our employees are on piecework.

Commissioner Commons. May I ask a question?

Mr. Thompson. Yes, sir.

Commissioner Commons. I think it is stated that the increased cost on account of changing hours was $400 a week.

Mr. Tait. No, sir; I wouldn't make that positive statement.

Commissioner Commons. What was it?

Mr. Tait. The increase of wages to the employees was based, you might say, on that. It is figured on the reduction of hours, as showing the increase. For instance, to explain that: If a girl was getting a dollar and a half a day for nine and a half hours, she would be paid under the ruling—she was paid a dollar and a half for nine hours, showing a half an hour daily loss to the employer, but still she received the same wages. There was no change in the wages on account of the reduction of hours.

Commissioner Commons. Then you figure that cost amounts to $400?

Mr. Tait. The figures there amount to $410.

Commissioner Commons. That must have applied only to the time-workers and not to the pieceworkers?

Mr. Tait. It would.

Commissioner Commons. So that the increased cost—assuming that the time-worker's output is reduced the same proportion that their hours are reduced, the figures would be $400 on account of shorter hours?

Mr. Tait. Yes, sir.

Commissioner Commons. Then you figured $157.50 on account of raising wages?

Mr. Tait. One hundred and fifty-seven dollars and fifty cents.

Commissioner Commons. So that the total increased cost, the two totals, is $557.50 per week?

Mr. Tait. No, sir.

Commissioner Commons. The total per month?

Mr. Tait. Per month.

Commissioner Commons. What is the total per week?

Mr. Tait. One-fourth of that, practically.

Commissioner Commons. I figure it makes about 15 per cent per week increase on the pay roll.

Mr. Tait. I haven't figured it. I could not certify to that figure. I would have to figure it out.

Commissioner Commons. That is all.

Mr. Thompson. I might ask you this question direct: What increase did you make in the prices to your customers?

Mr. Tait. A very slight increase.

Mr. Thompson. Well, how much?

Mr. Tait. Those figures I could not give you offhand. I didn't expect to be asked that question. But the items were very small. In some cases I can tell you what was affected practically to a certain extent.

In some cases sheets were raised 1 cent each. Some were doing them for 2 cents. and others were charging 3 cents. And collars were raised from 2½ to 3 cents. Those were the principal raises made on the prices by this advance in wages.

Mr. Thompson. Then the principal advance was just 1 cent for sheets and half a cent on collars. Upon that do you base your deduction that the patrons decreased their business with you on account of the increase?

Mr. Tait. They do. We know that to be a positive fact. We have had people refuse to send on account of that increase.

Mr. THOMPSON. Is there any other statement you care to make in regard to the operation and effect of the minimum-wage law?

Mr. TAIT. I am in favor of a minimum-wage law based on sound business methods. I can not say that this minimum-wage law is going to benefit the employee as it was expected, because it will have a tendency to bring a great many of them to the minimum wage.

It is not based on efficiency; it is based on age. There is an age limit. If a girl becomes 18 years of age, she is practically, under this law, entitled to what is known as the minimum wage. She has to serve an apprenticeship period of one year. Well, that is not always possible to learn a trade in one year. It is practically impossible to do it. It is based on that; it is not based on efficiency. And the reason why we prefer piecework in our plant in preference to the daily or hourly wage is that the efficient employee receives full value for her services and is benefited and does not have to carry the load of the inefficient employee.

Mr. THOMPSON. In so far as you have piecework, of course the law does not apply?

Mr. TAIT. It applies if our piece rate is not higher than the minimum-wage or amounts to the minimum wage.

Mr. THOMPSON. It has not been applied so far in that regard?

Mr. TAIT. No, sir; it has not been necessary, because the rate has been higher.

Mr. THOMPSON. What constructive suggestion would you make with reference to the minimum-wage law that would remedy the condition you speak of?

Mr. TAIT. The suggestion I would make if we want to benefit the working people and benefit the employers is to establish industrial schools, where every child is learned a trade and is self-supporting. The great trouble to-day, as I see it—I may be wrong, gentlemen, but this is my opinion, and I have made some little study of it—the main trouble to-day is that the most of our people have no knowledge, practically, of how to support themselves when they leave school, and I believe if we could train our children so that they have an industrial education—you take it from the years of 16 to 18—if they have to spend a part of the time in our industrial schools learning something it is going to benefit this Nation and make it an industrial Nation.

My reason for that is this, based on the theory that Germany to-day has got one of the greatest armies in the world, from the fact that during the period, as I understand it, from 17 to 21 every young man in the country has got to serve a part of the time in the army. They have got the foundation; they know what to do.

If our children—am a father myself, and I know what it is—if our children would learn some useful employment in our schools instead of spending from three to four years in the high school learning something which, in many cases, is not of practical use to them in their life work, it would be beneficial.

Industrial schools, I believe, will help and assist; and another thing, when they have learned that they can come out as experienced help or having a practical knowledge. They can enter into the different manufacturing businesses and command better wages, because all manufacturers are looking for experienced help and are willing to pay good prices for the same. It is not a question of wages, it is a question of ability.

Mr. THOMPSON. If such were carried out in this State—either industrial, vocational training, or part-time continuation schools for teaching industrial methods—would that be the thing which would make the law ideal, in your opinion, or are there other suggestions?

Mr. TAIT. I believe it would not be necessary to have that law. All these are thoughts of my own. My experience with the employees is this, that the experienced hand has no trouble in getting good wages, but it is the inexperienced hand who has the trouble, and it is the inexperienced hand who is causing to a great extent this unrest at all times.

Mr. THOMPSON. What you mean is you would give this law as a substitute for the minimum-wage law?

Mr. TAIT. Yes, sir. Well, it could be worked in conjunction. I don't think any employer objects, not my knowledge, to paying a minimum wage if it is based on sound business principles. It should be based on the earning capacity of the employee, not on a general rule in which it says all employees of a certain age should be paid this minimum wage.

Mr. THOMPSON. That is all, Mr. Chairman.

Chairman WALSH. Commissioner Lennon would like to ask a few questions.

Commissioner LENNON. Has there been a change in the number of people in the laundry employed by the piece since the enactment and enforcement of the law? Are there more or less people employed on piecework now than there was before the law went into effect?

Mr. TAIT. There would naturally be less on account of the shrinkage of the business.

Commissioner LENNON. Well, I don't mean that. I mean has there been any general change because of the law?

Mr. TAIT. There is an effort that way. You mean increase the.pieceworkers from what it is?

Commissioner LENNON. Yes, sir.

Mr. TAIT. I believe there has been. I can not speak positively on that question, because that is one of the questions I haven't taken up with the laundries of the city; but in our plant, as I say, we are gradually working into the piecework system entirely, because it is much more satisfactory to the employee in every respect. The employees who years ago were getting what was considered the highest wages under the daily or hourly basis are much better satisfied on the piecework, and you could not persuade them to go back to the daily or hourly basis under any conditions.

Commissioner LENNON. That is all.

Commissioner GARRETSON. What proportion of your employees work less than 54 hours a week?

Mr. TAIT. At the present time the whole of them.

Commissioner GARRETSON. All of them?

Mr. TAIT. All of them.

Commissioner GARRETSON. Then, if they work less than .that——

Mr. TAIT. They are paid for the time they work.

Commissioner GARRETSON. And are not paid under the minimum wage?

Mr. TAIT. The minimum wage ruling is a pro rata basis. It is on the hourly as well as weekly basis.

Commissioner GARRETSON. It is the 54-hour week?

Mr. TAIT. It is the 54-hour .week.

Commissioner GARRETSON. If they work 40 hours, then they are paid forty fifty-fourths·of the minimum wage?

· Mr. TAIT. They are paid forty fifty-fourths of the. minimum wage; yes, sir.

Commissioner GARRETSON. As a weekly proposition it does not apply at all?

Mr. TAIT. As a weekly proposition it does not apply at all practically on that 54-hour basis.

Commissioner GARRETSON. Has that worked any reduction in the earnings?

Mr. TAIT. Not in the earnings.

Commissioner GARRETSON. The fact is that more people have been working a less number of hours?

Mr. TAIT. It is not.

Commissioner GARRETSON. It has no effect?

Mr. TAIT. It has reduced the number of employees instead of increasing the time.

Commissioner GARRETSON. That is all. One minute. In regard to the amount of increase, I think you said that sheets that formerly were 2 cents were increased to 3 cents?

Mr. TAIT. In some cases; not in all.

Commissioner GARRETSON. Does that apply to all flat work?

Mr. TAIT. No, sir; it applies to what might be termed "the family flat work."

Commissioner GARRETSON. How do you do that, by the pound?

Mr. TAIT. No, sir; by the piece.

Commissioner GARRETSON. By the piece altogether?

Mr. TAIT. Yes, sir; by the piece altogether.

Commissioner GARRETSON. Then all family work is virtually increased 50 per cent?

Mr. TAIT. Not all family work; no, sir. Sheets—in some cases there were some laundries which were charging 3 cents for sheets previous to that time. Some were charging 2 cents, and there has been a general raising of prices to 3 cents on sheets. It does not affect it very materially, because the family sheet to-day is going in under the rough dry—to a great extent is going in under the. rough dry—which is based on the pound rate, and the pound rate was not affected by this price in any way.

Commissioner GARRETSON. What is your general per cent of increase on prices to the customers?

·Mr. TAIT. I could not tell you offhand on that.

Commissioner GARRETSON. Have you made any comparison of the per cent of increase in earnings and the per cent of the increase in prices to the public?

Mr. TAIT. The per cent of increase in earnings is going down, so much so that I have authority to make a statement here of a gentleman—it is not my own case; but I can tell you our own case.

Our per cent of profits has practically fallen away during the last year. In one case the operating cost of one plant was 99.2 per cent.

Commissioner GARRETSON. I am not talking of the per cent of profit; I am talking of the per cent on the market price.

Mr. TAIT. In what manner?

Commissioner GARRETSON. What has your regular per cent of charge to the customer increased?

Mr. TAIT. I could not tell you offhand, because any figures that I would have— I would have to know the number of pieces which we have handled along the line on which we raised the prices.

Commissioner GARRETSON. You would have to know what the total cost of a given number of articles was before you increase the price and the total cost now?

Mr. TAIT. Yes, sir.

Commissioner GARRETSON. The true relation is between the increase you have put onto the price and the increase that has come on your labor alone through this law, to get any fair comparison. Wouldn't that be the way?

Mr. TAIT. Offhand, the increased price has not taken care of the increased cost of labor.

Commissioner GARRETSON. That is all.

Chairman WALSH. Mr. O'Connell wants to ask a question.

Commissioner O'CONNELL. What are the weekly wages of your pieceworkers—your own firm?

Mr. TAIT. I am just studying. The weekly wages of the pieceworkers run from $10 to $15 per week.

Commissioner O'CONNELL. Well, now, what per cent of them make $15 per week?

Mr. TAIT. In answering these questions, it is very hard to answer them offhand, because in making a statement before this body I want to make a correct statement. I will file a report with you, if you wish me to do that, but I don't like to make a statement that may be contradicted.

Commissioner GARRETSON. Will you submit a copy of your pay roll?

Mr. TAIT. I can and will.

Commissioner GARRETSON. Be glad to have you do it.

Mr. TAIT. Yes, sir.

(See Tait exhibit.)

Commissioner O'CONNELL. How many white laundries in this city—that is, laundries other than those run by orientals?

Mr. TAIT. There are 15. I mean there are 15 steam laundries. There are quite a number of small hand laundries, which I could not tell you exactly.

Commissioner O'CONNELL. How many Chinese laundries in the city?

Mr. TAIT. Of that I can't tell you. I think there are somewhere about 40.

Commissioner O'CONNELL. What per cent of the laundry business in the city is done by the Chinese?

Mr. TAIT. That is a question I could not answer.

Commissioner O'CONNELL. Approximately 10, 20, 30, or 40 per cent?

Mr. TAIT. I could not approximate it. It would be very hard to answer that, not knowing the volume of business.

Commissioner O'CONNELL. Are the Chinese laundries increasing in number?

Mr. TAIT. No, sir; they are not.

Commissioner O'CONNELL. They are not?

Mr. TAIT. No, sir. The danger at the present time is the Japanese laundries. They are increasing, and increasing very rapidly.

Commissioner O'CONNELL. How many Japanese laundries?

Mr. TAIT. I don't know; there are quite a number scattered over the city, small places where they have barber shops and places of that kind.

·· Commissioner O'CONNELL. Their business is increasing?

Mr. TAIT. Their business is increasing.

Commissioner O'CONNELL. Does it have any perceptible effect on the laundries represented by you people?

Mr. TAIT. They have.

Commissioner O'CONNELL. So that growing increase of business on their part, is that having having some effect of decreasing the business that you speak of?

Mr. TAIT. Yes, sir; but the class of customers who as a general rule patronize steam laundries are not apt to patronize the Japanese or Chinese laundries. The decrease in the laundry business is due to the stringency of the times as much as anything else.

Commissioner O'CONNELL. Are the laundry workers organized?

Mr. TAIT. They are not.

Commissioner O'CONNELL. Have they ever been organized?

Mr. TAIT. Yes, sir.

Commissioner O'CONNELL. How long ago?

Mr. TAIT. From 1902 to 1903.

Commissioner O'CONNELL. Did they make a contract of any kind at that time with you as to wages and hours?

Mr. TAIT. They made a contract for one year as to wages and hours.

Commissioner O'CONNELL. Then disbanded, or what?

Mr. TAIT. No, sir; we refused to sign the contract the second year.

COMMISSIONER O'CONNELL. Have the laundrymen an association here?

Mr. TAIT. They have a club.

Commissioner O'CONNELL. They have a club?

Mr. TAIT. Yes, sir.

Commissioner O'CONNELL. The laundrymen hold membership therein?

Mr. TAIT. Yes, sir.

Commissioner O'CONNELL. In that club you discuss commercial affairs?

Mr. TAIT. We do.

Commissioner O'CONNELL. As to how business shall be conducted?

Mr. TAIT. Our club is educational in how business should be conducted and costs. We discuss the cost of operation and the per cent of cost in the different departments and all those things, and ways and manner in which to handle our work. It is educational.

Commissioner O'CONNELL. Have you ever discussed the question of whether you shall permit or not the employees to organize or recognize an organization they may have?

Mr. TAIT. We have discussed the question when it was forced upon us.

Commissioner O'CONNELL. Well, how are the piecework prices of the employees set? Who sets them?

Mr. TAIT. The manner in which we have set the piecework was based on taking a month's careful count of the number of pieces which the different employees handled and basing it on the wages which they were earning at that time.

Commissioner O'CONNELL. Were the employees consulted in any way and manner?

Mr. TAIT. They were.

Commissioner O'CONNELL. They were called into conference?

Mr. TAIT. They were called into conference.

Commissioner O'CONNELL. As a whole or just individuals?

Mr. TAIT. As a whole in that, and individuals. It was discussed.

Commissioner O'CONNELL. Then you dealt with them in a collective way in settling the piecework prices?

Mr. TAIT. In the different departments.

Commissioner O'CONNELL. Was there a bargaining back and forth whether it should be so much or less?

Mr. TAIT. No, sir; we made an agreement when we put them on as pieceworkers that we would guarantee them the same wages that they were earning at that time.

Commissioner O'CONNELL. Who set the prices?

Mr. TAIT. The prices were based on the actual cost of our operation one month previous to the time it was set—the number of pieces which they handled during that month and the cost for labor in handling that number.

Commissioner O'CONNELL. As I understand you, you went all over that and figured out what you thought would be a fair price, and then set down a rate of piecework prices for each piece?

Mr. TAIT. Yes, sir.

Commissioner O'CONNELL. And then called in your people and told them that was what you were going to do?

Mr. TAIT. Yes, sir.

Commissioner O'CONNELL. And if they accepted that you would guarantee they would make at least the minimum wage?

Mr. TAIT. Yes, sir.

Commissioner O'CONNELL. And their part in the conference or in the negotiations so far as the prices are concerned were simply making known to them what you were going to produce in the plant?

Mr. TAIT. Their part—they had a knowledge of this at the beginning; their part was to make the record as best they possibly could.

Commissioner O'CONNELL. What I want to get at is, did your employees go into it in the way of bargaining with you as to whether the price should be this or that, a higher or a lower price, but you set the price?

Mr. TAIT. We set the price. The result—do you wish to know that?

Commissioner O'CONNELL. What was the result?

Mr. TAIT. The result was an increase in their pay roll of from 20 to 30 per cent.

Commissioner O'CONNELL. What was the increase in production?

Mr. TAIT. About the same.

Commissioner O'CONNELL. Twenty to 30 per cent?

Mr. TAIT. In the production.

Commissioner O'CONNELL. That is all.

Commissioner COMMONS. Could you furnish us from your price lists data which would show the actual increase in prices charged to the consumer?

Mr. TAIT. Not from our price list. It would necessarily compel us to know the number of pieces which we are handling in those different lines; we would have to know that. We would have to know the number of sheets we are handling and know the percentage of our rates.

Commissioner COMMONS. You have not done that at all?

Mr. TAIT. No, sir.

Commissioner COMMONS. You state that the increase in production, however, has not been as great as the increase in wages?

Mr. TAIT. No; not from the returns which we are getting from our actual operating expenses. Of course the condition now of the business—it is in a peculiar position because it is—the hard times have affected the laundry business probably more than it has affected any other line of business. The homes are doing—they are doing considerable work which formerly went to the laundry. They are economizing.

Commissioner COMMONS. Does your association or club—has it done anything toward stiffening prices?

Mr. TAIT. In which way?

Commissioner COMMONS. Well, have the prices that your competitors charge been lower or higher; have they all come up?

Mr. TAIT. It is done through an educational—along educational lines, showing the cost per hundred pieces.

Commissioner COMMONS. You make a recommendation?

Mr. TAIT. We make a recommendation.

Commissioner COMMONS. Of the prices that should be charged?

Mr. TAIT. We make a recommendation of the price. We figure out, show the cost of those different things, the cost of production.

Commissioner COMMONS. So that the prices now charged are prices that the club has recommended to its members?

Mr. TAIT. It recommended—it has recommended to those; some prices are higher now; prices are not on a level; some prices are higher.

Commissioner COMMONS. Higher than recommended?

Mr. TAIT. Higher than recommended. We show from our club the cost of production on these different articles, and they can use their own judgment.

Commissioner COMMONS. So that all are not—all are not charging the same prices; some charge higher and some not. For instance——

Mr. TAIT. In regard to bedspreads, for instance, our prices on bedspreads is 10 cents, and a great many of our competitors are doing it for 5 cents.

Commissioner COMMONS. In that case what is the recommended price?

Mr. TAIT. The recommended price would be 10 cents on that, because if it is recommended on the cost you would find the cost of those spreads would be a great deal over the 5 cents charged.

Commissioner COMMONS. So there are some of the laundrymen who charge less than the recommended price?

Mr. TAIT. Oh, yes; there are some.

Commissioner COMMONS. And some charge more?

Mr. TAIT. Some charge more.

Commissioner COMMONS. It is purely a study of costs?

Mr. TAIT. Yes; it is a study of costs. It is based on the cost of labor, cost of material, overhead charges, and all those things are taken into consideration.

Commissioner COMMONS. When did you start this cost study?

Mr. TAIT. About five years ago.

Commissioner COMMONS. About five years ago?

Mr. TAIT. Yes, sir.

Commissioner COMMONS. It has not grown out of the minimum wage legislation?

Mr. TAIT. Oh, no; it has not.

Commissioner COMMONS. That is all.

Chairman WALSH. That is all. Thank you.

Mr. THOMPSON. Mr. Swigert. Is Mr. Swigert in the room?

Chairman WALSH. Call your next witness.

Mr. THOMPSON. Mr. Osborne.

TESTIMONY OF MR. BENJAMIN OSBORNE.

Mr. THOMPSON. Give us your name, please.

Mr. OSBORNE. Ben Osborne.

Mr. THOMPSON. And your business address.

Mr. OSBORNE. 162 Second Street.

Mr. THOMPSON. And your business.

Mr. OSBORNE. I am president of the building trades council; business agent for the structural-iron workers' union.

Mr. THOMPSON. What is the present condition of labor with regard to the structural workers and the unions?

Mr. OSBORNE. The building trades council, you mean; the building contractors and the unions—the building trades council? Why, the relation is fairly good. The majority of the contractors, building contractors, in the city of Portland employ union men.

Mr. THOMPSON. There is no organization, however, of building contractors, is there?

Mr. OSBORNE. No. There is what is called the builders' exchange, but it is composed of small contractors and subcontractors; not the general contractors.

Mr. THOMPSON. Referring for the moment to your own organization and your building trades council, is it similar to the building trades councils in other cities formed by the international organizaton?

Mr. OSBORNE. Yes.

Mr. THOMPSON. Have you a constitution and by-laws here?

Mr. OSBORNE. Yes.

Mr. THOMPSON. Have you them with you?

Mr. OSBORNE. Yes, sir.

Mr. THOMPSON. Would you mind letting the commission have a copy of it?

Mr. OSBORNE. Yes; here it is.

(A pamphlet entitled " Constitution and By-Laws of Building Trades Council of Portland and Vicinity," adopted December, 1913, was submitted in printed form.)

Mr. THOMPSON. What percentage of the men engaged in the building trades, if you know, in this city are organized?

Mr. OSBORNE. You mean as a whole? I should judge that there are 80 per cent organized.

Mr. THOMPSON. Did you hear the statement made here the other day in regard to the situation of the building trades?

Mr. OSBORNE. By whom?

Mr. THOMPSON. By one of your men—Mr. Sleeman.

Mr. OSBORNE. Well, I heard a portion of Mr. Sleeman's testimony; not all.

Mr. THOMPSON. Oh. Was there anything that you care to state now with reference to the condition of labor in the building industry in this city?

Mr. OSBORNE. Well, I would like to state the business of the building trades council in the city of Portland; it is one question you omitted to ask me that I notice you have asked most of the members representing different organizations.

Chairman WALSH. Go ahead and state it.

Mr. THOMPSON. Go ahead and state it.

Mr. OSBORNE. Well, the business of the building trades council is to bring about all the organizations that work in the building industry into one compact organization or federation known as the building trades council, for the protection of the organizations, one and all, and to bring about more harmonious feeling between the labor organizations and the contractors, and also to prevent jurisdictional trouble. The jurisdiction of the building industry is peculiar and has in all quite a number of trades that are closely allied, kindred trades, and we have an enormous lot of employers to deal with.

We have the general contractor, and each particular trade has its subcontractor. And in times past we have had a good many jurisdictional disputes. And the only way that we can eliminate those jurisdictional disputes was federating together.

Mr. THOMPSON. Now, Mr. Osborne, has your organization, the building trades council, or have any of the international unions that form a part of that, agreements, either verbal or written, with either the contractors individually or groups of contractors in the building trades in this city?

Mr. OSBORNE. You mean, has our building trades council agreements with their employers?

Mr. THOMPSON. Yes.

Mr. OSBORNE. Well, with some of them we have, and with some of them it is merely a verbal agreement.

Mr. THOMPSON. I see. What I want to get at is to see if you have any organization, any mediation, or any arbitration board, or any other kind of machinery by which you may adjust with the employers and the contractors jurisdictional strikes, such as they have in Chicago and New York, for instance, or even to settle ordinary labor disputes?

Mr. OSBORNE. No, sir. I will state that in our constitution of the building trades council we refuse to allow any organization to put the jurisdictional fight up to the employers to settle. We settle it ourselves.

Mr. THOMPSON. But in Chicago and in New York, where your unions are in business, they have an agreement with the employers' association by which they have an arbitration. Now, of course, you have nothing like that?

Mr. OSBORNE. No. We have no master builders' association here.

Mr. THOMPSON. Well, do you know of the existence of those agreements in New York and in Chicago in the building trades dealing with jurisdictional matters and other matters as well?

Mr. OSBORNE. Well, I haven't—it is just rumors that I have heard. I haven't heard——.

Mr. THOMPSON. Then you could not give us any statement as to whether that would be good for this city or not?

Mr. OSBORNE. Well, not without a master builders' association they would not be any good.

Mr. THOMPSON. Well, Mr. Osborne, will you tell us in your own way the condition of the building trades here, the condition of labor here, and such other information as you care to give to this commission in regard to your own trades?

Mr. OSBORNE. Well, I will state that the building trades council with its employers have got along on most favorable terms in the last few years—last four years. We had scarcely any trouble. The trouble that we have had if we—if there is a misunderstanding comes up occasionally between some trade that is affiliated with the building trades council and the contractor, and we start out to adjust this, and it gets rumored, the fault that we find and the trouble that we have with our contracts at that time in that we always find the employers' association with their business agent—that is what we call him. That is what he is—is a business agent. He is always on hand to inform the contractor to deny the unions the request that they are making in the adjustment of the trouble; that they have their labor exchange and they can furnish all the nonunion men that the contractor wants.

And, of course, some of the contractors who are new with us—that is, who want to operate what we call under open-shop conditions, and have signed agreements with us—they sometimes listen to this, and it is a little harder to adjust the matter.

The older and established contractor who has dealt with organized labor for any length of time pays no attention to it.

And I will state that the only trouble that we have had in the building industry, the only strike that I can call to mind, was that of the electrical workers. I believe in 1911 the electrical workers signed—drew up an agreement, and it was signed by the electrical contractors, or a majority of them, those that operated under union conditions.

The contract read that on May 1, 1911, the electrical workers should receive $4 per day, eight hours, and they should continue for one year at that rate, and on May 1, 1912, wages would be raised to $5 per day. But when May 1, 1912, came the contractors absolutely refused to pay, absolutely broke their contract, and I believe that a compromise was made at four dollars and a half per day. And they are still working at that rate, without any agreement whatever. The electrical workers refused to sign any more agreements because they had been broken by the employers. And I will state also that the employers' association was very busy at that time. And then we have sometimes a strike when some subcontract is let to a nonunion firm who refuses to employ union men. So we have a strike, but it has never lasted any length of time only once or twice that I remember of, and I dont' believe that it lasted over 30 minutes either time. It was fixed up satisfactorily.

Mr. THOMPSON. Mr. Sleeman gave us some figures here as to the wages paid in the various building crafts, as to the hours of work in the building trades here, and as to the growth of the unions in the building trades. He would know of those facts, would he not?

Mr. OSBORNE. Well, I presume unless he had—he might remember them offhanded. I know I can't. I didn't hear his statement in that.

Mr. THOMPSON. Well, have you a statement that you would care to make in regard to the wages paid, the hours of work, and the growth of the organizations?

Mr. OSBORNE. I will state that the carpenters and joiners receive $4 per day, eight hours work; five days and a half per week is the days that they work in a week. The painters and decorators receive the same money, same hours. The plumbers and steam fitters receive $6 per day, and the same hours. Steam fitters' helpers and plumbers' helpers receive $3 per day. Plasterers receive $6 a day, and the same hours, eight hours, and five days and a half per week. Bricklayers receive the same as the plasterers, $6. Tile setters, $6, eight hours, five days and a half per week. Marble setters, $5.50, eight hours, five days and a half per week. Cement finishers receive $5 per day, eight hours, for five days and a half. Hoisting and portable engineers receive the same. Structural-iron workers, $5, eight hours per day, five and a half per week. Lathers receive the same. Elevator constructors the same. Sheet-metal workers receive $4.50 per day; the hours and the week is the same, eight, and five and a half. The electrical workers receive $4.50 for eight hours, five days and a half. The building laborers have a graduated scale. The common laborer, the excavator, the man who cleans up in the building, receives $2.50 per day, and he works six days. The concrete mixer and wheeler and brick wheeler receive $3 per day, and the mortar mixer who tends plasterers receives $4 per day. The asbestos workers receive $3.50 per day. The composition roofers $3.25 per day. That is all based on an eight-hour day.

Mr. THOMPSON. Are those different lines pretty well organized in this city?

Mr. OSBORNE. Yes. Some of them a hundred per cent.

Mr. THOMPSON. Are these wages and hours you name the union scale?

Mr. OSBORNE. That is the union scale.

Mr. THOMPSON. And they are being paid in this city?

Mr. OSBORNE. They are.

Mr. THOMPSON. Referring to the jurisdictional matter, which you have touched on, have you many jurisdictional fights here in Portland?

Mr. OSBORNE. Well, we have had very few jurisdictional fights.

Mr. THOMPSON. How many cases have you had?

Mr. OSBORNE. The only one of any consequence was not with the organizations affiliated with the building trades council. The bricklayers was not in the council, and there was a jurisdictional fight between the stone setters and the bricklayers, and the stone setters was affiliated with the building trades council, and the building trades council supported them, and the work went ahead. The building trades mechanics all remained on the job and supported the organization that is affiliated with them.

Mr. THOMPSON. Have the bricklayers ever been affiliated with your council?

Mr. OSBORNE. Well, not to my knowledge. Not since I have been a resident of Portland. That is four years and a half.

Mr. THOMPSON. In cases of jurisdictional disputes occurring between members of your own council, what does your council do to settle them?

Mr. OSBORNE. Why, we have a—we call a meeting of the board of business agents of the various organizations and we discuss this matter. And sometimes we are sitting down there for two or three days discussing it, when it seems to get serious, without taking it to the job. And, as a rule, there are compromises made between the organizations that are involved.

Mr. THOMPSON. Have there been any cases where there have not been compromises; and then what hapened?

Mr. OSBORNE. Well, there was a case between the sheet-metal workers and the carpenters. We could not reach any satisfactory agreement, but the job was not molested.

Mr. THOMPSON. I see.

Mr. OSBORNE. The organization which was on the work remained there and finished up.

Mr. THOMPSON. Have there been any cases where a strike was called when you could not get together?

Mr. OSBORNE. Not to my knowledge in the last four years.

Mr. THOMPSON. Do the members of your crafts or your unions work with non-union men in this city?

Mr. OSBORNE. 'Not with nonunion men of its own craft. We at times—we work—all trades work a closed shop to their own trade.

Mr. THOMPSON. How about your own line of work?

Mr. OSBORNE. Well, my own line of work; we work a closed shop within our own trade. But there are times that we work on buildings where there is some other trade that is not organized, but not with our own organization. That is an understanding with the building trades council that we have, as I said before, all of the large contractors work union men. The work—and all subcontracts are let to union firms. There is only one large contractor in the city that operates nonunion; and, of course, there is some smaller contractors that operate nonunion. And we have got that understanding among ourselves that certain of those small contractors, if they let a subcontract to one of the union firms, we allow the members of that organization to go on and work there. That is in order to strengthen, and looking to that time when we can all work on all jobs or refuse to work on them.

Mr. THOMPSON. In regard to your line of work, who has the placing and bending of rods in reinforced concrete?

Mr. OSBORNE. The ironworkers organization, the members of the bridge and structural ironworkers.

Mr. THOMPSON. Is there any other organization here, or union, that claims that work?

Mr. OSBORNE. No, sir.

Mr. THOMPSON. Do you know what the wages and hours are of nonunion workers in this city of your trade?

Mr. OSBORNE. In my trade?

Mr. THOMPSON. I mean in the building trades.

Mr. OSBORNE. In the building trades? Well, it is anything they can get principally. There is no established rate of wages among them. I talked with the superintendent of the large nonunion contracting firm, and he told me that he paid from 35 cents to 50 cents per hour.

Mr. THOMPSON. For what?

Mr. OSBORNE. For carpenters. The union scale is a minimum of 50 cents per hour; but the majority of his men were working for less than 50 cents per hour; just a very few that was competent to receive 50 cents per hour. His building laborers were working for 25 cents per hour, and from that to 27½, and no overtime. They worked straight. Their hours may be six a day, if they get through with their work, and it may be twelve. And their ironworkers and rod workers, they receive from 25 cents per hour to 35 cents per hour. That is what the men who work with them, some two and three years, and who come and join the organization, informed me that that is what they got.

Mr. THOMPSON. Have you got any other knowledge of nonunion wages paid here in this town?

Mr. OSBORNE. Well, nonunion plasterers work for anything they can get, anywhere from $3 to $5 a day. I have never heard of them receiving more than that, except on one job. There was a job here some four years ago that went up by a large nonunion contractor who had come into the city and refused to employ any union men, and we didn't give him any union men at all. He advocated the open shop, and we give him the open shop. And I will state that the plasterers was brought in from outside cities, also the marble workers; and the man who was superintendent of the job told me that he heard the plasterer foreman say to the journeymen plasterers and the journeymen marble setters, he says, "Take your time. boys, we have got them over a barrel. They can't get the union men here, and we are getting the union scale, and let's make it last." And it was the last job the contractor ever done in the city of Portland.

Mr. THOMPSON. Any further statement you care to make, Mr. Osborne?*

Mr. OSBORNE. Well, I would like to state that there are some questions .in here. There is one here that is in regard to crafts or industrial—I am a trade-unionist and believe in it, and I believe in the building industry at the present time that we could eliminate certain trades. I believe that, and I understand that some of the international officers are in favor of this at the present time. I certainly am, because I know how hard it is at times to prevent jurisdictional fights between kindred trades of the metal workers, such as the ironworkers, sheet-metal workers. and metal lathers, should be in the same organization, and all the woodworking organizations, and all the mortar trades, and the finishing trades, and the pipe trades. And I believe that it will ultimately come to that shortly.

I want to say that I advocate it very strongly. Still it is trade-union, it is industrially, too; it is closer to industrial unionism, and I believe that the time will come, and it is not far, when we will be one organization in the building industry. I believe in that, but I don't believe that our members of the rank and file of organized labor are prepared for it yet.

There is another down here, of the limitation and standardization of output. That is something that the building trades know nothing of. They get the work for the members and tell them to perform it. There is no limit to what they can do or will do.

I heard the assertion here yesterday that when times were slack the building-trades mechanics worked harder, and when they were—when work was plentiful that they made more demands, and when work was slack they did not live up to the standard scale of wages. I want to say that the statement is not correct in any way that I have ever found out, and I have had a pretty good way of finding out these things. The building-trades organization demands the same wages when there is a cry for men and when there is no work to speak of at all. We have set a scale of wages, and there is no organization can raise its wages without bringing it to the building-trades council and getting the consent of all the trades and the organizations affiliated there before they can go out and demand a raise in wages. And when they make the demand and the building-trades council finds that the demand is just they support that organization and notify the contractor to that effect. And when the contractor agrees that he will pay those wages, why those are the wages paid, whether there are all the men in the city at work or whether there is just one job going.

Commissioner COMMONS. Mr. Thompson, I just had a question.

Mr. THOMPSON. That is all I had.

Commissioner COMMONS. I think you are probably referring to the testimony of Mr. Kroner yesterday.

Mr. OSBORNE. Yes.

Commissioner COMMONS. Well, I didn't understand him to make an assertion regarding wages.

Mr. OSBORNE. Yes; I heard him make it.

Commissioner COMMONS. Well, my understanding was this, that in the slack times the unions did not enforce their rules restricting the amount of work, or requiring extra work, or requiring more men, or limiting the amount of work that men should do. That, in other words, they worked faster and did not pay attention to their rules regulating output. But that in busy times they insisted on those rules, and did not work or did not speed up so much as they did in slack times. That was my understanding. Anyhow, what is your notion of that condition?

Mr. OSBORNE. Well, it is not true. The mechanics of the building-trades council usually go out to do a day's work. They know that if they don't do a day's work that they are not going to stay on the job, both when times are good and when times are slack.

Of course, I don't know; I am pretty well familiar with all the architects in the city, but I never heard of the gentleman until I saw him get on the stand here.

·◄And·I want to state that in regards the apprentice, or apprenticeship, there is no organization affiliated with the building-trades council, to my knowledge, except it be the building laborers, and they have a certain apprenticeship, too, in the common, what is known as the common laborer, that is the common work, wheeling and mixing cement and mortar is, to a certain extent, skilled. But all the organizations have an apprenticeship.· And the sheet-metal workers' organization, which he made the remark that he was a mechanic of that description, I will state that they use one apprentice to two journeymen in their shops at the present time, and also on the buildings. And the sheet-metal workers at times almost have.trouble, because they want to run in more apprentices than that. And.I will state that the ironworkers have an apprentice system that covers two or three branches of the trade. In the ornamental ironwork we have one apprentice to every two journeymen. He is required to learn that trade. It takes him three years. And in the structural work we have an apprentice, one to every seven men. There are not very many, there is not very much need of an apprentice in structural work. But in the last three years, to my knowledge, we have turned out something like twenty-three or four men through the apprenticeship. They are only required to serve one year. The carpenters and plasterers, and I think the steam fitters, have one to every three. The plumbers—I am not positive, I wouldn't say that. The tile setters have one to one. Electrical workers have one to every two journeymen. The cement finishers have one to every journeyman, to a certain number, three or four, and then they don't have so many. But the building-trades council don't bar apprentices. We encourage it in our organization.

Commissioner O'CONNELL. What is the average time in a year that a building-trades workman will be employed in the city? How much time will he get, 7, 8, or 10 months' work a year?

Mr. OSBORNE. Well, I should judge that if a building-trades mechanic averages seven months a year he is doing extraordinarily well.

Commissioner O'CONNELL. And if the wages of the building trades were on an average of $5 a day, which, according to your figures, they are not, their earnings for the year would not average much more than $2.50 a day, or $3 a day at the outside?

Mr. OSBORNE. Not very much. Of course I want to state, like last year, the men averaged more than seven months, but this year they will average less than six.

Here is another thing I want to call your attention to, and that is the closed shop. It is not the closed shop or open shop with us; it is union.and nonunion. The only closed shop that I know of is what the employers' associations calls the open shop. The doors are absolutely closed to a man who carries a card, if they know it. Absolutely closed. In my trade I have found there are—I have found contractors would get in a small way on a building, and when I went to the architect and contractor and taken the matter up with them they would say: "Well, I can't employ union men. I am forbidden. I am a member of the employers' association." Consequently they would have to—the contractor and all would have to leave the job at different times. I found even in my own trade three years ago we had some bridges up about 100 miles from the city, and the employers' association down there—had had their employment agency down in their headquarters—we used to go down there and hire out, and about every day some of us would, but there was always a request that it was absolutely nonunion; that the union men could not work. Last year—two·years ago it was—the ironworkers had a strike in Vancouver, British Columbia. I don't remember now whether it was last year or the year·before, but it seems to me it was last year. They have a list of all the nonunion workers on the Pacific coast and who they work for. A strike came on in Vancouver, British Columbia. I sent men to the employers' association, seeking work in Vancouver, British Columbia, because I knew they would be advertising for them; that is, there was not—yes, they did run an advertisement in the paper to apply 222 Commerce Building, I believe it was, chamber of commerce. I sent men down there, and they was not ready to ship, but they were going to ship them up there and pay their fare after they got up there across the line. But the strike was settled in a day or two in Vancouver, British Columbia, satisfactory to the ironworkers. Consequently we didn't get to send any men up there. Those things go on.

They shipped men here from the East in my trade about four years ago, until they had in the Northwest quite a few jobs going with them. At the present time I will state all those men are members of the bridge and structural·iron-workers' organization.

In our boycotts from the building-trades section we work—we send out a committee to investigate, to an owner when he is going to build a building, use our influence to have him let his contract to a union firm, and explain to him our mission and what our organization stands for, and our men are the most efficient men in the building industry, and we explain to him that the nonunion contractor does not uphold the standard of wages; and then, if he ·insists on' employing, giving his contracts to men who operate nonunion, we bring the matter before the building trades council, and before he is placed on the unfair· list we send him a communication to appear before our executive board and state what he has got to say. Sometimes they don't come; sometimes they do. Sometimes they are straightened out. Whenever they are not we usually prose-·cute a boycott against him firm. I also want to state that the employers' asso-ciation have their boycotts in a way. Here is a letter I have from the employers' association:

Commissioner GARRETSON. Is that the notice of letting of contracts to con-·tractors to employ union men?

Mr. OSBORNE. Yes. I would read this, if the committee desires it.

Chairman WALSH. All documents are to be submitted.

Mr. OSBORNE. I would like to keep this.

Chairman WALSH. Turn it over to the stenographer, and he will copy it be-fore he leaves the city and return it to you, unless the commission would like to hear it.

Commissioner GARRETSON. I should like to hear it.

Chairman WALSH. What is the substance of it?

Commissioner COMMONS. Just give us the substance.

Mr. OSBORNE. It says, " To our members." The employers' association calls attention——

Chairman WALSH. It seems that it is just a page. Go ahead and read it. 'I guess we will save time.

Mr. OSBORNE (reading) :

EMPLOYERS' ASSOCIATION OF OREGON,
Portland, Oreg., July 11, 1913.

To our Members:

At this time the Northwestern Electric Co. is soliciting your patronage for heat, light, and power. We thought you might be desirous of knowing that the Northwestern Electric Co. has leased from the Pittock Block (Inc.) the build-ing which is now being erected on Washington, Tenth, Stark, and West Park Streets.

The contract for this building was awarded to a contractor who has signed up with the unions in spite of the fact that a lower bid was submitted by an open-shop contractor whose responsibility is sufficiently attested by the fact that he was invited to bid on this work.

Several of those interested in this building are also in the management of the Northwestern Bank Buildings, where it was openly stated that only union men would be employed in its construction.

Yours, very truly,

EMPLOYERS' ASSOCIATION OF OREGON.

Commissioner GARRETSON. What is the difference between your placing em-ployers on the unfair list and the employer placing the men on the unfair list, or boycott list, if he deals with union labor?

Mr. OSBORNE. Well, the difference is that we are not·afraid to let the public-know that we do place them on the boycott. That is a natural right, we be-·lieve we have—to strike and to boycott a firm who is unfair. We believe we have a natural right to conserve our purchasing power, and we are not afraid to let the world know it.

Commissioner GARRETSON. You recognize the right of the other party to do it, in the same way?

Mr. OSBORNE. Absolutely, if he so desires.

Commissioner GARRETSON. But do you recognize the right of a man to do it himself and denounce another for doing it?

Mr. OSBORNE. No; it doesn't seem to me as though it is a square deal.

Chairman WALSH. That is all. Thank you.

Call your next witness

TESTIMONY OF MR. J. A. MADSEN.

Mr. THOMPSON. I wish you would make your own statement with regard to certain longshore conditions; it has already been stated on the stand here, but I understand you want to make some additional statement.

Mr. MADSEN. Yes. There was a statement made to the effect that the longshoremen's organization was responsible for driving some business away from this port. That is a misstatement, and I am prepared to show to the contrary. It is true that the longshoremen of this port are well organized and are receiving a fair wage, somewhat in excess of what is received on Puget Sound on some commodities; but the cost—the actual cost of loading a ship; the contract price of loading a ship—is greater on Puget Sound than it is in Portland, Oreg. As a matter of fact, everything here—it ranges about 10 per cent higher. Therefore the actual cost of loading a ship is cheaper in the port of Portland than it is on Puget Sound, the only difference being that the men who are actually performing the work receive a little more of that, of the profits, for loading that ship than they would in Puget Sound under the present circumstances. The figures are here. There is a regular schedule issued by the Portland Chamber of Commerce giving the prices, and I have here the Puget Sound scale, which on the face of it would seem to be small, but the conclusion of the rates adds a cost of 27 cents per ton, which aggregated makes the cost on Puget Sound for handling a cargo in general at least 10 per cent greater than on the Columbia River in the port of Portland.

There has been considerable business driven away from the city of Portland, but it has been owing to the fact that the docks were in the hands of a monopoly, and only those that were in position to get dock room would be able to do business of that character in this port. Recently we have added some municipal docks, and I presume that that part of the monopoly will be prevented from operating against the port. There are other causes, which I doubt it would be wise to bring out here just at this particular time, that work against the port. But the docks here and facilities for handling general cargoes are not near as good as they are in other ports. The docks here are what we might term man-killers; except those new docks that are being built by the municipality. The wheat docks are good and the lumber docks are good.

The difference in wages is, of course, caused by the form of organization we have on the Columbia River. The wages originally were as great on Puget Sound as they are here. Some 20 years ago they were higher, but about the same figure as they are to-day. There has been, practically speaking, no increase. The only ones that are continually harping about the cost of longshoremen in this port are the employers' association. They are continually endeavoring to butt in. They seem to be having a grudge against the organization of the longshoremen in this port. It has been able to accomplish a great deal for its members.

We have something like close to 1,000 members in this port, and in the 13 years we have been organized we have made moral and financial improvement, and improved every other standing of our prices and members in every other respect. Probably 80 per cent of them are men of families, own property, and nice in character. I presume our membership alone represents in actual capital and good citizenship a great deal more than the employers' association. [Laughter.]

Chairman WALSH. Excuse me, but we must keep order.

Mr. MADSEN. We are continually being subjected to criticism of this kind. I wish to state for the information of the commission that in 1910 an attempt was made to inaugurate a system similar to this prevailing on Puget Sound, in so far as hiring longshoremen was concerned, and reduction of wages, of course. But the longshoremen and stevedores held a joint meeting, invited the public press, and we compared those figures, and they were published, and it was shown that the cost for loading ships on the Columbia River at the port of Portland was really less than any other port on the coast. And that had the moral effect of quieting the continual outcry against the high price of labor on the water front of Portland.

The general unrest among labor that has been taken up a great deal comes to our notice probably more than any other craft. We are closely allied with the lumber industry, handling a great deal of that product, and we find that all of our unrest can be traced to one agency in this district, in this State, and that one agency is the employers' association.

There is a great deal of sentiment in favor of organization among the work-ingmen in this State, but the fear of being discharged for allying themselves with an organization is the preventive. That has been advocated, and, of course, enforced by the employers' association wherever they possibly can. They resort to all known and some unknown methods of preventing organization among the workers. Personally I am fully convinced that a Federal grand jury investigation would put them out of business, and thereby would be the peace that is so neces-sary between the employers and the employees. That is about the actual con-dition that exists in this district in particular.

Chairman WALSH. Prof. Commons would like to ask you a few questions.

Commissioner COMMONS. You have a central employment office of your own?

Mr. MADSEN. Yes, sir; we have more than one, we have three in this port—four.

Commissioner COMMONS. How do the dock managers get employees, then?

Mr. MADSEN. Simply call up the phone and want us to furnish men; they simply notify us how many men they want and the men are sent.

Commissioner COMMONS. And the men report to your office?

Mr. MADSEN. We use our headquarters as a rendezvous for the men, to keep them out of the saloons and other places, or otherwise they would have to congregate.

Commissioner COMMONS. Do you furnish them a room? What kind of a room is it that they have?

Mr. MADSEN. A large room—headquarters—where the men can sit down and read.

Commissioner COMMONS. Do they have a waiting list?

Mr. MADSEN. Sometimes work—slack time we have a waiting list.

Commissioner COMMONS. Other times how is it?

Mr. MADSEN. We have different branches of the work; sometimes they follow one and others another.

Commissioner COMMONS. Do the men get employment in the order in which they stand on the waiting list, or do they depend on the business agent for their jobs?

Mr. MADSEN. No. The waiting list would guide—would be the guide—not the business agent.

Chairman WALSH. That is all. Call your next.

Mr. THOMPSON. Mr. Spicer.

TESTIMONY OF MR. JOHN L. SPICER.

Mr. THOMPSON. Will you please give us your name?

Mr. SPICER. John L. Spicer.

Mr. THOMPSON. And your address?

Mr. SPICER. 294 Larrabee Street.

Mr. THOMPSON. And your business?

Mr. SPICER. General work.

Mr. THOMPSON. Were you connected with the unemployment committee in this city, or league?

Mr. SPICER. I was.

Mr. THOMPSON. Tell us briefly your connection with that.

Mr. SPICER. The first part of the employment here in the city—Mr. Gilbert can tell more about it than I can.

Chairman WALSH. Let us have Mr. Gilbert. We have only eight minutes left. You say that he knows all that you know and something in addition. Let us have Mr. Gilbert.

Mr. SPICER. I would just like to make one statement, if I could, and that is this: Of the men in the tabernacle about fifteen hundred were fed meals. Prac-tically every man was bitter in the denunciation of the employment agencies, and they stated that a good deal of the unrest was caused on that account—the robbery of the agencies—and they were very bitter on that line.

Chairman WALSH. You think something should be done to relieve that situa-tion by law?

Mr. SPICER. Yes, sir; I think the real cause of unrest, in the first place, is per-haps there. And I think that one of the real causes of unrest is that everybody is trying to get a greater share of wealth in the country and because of the intelligence of the workers. The workers recognize the damnable conditions and are trying to overthrow them. It is not ignorance, but intelligence, which is causing the unrest.

Chairman WALSH. That is all. Mr. Gilbert.

TESTIMONY OF MR. EDWARD GILBERT.

Mr. THOMPSON. Give us your name, address, and business.

Mr. GILBERT. Ed. Gilbert, 294 Larrabee Street.

Mr. THOMPSON. Your business?

Mr. GILBERT. I am a workingman, a laborer.

Mr. THOMPSON. You were on the committee of unemployed last winter?

' Mr. GILBERT. I was on the committee. I was here and organized the unemployed—helped organize the unemployed league.

? Mr. THOMPSON. .Will you state what they did?

Mr. GILBERT. I will make a very brief statement. I will try to make it all inclusive, as near as I can. Last winter, about December 1, there was a number of workingmen connected with no particular organization who realized that there was a large number of unemployed in the city; and not only that, but the greater part of them were absolutely destitute because of the conditions that prevailed in the camps and shops the season previous during the working season. They realized the necessity of doing something, and they called a meeting at the Plaza, which was attended by about eight or nine thousand workingmen then unemployed.

We organized what was called afterwards the unemployed league, and opened headquarters at No. 63 North Second Street, and gave publicity to the fact that there was such an unusually large number of unemployed in the city and took steps to secure work. We sent a committee to visit the governor, and also a committee to visit the various officials of the city and county, and we asked the cooperation of the labor unions in this town, which we did not get, and the various officers of the labor unions that we visited seemed to be more horrified over the fact that there would be a horde of hungry, starving men walking through the streets than they were concerned in that the good people—they were more concerned in what the good people of Portland would think about a horde of hungry men walking through the streets than they were about the hungry men. But we got cooperation from individual members of the various unions.. Mr. Hanson spoke at the meeting at the Plaza. I might say in passing that there was no charitable organization, or no church as an organization, in any way rendered assistance to the unemployed. Our main object and purpose for which we organized the league was to secure work at a reasonable living wage for the unemployed. We were unsuccessful, although we received promises from the immigration board and the governor and the various city and State officials, yet there was no work provided, with the exception of a little work that was provided out on the boulevard here. That was work cracking rock. It was relief work, it was designated as such. The men were paid 75 cents for cracking a yard of rock, and they were only allowed to work half a day at a time. That is, one man could only work half a day, in the forenoon, and then another man had to take his place. They only provided this work.

This work out on the boulevard, cracking rock, was designated as relief work, and even that—first they furnished us work for 200 men; later on they reduced that number to 150, and, in the course of a week or 10 days, the work was entirely shut down. There was no work then given to the unemployed by the city. The State, as far as I know, furnished no work at all for the men. They gave no work of any description. The county did nothing in regard to giving the men work, and this one effort by the city establishing the rock pile, was the only effort made to give the men work.

As I stated the main object of the league was not to seek charity; it was not to promulgate any particular doctrine; we didn't want the unemployed league to be a stamping ground for anyone who had a doctrine or philosophy to propagate. It was formed simply on the ground that men were hungry, out of work, destitute, and desired to work. Our one object was not charity, and our banner that we carried—we carried a banner—was: " We want work and not charity." That was the spirit that permeated the ranks of the unemployed at all times; but they were under the necessity, when work was not provided, to accept charity, and I, as a member of the unemployed league and of the unemployed last winter, think that so far as that was concerned it was an absolute failure. There was no work established. · There was no provision made for using the men. There was provision made for housing the men after a manner, and feeding them after a manner, but that is no solution to the unemployed problem. I guess that is about all on that. I would like to say about a word more, if you will extend my time?

Chairman WALSH. Certainly.

Commissioner GARRETSON. Have you any idea what would be a practical means?

Mr. GILBERT. What would be a practical means?

Commissioner GARRETSON. Yes, sir.

Mr. GILBERT. Of solving the unemployed problem?

Commissioner GARRETSON. Yes, sir.

Mr. GILBERT. Give the men work. Create work for the men, by using road work; clearing land; anything that would provide work at a reasonable wage— a living wage. The question of unemployment was given—a great deal of stress was laid upon what was so-called seasonal labor. I don't think that that is the cause of unemployment; in fact I know it is not. The seasonal labor or the climatic conditions in certain industries that have been classified as seasonal industries, simply during the time of the year when we are going to have those industries shut down, it does not necessarily mean it is because of climatic conditions. It is the force of the factory. Take the lumber industry, for instance. If we had a climate that it was possible, the same as it is now, favorable to work in the open the year round, we would find the lumber and logging industries would have a period in those industries where there would be slack times and dull times; that the camps would shut down. On the contrary, though, when the market was good and when there was a demand for lumber, we find that even in the winter months, in the worst kind of weather, that the logging camps continued to operate at full capacity. The same is true of the construction work.

I have in mind a north bank railroad that was built in 1904 or 1905 or 1906 or 1907. It was a well-known fact among the workingmen on construction work—railroad construction work—that this railroad took advantage of a situation created by the winter months, when the other contractors shut down; and they done the greater portion of their work in the winter months, because then there was a greater supply of labor on the market and very little demand for it and wages consequently would be lower, and they done their work even in what we call the rainy belt in the wintertime. This shows that even this occupation, which is generally classed as seasonal work and operates under climatic conditions, can be operated in the wintertime. This shows there is no large industry in the Pacific Northwest that I know of that the climatic conditions in this State is the cause of unemployment. The real fact of the matter of the cause of unemployment is the ownership—private ownership—of industries. Any time that there is a private ownership of industries, when we have private owners and employers of labor, we can find and we do find naturally that the industry is operated for profit, and that the thing that will determine the time when the industry will work is the demand for the commodity that the industry produces, and that the system of society, as it is organized at the present day, places it, in my opinion, for the worst for the unemployed in the Northwest and in all the country.

Chairman WALSH. Did you want to ask anything about this organization?

Commissioner COMMONS. I want to ask this one question: You spoke about furnishing work in the winter at a reasonable wage. Did that in your mind mean something less than the wage that you could get at other times of the years?

Mr. GILBERT. Well, at a reasonable wage, a living wage. Circumstances have a whole lot to do in dictating or determining just what a reasonable wage was.

Commissioner COMMONS. Suppose——

Mr. GILBERT. I can give you an illustration of that. There was a convention called in a hall upstairs, and in that convention delegates from all the representative bodies in the city were present. There was—it was called by the State federation of labor, and the proposition of securing work was taken up and one mad made the motion that no work would be considered by the unemployed that didn't take into consideration the union wage scale.

Now, there is a whole lot of work that the unorganized do that there is no scale set for by the various craft organizations. But, then, don't you see, that was saddling on the unorganized—although that motion passed and carried, it was saddling on the unorganized the necessity—of course, I would like to see every man get the union wage, and, in my opinion, the union wage is too small and not sufficient; yet you take the concrete industry, the laborers in the summer time—we find that there are men working for $2.25, and, in some cases, like this summer, $2 for 8 or 9 or 10 hours; and I believe the union wage is much higher than that, and that was saddling upon us the necessity of main-

taining something in a crisis, or particularly unusual situation, that the union could not do or does not do in ordinary times. And I believe that what is a reasonable living wage will be determined more or less by the circumstances.
Now, there was a case here that came from the O. W. R. & N. They had reduced wages from $1.75 to $1.50 a day. A dollar and a half a day, I don't believe, is a reasonable living wage, yet they were living under unusual conditions; they were sleeping on the floor and starving. Even with all of the charity, they were starving in the tabernacle, and $1.50 to them would mean a reasonable living wage.

Commissioner GARRETSON. In comparison with what they had?

Mr. GILBERT. In comparison with what they had. The circumstances must determine this.

Commissioner COMMONS. Your theory of a reasonable wage does not mean in hard times you should keep up the union scale of wages?

Mr. GILBERT. That isn't my theory at all. In hard times, more than any other, if possible, I would have the working man, if I possibly could, not only keep up wages but increase them.

Commissioner COMMONS. That is your theory?

Mr. GILBERT. I believe in meeting circumstances as they exist—facts as they exist. I have no theory about that particular thing. I gave you my theory. but we were under the necessity of doing something last winter—securing work for these men that we possibly could.

Commissioner COMMONS. Suppose you took a contract for clearing land in the winter and the landowners were not willing to pay two dollrs or two dollars and a quarter per day for clearing land. Suppose you could get a contract by which you could get a dollar a day in this dull season; would you consider that that would be a reasonable wage under the circumstances?

Mr. GILBERT. A dollar a day in the dull season, I don't think it is sufficient for a man to live on a dollar a day and work. You must taken into consideration that a man not working can possibly exist on a dollar a day, but a man who is clearing land—I have cleared some—they will need clothes. Your expenses will be so great you could not possibly exist on a dollar a day and supply yourself with food, clothing, and shelter.

Commissioner COMMONS. Well, if you were up against it and there was not anything else open to you, would you do it at a dollar a day?

Mr. GILBERT. Well, if I could not exist on a dollar a day—if I could not keep myself on a dollar a day, I think I would just as soon starve not working as working.

Commissioner COMMONS. Did you attempt to organize and taken any contracts for work at all of clearing land this last winter?

Mr. GILBERT. Well, there was a great deal of talk about organizing and taking contracts. We found this: That we could not even get the contract of splitting cord wood, not to mention clearing land. There was one man out here—there was a bunch of 100 men not connected with the unemployed league, although members of the unemployed, that thought they would pay a visit to Salem and hurry the governor up in doing something. After they got out in the suburbs there was a man out there who says, "I have some land and I can employ you, and I think it is my duty to do it, and I will do it, and I will pay you wages; I will furnish tents and cooking utensils and supply you with food, so that you can go ahead and go to work." They readily accepted the proposition, but then there was quite a few people in that vicinity in that town that went to this man and told him that if he employed those men, those vagrants, as they called them, they would run him out of town with the vagrants. That was the only offer we had of any consequence at all—taking a contract of any description.

Commission COMMONS. Did he get to the point of offering any particular rate of pay?

Mr. GILBERT. No, sir; he didn't get to the point that he had offered any particular rate of wages. But I think I talked to a man by the name of Carson, who was conducting the negotiations, and Carson said he was pretty sure the wages which he would offer would have been acceptable to the men, and I don't know if he did make any offer of wages, but that was understood, that it would be acceptable.

Commissioner COMMONS. You were willing to organize and take that kind of contract?

Mr. GILBERT. I don't know just what success they would have had if the unemployed in general would go into taking contracts to clear logged-off land.

I don't know just how successful that plan would operate, because a great many men are not fitted for that work; have no knowledge of that work, and still are unemployed in the wintertime and are men of various trades. We had tailors, and printers, and quite a few of skilled tradesmen, and men that work mainly at inside work. I know there was several tailors, and I, was personally acquainted with several printers. They were not physically fitted, and had no knowledge—they were unfitted for that work, they have never; done any of that work; they could not do it to advantage.

But on the other hand, there are men that understand that work, and I do know that a number of them were willing to take contracts splitting cord, wood and all that last winter, but the opportunity was not furnished them. There was endeavor made to secure this kind of work last winter and we had, no success. I can't say how willing they were or unwilling they were to take that work because the situation was not provided—the proposition was not provided.

Chairman WALSH. That is all, thank you, Mr. Gilbert. The commission will now stand finally adjourned.

Those witnesses who are here and have not been called may apply to the clerk, who will pay their witness fees, of course, the same as though they had been used as witnesses. We are sorry we could not hear all of you.

(Whereupon, at 12.45 o'clock p. m., Saturday, August 22, 1914, the commission adjourned to meet at San Francisco, Cal., on Tuesday, August 25, 1914, at 10 o'clock a. m.)

STATEMENT OF MR. GEORGE W. GORDON.

PORTLAND, OREG., *August 22, 1914.*

To United States Commission on Industrial Conditions:

GENTLEMEN: I have been a contractor and builder for the past 25 years in Portland, was the secretary of the Portland Master Builders' Association for many years, during which time we have been through three strikes and one lockout. During this period we had several meetings with delegates from the unions, and I have had a good opportunity to measure up some of the causes of the present unrest, which appears to be general.

When I first came to Portland there were no trade-unions. I found there were about 15 contractors here, most of whom seemed to have a thorough knowledge of construction and were posted as to values of different classes of construction and materials required, and the average cost of construction. These men were all successful contractors. The workmen, as a rule, were skilled, and the wages paid at that time ranged from $4 to $4.50 per day, according to the value of the services of the workman. Subcontractors got satisfactory prices for their part of the work, and everyone seemed satisfied with the conditions. The architects were also relieved of considerable responsibility, as they felt they had honest, reliable men to do their work, which lessened the need of their supervision.

The years that have passed since that time have brought many changes in the industrial world. Hundreds who at that time were carrying on a small business that gave employment to several, and at a satisfactory profit to themselves, have been driven out of business by the modern department store, and specialty-producing factories of one kind and another, which to a large extent eliminated the skilled mechanic and at the same time reduced their number according to the producing power of the machine, making it hard for the workman in regard to his earning capacity, the machine had put him in another class, and left many idle, besides. New methods of building were rapidly coming in vogue, which revolutionized the old methods, new buildings were being erected by contractors familiar with this class of work and the new appliances used in constructions, and skilled men were brought out who understood this new construction. This in a way handicapped the old contractor and he was unable to compete with the newcomer. In the meantime organizers were sent out to unionize the coast cities and, in their anxiety to build up the unions, did it by trying to get numbers instead of efficiency workmen and made excessive demands on the contractors, who had to contend with a new element in unionism—the employment of men who had no skill in the business, but who wanted the same wages as the skilled mechanic. Resenting this kind of treatment made the unions try another course, that of taking contracts themselves, which they did at prices below what they were worth, and they were unable to pay the workman the prices expected from the contractor and have a profit themselves. This method of procedure widened the breach between the contractors and the workmen.

During the interim food prices—controlled by a trust—were. advancing in prices. By this time the real-estate promoter was in evidence. By honeyed words and plausible-sounding stories of large sums made by advanced prices, it seemed easy to secure purchases at figures all out of proportion to the value of ground, but easy means of payments and future values landed the clerks and mechanics. The inducements that were put up to the purchaser were so alluring they did not hesitate to purchase. Following closely in the wake of the real-estate promoter came the good-roads promoters, who are aided by the newspapers in their schemes. Remunerative advertising was what they were after. Misleading articles were put in the papers lauding the virtues of their pavements, which have no real value over other pavements, but were covered by a trade-mark. These paving companies pay large salaries to promoters of their pavements, including all expenses added, and they also have men working on cammission. Their methods are to persuade if possible, coerce if they can, and when neither of these methods work they promise a rebate to signers of a petition which is presented to the council and which is accepted by them if signed by only 15 per cent of property owners, and it did not until recently take 80 per cent of the property holders' signatures to prevent them from forcing improvements against the wishes of the property owners.

These paving monopolists have fastened themselves so securely on the city that with the aid of the officials it seems almost impossible to shake them off. Royalties of 50 cents to $1.25 per surface yard for the privilege of laying their trade-marked products are exacted by these paving concerns. This effectually eliminates all competition and they then gouge the public unmercifully. The methods used by these people of enforcing improvements in outlying districts on property whose value was much less than the improvements assessed against them has resulted in thousands of poor people losing the homes they had been struggling for years to gain, but as property can not be bonded for more than the assessed valuation, which is 50 per cent of the actual value, it places the poor man in a position that he must pay cash for the excess of the assessments over the assessed value or he can not bond his property, and as he has not the means to pay this excess value his property is confiscated. These methods, which seem premeditated, have been the cause of more suffering and unnecessary privation than anyone can contemplate. Unless they investigate the system, the hard-earned money invested and the years of toil are gone for nothing. Under conditions of this kind the wonder to me is that the masses stand this abuse of their common rights, and yet for all his misfortune this man is afraid to assert his right by expression for fear the powerful interests who have deprived him of his home may deprive him of his job. But while there seems to be a calm on the surface, there has been engendered a deep hatred for the parties to his condition. Mr. Smith had better mingled among these people or got his information from some reliable source before he made the remarks that the unrest is imaginary. When a person has been deprived of his property by unscrupulous methods, you can not blame him for any action for reprisal at any time. Changes have been brought about so rapidly in the last few years that it seems impossible to combat them. The concentrated capitalists feel that their word is law, and they seemed to have no desire beyond accumulating more at the expense of the poor, half-starved workmen.

I never have had any sympathy with those who expect something for nothing, or agitators who,. many of them, are unfair and sell out the men they are expected to protect, but my experience is that a large majority of the workers, skilled and unskilled, are peaceable, law-abiding citizens who are happiest when working at wages that will insure them a living even with little margin for sickness and lack of employment. There is a multiplicity of causes for the unrest prevalent, but all have their source in the manipulation of the public utilities by a few people who, once they get control, only try the harder to obtain more public property without a proper recompense therefor. .

There should be a law enacted making it impossible for any person to force any kind of improvements against property in excess of 50 per cent of the value of the property. This would give the little fellow a chance to get a home, and I believe this system of forcing unnecessary improvements, which confiscate properties under the pretext of adding value to the same, is one of the principal causes for much of the present unrest.

Very truly, yours,

GEO. W. GORDON, *166 Eleventh Street, City.*

STATEMENT OF MR. W. C. FRANCIS.

The following statement was submitted in writing by Mr. W. C. Francis, manager of the Employers' Association of Portland (see p. 4579) :

1. I submit herewith declaration of principles and by-laws which will give more succinctly the purposes of our organization and its methods than I can by a verbal explanation. As to membership, we have between four and five hundred active factory members on our rolls, which means those who are engaged in industry.

2. To act as a clearing house for information pertaining to our members, such as activities of unions in different parts of the State and country. To give publicity to all of this and to conduct a labor bureau and list and furnish help as may be called for by anyone. We furnish to the laboring man assistance of this kind free of cost, and draw no line at his previous condition of servitude, his religion, or his nationality. We ask for references, however, merely to protect our bureau against men of vicious habits and ne'er-do-wells and those unfit, mechanically or otherwise, to perform the work.

(a) This association believes that laboring men or others have a right to organize. This goes without question, but it stands preeminently for the open shop.

(b) *Workmen's compensation.*—We have not indorsed this as an association, for our members are divided on the question. Personally I believe in some form of compensation for injured workmen, so as to protect society from the ambulance-chasing lawyers and the great amount of litigation that has been in our courts on account of damage cases.

(c) *Accident insurance.*—At some future time, when we evolve a better manner of selecting men to public office, selecting them for their honesty and efficiency, we perhaps can attach the State insurance feature to our compensation laws which will insure all workers, whether employee or not, against sickness, accidents, and death, in which, however, the workmen should pay the major portion of such protection, the same as he would to an insurance company, the State paying the cost of operation.

(d) *Promotion of industrial safety regulations and sanitation.*—We have not taken a stand as an association, so much as the metal trades association has on this matter, but many of our members are actively engaged in doing everything they can and in arranging safety regulation and sanitary methods, and some of our largest plants are models, so far as sanitary and safety regulations go, and do everything possible for their employees' welfare in this respect.

(e) There is a law now on the statute books of Oregon which provides for the regulation of time of service of female workers, and also prescribes a minimum wage for these.

(f) There is also a law on the statute books of Oregon which prescribes for child-labor regulation.

(g) Our association has taken no part in this as a body, but many of our most influential members believe in manual training as a vocational guidance, and have done much to further the aims and objects thereof in our public schools.

(h) Conciliation and arbitration may be one means of settling disputes, either labor or otherwise, but, measured by expressions, men are not much moved by the awards of such boards when a decision goes against them. In other words, men are not fair, and that is the reason we have warfare. This applies to all classes of men. I therefore believe this is not a panacea.

(i) The unemployment problem is a very important one, and the number of men without work in our country to-day is one of the leading causes of unrest. To relieve the situation there must be much constructive work entered into, much thought given to the subject after plans have been formulated. My personal views are that in times of stress to the common people, the Government might enter into projects of providing great reservoirs whereby flood waters could be stored, using the same for irrigation and at the same time preventing the rapid erosion of river banks by swiftly moving waters caused by floods. In this connection, the Government might undertake at the same time the deepening of the channels of rivers that could be used for navigable purposes so that the uses of inland waters by steamboats, barges, and smaller ocean-going vessels could be utilized and thus the people, particularly in the largely populated centers tributary to such rivers as the Ohio, Mississippi, and Missouri, would have competition of such nature as would bring about a reduction in rail rates at times when congestion of transportation lines took place by reason of crops or other commodities that have to be moved during seasonal rushes. The Government might, with profit to the people, undertake the construction of great arteries of travel from one end of the country to another, building several roads in the same direction at wide distances apart, if necessary, and then transversing these by others running north and south. These roads should be of hard-surfaced material, built for permanency, and to stand heavy wear and travel, and should be constructed so as to take heavy loads that might be placed upon them by reason of the people engaging in transportation with motor vehicles and trailers.

There is nothing, to my mind, that would assist the agriculturist and the man living in the country quite so much as good, hard-surfaced roads and one by which he could travel long distances with his horse-drawn or motor-propelled vehicles to market. The saving and the wear and tear to his equipment, the greater load he could carry and the longer distance it was taken to market would compensate the Government in building such a road, granting that a small levy for cost and operation of the road could be made. Then, there are our power systems to be developed of such magnitude that private enterprises could not well engage in. I have in mind particularly the harnessing of the Columbia River, both at the Celilo Rapids and at Cascades Locks, where hundreds of thousands of horsepower runs idle and to waste. I do not generally favor the Government going into the transportation business or the power business, as I believe that these are functions for private development. Something must be left to the citizen to engage in and to give incentive to impetus to create industry, and thereby competition, which is, when regulated, conducive to healthy business. Then, there is the question of large and unoccupied areas of land, both desert and partially timbered or logged off. This is the field for governmental endeavor, and during hard-times periods logged-off lands, particularly, could be profitably brought into a condition to be used for agricultural purposes with smaller cost when labor might be had for reasonable wages. The land problem is really one of the largest and most important that might be considered, and careful thought should be given to all of the suggestions herewith incorporated, for if followed in a practical manner, well planned and carried out with honesty and capability, as, for example, the building of the Panama Canal by and through Army officers, there can be no good reason why the country should not be much benefited and much of the unrest among the common people subdued through the employment of those now out of work.

(j) Welfare work is indulged in by individual employers, as, for instance, in the lumber industry, some of the laundries, and also some of the machine shops. The nature of this welfare work consists in the placing of reading and rest rooms for the interest of employees, and has, I believe, done some good. However, those who come in contact with this feature can tell more about it.

(k) Labor legislation is somewhat too recent to judge harshly or approvingly, and the principal defects that now seem on the horizon are the inclination on the part of the officeholders to be somewhat too zealous in enforcing laws that are but recent and new and have not yet become familiar to those whom it is intended for, and I should withhold any criticsm at this time, and will cover under another head the incompetence of officeholders.

(l) Minimum-wage legislation in this State has been passed affecting female and minor workers, and while in the abstract it is right that laws should be passed safeguardng the health of our future mothers as well as the child whom we want to become a sturdy citizen, the operation of the law has been so far somewhat cruel to the incompetents and misfits; in other words, those who can not come up to a certain standard.

The law of supply and demand as well as survival of the fittest is somewhat inexorable and seems to work regardless of restrictions placed by man-made laws, and in quite a few instances the writer has had opinions that a weeding process has been going on since the passage of the law of those unable to earn the minimum wage, and by reason of this many girls and women were now seeking something to do and willing to do it at almost any wage, but were deprived of engaging in the work that they were most familiar with because of their incompetence to come up to the standard. In other cases we find that there has been no appreciable change, and that the passage of the law has affected no increase in the regular weekly pay roll nor in the number of employees, particularly in the case of a large bag factory, the manager of which says he has not been obliged to discharge anyone because of the minimum wage. In other cases, such as in a large printing and bookbinding firm, complaint is made that provisions in the law should be made to care for emergency cases, for instance, in the binding of telephone directories printed three times a year, in which work many women and girls are employed. As this is a large publication and must be finished within a specified time, and while ample equipment to handle most work is installed, it is almost impossible to complete the work according to contract without running overtime; that during a period of three weeks in which the rush continues privilege should be permitted to work the female employees after the legal hours, which is 6 o'clock, the work to commence at 1 o'clock in the afternoon, extend to 6, an hour for luncheon, and then to 10 in the evening, when quitting. This would permit the fullest capacity of the machinery to be used and would not harm industry nor send work out of the State. I find from the opinions given that the candy factories and paperbox factories are the most seriously affected. But also find that the hotels have rearranged their female help so that none but strong women are now engaged who can do an allotted portion of work in the time—8 hours—required by law.

(m) Competition of the Oregon manufacturer with those in other States is something that several factors enter into besides the factor of labor; for instance, the cost of raw material, the cost of transportation, the cost of fuel, the distance from market. One factor, of course, favorably affects the whole Pacific coast region, and that is climate; but we can not go on to enact more and more stringent laws, affecting the employer, business man, and he who employs labor without most seriously hampering the worker, because of stagnation of enterprise and the lack of incentive on the part of him who would engage his money and talent to produce pay rolls were the laws less drastic. Our industries, aside from lumber, which is a native product in the raw, are as yet in a state of embryo, and anything tending to discourage enterprise through so-called progressive enactments will leave its impress upon the growth of the State in retarding effects that we will be a long time in overcoming, even though the pendulum swings the other way; that is to say, public opinion in favoring the passage of no more new laws.

(n) With the activities of trade-unions, particularly as to their methods, there is much fault to be found. With organization of the worker, no rightthinking person will find fault. With the administration of such organization, the general public has a right to scrutinize and criticize methods affecting not only the workers but those who engage in industry and those who consume the products of the other two. Much can be said against the methods of the trade-unions as officered and controlled under the American Federation of Labor jurisdiction. For instance, the closed shop means that no union man shall permit a man without a card or unaffiliated with his union to work in the same branch of trade on the same job with himself. There are cases where this is waived and the union is weak, but where the union is strong enough, a nonunion worker is deprived of making his living, and naturally friction and unrest ensues. This has got to be such a serious condition in the last few years and has caused so much friction all over the country, bringing into being employers' associations, generally, in all large centers, then later into smaller cities, and then by amalgamation of these into States and districts, that it now seems certain that a gigantic struggle will ensue between those who deem this privilege to act as sponsors for organized labor and the free workmen of the country who are not organized, also such friends as they may have among the employers who are thinking along the right lines and trying to be fair to those whom they employ. I will deal with concrete facts in some of the questions given to me to answer further on.

(o) The field for Federal intervention in industrial affairs seems to me, if carried on in interstate industrial matters, would bring up the question of State rights; and while Federal supervision, particularly of corporations who are doing an interstate business, might reasonably be expected to assist, still it is a question whether or not there would be some other plan, such as publicity and the formation of local adjustment boards, applying particularly to wages, hours, and sanitary conditions of labor, which would solve the problem much more satisfactorily. My own opinion is that when the question of minimum wage and reasonable hours is granted through some form of public activity, the trade and labor organizations of all kinds will have ceased to be a necessity for the workingman. It will then devolve upon some social or political organization to see that a square deal is given to all of those who may be affected, as workers or political factors under our system of carrying on our affairs.

3. This is a subject which opinions will differ upon, and I would subdivide unrest into three subheads of " Symptoms," " Causes," and " Remedies." We will deal first with the symptoms. I will divest myself in spots of personal opin-

ion, and will give the commission the benefit of my experience and the expressions that I get from others, workingmen as well as business men, members of
the unions as well as those unaffiliated.

Symptoms.—This head might by some be named "protests." Call it what you
may. We are being confronted with vast bodies of men, such as the Industrial
Workers of the World, the Socialist-anarchist, the anarchists pure and simple,
and various other bodies, tapering from mildly partisans to revolutionary propa.
gandists. All are the symptoms and all are voicing the cry of the oppressed.
The cry is becoming louder and louder as unemployment becomes more and more
prevalent and distress more and more acute. There can be no dismissing the
cry with a shrug of the shoulder or a wave of the hand, and the prudent man in
the different stations of life must needs give attention to those among us who
are suffering and who have a right to life and a certain portion of happiness.
Then, we have those of the higher type, who own property, the small home owners,
and the middle class, who are protesting against the high taxes and the increasing burdens placed upon them. And don't forget that the business man is not
immune from the causes that affect the working people, for he also is suffering,
as no one can escape, and must share in a general way to a greater or less degree
with any one class that does not obtain that to which it is entitled and does not
get under natural conditions.

Causes.—I would cite first of all bad administration of the law and lawyers
holding public office, many of them unfit by training for such positions; office.
holders in general not competent to carry on the work of the public in a business.
like and capable way; some who are unfitted by reason of having no courage to
make decisions, but who would favor a class of whatever kind through which
they might most easily profit. This is not said particularly to cast reflections
that officeholders in general are dishonest, but they can be such, however, without taking a bribe or money. For example, if a man caters to a class for the
votes he may get from them to the detriment of others who are not so strong
numerically, he is dishonest to the whole people, and stultifies his self-respect
by seeking emoluments to be delivered, present or in the future, by his attitude
of truckling to labor, or church votes, or those of whatever kind. Then, again,
we have newspaper and magazine publishers who proclaim wrong ideas at
variance with fundamental principles; who magnify and distort acts done by
one class and subdue and squelch things done by another class, however wrong
it may be. The yellow, muckraking publishers do this for the sole idea of
obtaining lucre therefor, and this is one of the evils of our republican civilization to-day.

I have in mind some of these influences which are bad, and would name
such writers as Creel, Sinclair, Steffens, who are constantly attacking business-
men and captains of industry and who magnify and distort and manufacture
stories that are at variance with facts generally. Then, there is the Socialist
press, which pours into its readers tales of happenings and attacks on not only
industry but Government. I have in mind a publication like the Washington
Socialist and the Appeal to Reason. Then again there is such a publication as
the Menace which has for its object the attack on a great and powerful religious
body and which it presumes to find fault with because of its political activity.
This is setting by the ears of a large portion of our people at the present time
and causing them to stop, look, and listen. Then, we have too many laws (the
country best governed is the country least governed); we have too many
lawyers in Congress and legislature, many only half-baked, and we have many
unscrupulous politicians who care nothing for the dear people except to gain
votes. We lack honesty among men and women; greed and rapacity, and the
desire for wealth is uppermost in most people's minds. They are obsessed with
the desire to acquire both riches and power. This is one of the underlying
causes that go to make up the sum total of our political and economic ills,
and the passing of laws will not cure the condition; the cure must come from
within and not from without. The citizen must improve as an individual before
the Nation will be better. No man can take that which he does not gain
honestly and by fair means from another without harming himself quite as
much as he does the other man, for the same reason that he undermines his
self-respect, respect as a citizen and man, and therefore becomes less fitted
to carry on the duties that go with such, and moreover sets an example
which is transmissible to others of like or weaker natures. Another case particularly is the idle rich who, by their example of ostentatious and profitless
spending, easily excite the passions of those of the lower class, and by their
example of vicious living may influence those who desire something they do not

have, to get it by questionable means, to gratify their taste for vain display. Methods of labor unions contribute largely to causes of unrest, and I refer more particularly to the boycott, picketing, closed shop, fines, blacklist against men who have seen fit to drop out of unions and who are hounded and followed wherever they go, and prevented from rejoining the union or from obtaining work. I do not blame the members of labor unions in general, but the vicious leaders, some of whom are ignorant of economic laws, some of whom are misguided, and some who are traitors to their followers and to their country.

The remedy.—If we must have unions, let us have open-shop unions, organizations which stand for efficiency of those who are members; which carry on a propaganda of education for those affiliated therewith and which will carry out a contract the same as is expected of any other body of men in a businesslike way and without deviation. For example, I would refer to the great Order of Railroad Brotherhoods, the Brotherhood of Locomotive Engineers, the Brotherhood of Firemen, the Brotherhood of Trainmen, and the Order of the Railroad Conductors. These are all open-shop unions, notwithstanding anything leaders of organized labor may say to the contrary. I know, because I have been one, having been affiliated with the Brotherhood of Railroad Trainmen, and master of one of its lodges, and in talking with railroad men, generally, and with officers of railway companies the expression is generally that these are open-shop organizations, and that there is no clause injected into the agreements between the brotherhoods and those by whom they are employed which states that none but members of their respective brotherhoods shall be employed. Moreover, at least, two of the brotherhoods have discussions in their lodge meetings as to the best method of conducting the work which they are engaged in. In this case, however, I refer to the mechanical end of railroad operation, and those who are not yet familiar with the fine points and the finesse of operation are instructed by the older ones and the ones more experienced. In this wise they become more efficient and therefore more valuable to their employers. Another thing that the brotherhoods all do, without exception, is to frown down upon the man who uses intoxicants, particularly to excess. In this way they keep up the standard of strength and ability to stand the strain of long and continued service, and therefore make themselves better and more capable so far as their employer is concerned. Then we have as another example the National Association of Stationary Engineers, who also come within the category of open-shop unions, and moreover do not believe in striking. This body of men also has test examinations in their lodges and meetings so that the employer who hires one of their men knows he is getting full value.

Then, we have in the process of formation in this country craftsmen organizations, the most notable of which is a body of men who have formed themselves into an engineers craftsman organization, and another one just starting which is composed of electricians, and I believe there is another contemplated taking in the carpenters. These are all formed upon similar lines as the National Association of Stationary Engineers, and I am quite reliably informed that the American Federation of Labor, at least the local branch of this body of the stationary engineers' union, has placed a fine upon each individual belonging to the craftsmen organization. A word might be said in this connection in favor of organizations based upon similar lines as the above. I would first of all mention the open shop; second, maintain a certain high standard of efficiency and morality of their members. I would make them responsible as a collective body, so that their agreements entered into between the employers and themselves would be carried out. All of these reasons would make most employers desire to do business with a body of this kind, which would carry out the idea of collective bargaining as being the best means by which a laboring man could sell the product of his brain and hand to the highest bidder. There is no man-made law that will subvert the natural law of efficiency for the desired end to be attained and place mediocrity above excellency as is being maintained through closed-shop unions. As already explained before conciliation boards will just be a temporary makeshift, and there is no reason why organizations of labor of the type of the American Federation of Labor and other closed-shop organizations should exist. No economic excuse can be found which would state that they were serving a useful purpose. They have outlived their usefulness and must of necessity be superseded by something better and more enduring. The same can be said of employers' associations, which are not necessary, but are the corollary only of labor unions which have brought them into existence because of the necessity for the employer to protect himself against the encroachments of unscrupulous bodies of men, who by their power have usurped many of the prerogatives and rights of the citizen· and individual for selfish purposes, as already explained.

· If'under a new dispensation of a labor organization of some kind, if it must be, we should have as·a most important factor·a means of publicity, pitiless publicity, if you please; applying to the greedy and rapacious and unscrupulous employer who would grind his workmen and seeks to declare dividends off of savings in wages. The same as publicity, pitiless again, against the leader of labor or religious society or·social society of whatever kind that attempts to usurp the rights of man under our republican form of Government, and such publicity under governmental supervision would serve to whip the recalcitrant into line of right doing.

· 5. This has been already answered under "I" (Measures for relief). It is hard to say where conditions are best, as suffering of the lower and middle class is most general all over this country. There are some localities which are favored perhaps by local conditions, such as bountiful crops, etc. In the main, times are quiet and stagnation of industry is very marked. I will say, however, that in cities operating under open-shop conditions the workers are best satisfied, because of an open and free field. I say this without any hesitancy, because I know the conditions to be true. I have had it told to·me in this'city a dozen times within the last month by union men themselves, men who are my friends and who believe in my sincerity, who come to me and say that they ■re debarred from working on open-shop jobs because of their affiliation and because of the rules of the unions. This is not a healthy condition, nor is it even a wise policy on the part of the leaders in present stress to hold their membership in line. I give one concrete example of a .job on one of our theater buildings in course of construction, where carpenters, plasterers, and other craftsmen were debarred from working because that was an open-shop job and· put up by an open-shop contractor with whom the labor unions had quarreled, and the men have chafed under these conditions.· This, I think, answers your question fully under head 6.

Referring to attitude· of courts and legal authorities in labor cases, I can say without fear of contradiction by anyone who is unbiased, that the laboring man generally, particularly that one affiliated with organization, has had most fair, and in some cases, most partial consideration from the courts and legal authorities who have looked upon the members of labor organizations as a valuable asset and ally in their political campaigns, present or prospective, and· as the employer has not been in politics to any great extent, he is rapidly learning and will soon have to be reckoned with on this score, and woe betide the dreamer or sycophant who would prostitute himself for the sake of votes.

Exhibit A.

CONSTITUTION.

I wish' to call your attention to some of the rules laid down in the Constitution and By-Laws of the. District Council of Carpenters of Portland and Vicinity.

Under constitution, section 23, page 11, we find a ruling governing initiation. The initiation fee is set at $15. If a member drops out for any reason, by nonpayment of dues, which he may be unable to pay by reason of sickness, lack of work, or other causes, he is dropped from membership in the union, and to be reinstated he must pay an entrance fee of $25, or $10 more than he originally paid for initiation when he first presented himself.

Section 35. System of fines. This is an arbitrary usurpation of power which unions generally use to whip their members into line, through fear of punishment and in some cases ostracism. Fines have been known to be very high and so exorbitant that the victim who came under the displeasure of an officer of the union or the members thereof could not pay and had to be dropped. The writer believes that this is an entirely un-American proceeding and believes that it should be stopped by and through the operation of law, as no one should have a right to usurp judicial functions.

By-laws and trade rules, section 4, page 15. "Union men shall in no case be allowed to work with nonunion men longer than one day who will not join the union, and shall report the names of any such cases to the business agent." Section 11, page 817. "Any member making a false statement as to the wages he receives or as to the hours he works or to any part, or the trade rules, or who refuses to show his wages or working card to the business agent or job steward shall, upon conviction thereof, be fined as per section 41."

Section 13. "Members shall not be allowed to file saws or sharpen tools on their own time while employed, and members doing so shall be fined."

Section 16. "Any foreman discharging a member without sufficient reasons shall be cited to appear before this council to show cause why he should not be fined, etc."

Section 17. This is one of the most urgent reasons given by employers generally why unions are not a success in different plants. This rule is followed by many other crafts. "Any carpenter can prefer charges against pacemakers, and any member found guilty of pace setting or rushing members with the view of holding his job and bringing up the other members employed to an excess standard of speed shall be fined."

Section 20. "Any member bringing his own stepladder, iron miter box, straightedge, sawhorse, or anything other than tools on the job shall be fined as per section 41." In this connection I desire to call your attention to a concrete instance of a case that came up in this city a few months ago on the Northwestern Bank Building, where three members of the carpenters' union were fined $25 each for violating this rule because they had brought iron miter boxes with them. They were skilled mechanics and naturally wanted to be efficient, and had provided themselves with the latest up-to-date appliances, but for some reason or other their union tabooed such a proceeding and it wanted them to use wooden mitre boxes or else the iron miter boxes furnished by the contractor on the building. .

Section 41. "All fines not otherwise provided for in these by-laws and trade rules shall not be less than $1 nor more than $50." I desire in this connection to say that men are fined for working on open-shop jobs, even when it is impossible to obtain work elsewhere. Several carpenters were recently fined $25 on the Broadway Theater, which an open-shop contracting firm is erecting, while others have been fined from $10 to $25 for a similar offense.

A banner carrier exhibiting a boycott levied by one of the unions in this city was discharged recently for getting shaved in an open-shop house, when it is well known that many members of unions are doing the same thing.

Men are unable to get work who do not stand in with certain business agents, or the ring which these business agents control, while others of the ring are kept at work the year around, in spite of the fact that 75 per cent of the men are out of work and ready and willing to do anything, but are deprived from doing so by reason of the arbitrary and exacting rules of the union.

Banner carrying is considered by the members of organized labor a disgrace, but is only tolerated by the increasing force of the foreign element in the unions and ring leaders who resort to violence and other un-American methods to gain their end.

The closed-shop methods are the cause of fines and trials, as men who have families must get work somewhere in order to keep the wolf from the door. Calls coming into the headquarters of the union from the contractors for men are supplied by the secretary, and as a rule only his friends or those of the business agent, by whom he is controlled, are furnished with work, thus building up a political machine that keeps the ring leaders in office. This is particularly the case now when jobs are scarce, and it seems a pity and a shame that many of our deserving workingmen are hampered and harassed by a policy of this kind.

Total number of wage earners in Oregon approximately, 200,000.
Number of millmen, labor commissioner's report 1913, 16,818.
Carmen, 150.
Order of Railway Conductors, 390.
Brotherhood of Locomotive Engineers, 217.
Brotherhood of Railway Trainmen, 320.
Brotherhood of Locomotive Firemen, 247.
Switchmen's Union, 95.
Order of Railway Trainmen, 150.
Railway machinists, 140.
Brotherhood of Railway Electricians, 1,180.

EXHIBIT B.

I wish to call your attention to some facts and figures relating to the lumber and logging camps of this section of the country, commonly known as the Columbia River section. It gives the wages and hours and other conditions in the mills and yards, and also the rate of wages and hours in the logging camps, as well as the average treatment of the lumberjack as to sanitary and housing conditions, as well as the food that is furnished him. Welfare work is not generally indulged in, but one or two camps have reading rooms and a sort of embryo Y. M. C. A. course:

Average wages paid in lumber mills.

Sawyers	$7. 50
Pony sawyer	4. 75
Engineer	3. 50
Millwrights	3. 75
Edger men	3. 25
Resaw men	3. 25
Trimmer men	3. 00
Setters, $2.50 and	2. 75
Other mill jobs ranging from $1.75 to	2. 25
Yard work	1. 75
Car loaders	2. 00
Teamsters	2. 00
Planer feeders, $2.25 and	2. 50
Graders	2. 00

Board, $5.25 per week.
Hospital, 50 cents to $1 per month. Some mills do not charge hospital fee.

EXHIBIT C.

I wish to give to this commission some facts which are a matter of record connected with the railroad strike of 1911, the strike commonly known as the railroad shopmen's union, which attacked the Harriman system of railways.

SOUTHERN PACIFIC CO.,
Brooklyn, Oreg., August 19, 1914.

Mr. W. C. FRANCIS,
Manager Employers' Association of Oregon, Portland, Oreg.

DEAR SIR: In compliance with your request for statement concerning conditions during the strike at Brooklyn shop and division shops on Portland division, I beg to submit the following facts: Previous to the strike, which took place September 29, 1911, we experienced no amount of trouble with our shop forces, especially machinists and boiler makers, in obtaining satisfactory service from all concerned. As to the dominating spirit of the men at that time, which was in evidence on all sides, it was extremely difficult to take decided action, due to the fact that no satisfactory results could have been obtained at that time. The spirit of the mechanics previous to the strike was unsatisfactory and the desired interest in doing their work was lacking very much in a general way.

When the strike took place no distinction was made by the unions between our older employees who had been in the service for 20 years and over and the apprentices, nor was any consideration shown to men that were physically disabled and taken care of by the company, with the result that out of 18 apprentices 3 of them remained with the company, and out of the older employees only a small number remained at work. These conditions show conclusively the aggressiveness of the unions to all classes and conditions.

The first few weeks of the strike we did not experience any serious trouble. However, shortly after this an element was brought in here that had no respect for law and order. Men were followed to their homes, beaten up, and molested in every way possible, and I am attaching statements from some of the employees that received rough treatment from the strikers. Every possible effort was made to obtain redress from the courts and authorities in charge of the situation, but very little, if any, better results were obtained thereby.

At outside points, such as Roseburg and Grants Pass, while the situation was not as serious, it was quite bad, as the striking element carried the movement to such an extent that when our employees commenced work at these points they were not able to obtain food until the matter was personally taken up with the merchants at both Roseburg and Grants Pass and better results obtained.

A number of cases came to my personal observation, but, due to the shortage of time permitted for particulars, I am not able to give specific data, although our records will bear out the fact that the tampering with power was carried on to a dangerous point, and while no lives were lost, considerable damage to equipment was done on many of the frame-up jobs. Every effort was made by shop forces to inspect engines very closely on arrival and departure from terminals to see that they were not tampered with, which might cause serious accidents. On numerous occasions we found engines were tampered with by some unknown persons and defect remedied before departure of engine. However, in some instances where engines were tampered with, engine failures occurred on the road, causing delay to trains.

During the entire trouble we were fortunate at all times to secure skilled mechanics, and the improvement in shop conditions shortly after the strike were quite noticeable, and to-day are not to be compared with former conditions, or previous to the strike, as we have no agitators or disturbing element raising discontent among our employees. Better feeling prevails among all shopmen, conducive to better results and better work. We received shortly after the strike applications from former employees. However, they were prevented from entering our service through the influence of the unions.

I am unable to fully state the causes leading up to the strike, but will state that from personal observation and from instructions received from our officials that the unreasonable demands made at the time and the disregard shown for contracts entered into with the different unions was one of the chief factors leading up to the trouble, notwithstanding that the company was willing at all times to treat the men in a fair spirit and repeatedly had advanced their wages from time to time. The conditions demanded by the unions at that time were such that it was impossible to consider them under any conditions. These facts you no doubt well know and do not require further discussion.

Our instructions from our officials, both before and after the strike, have always been to the effect that considerate and fair treatment be accorded all employees, irrespective of their affiliations, and these instructions are carried out to the fullest extent and no distinction whatever made if fair services are obtained from the men we employ; and due to this fact I would say that our present conditions to-day are more agreeable, more efficient, and more satisfactory in every respect.

BANNERING AND PICKETING.

A great deal has been said by union leaders and some union men in defending the position of the unions in their policy of bannering and picketing those with whom they come in conflict. I would like to state a concrete case of facts now existing in this city and show to the commission a boycott placed by the stationary engineers' union against the La Grande Creamery Co., of this city, and that in this boycott an entirely innocent party is being punished for something he had no connection with, but can get no redress either through the law or from the union, because the law provides no statute which makes bannering and picketing an offense.

About two years ago delegates from the stationary engineers' union called on the Liberty Ice & Coal Co. and asked them to sign up with the union and agree to hire none but union engineers and work them but eight hours per day. They told the Liberty Ice & Coal Co. if they would do this, the union would always supply them with competent engineers; all they had to do was to telephone union headquarters and competent men would be sent down.

At the time this took place the company had in their employ a head engineer who had been working for them for five or six years, but he did not belong to the union. They had also a night engineer who was a member of the union. The union officials asked that this head engineer be discharged and the night man be given his job and two other union men be hired to fill the vacancies. The company refused to do this and told them they would continue hiring men as in the past and would engage such men as met their requirements, regardless of whether they belonged to the union or not. The union officials then asked the company when hiring extra engineers to hire union men, which they agreed to do. There was nothing further said at this time.

When the busy season arrived the company decided to put on an extra engi- ¹ neer and telephoned to union headquarters for a man. The man the union sent was engaged and the first night on the job he became intoxicated and when the dayman arrived to relieve him he found this engineer asleep in a corner of the room while the engines were running wild. This man was discharged and the union did not say anything and neither did they come around to investigate. Nothing further was heard from them until two days before Thanksgiving, 1913, when several union officials walked into the La Grande Creamery Co.'s store and told Mr. Daniels if the Liberty Ice & Coal Co. did not sign up with the union his store would be boycotted and a banner placed in front of the same. Mr. Daniels claims he explained to them that he was not interested in the Liberty Ice & Coal Co., but his brother was, and he had an interest in the La Grande Creamery Co., and by boycotting his place of business they would be doing him an injustice. To this McGuire, one of the delegates, replied: "The innocent must suffer with the guilty at times."

Two days after this interview the banner was placed in front of the store and has been there ever since. The union officials have been in to see Mr. Daniels several times and on each occasion told him the matter could be settled by having Liberty Ice & Coal Co. sign up and discharge nonunion men.

When the banner was placed in front of the store Daniels told them if they did not remove same the union man at the plant would be discharged. As banner was not removed this union man was discharged after receiving a week's notice.

There have been other cases in this city of bannering and picketing of business houses, and there is now a case where a banner may be seen daily parading up and down in front of a large department store. The department-store managers do not know the reason for the boycott being placed against their firm, but the sign reads that the central labor council has declared the place unfair. Upon investigation and consultation with some of the labor leaders, the manager of the department store could not get any reason why his place was so boycotted and bannered, but assumed that perhaps there might be some business rival who was paying for it, and through the connivance of unscrupulous labor leaders could have this done.

The point I wish to make and bring to the commission's attention is that a union permitting bannering and picketing lays itself liable to a charge of graft; and this can easily be understood because numerous cases have come to light where dishonest business agents have levied blackmail against business concerns by threatening a banner and boycott, using as a pretext any fantastic reason, that the place was unfair or not following union rules.

It is usually pretty hard to prove these cases for the business men are intimidated, both with the fear of personal violence and business injury.

We have but to cite as a matter of evidence the publicity case of Chicago, and at the present time the Federal grand jury of that district is making an investigation into the affairs of some of the unions, and has found where union business agents and walking delegates have levied heavy cash assessments against different business concerns to such an extent that several of them have become immensely wealthy by reason of such piracy, and the culmination of the whole rotten condition came when a harrassed and distracted business man, who had been hounded for months by one of the business agents with a demand to kick in and come through with the cash, finally shot and killed the business agent, and that, of course, started the investigation.

These are all matters of record and can be proven by the records; names and amounts and dates can be given.

In conclusion I desire to call your attention to a different form of labor association from the A. F. of L., the National Association of Stationary Engineers, and offer as Exhibit D a copy of the constitution and by-laws of that organization.

I wish to call to your attention particularly the preamble on page 1, which reads:

"This association shall at no time be used for the furtherance of strikes, or for the purpose of interfering in any way between its members and its employers in regard to wages; recognizing the identity of interest between employer and employee and not countenancing any project or enterprise that will interfere with perfect harmony between them.

---

¹ Submitted in printed form.

"Neither shall it be used for political or religious purposes. Its meetings shall be devoted to the business of the association, and at all times shall be given to the education of engineers," etc.

In this connection I hand you a copy, which we will .mark "Exhibit E," of a rule of the International Union of Stationary Engineers, signed as approved by Matt Comaford, general president.

From a persual of this rule you will see that the A. F. of L. places a fine of $100 upon anyone connected with the National Association of Stationary Engineers, also belonging to the stationary engineers under the jurisdiction of the A. F. of L.

There are other cases where a fine of this kind has been levied against members who have a desire to join a craftsmen's union, and I can cite the case of the engineers craftsmen's association as well as the electrical craftsmen's association, both of which have locals in this city.

EXHIBIT E.

Article 1, section 4½.—No person is eligible to membership in this local that holds membership in any labor organization whose constitution conflicts ·with the constitution of the American Federation of Labor. Any member joining á labor organization whose constitution conflicts with the A. F. of L. upon conviction thereof shall be fined in the sum of not less than $100 or expelled from the union.

Approved.

MATT COMAFORD,
General President I. U. S. E.

STATE OF OREGON,
    County of Multnomah, ss:

I, W. C. Francis, being duly sworn, upon my oath depose and say: That I have read the above and foregoing statement of facts as to the labor conditions in this community, that I prepared the same, and I believe that the statements therein contained are true and show the present .labor conditions in this community.

W. C. FRANCIS.

Subscribed and sworn to before me this 19th day of August, 1914.

[SEAL.]

S. C. SPENCER,
Notary Public for State of Oregon.

EXHIBITS.

STATISTICS.

There are, according to the State labor commissioner, 729 lumber, shingle, and box manufacturing plants in Oregon in the period from October 1, 1910, to September 30, 1912. These were divided into the following classifications:

Box factories	13
Saw and lath mills	6
Planing mills	81
Shingle mills	28
Planers and box factories, combined	20
Sawmills	423
Sawmills and planing mills, combined	84
Sash and door factories	25
Saw and shingle mills, combined	10
	690

In these the labor commissioner reported there were employed 22,193 persons, about 582 being salaried individuals and the remainder wage earners. The wage earners, it is stated, received that year $12,673,858 and the salaried people $610,584, a total of $13,284,442. At the present time the number of plants is greater, and when they are running normally the pay roll is much above these figures.

The average wages and salaries paid in all the plants is given by the labor commissioner as follows: Female clerks, $2.37 per day; male clerks, $3.32 per day; men in the woods, $2.68 per day; skilled men, $3.32 per day; unskilled men, $2.26 per day; women, $1.79 per day.

Wheat exports from Portland and Puget Sound last year, or the equivalent of wheat in flour, were 524,180 tons from Portland and 586,405 from Puget Sound.

The live stock receipts at the Portland Union Stockyards for the preceding year were as follows: 80 cattle, 4,666 calves, 188,286 hogs, 295,730 sheep.

r   BANKS—(STATE).

Deposits year ending November:

1905	$62,334,190.00
1909	90,048,749.00
1911 (Dec. 10)	107,946,896.99
1912 (Nov. 26)	125,677,598.63
1913	132,762,156.87

Resources year ending November:

1908	106,894,974.00
1910	147,518,528.07
1913	165,000,000.00

BANK CLEARINGS—(PORTLAND).

These figures are given by the Portland Clearing House Association, wherein but 10 banks are included out of a total of 25 institutions.

1890	$9,439,224.51
1900	106,918,027.48
1905	228,402,712.00
1910	517,171,867.97
1911	557,933,736.69
1912	597,087,865.12
1913	627,818,344.10

1914: By months—

January	$49, 271, 242. 46
February	42, 297, 377. 00
March	55, 355, 019. 44
April	57, 520, 527. 33
May	47, 633, 567. 00 .
June	44, 721, 934. 60 ·

BUILDING PERMITS ISSUED—(PORTLAND).

	Number.	Valuation.
1900	392	$944, 985
1905	2, 318	4, 183, 368
1910	6, 523	20, 886, 202
1911	7, 686	9, 152, 370 ·
1912	10, 901	14, 850, 922 ·
1913	6, 694	13, 645, 015
1914: By months—		
January	503	444, 600
February	573	605, 530
March	708	882, 865
April	605	769, 500
May	542	643, 880
June	536	887, 585

CEREAL PRODUCTION—(STATE).

	Bushels.	Value.
1910:		
Wheat	17, 000, 000	$13, 750. 000
Oats	11, 000, 000	6, 000, 000
Barley	2, 500, 000	1, 250, 000
Rye	200, 000 ·	160, 000
1911:		
Wheat	15, 000, 000	11, 250, 000
Barley	3, 000, 000	2, 000, 000
Oats	12, 000, 000	5, 000, 000
Rye	300, 000	175, 000
1912:		
Wheat	21, 092, 274	15, 819, 205
Oats	14, 744, 046	5, 602, 737
Barley	4, 439, 374	2, 663, 624
Rye (estimated)	327, 000	305, 000
1913:		
Wheat	19, 150, 000	15, 325, 000
Oats	12, 500, 000	4, 900, 000
Barley	4, 000, 000	3, 380, 000
Corn	850, 000	525, 000
Rye	350, 000	310, 000
Total		24, 440, 000

FRUIT—(STATE).

	Value.
1910	$6, 662, 500
1912	6, 750, 000
1913	8, 550, 000

Oregon as a fruit State is rapidly forging to the front. The State's fruit-bearing area was about 40,000 acres; 125,000 acres were planted during the past five years. An ideal climate, soil of great fertility and variety serve to make the production in Oregon of high-grade fruits. Hood River took the sweepstakes at the National Apple Show, Chicago, for best apples, in 1910. ,

POTATOES—(STATE).

	Bushels.	Value.
1905	4, 453, 680	$2, 500, 000
1910	6, 000, 000	5, 000, 000
1912	8, 751, 685	3, 500, 674
1913	8, 750, 000	5, 250, 000

Potatoes yield from 100 to 200 sacks to the acre. They can be grown and marketed at a cost of 40 cents per sack of two bushels; the selling price ranging from 60 cents to $2 per sack. Potato crops net at least $60 per acre.

PAPER MILLS—(STATE).

At Oregon City there are three paper mills—one the third largest in the world—employing 1,000 men. They have an annual pay roll of $750,000, and produce yearly 72,850 tons of paper, and consume 75,000,000 feet of logs per annum. Total amount of raw material and finished products handled by these mills equals 400,000 tons per year.

POPULATION—(STATE).

1850	13, 294
1860	52, 465
1870	90, 923
1880	174, 768
1890	313, 767
1900	413, 536
1910	672, 765
1911 [1]	718, 000
1912 [1]	790, 000
1913 [1]	825, 000

PROBABLE LIST OF QUESTIONS THAT MAY BE ASKED OR INVITED.

1. What is the state of unrest in this region in respect to labor or capital?
2. What is the main cause of this unrest, with reference to the relations of labor and capital?
3. Would, in your mind, a State or Federal commission be best suited to the adjustment of differences arising from industrial unrest?
4. What is the trend of State legislation, what is the effect upon investment of the legislation being enacted, what have industrial enterprises seeking a location here said with reference to the laws and political conditions of the State, and is there any change toward a more conservative type of legislation in Oregon?
5. What is the effect upon labor of the State of seasonal employment, such as logging, fruit picking and packing, etc.?
6. Are industrial conditions of the State improving rapidly, have you many factories with large pay rolls, and are enterprises of this character growing or showing a tendency to remain stationary or decrease?
7. How are transportation conditions, are they affected by higher wages than are paid by competitors, and to what extent do these conditions influence the development of the community?
8. What are the conditions on the water front with reference to wages and costs of handling goods in trade, and are these conditions more repressive to business than are found in your rival cities, and if so what element is the cause?
9. Export and coastwise water-borne trade.
10. Atlantic seaboard trade competition, with reference to particular articles of commerce and industry.
11. European commerce, with reference to shipment by water direct, or by railway to the Atlantic and thence across the ocean.
12. Something on the conditions attending the handling of lumber, wool, fruit, etc., in the Atlantic and European trade.
13. Number of persons employed in the fruit producing and packing industry of the State.
14. Number of persons in general industries of the State.
15. Pay roll of the State.
16. Clearings of banks, with reference to increases or decreases for a considerable period.
17. Population growth for many years, as evidence of industrial conditions.

ANSWERS.

1, 2, and 3. No answer.
4. According to statements made by investment representatives coming to the chamber of commerce for data or assistance, there is a feeling that Oregon has experimented too far in legislation. These men, as a rule, insist that we have not been sufficiently conservative, that we are doing too much pioneer work, that

---

[1] Estimated.

we are a sort of political experimental laboratory, and that while some of the things we try and proclaim may have ultimate merit, we lose through undertaking to devote too much of our energies to the pure experiment. These investors have urged that capital does not like so much uncertainty in the legislative field, and wants a more stable atmosphere. We have secured many industries within recent years, but if the statements made to the staff of the chamber are correct, we have lost some through apprehension of our eagerness to adopt novel legislation. It is my personal belief that our experimental legislative work is growing less and that a more conservative tone is gaining among the voters, and that within the immediate coming years this tendency will become far more pronounced. It seems to me that a majority are coming to realize that business must have some fairly certain beacons, else it will not risk the channel of investment, and after business is established, it also appears to be a growing sentiment that it must have definite limitations within which it can operate for considerable periods without being compelled to spend most of its time and energies upon the task of determining whether it is legitimate. I might mention under the head of legislative influence upon business the effects that have come from what we know as our employers' liability law. This was championed by the leaders of union labor in the State. Their purpose was to remove some of the legal impediments that older statutes and the common law imposed when labor sought to establish financial liabilities of employers for injuries sustained by workmen. The measure became a law through the workings of our initiative amendment to the constitution. On the water front of this city, where the chamber's attention is most directed, because we are supposed to be a body of shipping or commercial men, we find that the suits instituted for injury and the judgments obtained have made a marked increase in our casualty insurance rates. Among longshoremen, where the rates were reported 3 per cent within recent times, my staff of the chamber now report that rates up to 6.5 per cent have been charged, and there was a grave fear that they would go much higher. In addition to this, I was informed that most of the casualty companies did not care to take these risks. This rate is on the pay roll of the stevedoring companies, and is not a large item in the total costs of shipping from a port, but when joined to many others, does make an important drawback to the business and progress of the community. These rates jumped, I have been informed, because of the large verdicts being secured under the employers' liability law, and I was also told that relatively little of the money so being secured in judgments went to the injured man or his family. We have secured adoption of the workmen's compensation law at last, after a most determined fight by the employers, business and some laboring men of the State, which we hope will ameliorate the severe conditions resulting from the other measure that came through the initiative. The workmen's compensation law was adopted by the legislature. There are many other details wherein legislative enactments of what are called an advanced or experimental nature have worked against what appears to me to be the sound, healthful progress of the community, but I will not undertake to enumerate all.

5. Our State is unfortunate in having so much seasonal work. Our heavy fruit production, which is gaining rapidly, requires employees for a relatively limited part of the year. The cultivation period and winter months need few persons compared to the short period when fruit is being picked and packed. This means that much of the help absolutely required in the fruit season must seek other work or is thrown into idleness during the remainder of the year. Logging operations also have periods, the exceedingly dry weather or worse months of winter usually seeing the camps closed down. Of the 45,502 farms of Oregon in 1910 it may be said that there is a heavy seasonal demand for labor, the peak load of course being reached in harvest days of late summer and fall. If we accredit about 7,000 men as working in the logging camps of the woods in this State; estimate 40,000 working days as the labor required for picking apples; that much or a little more for packing apples, and, say, 50,000 or 60,000 working days for the picking and packing of other fruits, and estimate that the 45,500 farms will require from one to two hired men on an average for some portion of the harvest period, it will be seen that with a State having in 1910 but 672,765 people the proportion engaged in seasonal work is very large. We have not, on the other hand, a very large percentage of industries requiring employees the year through as is found in the large eastern industrial centers.

6. Our industrial conditions are not developing satisfactorily. We do not manufacture enough. The price of certain needed raw materials, the sparse population adjacent to any manufacturing center, the higher price paid labor here than in the East, the long distances and high rates that must be paid in reaching large consuming centers have prevented rapid development here in manufacturing lines. We have found that the transportation rates favor movement of the finished product toward the West rather than the raw material to help our young industries, where we had to draw the raw material from the East. Most all inquirers who come to the chamber tell us that the wage scale of this territory is considerably above that of the large eastern centers, and that we must have considerable advantages in other lines to warrant location in the Northwest. In the case of lumber, of course the raw material makes the business possible. We have figures on glass industries, the manufacture of nitrates from the air, hat factories. pipe-casting plants, machine factories for the woodworking constructions, etc., and have lost most of them, if not nearly all. So long as New York, Pennsylvania, Massachusetts, Connecticut, Ohio, and Illinois get low-priced labor for their mining operations and factory help and we have to abide by a much higher scale here, we will be unable to compete until rather unusual opportunities are developed in connection with a limited number of industries. As our agricultural population increases, giving to the local factory more consumers near home, we will slowly work out of this condition. If immigration through the Panama Canal has a tendency to equalize conditions on the Pacific with those on the Atlantic seaboard we may make more rapid industrial progress. Laboring men and leaders of organized labor are eager to prevent any great inrush here that would have the effect of reducing materially the wage scale now prevalent, and have often advised people throughout the country not to come here in the expectation of securing labor jobs.

7. Our transportation charges in the West are higher than in the East, due, so the railway companies tell us. to the fact that there is less density of traffic here, we have more mountain sections, fuel as a rule costs more, and wage scales in the railway lines are higher. On the water we are again confronted with somewhat higher charges, at least so far as handling goes. The water-front charges along the Pacific are reported to me by the steamship companies to be higher than on the Atlantic, the efficiency of work less, and the time for handling cargo greater. The exact percentage of difference is not stated, varying somewhat, of course, in different ports. The effect of this will be felt most in the lumber trade. Western Douglas fir will soon be sharply competitive with southern yellow pine in North Atlantic seaboard and European markets. Our ability to manufacture cheaply and get the product to the consumer at the lowest possible transportation charge will be the controlling factors in our progress. We could easily produce for the export trade 3,000,000,000 to 4,000,000,000 feet more of the fir lumber, if we could reach the market at a living figure. The higher charges our longshoremen have been compelling our Portland mills to pay, we feel, will be barriers to our progress, unless we are able to equalize these and other conditions that weigh against us. We have had in this port for many years no organized body along the water front among the employers to meet the organized bodies of the laborers, with the result that shipping men constantly complain that we are the highest-priced port of the Pacific. We have not kept pace with our rival ports in development of our shipping, and the steamship company managements declare that this is one of the serious drawbacks with which we have been burdened. In reaching out for a much greater market, through the Panama Canal, where the margin will be very close, all these elements are being placed against us, and we feel that we will have to get down nearer a common standard or lose in the contest.

8. Our water front, as compared with rivals of the Pacific coast, has been for years paying the highest wages. When a scale for Puget Sound was fixed in 1913, general cargo there was put at 45 cents an hour regular time and 55 cents overtime. At the same time Portland was paying 55 cents an hour regular time and $1 overtime for all offshore business, in handling general cargo. When we bid to have steamship lines enter this port, and were in rivalry with Puget Sound, these rates were always held against us. Although the stevedoring companies undertook to equalize conditions in the two ports by making contracts for something near the same figure per ton, shipping agencies insisted that in overtime and in the more drastic regulations here they uniformly had to pay more in Portland than in our rival port. Frequent complaint is made to the chamber of a disposition among the longshoremen to drag the work out so as to

get overtime, to retard operations by having a tired crew·that has done¹a full shift ·regular time take an overtime shift, and to attempt·to regulate·the size of the·sling loads so as to make operations intolerably slow. ' Our shipping men have been informed that a coast-wide organization of longshoremen has been effected, and but recently voted upon an extensive ballot, several items of which would prove a profound detriment to Pacific coast shipping if they were put into practice. These and many other facts experienced along the water front of Portland have convinced the shipping men that they must have an effective shipping association that is as strong as the organization of laborers, and which will be charged with the constant duty of preventing the labor bodies from advancing their cause here so fast that we will be largely put out of competition with our rivals where the employers have been more aggressive on the water front. Most of the shipping men of the community feel that they and the whole port have suffered from permitting unrestrained adoption of water-front wage scales and regulations.

9. Portland's water-borne trade for the year 1913 was as follows:

Domestic:	Tons.	Value.
Export	741, 317	$18, 109, 976
Import	1, 128, 493	23, 686, 212
Foreign:		
Import	55, 133	1, 566, 634
Export	658, 664	14, 470, 174

Against this showing our chief competitor on the north, Seattle, is credited with the following water-borne trade:

Domestic:	
Imports	$38, 382, 283
Exports	39, 932, 788
Foreign:	
Imports	25, 898, 466
Exports	19, 917, 317

Tacoma, the second Puget Sound port that is a Portland rival, has about the same foreign imports and exports as Seattle. Both these ports have been working for years under more favorable water-front conditions than Portland. While we recognize that labor conditions alone have not controlled the results stated, they have been a contributing factor, and one of the several factors which we believe a patriotic community ought to insist should be 'righted.

10 and 11. Our commercial future growth depends upon our ability to get down to close margins, in competition with those persons supplying raw materials and agricultural and horticultural products to the Atlantic seaboard and European markets. I have mentioned lumber. We have tremendous possibilities in this development. We have been prone to view the Panama Canal as at last opening a transportation avenue that would enable us to make big expansion of the lumber manufacturing industry and commerce. We face, first, the competition of our neighbor, British Columbia, which is credited with having about one-third as much soft woods in her forests as Oregon, Washington, and Idaho, or 330,000,000,000 feet, against our approximately 1,000,000,000,000 feet. Steamship experts tell us that, through British Columbia having the privilege of shipping to Europe and the Atlantic seaboard on British bottoms, she will have an advantage in about one-third of the transportation costs in reaching our own Eastern States. Then we next meet the southern pine manufacturer, who has low wage scales, and rates that range from 12 cents to 35 cents per hundred in reaching most of the North Atlantic markets. If our coastwise shipping has high wage or labor requirements. if it labors under inequalities in measurement and other requirements, and then on top of this, if our longshoremen charge us materially higher rates for handling, and the local mill man must pay higher wages in his manufacturing plant, we will have multiplying difficulties in attaining a fair development of the great lumber industry. We occupy the same general position in respect to fruit. We have planted enormous numbers of apple, pear, peach, and apricot trees and berry bushes. Whereas in the Northwest we will have this year about 15,000 carloads of apples, if only a limited portion of the actual nonbearing plantings reach maturity in the next decade we could produce 50,000 to 80,000 carloads, each carload containing 650 boxes. We can not get a living market for this fruit, unless it may be handled

very .cheaply. It will have to get low transportation charges, also. Our struggle is to see that these charges are kept within living limits, to save the prospective industry from collapse. Our woolgrower is also deeply interested in getting his fleece to the Atlantic seaboard at a low cost. Australia has been able to reach the same points at a less transportation charge than the average northwestern producer. If we can get this wool to the Pacific seaboard at low cost, have it handled here at the minimum, and then have the steamships take it through the Panama Canal at a very low charge, we may be able to compete with Australia and live. All of our other industries hang on the same thread, where the export trade or distant market are their lifeblood. For this reason the wage scale, the transportation rate, and all the intermediate charges are of the utmost interest. Unless we can get low handling charges by water, we will profit little by the canal, and may have to ship the few commodities sent to Europe across the continent by railway and thence across the Atlantic, where more inviting rates are found on water and in handling.

SCALE OF LONGSHOREMEN'S WAGES (CENTS PER HOUR), JUNE 10, 1913.

PUGET SOUND.

	Straight time.	Overtime.
General cargo	45	55
Wheat, barley, oats, and third and first flour	50	75
Lumber	50	75
Creosote lumber	60	90
Fertilizer, lime, sulphur, explosives, and cements	50	75

PORTLAND.

General cargo	55	100
Grain	55	100
Flour, small sacks	50	100
Lumber	50	75
All other cargo loaded and all classes of cargo discharged	55	100
Hatch foremen	65	110

DOWN RIVER, BELOW ST. JOHNS.

Lumber	50	75
Hatch tenders, engineers, and raft men	60	90
Foremen	65	100

ASTORIA.

Lumber	50	75
Hatch tenders, engineers, and raft men	60	90
Foremen	65	97½

SWETT EXHIBIT.

BY-LAWS OREGON CIVIC LEAGUE.

ARTICLE I.

MEMBERSHIP AND DUES.

Any qualified elector of the State of Oregon shall be eligible to membership upon declaration of intention by enrollment and payment of the dues of $2 per year.

ARTICLE II.

OFFICERS AND EXECUTIVE BOARD.

The president shall be elected by the league and shall be one of the directors. Six other directors shall be elected. The president and the directors shall constitute the executive board. The president shall apportion the work among the directors and among any standing committees created by the board. The directors shall have all the powers of this organization not expressly reserved by these by-laws or by the articles of incorporation. The chairmen of standing committees, heads of departments, and the treasurer shall be entitled to meet with the board and to have a vote in matters affecting the general work of the league.

The executive board shall choose the treasurer and the executive secretary.

ARTICLE III.

DUTIES OF THE OFFICERS.

1. It shall be the duty of the president to preside at all meetings of the league and of the executive board, to have general supervision of all business of the league, and to sign all orders upon the treasury, and to appoint all committees of the league unless otherwise ordered. He shall be ex officio a member of all standing committees and shall make an annual report to the league.

2. The executive board shall choose from their number a chairman who shall preside in the absence of the president.

3. The executive secretary shall be the executive officer of the league, acting under the direction of the executive board. The secretary shall attend all meetings of the league, of the executive board, and of the committees; and he shall keep a record of the proceedings of these bodies. He shall conduct the correspondence of the league and do such other things pertaining to the work of the league as shall be designated by the executive board.

4. The treasurer shall be the custodian of the funds of the league, and shall disburse the same only upon orders approved by the president or the chairman of the executive board and countersigned by the secretary. The treasurer shall give bonds in such sum as the executive board may direct. The treasurer shall make monthly reports to the executive board, and shall make at the annual meeting a full report for the year.

ARTICLE IV.

ELECTIONS.

1. The executive board shall appoint, 30 days before the annual meeting, a nominating committee of five members, none of whom shall be members of the executive board, for the nomination of members of the executive board, and this committee shall make known its nominations to the members of the league at least 15 days before the date of the annual meeting.

2. Any member of the league may be nominated for membership on the executive board upon the written petition of 10 members of the league, sent to the secretary at least three days before the date of the annual meeting. If there are such nominations in addition to the report of the nominating committee, then the secretary shall print a ballot containing all nominations, which shall be voted upon at the annual meeting.

3. Nominations may be made from the floor at the annual meeting.

4. The first annual election, after the adoption of these by-laws, for president and directors of the executive board, shall be held in December, 1914.

ARTICLE V.

STANDING COMMITTEES AND DEPARTMENTS.

1. The president shall annually appoint the following standing committees:
   (a) Membership.
   (b) Finance.
   (c) Education.
   (d) Publicity.
   (e) Legislation.
   (f) Cooperation.

2. The league shall be divided into six departments as follows:

1. State government.
2. Municipal government.
3. Social service.
4. Suffrage and women's welfare.
5. Schools and child welfare.
6. Public welfare.

3. The president shall, with the consent of the executive board, appoint such other committees as may be found necessary to carry on the work of the league.

4. On petition of 10 members a new department may be organized.

ARTICLE VI.

MEETINGS.

Besides the annual meeting in December, the league shall hold at least one meeting per quarter. Other meetings may be held at the order of the executive board. A meeting shall be called by the president upon a petition signed by 8 per cent of the members of the league, provided that not to exceed 20 in any case shall be required. A quorum shall consist of 30 per cent of the membership, or not to exceed 30 members.

ARTICLE VII.

RULES OF ORDER.

Roberts's Rules of Order shall govern the proceedings of all meetings of the league, of the executive board, of the committees, or of the departments in so far as they do not conflict or are not inconsistent with the provisions of these by-laws.

ARTICLE VIII.

AMENDMENTS.

These by-laws may be amended at any annual or called meeting of the league by a majority vote of those present, the proposed amendments having been first submitted a week in advance to the members of the league. The articles of incorporation may be amended at an annual or a called meeting by a two-thirds vote of the league, the proposed amendments having been first submitted a week in advance to the members.

ARTICLE IX.

RECOMMENDATIONS.

The executive board may recommend measures to the league for action. No position shall be officially taken on legislative matters except upon a vote of the league (at a meeting called for the purpose or at a regular meeting).

A. E. WOOD EXHIBIT.

A Study of the Unemployed in Portland, Oreg., January–February, 1914.

During the winter of 1913–14, Portland, Oreg., like other large cities all over the country, was the center of a large group of unemployed men. Overcrowding the lodging houses and relief stations, such as the Men's Resort, Salvation Army, Portland Commons, the men finally organized themselves into an unemployed league, and petitioned the city officials to open for their use a large building formerly used for revival meetings, and known as the Gypsy Smith Tabernacle. After much difficulty and parleying, in which public-spirited citizens used their influence on behalf of the men, permission to use the tabernacle was finally granted, and in addition the city council appropriated $500 for the purchase of blankets and a small number of meal tickets. After these tickets were gone the men were sustained through contributions of food and money, solicited by the men, with the help of the Oregon Civic League, and given by well-disposed citizens. While the hall was open the men themselves were responsible for the management and discipline, and it is to be said to their great credit that, under peculiarly trying circumstances, things proceeded with exemplary order, and the general morale of the city was so favorably affected that the crime rate was lower than it had been for years.[1]

The tabernacle was open from January 1 to April 1, excepting for a few days when it was closed and fumigated on account of a smallpox scare. During this time an average of 900 men were housed each night, and from 1,200 to 1,500 men were fed two meals a day. Reports were rendered each day to the secretary of the Oregon Civic League concerning the number of men who had been housed and fed and those who were sick; also, reports included lists of donations. The following is a specimen report:

Specimen report for January 18, 1914.[2]

SICK LIST.

	Temperature.
John Brandon	99. 6
John H. Murphy	103. 2
Charles O'Leary	98. 6
Thomas Clark	103. 2
Harry Anderson	100. 2

BED REPORT.

	Number.
Men furnished with beds	394
Men furnished with blankets	150
Men furnished with their own blankets	72
Men sleeping on floor without blankets	330
Total number of men sleeping in the tabernacle	946
Men fed for breakfast	1, 384
Men fed for supper	1, 550

The presence of these men out of work and sheltered in the center of the city gave rise to much discussion. Were they genuine workingmen or tramps and hoboes? Could they not find work if they had wanted to? Were they improvident with the money they had earned? Were they "agitators"? Was not the tabernacle drawing men to Portland who otherwise would not come here? Why are they out of work? These and many other questions were asked by the community, which at last in a somewhat spectacular way was compelled to consider the problem of the unemployed.

The following study is an attempt to answer some of these questions, not from the standpoint of any theory, but by the testimony of the men themselves. The occasion of the survey was the National Conference on Unemployment that had been called under the auspices of the American Association for Labor Legislation, to meet in New York City February 28, 1914. With the help of members of the executive committee of the Unemployed League, a questionnaire was drawn up for submission to the men. A specimen questionnaire is to be found below. The questionnaires were given to the men and filled out either by the men themselves or by men who were selected as clerks. There was no compulsion about the matter. The men were told that information was wanted for use at the conference in New York, the object of which was to secure legislation in regard to employment agencies and other matters affecting the problem of unemployment. The writer, together with Reed College students, mingled with the men as the questionnaires were being filled out and is satisfied that the 449 men from whom answers were secured were chosen generally from the total number of men frequenting the tabernacle, and that there is no reason for doubting the truth of their statements.

[1] A fuller account of the tabernacle and its opening is to be found in the April number of Welfare (Seattle).
[2] After the tabernacle had been open for a few days, the city health department sent a physician there each day.

Questionnaire as filled out by J. Reynolds.

· Name: J. Reynolds. Age: 60. Birthplace: Springfield, Mass.
Married or single: Single. Residence: Tabernacle.
Trade or occupation: Laborer. Why did you come to Portland? For work.
Where did you come from and when? White Salmon; November 20, 1913.

QUESTIONS FOR MECHANIC.

Do you work at your trade exclusively? What is the average length of time
each year your trade furnishes employment?
What work, if any, besides your trade do you do? Has there been as much
work in your trade this year (1913) as last?
As in previous years?
Number of days employed January 1 to April 1, 1912: 30. Average wage per
day: $2.50.
Number of days employed April 1 to December 31, 1912: 150. Average wage
per day: $2.50.
Number of days employed January 1 to April 1, 1913: None. Average wage per
day: None.
Number of days employed April 1 to December 31, 1913: 90. Average wage per
day: $2.50.
What were your living expenses while working? $1.10. What were your
living expenses while not at work? .How much money did you have when you
last quit work? $105. How was it spent? Food, shelter, clothing.
Why have you not money to keep you through the winter? Not enough work.
How long out of work? 90 days.
Give the last three places you were employed and why you quit.
   (*a*) Kennedy Construction. (*a*) Job finished.
   (*b*) North Western Electric Co. (*b*) Job finished.
   (*c*) North Eastern Railroad. (*c*) Bad weather.
What are your views on employment agencies? No earthly use for them;
ought to be closed up.
Remarks: Portland sends out a lot of pamphlets about the opportunities, but
I have never been able to get work in the city.

I. Why are the men out of work?
The answer to this main question is discovered through replies to the following inquiries:
.A. Why did the men leave their last jobs?
As can be seen on the questionnaire, the men were asked to name their
last three places of employment and the reason for leaving each place. Altogether there were 1,284 reasons given for quitting work. They were as
follows:

1. "Laid off" (includes "work shut down," "job finished," "bad
   _ weather," "no more work")_____ 810
2. "Bad conditions" (includes "low wages," "poor food," "long
   hours")_____ _____ 189
3. "Quit" (no further reason given)_____ 109
4. "Sick or injured"_____ 52
5. "Discharged"_____ 109
6. "Strike"_____ 10
7. "Business failed"_____ 1
8. "Placer exhausted"_____ 1
9. "Mexican revolution"_____ 1
10. "Served time"_____ 1
11. "Deported from Florence, Oreg."_____ 1

      Total_____ 1, 284

Altogether, among the 1.284 men, 810, or 63 per cent, left their jobs because they were laid off; 298, or 23.2 per cent, just "quit," or left because of bad conditions; 109, or 8.4 per cent, left because they were discharged; 52, or 4 per cent, left because of sickness; and 10, or under 1 per cent, left because of strike. · From this is can be seen that among these men involuntary unemployment is far · more prevalent than voluntary unemployment.

B. What is the relation between the reasons men gave for being out of work and the length of time they are out of work?

The following correlation is made with a view of determining whether the men who leave their jobs because of alleged bad conditions of labor are out of work for a longer period than those who are just "laid off":

Correlation of the reasons why quit last place of work and the length of time out of employment.

Time unemployed.	Laid off.	Bad condi- tions.	Quit.	Strike.	Sick or injured.	Dis- charged.	Mexi- can revolu- tion.	Failed.	Total.
Under 1 month	16	10	3	1		1			31
1–2 months	52	16	2		3	2	1		76
2–3 months	72	11	9		3	4		1	100
3–4 months	79	19	9		6	3			116
4–5 months	40	6	8	2	4	1			61
5–6 months	12	2	1						15
6–7 months	5	1	2		1				9
7–8 months	1				1				2
8–9 months	3								3
9–10 months			1						1
10–11 months	1				1				2
11–12 months									
Over 12 months	1			1					2
Total	282	65	35	4	19	11	1	1	418

From the foregoing table it does not appear that those who leave work because of "bad conditions," or who quit for no assigned reason, are out of work for longer periods than those who are laid off. Cnsidering the groups according to months unemployed, the largest single group are those who are out of work from three to four months, numbering 116. Of these, 79 were laid off, whereas only 80 quit because of bad conditions or for no given reason.

C. What does the United States census tell us about unemployment in Oregon?

According to the 1910 census there is an average number of wage earners employed in Oregon manufactures of 28,750. In January (1909), the month of minimum employment, this average falls to a minimum number employed of 23,354, while in September this number rises to 30,978, because September is the month of maximum employment in Oregon manufactures. There is, then, a difference of 7,624 in the number of wage earners employed in the months of maximum and minimum employment. If these men found no new jobs they then remained unemployed during the slack months. Moreover, these 7,624 men do not include those who are employed in nonmanufacturing industries— e. g., construction work—who are periodically unemployed because of the seasonal and fluctuating character of their employment.

The following table, taken from the 1910 census, shows the seasonal differences in employment in Oregon industries:

Statistics in regard to wage earners in Oregon manufactures.

[Abstract of 1910 census.]

Industry	Average number.	Maximum. Month.	Maximum. Number.	Minimum. Month.	Minimum. Number.	Number Dec. 15— Over 16. Male.	Over 16. Female.	Under 16. Male.	Under 16. Female.
Artificial stone	26,750	Sept..	61	Feb...	34	64			
Baking powder, yeast	6	Nov...	8	May..	2	5	3	1	
Boots, shoes	56	July...	59	Jan...	53	54	4		
Brass, bronze	42	Jan...	43	Aug...	39	42			
Bread	613	Oct...	666	Jan...	575	477	191	2	
Brick, tile	385	July...	747	Jan...	78	729	1	5	
Butter, cheese, condensed milk.	420	June..	515	Jan...	344	365	30	4	
Canning, preserves	661	Sept..	1,588	Feb...	113	866	535	15	36
Carpets, rugs	11	July...	13	Jan...	9	9			
Carriages, wagons	62	July...	65	Feb...	57	62			
Car-shop construction	777	Dec...	856	Feb...	684	856			
Men's clothing	544	May...	599	Sept..	487	55	485		
Confectionery	283	Dec...	336	Jan...	257	108	229		
Cooperage, wooden goods	23	May...	30	Oct...	12	30			
Copper, tin, iron	431	Aug...	520	Jan...	320	411	34		
Cutlery, tools	23	May...	25	Jan...	23	23			
Dairyman, etc., supplies	7	Mar...	12	June..	4	11			
Flour, grist, mills	394	Sept..	469	Mar...	349	470	1		
Foundry, machine-shop products.	1,055	Apr...	180	Jan...	925	1,072			
Fur goods	51	Sept..	65	June..	36	25	47		
Furniture, etc	552	Oct...	593	Jan...	474	578	7		
Gas, electric fixtures	59	Nov...	71	Apr...	46	50	9		
Hand stamps, stencils	16	Feb...	17	Jan...	15	14	2		
Ice manufacturing	69	Aug...	111	Jan...	42	70			
Jewelry	31	Nov...	36	Jan...	29	34			
Leather goods	353	Dec...	367	Jan...	332	356	13		
Leather, tanned, finished	49	June..	53	Jan...	46	49			
Malt liquors	204	July...	222	Jan...	183	191			
Lumber, timber	15,066	June..	16,462	Jan...	11,545	17,501	59	12	
Marble, stone	76	May...	90	Jan...	63	74			
Mattresses, springs	83	Dec...	105	Jan...	65	92	13		
Models, patterns	12	Mar...	13	July...	9	11			
Patent medicines	20	Jan...	38	June..	9	33	5		
Printing, publishing	1,459	Dec...	1,505	July...	1,424	1,279	219	25	5
Shipbuilding	212	July...	271	Sept..	153	188			
Meat packing	366	Dec...	418	Mar...	346	414	3		
Steam packing	23	Oct...	24	Jan...	22	23	1		
Stoves, furnaces	86	Oct...	122	Mar...	61	118		1	
Surgical supplies	5	Nov...	7	Jan...	5	4	2	1	
Tobacco	187	Nov...	198	July...	174	165	25	3	
Umbrellas, canes	6	Jan...	6	Apr...	5	2	4		
Woolen, worsted, felt	469	Dec...	573	May..	420	339	214	16	4
All other industries	3,456								
All industries	28,750	....	30,978	....	23,354				

D. What is the testimony from employers themselves regarding unemployment in Oregon?

In a questionnaire sent out to employers by Prof. William F. Ogburn, of Reed College, concerning the laying off of men, 14 timber and construction companies replied that each year, as a usual thing, they laid off a total of 2,733 men for an average of three and one-half months. These companies that replied constitute only a small proportion of the total number of construction companies in the State.

E. What is the length of time that the occupations of the men in the tabernacle furnish employment during each year?

Three hundred and twenty-five men answered this question. The following table shows the distribution of the men with reference to the time their trade usually furnishes employment:

Time occupation employs.	Number of men.	Per cent of men.	Time occupation employs.	Number of men.	Per cent of men.
2 months or under............	2	−1	10 to 12 months............	119	36.6
2 to 4 months.................	33	10.1	Uncertain or no work in		
4 to 6 months.................	88	27	trade here.................	9	2.7
6 to 8 months.................	53	16.3			
8 to 10 months...............	21	6.4	Total...................	325	100

It is to be noted that 37 per cent of the men find regular employment at their trades or occupations for only six months or less, and that 53 per cent of the men find such employment for eight months or less each year.

F. How did the amount of employment in 1912 compare with the amount in 1913?

It was the almost unanimous testimony of the men that there was less employment in 1913 than in 1912. In answer to this question as to the relative amounts of employment, the replies gave the amount of employment in four divisions as follows:

The number of days employed from January to April, 1912, and the corresponding number for 1913; then the number employed from April to December, 1912, and the corresponding number for 1913. The tabulated results may be seen as follows:

Number of days employed in 1913, compared with number in 1912.

Days.	1912—Jan.-Apr.	1913—Jan.-Apr.	Days.	1912—Apr.-Dec.	1913—Apr.-Dec.
90–80..............................	129	53	270–240..........................	59	23
80–70..............................	13	16	240–210..........................	25	29
70–60..............................	9	8	210–180..........................	35	28
60–50..............................	57	57	180–150..........................	82	67
Number of men over 50 days......	208	134	Number of men over 150 days....	201	147
50–40..............................	21	38	150–120..........................	75	81
40–30..............................	26	23	120–90...........................	54	91
30–20..............................	74	103	90–60............................	36	62
20–10..............................	13	25	60–30............................	21	45
10 or under.......................	9	6	30 or under......................	5	21
Total replying...............	351	329	Total replying...............	392	447

From this table it may be seen that taking the short period—January to April—with a maximum of 90 days, a greater number of men were employed for more days in 1912 than in 1913; that is, a majority of the men were employed for over 50 days during this period in 1912, and a majority for under 50 days in 1913.

Again considering the long period—April to December—with a maximum of 270 days—a majority of the men were employed for over 150 days in 1912, and for under 150 days in 1913.

The divisions of the year into industrial periods, January to April, and April to December, was made upon the recommendation of the men themselves.

G. What does the Fifth Biennial Report of the Bureau of Labor Statistics of the State of Oregon have to say about unemployment in Oregon?

The 1913 report of the Oregon Bureau of Labor Statistics has little directly to say about unemployment. However, hidden away in the tabulation of industries is to be found data showing the number of male wage earners each industry employs, and the days per year during which many of the industries operate. From this data it can be seen that in 16 industries, employing 26,116 men there is an average unemployment per man of 124.7 days per year, unless the men in these industries found other jobs. The worst industries with respect to seasonal character, and resulting unemployment of their wage earners, are the fruit packing industries, operating only 78 days and employing 340 male wage earners; the salmon canneries, operating only 127 days and employing 850 white employees, and 185 Japs and Chinese; the lumber industry, operating only on the average of 182 days per year, and affecting 21,613 men; brick and tile manufacturing, operating only 175 days per year, and affecting 722 men. The list of 16 industries, and their slack periods are to be seen in the following table:

Male wage earners and days operating among 16 Oregon industries.

[From the Fifth Biennial Report of the Oregon Bureau of Labor Statistics.]

Industry.	Male wage earners.	Days operating.	Days not operating.[1]
Artificial stone...	61	200	112
Barrels and kegs...	24	240	72
Bricks and tiles..	722	175	137
Carpenters (not including independent workers)....................	1,428	240	72
Cider and vinegar..	90	200	112
Dyeing..	86	304	8
Grain elevators..	31	300	12
Fruit packing (omitting pieceworkers)............................	340	78	234
Mandill manufactures...	17	234	78
Ice...	299	275	37
Coal mining...	165	251	61
Paper boxes...	39	300	12
Salmon canneries (omitting pieceworkers):			
Whites.......................................	850	....	....
Japs and Chinese.............................	185	127	185
Sewer pipe..	115	200	112
Soap..	51	300	12
Lumber..	21,613	182	130
Total..	26,116	....	....

[1] Based on a total number of working days of 312 per year.

Average number of days of unemployment for each man, 124.7.

There is a discrepancy of over 5,000 men between the average number of men in the lumber industry according to the Federal census (15,066) and the number according to the Oregon labor commissioner (21,613). This discrepancy is probably accounted for by the fact that the Federal census does not include 5,000 men in the woods (as it is a report on manufactures solely), whom the labor commissioner's report does include.

In regard to agricultural labor, the following meager but important data is included in the report of the bureau of labor statistics:

Cabbage industry, 428 wage earners employed for 60 days of the year.

Pruning and spraying trees, 635 wage earners employed for 252 days.

Rhubarb industry, 39 wage earners employed for 8 months.

Strawberry industry, 9,580 wage earners employed for 3 weeks.

The foregoing facts bearing upon the seasonal character of Oregon industries, including statements from the unemployed men, from employers, from the Federal census, and from the report of the Oregon Bureau of Labor Statistics, answer in part the question, Why men are out of work? But besides seasonal work another cause of unemployment is casual work. To show to what extent this was a factor in the problem of unemployment among the men in the tabernacle, it was ascertained what proportion of the men had trades and what proportion were common laborers. The presumption is that casual work would be more prevalent among common laborers than among men who claimed to have some trade. By a casual worker we mean not so much one who is unemployed as one who is underemployed, and whose usual reliance is upon work of an unskilled character that can be found here and there.

H. What proportion of the men were laborers?

Of the 445 men replying as to their occupation, 145 designated their occupation as "laborer," and 73 designated some form of unskilled labor; 227 men claimed some form of skilled labor, and among these 86 trades were represented. The list of occupations, skilled and unskilled, are the following:

Occupations of 445 men in the tabernacle.

SKILLED WORKERS.		SKILLED WORKERS—continued.	
Machinists	11	Motorman	1
Later	1	Clerks	5
Silversmith	1	Packer	1
Miners	11	Varnish mixer	1
Cooks	25	Paper-mill worker	1
Engineers	14	Papier-mâché worker	1
Stonecutter	1	Glass worker	1
Bookkeepers	2	Bakers	4
Bolt maker	1	Sign painter	1
Linemen	2	Ship rigger	1
Trainmen	3	Pressman	1
Blacksmiths	4	Jeweler	1
Nurse	1	Drill runner	1
Painters	9	Watchmaker	1
Molders	6	Sack sewer	1
Roofers	2	Toolmaker	1
Chauffeur	1	Architect	1
Barbers	4	Candy maker	1
Steamfitters	4	Cleaner and presser	1
Plumbers	4	Tailor	1
Cement workers	4	Film operator	1
Bricklayers	2	Furniture finisher	1
Telegraph operators	2	Nickle plater	1
Box maker	1	Solicitor	1
Boiler makers	5	Marble worker	1
Millwright	1	Hotel workers	2
Shipwright	1	Draftsman	1
Oil worker	1	Upholsterer	1
Brakemen	2	Gas fitters	2
Musician	1	Salesman	1
Ironworkers	3	Stage carpenter	1
Butchers	3	Edge man	1
Timekeeper	1	Paper hanger	1
Cigar makers	2	Plasterer	1
Switchmen	4		
Printers	2	Total	227
Linoleum printer	1	UNSKILLED WORKERS.	
Firemen	11		
Waiters	4	Hod carriers	2
Mill hand	1	Gardners	2
Carpenters	5	Ranchmen	4
Cranemen	2	Sailors	5
Skinners	3	Loggers	22
Electricians	3	Railroad construction men	10
Tallyman	1	Teamsters	22
Metal workers	3	Flunky	1
Car repairer	1	Stableman	1
Shoemaker	1	Hotel workers	2
Druggist	1	Kitchen workers	2
Auto mechanics	2	Laborers	145
Carriage painter	1		
Bridgemen	2	Total	218

Two hundred and twenty-seven men in 85 trades and 218 unskilled workmen and "laborers."

I. What proportion of the men follow one occupation exclusively?

Three hundred and thirty-five men answered this question; 123 stated that they followed one occupation exclusively and 207 stated that they did not. The presumption would be that those who worked at one occupation exclusively would be unemployed when they did not find their regular work.

J. How many men have alternative occupations?

Eighty-four men gave alternative occupations; the 363 remaining in the whole group either gave no alternative or stated that it was common labor.

This fact, combined with the fact that 53 per cent of the men find work at their regular occupations for only eight months of the year or less, would indicate that there are always at certain times of the year in Portland a large number of laborers who, whether or not they have trades, are forced to take what they can get. In dull seasons the usual army of casual workers is increased by skilled tradesmen who find no work in their regular employments and who must therefore take to common labor.

That this is so is confirmed by the number of men who apply for work at the municipal free-employment bureau, 50 per cent of whom, according to the manager of the bureau, would be classed as casual workers. The bureau keeps no record of applications for jobs. Its record of jobs filled for the first eight months of 1914 is as follows:

Male help for whom jobs were secured, January–August, 1914.

	Total number of men given jobs.	Number of jobs inside the city.	Number of jobs outside the city.	Number employed by the city.
January	1,135	1,076	59	429
February	963	936	27	500
March	757	729	28	291
April	676	598	78	....
May	585	573	12	....
June	580	560	20	....
July	639	611	28	....
August	889	854	35	....

K. What was the evidence from the public press and from the unemployed themselves concerning unemployment?

Additional evidence as to the presence of large numbers of common laborers in the city last winter is contained in a statement in the Oregonian for December 16, and is of value because of the general conservative tone of this newspaper. The statement is as follows:

STATEMENT FROM THE OREGONIAN FOR DECEMBER 16, 1914, AS TO UNEMPLOYMENT IN PORTLAND.

" Demand for labor was never so scarce in Portland as it is at present. On account of the wonted unactivity in lumber and logging camps, railroad construction, and public-improvement work thousands of men in various parts of the territory tributary to Portland have been laid off. Many of these men are now walking the streets of Portland looking for work. Other large numbers have left the city, but labor agencies say that for every man who has left another has come.

" In addition to the thousands of idle workingmen, there are in the city the usual quota of loafers, men who never work, who take advantage of the existing inactivity to enlist in the ' army of the unemployed.'

" Employment agents, who usually have more orders for help than they can fill, now are unable to provide work for a single individual. One of the biggest agencies in town, one that had places for 2,909 men six months ago, yesterday was without a single order. Its big blackboard, on which the jobs in more active times are listed, was clean.

" In one or two instances men were wanted for such places as dishwashers or porters, and these were quickly filled. One agency needed 20 men to work in a lumber camp on Coos Bay, but the steamer fare is more than $7, and no man who applied had that much money.

" And no relief is in sight. Not until weather conditions permit will activity in construction camps and logging districts be resumed. Most labor men look for little or no demand for men until April."

STATEMENT CONCERNING LABOR CONDITIONS IN PORTLAND JANUARY–FEBRUARY, 1914.

[From Dan Emmett, a member of the executive committee of the Unemployed League.]

" I began to get data on the labor conditions in this part of the State about the middle of January. The Terwilliger Boulevard rock pile and the city work in the streets and in the parks was about all the work there was. There was a little building going on at that time, but mostly tradesmen were hired. Mr. Brewster gave us 200 tickets good for a job each day on the rock pile, where a man could make 75 cents by breaking one-half yard of rock. He was only allowed 75 cents each day. All the other city work was for married men. I interviewed a great many sawmill and logging companies during the month of January and the first part of February, and was told by most of them that it would be 30 or 60 days before there would be much work to do. They all had more applicants for work than they could use, but most of them told me that they would be glad to help us in any way that they could. I kept in communication with the city and county commissioners who told me that they would recognize the Unemployed League when work was started. Mr. Daly, of the city commissioners, said that he would rush the municipal wood yard as soon as possible and give some of us work, but nothing has been done as yet. So a great many people continue to call us bums and tramps and say that we will not work. Mr. Yeon, who is interested in the Sandy River work which will be done by the county, told me it would be only a short time till they would start up a camp of 100 men from the tabernacle. A few jobs have come in lately, but they were only short ones. There have been a number of parties interested in annoying us. We have been notified that men were wanted at a certain place. We have sent them out where there was no job to be had. We sent 15 men out to Taggert to cut cordwood. There was a man there who had been hiring men, but needed none just then. A man who had a grudge against him had told us about the work. I have interviewed numerous contractors, who tell me they would be glad to remember us when they start work. Some of the logging companies told me they let the foreman do all the hiring. Anyone going out in the country would have to take his chances with another man who might have money to keep him in case he found no work. A great many prefer to hire from the paid employment agencies, where they have a standing order for men. One of the tabernacle men would have to walk or beat his way, for none of them have any money. That is the reason I wanted some of the companies to give some of our men a letter or something which would insure them a job when they arrived. With the exception of Larkin and Green, the Silver Falls, Hammond, and a few more companies, they seemed to think business would be very dull until they got a better price for their logs."

L. Would the men in the tabernacle have worked if they had had the opportunity?

All the evidence went to show that most of the men in the tabernacle would have worked if they had had the chance. Before the opening of the tabernacle the city council had begun to employ idle men in parks, and rounding street curbs, at $3 per day, working each man two days per week, and giving first preference to married men and to men who were on the civil-service list. According to the Oregonian of December 19 there were 5,000 applications for such positions. After the tabernacle was opened the city council then put men to work at the rock quarry on the Terwilliger Boulevard, paying 75 cents for breaking one-half cubic yard of rock. The experience with the men there was that there were not tools enough for all who wanted to work, and in less than a month, after 4,500 cubic yards of rock had been broken, the city officials felt obliged to close down the quarry. Altogether on relief work up to January 26, 1914, the city paid out in wages over $23,000.

On one occasion 80 men were sent out from the tabernacle to Cascade Locks to work for the Oregon-Washington Railroad & Navigation Co. Upon arriving at their job these men discovered that they had been sent out as strike breakers, and refused to work. The road had reduced the daily wages of 115 Italians and Greeks from $1.75 to $1.50, and the men struck to maintain the higher wage. Whether or not the men from the tabernacle were justified in refusing to replace the strikers each one must decide for himself. The facts of the case were printed in the Oregon Journal for March 15, and were ascertained by the secretary of the Oregon Civic League.

M. Were there then no "hobos" among the men in the tabernacle?

During its occupancy by the unemployed men the tabernacle was referred to as the "tramps" or "hobos" hotel. To large numbers in the community it is still inconceivable that worthy men should be out of work. The data heretofore presented should convince any open-minded person unemployment is a factor to be reckoned with by thousands of Oregon wage earners. The question remains, however, as to whether there were not among the legitimate workingmen some men who were not looking for work. If there were any such the community is prone to cover its own responsibility in judging the whole group by the few who possibly could be held personally responsible for their unemployment.

But let us examine this question of personal responsibility. Students of the question are aware that in any group of unemployed men there are various classes, each of which is a product of social and individual circumstances differing from those affecting other classes. For example, besides the unemployed there are the unemployable. And who are the unemployable? Some are so because of no fault of their own, but because of sickness, old age, injury, or mental deficiency. Again, some may be held to a degree personally accountable because of intemperance, indisposition to work, or of viciousness. No possible classification can be made of these various groups until a study of them has been made and a work test submitted. Above all, the test should be a fair one. It is not fair to offer broken-down, underfed men work at crushing rock, and then to condemn them if they do not stick to the job. As one observed the slow file of men coming to and from the tabernacle one could see that the first need of many of them was medical care.

Eliminate the able-bodied willing workers, who constituted the great majority of the men; the sick, the infirm, and the mentally deficient, all of whom were entitled to relief and care; and the alcoholics, who were excluded from the tabernacle by the men themselves, and whom do we have left to hold personally accountable? A very small number of men—5 per cent perhaps—who have become indisposed toward work and who are not discomfited at having to live upon the community. Even in the case of these men society can not disclaim responsibility for their existence. The man who can find no work or who finds it only occasionally easily drifts into the class of those who are not anxious to work. Several men in the tabernacle declared that in coming West looking for work their funds had become exhausted and for the first time in their lives they had been compelled to take to the freight cars. It is easier to take the second ride than the first and the third than the second; so gradually the man who wants to work becomes the man who cares not whether he finds it or not. Probably there were a few such men in the tabernacle, but they constitute a grave problem for society to solve; no less than the able-bodied men who are looking for work.

N. Were there any "agitators" in the tabernacle?

Waiving the consideration that there is something wrong with an able-bodied man who wants work and can not find it, if he does not become an "agitator," a census was taken of 326 men as to whether they were union men or members of the I. W. W. Their replies are contained in the following table:

Not members of union	126
Members of union	102
Formerly members of union	12
Have union belief	21
Want one big union	5
I. W. W	14
No reply to question	46
Total	326

As a matter of history it was interesting to note that the executive committee of the Unemployed League had not long been organized when it became apparent that there was a struggle between radical and conservative members. The outcome of this struggle was that the I. W. W. element was either put out of the tabernacle or made to cease creating disturbance.

II. Why did the unemployed men come to Portland, and what was the effect of the tabernacle?

A. Testimony of the men as to why they came to Portland.

The men gave two chief reasons for coming to Portland:

(1) Three hundred and seven of the four hundred and forty-two men who replied to the question stated that they came to Portland in search of work. The "inland empire," which is tributary to Portland, creates a labor supply tributary to Portland. In this city are 18 male employment bureaus operated for private gain. If a man is in southern Oregon in search of work, he must come to a labor agency in Portland, even though the agency collects fees and sends the man back to a job in the district from which he came. In the Northwest, where the distances between industrial centers are so great, a man with-

out work frequently has the alternative of consuming a large part of his income in traveling to the nearest industrial center or of resorting to the illegal practice of riding the freight cars. One course leads to destitution and the other to vagrancy.

(2) Eighty-four of the four hundred and forty-two men stated that they came to Portland to "better their condition" or that they were attracted by the advertisements of the advantages of living in this State. Commercial clubs, the State immigration commission, and railroad companies send broadcast pamphlets about the opportunities in Oregon. Doubtless the purpose of this advertising is to attract persons who have sufficient capital to make an economic success; nevertheless it is an incontestable fact that these publications reach hundreds of workingmen who have nothing to offer but their labor and who are misled by the inexplicit and vague phrases of the advertisers. Once here they may come to realize, though only too late, that as wage earners they meet with the same fluctuating conditions of employment in Oregon as elsewhere.

Much wiser is the statement to be found on page 6 of the Fifth Annual Report of the Bureau of Labor Statistics, "By the automatic action of the law of industrial supply and demand, however, Oregon, as well as other States, rarely holds out any exceptional inducements to wageworkers, and all such who are comfortably situated elsewhere should be very sure of their ground before deciding to leave position and friends for uncertainties in a strange land."

The 51 men remaining gave various reasons for coming to Portland, of which many have to do with economic circumstances. For example, men come "to get paid off," "to get a ship," "to work for the Standard Oil Co.," "to work for the Oregon-Washington Railroad & Navigation Co.," "to settle in Oregon," "to get work in a sawmill."

The sum of the evidence as to why men come to Portland bears witness to the fact that Portland as the center of an extensive territory, reaching into Oregon, California, Washington, and Idaho, is of necessity a center for an army of migratory workers who depend upon hearsay and upon unscientifically managed labor agencies for their information concerning opportunities for work. If no work is found, then men must remain in the city until work turns up, and if their stakes are spent they become entirely dependent upon the community for the necessities of existence.

B. Did the opening of the tabernacle attract men to Portland? After what has been said concerning the fundamental reasons for men coming to Portland, the question stated above assumes less importance. However, inasmuch as it was alleged that in giving shelter to the shelterless the community would be in danger of caring for more than its share, it is pertinent to inquire as to the effect of the tabernacle in drawing men to the city.

Three hundred and seventy-six men replied to the question as to how long they had been in Portland. Remembering that the tabernacle was opened January 1, and that the survey was made between February 10 and February 21, the following table shows how long the men had been in Portland:

	Over 6 months.	6–5 months.	5–4 months.	4–3 months.	3–2 months.	2–1 month.	Under 1 month.	Total.
Number of men......	84	29	18	27	62	80	76	376
Per cent.............	22.3	7.7	4.7	7.1	16.4	21.2	20.2	100

From this it will be seen that 58.2 per cent, or 220 of the men, had been in Portland over two months; 80 men, or 21.2 per cent of the men, had been here from one to two months. As it would have taken a few days for notice of the opening of the tabernacle to reach men outside of Portland, some of these 80 men, say 50 of them, would, in any case, have been in town. This approximates 70 per cent of the men who would have come to Portland whether or not the tabernacle was open.[1] As for the remaining 30 per cent who came to Portland after the opening of the tabernacle, it is difficult to prove that the tabernacle brought them here. The presupposition is in favor of their being here in any case, and of their being dependent upon the various overworked

---

[1] By actual count of 411 replying to question as to when they came to Portland, 134, or 32 per cent, said they had come since the 1st of January.

philanthropic agencies,[1] or living in the insanitary lodging houses, where in case of plague the community would have been far less protected than if the men had been under public supervision in a place like the tabernacle.

As additional evidence concerning the alleged effect of the tabernacle in drawing men to Portland, it will be well to note what places men came from.

Of the men who came to Portland from large cities on the coast between January 1 and February 10, 21 came from Seattle, 7 from Tacoma, 9 from Spokane, 2 from San Francisco, 2 from Los Angeles, and 3 from .Vancouver, British Columbia.

Concerning the 21 who came from Seattle, it can be said that there was no need of their coming to Portland on account of the shelter that was offered here, inasmuch as Seattle had a shelter like the one in Portland, which was largely supported by the merchants in the community. (See Welfare for April, 1914.)

The outstanding fact concerning the question as to where the men came from is that 20 States and 100 towns and cities outside of Oregon were represented by the men in the tabernacle. It is hardly likely that the accommodations in the tabernacle were so comfortable as to attract men from New York, Salt Lake City, Denver, and Winnipeg.

Finally, if the tabernacle had been a leading cause of drawing men to Portland, one would have expected to find an increasing number of men frequenting the place. . The fact is, however, that after the tabernacle was opened about the same number came there each day during January and February, and toward the end of March the numbers began somewhat to decrease. The following table, taken from the daily reports of the Unemployed League, makes this clear:

Number of men on the roster of the Unemployed League, December 29, 3,500.

Number of men eating and sleeping in the tabernacle.

Date.	Eating.		Sleeping.	Date.	Eating.		Sleeping.
	Morn.	Night.			Morn.	Night.	
Jan. 15 [2]	1,340	1,363	897	Feb. 4	1,140	1,390	790
Jan. 19	1,325	1,340	903	Feb. 8	1,340	1,580	852
Jan. 22 [3]			310	Feb. 12	1,280	1,480	903
Jan. 24	650	590	838	Feb. 19	1,355	1,480	893
Jan. 28	900	1,160	800	Mar. 12	1,120	1,190	910

III. Were the men improvident?

A. How much money did they have when they last quit work?

Among 430 men, who also stated the length of time they were out of work, the amounts they had when they last quit work were as follows:

Amounts.	Number of men.	Cumulative per cent.	Amounts.	Number of men	Cumulative per cent.
Nothing	6	1.3	Under $200	391	90.9
Under $25	130	31	$200–$224	11	93.4
$25–$49	76	49.3	$225–$249	3	94.1
$50–$74	66	64.6	$250–$299	8	96
$75–$99	37	73.2	$300–$399	6	97.4
$100–$124	34	81.1	$400 or over	11	100
$125–$149	18	83			
$150–$174	19	89.7	Total	430	
$175–$199	5				

Average amount each man had among whole group of 430... $80.10
Average amount each man had among the 391 who had less than $200............................. 54.21

[1] According to statements by W. G. MacLaren, of the Portland Commons, and Capt. Andrews, of the Salvation Army, these organizations did three- times the amount of relief work during the winter of 1914 than they had ever done in any previous winter of their history.

[2] When reports first began to be filed with Oregon Civic League secretary.

[3] The small number using the place on this day is accounted for by the fact that the odors from the fumigation after the case of smallpox were still strong.

It is to be noted that the 391 men who had less than $200 constitute 90.9 per cent of the whole group.

B. What did they spend their money for?

Altogether 440 men replied as follows in regard to what the money was spent for:

1. Living expenses (including board, lodging, traveling expenses, fees to employment agencies) _____ 348
2. Sickness_____ 52
3. Support of others_____ 17
4. Drink _____ 17
5. Recreation_____ 2
6. Robbed_____:_____ 2
7. Miscellaneous_____ 2

Total number of men replying_____ 440

It is to be observed that 348 of the 440 men, or 79 per cent spent their savings while out of work for living expenses. No detailed statement was obtained as to amounts spent for each item under "living expenses." "Traveling," as an expense, however, was mentioned ―――― times. In the West especially, the long distances between industrial centers force upon migratory workers the undersirable alternatives of spending all their funds for traveling expenses, or of resorting to the freight cars. While spending the summer at a point between Portland and Spokane the writer has had opportunity to see the freight trains pass, and passenger trains, too, for that matter, with men stealing rides in every conceivable place in and on the cars. In talking with these men, as they would sometimes be put off by the trainmen, they all told the same story of their attempt to reach the harvest fields, where they hoped to find work. Apparently, "our bumper crops" are gathered, in part at least, by wandering, homeless men who are forced to beg by the roadside bread that comes from the grain which they are eager to harvest.

Another fact to be observed is the number of men who spend their savings for sickness. "Sickness" was mentioned by 52 men as an expense. It is well known to all students of social conditions that among wage earners and their families sickness is one of the leading causes of destitution, to say nothing of the waste of human resources. The economic waste through sickness could be largely prevented if wage earners could take easy advantage of the means which science has discovered for the prevention and cure of disease.

It is further to be noted that 17 of the 440 men stated that they had spent their money for "drink." Drunken men and saloon loafers were not ad-. mitted into the tabernacle, and judging from the looks of the men and the general businesslike conduct of affairs in the tabernacle, the probability is that there was not a larger number of excessive drinkers among them.

C. How long were the men out of work?

This question is answered in two divisions:

(1) The length of time the group as a whole were out of work, and the correlation of this time with the average stake of the group as a whole.

(2) The length of time out of work of the 391 men whose stakes were less than $200, and the correlation of this time with the average stakes of this group.

Time unemployed of the group as a whole.

	Time unemployed.									Total.
	Under 1 month.	1-2 mos.	2-3 mos.	3-4 mos.	4-5 mos.	5-6 mos.	6 mos.	6-12 mos.	Over 12 mos.	
Number of men.....	29	83	103	115	63	16	8	9	4	430
Per cent of men.....	6.7	19.5	23.0	26.7	14.6	3.7	1.8	2.0	—1	100
Cumulative per cent.	6.7	26.2	50.1	76.8	91.4	95.1	96.9	98.9	100	....

It is to be noted that the largest single group—115—were out of work from three to four months.

The average unemployment for each man since his last job in the group was 2 months and 22 days. This average is probably a little low, for the reason that in the few instances where fractions of months were designated (as when a man said that he was out of work for 5 weeks or for 2¼ months) these fractions were disregarded and the average ascertained only on the basis of whole months.

(a) How fast did they spend their money?

Remembering that the average amount of money possessed by each of the 430 men when he quit his last job was $80.10, each man would have spent his money up to the time when he came to the tabernacle at the rate of about $29 per month.

Time unemployed of the 391 men whose stakes were less than $200.

	Time unemployed.									
	Under 1 month.	1–2 mos.	2–3 mos.	3–4 mos.	4–5 mos.	5–6 mos.	6 mos.	6–12 mos.	Over 12 mos.	Total.
Number of men.....	29	80	94	108	55	15	7	3	....	391
Per cent of men.....	7.4	20.5	24	27.6	14	3.8	1.7	−1	....	100

We should remember that these 391 constituted 90 per cent of the whole group of 430.

(a) How fast did the 391 men spend their money?

The average unemployment among these 391 men was 2 months and 14 days. Remembering that the average amount that each of these 391 men had when he last quit work was $54.21, the rate of expenditure of their savings for these men, from the time they quit their jobs until they went to the tabernacle, was $21.85 per month. This would amount to about $5.46 per week. Considering that $8.64 is the minimum amount that, according to the Oregon Minimum Wage Commission, a factory girl can live upon in decency and comfort, it does not appear that these men were improvident in the use of their savings during the period of their unemployment.

D. But were the 39 men who had over $200 improvident in the use of their money?

The following table shows facts concerning the 39 men who had $200 or more when they last quit work, including data concerning where they came from and when, trades, the age of each man (except in a few instances where the age was not given), the amount of each man's stake, and the time he was unemployed:

Table showing age, where from and when, trade, amount of money when last quit work, how the money was spent, marital state, and time unemployed in case of 39 men whose stakes amounted to $200 or over.

Age.	Where from.	When.	Trade.	Stake.	How spent.	Time unemployed.	Married or single.
	Genture, Oreg.	Mth, 1913	Cook	$250	Clothes, food, shelter, traveling, sickness	2 months	
33	California	October, 19..	Trainman	200	Support mther, traveling	do	
	San Francisco	August, 1913	Molder	200	Railway fare, clothes, hotel expenses	3 months	
26	Nome, Mka	December, 1913	Roofer	275	Lost it prospecting	3 days	
	Idaho, Mka	November, 1913	Lineman	200	Food, shelter, clothing, rilway fare, sickness	63 days	
26	Hoquiam, Wash.	February, 1913	Stationary engineer	200	Clothes, do	4 months	
45	Nevada	Mar, 1913	Miner	400	Living expenses, traveling, sickness	3 months	
33	San Francisco	January, 1913	Paper mill	325	Hospital doctor's bills	5 months	
46	do	August, 1913	Cook	784	Hospital	14 months	
32	Montana	Mar, 1913	Roofer	310	Clothes, food, Mr, whisky, women	3½ months	Married.
35	Milwaukee	1912	Molder	300	Living mes	6 months	
35	Salt Lake	January, 1914	Timekeeper	230	Living : mes and support of 1 m.	4 months	
25	Seattle	Member, 1913	Miner	400	Railway fare and living	3 months	
35	Chicago	May, 1911	Engineer	200	Doctor's m.	6 months	
	Spokane	Mar, 1913	Fireman	350	Mes and other necessities	7 months	
29	Wenatchee, Wash.	Mar, 1913	Waiter	335	Support of mother, clothing, shelter, food, railway fare.		
47	Utah.	Mar, 1913	Railroad work	500	Looking for work	3 months	
46	Seattle	February, 1913	Boiler maker	225	Fare to Canada to look at land	2 months	
29	Gavra	1912	Cook	425	Doctor's bills	1 month	Do.
34	New York City	April, 1913	Mechanic	750	Hillsboro land deal, auto repair shop	2 months	
42	Mnd, Cal.		Engineer	490	Traveling, board, helping sick friend	9 months	
29	Seattle	October, 19..	Miner	540	Hospital fees, board	2 months	
55	Idaho.		Logger	350	Traveling, drinking	do	Do.
24	San Francisco	July, 1913	Sign painter	250	Sent to family	do	
25	Umatilla.	February, 1914	Sailor	200	Traveling and living	13 months	
32	Denver	do	Laborer	200	Railway fare, living	2 months	
24	Seattle	Mar, 1913	Candy maker	220	Traveling, living, sickness	1½ months	
50	Wisconsin	1888	Butcher	225	Clothes, living expenses	4 months	
	Mgo	1907	Machinist	200	Living (been on 3 years' strike)	do	
32	Tacoma	December, 1913	Foreman	280	Clothes	3 years	
32	Seattle	October, 1913	Marine fireman	286	Traveling, sickness	6 weeks	
28	Imperial, Oreg.	December, 1913	Barber	250	Traveling	½ month	
41	Pittsburgh	do	Machinist	250	Machinist	12 months	
45	Lewiston, Mont	February, 1913	Laborer	921	Booze and clothing	10 months	
35	Mal, Mia	February 1, 1914	Cook	400	Hospital	18 months	
	Tacoma, Wash.	January 15, 1914	Laborer	400	Clothes	3 months	
20	San Francisco		Salesman	400	Traveling, clothes	4 months	
20	Port Richmond	February 1, 1914	Stage carpenter	230	Clothes, money stolen	do	
27	Salt Lake City	October 1, 1913	Cook	283	"Blowed it in."		

The following facts are to be noted:
1. Of the 35 men who stated their age 26 are under 40 years of age.
2. Excluding as abnormal the man who said he had been out of work for three years, the average unemployment of 37 other men who answered to the question was 4 months and 21 days.
3. The average stakes of 39 men was $330.
4. The average rate of expenditure would then be $70.23 per month.
5. Sickness was mentioned as an expense 12 times; support of others, 3 times; dissipation, 4 times; traveling, 16 times.
6. Thirty-six of the 39 men came to Portland from States outside of Oregon, Canada, the Atlantic coast, and the Middle West being mentioned as starting points.
7. Twenty-seven of the 37 who stated when they came to Portland said that they had been here over two months; 5 had been here over a year.

Judging solely from the statements of the men, without more detailed inquiry, and allowing for amounts expended for sickness, necessary traveling, and support of others, there do appear to be indications of improvidence among this group with comparatively large savings. Of course the men who admitted having squandered their " stakes " were improvident. But even among some of the others it does not appear why No. 37, for example, who has been out of work three months and who had $400 to spend on clothes and traveling, could not have kept himself from destitution within that time. Or again, No. 6, who had $200 and was out of work for four months, could, unless there were expenses which he did not mention, have lived upon his " stake." Only four of the group were married, viz, Nos. 11, 20, 24, and 39. Over against the instances of improvidence, however, should be set the case of the sign painter, No. 24, who was married and had sent his savings to his family, and who for some reason or other had been out of work for over a year. Among every group of 39 men there will be some who are improvident. Whether an especially larger proportion of those under discussion are so could be determined only by a more thorough investigation than is involved in this survey.

E. What were the earnings of the men during 1912 and 1913? Improvidence could be determined only on the basis of the earnings of the men. These it was possible to compute because the men gave the number of days employed and the wage per day from January to April and April to December, 1912, and the same for 1913. The results of this portion of the question are shown in the following table:

Earnings of 421 and 425 men in 1912 and 1913, respectively.

	1912	Cumulative per cent.	1913	Cumulative per cent.
Under $50	1	−1.0	5	1.1
$50–$99	4	1.1	6	2.5
$100–$149	9	3.3	12	5.4
$150–$199	13	6.4	30	12.4
$200–$249	16	10.2	35	20.7
$250–$299	23	13.3	37	29.4
$300–$349	26	22.3	42	39.2
$350–$399	27	28.7	44	49.6
$400–$449	31	36.1	36	58.2
$450–$499	42	46.0	39	67.2
$500–$599	49	57.7	36	75.7
$600–$699	60	71.9	44	86.1
$700–$799	41	81.7	27	92.4
$800–$899	23	87.1	10	94.7
$900–$999	18	91.4	7	96.4
$1,000–$1,199	10	93.8	6	98.3
$1,200–$1,499	19	98.3	5	99.5
$1,500–$1,999	5	99.5	2	100
$2,000 and over	2	100.0		
Total number of men	421		425	

Average earnings, 421 men in 1912.. $591.58
Average earnings, 425 men in 1913.. 439.81

That over 400 men in the Northwest should earn only $591 on the average during 1912, and $439 on the average during 1913, compares with the statement of Scott Nearing,.in Wages in the United States, that the average annual wage of adult male workers in that section of the country north of Mason and Dixon's line and east of the Rockies is $650; that sometimes this average goes to $750 and sometimes as low as $350.

The earnings of the men in the tabernacle for 1912 and 1913, if distributed evenly over these years, would have meant $11.83 per week in 1912 and $8.79 in 1913. They do not seem to permit of any considerable degree of improvidence.

APPENDIX.

A. What were the ages of the men?

Four hundred and sixteen men replied to the question as to age, and their replies are as follows:

Age.	Number of men.	Per cent of men.	Age.	Number of men.	Per cent of men.
16–20 years	16	3.8	41–45 years	26	6.2
21–25 years	86	20.6	46–50 years	36	8.6
26–30 years	82	19.7	Over 50 years	36	8.6
31–35 years	80	19.2			
36–40 years	54	14.1	Total	416	100.0

From the above it can be seen that 44 per cent of the men are under 30 years of age and 63 per cent are under 35 years of age; that is, the majority are young men who ought to be adding to the productive resources of the Nation as well as to their own success and happiness.

What per cent of the men were foreign born?

Of 437 who replied to the question as to country of birth, 158, or 36.3 per cent, were foreign born. Portland has a present foreign-born population of about 21 per cent; that is, there were more foreigners among this group than among the population of the city as a whole. It is certain that when the Panama Canal will have been open 10 years the per cent of foreign born among wage earners coming to Portland will be much larger.

B. What proportion of the men were married?

Forty men said they were married; this is about 9 per cent. Married men who were residents of the city were the first who were given relief work in the various city departments. The associated charities were also active in helping the families of married men living in Portland. Generally speaking, the tabernacle was the resort of migratory workers who were not married, and whose only Portland address was the tabernacle.

C. What can be learned from personal histories of the men?

The following personal stories were secured through conversations with the men. All but one of them were obtained by a Reed College student who spent several nights sleeping at the tabernacle:

No. 1. This man was a fine-looking Swede, 32 years old, and weighing about 180 pounds. He had been employed at Wilsonville, Oreg., logging and wood cutting. He had come to Portland and spent all his money on a good time, and wanted to earn enough to pay his way back. He had been obliged to go to the place in the first place on a freight car.

No. 2. This man had come from California in November. He said that during the summer he had waited, with about 400 "white" laborers, near one of the California hop yards, expecting work, when the company brought in two carloads of Japs and sent the "white" laborers away. This man seemed to be fairly well educated. Recently he had worked several days at casual jobs, and one day on the city rock quarry. He "beat" his way out of town to take a job cutting wood, but when he got there he found that the man was paying only board and no wages. This made the unemployed man indignant. and he cursed him. He seemed very rebellious, and said that if he had a family he would shoot a man before he would let his wife and children starve. Coming from California he had stolen a ride for over 200 miles on the "Shasta Limited," riding the "blinds." He said that conditions were worse in California than in Oregon, because many men stay the winter in California on account of the climate. He said that in California the roads and creeks were lined with men who were living on walnuts and "spuds." He said that six years ago he had come West from Florida, attracted by advertisements of the country. Once he had made $300 in the woods in six months, but had spent it all in a short time. This had occurred a long time ago, and he was still brooding over his folly. He was in wrath over the employment agencies that are in collusion with the foremen in order to get fees from the men, discharge them, and then divide the "stakes."

No. 3. This was a lad still in his teens. On account of his health he had come to Oregon from the Middle West where the doctors told him that he must get into a milder climate. He had been employed at agricultural work until the man whom he was working for gave the job to a relative. The boy then drifted to Portland, and being unable to find work drifted into the tabernacle. He spent one evening at a reading room in the North End that has been established by the Episcopal diocese. There a clergyman of the diocese talked with him and found that the boy wanted to take a job with the telegraph company, but had no money with which to buy a bicycle. The clergyman loaned him the money, and the boy got the job. A place was then got for the lad in one of the banks of the city, and he then also worked nights with the telegraph company. The boy has the job at the bank at the present time, and has repaid all the money that was loaned him. His wages at the bank have been raised thrice. He has since declared that during the winter when he was out of work he would have killed himself if he had not been afraid to do so.

No. 4. An Italian barber who had come to Oregon from Pittsburgh. In different cities all the way to the West he had tried to get work in his line, but was unsuccessful, possibly because he was not a union man. His clothes now were so worn that he could not make a good appearance. Said that he could not work on the rock pile, as the tools were poor and the work was too heavy for him. He said that the last three months he had been able to get only 10 or 15 days of work. He had been begging at the doors for dry bread until the opening of the tabernacle.

No. 5. Man of Irish and German descent about 43 years of age. Lost his wife and three children in the San Francisco earthquake. Lost his paper hanging and painting business. He tried to get his insurance from the insurance company, but did not succeed. This man looked sober and worried. He said that at one time he had made some money on an onion crop in California, but had paid it all out for sickness. Again he had had work in a lumberyard, when his leg was broken by a falling log, and the money he had saved was all gone before he got out of the hospital. He had attempted to start a paper-hanging business in Marshfield, Oreg., but came away from there and wanted to go to Australia. He brooded over his ill luck continually.

No. 6. A young Jew, aged 21, who had worked in a gold mine in Oaxaca, Mexico, until he got notice from the American consul to get out of the country. He had. "beaten" his way up the Pacific coast, and wanted to go to his home in Chicago. He seemed not to be disturbed at the prospect of having to find a job and make his way without any money.

No. 7. An Englishman, 27 years old, whose home was in Liverpool. He was a photographer by trade, and had his camera materials in a trunk somewhere. He came to this country with money made in a camera exhibit. Came first to the United States and then went to Canada, where he went broke. Came back into the "States" in the "crow's nest" (cowcatcher). Has no hopes for the future. Used to worry about it, but now takes things as they come. Had worked in the harvest fields in Canada, but had acquired the wandering spirit, and wanted always to move on. At this time he was getting most of his meals by cutting wood and general work. At the rock pile he could not finish his one-half cubic yard in four hours; so he went back the next day. He said that he would go back to Liverpool again if he had the money.

LORNTSEN EXHIBIT.

UNITED STATES COMMISSION ON INDUSTRIAL RELATIONS.

GENTLEMEN: At the hearing in Portland, Oreg., on the 21st instant I was requested to submit in writing a brief statement on the four questions mailed to me, especially to give the figures I quoted:

1. *General labor conditions in fishing.*—To enable you to get at the facts, I must take you back as far as to 1866, when canning commenced on the Columbia

River, and quote some figures taken from the report of United States Commission on Fish and Fisheries:

Year.	Price paid per salmon.	Charged per case.	Year.	Price paid per salmon.	Charged per case.
1866	$0.15	$16.00	1873–1879	$0.25	$0.50–$7.00
1868	.20	13.00	1880	.50	4.60– 4.80
1868	.20	12.00	1881	.60	5.00
1869	.20	10.00	1882–83	.75	5.00
1870	.20	9.00	1884	.50	4.70
1871	.20	.50	1885	.75	4.00
1872	.22½	8.00			

Which proves that there was no relation between the price paid for salmon to the fishermen and the price charged the public for canned salmon. They paid as little as possible and charged all they could get.

In 1886 the packers offered 45 and 55 cents per salmon, the former for salmon caught by cannery gear and the latter for salmon caught by private gear. This offer was quietly but firmly refused, and on April 11 that year the Columbia River Fishermen's Union was organized and the price asked was 55 and 65 cents, resulting in a strike until May 15, when the union price was agreed to by the packers.

In 1887 the price was set to 80 and 90 cents and obtained without any trouble, and the following year the price was $1 and $1.25.

In 1889 $1 and $1.25 was the price set and obtained. The union thought it a fair price and would not ask for an increase that year, but the packers must have felt very generous, because they gave the fishermen free boats, and those who had their own boats received $40 in cash.

Thus with the union's assistance the fishermen in four years had received over $1,500,000 in clear cash over and above what they would have received had they remained unorganized. But this was not all. The fishermen had before been traveling from place to place; many of them settled down in Astoria, and on the banks of the Columbia. Feeling secured in their endeavor to earn an honest living and could see their way clear to support a family, many of them married, as men of common sense usually do.

As stated before, the fishermen through their union had reached as high a price as they thought was reasonable, and although the packers the previous year had given $40 to each boat, above the price set, they did not want to ask any increase for the season of 1890, and set the price at $1 and $1.25. However, the packers refused to pay the price set and a strike was the result.

The union was not as powerful as in former years on account of so many men getting on the river, of which the greatest part did not see fit to join the union, and probably was paid by the packers to stay out and assist the packers to break up the union. A compromise was agreed on and the men received $1 per salmon, and later on 75 cents was the ruling price; then to cap the climax the packers would not pay full price for a salmon unless it was at least 15 pounds.

In 1891–92 90 cents and $1 was the price; 1893 the price was 5 cents per pound, which we had for seasons 1894–95, the same price was also asked in 1896, but not obtained. A certain Mr. Norris, from the A. Booth & Co., Chicago, came to Astoria that spring and managed to organize the packers, presumably with the object in view to disrupt the union. It was said that said Norris got each packer to put up $10,000 in cash as a bond to not pay 5 cents per pound, and there must have been some such action taken according to statement made by one of the packers to myself sometime after the commencement of the strike, to wit: "I can promise and guarantee you 4½ cents, yes, 4¾ cents per pound and a little more, but you will never see 5 cents this season."

The strike was lost, compromised on 4 cents, and later that was cut to 2 cents per pound, and the leaders in the strike should not be able to deliver fish to any cannery on the river the following year.

2. Operation of cooperative canneries.—Cooperative cannery built: The leaders in the strike in 1896 and others, many of them with families and little homes of their own in Astoria and along the banks of the Columbia River, were not to be driven away by the packers, but they set to work and organized the "Union Fishermen's Co-op Packing Co." with a capital of $20,000, built a $33,000 plant, and put up 44,000 cases of salmon during season 1897.

The other packers certainly did the best they knew how to burst that company, every conceivable scheme from blocking the market to keeping supplies from that company, but thanks to a certain banker in town the packers did not succeed.

The cooperative company is the greatest blessing that ever came to the Columbia River. There never has been a strike on the river since it was organized in 1896–97, and the price has through the effort of the union and that cannery advanced from 4 cents per pound in 1896 to 6 cents per pound for salmon less that 25 pounds and 7½ cents per pound for salmon 25 pounds and over.

The following table will show the price paid for salmon on the river and the price obtained for the canned goods since that cannery was built:

Year.	Tall.	Flats.	Halves.	Ovals.	Half ovals.	Per pound.	Dividend (per ton).
1897	$4.60	$5.20				4 cents	
1898	5.20	5.60				4 cents	
1899	5.00	5.60				5 cents	$5.00
1900	6.40	6.80				....do	
1901	6.20	6.60				5 and 6 cents	2.50
1902	5.40	5.80				....do	2.50
1903	5.40	5.80				....do	10.00
1904	5.80	6.20	$3.60	$8.	$5.	....do	10.00
1905	5.80	6.20	3.60	8.	5.	....do	14.00
1906	6.00	6.40	4.00	8.	5.	....do	16.00
1907	6.60	7.00	4.20	9.	6.	5 and 7 cents	16.00
1908	6.60	7.00	4.20	9.	6.	....do	12.00
1909	6.60	7.00	4.20	9.	6.20	....do	15.00
1910	7.60	7.60	4.40	9.	6.60	5, 5 and 7, 5 cents	15.00
1911	7.60	8.00	4.80	10.	6.80	....do	20.00
1912	7.80	8.00	5.00	10.	6.8	....do	10.00
1913	7.40	7.60	4.70	10.80	6.0	....do	5.00
1914	7.80	8.40	5.00	10.80	7.80	....do	

And this is not all; the other packers to keep their fishermen had to pay a certain bonus to them above the union prices on the river.

There is only one such company on the Columbia River and it has made good, its property could not at this date be duplicated for less than $250,000. Every fisherman fishing for this cannery receives the same for his fish, whether he be a shareholder or not. A shareholder gets 6 per cent interest for cash invested in stock, and there is no water in that stock.

3. *Labor conditions in cooperative canneries as compared with other canneries.*—The question of wages to the cannery workers received serious consideration and study during the first two years, and the conclusion reached was to pay as other canneries paid, sometimes a little more and also aimed to reduce the hours.

Up to the time of the introduction of the sanitary can, Asiatic labor was chiefly employed. This labor is still employed in other canneries and under a contract system; the contractor agrees to pack complete the entire production of canned goods for a fixed amount, say about 44 or 45 cents per case of 48 cans. The cannery guarantee the contracting firm a certain amount of cases and must pay for the stipulated number whether packed or not, the contracting firm in turn guarantee the packing company that he will furnish sufficient help to put up a certain number of cases per day. To put up 1,000 cases per day would require about 40 people, outside of labeling.

The cooperative company hire white help only; they are classified as follows: General labor, consisting of all office help, cannery superintendents, and foremen, fish receivers at cannery and all stations, and all launch crews. Canning labor, consisting of butchers, slimers, fish graders, gang-knife men, fillers, salters, cleaners, machine operators, workers about coolers and retorts, firemen, and salmon cooks.

Cold-storage labor: Butchers, splitters, slimers, salters, and general labor.

Can-making department labor: Superintendent, machinists, and general help required in the line of can making, which is all machine work.

The average pay for the spring season of four months in 1913 was as follows:

	Employees.	Per month, each.
General labor	30	$75.00
Cannery labor	57	53.56
Cold storage labor	19	57.57
Can-making labor	21	52.65

In addition to this there is labeling, box making, and barrel making, all of which are piecework. The fastest labeler may earn from $3 to $3.75 in nine hours and the slowest 50 cents, box makers from $5 to $7, and barrel makers about the same amount per day. The general average wages paid for the period mentioned covering all employees was $2.25, the highest $3.75, and the lowest $1.25 per day, the hours of labor being for the greatest portion nine, which is a reduction of one hour less than other establishments of same nature.

The sanitary and working conditions in the cooperative plant are incomparable with conditions where Asiatics are employed. This plant is the only one on the Columbia River in which you will find electric fans installed—this to keep the flies away from the fish. There are two large overhead and two smaller fans, one on each end of the filling table.

There is no aim at speeding up in this plant; the cost of production per case is equal to and at times more than it would cost to turn the packing over to a contractor.

4. *Obstacles to extension of cooperative movement.*—Chiefly lack of funds. A couple more cooperative plants on the river would solve the problem.

The Columbia River Fishermen's Protective Union very early realized that to perpetuate the salmon supply and through it the salmon industry proper protective measures, such as has been adopted for other salmon streams and proved of greatest benefit, must be adopted for the Columbia River, and to that end has spent a great deal of money and energy, but so far those who have become rich on the ruination of the industry have always managed by means best known to themselves to continue their destructive work.

During the 1901 legislative session a measure was passed in both houses prohibiting stationary fishing appliances in every river in Oregon and no commercial fishing permitted above tidewater—true salmon protection. But overnight it was juggled and Columbia River was out. The result of that law saved the salmon in every river in Oregon, except Columbia.

The salmon catch in the coast river had dwindled down to almost nothing. In 1901 the total catch of Chinook salmon in the coast streams of Oregon was less than 700,000 pounds and the silver salmon catch less than 3,000,000 pounds. However, through the law passed the Chinook catch in the same streams in 1906 had increased to 3,019,000 pounds and the silver catch to about 5,000,000 pounds, and this can not be laid to hatcheries, as it was too early to have any result from hatchery work; it was common-sense regulation; that is all. And since that cannery after cannery and cold storage has been built and they are all doing well.

In December, 1906, when in Washington, D. C., together with another gentleman, we called on United States Commissioner of Fish and Fisheries Mr. Bower, endeavoring to get his assistance in our effort to save the Columbia River Chinook salmon from the greedy wheelmen. It, however, did not take long to find out that he was on the other side of the fence; his action proved that he was more interested in saving the wheelmen than the salmon.

In 1908 a salmon protective measure was submitted to the voters of Oregon by initiative. It provided for the prohibition of all commercial salmon fishing in the Sandy River and in the Columbia River east of its confluence with the Sandy River. This measure carried by a majority of almost 26,000, and would have been the law had it not been for a conspiracy between the wheelmen and the State officials. Why, it seemed as if the whole State machinery from the governor down was set in motion to defeat the people. The attorney general applied to the Federal court for an injunction against a measure carried by the people, to enable them to tie up the whole salmon legislation enacted by the people until the legislature met—to have it all annulled there.

During the 1909 legislative session the destroyers of the salmon, with the governor and all his influence and all the influence that could be gathered together, managed through the manipulation in the legislature to pass a new salmon law. Its heading was, "For the protection of the Columbia River salmon industry." It should have been headed as follows, "For the benefit of the stationary fishing-appliance owners, especially the wheelmen, and for the sure destruction of the salmon industry on the Columbia River," because in that measure it provided first to, legalize "purse seines," a class of gear which is prohibited in every river in the civilized world, and in some countries not allowed within 7 miles of shore. Purse seines were prohibited in Oregon during the 1907 session. Traps and seines, with their small meshes and wheels, were allowed, just the opposite to what are allowed where salmon protection is in force. Yes, for the protection of the salmon such gear as have been condemned in every salmon river is legalized. Not satisfied with that they had to provide for more salmon for the wheelmen, as they are the ones who put up the great dinners for legislators, you see, as well as for others high up—something the fishermen could not do and would not do if they could. So to get more fish to the wheelmen the closed season had to be extended "for the protection of the salmon." So they agreed to close all fishing from March 1 to May 1; that is, no salmon can be taken during those two months, and the salmon goes up toward the spawning grounds. But they never get that far, unless there should be a freshet in the river, which, as a rule, there is not that time of the year, and the result is that Mr. Wheelman or his seines under Cilllo Falls get the full benefit of the protection provided for for the salmon. But this is not all. A weekly closed season, from Saturday 6 p. m. to Sunday 6 p. m., during the spring season, when the bulk of the salmon is supposed to be caught by gill nets, was needed, but during the fall season, when the bulk of the salmon is caught by traps, seines, and wheels, there is no closed season during the week.

The United States War Department is also doing its share through the engineer's office in Portland, Oreg., toward unrest on the Columbia River. It is against the common law, according to court decisions, to place any stationary fishing appliances where they will interfere with the common right to fish. Copy of such decisions have been filed with the engineers, and they have been asked to not issue permits for trap locations on the common drifting grounds, and to submit to this union any requests for trap locations, so it could be ascertained first whether such trap would interfere or not. But to no avail. The gill-net men have, through the traps permitted by the United States Engineers on the Columbia River, been forced from some of their best fishing grounds and now have to fish in the channels and at the mouth of the river, but that is not all; an attempt was made some years ago to drive the gill-net men from the river; charges were filed with the War Department that the gill-net men obstructed navigation. A man was sent out from Washington, D. C., to investigate, with the result that the charges fell flat, and that the complainants were found to be a party interested in traps and fish wheels and a captain in the Army who has always been found to favor the trap men, and that the vessel delayed by nets was a Government boat out with a dancing party. That was in 1907.

During season of 1911 $75,000 will not cover the loss of the gill-net men caused by the War Department planting mines outside of Fort Columbia on the gill-netters' drifting ground. This was, however, stopped, and it was agreed that there should be no more mine practice during the fishing season, and there was none last year, but this spring mines were planted on the, or rather near the, Peacock Spit, at the mouth of the river, on one of the best fishing grounds on the river as well as the most dangerous.

The commander at Fort Stevens was asked to have said mines removed before the fishing commenced, May 1, because they constituted a menace to the lives and property of the gill-net men. That was early in April, but no answer. The mines remained, the fishing season opened, and with that the ripping and tearing commenced. Complaints were filed, and when they were to remove those mines it was found out that Uncle Sam did not have the wherewith to do it; two mines were removed, but the third remained to the end of the season, and $50,000 does not cover the loss to the men on their gear alone; then, add to that the time and fish lost.

This season an order was received from the Secretary of War prohibiting fishing on a certain area of the river, because a captain of a steamboat did not have common sense enough to keep a course along the river staked out with buoys, but had to run his vessel where the nets were the thickest.

An order was promulgated by the custom department applying a certain paragraph of the pilot rules to the gill-net boats, notwithstanding the fact that such boats are not mentioned in the paragraph, but only " vessels when trawling, dredging, or fishing with any kind of drag nets or lines." This paragraph when lived up to by those who operate such gear as are mentioned in it will receive protection, but it has the opposite effect on the gill nets. And I can not understand how men with common sense could make such a rule as referred to, unless it was made to assist lantern merchants to make some money; it has surely not proven to be of any protection to the gill nets, and it has not prevented careless navigators from running down a fishing boat and sinking it, the man saving his life by getting hold of a rope's end hanging over the bow of one of the barges in tow by the steamer.

In other countries you will always find that the Governments are doing their very best to assist the fisheries and the fishermen, but not so here; here, apparently, the Government, State and Federal, is doing its best to assist special privileged parties, such as trapmen and wheelmen, although it is well known that such gear as traps and wheels will in time destroy the fisheries in any river if permitted to operate long enough, while it seems to hound the gill-net fishermen, notwithstanding the fact that gill nets are the only gear recommended by men who have made a study of the fish question.

Congressman Minor, a member of the Congressional Merchant Marine Commission, said in Seattle, Wash., on July 26, 1904: " The traps will do for you here to your salmon what they did on the Great Lakes to our white fish— practically exterminate them."

Very respectfully, yours,

H. M. LARNTSEN,
Secretary Columbia River Fishermen's Protective Union.

C. E. S. WOOD EXHIBIT.

PORTLAND, OREG., *August 22, 1914.*

To the COMMISSION ON INDUSRIAL RELATIONS:

At the suggestion of Mr. Thompson I supplement my testimony with the following:

I have had so many appeals to me from laborers from the various railroad, lumber, construction, and other camps that I am convinced an arrangement was understood between the private employment agencies and the foremen of the camps to the effect that the private agency would receive its fee from the man who would be sent to the camp and employed for a day or two and then discharged upon some pretext, making room for another to go through the same process.

In expressing my anarchistic view that the possession of land ought to depend on its beneficial use, perhaps I did not make it clear that I quite understand that the more natural evolution and the easier to accomplish is the single tax or Henry George theory of the State taking the ground rent, or so much as it needs. I want to make it plain that I appreciate that these social changes proceed in the line of least resistance, and, in my opinion, the single tax is the line of least resistance, though I think finally the time must come when human society will depend on a voluntary cooperation impelled by an intelligent self-interest. It also occurs to me to suggest, as perhaps having some practical value for the commission, that the United States could make future grants of land permanently depend upon beneficial use and possession, with no possibility of acquiring a title permitting speculation in idle land.

A friend regretted that I did not express my views on strikes and boycotts. I will therefore say here briefly that the very fundamental principle of anarchism is the absence of force by any person or power toward any peaceable person, and the securing of the utmost personal liberty by peaceable people; therefore, I believe strikes, when peaceably conducted, are only the exercise of the absolute right of free men, and the same as to boycotts. If I have a right, for any reason that pleases me, not to patronize any dealer or industry, I have the right to persuade others to do likewise, and to my mind it is utterly impossible in true theory to make wrong a thing peaceably done by a number conspiring together if that thing was right when done by an individual, and if wrong when done by single individuals, the fact that a number do it does not make it right, not even murder. In short, numbers and so-called conspiracy have nothing whatever to do with the inherent right or wrong of a thing.

Yours, very truly,

C. E. S. WOOD.

The commission also will be doing good work if it can produce a popular understanding that "free speech" means the right to freely express an opinion on any subject whatever, the speaker being held personally responsible for his utterances—slanderous or riotous—but that no subject is sacred from discussion. The Government, the flag, God—where sacredness begins and the right to speak is qualified or permission must be asked free speech is at an end.

I have had an interminable and most disagreeable practice in legally fighting in the police courts for men arrested under all manner of pretexts—usually "obstructing the streets," false in fact; or "violence to an officer," false. The real crime being they were "preaching unrest."

C. E. S. W.

TAIT EXHIBIT.

Troy Laundry Co. report of employees week ended May 9, 1914.

Name.	Sex.	How paid.	Hours worked.	Wages.	Duties.
M. E. Howatson	Female	Weekly	54	$20.00	Office.
F. Elling	do	do	54	13.50	Do.
M. Howerton	do	do	54	10.00	Do.
C. V. Bauman	do	do	54	15.00	Do.
M. H. Becker	do	do	54	17.50	Do.
Ella Bowe	do	do	54	12.00	Do.
E. Peterson	do	do	54	13.50	Do.
R. Peage	do	do	54	15.00	Do.
G. Howerton	Male	do	52	20.00	Do.
Arthur Ball	do	do	52	30.00	Foreman, distributing room.
J. Martin	do	do	52	17.00	Marking and distributing.
J. Clary	do	do	52	18.00	Do.
Mrs. Patterson	Female	do	52	12.00	Do.
M. Frenna	do	do	52	12.00	Do.
W. Wint	Male	do	52	20.00	Do.
Mrs. Applegate	Female	do	52	15.00	Do.
C. Hattery	Male	do	52	16.50	Do.
R. Brower	do	do	52	20.00	Do.
A. Andrich	Female	do	52	15.00	Do.
B. Aldrich	do	do	52	10.00	Do.
Nora Casey	do	do	45	13.00	Rough-dry marking and distributing.
F. Fessler	do	do	43½	10.70	Do.
K. Maher	do	do	45	9.00	Do.
M. Miller	do	do	45	10.00	Do.
P. Metzger	Male	do	53½	35.00	Foreman, lower floor.
A. Hiersche	do	do	51	16.50	Rough-dry washer.
G. S. Casey	do	do	50½	18.00	Washer.
F. Hiersche	do	do	52	18.00	Do.
C. Chase	do	do	49½	15.00	Sorter.
D. Steigler	do	do	52½	10.00	Elevator boy.
O. Natemier	do	do	52	15.00	Wringer man.
N. W. Olsee	do	do	51½	16.50	Washer.
O. McBee	do	do	50	13.50	Wringer man.
R. Franklin	do	do	49½	15.10	Hand washer.
Mrs. Kavanaugh	Female	16⅔ cents; by hour	43½	7.50	Do.
R. Sanders	Male	Weekly	52	15.00	Mangle checker.
H. Burns	do	do	52	15.00	Mangle counter.
J. Slowick	do	do	51½	12.00	Mangle department.
A. Gerolo	Female	14 cents; by hour	50	6.95	Mangle shaker.
R. Smith	do	16⅔ cents; by hour	50½	8.40	Mangle stacker.
M. Jacoby	do	14 cents; by hour	50	6.95	Mangle shaker.
A. Knox	do	15⅓ cents; by hour	47½	7.30	Mangle stacker.
E. Lenhardt	do	14 cents; by hour	50	6.95	Mangle side feeder.
R. Donovan	do	15⅓ cents; by hour	50½	7.75	Mangle shaker.
L. Stark	do	16⅔ cents; by hour	50½	8.40	Mangle folder.
L. Archer	do	15⅓ cents; by hour	47½	7.30	Do.
L. Dyer	do	do	47½	7.30	Mangle stacker.
M. Feigler	do	do	50½	7.75	Mangle folder.
S. Donovan	do	16⅔ cents; by hour	50½	8.40	Mangle feeder.
L. Webber	do	14 cents; by hour	47½	6.60	Mangle shaker.
L. Halgen	do	16⅔ cents; by hour	47½	7.90	Mangle feeder.
J. Meyer	do	14 cents; by hour	27	3.75	Do.
E. Schumock	do	16⅔ cents; by hour	47½	7.90	Mangle folder.
Ellen Bachman	do	18⅓ cents; by hour	47½	8.70	Mangle feeder.
Elin Bachman	do	15⅓ cents; by hour	47½	7.30	Mangle folder.
D. Klatt	do	do	50½	7.75	Mangle shaker.
L. Webber	do	14 cents; by hour	27	3.75	Do.
L. Wilger	do	16⅔ cents; by hour	47½	7.90	Mangle feeder.
M. Marquardt	do	15⅜ cents; by hour	47½	7.30	Mangle folder.

Troy Laundry Co. report of employees week ended May 9, 1914—Continued.

Name.	Sex.	How paid.	Hours worked.	Wages.	Duties.
P. E. Golden	Male	Weekly	54	$35.00	Foreman, upper floor.
Geo. Hodel	do	do	52	20.00	Foreman, shirt department.
F. Atwood	Female	do	53½	9.00	Starch ladies' clothes.
E. Parenti	do	Piecework	42½	10.30	Starch shirtbands and cuffs.
T. Davis	do	do	47	8.70	Starch shirt bosoms.
B. Hanson	do	Weekly	51	12.00	Rough-dry starch ladies' clothes.
Mrs. Bershauer	do	16⅔ cents; by hour.	48½	8.10	Starch collars.
A. Singer	do	15⅓ cents; by hour.	52	7.95	Rough-dry starch room.
Mrs. Dennemin	do	16⅔ cents; by hour.	52	8.10	Starch collars.
L. Krause	do	20 cents; by hour.	48½	9.70	Collar finishing.
A. Boesch	do	16⅔ cents; by hour.	52	8.65	Do.
Mrs. Pruka	do	15⅓ cents; by hour.	46½	6.45	Do.
Mrs. Melvin	do	Piecework	47½	7.05	Shirt finisher.
J. Mapes	do	do	48	12.85	Do.
T. Peterson	do	do	48	10.85	Shirt sleeves.
M. Facino	do	do	48	11.00	Shirt press.
F. Facino	do	do	48	10.30	Shirt sleeves.
Mrs. Yost	do	do	47½	11.15	Neckband and yokes.
C. Hanson	do	do	48	9.35	Neckband press.
J. Boyer	do	do	48	9.80	Neckband folder.
A. De Witt	do	do	48	11.50	Bodies and sleeves.
B. Gagen	do	do	44	7.75	Do.
M. Gardner	do	14 cents; by hour.	45	6.25	Shirt dampener.
Mrs. Bolton	do	Weekly	51	9.00	Seamstress.
M. Zanella	do	15⅓ cents; by hour.	52	7.95	Body ironer finisher.
Mrs. Prior	do	16⅔ cents; by hour.	52	8.65	Do.
M. Reese	do	do	51	8.50	Underwear and socks department.
E. Voss	do	15⅓ cents; by hour.	47	7.20	Do.
L. Facino	do	18⅓ cents; by hour.	51	9.45	Handkerchief mangle.
M. Rutto	do	16⅔ cents; by hour.	50½	8.40	Do.
M. McBeath	do	Weekly	52	13.50	Forelady, ladies' clothes.
Mrs. Gresham	do	16⅔ cents; by hour.	46½	7.75	Seamstress, ladies' clothes.
Mrs. Albrecht	do	15⅓ cents; by hour.	48½	7.45	Hand ironing.
C. Boesch	do	16⅔ cents; by hour.	48½	8.10	Lace curtains.
L. Tucholke	do	Piecework	48	11.85	Ladies' clothes ironing.
A. Tucholke	do	do	48	12.10	Do.
Miss Ross	do	do	45	7.85	Do.
B. Sells	do	do	48	10.65	Ironer.
Mrs. Scott	do	do	13½	1.55	Do.
Mrs. Peters	do	do	18	2.45	Do.
A. Harju	do	16⅔ cents; by hour.	51½	8.60	Body ironer.
R. Erickson	do	15⅓ cents; by hour.	50½	7.75	Do.
E. E. Hammell	Male	Weekly	54	22.50	Engineer.
C. E. Gerguson	do	do	54	21.00	Do.
A. P. Condray	do	do	60	16.00	Watchman.
E. B. Howerton	do	do	60	15.00	Do.
H. Johnson	do	do		18.00	Hostler.
F. S. Dimmitt	do	do		15.00	Do.
E. R. Hall	do			[1] 12.00	Driver.
F. P. Brown	do			[1] 12.00	Do.
C. F. Williamson	do			[1] 12.00	Do.
G. W. Fultz	do			[1] 12.00	Do.
George Callahan	do			[1] 12.00	Do.
J. C. Fox	do			[1] 12.00	Do.
A. Rosenthal	do			[1] 12.00	Do.
E. D. Watson	do			[1] 12.00	Do.
W. J. Loeber	do	do		15.00	Do.
H. Heise	do	do		[1] 12.00	Do.
C. B. Lance	do			[1] 12.00	Do.
T. V. Harnden	do			[1] 12.00	Do.
C. W. Lyons	do			[1] 12.00	Do.
C. T. Hale	do	do		23.10	Do.
E. Touhey	do			[1] 12.00	Do.
J. Hohman	do			[1] 12.00	Do.
C. Westervelt	do			[1] 12.00	Do.
N. T. Powell	do			[1] 12.00	Do.
W. Gardiner	do			[1] 12.00	Do.
E. Hopkins	do			[1] 12.00	Do.

[1] And 5 per cent.

ED SHOP CONTROVERSY
OCKTON, CAL.

this subject, see pages 4904 to 4909.)

4771

COMMISSION ON INDUSTRIAL RELATIONS.

SAN FRANCISCO, CAL., *Tuesday, August 25, 1914—10 a. m.*
Present: Chairman Walsh, Commissioners Lennon, O'Connell, Garretson, O'Connell, and Weinstock; also W. O. Thompson, counsel.
Chairman WALSH. You may proceed now. The witnesses are here.
Mr. THOMPSON. Mr. Irish.
Commissioner WEINSTOCK. Mr. Irish is here. He was in here a moment ago. He must be outside somewhere now.

TESTIMONY OF MR. JOHN P. IRISH, JR.

Mr. THOMPSON. Please give us your name.
Mr. IRISH. John P. Irish, jr.
Mr. THOMPSON. And your address?
Mr. IRISH. Stockton Chamber of Commerce.
Mr. THOMPSON. And your occupation?
Mr. IRISH. I am secretary of the Stockton Chamber of Commerce.
Mr. THOMPSON. How long have you been secretary of the Stockton Chamber of Commerce?
Mr. IRISH. With your permission—it was my understanding—I do not know how many of these formal questions are necessary; but it was my understanding I was to be permitted to make an uninterrupted statement.
Chairman WALSH. Just answer the questions, please, until we get to that, Mr Irish.
Mr. IRISH. Yes; surely. I beg pardon.
Mr. THOMPSON. Just laying the foundation to establish who you are.
Chairman WALSH. Go ahead and ask him the questions.
Mr. IRISH. What was the last question?
Mr. THOMPSON. How long have you been secretary of the Stockton Chamber of Commerce?
Mr. IRISH. A year and three months.
Mr. THOMPSON. Prior to that, were you engaged in business in Stockton or on the coast?
Mr. IRISH. Prior to that time I was connected with the United States Department of Agriculture, and had my residence in Stockton in connection with that work.
Mr. THOMPSON. For how long a time?
Mr. ITISH. A period of two years.
Mr. THOMPSON. Two years?
Mr. IRISH. Three years.
Mr. THOMPSON. How long have you been a resident on the coast here?
Mr. IRISH. All my life.
Mr. THOMPSON. All your life?
Mr. IRISH. Yes, sir.
Mr. THOMPSON. Now, Mr. Irish, you may go ahead and tell the story of conditions industrially at Stockton as you understand them.
Chairman WALSH. Say, first, I think the commission would like to hear about the organization, the aims and objects, and the length of time it has been in existence, etc.
Mr. IRISH. With your permission, I will reach that in the regular course of the——
Chairman WALSH. Well, would it disturb you too much just to state it now? We are trying to get this logically, as we have at other hearings.
Mr. IRISH. The length of time that the organization has been in effect?

4773

Chairman WALSH. The aims, objects, and the length of time of its being.

Mr. IRISH. The organization has been in being for a period of a year. Its aims and objects I would prefer to file with you rather than to attempt to state myself. They have been very concisely drawn up.

Chairman WALSH. Have you them with you?

Mr. IRISH. Col. Weinstock has them. No; I don't think I have. With your permission I will read them. I don't want to let my memory transgress the written record; that is all. [Reading:]

"This association is formed to protect the industrial interests of Stockton and general territory; to establish equitable industrial conditions for employers, employees, and the general public; to prevent and avert industrial disturbances; to harmonize differences between employers and employees with justice to all concerned, and to assist in the enforcement of the laws of the land; to oppose restriction of output, sympathetic strikes, lockouts, boycotts, and illegal persecutions of individuals, all of which are a menace to the industrial progress of our community and our country, and tend to the undermining of constitutional rights; to secure for employers and employees the freedom of individual contract in the matter of employment, and to insure everyone in his right to earn a living, regardless of his membership or nonmembership in any organization; to prevent any interference with persons seeking through honest effort and work to earn a living; to protect everyone in his lawful right to conduct his business or affairs as he deems proper so long as he does not encroach on the rights of others."

We have pledged ourselves to stand firmly for the open shop and to lend our united and individual support without reservation to the maintenance of the same. We understand the open shop to mean the exclusion of the use of the union label, the union stamp, and union display card from our places of business and our products, and the elimination of the signing of other agreements between our members and labor organizations. We have guaranteed our hearty support in all honorable ways to the members of the association and officers and committee in the handling of all labor controversies. We are unalterably opposed to low wages, long hours, and insanitary conditions.

Chairman WALSH. You may proceed with your statement.

Mr. IRISH. That covers it at this point fully, as I understand it.

Chairman WALSH. Proceed with your statement, then.

Mr. IRISH. As I understand it, the matter the commission is interested in is, the causes which led up to the present situation in the city of Stockton. Those causes are of somewhat long duration. I don't propose to multiply instances, but with your permission, to file the matter under the three most prominent heads and to cite at least one instance in each case to prove my point.

Now, the matter seems to put itself in this way: First, as to the attitude of organized labor in the city of Stockton toward the business interests of the employers, and as to that I will cite you one single instance in the case of the five-and-a-half-day week with six days' pay. This is a stipulation which has been enforced against the planing mills in the city of Stockton as well as against the carpenters and others engaged in building-trade lines. At the time that this was put into effect in Stockton there was no objection on the part of the contractors particularly—any of the building contractors. The objection came from the planing mills because they were shipping goods into competitive territory with San Francisco and that zone lying between San Francisco and Oakland, and Stockton. Their protest was voiced in this way. They said they had no objection to the installation of this rule if it was enforced equally against competitors who were operating under closed-shop conditions. In other words, they wished, if this thing was to be enforced, that it be enforced against all men selling goods in the competitive territory in order that they might not be put to a disadvantage in the competition.

The answer they received was that it didn't make any difference whether it was enforced in San Francisco or Oakland or not; it was going to be enforced in Stockton. The fact was that for a considerable part of the time after the Stockton Planing Mills—under the closed shop Stockton Planing Mills have been operating to disadvantage with competitors in the same territory and under the same labor jurisdiction. The effect of that has been to hamper, cripple, and increase materially the cost of output and put them materially to disadvantage with competitors. I might cite instance after instance of that sort. If the commission desires, we are perfectly willing to file other instances, but I am not going to cite them at this time.

Chairman WALSH. Perhaps you might suggest two or three more.

Mr. IRISH. I prefer not to do that, because if I do there are so many instances that we will have to multiply, and we might file them with the commission, if you so desire.

Chairman WALSH. Probably you better give two or three more.

Mr. IRISH. Let me cite another instance along the same line. The electrical workers' union of the city of Stockton is composed approximately of 47 members, if I am not mistaken, nearly half of whom are in the employ of one electrical contractor.

Some time ago—some three years ago, I believe; but I am not quite sure as to dates; it can be made a matter of record if you will—there was a question as to hours and wages raised between the carpenter contractors and their employees and the electrical contractors and their employees. The demand of the men was for an increase in the scale of the carpenters from $4 to $4.80; for an increase in the scale on the part of the electrical workers from $4 to four dollars and a half. These demands, after some little trouble, were granted.

Immediately subsequent to the granting one of the electrical contractors in town bid on a $27,000 job in the city of Stockton, and he bid on the basis of the new scale. The day after his bid was accepted and his bond was posted he was informed that the electrical workers' union had made another increase in the scale from four dollars and a half to $5 a day, which he would have to pay. He told the business agent that he had made his bid and filed his bond on the assumption that the scale was still in effect; that he had had no notice. But they said, " It does not make any difference; you will have to pay the scale." He said, " Can't you show me some way out of this? " They said, " No; the scale is on; it will have to be paid." The net result was that, by his own statement, on a $27,000 job, his increase amounted to $2,700—$2,900—a little over 10 per cent. Ordinarily you figure—I don't know just how some contractors figure their profit; but I take it 10 per cent is a fair profit. In this case, then, if the profit be 10 per cent, he forfeited his profit and paid $200 for the privilege and pleasure of affording his men an opportunity to work. Now, that is a citation along the same general lines. So much for that phase of it. As to the relationship or attitude of the union——

Chairman WALSH. Will that give us a fairly good view of those things which seem to make it impossible to exist under those conditions? Does that give a pretty fair idea?

Mr. IRISH. That gives a pretty fair view.

Chairman WALSH. Will you cite any other instances?

Mr. IRISH. I do not think it is necessary, because that concerns both the attitude of the union toward the interest of the employer on the job and toward the interest of the employer in the distribution of his fabricated product over the territory in which he deals, if you please, which I think covers.

Chairman WALSH. That satisfies you?

Mr. IRISH. That satisfies me as a broad enough statement to cover that phase of the condition, if you please. Now, as to the attitude of organized labor toward the relationship between the employer and the men with whom he does business. Again I might multiply instances, but I will cite one in point, which, I think, fairly covers that phase of the situation. Again with the electrical workers' union. I am not citing or singling them out particularly, because they are no better or no worse than the rest of them, but simply because the incident occurs to my mind. In the electrical workers' union, an employing electrical contractor needed two more men on a certain job. In order to secure these men, as he was under the closed shop, he went to the business agent and said: " I want two more men." He said that he could get two men, and gave him their names. He said, " I don't want those two men; I won't employ them, because I have twice discharged one of them for failing to give me a day's work for a day's pay—for malingering on the job; and the other man I hired to do some inside wiring in a house that was already in occupancy—some repair work—and when he went down to work the lady of the house was alone, and he asked for a drink of water. She told him that he could find all the water he wanted in the refrigerator, where it was cool, on ice. He went to the refrigerator, and the man who kept the house was of a convivial habit, and he found a bottle of whisky also in the refrigerator, and he yielded to the temptation lots of us have yielded to, and he proceeded to consume that bottle of whisky, with the result that he got disgustingly drunk on the job, frightened the lady of the house nearly to death, messed the wiring all up, and generally made hash of things.

With the net result that the next morning the man who had employed his employer to do that job came down to the office and made things mighty unpleasant, with the net result that the man was discharged, as I think he should have been. Now, very naturally that contractor doing the work in the houses of various people about town did not desire to have a man of that type in his employ and he told them so. And they said, "Well, they are all the men that we have got available at this time." So the man said, "Well, I will send out of town." And they said, "You can try it if you wish." He sent out of town and brought two electrical workers up there, both union men, both with union cards; got them from San Francisco or Oakland, I am not sure which at this time. And they were met by the business agent and told that two brother electricians in town were out of work and that no outside workers naturally could be allowed to come in until those two members in good standing had work. The result was he was forced to drag along that job and make excuses and that sort of thing, because he could not get the men to do the work.

Now, one step further, the attitude of the labor organizations in Stockton as it has exemplified itself toward the relation existing between employer and employee, and this, gentlemen, really is the most important phase of the situation as it affects us in some ways: The Sperry Flour Co., operating on the same basis that every flour company on the coast is operating, were approached by the unions and told that their five engineers must join the union. The Sperry Flour Co. told them that they had no objection to the men joining the union, if they so desired, and they were perfectly willing to call them in the office and tell them so, and they meant it. The union said that they had been endeavoring for a considerable length of time to get these men to join the union and they had refused to do so, and that they must join the union or the Sperry Flour Co. would be boycotted. The Sperry Flour Co. said, "We have nothing to do with the affiliations of these men. If they choose to join a labor organization they are perfectly free to do so. We put no stone in their path if they do join, nor will we compel them to join." The labor organizations met and declared a boycott on the Sperry Flour Co., placed a picket in front of their place, and put a State-wide boycott in effect against the Sperry Flour Co.

Now, it was apparently a matter of indifference to organized labor that these men were working the hours, were receiving the scale, and in some instances better than the scale, were working under better conditions than were demanded as a fundamental by the unions, and were perfectly satisfied with their work. It was a matter of indifference to the unions that those men were perfectly satisfactory to their employers. They demanded the signature of an agreement under which the Sperry Flour Co. would not employ anyone but union men, and the Sperry Flour Co. refused to discharge those men for refusing to join the union, and therefore were boycotted. Now, all this leads up—and pardon me for trespassing on your time, all this leads up to the underlying conditions which led to the formation of our organization. It came to this—these conditions came to a crux with the boycott on the Sperry Flour Co. Now, not in a professional way at all, but merely for your information, let me say this, that the principal industries in the city of Stockton are its flour mills, its machine shops, its warehouses, and its various distributing and jobbing plants. The two largest pay rolls in the city of Stockton are paid by the Holt Manufacturing Co. and the Sperry Flour Co. Conditions at the time this boycott was levied by the unions against the Sperry Flour Co. had become such that the larger employers of labor were reaching that point where they refused further to be put under the unfair domination that they had been under, and where the Holt Manufacturing Co., which was not operating a union shop, was practically in a mood to decide that they would go elsewhere, where they were not subject to the continuous attack that they were subjected to in the city of Stockton. In other words, the continuance of this method and policy which I have attempted very briefly to outline to you, meant the withdrawal ultimately, and perhaps immediately, from the city of Stockton of two of its most important industries, upon which an enormous number of subsidiary companies depended.

For instance, with the Holt Manufacturing Co., a great deal of their casting was done by small, independent foundrymen of the city of Stockton, who depended very largely on them for a livelihood. The same matter to a degree applied to the other small manufacturing plants in town. The building contractors and erectors depended indirectly on the continuance of the Sperry pay roll and the expenditure of that money by the men. Their removal from town meant a very heavy drop in the building contracting business. The building contractors themselves were not altogether satisfied with conditions—none of us were—but the underlying and contributing cause to the formation of the organization was not only our exemption from unfair exactions, not only the restoration to us of the power to have some liberty and latitude in the type of men that we hired, but our relationship to them; and fundamentally, and under all that, it was the perpetuity and growth of the city in which we live. Now, I will go just one step further and then I will come at the formation of the organization which you asked for. One of our principal objections, which I have not touched on, to the continuance of this condition in the city of Stockton, lay in the fact that whenever any question arose between employer and employee and was carried to the local union, and there was a question of some little difficulty of coming to an agreement, we were immediately met with the condition of outside men, who had no interest in the city and no stake in the city—not property owners, not taxpayers—to whom the growth and prosperity of the city meant nothing; they were brought in to settle the dispute and the matter taken out of the jurisdiction of the local union, which left us in the position of being under alien judges and under their thumb. It was a condition which rapidly became insupportable. So, following the Sperry trouble, came a dispute with the bartenders over at the Hotel Stockton—not with the bartenders, but with the bartenders' union. They had always operated as an open-shop plant. The bartenders, of their own volition—they were all good men in their trade and could have gone elsewhere and gotten positions; some of them were recruited from first-class hotels in other places and would have had no difficulty in going elsewhere and getting a position. They were working seven days a week and under conditions which gave them time off when they wanted it, and they were satisfied to remain under that condition.

One of the bartenders was discharged for cause, after a dispute with other bartenders at the bar, and as a result—not, I think, to spite Mr. Wagner, the proprietor, but for the purpose of venting his ire against the other bartenders with whom he had quarreled—of course this is all surmise on my part, but I think the circumstances bear me out—this bartender went and complained to the union that these men were working more than the union hours per week. The demand was made of Wagner that he force them to work union hours or discharge them, which he refused to do. The natural result was that the Hotel Stockton, which had been built by popular subscription in order to get a first-class hotel in the city of Stockton—a hotel in which we not only had a pride but in which a great many of the citizens had an interest, large or small—was boycotted, and that took this phase: They had a black banner with a yellow rat on it, and they had one man constantly parading up and down the curbstone in front of the main entrance to the hotel. Whenever a bus arrived from the train—at that time all the tourists came to the Stockton Hotel, because it was the first-class hotel in town—they were confronted with the banner; they always had two men there then, who walked back and forth in front of the bus in order to disturb the passengers to the hotel.

Not from the standpoint of Mr. Wagner or the standpoint of the hotel that we felt this thing was an outrage, but it put our city in a very unfavorable light to incoming men who might or might not be prospective investors or settlers. They picketed the bus at the depot; they applied at time vile epithets to the men and women for getting into the bus and going up to what they called "a scab hotel." This wasn't pleasant. It wasn't conducive to our pride in our city or conducive to a favorable attitude on the part of the stranger coming in, the use of those two banners. The Sperry boycott and the trouble at the Stockton—from these came the inception and formation of the organization which has been formed since, the merchants, manufacturers, and employers' association. It was not formed by an imported outside agitator. I say that for your information and I know, because I was present at every meeting that led to its formation. It was formed by citizens and employers of the city of Stockton. Its constitution and by-laws were adopted and platform and principles were outlined before we even had a paid man to take general directory charge of the detail work in the organization, and ultimately when the organization came along we brought in Mr. Calkins, of Sacramento, an old newspaper man, and a man of reputation, who had a standing as being able to talk intelligently and present matters in an intelligent way. We brought him to assist us in the detail work of the organization. As to our platform, as to our principles and by-laws and organization, they were formed and have been carried on without exception by the citizens, property owners, taxpayers, and employers of the city of Stockton. Now, so much for our organization. Do you want me to talk on further? And with your permission I am not going beyond the 8th of July.

Commissioner COMMONS. May I ask a question?

Mr. IRISH. Surely.

Commissioner COMMONS. Is there a chamber of commerce and also an employers' association?

Mr. IRISH. There are both. The merchants, manufacturers, and employers' association—let me explain just a minute. The chamber of commerce was organized some seven or eight years ago, coming out of the old county board of trade. The merchants, manufacturers, and employers' association is an entirely separate organization, formed for a separate purpose, and with, to a degree, a separate object in view. It is a protective association of employers. It has no direct or indirect connection with the chamber of commerce. · It happens as a matter of coincidence that I am both secretary of the chamber of commerce and a director of the merchants, manufacturers, and employers' association, but that is merely a tribute to the bad judgment of a lot of people and has no significance beyond that fact.

Things went along very peacefully, fairly peacefully, until this spring when the new contract—the new agreement—came up to be signed between the retail clothiers' association and shoe men and the clerks' union. Conditions had not been altogether satsifactory, although in that case as in all the others, no question of hours and wages were involved, and no sanitary conditions. It was merely restricted shop rules and that sort of thing. The same general condition I have outlined to you, more the attitude of mind than anything else. The clerks' union was orginially formed through coercion and duress on the part of the employers upon the employees at the instance of organized labor. That may seem complicated, but I can't simplify it. That this is true is shown by the fact that in most instances it was absolutely necessary that the employer collect the dues and turn them over to the union, because if they didn't do that, the clerks got behind in their dues and were fined. The most of the men and women had no heart in the organization.

The new agreement came up to be signed, and the retail clothiers and shoe men got together themselves, as is our method, and decided that they didn't want to sign a new agreement with the union, following out the line of this agreement and this declaration of principles. They came to us and we told them they were entirely justified in this stand, if the chose to take it, and we would protect them in it so far as our organization could. So they refused to sign the agreement. Well, nothing much was done at that time and for a day or two; then the business agent came around and removed the union display card. I don't know that I need to amplify all that, you all know what it is. It is a card which is displayed in the windo which says, "This is a union shop." Mind you, they were still operating under closed-shop conditions and with nothing but union men; no difference as to hours or wages; no difference in the scale of working conditions, but they had refused to sign an agreement. So that the cards were removed and they assented to that removal. A good many of them had not had them ond on display for some time and said they didn't care whether they were removed or not; they were perfectly willing that they should be removed.

About two weeks after that they came back and demanded the cards be replaced. Again the clothiers decided they did not want to replace, and came to us and said they did not want to put the cards back, and asked if we would protect them if they were not replaced. We said we would. So then they told the clerks' union that as they had taken the cards away of their own volition they could keep them. Then we received—that is, the shoe men and dry goods men in town, clothiers, received a communication from various unions to the effect that unless—that a fine had been levied against their members for patronizing these stores and that that fine would stand until the stores took back the union cards and signed the agreement, and became fair, I believe, was the term that they used.

We were confronted, then, with this condition: Here are a lot of men who are receiving salaries as clerks in the stores, who through the conduct, their union had demanded, or the other unions demanded that they don't sell their employers' goods to them. And we even had one case where a man came in a store and a clerk who was there, who was not looking out for his employer, said, "What are you doing here? You can't patronize this store. It is unfair." The man said he had forgotten it, and turned around and walked out. You can yourself see it is rather an anomalous condition for an employer to be in, and one that can't continue long.

Commissioner O'CONNELL. Have you got the name of that party?

Mr.·IRISH. I can get it for you; yes.

Commissioner O'CONNELL. And furnish it to us this afternoon?

Mr. IRISH. I am afraid I can not do it as soon as that; no.

Commissioner O'CONNELL. To-morrow morning?

Mr. IRISH. I might possibly be able to do it by then. I can not give you any definite time. I can give you the name. Then, while this condition was still going on, while these boycotts were still being levied, while the pickets were being placed in front of the stores—and, by the way, that is an amusing thing; men were placed in front of these various stores with red tags on and they walked up and down in front of the stores trying to get people not to go into them, and there were some stores still operating under a signed agreement. They told the members of our organization—some of them were not members of our organization, two of them were, three, I think, I have forgotten exactly; one shoe store, I believe, at that time—they handed these cards, "Don't patronize" or "Do patronize" on them. Well, the men walked up and down the side walk and gave them away and very often would tell a man not to go in that store, that place was unfair. I know that is true because it was done to me once by a man who did not happen to know me. As a rule, they knew me and did not bother me.

While all this was going on there began the same trouble with the cooks and waiters' union, who demanded the signing of two new agreements on the part of the restaurant keepers' association in Stockton. And that new agreement provided among other things—in this sense it is significant—it provided among other things that in all cases, with every place that sold cooked food, and therefore was eligible to have men there unionized, that a janitor should be employed for the purpose of cleaning up the tables, replacing the sugar in the sugar bowls, and all that sort of thing. And you gentlemen know, and anybody knows, that in a first-class hotel where the time of the waiter is completely occupied that is all right; but the spectacle in a lunch room of a separate man taking the goods away from the table, the dirty plates away from the table, and the glasses of water, and all that sort of thing which goes a good ways toward cutting down the profits of the merchant, was perfectly absurd and inane.

Well, the restaurant keepers' association declined to sign the agreement. They came to us and told us they were going to decline to sign the agreement, and we said we would back them. We backed them. And they were boycotted, their cards were withdrawn, and the pickets walked up and down in front of their places. And the same condition obtained there that obtained in the retail clerks, except that the men walked out immediately.

The net result in the clerks' union was that most of the men sent in their union cards, resigned from the union, and the employer took the stand he could not employ men who were working against his interests, and he told them in advance. So they sent their cards back and very few of the clerks, so far as I know, left the employ.

The cooks and waiters walked out in a body just about 12 o'clock in order that they would place the greatest possible burden on the employer in replacing them. We were able to replace the men and go on with the work. So here were two sets of members of our association who were being boycotted by all of the unions in town. We made every honorable effort· to avoid drawing anybody else into this controversy. We did not want trouble. Our motto was defense and not defiance. We were not in the attitude of precipitating trouble all down the line, but we proposed to meet conditions as they came; not to force them. We had a committee at one of the meetings with the building-trades council—that is, they had a consultation with one of the members of the building-trades council—and he suggested to this committee, which was composed of millmen and lumbermen and contractors that we talk with the employees, and the building trades said, "We don't want to be drawn into this." Our committee said, "We don't see any necessity that you should be drawn into this, because your people are boycotting these stores, and we would not mind if you put a boycott if you advise your men not to trade, but when you put a fine on them you are exercising unfair coercion over those men in keeping them away from the stores. If you will simply say that they are unfair and let them patronize or not as they like, you can keep the boycott and let it stop right there, but don't levy a fine."

Now, we wanted to talk to the building-trades people. Well,·they arranged for the thing, and when we came both members of the building-trades council and members of the Centrla Labor Council came, which, of course, made it impossible to discuss the matter between the two, employers and employees, and nothing came of it. One of the men I believe said he would sooner see his men lying dead in the open street than operating under open-shop conditions. Of course that was a statement that came out in heat. I do not quote it as being the calm judgment of that man perhaps, but it simply shows the attitude in which they went into the conference.

Mr. McLaughlin and Mr. Tracy came up—Tracy was president of the typographical union at San Francisco, I believe, and McLaughlin State labor commissioner and formerly connected with the teamsters' organization here. They came and they wanted to know if there was any way in which trouble could be avoided. I was present at that conference, and we told them at that time that we were not seeking trouble; that it was our last desire to start any turmoil; on the other hand, we would not abandon our principle or discuss ‚the objects which by that abandonment would be done, and we suggested this to them—at that time we were very conciliatory—we said there was just one fundamental thing we stood on here, and that was the situation in which—this, gentleman, is really the fundamental—the situation in which a lot of employers were being coerced into forcing men into organizations against their will, and that that was one thing we would not assent to.

We would not permit—in that sense we would give any man all of our assistance to prevent that condition coming about if he chose to fight it. That was one question that there was no question of arbitration and mediation on at all. Mr. Tracy—and we drew that up in the form of a letter, and we asked them to write us a letter. We said, "If you can get the building trades to get out of this and get this thing cleaned up on that basis, why there won't be any trouble." And they said they thought it could be arranged and that they would call a meeting the following Sunday. Well, they told us at that·time that all of their·men were—pardon me, they told me that all of their men were within convenient reach except the men down at Los Angeles and that they could get them by telephoning and get the men together on Sunday. I believe this was on Thursday, if I am not mistaken. So we agreed that before taking any further steps, as we wanted to avoid trouble, we would wait. We waited until Sunday, and we heard nothing. We waited until Monday, and we heard nothing. And finally we got word from them that it had been impossible owing to the distance over which their men were scattered to get together. Well, we had been confronted with that thing right straight along for months, and we were satisfied it was not so. And to be perfectly frank, we felt it was merely a play for time. So we called our people together and we made a declaration for open shop in consonance with the principles that were outlined and which I have read you. And the next morning, which was the 8th of July, that was read in every shop. Notice was served on the men that hereafter that plant would be operated under the open-shop conditions.

Now, that brings it down to July 8, gentlemen, and with your permission, gentlemen, we will leave it right there. Now, if there is any question that will tend to enlighten you further that I can answer, I would be very glad to.

Chairman WALSH (addressing Mr. Thompson). You are not through yet?

Mr. THOMPSON. I am not quite through yet.

In that part of your aims and objects where you say that you are against the signing of any agreement with any organization or union, would you state to us the reasoning or basis upon which you came to that conclusion? Is that a temporary or it is a permanent view?

Mr. IRISH. That is just as permanent as anything else in that‚statement,‚and it has its basis in the matters which I have already outlined to you in my preliminary statement. Those are the reasons. There is no use going over them again.

Mr. THOMPSON. That is all you have to ˙say on the subject of collective bargaining, I take it?

Mr. IRISH. I have this to say, that—that, as I said before, that we did not propose to sign an agreement with people which places us in‚a position ˙that when a matter comes up for discussion it is not discussed between ourselves and our employees, it is not even discussed between ourselves and the local members of the organization to which our employees belong, but in the ultimate it falls in the hands of irresponsible outsiders who have no interest in the perpetuity and growth of our city. Now, that is the reason, flatly.

Mr. THOMPSON. Now, I would like you to state, so we can have it definitely—in the category of irresponsible outsiders, whom do you include?

Mr. IRISH. I include those people not residents of Stockton, not citizens of Stockton, not taxpayers in Stockton; men who have no interest in the city, who come there to settle these disputes. I think that is full enough.

Mr. THOMPSON. Well, that is to say, perhaps I can put it a little bit more definitely.

Mr. IRISH. If you please, I would prefer to make my own statements.

Mr. THOMPSON. Well, I will put the question to you.

Mr. IRISH. Very well.

Mr. THOMPSON. And you can do as you please about it. Do the representatives of organized labor or of unions, State officials, for instance, or the officials of the international unions, which spread across the country, come within the class of objectionable people?

Mr. IRISH. Did I say objectionable people? Now, just kindly amplify that statement, because if I am going on record I want to go on record correctly, if you please.

Mr. THOMPSON. Well, so we won't have any quarrel about words, taking such a phrase and such language as you used, would the State representatives of unions and the representatives of the international unions come within the designation which you gave?

Mr. IRISH. They would come within that designation. And with your permission I will amplify that just a little bit. They would come within that designation in the sense that they were irresponsible as to our Stockton conditions. They are not local men and they have no local interest there, and in that sense they are irresponsible. Now, just one more thing as to the signing of agreements: Remember this, that the demand is always made in any agreement that is signed that none but union men shall be employed, and that if nonunion men are employed they shall at their earliest opportunity join the union. That is another reason why we won't sign an agreement, but that is only one of them.

Mr. THOMPSON. Well, I would simply ask you for the time being, at least, to answer the definite questions that I put to you. I am perfectly willing you should make any explanation after that, if you please.

Mr. IRISH. I have answered that, I think. I think the record will show that I have.

Mr. THOMPSON. Now, is your organization affiliated or does it have any understanding of any kind or character with any other body of employers in this State?

Mr. IRISH. With your permission, I have stated the method of our organization. I have stated how our organization came about and what it stands for, and I will answer no further questions along that line. That is a matter which does not concern you, sir.

Mr. THOMPSON. Well, then, for the purpose, Mr. Irish, of making a record here in regard to questions or facts which, perhaps, the commission would care to hear about, I will ask you some further questions, and you can let your present answer stand, if you please, as to them. Is there a State employers' association in this State?

Mr. IRISH. That is a matter about which you can secure information if you will. You won't secure it from me. I will say this much now: I can see where your questions are pointing, and they are pointing in an unfair direction.

Chairman WALSH. Say, we are going to try to carry on the hearings without characterizing motives or anything of that sort.

Mr. IRISH. Well, they simply impress me as being carried on in an unfair direction. Let me say this——

Chairman WALSH (interposing). Say, one moment, please. Try to refrain from characterizing, if you think that way. You understand.

Mr. IRISH. I will do my best, sir; but will not give any guarantee.

Chairman WALSH. I didn't catch the last. You won't do what?

Mr. IRISH. I will try my best. I will not give a guarantee.

Chairman WALSH. I think you are a very intelligent person. I think you could do that.

Mr. IRISH. Thank you for the tribute. Now, if the tendency of your questions is to put our organization in the position of demanding for themselves, through the affiliation with outside interests, assistance to come in and settle questions, without our consent, while we deny that right to organized labor, as it affects us in Stockton, I will say that that is not so; that our operations are conducted by ourselves; that any settlements that are made are made by our organization without any outside dictation from anybody or anywhere. Does that cover it?

Mr. THOMPSON. Well, I will put my questions, Mr. Irish, and you can make your answer as you please. If such as organization exists, does your organization have any understanding with it, definite or indefinite, written or unwritten?

Mr. IRISH. That is a matter, sir, which does not concern you, and which I must decline to answer.

Mr. THOMPSON. Is there an employers' association in the city of San Francisco?

Mr. IRISH. That is another question which does not concern this inquiry, and which I decline to answer. You can question those people. You have the power of subpœna.

Mr. THOMPSON. If there is such an organization, has your organization either generally or specially got any kind of an agreement or understanding, verbal or written, with it?

Mr. IRISH. That is also a question which I decline to answer. I have stated—I have said this, and it stands for any organization that you choose to name—that as far as the conduct of our industrial affairs in the city of Stockton are concerned they are guided, directed, limited in no way by any man, by any organization, or by anybody outside of our own organization in the city of Stockton, composed of employers, merchants, manufacturers, and professional men in that city.

Mr. THOMPSON. Just to make one more question of that character in the record, I will combine several associations. Has your organization any kind of an understanding or an agreement with the National Erectors' Association, with the National Founders' Association, with the National Association of Manufacturers of this country?

Mr. IRISH. Will you kindly state just what the type of agreement you have in mind—or do you care to state that?

Mr. THOMPSON. Any kind of an agreement. I asked you if you had any. You can answer it yes or no—any verbal or written understanding or agreement of any character with any of those organizations or the officers of those organizations?

Mr. IRISH. May I ask—not that I want to answer a question with a question——

Mr. THOMPSON (interposing). Well, I prefer to have you say yes or no to that if you will.

Mr. IRISH. Well, as I understand it, this is an unfair attack; these questions have no bearing upon the inquiry into industrial conditions in Stockton. And I have made this statement, that we are directed, controlled, limited in no way by anyone outside of Stockton. Now, if you desire—if you desire by your questionings to attempt to establish the fact that there is any sort of an agreement, or working agreement of any sort or any arrangement, such as exists in the labor unions through which power is delegated up and up and up and up to other sources, I would say to you frankly that there is no agreement of that kind in the city of Stockton, never has been, and never will be.

Mr. THOMPSON. Mr. Irish, I didn't ask you that question, and you know it.

Mr. IRISH. I know you haven't.

Mr. THOMPSON. I would like the reporter to read the question, and I would like you to answer yes or no. And if you don't care to, say you don't care to answer. That will be perfectly satisfactory to me, and I will drop the subject.

(Record read as follows:)

"Mr. THOMPSON. Just to make one more question of that character in the record, I will combine several associations. Has your organization any kind of an understanding or an agreement with the National Erectors' Association, with the National Founders' Association, with the National Association of Manufacturers of this country?

*   *   *   *   *   *   *

"Any kind of agreement. I asked you if you had any. You can answer it yes or no—any verbal or written understanding or agreement of any character. with any of those organizations or the officers of those organizations?"

Mr. IRISH. You really want that question answered yes or no?

Chairman WALSH. Say, one minute, Mr. Witness. Now, I wish to say that we want to have an understanding. Of course, this inquiry has gone over a wide range and the commission has determined in advance what is pertinent to the inquiry.

Mr. IRISH. Yes.

Chairman WALSH. And Mr. Thompson here voices our questions, of course, and he will not ask any question that is not pertinent.

Mr. IRISH. Exactly.

Chairman WALSH. And please assume that they are all pertinent, and if there are any that for any reason you refuse to answer we will not insist upon an answer if it can be obtained elsewhere. We would like you to assist us by giving the answers frankly and fully as far as you know. It will expedite our hearing.

Mr. IRISH. Yes——

Chairman WALSH. If we can get them at different places and you decline to answer, why that will be perfectly all right with us. And then if we can't get them, we may recall you.

Mr. IRISH. Let me say this, if you will pardon me just a minute, in response to what you have said.

Chairman WALSH. Yes.

Mr. IRISH. There is no particular weighty reason why these questions should not be answered. The only thing is this, that those are questions which would concern very intimately the status of affairs since—that is, which might concern us in the minds of some people, in Stockton, since July 8.

Chairman WALSH. You may decline to answer those, and we will take our own means of ascertaining conditions since that time.

Mr. IRISH. That is perfectly satisfactory to me, and that is the reason for my refusal.

Mr. THOMPSON. Just one more question, Mr. Irish. This is from Mr. Drew. As counsel of the organization you name, I ask Mr. Irish, as a matter of courtesy, to answer that question.

Mr. IRISH. I am perfectly willing to do that.

Chairman WALSH. One minute. What is this?

Mr. DREW. I have asked Mr. Irish to answer the question.

Chairman WALSH. There is a request for what, Mr. Drew?

Mr. DREW. On behalf of these organizations, the erectors and manufacturers and founders, that he answer the question.

Chairman WALSH. Very good, on the request from Mr. Drew.

Mr. IRISH. On that I am perfectly willing to say that there is no agreement, either verbal or written, with any of these organizations or in any other way.

Mr. THOMPSON. Now, Mr. Irish, do you know Mr. Zeehandelaar, secretary of the Merchants' & Manufacturers' Association of Los Angeles?

Mr. IRISH. I don't. I have never had the pleasure of his acquaintance. I would like to know him.

Mr. THOMPSON. Have you heard of a man by that name?

Mr. IRISH. Oh, yes.

Mr. THOMPSON. Have you or your association any connection with him?

Mr. IRISH. Not to my knowledge.

Mr. THOMPSON. So far as you know. You are secretary of this organization and handle its correspondence?

Mr. IRISH. I don't. I have nothing to do with its correspondence.

Mr. THOMPSON. Do you know whether he as secretary of that association was asked to take part in that Stockton matter?

Mr. IRISH. I don't.

Mr. THOMPSON. Or dispute with organized labor?

Mr. IRISH. I don't.

Mr. THOMPSON. Would you say now that he was not asked?

Mr. IRISH. So far as my knowledge goes, he was not.

Mr. THOMPSON. And would you say that the association of Los Angeles was not asked to take part in that?

Mr. IRISH. So far as my knowledge goes, it was not.

Mr. THOMPSON. I think that is all.

Chairman WALSH. Do you wish to ask any questions?

Commissioner COMMONS. I would like to ask a question.

Chairman WALSH. Prof. Commons.

Commissioner COMMONS. I would like to ask if prior to this time, when you formulated this final determination not to make agreements while these negotiations were on with reference to the Sperry Co. and the Hotel Stockton, and the clerks and restaurant workers, was any attempt made to create any board of mediation and conciliation at Stockton, or anything of the kind which could be appealed to for final decision or in any way, to settle this class of questions?

Mr. IRISH. In so far as the Sperry and Hotel Stockton troubles were concerned, they were long prior to the formation of this organization, a long time.

Commissioner COMMONS. That is, the Sperry and the Stockton?

Mr. IRISH. Yes; and no attempt has been made since that time to form any board of mediation or conciliation.

Commissioner COMMONS. That is, with reference to the clerks and restaurant trouble?

Mr. IRISH. No. Let me—if I may be permitted to just add a word to that question. Understand, that in none of these cases was any matter of hours, wages, or working conditions involved. It was a matter of the recognition of the union and the recognition of the principle that none but nonunion men—recognition on their part of the principle that union and nonunion could not work together, and from there the rest of the trouble started. It is merely in the signing of an agreement, that the only question to arbitrate was as to whether that agreement should be signed or not. There was no question of hours, wages, or working conditions involved, and never has been. Does that make it clear? I didn't mean to cut across.

Commissioner COMMONS. I was trying to get at the nature of the issue that arose there, the question would be—first, I would like to know whether either side or its representatives that came from outside made any proposition to create—to arbitrate, to leave it to a disinterested third party.

Mr. IRISH. Not so far as I know. No. And understand, all the time—you say you are not quite clear as to the issues involved. The only issue that has been involved from start to finish is the matter of the signing of an agreement, and the matter of union and nonunion men working together in the same shop.

Commissioner COMMONS. Then I take it that the signing of the agreement always in your case, in the Stockton case—in those two cases—involved the signing of a closed-shop agreement; that that is the way in which it always came to you.

Mr. IRISH. Nothing but a closed-shop agreement has ever been presented there for signature, as far as I know.

Commissioner COMMONS. And they simply decline to sign it?

Mr. IRISH. They decline to sign it.

Commissioner COMMONS. Now, in your opinion, that would also prevent the establishment of any board, local board of arbitration, between the employers' association and the unions of Stockton?

Mr. IRISH. Well, now this situation exists—I may seem awfully tedious in answering these questions, but it is awfully hard, because some of them require explanation. At the time that the open-shop statement was definitely sent out and the announcement was read in the various shops, in order to divorce from the minds of the men any question as to what that involved, we passed a statement which every man in our organization has signed, to the effect that no man would alter the scale, in order that there might be no question that the scale was involved. And we further said that if any man attempted to lower wages or increase hours, except by application to a committee of our organization, he would be forthwith expelled from the organization.

Now, there was the basis for a working out of any question of hours or wages. It has only gone that far because the question has not been involved so far.

Commissioner COMMONS. But take this case of the electrical contractor; that didn't come up until later.

Mr. IRISH. Oh, that came away before, away before there was any organization at all.

Commissioner COMMONS. The question whether a man was being discriminated against might not that have been considered as an arbitrable subject?

Mr. IRISH. Discriminated against just how, please?

Commissioner COMMONS. That he was being discharged because he was a union man, or being discharged because of inefficiency.

Mr. IRISH. As to that, the attitude of our association is that the individual man runs his individual business. We no more attempt to dictate to him as to his policies than we permit anyone else to. The only thing is this, that we are a protective organization. If a man gets into trouble and comes to us for protection, he must show a good cause, don't you see? Now, this is true. I know men in the city of Stockton, members of our organization, who have come 'into the organization before this trouble started, who were operating closed shops before this trouble came—one of them right over here, a gentleman who was visited by 125 gentle workers and knocked down and kicked and had his cheek bone broken and his eye cut. Now, I don't believe that he probably would care to employ any union men after this trouble is over. Now, this is the thing, if he comes to us for protection from trouble which comes from discrimination between union and nonunion men, we simply say to him: "That is your own business." At least that is my understanding of the association. Do you see?

Commissioiner COMMONS. Well, I was thinking before the final ultimatum was reached, whether any provision for taking care not only of wages and hours, but of all questions of dispute, had been considered at all.

Mr. IRISH. We recognize the right of free contract.

Commissioner COMMONS. That is, your organization started out with the idea of individual bargaining from the start, that was in the foundation?

Mr. IRISH. Exactly. I was just looking for that. May I replevin this a moment [indicating written statement heretofore read by the witness]?

Commissioner COMMONS. Well, I take it that that statement you read to us was one that was formulated in 1908.

Mr. IRISH. No. This document was formulated last August, a year ago, and has stood ever since. This was formulated prior to any trouble at all. This was the foundation statement out of which our organization grew.

Commissioner COMMONS. When you organized at the start you put yourself into a position where you could not enter into any agreements which would take into account all questions of dispute between the unions and the others?

Mr. IRISH. Exactly. We simply took this stand, that any man was free to join any organization, the Masons or the Catholics or any organization.

Commissioner COMMONS. From the very start, then, it was the issue of the open shop?

Mr. IRISH. Absolutely.

Commissioner COMMONS. And nothing was left open in order to build up if possible any different system by which even that question could be arbitrated?

Mr. IRISH. Not as between our association and the labor unions; no.

Commissioner COMMONS. No.

Chairman WALSH. Mr. Commissioner Lennon would like to ask you a question or two.

Commissioner LENNON. Mr. Irish, did I understand you correctly that all the agreements entered into at Stockton contained a provision that none but union men should be employed?

Mr. IRISH. Not quite that.

Commissioner LENNON. Or union women?

Mr. IRISH. So far as I know every agreement that I have ever seen carried the provision that none but union men should be in permanent employment; that if a man joined—that if a man were employed who was a nonunion man, he should join the union at the first opportunity or cease employment.

Commissioner LENNON. Did that agreement ever contain the provision that none but union people should be employed?-

Mr. IRISH. Yes; all that I have seen.

Commissioner LENNON. How many unions are involved in the controversy as it now stands at Stockton?

Mr. IRISH. I know of none that are not. Not all of them are out on strike.

Commissioner LENNON. Will you furnish the commission with a copy of the agreements as they existed prior to the controversy?

Mr. IRISH. I will endeavor to have our secretary do that. I haven't them in my possession. I imagine he could secure those copies and would be glad to furnish them.

Commissioner LENNON. I asked this because there are some unions in Stockton that never put that provision that I know of in any of their agreements. I want to see the agreements. Is the Holt Manufacturing Co. a corporation or individual?

Mr. IRISH. As to that you would have to ask the Holt Manufacturing Co.; I don't know.

Commissioner LENNON. Is the Sperry Flour Co.—I may not have the name exact——

Mr. IRISH. Sperry.

Commissioner LENNON. Is that a corporation or a firm?

Mr. IRISH. You will have to ask them as to that; I don't know.

Commissioner LENNON. Did I understand you at one point to say that the bartenders were employed seven days a week?

Mr. IRISH. Yes, sir.

Commissioner LENNON. At one time?

Mr. IRISH. No, sir; not generally in town. This applied to the one local condition in one particular bar where they were working seven days of their own volition.

Commissioner LENNON. Do you know whether or not the wages and conditions of labor in Stockton have been brought about by the organization of labor or by some other process?

Mr. IRISH. Well, that is a matter which I am not competent to go into at this time, with your permission. There are others here who possibly can, who will be on the stand.

Commissioner LENNON. That is all.

Chairman WALSH. Commissioner Weinstock would like to ask some questions.

Commissioner WEINSTOCK. Among the causes which I have heard, Mr. Irish, given for the present situation in Stockton is what is known as the Totten case. I think you related that case to me when I was in Stockton the other day.

Mr. IRISH. Do you want me to go into that?

Commissioner WEINSTOCK. I think the commission would be interested in hearing that particular case.

Mr. IRISH. That was merely one of the samples I didn't cite, because I am trying to relieve you of me as soon as I can. The situation was this: It was not one of the fundamental causes of this trouble at all; by comparison it was a mosquito bite as against the goring of a bull, but it illustrates the attitude and as such may be of interest. As you know, in the closed-shop planing mill the union stamping is in charge of the shop steward, and the proprietor has no art, part, or interest in it except as he pays the salary of the man who puts the stamp on the closed-shop goods. He has no control over the placing of this stamp; the union retains that to themselves, because they don't want that man to be under anybody except their own control. Mr. Totten had a job of cabinetwork to deliver on the third story of a building. This cabinetwork was of all kinds and sizes and was hard to handle, and the stuff went out of the mill and was delivered on the third story of this job. The business agent of the carpenter's union rang up—the business agent of the building trades, I guess it was—rang up and said there was some unstamped stuff went up to the job. Mr. Totten says, " I am sorry, but that is the fault of the man that does the stamping, and I haven't anything to do with that. You know I am working union hours and paying the scale, and I run a closed shop and am fair," but he said, " I am perfactly willing to do what is right, and I will send the steward for his time and pay him to go up there and stamp it. And they said, " No, you dont; nothing is stamped after it leaves the mill. You will send your team down, go up on the third floor, and haul the stuff down and put it on the wagon and take it back to the mill and let the steward stamp it, and then haul it back to the building and deliver it on the third floor again." " Well," Mr. Totten said, " it is rather unfair to put me in that position. I am not responsible for it being unstamped. You haven't got any conditions in the mill to complain of, and to compel me to go to all this expense and trouble——" " It has got to be done; don't make any difference." Mr. Totten had to do it, and did it; he hauled it clear back to the mill; the stamp was put on without any question. Then he had to haul it back and put it, on the third floor. Mr. Totten will be on the stand, and you can interrogate him more fully about it if you care to. It simply has been cited, just as other cases have been, as an evidence of the unreasonable attitude of those people; that is all.

Commissioner WEINSTOCK. One point here that I think the other commissioners, in common with myself, would like to have made clear. This statement here. among other things, says this: " We pledge ourselves to stand firm to the open shop and the elimination of signed or other agreements between our members and labor organizations." Does that mean that the organization is opposed to the signing of any agreements, or certain kinds of agreements?

Mr. IRISH. Any agreements.

Commissioner WEINSTOCK. Any agreements?

Mr. IRISH. Yes, sir.

· Commissioner WEINSTOCK. Regardless of the fact whether those agreements stood for the closed shop or whether those agreements permitted the employer to engage anybody he pleases?

Mr. IRISH. Irrespective?

Commissioner WEINSTOCK. Irrespective.

Mr. IRISH. Yes, sir.

Commissioner WEINSTOCK. That is, it is a sweeping blanket statement?

Mr. IRISH. Yes.

Commissioner WEINSTOCK. Substantially, it means, I take it, that the association is opposed to recognizing or dealing with unions?

Mr. IRISH. It is opposed to dealing with unions; yes.

Commissioner WEINSTOCK. Or recognizing them as unions?

Mr. IRISH. In the making up of agreements between individual employer and the unions; yes.

Commissioner WEINSTOCK. That is all, Mr. Chairman.

Chairman WALSH. Commissioner Garretson would like to ask you a question.

Commissioner GARRETSON. I want to ask your opinion as to a certain attitude, as between the association and the union. Bear in mind it is on a point that as a union man I have no interest in; I am speaking, as the union, I believe, represents, because neither the sympathetic strike nor the insertion of a clause in an agreement that only union men will be employed has never in any single instance been charged against my union. But I want to know what your opinion is as to the consistency of a position—what is the difference between the attitude of your organization, as outlined there, in all upholding any one of its members whom they decide to protect, and the sympathetic strike which you condemn on the part of the union? What is the difference ethically, practically, between your attitude, of 40 different employers—I am just using that number—of 40 different employers combining, all in different pursuits, to fight any one union, and 40 unions combining to fight any one employer?

Mr. IRISH. You refer to a sympathetic strike?

Commissioner GARRETSON. Yes; either a sympathetic boycott or sympathetic war on the other hand?

Mr. IRISH. Yes. Well, our attitude might be on all fours if whenever one of our employers was being attacked by a union for refusing to sign an agreement we discharged all of our men and refused to give them any further work; we would be on all fours. Our protection in that manner means simply this, that if a man gets in trouble——

Chairman WALSH. A little louder, please.

Mr. IRISH. Pardon. If a man gets in trouble with a union—that is, to fight a union organization through refusal to sign an agreement—that is, our organization will protect him by legal advice and counsel, by any fair and legitimate means in our power. It does not mean——

Commissioner GARRETSON. Money and moral support?

Mr. IRISH. Money and moral support, exactly.

Commissioner GARRETSON. That is it.

Mr. IRISH. If those matters can confine themselves to money and moral support in all cases, I do not think there could be the objection that there is to-day; on the other side, I simply submit that as my——

Commissioner GARRETSON. On the other hand, you give him the best weapon you have?

Mr. IRISH. Oh, no.

Commissioner GARRETSON. Oh. What is the best?

Mr. IRISH. We could use coercion of various sorts.

Commissioner GARRETSON. Isn't that, the contributing of money, as strong a form of coercion as the union man contributing his time, which is his money?

Mr. IRISH. Well, now, no. Let me put it this way. Let us get down to brass tacks, of you will pardon the term.

Suppose, for instance, that here is a subcontractor and he has got a subcontract on a building. Now, that contract when it was signed did not stipulate that he should employ union or nonunion help, or anything of the kind. He got the contract on a bid. Very well. The building trades come in and say that that man is unfair, will unfair the whole job unless the chief contractor who he subcontracts under forces him to cancel the contract. All right. What would we do? In the first place we would make sure that the man had a legal contract; and in the second place we would protect him legally in taking his stand, because he is entitled to that; in the third place we tell him that if he insisted, as he had a legal right to do, on finishing that job and the matter gets in the courts and he lost, that we would protect·him in his loss. In other words, we put him in a position, just as near as we can—I·want to show you how I see it, I may be all wrong, I am not infallible; but we put him in a position where he is equally as strong as the people that are opposing him; no more. We do not go out on sympathetic strikes, but we say, "If you have a legal right"—a legal right, mind you.

Commissioner GARRETSON. Yes.

Mr. IRISH. If you have a legal right to finish this job, we will see, as an organization, that you are protected in your legal right; that much, and no more.

Commissioner GARRETSON. "And if you lose, reimburse you for your loss?"

Mr. IRISH. Exactly. Because we would not take those things unless a· man has a legal right, because we have got to give him that protection.

Commissioner GARRETSON. Is there, in your opinion, any difference between that protection and the protection which the men will give to· these who are serving that contractor? They will give him the industrial protection ·that they can give him, because they can not furnish those things that you have agreed to; in other words, you contribute your influence sympathetically and practically to the employer: they contribute their time by ceasing work in·the behalf of those who are striving against him and his employee. Is it not a fact that ethically the two questions are on exactly the same plane?

Mr. IRISH. I am afraid our poles are too far apart to answer that. I can't see the argument, but you will pardon me—I have to say that.

Commissioner GARRETSON. Now, you do not discriminate against the employment of union men?

Mr. IRISH. No.

Commissioner GARRETSON. You have seen a good many employers who did?

Mr. IRISH. Yes; some of them are members——

Commissioner GARRETSON. What, in your opinion, is the difference between a boycott by the union of the products of an institution with which they are at strife and the boycott of a man bearing the union brand by an employer? ·

Mr. IRISH. Just this difference: If any boycott—any boycott, I don't care what it is or where it is——

Commissioner GARRETSON. Whether of men or products?

Mr. IRISH. Men or products; any boycott that is a boycott based on a moral basis, not the penalty of a fine, that is one thing—that is your free right as a purchasing agent—but any boycott which is forced on a man when he is afraid of using that stuff because he is going to be fined for it, is not a moral boycott; that is the exercise of coercion against the free right of that man. There is a difference, as I see it. Am I plain?

Commissioner GARRETSON. I see your point. You never·belonged to a union?

Mr. IRISH. No.

Chairman WALSH. We must preserve perfect order, ladies and gentlemen.

Mr. IRISH. As I take it from the colloquy, continuing the colloquy—I have never belonged to a union, but I have earned my living in the biblical term, "By the sweat."

Commissioner GARRETSON. By the sweat of your brow?

Mr. IRISH. Yes.

Commissioner GARRETSON. Let me ask your·opinion, predicated on this: You get exactly the same result in an association like that of which you are a member now—which would you regard the most heavily——

Mr. IRISH. I didn't get that.

Commissioner GARRETSON. Which would you regard the most heavily, taking the rule of the association of which you are a member, or the greater condemnation that would come on you from your associates in that association?

Mr. IRISH. Well, that would depend entirely on whether I thought I was right or not. I never——

Commissioner GARRETSON. If you felt you were right?

Mr. IRISH. This is a personal question?

Commissioner GARRETSON. Yes.

Mr. IRISH. If I felt I was right I wouldn't care a rap for the .moral· condemnation. On the other hand, if I felt the employer was penalizing me in that regard—I take it the man cares more for ·the support of his family than he does for the moral condemnation. I will cite an instance on this·matter: Here is a painter that comes to Stockton and he goes to work under open shop, and the question was asked him, and he said he had been· a member of the painters' union in San Francisco. I have only his hearsay testimony, but it has been—I have known of other cases of the same kind. Now he was a union painter in the city of San Francisco and there were two nonunion men on that job, and he didn't go around looking at the other men, he was slapping paint on the wall, that is what he was paid for, and he is a good workman. The two nonunion painters are on the job, and the other fellow is working for the wages, and whatever it was worth to him. Now, that man comes to Stockton and works under the open-shop conditions and some amiable gentleman up there that disagreed with his views got after him as he was out of the union, because he told me that he had been so penalized—he had been fined $25 two or three times for working with those nonunion men—and he couldn't continue under those conditions. That is an instance.

Commissioner GARRETSON. Would you call that a moral or an immoral obligation that had been placed on him?

Mr. IRISH. I prefer not to commit myself.

Commissioner GARRETSON. That is all.

Chairman WALSH. Mr. O'Connell wishes to ask you some questions.

Commissioner O'CONNELL. I understand you to say you are not an employer?

Mr. IRISH. No, sir; you are wrong in that assumption. I have been.

Commissioner O'CONNELL. When?

Mr. IRISH. Well, for about 10 years.

Commissioner O'CONNELL. Where?

Mr. IRISH. Well, most all over the State of California; employing both skilled and unskilled labor.

Commissioner O'CONNELL. What particular business were you engaged in?

Mr. IRISH. In agriculture and reclamation work; in irrigation development both by pump and otherwise, in the course of which——

Commissioner O'CONNELL. Contractor?

Mr. IRISH. No, sir; operating for myself, or operating as superintendent and general manager for other people. During that time I employed both skilled and unskilled labor; that is, varying all the way from highly skilled mechanics down to common laborers.

Commissioner O'CONNELL. How large a force can you now recall you were ever in charge of?

Mr. IRISH. Oh, I think the biggest force was about 400 men; in that neighborhood; the large portion of them being unskilled labor, with a considerable portion skilled labor.

Commissioner O'CONNELL. Have you a knowledge of conditions existing in your city as to wages, hours, etc., prior to the time of the so-called closed shop?

Mr. IRISH. That is a matter you can go into very definitely with some of the people who will appear later and have more intimate knowledge of that condition than I.

Commissioner O'CONNELL. Who, for instance?

Mr. IRISH. I imagine Mr. Holt, probably.

Commissioner O'CONNELL. Mr. Holt?

Mr. IRISH. Mr. Holt; yes, sir.

Commissioner O'CONNELL. What are the number of the members in your association?

Mr. IRISH. Four hundred and three, I think. I counted them the other day. I am not quite positive as to that part—403, I think.

Commissioner O'CONNELL. What is the cost of membership?

Mr. IRISH. It is on a sliding scale. That is a matter I prefer not to go into at this time.

Commissioner O'CONNELL. Does your constitution and by-laws cover that requirement?

Mr. IRISH. Will you pardon if I ask; Mr. Bird, does the constitution cover the assessment? I am not quite clear in my mind.

Mr. BIRD. No, sir.

Mr. IRISH. You can secure that information from later witnesses. It is a matter I have not concerned myself with particularly, and don't feel competent to go into that.

Commissioner O'CONNELL. Don't you know the cost of membership in the association, as its secretary?

Mr. IRISH. I am not secretary of the association; I have said that three times. I beg pardon for seeming a little bit irritated, but I have answered that question several times.

Commissioner O'CONNELL. That is all.

Chairman WALSH. That is all, unless you have some other statement to make, or something you haven't fully covered that you desire to make a voluntary statement in regard to. If so, we should be glad to hear it. ·

Mr. IRISH. Nothing more that I think of.

Chairman WALSH. That is all.

Mr. THOMPSON. Just one more question.

Chairman WALSH. Go ahead.

Mr. THOMPSON. Do the answers you have previously given with reference to" the affiliation or understanding of your organization apply to the Federation of Employers' Associations of the Pacific Coast?

Mr. IRISH. ·I decline to answer that question entirely, ·referring to my original statement.

Mr. THOMPSON. Did you mention a man named Calkins or any man of that. name belonging to your organization or employed by it?

Mr. IRISH. Mr. Calkins is manager of our organization.

Mr. THOMPSON. That is all. Thank you.

Chairman WALSH. That is all. Call your next.

Mr. THOMPSON. Anton Johannsen.

TESTIMONY OF MR. ANTON JOHANNSEN.

Mr. THOMPSON. Give us your name, please.

Mr. JOHANNSEN. A. Johannsen.

Mr. THOMPSON. And your business address. .

Mr. JOHANNSEN. Stockton, Cal.

Mr. THOMPSON. And your business.

Mr. JOHANNSEN. General organizer of the United Brotherhood of Carpenters and Joiners of America.

Mr. THOMPSON. How long have you been in that work?

Mr. JOHANNSEN. About six months.

Mr. THOMPSON. What business were you doing before that?

Mr. JOHANNSEN. I was State organizer for the Building Trades of California.

Mr. THOMPSON. How long were you doing that work?

Mr. JOHANNSEN. Four years and six months.

Mr. THOMPSON. How long have you been on the Pacific coast, Mr. Johannsen?.

Mr. JOHANNSEN. A little over six years; not quite seven.

Mr. THOMPSON. And have you been connected with labor matters during that time?

Mr. JOHANNSEN. Yes, sir.

Mr. THOMPSON. Are you familiar with the situation at Stockton to-day? ·

Mr. JOHANNSEN. I am.

Mr. THOMPSON. Will you tell us briefly the facts as you view them?

Mr. JOHANNSEN. The city of Stockton has had no labor trouble for the past 12 years with the exception of a strike that took place 4 years ago .which involved an increase of wages for the carpenters of 50 cents a day. That strike lasted several weeks and was compromised. An adjustment was finally brought about satisfactory to both employers and employees. In place of the, carpenters getting $4.80, they agreed upon a $4.40 scale, which ·is now the prevailing wage. A year ago, or a little over a year ago, the Saturday half holiday was demanded by the millmen at Stockton, and granted. It is true that the millmen get the same wage for five and a half days now that they formerly received for six days. The wages of the millmen in Stockton is approximately: 50 cents a day less than the wages of the millmen in San Francisco. The mills in Stockton are of considerably smaller character and nearly all of their work. is confined to Stockton and its surroundings—immediate surroundings. ·,

The Building Trades Council of Stockton has jurisdiction over the organization I represent, the carpenters, and all other organizations in the building industry, including the electricians. The building trades council at no time to my knowledge has acted in a manner that would be contrary to its laws.·. One. of the laws is that any organization who desires a change of working condi-; tions which will affect the cost of a building, in the way of increase in wages or reduction of hours, it is necessary that such a demand shall first.be.made by the craft union to the building trades council, and then the contractor·or employer shall receive 90 days' notice. That is the law—90 days' notice—and only after this 90 days' notice expiring will the increase in wages be demanded,: and not then if the contractor is tied up on any job that he contracted for prior to the increase in wages.

In other words, if the job he contracted for was before the demand was made it will be completed at the old scale. That is the rule in every building trades council in this State, including Stockton. The electrical workers' union in Stockton has not any business agent; its business is done through the business agent of the building trades council. The building trades became involved in this Stockton situation by no fault of their own, and by deliberate coercion on the part of the M., M. and E. A conference was held at its direction. The president of the council was requested to appoint a committee to meet with a like committee from the M., M. and E., which was done. The building trades council was infromed that unless they would cease their attitude of opposition to the stores controlled by the M., M. and E. that they would be locked out, and they were informed in the event that the building trades-unions did agree to keep their hands off from the fight so far as the clerks were concerned and the cooks and waiters, that the building trades as such would not be molested. This the council promptly refused to do. As far as the building trade is concerned in Stockton, we haven't seen much of a fight yet. The firm of Sherhart & Neisted, who have sued for an injunction against our organization and individuals—Mr. Neisted informed me personally on his building, on the Lincoln High School, a week ago last Saturday, if we would agree to turn down the millmen he would fire all scabs off the job and unionize his entire work in the building industry. That the only thing he was afraid of was the mill end of it. That is one of the firms.

Mr. Sherhart has informed, not me personally, but others, that the merchants, manufacturers, and employers' association have sued for this injunction without either his consent or knowledge of same being applied for. The Merchants, Manufacturers and Employers' Association of Stockton have boycotted the hotel in which all general organizers are located, the Clark Hotel, and have advised the different merchants in the city that when a drummer comes to sell goods they ask him what hotel he is stopping at, and if he says the Clark Hotel, they will tell him to peddle his paper, to be on his business, that they can't do any business with him. The declaration for the open shop was made July 8. Not one international organizer was sent to Stockton upon either the volition of the organization, the international organization, or of the organizer. No one was sent there until they were requested by the local men in Stockton. If the local membership in Stockton was permitted to outline the course of action, every union man and every union woman in every store, in every factory, and on every building would now be on strike. In other words, the local sentiment was for a general declaration to tie the whole town up the same as the I. W. W. program of the merchants, manufacturers, and employers' association. The international organizers have prevented the consummation of that kind of situation.

We find that the firm of Totten & Brant, mill owners, had entered into a contract with some of the general contractors who are now and always have been fair, and who are at present fair. For instance, there is a building under construction there called the East Side School. The general contractor's name is Acerman; his home is in Oakland. There is an annex being built to the insane asylum, and the general contractor is Bergen & Son, San Francisco. These two general contractors contracted for the millwork with Totten & Brant prior to the declaration of the open shp. Mr. Totten is a member of the strike committee of the M., M. and E. These firms were permitted by the building trades' council to accept this unfair millwork with the proviso that on all future work they would only employ only union millwork, because of the lack of a desire upon our part to jam any man into a situation over which he had no control.

The M., M. and E. have made every effort to provoke us into declaring those union jobs that are now union jobs unfair. For instance, there is a large bank building, the largest building in Stockton now under construction, and the contractor—I can't think of his name—Walker Bros., they are the general contractors. That is a 10-story building. Everything is fair on the building—that is; what we call fair—everything union.

Mr. Walker had occasion to have some lumber delivered on that job. He notified the team owner, who was a union team owner, and in the interval some member of the M., M. and E. influenced the team owner to send a nonunion team on the job in order to get us to declare a strike on the building. Of course, we didn't fall for the dope, and didn't strike the building.

The condition as to the attitude of the clerks which brought about this trouble: The clerks' union on the expiration of their agreement sent a statement to the retail clothiers' association requesting a conference for the purpose of considering the new agreement or the extension of the old agreement. There was no demand made by the clerks of any description, and when the clerks' representative, together with the representative of the labor council, went to the clothiers' association, they were informed that the retail clothiers' association had no power to act; that they must go to Mr. Calkins, the secretary of the merchants, manufacturers, and employers' association.

The union cards in the restaurants were not taken down by the business agent, but were taken down—were ordered down by the agent of the M., M. and E. The merchants, manufacturers, and employers' association, has had a standing advertisement in the daily press inviting police officers to arrest men and offering a reward regardless of whether such arrests bring about convictions or otherwise.

The building trades council and its affiliated organizations, including the millmen, are prepared to enter into an adjustment or arbitration or otherwise of any controversy that is complained of by the merchants, manufacturers, and employers' association except the elimination of our organization. The attitude of labor toward the employer is perhaps best manifested in the fact that the Totten & Brant mill, one of the concerns which is of some moment in the fight up there, the employees of that mill just a very short while previous to this declaration of general lockout donated a week's pay or week's labor to Mr. Totten to help him out in building his new mill which had been burned down.

The merchants, manufacturers, and employers' association have advertised in this city and in Los Angeles, contrary to the law, for nonunion men. That is to say, without informing them as to the war up here. Mr. Clark, the owner and proprietor of the Roberts & Clark planing mill, was in Los Angeles engaging men, employing nonunion men to come to Stockton. Those men were not informed as to the conditions, and were deliberately misled. Some of them went to work, others have ceased to work and refused to go to work. Two of them never went to work at all, and gave us their affidavit, and the matter is now pending before the labor commissioner.

Two nonunion hod carriers came to work with shotguns. They were arrested, charged with carrying concealed weapons, plead guilty, and the attorney for the M, M. and E. paid their fines.

The M, M. and E. have imported into Stockton 20 gunmen, many of whom are ex-convicts. They fall for the bait, of course, the same as they always do, and we had 20 women pickets on one of the schoolhouses, called the West Side School. Thirty men were around that building. There were eight nonunion bricklayers and six hod carriers and two plumbers working on the building. Within five minutes after the women had arrived on that building or in the street, the patrol wagon came with two officers in it, rode by our crowd about 100 feet, and then came a seven-passenger automobile, "A310 California," in which were five gunmen and the chauffeur. They stopped in the middle of our crowd, but the men did not say a word to them, and they could not stand the tongues of the women, and they kept running around the block like a lot of maniacs. When the scabs stopped work our people were speaking to them in the hope of influencing them to quit work, and the uniformed policemen on the job was afraid there might be some trouble, and requested me to disperse the crowd, which I did. We then demanded the arrest of these gun men, and searched them. They were promptly arrested, and in the automobile was found 14 brand new pick handles, 12 blackjacks, and each one had a 38 Colt's revolver. They were placed under arrest and put under bond of $100, and the attorney for the M., M. and E. immediately responded, within less than 10 minutes, which, in our judgment, is conclusive evidence that the whole thing was programmed by the M., M. and E. previous to those men being arrested. At any rate the attorney for the merchant, manufacturers, and employers' association came to the jail and put up cash bonds, and the men were released on bail, and are still in Stockton.

The union pickets have been instructed by our organization like this: First, there must be absolute sobriety; second, there must be no violence indulged in, or tolerated; third, there must be no strong language tending to provoke violence; fourth, any uniformed officer on the beat anywhere who makes any request or offers any suggestion, such request and such advice must be heeded by the picket; fifth, the pickets are to interview nonunion men peaceably and in an orderly manner in the hope of winning them over to our side and away from the M., M. and E.; last, no union man is permitted to carry concealed weapons.

Any picket failing to comply with these instructions will receive no protection from the organization.

. There is not one single building contractor in the city of Stockton, whom I have come in contact with, that has offered any objection to any of the rules of the building trades organization, but all of them seem to be cowed by the display of financial support by the M., M. and E.

. As to the employment of outside men, I had occasion to adjust a job for a man named Wilson, who is a plumbing contractor of San Francisco. He has the steamfitting and plumbing of the insane asylum. He employed a steamfitter from San Francisco, and the union in Stockton exacted $1 a day from this man for three and a half days, and then wanted him to cease work yesterday morning. The contractor got in touch with me yesterday, and I took him in a machine and went out and investigated the job, and found that the only steamfitter that was available in Stockton, who could do that work and was a union man, did not want to go on the job. I immediately informed the contractor he could go ahead with any union man from any city anywhere, so that that was adjusted the same as we have always adjusted them.

We had one contractor by the name of Hirshman, a painting contractor. He had a contract for what is known as the high school in Stockton, and several other jobs I can't remember just now, but anyhow the high school. He came before our executive board and requested the privilege of completing all of his painting work on all the jobs that were declared unfair. He didn't ask for the employment of nonunion painters. I told Mr. Hirshman he could employ his union painters, he could employ his old crew of union painters, and could go on and do all those jobs where scabs were and could finish his work provided on all future work he would only accept contracts where all work was union. When he proceeded with his union painters on the high school the agent of the merchants, manufacturers, and employers' association, according to his own statement from his own lips to me, insisted that he employ at least one or two nonunion men, so that we would be provoked to take the balance of the union men away from him. In other words, by the acts of the M., M. and E they have been and now deliverately making efforts to tie up the entire industry in that city.

The secretary of the merchants and manufacturers' association, Mr. Calkins, with the assistance of another man engaged a man by the name of Graham to act as a personal bodyguard. This man Graham was taken over to the police department for the purpose of swearing him in as a deputy. The police department refused to swear him in as a deputy. He was then sworn in as a deputy by the merchants, manufacturers, and employers' association, and this man was led to believe that his star and his blackjack that they gave him—they gave him a piece of hose 18 inches long and put buckshot in it and told him he could protect Mr. Calkins even at the cost of human life. This man was an ex-convict, he had been in San Quentin Penitentiary three years. He was a young man of no great intelligence, and walking down the street one night he was arrested, and he told the police officer he was an officer and had the right to carry concealed weapons. He was arrested and plead guilty and made an open statement of the whole business. He was fined $100, and since that time Mr. Calkins has disappeared and nobody knows where he is.

The M., M., and E. don't believe in violence, but they evidently believe in murder from the way they imported the gunmen in there——

Chairman WALSH. Just please state the facts.

Mr. JOHANNSEN. Those are the facts.

Chairman WALSH. Without any characterization, you understand.

. Mr. JOHANNSEN. All right. There is not one member of the merchants, manufacturers, and employers' association to my knowledge within the past four weeks who has given any utterance to any man or any women in that city, or those who have come into the city, which would indicate that they have any purpose except the annihilation and the destruction of organized labor or labor organizations.

The statement about Mr. Totten and the control of the stamp: The United Brotherhood of Carpenters, of which I an general organizer, issues a stamp to be furnished to the employer for his protection; that is, protection against unfair competition. And the building mechanics refuse to handle material manufactured or dressed or planed or sized unless it bears that stamp. The stamp is in the control of the shop steward. The shop steward, of course, is in the employ of the employer. The statement made about material going to the third story of a building without being stamped and being compelled to take the material down again is a good story, but it does not happen to be true.

The further statement made that the building trades council declares an entire job unfair because some subcontractor violates the rules or in some way exacts an infraction, that is not true. The truth is that the law of the building trades council both in Stockton and elsewhere in this State provides this: If I as a subcontractor engaged in the plumbing business, or plastering, or brickwork, or painting, or electrical work, or any branch of the building industry, take a job from a general contractor, and the entire job is fair and for some reason I am declared unfair by the plumbers' union, if I happen to be a plumbing contractor and I refuse to comply with the rules, the general contractor's job is not stopped, but the contract is allowed to be completed with the understanding that he does not in the future employ that kind of men. There has never been a strike in the building trades' organization in Stockton over the question of jurisdiction of one union with another union. Those matters are always adjusted and dealt with by the building trades and the international representatives.

Mr. THOMPSON. Mr. Johannsen, you say that the——

Mr. JOHANNSEN. I want to say something more about the hours and wages, if you please.

Mr. THOMPSON. All right.

Mr. JOHANNSEN. The merchants, manufacturers, and employers' association have a sign in all the stores in Stockton over which they have control. The sign is very neatly gotten up, looks like an artist must have done it. It has a big heading on it, "Hours and wages," and a resolution passed by the merchants, manufacturers, and employers' association:

"*Resolved*, That we are unalterably opposed to any decrease in wages or increase in hours unless the committee of the merchants, manufacturers, and employers' association agrees to it."

The building trades council and its affiliated organizations at no time in the history of this strike have exacted any fine of any of its members for failure to comply with its advice as to the nonpatronizing of nonunion stores; that is to say, no fines have been placed against any member of any building trades' organization in the city of Stockton to my knowledge.

Mr. Tyson, of the Nelson Lumber Co., and Sunset Lumber. Co., of the city of San Francisco and Oakland and other places, was a prominent guest of the merchants, manufacturers, and employers' association, and made a great speech at their banquet showing the indorsement and support of the merchants, manufacturers, and employers' association, and particularly the lumber handlers and dealers of San Francisco and other localities. The merchants, manufacturers, and employers' association have threatened to recall the mayor of Stockton because he refuses to issue an order clubbing our pickets with or without reason.

I don't know of anything else, unless you want to ask some questions.

Mr. THOMPSON. I do, Mr. Johannsen. You stated in the early part of your statement that the employers' association asked for a meeting with the building trades council in Stockton?

Mr. JOHANNSEN. That is correct.

Mr. THOMPSON. At that meeting did the employers' association bring up the question of the boycott by the building trades on the retail stores or any other proposition?

Mr. JOHANNSEN. Yes, sir.

Mr. THOMPSON. What did they say about that boycott and what was said on your part?

Mr. JOHANNSEN. They requested the building trades council and its affiliated unions to remain neutral and permit the M., M. and E. to lick the little union first.

Mr. THOMPSON. What kind of boycott was being carried on which they wished you to desist from?

Mr. JOHANNSEN. We had resolved—passed a resolution pledging our moral support to the union affected.

Mr. THOMPSON. And asked your members not to trade with the unfair stores?

Mr. JOHANNSEN. Something to that effect.

Mr. THOMPSON. You say that no member of your organization or the building trades has been fined for trading with unfair stores?

Mr. JOHANNSEN. No, sir; they didn't need to be, because they wouldn't trade with them.

·Mr. THOMPSON. Was there any statement made to you or the building trades council at the time, or the committee of it, that the employers' association considered the boycott an unfair thing?

Mr. JOHANNSEN. No, sir.

Mr. THOMPSON. In regard to the organization of the building trades, have you a board before which the employees—I mean members of the union are summoned to appear to show cause why they should not be fined or penalized?

·Mr. JOHANNSEN. They have.

Mr. THOMPSON. For failing to carry on a boycott?

Mr. JOHANNSEN. For the individual members?

·Mr. THOMPSON. Yes, sir.

Mr. JOHANNSEN. No, sir.

Mr. THOMPSON. Well, do you have a board before which you subpœna or summon contractors?

Mr. JOHANNSEN. Yes, sir.

Mr. THOMPSON. To show cause why they could not be fined or penalized?

Mr. JOHANNSEN. Declared unfair.

Mr. THOMPSON. And now you might tell us in your own language what the method of that is and its purpose.

Mr. JOHANNSEN. That is the executive board· of the building trades council. The executive board·comprises one member of each affiliated local union. Such members are selected by the local union to act as an executive board. When a craft—▮or instance, the plumbers or plasterers or brickmen or carpenters or any particular craft—enters a complaint against any contractor, either general or·subcontractor, such complaint is not acted upon, but is referred to the executive board. The executive board directs its agent to summon such contractor to appear before that board and show cause or give reasons why a declaration of unfairness should not be made against him. In other words, it acts as a board of inquiry as to the facts and circumstances, and then makes its findings to the regular meeting of the council.

· Mr. THOMPSON. Sort of a board of adjustment?

Mr. JOHANNSEN. Exactly.

Mr. THOMPSON. Of complaints?

Mr. JOHANNSEN. That is correct.

Mr. THOMPSON. Does such a board or has such board ever assessed fines against employers and, if so, in what cases and what was the reason for it?

Mr. JOHANNSEN. Not lately. We formerly used the policy some years ago. If a man got tied up and was unfair and done something that he should not have done, and ought to have known he should not have done,.and that he did know he should not have done, and the job was practically completed, we would exact a fine of $200 or $300 or $500 as the case might be against him, that he had to give to some charitable association.

Mr. THOMPSON. How long since that form——

Mr. JOHANNSEN. That has been discontinued for the past four years.

Mr. THOMPSON. Since that time have such fines been collected, if you know?

Mr. JOHANNSEN. He was declared unfair until the charitable institution showed us the receipt, or showed us he had paid the fine.

Mr, THOMPSON. By unfair, you mean the union men were called off the work?

Mr. JOHANNSEN. They refused to work for him.

Mr. THOMPSON. You made some statement of how you came to go to Stockton, or how the international union got involved in it. Will you tell us how you came to go there, and whether or not you are now living there?

Mr. JOHANNSEN. The members and officers of the carpenters' union in Stockton petitioned the general officers, the United Brotherhood of Indianapolis, and requested specifically that I be sent to Stockton to help conduct their end of the fight.

Mr. THOMPSON. And since that time you have been living there?

Mr. JOHANNSEN. Sure; I am up there.

Mr. THOMPSON. I might ask another question along that line. Something has been said here to-day about home protection and people of a town taking care of their interests. State to the commission, if you will, how you view the participation by the officers of the international union in the industry or union affairs in Stockton.

Mr. JOHANNSEN. There is no interference of any description whatsoever by either the State officers or officers of the international union in the conduct of· the affairs of the local union or a local building trades council until they make a request for some assistance either financially or advisory. or otherwise.

Mr. THOMPSON. And that request had been made in the Stockton case?

Mr. JOHANNSEN. Yes, sir.

Mr. THOMPSON. And you came as a result of that request?

Mr. JOHANNSEN. I did.

Mr. THOMPSON. How many jobs or establishments are being picketed in Stockton now, if you know?

Mr. JOHANNSEN. All the building jobs that are unfair, and the planing mills and the Stockton Iron Works.

Mr. THOMPSON. Could you be more specific and tell us the jobs? That information is desired.

Mr. JOHANNSEN. The Stockton Iron Works, the Totten-Brant Planing Mill, the Roberts & Clark Mill, Union Planing Mill, Lincoln School, Jackson School, the job at Center and Market—I don't know the name of the job.

Mr. THOMPSON. Would you mind telling what was the purpose of the picketing that has occurred?

Mr. JOHANNSEN. To appeal to a sense of shame of the scabs, if they have any.

Mr. THOMPSON. Who has general charge of the picketing?

Mr. JOHANNSEN. I have.

Mr. THOMPSON. What are the pickets paid and by whom are they paid?

Mr. JOHANNSEN. They are not paid anything. They receive the same as all other men, $6 a week strike benefits, from their international organization.

Mr. THOMPSON. I believe you said something, Mr. Johannsen, about ex-convicts or others being employed as gunmen, etc. Are there any ex-convicts in official positions in labor unions, to your knowledge?

Mr. JOHANNSEN. I don't know.

Mr. THOMPSON. That is all, Mr. Chairman.

Chairman WALSH. Mr. Weinstock wants to ask you some questions.

Commissioner WEINSTOCK. You were telling the commission, Mr. Johannsen, of a practical boycott that had been started by the M., M. and E. against certain unions. Which side was the first to initiate the boycott in Stockton in this controversy?

Mr. JOHANNSEN. The M. and M.

Commissioner WEINSTOCK. Will you explain how and when?

Mr. JOHANNSEN. They interfered with the clerks' union; they prohibited them from doing business with the retail clothiers' association. Without their interference there would have been an adjustment and no trouble at all.

Commissioner WEINSTOCK. Just state, if you will, a little more specifically the attitude of the M., M. and E. in that particular case. Just what they did and how they did it.

Mr. JOHANNSEN. It is in their declaration, namely, that no association, the employers of labor of any description, shall deal with any labor union.

Commissioner WEINSTOCK. Prior to that, in the present controversy organized labor had not levied any boycott on the employers?

Mr. JOHANNSEN. Not to my knowledge.

Commissioner WEINSTOCK. Was that period before or after the Sperry flour boycott?

Mr. JOHANNSEN. You understand that when the agent for the clerks and the agent for the labor council was advised by the employers' association that they could not deal with them because they dealt with the storekeepers individually, they went to each individual to ascertain as to whether or not the conditions were satisfactory, and so on and so on; and all those merchants who agreed, of course, retained their union store card, and all those who did not agree they removed the union store card. They did not take the union out; they took the union store card out.

Commissioner WEINSTOCK. When did this circumstance happen that you speak of, where the storekeepers refused to deal with the union?

Mr. JOHANNSEN. I think that was along in the latter part of May.

Commissioner WEINSTOCK. This present year?

Mr. JOHANNSEN. Yes.

Commissioner WEINSTOCK. 1914?

Mr. JOHANNSEN. Yes. The Sperry boycott levied against labor: I believe it was not levied until recently, until the declaration of the unfairness.

Commissioner WEINSTOCK. But there was some statement made here by Mr. Irish, I think, this morning, that there had been a boycott levied on the

Sperry flour mills due to the flour mills refusing to unionize their engineers. Now, when did that take place?

Mr. JOHANNSEN. Mr. Irish can afford to be more careless with his statements than I can. I don't know anything about it.

Commissioner WEINSTOCK. That is, you don't know when the——

Mr. JOHANNSEN. All I know——

Commissioner WEINSTOCK. You don't know when the boycott was levied? Do you know whether there was a boycott levied against the Sperry flour mills because they declined to unionize their engineers?

Mr. JOHANNSEN. Well, so far, as I know, the Sperry Flour Mill Co., in the first place, is not union; only recently the State federation and building trades issued a boycott against them throughout the State.

Commissioner WEINSTOCK. How recently?

Mr. JOHANNSEN. In the last two or three weeks, so far as I know.

Commissioner WEINSTOCK. Has there been no boycott on the Sperry Flouring Mill?

Mr. JOHANNSEN. I suppose; there may have been; I don't know; I presume that was local in Stockton.

Commissioner WEINSTOCK. Well, if there had been a boycott levied against the Sperry Flouring Mills before this last May, then I suppose you would want to correct your statement that the first boycott was initiated by the M., M. and E.?

Mr. JOHANNSEN. Oh, not necessarily.

Commissioner WEINSTOCK. That is, your statement would still stand that they were the first to initiate the boycott?

Mr. JOHANNSEN. I am assuming now, of course, that the Sperry Flour Co. is a minor consideration in this, as far as the open shop—that is, the present status of the company in Stockton.

Commissioner WEINSTOCK. That is not the point. The point I want to get at is, by which side was the boycott initiated? Was it initiated by labor or initiated by the M., M. and E.?

Mr. JOHANNSEN. Well, I am afraid we will have to go back too many years; I don't know. I really don't know. I can't answer that. I don't know.

Commissioner WEINSTOCK. Your answer is you don't know?

Mr. JOHANNSEN. I am not familiar enough with the Sperry flouring business.

Commissioner WEINSTOCK. In the instructions given to the pickets, Mr. Johannsen, over your name—I have a copy of the card that was handed to me the other day—among other things I notice this: " Strong language tending to provoke violence must be abstained from." This, of course, makes it clear that so far as the instructions are concerned, you, as the captain in chief of all the pickets, are opposed to violence in this trouble—labor trouble?

Mr. JOHANNSEN. Yes.

Commissioner WEINSTOCK. Has there been any violence in Stockton?

Mr. JOHANNSEN. Oh, there has been a couple of little scraps, you know. That is all.

Commissioner WEINSTOCK. Will you tell any more of the violations that have taken place, that have come to your knowledge?

Mr. JOHANNSEN. I haven't seen it.

Commissioner WEINSTOCK. Do you know whether there has been violence?

Mr. JOHANNSEN. Oh, I understand there was a little scrap at Totten & Brant's mill.

Commissioner WEINSTOCK. You were not present?

Mr. JOHANNSEN. I was not present.

Commissioner WEINSTOCK. So, that whatever knowledge you have of that case would be entirely hearsay?

Mr. JOHANNSEN. Yes; entirely hearsay.

Commissioner WEINSTOCK. Has there been any violence that you know of?

Mr. JOHANNSEN. No. If there had been, I wouldn't testify to that; so what is the use of asking that question?

Commissioner WEINSTOCK. Why wouldn't you testify?

Mr. JOHANNSEN. Because I wouldn't tell everything; I wouldn't tell if I did know; you might as well have the facts about it.

Commissioner WEINSTOCK. That is, if there had been violence and you knew of it, you wouldn't tell the commission?

Mr. JOHANNSEN. No; but there hasn't been any, so far as I know.

Commissioner WEINSTOCK. You gave the commission explanations, Mr. Johannsen, of the various cases that Mr. Irish had cited as to what he believed to be the underlying causes for the present trouble. Among them he cited what I presume has become known as the Totten case, where a certain amount of lumber had been delivered to a certain building without the union rubber stamp placed thereon; and, at the insistence of the union, despite the fact, as he states, that the oversight was due to a union employee at the planing mill, the lumber had to be carted back to the mill and stamped and then recarted to the building. Your explanation for that was that that statement was not a true statement on the part of Mr. Irish.

Mr. JOHANNSEN. My statement was I don't believe it.

Commissioner WEINSTOCK. Do you know anything of the case at all?

Mr. JOHANNSEN. Not of that particular case, but I know of our rules in general.

Commissioner WEINSTOCK. I see. Then you could not give a counter statement to the commission of that particular case?

Mr. JOHANNSEN. No; not right now. I might perhaps to-morrow. He was very careful not to mention the name of the building, the location, and so it is difficult to trace it.

Commissioner WEINSTOCK. Were the contractors, the building contractors in Stockton, organized before this trouble arose?

Mr. JOHANNSEN. That I couldn't say. I do not know. I do not think they were as a building contractors' association.

Commissioner WEINSTOCK. I see. Do you think it would have made any difference in the situation to-day if the contractors had been organized, so that any grievances arising, such as Mr. Irish told about, could have been adjusted right there and then?

Mr. JOHANNSEN. That would depend, of course. If the contractors had been organized, and at the same time would have sufficient independence financially of the banks, the chances are they would have told the M. and M. to go to hell.

Commissioner WEINSTOCK. I am not speaking about the present situation.

Suppose the contractors had been organized a year ago, or two years ago, or three years ago, so that these cases that then have been cited as causes of irritation could have been taken up right there and settled and adjudicated, had a conference?

Mr. JOHANNSEN. Yes; there would be less, you mean—I think I see what you are driving at. If the power, the relative power compared?

Commissioner WEINSTOCK. Yes.

Mr. JOHANNSEN. Of course that is true.

Commissioner WEINSTOCK. Then, on account of the split in the situation at Stockton, at least so far as the building trades are concerned, is the fact only one side was organized?

Mr. JOHANNSEN. Well, that is a matter of speculation. Of course I don't know.

Commissioner WEINSTOCK. You can express your opinion about it. You are familiar with the organizations and the conditions in other cities where there is a mutual organization of both sides and you know how that works out?

Mr. JOHANNSEN. I might give my opinion. If everything was efficient through the whole country—things are varied, so that I could give a very varied opinion on those things, and I don't care to give an opinion on those things. I do not know, it might have turned out different.

Commissioner WEINSTOCK. Is it customary where both sides are organized in the building trades to have a grievance committee?

Mr. JOHANNSEN. Yes; they generally have committees.

Commissioner WEINSTOCK. Then, when an issue arises, is it customary to submit that issue to your grievance committee, to representatives on both sides?

Mr. JOHANNSEN. It all depends upon the nature of it. For instance, there are certain rules mandatory. For instance, there are certain conditions which the plumbers work under and the other trades agree to. Then the building trades' only function is as an agent to enforce those rules for both sides. If the employer contends that the union is arbitrary, or otherwise, the building trades does not allow it, that particular local union, to adjust its difficulty, because it would be biased through its selfishness.

Commissioner WEINSTOCK. Is it true, Mr. Johannsen—the point I had in mind was this: I happen to know in the Metal Trades' Association they have what I think is called a grievance committee, where when either side has a grievance it is submitted to this grievance committee, and they investigate and determine it.

Mr. JOHANNSEN. I see what you are driving at. There is, of course, an equality of power there. There is not that in the building trades.

Commissioner WEINSTOCK. There is not?

Mr. JOHANNSEN. No.

Commissioner WEINSTOCK. But isn't there an equality of power where both sides are organized?

Mr. JOHANNSEN. If you have a stick of dynamite in your hand, and I have a stick of dynamite in my hand, it would be foolish for us to throw at each other, because we have both got the same kind of power and we both want to live. Is that what you are driving at?

Commissioner WEINSTOCK. Yes.

Mr. JOHANNSEN. Certainly, I agree with that.

Commissioner WEINSTOCK. In other words, what I want to find out is this, whether, if the building trades in Stockton had been organized, strongly organized, so they could have dealt collectively with the union in place of the union dealing with each employer separately, whether it might not have brought about a better condition and obviated the present situation?

Mr. JOHANNSEN. That is quite possible; yes.

Commissioner WEINSTOCK. That is all, Mr. Chairman.

Chairman WALSH. Did you want to ask any questions, Mr. O'Connell?

Commissioner O'CONNELL. Yes. You made a statement this morning that the declarations for the open shop carried with it that there was to be no discrimination of any kind between the union and nonunion employees; in other words, to be the right of an employee to judge for himself whether he should belong to the union or not. Do you know of any discriminations that have taken place in Stockton in the way of employers calling employees into their offices and asking them to surrender their cards of membership in their unions, or foremen or superintendents of any firms taking like action?

Mr. JOHANNSEN. That happened. That is the way they did with the clerks.

Commissioner O'CONNELL. Have you any particular cases in mind of any firm calling in its employees?

Mr. JOHANNSEN. I have not, but I could get them.

Commissioner O'CONNELL. Will you furnish the commission——

Mr. JOHANNSEN. I will try to.

Commissioner O'CONNELL. With specific information?

Mr. JOHANNSEN. I will try to get it for you this afternoon; yes.

Commissioner O'CONNELL. That is all.

Chairman WALSH. Mr. Commons would like to ask you some questions.

Commissioner COMMONS. You spoke about certain things that you would not arbitrate; that is, certain things such as eliminating the union out of existence, and that there are certain rules that are mandatory—that are not arbitrable. What are they?

Mr. JOHANNSEN. There are no rules mandatory that I know of. What I meant by that is if the employers should decide my union has got to be strangled, I would rather fight than get strangled.

Commissioner COMMONS. But they would not do that, as an abstract proposition. They would do that by dealing with each situation as it arises. What is this situation that could arise that you consider essential?

Mr. JOHANNSEN. I do not know. We feel in the absence of power all of our declarations for justice is so much wind.

Commissioner COMMONS. Would you arbitrate the question of discrimination?

Mr. JOHANNSEN. What do you mean?

Commissioner COMMONS. As to whether a man is rightfully discharged or not, or whether it is on account of——

Mr. JOHANNSEN. No; we never question as to—unless we have positive proof that he is discriminated against because of the fact of his union affiliation, and we could prove that, and that is a difficult thing to prove—whether or not the employee has a right, if he desires; it is up to him.

Commissioner COMMONS. In other words, the charge is made here that the unions in Stockton refused to allow an employer——

Mr. JOHANNSEN. That is, an employer; the laboring man hasn't made that condition; that is the unfortunate part of it. So far it has come to our attention——

Commissioner COMMONS. What I want to know is whether you would submit a case like that to a joint committee?

Mr. JOHANNSEN. Why, certainly.

Commissioner COMMONS. Have the unions of Stockton offered to do so?

Mr. JOHANNSEN. That is our open declaration, certainly.

Commissioner COMMONS. Then what are the questions that you refuse to arbitrate?

Mr. JOHANNSEN. The question as to whether our union shall live or not. The issue in Stockton is either the M. and M. dies or we die.

Commissioner COMMONS. The issue, as I understood it to be stated a while ago, was in regard to this ultimatum in the last year; if you will notice it, they insisted that the agreements should be closed-shop agreements. Is that true of all the agreements that have been proposed by the unions—that they should only be union men who were employed?

Mr. JOHANNSEN. Why, certainly. I can't speak for all the unions, but so far as the building trades are concerned we refuse to work with nonunion men. But he can hire all the nonunion men he wants; but if he wants our services he will have to employ union men.

Commissioner COMMONS. Consequently he is acting on the same principle when he refuses to employ union men?

Mr. JOHANNSEN. That is up to him. We have no objection, if he wants to fight it out on those issues.

Commissioner COMMONS. He can generally fight on the other?

Mr. JOHANNSEN. We haven't any objection to the M., M. and E.; we are not worried about them. They can organize all they want.

Commissioner COMMONS. Can you speak for the union people; you wouldn't consider that that ever could be settled by a board of arbitration?

Mr. JOHANNSEN. Well, as to whether or not the union shall operate on what they call the closed shop—what we call the union shop.

Commissioner COMMONS. Suppose they didn't mention that question at all about having a provision in the agreement that there should be no discrimination against union men, which would be an arbitrable question; would the union stand for that?

Mr. JOHANNSEN. Well, I would prefer that that should be put up to them first; I don't know.

Commissioner COMMONS. Would you, as representing the union, say that they should not accept that?

Mr. JOHANNSEN. I don't quite understand what you mean at all. I am confused. I can't get what you are driving at.

Commissioner COMMONS. Commissioner Lennon asked a question a moment ago on that point. He stated that there are certain agreements which do not mention the question of the open and closed shop, but they had in them a provision there should be no discrimination against the union.

Mr. JOHANNSEN. Well, that means the same thing, you know; in the end it means the same thing.

Commissioner COMMONS. Is that an arbitrable question?

Mr. JOHANNSEN. They have no agreements at all—the building trades; the building contractors don't make any agreements at all.

Commissioner COMMONS. Is that a question that could be submitted to a third party for decision in case there was an alleged discrimination?

Mr. JOHANNSEN. I don't know.

Commissioner COMMONS. The proposition I am getting at is this: If you stand for the closed shop, then the employers stand for the closed shop, too?

Mr. JOHANNSEN. I am perfectly willing they shall stand for the open shop.

Commissioner COMMONS. There is no middle ground?

Mr. JOHANNSEN. I am perfectly agreeable to that, too. That is up to them.

Commissioner COMMONS. That is the situation that the unions have brought on at Stockton through a period of several years, and the employers now are simply taking the stand the same as you have been taking for a number of years; is that not the situation?

Mr. JOHANNSEN. That is correct in some cases.

Commissioner O'CONNELL. Did I understand there are no signed contracts at all between the building trades, the building trades employers, and the building trades workmen?

Mr. JOHANNSEN. None; never have been.

Commissioner O'CONNELL. Covering hours, wages, union, and nonunion?

Mr. JOHANNSEN. There is an understanding, of course; for instance, what the wages shall be for plumbers. There is an understanding between the plumbers and the trades, they understand what it is before——

Commissioner O'CONNELL. But no agreements in writing?

Mr. JOHANNSEN. No agreements at all. If, for instance, any department had a question of wages, that organization comes to the building trades for their proposition, and if it is covered by the building trades it is brought up to the attention of the employers and reasoned out with them, and if that is agreed upon that is all there is to it, just verbally. No agreement at all except that kind of an agreement—a verbal agreement; an understanding.

Commissioner COMMONS. There is an understanding?

Mr. JOHANNSEN. An understanding.

Commissioner COMMONS. And that is always understood?

Mr. JOHANNSEN. Certainly.

Commissioner COMMONS. So that whether or not it is put down in writing, from your standpoint that does not make any difference?

Mr. JOHANNSEN. Oh, no.

Commissioner COMMONS. And if that is not understood, you make it understood?

Mr. JOHANNSEN. Yes, certainly.

Commissioner COMMONS. That is the fact?

Mr. JOHANNSEN. Yes.

Commissioner O'CONNELL. But there is not any signed contract to that effect?

Mr. JOHANNSEN. No.

Commissioner O'CONNELL. No document of any kind signed?

Mr. JOHANNSEN. No, none whatever.

Commissioner O'CONNELL. Simply a question of whether he wants all union men or all nonunion men?

Mr. JOHANNSEN. Yes.

Commissioner O'CONNELL. And he decides it for himself?

Mr. JOHANNSEN. He decides that for himself, exactly; that is his choice.

Commissioner LENNON. Just a question, Mr. Johannsen. Take, for instance, the building trades; take your own trade. If there is any scarcity of men in the town doing carpenter work, can the employer hire nonunion carpenters?

Mr. JOHANNSEN. Certainly.

Commissioner LENNON. To help out?

Mr. JOHANNSEN. If we can not furnish the men, certainly.

Commissioner LENNON. Now, I want you to make clear; perhaps you did, but I want you to make clear as to the right of the employer to discharge men for poor work, for drunkenness, or incompetency, or inefficiency, or for no reason, for that matter.

Mr. JOHANNSEN. I think that perhaps the best evidence of that is I have never known of a case in my experience in the movement in this State where any union has ever demanded reinstatement of a man who had been discharged.

Commissioner LENNON. Unless he had served upon a committee and it was almost clear that his discharge——

Chairman WALSH. He says he don't know.

Mr. JOHANNSEN. I haven't any knowledge of that.

Commissioner LENNON. You haven't that knowledge, then?

Mr. JOHANNSEN. Most of that charge by the employers is all bunk.

Commissioner LENNON. That is all, Mr. Johannsen.

Commissioner COMMONS. I would like to ask a few questions.

Chairman WALSH. That is all, thank you; unless you have some statements you desire to make.

Mr. JOHANNSEN. No, I have not anything more.

Chairman WALSH. We will take a recess until 2 o'clock. Mr. Johannsen, please return at that time. Prof. Commons would like to ask you some questions.

(Whereupon, at 12.30 o'clock p. m. on Tuesday, August 25, 1914, an adjournment was taken until 2 o'clock p. m. of the same day.)

AFTER RECESS—2 P. M.

Met pursuant to adjournment. Present as before.

Commissioner WEINSTOCK. In the absence of Chairman Walsh, he has asked me to preside until his return. Call your next witness, Mr. Thompson.

Mr. THOMPSON. Mr. Johannsen had not finished, Mr. Chairman.

Mr. Johannsen, will you please take the stand?

TESTIMONY OF MR. ANTON JOHANNSEN—Continued.

Mr. THOMPSON. You were not quite through with your questioning, Mr. Commons.

Commissioner COMMONS. I had a question, Mr. Chairman. The statement was made here this morning, I think it was about the electrical workers, in which certain members of the union were brought in by the employer from San Francisco, and they were not allowed to work. What are the rules between unions, we may say, of the same trade in different cities in this State? Can a union man come from San Francisco to Stockton and get employment, if he carries a card, without having previously joined the Stockton union or gotten a permit or something?

Mr. JOHANNSEN. He can, providing that there are no union men in Stockton out of employment.

Commissioner COMMONS. Well, if you will notice what was stated this morning—it was charged that there were only two union men that were out of employment, and they were men that had been discharged by this employer, and were not satisfactory, for reasons, which, if true, were good. Now, what would be the situation in such a case? Would the union there insist that those two men should be employed in preference to an outsider?

Mr. JOHANNSEN. That would depend, of course, upon the nature of the contention of the employer for discharging those men. I say unless the union is in a position to prove that those men are discharged and discriminated against because of their activity in the union as such, then the union would not permit their discharge.

Commissioner COMMONS. In such a case as was stated this morning, assuming that that was the grounds of discharge, and that they were ascertained?

Mr. JOHANNSEN. Of course, that statement comes from such an unreliable source. If you get that statement from the contractor who really employed those men who did the discharging, who really had the complaint, it might then be investigated. I could then ascertain the nature of the thing, whether the union was justified in that or not. But it comes from such an unresponsible source, the chamber of commerce——

Commissioner COMMONS. Let it go. If he comes from San Francisco to Stockton, can he go to work on the day he arrives?

Mr. JOHANNSEN. He can.

Commissioner COMMONS. Could he go right on the job?

Mr. JOHANNSEN. There isn't anything required of him except to show that he is in good standing in some union in the jurisdiction of his international union, whether he comes from 'Frisco or any other place.

Commissioner COMMONS. That is true of any man that comes from any part of the country?

Mr. JOHANNSEN. That is the rule; yes, sir.

Commissioner COMMONS. Is there any local rule that interferes with that at all?

Mr. JOHANNSEN. There is no local rules except that we give the local men preference over outside men.

Commissioner COMMONS. They have the decision on that point, the local, have they?

Mr. JOHANNSEN. They do until it is called to the attention of the building trades; that is to say, if an electrical contractor desires to employ a given number of men who come from a different locality than Stockton, or any other city, and the electrical workers' union refuses to allow those men to work, or succeeds in having them stop work, then that contractor can get redress by making application to the building trades, and the building trades lets those men work pending investigation. Those men remain to work, providing that it is shown that the employer could not get competent help. In other words, there is no excuse except that of being unable to supply the competent help. If a given union can not guarantee competent help, the employer is at liberty to hire men wherever he can get them.

Commissioner COMMONS. The building trades is final, then—this executive committee you described, I think it was?

Mr. JOHANNSEN. Yes, sir.

Commissioner COMMONS. Of the building trades is final?

Mr. JOHANNSEN. Yes, sir.

Commissioner COMMONS. No appeal to the union of the craft involved?

Mr. JOHANNSEN. There is an appeal, but not to the local union.

Commissioner COMMONS. To the international?

Mr. JOHANNSEN. There is an appeal to the international, but in the meantime the contention of the employer is agreed to at that time. That is, they are allowed to work pending the appeal.

Commissioner COMMONS. Is there an appeal of the building trades council to the international?

Mr. JOHANNSEN. To the building trades council, and from that to the federation of labor.

Commissioner COMMONS. And in the meantime the men are allowed to work?

Mr. JOHANNSEN. The men are allowed to work and the job is completed. That is very seldom resorted to.

Commissioner COMMONS. In the meantime the man has the men and continues the work?

Mr. JOHANNSEN. I don't know of any case, and there was no contention made this morning that the building trades as such ever had their attention called to a situation of that kind. If they did, they would have adjusted it just like I described.

Commissioner COMMONS. I don't know whether you were informed about the Sperry boycott. Has that boycott been extended beyond the limits of Stockton?

Mr. JOHANNSEN. Sure; throughout the State.

Commissioner COMMONS. Do you know what date that was?

Mr. JOHANNSEN. I could not state what date, but it is recently, at any rate.

Commissioner COMMONS. Since July 8?

Mr. JOHANNSEN. Since July 8; yes, sir.

Commissioner COMMONS. What authority extends the boycott beyond the limits of a place like that? State federation?

Mr. JOHANNSEN. The State federation of the State building trades. The State federation.

Commissioner COMMONS. How often does that meet, or can it be done by the executive council?

Mr. JOHANNSEN. It can be done by the executive council by referendum vote by mail.

Commissioner COMMONS. Is the action of the State federation binding on the building trades?

Mr. JOHANNSEN. In cases of that kind; yes, sir. It is not exactly binding, but there is a moral understanding it will be complied with.

Commissioner COMMONS. Are the building trades members of the State federation?

Mr. JOHANNSEN. Yes, sir.

Commissioner COMMONS. Can the building trades also independently declare a boycott for the State?

Mr. JOHANNSEN. They can't declare it independently. If they do, the State federation is under no obligation to support them. In other words, the building trades, if they want a State boycott, must make request to the State federation.

Commissioner COMMONS. There is a State federation of the building trades?

Mr. JOHANNSEN. Yes, sir; State building trades.

Commissioner COMMONS. Which includes all building trades councils?

Mr. JOHANNSEN. All building trades councils and all building trades unions.

Commissioner COMMONS. How is that State building trades constituted?

Mr. JOHANNSEN. Each county has what they call a county building trades council. That council is comprised of all the crafts which are engaged in the building industry—bricklayers, carpenters, plumbers, steamfitters, hod carriers, plasterers, and so on. It includes, in other words, all mechanics and laborers engaged in the building industry; they have their respective unions, and they form a council, and each local union has representation, according to membership, in that council, and that council acts as agent to enforce the rules of each local union.

Commissioner COMMONS. Then there is representation in the State federation——

Mr. JOHANNSEN. Each local council, you understand, in the different counties has representation in the State building trades. They have a conference once a year and each local union in each city or county is entitled to one delegate, and that convention assembles once a year, and that convention deals with matters that may come up from time to time, and during the interval of the convention the executive council transacts the business.

Commissioner COMMONS. Now, this executive council of the State building trades would be able to pass upon, has authority to pass upon——

Mr. JOHANNSEN (interposing). Certainly.

Commissioner COMMONS. A boycott or a strike on an unfair employer?

Mr. JOHANNSEN. Not upon a strike.

Commissioner COMMONS. Yès; that is what I was trying to get.

Mr. JOHANNSEN. Not upon a strike.

Commissioner COMMONS. What is its authority?

Mr. JOHANNSEN. There is no authority vested in the State building trades' officers to call a strike in any given locality.

Commissioner COMMONS. Well, then, they can not call a strike, but what can it do—can it do anything toward the settlement of a strike?

Mr. JOHANNSEN. It can prevent a strike, and it can adjust a strike after it is started.

Commissioner COMMONS. Has it any power to order them to return to work?

Mr. JOHANNSEN. Certainly, it has the power to order them to return to work, providing, upon investigation, they find that the rules, the ordinary rules, have not been complied with—the laws have not been complied with.

Commissioner COMMONS. In that way it has jurisdiction over any local?

Mr. JOHANNSEN. For instance, I will give you an illustration.

Commissioner COMMONS. Yes.

Mr. JOHANNSEN. About four years ago the lumber handlers' union in Oakland called a strike in one of the lumberyards there—called their men all off because there was a nonunion man working there. That would mean, of course, to involve all the planing mills, and the planing mills, naturally, of course, would involve all the building trades. In other words, all the trades would become involved by reason of the strike. And the building trades have a working arrangement that if an individual or an individual union has the means of involving all the other trades into a strike, then that union should agree to consult, to advise with, and to accept the judgment of those unions so affected. In other words, no strike can be called unless it is called by the consent of all of the trades. This union called a strike. I was over in Oakland at that time. I went to the business agent of the union and demanded——

Commissioner COMMONS. Is that union a member of the building trades?

Mr. JOHANNSEN. A member of the building trades.

Commissioner COMMONS. It is the lumber handlers you say?

Mr. JOHANNSEN. The lumber handlers.

Commissioner COMMONS. Yes.

Mr. JOHANNSEN. I demanded that he immediately order his men back to work pending an investigation by the officers of the building trades.

Commissioner COMMONS. And you represented the State?

Mr. JOHANNSEN. I represented the State building trades at that time.

Commissioner COMMONS. I see.

Mr. JOHANNSEN. And the men were ordered back to work.

Commissioner COMMONS. Well, then, the local strike becomes the property of the State building trades?

Mr. JOHANNSEN. Oh, no; you don't seem to catch it.

Commissioner COMMONS. No; I don't.

Mr. JOHANNSEN. There are certain laws, rules, and regulations which govern the local building trades council, and whenever they act independently of the State building trades and conform with those rules—those regular regulations—why, then, the State building trades does not interfere. But if they do anything contrary to the ordinary rules and regulations; for instance, supposing that a local union would ask for an increase in wages from their employers, and supposing they did not give the 90 days' notice, which is required by law, and supposing the local building trades was influenced extraordinarily by that local union to consent to it, then the matter becomes the function of the State building trades to tell that local council, "You are in the wrong here, you have violated the law. The men have got to go back to work pending such a notice." Like they did in Bakersfield. There had been a lockout in Bakersfield, and I was ordered to Bakersfield to enforce the law. To enforce the law meant that the men had to go back to work and to give the regular 90 days' notice. That, in that case, was the plumbers.

Commissioner COMMONS. In this Stockton case, are you in that case representing the State building trades?

Mr. JOHANNSEN. I am representing the carpenters.

Commissioner COMMONS. What authority have you got over the other unions?

Mr. JOHANNSEN. I have got none except what authority was granted me by the Stockton unions.

Commissioner COMMONS. Oh, the Stockton Building Trades Council invited you?

Mr. JOHANNSEN. Well, the Stockton unions—why all of them have selected me to have charge of all the picketing. That is all the authority I have got.

Commissioner COMMONS. You are the agent for them?

Mr. JOHANNSEN. Yes.

Commissioner. COMMONS. Now, in the case of boycotts, that is the point I was asking you about, about the practice there of the State building trades council in declaring a firm unfair. That means declaring a boycott on its products, as I understand it?

Mr. JOHANNSEN. Yes.

Commissioner COMMONS. Does it go through the same——

Mr. JOHANNSEN. It goes through the same channel. First, it comes from a local union that is affected, and they bring it to what we call the building trades, or the labor council, and it is indorsed there. Then it comes to the State office, and in some cases goes to the A. F. of L. for their cooperation.·

Commissioner COMMONS. How can the boycott extend beyond the State of California? How can it be made—what is the system of attack there?

Mr. .JOHANNSEN. Well, if you are running a business, if you are running a business, for instance, that sells its product all over the country, why, of course, we would fight you all over the country if we could, that is all.

Commissioner COMMONS. I mean how would you bring it about, according to your laws; how would you authorize a boycott all over the Pacific coast?

Mr. JOHANNSEN. Well, you can't authorize a boycott all over the Pacific coast. We can't authorize no boycott all over the Pacific coast.

Commissioner COMMONS. There is no federation that takes in the Pacific coast?

Mr. JOHANNSEN. Why, of course not.

Commissioner COMMONS. Well, how about over the country, then?

Mr. JOHANNSEN. If we do that we make application to the A. F. of L.

Commissioner COMMONS. So that your jurisdiction is how far?

Mr. JOHANNSEN. The State of California.

Commissioner COMMONS. There has been no attempt to federate the unions of the Pacific coast into a separate central council?

Mr. JOHANNSEN. Oh, no; that has not been necessary yet.

Commissioner COMMONS. In this central labor council in Stockton, are the common laborers organized also?

Mr. JOHANNSEN. The labor council?

Commissioner COMMONS. Yes.·

Mr. JOHANNSEN. Neither the labor council nor the building trades and callings except the building trades; everything else, for instance, machinists, boiler makers—there are several mechanical trades in this, the printers, everything except those who are engaged in the building industry.

Commissioner COMMONS. I am trying to get at the extent to which common labor and unskilled labor are organized and recognized as organizations in Stockton.

Mr. JOHANNSEN. Well, there is a building laborers' union, which is confined to the building line. They generally have better conditions than other labor,· ordinary labor, does; that is, less hours and better wages, as a rule. There are in the building trades council what is known as a building helpers' union, with headquarters like in Stockton, that includes hod carriers, in the building trades, and common labor.

Commissioner COMMONS. Is that a closed-shop union?

Mr. JOHANNSEN. Closed-shop union; certainly.

Commissioner COMMONS. Same as the others?

Mr. JOHANNSEN. Yes.

Commissioner COMMONS. What is their scale?

Mr. JOHANNSEN. Their scale is four and four and a half.

Commissioner COMMONS. That is all laborers?

Mr. JOHANNSEN. Yes.

Commissioner COMMONS. Hod carriers?

Mr. JOHANNSEN. Hod carriers.

Commissioner COMMONS. What is the scale for common labor?

Mr. JOHANNSEN. Two and a half for eight hours.

Commissioner COMMONS. Unorganized?

Mr. JOHANNSEN. No; organized; they are not unorganized.

Commissioner COMMONS. Well, take unorganized labor in Stockton, what would be the pay of unorganized common labor?

Mr. JOHANNSEN. Two fifty for eight hours.

Commissioner COMMONS. You mean to say that all common labor in Stockton is organized?

Mr. JOHANNSEN. Certainly.

Commissioner COMMONS. There is no nonunion common labor in the town?

Mr. JOHANNSEN. Oh, there may be some here and there, but not to speak of.

Chairman WEINSTOCK. Only in the building trades.

Commissioner COMMONS. I am speaking outside of the building trades, such as in the factories and in shops.

Mr. JOHANNSEN. Oh, there are some there; yes. There are some sweepers and such stuff as that.

Commissioner COMMONS. Yard laborers, loaders, and things of that kind?

Mr. JOHANNSEN. They are all organized.

Commissioner COMMONS. They would be represented in the labor council, wouldn't they?

Mr. JOHANNSEN. Not in the lumber yards. They are all in the building trades.

Commissioner COMMONS. Oh, I see.

Mr. JOHANNSEN. Because the lumber is supplied to the building.

Commissioner COMMONS. Take these machinery trades, then.

Mr. JOHANNSEN. The machinery trades? There are not many there, except in the metal trades.

Commissioner COMMONS. Do you know whether they are organized?

Mr. JOHANNSEN. No; there is not enough there for them to form an organization.

Commissioner COMMONS. How about city labor?

Mr. JOHANNSEN. I don't know anything about the city labor.

Commissioner COMMONS. If common labor comes into Stockton from any other place, what is his method of getting work?

Mr. JOHANNSEN. He is up against it no matter where he goes or where he comes from—common labor.

Commissioner COMMONS. Well, up against what?

Mr. JOHANNSEN. Because people don't recognize anything except power; they don't recognize justice and right. He hasn't got much power if he hasn't got a trade and hasn't got influence and hasn't got money and friends. That depends upon who he is, where he is going to, where he comes from.

Commissioner COMMONS. Suppose he wants to get work in the building trades, common labor in the building trades, what would he have to do there?

Mr. JOHANNSEN. The requirements made of him?

Commissioner COMMONS. Yes.

Mr. JOHANNSEN. He has to join the union.

Commissioner COMMONS. What would be the initiation?

Mr. JOHANNSEN. Ten dollars.

Commissioner COMMONS. And dues?

Mr. JOHANNSEN. Seventy-five cents, and a dollar a month, depending upon what he does. If he goes to work and is classed at $3 a day, he pays 75 cents; if $4 a day, a dollar; and if he earns more than $4, he pays a dollar and a quarter.

Commissioner COMMONS. What classes of labor get these different scales; what class gets $3?

Mr. JOHANNSEN. The commonest labor—wheeling brick and just ordinary work.

Commissioner COMMONS. And $4?

Mr. JOHANNSEN. The men that prepare mortar for the brickmen and hod carriers; the men that prepare mortar for plasterers, four dollars and a half.

Commissioner COMMONS. And helpers in the latter two cases, are they?

Mr. JOHANNSEN. There are not any helpers.

Commissioner COMMONS. Suppose he wants to get to work outside of the building trades, in the planing mill—what should he have?

Mr. JOHANNSEN. There is not anything required of him.

Commissioner COMMONS. Does he have to join any union?

Mr. Johannsen. No; there is no organization.

Commissioner Commons. Common laborers?

Mr. Johannsen. No.

Commissioner Commons. In the planing mills? The planing mills, then, includes what kind of labor?

Mr. Johannsen. Well, that is, I don't know what you would call it. We do not take in anybody except mechanics in planing mills and apprentices.

Commissioner Commons. What proportion of the planing-mill force is eligible to your organization?

Mr. Johannsen. Well, perhaps, 7 or 8 or 10 per cent.

Commissioner Commons. Then there would be from 90 to 93 per cent that are not eligible?

Mr. Johannsen. No; that are eligible to join the union, I mean. What I meant to say was 10 and not over 12 per cent of the employees in and around the mills are what you would call common labor and not eligible to join the union.

Commissioner Commons. All the rest are classed as mechanics and eligible?

Mr. Johannsen. Yes; they are.

Commissioner Commons. That is all.

Acting Chairman Weinstock. What is the initiation fee, Mr. Johannsen, for the carpenters' union?

Mr. Johannsen. In Stockton?

Acting ■hairman Weinstock. Yes.

Mr. Johannsen. Twenty dollars—no; $30.

Acting Chairman Weinstock. Do they have one uniform fee throughout the State, or does each local establish——

Mr. Johannsen. Each local establishes its own scale, its own initiation fee—each locality.

Acting Chairman Weinstock. What initiation fee is there in San Francisco?

Mr. Johannsen. Thirty dollars.

Acting Chairman Weinstock. The same rate?

Mr. Johannsen. Yes.

Acting Chairman Weinstock. Are you familiar with the initiation fee in the other crafts, like the bricklayers. the plumbers, and the plasterers?

Mr. Johannsen. I couldn't say exactly, but it is about the same as in 'Frisco.

Acting Chairman Weinstock. Could you furnish this commission with a list?

Mr. Johannsen. Sure; I could do that.

Acting Chairman Weinstock. Of the initiation fees in the various building-crafts trades?

Mr. Johannsen. Oh, yes; I could do that.

Acting Chairman Weinstock. Will you do that?

Mr. Johannsen. I will do that; yes.

Acting Chairman Weinstock. What are the monthly dues in the carpenters' union?

Mr. Johannsen. They are paying a dollar up there.

Acting Chairman Weinstock. And the maximum is how much?

Mr. Johannsen. There is not a maximum; they can pay as high as they decide amongst themselves.

Acting Chairman Weinstock. How are these initiation fees payable, payable in one lump sum?

Mr. Johannsen. No. They are payable in four weekly——

Acting Chairman Weinstock. Four weekly installments?

Mr. Johannsen. Four weekly installments.

Acting Chairman Weinstock. What happens if a worker is unable to meet an installment, if he has personal claims from other sources, is there any grace allowed him?

Mr. Johannsen. Well, that depends on a good many things. Suppose——

Acting Chairman Weinstock. In case of sickness in the family, or if he meets with misfortune.

Mr. Johannsen. We don't judge a man's misfortune, a man's sickness, a man's " up against it " with other men. For instance, we have got 200 men in the union, and one man comes along and says he is up against it. We might have 100 men in that union up against it also, and we act accordingly. That depends upon the circumstances. But those things, if they are facts, if it is true that that man is up against it, he generally gets considerable allowance made.

Acting Chairman WEINSTOCK. That is, the rule is not ironclad?
Mr. JOHANNSEN. No; it is not.
Acting Chairman WEINSTOCK. It is not absolutely enforced?
Mr. JOHANNSEN. No.
Acting Chairman WEINSTOCK. It is elastic?
Mr. JOHANNSEN. Yes; it is elastic.
Commissioner COMMONS. Did you hear the statement made this morning, by Mr. Irish to the effect that a number of men beat up an employer at Stockton? A hundred men or a hundred and twenty-five, I think he said. I don't know if he went any further into it.
Mr. JOHANNSEN. Well, of course——
Commissioner COMMONS. What was that incident he referred to?
Mr. JOHANNSEN. Well, of course, men have different interpretations of the truth.
Commissioner COMMONS. What was that incident?
Mr. JOHANNSEN. There was a little fight down at Totten & Brant's mill. It was all hearsay as far as I know. There was about 20 men engaged in it; I think they were about equally divided. Mr. Totten raised a chair and hit one of our pickets over the head with a chair, and they got into a fight, the whole bunch of them. It didn't amount to anything. It was what you could see anywhere.
Commissioner COMMONS. It was testified here he had his jaw broken.
Mr. JOHANNSEN. Who had?
Commissioner COMMONS. The employer.
Mr. JOHANNSEN. No, sir; he didn't. He had a little black eye. Kind of humiliated him, was all.
Commissioner COMMONS. Was this fight with the pickets?
Mr. JOHANNSEN. Yes, sir.
Commissioner COMMONS. Were these pickets under your direction?
Mr. JOHANNSEN. In doing that they wasn't. Unfortunately, I happened to be in the city.
Commissioner COMMONS. Were they acting under your direction when they did that?
Mr. JOHANNSEN. They were not acting under my direction when they did that. I wouldn't direct men to do that in daylight.
Commissioner COMMONS. You mean to say you do direct men to do it in the nighttime?
Mr. JOHANNSEN. No, sir; I don't mean that at all. But if I was going to direct them to do that, I would certainly direct it under cover of darkness, if I was going to direct it. I would do like the business men do, and try and evade the law, if I could, if I thought it was necessary.
Commissioner COMMONS. This happened in the daytime?
Mr. JOHANNSEN. It happened in broad daylight; policemen there and everything else.
Commissioner COMMONS. Have any since happened in the nighttime?
Mr. JOHANNSEN. No, sir; nothing happened in the nighttime.
Commissioner COMMONS. Your idea is that it is practicable and necessary to meet force with force; if the employer is organized, you should organize in the same way?
Mr. JOHANNSEN. Well, men do those things whether we like it or not, in the fight.
Commissioner COMMONS. What is your discipline of pickets if they decline to—if they disobey?
Mr. JOHANNSEN. The discipline, if a man does anything contrary to the instructions, he has no guaranty of organized protection. On the contrary, he is informed the organization will not protect him.
Commissioner COMMONS. Have you disciplined any pickets?
Mr. JOHANNSEN. No, sir; there has been no occasion for it. Just those few little outbursts is all. There has been no occasion for it, so far.
Commissioner COMMONS. No claim has been made to you by anybody?
Mr. JOHANNSEN. These things were perfectly human outbursts. Human indignation, which you can't help in men who are undisciplined. The average workingman has not been accustomed to discipline, except the discipline of the boss who made him do what he pleases. It is not so easy to discipline them in our direction. It takes a little time.
Acting Chairman WEINSTOCK. Call your next.
MR. THOMPSON. One more question, Mr. Chairman.

In regard to the boycott, some statements have been made here with reference to the enforcement of it by means of fines. Were any fines threatened or levied by the local union against its members to enforce the boycott order?

Mr. JOHANNSEN. Not that I know of.

Mr. THOMPSON. Would you be apt to know if there were such?

Mr. JOHANNSEN. I think I would. There might have been before I came here, that I don't know anything about.

Mr. THOMPSON. That is all, Mr. Chairman.

Acting Chairman WEINSTOCK. That is all, Mr. Johannsen. Thank you very much. Will you call your next witness?

Mr. THOMPSON. Mr. Bird.

TESTIMONY OF MR. C. G. BIRD.

Mr. THOMPSON. Will you please give us your name?

Mr. BIRD. C. G. Bird.

Mr. THOMPSON. And your business address?

Mr. BIRD. Stockton.

Mr. THOMPSON. And your business?

Mr. BIRD. Lumber.

Mr. THOMPSON. What company are you connected with?

Mr. BIRD. Simpson-Gray Lumber Co., at Stockton.

Mr. THOMPSON. How long have you been connected with it and where does it do business?

Mr. BIRD. At Stockton, 124 West Weber Avenue. I have been connected with the company about two years.

Mr. THOMPSON. How long have you been located in Stockton?

Mr. BIRD. About the same length of time.

Mr. THOMPSON. Are you acquainted with the industrial situation there?

Mr. BIRD. Somewhat.

Mr. THOMPSON. With what has been testified to to-day here by the witnesses on both sides. You have heard what has been testified to?

Mr. BIRD. I have.

Mr. THOMPSON. What have you got to say to the commission with reference to those matters?

Mr. BIRD. Well, in the first place, I would like to know if I fully understand why I am here. It was given to me by the gentleman who subpœnaed me—I was told I was desired to appear before a board of men appointed by President Wilson to investigate into the cause of labor disturbances throughout the country, to the end that they might legislate in order to prevent these troubles. He stated that this board consisted of nine members, representing three from the laboring classes, three supposed to represent the employers, and three from the general public, and that this investigation was going to take in simply the causes and events that led up to this trouble in Stockton. Is that correct?

Mr. THOMPSON. Well, I don't know, of course, what was told you.

Mr. BIRD. Is that what I am supposed to testify to?

Mr. THOMPSON. I would prefer that the chairman should answer your question in regard to that matter.

Acting Chairman WEINSTOCK. You are substantially correct.

Mr. BIRD. Well, in the first place, I would like to state that I don't care to enter into any debate with any member of the board on any question that may come up here at all, and I also am not going to enter into a detailed denial of the statements made by the preceding witness—statements which in regard to the conditions and events at Stockton, most of them are absolutely false; he knows them to be false, the business men of Stockton know them to be false, and any thinking man who has gone into the conditions there at all knows those statements to be false. And I hesitated after hearing his statement, about coming on the stand here at all, or giving any testimony unless I was assured that the board would take into due consideration the character of the witnesses here, their past records, and in some instances their national reputations.

Mr. Irish has gone very carefully over the conditions in Stockton. I know of nothing that he said that I could not indorse. I think he has gone over them very carefully, indeed, and very fully, and probably the only thing I can do is to give you my personal views, what I have seen personally, as to the conditions there that led up to my taking any part in this matter. To do so I may have to go back somewhat prior to the time that I went to Stockton.

Prior to 1908, April 11, and some time thereafter, I was secretary-treasurer of the Pacific Coast Lumber & Mill Co., of Oakland. Prior to April 11 we were running what is known as a closed shop, and I think I know pretty well what closed-shop conditions are; their restrictions of output, their unreasonable demands, their refusal of allowing men who do not belong to their union to earn their bread and butter, their fines for the breaking of their rules—not only fines against their members, but against any merchant who is under their control—their unreasonable agreements, and in some instances what I think ought to be, if they are not, unlawful agreements that they compel employers of labor to sign and follow out.

On April 11, 1908, after enduring these abuses and unreasonable demands for years and years, events occurred which had nothing whatever to do with the question of hours and labor that made it necessary for us to refuse absolutely to treat longer with them, and from that date we declared for the open shop. We knew what their methods were prior to that date, their means of obtaining their ends through coercion and threatening, but we had no idea of what those things really meant until after April 11.

They then commenced their picketing and boycotting and the destruction of property—our property; property we sold to other people and shipped out on jobs we had on hand; their threatening our lives and the lives of our workmen and the attempt at carrying out those threats by beating them up and following them from place to place; their injury to our stock and our teams; their threatening to burn, and attempting three times to burn, our plant; their threatening to dynamite, and finally dynamiting, our plant and blowing it up. We knew what those things meant. We found out, but with all of that we stood pat in our determination to not be guided by such leaders as they had at that time fighting us. ·

In October, 1912, I, with some others, bought out the old firm of Simpson & Gray, of Stockton. I was told by my friends that I could not endure the conditions I would have to be working under at Stockton. I asked them why and they said owing to the strict union rules in vogue at Stockton, that it was an absolutely closed-shop town. I told them I thought if other business men could stand it I could, and that when it became unbearable there was always a remedy, and that if it did become unbearable I was sure the people of Stockton wouldn't stand for it. But it was not long after I went to Stockton that I commenced to feel the influence of the closed-shop conditions. In the first place, I was not allowed to bring in any lumber that was sized or planed on four sides or worked in any manner, such as rustic and tongue and groove, that could be worked in the mills of Stockton, with few exceptions of stock patterns. Large timbers that could not be worked in Stockton they allowed to be brought in worked. Surfaced four sides or however it happened to be.

They refused to allow my foreman to touch a piece of lumber; they refused to permit me—at least, they tried to prevent me—from bringing in any workmen from the outside after I had tried tallymen or yard clerks, as they are called—tried them at Stockton and found them inefficient. When I attempted to bring men into Stockton that were willing to join their union, they stated in their meeting that they would not accept the man or men I would bring in; that there were plenty in Stockton that I could hire. I did hire all those that I could find available, and discharged most of them owing to drunkenness and inefficiency. Not only that, but there are hundreds of instances I could name if I had time. Another one is that they demanded instead of paying my men on Monday night, as was my custom, that I pay them on Saturday night. I asked the walking delegate the reason for it, and he said because it was inconvenient for him to come around and collect their dues on Monday night.

They would come to my men when they were working on the yard and take them from their work and bring them up to the office and demand that I pay them money or that the bookkeeper pay them money with which to pay their initiation fees and their dues.

In the instance where they demanded that I—or stated that I could not employ outside men, I took up with the other lumber yards, and after convincing them that if they put the screws to me in that manner that it would only be a short time until they put the screws to them, the other yards notified their stewards, and notified mine, that that man was going to work whether they accepted him in the union or not.

After I had been there a short time, and before coming, I looked over the field at Stockton. It looked good to me. It looked like a good town and well located. I commenced to inquire from the different merchants and business men of the town why it was that there were not more new factories and industries entering Stockton, why it was that Stockton with all its facilities was not able to bring in outside capital to invest there, eastern capital for factories and such.

I was informed by the chamber of commerce and others that there had been numerous inquiries as to conditions in Stockton, all of which were answered satisfactorily, with the one exception of the labor conditions, that they could not guarantee to outside capital freedom from strife and trouble in Stockton owing to its reputation as being the strongest union town west of the Rockies.

It was about a year ago that the trouble which has been detailed to you by Mr. Irish, and will be further detailed I presume by other witnesses, came about at the Sperry mills. They also had a boycott on the Hotel Stockton, as has been detailed to you, which is not necessary to go any further into.

And shortly after that, or during that trouble, the merchants' and manufacturers' association was formed, principally by some of the warehousemen on the water front. That was the nucleus. It was formed not for the purpose of running out unionism, not for the purpose of destroying unions or of lowering wages or of lengthening hours. It was formed with the sole purpose of combating such disturbances and such acts of the labor unions as were illustrated in the Sperry mills trouble and also the Stockton Hotel.

It was not long after the association was formed, and I believe it was due to the formation of the association, that they took the boycott off of the Sperry flour and removed the obnoxious picket from in front of the Stockton Hotel.

It was our determination from the start that we would simply, when these things came up, meet them and try to overcome them. We did not intend in starting to make Stockton absolutely open shop. But we did intend to have something to say in regard to the conduct of our business and the manufacturing interests of the city and put Stockton in a condition where it could invite outside capital to come and invest without fear of molestation.

Shortly after the boycott and picketing were taken off of those two establishments they went to the city commissioners and made a demand upon them that all of the employees of the city of Stockton be compelled to join the unions. We went before the commissioners, stated who we were, who we represented, and demanded that in justice to the free workmen of Stockton and the business interests of Stockton, that such a rule be not made. And it was not.

Further investigation revealed to me this fact, that if the boycott had continued on the Sperry flour, that if the continuous warfare on the Holt Manufacturing Co. continued, and if other warfares were started in other lines of business, that it would mean absolutely the Sperry flour and the Holt Manufacturing Co. were going to shut up their plants in Stockton and leave.

We felt that the leaders in charge of the fight, who are now in charge of the fight, had absolutely no interest—that they had no interest in the business welfare or the conditions of Stockton. They cared not a whiff whether these concerns closed their doors or not. But we, as business men, did. And we were determined that, come what would, we would see that those establishments stayed in the town and that Stockton was put in a condition where she could invite others to come there and be protected.

As I have stated, the question of hours or wages has never entered into this argument whatever, has never entered into the fight except as it has been thrust into the fight by the other side in order to influence public opinion.

Now, in summing up, if, as the preceding witness states, this is to be a fight to the finish, if it is to be as he has stated—as he has been reported to have stated in the press—if it is to be a fight until every hospital in Stockton is filled, if he is going to continue, if they are going to continue the beating up as it has been going on there almost daily for the last two weeks, ever since that witness has entered the town and taken charge of the fight, if those things are to continue, if their threats are to be carried out of maiming workmen, of running them out of town, as they have done, if it is to be a war to the finish until the M., M. and E. or the union labor element is driven out of Stockton, then I wish to assure that gentleman that it will not be the M., M. and E. that is driven from the field.

We are not there to drive the labor unions from Stockton or from any other place. We admit their right to organize and have their unions, but we also claim the right to have our organization and to run our separate businesses as we think best, providing we keep within the law.

Mr. THOMPSON. Mr. Bird, is your association receiving any financial support from associations in San Francisco or any other cities, directly or indirectly?

Mr. BIRD. It is not.

Mr. THOMPSON. Has any agent of the San Francisco manufacturers and merchants interested himself in the Stockton controversy?

Mr. BIRD. Not to my knowledge.

Mr. THOMPSON. Would you know, or be apt to know?

Mr. BIRD. I certainly would.

Mr. THOMPSON. Has your association used any pressure direct or indirect to get Stockton manufacturers to enter the M., M. and E.?

Mr. BIRD. Have we used what?

Mr. THOMPSON. Any pressure, direct or indirect.

Mr. BIRD. Absolutely none, to my knowledge.

Mr. THOMPSON. That is all, Mr. Chairman.

Chairman WALSH. Any questions, Mr. Garretson?

Commissioner GARRETSON. No; I don't believe I have.

Chairman WALSH. Mr. O'Connell, do you care to ask any?

Commissioner O'CONNELL. Yes.

Chairman WALSH. Commissioner O'Connell would like to ask you a question or two.

Commissioner O'CONNELL. I understand you are president of this association known as the M., M. and E., is it?

Mr. BIRD. Yes, sir.

Commissioner O'CONNELL. What is the membership of that association composed of, of manufacturers, of business men in the city?

Mr. BIRD. Manufacturers, business men, professional men.

Commissioner O'CONNELL. What percentage of those that are eligible hold membership in the city?

Mr. BIRD. Sir?

Commissioner O'CONNELL. What percentage of the entire number of eligible business men, manufacturers, etc., in your city, hold membership in the association?

Mr. BIRD. That I am not prepared to say.

Commissioner O'CONNELL. Approximately?

Mr. BIRD. No; but I can state that they represent—the employers in the association represent 95 per cent of the employed in the city of Stockton.

Commissioner O'CONNELL. Ninety-five per cent of the employed?

Mr. BIRD. Yes, sir.

Commissioner O'CONNELL. What are the requirements of membership in the association?

Mr. BIRD. What are the requirements?

Commissioner O'CONNELL. Yes.

Mr. BIRD. No special requirements other than what is stated on our pamphlet.

Commissioner O'CONNELL. A man must be in business and must be employing somebody?

Mr. BIRD. Not necessarily.

Commissioner O'CONNELL. Any reputable citizen without a calling may become a member?

Mr. BIRD. Yes, sir.

Commissioner O'CONNELL. What are the initiation fees?

Mr. BIRD. There are none.

Commissioner O'CONNELL. What are the dues?

Mr. BIRD. It is a sliding scale, 25 cents a head for each employee. That is, if I have 10 employees my monthly dues would be $2.50. If I have one employee, there is a minimum of $1 a month.

Commissioner O'CONNELL. Do you provide for the levy of assessments, or special collection of funds in a special way?

Mr. BIRD. No provision that I know of.

Commissioner O'CONNELL. As necessity requires it?

Mr. BIRD. No provision that I know of.

Commissioner O'CONNELL. Does the law provide for compensation to an employer for loss occasioned by a strike?

Mr. BIRD. How is that?

Commissioner O'CONNELL. Does your law provide for a compensation in any way of an employer when he suffers loss by a strike—loss of business?

Mr. BIRD. I don't know that it does.

Commissioner O'CONNELL. You don't know that it does?

Mr. Bird. I don't know that it does.   I know we would compensate them, I am pretty sure of that.

Commissioner O'Connell. Has there been any compensation so far in these recent troubles you are having there?

Mr. Bird. There may and there may not be.   I am not positive as to that.

Commissioner O'Connell. If there were moneys paid out by your association, as the president of that association, would you have to indorse the payments, sign the check, voucher, or whatever it might be?

Mr. Bird. I don't think that is pertinent to this investigation.   [Laughter.]

Chairman Walsh. Be in perfect order, please, ladies and gentlemen.

It is pertinent.   If you have any other reason for declining you may give it; but it is pertinent.

Commissioner O'Connell. The commission will decide.

Mr. Bird. Well, I am free to say that it is not necessary for me to sign the checks of the association.

Commissioner O'Connell. Then, who is the authorized party to sign the checks for payments to the members of your association?

Mr. Bird. The secretary and treasurer.

Commissioner O'Connell. And the president of the association would not know anything about it?

Mr. Bird. Not necessarily.

Commissioner O'Connell. You are the executive of the association?

Mr. Bird. Sir?

Commissioner O'Connell. You are the executive of the association, the president of the association?

Mr. Bird. I am president of the association.

Commissioner O'Connell. Does your association pay for the bringing in of men to take the places of those on strike, or locked out, as the case may be—importing men?

Mr. Bird. How is that?

Commissioner O'Connell. Does your association pay the expenses of importing men to come to your city for the purpose of taking the place of those on strike, or locked out, as the case may be?

Mr. Bird. There were no lockouts.

Commissioner O'Connell. Well, for the sake of the argument, a strike?

Mr. Bird. They may and they may not.   It depends upon the conditions.

Commissioner O'Connell. They provide, however, that they can do so, I suppose?

Mr. Bird. What provides?

Commissioner O'Connell. Well, your rules and regulations.

Mr. Bird. No such rules or regulations having that provision at all, nor providing for that.

Commissioner O'Connell. Does your association arrange to bring men to Stockton for the purpose of taking the places of men on strike?

Mr. Bird. It can if it sees fit.

Commissioner O'Connell. Have you done so in these recent affairs?

Mr. Bird. I don't know that it has.

Commissioner O'Connell. Is there any person that you know of connected with your association that does know these things?

Mr. Bird. Possibly; yes.   The secretary may know.

Commissioner O'Connell. Well, I made inquiry—oh, it wasn't the secretary. You say that you declared for the open shop and the freedom of employment. As a practical man, I take it you are a man of business having to deal with labor, can you tell this commission, or give it your idea, at least, as to what men might do, how they might associate, or how they might cooperate together for the purpose of improving conditions of employment, perfectly legally and within the law, within their rights; what method they are to proceed upon to bring about that result?   Is it your idea that they can do that best individually as dealing with the employer as such?

Mr. Bird. To bring out their better conditions for them?

Commissioner O'Connell. Yes; reduce the hours of labor, for instance. Supposing they were working 10 hours and they wanted 8, how would an individual proceed to bring that about in your factory, say you employ a hundred people?

Mr. Bird. I don't know, I am sure, how he would bring it about.

Commissioner O'Connell. Do you think it would be possible for the individual to do it?

Mr. BIRD. I should—under some conditions; yes.

Commissioner O'CONNELL. And what conditions would it be possible under which he could do it?

Mr. BIRD. As I stated to you before, I don't care to enter into any debate or category with regard to this.

Commissioner O'CONNELL. I don't desire to enter into any debate.

Mr. BIRD. The conditions that brought up the trouble in Stockton—that is the matter for which I was brought here.

Commissioner O'CONNELL. Forget Stockton for a minute.

Mr. BIRD. All right.

Commissioner O'CONNELL. As a man employing labor, I don't care where you are, and you stand for what you say your association now stands for at Stockton, the open shop, what is called the open shop—we are now in San Francisco—in which you say you prefer to deal, and do deal, with only the individual, you will not deal collectively, could not deal with organized employees, associations of them, hence they must deal with you as individuals. Now, we are located in San Francisco—all of us. How can the individual also in San Francisco, as an individual, bring about, for instance, reduction of the hours of labor in the factory? How is he to improve his condition, so far as that is concerned?

Mr. BIRD. As I stated, it depends upon conditions.

Commissioner O'CONNELL. Can you cite us an instance?

Mr. BIRD. I am not here for debate.

Commissioner O'CONNELL. Mr. Chairman, unless there is some other arrangement about witnesses, unless the witnesses who appear before this commission——

(Chairman Walsh and Commissioner O'Connell conversed a few minutes off the record.)

Chairman WALSH. Mr. Lennon would like to ask you a few questions.

Commissioner LENNON. Mr. Bird, do you know whether or not any workmen in Stockton are employed under union conditions, under union agreements?

Mr. BIRD. I think there are; yes.

Commissioner LENNON. About how many?

Mr. BIRD. I am not prepared to state.

Commissioner LENNON. Are there as many as there are involved in the lockout or strike?

Mr. BIRD. Repeat that question—are there as many?

Commissioner LENNON. Are there as many working under union conditions in Stockton, union regulations, as there are involved in the lockout or strike who are not employed?

Mr. BIRD. I think not. I don't think there are as many employed under union conditions as are locked out at the present time. I may be wrong.

Commissioner LENNON. Do you know whether there is——

Mr. BIRD. I want to correct that—as are striking at the present time.

Commissioner LENNON. Well, involved in the difficulty. We are not particular as to the words in this case. Are the printers employed by the newspapers in Stockton involved in this controversy?

Mr. BIRD. Not that I know of.

Commissioner LENNON. And the other trades in the printing offices?

Mr. BIRD. I don't know.

Commissioner LENNON. Are proprietors of newspaper offices eligible for membership in your organization?

Mr. BIRD. They are.

Commissioner LENNON. Are any of them members?

Mr. BIRD. They are not.

Commissioner LENNON. Are there any cigar makers in Stockton—do you know whether there are?

Mr. BIRD. Cigar makers?

Commissioner LENNON. Yes.

Mr. BIRD. I don't know whether there are or not.

Commissioner LENNON. Do you know of their being involved in this controversy?

Mr. BIRD. Not that I know of.

Commissioner LENNON. Do you know whether the principal buildings that are being constructed in Stockton are being constructed by union men or nonunion men?

Mr. BIRD. Well, according to what you class as principal buildings. The school buildings are being constructed principally by nonunion men. There is one building that is being constructed by an outside contractor, who is running his work as a closed shop. There is also a bank building which is being constructed at the present time, closed shop.

Commissioner LENNON. I might ask one question as to your opinion. Of course, I realize, as the chairman says, you have a right to refuse to answer if you want. Do you believe that workmen have the same right of organization that employers have?

Mr. BIRD. Certainly.

Commissioner LENNON. Are they permitted to exercise that right at the present time in Stockton?

Mr. BIRD. Yes; as far as I know; as far as I have any knowledge of it, they are.

Commissioner LENNON. This contest that is on there is not then fundamentally for the purpose of eliminating organization?

Mr. BIRD. Absolutely not.

Commissioner LENNON. That is all I care to ask.

Chairman WALSH. Did you want to ask some questions, Mr. Weinstock?

Commissioner WEINSTOCK. Yes.

Chairman WALSH. Commissioner Weinstock wants to ask some questions.

Commissioner WEINSTOCK. This commission, Mr. Bird, is very much interested in getting the fullest possible information concerning violations in labor troubles. Now, in the course of your statement, you mentioned the fact, as you claimed it to be, that there had been many acts of violence in recent weeks in Stockton, in connection with the present labor disturbance. Will you tell this commission when the last act of violence happened, so far as you know?

Mr. BIRD. So far as I know positively, probably last Wednesday, I think it was; but from what I know from hearsay, which you have to discount quite a bit, it was Saturday.

Commissioner WEINSTOCK. There was an act of violence committed Saturday in connection with the labor trouble?

Mr. BIRD. I was told there was; yes.

Commissioner WEINSTOCK. Can you give us some idea of the character of that act of violence?

Mr. BIRD. It was on Market Street; a man was beaten up in front of one of the saloons there. The matter was reported to our committee, I think, on yesterday noon—Monday noon.

Commissioner WEINSTOCK. Was the injured party a nonunion worker?

Mr. BIRD. He was.

Commissioner WEINSTOCK. Was it known by whom he was assaulted?

Mr. BIRD. Not when I left; it had not been found out.

Commissioner WEINSTOCK. The assaulting parties are unknown?

Mr. BIRD. At the time I left Stockton they were unknown.

Commissioner WEINSTOCK. Well, how long has this disturbance been going on—these disputes?

Mr. BIRD. Violence?

Commissioner WEINSTOCK. No; this whole trouble.

Mr. BIRD. Since the declaration, I presume, of the open shop. The violence did not commence to any extent until Johannsen came to town and made the declaration, the fight had been a kid-glove matter, but he would show Stockton what a real labor war was.

Commissioner WEINSTOCK. You refer to Mr. Johannsen?

Mr. BIRD. I do.

Commissioner WEINSTOCK. When did Mr. Johannsen come to Stockton?

Mr. BIRD. I think it was a week or two weeks ago to-day.

Commissioner WEINSTOCK. Then the acts of violence that have been committed have been committed within the past two weeks?

Mr. BIRD. Almost altogether.

Commissioner WEINSTOCK. Are you familiar with this card of instructions that has been issued by Mr. Johannsen?

Mr. BIRD. I have seen it.

Commissioner WEINSTOCK. Have you seen it?

Mr. BIRD. Yes.

Commissioner WEINSTOCK. Have the instructions on that card, so far as you know. been observed by the union men?

Mr. BIRD. Absolutely no.

Commissioner WEINSTOCK. They have not? Does your association keep a record of all the instances where violence has been committed?

Mr. BIRD. We have, I think, a fairly complete record of it.

Commissioner WEINSTOCK. How many cases have happened according to your records?

Mr. BIRD. That I could not say.

Commissioner WEINSTOCK. Well, approximately.

Mr. BIRD. Well, at least 15 or 20.

Commissioner WEINSTOCK. Have any steps been taken on either side to bring the wrongdoers to justice?

Mr. BIRD. Wherever we could get evidence; yes.

Commissioner WEINSTOCK. Now, who have been the injured parties in those cases? Have they been union or nonunion men?

Mr. BIRD. I do not know of one case where a union man was assaulted.

Commissioner WEINSTOCK. I take it, then, that your statement is that all the assaulted parties were nonunion men?

Mr. BIRD. Were nonunion men who came in there to work—not all of them—the case of Totten and Brandt; it was three of the—two of the owners of the mill and some of the office employees assaulted.

Commissioner WEINSTOCK. And I take it further that your association undertakes to give its protection, whatever protection can be given to the nonunion men who are asked to go to work?

Mr. BIRD. Surely.

Commissioner WEINSTOCK. What steps has your association taken to protect these men and to bring the wrongdoers to justice?

Mr. BIRD. Done everything we could with the city administration and the police force.

Commissioner WEINSTOCK. In what way, tell us?

Mr. BIRD. Asking them to give us protection.

Commissioner WEINSTOCK. Has the protection been given?

Mr. BIRD. They claim it has.

Commissioner WEINSTOCK. Well, that is hardly an answer to my question.

Mr. BIRD. Well, I am answering the question that way because after they claimed they were giving the protection—all the protection they could—the acts of violence continued.

Commissioner WEINSTOCK. Then I judge that your opinion is that the authorities have not given the necessary protection?

Mr. BIRD. That is my opinion, most decidedly.

Commissioner WEINSTOCK. What means do the employers of nonunion workers take to protect them—to protect nonunion workers?

Mr. BIRD. That is going into events after the eighth of June?

Commissioner LENNON. After the eighth of June, or July?

Mr. BIRD. July.

Commissioner WEINSTOCK. You do not care to answer that question?

Mr. BIRD. I do not care to go into that phase of it at all.

Commissioner WEINSTOCK. This card issued by Mr. Johannsen reads: "All pickets are prohibited from carrying concealed weapons." Have there been any instances that have come under your notice, within your hearing, where strikers or nonunion workers have carried and used concealed weapons?

Mr. BIRD. That also is subsequent to July 8, but I am willing to state that not under my personal observation, but under the observation of those who have given me signed statements, they have carried and exhibited what I would call concealed weapons. There is one matter I would like to give you my opinion on and that is, those instructions there are a farce.

Commissioner WEINSTOCK. Now, let us see how far they have observed, so far as you know? The first instruction is that absolute sobriety must prevail. What has been your observation on that point?

Mr. BIRD. I have not been out observing them. It is, I think, a good rule to give if they didnt' want to get into trouble.

Commissioner WEINSTOCK. "That strong language tending to provoke violence must be abstained from." Have any come under your notice here where strong language has been used?

Mr. BIRD. Too numerous to mention.

Commissioner WEINSTOCK. "That pickets shall not congregate in large crowds." Has that instruction been observed, so far as you know?

Mr. BIRD. It has not to my own observation.

Commissioner WEINSTOCK. That "any advice or request from a uniformed officer must be heeded and complied with"?

Mr. BIRD. I guess they would be perfectly willing to comply with the instruction they received from the uniformed officers and also from the special officers, some of whom have been selected from the strikers' ranks.

Commissioner WEINSTOCK. That "pickets are to abstain if possible from speaking or interfering with men and persuading them in an orderly manner from misleading compromises of the M., M. and E. and offering hope of the future which organized labor stands for." So far as you know, has that order been carried out—that is, persuasion has been done in an orderly manner?

Mr. BIRD. Absolutely not.

Commissioner WEINSTOCK. That is all, Mr. Chairman.

Chairman WALSH. Mr. Garretson would like to ask a few questions.

Commissioner GARRETSON. Mr .Bird, in answer to a question from Mr. Weinstock, you waived the date of July 8 to state that in your opinion what you considered concealed weapons had been used by some of these men?

Mr. BIRD. Yes.

Commissioner GARRETSON. Did you hear the statement of Mr. Johannsen in regard to this automobile, that the men were convicted in the courts——

Mr. BIRD. No; I didn't hear that he said that they had been convicted in the courts.

Commissioner GARRETSON. Beg pardon—arraigned in the courts and let out on bail; did you hear that statement?

Mr. BIRD. Well, there have been other cases where they have been arraigned in court and let out on bail also.

Commissioner GARRETSON. Was the story as he told there substantially correct?

Mr. BIRD. I think it was not correct.

Commissioner GARRETSON. In what respect?

Mr. BIRD. I don't care to discuss it.

Commissioner GARRETSON. Do you know whether those men who had the talk with these representatives were discharged?

Mr. BIRD. I don't know.

Commissioner GARRETSON. Is it true that bail was furnished for them by the attorneys of the association?

Mr. BIRD. I don't know.

Commissioner GARRETSON. That is all, Mr. Chairman.

Chairman WALSH. Anything else? Mr. Commons would like to ask you a few questions.

Commissioner COMMONS. You state that special policemen were appointed from the ranks of the strikers.

Mr. BIRD. I stated so.

Commissioner COMMONS. Do you know how many?

Mr. BIRD. I have been told three or four. I know of one who was a striker from Totten & Brandt's mill. Prior to the day of his appointment he passed down by our place of business, accosted our foreman with these words: "How do you like to be a rat tail? We will get you yet." The following day he was appointed a special officer on the Stockton police force. The police commissioner was notified of that. Yesterday he was still on the force. That occurred about two—about a week ago.

Commissioner COMMONS. Do you know how many special policemen have been appointed, how many altogether specially?

Mr. BIRD. I do not know. I know of 8 or 10.

Commissioner COMMONS. Can you give the name of this particular man you refer to?

Mr. BIRD. Yes; I think I can. [Referring to memorandum book.] Fred A. Rogers.

Commissioner COMMONS. Have you other names?

Mr. BIRD. I have the names of some of the special officers here, yes; memoranda of them.

Commissioner COMMONS. All those outside?

Mr. BIRD. I can't say.

Commissioner COMMONS. You can't say whether any other?

Mr. BIRD. I have an opinion that several of them here were very rabid union sympathizers.

Commissioner COMMONS. But you don't know whether they were strikers or were locked out in any respect?

Mr. BIRD. No; I don't-know whether they were strikers or were locked out. I know they weren't locked out. I don't know whether strikers or not, but they have been workers in the union-labor movement.

Commissioner COMMONS. That is, you do know that others besides this one that you have mentioned?

Mr. BIRD. Yes; by information. This man I know actually, because I came in personal contact with him, that is, in personal sight of him every day—the man who made this remark to our foreman.

Commissioner COMMONS. Did your association or the employers ask for special policemen to be employed?

Mr. BIRD. Have special police to be appointed?

Commissioner COMMONS. By the city authorities.

Mr. BIRD. Well, ask for it? They offered to, that is, the mayor offered to, to me.

Commissioner COMMONS. He offered to appoint special policemen?

Mr. BIRD. Yes, of our naming; but he never did so, to my knowledge.

Commissioner COMMONS. Did he ask you to name special nominees for special police?

Mr. BIRD. No; I don't know. He never asked me, but after the Totten & Brandt record there I asked the mayor what he was going to do about it, and he said they were going to appoint special police. He says: "You name men you want appointed." He did at that time say to name the men, name the men we wanted appointed. I did name some men—I didn't name them myself, but one of our committee, I believe, named men; but I don't know whether or not any of them were appointed. None of them that I know of appear on the list that was published in the papers as having been appointed.

Commissioner COMMONS. In the cases in court, arrests that have been made, what has been the disposal of the cases, so far as arreests have been made?

Mr. BIRD. Arrests in cases of violence?

Commissioner COMMONS. Yes.

Mr. BIRD. I do not know that any disposition has been made of them. They have been put over until after election.

Commissioner COMMONS. Are they all out on bail?

Mr. BIRD. I think they are; I am not positive as to that.

Commissioner COMMONS. They were put over until after election?

Mr. BIRD. You can take that for what it means—for what you think it means.

Commissioner COMMONS. Have you any idea at whose request they were put over?

Mr. BIRD. No.

Commissioner COMMONS. You have no information about that?

Mr. BIRD. No.

Commissioner COMMONS. Has there been any use of the injunction so far in this case?

Mr. BIRD. Yes.

Commissioner COMMONS. What is the situation about that injunction? What court issued it?

Mr. BIRD. How far do you want to go into that? This is still continuing on matters subsequent to the 8th of July. There have been injunction suits and injunctions granted, temporary and permanent.

Commissioner COMMONS. That is one of the most fundamental things we have to go into—the attitude of the courts and the governing authorities toward this question. And it seems to me that personally I should like to have such information as will help us in that matter.

Mr. BIRD. I say there have been injunctions granted, temporary and permanent, in several cases. It is difficult, you understand, to get evidence where union labor representatives claim that pickets are not pickets and boycotts are not boycotts. When pickets are advertising agents you have got to get considerable evidence to prove that they are not what they are called.

Commissioner COMMONS. Are those injunctions outstanding now?

Mr. BIRD. There are some of them outstanding that have not been decided yet.

Commissioner COMMONS. There are temporary injunctions now pending here? What is the status?

Mr. BIRD. In this case?

Commissioner COMMONS. Yes. There have not been any trials for contempt yet, have there?

Mr. BIRD. No.

Commissioner COMMONS. What court is it that has issued these injunctions?

Mr. BIRD. The superior court; I suppose that is where it was brought.
Chairman WALSH. I did not catch that.
Mr. BIRD. The superior court. You mean whose court?
Commissioner COMMONS. Yes. It would be the superior court, the local judge—the judge of the county?
Mr. BIRD. Oh, yes.
Commissioner COMMONS. State courts?
Mr. BIRD. No; county courts.
Commissioner COMMONS. County courts?
Mr. BIRD. Yes.
Commissioner COMMONS. That is all.
Commissioner GARRETSON. Are those injunctions that have been issued, both the permanent and temporary, issued by one court?
Mr. BIRD. That I can't say.
Commissioner GARRETSON. Well, that would simplify getting the records.
Mr. BIRD. I don't know.
Commissioner GARRETSON. In that case we might have to go over several.
Mr. BIRD. I do not know if one court or not.
Chairman WALSH. That is all. Call your next witness.
Mr. THOMPSON. Mr. Woods.

TESTIMONY OF MR. J. T. WOODS.

Mr. THOMPSON. What is your name?
Mr. WOODS. J. T. Woods.
Mr. THOMPSON. And your occupation?
Mr. WOODS. Electrical worker.
Mr. THOMPSON. And your address?
Mr. WOODS. 1138 East Miner, Stockton.
Mr. THOMPSON. You are located there?
Mr. WOODS. Yes, sir.
Mr. THOMPSON. What other position have you?
Mr. WOODS. In Stockton?
Mr. THOMPSON. In connection with labor.
Mr. WOODS. As president of the Stockton Building Trades Council.
Mr. THOMPSON. How long have you held such position?
Mr. WOODS. Two years.
Mr. THOMPSON. You are acquainted, naturally, with the conditions in Stockton?
Mr. WOODS. Yes, sir.
Mr. THOMPSON. What have you to add to what has already been said by the witnesses here to-day with regard to that situation?
Mr. WOODS. The situation at Stockton?
Mr. THOMPSON. Yes.
Mr. WOODS. Well, the situation at Stockton for the last two years—I have been president of the building-trades council—I have been in the Stockton Building-Trades Council for nearly 12 years. The building trades, with the exception of four years ago, where there was a strike of three months, in which the carpenters were involved, an adjustment was made; they struck for four-eighty, and it was compromised for four-forty—since that time the building trades and their employers have been working in harmony and with but very little friction.

We have had two very small—very little trouble to settle, and practically all the trouble that has come up locally from the local organization with their employers has been settled amiably and peaceably by the building-trades council, and everything has been satisfactory. The contractors, the builders I am speaking of, were satisfied, so far as they were concerned, with our business dealings. And everything was working nicely. We had no trouble nor anticipated any trouble until about a year ago nearly; the merchants, manufacturers, and employers' association formed an organization in the city of Stockton, claiming that it was formed for the betterment and to counteract the abuses of the business in the city.

Immediately they were formed, any little controversy that came up in the building trades, why, we were referred to the secretary of that association, Mr. Calkins, and he refused to have any dealings with us with regard to that or with regard to any trouble or to notify the contractors at any time any trouble came up, and they asked him, and he said, " Pay no attention to the building trades"; go ahead with your business, union or nonunion. Well, we usually reached those contractors and settled with them. Now, up until the time that that association was formed everything went along peaceably, and for some time afterwards, so far as that is concerned, because the contractors, the majority of the building contractors, did not want to join the association, and did not join it until such time as pressure was brought to bear, and they informed me that they had—and then even after they had joined the association they were fair to labor, every one of them. But it did not suit Mr. Calkins. Mr. Calkins had made the statement to the people, to our people in particular, that he came there to make Stockton an open-shop town from the day he organized. And the contractors whom I interviewed who had joined the association, each and every one told me the same, made the said statement to me—that the reason that they were in that association was because they had to be there. An automobile had come around with three of the committee from the employers' association. Those of them who held out were told that they must either get into the association or they would take steps to force them into the association, and they were forced in in that way. Then the contractors who did not believe in the association, did not want to go into the association, and who still continued to accept and employ our people, when the trouble started with the clerks' organization; the clerks were locked out, their cards were demanded, and our boys, members of the building trades, naturally after they were—after the clerks were locked out—I suppose that the majority of them traded at stores who employed union men, the same as men who were employing us, a natural right—they did.

Well, it went along for some little time and the issue was forced on the contractors. They came and told me they were—the proposition was put up to them that they must put nonunion men on the job; that they would have to come out for the open shop. That went on for some little time, and they didn't do it.

The next trouble that came up was with the cooks and waiters. The cooks and waiters had made no demands. The agreement, I believe, had expired, but they didn't ask for a renewal of the agreement. They were just simply working along under the old agreement without any renewal. Mr. Calkins called a meeting of the restaurant keepers and hotel keepers and demanded that they take the cards out of their restaurants, and some of them took them out and then put them back again, as it didn't suit them. Mr. Calkins has consituted himself as a chairman and appointed a committee of restaurant keepers to go around and wait on the different restaurants to take their cards out, which they did, and had them in their offices. That brought on trouble with the cooks and waiters. When some of those restaurant keepers were forced to take this action or were told their supplies would be cut off they had to leave the cards out, and the cooks and waiters were forced through this attitude into the street. They were told they had to either give up their cards or quit; that from that day on it was an absolutely nonunion shop.

Well, the cooks and waiters came out and the clerks were out prior to that. The building trades had not been in this fight. The building trades had no trouble with any of its employers, but the building-trades mechanics, while they did not declare any boycott on any person or firm in the city of Stockton, our people were evidently trading with their own friends, because Mr. Calkins had absolutely refused to meet any of the miscellaneous crafts. Refused to talk with them or have anything to do with them, and they could not get a meeting. They asked for meetings, but they could not get them.

. Well, some time after the cooks and waiters were out, I believe it was about a week or such matter, or 10 days, there was a committee came to me out to the Jackson School Building where I was working, and they came out there and came in the building and asked if I would come out and have a talk with the committee. I told them I would, so I went out.

They asked me for a meeting of the building-trades mechanics—a committee of three to meet their committee that evening at 7 o'clock, to see if we could come to some agreement or adjustment on the matter. And in that conversation I was told by the gentlemen of the committee that we would have to take some action. They made a demand on me that we force the members of the building trades, who were not trading with the stores who had locked their union clerks out, claimed there had been letters written fining some of our members if they traded with any of these unfair stores. That if we didn't force this organization to rescind the letter and if we didn't immediately take steps to force members of the building trades to trade with the members of their association, that they would have to take action against us, and that was the sum and substance of the matter.

.I told them, "Gentlemen, if that is your attitude and your demand there is no use of us having a meeeting, because we can not consider that part, and we will not, but we will meet you this evening with a committee of three from each organization," which was agreed upon.

.The committee met at 7 o'clock, and as in all other meetings there was a great deal of preliminary and useless argument brought up, pro and con, before we came to any sort of understanding at all.

. The first proposition that was put up to us by Mr. Totten was the same thing that he had repeated to me out at the school house—made the demand on us that we immediately notify the members of the building trade-unions that they must trade at the stores that were in their association, whom they had not been trading with since the trouble; and we could not get anywhere, and it was practically a dead end; and finally I made the suggestion that we meet the people who were directly involved in the trouble, and that we get the members of the clothiers' association and members of the hotel and restaurant keepers, and members from the building trades, and a like committee from the miscellaneous crafts, and have another meeting to see if we could not come to some adjustment of the trouble in some manner.

.That was finally agreed on, and the next night we had the meeting of all those committees. Now, at that meeting they were all represented, and every phase of the question was gone into, and the building trades made the statement again that they had no trouble with their employers; that their employers had no grievance against us, and it was admitted by members of the committee—Mr. Totten admitted it himself on that committee that evening, that he did not have any trouble with his employees, and he didn't want any trouble. Mr. Inglis, another one, said the same thing, and Mr. Viebrock, who was on the committee also, admitted he did not have any trouble with his employees and didn't want to have any trouble, and believed we could adjust the matter, which we were willing to do.

The proposition was brought up again. The building trades had no official boycott on any person or firm in Stockton. They claimed we were boycotting them; that we were not trading with their people, and they demanded again that we force our members to trade with the stores who were not employing union men, and force the rescinding of any letters which had been written; that they must make a public statement to the effect that they would trade at those stores—rescind the letter in effect publicly. And when that came up, the question was asked Mr. Totten, "Do you make a demand of the building trades that they force the members of the building trades to trade with the stores who are employing nonunion clerks and that they force the members of the building trades to rescind their letters publicly that there is a fine on their men trading with any of these stores; that if they don't comply with these demands, would they put the building trade members into the street?"

Mr. Totten's answer was "Yes." The building trades wouldn't comply with that demand under those circumstances.

Now, in regard to the assertion that was made on the stand this morning of whether we would not allow employees to work on certain electrical work. That two electrical workers were forced into a shop at Stockton. That one of those electrical workers who was working in that shop went out to a building, a private house where there was some repair work being done—and this man went out there and got drunk and frightened the lady of the house—and she called her husband to that effect—that this man was out there drunk.

Now, there is a firm, the Stockton Electrical Machine Equipment Co., who had a man in their employ who did go out to a house to do some work and who found some liquor in the basement and did get drunk; and they telephoned in and Mr. Eudall went out and brought him in and fired him. It came to our knowledge, and came up at the electrical workers' union, and he was put on the carpet and asked if that was true, and he admitted it was. He was given a talking to. He was reprimanded by the chair and by the executive board of the electrical workers' union, and told that only for his wife and two children his card would be taken away from him, and that he would be suspended for 60 days.

For some little time he wasn't able to get employment in Stockton, and we finally had to take and assist his wife and children from our treasury to keep them going until such time as we could get this man work. Then he started in to drink, and I went to him and told him I would use the law of the State of

California if he kept on drinking and have him put in the asylum for inebriates,· and scared him so badly that he went to work, and has been working ever since.

In regard to the other case, the case of the other man that they claimed was forced on this employer: The electrical workers have no business agent, and· have no authority to force anybody on anybody, and it was not done.· The· employers of the building trades have the right to hire whom they please, if they have a card. Any man who is not efficient, if he is slow, or his work is not good, if he is not a mechanic, it is up to the employer to discharge that man and·let· him go, and he has no protection. A man in our business, in the electrical busi-· ness, must be a mechanic. and if he can't fill the bill, he is discharged and no· questions asked.

Now, the business men were not satisfied, a great many that joined the asso- ciation. A great many of the business men were satisfied with the conditions· that prevailed in Stockton under union conditions. Those men have told·me that they were perfectly satisfied; that their business had been better under· union conditions for the last eight or nine years than it had ever been before· in the history of the city of Stockton, when wages ran anywhere from a dollar and a quarter to two dollars and a half a day; that their business had built up, and that Stockton was a better town financially and otherwise than it had ever been before, under absolutely union conditions.

Now, the building contractors: The majority of those men, I had personal interviews with each and all of them. This association was forced upon them and they were forced to abide by the rules of the merchants and manufacturers' association. Those men did not want to go into an open-shop controversy. Those men all admitted all their money had been made, and all their success as contractors had been made under union conditions; prior to the time that the building trades council was formed and union conditions prevailed that there was absolutely no money in the building business in Stockton. And it was the same with the business men. They made the same statement to me, that before· organized labor had made a better condition of wages that the business was not' good.

Now, we have men who came to me for permission to work since the trouble came on, members of the association, their names are on the roll, and they tell me that they can't take it off for the very fact they are afraid it will jeopardize their credit.

One man came to me the other day and he wanted to complete some work— well, it was not to complete, it was to put in some new work in a building. The lumber bill would amount to about $350, and he wanted to know if we would allow him to buy his lumber in any of the yards in Stockton, if everything else would go through with organized labor; and he stated to me as the reason why, that he owed a note of $1,700 to a party, and if he bought the lumber out of Stockton the man would immediately foreclose on the note and he would be put out of business. We didn't want to put anybody—jam anybody up into a hard position. We want to treat our friends all right, and want to be just with everybody, and he was granted that permission.

Mr. THOMPSON. Are you through with your statement now?

Mr. WOODS. No, sir; I am not just yet.

I would like to state that in the committee meeting, the second meeting of the committee, Mr. Totten, who was chairman of that committee, made the statement that he didn't want any trouble and that he would like to keep out of trouble if he could, but he could not do it by the very fact he wasn't run- ning his own business. In other words, that the people who were back of him, demanded the open shop.

I would like to state also that the majority of the people who are responsible for the formation of the merchants and manufacturers' association have been really, from the best knowledge we have—were not citizens of. Stockton, and did not represent their own business. Mr. Calkins and Mr. Irish do not repre-; sent the citizenship of Stockton nor the business of Stockton. They were from the outside. The people who came there in the formation of that association, were practically all from the outside, so far as we can find out, from Los Angeles, from Portland, from Seattle, and San Francisco. And quite a number of the men on the executive committee that are there now don't represent their own money. They represent other interests, a great many of them, out-of-town interests, such as lumber interests, out of the city of. Stockton, and other interests that are outside of the city.

I guess that is about all of the statement that I have.

Mr. THOMPSON. ¨Mr. Woods, could you be a little bit more definite with reference to the names of those you say are on the board of directors of this manufacturers, merchants and employers' Association who are not residents of Stockton, or, at least, who were not originally residents when this association was formed?

Mr. WOODS. Well, the men who were not directly interested in Stockton in the formation of this association were Mr. Irish and Mr. Calkins and Mr. Irish, sr., of San Francisco, was one of the principal organizers of the association in Stockton.

Mr. THOMPSON. Where did they come from, if you know?

Mr. WOODS. Well, I don't know where Calkins comes from, from everywhere, I guess.

Mr. THOMPSON. Did the members of the unions look upon Mr. Calkins as an objectionable person in the industrial affairs of Stockton?

Mr. WOODS. They look upon Mr. Calkins as an objectionable person in this respect, that Mr. Calkins went there and misrepresented to the people of Stockton the real motive of the organization. He told them it was for the boosting of Stockton and it was not against labor. And he misrepresented absolutely all the way through, because we had information and the copies of letters from the very start, that he was working absolutely against the organizations of labor in that town.

Mr. THOMPSON. Is the feeling against him pretty strong?

Mr. WOODS. Well, the feeling was pretty strong; yes.

Mr. THOMPSON. Mr. Johannsen testified this morning that a union man with a union card and dues paid up could not get a place in Stockton, providing outher union men of the same craft in good standing were out of work. What have you to say, if anything, Mr. Woods, in that connection?

Mr. WOODS. Well, that would depend entirely on conditions. In the few years' experience that I have had as president of the building trades council, there has not been any man turned down for a job in Stockton who had a good, paid-up card.

Mr. THOMPSON. Well, is there any such rule of the union, do you know, of the kind named?

Mr. WOODS. There is not any such rule; no; because we have had men in my own particualr line—we have had some of our boys walking the street when men from Sacramento and San Francisco were busy working in the town on big jobs.

Mr. THOMPSON. Without objection from the union?

Mr. WOODS. Without objection. There was no kick made.

Mr .THOMPSON. In regard to the contractors being forced into the M., M. and E., yo usay statements were made by them that steps would be taken to force them in. Is there any definite kind of steps that it was alleged would be taken?

Mr. WOODS. The steps that were alleged would be taken were that they would be shut off on their material, and they would have to pay their bills.

Mr. THOMPSON. In what lines of industry, or in the building trades—in what lines was that statement made?

Mr. WOODS. That is the general builder, the general contractor.

Mr. THOMPSON. Would you care to name here any individual who made that statement to you?

Mr. WOODS. I would not like to for fear that it might injure him.

Mr. THOMPSON. Is there anybody that you know of who would be able to give us, perhaps, more testimony in that regard?

Mr. WOODS. I think so. I think I can get the name. I would not want to mention the names without their consent.

Mr. THOMPSON. I see. That is all, Mr. Chairman.

Chairman WALSH. Mr. Weinstock would like to ask you some questions.

Commissioner WEINSTOCK. You are familiar, Mr. Woods, with the contents of this card issued by Mr. Johannsen to all the pickets in Stockton, which makes for law and order?

Mr. WOODS. Yes.

Commissioner WEINSTOCK. In how far, to the best of your knowledge and belief, have those instructions been observed by the pickets?

Mr. WOODS. Well, to the best of my belief, the union pickets and the union men of Stockton have adhered to that as closely as possible. If there has been any trouble with union men I don't know it.

Commissioner WEINSTOCK. You heard the statement made on the witness stand by Mr. Bird, the president of the manufacturers'—the M., M. and E.?

Mr. Woods. Yes.

Commissioner Weinstock. Wherein he gave it as his opinion that those instructions were a mere farce and were not observed, and that there had been numerous cases of violence against union workers, or rather nonunion workers, since this card had been issued. What are the facts as you know them?

Mr. Woods. Well, all I know is the reports that I have heard. I have no knowledge that there has been any violence of our people.

Commissioner Weinstock. Have any union workers been placed under arrest since this card has been published?

Mr. Woods. Not to my knowledge; there has not.

Commissioner Weinstock. None have been arrested?

Mr. Woods. Not to my knowledge; I don't remember of any.

Commissioner Weinstock. Are there any union men who are to-day under arrest in Stockton for acts of violence in these labor troubles?

Mr. Woods. There are men who have been suspicioned, been arrested on suspicion of violence.

Commissioner Weinstock. Are they out on bail?

Mr. Woods. Yes, sir.

Commissioner Weinstock. May we ask who furnished the bail?

Mr. Woods. Well, the bail was furnished by—in a good many instances by their friends.

Commissioner Weinstock. Has there been any bail furnished by the unions or representatives of the unions?

Mr. Woods. That I—in one or two instances I think there has.

Commissioner Weinstock. Can you name the instances?

Mr. Woods. No; I can't.

Commissioner Weinstock. But, so far as you know, there have been one or two instances where bail has been furnished by unions or representatives of unions?

Mr. Woods. Yes, sir.

Commissioner Weinstock. I understood you to testify, Mr. Woods, that there are employers who are members of the M., M. and E., as it is called, and who are members unwillingly?

Mr. Woods. Yes, sir.

Commissioner Weinstock. Do you know of any reason why they can not withdraw if they are not in harmony with the purposes of the M., M. and E.?

Mr. Woods. Why, the reason that they can not withdraw, as they have told me themselves, because that they won't be able to buy material; in other words, that their credit will be hurt in such a way that they can't go along with the business.

Commissioner Weinstock. Well, now, do you know whether that statement was made on their part simply as a pretext for continuing in the organization, or whether it is a bona fide statement?

Mr. Woods. I have every reason to believe it is a bona fide statement.

Commissioner Weinstock. May we ask how you have reached that belief? What makes you believe that?

Mr. Woods. From my personal knowledge of the men and for the reasons that I practically know that they are in there. In fact, there are four—four or five contractors who I am absolutely positive that is the only reason they are there, because they have to be there.

Commissioner Weinstock. You mean that they are not financially independent?

Mr. Woods. They are not running their own business.

Commissioner Weinstock. That is all, Mr. Chairman.

Chairman Walsh. Mr. Garretson, any questions?

Commissioner Garretson. No.

Chairman Walsh. Any questions, Prof. Commons?

Commissioner Commons. No.

Chairman Walsh. That is all; thank you. Call your next.

Mr. Thompson. Mr. Stewart.

Chairman Walsh. He is not on this program?

Mr. Thompson. He has been subpœnaed, but I understand he can't be here to-morrow, and having subpœnaed him we thought we would put him on to-day.

TESTIMONY OF MR. CLAUDEIOUS EDWARD STEWART.

Mr. Thompson. Mr. Stewart, will you give us your name, please?

Mr. Stewart. Claudeious Edward Stewart.

Mr. THOMPSON. You may sit down, Mr. Stewart.

Mr. STEWART. Yes, sir.

Mr. THOMPSON. And your business address, please?

Mr. STEWART. 627 East Senora Street, Stockton.

Mr. THOMPSON. And your business?

Mr. STEWART. House painting, decorating, and so forth.

Mr. THOMPSON. House painting?

Mr. STEWART. Yes.

Mr. THOMPSON. You are a master house painter?

Mr. STEWART. Yes, sir.

Mr. THOMPSON. Have you heard the testimony that has been given here to-day with reference to the situation in Stockton?

Mr. STEWART. Well, not all of it. I was told to stay there in the hall of the hotel, and I stayed there from 10 o'clock until halft past eleven before I knew it.

Mr. THOMPSON. Will you give us your view of the facts as they are in Stockton with reference to the labor problem?

Mr. STEWART. Well, this man, Calkins, wrote me a letter, and I went up to his place and seen him, up in the Elks Building, and he wanted me to join this M., M. & E. He said I could get work right away, and give me a big talk that way, that I could get work and all the work I wanted. And I waited for—let's see, that was one, two—and the third month he sent me a bill for dues. Well, I went up there and told him I hadn't done no work; I couldn't pay him any dues. "Well," he says, "we will leave it go on, leave it go on.", Well, August 5 or 4 I got a job around the corner there from the Elks Building, and I went to pay him up the $4 I owed him. And when I got up there, why it seems they make out a small receipt for each month. He made out four of them, and I told him before I would pay him that I wanted my name off of the big book, as they call it, or he would not get the $4. We went on talking, and he said I must be a coward or something to that effect. I says, "I ain't afraid nobody." He said he wasn't. "Well," he says, "them people down there are nothing but a lot of cowards." He pointed down the street. It got like that so——

Mr. THOMPSON. Who do you think he meant when he pointed down the street?

Mr. STEWART. Why, that is the labor-union people. So being called a coward and saying he was afraid of nobody, and he said a dirty remark to me besides, I don't care about repeating it right here, and I didn't like the sound of it. I told him I had this job next door and it was a union job, and I had to have union men on it. But they would not work unless I was clear in this M., M. and E. business. "Well," he says, "I will give you a temporary card, but your name will remain on the big book." "Well," I says, "I don't want it on the big book. I want to pay up and get out of the big book." I had my money to pay it. He says, "Well, I think you are a coward like the rest of them," as I turned to go out the door.

So, I went down near the job, and I sat there about 10 minutes, thinking it over about being called a coward. That didn't sound good to me. So I made up my mind I would go down to the union and tell them how it stood; that they would furnish me four or five men; if he didn't give me a receipt I would make him give me a receipt. They all sat in a place like this, so I went down, and there was four or five volunteered to come up there. He had bragged so he was afraid of nobody, I though probably he had a gun in the corner, because he made for the corner when I got there. But anyhow them men come up with me. I says, "I don't want none of your help; I will tend to him myself unless in case somebody else jumps onto me." They said they would. They wanted to know if they should take any guns along. I said, "No; don't take any gun. I don't want any gun myself." So we marched up there and we came in the door here [indicating], and he has a desk like that [indicating], and he jumps up there and comes around here [indicating], and there was a corner over here [indicating]. I went in first and I got the other side of him, so by him coming, I come over there for that corner, and I suppose he had a gun or something, he wasn't afraid of nobody, he said. So when he got along over there I grabbed him by the neck and hit him a smack with my fist, put him in the corner, and I give him what I thought was satisfactory, and got up to go out. And I stubbed my shoe on the runner in the halls they have, and I fell down. And I see one man coming, and all my men gone with the exception of one. And this fellow was coming. I was trying to get up as quick as I could, and here this fellow that had stayed—the last one—went over and fixed him. I don't know what he done to him, hit him a lick in the jaw or something. I didn't stop to·see. I was trying to get out of there. And that is all I know about it. So I ran down the stairs and down around into the place where I was working.

Mr. THOMPSON. Do you care to make any further statement about the condition of affairs in Stockton?

Mr. STEWART. No; that is all I know of. I never done no work waiting for him.

Mr. THOMPSON. What representations were made to you when you joined the M., M. and E.?

Mr. STEWART. Well, he gave me to understand I would get work right away. I kept waiting and waiting and waiting until the three months was up, and he sent me a notice for my $2 bill; and I went up there and told him I hadn't done no work to get it. "Well," he says, "we will let it go on," until it run up to the 5th of August, that was the day we had trouble; that was five months, all told.

Mr. THOMPSON. That is all, Mr. Chairman.

Chairman WALSH. Any questions, Mr. Weinstock?

Mr. WEINSTOCK. You are a master painter, Mr. Stewart?

Mr. STEWART. Yes, sir.

Commissioner WEINSTOCK. Do the master painters of Stockton have an organization?

Mr. STEWART. Well, they have had one; but I got out of there. There was some trouble that they had in there, and they told—I don't know, they got some word·around that they would let me do all the old work if they could do the new work.

Commissioner WEINSTOCK. Now, when was this master painters' association organized?

Mr. STEWART. Oh; that must be four or five years ago.

Commissioner WEINSTOCK. Is it still in existence?

Mr. STEWART. Well, I could not tell you that.

Commissioner WEINSTOCK. When did you drop·out?

Mr. STEWART. Oh, I dropped out—well, it was quite—yes; it has been quite a while now. They took me in——

Cmmissioner WEINSTOCK (interposing). About how long ago, approximately?

Mr. STEWART. Let's see, it must be—see, I went away for a·little while, and then I came back. It must be four or five years.

Commissioner WEINSTOCK. Since you dropped out?

Mr. STEWART. Yes, sir; they collected a lot of money, and then they would go down to Madden's and have a big feed. I thought I could have a better feed at home with my wife and children. So I told them I didn't propose to pay money in there to do that way.

Commissioner WEINSTOCK. You have been out of the employers' association?

Mr. STEWART. I have been out of there.

Commissioner WEINSTOCK. Four or five years?

Mr. STEWART. Yes, sir.

Commissioner WEINSTOCK. Do you remember how long you were a member?

Mr. STEWART. Well, let us see, it will be—it has been about a year, I guess. Somewhere around there, probably a little over.

Commissioner WEINSTOCK. You joined about four or five years ago and dropped out about a year ago?

Mr. STEWART. Somewhere.

Commissioner WEINSTOCK. You were a member about three years?

Mr. STEWART. I was in there——

Commissioner WEINSTOCK (interposing). Yes.

Mr. STEWART. About three years ago I went away for eight weeks and come back.

Commissioner WEINSTOCK. When disputes would arise between the journeymen on the one hand and the master painters on the other hand, how were those disputes settled? Did they have a grievance committee that they submitted them to?

Mr. STEWART. Well, I don't know; they didn't seem to. They took in·men there that were supposed to be—say like you and me was a partner, you would be in the union and I would be in the bosses—that sort of·stuck them the worst, because I knew that. They swore it was a falsehood on that part of it, because I sold out all of my tools to two parties.

Commissioner WEINSTOCK. What I wanted to know, Mr. Stewart, was this, whether the master painters, who you say were organized——

Mr. STEWART (interposing). Yes, sir.

Commissioner WEINSTOCK. Whether there was a grievance committee, as there is in many instances?

Mr. STEWART. No.

Commissioner WEINSTOCK. Representing both sides to settle any disputes that might come up?

Mr. STEWART. No.

Commissioner WEINSTOCK. They had no such committee?

Mr. STEWART. No.

Commissioner WEINSTOCK. That is all, Mr. Chairman.

Chairman WALSH. Any other questions? That is all; thank you, Mr. Stewart. Call your next.

Mr. THOMPSON. Mr. Luke.

TESTIMONY OF MR. E. J. LUKE.

Mr. THOMPSON. Mr. Luke, will you give us your name?

Mr. LUKE. E. J. Luke.

Mr. THOMPSON. Your business address?

Mr. LUKE. Stockton.

Mr. THOMPSON. Your business?

Mr. LUKE. Flour miller.

Mr. THOMPSON. I didn't get that.

Mr. LUKE. Flour milling.

Mr. THOMPSON. Are you connected with the Sperry Flour Co.?

Mr. LUKE. Manager of it.

Mr. THOMPSON. How long have you been manager of that company?

Mr. LUKE. Very near five years.

Mr. THOMPSON. Five years. You are acquainted with the conditions that exist to-day in Stockton?

Mr. LUKE. I am.

Mr. THOMPSON. You have heard the testimony of the witnesses here also to-day?

Mr. LUKE. Yes.

Mr. THOMPSON. Will you tell us the facts as you view them; if you view them different from what the other witnesses have stated?

Mr. LUKE. About May, 1913, I was approached by a representative of labor in Stockton, who informed me that there had been a union formed of the warehousemen and packers and a demand made for the closed shop and shorter hours than they were then having. The same demand was made upon the other mill and all the warehousemen in Stockton. There was a warehousemen's association in Stockton several years ago, and this was re-formed to take up this question. We had several meetings, went over all the phases of the situation, and decided to not accede to the demands that were made upon us. It went along, then, for a short while, and while these things were under discussion they made another demand upon us from the engineers, wanting our engineers to join the union; in other words, the closed shop. The wages and hours which we were paying the engineers in some instances were better, and in all instances were just as good, as the union demanded. Our engineers refused to join the union. They then demanded that we make them join the union. I took the stand that we always had maintained there, that we didn't care whether a man belonged to the union or not. We had union men working for us in very near all lines, and we had nonunion men working for us in all lines. They then declared the boycott upon—the engineers then declared the boycott upon the Sperry Flour Co., and it was about—I guess it was about the last of August. That went along for about four months when it was withdrawn. We had several conferences with quite a few of the leaders, but nothing came of it. We still stuck to the proposition that we were running an open shop and had union men and nonunion men working for us, and we didn't care whether they were union or nonunion.

That went along all right during the—the warehousemen and packers union would only have taken 10 to 15 per cent of our men anyhow. When the engineers placed the boycott upon us, the warehousemen's union that had made the demands upon us still continued to work. We then informed the officers of the warehousemen's and packers' union who were working for us; that that boycott would have to be withdrawn or they would have to sever their connection with the Sperry Flour Co. They didn't do that. The boycott was not withdrawn. And we shut down until we got another crew and started up again and have been running continually ever since. Most of these men are back working for us. The engineers that they wanted to force into the union had been, as I understand it in an indirect way—I never asked them—members of the union at one time. Two of them had been with us over 20 years, and I think one of them has been with us 12 years, and the others have been with us 2 or 3 years. Things went along all right until a short time ago, when this trouble occurred up town with the clerks. And we were then requested by some of the labor representatives in San Francisco to withdraw from the M., M. and E. We refused to do so, and a boycott was placed upon us. The same men are working for us to-day as have been working for us right straight along. No demands have been made upon us as regards hours or wages or conditions. That is the situation to-day. We were boycotted for, I should say, about three weeks, three weeks or a month, the first time the boycott was placed upon us.

Mr. THOMPSON. Do you subscribe to the by-laws and the objects and aims of the M., M. and E.?

Mr. LUKE. Yes, sir.

Mr. THOMPSON. That states your view of the manner of dealing with labor?

Mr. LUKE. Very nearly so.

Mr. THOMPSON. What I meant more specifically is this, you are not a believer in collective bargaining?

Mr. LUKE. No.

Mr. THOMPSON. Would you care to give to the commission more extendedly your reasons for not believing that?

Mr. LUKE. I would rather answer——

Mr. THOMPSON. Or have you stated it already?

Mr. LUKE. I would rather answer questions that were asked me than to make any extended remarks. I think that has been gone over very thoroughly here to-day.

Mr. THOMPSON. That is all, Mr. Chairman.

Chairman WALSH. Any questions?

Commissioner WEINSTOCK. Yes.

Chairman WALSH. Mr. Weinstock.

Commissioner WEINSTOCK. You were present, Mr. Luke, this morning when Mr. Johannsen gave his testimony?

Mr. LUKE. Yes, sir.

Commissioner WEINSTOCK. You heard the question put to him as to which side of this controversy in Stockton had taken the initiative in the matter of boycotting, and you heard his answer that it was the M., M. and E. who had initiated the boycotting?

Mr. LUKE. Yes, sir.

Commissioner WEINSTOCK. Is that statement correct?

Mr. LUKE. That statement can not be correct, because the Sperry Flour Co. was boycotted before the M., M. and E. was formed.

Commissioner WEINSTOCK. So that your testimony is that organized labor took the initiative in the matter of boycotting in the city of Stockton?

Mr. LUKE. Well, I won't say the city of Stockton. I will say the Sperry Flour Co. We were singled out, amongst all that the demands were made upon, to be placed upon the boycott list.

Commissioner WEINSTOCK. Your mill is located in Stockton, is it not?

Mr. LUKE. Yes, sir.

Commissioner WEINSTOCK. Well, have there been any other boycotts levied by organized labor during this trouble?

Mr. LUKE. The first trouble, or this trouble that is going on now?

Commissioner WEINSTOCK. This present trouble, yes.

Mr. LUKE. I believe some of the stores uptown are being boycotted.

Commissioner WEINSTOCK. Can you recall when the first boycott was established in this present trouble?

Mr. LUKE. No, sir.

Commissioner. WEINSTOCK. What boycotts, if any, have the members of the M., M. and E. placed against the workers?

Mr. LUKE. I don't know.

Commissioner WEINSTOCK. The union workers?

Mr. LUKE. I haven't been active in the M., M. and E.

Commissioner WEINSTOCK. You are not informed?

Mr. LUKE. No, sir.

Commissioner WEINSTOCK. Are there union men now in your employ, Mr. Luke?

Mr. LUKE. Mr. Weinstock, in answer to that I will say this, that I have never asked any man in our employ whether he has been a union man or nonunion man.

Commissioner WEINSTOCK. So you really don't know?

Mr. LUKE. No; I know all this time I have been informed by outsiders that there have been. We have had the teamsters working for us, and we have had longshoremen and lumber handlers, which I have been told were union men, but I have never asked one, either in a direct or indirect way, about it.

Commissioner WEINSTOCK. So that you really don't know to-day whether your people are union people or nonunion people?

Mr. LUKE. No, sir.

Commissioner WEINSTOCK. Is that question put to any applicant for employment?

Mr. LUKE. No, sir.

Commissioner WEINSTOCK. That is, you are indifferent as to whether the applicant is a union or nonunion man?

Mr. LUKE. Yes, sir.

Commissioner WEINSTOCK. You have never discharged any man because he was a member of the union?

Mr. LUKE. No, sir.

Commissioner WEINSTOCK. You have never asked any union man to give up his card to enter your employ?

Mr. LUKE. No, sir.

Commissioner GARRETSON. Your attitude has been the same before the trouble and since the trouble in that respect?

Mr. LUKE. Yes, sir.

Commissioner GARRETSON. That is all.

Commissioner LENNON. What hours do you work in your mill, Mr. Luke?

Mr. LUKE. Ten hours.

Commisssioner LENNON. Ten hours.

Mr. LUKE. In the flour mill we work 12 hours, but the men only work 10 hours, change shifts. Some go on early and go home early, and others come on late and go home late.

Commissioner LENNON. Well, do they have to be ready for service 12 hours?

Mr. LUKE. No.

Commissioner LENNON. Ten hours?

Mr. LUKE. Yes, sir.

Commissioner LENNON. What is the general rule for a day's work in your city?

Mr. LUKE. Wages?

Commissioner LENNON. No; what is the rule, usual rule in Stockton as to the hours of labor for a day's work?

Mr. LUKE. Oh, some of them are working 9 and some 10. Ten hours is the rule generally in the milling business.

Commissioner LENNON. Ten hours is the general rule. You know there are mills, at least one mill in the United States where they have the eight-hour day?

Mr. LUKE. I don't.

Commissioner LENNON. There is.

Mr. LUKE. I know they tried it in Minneapolis.

Commissioner LENNON. There is such a mill, and a highly successful one. That is all.

Commissioner WEINSTOCK. Just one more question, Mr. Chairman, if it is permissible.

Chairman WALSH. Go right ahead, Mr. Weinstock.

Commissioner WEINSTOCK. Have any of the men who were in your employ, Mr. Luke, when this trouble first began, have any of them dropped out since then on account of this trouble?

Mr. LUKE. This last trouble?

Commissioner WEINSTOCK. Yes.

Mr. LUKE. No.

Commissioner WEINSTOCK. Not any?

Mr. LUKE. No.

Commissioner WEINSTOCK. So far as you know, have you acts of violence been committed against any of your men?

Mr. LUKE. Not against our men.

Commissioner WEINSTOCK. Not against your men. That is all, Mr. Chairman.

Chairman WALSH. Prof. Commons?

Commissioner COMMONS. Can you tell if this boycott first extended outside of the limits of Stockton; that is, when the State organization first took it up?

Mr. LUKE. When they first took it up?

Commissioner COMMONS. Yes.

Mr. LUKE. The State organization, I believe, indorsed it at their meeting in Fresno just about a year ago; I think it will be a year in September or October.

Commissioner COMMONS. What was that, the building trades or the State federation?

Mr. LUKE. No. The labor council.

Commissioner COMMONS. State labor council?

Mr. LUKE. The federated—the building trades council I don't believe ever did indorse it.

Commissioner COMMONS. It is called the State federation of labor, I take it.

Mr. LUKE. That is it.

Commissioner COMMONS. Did you first feel the effect outside of Stockton at that time?

Mr. LUKE. Well, we felt it; yes; in the large cities.

Commissioner COMMONS. In the large cities?

Mr. LUKE. Yes, sir.

Commissioner COMMONS. You have been feeling it, then, in the large cities for a year?

Mr. LUKE. Yes, sir.

Commissioner COMMONS. Has it extended outside of the State of California?

Mr. LUKE. I don't think it has. I believe they tried to up at Washington, but I don't think it extended that far.

Commissioner COMMONS. Have the employers throughout the State come to your support in turning purchases in your direction?

Mr. LUKE. Not in my territory they haven't.

Commissioner COMMONS. How have you met that boycott? In other words, the boycott of the labor unions would tend to shut off their sympathizers from purchasing of you. What I am getting at is, have the sympathizers with the employers turned purchases toward you to offset that?

Mr. LUKE. I don't—I am glad you asked that question because I would like to make a little addition to that statement. I don't think the first boycott that was placed upon us was very heavily indorsed by the outside labor councils because I had meetings with labor leaders from Sacramento and from Oakland and from San Francisco.

My argument all through that controversy was this, that we were paying more money in wages, giving them better conditions in such as your compensation act partly covers now; in other words, we were paying the men from the minute they got hurt, doctor and medicines, and full wages, until they were well enough to go back to work, and if they weren't in condition to come back and do the same work they were doing why we kept them around the mill doing very light work. We were paying $3 a day to our men. We are to-day. Sacramento, on one side of us, 50 miles away, is paying two and a half to most of their men; some $3. We are paying $3 to all our men, warehousemen and packers. San Francisco, on the other side, was paying two and a half to most of their men. And I argued then that it wasn't fair to ask us to pay more than we were paying until they had succeeded in getting the two competitive points up to where we were.

Commissioner COMMONS. Well, then, am I to understand that this boycott of a year ago at Fresno was not a real boycott, then?

Mr. LUKE. Oh, yes. After they tried to make it effective.

Commissioner COMMONS. Well, how long ago did they try to make it effective?

Mr. LUKE. Well, right after that meeting at Fresno.

Commissioner COMMONS. Oh, I see. Then when did the employers first begin to support you to offset the union boycott?

Mr. LUKE. Personally, I don't know of any case where they have supported us.

Commissioner COMMONS. Have they made purchases of you?

Mr. LUKE. Not any others than always did purchase of us.

Commissioner COMMONS. You haven't gained any new purchasers since the boycott?

Mr LUKE. Not that I personally know of.
Commissioner COMMONS. Have you?
Mr. LUKE. The company might in the different sections that they are in, but I would not have any knowledge of that because I am only situated there in Stockton in the San Joaquin Valley.
Commissioner COMMONS. You did not have charge of the sales?
Mr. LUKE. No, sir; only in my territory. That is my own territory up there.
Commissioner COMMONS. Just around there. Where is your sales headquarters?
Mr. LUKE. San Francisco.
Commissioner COMMONS. You work seven days a week?
Mr. LUKE. No, sir. We are now; yes, sir.
Commissioner COMMONS. When did you start working seven days?
Mr. LUKE. About two weeks ago.
Commissioner COMMONS. You had been working previously six days?
Mr. LUKE. Yes, sir; we are working 17 hours now.
Commissioner COMMONS. How is that?
Mr. LUKE. Working 17 hours now—overtime.
Commissioner COMMONS. That is in the week?
Mr. LUKE. No, sir; a day.
Commissioner COMMONS. I don't quite get how you get 17 hours overtime.
Mr. LUKE. Not overtime. We are working now 17 hours during the last week or so.
Commissioner COMMONS. You shut down the other seven hours in the day?
Mr. LUKE. At night, from 11 to 6.
Commissioner COMMONS. You are running two shifts?
Mr. LUKE. No, sir; we are changing the shifts around.
Commissioner COMMONS. How do you get in 17 hours. Explain that shift system.
Mr. LUKE. We start at 6 o'clock in the morning, some of the men, and some start at 7 o'clock.
Commissioner COMMONS. And each works 10 hours?
Mr. LUKE. No, sir; they are working overtime.
Commissioner O'CONNELL. Are they working 17 hours?
Mr. LUKE. No, sir; they are not working no more than 16 hours.
Commissioner O'CONNELL. There are some of them working 16 hours?
Mr. LUKE. Yes, sir; but getting overtime for every hour over 10.
Commissioner COMMONS. What is the rate for overtime?
Mr. LUKE. Forty cents an hour.
Commissioner COMMONS. What is straight time?
Mr. LUKE. Thirty cents.
Commissioner COMMONS. Prior to two weeks ago you were working 10 hours, without any overtime at all?
Mr. LUKE. In one mill, and the other mill was working 24 hours.
Commissioner COMMONS. Two shifts of 10 hours each?
Mr. LUKE. The millers change around. The two millers work 10 hours, but the others are 12. Some come on early and go home early and others come late and go home late.
Commissioner COMMONS. Is there any force working 12 hours?
Mr. LUKE. No, sir.
Commissioner COMMONS. But the mill is working continuously 24 hours. The four hours' difference is made up by overlapping. You stock up your bins for packing?
Mr. LUKE. Yes, sir.
Commissioner GARRETSON. You use men to break the shifts by early calls for certain men?
Mr. LUKE. Yes, sir; that is right.
Commissioner COMMONS. Are there union mills in this country—in this State?
Mr. LUKE. Not that I know of.
Commissioner COMMONS. All these competitors, of course, are nonunion; they are not organized?
Mr. LUKE. Yes, sir.
Commissioner COMMONS. What are their hours?
Mr. LUKE. Ten hours. If they work full time—24 hours—they shift just about the way I explained a moment ago. Ten hours is generally the work of a packer.

Commissioner COMMONS. They have been paying——
Mr. LUKE. Two dollars and a half and three dollars a day.
Commissioner COMMONS. Two dollars and a half to three dollars for 10 hours. That is 25 to 30 cents an hour. You have been paying 30 cents and are now, paying 30 cents, and 40 cents for overtime?
Mr. LUKE. Yes, sir.
Commissioner COMMONS. How many men have you?
Mr. LUKE. Pretty nearly 200.
Commissioner COMMONS. How many men are engineers?
Mr. LUKE. Five. The number on this double time is seven.
Commissioner COMMONS. In the case of these warehousemen and packers, is that a new organization?
Mr. LUKE. Yes, sir.
Commissioner COMMONS. That has not been in existence in this State before?
Mr. LUKE. Yes, sir; it had been in existence in this State seven or eight years ago.
Commissioner COMMONS. Was it created anew?
Mr. LUKE. Yes, sir; in Stockton. Yes, sir; that is my understanding.
Commissioner COMMONS. And what is the highest wages paid?
Mr. LUKE. In the mill?
Commissioner COMMONS. Yes, sir.
Mr. LUKE. Any man?
Commissioner COMMONS. Yes, sir.
Mr. LUKE. Two hundred dollars.
Commissioner COMMONS. He is the head miller?
Mr. LUKE. One of them.
Commissioner COMMONS. What is the lowest?
Mr. LUKE. Oh, we employ boys for a dollar and a quarter to a dollars and a half a day.
Commissioner COMMONS. The lowest adult, what do you pay?
Mr. LUKE. The lowest adult would be two and a half.
Commissioner COMMONS. How many boys would you have?
Mr. LUKE. Oh, I guess we have about six or seven; somewhere there.
Commissioner COMMONS. That is all.
Commissioner GARRETSON. Did you ever consider leaving Stockton on account of labor conditions you were confronted with there?
Mr. LUKE. We did.
Commissioner GARRETSON. That is all.
Chairman WALSH. That is all.
Commissioner O'CONNELL. I would like to ask a few questions.
Chairman WALSH. Mr. O'Connell would like to ask some questions.
Commissioner O'CONNELL. What has been the cause of your increasing the hours from 12 to 17?
Mr. LUKE. Trying to fill orders.
Commissioner O'CONNELL. Then the boycott is not affecting you now?
Mr. LUKE. Well, there has been a rush of orders of late, because every groceryman expects an advance in the price of flour. We haven't advanced the price of flour, notwithstanding the advance of wheat.
Commissioner O'CONNELL. What is your production per day in barrels?
Mr. LUKE. A thousand barrels for 12 hours.
Commissioner O'CONNELL. What is the highest you ever had?
Mr. LUKE. You mean in barrels?
Commissioner O'CONNELL. Yes.
Mr. LUKE. I think one month we ran 32,000 barrels.
Commissioner O'CONNELL. What is the difference just prior to this war scare we have on now—your production then and your production prior to the boycott being issued?
Mr. LUKE. Well, that could be answered better by saying we were working overtime five hours.
Commissioner O'CONNELL. Then the boycott has not affected you during that time?
Mr. LUKE. I can't tell that, because we don't know how many of these orders are just stocking up
Commissioner O'CONNELL. What I catch is your production is as large, if not larger, than it has been at any time during the trouble?
Mr. LUKE. Yes, sir; but I am trying to get you to understand we can't tell how much of that is added business, if any of it is added business, because

every merchant expects a raise in flour and he is putting in all he can take care of and pay for.

Commissioner O'CONNELL. As I understand, the so-called boycott has been levied some time ago?

Mr. LUKE. This last one only about four weeks ago.

Commissioner O'CONNELL. This last one about four weeks ago. The first one was not effective at all, as I understand?

Mr. LUKE. Oh, slightly.

Commissioner O'CONNELL. Then it takes some time before you would be in position to ascertain whether the recent one is really effective or not?

Mr. LUKE. Yes, sir.

Commissioner O'CONNELL. You say your mills are running 17 hours, but some of the men, or none of them, are working over 16 hours?

Mr. LUKE. Yes, sir.

Commissioner O'CONNELL. That comes because of starting them earlier and later?

Mr. LUKE. Yes, sir.

Commissioner O'CONNELL. Making the shifts, that hour that the mill is running and that the men are not, operating 17 hours. How long have they now been working 16 hours?

Mr. LUKE. I started two weeks ago to work every other night. Last week we commenced and worked every night and worked Sunday.

Commissioner O'CONNELL. Including Sunday? Sixteen hours a day for seven days, and that has been going on two weeks?

Mr. LUKE. Yes, sir.

Commissioner O'CONNELL. And the possibility of continuing that. There is no way that the number of employees might be increased in order that the excess number of hours might not be necessary?

Mr. LUKE. If we could get skilled packers—yes, sir—or millers.

Commissioner O'CONNELL. That is all.

Mr. THOMPSON. Just one question, Mr. Chairman. Do you know, Mr. Luke, whether or not any pressure, directly or indirectly, has been used to induce merchants and manufacturers to join your association at Stockton?

Mr. LUKE. I don't. I haven't been active in that.

Mr. THOMPSON. That is all.

Chairman WALSH. That is all.

Mr. Irish, will you please take the stand a moment? Mr. Weinstock wants to ask Mr. Irish a question.

TESTIMONY OF MR. J. P. IRISH, JR.—Recalled.

Commissioner WEINSTOCK. You are secretary of the Stockton Chamber of Commerce?

Mr. IRISH. Yes, sir.

Commissioner WEINSTOCK. And I take it that the Stockton Chamber of Commerce, in common with other chambers of commerce, has what might be called a promotion department?

Mr. IRISH. Yes, sir.

Commissioner WEINSTOCK. Reaching out and trying to get——

Mr. IRISH. In common with most all of them, it is mostly all promotion department.

Commissioner WEINSTOCK. You have no object in view; that is, to bring new industries to Stockton?

Mr. IRISH. Yes, sir.

Commissioner WEINSTOCK. Do you keep a record of those prospects?

Mr. IRISH. Yes, sir.

Commissioner WEINSTOCK. Could you tell this commission how many such prospects you have had, say, within the past year?

Mr. IRISH. It is a matter of some difficulty to analyze just how many of them are prospects and just how many are impelled by mere idle curiosity in looking from place to place with an ultimate view of locating. I can say, this, however, and I am glad to have an opportunity, if you will permit me, to read it into the record. When I first assumed my connection with the chamber of commerce I made it my business to get in touch with the various manufacturing plants that were either contemplating a move, or, more often, were expecting to open a branch plant on the Pacific coast; and I made it my business with any such that I could find to get into correspondence with them through a rather orderly system of follow up, and told them I could furnish them with information that would be of interest to them, and tried to interest them; if they were going to locate, to come to Stockton. Our actual prospects in 10 months, when they were boiled, cleared down by a follow up, were zero. We had none. The usual course that they took was that we got to the point finally where they began—taking an individual business, after they asked about transportation and other general matters, and finally got boiled down to a place where they would inquire as to the amount of thermal units in the oil, and the prices at which oil could be bought, insurance rates and cost of building and cost of the raw material, and those fundamentals that a manufacturer gets down to when seriously considering a location—invariably with the location of some plants, I don't know anything about all, but invariably the question boiled down to the question as to labor conditions in Stockton, and that almost invariably boiled down to whether the manufacturer or employer of labor was in a position to receive any protection through organization against unfair demands on the part of labor unions, and in many cases, coming from open-shop towns, whether the right of free employment could be had in the city of Stockton.

The answer was always this, that two of our largest manufacturing concerns were operating on the open-shop basis. But immediately, apparently, those people would put their independent investigators on, and the natural result was, I was never able to get any further. It took that course in case after case, covering a great line of industries.

Since the recent developments and for once I am perfectly willing to go later than the 8th of July. Since this development I have had five manufacturing firms who are actually and legitimately prospects, looking for a location, and, in some cases, seeking options on sites, and they have come into the town for the purpose of locating. Mind you, they are not located yet, but they have gone further than they ever did before. And without exception they have told the same story, that they came because they would be able to work under open-shop conditions, and in every case we told them that they must understand that the schedule of hours and labor was not altered by this condition. They said that was a matter of indifference to them. It was protection against unfair demands that they were looking for and they thought they would get it there. I guess that covers it. I didn't aim to take up so much time.

Commissioner WEINSTOCK. Let me put it in this form. It would be of interest and, in fact, pertinent to the investigation that the commission is making; to know of specific instances where prospective manufacturers decided against Stockton on account of labor conditions. Could you give the commission any such specific instances?

Mr. IRISH. Unfortunately, the type of the matter I got did not specify their reason for lack of interest. The query came simply as to labor conditions in the city of Stockton, and thereafter I was unable to extract any further correspondence from them. It ceased right there.

Commissioner WEINSTOCK. There was testimony to-day, I don't know whether by you or some other gentleman from Stockton, to the effect that prospective manufacturers had been frightened away from Stockton because of labor conditions, and if that could be demonstrated, it would be an important point.

Now, if it is possible for you—if not at this moment, then at your earliest convenience—to furnish this commission with testimony, authenticated testimony, showing instances where prospective manufacturers have been kept away from Stockton because of labor conditions, that would be an important matter for the record.

Mr. IRISH. May I put my answer to that in this way: I will be very glad to go back through my files, and be very glad to take the matter up with the individual concerns that I have correspondence with in my files and ask them if they are willing that that correspondence be placed in the record here. In our relations with the prospective manufacturer or investor we are naturally in a position where their confidence must be held as sacred by us, not only for this reason but because they don't want to know they are coming to a place because, as a rule, real estate values go up on that knowledge, and all our correspondence is confidential.

If I am able to furnish that, I will be glad to do it. I can only say this definitely, we have never had a prospect of an industry locating, what I would call a prospect, until after the open-shop declaration, and since then we have had five that have been on the ground.

Commissioner WEINSTOCK. At this time you could not give the commission any definite case that the prospect was kept away because of labor conditions? ·Mr. IRISH. I could not do that without taking the matter up with them.

Commissioner WEINSTOCK. That is all.

Commissioner GARRETSON. Let me ask one question. Bear in mind we have heard that in every town on the Pacific coast.

Mr. IRISH. I have no doubt.

Commissioner GARRETSON. Isn't it a fact that every applicant you had probably also was an applicant to a score or less of other towns, asking what they had to offer. Isn't that the universal practice, virtually?

Mr. IRISH. Not universally.

Commissioner GARRETSON. Generally, then?

Mr. IRISH. In many cases, but in certain specific cases, three at least to my knowledge, that was not true.

Commissioner GARRETSON. There are not other chambers of commerce with like mission, doing just the same style of investigation as yourself, and working their prospects and presenting the advantages of their paradise, just as you were of yours?

Mr. IRISH. Did you ever run a chamber of commerce? ·

Commissioner GARRETSON. I have been particeps criminis.

Mr. IRISH. I see. I thought so. I can only say this, that of course that is true in a great majority of cases. Of course there are specific cases where you find a man who is looking for a specific type of location, and you are lucky enough to get to him first and finish before the other man butts in. Three of those cases I know of.

Commissioner GARRETSON. All of the propositions from the town as a whole usually go into one jack pot for the determination of the case?

Mr. IRISH. Yes, sir. As a fellow criminal, you have me at some disadvantage.

Chairman WALSH. The hearing will now adjourn until to-morrow morning at 10 o'clock.

(Whereupon, at 4.40 o'clock p. m. on Tuesday, the 25th day of August, 1914, an adjournment was taken until the following day, Wednesday, August 26, at 10 o'clock a. m.)

SAN FRANCISCO, CAL., *Wednesday, August 26, 1914—10 a. m.*

Present: Chairman Walsh, Commissioners Weinstock, Garretson, O'Connell, Lennon, and Commons. William O. Thompson, counsel.

Chairman WALSH. You may go ahead, Mr. Thompson, please.

Mr. THOMPSON. Mr. Dale.

TESTIMONY OF MR. J. B. DALE.

Mr. THOMPSON. Mr. Dale, will you give us your name?

Mr. DALE. J. B. Dale.

Mr. THOMPSON. Your business address?

Mr. DALE. General delivery, Stockton, Cal.

Mr. THOMPSON. And your business?

Mr. DALE. I am an organizer for the American Federation of Labor and the California State Federation of Labor.

Mr. THOMPSON. How long have you been the organizer for those two bodies?

Mr. DALE. Four years and a half.

Mr. THOMPSON. Four years and a half on the western coast here?

Mr. DALE. Yes, sir.

Mr. THOMPSON. Are you familiar with the conditions in Stockton?

Mr. DALE. Yes, sir; somewhat.

Mr. THOMPSON. Will you tell us in your own way, briefly, if you will, what you have to add to that which the witnesses have already testified to?

Mr. DALE. Well, about the middle of April this year, 1914, I was instructed by Secretary Scharrenberg, of the California State Federation of Labor, to proceed to Stockton and assist Stockton Labor Council in an open-shop war that had been inaugurated by the M., M. and E., known as the merchants, manufacturers, and employers' association, at the city of Stockton.

Now, leading up to the trouble——

Mr. THOMPSON. I will ask you one question there. Do you know why that word was sent to you?

Mr. DALE. Yes, sir. By the solicitation of the Stockton Central Labor Council; their representative, a man by the name of Vitaich, T. J. Vitaich, business agent for the Stockton Central Labor Council and executive board member of the California State Federation of Labor, made that demand upon the executive board of the California State Federation of Labor; hence my visit to Stockton.

Mr. THOMPSON. You may go ahead, Mr. Dale.

Mr. DALE. The clerks' agreement expired, as near as my memory serves me, along in the month of March, 1914. At the time for the re-signing of the agreement the representative of the clerks, which was the business agent of the central labor council, called on the various merchants, and he found this condition of affairs: That the clothiers' association had been voted bodily into the M., M. and E., and when the business agent approached the merchants asking for their signatures to another agreement he was referred to Mr. Calkins, secretary of the M., M. and E., with offices in the Elks' Building, Stockton. And Mr. Calkins told him this: "We have concluded to not sign any agreement with any organization of labor."

The representative of the clerks made this request: "Will you give me that statement in writing?" Mr. Calkins said: "It is not necessary. That is the conclusion of our association, and we will not give you any written statement why we have entered into this agreement."

Then the representative of the clerks, the business agent of the central labor council, started in on a campaign with the various merchants. Many of the cards he had to remove from the stores, the proprietors of which had always been at peace with the clerks. Now, there is one point that I want to emphasize. The clerks were asking for nothing. They had, about four months prior to this—one of the large stores in the city had suggested—the manager of said store had suggested to his help that they use their influence in the clerks' union to bring about a 6 o'clock closing movement. That was to our mind, after developments had convinced us that that was simply an attempt on the part of the merchants, some of them at least, to start a campaign of discontent or dis-. organization, if I may use that word, in the clerks' organization, and when that was discovered that request was eliminated from the clerks' agreement, and there was nothing more said about it. Hence, the clerks were asking for nothing, no increase in pay, no decrease in hours, nothing at all; simply wanted their agreement re-signed, which they refused to do.

When I reached Stockton we looked over the situation, and we concluded to inaugurate a campaign of this nature—to go from union to union, night after night, urging the members of organized labor and their friends to use their purchasing power, patronizing the stores that displayed the card, patronize the restaurants that displayed the card, spend their money with their friends and let their enemies alone.

The statement has been made here that we issued an edict of boycott. I wish to tell this committee that that is absolutely false. You can go to Stockton and get every minute book of every organization in Stockton, and if you can find one sentence that looks like the authorization of a boycott I will surrender my commission and quit work for the State federation of labor.

There was no boycott declared. A man that smokes a Natividad cigar boycotts the St. Elmo, if that is a boycott. Do you "git" me? That is what we mean, and that is what we—that was our policy.

Now, then, the first blow that was struck in the industrial war in Stockton was struck by a member of the M., M. and E. There was a card passer in front of a shoe store—Mr. Dunn's. Mr. Dunn deliberately walked out after the— the man hadn't been there 10 minutes, and struck him a blow in the face. He carried a black eye for eight days from the effect of it. And there is a little incident to that that I want to tell the commission. It is this: Mr. Dunn was arrested for battery. He demanded a jury trial. Mr. Dunn swore under oath that he struck the blow. Mr. Dunn's son swore that he seen him strike the blow. Mr. Lynch, their hired man, swore likewise. Two disinterested men standing within 5 feet of the occurrence swore they saw the blow struck. And the jury brought in a verdict of not guilty. That is the court record. That is the truth. I simply relate this to let you know the conditions that obtain in Stockton. When men come before this commission and tell you that their objects are square and above board with labor it is necessary to analyze their actions, for actions speak louder than words.

Now, there was at that time, I believe, 16 stores displaying cards—retail clerks' store cards. You know what they are. And I think there was about 18 or 20 stores that had no cards.

Now, the M., M. and E. advertised in the three daily papers the stores that did not display the cards, and they made this appeal to the public: "These are the stores that stand for industrial freedom. If you believe in industrial freedom, patronize these stores." And the list of the stores was in the papers. We did likewise. It had settled down to a fight, a rough and tumble fight, if I may use that term. We were appealing to our people to patronize the merchants and the restaurant people that displayed the cards. They were appealing to their people, using their influence, to patronize the stores that did not display the cards.

And I contend, and I want this commission to get the point, and I believe you will without my mentioning it to you, but I want to make it plain, that they were boycotting the stores that had the cards, and we were boycotting the stores that had no cards.

Now, if anyone is guilty, we are all equally guilty. I have nothing to shun. I have nothing to side-step, nothing to keep under cover from this commission. I want you to know the full and complete facts.

About the 17th or some time in the latter part of April or May the Holt Manufacturing Co. gave a big demonstration. Every man in their employ was given a day's pay to march in a parade—the first time in the history of that organization that anything of that kind had ever occurred. I took occasion to make the remark that in my opinion the parade had been pulled off for effect—to get public opinion on their side. Some reporter overheard what I said, and I ■lieve it appeared in the Sacramento Bee. I am still of that opinion. I am not taking back anything that I said then. I still believe that to be true.

Later the card passers were enjoined. Now, those people—and I want this commission to get this point—that we contend that those people we had at that time were not pickets; they were card passers; they were advertising stores and restaurants and people that were fair to labor. We were not able to buy space in the newspapers as the M., M. and E. They advertised theirs in the newspapers. Our medium of advertising was by handing out cards. They enjoined the card passers. The injunction was made permanent.

Later there was a couple of innocent-looking little donkeys placed on the streets, with a blanket over them telling the story that certain restaurants were unfair; and the judge enjoined the donkeys, mark you, and he made that permanent. The donkey can't coerce, he can't threatent, he can not malign any one. The only thing that he can do is to kick, and any man that has got any sense knows which end he kicks from and to keep away from that end of it. That is all. The donkey was enjoined, the two of them; took off the streets, and I don't know where they are at.

Now, that shows again the disposition of some of the citizenship of Stockton relative to organized labor. The bankers, every one of them, belong to the M., M. and E. Now, I don't know whether they have used their financial influence to coerce anyone or not. There will be other men, other people here to tell that story. But in my opinion they have. Rumor is current on the streets of Stockton that those men have gone the limit to seal the lips and tie the hands of the men of labor and merchants and contractors that want to be friendly to labor.

Now, I make that statement to your unqualifiedly. I am telling this commission that that rumor is current, and I believe that there will be men who will follow me and will emphasize that more fully and be more clear on the proposition.

They even went so far in their efforts as to try to muzzle the newspapers, and tried to frighten the pulpit from speaking their minds, and still they have the immaculate nerve to come before the commission and tell you their action was in keeping with right and fair play. If that is fair play, I don't have the right understanding. I don't understand the meaning of the word.

There was a statement made yesterday, I believe, by Mr. Irish relative to a Mr. George Tracy.

Chairman WALSH. Mr. Dale, will you please pitch your voice a little higher. It is very hard to hear in this room. After the adjournment yesterday some of the audience spoke to me and said they were unable to hear the witnesses, and as they are very much interested in the proceedings here I wish you would try and speak a little louder, so that we all can hear.

Mr. DALE. There was a statement made yesterday by Mr. Irish, I believe—if I am wrong in the witness I will beg his pardon—to the effect that Mr. Tracy, president of the San Francisco Typographical Union, and Mr. McLaughlin, State labor commissioner, visited Stockton and endeavored to use their influence in bringing the warring factions of the industrial war in Stockton together. They asked time until the executive board of the California State Federation of Labor met in executive session, which was in April; no, May 12 or June 12—June 12.

Mr. Irish left the impression and, I think, intentionally so, with this commission that that was a bluff on the part of labor; that they didn't mean it. That it was our intention to simply play and spar for time. I want to tell this commission that that was a bona fide proposition on the part of labor. We meant it. We wanted them to wait. We begged them to wait until June 12, when the executive board of the California State Federation of Labor met in executive session, when they could take up the matter of the Stockton situation.

Now, prior to this there had been a committee that had called on the mayor and the board of commissioners in the city of Stockton, and the committee had this to say to the mayor:

"If you will use your influence as the executive officer of the city of Stockton; if you will make a statement in the papers of Stockton to the effect that in behalf of the third party, the public, you demand that the two warring factions in the city of Stockton come together, if you will do that, Mr. Mayor, I believe you will be instrumental in preventing an industrial war in the city of Stockton."

He was told in the event of the trouble continuing that the streets of Stockton would be filled with blacklegs, yeggmen, gunmen, and ex-covicts, and that prediction was verified and there are now in the city of Stockton, such men.

In Stockton this morning they are there with their blackjacks and guns and billies. As Johannsen told you yesterday, five of those fellows were arrested. They had the automobile, the whole bottom of it, covered with pick handles, blackjacks, and guns, and I was present when the city attorney, Carlton Case, from the M., M., and E., put up a check for $500 for those men, and when they signed the roll in the police court, they signed it Mr. Miller, and Jones, and Smith, strike breakers. That is the way they signed themselves at the police court. The signatures are there and you can send and get the books. They made no bones of it. Strike breakers, that was their occupation, that was their business; that was what they were brought to Stockton for, to break the strike and break men's heads, and that is what they came there for. And labor has from the beginning of this asked and begged that the matter be arbitrated, and we are ready now—I want to say to this commission as a representative of the American Federation of Labor, that organized labor stands ready now to arbitrate this matter. The mayor was told by this committee I have just mentioned to you that organized labor would pay half of the expenses of bringing men to Stockton who have no interest in the affair and know nothing about the facts, and whatever the finding of the arbitration board might be, organized labor would bow and take its medicine.

I was with the committee that met with a committee from the M., M., and E., and conditions were thrashed over for probably three hours, and Mr. Totten, who will follow me probably, made this statement: "You fellows have got to call your dogs off of our people." That isn't the language he used, but that was the meaning.

"You have got to cease boycotting the members of our institution or we will discharge your people." Now, this is a very important point—"or we will discharge your people and we will put men in their places that will take orders from us and not from you."

That was Totten's statement. If he denies it here, why, it is up to him. There were 20 men listening to him at that time, and that is what he said.

A plain declaration of "You do what I tell you to do, spend your money with the people that I tell you to spend it with, or we will put your people on the streets; we will fill the town with strangers, we will put the taxpayers, the fathers and the mothers, and the children out of the schools." That is what the declaration meant, and that is just what they are doing.

I want to emphasize to this commission once more that from the beginning of the trouble, since my advent into Stockton, that it has been my endeavor all the time, every hour in the day and every day in the week, to get the factions together and bring about a settlement. We want to do that now, but we can't. As Johannsen told you, we can not, and we will not arbitrate the right to live as an organization. That is sacred. The law of the land says we have a right to organize. That we will do. Any proposition as to hours, any question of hours or wages, those questions we are willing to submit to a board of arbitration. We will tell our story and they can tell theirs, and let fair men reach a conclusion, and we will abide by the decision.

Now, that is about all I have got to say on the question.

Mr. THOMPSON. Mr. Dale, in regard to the matter of a boycott. When this trouble arose in Stockton you asked people, of course—your organization did—to deal with the stores that showed the signs?

Mr. DALE. Absolutely; yes, sir.

Mr. THOMPSON. And you asked the friends of organized labor to deal with those stores, too?

Mr. DALE. Yes, sir.

Mr. THOMPSON. And the public generally to do the same thing?

Mr. DALE. Yes, sir.

Mr. THOMPSON. And on the other hand the M., M., and E. asked the same thing?

Mr. DALE. Yes, sir.

Mr. THOMPSON. And the people who were friendly to them?

Mr. DALE. They published it in the papers.

Mr. THOMPSON. And the public in general?

Mr. DALE. Published in the daily papers, the three daily papers.

Mr. THOMPSON. So far, then, the attitude and acts of both were similar?

Mr. DALE. Yes, sir.

Mr. THOMPSON. Now, will you tell the commission at what point the acts of the M., M. and E. were different in principle from the acts and methods that your organization pursued in its development of the struggle there?

Chairman WALSH. Say, excuse me. The commission, I think, will draw the conclusion. Let the commission draw that conclusion. We want to hurry through. He has stated now what was done by both sides, and they have stated largely, and I think maybe the commission will be prepared to draw their own conclusion, and thus keep out of the realm of argument.

Is there anyone who wants to ask Mr. Dale any question?

Commissioner WEINSTOCK. Yes.

Chairman WALSH. Mr. Weinstock wants to ask you some questions.

Commissioner WEINSTOCK. Will you be good enough to explain to the commission, Mr. Dale, what your interpretation of a boycott is—what constitutes a boycott?

Mr. DALE. Well, I believe it was Dean Swift, a good many years ago, who was having a fight in Ireland with England, and he told them to burn everything that came from England except the coal. "Don't burn the coal, but burn everything else, not the coal."

Now, my explanation of a boycott is simply that to let the other fellow's goods alone——

Chairman WALSH. A little louder, please. Your conception is what?

Mr. DALE. It is simply to let the other fellow's product alone. I make this contention, that the greatest employer of labor is labor; it is not the merchant that employs the clerks, it is the people that patronize the store of the merchant that employs the clerks. Now, that is my position—the greatest employer of labor is labor, and when labor learns to demand the goods that bear the label; when labor learns to patronize the man and the woman that displays the card; when labor learns to attend strictly to its own business, the fight is settled. There will be no job for you fellows, and there will be no job for me. There you are.

Commissioner WEINSTOCK. Does that men, Mr. ——

Chairman WALSH. Please preserve complete order. Please do not give expression to anything like that.

Mr. DALE. If I ask my friends to withhold their patronage from you, that would be a boycott; that is the interpretation of a good many men relative to a boycott; yes.

Commissioner WEINSTOCK. I see. I can not quite reconcile that definition of a boycott with a statement you made in the beginning of your testimony to the effect that you deny any boycott was declared by the Stockton——

Mr. DALE. Officially. Officially. I think I said, Mr. Weinstock, officially, that you could bring the minute book of every organization in the city of Stockton.

Commissioner GARRETSON. You draw the line between a natural and an official boycott?

Mr. DALE. Yes, sir.

Commissioner WEINSTOCK. Well, what is the difference, after all, in effect, Mr. Dale, between passing a resolution at a meeting of the unions, or appealing to the unions at their meetings to withhold their patronage from certain people?. Isn't the effect precisely the same?

Mr. DALE. Yes, sir; yes, sir.

Commissioner WEINSTOCK. So that while technically there was no boycott levied, practically there was a boycott levied?

Mr. DALE. From both sides; yes. I want that understood, from both sides. We were going after each other—we had an earning capacity, labor contended at that time they had an earning capacity of in the neighborhood of $14,000 a day, of men and women who we could largely control in the spending of their money. The M., M. and E. had less than $4,000 a day of earning capacity of the working people, whom they could control, who would take orders from them. Now, then, the rank and file of the uninterested public sympathy is usually with the under dog in the fight. And labor was the under dog in the fight. And we got much the best of that fight. They will admit that. They may try to hide it here in their statements before the commission, but it is nevertheless the truth. We simply backed them off the boards, in the language of the street.

Commissioner WEINSTOCK. You also made use, Mr. Dale, of the expression " card passers." That is not quite clear to me. What is the distinction between a picket and a card passer? Where does the picket end and the card passer begin, or vice versa?

Mr. DALE. Well, one is called a picket and the other is called a card passer. One is an advertiser, handing out the cards, the same as you, Mr. Weinstock. if you were advertising your store. You have so many handbills struck off. You get a boy or you get a man to strike out over the city of Sacramento or over the State of California and distribute those handbills—Mr. Weinstock has got a sale of goods on such and such a day at such and such a place. Now these cards simply stated the fact, here are the stores that display the union-label card; there are the restaurants that display the house card of the restaurants, etc.

Commissioner WEINSTOCK. Now, did these card passers, as you call them, walk up and down the streets generally, or did they stand in front of some particular shop?

Mr. DALE. Well, in a few instances they probably walked up and down in front of two restaurants—or three, and a few stores. And they did walk all around town.

Commissioner WEINSTOCK. But primarily they stopped in front of certain shops and stores?

Mr. DALE. Well, I don't know whether I am clear in making that admission or not. The men simply came of their own volition to headquarters and would pick up the cards that was there.

Commissioner WEINSTOCK. What would those cards say?

Mr. DALE. Well, they would say—they had a facsimile of the store card of the clerks, and they had the name of the store—the Arcade, the Chamberlain, and so on down the line, stores that were fair to labor. And that told the story to a trade-unionist, or it told the story to anyone that was in sympathy with us, where to go to patronize the stores that were fair to labor, and keep away from stores that were unfair to labor.

Commissioner WEINSTOCK. Let me see whether I understand that clearly. These cards did not say, " Don't patronize A or B " ?

Mr. DALE. No, sir.

Commissioner WEINSTOCK. But they simply said, " Do patronize C, D, and E " ?

Mr. DALE. No; it didn't say that. It simply told the stores that were fair. That is all it told.

Commissioner WEINSTOCK. Gave a list of the so-called fair stores?

Mr. DALE. Yes, sir.

Commissioner WEINSTOCK. Didn't mention the unfair houses?

Mr. DALE. No, sir. Absolutely no.

Commissioner WEINSTOCK. You cited the case, Mr. Dale, where one of those card passers was assaulted by the proprietor of one of the stores?

Mr. DALE. Yes, sir.

Commissioner WEINSTOCK. And the case was brought into court?

Mr. DALE. Yes, sir.

Commissioner WEINSTOCK. And that the defendant admitted that he had struck the card passer?

Mr. DALE. Yes, sir.

Commissioner WEINSTOCK. And there was corroborating testimony to that effect?

Mr. DALE. Yes, sir.

Commissioner WEINSTOCK. And that despite that fact he was discharged, or that is, a verdict was brought in by the jury of not guilty?

Mr. DALE. Of not guilty; yes, sir.

Commissioner WEINSTOCK. Well, now, are we to understand—we must infer one of two things from that—either that the jury was a packed jury or that the sentiment of the community was not in sympathy with the strikers. Now, what was your opinion on that?

Mr. DALE. Well, Mr. Weinstock, I am loath in a measure to give an opinion. Of course, I have got a very strong opinion upon that proposition, but I don't know that it would advance the conclusions that this commissin wishes to arrive at for me to express that opinion.

Commissioner WEINSTOCK. You brought that out as a point, Mr. Dale?

Mr. DALE. Yes, sir, I did.

Commissioner WEINSTOCK. And I want to see along what lines you want that to be considered?

Mr. DALE. Well, I believe you have got the idea pretty clearly. I think you have got just which I mean.

Commissioner WEINSTOCK. I don't know which is the case.

Mr. DALE. Both of them. I don't think there is any way of getting away from the inference.

Commissioner WEINSTOCK. Well, there is a big difference between a packed jury and public sentiment.

Mr. DALE. Well, in order to pack a jury, public sentiment must be pretty well crystallized before a man will undertake to pack it.

Commissioner WEINSTOCK. Not necessarily.

Mr. DALE. Well, probably not. But in this case I believe it was. Of course, I am not in a position to prove that. It is only an inference on my part.

Commissioner WEINSTOCK. You were here yesterday, were you not, Mr. Dale?

Mr. DALE. Yes, sir.

Commissioner WEINSTOCK. You heard all of the testimony that was presented?

Mr. DALE. Most of it; most of it.

Commissioner WEINSTOCK. Have you heard the statements made about violence having taken place in Stockton during these recent troubles?

Mr. DALE. Yes, sir.

Commissioner WEINSTOCK. Will you give us your statement on the question of violence, what your observations have been, and what you know of the facts?

Mr. DALE. Well, I have seen no violence.

Commissioner WEINSTOCK. Well, have you heard of violence taking place?

Mr. DALE. I have heard it discussed; yes, sir.

Commissioner WEINSTOCK. How many instances of violence have you heard of taking place, either through the public press or through word of mouth?

Mr. DALE. Well, I have heard of nonunion men striking union men, and I have heard of union men striking nonunion men, and I have seen men with black eyes. I heard a story, I think it was three or four weeks ago—yes, yesterday was—to-day is Tuesday, isn't it? No, yesterday was Tuesday—three weeks ago, I think, yesterday afternoon there was some men visited a planing mill, Totten & Brandt's, and the story has it, the street rumor, that Mr. Brandt, I believe it was, received his visitors with a chair, and a free fight followed.

Commissioner LENNON. A chair to sit on, or——

Mr. DALE. No; a chair, I think he meant to make him a present over the head with it. And the chair was broken to pieces in the fracas, and he used the handles of it to very good advantage over the heads of some of the men. That was one of the proprietors of the mill. Now, that is the story that is told. I am not here to verify that at all.

Commissioner WEINSTOCK. Do you know of any instances, Mr. Dale, where union men were assaulted by nonunion men, or by the emissaries of nonunion men?

Mr. DALE. I have heard of that; yes, sir, but I don't know of it.

Commissioner WEINSTOCK. How many such instances do you know about?

Mr. DALE. Well, I don't know that I could enumerate the number. I have heard it, you know. I presume you understand pretty thoroughly when you get men in town not carrying the cards, and the citizens of the town walking the streets, you know usually what follows—usually trouble.

Commissioner WEINSTOCK. Have there been any cases reported at the union headquarters where the union men were assaulted by nonunion men?

Mr. DALE. I think I remember of one instance where a man climbed on a dray to talk to the driver, and the driver hit him over the head with a hay hook, and knocked him down, and the dray ran over him. I believe that is the only one that I can call to mind.

Commissioner WEINSTOCK. Now, do you know of any instances where nonunion men were assaulted by unionists?

Mr. DALE. I don't know of it; no, sir. I have heard of it.

Commissioner WEINSTOCK. Have there been any arrests made in the city of Stockton?

Mr. DALE. There was.

Commissioner WEINSTOCK. There was? About how many?

Mr. DALE. Well, probably ten or a dozen.

Commissioner WEINSTOCK. Who were the parties arrested, unionists or non-unionists?

Mr. DALE. Both.

Commissioner WEINSTOCK. Unionists and nonunionists?

Mr. DALE. Yes, sir.

Commissioner WEINSTOCK. The cases haven't yet been brought to trial?

Mr. DALE. Well, I think a couple of hod carriers pleaded guilty, who were caught with the goods on them, carrying concealed weapons, and their fine was paid by the attorney of the M., M. and E., and they were turned loose.

Commissioner WEINSTOCK. Those were nonunionists?

Mr. DALE. They were nonunionists.

Commissioner WEINSTOCK. Convicted of carrying——

Mr. DALE. Carrying concealed weapons.

Commissioner WEINSTOCK. Concealed weapons?

Mr. DALE. Yes, sir.

Commissioner WEINSTOCK. Now, how many unionists have been arrested?

Mr. DALE. Well, that I could not say, Mr. Weinstock.

Commissioner WEINSTOCK. Approximately.

Mr. DALE. In the neighborhood of ten or a dozen.

Commissioner WEINSTOCK. Are they out on bail?

Mr. DALE. Yes, sir.

Commissioner WEINSTOCK. May we ask who furnished the bail?

Mr. DALE. I did.

Commissioner WEINSTOCK. That is, you did personally or representing the unions?

Mr. DALE. Representing the unions, probably. I am the representative of the unions. It is hard to separate me from that. I am at work for them.

Commissioner WEINSTOCK. In your testimony, Mr. Dale, you pointed out that organized labor stands ready now, and has been ready at all times since this difficulty has arisen, to arbitrate.

Mr. DALE. Yes, sir.

Commissioner WEINSTOCK. The issues.

Mr. DALE. Yes, sir.

Commissioner WEINSTOCK. But the other side has declined to?

Mr. DALE. Absolutely.

Commissioner WEINSTOCK. Arbitrate the matter. Now, you stated that there was one thing that labor would not arbitrate, and that was its existence?

Mr. DALE. Yes, sir; the right to organize.

Commissioner WEINSTOCK. Well, now, I want this made clear to myself; it doubtless is to the other members of the commission, who may not be as murky on the situation at this moment as I am; and that is this, is it the contention of organized labor that it can not exist without the closed shop, or is it possible for organized labor to exist and to be recognized and to be dealt with without the use of the closed shop?

Mr. DALE. We care nothing about whether you call it a closed shop or pawnshop or what kind of a shop you call it, but when you discharge our people because they have a card, then we have to get busy.

Commissioner WEINSTOCK. You know, of course, Mr. Dale, there are two kinds of labor agreements, some of them probably right in this very city. One kind of agreement that stipulates that only union men shall be employed; another sort of agreement where that issue is omitted entirely, and where the employer is at liberty to employ whomsoever he pleases, union or nonunion. I think that is the situation, unless I am incorrectly informed, of the metal trades in San Francisco. They have had their written agreements and oral agreements which stipulate the hours and wages and conditions of labor, but nothing is said about the employer confining himself exclusively to union men. That would be an instance where organized labor is recognized and dealt with and yet the employer is not compelled to confine himself strictly to union labor. Now, in the Stockton situation is it the attitude of organized labor that it will not permit the question as to whether the employer is or is not to employ union labor to be arbitrated, or is organized labor taking the position that it will arbitrate that question as long as organized labor is recognized and dealt with?

Mr. DALE. I think you are right. I want to say this, that if they will permit the business agent, the representative of the various unions, to enter the planing mills, go on the buildings, visit the stores, restaurants, machine shops, or factories, and interview the men who are not union men, and use their influence to get them to join the organization, I think that would satisfy labor. But the position of the open shop in Stockton is that the stamp must go, the union label must go, the business agent must be run out of town; they will have absolutely nothing to do with labor that bears the color of organization. That is their declaration.

Commissioner WEINSTOCK. Let us see if I understand that correctly, Mr. Dale. Your statement is, and I take it that you speak authoritatively, that organized labor does not insist that the employer shall confine himself to union men?

Mr. DALE. Well, organized——

Commissioner WEINSTOCK. That is, he is at liberty to employ anybody that he pleases, but he must give the union an opportunity to invite the nonunionist to become a member of the union? Have I understood it correctly?

Mr. DALE. Well, I do not know whether I care to go on record as saying that organized labor does not insist on the union shop. We do insist on the union shop. Of course, we do. Of course, we do that. But, of course, that is a matter that I would want to submit to an arbitration board rather than pass loosely on it here before this commission. But that is one of the things that we would be willing to talk about.

Commissioner WEINSTOCK. You would assume that to be a debatable question?

Mr. DALE. Yes, sir.

Commissioner WEINSTOCK. That is, your attitude is not ironclad?

Mr. DALE. No, sir.

Commissioner WEINSTOCK. That is, under no circumstances will you consider that phase of the question, you are willing to debate it?

Mr. DALE. Yes, sir.

Commissioner WEINSTOCK. And you are willing to abide by the judgment of a fair arbitration board in the matter?

Mr. DALE. Yes, sir.

Commissioner WEINSTOCK. Suppose that the board of arbitration should say, "In our judgment the employer ought to be permitted to employ anybody he pleases, union or nonunion; that the unionist ought to be permitted in the case of nonunion men to persuade them by peaceful methods and in any way that would not interfere with their work or their business to join the union." Would an arbitration of that kind be accepted by the unionist?

Mr. DALE. Well, now, it is owing to what construction you would put on "interfering with their work." Now, the business agent usually wants to visit the buildings when the men are present in the buildings.

Commissioner WEINSTOCK. You can easily understand, Mr. Dale, that you would not want men to come, if you were an employer and working under pressure, you would not want men to come in and disturb your men while they were at work?

Mr. DALE. No.

Commissioner WEINSTOCK. Perhaps that would lead to a row or friction.

Mr. DALE. The average business agent wouldn't do that. The average business agent is a tolerably diplomatic fellow, with all the statements to the contrary; he has been an absolutely fair fellow and has pretty fair sense, and he is working for a bunch of men that are pretty hard to please, and he has got to use good horse sense in getting by. I know you read of lots of things the business agent is accused of that are not true.

Commissioner WEINSTOCK. That is all, Mr. Chairman.

Chairman WALSH. Commissioner Lennon would like to ask you some questions.

Commissioner LENNON. Can you inform us as to how juries are drawn in the State of California?

Mr. DALE. Well, I think there are so many—the bailiff or the constable goes to the register, I presume, and takes the names, and subpœnas the men, and their names are read off by the judge, or the names are put in a box and he draws out the names.

Commissioner LENNON. You mean to say that the bailiff of an inferior court would have the power to select the names that are to go on petit juries, or the juries?

Mr. DALE. Counsels usually examine the jurymen.

Commissioner LENNON. Do they not——

Mr. DALE. Of course, they can reject a certain number of jurymen.

Commissioner LENNON. Have they not in this State a system of placing in a box the names of all the qualified voters, and then from the box a regular drawing is had to secure jurors to get the panel?

Mr. DALE. Why, as I understand it, the names are selected by the bailiff or by the constable, so many names, say, 40 names, and those 40 names are put in a box, and the judge draws the names as he puts his hand in, as he gets hold of a piece of paper, and he draws it out, bearing the name of John Smith, or George Smith, or whoever it may be, and he is placed in the box, and he is interrogated by the attorneys.

Commissioner LENNON. Then, as you understand it, the bailiff has the power to select from the citizenship a limited list of those who are to be drawn as jurors?

Mr. DALE. Yes, sir.

Chairman WALSH. I want to inquire about this: Take the case of the jury which you say acquitted Mr. Dunn. Was it a jury that you would call democratic in its composition? Did it represent all classes. Was there a number of working people upon it commensurate with the population of the city of Stockton?

Mr. DALE. I hardly think so.

Chairman WALSH. What court was Mr. Dunn tried in, please?

Mr. DALE. Judge Parker's court.

Chairman WALSH. Is that a superior court?

Mr. DALE. No; police court.

Chairman WALSH. A magistrate's court, as it were.

Mr. DALE. Police court.

Chairman WALSH. How many jurors?

Mr. DALE. Twelve.

Chairman WALSH. Twelve jurymen?

Mr. DALE. Yes.

Chairman WALSH. Did you notice the composition of them,- whether they were partially workers, or employers, or farmers, or what?

Mr. DALE. I think there was some farmers among them. I do not think there was a workingman on the jury.

Chairman WALSH. How did that happen? Is it on account of the way jurors are selected? How many workers, would you say?

Mr. DALE. I do not know anything else to attribute it to.

Chairman WALSH. How many workers would you say there are in Stockton—adult workers, eligible for jury service, respectable men?

Mr. DALE. Why, there is between three and four thousand people in Stockton belong to organized labor, and there is probably that number or more than that outside of the organization.

Chairman WALSH. And were none of those gentlemen drawn on the jury to try this gentleman?

Mr. DALE. No, sir; not in my opinion. I was present. I was not personally acquainted with the men, not living in Stockton.

Chairman WALSH. Were the labor organizations represented by counsel?

Mr. DALE. Yes, sir.

Chairman WALSH. Upon what date were these men arrested in the automobile that you claim had been carrying concealed weapons on their person?

Mr. DALE. I don't know that I can give you the date. I think it was two weeks ago Monday.

Chairman WALSH. Ordinarily how soon is a case of that sort tried in a police court in Stockton?

Mr. DALE. Men carrying concealed weapons?

Chairman WALSH. Yes; when no labor dispute is on.

Mr. DALE. I could not answer that question. Those men, of course, were caught with the goods on them, and there was no trial to it.

Chairman WALSH. Don't they try police court cases in Stockton on the morning after the men are arrested, usually, when there is no labor dispute?

Mr. DALE. In many cases, I think so—cases of vagrancy and probably battery. But the case of Mr. Dunn, I think, was postponed in the neighborhood of a month; not quite that long.

Chairman WALSH. Leaving Mr. Dunn out, was protest made by your counsel over the delay in the trial of these men arrested in the automobile?

Mr. DALE. We had no counsel. The men that were arrested in the automobile, they simply plead guilty.

Chairman WALSH. They plead guilty?

Mr. DALE. Yes, sir; they had the goods on them.

Chairman WALSH. They have been fined?

Mr. DALE. They put up the fine, and I don't know whether the thing came on to trial yet or not. I have been out of Stockton last week; I was sent to Fresno.

Chairman WALSH. You say they plead guilty, and the trial is over?

Mr. DALE. Sure; and the fine paid.

Chairman WALSH. Your information is very meager.

Mr. DALE. I can speak for the two hod carriers.

Chairman WALSH. I am speaking about these you say were arrested, and nail given by the attorney of the M. M. and E., and found to have, so somebody testified, pick handles and revolvers and blackjacks in the automobiles. Did those men plead guilty, or do you know?

Mr. DALE. Why, they plead guilty; yes, sir.

Chairman WALSH. What was their punishment?

Mr. DALE. A fine, I think, of $100, or a hundred days in jail.

Chairman WALSH. And was the fine paid, or are they serving their term?

Mr. DALE. Those men were arrested and brought into Judge Von Ditten's court, and they were sentenced to—a bail of a hundred dollars, then the attorney——

Chairman WALSH. Were you present?

Mr. DALE. I was. And the attorney of the M. M. and E., Mr. Carlton Case, put up a check for $500 for their appearance in court.

Chairman WALSH. In a superior court of some sort?

Mr. DALE. No, sir; I think it was in that same court, Von Ditten's court, and I was ordered then to Fresno. I was in Fresno probably 10 days. What disposition has been made of that case I am not in position to tell you, but the court record would tell you.

Chairman WALSH. That is all. Any other questions? That is all.

Mr. THOMPSON. One question: Did the M. M. and E. issue any order or request to the members or others to boycott any firm, if you know?

Mr. DALE. I am not in position to say that other than they advertised in the papers——

Chairman WALSH. He has explained that.

Mr. THOMPSON. Did they threaten to impose any fine for patronizing any store?

Mr. DALE. Not to my knowledge.

Chairman WALSH. His answer to that was no, and his whole statement shows it. Anything else?

Mr. THOMPSON. That is all.

Chairman WALSH. That is all, Mr. Dale.

Call you next.

Mr. THOMPSON. Mr. Totten.

TESTIMONY OF MR. CHRIS. TOTTEN.

Mr. THOMPSON. Mr. Totten, will you give us your name, business address, and your business?

Mr. TOTTEN. Chris. Totten; Stockton, Cal

Mr. THOMPSON. And your business, please?

Mr. TOTTEN. Planing mill.

Mr. THOMPSON. How long have you been engaged in that business there?

Mr. TOTTEN. About three of four years—four years.

Mr. THOMPSON. Are you acquainted with the industrial trouble in Stockton?

Mr. TOTTEN. Yes, sir.

Mr. THOMPSON. Will you give us your views of it, if you have any, if you have anything to say in addition to what has already been stated.

Mr. TOTTEN. Well, I think the ground has been fairly well covered by Mr. Irish and Mr. Bird. However, I might add that there is a merchants, manufacturers, and employers' association in Stockton. They have told you why it was necessary for us to have that kind of an organization there. We belong to that organization. We employed up until about a month or six weeks ago, I have forgotten now what date, I think it was July 8, somewhere along there, we employed all union men except the helpers in the mill.

We found that the unions, from time to time, exacted—made unreasonable demands and unreasonable exactions, and I might state that in regard to that stamp business that Mr. Johannsen says we gave no names, that material was delivered to Littlefield-Corbett furniture store. It was not a new building. It was delivered on the third floor, and they compelled us to return that material to the mill. They threatened unless we did do that they would cause us trouble. Take about four months ago, we had five or six cars of lumber come in at one time. We asked the lumber handlers' union to send us down lumber handlers. They sent us all they had—I don't know just exactly how many they did send—they sent us all they had. There were barges in at that time, and they did not have enough. We were about to get stuck on the last car for demurrage. The man in the mill that has charge of the stickers—a young man who takes a general interest in things, he was, you might say, assistant to the foreman—he saw that we were going to get stuck for the demurrage, and he got in the car and began to help unload. The business agent told him unless he got out of the car he would see that a fine was placed on him. That man got $30 a week. His wages, I think, was $4.50 a day, but he got $30 a week straight time because he was a good man and took an interest in the business. However, the business agent told him to get out of there.

It was brought out that—Mr. Johannsen says that the wages in Stockton were 50 cents a day less than San Francisco. I am not sure—I haven't a copy of the wage scale in San Francisco, but I understand the minimum wage scale in Santa Clara is $3.25. Our minimum scale is $3.50. Mind you, $3.25 for six days, eight hours each. Our minimum wage scale is $3.50 for five and a half days. That is, we pay for six days; that is, pay $3.50 a day, and divide it, $21—$3.50 is $21 a week for five and a half days. The maximum, I think, in Santa Clara is $5 a day, or $30 a week. Our maximum is $4.50 a day for five and a half days, which is $27 a week.

I might say that it was necessary for Mr. Neisted to sign that bill of complaint before he could have instituted any suit whatever, so that he must have known it.

One thing I was very glad that they brought out, Mr. Johannsen especially: About a year ago we had a fire. Our firm, as I said, we have only been in business about four years. About a year ago we had a fire, and our plant was totally destroyed. The fire was at the time of the Pacific Gas & Electric Co.'s strike, or right at the heat of that strike. They had some large power lines that ran right by our place that belonged to the Pacific Gas & Electric Co.

Chairman WALSH. I can't hear you.

Mr. TOTTEN. The Pacific Gas & Electric Co. has some large power lines that ran right by our place. Our fire was at the time of the strike of the Pacific Gas & Electric Co. However, we were not affected by the strike; but, as I say, we had some large power lines; that is, the Pacific Gas & Electric Co.'s large power lines ran right by our place, and our plant was destroyed. About a week after that we had another place—three or four days, probably, after that we had another mill burn. Both mills were not in operation, however. The Pacific Gas & Electric Co. had power lines in both places. Our employees met a few days after that fire—of course, we were hit hard; it was almost a solar plexus—they met a few days after the fire and got together, I think, at union headquarters and agreed to give us one week's wages gratis. They came out in a signed statement in the paper, a published statement, that they would do that. The public gave them credit for it. Our pay roll at the time before the fire, the week before the fire, was approximately $2,000 a week. I think it was August 16—our fire was on July 13—August 16 we got our new mill practically started. We did not have to build a mill; we found one already built.

We got it started, and I wrote a letter—I have a copy of that letter; I telephoned up for it this morning, but the girl could not find it; but I know where it is myself, and I would like to file it with the commission.

Chairman WALSH. We would be very glad to have it.

(The letter referred to is printed as "Totten Exhibit No. 1," at the end of this subject.)

Mr. TOTTEN. I wrote a letter to our employees and told them that I thanked them for doing that, and that it showed a good spirit and came at a time when help was needed, and told them that I appreciated the fact also that they had been out of work for 30 days, and probably some of them were not in position to make that sacrifice immediately, and I would leave it strictly up to them; I would not set apart any certain week or time that they could make this payment. They could pay it any time they pleased. When this trouble came up I went and got the letter out of the mill, because I presumed that that would be sprung on me some day. The old flyspecks and the four corners are torn off of the letter that shows where it was packed in the mill. I said, "Below is a list of all the employees who signed the agreement, and as you comply with your part of the agreement we will scratch your name out or cross it out," something to that effect. I asked the bookkeeper to tell me exactly how much was paid. There was $310 paid.

The office force does not belong to the union. They, all of them, paid. There are a great many, as I said at the outset, helpers in the mill that do not belong to the union. All of them paid. If the commission or Mr. Johannsen desires, I can furnish him the names of those who paid. Notwithstanding the fact the public has given them credit of paying a week's wages, they paid $386, I think.

Commissioner WEINSTOCK. Three hundred and eighty-six dollars out of how much?

Mr. TOTTEN. Out of a pay roll of $2,000; and I would judge—take the office and nonunion help out of it, and the unions would have paid me about in the neighborhood of about $225.

Commissioner WEINSTOCK. Two hundred and twenty-five dollars. What wages did the unions get?

Mr. TOTTEN. What wages?

Commissioner WEINSTOCK. Did the union men get collectively for the week? You say you have a $6,000 weekly pay roll?

Mr. TOTTEN. No, sir; I said $2,000.

Commissioner WEINSTOCK. Well, out of $2,000 what proportion of it is paid to your union labor or was paid to your union labor?

Mr. TOTTEN. Well, I said out of what was paid to us there was probably $225 paid to us by the unions, and the proportion of our pay roll that goes to the unions I would judge was, say, $1,600 out of $2,000.

Commissioner WEINSTOCK. Sixteen hundred dollars?

Mr. TOTTEN. Yes, sir; something like that.

Commissioner WEINSTOCK. That would be about 14 per cent; that is, the contributions of your union employees was about 14 per cent of the week's pay?

Mr. TOTTEN. Yes, sir; something like that. The Sperry Flour Co., that boycott was started along in May or June. There was no merchants and manufacturers' association then—1913. Mr. Johannsen spoke of a little scrap at our mill. Also said he was out of town. I don't know whether he was or not, but it was no little scrap, because I was there. It was a big scrap. There was about 125 men came down there, somewhere in the neighborhood of 125. A lot of those men were strangers; I never saw them before; a lot of them were our old men. He stated I got mad and hit somebody with a chair. I hope the commission will give me the credit of having more sense than to jump on a crowd of 125 men with a chair, especially if they could have seen some of them. They knocked one of our men down, I forget his name, he is a middle-aged man, probably 45 or 50. They knocked him down and fractured his cheek bone. I didn't know that they fractured the bone until about a week afterwards. They closed that eye up. He got hurt in the mill and closed the other eye up. He was in bad shape, and I sent him to the hospital and had him examined, and they told me that this bone was fractured. When they knocked this man down, then is when the chair came in. Mr. Brandt picked up a chair and started toward the man who knocked him down, but he never got there. About six of them jumped on Mr. Brandt and beat him and cuffed him, and I started to help Mr. Brandt, and I had probably five or six on me. My two brothers came to my rescue, and they were kept equally busy. We were told that they were coming down there that afternoon to raise trouble. He says—I think he said—that the police were on the ground. The police were not there. They were telephoned to and asked to be there, but they were not there. They did not come until the fight was entirely over. We swore to—I did—and I swore to warrants for those who I knew—absolutely knew—and could prove that did take a part in the fight and struck me. They were arrested, and, as Mr. Dale says, he put up the bail.

I remember very well another man that was arrested on suspicion. They telephoned to me to come down to the police office to see if I could identify him. Mr. Dale was there to put up the bail.

Mr. Dale said that I told him that we were going to run our own business. That is a fact. We are going to try to. I think we will succeed.

Mr. THOMPSON. Mr. Totten, I would like to ask you a question or two.

Mr. TOTTEN. Go right ahead.

Mr. THOMPSON. Something has been said here about some men in an automobile being arrested, with pick handles and blackjacks and other instruments of personal warfare were found in the automobiles. Have you heard of that incident?

Mr. TOTTEN. Yes; yes, sir.

Mr. THOMPSON. And it has also been said that the attorney for the M. M. and E. bailed those men out?

Mr. TOTTEN. That is a fact, absolutely.

Mr. THOMPSON. Do you know who those men were employed by—for whom employed?

Mr. TOTTEN. The men were employed by the merchants and manufacturers of Stockton. They are our men. However, Mr. Dale, I think, told you that they were fined. They have had no trial. They were not found guilty. The arms that they had were not on them, either. I would not blame them—if you could have seen the men that came to my place looking for trouble, you would not go in an automobile without you had something along, because they won't fight fair; there never one jumps on a man—there are six or eight; and those men did have clubs and they might have had revolvers. I did not see them. I think they used good judgment if they did take them along with them. I do not think they had 15 blackjacks or 15 pick handles. I don't think so, because there would have been no occasion for five men to have that many.

Mr. THOMPSON. What was the object of the men? What was their duties.

Mr. TOTTEN. Well, I will tell you. There were so many of those crimes committed by Mr. Johannsen's organized gangs, and the police showed very clearly that they could not cope with it. The fact of the matter is, they did not seem to want to. So it was absolutely necessary for us to bring in somebody that would protect our men, and it has had a fairly good influence.

Mr. THOMPSON. Where were they procured, if you know?

Mr. TOTTEN. I think they were gotten in San Francisco. I do not think there was any of them that were ex-convicts. If I did, I would see that they were discharged. I do think that the unions slipped us a man named Graham that is an ex-convict. But we also slipped him back to them when he got arrested; we let them pay his fine, because we were not knowingly keeping any crooks in our employ. Neither have we any ex-convicts that we know of that are in our employ or are officers of our organization.

Mr. THOMPSON. Do you know how they were gotten?

Mr. TOTTEN. No; I do not. I do not think, though, that any of them are ex-convicts. They are all—they look like they could put up a fairly good scrap.

Mr. THOMPSON. What was their purpose?

Mr. TOTTEN. What was their purpose?

Mr. THOMPSON. What was the purpose of the men in Stockton? What did you intend to use them for?

Mr. TOTTEN. In case of another riot—in case another riot should come to my place. For instance, if I should go back home to-night, and I should have reasonable information—that is, if the information came to me that I was going to have a riot, and I believed it—I think I would have a few of these men planted in there to help my men. I think I would, in fact, I know I would, because the police, as I said, don't amount to much.

Mr. THOMPSON. That is all, Mr. Chairman.

Chairman WALSH. Any of you gentlemen desire to ask any questions?

Commissioner O'CONNELL. Yes.

Mr. TOTTEN. Go right ahead.

Commissioner O'CONNELL. Mr. Totten, I understand you are chairman of the employers' strike committee?

Mr. TOTTEN. Yes, sir; that is correct.

Commissioner O'CONNELL. Will you please explain to the commission the purpose of that committee?

Mr. TOTTEN. Well, that committee is just simply formed to carry on the business of the Merchants and Manufacturers' Association.

Commissioner O'CONNELL. What is that business? What is the committee supposed to do? How is it made up? How is it selected?

Mr. TOTTEN. The committee, I think, the night that the declaration was made for the open shop, there was a motion made that a committee of five be appointed.

Commissioner O'CONNELL. By the president?

Mr. TOTTEN. By the president. That is how it was to be appointed.

Commissioner O'CONNELL. The president selected five men to act as the strike committee?

Mr. TOTTEN. Yes, sir.

Commissioner O'CONNELL. To have full charge of handling the strike?

Mr. TOTTEN. Yes, sir.

Commissioner O'CONNELL. On behalf of your association?

Mr. TOTTEN. Yes, sir.

Commmmissioner O'CONNELL. Who were the others that were selected by the association?

Mr. TOTTEN. Well, I really do not know whether the other gentlemen on that committee would like for their names to be given out. You see the unions know me, and you know what happened to me. And I would rather have the permission of the other four, because I would not care to put them up as a target.

Commissioner O'CONNELL. Then it is not publicly known of whom your strike committee is composed?

Mr. TOTTEN. I don't know whether it is or not. Our whole association knows who it is, and it is not hard to find out. I, personally, would not conceal it. We have nothing to conceal that I know of.

Commissioner O'CONNELL. This committee has full power to carry on the strike in behalf of your association in Stockton?

Mr. TOTTEN. Yes, sir.

Commissioner O'CONNELL. Whatever action is taken by your committee for what you might consider the best interests of your association is approved by the association?

Mr. TOTTEN. Yes, sir.

Commissioner O'CONNELL. You employ—as I understood you to speak about the men you were bringing to your plant—your committee employed the men to look after the other plants in the same way?

Mr. TOTTEN. Anybody that needs help, we will send them men.

Commissioner O'CONNELL. The purpose of your committee is to select men whom you think are capable physically to protect the men in the plants?

Mr. TOTTEN. Yes.

Commissioner O'CONNELL. To the extent of licking or shooting to protect?

Mr. TOTTEN. No; I would not advise any man to shoot. It would have been perfectly justifiable, though, in my own case at my place, if I had done some shooting. I would have been absolutely justifiable in it. As a matter of fact, I want to tell you I had a talk with one of the men that you might say is a kind of captain over those that were in that machine, and I told him that I would not, if I were they, I would not carry a gun, even in the machine. But I will say, though, that they showed good judgment, knowing what they had to go up against.

Commissioner O'CONNELL. Is your committee authorized to expend funds for the employment and payment of these men?

Mr. TOTTEN. Yes. Yes, sir; we pay them.

Commissioner O'CONNELL. Who furnishes and provides the arms and weapons for these men?

Mr. TOTTEN. I could not tell you. We do not purchase.

Commissioner O'CONNELL. Are they supposed to bring them themselves?

Mr. TOTTEN. Well, we never asked them. In fact, we didn't know that they had guns. I didn't know that they had any guns on them until they were arrested. They didn't have the guns on. They were in the machine.

Commissioner O'CONNELL. Do you provide weapons of any kind for your employees?

Mr. TOTTEN. No, sir.

Commissioner O'CONNELL. For the employees of the association?

Mr. TOTTEN. No. Except in this case where Graham, as I told you, this man that I say I think we had slipped to us, an ex-convict—I understand that the association or some one at the association gave him an order on a hardware store for a gun. I never saw that order, don't know whether he did or not; but I understand it indirectly.

Commissioner O'CONNELL. Where did these men get these guns and pick handles and weapons of destruction that they had with them?

Mr. TOTTEN. Well, I could not tell you.

Commissioner O'CONNELL. How many men has your committee employed?

Mr. TOTTEN. Well not—I think we have got in the neighborhood of 20.

Commissioner O'CONNELL. Are these men employed, brought into the city from the outside?

Mr. TOTTEN. Yes, sir.

Commissioner O'CONNELL. How were they employed?

Mr. TOTTEN. We sent a man to the city to get what we would term guards.

Commissioner O'CONNELL. You mean to San Francisco?

Mr. TOTTEN. Yes, sir; to San Francisco.

Commissioner O'CONNELL. Where did he go to get them in San Francisco?

Mr. TOTTEN. I could not tell you. I never asked him.

Commissioner O'CONNELL. Employment agencies?

Mr. TOTTEN. I could not tell you that.

Chairman WALSH. He says he don't know.

Commissioner O'CONNELL. Or detective agencies?

Mr. TOTTEN. If I had know that, I would have answered you in the first place.

Commissioner O'CONNELL. Is your committee dealing directly or indirectly with detective agencies in Stockton or in San Francisco or elsewhere?

Mr. TOTTEN. Well, I don't feel that I should answer that question. I will say this——

Chairman WALSH. Now, one minute, Congress has required and directed us to specifically find that out. Now, why don't you wish to answer it?

Mr. TOTTEN. I don't know that it would be any particular harm; yes.

Chairman WALSH. I wish you would.

Mr. TOTTEN. We have ways of getting information, and we get them through the usual channels, we get it through the usual channels.

Chairman WALSH. That is not quite an answer to the question.

Mr. TOTTEN. All right. Ask it again.

Chairman WALSH. You employ detectives for that purpose and do business with detective agencies?

Mr. TOTTEN. Yes.

Commissioner O'CONNELL. Have you detectives now in your employ at Stockton?

Mr. TOTTEN. Well, I don't know. I don't hardly think we have any just at this particular moment.

Commissioner O'CONNELL. What sums of money have your committee expended in carrying on the strike in Stockton?

Mr. TOTTEN. I could not tell you.

Commissioner O'CONNELL. Doesn't the money pass through your committee, you say?

Mr. TOTTEN. Yes, sir. Well, no; it doesn't pass through our committee.

Commissioner O'CONNELL. Whose hands does it pass through?

Mr. TOTTEN. It passes through the treasurer's and the secretary's hands.

Commissioner O'CONNELL. Does the president have anything to do with it?

Mr. TOTTEN. I don't know whether the president signs the checks or not.

Commissioner GARRETSON. Who O. K's the bills?

Mr. TOTTEN. Whoever orders the goods.

Commissioner GARRETSON. If your committee ordered the expenditures, you would O. K.?

Mr. TOTTEN. If our committee ordered anything, I would O. K. it; yes.

Commissioner O'CONNELL. Are you advised, or in seeking advisement, do you confer in any way with the officers or the legal advisers of the National Manufacturers' Association?

Mr. TOTTEN. No, sir.

Commissioner O'CONNELL. Or the National Metal Trades' Association?

Mr. TOTTEN. No, sir; no, sir.

Commissioner O'CONNELL. Or the founders' association?

Mr. TOTTEN. No, sir; the National——

Commissioner O'CONNELL. Any other association outside of Stockton?

Mr. TOTTEN. The National Manufacturers' had a representative in Stockton not long ago and asked me—my firm to become a member, but I did not. That is all I know about the National Manufacturers.

Commissioner O'CONNELL. You said a moment ago that the statement made by Mr. Irish regarding some particular material being taken into a building without the label on and then being ordered back to the factory and rehandled was not true.

Mr. TOTTEN. Did I?

Commissioner O'CONNELL. You said that it was some other——

Chairman WALSH. I think he just gave the specific name of the place which Mr. Irish didn't give. Is that correct?

Commissioner O'CONNELL. You say it was furniture material?

Mr. TOTTEN. No.

Commissioner O'CONNELL. Will you please make a statement?

Mr. TOTTEN. Let me say it just exactly as it was. Mr. Irish told the truth. However, it was a furniture store that was not—it was not a new building. It was a furniture store. This furniture store ordered a lot of shelving cut up in small pieces, the Littlefield-Corbett furniture store. They are there now. We delivered the material to that building, and put it on the third floor. After we got the material there and got it on the third floor, the business agent—I don't know how he found it out, but he called us up and told us there was no stamp on the material. And we were compelled to go and get the material and bring it back to the mill and put it into the mill and put the stamp on it and take it back to the store and put it on the third floor.

Commissioner WEINSTOCK. A statement was made by somebody, Mr. Totten, I can't recall just who, that you had at times ordered the steward, as I think he is called, not to use the stamp on lumber.

Mr. TOTTEN. No; I will tell you. When we declared for the open shop I went out in the mill and called all the men together.

I said: "Boys, on and after this date we will not use any stamp on any goods in this mill. Neither will we recognize you as shop steward, only recognize you as a workman."

Commissioner WEINSTOCK. I am speaking, Mr. Totten, of the period before that.

Mr. TOTTEN. No; that is not true. We never told a man not to.

Commissioner WEINSTOCK. You never instructed the steward not to use the stamp?

Mr. TOTTEN. No.

Commissioner WEINSTOCK. On this particular occasion that you have just been telling about where shelves were taken to a furniture store, had you told the steward not to use the stamp?

Mr. TOTTEN. No, certainly not; certainly not.

Commissioner WEINSTOCK. The testimony has brought out two facts: One, that there has been violence in Stockton during these recent labor troubles; and secondly, that the M. M. and E. have employed guards.

Mr. TOTTEN. Yes.

Commissioner WEINSTOCK. Now, what the commission would be interested in to know is which was the cause and which was the effect. Did the riots lead to the M. M. and E. employing guards?

Mr. TOTTEN. Absolutely.

Commissioner WEINSTOCK. Or did the employment of the guards lead to the riots?

Mr. TOTTEN. No; because the guards have not to this date struck a man.

Commissioner WEINSTOCK. When did the violence begin, as near as you can recall?

Mr. TOTTEN. The first blood, as Mr. Dale so aptly puts it, is when Mr. Dunn— Mr. Dunn is an old Irish citizen, a mighty nice man. There was a picket in front of his store. The picket did something to justify Mr. Dunn—that is, he felt justified. I think the picket come in the store quite aways and pulled a customer out, or something like that, I am not sure. Mr. Dunn struck that man—, gave him a black eye. Twelve men let him go. He was tried—the unions have an attorney there. He was tried, and I am inclined to think that he was given a fair and impartial trial, because San Joaquin County—Stockton is a small place.

Commissioner WEINSTOCK. Was that the first case of violence?

Mr. TOTTEN. That was the first case that I know of.

Commissioner WEINSTOCK. Now, can you recall the second case that happened?

Mr. TOTTEN. The second case is—there was a contractor by the name of Smith & Buck, who were building in the northern part of the city. The fact of the matter is, I think, it, at that time, was outside of the city limits. There was a gang went out there; I don't know how many. Mr. Smith estimated it at 40 to 60. They went out and went right onto the premises. The foundation had just started, and I believe that they were mixing concrete. And they took shovels and beat Mr. Smith and Buck up fairly well. They were union men.

Commissioner WEINSTOCK. That was on or about what date?

Mr. TOTTEN. Well, that, I believe, was on the morning of the Tuesday that they came over to our place and done such an admirable job.

Commissioner WEINSTOCK. Well, that was on or about what date?

Mr. TOTTEN. Well, that was three weeks ago—I believe it is three weeks ago from yesterday. Yesterday was Tuesday, wasn't it?

Commissioner WEINSTOCK. Yes; that would be three weeks ago yesterday; that would be about the 3d of August.

Mr. TOTTEN. I think—I am not dead sure of that date.

Commissioner WEINSTOCK. It was on or about that date?

Mr. TOTTEN. Oh, it was about—along about that time.

Commissioner WEINSTOCK. And about what date did the trouble happen at your place?

Mr. TOTTEN. The same date that Mr. Smith was——

Commissioner WEINSTOCK. Now, when were these guards employed?

Mr. TOTTEN. Well, probably a week after that date.

Commissioner WEINSTOCK. A week after that?

Mr. TOTTEN. Yes.

Commissioner WEINSTOCK. Your point then is that the assaults and the violence was the cause?

Mr. TOTTEN. Absolutely.

Commissioner WEINSTOCK. And the employment of the guards was the effect?

Mr. TOTTEN. Yes; that is absolutely it. And if I went through this trouble again, I think I would have the guards in the first place. I would get them first.

Commissioner WEINSTOCK. You mean you would anticipate the trouble?

Mr. TOTTEN. Yes; I would anticipate and get them on the ground first.

Commissioner WEINSTOCK. But in this case you did not anticipate?

Mr. TOTTEN. No; we didn't.

Commissioner WEINSTOCK. And they were brought in after trouble had been created?

Mr. TOTTEN. Yes, sir.

Commissioner WEINSTOCK. And to protect you against further possible trouble?

Mr. TOTTEN. Yes, sir.

Commissioner WEINSTOCK. Have you heard the statement of Mr. Dale this morning, Mr. Totten, in the matter of arbitration?

Mr. TOTTEN. Yes.

Commissioner WEINSTOCK. To the effect that so far as insisting upon employers confining themselves altogether to union men—I take it that he spoke for the unions—that they would be willing to treat that as a debatable question, have it discussed, and to have it passed upon by some disinterested body. What is the attitude of the M. M. and E. on that score? Would they be willing to consider that a debatable question?

Mr. TOTTEN. The M. M. and E. would refuse to be put in a position where they are compelled to use coercion to get any of their employees to join any kind of an organization.

Commissioner WEINSTOCK. Yes; that is, the M. M. and E. would not consider any proposition which would make it imperative on the part of the employers to force their employees to join the union?

Mr. TOTTEN. That is correct. And I will say this, that even now in my employ—I hope the men won't be singled out and hurt—but now in my employ there are a couple of union men, cabinet makers. I knew that they were union men when they came there. They have only been there a short while. They came and they asked for work, and I knew that they were union men. They are there now, unless they have been frightened away since I have been gone.

Commissioner WEINSTOCK. Well, coming back to the question that I raised, Mr. Totten, if the attitude of the unions should be that they are willing to debate the question as to whether the employer shall be compelled to force his men into a union or to employ only union men, and that if it should be decided by a disinterested body that the employer should not be compelled to employ only union men, and he should not even be compelled to oblige his nonunion men after they were in his employ to join the union, would the M. M. and E. be prepared to discuss that question with organized labor?

Mr. TOTTEN. Oh, certainly. The M. M. and E. has never refused to discuss any question whatever and to meet them at any time. And they would of course be—in my opinion, they would discuss that with them.

Commissioner WEINSTOCK. Well, would the M. M. and E. then be willing to recognize representatives of organized labor as organized labor?

Mr. TOTTEN. No; we would not deal with them collectively as a union.

Commissioner WEINSTOCK. That is, the attitude of your association is that you will not recognize or deal with organized labor?

Mr. TOTTEN. No; we will not.

Commissioner WEINSTOCK. Well, then, if the association will not recognize and will not deal with organized labor, how could you get together to even discuss this debatable question?

Mr. TOTTEN. Well, I don't know. But it is a fact; we would not. If the unions wanted to go to work to-morrow, if their men wanted to go to work to-morrow and work along with the men we have, we would raise no objection to it.

Commissioner WEINSTOCK. That is, you would deal with them individually?

Mr. TOTTEN. Oh, certainly, certainly.

Commissioner WEINSTOCK. But not collectively?

Mr. TOTTEN. No, sir.

Commissioner WEINSTOCK. That is all, Mr. Chairman.

Chairman WALSH. Mr. Garretson would like to ask you a question or two.

Commissioner GARRETSON. Then on the basis of that answer, you assert the right of the employers to organize and have a spokesman, and deal collectively in all these matters with the individual laborer, but you refuse the right to the laborers to follow the same method that you do?

Mr. TOTTEN. No; we don't refuse him the right. He can organize all he pleases. We don't care how much he organizes. We don't care if every man—if he organizes a hundred per cent, that doesn't make any difference.

Commissioner GARRETSON. The statement has been made here and not denied, that in the instance of the clerks' union, when they went to their employers they were told by their employers that they would have to settle with Mr. Calkins.

Mr. TOTTEN. Well——

Commissioner GARRETSON. Is that correct or incorrect?

Mr. TOTTEN. I could not tell you whether that is correct or not; but I will say this, that the organization was not very old at that time, and that might have been the case.

Commissioner GARRETSON. Is that a consistent position from your standpoint——

Mr. TOTTEN. I could not say.

Commissioner GARRETSON (continuing). To arrogate a right to yourself that you deny, to your employees?

Mr. TOTTEN. No; that would not be consistent.

Commissioner GARRETSON. You used the phrase a few moments ago that you thought these men in the automobile, if they had guns, that they used good judgment. Do you mean to convey the idea that when one's idea of what is good judgment comes into contact or conflict with a little matter like the law of the land that the good judgment should take precedence of the law?

Mr. TOTTEN. Were you ever in a mob?

Commissioner GARRETSON. Yes.

Mr. TOTTEN Did you ever get your face all pounded up about six times?

Commissioner GARRETSON. No; I was too smooth.

Mr. TOTTEN. Well, unfortunately I am not as smooth as you are.

Commissioner GARRETSON. Thank you.

Mr. TOTTEN. I am sorry that I am not. I wish I was smoother. I would do my best to put it over on you. But if you ever do get into a place where there is five or six jumping on you at once and hammering on you, you will then see the necessity of having somebody there with a Gatling gun.

Commissioner GARRETSON. Don't you stand in a different relation to that, to what your hired man does? Do you or do you not, when you are talking about personal self-defense and hiring a man to go through the forms of self-defense—is there a difference?

Mr. TOTTEN. I explained to you in the outset that after the police had refused or——

Commissioner GARRETSON. Had failed?

Mr. TOTTEN. Had failed.

Commissioner GARRETSON. As you thought.

Mr. TOTTEN. We brought in people as guards to protect us.

Commissioner GARRETSON. Do you believe in the right of either a private individual or a corporation or a partnership to maintain armed forces?

Mr. TOTTEN. Well, I told you a while ago that I had told—if it is necessary, certainly. But I told you a while ago——

Commissioner GARRETSON. Who decides when it is necessary, Mr. Totten?

Mr. TOTTEN. I would.

Commissioner GARRETSON. Oh, you are above the tribunals of the land in that respect?

Mr. TOTTEN. No, sir; no, sir; absolutely not.

Commissioner GARRETSON. That is all, Mr. Chairman. By the way, who owned the auto?

Mr. TOTTEN. Who owned it?

Commissioner GARRETSON. Yes.

Mr. TOTTEN. I could not tell you. We own one.

Commissioner GARRETSON. You own one?

Mr. TOTTEN. Yes, sir.

Commissioner GARRETSON. Do you know whether it was your car or somebody else's?

Mr. TOTTEN. No; I don't know.

Chairman WALSH. Mr. Lennon.

Commissioner LENNON. Mr. Totten, were these guards deputized by the sheriff as officers of the law?

Mr. TOTTEN. No.

Commissioner LENNON. Were they deputized by the chief of police as special officers?

Mr. TOTTEN. No.

Commissioner LENNON. Are you aware as to whether they are citizens of the State of California or not?

Mr. TOTTEN. No; I don't know whether they are or not.

Commissioner LENNON. That is all.

Commissioner COMMONS. I would like to ask a question.

Chairman WALSH. Prof. Commons.

Commissioner COMMONS. I would like to ask about the guards or the pickets which the unions have. Do you know how many they have?

Mr. TOTTEN. Well, I should judge two or three hundred.

Commissioner COMMONS. Do you know about their organization, how they were organized and marshaled?

Mr. TOTTEN. No; I don't. I don't know how they are organized at all. I know that they can—they have ways of summoning and getting help awful quick; that is, collecting a crowd.

Commissioner COMMONS. Do they have a number stationed in front of your place and other places?

Mr. TOTTEN. Yes, sir. Not at all times, but——

Commissioner COMMONS. Do these pickets carry any emblems, or anything?

Mr. TOTTEN. No.

Commissioner COMMONS. What do they do?

Mr. TOTTEN. Well, they walk up and down in front of the place, maybe; I have seen as high as a hundred walking up and down. They will get in front of a job and they will holler "scab." And I have even seen them go so far as to even where a man was mixing concrete in the street to punch him in the side as they walked by hollering "scab"; and then they call them very violent names.

Commissioner COMMONS. Do they pass out cards?

Mr. TOTTEN. Well, not the pickets on the jobs in the building trades, that is, what you would call the building trades' council does not pass out any cards.

Commissioner COMMONS. There is another class of pickets, men that are picketing stores, is there?

Mr. TOTTEN. Well, yes. I don't really think—I haven't noticed any pickets in front of the stores recently.

Commissioner COMMONS. Well, who are those that pass out cards?

Mr. TOTTEN. Well, that was in the outset; in the start of the trouble, the Central Labor Council, I think. It was proven in an injunction case there, that the Central Labor Council appointed these pickets, and, I believe, paid them 75 cents a day to pass out cards in front of a man's store or restaurant, as the case may be.

Commissioner COMMONS. Do you know whether these two or three hundred pickets that you speak of now are paid?

Mr. TOTTEN. No; I don't know whether they are paid or not. I have understood that they were, but I don't know whether they are or not.

Commissioner COMMONS. Do you know where they come from, from Stockton or from the outside?

Mr. TOTTEN. Well, some of them are Stockton people; yes. Some of them are strangers, but I don't know whether they live in Stockton or not; I don't know everybody in Stockton.

Commissioner COMMONS. You don't know all of the pickets, and you don't keep any record of the pickets that they have?

Mr. TOTTEN. No, sir.

Commissioner COMMONS. Or have any further knowledge?

Mr. TOTTEN. No, sir. I am reasonably sure, though, that there are at least 75 or 100 strangers in town and have been there for some time, that have mighty tough looking faces. I don't know how they came there.

Commissioner COMMONS. Well, are they acting as pickets?

Mr. TOTTEN. Yes, sir.

Commissioner COMMONS. Your theory is that——

Mr. TOTTEN. I think they are the ones that does the most of the fighting.

Commissioner COMMONS. You think they are brought from out of town?

Mr. TOTTEN. Yes, sir.

Commissioner COMMONS. You think they brought in there 75 out-of-town people to do this picketing?

Mr. TOTTEN. Yes, sir.

Commissioner COMMONS. And this rough work that you have in mind?

Mr. TOTTEN. I think it.

Commissioner COMMONS. You have no knowledge of it, though?

Mr. TOTTEN. No; no direct proof right at this minute.

Commissioner COMMONS. Well, have any of your detectives furnished you any proof?

Mr. TOTTEN. Yes, sir.

Commissioner COMMONS. To what extent have they?

Mr. TOTTEN. Well, they have told us at different times when these men came in, squads of them at different times; they have told us when squads of them came in.

Commissioner COMMONS. Told where they got them?

Mr. TOTTEN. No; we have never found where they got them.

Commissioner COMMONS. Just located them when they were brought in?

Mr. TOTTEN. Well, may be they would come up on the train with them, that is, they would find them on the train or boat, as the case may be.

Commissioner COMMONS. Did you slip over anybody on them in those pickets?

Mr. TOTTEN. No, sir.

Commissioner COMMONS. Didn't go along the same line?

Mr. TOTTEN. No.

Commissioner COMMONS. And it is upon the basis of what the detectives report to you, that you think that they had abou 75 brought in?

Mr. TOTTEN. Yes, sir.

Commissioner COMMONS. That is all.

Chairman WALSH. Have you some letters written; sent out to the merchants?

Mr. TOTTEN. I have.

Chairman WALSH. Respecting this boycott?

Mr. TOTTEN. Yes.

Chairman WALSH. Will you kindly file them with the commission?

Mr. TOTTEN. These are the letters that Mr. Dale. told you that there was no boycott, these are the letters.

Commissioner WEINSTOCK. Read one or two.

Mr. TOTTEN. To Rosenbaum——

Chairman WALSH. Kindly submit those. We were compelled to make a rule before we arrived here on account of the voluminous character of the documents, all documents must be submitted. We will read them. You may hand them to Commissioner Weinstock.

Mr. TOTTEN. Letter directed to Rosenbaum where he says that any member of this union found patronizing such stores that do not display union store cards will be fined $5.

(The letters so presented were marked "Totten Exhibit No. 2," and are printed at the end of this subject.)

Chairman WALSH. Now, have you studied the relative efficiency as between the open shop and the union shop?

Mr. TOTTEN. Well, not a great deal.

Chairman WALSH. Then I will not ask you the question. We will ask some one else. I do want to ask you a question or two: Have you given the experience which you had in your own business, which led you to the attitude which you take to-day with reference to the unions?

Mr. TOTTEN. Put that again, please.

Chairman WALSH. Have you fully stated the experience which you had in your own business which led you to the attitude which you take to-day?

Mr. TOTTEN. I have not stated all of it.

Chairman WALSH. Well, now, is there anything else you would like to state voluntarily in that respect?

Mr. TOTTEN. There seems to be a disposition on the part of the union to curtail output. For instance, I had a man that was what you would call a straw boss. His name was George Shepherd. He was a Scotchman, and he was a very nice man—nice boy. And there were two Germans that worked right close to the office. The office is glass, and I can see out there very plainly. Work got slack. This was something like probably seven or eight months ago. I asked one of these German boys, I said, "I think I will have to let you off at the end of this week, or probably your partner." He spoke up and he said, "I am sorry you are going to let me off." He spoke of some expense he had gone to recently, how he would like to hold his job. He said, "Why do you single me out" I told him because he was rather slow. "Well," he said, "the reason of that was that the straw boss had told him to slow up, not to work so fast." "Well," I said, "did he tell anybody else that?" He said, "He told my partner." I called he and his partner in the office, and they both told the same story. I sent for the straw boss and asked him if he had told these boys to slow up. He said—he acknowledged that he had, and said since work had gotten slack he told the boys not to turn out so much work.

Chairman WALSH. Anything else, Mr. Totten?

Mr. TOTTEN. No.

Commissioner COMMONS. I would like to get the explanation of this stamp that you have spoken of, what that implies, what class of work must have the union stamp in your establishment.

Mr. TOTTEN. Everything that goes out must have a stamp on it.

Commissioner COMMONS. How much work does that entail?

Mr. TOTTEN. Well——

Commissioner COMMONS. What operations?

Mr. TOTTEN. Take a mill our size, it would require, say, a man probably one-half of his time a day to put that stamp on.

Commissioner COMMONS. I am speaking not of the time taken to put the stamp on, but what kind of work has to be done? Of course, this lumber comes in rought to you, does it not?

Mr. TOTTEN. Yes, sir.

Commissioner COMMONS. Well, then, what is it that——

Mr. TOTTEN. After the lumber is surfaced, after a piece of cabinetwork is made, after a frame is made or a window or a door, that stamp is applied to that piece of work.

Commissioner COMMONS. Could you put that in matters of cost or expense, how much added work is done in your mill above what would be done by an outside mill if they sent their lumber direct to the building?

Mr. TOTTEN. Oh, that wouldn't amount to anything, that additional cost of putting the stamp on the material.

Commissioner COMMONS. I am not talking about the stamp. I am speaking of the lumber after it comes in.

Mr. TOTTEN. No; I could not, because I have not—I could not answer that intelligently now.

Commissioner COMMONS. My point is this, this wood might be made in mills away from Stockton and sent directly to contractors to put in the building, could it not ?

Mr. TOTTEN. Yes.

Commissioner COMMONS. And it would be done except for this stamp?

.Mr. TOTTEN. Yes.

Commissioner COMMONS. So that the stamp in one way was a protection in your mill against competitors outside?

Mr. TOTTEN. Yes; to a certain extent it was a protection against competitors; at the same time you have outside competition just the same like—you take San Francisco mills and the Santa Clara mills, they ship some stuff in there just the same.

Commissioner COMMONS. Will the building trade in Stockton put up material that comes from outside that does not have the stamp?

Mr. TOTTEN. Well, no; not generally; in some cases I have known where they have; not generally.

Commissioner COMMONS. Well, generally, then, your mill would have the field as long as the unions enforced that rule, the building trade unions, of not putting up unstamped timber or lumber?

Mr. TOTTEN. Well, now, as I said before, we have competition just the same; that is, San Francisco and Oakland and even Sacramento ships in there.

Commissioner COMMONS. Those are stamped?

Mr. TOTTEN. Stamped.·

Commissioner COMMONS. Under your rule unstamped lumber can go into any building?

Mr. TOTTEN. Yes.

Commissioner COMMONS. Now, does that make any difference in cost to you? Will your competitors, must they reduce, or must you reduce your price to meet outside competition of unstamped material?

Mr. TOTTEN. Well, I may have to reduce prices some; yes; I might have to do that.

·Commissioner COMMONS. You figure that the difference in cost between the cost of producing the stamped material under union conditions and unstamped material under nonunion conditions is a matter of sufficient importance to make it a point in the competition in the building trades?

Mr. TOTTEN. Yes; I figure that we will—by not having this stamp we could manufacture, run our business at a good deal better advantage by not having to deal with the unions, or to have any stamp.

Commissioner COMMONS. Have you figured out how much you could cut prices?

Mr. TOTTEN. No, sir.

Commissioner COMMONS. Can you cut·them 10 per cent?

Mr. TOTTEN. I could not tell you now.

Commissioner COMMONS. You must have figured out what competitors will be able to send in unstamped lumber to compete with you from the outside. How much would they have to cut prices below what you have been in order to get into the buildings?

Mr. TOTTEN. Well, I can't tell you that.

Commissioner COMMONS. That has not been figured out to your knowledge?

Mr. TOTTEN. No, sir.

Commissioner COMMONS. Could it be figured, out?

Mr. TOTTEN. I think so; yes, sir.

Commissioner COMMONS. Could you figure it out?

Mr. TOTTEN. Well, I couldn't figure it out now. Icould at some future time.

Commissioner COMMONS. Would you be willing to figure?

Mr. TOTTEN. Yes, sir.

Commissioner COMMONS. You see what I am after.

Mr. TOTTEN. Yes; I would be willing to give you that.

Chairman WALSH. That is all, Mr. Totten. Thank you.

Call your next witness.

Mr. THOMPSON. Mr. Duffy.

TESTIMONY OF MR. JOSEPH P. DUFFY.

Mr. THOMPSON. Will you give us your name?
Mr. DUFFY. Joseph P. Duffy.
Mr. THOMPSON. And your business address?
Mr. DUFFY. San Francisco.
Mr. THOMPSON. Your business?
Mr. DUFFY. Third vice president of the Bricklayers and Masons and Plasterers' Union of America.
Mr. THOMPSON. How long have you been interested in the labor problems on the coast here?
Mr. DUFFY. About eight years.
Mr. THOMPSON. As an officer of the union?
Mr. DUFFY. Yes, sir.
Mr. THOMPSON. Are you acquainted with the Stockton situation?
Mr. DUFFY. To a certain extent.
Mr. THOMPSON. You have been here and heard the witnesses yesterday and to-day?
Mr. DUFFY. I wasn't here yesterday; no, sir.
Mr. THOMPSON. Tell us your views of the Stockton situation.
Chairman WALSH. As applied to his own craft and developed along the part of your work, please.
Mr. DUFFY. The situation pertaining to my organizaiton developed about four weeks ago. I received a communication from the building trades council asking me to get our organization to support the rest of the trades in so far as there was a declaration for open shop in the city of Stockton by the M. M. and E. I took the matter up with the executive board of my organization, whose headquarters are at Indianapolis, and gave them the particulars pertaining to the situation with regard to the open-shop methods practiced by the M. M. and t. in the city of Stockton, and they forthwith issued an order for me to proceed to Stockton at once and to call out the members of our organization to support the rest of the trades in the building industry. Having received those orders I forthwith carried them out. After arriving at Stockton I investigated the situation very thoroughly, and, as the principles of organized labor were involved, it was up to me to call my men out in support of the rest of the trades. At that time we were not affiliated with the building trades council of the city of Stockton.

The committee of the brick contractors who belonged to the M. M and E. waited on a committee of our organization and offered to sign an agreement with them for a certain period—two or three years; that if they would not participate in this trouble in the city of Stockton they would agree to sign an agreement with them and give them any condition they might ask for, if they would stay on the job and work with nonunion men. In other words, they wanted to use the bricklayers' organization in order to try to crush the rest of the trades in this fight. They had before offered inducements in other places where we had open-shop fights in this State, but we absolutely turned them down. They even went so far as to offer us $1 a day extra in order to induce us not to support the rest of the trades and assist them to crush the weaker unions.

We are a pretty strong organization, at least we are conceded to be, and we are nearly 100 per cent organized all through the State. In fact, the whole Pacific coast is well organized and at every opportunity, when there are labor troubles, they try to use the bricklayers if they can, in order to try and crush the smaller unions; and I want to state further that after our men came out in the city of Stockton the merchants and manufacturers' association proceeded to bring nonunion men from the city of Los Angeles into that city to take the places of our members. They employed, I believe, something like 10 or 12 men that they brought in from outside districts, presumably from Los Angeles. I know myself most of them did come from Los Angeles. We interceded with those men and tried to get them to come off of the work, and we were successful in five or six instances whereby we got the men to come off of the work without any trouble whatsoever, by a little persuasive talk. We talked kindly to the men; we didn't use any abusive language of the sort that has been told you by different members of the M. M. and E. There was no violence used whatsoever at any time to my knowledge.

Since I have been in Stockton the last four or five weeks I have never seen at any time any violence used on any job. I have heard of instances where it has been done, but I believe it was caused mostly by the attitude and actions of the members of the M., M. and E. Mr. Totten, I believe, was the first man that started violence. I believe he runs a planing mill in the city of Stockton, and his men, of course, were all out in his mill. He had something like 25 or 30 men employed there that they brought in from outside districts, and the pickets that were down there near his planing mill were trying to talk to these men to get them to come off the work; that is, to quit the job and come back in the union. Some of them, I believe, were formerly union men, but there were no desertions from the ranks locally.

Chairman WALSH. Were you there at the time?

Mr. DUFFY. Yes, sir; I was there.

Chairman WALSH. We are trying to limit this now to the part you might have that is reasonably pertinent to the investigation. We have heard both sides, and considerble concessions have been made by both sides. If you will, kindly confine yourself to things you think are pertinent in your own judgment.

Mr. DUFFY. Then I would only be repeating what other witnesses have stated.

Chairman WALSH. Then eliminate that.

Mr. DUFFY. I get your point.

Chairman WALSH. Here is the whole story about the automobile. It has been conceded on both sides so that we can now draw our own conclusions. Statements have been made that a certain thing was a boycott and a certain thing was not, and correspondence has been submitted, so that we can get at that. If there is anything else in dispute or anything new——

Mr. DUFFY. There is nothing new that I could speak of except that which I was going to state about Mr. Totten.

Chairman WALSH. Go ahead.

Mr. DUFFY. That he was the one that started the trouble in the city of Stockton as far as I know from my own personal knowledge, when these men were down at his mill trying to pursuade these other men to come off of the work, he got so wrought up over the idea and as they succeeded in enticing several men to come out of his mill, he came out of his office with a chair and went over and struck one of the pickets over the head with it, and, of course, the picket reciprocated and handed him a bunch of fives, as you would term it, and that started the riot. They all got mixed into it. That is about as far as I know in regard to that matter.

As I stated before, I would only be repeating what some other witness has stated in any further testimony I may give.

Chairman WALSH. Anything else?

Mr. THOMPSON. One question. Did your organization have a contract with the mason contractors at that time?

Mr. DUFFY. No, sir.

Mr. THOMPSON. No agreement of any kind?

Mr. DUFFY. No agreement whatsoever.

Chairman WALSH. Any questions? Mr. Garretson would like to ask a question.

Commissioner GARRETSON. Can you name this committee of the M., M. and E. that came to you with the proposition?

Mr. DUFFY. No, sir; the committee came to me through some members of my organization. It emanated from the brick bosses who belonged to the M., M. and E. Mr. Cowell is one of them. He said, " Why didn't you come to me and we could have sat down and done business; you did not need to put your organization to this trouble here." He says, " We have always got along fine with the bricklayers' union, and they have got no grievance whatever." I told him, " Do you suppose the bricklayers' union are going to allow themselves to be disgraced with the rest of the trade-union movement and stand idly by and see a lot of nonunion men come in on these buildings and work alongside our union men? "

Commissioenr GARRETSON. Then the attitude of the brick contractors who were members of the M., M. and E. was the direct opposition in this instance to the attitude of the clerks employers' association who referred their employees to Mr. Calkins?

Mr. DUFFY. Absolutely.

Commissioner GARRETSON. That is all.

Chairman WALSH. That is all. Thank you, Mr. Duffy.

Call your next.

Mr. THOMPSON. Mr. Holt.

TESTIMONY OF MR. PLINY.E. HOLT.

Mr. THOMPSON. Give us your name and business address and business, Mr. Holt.

Mr. HOLT. Pliny E. Holt; I am vice president and general manager of the Holt Manufacturing Co. I will have to ask your pardon a little bit, as I suffered a severe nervous breakdown about two years ago and my voice is very low.

Chairman WALSH. That is all right. Do the best you can.

Mr. THOMPSON. You have been here the last two days?

Mr. HOLT. Yes, sir.

Mr. THOMPSON. You have heard the testimony given in regard to the Stockton situation?

Mr. HOLT. Yes, sir; I have heard quite a bit of it.

Mr. THOMPSON. What can you give us in addition to what has been stated?

Mr. HOLT. My attitude is more of an interested outside spectator. My company has not been mixed up in this fight in any way. You understand, we run a nonunion institution, and of course our men have not been affected by this trouble, and we are interested and are members of the association, but not active.

Mr. THOMPSON. Are there any facts you could add to those already stated by the other witnesses?

Mr. HOLT. Why, of course there are lots of facts leading up to this trouble. It is a long story.

Chairman WALSH. If they have not been gone over and you consider them significant to the inquiry, please state them as concisely as you can.

Mr. HOLT. I hardly know how to do that without dragging into this a great deal of our own personal history in connection with the labor situation on the coast, which is not really pertinent to this—just this particular inquiry—just now.

Chairman WALSH. I am letting you judge it. If you think it is not pertinent to the Stockton inquiry, please omit it and give us something else.

Mr. HOLT. It has been brought about, of course, by a long series of troubles. I have heard it hashed over a good many times. Men have come and expressed themselves to me personally about the trouble they were having and the continued unjust demands, as they considered it, being presented to them. Their output was restricted——

Chairman WALSH. Have you any personal knowledge of restriction of output on the part of employees?

Mr. HOLT. I have a great deal of that.

Chairman WALSH. Briefly state it.

Mr. HOLT. For instance, in connection with our business we have a great deal of work done in the shops in the city of Stockton—the foundries, for instance. Our foundry is not adequate to supply the material that we use. We have some of it come from our factory in Peoria, but even then we buy a good deal outside at a much greater price than we could produce it ourselves, but in order to get it we buy from the local company.

We have one instance particularly that was the source of a great deal of dissatisfaction this year. One of the owners of the foundry we are getting these engine cylinders from is the Monarch Foundry Co., and they did quite a good deal of our gas-engine castings per year, and their output of cylinders was eight cylinders per day per man. Our work got a little slack and we started making those cylinders in our own factory, and our regular men, working along at the regular gait—not forcing them—made 18 cylinders a day. To offset that we worked nine hours against their eight hours, for which you would have to deduct, say, 15 per cent of what it was. When it was called to my attention I went out to see if our foreman was forcing the men. He said no, absolutely; that the man could have turned out 25 if he had worked hard; it was just the regular routine work. That is one particular instance. It was called to the attention of the man that was making the castings, and I asked him if that was why he charged us so much, and he said it was, because he could not make them any lower. We paid him 5 cents a pound, and we make the same castings in our plant for 3½ cents, and make the same castings at Peoria for 2½ cents. Simply the difference in the labor conditions and material conditions at the different places.

Chairman WALSH. Have you any other instances of that character?

Mr. HOLT. Not that I can give such concrete cases except in our own instance, where when we had trouble with the union and when we were forced to eliminate the union from our plant, that was about 10 or 12 years ago, and our plant has been run on that basis since that—there has been no change in our attitude at all.

Chairman WALSH. You may state those even if not so specific as this. Anything you could say was restriction of output. Of course you are not confined to personal knowledge.

Mr. HOLT. This case was personal knowledge from our superintendent of the plant at that time.

Chairman WALSH. I see that was, but any others you have.

Mr. HOLT. This other case I want to state here—our attitude to the union at that time was very friendly; in fact, we helped organize one union so as to take in some of the men who were not placed. We have a variety of work, and we operated for two or three years under union conditions, and the last year we operated we found we could not exist under those conditions; that the reduction in output was such that we were operating at very close to a loss, and if it continued, we knew we could not continue. That was our reason for eliminating it. The particular case is we have what we call a wheel gang welding tires for large wheels for harvesters. These men in running their regular day's work would weld from 60 to 65 tires a day. After the shop committee got real busy they cut that down to 25 tires a day. We had numerous cases of the same thing. That, of course, led to our eliminating the unions— that was 10 years ago and we haven't had any experience with unions since that time because we wouldn't allow them to dictate our affairs.

Chairman WALSH. Is there anything else, as I stated when you began, that you think is significant, or that you think is pertinent to the inquiry, that has not been gone into?

Mr. HOLT. Mr. Dale made a remark this morning saying we had a picnic here some months ago, about two months ago, and said it was pulled off to influence this situation at that time. That is absolutely false. Our picnic was decided on six months before it was given, and the parade was planned by the men. It was handled by the committee of shop men of their own, and we had nothing whatever to do with it. We donated them the day's wages, furnished them all the supplies, and gave them money to spend and told them to spend it any way they pleased. It was in lieu of the annual dinner we had always had previous to that time for heads of departments, but we have decided now to make it annual and take in every man in our employ, and it had nothing to do with the local situation. That is all, unless you want to go into other matters.

Chairman WALSH. That is all, unless there are some questions. Mr. O'Connell wants to ask a question.

Commissioner O'CONNELL. I understand you to say you are not in any way connected with the present situation——

Mr. HOLT. Except as a member of the association, but not active.

Commissioner O'CONNELL. The policy therefore—the policy as advocated by the association—must meet with your approval in conducting the affairs of your plant?

Mr. HOLT. Oh, certainly—no; it is in this way, our attitude is this, we will help them all we can morally and by our regular dues, as long as they live up to the principles we have set down and lived under some 10 or 12 years. If for any reason they would compromise with the unions or compromise in any way that would affect our policy, that minute we draw out of the merchants, manufacturers, and employers' association, or draw out of any other organization we are connected with. Our attitude is absolutely independent.

Commissioner O'CONNELL. Your policy is operation of the open shop?

Mr. HOLT. No, sir; nonunion.

Commissioner O'CONNELL. Nonunion?

Mr. HOLT. Yes, sir.

Commissioner O'CONNELL. Nonunion shop absolutely?

Mr. HOLT. Yes, sir.

Commissioner O'CONNELL. That is not the policy of the association.

Mr. HOLT. No, sir; their policy is the open shop.

Commissioner O'CONNELL. And you won't employ union men at all?

Mr. HOLT. No, sir. We have at times; yes, sir; I will take that back; we have at times, but we don't make a policy of it. We find they are not as reliable men and don't give us anywhere near the satisfaction. They don't be-

come the steady, reliable men. Our men have been in our employ some of them
33 years, and some of them anywhere from 10 to 20 years. We pay them good
wages and try to build up a strong organization—independent workers.

Commissioner O'CONNELL. Then, if it is discovered a union man has secured
employment in your plant by some means or other, what becomes of him after
that?

Mr. HOLT. He is dropped.

Commissioner O'CONNELL. Dropped?

Mr. HOLT. No, sir; he is given the opportunity of withdrawing· from¹ the
union. I tell him that it is against our policy, and that if he wants to stay
with us he can withdraw and stay with us. Otherwise we drop him and replace him with another man.

Commissioner O'CONNELL. Then you boycott him because he is a member
of the union, as fas as employment with your firm·is concerned?

Mr. HOLT. Yes, sir.

Commissioner O'CONNELL. That is all.

Chairman WALSH. Any other questions?

Mr. THOMPSON. Just one other question. What wages do you pay, and what
hours do you have?

Mr. HOLT. We have nine hours, and our wages run from $2 to $5, depending
upon the man. We have no scale of wages.

Chairman WALSH. Will you kindly submit to us your pay roll?

Mr. HOLT. I would be very glad to.

Chairman WALSH. We will have an investigator pick out the· dates, and the
commission would like to go over it.

Mr. HOLT. Very gladly. We give you a very cordial invitation to .visit us
if you want to come to Stockton.

(The information requested was later supplied and is printed as. " Holt
Exhibit.")

Chairman WALSH. That is all, Mr. Holt. Thank you.

Call your next.

Mr. THOMPSON. Mr. Kennedy.

TESTIMONY OF MR. FRANKLIN H. KENNEDY.

Mr. THOMPSON. Will you give us your name, your business address, and your
business?

Mr. KENNEDY. Franklin H. Kennedy ; manager of the California Moline Plow
Co., Stockton, Cal.; jobbers of agricultural implements.

Mr. THOMPSON. How long have you been located at Stockton?

Mr. KENNEDY. About 19 years.

Mr. THOMPSON. You are acquainted. with the situation there?

Mr. KENNEDY. Somewhat. More largely by hearsay, however ; I have not
been there all of the time.

Mr. THOMPSON. Have you been here yesterday and to-day?

Mr. KENNEDY. No, sir ; I just heard the last three witnesses and part of the
fourth.

Mr. THOMPSON. Well, you may tell the situation in Stockton as far as you
know it, and that does not cover the ground that you have already heard the·
witnesses testify about to-day.

Mr. KENNEDY. Well, as I said, I only know it through hearsay. I haven't
taken any active interest in it. I haven't attended any meetings of the merchants, manufacturers, and employers' association, and our company is not·a
member of it, although our name appears there, but it is contrary to my instruc- ·
tions.

Chairman WALSH. Their name appears where?

Mr. KENNEDY. In the list they have published of their membership.

Chairman WALSH. It is contrary to what instructions?

Mr. KENNEDY. To my instructions. We are not allowed—as manager of·
our institution we are not supposed to go into labor disputes.

Chairman WALSH. Have you gone into this and joined this organization? :

Mr. KENNEDY.· No, sir.

Chairman WALSH. And you do not wish, then, as I take it, to discuss their ·
reasons for forming it or their trouble with the opposing organizations? ` ,

Mr. KENNEDY. Absolutely not, because I have no knowledge of it. · · · ·

Chairman WALSH. Then, I move that we just excuse this witness as not
being enlightening, if there is no objection by the commission. He says his
name was put on there without authority.

Mr. KENNEDY. I mean the name of the California Moline Plow Co.

Chairman WALSH. That is, he has no personal knowledge of anything. Do you want to ask him any questions?

Commissioner WEINSTOCK. Yes, sir; I think Mr. Kennedy can give us some information that will be of value.

Chairman WALSH. Very good. Go ahead.

Commissioner WEINSTOCK. You have been employed a great many years?

Mr. KENNEDY. Yes, sir.

Commissioner WEINSTOCK. You are connected with some large enterprise in the East?

Mr. KENNEDY. Yes, sir; our house is a branch, and distributes.

Commissioner WEINSTOCK. You have had experience with labor?

Mr. KENNEDY. Somewhat.

Commissioner WEINSTOCK. Under various conditions?

Mr. KENNEDY. More indirectly than directly.

Commissioner WEINSTOCK. You have handled union labor and nonunion labor?

Mr. KENNEDY. Not directly. Our employees as far as they can be classed as laborers are not members of any union. I don't know that there is any union provided for them. We make no distinction and ask no questions. but as far as I know we have no labor-union men in our employ at Stockton.

Commissioner WEINSTOCK. You have no union men in your employ; is that what you mean?

Mr. KENNEDY. Yes, sir.

Commissioner WEINSTOCK. Are you familiar with the law under which this commission is working?

Mr. KENNEDY. No; except in a general way, as it is given in the newspapers; I have that.

Commissioner WEINSTOCK. One of the things Congress has given this commission to do is this: "To inquire into the methods for avoiding or adjusting labor disputes through peaceful and conciliatory mediation and negotiations; into the scope, methods, and resources of existing bureaus of labor," and so on. Well, now, from your broad knowledge as an employer and a business man, what suggestions can you make to this commission as to the best way to establish and maintain mutually satisfactory relations between employers and employees?

Mr. KENNEDY. Well, to answer that question, I doubt my ability to make suggestions. I can offer an opinion.

Commissioner WEINSTOCK. We would be very glad to have it.

Mr. KENNEDY. I think that unquestionably labor unions are a necessity, not only for a protection to the employee, but also as a protection to the employer against himself. I do think that either party when they get control is dangerous. And I might add, incidentally, that, I think, is originally the cause of the trouble at Stockton. Now, I am saying that purely from an outsider's view, because I do not come directly in contact with the labor condition there, but I am acquainted with it, though, in talking with labor-union men on it, and also outsiders—that the labor unions were too powerful in Stockton, that they had too great an influence there. And the same thing would apply anywhere else. The same thing will apply with employers who get too great power. Therefore, I think they are both necessary, but I do not think——

Commissioner WEINSTOCK. Pardon me. When you say "both necessary," are we to understand that in your judgment both sides ought to be organized?

Mr. KENNEDY. I think both sides have the right to organize, and I think perhaps that it would be necessary for both sides to organize; but it would seem to me if labor unions or organizations for the protection of laboring people would not dictate to the employer that he should not hire anybody but their people; and, on the other hand, the people that had the interests of the labor to take care of would look after the hours and pay—that that would be a reasonable division of two great contentions between labor and employer.

Commissioner WEINSTOCK. You mean that you think that it is unwise for organized labor to insist upon the employer employing only union men, on the one hand, and, on the other hand, you believe that the worker ought to have a voice in determining the wage and the hours?

Mr. KENNEDY. Yes, sir.

Commissioner WEINSTOCK. And the working conditions?

Mr. KENNEDY. Yes.

Commissioner WEINSTOCK. You believe that wherever those conditions prevail there is greater likelihood of industrial peace than where either one side or the other is alone strongly organized?

Mr. KENNEDY. Unquesionably. And we have proof of that in cases where such condition exists.

Commissioner WEINSTOCK. That is, whichever side happens to be organized effectively will take advantage of the disorganized conditions of the other side?

Mr. KENNEDY. It is a natural conclusion because selfishness is not eliminated.

Commissioner WEINSTOCK. So that really, summing up, I would take it to be this, that for the highest—if the highest degree of industrial peace could be established and maintained, it would be, in your opinion, by mutual organization, mutual recognition by the employer, both the employer and the employee in all matters, by giving the workers a voice in fixing hours, wages, and working conditions?

Mr. KENNEDY. Yes, sir.

Commissioner WEINSTOCK. That is to accord industrial democracy? That would make it largely a question of industrial democracy?

Mr. KENNEDY. Well, I do not take it exactly to that point. I do, though, as a business proposition, go just that far. I am not a philanthropist in this matter at all. It is a question purely of business, of costs, and for that reason it had better be in the position that neither party has absolute control of the other. Everything in nature has a controlling or compensating force. Why should industrial affairs not be so provided?

Commissioner WEINSTOCK. That is all, Mr. Chairman.

Chairman WALSH. That is all.

Call your next witness.

Mr. THOMPSON. Mr. E. C. Dickinson.

TESTIMONY OF MR. E. C. DICKINSON.

Mr. THOMPSON. Mr. Dickinson, give your name, business address, and business.

Mr. DICKINSON. E. C. Dickinson. My business address is 1214 West Weber Avenue, Stockton, Cal.

Mr. THOMPSON. Have you been here yesterday and to-day?

Mr. DICKINSON. Yes, sir.

Mr. THOMPSON. Have you heard the testimony given?

Mr. DICKINSON. Yes, sir.

Mr. THOMPSON. What can you add to that which has already been testified?

Mr. DICKINSON. I think the subject has been pretty thoroughly gone over. I do not know anything I can add that will assist this commission in their work, except I am acquainted and quite familiar with the early organization of the merchants, manufacturers, and employers' association in Stockton.

Mr. THOMPSON. Would your testimony be different from Mr. Irish's in that respect?

Mr. DICKINSON. Except the early part; he did not go into the early part of the organization. I will say that it was absolutely a local organization. I was quite familiar with that. The objects were as he stated. Outside of that everything that he stated is, I think, correct with regard to the organization.

Mr. THOMPSON. That is all, Mr. Chairman.

Chairman WALSH. Is there anything that you would like to say, Mr. Dickinson, from the standpoint of the general public? You are a grain dealer, as I understand it.

Mr. DICKINSON. Yes, sir.

Chairman WALSH. Are you a large employer of labor in your business?

Mr. DICKINSON. No, sir; not a large employer. We are not in this controversy at all.

Chairman WALSH. Have you an elevator?

Mr. DICKINSON. No, sir; we have not. We handle our grain here in sacks.

Chairman WALSH. You think the subject has been quite well covered?

Mr. DICKINSON. I think it has been very well covered; yes, sir.

Chairman WALSH. That is all.

Mr. THOMPSON. Just one question, Mr. Chairman. Has your policy—I presume it is the policy of your association—at any time been influenced or controlled by outside persons or associations?

- Mr. DICKINSON. No; it is purely a local organization, originated in Stockton. The purposes have been thoroughly stated here by Mr. Irish and Mr. Bird.

Commissioner WEINSTOCK. I would like to ask a question, Mr. Chairman.

Chairman WALSH. Mr. Weinstock would like to ask you a question.

Commissioner WEINSTOCK. You have been an employer, Mr. Dickinson, for many years, have you not?

Mr. DICKINSON. Yes, sir.

Commissioner WEINSTOCK. And your opinion, therefore, ought to be of value to this commission in helping it to reach its conclusions. May I ask you how far, as a result of your experience and your knowledge of things and judgment, you have given accord to the sentiments expressed by the preceding witness, Mr. Kennedy, when he said that. in his judgment, the best possible industrial peace would be where both sides are organized, where the employer recognizes and controls the labor organization and gives labor a voice in fixing hours, wages, and working conditions, but reserving the right to employ union or nonunion men as he chooses?

Mr. DICKINSON. That coincides with my views pretty closely.

Commissioner WEINSTOCK. You would be in harmony with his point of view?

Mr. DICKINSON. Yes; I would be in harmony with his point of view.

Commissioner WEINSTOCK. That is all.

Chairman WALSH. That is all. Call your next witness.

Mr. THOMPSON. Mr. Martin.

TESTIMONY OF MR. IRVING MARTIN.

Mr. THOMPSON. Give us your name, your business address, and your business, please.

Mr. MARTIN. Irving Martin; Stockton, Cal.; newspaper publisher.

Mr. THOMPSON. What paper do you publish?

Mr. MARTIN. The Record.

Mr. THOMPSON. How long have you published that?

Mr. MARTIN. For 18 or 19 years.

Mr. THOMPSON. Are you a member of the M., M. and E.?

Mr. MARTIN. I am not.

Mr. THOMPSON. You are not?

Mr. MARTIN. No, sir.

Mr. THOMPSON. Are you acquainted with the situation in Stockton?

Mr. MARTIN. In such a general way as a newspaper man might become without being a member of the organization. Be a matter of hearsay, of course.

Mr. THOMPSON. Well, have you been here yesterday and to-day?

Mr. MARTIN. I heard the testimony of nearly all the witnesses; yes, sir.

Mr. THOMPSON. Will you kindly give us such views of the witnesses which you have heard which adds to what has been testified?

Chairman WALSH. Let me get a fact or two right at this point. Now, so far as these troubles are concerned, have you had any public expression—you have, naturally, in your newspaper, have you, published it?

Mr. MARTIN. Pretty fully; yes, sir.

Chairman WALSH. And you have taken the means that newspaper men ordinarily take to ascertain the facts and give publicity to them?

Mr. MARTIN. Yes, sir.

Chairman WALSH. And have you endeavored to get the facts from both sides whether they reflected upon one side or the other?

Mr. MARTIN. We have; yes, sir.

Chairman WALSH. And you endeavored to publish the news with reference to the matters that grew out of this industrial dispute in Stockton?

Mr. MARTIN. So far as I am conscious we have obtained those things that affect the public mind so deeply.

Chairman WALSH. Now, are you proprietor of the paper?

Mr. MARTIN. I am the principal stockholder.

Chairman WALSH. The principal stockholder. It is run, then, by a corporation, I take it?

Mr. MARTIN. Yes.

Chairman WALSH. And are you an editorial writer? Do you write some of the editorials?

Mr. MARTIN. I write some, not all of them.

Chairman WALSH. Are you the one in charge of it—to supervise the writing of all the editorials?

Mr. MARTIN. Yes, sir.

Chairman WALSH. Who is the business manager of your paper?

Mr. MARTIN. Mr. A. A. Seaver.

Chairman WALSH. Are you in touch with the business management?

Mr. MARTIN. Pretty closely; yes, sir.

Chairman WALSH. In addition to being the principal stockholder, are you an officer in the corporation that runs the paper?

Mr. MARTIN. I am president of the company.

Chairman WALSH. The name of the paper is the Stockton Record?

Mr. MARTIN. The name of the paper is the Stockton Daily Evening Record.

Chairman WALSH. Now, you may go on and tell the facts—particularly with reference to any new facts that you care to give. It might be well for Mr. Martin to give a general sketch, beginning at the very beginning of the whole trouble, from the standpoint of the citizenship of the community and all those that are not directly involved, one of whom I take you to be.

Mr. MARTIN. Gentlemen of the commission, I have been very much interested in the hearings, and to a certain extent you seem to have gotten the attitude of the witnesses. I wish to state that from my standpoint some of the objects of the M. and M. in Stockton, I think, you have pretty well cleared up by the investigation. There has been a great deal of misunderstanding in regard to the objects of the organization. If you will just permit me, I would just like to read a line or two of Mr. Irish's testimony. I refer to a question by Commissioner Commons:

" Commissioner COMMONS. When you organized at the start, you put yourself into a position where you could not enter into any agreements which would take into account all questions of dispute between the unions and the others?

" Mr. IRISH. Exactly. We simply took this stand, that any man was free to join any organization, the Masons or the Catholics or any organization.

" Comissioner COMMONS. From the very start, then, it was the issue of the open shop?

" Mr. IRISH. Absolutely."

That expresses my idea of the situation, and the testimony of the other witnesses to the effect that the association declined to recognize the unions is also borne out by my observations and experience as far as it extends, that the association was formed for the specific purpose of making the open-shop fight and to not recognize the unions.

Chairman, WALSH. One minute, please. At this point the commission will stand adjourned until 2 o'clock.

I have been requested to make this statement: That this table here is reserved for working newspaper men, and the fact that the chairs are not always occupied does not indicate that they are not needed, because they come and go. So I have been asked to make the request that no person occupy the chairs at the table except working newspaper men here on that business.

We will adjourn until 2 o'clock.

(Whereupon, at 12.30 o'clock p. m. on this Wednesday, August 26, 1914, an adjournment was taken until 2 o'clock p. m. of the same day.)

AFTER RECESS—2 P. M.

Met pursuant to adjournment. Present as before.

Chairman WALSH. Well, we will proceed now, Mr. Thompson.

Mr. THOMPSON. Mr. Martin, will you please take the stand again?' Is Mr. Martin here?

Chairman WALSH. I noticed him out in the anteroom. Call Mr. Martin, Mr. Sergeant at Arms. Where is the sergeant at arms and the assistants? We are ready to start now.

TESTIMONY OF MR. IRVING MARTIN—Continued.

Mr. THOMPSON. You were in the midst of a statement, Mr. Martin. Will you just take up your thread where you left off and go ahead?

Mr. MARTIN. Well, I guess the easiest way is to begin all over again.

Chairman WALSH. Mr. Martin, it has been suggested that there is another gentleman here whose testimony they think would be more logical before yours. And if it is convenient to you you may retire until we hear that.

Mr. MARTIN. That would be all right. I haven't really started yet, anyway. Chairman WALSH. Very good. Then just retire, please, until we get through with this other witness.
Mr. THOMPSON. Mr. Kincaid.

TESTIMONY OF MR. FRED L. KINCAID.

Mr. THOMPSON. Will you give us your name, your business address, and your business, please?
Mr. KINCAID. Fred L. Kincaid; my present business address is 930 North San Joaquin Street, Stockton; my business at the present time is that of speculator; sometimes I loan money and things of that sort.
Mr. THOMPSON. Well, what subject, what material do you speculate in?
Mr. KINCAID. Buy lands and sell them. Now, own some farm lands in San Joaquin County, and am interested and have been for a great many years in the welfare and progress in the city of Stockton and its people.
Mr. THOMPSON. How long have you lived there?
Mr. KINCAID. Twenty-one years.
Mr. THOMPSON. Are you acquainted with the present situation in Stockton in industrial matters?
Mr. KINCAID. Yes, sir; and the causes leading up to it, do you mean?
Mr. THOMPSON. Yes, sir.
Mr. KINCAID. Yes, sir.
Mr. THOMPSON. Have you heard the testimony given here yesterday and to-day?
Mr. KINCAID. Yes, sir.
Mr. THOMPSON. Will you tell us briefly and in your own way such facts as have not been given to the commission?
Mr. KINCAID. My views necessarily will be along different lines than perhaps those of any other of the witnesses that have been here, because as I have heard the testimony, it has represented the personal views of those interested in one side or the other; while mine will probably largely be from a humanitarian standpoint rather than that of the employer or employee.
As I have said, I came to Stockton 21 years ago, leaving San Francisco somewhat prejudiced against unions, because I had been in business in San Francisco for eight years previous to that and left there largely because I felt I was somewhat hampered by unions.
I went to Stockton and I found there what at that time seemed to me ideal conditions, because there were practically no unions there. I went into business at Stockton, in the manufacture of combined harvesters, in the fall of 1892, or in the winter of 1892–93. Conditions at that time were, as I have said, to me, apparently ideal.
I remember along in the early years that one man in particular or in fact several, but one in particular, a Mr. McCall, was about to retire from business and invest his money in buildings, and he was able to hire carpenters, finished mechanics, for the nominal sum of $2 and $2.50 per day, and he commented upon it quite a great deal; in fact, I have heard him say a dollar and a quarter a day was enough for mechanics. And then I commenced perhaps to change my views as to what were ideal conditions. Perhaps I was getting along to a riper time of life and I did change them materially.
I have since that time seen those same mechanics that were getting from $2 to $2.50 a day, owing to their organization get themselves onto a living basis.
Carpenters are getting, as you have heard testified, $4.40 per day, and, it is quite apparent, are more able to take care of their families and give them the education that is due them.
I have seen other matters change in Stockton that have been benefited by those same conditions. But for the first 10 years of my life in Stockton it was practically at a standstill. Since then it has always been on the increase, and it has grown almost to a boom until the conditions caused by the late trouble came up.
Everybody was prosperous in Stockton up to about a year ago or such a matter. I say everybody; I am speaking generally.
In all the years I have lived there I have never found labor unions taking any very drastic measures. They have at times had some strikes. I have been in a way involved in some myself. I have even sometimes allowed myself to be a little annoyed by some of the measures they have taken. I remember at one time that I had a number of machines that were necessary—a number of

harvesters—that belonged to myself, and it was necessary that they be repaired and put on the market before the harvest season, and in order to do so I was enabled to hire union labor; but I had to buy material from the Holt Manufacturing Co., castings, particularly, because they could not be gotten anywhere else, and my union men refused to handle them. At that time, as I say, I allowed myself to become a little annoyed. I say this only to show I am in the middle of the road; I do not represent either side, I want you to understand. That I have been myself—do not feel now that the unions have always done things right in the community; they have made mistakes like everybody else, but they have never, in my judgment and knowledge, created a situation that was so absolutely untenable as the present situation in Stockton.

My first connection with the present situation was perhaps in May or June of this year. Up to the 1st of July, I will state, and for six years previous thereto I had been the manager of the California Anchor Fence Co., an employer of labor in Stockton; and about that time, when a Mr. Calkins—he said his name was Calkins, at least—came into my office to talk to me about the prospects of the organization known as the merchants, manufacturers and employers' association. He outlined the objects of it about as here testified to, and I told him that—oh, he supplemented that by saying that they proposed to shake off the yoke of union labor in Stockton forever. Well, I said, "If that is your object I am not in accord with it, and I do not believe in it." I told him that under the present situation of society that unions are absolutely necessary, "and therefore I will not go into your organization." He became angry and said he did not care, as it seemed as though I was not in the right frame of mind to go into their organization and they didn't want me. I told him I was very glad of that, and consequently I did not go in. I have been a member of the chamber of commerce, however, for many years, and am yet.

My next connection, that will be of interest to this commission, with the present situation of affairs was along the latter part of July, after the lockouts had been declared, after the merchants had practically notified their unions that they must take their cards out and cease their boycotting, etc., when I was asked to go down to one of the banks in Stockton, the one where I have done business for some years. I didn't know the object of it, and I didn't respond, in fact, to the first notice or first request; and then I got the second one, through my wife, who was met by the president of the bank, and she was requested to have me come down and see them.

I went down absolutely in ignorance as to what was required of me or what was wanted of me, but it soon developed. I was informed that in the judgment of the banker I was closely in touch with Mr. Martin, of the Stockton Record. I think I was accused, in fact, or asked if I did not have some interest in the Record. I told them that I had none; that I was very friendly to Mr. Martin, so far as that was concerned.

I was informed that the policy of the Stockton Record was distasteful to the merchants and manufacturers' association. I had read he Record pretty regularly—in fact, absolutely all the local news that was in it every night—and it was quite astonishing to me. I could not see that there was any reason for its being distasteful to any side. The news was published; that is all I could see. But the outcome of it was that they required, or desired, that I see Mr. Martin and request him to change his policy.

And I said to them, "Well, Mr. Martin's policy is one of absolutely neutrality. How would you want him to change it?" Well, they wanted him to be neutral; they didn't want him to publish these items about strike breakers coming to town. That was one thing; and they said he had refused, or did not publish, rather, news favorable to the M., M. and E., and that if he didn't change his policy that we proposed—meaning the merchants and manufacturers who the banker was at that time representing—to withdraw our support from the Stockton Record; that we were furnishing the lifeblood for that paper, and that without it the paper could not exist, and that every merchant in town would withdraw that support in the form of advertising; and furthermore that he better look out for his interests financially.

And I was asked to see Mr. Martin and tell him this. At first thought I refused. I told them that I would not assume on account of friendship to Mr. Martin to carry any such a message to him; that Mr. Martin was capable of running his own business. and I didn't see it that way.

The statement was made there that although that bank to my personal knowledge had no hold on the Stockton Record or on Mr. Martin, the statement was made there that if that banker had the power, he would put the screws to Mr. Martin, as it was expressed, and his Stockton Record, which was to me an intimation that any other bank that might have the power would do so.

Personally I happened to know that there was more or less business as between the Stockton Record and one of the other banks, and so after some consideration I concluded that I would see Mr. Martin about it, and I did so.

During that, by the way, though I have heard it testified to here that there would be no coercion of any kind permitted by the M., M., and E., and therefore it seems that it would be pertinent to speak of another matter that came up during the time that I was in that particular bank.

The banker said to me, "There was a man in here this morning to see me. I asked him if he would join the M., M., and E. association, and he said he could not. And I asked him why, and he said 'Well, I am just the manager of a little small corporation here. The president of our corporation is interested in business in San Francisco that depends very largely on union patronage, on the patronage of union people, and it would be ruinous to the president of my company if we allowed our little laundry association to be drawn into this affair, and therefore I can't do it.'" And Mr. ———, the banker, said, "I informed him that his president could come in here and pay the overdraft, or the money that they owe this bank immediately." And I said, "Did you do that?" And he said, "Yes; I did." And I said, "I am very sorry to hear that."

However, I didn't know anything about the outcome of that until a day or two later. It so happened that this very man, the president of this little corporation, owed me a few notes. And he came to me the next day and he said, "I am going to have trouble," and he said, "I may not be able to pay you those notes when they are due." And he said "Will it be all right?" And I said, "Yes; I know of your trouble. I heard of it." And he said, "Who told you?" and I told him the banker. And I said, "How are you coming out of that?" "Well," he said, "I don't know." He said, "The corporation isn't very well fixed. We owe some money, but I don't know. I think we will be able to meet the small amount that we owe the bank if they don't bother us any further." A day or so later he did inform me that they had paid the amount in the bank. And a day or so after that he again informed me that his corporation had been called upon, he presumed through the efforts of the merchants and manufacturers' association, for a larger indebtedness that he did not believe his company could meet, an amount of $1,900, which they owed a laundry-machinery company, and which they were presumed to be paying on installments.

But he said he was in touch with their president in San Francisco, but he had not yet decided whether they could or not. I saw him several times in the next few days, and he was in great distress. He asked me if I could not let his company have this $1,900. I told him I wasn't in a position to do that just then, but that there was a banker in town who had frequently asked me to get accounts for him—help him get accounts—and I would go with him to this bank and see at least how far-reaching their agreements were. I did not hold out any inducement that anything could be done. We did go to the second bank, a smaller bank than the first one I referred to, and I asked the president of that bank, after making the statement to him that he had frequently asked me to help him get accounts, and I was then prepared perhaps to help him to get one I considered was all right and told him of this case and of the requirements of it, and as to why my man desired to change his account from one bank to the other.

By the way, I was personally interested in both banks to the extent of carrying deposits in both, so that it was not a matter of personal feeling on my part of getting him to change. It was one merely of a desire to have him do what was for the best interests of himself.

The second banker promptly informed me that owing to the agreement among the bankers he could not put on any accounts of that kind. In fact, he also told me that their agreement was rather more drastic than I had heard. He told me that the unions as unions had withdrawn their accounts from the banks—by the way, I speak of these incidents not in any way but grief; I am sorry it is so; I wouldn't speak of it in anger or feeling of any kind, but it has been declared often in Stockton that this condition prevailed and just as often been denied, and I merely speak of this as perhaps proof of the fact, and that is all. You can take it for what it is worth.

The second banker told me that union after union as unions had withdrawn their accounts from the bank, and now the union men as individuals were withdrawing their accounts, and that it had been agreed among the banks that if that continued they proposed to call every loan in Stockton that had to do in any way, directly or indirectly, with any union man, be it mortgage or a loan, and they would do it without notice.

I afterwards, in speaking with a man who was a director of another bank, mentioned that fact, and he said, " Well, I don't believe it, because "—I say this in fairness, too—" because I am a director of one bank, and if there had been any such agreement as that I know I would have known it." But you can take that for what it is worth. Those were mere statements. The outcome of the matter that I spoke of, a small laundry corporation subsequently developed. That may be of interest to you, and I might as well mention names as I go along. The corporation I speak of was the New Method Laundry, the manager of which was Mr. Eaves.

Chairman WALSH. Who was the first banker?

Mr. KINCAID. I am very sorry to say it was Mr. Hough, of the First National Bank.

Chairman WALSH. What are his initials?

Mr. KINCAID. J. H., I believe.

Chairman WALSH. H-o-u-g-h?

Mr. KINCAID. Yes, sir.

Chairman WALSH. J. H. Hough, of the First National Bank. Proceed.

Mr. KINCAID. I don't want it understood that I have anything but the highest regard for Mr. Hough.

Chairman WALSH. We want to get at the facts, and we will appreciate it if you will give us the facts.

Mr. KINCAID. I don't want to speak condemnatory of Mr. Hough.

Mr. Eaves, not being successful in any way in getting his loan to meet this $1,900 indebtedness, and I not being able to help him, was eventually forced into joining the M., M. and E. to get it. I know this fact from two instances. Mr. Hough himself told me in the first place that this Mr. Eaves had come back to him and asked him if he would join the M., M. and E. if he would let him have the $1,900 to stave off his disaster. He told him promptly he wasn't buying new accounts, but he didn't say he didn't let him have any money.

Mr. Eaves the next day I met him, and I said, " How are you getting along, Eaves?" " Well, I had to do it." " Do what?" I said. " I had to join the M., M. and E." I said, " Why?" " I went to Hough and asked him if he would let me have that money if I would join the association, and he let me have it." So that is one case, of course, that I can absolutely speak of.

In the case of the Stockton Record, Mr. Martin, I took particular pains because he is a personal friend. I told him I wasn't bringing this as a matter of news to him—just as a matter of protection if it was necessary. He said it wasn't necessary; that he should pursue the policy that he had pursued at all times, and he has done so. If that is of any benefit to you.

Chairman WALSH. Is that all?

Mr. KINCAID. That is all the statement I have to make.

Chairman WALSH. Did you wish to ask the witness some questions, Mr. Weinstock?

Mr. WEINSTOCK. Only this: I should judge from the statement you make, Mr. Kincaid, that it is a case of war on both sides.

Mr. KINCAID. It looks very much like it.

Commissioner WEINSTOCK. That the members of the M., M. and E. have followed the tactics of organized labor in boycotting their enemies and helping their friends.

Mr. KINCAID. They certainly have, to the most bitter extent. There never has been such a bitter condition in Stockton or anywhere else that I know of as exists there to-day, brought about, apparently, from no earthly reason— for the unions were not aggressive. They did, I think, do some foolish things. We all do. I don't think any of us are perfect. I think, perhaps, they have annoyed all employers at times; as I said, or started to say, they have annoyed me at times, and some persons have said to me, " I don't understand you ; you have been connected with business in conflict with the unions, and they have bothered you in the past." I am ready to define my position as feeling that one's own personal interest should be rather squelched at times in the interest of broad humanity; while I don't pose as an angel, I do hope that I will be understood as having a greater interest in humanity than I have in making a few dollars.

Commissioner WEINSTOCK. The situation, then, I take it, is largely regarded as a matter of war, and that mutual reprisals seem to be in order?

Mr. KINCAID. Yes. If I was situated as Mr. Totten is—I have a high regard for him as a man—probably if I were in his position, a large employer of labor, just looking at it from my own selfish or interested standpoint, I should feel I should be better off if I could eliminate the unions. I haven't any doubt that the manufacturers of Stockton do feel that way, but nevertheless the fact remains that it has been possible in Stockton for.the large manufacturers, if they so desired, to run open shops, nonunion shops, or do about as they pleased. It has been said that Stockton was a strongly organized union town. I deny the fact, for in the 21 years I have been there what strikes they have had have been conducted along gentlemanly lines. There has been no violence, unless it has been within the last three weeks, in which time I have been away from there. It has been possible at all times, as I have said, to conduct any sort of business anybody wanted. And the statement that manufacturers have been kept away from Stockton because of labor conditions I believe is absolutely unfounded, because I don't think there is a place, I know there is not a place on the Pacific coast, where conditions could have been any better than they have been in Stockton the 21 years I have lived there for. a manufacturer to conduct his business in his own way.

I don't refute, don't care to refute, the statements of these men who have come on the stand and have said they had been annoyed by labor conditions. Individuals have. I speak of it from a broad standpoint. Personally, as I have said, for six years I have managed the California Anchor Fence Co., and at. times we have as high as 200 men, and that down to 1. I have never had but very little trouble with unions. Sometimes our men—we, by the way, have conducted, perhaps not from choice but from necessity, a nonunion shop, because our men largely working in the field where there were no unions.

Commissioner WEINSTOCK. Do you employ any men now?

Mr. KINCAID. No; I resigned my position on the 1st of July of this year.

Commissioner WEINSTOCK. I take it, then, that you have been an observer of economic conditions and a student?

Mr. KINCAID. I have been an observer and a lover of it; yes, sir.

Commissioner WEINSTOCK. What is the remedy for these industrial troubles, as you see them? Do you believe that unionism is essential to the welfare of the workers?

Mr. KINCAID. Under the present conditions, yes; as deplorable as it may seem, without unions labor conditions would be more deplorable; the selfishness of the human, family will not permit working people to retain a living wage unless they do have unions, because of that same statement I made awhile ago about Mr. McCall—he is not a bad man—just a man who had the opinion that a dollar and a quarter a day was enough for a laborer; and that is, unfortunately, the sentiment held by many individuals.

· Commissioner WEINSTOCK. In view of your opinion, Mr. Kincaid, that unions are essential to the welfare of the worker, what remedy would you suggest for these industrial troubles? How would you minimize them? How would you meet them? How would you prevent them?

Mr. KINCAID. It looks to me very much as though Government control—I am not a Socialist by any means—but that Government control would be the only remedy unless it were that of broader education for both the employer and the employee.

Commissioner WEINSTOCK. You mean Government control for private enterprises?

Mr. KINCAID. Yes, sir; it looks to me as though——

Commissioner WEINSTOCK. Isn't that socialism pure and simple? .

Mr. KINCAID. It is as to that part of it, and to that extent possibly I may believe in socialism.

Commissioner WEINSTOCK. You mean you would have Government owned and operated enterprises in the country?

Mr. KINCAID. At least control these industrial conditions to such an extent that we should not have the necessity for these perpetual wars; and a commission that would do that would really be a part of those relationships of the human family which would be essential for our welfare and prosperity.

Commissioner WEINSTOCK. Well, experience shows, though, that even Government control does not prevent strikes and lockouts, that they occur in Europe where they operate the railroads and the post office and the telegraph and. telephone and all that sort of thing, and in Australasia they operate the street cars, and yet there have been strikes and lockouts among those very people—not lockouts, but strikes.

Mr. KINCAID. I still believe stringent measures preventing injustice on either side is possible by Government commission.

Commissioner WEINSTOCK. By Government commission?

Mr. KINCAID. Yes. Well, that is what I mean by Government control, by a commission.

Commissioner GARRETSON. Supervision.

Mr. KINCAID. Yes; supervision and control is still possible, and I believe it is possibly the only solution, because if you leave these matters to individual control we are too selfish yet. We may develop into it some time—I hope we will; but there should be a universal, brotherly love that should extend from the lowest laborer in the field to the highest capitalist, and it does not exist at the present time.

Commissioner WEINSTOCK. You have lived in Stockton 20 years?

Mr. KINCAID. Twenty-one years.

Commissioner WEINSTOCK. I presume you are fairly familiar with conditions there in the building trades and other industries?

Mr. KINCAID. Yes.

Commissioner WEINSTOCK. And you have doubtless heard the testimony here the building trades were thoroughly organized on the one side and the building contractors were not organized?

Mr. KINCAID. Yes.

Commissioner WEINSTOCK. And you may have heard the recital of all the different incidents which have occurred which, from the employer's point of view, were aggravated, were accumulative, until, according to their statement, it had reached the point where it had become unbearable, and they determined to throw off the yoke. Now, had there been a contractors' association that would recognize and deal with the unions so that these grievances could have been taken up one at a time and adjudicated so far as the present situation is concerned, do you think the present situation would have been brought about? In other words, if these grievances could have been settled when they happened, in place of being permitted to accumulate, would it have had—

Mr. KINCAID. There are so many conditions enter into that. Personally, I was in the planing-mill business for eight years in San Francisco. I had to do with contractors and building contractors' associations. I belonged to the millmen's association at that time, in San Francisco, and we were all new. We all had crude ideas. We proposed to regulate all kinds of matters, particularly the aggressive union matters. But we did not, for various reasons, principally in that case, perhaps, because of the fact that contractors are persons generally who have no financial interest at stake, like large manufacturers who have thousands and hundreds of thousands sometimes invested in their plant, and therefore the incentive to protect that investment was not present so strongly with these contractors. In other words, they were merely standing as between the consumer and the producer, the laborer to the house owner, and as to whether the unions demanded a greater or less amount did not enter into their calculations, unless they were interested in the human family to some extent. In other words, it didn't make any difference to them whether they paid $5 a day or $4 a day, because the consumer——

Commissioner WEINSTOCK. It was passed on.

Mr. KINCAID. Simply passed on. The consumer ultimately paid it. Therefore, there was no very strong fight made in our organization here as against the unions. I have never known a strong fight to be put up by contractors as against unions, and for that reason labor unions have been able, in my judgment, to make a great deal more progress in building-trade lines than along any other line where large amounts were involved in the matter of manufacturers' plants.

So far as your question now is concerned as to the possibility of those things being settled, there is almost as much selfishness on the one side as on the other, and whichever side gains the victory it would only be temporary. A victory means more aggressiveness, more demands on either side, I think—if that answers your question. This is simply my opinion, however.

Commissioner WEINSTOCK. It does not exactly answer my question.

Mr. KINCAID. If you will repeat it.

Commissioner WEINSTOCK. The thought I had in mind was this, Mr. Kincaid, whether in place of there being organization only on one side of the building trades there had been organization on both sides, so that these alleged grievances could have been taken up one at a time and adjudicated—whether it would have—whether the present situation would have been likely to have happened as it has? Would it not have prevented that?

Mr. KINCAID. If the result is to depend upon the strength of organization on both sides and it has got to be a case of the survival of the fittest as to which is the strongest. If this organization of the present business men of Stockton, that they call the M., M. and E., is strong enough to browbeat and frighten the unions, why probably the unions will accede to any demand that they may make. But, on the other hand, if the unions' organization is the strongest why they will make the other fellow lay down, as it were.

Commissioner WEINSTOCK. You heard the story or the illustration given here yesterday by Mr. Johannsen. I think the corresponding question was put to him. And in his own peculiar way he pointed out that when two fellows each had a stick of dynamite, that neither one would throw it; which I interpreted to mean that where both sides are organized they respect and deal with each other.

Mr. KINCAID. I think that is very apt, probably a very apt illustration, a deplorable one though it may be. Quite likely it would result in good. There is this much to it, however, I think that the citizenship of any community should expect more from its merchants and manufacturers than it should from the labor unions. In other words, I don't think that any community of business men or any set of business men have the moral right to organize, even though they have the financial power to do so, in a way that would browbeat the laborers. They have every advantage, that of environment and education, and every other advantage. They should be more generous, in my opinion, if opinion is of any use.

Commissioner WEINSTOCK. That is all.

Chairman WALSH. Do you want to ask any questions? Mr. Garretson would like to ask a question or two.

Commissioner GARRETSON. Mr. Kincaid, in answer to a question a moment ago, as to whether or not the employers hadn't taken a card from the employees' book in the methods that they had used, that you have described, what, in your opinion, would be the comparative power that the M., M. and E. association was able to exert in that direction as compared with the power that the union men could exert in the city of Stockton?

Mr. KINCAID. The power that they might exert is unlimited and deplorable.

Commissioner GARRETSON. You mean which?

Mr. KINCAID. That the power of the M., M. and E. with the financial backing of the banks, is unlimited and deplorable. There are few men in the city of Stockton, and I presume any other city, that would be situated just exactly as I am. I can come to you freely and express my opinion without fear or favor, for I have none to ask of any man.

Commissioner GARRETSON. You are absolutely independent of any kind of pressure?

Mr. KINCAID. Absolutely; of any kind of pressure from either side, and I will state I presume I occupy almost a unique position. I believe if this Mr. Eaves I spoke of was asked to come before you to-day to corroborate my statement, he would be afraid to do it.

Commissioner GARRETSON. On account of after results?

Mr. KINCAID. I believe he would. I don't know; he has not said so to me. I wish he would try it.

Commissioner GARRETSON. Then the real caliber of the two weapons is a 9-inch gun to a popgun?

Mr. KINCAID. Yes, sir.

Commissioner GARRETSON. Do you believe that that system is a fine illustration of what has been described by another as the invisible government?

Mr. KINCAID. I could not say. It seems to me to be the system prevailing in Stockton. I hope it does not prevail anywhere else, and never there again.

Commissioner GARRETSON. Do labor men conduct their campaign openly and without secrecy?

Mr. KINCAID. Up to five weeks ago I had not seen anything obnoxious other than those small and petty things that have annoyed individuals, and have at some times annoyed me.

Commissioner GARRETSON. Their campaign must, of necessity, where they use weapons of the boycott or anything of that kind, be open?

Mr. KINCAID. It is their only weapon; we recognize that fact.

Commissioner GARRETSON. And it is open and aboveboard?

Mr. KINCAID. It has been:

Commissioner GARRETSON. That is all.

Commissioner LENNON. Has the prosperity of the city of Stockton improved and increased as the unions have developed and have raised wages?

Mr. KINCAID. The city has; yes, sir. Now, I don't care to stand on record as saying that that was the sole cause of it, but as an illustration as to the prosperity——

Commissioner LENNON. As a matter of fact?

Mr. KINCAID. As a matter of fact, it has, whatever the cause may be:

Chairman WALSH. What was your illustration?

Mr. KINCAID. Eleven years ago a building in the city of Stockton was offered for sale. It had been occupied by the grangers' union, that had become defunct. A friend of mine in the real-estate business came to me and suggested that we go in together and buy that building, which was offered for $34,000, and in looking into it with him I found it had not paid interest hardly on $3,400 since the grangers' union had gone out of it. It was occupied in the upper story—it was a brick building, by the way, that cost nearly $60,000, and with its lot should have been reasonably worth close to $100,000. It was offered for $34,000 because of the conditions prevailing in Stockton at that time. There was no business for it. The only occupants in the building at that time were some artists and householders living in the upper story, which was not finished off, by the way. They had strung tents, or at least burlap, to partition off part of that, and were living up there and paying nominal rent. There was a little storage in the basement and that is all that was rented, and for that reason I refused to go into it.

That building has increased in value and still stands, and I venture to say that to-day $150,000 would not buy it. If I had it, it wouldn't. I didn't buy it.

Commissioner LENNON. Is it your experience that where the working class receives a high wage that the business men of the city are more or less prosperous than where they receive a less wage?

Mr. KINCAID. The business men of the city of Stockton have certainly been very much more prosperous during these last 10 years when men were getting fair wages than they ever were before. Men were able to buy and pay for shoes for their babies that could not have done so on the $2.50 that they formerly got.

Commissioner LENNON. I was going to ask you as a matter of opinion; I don't know that you will want to answer: Do you believe that if this contest goes on and should terminate disastrously to the unions, that the wages are liable to go down again?

Mr. KINCAID. If it were not purely a local matter, they would. Being local, however, the union men could leave, fortunately, and go somewhere else where conditions of that sort did not prevail.

Commissioner LENNON. Yes; but some one would take their places. What do you think the effect would be on their wages?

Mr. KINCAID. Undoubtedly they would be forced down. It is human nature to get the most you can apparently for the least money, and our business men of Stockton are not above that.

Commissioner LENNON. That is all.

Chairman WALSH. That is all, thank you.

Mr. THOMPSON. One more question, Mr. Chairman.

Chairman WALSH. Oh.

Mr. THOMPSON. Do you know if any bank in Stockton showed a disposition to call Mr. Martin's loans, if he had any?

Mr. KINCAID. I do not, except as was said by one banker there, that if he had the loan, as I have said, and had the power, he would put the screws to him.

Mr. THOMPSON. That is all.

Chairman WALSH. That is all, thank you, Mr. Kincaid. Call your next.

Mr. THOMPSON. Mr. Martin.

Mr. KINCAID. May I be excused now?

Chairman WALSH. You may be excused finally.

TESTIMONY OF MR. IRVING MARTIN—Recalled.

Mr. THOMPSON. Mr. Martin, you may resume your statement.

Mr. MARTIN. Gentlemen, I think it has been abundantly demonstrated that a state of organized warfare exists in the city of Stockton. I think the causes leading up to the situation have been pretty thoroughly gone into. I might add that, in my judgment, the reorganization of the directorate of the chamber of commerce which took place about a year ago, at the time that Mr. John P. Irish was elected as secretary—that the organizing for the fight which afterwards developed entered quite a little into the reorganization of that directorate. Up to the time that Mr. Irish became secretary of the chamber of commerce organized labor in the city of Stockton had had representation on the directorate of the chamber, the idea being that the chamber of commerce represented not merely the business life of the community but the collective life of the community, and that organized labor was entitled to representation on that body. And from that standpoint unionmen had been on the directorate for some years.

Mr. Irish personally told me that one of the considerations of his election as secretary was that no labor men were to be on the directorate. It is probably very apparent that before this situation developed into warfare, that a great many moves had been made in preparation for it. The formation of the association in August last and their declaration of principles which have been offered in evidence shows that that as one step leading up to the events which afterwards developed.

The boycott on the Sperry Flour Co.—and bear in mind that there have been two boycotts, one declared last year, and that trouble was settled before the present industrial warfare in Stockton commenced; and there is no connection, I don't believe, between the two boycotts. The recent boycott on the Sperry Co. dates back three or four weeks and is a separate matter from the boycott last year. But at the time of that boycott the Sperry Flour Co. made a very active fight and influenced to a great extent public sentiment, claiming that they were a large employer of labor, an institution of the city of Stockton, deserving of consideration; that they had been located there for a great many years and were a very prominent manufacturing enterprise. And they went pretty thoroughly into the matter, and a great deal of sentiment, I think, was developed along that line at that time against the use of the boycott.

Later on the trouble at the Hotel Stockton, which has already been developed in the testimony, where picketing was done and where the union pickets carried a banner depicting thereon a long-tailed rat, inflamed public sentiment again and was another cause which led up to the conflagration.

In other words, there were a great many moves made which entered into the trouble which finally commenced after the organization of the merchants and manufacturers' association had been fully perfected, after a great many months of work on the part of the organizer, Mr. L. S. Calkins.

Mr. Calkins was brought to Stockton and remained—had been there quite a few weeks before even the newspapers were aware of his presence. The organization was very carefully formed, and finally succeeded into gathering into its membership—I think their statement claims 90 per cent of the business and employers of Stockton. And there is no question but what they have that comprised in their membership.

The particular line of business that I am engaged in—I don't think any of the newspaper men were asked to join. Certainly I was not. And I don't think it would have been possible for any of the newspapers of Stockton to have joined and upheld the principles of the organization. In other words, I don't think it would be practically possible to run an open-shop newspaper in the city of Stockton at the present time.

After the formation of this organization, and just for the purpose of illustrating the great care and thoroughness with which the organization was formed and the success that they had in getting individuals and institutions in it, I desire to state that I am a director of a building and loan association— one of nine directors. They desired our association to join. Some of the directors did not desire the association—the building and loan association—to join the other association. And a very warm fight developed among the directorate, the members of which had been warm personal friends and business associates for years.

The building and loan finally affiliated with the M., M. and E. by vote of its directorate of 5 to 4, after a protracted and very acrimonious session. Speaking for myself personally, I very strongly opposed the going of our association into the merchants, manufacturers and employers' association, claiming that it was neither a manufacturer, a dealer in mercantile goods, nor an employer; that we largely dealt with the poorer class of people, the aim and object of our association being to loan money in small amounts to actual home builders, and that we had something like, I think, in the neighborhood of 50 loans at that time, the bulk of them being to small home owners.

However, the association entered the main association. One of the arguments made was that this was a broader matter than any individual or any association, and we all ought to be patriotic enough to join a movement which was for the benefit and interest of the city of Stockton.

Just there I wish to digress long enough to say that I feel that the majority of the members of the merchants, manufacturers and employers' association are sincere in their proposition that the association is for the benefit of the city. I think that they are entirely wrong in that viewpoint, but I think that they are sincere. I could wish that they would be as charitable in connection with myself.

A great many of the members of the association I think did not—I am satisfied did not—understand the objects of the association. I have had repeated discussions with members of the association who told me that the association was not for the open shop, and that it was not against the recognition of the union. And I am satisfied that when those members made those statements to me that they absolutely believed them—statements which it has subsequently developed, according to the testimony taken here, were at least erroneous.

My first connection—if that is the proper word to use—with the operations of the merchants and manufacturers' association came some time in last May. I was attending a picnic at Lockford in the northern part of San Joaquin County, and a gentleman friend of mine who is an active member of the M., M. and E.—and, by the way, I wish to state that in these matters I do not desire to embarrass anyone—a great many of the things that I get must necessarily come from friends who are allied with the other side and who tell me things in confidence, and whose confidence I could not betray.

Chairman WALSH. We will leave that to you whether to mention any of the names or not. Just go ahead.

Mr. MARTIN. Yes. This gentleman told me that he came—he took me aside from the picnic gathering. The picnic was held in a large grove of oak trees. He took me aside from the picnic gathering in his automobile and had a talk with me of about an hour's duration. He said he wanted to give me a tip; he didn't think that I knew what was going on, and that he wanted to warn me. He said: " A great deal of talking has been done by the members of the association in reference to the attitude of the newspapers." He said, " In this matter we propose to win. We are going to win. We are going to stop short at nothing." He said, " We don't see why, as merchants and as advertisers, we should give our support to those who are not with us in this fight." He also said that the association was so thoroughly organized that any one who owed obligations was on dangerous ground. To make a long story short, he emphasized in his talk with me the two things, advertising patronage and financial obligations, both of which apply very forcibly to my business enterprise. One of them is necessary for its continuance, and the other, owing to the organization of the business and the fact that about three years ago I put up a large building and put a very expensive plant in it, and still owe quite a little in the way of obligations, meant that the thing applied pretty emphatically to me.

I received other intimations from other friends to the same effect at various times. I was also told by this gentleman that the matter had been taken up and that a committee was going to call upon me to take the matter up with me. I asked him if I was the only newspaper concerned in the matter, and he said no, that all of them were going to be called upon the carpet.

In due course of time a committee of seven business men, all of whom are in the mercantile business, called upon me at my office, and, in the presence of my business manager and my advertising manager, had an extended conference with me.

One of their members had been selected as spokesman, and, at considerable length, but in a very rambling, indefinite way, talked along the line of patronage and what kept the newspapers going, and things of that kind, but made no specific statement and no specific threat. Other members of the committee then joined in the conversation, but none of them made any specific statement.

After listening to them and getting from them whatever they had to offer, I made my reply and told them that I had heard a great deal of certain things that were going to be done, by individuals telling me so; but that their committee had not specifically touched upon them, but that I presumed they knew at that time that those things had come to my knowledge, and that in my reply I would make the reply the same as if they had come through with their statements.

< The only specific thing that they had touched upon in their statements was that they desired me to attend a meeting to be held at the Hotel Stockton on a Wednesday evening. The date of this conference with me was on a Monday morning. I joshed with them and told them I was very pleased to meet them as individuals, but I could not understand why seven men, who were presumably all busy, should leave their places of business and come to my office for the purpose of inviting me to attend a meeting, when one of them might have done it over the phone.

' I then told them I was glad to meet them and to meet them in conference. I was glad to get their ideas and suggestions, but that I was going to be a little bit more frank with them than I thought they had been with me. I told them that if I went into their places of business and undertook to tell them the conduct and policy of their stores had been wrong—they had intimated that to me about the policy of the paper, but not making any definite proposition—and if I undertook to tell them that they were conducting their stores wrong they would know I didn't know anything about the mercantile business, and, furthermore, that I would not have any right to come to them and interfere with their business and they would probably politely tell me so and invite me to leave the store.

' I told them that when they came to me in a line of business that is a very peculiar one, and which, I think, isn't very generally well understood by men in the mercantile business, that they were then speaking to me about a business which I knew that they knew nothing about, and that I must reserve the right to conduct the business according to my best judgment, presumably the same way they were conducting their stores; and, in order to forestall any future trouble, which I at that time instinctively felt was approaching, I told them that, come what might, I must continue to run my business according to the best of my judgment.

I want to say that from my own standpoint—and not from theirs, possibly—that I had been endeavoring to steer a clear course in the industrial warfare which was then developing in the city of Stockton. My interests are all there; my home has been there and will continue to be there; my friends and associates have been to a large extent naturally among the same people that were in this organization. I have been intimately associated with them in fraternal. social, and political matters and all matters that enter into a community life. There is not anything that I wouldn't do if I could do it from my standpoint—and I must be the judge of that—to remain in touch with those men.

But that in this matter, which I thought I saw was going in certain directions, I thought I saw what would be the ultimate outcome of it, and, seeing, as I thought I did, far beyond what they saw; knowing I would have to align myself; knowing where my sympathy would be and where it must be in the final show-down in any matter of that character, I wanted once and for all to place myself where they would have no occasion in the future to misunderstand me. I thought I did succeed in doing so.

In the course of this conference a great many matters were gone into and the conference ended very satisfactorily to us. Some things were brought out and discussed, which they said they were glad had been brought out; and all left the office feeling better and said they thought we would be able to get along all right.

That same committee, I afterwards ascertained, called upon the other newspapers of Stockton and presumably had talks with them.

The situation continued for a while with all of the newspapers attempting to do all they could in the papers at that time not to incur the ill will or displeasure of either side. That I know was my endeavor, and from a newspaper standpoint, I could see very plainly that it was the endeavor of the other newspaper publishers.

But it appeared that that course was not satisfactory, and I don't know just how long, but probably two or three weeks after this initial conference all the newspapers of Stockton were summoned to appear before a meeting held in one of the rooms of the Hotel Stockton at which there were about twenty of the business men present. members of the M., M. and E., with one member presiding as chairman; and at that meeting, from a newspaper standpoint, there were present J. L. Phelps, C. L. Ruggles of the Independent; Cyril Nunan of the Mail and M. G. Woodward of the Mail; Dave S. Matthews and myself from the Record. There are three daily newspapers in Stockton, and this conference comprised the editors and publishers of the three newspapers.

The conference was quite an extended one. The burden of complaint that they advanced to us was that we hadn't given them, to use the current slang expression, "fifty-fifty"; that they felt they were not getting a fair shake in the news columns of the newspapers. At this time no Stockton paper had contained a line of editorial on the situation. None of the Stockton papers, with the exception of the Record, have yet contained editorial views on the situation. They complained specifically of the publicity that was being given to the union side of the matter and instanced particularly a meeting held under union auspices where a women's label league was formed. This meeting was reported in all the newspapers to the extent, I think, of something like a column and a half. It detailed the speeches that were made and the complete formation of that organization.

This organization, by the way, was formed for the purpose—I guess boycott would be the right word to use for it—for the purpose of boycotting the stores that did not display the union card. They said—the employers said at this conference, "you should not give publicity to the union, it is having a bad effect. We are your advertising patrons; these people are not patronizing us, and therefore you should not lend encouragement to them." Up to that time the association had not desired very much in the way of publicity. The city editor of our paper, and I presume that was true of the others, found great difficulty in getting anything at all from the authorized members of the association, and, by the way, I wish to state here that I have never in my experience known of any association or organization that has been enabled to so effectively guard secrecy as this M., M. and E. association. It is certainly an eye opener to the newspaper men of Stockton, the way they have been able to keep their affairs pretty close.

But we tried. The city editor would repeatedly come to me and say, "I can't get anything from them," and was very much put out at it. I instructed him very emphatically to telephone to headquarters every day, never to let a day slip by, and to state he had telephoned, and if they had nothing to give to make that statement in the paper that they had nothing to give. I was doing that in an endeavor to try, as I said before, to steer a middle course.

On the other hand, the union representatives went out of their way to come to the newspaper offices and give statements of their doings. They made it a point to cultivate the city editors and reporters and give them their statements.

Mr. Calkins, in his treatment of the reporters of the Record, was very arbitrary, and as they told me, insulting; and I am satisfied that later on, in the development of the situation, that some of those human interest incidents entered into matters in such a way that, possibly unknowingly to themselves, the reporters, to a certain extent, might have been a little bit prejudiced or biased in favor of the unions; because their representatives, as I said before, made every effort to give them news and to keep in touch with them. I endeavored to get the reporters to be careful in verifying statements, but I fear that the person who comes and gets in touch with the reporters and treats them halfway decently, if there is such a thing as getting the best of the shake, is likely to get it.

Now, to go back to this conference again: After considerable discussion I put this thing specifically to the chairman of the meeting. I said, "Isn't it a fact that up to the present time this association has not desired publicity, and not desiring publicity yourselves, you do not desire the other side to have it?" I repeated the statement, and said, "If that statement isn't true, isn't right, I want it challenged." I wanted to get somewhere in the conference, and I wanted to get a basis. "If that isn't true, let us have an understanding."

The statement was not challenged, and by the smiles and nods of their heads the conclusion, I think, was warranted that they admitted the corn. In other words, that their complaint had been against the newspapers, that the newspapers were giving publicity to the union side and that they thought the newspapers should not give the publicity to that side.

The matter of advertising was gone into, and they specifically stated that the typographical union had passed a resolution assessing a fine of $25 on any member of the union who traded at any store not displaying a union card. Up to that time I had not heard of that action. The action was taken at the meeting of the union, and we promised this conference of business men we would take the matter up with our employees and see if we could not get that resolution rescinded.

The endeavor was made to get it rescinded, and Mr. George A. Tracy, president of the San Francisco Typographical Union, made a visit to Stockton and the matter was taken up with him and reported back to us to this effect: "We don't thing that the matter cuts much figure. We could rescind the resolution imposing the fine of $25," he said, "but we could not get our members to trade at those stores."

That conference broke up about the same as the other conference had, with the business men stating they were glad the conference had been held and they thought they had accomplished something.

A week or so after that conference a gentleman came to my office one afternoon and inquired for the managing editor, and some of my staff were talking with me, and they waved their hands at me, and he wanted to know if I was editor of the paper, and I told him I was. He said, "My name is Bailey." I said, "Pleased to meet you, Mr. Bailey." He said, "I want to summon you to attend a meeting to-night," at what I thought he said was the executive committee of the M., M and E. It later on developed in the conversation that it was the strike committee, and that interested me mightily. And I said, "By the way, Mr. Bailey, I haven't had the pleasure of meeting you before; how long have you been here?" He said, "Two or three weeks." And I said, "Well, just what is your connection with the association?" And he said "Well, I am adviser and counselor." I said, "Well, what do you do?" "Well," he said, "I am adviser and counselor, and that is what I do." I said, "Where do you come from, Mr. Bailey?" He said, "From Portland." And I was greatly puzzled about the matter, and I said, "Did you ever have anything to do with the printing business?" He says, "Oh, yes; that is my business, I have had something to do with it."

We had a general discussion about the printing business. And in the course of the conversation he spoke about having on tap five or six nonunion linotype operators that he was in touch with, and so forth. I said, "You don't have any idea that anything of that kind could be done in the city of Stockton." I had heard the intimation—had been told by friends that discussions were being had about the starting of another paper in the city, and so forth, or the buying of one of the papers then issued. I said. "You don't have any idea that would have any bearing on the Stockton association, that you could do anything like that in Stockton, do you?" He said, "I do. We could put all these papers on a nonunion basis within two weeks." I said, "I beg to differ with you there. I don't think that could be done. But," I said, "I don't see that that has anything to do with this other matter." I said, "I had intended to-night to attend a political meeting at which Mr. Keesling, candidate for governor, speaks in Stockton." He said, "That is unfortunate," and, he said, "This matter to-night is a very important one, and you better attend." I said, "What is the object of the meeting to-night?" He said, "I am not at liberty to divulge it." I said, "Well, I think I have met all of these gentlemen before on two occasions and gone over matters with them, so I do not see that any good purpose could be served by going over it again." He said, "No; you have not met this committee before." I said, "Well, all right, who are they?" He said, "Well, I am not at liberty to state." He then said, "You will be present at the conference, will you?" I said, "I don't think I shall, Mr. Bailey. I won't say positively. I will think it over this afternoon. If I thought that was a conference of citizens of Stockton, considering some matter of general interest to the city, and they desired my cooperation or counsel, I would be pleased to go. I would be pleased to attend any meeting of that kind. But if it is a matter of my meeting some gentlemen who propose to tell me how they think I ought to conduct my business, and intimating to me what is liable to happen to me if I don't conduct it as they think I ought to, why I don't think that it would be a good thing, either for me or them, for me to attend that conference." He said, "Well, if you are not there to-night, I will report that you are attending a political meeting." I said, "You will report nothing of the kind. If I am not there, it will be because I don't care to go."

After he left the office I got to thinking the matter over, and, after waiting a little while, I telephoned to the offices of the other two Stockton papers, the Mail and the Independent—oh, by the way, I had asked him if I was the only one of the newspaper publishers that were summoned to this conference. He said no; they were all going to be included. I telephoned to the other newspaper offices and found that he had been to each of their places making the same request that he had to me. Three of them—that is, the two Nunan brothers, of the Mail; Mr. Ruggles, of the Independent; and myself—met at Mr. Ruggles's office pursuant to our telephonic conversation. And we compared notes and told each other what he had said to each of us, and he had said some things to the others which he hadn't said to me, and we were all quite a little stirred up over the matter; we had all been, from our standpoint, taking extraordinary pains both to give the news and keep clear of trouble. We got stirred up and decided that the time had about arrived for us to refuse to accept service of summons, and we decided not to go, and none of us did.

The next morning about 10 o'clock I was telephoned to by a merchant, a friend of mine, and he said: "You weren't at that meeting last night." I said, "What meeting is that?" "Oh," he said, "you know what meeting I mean." He said, "You ought to have been there." He said, "You don't know what is going to be the result." He said, "I think if you understood that you would have been there." I said, "I don't get the point." He said, "Quit that. You know what I mean." "Now," he said, "we are going to admit that possibly we got off wrong; that we got at that in the wrong way." And he says, "Therefore, forget that, and we will start in over." He said, "Will you take lunch with us to-day?" I said, 'Am I to be the sole guest of honor?" He said, "No; all the others." I said, "Yes; if the other newspaper men will be there, I will come." He told where the meeting was to be held; where the luncheon was to take place, Mr. Ruggles, Mr. Cyril Nunan and myself took lunch with the strike committee of the M., M and E. We spent about two hours in conference with them, after the luncheon had been disposed of, Mr. Ruggles having departed by that time and Mr. Nunan and myself remaining. Mr. Totten, who testified on the stand that he was chairman of the strike committee, presided. I do not feel free to go into the membership of the committee any farther, but since Mr. Totten has admitted that he was chairman of the committee, I see no particular harm in mentioning that fact.

The discussion hinged upon the same proposition. In other words, the news reports in the papers, that the news reports were not fair to the M., M. and E., that they were being colored and biased and in favor of the union. We went over the thing quite extensively, and, finally, a suggestion was made that a publicity committee be appointed to give the newspapers each day whatever there was of news from the association standpoint to be given out. They stated that they would appoint that committee, and subsequently we were informed that Mr. Totten was a member of that committee.

I wish to state right here that from a newspaper standpoint in the conduct of the news of this situation, that at the outset I gave the city editor these instructions: That the proposition was a ticklish one, and he would have to be very careful; that almost any statement or occurrence that he reported would be the subject of misconstruction and misinterpretation, and would be pulled to pieces by either side. I warned him that he must get specific statements signed, or use quotation marks if we quoted anybody. That that policy would have to be absolutely adhered to. That he could not say that "it was said," "it was a report," or "it is reported," etc.; that he must pin things upon pegs; that somebody would have to stand for the statements. That policy was adhered to for awhile. And it led to this result—and, by the way, that policy was followed in the main by the other papers—it led to this result:

That Mr. Totten, or Mr. Calkins for the association, whoever it might be, would put forth statements, long, signed statements; then Mr. Dale, or some of the other union side, or Mr. Woods, Mr. True Woods—and it early developed into a proposition of each side jockeying back and forth for position, and both sides coming through with statements, placing their own interpretation on things, and endeavoring to place the other side in wrong. It got to be a farce from that standpoint.

Finally it got to be intolerable from the newspaper standpoint, and one day when trouble developed at the Commercial Bank, which is the largest building being erected in Stockton at the present time—a 10-story building—they had some trouble there over some lumber that was delivered—Mr. Totten came through with a statement from the employers' side, and Mr. True Woods from the union side; and Mr. Reynolds, city editor of the Record, brought the statements in and handed them to me. The statements, it appeared to me, were an attempt to jockey, each side endeavoring to place the other in wrong.

I told Mr. Reynolds, I said, "You go down to the job, you find the foreman, the superintendent, or somebody, and ask him what actually happened."

He went down there and came back, and he said, "Well, I didn't get much."! He said, "I found there a man named Murphy that was a foreman, and Murphy §ays, 'Now, here, we didn't have any trouble here.' He said, 'There was a little misunderstanding, but it .was all straightened out, and work is going on on the job.' "

I said to Mr. Reynolds, "You publish just that." I took the two statements that had been lying on my desk, tore them up, and threw them in the waste-basket.· I said, "Hereafter, in handling this situation, you get your own size-up of what took place, get it as correctly as you can, and publish it just that way. But in the future disregard any signed statements from anyone that seem to be in their nature designed to provoke more trouble and more bitterness and to jockey for position; absolutely disregard them, but try to get the facts as near straight as you can." And that has been adhered to since.

I want to refer again to the fact, and I want to make that plain and em-phatic, that I do not claim that it has been humanly possible for a newspaper to handle this situation and be entirely fair. I am willing to admit, as I stated before, that possibly the human equation coming in, with the union men trying to give their situation to the reporter, that they may have got a little bit the best of it. But I don't think that referred to the acts of violence which developed later on, because in that matter I think that they have been as fairly set forth and with as little desire to ·provoke trouble as would be possible to observe and still give the news. At least that has been our design.

. Now, to go back again to this conference with the strike committee, at the time that they were going to appoint a publicity committee.

After the luncheon was over, and sitting around the table we had quite a free and easy talk. In that conference the whole burden of the talk seemed to be little troubles, little petty annoyances that different members of the committee had been subjected to in the conduct of their businesses. One man would tell his trouble; another man would tell his; another man would tell his. That was the whole burden of the talk. It was not a proposition of endeavoring to straighten them out, to get at and settle them, but first one man and then another—it was not an endeavor to get at them as between man and man, but it was to bring up those things and magnify them, and have a sort of mutual sympathizing association. I rather chafed under that, because it is rather—it makes me rather impatient to—for instance, for men in mercantile lines of business to talk to me about union troubles. They don't know any-thing about this from my standpoint. I have got four of them in my line of business; the typographical, the pressmen, the stereotypers, and the book-binders. Two of them are not local unions; Sacramento claims jurisdiction over the bookbinders and stereotypers. I have had some union troubles in the conduct of my own business. I know what the annoyances are, etc. And to have merchants tell me about union troubles where they just employ a few clerks—oh, well, it was something that made me, as I said, rather impatient.

But, however, after getting through that they then put me on the grill and told me I didn't understand the situation—men that I had known for years, chummed with, been raised with, and so forth. They said, "Now, here, you don't understand this situation. If you did understand it you would look at it just the same as we do." I told them it was probably true I didn't understand the situation; that I had a few business details to handle and did not have all my time for study, and thought, and reading, but I thought I understood some-thing about general industrial conditions; I was willing to admit I didn't understand all that might be known about it. They kept repeating that until it kind of got of my nerves—"that I didn't understand, and if I did understand I would .look at it just the same as they did." Finally a member of the com-mittee whom, as I said before, I have known from boyhood, sitting right by me said, "Now, here, you have got a mistaken idea about this. You think we intend to lower wages." I said, "I never thought anything of the kind; I have never said anything of the kind, either· personally or through the paper." "Well," he said, "but you think so." I said, "I don't see what right you have to say I think so." "Well," he said, "you do." He said, "You don't under-stand it." I said, "Well, I don't care to discuss the matter with you. I have got my own ideas of what brought up wages; I have also got my ideas of what might happen under certain conditions; but I don't see that that is relevant to the matter, and I don't care to go into it." He said. "Well, all right." He said, "When I drew up that resolution "—the resolution they drew up setting forth their platform, their declaration about not lowering wages—

he' said, "That resolution, I drew that, and I drew it carefully and I drew it' right." He said, "It was a hard resolution to draw." He said, "We could not in that resolution put anything which could be construed as a recognition of unionism."

That got a rise out of me. Up to that time they had been endeavoring to tell me that they were not against unionism; that they were not for the open shop except only in so far as they had been compelled to declare for it; and I tried to tell—I had tried to tell them that their original declaration of principles meant the open shop, freedom of contract, and so forth, and it has since been admitted here on the stand that it did mean just that; but individually they had been telling me that it did not mean that, claiming they were friendly to unions and just simply wanted to straighten out some of the exactions. By the way, if they have endeavored to straighten out any of the arbitrary features of unionism they have done so without my knowledge. It has not been made public. But that made me hot, and I broke out and gave them some of my own ideas on the situation. I told them it was perfectly plain to me why they could not understand me, and that I didn't think I would be able to make them understand me; that being an employer, such as they were, not taking just the same view of it that they did, that they undoubtedly considered me a traitor to my class. They have acted as though they did consider me that. I said, "The reason for it is that you do not seem to be able to comprehend that a man who is a newspaper men has got two sides—that he is an employer, a business man, the same as yourselves, and, in addition to that, he has a newspaper capacity—and very often, as a newspaper man, he may do the very things that may be in direct conflict with his selfish personal business interests. As a newspaper man he is a sort of receptacle for all the things that go on in the community; the crimes, the hopes, the aspirations, the struggles, and everything that enters into the make-up of the community life pour in every day into the newspaper office, and if a man is a newspaper man at all those things enter into his very life; they enter into and unconsciously color his conduct of the newspaper, and when a newspaper is put forth it is no longer—it has not the ideas simply of the man running it, but it is a reflex of whatever enters into and affects the life of the community; and if it is not that, then it is not what the public have a right to expect from a newspaper."

I told them that and some other things along that line. And when I got through they waited awhile and then said, "Well, we didn't know before that you were a Socialist." I said, "Well, I am not." They said, "Well, that looks like as if you were." That conference—because I went a whole lot further than that, I don't care to go further into that in detail, but I went pretty far—that conference then was the last conference that they ever held with me. After stewing about that for a day or two, I told Mr. Banks, my editorial writer, that I guessed it was no longer possible to keep quiet on the situation; that the time had arrived from a newspaper standpoint when it would be absolutely cowardly to longer remain silent, and that we must have something editorially to say on the subject. An editorial was framed up which made a plea for a settlement through arbitration; a plea that both sides to the controversy get together, put aside their paid agents and talk to each other as man to man and try to bring about an adjustment of the intolerable conditions. The publication of that editorial, of course, so far as the record was concerned, placed it, from the employers' standpoint, beyond the pale. That evening at my home I received a telephone message from one of the prominent members of the strike committee who said he wanted to know if I could see him if he came out to the house, and I told him yes. He came out to the house and we had a talk about the editorial, because that is what he wanted to see me on. He said, "That editorial has done a great deal of harm." I said, "Well, I am sorry if it has. I don't think it has. I don't think that it could be possible to do any' more harm than has already been done." He said, "Well, you will find that it will result in a great deal of harm." "However," he said, "I wanted to see you on that. I gathered from that editorial that it was inspired." I said, "What do you mean by inspired?" He said, "Well, you have been in conference with the labor men."

I want to digress here again just a moment and state that friends of mine, members of the M., M. and E., have told me that it has been reported among the members that I have been in constant touch with Mr. Johannsen, and that I have daily secret conferences with the labor forces, and that they have affidavits to that effect.

I desire to state that I have had no conference with Mr. Johannsen. I scarcely know the man. He comes to the office and talks with the city editor. Probably before I saw him on the witness stand here and studied his face I would not have known him on the street. I have held no conference whatever with any labor representatives, unless by conference would be construed a visit to my office My Mr. Dale or Mr. Griffin, or somebody like that. Mr. Dale **was there** frequently in the early stages of this trouble and talked with the **city editor,** and would come into my room.

The door of my room stands open. I am pretty accessible to the public. Anyone can come there and talk with me at any time. Whatever talking I have had with them has been right there. I have never in my own home, in any place outside of my office, or anywhere, held any conference with any labor leaders.

Therefore, when this gentleman told me that the editorial was inspired, that he understood that I was in conference with the labor leaders, I simply told him that I didn't understand what he meant by being inspired. He said, "Well. I think that that was put forth by the labor men as a feeler for a settlement." I said, "Get that idea out of your mind. No labor man or anybody else knew anything about it." The copy for the editorial was turned over to the foreman with instructions to give it to one of the linotype operators and keep the copy so that nobody would see it; that as soon as the editorial was in type, to bring the copy and the proof of it immediately into my room and take the linotype matter itself and put it away so that nobody could see it; that I wanted nobody to know anything about the editorial until it appeared in the paper.

The gentleman told me that the editorial would do a great deal of harm. And he said, "I think that you will find that the more it is studied into and thought over by either side, the more you will find that neither side is pleased by it." And I shot back at him that if that was true, it would be the best proof possible to my mind that the editorial was about right.

He then went into things rather elaborately and told me about different conferences that had been held between members of his association and members of the unions. He is a man that I have known for years and years. His word is absolutely truthful. He was not on this stand in this investigation. He would say to me, "Now, you believe me when I tell you a thing, don't you?" I would say, "Absolutely, no question about it at all." So he put up to me things from his standpoint, what he had said and done, and what had been said and done, and then wanted to know if I didn't believe him. And I replied every time that I did believe him. Then when he got through with this statement, after having put the things up to me and my having affirmed that I believe what he said, he said, "Now, don't you see it?" I said, "I don't see it. Do you want me to tell you something on the other side?" He said, "I don't care to hear it." I said, "All right, nothing more to be said."

The conference ended in that way. In other words, in that conversation came out the point that because I could not see things just as he saw them, because he is truthful and honest in his attitude, etc., why, then, if I could not agree with him, why there must be something wrong.

After that editorial we continued along the line of the news situation——

Chairman WALSH. You are not talking quite loud enough.

Mr. MARTIN. How is that?

Chairman WALSH. You are not talking quite loud enough.

Mr. MARTIN. We continued along the lines of the news situation, and when the acts of violence developed, again a very serious problem from a newspaper standpoint was presented.

I wanted to give the news, but I didn't want to do anything that would create more trouble. I didn't want to send out to the outside world the real seriousness of the conditions in Stockton. So when the first outbreak of trouble came at the Totten & Brandt planing mill, it came in the afternoon or evening at quitting time. Our paper is an evening paper. The occurrence was reported the next morning in the morning paper, the Independent, and in great big headlines they used the words "riot," "bloodshed," and it jarred me. And I told Mr. Reynolds, our city editor, I said, "Be very careful in your statement, and especially in your headings. Don't use the word 'riot.'" He said, "Well, what shall I use?" I said, "Well, use something else; use 'trouble'; use 'encounter'; use any word that you want to; but don't use 'riot.'" I said, "Stockton is getting hit badly enough at the present time, and we don't want to do anything to aggravate the situation, and especially we don't.want to have it go abroad what condition of affairs the city is in at the present time."   , .

Now, in the matter of the violence, taking the different things that have happened, and not handling them personally from a newspaper standpoint, and with my main attention being given to other matters,·I am prepared to say that I am not competent to give just the best opinion in the world in regard to the extent of the violence. But so far as my opinion does go, I want to record it to this extent, that I don't think that the features of violence are as bad as has been represented on the stand here, or as they are generally understood to be.

The encounters have not got beyond the stage of fistic encounters to a general extent—I don't mean the grabbing up of a chair or something in that way. And in the present disturbed conditions in the city of Stockton, with 900 men either òn strike or locked out, with other people from the outside taking their jobs, I think the situation is not as bad along that line as it might be. .

Inevitably, idleness and bitterness and whisky are going to cause more or less trouble. And that has been the groundwork of the trouble there. If you have got 900 idle men whose hearts are filled with bitterness, and if you have·got people on the other side whose hearts are filled with bitterness, and if you have got other people coming in and taking their positions, etc., why, it is inevitable that there will be more or less trouble. And I don't think you could get peace officers enough on the job to prevent more or less trouble.

And, by the way, the trouble possibly is not much worse than some troubles that we have nearly every night. There are men beaten up in the saloons there, and so forth, through liquor every night, and not much attention is paid to it. But where you have that combination, as I said before, of idle men whose hearts are filled with bitterness, and with open saloons on every hand, you are going to have trouble.

I want to say further, in my opinion, and I think I can say this with fairly good grace, because I fought very strenuously personally and from a newspaper standpoint, against the present administration in the city of Stockton—tried very hard to get the chief of police out of his job—still trying. I .think, from that standpoint at least, that I would be unprejudiced.

But I want to state that I think they have handled the situation pretty fairly well. It has been published in the newspapers that a policeman has been caught in the crime of playing cards and eating watermelon with pickets. Now, if that condition made for peace rather than for trouble, and I think it did, I don't see any particular harm in it. But it was thought.to be an awful condition of affairs by some.excellent gentlemen in our city.

Now, all the time that those things were going on there have been individual friends coming to me and telling me about the things that were being.said privately in reference to the boycott on the Record, and what was going to be done to it. And as an illustration, just to show you how prevalent these things were in the community, one Sunday evening—I had been at home during the day and I hadn't been feeling very well—I was telephoned to by one of our linotype operators. He said, " We want you to come down town. We want to meet you to-night, you and the other newspaper men, on a very important matter." He said, " We want you to meet the executive committee of the typographical union." I said, " Well, can't you wait until the morning? I am not feeling very well and I would rather take it up then." He said, " No; it is too important a matter. We have got to see you to-night." I said, " Well, if it is that important I will come down." I put my clothes on and went down to the Record office, and meanwhile he had arranged a meeting with the other newspaper men, Mr. Ruggles of the Independent, Mr. Numan of the Mail, Mr. Seaver, my business manager, and myself. We met the executive committee of the typographical union. The chairman of the committee stated to us ,that they had met that day and that they had knowledge and information that our advertisers were going in a body to discontinue their advertising. The union men·had got considerably worked up over it, and said if that thing took place that they would be willing to work as long as necessary for nothing, even if they had to draw strike benefits from their international union.

We thanked the men for that offer, but told them we could not believe that things were that serious, and we questioned the correctness of their·view, of their size-up of the situation. They maintained that they had got.it and got it straight, and that that thing was going to be done. And I still maintained that I thought they were wrong;.that while some advertisers might withdraw, and while they had a right to do it as individuals, and the right could not be ques⁻

tioned—and can't be questioned—that I didn't think the thing was as serious as they stated, and I didn't think the business men would do that.

But all the time I heard these reports of threats; and friends of mine came to me and told me that there was a very serious condition, that I ought to change the policy of the paper. Meanwhile after this violence, the first outbreak at Totten & Brandt's, we took another editorial stand on the matter. The first editorial stand was for peace and arbitration—setlement. We then took a strong editorial stand for the maintenance of order, for peace first and arbitration afterwards, making the editorial just as strong as I think it could be written.

Later on we took another editorial stand, that was for the free expression of opinion on the part of the paper, setting forth that we thought that later on, when the trouble was over, that some of the business men themselves would be fair-minded enough to admit that what they had attempted to do in controlling the publicity of the paper in its tendency, would be more harmful in its effect—if they could succeed in coloring the news or of controlling the publicity—it would be a very bad condition of affairs in the community. We also set forth that the two mediums of public expression, the newspapers and the pulpit—that no attempts should be made to restrain them.

Those are the only three things that we have advanced editorially, arbitration, the maintenance of order, the free expression of opinion. There has never been any article, either editorial or local, in the paper, that I think anyone could have a reasonable right to object to. We have not criticized, we have not abused the members of the association. We have not gone further into the matter than the three things that I have told you.

I also do not object to stating the reason why we have not gone further. And the reason is this: In the present inflamed condition of the public mind there, realizing that possibly there might be more trouble, more violence, not desiring the union men to be able to take anything that we have written or published, as an encouragement or as an incitement, we have carefully refrained from giving them any chance or any hope or encouragement by thinking that we were absolutely with them in this matter.

What we have done has been from the desire to be fair, to recognize that they have rights, and that the employers have rights, and that any settlement that is brought about must be a settlement with honor on both sides. If it is not a settlement of that kind that it will not be a settlement. That if either side is absolutely to be licked to a standstill by the other, that then the "industrial equilibrium" which these gentlemen having been pleading so strongly for, or have been endeavoring to bring about, will not be brought about. Because my idea of unionism is that the union man views his union as something very vital and very essential—that they would sacrifice anything for it, almost their lives; that their women folks feel just the same about it—in fact, I think, more intensely.

I get that from all directions. It pours into me personally in talks, letters, telephonic communications, and so forth, from men and women of the city, many of whom I know. I have listened to their conversations and talk among themselves as I ride on the street cars or as I get around in public places, and I am satisfied that they believe that unionism is very vital to them.

And as they believe that, I believe that they have the same right to do everything that they can to protect that right, and that it is just as much their province and their duty and their right to protect it as it is the part of the business man to protect his business; that the job of a workman is just as important as the $100,000 business of a business man; that it is entitled to just as much consideration from the Government and from the community.

And it is pursuant to those ideas and those thoughts that I have been endeavoring to conduct the paper. The incident that Mr. Kincaid has related here this afternoon in reference to the banker, he came and told me that. And while I have heard other things, and so forth, I don't believe anyone will go to the extent of doing the things that were threatened or intimated there. Certainly, up to the present time, nobody has attempted to disturb me along financial lines. Quite a little advertising has been withdrawn from the paper, but I concede it to be the right of the merchant and business man to withdraw it. It has not been done as a concerted action; it has been done individually. Just along the line of the financial part of it, but just a little by way of explanation, I desire to state that in the operation of my business and the building of it up and the putting up of a building and installing the plant and so forth, I became rather heavily involved. I have been in the process of paying for those obligations, but still owe some, and I will admit it is a very tender, vital matter with me.

I have endeavored to keep absolute faith with the people I borrowed money from, and I borrowed it in considerable quantities; and I think up to the present time, and irrespective of this present trouble—I feel that that condition will be true when the present trouble is settled as it must be—that I may still be in the confidence and good graces of those people who in times past had confidence enough in me to loan me money in large quantities. I have certainly tried in every way to repay that confidence. I would have done anything I could have done at the present time to remain in touch with them, but I have and must continue to do the thing I think ought to be done from a newspaper standpoint.

Now, I have gone over those things, and I appreciate the work you gentlemen have on hand, the importance of it, and the burden it is to you to give up your time to these matters; and if there is anything, any questions I can answer, or anything to further enlighten the situation, I would be very pleased indeed to do it. I haven't mentioned names because, as I said before, I don't wish to embarrass anyone. Whatever trouble I have now or may have in the future, I will try and meet it as best I can.

Chairman WALSH. That is a very full and complete statement, and I thank you for it. There are no questions?

Mr. THOMPSON. There are some questions I want to ask.

Commissioner WEINSTOCK. One question.

Chairman WALSH. Commissioner Weinstock would like to ask some questions.

Commissioner WEINSTOCK. As a student of economic problems, what is your remedy? What suggestion have you to make to this commission as to how to deal with the situation such as you are laboring under at Stockton? How could that be prevented and minimized?

Mr. MARTIN. I don't feel that I am able to advise you, Mr. Weinstock. I feel you and the other gentlemen of the commission are better posted than I am about such matters, and I have simply given you my ideas of the situation there.

Commissioner WEINSTOCK. The only way we can hope to be able to handle the problem is by getting the advice and suggestions and opinions of men whose opinions are worth having. We value your opinion and would be very glad to have it.

Mr. MARTIN. I will tell you what I think has got to be done as a basis. I can't tell you how to do it, but before anything can be accomplished at all, you have got to do away with the bitterness and get a better feeling into the hearts and minds of men than exists at this time. I can't tell you how to do it, but it has to be done before anything can be accomplished. Our local situation is a very deplorable one; it arrays brother against brother and father against son. One brother is in business and the other brother belongs to the union. It is certainly a very bad condition and can only be remedied by doing away with the feeling of bitterness which exists at the present time.

Commissioner WEINSTOCK. Among the suggestions which have come to the commission from various sources is one for the creation and maintenance of a Federal industrial commission, a permanent Federal industrial commission very much along the line of the present mediation board that deals with railroad labor troubles. Do you think any such permanent commission would be an advantage or would be a possible remedy?

Mr. MARTIN. I think so, Mr. Weinstock. I believe so and hope so; certainly something has got to be done, and certainly that ought to be tried.

Commissioner WEINSTOCK. If there was such a Federal commission in existence at this time, how could it have been of service in the Stockton situation?

Mr. MARTIN. I think it could have been of service in the Stockton situation, Mr. Weinstock, by the creation of public opinion.

For instance, in the Stockton situation, according to the statement of the M., M., and E., they claim a membership, I think somebody testified yesterday, of 403. I don't know the strength of the unions in Stockton, but probably two or three thousand or thereabouts.

Now, the population of the city of Stockton, including the city proper and the suburbs which are a part of the city, is probably in the neighborhood of 40,000. In other words, there is a great third party involved in this matter whose interest is absolutely being lost sight of by the combatants, but whose interest is very vital and whose interest ought to be considered; and that great third party, if it had proper organization and a rallying force and directing force such as this commission could be, to shape up public sentiment, would probably have a very wholesome influence on the members of the union, so far as their arbitrary actions and restrictions are concerned, and also on the employers. I think it would have a very wholesome effect in creating public opinion, which, by the way, after all, must be the force which is going to settle this thing; it can't be settled by either party to the trouble.

Commissioner WEINSTOCK. You think, then, such a proposed Federal commission would be an advantage?

Mr. MARTIN. I think so, Mr. Weinstock, and something must be done or tried, and it seems to me that that is a good thing to try. If it is tried and not found successful, then search must be made further for a remedy.

Commissioner WEINSTOCK. You were present this morning when Mr. Kennedy, I think the name was——

Chairman WALSH. Yes.

Commissioner WEINSTOCK (continuing). When Mr. Kennedy testified?

Mr. MARTIN. Yes, sir.

Commissioner WEINSTOCK. You heard his suggestion?

Mr. MARTIN. I heard it partially; I was sitting back a little ways.

Commissioner WEINSTOCK. In his opinion the best possible industrial conditions are likely to prevail where both sides to begin with are organized. Second, where the employers recognize and deal with labor unions and give them a voice in fixing hours and wages and working conditions, but reserving the right to employ union or nonunion men. Are you in accord with the opinion of Mr. Kennedy? Do you think those conditions would tend to a higher degree of industrial peace?

Mr. MARTIN. I used to think that, and it seemed wrong for any man or set of men to insist—if that is the correct word to use—that they would only work with men that belonged to their union. I used to think it ought to be right for a man to work with another whether he belonged to a union or not. But in the present industrial phase of things, with the way the welfare is developing, etc., and the way the unions seem to hold so firmly to the closed-shop proposition—and knowing that they themselves have studied more deeply over this matter and have gone into it more practically than I, and as they seem to consider the closed shop so vital to the permanence of the union, I am free to say I am rather changing my opinion upon that matter; that the closed-shop conditions may seem to be the only way of maintaining their unions; and if the maintenance of their unions depends upon the closed shop, rather than see the unions absolutely destroyed I would see the closed shop maintained. I think if the unions were destroyed, that we would have a far worse condition—I am afraid we would have a far worse condition than that which we now have.

Commissioner WEINSTOCK. Does the closed shop prevail in the publishing business?

Mr. MARTIN. In Stockton?

Commissioner WEINSTOCK. Yes, sir.

Mr. MARTIN. Yes, sir.

Commissioner WEINSTOCK. That is, you employ only union men?

Mr. MARTIN. Yes, sir.

Commissioner WEINSTOCK. You do not employ a nonunion man, even though he is qualified to do the work?

Mr. MARTIN. We could not, Mr. Weinstock. Even if we desired to, we could not.

Commissioner WEINSTOCK. Then, as an employer who is working under closed-shop conditions, will you tell this commission what you find to be the advantages and the disadvantages from the employer's point of view?

Mr. MARTIN. I find the disadvantage to be that I have practically no control over employment. A man can not come to me and apply for employment, he must apply to the foreman of whatever department in which he desires employment. Should he apply to me, a fine of $25, I believe, would be assessed against him by the union.

I have the right to discharge only for absolute incompetency or drunkenness or something of that kind. But practically I have not the right of employment or of discharge. Now, I am not prepared to say that I ought to have that right, I am simply saying I haven't it. I used to think that was unjust and that it was wrong; but we get along pretty fairly well with the foreman handling those things for us. The foreman, by the way, must be and is a member of the union. That is in the past what I have considered one disadvantage. Another disadvantage, I think, is the rstriction of apprentices. Competent men don't seem to be developed in the printing business rapidly enough to keep pace with the growth of the business; that the output or source of supply of competent printers is very limited. We have had within the past couple of months great difficulty in getting linotype operators. Now, that may not be owing to the restriction of apprentices, but I have thought possibly it was. There are various working regulations that I have thought operated rather detrimentally, but I am beginning to find, Mr. Weinstock, that if I take those matters up with the boys and talk the matter over with them, that as a general thing I have been able to get them adjusted.

For instance, if I would say, Now, here is something in which you are handicapping me; you don't understand this, and I am running the business, and I am better prepared to know where I am handicapped than you are, and you are handicapping me in this direction, and I don't think it is just right. I have found them in the past year or so quite amenable to reason along that line. I can't tell you just how it is coming about. I can't tell you whether it is going to be permanent, but in my individual experience as an employer I have found my men considerably more amenable in getting together with me than they formerly were, and I think that is a general condition; I hope it is.

Commissioner WEINSTOCK. What other disadvantages do you find?

Mr. MARTIN. I think those are the principal ones.

Commissioner WEINSTOCK. How about the advantages?

Mr. MARTIN. The advantages—the principal advantage I find Mr. Weinstock, and I consider it a very material advantage, is the fact I am absolutely certain that everybody else in my line of business is complying and must comply with exactly the same regulations I have to comply with.

The reason I am emphasizing that is that several years ago, when I first got into the business, they had wage scales and so forth in those days, but they were not being complied with; and it was generally understood that they were not being complied with, and the result was that the employer who had a disposition to drive a hard bargain could drive a hard bargain, and I felt, under those circumstances, that competition would come down to the question of a man who could drive the best bargain with his help, getting the best of it, and, under those condtions, I have felt I would be handicapped. I have always thought it was somewhat of a protection to know that other men in the same field had to comply with the same conditions I had to comply with; knowing what those conditions were, it was up to me to so handle my business that I could handle it successfully and profitably, and also knowing those conditions had to be complied with by everybody else in my line of business.

Commissioner WEINSTOCK. In other words, you feel when it comes to the labor cost you are protected against what might be called the unfair employer?

Mr. MARTIN. Yes, sir.

Commissioner WEINSTOCK. And in the labor cost you start out on an absolutely even footing with your competitor?

Mr. MARTIN. Yes, sir.

Commissioner WEINSTOCK. In the fixing of wages and hours and working conditions are those things fixed arbitrarily by the union or have you an even voice?

Mr. MARTIN. Have no voice at all and have had no voice, absolutely none.

Commissioner WEINSTOCK. These things are determined absolutely by the union?

Mr. MARTIN. Yes, sir.

Commissioner WEINSTOCK. And you must submit to any wage they name and any hours they fix and any condition they may determine upon?

Mr. MARTIN. We have always done so and felt we had to do so.

Commissioner WEINSTOCK. Well, is that a desirable situation, to rob the employer absolutely of his voice in the matter?

Mr. MARTIN. Possibly not, Mr. Weinstock.

Commissioner WEINSTOCK. I could understand how labor has a grievance where it has no voice in determining the wages and hours and conditions under which they shall work, but that is simply shifting the grievance from one side to the other. The grievance remains just the same, except it is a grievance on the part of the employer instead of being a grievance on the part of the worker. Are the publishers organized, for example?

Mr. MARTIN. We have at the present time a printers' association, which was organized for the specific purpose of determining cost of production, but it has not gone into other matters. It was not organized for the purpose of handling labor matters, and we specifically declared we did not intend to go into labor matters.

Commissioner LENNON. Don't you belong to the newspaper proprietors' association?

Mr. MARTIN. We affiliate with that. We just commenced affiliating with that a few months ago. We sent in whatever the fee was. I haven't had any active connection with it and haven't been a member long enough to really know. We get certain information about bad pay among eastern advertisers that I consider worth whatever it was; I don't remember now.

Commissioner LENNON. Are you not aware of the fact that there is bargaining between the newspaper proprietors and the International Typographical Union as to the wages and hours that shall be worked and the conditions under which employment shall be had, and that their committees meet and make agreements covering the country?

Mr. MARTIN. I am aware they have joint conferences and so forth, but they have had absolutely nothing whatever to do with our Stockton situation. The Stockton situation has been handled by Stockton Typographical Union, No. 56, no question about that at all; and whenever the time came for a readjustment of wages or of hours, we were not invited into conference; we were simply served with official notice that at a certain day the hours will be so-and-so and the wages so-and-so.

Commissioner WEINSTOCK. You have no choice but to submit?

Mr. MARTIN. We never have done otherwise than submit, Mr. Weinstock. I don't think we could have done otherwise.

Commissioner WEINSTOCK. Is that situation a local situation, or a common situation in the publishing business?

Mr. MARTIN. I am referring to the local situation.

Commissioner WEINSTOCK. Do you know what situation is general in San Francisco and eastern points?

Mr. MARTIN. I do not, except in a general way.

Commissioner WEINSTOCK. To the best of your knowledge and belief, what is the common condition?

Mr. MARTIN. Well, the last time our wage scale was raised I objected very strongly, not to the raise in the scale, but to the way in which it was done, and took it up with my men. I told them I wouldn't feel so badly about it if they had come around and talked the matter over with me and given me a chance to be heard. But they served notice on me that they were going to do a certain thing and they did it, and I didn't like it. I said, " You boys all know me, and if you want to do a certain thing why don't you come in and talk it over with me? You know where I am, and I am very approachable." They said, " Because we thought it would lead to trouble." I says, " What do you mean by that? " And it narrowed down to the proposition that they had decided what the proposition was going to be, and there was no back talk on the matter.

Commissioner WEINSTOCK. I suppose you feel as the worker would feel, or might feel, if you arbitrarily cut the wages without consulting them.

Mr. MARTIN. I want to state that in this matter now affecting the city of Stockton that I don't assume that my individual proposition cuts much figure, only in so far as it relates to the general situation. I am not conceited enough to think I cut an important figure in the proposition, but I have taken the general broad view of it. I had thought in times past I probably had suffered a little bit through unionism myself. I am inclined to think I did. But when the situation develops as it has developed now, and when I could see it developing and when I knew at the start what it meant, and when I know some other things that I don't care to go into here, and I don't think ought to be spoken of at all along industrial lines, then it seems to me that the little individual matters of restrictions or annoyances were so small or so petty in connection with the big question that they ought to be absolutely disregarded, and that is the only way I view it. In other words, to put it in a more definite way, Mr. Weinstock, I feel this way: I would not be justified, irrespective of how much I had suffered—if I had suffered in my individual business—that I would not be justified in precipitating upon a community like Stockton the condition of affairs that exists at this time; that I would not have any right to do it, no difference how much I had suffered individually. Even if I had been ruined in my business, that I still would not be justified in bringing the community to the condition that exists in Stockton at the present time—the bitterness and heartburnings and ill will and feeling. That may not be the correct way to look at it, but I am trying to tell you how I have arrived at the point where I am. In other words, when the big fight come on, just the same as the war in Europe, the little questions that led to it are disregarded.

Commissioner WEINSTOCK. Was that a little question, that the employers shall be robbed of a right of a voice in fixing hours and wages and labor conditions? Is that any smaller thing, that the employer shall be robbed, than that the employee shall be robbed of a voice in fixing hours and wages and working conditions? Isn't that a big question?

Mr. MARTIN. Yes, sir; it is, and I have talked to my men along that line. I told them I am satisfied that some day they themselves would see it or public opinion would so operate to show them that that way of getting at it wasn't right. I haven't made any bones about it; I have talked that over with them repeatedly.

Commissioner WEINSTOCK. Does the condition that exists in your community establish not a true industrial democracy, but an industrial autocracy, a one-sided arrangement?

Mr. MARTIN. That may be so.

Commissioner WEINSTOCK. Would you consider that the ideal condition?

Mr. MARTIN. Well, my experience has been, we don't have those ideal conditions. I haven't found them. In other words, it is a condition and not a theory that is confronting us. In matters of this kind, as I said before, I felt those things were so small I haven't allowed them to enter into the matter as far as I was concerned in the conduct of this paper at all. I irked under them at the time, and felt under restrictions and grumbled and growled at my boys, and never lost an opportunity to poke it into them and tell them how I felt about it, and I furthermore told them that some day they would see it, and that it would be changed some day. In fact, I think the entire relations between employer and employee will be changed some day.

Commissioner WEINSTOCK. In other words, in the interest of peace you are willing to give up your rights?

Mr. MARTIN. By the way, Mr. Weinstock, this situation in Stockton, in my judgment, isn't a union and nonunion situation; it is far deeper and broader than that. It is absolutely a class situation. It is absolutely the employers and financiers on one side and those who work on the other. The class lines are just as absolutely drawn as anything can be. It is far beyond union and nonunion. Just to illustrate. There is a little storekeeper who took the union side of this matter after considerable perturbation and being "up in the air" quite a while. I had a talk with him and asked how he had been getting along. He said he had the best month's business in his history. He says, "I am surprised, I can't understand it." He says, "I thought I would get considerable union trade but" he says, "I find I am getting a lot of trade from the nonunion men, from some of the people who work at Holt's," which is a nonunion shop. In other words, that illustrates that it is an absolute class proposition.

And, by the way, the M., M. and E., while its objects are for industrial equilibrium and things of that kind, it is an organization exclusively of class. The employees of Mr. Holt, nonunion men, are not asked to join the association. I don't assume they would be permitted to join. In other words, it is absolutely a class association. That is a fight of class against class.

Commissioner WEINSTOCK. That is all.

Chairman WALSH. Commissioner O'Connell would like to ask a question or two.

Commissioner O'CONNELL. Is not one of the most valuable assets in connection with the publication of a newspaper the assurance it is going to be issued each day on time?

Mr. MARTIN. It unquestionably is; yes, sir.

Commissioner O'CONNELL. What is your opinion or experience as to that assurance under union and nonunion conditions?

Mr. MARTIN. I understand that the typographical union does not call a strike without giving, I think, 90 days' notice, and it must come from the international union. That is my general impression of it. In other words, they do not walk out on you. Before trouble comes you would have 90 days' notice of the trouble, and from that standpoint it is quite a protection.

Commissioner O'CONNELL. I understood you to say you had just recently joined the National Newspaper Association.

Mr. MARTIN. We simply sent in the fee, whatever it is. It was handled through the business office, and I not well informed enough on it to talk intelligently on it.

Commissioner O'CONNELL. In order that Mr. Weinstock may catch this, it may interest him. The arrangement between the National Newspaper Publishers' Association and the International Typographical Union is that no increase can be demanded of the employer and put in force if the employer objects to it until it has been submitted to a board composed of an equal number of both national organizations, and they shall decide on the justice of it.

Mr. MARTIN. Yes, sir.

Commissioiner O'CONNELL. So that there is no such thing, if you are now in the national association, as a compulsory wage being forced upon you without you having a say through your association?

Mr. MARTIN. I understand that is right upon that line. And right on that line I might state this, that I feel that a great many of these restrictions and things that have annoyed and bothered us in times past, if, instead of grumbling and feeling put out at them, we would join in and cooperate with others in the same line of business as ourselves and take them up with the international union and undertake to have them adjusted through the international body, we could have done so. But we haven't done so. We have scrapped among ourselves and allowed our petty jealousies to interfere, and we have simply sat down and taken what was handed to us.

Commissioner O'CONNELL. In addition to the assurance of the daily issue of your paper, as these two associations agree to do, if by any means your publication is inconvenienced, they will see to it that it is gotten out by members of this organization, and a sure guaranty that you publication will not be stopped, which is the greatest asset you must have in the publication?

Mr. MARTIN. Yes; undoubtedly.

Commissioner O'CONNELL. That is all.

Chairman WALSH. Have you any agreement with the union in the printing trade, written agreement?

Mr. MARTIN. No, sir; not in Stockton. We never have had a written agreement with them to my knowledge.

Chairman WALSH. Approximately how many editorials has your paper written on this strike subject now?

Mr. MARTIN. There have only been the three main editorial points advanced, and we have written, incidentally, maybe kind of along those lines, but the three main propositions advanced were " Peace," " Settlement," and "Arbitration," and by the way, along the line of arbitration, " obnoxious " is the word they have used. They consider I have made myself obnoxious by editorials in favor of arbitration when they say " there is nothing to arbitrate." I have only made those three main editorial points, " Peace," " Settlement," and "Arbitration," through the paper.

Chairman WALSH. Will you please file the three copies of those editorials with the commission, if you have extra copies?

Mr. MARTIN. I would be pleased to do that, and beyond that, if it would not be piling you up too much, I would like to submit a complete copy of the files of the paper since this trouble has started, with the commission. File them with you.

Chairman WALSH. I wish you would do that, and we will have some of our staff select whatever is in there for our record.

Mr. MARTIN. I would be pleased to do that.

(The editorials referred to, entitled " Peace first, then arbitration," " Free expression of opinion," and " Let us have peace," from the Stockton Daily Record, dated, respectively, August 6, 11, and 21, 1914, were later submitted in printed form.)

Chairman WALSH. Those are all the questions we care to ask you, and you may be excused.

The commission stands adjourned until to-morrow morning at 10 o'clock.

(Thereupon, at 4.45 o'clock p. m., an adjournment was taken until 10 o'clock a. m. of the following day, Thursday, August 27, 1914.)

SAN FRANCISCO., CAL., *Thursday, August 27, 1914—10 a. m.*

Present: Chairman Walsh, Commissioners Commons, Garretson, O'Connell, Lennon, and Weinstock; also William O. Thompson, counsel.

Chairman WALSH. The commission will please come to order.

Mr. THOMPSON. Mr. Hough. Is Mr. Hough, from Stockton, in the room? Mr. Byrd.

TESTIMONY OF REV. J. W. BYRD.

Mr. THOMPSON. Give us your name, your address, and your profession, please.

Rev. BYRD. J. W. Byrd, B-y-r-d; my address is No. 132 North Stanislaus Street, Stockton; I am pastor of the Grace Methodist Church South of that place.

Mr. THOMPSON. How long have you been there, Mr. Byrd?

Rev. BYRD. Slightly over two years.

Mr. THOMPSON. Are you familiar with the situation in Stockton—the industrial affairs?

Rev. BYRD. To some extent.

Mr. THOMPSON. Will you tell us in your own way the facts as you view them?

Rev. BYRD. I do not wish to go over any of the testimony to any great extent that has been thus far given before this commission. However, I do wish to recite something of my own personal relation with the Stockton industrial situation. As I have just stated, I have been in Stockton slightly more than two years. During particularly the past year I have been to a considerable extent associated with the business clement of the city, friendly and otherwise, hnd naturally the things that I have heard, when discussions were brought up in our conversations with regard to the labor situation in Stockton, have been such as to prejudice my mind against labor unions. I must confess that when I heard of the movement among the merchants, manufacturers, and employers' association I was somewhat in favor of it, because I really did think there were certain abuses on the part of labor unions that should be corrected, and if this movement was simply for that purpose I thought it was certainly worthy.

Being of that state of mind with regard to this movement, I did not exercise any effort in order to find out just what were the features of the organization because I did not feel very much concerned in it. Later on, however, it was brought to my attention, as the situation become more acute, and I took it upon myself to inquire as to whether or not a settlement might be brought about. So .I went to a friend of mine, a man who is in business in Stockton, who as I thought at that time occupied an influential position in the merchants, manufacturers, and employers' association, and asked him if he was willing to talk to me about it. He was very cordial and said he was perfectly willing. .And he told me of the genesis of the organization, and the relations existing between the clerks and the clothiers—the clerks of the shoe and clothiers' stores. And I asked him at that time if it were not possible to bring these things to a settlement by arbitration or otherwise. He answered me very immediately that he did not think so, that he thought the movement would issue in an open town—open-shop town. I did not consider it worth while to talk with him further, as that seemed to be his attitude of mind, and I wish here to emphasize that this seems to me to have been the purpose of the organization so far as I have been able to find out. That it was simply for..the destruction of unionism in the city.

He at the time showed me certain letters that had come to him and to his firm from certain labor unions suggesting the boycott, in fact, threatening the boycott; and he also told me that at that time, by reason of the fact that the boycott had also been carried so far that clerks in one establishment were soliciting the nonpatronage of people who would come in to trade with those stores, because they were unfair. The result of that situation was that, on a certain day, the employers in the shoe stores and in the clothing and dry goods stores called their clerks together and told them that they must either withdraw from the union or get out of their employment. The result, as he said to me, was, that they practically all withdrew from the union.

The agreements that were shown to me more than one time and by more than one person, the agreements that were asked to be signed—that the merchants were asked to sign by the clerks, did not seen to me to contain any very grave demands. In fact, I did not see anything in them myself to warrant any such uprising on the part of the merchants. However, at the time I did not say anything to them about it, just forming my own opinion privately.

I recite this simply for this point, that I think, as I have just stated, that the organization must have been formed to destroy unionism, and they were simply trying to use these agreements as a point of justification for their organization.

Then, later on, I decided I would take up the question in my pulpit and discuss it, and I had various reasons for so doing. One of them was that my conclusion that they had determined to make Stockton an open-shop town. Not only an open-shop town, but that it was for the destruction of the unions.

I took this stand from my pulpit, not because of any desire to get into the good graces of the union men of Stockton, but because I thought I would be aiding unionism not simply in Stockton, but elsewhere.

I think this is a point that should be emphasized, that the movement is not local. The organization as such in Stockton may not have any direct connection with any other like organization in any other city, but I am very firmly convinced that its purpose is probably a nation-wide movement, and that if unionism fails in Stockton or if the M., M. and E. succeeds there, it will simply strengthen the purpose of the organization in other places. In fact, I have the direct statement from the president of the association in Stockton, that if it were not for the fact of the oncoming exposition here in the city of San Francisco, this city would be in the same battle now, and he also made the same statement that it would be carried throughout the State. He made this in connection with the declaration that they were opposed to the reduction of wages and the increase of hours. As you have doubtless had called to your attention, there was a resolution passed by the association that they would stand—that they were unalterably opposed to any reduction in wages or any increase in hours unless such a case were brought before a committee which would investigate and report upon it.

At the time I was planning my sermon the president of the association came to me, asking me not to preach—spent an hour and a half in my study talking with me on the question, and I confronted him with that point in the resolution that it was possible for them to reduce the hours—to reduce the wages and increase the hours. And in explaining that point he made what I considered a very damaging admission, and that was that it was not a local movement simply, and that if the movement succeeded throughout the State and throughout the country somebody somewhere would naturally lower wages and increase the hours, and they would have to compete with those who did such, and that they wanted a possibility of doing the same themselves. That was the admission of the president. I have never so far divulged it, did not divulge it in my sermon, because he claimed afterwards that it was a personal confidence. But I feel that this commission ought to know that, and therefore I have been willing to state it.

Another point that should be emphasized in this is that the question of hours and wages as such in Stockton probably may not enter into the controversy. It would not make much difference if the employers of Stockton did not reduce wages or increase hours.

Probably they do not intend to; probably they are sincere in that, but the point is the detriment to unionism; if unionism fails there it must fail in other places, because it is weakening all along the line. And that was one of my strong reasons for taking my stand with regard to unions. Not that I agreed with a great many things that were demanded by unions, but because fundamentally I considered that the unions needed assistance, that assistance, and should have the support of the better element of the community.

I was further led to my conclusion by reason of the methods that were employed by the merchants, manufacturers, and employers' associations in securing members. This point has been brought to your notice, and I simply wish to emphasize that. There have also been questions directed in certain witnesses here with regard to the difference between the forcing of merchants to join an association by reason of the closing in of indebtedness or the refusing of credit and the forcing of union men to join.

I wish to give you what I esteem as important in that difference, and that is that the unions, the way they force the individual is simply a matter of individual concern; it does not have very great immediate social consequences. But by reason of the great part that credit plays in industrial and commercial relations in the country to-day any unwarranted tampering with it is certainly detrimental to human society to a very far greater extent than anything that can be exercised by the union, man to man. I think that is an important point. And here also is a point I would like to call to the attention of the commission; that is it seems to me that if there is no law covering this point there certainly ought to be a law forbidding any bank, an institution as public as a bank, entering into any such controversy as this situation in Stockton to such an extent, to the extent that the banks have been persistently rumored to have entered into this situation in Stockton.

I wish to corroborate the statement of Mr. Kincaid with regard to one person who was certainly forced into the association through this method. He recited the instance of the New Method Laundry, of which Mr. Eaves is manager. I had heard that the association had been forcing in merchants by this method, and I desired not to take second-hand information, but to find out for myself. So I went directly to Mr. Eaves and asked him the direct question. That was before he was forced in. I heard that they were bringing great pressure to bear upon him. And he told me the situation—that he was being pressed. He said they had gone so far as to come to San Francisco, find out his bills and his indebtedness, get them, and threaten to close in on him at once if he did not make satisfaction for them. He was hoping then he would be able to make some arrangements by which he could keep out. But in a few days I heard that he had joined the association. I did not go back to him, feeling sure that he was forced in by the methods that he had recited to me. And I feel sure that that is the way.

I was rather led to the conclusion because I realized the temporary necessity, temporary at least, of the union labor. I feel that it is certainly necessary that labor should organize in order to protect itself from the oppression and the aggression of capital. This has been, of course, a matter of history—the relation existing between the two; and certainly they have no assurance to-day that they will be any better protected than they were in past years, or past ages, for that matter.

I was further led to my decision on this point by reason of the fact that I did not feel that any adequate effort had been made to settle those differences. Here is an important point. The complaints of the members of the 'M., M. and E. are not against unionism as such. They say so. They are against certain abuses, and they are ready to recite for hours and hours certain abuses that have been—to which they have been subjected by labor unions. But they are fighting labor unionism. They are trying to destroy labor unionism.

After I had met the president of the association and had my long discussion with him, the next day he called me up, asking me to meet their committee, their strike committee, about which you heard yesterday. So I went and met them. We discussed the proposition for something like three hours, and they seemed to assume that I would not tell the truth, or the truth would hurt them. Their attitude was that I should not preach upon the proposition at all, that is was not my province, that it wasn't any of my business, in fact, and that I didn't know anything about it; and that I should not, assuming that I would not tell the truth, or that the truth would hurt them.

And I made this proposition to them, that I would consent not to preach if they would consent to write out their grievances, stating them clearly as it was possible, and as strongly as it was possible for them to do so, and submit it to a board of arbitration to adjust the matter between themselves and the union, leaving out of discussion the proposition of the open shop.

They answered me that they would not be forced. I don't know how they thought I was trying to force them, but that was their answer that they would not be forced, and they would not do it. The outcome of it was that I did preach a sermon that aroused some interest in the city, treating, not exhaustively, of course, but typically, as I judged, certain of the arguments of the M., M. and E., and stating certain of my reasons why I took the stand that I did.

Those are briefly my relations with the present situation in Stockton.

Chairman WALSH. Any questions?

Commissioner GARRETSON. Yes.

Chairman WALSH. Mr. Garretson would like to ask you a question.

Commissioner GARRETSON. Mr. Byrd, their attitude that they would not be forced, was that in consonance with their position that they wanted to force you not to do a certain thing?

Rev. BYRD. Well, I don't know as they wanted to force me not to do it. They didn't have any way to force me.

Commissioner GARRETSON. But as to intention?

Rev. BYRD. Well, I don't know that their intention was to force me. They wanted to persuade me not to.

Commissioner GARRETSON. Oh, it was moral suasion?

Rev. BYRD. I don't know what. You can call it——

Commissioner GARRETSON. Or immoral suasion, as one looks at it?

Rev. BYRD. Call it what you like.

Commissioner GARRETSON. Have you heard all of the testimony that has been given during this hearing?

Rev. BYRD. The major portion of it.

Commissioner GARRETSON. Did you hear the statement made yesterday morning, where it was pressed upon the attention of this commission, that in weighing the testimony—not evidence, but testimony that might be given, that the commission should take into consideration the man that gave it?

Rev. BYRD. I heard that statement; yes, sir.

Commissioner GARRETSON. From your experience of the situation in Stockton, do you believe that the man who has a thousand dollars is entitled to more credence in testimony than he gives than the man that has $1 or that has none?

Rev. BYRD. I don't think the question of money enters into it.

Commissioner GARRETSON. You don't?

Rev. BYRD. No, sir.

Commissioner GARRETSON. It is man for man from your standpoint?

Rev. BYRD. Yes, sir.

Commissioner GARRETSON. The man is worth more than the dollar?

Rev. BYRD. Yes, sir.

Commissioner GARRETSON. That is all, Mr. Chairman.

Chairman WALSH. Prof. Commons.

Commissioner COMMONS. You stated that your suggestion was to them that they arbitrate everything except the open-shop question?

Rev. BYRD. Yes, sir.

Commissioner COMMONS. Why did you make an exception of the open shop?

Rev. BYRD. I made the exception of the open shop, I made the statement in my sermon, using this illustration—rather rough—that you might just as well speak of growing a goop crop of potatoes without soil, as of a strong union without the closed shop; that is, that the union would not be in a position to make any demands, possibly, even reasonable demands, unless it had a closed shop. That is my position. I am further led to that conclusion from this standpoint. I don't believe that any man ought to stay out of the union. It is somewhat like eating bread in the sweat of another's brow. I am almost led to the decision that it is a just proposition where men are forced into the union, because I don't believe any man should claim the privileges and the good conditions and the good wages that have been brought about by union effort and the sacrifices of union men, without also giving a corresponding service in return; that is, in money and his own sacrifice in that particular. Of course, here should be stated that the union should always be open. It should not exclude any man who wanted to come into the union.

Commissioner COMMONS. Did you put this argument up to this committee?

Rev. BYRD. I didn't state that argument, no, to the committee. I put the argument as to the closed shop to them; yes.

Commissioner COMMONS. Well, did you put up the argument to them, the proposition of their forcing employers to come into their organization?

Rev. BYRD. Yes, sir.

Commissioner COMMONS. How did they justify that?

Rev. BYRD. They denied it.

Commissioner COMMONS. Denied it?

Rev. BYRD. Denied that they were doing it.

Commissioner COMMONS. Did you take the ground with them that is was improper for them to force employers to come into their organization?

Rev. BYRD. Yes, sir.

Commissioner COMMONS. Did they justify that as compared with your justification of the unions enforcing men to come in?

Rev. BYRD. On that point I did not argue with them, because they simply denied that they were doing any such thing, when I had the names of men and the testimony of men upon whom pressure was brought to bear. They seemed to get around it in this way: They were not doing it as an organization. I don't know how they were doing it; it was being done. I told them I could give them the names of the men.

Commissioner COMMONS. You are rather attempting to analyze the whole situation there. Does it appear to you that on each side, each side is fighting for a closed-shop proposition. The employers are forcing all of the employers into their organization, and the unions are forcing all the employees into their organization. Is that the way the issue has finally worked itself out?

Rev. BYRD. Well, I don't think that is exactly the situation in Stockton. It is my understanding that it is the effort of· union men at all times to secure all workers as members of their union. I am not quite sure there is the effort——

Commissioner COMMONS. Then, this is the first effort of the employers to force all employers into their association?

Rev. BYRD. This is the first I have ever known of such organization in Stockton.

Commissioner COMMONS. Now, you proposed a remedy. This remedy that you propose is not to prohibit the employers from forcing all employers into their organization, but it is to force the banks to keep out of the situation, is that the idea?

Rev. BYRD. Well, I would suggest that, too; yes, sir.

Commissioner COMMONS. That is, you would consider it would be proper if legislation were adopted to allow employers perfect freedom to force all employers into their association, but you would have legislation that would keep the banks from backing them up?

Rev. BYRD. Yes, sir; I would; so that they might not use the credit at the bank as a club over their heads. I think that would be an unwarranted interference in the credit system.

Commissioner COMMONS. But as far as the employers' association is concerned, that it would be perfectly proper for them?

Rev. BYRD. I think it is perfectly proper for them to use all just means to secure members of their association.

Commissioner COMMONS. Well, could they use the boycott means?

Rev. BYRD. I think·the boycott is perfectly justifiable.

Commissioner COMMONS. Both sides could use the boycott?

Rev. BYRD. I do. I took that position in my sermon, that the boycott is justifiable. I don't think there is anything there to be ashamed of.

Commissioner COMMONS. Then if they want to get other manufacturers who are furnishing raw material to certain manufacturers or contractors—if they wanted them to refuse to furnish raw material to those manufacturers, that would be proper? That would be a boycott?

Rev. BYRD. Yes. I realize that the merchants have a means much more extended, or a more extensive weapon, to fight with along that line than the unions can ever hope to have—more complicated.

Commissioner COMMONS. That is, you recognize that they can boycott more effectively than the unions?

Rev. BYRD. Yes, sir.

Commissioner COMMONS. And yet you think both sides have the legal right to boycott?

Rev. BYRD. When I was thinking of boycotts I was thinking merely in the matter of trade, purchasing; that is, purchasing as it is ordinarily carried on in the stores.

Commissioner COMMONS. That would be the way the unions would boycott?

Rev. BYRD. That is about the only way they could.

Commissioner COMMONS. But the employers would boycott at the source?·

Rev. BYRD. Yes, sir.

Commissioner COMMONS. They would bring pressure to bear on the materialmen?

Rev. BYRD. Yes, sir.

Commissioner COMMONS. Also wouldn't they bring pressure to bear on the banks?

Rev. BYRD. Well, they might bring pressure to bear on the banks; yes, sir.· ·

Commissioner COMMONS. If the unions withdrew their deposits, and all the union men withdrew their deposits from the banks, that would be a boycott on the banks by the unions, wouldn't it?

Rev. BYRD. That would be to some extent. I do not believe they care very much about that. A banker said to me in Stockton several days—well, several months ago, in fact, that a certain union man approached him in the bank and asked him if he had taken his stand with the M., M. and E. That was along toward the beginning of the growth of the organization. And he said, "No; not yet." They said to him, "We just want to tell you if you do, we, the union men, are going to withdraw our deposits." And he said to them, "Well, we have not taken any stand yet, but you may be sure when. we take any stand it will be with the M., M. and E. That is where we loan our money. That is where we look for our profits."

Commissioner COMMONS. If both the M., M. and E. and the unions would boycott any bank and they could force the bank to close, to quit, couldn't they? I am simply analyzing your remedy—you proposed a remedy—and I wanted to see how far.

Rev. BYRD. I didn't propose that as a remedy. I do feel that the bank should not take that stand.

Commissioner COMMONS. But still it is perfectly legitimate for both sides to boycott the banks?

Rev. BYRD. Well, I say this: A man has a right to put his money where he chooses, to do business with the man he likes. In our church, for instance, that is, give preference over others. That is the case in every club, lodge, there is this in the rules of our church, this statement that we shall trade with those who are of our denomination where it is a reasonable condition; or anything else, that you trade with those who are of your way of thinking, who are sympathizing with you.

Commissioner GARRETSON. Can't you go further with that doctrine and say that every system of religion has been founded on a boycott, and that if you do not believe in that system you would be damned?

Rev. BYRD. I wouldn't exactly state it as strongly as that.

Commissioner GARRETSON. But the result would be the same. It isn't fashionable to say a man would be damned now; it is better to say he is lost.

Rev. BYRD. You are modern.

Chairman WALSH. Prof. Commons has not finished.

Commissioner COMMONS. What I was getting at was this:

In carrying out the idea of a boycott you would not say that the kind of preference that you have mentioned will be a boycott in the case of the churches?

Rev. BYRD. It is the same principle.

Commissioner COMMONS. Suppose you should excommunicate a member who traded with a nonmember?

Rev. BYRD. I wouldn't do that; allow liberty there, of course.

Commissioner COMMONS. That would be a boycott, would it not?

Rev. BYRD. It would be carrying it——

Commissioner COMMONS. The church has excommunicated people?

Rev. BYRD. That would be carrying it to a great extreme.

Commissioner COMMONS. I do not want to bring up the religious question at all, of church organization, but——

Rev. BYRD. That is all right. Your question is perfectly legitimate.

Commissioner COMMONS. My point, as I see it, is this, that in Stockton, and possibly other places, the community, or the interests on both sides, have recognized the legitimacy of a complete boycott.

Rev. BYRD. They seem to have done so; yes.

Commissioner COMMONS. And when that is recognized, both sides are entitled to carry it just as far as they choose?

Rev. BYRD. Well, I do not think you are entitled to carry anything so far as you choose, when it is merely personal or selfish ambition that is entering into it.

Commissioner COMMONS. Well, that is the actual situation.

Rev. BYRD. It seems to be; yes.

Commissioner COMMONS. I do not care to argue the question. I just want to get at the actual situation. Both sides have fallen back practically on the boycott—on the coercive boycott—not simply the voluntary talking amongst the friends as to what they must do, but they are bringing pressure to bear on outsiders to force them into line.

Rev. BYRD. It seems to be.

Commissioner COMMONS. That is the situation, is it?

Rev. BYRD. That seems to be the situation, to a large extent, at least.

Commissioner COMMONS. And both sides are using that method, and the question then arises whether that is from the standpoint—the general standpoint—that each side should be permitted to use that method, or whether it should be limited by law. That is your——

Rev. BYRD. Yes. The question of the bank——

Commissioner WEINSTOCK. I take it, Mr. Byrd, that from what you have said that your attitude is that the closed shop is vital to unionism?

Rev. BYRD. That is the way I feel; yes, sir.

Commissioner WEINSTOCK. That is, without the closed shop unionism can not stand?

Rev. BYRD. Well, it is possible for unionism to stand to a certain extent, I think, without the closed shop; but as far as being in a position to make any demand, even just demand, I do not see how it can.

Commissioner WEINSTOCK. Without the closed shop?

Rev. BYRD. Yes.

Commissioner WEINSTOCK. Well, are you aware of the fact, Mr. Byrd, that the railway unions of this country are among the strongest unions in the world; that they have a membership of 150,000; and that they have the open shop?

Rev. BYRD. That has been called to my attention; yes, sir.

Commissioner WEINSTOCK. And are you also aware of the fact that in the city of San Francisco the iron trades council, representing between four and five thousand workers, have the open shop?

Rev. BYRD. No; I am not.

Commissioner WEINSTOCK. And the employers are at liberty to employ anybody they choose?

Rev. BYRD. I am not acquainted with that condition; no, sir.

Commissioner WEINSTOCK. Well, I think if you will make some further inquiry, then, you will find that the Iron Trades Council of San Francisco is a very powerful organization.

Rev. BYRD. But is it recognized as a union; the point is, is it recognized as a union?

Commissioner WEINSTOCK. Yes; it is recognized as a union, and the employers—that is, the metal trades association, who represent the employers, recognize the iron trades council, deal with it, enter into agreements with it; but they have the open shop.

Rev. BYRD. As a matter of fact, the open shop is not very extensive, though. That is, there are not many employees who do not belong to the union.

Commissioner WEINSTOCK. Well, that may or may not be, but the fact remains that the employer is at liberty to employ anybody he pleases, whereas, under the closed shop management, as you have it in mind, the employer would be obliged to employ only union men.

Rev. BYRD. Well, I still maintain my position that even in that condition if the employer is strong enough to do it he can absolutely drive out those unions and employ nonunion men. They have absolutely no recourse.

Commissioner WEINSTOCK. But the fact will also have to be admitted then, Mr. Byrd, that it is entirely possible for unions to exist and to be powerful, to be recognized, to have a voice in fixing wages and hours of labor, and conditions, and still have the open shop; and if that is so then the closed shop is seemingly not vital to unionism. It is an advantage to be, but not vital.

Rev. BYRD. Well, that is a point, of course, that remains to be established, whether or not that is true.

Commissioner LENNON. Mr. Byrd.

Commissioner WEINSTOCK. Just one more question.

From your investigation and study of the problem, Mr. Byrd, if you had the power how would you prevent a repetition of the conditions prevailing in Stockton, and from being repeated elsewhere, for example?

Rev. BYRD. Well, I do not know just how I would prevent it. I wish to be understood that I am not opposed to the organization of the merchants, manufacturers and employers association. I think they ought to retain their organization. It seems to me that that is necessary.

Commissioner WEINSTOCK. That is, for the employers to retain their organization?

Rev. BYRD. Yes; so that they as an organization may deal with the unions as an organization through proper committees, and that any disputes that arise ought to be referred to the proper committees, the proper powers to act.

Commissioner WEINSTOCK. Were you here yesterday when Mr. Kennedy testified?

Rev. BYRD. Yes.

Commissioner WEINSTOCK. Do you recall the suggestions that he made to the commission?

Rev. BYRD. I do not recall them definitely; in a general way.

Commissioner WEINSTOCK. Briefly they were these: That in his judgment the best possible industrial conditions are where both sides are organized, where the employer recognizes and deals with organized labor, and gives it a voice in fixing hours, wages, and working conditions, but reserving the right to employ union or nonunion men as he chooses.

Now, how far could you agree with Mr. Kennedy in his suggestions?

Rev. BYRD. I disagree with him in the matter of the employment of nonunion men.

Commissioner WEINSTOCK. That is, you would rob the employer of the right to employ nonunion men?

Rev. BYRD. Yes, sir.

Commissioner WEINSTOCK. In all things else you would agree with him?

Rev. BYRD. I think so; yes. As to the employment of nonunion men, as I said awhile ago, if I were a laboring man I should feel myself morally bound to unite with a labor union. That would be a sufficient reason. There are other considerations, but that would be a sufficient reason with me.

Chairman WALSH. Is that all?

Commissioner WEINSTOCK. Yes.

Commissioner O'CONNELL. I want to ask you if you understand the difference between the open shop that Mr. Commissioner Weinstock has been asking you about, and the open shop that is proposed at Stockton?

Rev. BYRD. Yes; I think I understand.

Commissioner O'CONNELL. You understand the open shop that Mr. Weinstock speaks about, the railroad organization, is an open shop in which the company makes a contract with the union men covering the employment of all people on the railway system over which they have jurisdiction?

Rev. BYRD. Yes.

Commissioner O'CONNELL. The company does not deal with individuals, with nonunion men.

Rev. BYRD. Yes.

Commissioner O'CONNELL. In making their hours and wages and conditions. That is the open shop in the railway system. That is not the kind of open shop that is proposed in Stockton.

Rev. BYRD. No; it is not.

Commissioner O'CONNELL. That is all.

Chairman WALSH. Mr. Lennon would like to ask you some questions.

Commissioner LENNON. Mr. Byrd, I understood you to say that you saw the agreement that had been presented by the clerks to the merchants. Did that contain a demand that no clerk could be employed permanently unless they were members of the union?

Rev. BYRD. I can not tell you what were the provisions of the agreement. In fact I did not pay so much attention to it so far as the details are concerned. I simply read it. I did not see anything in it to my mind that was objectionable. That is all I can say to that, because I do not know, did not read carefully the stipulations, do not know what the stipulations were now.

Commissioner LENNON. What do you believe is the tendency of individual contracts for labor in industry? Is it toward higher wages, less hours, and better conditions, or is it taken advantage of to create a tendency in the other direction?

Rev. BYRD. Well, I should certainly have to have a stronger faith in human beings if I thought it was tending to better conditions for the worker.

Commissioner LENNON. Have you a personal acquaintance with more or less of the union men of Stockton prior to this trouble?

Rev. BYRD. How is that question?

Commissioner LENNON. Did you have a personal acquaintance with some of the union men of Stockton prior to this contest?

Rev. BYRD. My acquaintance with the union men of Stockton was very, very limited; it is to-day.

Commissioner LENNON. You didn't know many of them individually?

Rev. BYRD. No, sir; I have two or three members of the union, members of my church.

Commissioner LENNON. Do you know whether in the community they were recognized as being respectable, decent citizens?

Rev. BYRD. I think they were; yes, sir.

Commissioner LENNON. Have you an idea as to whether Stockton stands on a par with other cities as to general morality and general conduct of the citizenship?

Rev. BYRD. I don't know. I am not acquainted in other cities as to the general morality, as I could not be unless I lived in those other cities. I think as far as the citizenship of Stockton is concerned we have as substantial a citizenship as anywhere.

Commissioner LENNON. Did you hear the testimony that Stockton was the most strongly organized city, as far as unionism was concerned, on the coast?

Rev. Byrd. I have heard that statement; yes, sir.

Commissioner Lennon. Then that organization didn't seem to have destroyed the character of the citizenship of that city, as far as you could observe? .

Rev. Byrd. No, sir; I don't think it did.

Commissioner Lennon. What would be the consequence as to the homes of the workingmen of the city of Stockton if their organization is destroyed? ..,

Rev. Byrd. Well, the organization of course has some tendency—a great tendency—to affect the homes, in that the mere fact of the laboring men organizing and getting together, discussing the subjects that are vital to them, certainly heightens the manhood and general social conception of the individual members of the union, which would naturally react upon the home.

The wage has, of course, another very vital relation to the condition of the home.

Commissioner Lennon. You believe that where men and women take a wide, strong interest in the welfare of their fellows that they, by so doing, raise their own standards?

Rev. Byrd. I did not catch the first part of the question.

Commissioner Lennon. Where a man tries to be useful in the world, where he tries to render service in the world, where he takes an interest in the welfare of his fellows, that it reacts for his own betterment?

Rev. Byrd. I think that is the fundamental condition in one's own betterment.

Commissioner Lennon. Would the destruction of the unions in Stockton have any probable effect as to breaking up the school life of the families, if the father had to leave the city?

Rev. Byrd. I think it would.

Commissioner Lennon. I think that is all, Mr. Chairman.

Commissioner Weinstock. Just another question, Mr. Chairman—another question.

Chairman Walsh. Very good. Mr. Weinstock wants to ask you some questions.

Commissioner Weinstock. If, with your present opinions, Mr. Byrd, you were a wage earner and a unionist and a believer in the closed-shop principle being vital to unionism, how far would you go along the lines of establishing the closed shop? How far would you go with other wage earners who did not agree with you in the importance and the necessity of becoming a unionist?

Rev. Byrd. I would go about as far as I go in my present position when I meet men who do not agree with me.

Commissioner Weinstock. That is, you would stop at persuasion?

Rev. Byrd. Yes, sir; I would do that, stop at persuasion.

Commissioner Weinstock. Would you think that coercion and intimidation, and, if need be, force, were justifiable on the part of unionists in endeavoring to get their fellow workers to become unionists?

Rev. Byrd. I do not think that is ever justifiable.

Commissioner Weinstock. Then you would draw the line at coercion and intimidation and force?

Rev. Byrd. Yes, sir.

Commissioner Weinstock. You would establish the closed shop by persuasion?

Rev. Byrd. Yes, sir.

Commissioner Weinstock. Pure and simple?

Rev. Byrd. Yes, sir.

Commissioner Weinstock. You would establish the closed shop by persuasion, if your fellow workers could not be persuaded, then what?

Rev. Byrd. Well, I should have to subject myself to the conditions that were entailed by that situation.

Commissioner Weinstock. I see. Then you are in favor of the closed shop only when the closed shop can be established by moral suasion?

Rev. Byrd. Sure.

Commissioner Weinstock. And not by any other means?

Rev. Byrd. Not by any other means; no, sir. I can understand the spirit by which force is used. I have a very keen understanding of that spirit, I think, and am somewhat in sympathy with it in my personal views, though I can not of course justify it.

Commissioner Weinstock. You have kept yourself informed, I take it, Mr. Byrd, of the conditions prevailing in Stockton since this trouble has arisen? ˙:

Rev. Byrd. So far as I could; yes, sir.

Commissioner WEINSTOCK. Well, from your knowledge of the conditions, has there been violence since these industrial troubles have arisen?

Rev. BYRD. Yes, sir; there has been some violence.

Commissioner WEINSTOCK. Have you investigated the matter of violence there?

Rev. BYRD. No; I have not.

Commissioner WEINSTOCK. Well, to the best of your knowledge, who is responsible for this violence?

Rev. BYRD. I am not able to say who is. I have my opinion. That is probably not based on actual facts.

Commissioner WEINSTOCK. You have no personal information?

Rev. BYRD. Just general information would be all that I could say.

Commissioner WEINSTOCK. That is all.

Chairman WALSH. Any other questions?

Commissioner GARRETSON. I have a few more.

Chairman WALSH. Go ahead.

Commissioner GARRETSON. Doctor, on this question of banks a little further. Some questions were asked you a few moments ago, and I want to ask you one or two on the other side of that. I understood that you merely threw out the suggestion of legislation controlling the action of banks as one of the incidents of this campaign, and not as a general corrective, that it should be prohibited as a general proposition.

Rev. BYRD. I feel this, that the bank should be, if possible, hedged about by law, and with regard to it there should be created on the part of the people, or in the minds of the people, such an attitude that they will not expect the bank to take one side or the other, and therefore it would not be subject to the boycott.

Commissioner GARRETSON. The fact is the bank is a quasi-public institution in its nature, like the railroads?

Rev. BYRD. Yes, sir.

Commissioner GARRETSON. And isn't the exact parallel, the precedent for that found in existing legislation that prohibited railways from issuing rebates which were a discrimination in the industrial war between firms?

Rev. BYRD. Yes, sir; it is pretty near a parallel. I am not able to say that it is an exact parallel.

Commissioner GARRETSON. Taking it then as a public institution or a quasi-public institution to render public service to anyone, it would be a perfectly legitimate piece of legislation?

Rev. BYRD. Yes, sir.

Commissioner GARRETSON. Are you of the opinion that the employer as well as the employee owes a duty to society in general?

Rev. BYRD. Yes, sir.

Commissioner GARRETSON. You don't lean to the idea that the man who holds property and who employs men is society?

Rev. BYRD. No, sir. In my sermon, if you will allow me to make the statement, I took the position that the laborer was a part of the business just as much as—at least in quality, as much as the employer is.

Commissioner GARRETSON. In result, could all the capital on earth produce anything without the labor?

Rev. BYRD. No, sir; it could not.

Commissioner GARRETSON. And, then, would it be a calamity to society in general to place labor back where it was, we will say, only 40 years ago, prior to the influence of unionism?

Rev. BYRD. I think so. That is my unquestioned opinion.

Commissioner GARRETSON. You proceed on the basis, I believe, that if associations like the M., M. and E. were successful, that it would leave laboring men as thoroughly at the mercy of the employer as they were before the rise of unionism?

Rev. BYRD. Yes, sir; I think so.

Commissioner GARRETSON. That is all, Mr. Chairman.

Chairman WALSH. Prof. Commons has one more question.

Commissioner COMMONS. I wanted to ask you about that—in Stockton are the methods which you call voluntary in requiring men to join the union—now, you would stop at the point where persuasion ends?

Rev. BYRD. Yes, sir.

Commissioner COMMONS. That is the proposition. Now, in Stockton, is that the point where the union stops?

Rev. BYRD. I am not acquainted enough to know to state.
Commissioner COMMONS. You don't know what methods they use?
Rev. BYRD. No; I don't.
Commissioner COMMONS. To bring men into the organization?
Rev. BYRD. No, I don't.
Commissioner COMMONS. Do you know whether they refuse to work with non-union men?
Rev. BYRD. I think they do.
Commissioner COMMONS. Would they strike if there was a nonunion man on the job?
Rev. BYRD. That seems to be their position. I don't know.
Commissioner COMMONS. And would you include that under the idea of persuasion?
Rev. BYRD. Sure.
Commissioner COMMONS. That is one kind of persuasion you have in mind?
Rev. BYRD. One kind of persuasion, I think it is; yes, sir.
Commissioner COMMONS. And so if the employers——
Rev. BYRD. I think it is perfectly legitimate.
Commissioner COMMONS. If the employers say that they will not deal with an employer who deals with unions, they withdraw their patronage from him—now, leave out of account this question of the banks, leave the bank question out—that would also be voluntary on their part?
Rev. BYRD. Yes, sir.
Commissioner COMMONS. Voluntary persuasion?
Rev. BYRD. Yes, sir; they might do that.
Commissioner COMMONS. And that is the situation in Stockton, that both sides are using voluntary persuasion up to the point of withdrawing their patronage as a body in order to induce those who are not members of either organization to come in?
Rev. BYRD. I don't know that that is the point now. The things that are being done now are simply to win the fight.
Commissioner COMMONS. Does not it inevitably lead to that issue? It is now a question of whether the union will have all people in the union, or the employers have all people out of the union?
Rev. BYRD. That may be the issue.
Commissioner COMMONS. That is the reason there is a fight, because both sides have adopted that method of persuasion. That is an argument or inference, the chairman tells me, so that I will not press it any further.
Chairman WALSH. I just have a question to ask you: Are there any specific facts in your knowledge that you could give the commission tending to amplify or support your statement that it is the intention of the M., M. and E. to extend their organization outside of the city of Stockton?
Rev. BYRD. If I made that statement I wish to correct it, that it was their intention.
Chairman WALSH. Probably I didn't state it correctly—fairly—but I understood you to say that it was your opinion, or that you had gathered facts that led you to believe it was a broader movement than a movement in the mere city of Stockton; that it was a fight on unionism every place. Now, outside of that being your opinion from what you saw in Stockton, have you any other facts? Were any statements made to you with reference to what might be done in San Francisco or Los Angeles, or any other place?
Rev. BYRD. Yes, sir; I recited the statement of the president of the M., M. and E. that if it were not for the fact the exposition was upon San Francisco that this city would be in the fight.
Commissioner COMMONS. Did he say upon what he based that?
Rev. BYRD. He did not say. We were discussing the clause in regard to the hours and wages, that they would not be changed without being referred to a committee, and he was explaining why that clause was in there.
Chairman WALSH. He said while there was one condition in Stockton in relation to hours and wages that that might come about in a general way, and that Stockton desired to be in a position where they could meet such competition?
Rev. BYRD. Yes, sir.
Chairman WALSH. That is all.
Mr. THOMPSON. Just a minute.
Chairman WALSH. All right. You may proceed.
Mr. THOMPSON. I believe you testified while you were making your first statement that while you believed all men should join the union, you also believed the union should be open. Will you tell us just what you meant by that?

Chairman WALSH. He stated what he meant by that, that no man should be excluded from the union. Let's let it go at that.

Mr. THOMPSON. I would like to ask another form.

Chairman WALSH. Not on that subject, please, Mr. Thompson.

Commissioner WEINSTOCK. Just one moment.

Chairman WALSH. One moment. Mr. Thompson hasn't finished yet.

Commissioner WEINSTOCK. Pardon me, I though he had finished.

Mr. THOMPSON. Another question Mr. Drew has handed up: What union did you refer to when you spoke of union abuses?

Rev. BYRD. I didn't refer to any union—any particular union.

Mr. THOMPSON. What kind of abuses?

Rev. BYRD. Well, those abuses that have been recited here on this stand by previous witnesses. I believe there was one particular case that has been referred to more than once—the instance of Mr. Totten's case, where lumber was required to be taken down from the third floor and hauled back to the shop and restamped. I think there are other ways to remedy that which are just as effective and more reasonable.

Mr. THOMPSON. That is all.

Chairman WALSH. That is all. Thank you.

Commissioner WEINSTOCK. Just one moment. I want to make sure we understand the witness thoroughly.

Chairman WALSH. Oh, yes; I forgot.

Commissioner WEINSTOCK. Do I take it that summing up your ideal condition or ideal of the labor condition, so far as labor is concerned, would be the closed shop and the open union?

Rev. BYRD. Yes, sir. With every effort possible to induce every laboring man to join the union, then, of course, on my part, that includes the idea that it shall—that there shall be every effort on the part of the union to secure instructions for themselves and all of their members with regard to their duties and responsibilities in an industrial society, and that like instructions shall be given to the organization on the other side, because they are just as needy in that particular as are the union men or laboring men.

Chairman WALSH. Is that all, Mr. Weinstock?

Commissioner WEINSTOCK. Yes, sir.

Chairman WALSH. That is all. Thank you, Doctor. Call your next.

Mr. THOMPSON. Mr. Bentley.

Chairman WALSH. Is Mr. Hough here now?

Mr. THOMPSON. Mr. Hough.

Chairman WALSH. Just have the sergeant at arms ascertain where Mr. Hough is, and then go ahead with the other witness. Mr. Sergeant at Arms, find out where the other witness is who is not present. Proceed.

Mr. THOMPSON. Mr. Bentley.

EXHIBITS.

TOTTEN EXHIBIT NO. 1.

TOTTEN & BRANDT PLANING MILL CO.,
Stockton, Cal., August 27, 1914:

Col. HARRIS WEINSTOCK,
San Francisco, Cal.

DEAR MR. WEINSTOCK: I am inclosing you herewith copy of a letter that I referred to in my testimony yesterday. As I said, our pay roll at that time was $2,000 per week. The total amount received from the entire crew was $358.15; $146 of this amount was paid by nonunion and office employees, making a total amount paid by the union employees $212, or approximately 14 per cent of the union men who signed this agreement made good their promises.

I am not sending you the original document, for the reason that I might have occasion to use this later on. However, if it is necessary, I can go before notary public and have a true copy of this attested and mail same to you.

Yours, truly,

TOTTEN & BRANDT,
By C. TOTTEN.

TOTTEN & BRANDT PLANING MILL CO.,
Stockton, Cal., August 16, 1913.

To our employees:

We wish to take this occasion of expressing our gratitude and good will to our employees who have so kindly offered one week's service gratis. We hope to be able to show to our employees at some future date that we thoroughly appreciate and are thankful for this act of kindness. Wish to say furthermore that it came at a time when help was needed. While this in no way covers our loss, at the same time it does show to the public that there was a kind feeling existing between our employees and ourselves.

After thoroughly considering the matter we have decided that each of you would be the best judge when you could afford to fulfill your part of the agreement, and under these circumstances we are not going to set aside any special week or we are not going to demand any time of payment; we will leave it strictly up to you. You will receive your checks regular as before, and when you feel as though you can best afford to fulfill your part you will be at liberty to do so.

Below are the names of all employees, and those having the line drawn through the name have paid in full, and as fast as the payments are made the lines will be drawn through the names.

Yours, truly,

TOTTEN & BRANDT.

TOTTEN EXHIBIT NO. 3.

BARTENDERS' INTERNATIONAL LEAGUE OF AMERICA,
LOCAL NO. 403,
Stockton, Cal., May 16, 1914.

SIR: I was instructed at our last regular meeting, held on the 13th instant, to inform you that our members will be warned to withdraw their patronage from your place of business and also their families till you can see your way clear to display the union card.

4904

We regret this very much, as we have always felt that your firm was friendly to organized labor.
I am, sincerely, yours,

E. H. MURPHY, *Secretary.*

[United Association Journeymen Plumbers, Gas Fitters, Steam Fitters, Steam Fitters' Helpers of the United States and Canada.]

STOCKTON, CAL., *May 28, 1914.*

DEAR SIR: It was brought to the attention of this local union at its last meeting that there were certain retail merchants in this city who had refused to recognize the retail clerks' union, and were consequently not displaying the union store card.

As we believe that what affects organized labor as a unit affects the whole cause, this local union went on record as discouraging, as far as possible, the patronizing by members and their families of any store which does not display the retail clerks' store card, and is consequently not wholly fair to organized labor.

Respectfully, yours,

PLUMBERS' LOCAL UNION No. 492.

BARTENDERS' INTERNATIONAL LEAGUE OF AMERICA,
LOCAL No. 403,
Stockton, Cal., May 16, 1914.

HUDSON & KING.

GENTLEMEN: I was instructed at our last regular meeting, held on the 13th instant, to inform you that our members and their families will be warned to withdraw their patronage from your place of business till you can see your way clear to sign the agreement of the clerks' union and display the union store card.

We regret this very much, as we have always felt that your firm was friendly to organized labor. I beg to remain,

[SEAL.]   E. H. MURPHY, *Secretary.*

STOCKTON, CAL., *May 18, 1914.*

ROSENBAUMS & SONS.

GENTLEMEN: We are compelled to call your attention that after repeated attempts to get the retail merchants of Stockton to reconsider their former action and sign up with the Retail Clerks' Local 197, of Stockton, Cal., that I have been instructed by this Local 22, International Brotherhood of Teamsters, of Stockton, to inform you that we have found it necessary to notify you that until such time as you see fit to sign up with the retail clerks and display the union store card in your windows you can not expect to receive any of the patronage from members or their families of this local.

Any member of this union found patronizing such stores that do not display union store cards will be fined $5.

Hoping you see fit to sign the agreement and get a union store card, we remain,

Yours, respectfully,

TEAMSTERS' UNION 22,
[SEAL.]   C. S. NUNLEY, *Recording Secretary.*

BARTENDERS' INTERNATIONAL LEAGUE OF AMERICA,
LOCAL No. 403,
Stockton, Cal., May 16, 1914.

SIR: I was instructed at our last regular meeting to inform you that our members and their families will be warned to withdraw their patronage from your place of business till you can see your way clear to display the union store card.

We regret this very much, as we have always felt that your firm was friendly to organized labor. I beg to remain,
Sincerely, yours,

E. H. MURPHY, *Secretary.*

HOLT EXHIBIT.

HOLT MANUFACTURING CO. (INC.) OF CALIFORNIA,
Stockton, Cal., December 9, 1914.

Mr. LEWIS K. BROWN,
Secretary United States Commission on Industrial Relations,
Chicago, Ill.

DEAR SIR: Referring further to my letter of December 4, I presume you will understand that the rate of wages scheduled in my recent report to you for the Holt Manufacturing Co., in amounts less than $2 per day, must necessarily apply to apprentices, but to be sure that such classification of wages will not be misunderstood I now call such fact specifically to your attention.

Yours, very truly,

HOLT MANUFACTURING Co.
P. E. HOLT, *General Manager.*

The Holt Manufacturing Co., pay roll for the week ending November 14, 1914.

FOUNDRY.

Shop No.	Wage rate.	Shop No.	Wage rate.	Shop No.	Wage rate.
C2	$5.25	C27	$4.00	C52	$2.60
C3	3.50	C28	4.00	C53	2.00
C4	3.50	C29	2.25	C54	2.25
C6	3.00	C30	2.25	C55	2.00
C7	2.60	C31	4.00	C56	2.25
C8	4.50	C32	3.25	C57	2.50
C9	2.25	C33	2.75	C58	4.00
C10	3.00	C34	2.60	C59	2.25
C12	3.25	C35	4.00	C60	2.25
C13	4.00	C37	3.00	C61	4.00
C14	2.25	C38	2.50	C62	2.50
C15	2.25	C39	4.00	C64	4.00
C16	4.00	C40	3.25	C65	4.00
C17	2.50	C41	2.25	C66	4.00
C18	1.75	C42	2.25	C67	2.00
C19	2.25	C43	4.00	C68	4.00
C20	2.25	C44	2.25	C69	2.25
C21	2.25	C45	2.25	C70	3.25
C22	3.50	C46	2.25	C71	2.35
C23	4.00	C47	2.25	C72	2.50
C24	4.00	C49	2.00	C73	3.50
C25	3.00	C50	4.00	C74	1.50
C26	2.50				

TRACTION ENGINE SHOP.

Shop No.	Wage rate.	Shop No.	Wage rate.	Shop No.	Wage rate.
E4	$2.25	E18	$2.75	E31	$2.25
E5	2.50	E19	2.75	E32	2.25
E6	2.50	E20	3.00	E33	2.25
E7	3.50	E21	3.50	E34	2.25
E8	2.75	E22	2.75	E35	2.75
E9	2.50	E23	3.25	E37	2.25
E10	2.25	E24	2.00	E38	2.25
E11	2.25	E25	2.25	E39	2.25
E12	3.25	E26	2.50	E42	2.50
E14	2.25	E27	2.25	E43	2.50
E15	3.50	E28	2.75	E44	3.00
E16	2.25	E29	3.00		
E17	2.25	E30	2.50		

The·Holt Manufacturing Co., pay roll for the week ending November 14, 1914—
Continued.

BLACKSMITH SHOP.

Shop No.	Wage rate.	Shop No.	Wage rate.	Shop No.	Wage rate.
H2	$4.80	H30	$2.75	H58	$3.50
H3	4.00	H31	2.50	H59	2.25
H4	3.50	H32	2.75	H60	3.00
H5	2.25	H33	3.25	H61	2.25
H6	2.25	H34	2.50	H62	2.00
H7	3.00	H35	2.50	H63	3.50
H8	2.00	H36	3.75	H64	2.50
H9	3.00	H37	2.25	H65	2.50
H10	2.75	H38	2.25	H66	2.25
H11	2.25	H39	3.00	H67	2.00
H12	3.50	H40	3.75	H68	2.00
H13	3.50	H41	2.50	H69	2.00
H14	2.50	H42	2.25	H70	2.25
H15	3.00	H43	3.00	H71	2.25
H16	2.50	H44	3.50	H72	2.25
H17	1.75	H45	2.50	H73	2.25
H18	3.00	H46	2.25	H74	2.25
H19	3.25	H47	2.50	H75	2.25
H20	2.00	H48	4.00	H76	2.25
H21	2.25	H49	4.00	H77	2.25
H22	3.50	H50	2.75	H78	2.50
H23	3.00	H51	2.25	F3	2.25
H24	3.50	H52	3.00	F4	3.00
H25	2.50	H53	2.25	F5	3.25
H26	2.50	H54	2.25	F6	2.25
H27	2.00	H55	2.25	F7	2.25
H28	2.50	H56	2.75		
H29	3.25	H57	2.50		

MILL.

I2	$3.75	I6	$3.50	I11	$3.00
I3	3.00	I8	3.50	I15	2.25
I4	2.75	I9	3.25		
I5	2.75	I10	3.50		

HARVESTER CONSTRUCTION.

J3	$3.00	J13	$2.75	J23	$3.00
J4	2.50	J14	2.75	J24	2.50
J5	3.00	J15	3.00	J25	3.00
J6	2.50	J16	3.00	J26	2.50
J7	2.00	J17	3.00	J27	3.00
J8	2.00	J18	2.50	J28	2.50
J9	3.00	J19	3.50	J29	3.00
J10	2.75	J20	1.50	J30	3.00
J11	2.50	J21	3.00	J31	3.50
J12	3.00	J22	3.50	J34	2.50

PLOW ASSEMBLING.

K2	$3.50	K5	$2.75	K9	$2.50
K3	2.25	K6	2.25	K10	2.25
K4	2.50	K8	2.00	K11	2.25

PAINT SHOP.

L2	$3.00	L7	$2.50	L12	$2.50
L3	2.50	L8	2.50	L13	2.50
L4	2.50	L9	2.50	L14	2.25
L5	2.50	L10	2.50	L15	2.50
L6	2.75	L11	2.50		

The Holt Manufacturing Co., pay roll for the week ending November 14, 1914—
Continued.

SHEET METAL.

Shop No.	Wage rate.	Shop No.	Wage rate.	Shop No.	Wage rate.
N2	$2.25	N6	$2.25	N9	$2.25
N3	3.00	N7	2.25	N10	3.00
N4	2.25	N8	2.50	N11	2.25
N5	2.50				

DRAPER ROOM.

M2	$2.50	M4	$2.00	M8	$1.75
M3	2.00				

SCREEN DEPARTMENT.

O1	$3.00				

SICKLE BAR DEPARTMENT.

P1	$3.25	P2	$2.50		

CASE HARDENING DEPARTMENT.

G1	$3.50	G4	$2.75	G6	$2.75
G2	2.25	G5	2.75		

PLUMBERS.

T2	$2.75	T4	$2.75	T5	$2.50
T3	3.00				

MACHINE SHOP.

S2	$4.80	S35	$4.00	S68	$3.75
S3	3.75	S36	3.00	S69	1.50
S4	3.00	S37	3.50	S70	1.50
S5	1.25	S38	2.75	S71	2.00
S6	3.75	S39	2.50	S72	2.00
S7	2.00	S40	3.75	S73	3.75
S8	2.00	S41	1.00	S74	3.50
S9	3.00	S42	2.25	S75	3.25
S10	4.00	S43	3.75	S76	3.50
S11	3.50	S44	3.50	S77	3.25
S12	1.25	S45	3.50	S79	3.50
S13	3.75	S46	2.75	S80	1.50
S14	2.50	S47	3.50	S81	3.75
S15	3.50	S48	2.00	S82	2.50
S16	3.50	S49	1.25	S83	2.75
S17	3.75	S51	3.50	S84	1.25
S18	2.50	S52	4.50	S85	2.50
S19	1.75	S53	2.00	S86	3.50
S20	4.50	S54	3.75	S87	2.25
S22	3.50	S55	2.75	S88	3.50
S23	2.50	S56	3.50	S89	2.75
S24	2.25	S57	3.00	S90	3.50
S25	3.50	S58	2.00	S91	3.50
S26	3.00	S59	3.75	S92	1.25
S27	3.00	S60	3.50	S93	1.00
S28	2.25	S61	2.75	S94	3.50
S29	3.50	S62	2.25	S95	1.50
S30	2.50	S63	2.75	S96	2.50
S31	2.00	S64	3.50	S97	2.25
S32	3.50	S65	1.50	S146	2.25
S33	3.50	S66	3.25	S98	3.50
S34	2.25	S67	1.75	S99	2.25

The Holt Manufacturing Co., pay roll for the week ending November 14, 1914—
Continued.

MACHINE SHOP—Continued.

Shop No.	Wage rate.	Shop No.	Wage rate.	Shop No.	Wage rate.
S100	$2.25	S118	$3.50	S134	$3.50
S101	3.00	S119	2.50	S135	2.50
S102	$2.00	S120	2.25	S136	2.50
S103	3.50	S121	2.25	S137	3.25
S104	3.75	S122	3.50	S138	2.50
S105	3.50	S123	1.00	S139	3.50
S107	1.00	S124	1.00	S140	3.50
S108	2.50	S125	3.75	S141	3.00
S109	2.50	S126	3.00	S142	2.50
S110	2.75	S127	1.00	S143	3.50
S111	3.25	S128	2.00	S144	2.25
S112	2.75	S129	3.50	S145	3.00
S113	2.00	S130	2.25	S147	3.25
S114	3.75	S131	2.50	S148	1.00
S115	1.00	S132	3.50	S149	2.25
S116	2.50	S133	3.50	S150	2.00
S117	3.50				

TOOL ROOM.

X1	$4.50	X5	$3.75	X10	$3.00
X2	3.75	X6	3.50	X11	1.00
X3	1.00	X7	1.00	X12	1.00
X4	4.00	X9	3.85		

GAS ENGINE ASSEMBLING.

Y2	$2.75	Y9	$2.50	Y17	$3.00
Y3	2.75	Y10	2.25	Y18	2.50
Y4	3.00	Y11	3.75	Y19	2.75
Y5	2.50	Y12	3.75	Y20	2.75
Y6	2.50	Y13	2.75	Y22	2.75
Y7	3.00	Y14	3.00		
Y8	3.00	Y15	3.00		

ONAL LABOR PROBLEM
AGRICULTURE

its under this subject, see page 5027.)

4911

COMMISSION ON INDUSTRIAL RELATIONS.

SAN FRANCISCO, *Thursday, August 27, 1914—10 a. m.*

Present: Chairman Walsh, Commissioners Lennon, O'Connell, Garretson, Commons, and Weinstock; also W. O. Thompson, counsel.

TESTIMONY OF MR. R. I. BENTLEY.

Mr. THOMPSON. Will you give us your name, business address, and business, please?

Mr. BENTLEY. R. I. Bentley; business address, 120 Market Street. Is there another question?

Mr. THOMPSON. And your business?

Mr. BENTLEY. I am general manager of the California Fruit Canners' Association.

Mr. THOMPSON. Will you tell us briefly the nature of that organization?

Mr. BENTLEY. The organization is a corporation which owns and operates plants all over the State for the canning of fruits and vegetables. We also handle more or less dried fruit; that is, packing it after it is dried.

Mr. THOMPSON. To get more clearly what I want, is this an association of canneries and firms or is it a corporation itself?

Mr. BENTLEY. It is a regular corporation.

Mr. THOMPSON. It is?

Mr. BENTLEY. Yes, sir.

Mr. THOMPSON. But with the name of association?

Mr. BENTLEY. Yes, sir.

Mr. THOMPSON. In addition to packing and canning your own goods, do you do work for other fruit raisers or shippers?

Mr. BENTLEY. We grow some of our own products which we can, but the bulk of the products that we can are contracted with growers.

Mr. THOMPSON. What other products—but what you do produce you produce for your own company?

Mr. BENTLEY. Yes, sir.

Mr. THOMPSON. I mean what you can?

Mr. BENTLEY. Yes, sir.

Mr. THOMPSON. Where are your canneries located, Mr. Bentley?

Mr. BENTLEY. Those we are operating in California are: Two in San Francisco, one in Oakland, one in San Jose, one in Stockton, one in Sacramento, one at Marysville, one at Hanford, one at Visalia, one at Los Angeles, one at Santa Rosa, one each at Leandro, Milpitas, Vorden, and Pittsburg.

Mr. THOMPSON. Now, could you tell us briefly the kind of fruits you put up or other stuff you can—vegetables and fruits?

Mr. BENTLEY. We can nearly all varieties of fruits and vegetables grown in the State of California.

Mr. THOMPSON. What volume of business does your company have during the year?

Mr. BENTLEY. In dollars?

Mr. THOMPSON. In dollars.

Mr. BENTLEY. About $12,000,000.

Mr. THOMPSON. What amount of labor do they employ in that work, if you know?

Mr. BENTLEY. In the height of the season I think we have in the neighborhood of 7,500 people.

Mr. THOMPSON. What is the character of the demand for labor in your industry? What kind of labor is needed?

Mr. BENTLEY. The character of the demand?

4913

Mr. THOMPSON. What sort of labor?

Mr. BENTLEY. You mean is it stable?

Mr. THOMPSON. No. What kind of labor, skilled or unskilled? Ordinary labor—or what is your classification?

Mr. BENTLEY. I should say 10 per cent of our labor is skilled, and 90 per cent unskilled. Of the 10 per cent they are all males, of the skilled labor.' Of the unskilled, I should say that there are 10 or 15 per cent males, and the balance females.

Mr. THOMPSON. What kind of work is the labor used for—that is, take the unskilled labor, what kind of work does it do?

Mr. BENTLEY. The preparation and packing of fruit and vegetables.

Mr. THOMPSON. How would you classify that—separately, or do you classify it?

Chairman WALSH. How many packers and how many canners, and so on?

Mr. BENTLEY. Well, of course, that varies with the product we are handling, Some varieties will take more canning than preparing and other varieties take more preparing than canning.

Mr. THOMPSON. If you can do it readily and briefly, take the different kinds of products you put up and give us that statement.

Mr. BENTLEY. Well, take the first product which we handle, which is asparagus. The proportion which can would be greater than those preparing. Take the next product we handle, peas, which is almost all mechanical; that is, the hulling of the peas and sorting, with the exception of a little grading which is done by hand—rather, not grading, but a little sorting after they are graded by machinery is done by hand—and the balance of it practically all machinery. The next product we handle is strawberries. The proportion of those preparing would be in excess of those canning. The cherry, the proportion of those preparing would be in excess of those canning.' The apricot, the proportion of those canning would about equal those preparing. Peaches and pears, the proportion of those preparing would exceed those canning.' The same would apply to other vegetables which come in order, like string beans and tomatoes. The proportion of those preparing would exceed those canning. I think that practically covers the whole field.

Mr. THOMPSON. Are there any branches of this canning work or any of these particular fruits or vegetables you have named that give continuous work throughout the year, or is it seasonal and comes in every case for the season?

Mr. BENTLEY. It is seasonal. No one variety are we able to can the year around. Our season begins in April on asparagus, and that season lasts until about the 1st of July. The strawberry is probably a variety that runs a longer period of time than any other one. It begins usually in May and sometimes lasts until the 1st of November. Peas is a very short season, not lasting over a month. Apricots and all the other varieties of deciduous fruits, excepting peaches, the season is about three weeks. The peach season begins July 15 and winds up about October 1. It is the variety we have the largest demand for, and more of an effort has been made to extend the season in that variety than any other, which accounts for the length of the season. I made one statement there that all other varieties would be about three weeks. I want to qualify that—any one variety in any one district. We have early districts in the State where apricots will come in the latter part of June and wind up shortly after the 4th of July, and by the 15th, anyway, and we have another section that don't begin until the 10th or 15th of July, and in that way the season is extended on the variety beyond the time I mentioned of about three weeks. Three weeks is the period that will exhaust any one kind of a variety in any one district

Some districts, however, grow more than one kind of a variety that mature at different times. In such districts the season will be longer than three weeks. Six weeks would probably be the maximum for every variety of deciduous fruits, excepting peaches.

Mr. THOMPSON. Take these varieties. You have in some of the canning and packing places, places that you put up many varieties of stuff?

Mr. BENTLEY. Yes, sir.

Mr. THOMPSON. To what extent will the force you use in such a place be kept from one fruit or vegetable to the other, or about what proportion? What I am trying to have you tell is how long will they have work in the place where they work the longest in an industry.

Mr. BENTLEY. Well, the largest plant we have is located here in San Francisco, and we begin here about the 1st of April and wind up about the 1st of December; sometimes run into December to some extent.

Mr. THOMPSON. Then the plant is shut down?

Mr. BENTLEY. Yes, sir.

Mr. THOMPSON. Are those employees there taken elsewhere, or just simply the relation terminated and that ends it?

Mr. BENTLEY. Yes, sir. That ends it so far as we are concerned. In many sctions where we operate, however, large acreages of deciduous fruits and olives are grown. The season on both citrus fruits and olives begins about the time that we close down, so that a large proportion of the labor we use is used in the harvesting and marketing of these products.

Mr. THOMPSON. Take the place where you have the shortest work in the year.

Mr. BENTLEY. Yes, sir.

Mr. THOMPSON. How long do they work, and where does that labor come from?

Mr. BENTLEY. The shortest period, I presume is our pea-packing plant. That only lasts three weeks. This is in a district in the Santa Clara Valley, where we have other plants and where the labor is used in other plants. In fact, we usually send our skilled labor from one of the big plants to the smaller plants to operate it. The same is true of some of our other smaller plants, like asparagus plants, that work exclusively on asparagus. We send skilled labor there to operate those plants, and bring them back after we have closed up.

Mr. THOMPSON. Take the places of peas and asparagus, where does the 90 per cent of labor come from—from the neighborhood?

Mr. BENTLEY. Yes, sir; for the most part.

Mr. THOMPSON. Do you divide your labor as to whether foreign born or native born?

Mr. BENTLEY. That varies in localities. I presume in San Francisco the proportion of foreign born is quite large. It is quite hard for us to distinguish—that is to say, what proportion are native born—because in our plants in San Francisco the bulk of the employees are Italians or of Italian descent. Just what proportion are native born it would be difficult for me to say, but I should say at least 75 per cent, counting the descendants who are born here as native born, were foreign born. We have other plants where they are practically all native born. It depends a good deal on the locality.

Mr. THOMPSON. You got a list of questions, didn't you?

Mr. BENTLEY. Yes, sir.

Mr. THOMPSON. Have you got them with you?

Mr. BENTLEY. Yes, sir.

Mr. THOMPSON. Could you take those questions and run them right down and answer them one after the other?

Mr. BENTLEY. Yes, sir.

Mr. THOMPSON. You might do that, then, please.

Chairman WALSH. Begin at question 2, I would think. You have already given us the proportion of skilled and unskilled. Now, begin with the second question. If foreign born, adults and minors, natives, and answer them right down as concisely and exhaustively, of course, as the question calls for.

Mr. BENTLEY. Question 2: What is the character of the supply of labor in your industry? Is that it?

Mr. THOMPSON. I think it would be question 3.

Chairman WALSH. It is the subdivision of that question 2, under the same head. Give the number as to how many males and how many females.

Mr. BENTLEY. Twenty per cent males, including skilled labor, 80 per cent females.

Chairman WALSH. Adults and minors?

Mr. BENTLEY. About the same proportion, 80 per cent adults and 20 per cent minors. Native or foreign. As I have stated, it varies in the locality.

Chairman WALSH. You have stated that, but can you give us anything more definite on that now? That varies in localities. If you can, give localities, give us what the proportion is, if you can?

Mr. BENTLEY. I have given you San Francisco. I should say at San Jose, which is our next largest plant, the proportion of foreign born would be 25 per cent.

Chairman WALSH. What nationalities?

Mr. BENTLEY. Of all kinds, I should say.

Chairman WALSH. Asiatics?

Mr. BENTLEY. With the Italian predominating.

Chairman WALSH. Asiatics?

Mr. BENTLEY. No Asiastics, sir. Take our San Joaquin Valley plant and Sacramento Valley plant, I should say that the proportion there was about 75 per cent native born and 25 per cent foreign born.

Chairman WALSH. When is this demand for labor lightest? Has that been covered?

Mr. BENTLEY. It is lightest in the months we don't operate, and those are December, January, February, and March.

Chairman WALSH. Heaviest in the other times?

Mr. BENTLEY. Heaviest during the other period, during July, August, and September; that is what we call our rush season.

Chairman WALSH. What methods are used in your industry in getting the job connected up with the man or woman?

Mr. BENTLEY. We use advertising, soliciting, and, in a limited way, the employment agency.

Chairman WALSH. What method have you found most satisfactory?

Mr. BENTLEY. The method we used to the greatest extent is just simply that of an informatory character; to let the people know we are operating is advertising.

Chairman WALSH. Where do you advertise?

Mr. BENTLEY. In the local papers.

Chairman WALSH. Any outside of California?

Mr. BENTLEY. No, sir.

Chairman WALSH. What can yon say, if you have anything to say, of the practical working of the private employment agency as at present used in your work?

Mr. BENTLEY. We found that the employment agencies in most cases are sadly deficient, for the reason that if we want the man to do a certain work, even take farm work, if we want a teamster, for instance, he don't always ascertain whether that man has ever handled a horse, so sometimes instead of getting a man who can handle a horse, we get sombody who is of no earthly account and have to return him. In other instances, where people in the employing agency either see the necessity of taking better care of their clients, or for some reason they pay more attention to our requirements, and in such cases it is a great help to us.

Chairman WALSH. Who pays the employment agency for this securing of labor?

Mr. BENTLEY. The laborer, as a rule, although sometimes we have offered the employment agency, where it was an urgent case, something to pay particular attention.

Chairman WALSH. So, mainly, you have no information of what the agricultural labor pay to get employment?

Mr. BENTLEY. No, sir.

Chairman WALSH. Have you been advised of any abuses in private employment systems—that is, of sending persons to employment purposes made temporary—so as to collect additional fees?

Mr. BENTLEY. I do not know of my own knowledge of anything of that kind. I have heard of such things.

Chairman WALSH. Can you tell us where you have heard of it, so that we may pursue the investigation?

Mr. BENTLEY. No, sir; I could not.

Chairman WALSH. Have you considered the possibility of spreading a demand for agricultural labor more evenly throughout the year, such as by diversifying crops, or some other method, or some other invention?

Mr. BENTLEY. Yes, sir; we naturally, from an economic standpoint, want to operate our plants as long as we can, and we do everything that we can to extend the seasons in all of our plants, and are working along those lines all the time.

Chairman WALSH. Could you state briefly what your present plans are for doing that, for making the occupations less seasonal?

Mr. BENTLEY. Well, one illustration of that is in the matter of the variety of peaches, which I have just mentioned. That variety has been extended now over the season from the latter part of June until the 1st of October. It shows what can be done with that variety, and while with other varieties we may not be able to extend the season to the same extent, we can undoubtedly lengthen them.

Chairman WALSH. Have you any organization on that particular subject?

Mr. BENTLEY. No, sir.

Chairman WALSH. Or is it desultory, just as you think of it yourself?

Mr. BENTLEY. There is no organization outside of our own business or inside either that deals exclusively with this problem, yet all canners and growers are giving a great deal of thought to the subject and steadily accomplishing something.

·. Chairman WALSH. There is no organized effort being made to make occupations less seasonal in your industry?

Mr. BENTLEY. No, sir.

' Chairman WALSH. What is your attitude toward agricultural and migratory labor unions?

Mr. BENTLEY. I don't think they are seasonal.

Chairman WALSH. For what reason, briefly?

Mr. BENTLEY. Well, efforts have been made to organize the cannery labor, and they have not succeeded. That is one reason. Another reason is this, in the handling of perishable products; as far as I am concerned, I certainly would want to get out of the business if we were in such a position in the handling of perishable products that we would have to yield to demands or go out of business. That is, it is entirely different from most manufacturing businesses, in that the product does waste if you do not handle it immediately; that is, you are bound to be damaged. In our product, of course, any delay, anything that is not canned the day it comes in, it is deteriorating immediately.

It is my opinion that all employers of labor, including those that handle perishable products, would welcome unionizing, provided the abuses which union-labor organizations practice could be corrected. The first thing to do would be to make all such organizations responsible, both legally and financially, so that if they entered into a contract they would be legally bound to carry the same out. If the same attention was paid to correcting the abuses of unions and hedging them in with regulations that is now being paid to business by our State and Federal legislatures, I am satisfied that it would be to the material benefit of all concerned.

Chairman WALSH. Has there been any organization among the employees in your industry of the I. W. W.?

Mr. BENTLEY. There have been attempts at it.

Chairman WALSH. Is it spreading or not?

Mr. BENTLEY. I do not think it is.

Chairman WALSH. Are there any signs of activity at the present time among them?

Mr. BENTLEY. Well, there was an attempt made to organize at several different points this summer.

Chairman WALSH. And was any organization effected?

Mr. BENTLEY. No.

Chairman WALSH. Any disturbances growing out of it?

Mr. BENTLEY. Yes.

Chairman WALSH. Prosecutions?

Mr. BENTLEY. No; no prosecutions. We had a strike at San Jose, which lasted one day.

Chairman WALSH. How many persons were engaged in it?

Mr. BENTLEY. Oh, I think—I couldn't tell you exactly. There were enough engaged in it so that we shut up the plant for one day.

Chairman WALSH. How was it ended?

Mr. BENTLEY. We opened the plant the second day, and the bulk of them came back to work.

Chairman WALSH. I would like you to give a description of the general living conditions in your industry in your plants.

Mr. BENTLEY. In the plants themselves?

Chairman WALSH. Just describe as briefly as you can how the employees live. This is question 6, and you have probably considered that.

Mr. BENTLEY. As to their living conditions, of course, the bulk of the employees in the canneries are local people, and the bulk of them are not dependent upon what they earn in the canneries for their livelihood. Most of them are wives and daughters of men who are working. The result of it, I think, is the conditions are very good. Outside of that it is difficult for me——

Chairman WALSH. Do you have company stores any place?

Mr. BENTLEY. No, sir.

Chairman WALSH. And is there any place in which you have boarding houses or places where you board your employees?

Mr. BENTLEY. Yes, sir.

Chairman WALSH. And how are they conducted? First, what is the charge made for board?

Mr. BENTLEY. Where we have boarding houses, there is no charge made; that is, some of our—we are conducting some ranches, and in those places we pay them all so much a month and board them.

Chairman WALSH. Well, in the boarding houses you say there is no charge made, do you not take into consideration that in the rate of wage paid the worker?

Mr. BENTLEY. Well, it is, of course, taken into consideration as an expense, but it is not customary here.

We simply pay them whatever the going rate is per month, and the board is that additional expense.

Chairman WALSH. What is the adult male worker given, common laborer, in your industry?

Mr. BENTLEY. On our orchards, and so on, I think it is about a dollar and a half a day and board. Of course, sometimes during the harvesting season the demand for labor is such that we have to pay more than that.

Chairman WALSH. And a dollar and a half is the lowest—a dollar and a half and board?

Mr. BENTLEY. I think so, excepting in some cases where we have employed orientals. Then the rate is a little lower than that.

Chairman WALSH. And for a woman?

Mr. BENTLEY. The bulk of the women are on the piecework basis.

Chairman WALSH. And what do they make?

Mr. BENTLEY. I should say they average, when they are working steadily, about $10 per week.

Chairman WALSH. How many hours per day?

Mr. BENTLEY. Well, during the height of the season they average about 10 hours a day

Chairman WALSH. And the men?

Mr. BENTLEY. About the same.

Chairman WALSH. And when it is not in the height of the season, are there less hours or more?

Mr. BENTLEY. Yes, sir; less.

Chairman WALSH. How low do they run?

Mr. BENTLEY. I should say during the—about an average of eight.

Chairman WALSH. Do the men work on piecework also?

Mr. BENTLEY. No, sir.

Chairman WALSH. That is all day work?

Mr. BENTLEY. Yes, sir.

Chairman WALSH. Is the board included in the women's wage?

Mr. BENTLEY. No, sir.

Chairman WALSH. In any instance at all?

Mr. BENTLEY. No, sir.

Chairman WALSH. In any of those boarding places do women board, or girls?

Mr. BENTLEY. I beg your pardon.

Chairman WALSH. In any of your boarding places, do you have women or girls?

Mr. BENTLEY. No, sir.

Chairman WALSH. Are all of the women and girls in your industry living in their own homes?

Mr. BENTLEY. No, sir.

Chairman WALSH. Well, where?

Mr. BENTLEY. In some of our plants we have little cottages where they live.

Chairman WALSH. Women and children?

Mr. BENTLEY. Yes, sir.

Chairman WALSH. What pay do you give children?

Mr. BENTLEY. The same as the women. It is all on piecework basis.

Chairman WALSH. Are the children all on piecework?

Mr. BENTLEY. Yes, sir.

Chairman WALSH. And what is the eldest and what is the youngest?

Mr. BENTLEY. Well, we are working under a State law. I have forgotten just what; I think the limit is 14, with school certificates during the vacation time. Then, after that, my recollection is that either 16 or 18 is the limit.

Chairman WALSH. Is that law strictly observed in your industry?

Mr. BENTLEY. Yes, sir.

Chairman WALSH. And is there any inspection on the part of the State officers over your industries as to the ages of these children?

Mr. BENTLEY. Yes, sir.

Chairman WALSH. How is it carried out, please?

Mr. BENTLEY. There are deputies going over the State. I don't know how often. I don't know as they have any regular periods, but they are constantly going around.

Chairman WALSH. What ranch do you have more particularly under your personal observation?

Mr. BENTLEY. Well, we have quite a large fruit ranch in the San Joaquin Valley and another one skirting the bay.

Chairman WALSH. Do children work there?

Mr. BENTLEY. No, sir.

Chairman WALSH. Or minors?

Mr. BENTLEY. No, sir.

Chairman WALSH. What is the closest plant that you have, or cannery, that is closest to your observation?

Mr. BENTLEY. We have two here in San Francisco.

Chairman WALSH. And those are inspected in the way that you have stated?

Mr. BENTLEY. Yes, sir.

Chairman WALSH. When was the inspection made the last time?

Mr. BENTLEY. I could not tell you.

Chairman WALSH. How frequently is it made in the plant in San Francisco?

Mr. BENTLEY. Oh, I should say three times during the season.

Chairman WALSH. You have that of your own knowledge, do you?

Mr. BENTLEY. That is, that we know of. It may be oftener.

Chairman WALSH. Are there times when the supply of labor exceeds the demand?

Mr. BENTLEY. Yes, sir.

Chairman WALSH. To what extent?

Mr. BENTLEY. Well, of course, as I have stated, during the four months in the year when we are not operating there is a large supply of labor, but the bulk of that goes back—being women, they go to their homes. The men have to find other employment.

Chairman WALSH. Have you observed so that you could make any comparison between the efficiency or lack of efficiency in the various types of agricultural labor; that is, as to nationalities, as to places they are recruited from, whether through advertisements or employment agencies; any observations you could make on that we would be glad to have.

Mr. BENTLEY. Well, as to the efficiency, I don't think that nationality has very much to do with it. And as to recruiting them, I don't quite fully understand what you wanted there.

Chairman WALSH. Well, for instance, do you find that the people you get from private employment agencies are efficient people, or do they lack in efficiency; are they permanent in their work, stay with you, or do they just come for a day or two? I don't know whether that makes it clear.

Mr. BENTLEY. Well, as I stated before, with employment agencies sometimes we have a great deal of trouble; but we have got down now so that there are certain ones that we go to that know that we don't deal with them unless they do pay some attention to our requirements and our affairs. And so far as during the three months in the year when we are crowded with work, of course we take anything, efficient and inefficient. We don't get enough to do all the work, to handle all the fruit that we could handle during that period of time. There is hardly a year but what we have to resort, for instance, to cold storage in order to save the fruit.

Chairman WALSH. Have you some questions, Mr. Weinstock?

Commissioner WEINSTOCK. No.

Chairman WALSH. Any other questions?

Commissioner COMMONS. I would like to ask: You spoke of operating ranches as well as canning. What is the nature of that; do you control growers or do you have your own ranches that produce all the product?

Mr. BENTLEY. We have two ranches; one in the San Joaquin Valley and one in Contra Costa County. One is a fruit ranch and the other is an asparagus ranch that we own outright. We, of course, control those, but beyond that we control nothing except by contract.

Commissioner COMMONS. You make contracts at the beginning of the season?

Mr. BENTLEY. Sometimes. Sometimes we make term contracts covering a period of years.

Commissioner COMMONS. Well, in those contracts do you control the seasonal; that is, through those contracts do you make an attempt to extend the season, say, to get the growers to distribute their crop in such a way that you could lengthen out your season?

Mr. BENTLEY. Of course in deciduous fruits you could not make the growers extend the season, because it would have to be harvested when it gets ripe. We aim to have annuals, vegetables that we handle, to have them planted so as to extend the season as much as possible.

Commissioner COMMONS. Well, on your ranches—I suppose they are typical of ranches in the State, are they not?

Mr. BENTLEY. Yes, sir.

Commissioner COMMONS. How large, take one of the ranches, the largest one?

Mr. BENTLEY. Well, the largest fruit ranch is about a thousand acres.

Commissioner COMMONS. What do you grow on that?

Mr. BENTLEY. Principally peaches.

Commissioner COMMONS. How many employees do you have on the ranch?

Mr. BENTLEY. Why, the year around, I should say probably 40 men; during the harvesting period probably three times that many.

Commissioner COMMONS. Those 40 men are the men that are paid this dollar and a half per day and board?

Mr. BENTLEY. Yes, sir.

Commissioner COMMONS. Those are steady men?

Mr. BENTLEY. Yes, sir.

Commissioner COMMONS. Do they have homes there and families?

Mr. BENTLEY. Well, some of them. We have cottages there for those who do have families, and the unmarried men have a house where they——

Commissioner COMMONS. What proportion of them are married and have families?

Mr. BENTLEY. Oh, a small proportion.

Commissioner COMMONS. Are they mostly changeable, migratory?

Mr. BENTLEY. No; that class of help that we run the year around are fairly steady.

Commissioner COMMONS. How many men would you have to hire in the year to keep up that force of 45?

Mr. BENTLEY. We have no statistics on that point at all, and I don't think that I could answer that intelligently, but I don't think that it is large. I don't think that we would—I should say of the 45 men, probably 80 per cent that started out at the beginning of the year would be there at the end of the year. The other 20 per cent would go and come, but how often they would go and come it would be difficult for me to say. In fact, I am guessing at it anyway. It is a point that hadn't occurred to us, and we have no facts to deal with that. I probably can get something on that.

Commissioner COMMONS. Well, then, the other hundred that you have to employ in the picking, they are also men?

Mr. BENTLEY. Yes, sir.

Commissioner COMMONS. And what do you pay them the season?

Mr. BENTLEY. The same. During the harvesting period sometimes we pay more. It depends upon what the going rate is.

Commissioner COMMONS. When do you increase the force above 45, at what date?

Mr. BENTLEY. Well, the harvesting period in this particular place begins in June and winds up about the middle of September. We have that force during that period.

Commissioner COMMONS. They are engaged in picking and shipping?

Mr. BENTLEY. Yes, sir.

Commissioner COMMONS. Now, would that be typical then of the peach——

Mr. BENTLEY. Yes, sir.

Commissioner COMMONS (continuing). Growing all over the State?

Mr. BENTLEY. Yes, sir.

Commissioner COMMONS. That about one-third are steadily employed during the year?

Mr. BENTLEY. Yes, sir.

Commissioner COMMONS. And two-thirds there is an extra demand for—I think it is about four months you figured it out?

Mr. BENTLEY. Yes, sir.

Commissioner COMMONS. What do you grow on the other ranch?

Mr. BENTLEY. Principally asparagus.

Commissioner COMMONS. Well, now, how does that work out? How large is that ranch?

Mr. BENTLEY. The acreage in asparagus is about 750. The balance of the land is not particularly good. We begin there, depending upon climatic conditions, sometimes in March, sometimes early in March, and sometimes the middle of March, and we wind up about the 1st of July, the cutting.

Commissioner COMMONS. How many steady people the year around?

Mr. BENTLEY. Well, about the same proportion.

Commissioner COMMONS. The same proportion?

Mr. BENTLEY. Yes, sir.

Commissioner COMMONS. They get, then, about three or four weeks, I think you figured?

Mr. BENTLEY. Well, say, from the middle of March to the 1st of July, that is longer than that—nearly four months; three months and a half, say.

Commissioner COMMONS. The wages and other terms are all the same, are they?

Mr. BENTLEY. Yes, sir.

Commissioner COMMONS. In those cases. And that would be in general the way the asparagus business is conducted over the State?

Mr. BENTLEY. Yes, sir.

Commissioner COMMONS. Does your company own these canneries, or is it an association of owners?

Mr. BENTLEY. We own them. The name "association" is a misnomer, in a way; we are a regularly incorporated company, and own them.

Commissioner COMMONS. You are incorporated?

Mr. BENTLEY. Yes, sir.

Commissioner COMMONS. Under the California laws?

Mr. BENTLEY. Yes, sir.

Commissioner COMMONS. Do you have figures that would give us an idea of the extent of the business in the State of others outside of your company?

Mr. BENTLEY. Oh, yes; yes.

Commissioner COMMONS. Could you state those?

Mr. BENTLEY. You mean what the——

Commissioner COMMONS. How many others; you have given us a list, quite a large list.

Mr. BENTLEY. I gave a list of the plants that we had.

Commissioner COMMONS. Do you know what the extent of the industry is in the State for all others outside of yours?

Mr. BENTLEY. Well, we probably represent 40 per cent of the canning business in the State. That is, we pack probably 40 per cent. Is that what you mean?

Commissioner COMMONS. Yes. Yes, that is what I wanted to get at.

Mr. BENTLEY. Yes.

Commissioner COMMONS. Forty per cent?

Mr. BENTLEY. Forty per cent of the output.

Commissioner COMMONS. What is the capitalization of your company?

Mr. BENTLEY. Three million dollars.

Commissioner COMMONS. And the turnover is twelve million?

Mr. BENTLEY. Yes, sir.

Commissioner COMMONS. Now, the other 60 per cent; are they organized in a similar way with yours, in combinations?

Mr. BENTLEY. We are the largest company in the business. There are others varying in size that have plants scattered around in different localities the same as we have, but there are none of them as large as we are.

Commissioner COMMONS. Is there any association of all canners?

Mr. BENTLEY. No. There is an association to the extent that we meet once a year, more in a social way than any other. There is no organization other than that. It is social.

Commissioner COMMONS. Well, what do they take up? the type of questions that they take up?

Mr. BENTLEY. Oh, occasionally there is an executive committee that takes up a question of general interest. For instance, in the present situation, those interested in the export business—looking after freight and war risks and so on, which is of general interest.

Commissioner COMMONS. Do you have a general selling agency at all?

Mr. BENTLEY. No, sir.

Commissioner COMMONS. Each company sells its own?

Mr. BENTLEY. Each company sells its own product.

Commissioner COMMONS. Do you take up—is your association represented in any way before the State boards or commissions that fix hours and wages? Do you appear before them?

Mr. BENTIEY. Well, if there is any legislation that we think is detrimental to our interests, we of course have somebody on the ground.

Commissioner COMMONS. That is in the legislature?

Mr. BENTLEY. Yes, sir.

Commissioner COMMONS. But in the welfare commission or commissions of that kind that fix hours?

Mr. .BENTLEY. When we are interested we appear ·before it, of course—any commission.

Commissioner COMMONS. Have they fixed any hours?

Mr. BENTLEY. No, sir.

Commissioner COMMONS. Or wages or anything in your industry?

Mr. BENTLEY. Not as yet. The welfare commission have required us to fill out blanks this season, which will give them some data to work on, but other than that they have made no move as yet.

Commissioner COMMONS. That is all.

Chairman WALSH. Mr. Garretson would like to ask some questions.

Commissioner GARRETSON. You build your plants or acquire them?

Mr. BENTLEY. Our organization absorbed a good many subsidiary companies in its start. Of course since that time we have built some plants.

Commissioner GARRETSON. And under the present name it dates from that absorption, or was it the old name?

Mr. BENTLEY. It dates from the time of the absorption; yes, sir.

Commissioner GARRETSON. This association that you refer to, does its executive committee ever confer in regard to the price to be paid for material· to those you buy from?

Mr. BENTLEY. No, sir.

Commissioner GARRETSON. Nor the output?

Mr. BENTLEY. No, sir.

Commissioner GARRETSON. Nor the labor?

Mr. BENTLEY. No, sir.

Commissioner GARRETSON. That is all, Mr. Chairman.

Chairman WALSH. That is all; thank you.

Chairman WALSH. Call Mr. Horst. Is he the next one?

Dr. PARKER. Mr. Horst.

TESTIMONY OF MR. E. CLEMENS HORST.

Chairman WALSH. Take that chair, please, Mr. Horst. You have been served, Mr. Horst, with a copy of the questions under which the commission would like you to direct your answers?

Mr. HORST. Yes; I got a copy yesterday; but I don't know what I did with it.

Chairman WALSH. Did you look it over before you lost it?

Mr. HORST. Yes; I looked it over.

(The list of questions was handed to Mr. Horst.)

Chairman WALSH. I wish you would please follow that, Mr. Horst, and answer those questions as exhaustively and as concisely as you can.

Mr. HORST. The first question: "What is the character of the demand for labor in your industry, and what sorts of labor are needed?" Well, all adult labor; and all sorts—that is, all nationalities.

Chairman WALSH. Skilled and unskilled?

Mr. HORST. Outside of the head men; that is, all unskilled. Probably 5 per cent skilled and 95 per cent unskilled.

Chairman WALSH. What do you call the head men, please, Mr. Horst?

Mr. HORST. Well, the superintendents.

Chairman WALSH. Foremen?

Mr. HORST. And the foremen.

Chairman WALSH. Now, as to sex.

Mr. HORST. The sex, all men up to harvest time. And then during harvest time in our particular business, in our company's business, in California, there would be 90 per cent men and 10 per cent women.

Chairman WALSH. Adults or minors?

Mr. HORST. Well, all adults in our business.

Chairman WALSH. Have you any preference for any particular nationality?

Mr. HORST. No, sir.

Chairman WALSH. I will get you to state, Mr. Horst, the name of your company.

Mr. HORST. The E. Clemens Horst Co.

Chairman WALSH. And it is a corporation, is it?

Mr. HORST. It is a corporation; yes, sir.

Chairman WALSH. Of what State—incorporated in what State?

Mr. HORST. New Jersey.

Chairman WALSH. And the capital stock?

Mr. HORST. One million one hundred thousand dollars.

Chairman WALSH. And its lines—the lines of its product?

Mr. HORST. Hops—hop growing.

Chairman WALSH. Altogether?

Mr. HORST. Yes, sir.

Chairman WALSH. And how long has it been in existence?

Mr. HORST. Well, that particular company 11 years; but it is a continuation of another company that has been in business for about 25 years.

Chairman WALSH. What proportion of the business of the industry does your company do, what percentage would you say, in the State?

Mr. HORST. About 10 per cent of the business of the coast.

Chairman WALSH. That includes what States?

Mr. HORST. California, Oregon, and British Columbia. About 20 per cent of the business of California.

Chairman WALSH. How much of Oregon?

Mr. HORST. About 4 per cent.

Chairman WALSH. And British Columbia?

Mr. HORST. A hundred per cent—90 per cent; about 95 per cent.

Chairman WALSH. And what is the extent of your business in British Columbia per year in money?

Mr. HORST. About $200,000.

Chairman WALSH. And in Oregon

Mr. HORST. About a hundred and fifty thousand.

Chairman WALSH. And in California?

Mr. HORST. About five hundred to six hundred thousand dollars.

Chairman WALSH. Now, then, take question B to begin with: "What is the extent of the demand for labor in your industry—its seasonal character? Describe the season of fluctuations in the demand during an average year."

Mr. HORST. Well, there are very few people engaged in the wintertime, and our regular season is from about February to harvest time, and then during the harvest time we have our big season.

Chairman WALSH. And what is that time of the year?

Mr. HORST. From the middle of August to the 1st of October. In California from the middle of August to the middle of September.

Chairman WALSH. What is the character of the supply of labor in your industry? What sorts of labor are available?

Mr. HORST. Well, all sorts of unskilled labor.

Chairman WALSH. Does the supply sometimes exceed the demand, or vice versa?

Mr. HORST. Well, for the last two years the supply has greatly exceeded the demand.

Chairman WALSH. What nationalities do you have from which to pick your help?

Mr. HORST. All nationalities.

Chairman WALSH. Well, are there many native born? What proportion do the other nationalities bear to the native born?

· Mr. HORST. Well, it is continually varying. Sometimes we have a lot of Americans and sometimes we do not. It is varying all the time. It would not be the same one week after the other or one year after the other.

Chairman WALSH. What nationalities are employed; is there any particular one predominates?

Mr. HORST. Well, what we call the itinerant laborers, they would predominate.

Chairman WALSH. Yes; but what nationalities—Italians?

Mr. HORST. No.

Chairman WALSH. Germans or——

Mr. Horst. They are what we call the "hobo" element.

Chairman Walsh. Yes; but what nationalities?

Mr. Horst. Well, I guess they are mostly Americans.

Chairman Walsh. Mostly Americans. What methods are used in getting the job connected with the man in your industry?

Mr. Horst. Most of them come along with their blankets and apply for the job.

Chairman Walsh. Do you advertise?

Mr. Horst. No more now. We used to advertise, say, a few years ago.

Chairman Walsh. Do you use employment agencies, private or public?

Mr. Horst. We use them to some extent; yes.

Chairman Walsh. Now, just describe how it is done and what.

Mr. Horst. We telephone to the employment agent to send a certain number of men for a certain class of work, and they send the men out.

Chairman Walsh. Who pays them?

Mr. Horst. The man employed.

Chairman Walsh. Could you suggest any way or any method of getting employees in your industry?

Mr. Horst. Well, it might, it seems to me, make better working conditions for the men.

Chairman Walsh. Well, are you doing that?

Mr. Horst. Yes; we are making—yes, we are improving the conditions. But there is an oversupply of men, anyhow.

Chairman Walsh. What are the possibilities of spreading the demand for agricultural labor of your character more evenly throughout the year? Is there any possibility of a thing of that sort?

Mr. Horst. In the hop, particularly; the hop industry?

Chairman Walsh. In your industry, yes; in the hop industry.

Mr. Horst. No; you can't make any improvement in the demand for labor in that particular industry.

Chairman Walsh. It can not be made more elastic? There is no other use the land can be put to or anything of that sort?

Mr. Horst. Oh, yes; but that would not be in the hop industry, then.

Chairman Walsh. I know; but, as a person chiefly in the hop industry, couldn't you do anything else at all to take up more labor during the year?

Mr. Horst. We could grow other crops at other times.

Chairman Walsh. Has any attention been given to that? Is it being done?

Mr. Horst. To some small extent.

Chairman Walsh. Well, would it be economically advantageous to you to do that?

Mr. Horst. I don't think so.

Chairman Walsh. And therefore it has not been done?

Mr. Horst. It is not done.

Chairman Walsh. What is your attitude concerning agricultural and migratory labor unions?

Mr. Horst. In what way?

Chairman Walsh. Your entire attitude toward them? Can the men working in your industry be organized as a matter of advantage to either the workers or yourself?

Mr. Horst. I think it is possible that the men can be organized, but not probable; that is, not as far as white men are concerned. The organization is carried on pretty effectively as far as the Asiatics are concerned. The Asiatics have organizations, and they work satisfactorily.

Chairman Walsh. Just describe their organization.

Mr. Horst. Well, they don't have any organization by name. They have societies and—for instance, you take the Hindus; they run in bands. They run in lots of 15 to 50.

Chairman Walsh. Do you deal with them collectively?

Mr. Horst. You deal with one Hindu, who will furnish you the whole crew. You go to the Japanese and they will furnish you with a hundred or two hundred, and you go to one man and he will furnish the number of men. You go to a Chinaman and he will do the same thing, furnish any number you want.

Chairman Walsh. Is your rate of wages stable? Do you pay the same rate to all nationalities?

Mr. Horst. No. I have my rates of wages here for California, Oregon, and British Columbia.

Chairman Walsh. Very good. Give them to us.

Mr. Horst. In California in fall and winter, nine and a half hours' work, $1.85 pay, no board; in the summertime, 10½ hours, $1.85 pay, no board; in the harvest time, 11 hours, $2.60, without board. Now, I have got the figures here for Oregon and British Columbia, if you would like to have them.

Chairman Walsh. Go ahead and give them.

Mr. Horst. In Oregon, nine and one-half hours, $2 a day—that is, in the winter; in the summer, 10 hours, $2 to $2.25; in the harvest time, $2.75; in British Columbia, nine hours, 22½ cents an hour in the wintertime; 10 hours, 22½ cents per hour, in the summertime; harvest time, 22½ cents per hour. Now, the white women in Oregon during harvest time, 25 cents per day cheaper than men, or $2.50 per day. White women during other times about 25 cents per day cheaper than men. White women during harvest time, $2 to $2.25 per day, against men at $2.60 per day.

I have here the rate of wages for the Hindus and Japs. Do you want that?

Chairman Walsh. Yes.

Mr. Horst. Hindus, California, winter and spring, $1.50 to $1.75; Japs, $1.60 to $1.85; Japs, summer time, $1.75 to $2.25; Japs, harvest, $2.25 to $2.50; Hindus, in summer, $1.85 to $2; Hindus, in harvest, $2 to $2.25; Mexican rates same as Hindus; Greeks same as Hindus, but at times as high as Japs; Chinese rates same as Hindus. In Oregon—Japs, the same rates as white men at practically all times; very few Greeks and Mexicans in Oregon on ranch work. In British Columbia Hindus get 15 cents to 17½ cents an hour in winter and 17½ cents per hour in spring and summer; Hindus get 17½ cents to 20 cents per hour in harvest time; Chinese rates same as Hindus; no Japs on ranch work in British Columbia.

Chairman Walsh. What proportion of white men do you have to these ranches?

Mr. Horst. Well, we get as many white as we can, and fill up with orientals.

Chairman Walsh. Then, you can not get enough white labor—you say that is the reason?

Mr. Horst. You can get enough white labor, but it changes too frequently; you can't get steady. You get as many white people as you can safely get and count upon to work, but you can't count upon the white men—the white element—that works in the hop fields during the harvest season.

Chairman Walsh. Could you take the average year and approximate the relative numbers of the orientals and white men?

Mr. Horst. Well, in the wintertime there are no orientals employed. I am talking of the hop industry as an entirety.

Chairman Walsh. Yes.

Mr. Horst. In the wintertime there are no orientals. In the spring work—that is, the training work—taking the State as an entirety, I presume the orientals would figure about 25 per cent.

Chairman Walsh. Describe how you board your people.

Mr. Horst. The orientals board themselves. The whites we board up to harvest time, and where we have hop-picking machines we board them during harvest time, and where the people pick hops by hand they board themselves.

Chairman Walsh. And there is no charge for board in any instance?

Mr. Horst. No; these prices I gave you are without the board.

Chairman Walsh. Without the board?

Mr. Horst. The board deducted.

Chairman Walsh. Just describe how your boarding houses are operated?

Mr. Horst. Well, the men can board there; they can either get the board or get the 60 cents. The boarding houses are run on a basis a man can take his pick—board himself or not board himself.

Chairman Walsh. What do they do generally?

Mr. Horst. They generally don't board themselves.

Chairman Walsh. They don't board themselves; they generally board in your boarding houses?

Mr. Horst. Yes, sir.

Chairman Walsh. How is your commissary recruited—how do you get your provisions?

Mr. Horst. We buy them in the——

Chairman Walsh. Do you have a commissary department?

Mr. Horst. Each ranch buys its own food supplies.

Chairman Walsh. How many ranches has your company?

Mr. Horst. Oh, about a dozen.

Chairman WALSH. Just describe where they are, please, and the number of men employed—the number of persons employed on each.

Mr. HORST. I can tell you the ranches, but I can't tell you offhand the number employed on each place.

Chairman WALSH. Give it as close as you can, approximately, or else say you can not.

Mr. HORST. I can get the figures after lunch, if you wish.

Chairman WALSH. I wish you would supply them after lunch. Just describe at the present time where they are located.

(See Horst exhibit.)

Mr. HORST. Ranches at Agassic, British Columbia; Sardis, British Columbia; Salem, Oreg.; Independence, Oreg.; Los Molinas, Cal.; Wheatland, Cal.; Ben Ali, Cal.; Perkins; two ranches on the Consumne River in Sacramento County, and one in Mendocino County, Cal.

Chairman WALSH. Is there any organization among your employees at the present time?

Mr. HORST. No, sir.

Chairman WALSH. Have any complaints ever been made as to wages and conditions of labor upon your ranches?

Mr. HORST. No.

Chairman WALSH. None that have been brought to your attention at all during the past year or two?

Mr. HORST. No, sir.

Chairman WALSH. Any other questions?

Commissioner GARRETSON. Yes. Among the Hindus, Japs, and Chinks, the same result works out as if they had a labor union—you deal with the head man?

Mr. HORST. Yes.

Commissioner GARRETSON. The padrone or boss or whatever you call him?

Mr. HORST. Yes.

Commissioner GARRETSON. And he adjusts any questions or complaints that arise, he adjusts them himself?

Mr. HORST. Yes.

Commissioner GARRETSON. And if satisfactory conclusions are not reached, if they leave, they leave in a body?

Mr. HORST. Yes, sir.

Commissioner GARRETSON. And the result is exactly the same, as far as they are concerned, as if organization by name, which I suppose they never hear of, did exist among them?

Mr. HORST. Yes, sir.

Commissioner GARRETSON. That is all.

Commissioner COMMONS. In this State, what is the largest number of men you employ at the height of the season?

Mr. HORST. Our company, or the hop growers in general?

Commissioner COMMONS. Your company.

Mr. HORST. Oh, about, in the height of the season, I guess about 1,500.

Commissioner COMMONS. That is for one month?

Mr. HORST. Yes, sir.

Commissioner COMMONS. And how many men steadily through the year?

Mr. HORST. Beg pardon?

Commissioner COMMONS. At the other times of the year, what is the number that is employed?

Mr. HORST. Well, I guess in the wintertime probably about 150 in California, and in the springtime probably 300 or 400; then in harvest time about 1,500, and that is—we have very few people engaged in the harvest season on account of having machines with which to pick the hops; by hand picking it would take proportionately during the harvest season very, very many more.

Commissioner COMMONS. Is the hand picking the prevailing manner in the State?

Mr. HORST. Yes, sir.

Commissioner COMMONS. How would that compare with the 1,500—you have 1,500 doing your picking?

Mr. HORST. It takes about five times as many hand pickers as machine pickers, in round numbers.

Commissoner COMMONS. How long has this machine been practicable?

Mr. HORST. The last few years.

Commissioner COMMONS. What year did you first use it?

Mr. HORST. We used the first machine in 1908, but it has been developed since that time.

Commissioner COMMONS. Is all of your picking machine picking now?

Mr. HORST. In California; yes.

Commissioner COMMONS. When did you first get on the basis, that basis of all your picking—machine picking?

Mr. HORST. About 1910.

Commissioner COMMONS. You are the pioneers, then, in the use of the machine?

Mr. HORST. Yes.

Commissioner COMMONS. The rest of the business is mostly hand picking?

Mr. HORST. It is all hand picking, practically all.

Commissioner COMMONS. Are these machines operated by men?

Mr. HORST. Beg pardon?

Commissioner COMMONS. Are these machines operated by men?

Mr. HORST. Yes, sir.

Commissioner COMMONS. Do you have any women at all?

Mr. HORST. Well, just a sprinkling.

Commissioner COMMONS. What do they do?

Mr. HORST. Beg pardon?

Commissioner COMMONS. What work do the women do?

Mr. HORST. They work on conveyor belts, pick out stems, and all such things, from conveyor belts.

Commissioner COMMONS. Just sort?

Mr. HORST. Yes.

Commissioner COMMONS. How is your packing done?

Mr. HORST. That is all done by men; everything else done by men.

Commissioner COMMONS. Now, take the men that work during the year, are they steady employees?

Mr. HORST. No, sir.

Commissioner COMMONS. Do they change?

Mr. HORST. They are changing; there are a few on each place that stay the year around, but the labor floats a good deal.

Commissioner COMMONS. You said about a hundred and fifty in the winter?

Mr. HORST. Yes.

Commissioner COMMONS. Are those that stay in summer there on steady jobs?

Mr. HORST. Yes.

Commissioner COMMONS. Is that a floating element? Do they have their families and stay there?

Mr. HORST. No.

Commissioner COMMONS. With their families?

Mr. HORST. No; very few men in our line of business have families.

Commissioner COMMONS. Not even this hundred and fifty that have permanent jobs?

Mr. HORST. No even they.

Commissioner COMMONS. There is no such thing as a permanent job?

Mr. HORST. They have a permanent job, but they don't have the family.

Commissioner COMMONS. Take that hundred and fifty; you have a hundred and fifty permanent jobs, how steady are the men who work on those jobs?

Mr. HORST. Well, I guess around the year perhaps 75 per cent of that lot of men probably does not change, 50 to 75 per cent of them does not. But those that we have during the harvest season, they come and go, a continual procession coming in and going to work a day or two or three, and going out.

Commissioner COMMONS. Take the planting and what do you call it, the training?

Mr. HORST. Yes.

Commissioner COMMONS. Where you have three or four hundred—is that also a changeable number of people?

Mr. HORST. Well, they don't change around very much. Their season is so very short, the training season is not very long.

Commissioner COMMONS. It is not?

Mr. HORST. Yes; it is in a way, it runs a couple of months, or runs three months.

Commissioner COMMONS. Runs up to the harvest?

Mr. HORST. But at that time of the year the people don't change around as much as they do during harvest time. The demand for labor during harvest time is so much greater than at other times of the year that the people move around much more. It is so easy for a man to get a job during harvest time that there is not the same——

Commissioner COMMONS. All of these people that come, both for the training season and the harvest season, they come with their own bedding and blankets?

Mr. HORST. Practically all of the people that work on the ranch come with their blankets; all of the white people, practically all of them, come with their blankets.

Commissioner COMMONS. And I suppose the orientals come in gangs as well as the others?

Mr. HORST. Yes.

Commissioner COMMONS. What are your housing accommodations?

Mr. HORST. They have bunk houses, regular bunk houses, and during the picking season we have tents in addition to the bunk houses. Then all of the ranches are taking up and fixing according to the terms of the State Board of Immigration and Housing; we followed out their directions with regard to housing the men, baths and so on.

Commissioner COMMONS. What are these standards? Are they different from what have been heretofore?

Mr. HORST. They made a change. They never made a standard until last year. There was no standard at all. Now they have made a standard for sanitary arrangements and for housing, and for baths for the employees.

Commissioner COMMONS. Shower baths, are they?

Mr. HORST. Yes, sir.

Commissioner COMMONS. Are they used by the men?

Mr. HORST. They are not used as much as they ought to be.

Commissioner COMMONS. Are there enough of them to go around?

Mr. HORST. Yes; more baths than people use. The requirements for baths are in excess of the demand for their use. Probably in another year people will get used to bathing.

Commissioner COMMONS. Well, I suppose it is too early to say whether these improved housing arrangements make your work more steady, or rather the number of men more steady, the employment more steady?

Mr. HORST. Well, I couldn't tell you that.

Commissioner COMMONS. Do you keep any figures that would show the number of different individuals that you hire in the course of the harvest season? You say you have 1,500.

Mr. HORST. We keep the list of the men that come and go; yes.

Commissioner COMMONS. How many? Fifteen hundred in four weeks?

Mr. HORST. Of the people that come during the harvest season, you can figure roughly that 50 per cent of them will stay during the harvest season; 50 per cent that start at the beginning stay during the season.

Commissioner COMMONS. That is 750 out of the 1,500, we will say, that start in, stay through?

Mr. HORST. Stay during the season. The other 50 per cent will be the floating element. They come and stay a couple of days and move along, work in the next place. Maybe some man will leave a job on one of our ranches and go to another of our ranches; they just keep going from ranch to ranch on maybe our own property. It is a sort of gypsy spirit within them.

Commissioner COMMONS. Do these oriental contract gangs do that?

Mr. HORST. They don't move around.

Commissioner COMMONS. They start in and stay?

Mr. HORST. They start in and stay.

Commissioner COMMONS. Of these hundred and fifty, what proportion would come under these oriental gangs that work together, how many of those would be in this——

Mr. HORST. I don't know which hundred and fifty you refer to.

Commissioner COMMONS. Out of the 1,500 that are there in the harvest season, how many of them will belong to these oriental gangs?

Mr. HORST. Oh, perhaps a third of them.

Commissioner COMMONS. Five hundred?

Mr. HORST. Yes.

Commissioner COMMONS. Now, the rest are what you call hoboes, all nationalities?

Mr. HORST. Yes, sir.

Commissioner COMMONS. They are what you call the whites?

Mr. HORST. They are whites, they are all whites.

Commissioner COMMONS. They come as individuals with their blankets?

Mr. HORST. They come as individuals.

Commissioner COMMONS. Now, of that half that come that are not orientals, how many of them stay through the season?

Mr. HORST. Well, I say of them, those that come in at the beginning, perhaps 50 per cent of them don't move; they will stay through the season, and the other 50 per cent come and go.

Commissioner COMMONS. The orientals stay all through the season; 50 per cent of the others stay through the season?

Mr. HORST. Yes, sir; but you don't know which lot of the whites are going to stay. If there could be some method devised so they could be made to stay and you wouldn't have to change around all the time, the employers' position would be very much better; but how to accomplish that I don't know.

Commissioner COMMONS. Suppose they would organize the way the orientals do, have an agency?

Mr. HORST. It would be a good thing for the employer, I believe.

Commissioner COMMONS. If they had an agency and organized, and you would hire them the same as you do orientals, and they would agree to furnish help during the season?

Mr. HORST. I think it would be a great improvement for the employer, if the leaders were responsible men; that is, reliable men; if they were workers rather than agitators.

Commissioner COMMONS. When you come to contract with these oriental gangs, is that made by the day for so much work, or for each man that is employed, and do you keep the time of his employment?

Mr. HORST. Pay them so much per day per man; pay so much per day per man to the Chinaman or the Japanese, or the Hindu, who keeps his time—and we keep the time at the same time, and compare notes every noon and evening.

Commissioner COMMONS. Do they make use of your boarding house?

Mr. HORST. No; they always board themselves.

Commissioner COMMONS. How do they arrange that? Do they have tents or what?

Mr. HORST. Well, they have tents and they have cooks, and they take care of their own commissary.

Commissioner COMMONS. Now, the whites, how about them? Do they board themselves?

Mr. HORST. No. On our place we board all the whites; on all the other places the whites, one class of·them is boarded by the employers and the other class boards itself.

Commissioner COMMONS. What is it that determines that?

Mr. HORST. Well, those people that work on piecework, they board themselves. Those people that don't work piecework are generally boarded by the employer. For instance, hand picking, they get so much per 100 pounds, and those people will board themselves. But teamsters and gleaners and all the other classes of people that work on a ranch where hand picking is done, those people are boarded by the employers. But those men generally have the option of either boarding themselves or being boarded. If they board themselves, they get the board allowance.

Commissioner COMMONS. Your ranch is being picked by machine picking, then?

Mr. HORST. They are conducted differently.

Commissioner COMMONS. There is not any piecework in it?

Mr. HORST. We have got no piecework; no, sir.

Commissioner COMMONS. So they all board with the companies?

Mr. HORST. Yes.

Commissioner COMMONS. In the companies?

Mr. HORST. Yes, practically all; those that want to board themselves can do it, and get their allowance, and some take-advantage of it; but not many.

Commissioner COMMONS. That is all.

Chairman WALSH. Commissioner Garretson would like to ask you some questions.

Commissioner GARRETSON. The institution of these standards by the State turns you into a mission of cleanliness, virtually, because people have not caught up with the institution yet; is that it? They have not commenced bathing yet—do not avail themselves of that?

Mr. HORST. They do to some extent.

Commissioner GARRETSON. I say not generally yet?

Mr. HORST. We had bathing—bath houses—on our ranches 10 years ago, but nobody ever used them.

Commissioner GARRETSON. Did you have to go out and put any additional expense to get these standards?

Mr. HORST. Yes.

Commissioner GARRETSON. How much change did it make on your ranches, the establishment of these standards?

Mr. HORST. How much difference in what respect?

Commissioner GARRETSON. In the institution of the plant that was required?

Mr. HORST. Oh, I don't know; certain standards; a certain number of toilets for a hundred people engaged; I don't know the number; a certain number of bathing places per hundred.

Commissioner GARRETSON. Did it make any great difference in your housing facilities, the establishment of the standards, over what you had before?

Mr. HORST. A comparatively small expense.

Commissioner GARRETSON. These machines that you have, is it necessary to glean behind them?

Mr. HORST. Yes, sir; to some extent.

Commissioner GARRETSON. And this service that is performed by women on the transmitting belt, is that an outgrowth of the use of the machine, or did it occur also, and was it necessary in hand picking?

Mr. HORST. It is not necessary in hand picking; no, sir.

Commissioner GARRETSON. Both of those are the outgrowth of the use of the machine?

Mr. HORST. Yes.

Commissioner GARRETSON. This gypsy spirit that you referred to as existing among a large number of these workers—the wanderlust?

Mr. HORST. Yes.

Commissioner GARRETSON. Do you believe that that has been developed in any degree by the prevalence of seasonal employment?

Mr. HORST. Well, I tell you, the trouble is, people don't—there is not enough work to go around, and the people get in the habit of moving, and they keep moving.

Commissioner GARRETSON. That has been developed largely by the fact that they were never able to secure steady employment?

Mr. HORST. I believe so. I believe if there was more steady employment we would have less of that wandering sort.

Commissioner GARRETSON. In other words, if the boy, when he comes from school, entered on the service that was regular he would develop regular habits, probably, instead of having the wandering spirit developed by his being employed a little while and then having to hunt work?

Mr. HORST. That is it. There is an overabundance of labor in California to-day. There is no getting over that fact to-day.

Commissioner GARRETSON. You are laboring, then, under exactly the same difficulty that confronts the north coast, as it is stated there, a superabundance of men as against the opportunities for labor that exist.

Mr. HORST. Yes, sir.

Commissioner GARRETSON. Do you believe that has been contributed to in this country in any appreciable degree by the continent-wide blazing of the opportunities for employment and of the climatic advantages?

Mr. HORST. Well, I feel this, that the situation has been very materially changed by the new tariff bill, and, of course, I don't want to go into any political question; but I can not help but feel that we are making a mistake in increasing our imports. As it decreases the amount of labor available it decreases the amount of work available, and we ought to do everything we can to import the least amount of stuff, because our population is so rapidly increasing we have to look out for them and take care of the gradually increasing population of this country.

Commissioner GARRETSON. Now, have you been able to note any appreciable increase in unemployment since that tariff went into effect?

Mr. HORST. I think it has been very noticeable.

Commissioner GARRETSON. You didn't suffer in the same degree from a surplus of men prior——

Mr. HORST. We don't suffer from a surplus of men; the men suffer.

Commissioner GARRETSON. I am speaking of the body as a whole. The employer, I don't think, ever suffers directly from a surplus of men. Indirectly,

I think that he might; but have you noticed that prior to the passage of this tariff the laboring people did not have that trouble?

Mr. Horst. The laboring man did not have the trouble—well, just before the tariff passed; the unsettled conditions took place just before the passage of the tariff—perhaps a year before—but since that time there has been the general fear of the tariff, and then the actual fact of increased importations, coupled with increased population in this country, has made the thing bad, and we have a surplus of workers; and that condition, to my mind, needs remedying more than these outcroppings you appear to be touching between organized labor and employers.

Commissioner Garretson. Bear in mind I am not sensitive on the tariff, because what little politics I have is Republican; but I am not working very hard at it. That is all, Mr. Chairman.

Chairman Walsh. What is your acreage this year of hops?

Mr. Horst. We have about 3,000 acres in hops.

Chairman Walsh. How are crop conditions generally; are you getting a full year?

Mr. Horst. Well, it is about—it is a fair year; not a full year.

Chairman Walsh. How does it compare with last year?

Mr. Horst. About the same—a little short of last year.

Chairman Walsh. A little short of last year?

Mr. Horst. Yes, sir.

Chairman Walsh. What was your acreage last year?

Mr. Horst. The same acreage.

Chairman Walsh. Approximately the same?

Mr. Horst. We had approximately the same.

Chairman Walsh. This rate of wages you submit here was the prevailing rate last year as well as this year?

Mr. Horst. The wages haven't been reduced; only the labor has been more plentiful.

Chairman Walsh. The wages have not been reduced and the acreage has not been reduced any?

Mr. Horst. In Oregon the wages have been increased in the last few years. Up until about three years ago the Oregon wages were below the California wages.

Chairman Walsh. You observed——

Mr. Horst. Now, it is the other way.

Chairman Walsh. Now your observations relative to the tariff apply to other commodities than hops?

Mr. Horst. If there is a surplus of labor in one line, it reflects on other lines.

Chairman Walsh. So that it is in this indirect way you think you observe the operation of the tariff in causing a surplus of labor. It has not occurred in your industry; you have raised just as much and wages are better.

Mr. Horst. It hasn't occurred in our particular line, only we have felt the surplus of labor as the result of other lines.

Chairman Walsh. You have had just as much crop gathered?

Mr. Horst. Yes, sir.

Chairman Walsh. That is all.

Commissioner Commons. How about the prices of what you sold during the last year?

Mr. Horst. Well, our prices are governed by foreign crops. If the foreign crops are large, we have low prices; if the foreign crops are short, we have high prices.

Commissioner Commons. Any tariff on your product?

Mr. Horst. Yes, sir; there is a tariff on the product.

Commissioner Commons. Has that been changed?

Mr. Horst. It was advanced. It was advanced in the Payne-Aldrich bill, and left the same in the Wilson bill—left the same in the last bill.

Commissioner Commons. But the bulk of the product is shipped abroad?

Mr. Horst. No, sir.

Commissioner Commons. Then the tariff does not benefit you?

Mr. Horst. The tariff—it does benefit us. If it was not for the tariff we would all quit.

Commissioner Commons. How is the price fixed by the foreign market, then?

Mr. Horst. Because they ship their hops in here. We have got a funny situation. We import and we export. While we export more than we import, still the size of the foreign crop fixes the price in America.

Commissioner Commons. Notwithstanding the tariff?

Mr. Horst. It fixes the price in America; yes, sir.

Commissioner Commons. Notwithstanding the tariff? If you have a satisfactory tariff?

Mr. Horst. We have a satisfactory tariff; but notwithstanding the tariff the size of the foreign crop fixes the price in America.

Commissioner Commons. Are the prices of hops low this season compared with what they were last year?

Mr. Horst. The prices this season are about the same as they were last season in the middle of the season. They were higher at an early date last year than they are this year; very much higher.

Commissioner Commons. What has been the tendency the last three or four years?

Mr. Horst. We have high prices and low prices; it is a widely fluctuating article.

Commissioner Commons. Depends largely on the crop?

Mr. Horst. The price depends largely on the foreign crop; yes, sir.

Chairman Walsh. Could you conduct your industry with an eight-hour day?

Mr. Horst. Yes, sir.

Chairman Walsh. That is all; thank you.

Commissioner Weinstock. Just one question. Have you made any forecast as to what effect on the labor conditions the European war would have if it is prolonged?

Mr. Horst. I believe as soon as the war is over we will have an enormous immigration, and labor conditions here will be made a lot worse.

Commissioner Weinstock. If the war should be prolonged for several months or a year, what effect would that have upon the labor conditions?

Mr. Horst. I believe as long as the war lasts it is going to be a good thing for America, and as soon as the war is over we will have an enormous amount of immigration, and it will be a bad thing.

Commissioner Weinstock. We will have a surplus of labor?

Mr. Horst. We have an oversurplus now.

Commissioner Weinstock. It will be intensified?

Mr. Horst. Yes, sir.

Chairman Walsh. At this point we will adjourn until 2 o'clock.

(Whereupon, at 12.30 o'clock p. m. on this, Thursday, the 27th day of August, 1914, an adjournment was taken until 2 o'clock p. m. of the same day.)

AFTER RECESS—2 P. M.

Met pursuant to adjournment. Present as before.

Chairman Walsh. All right. Proceed.

TESTIMONY OF DR. CARLETON H. PARKER.

Mr. Thompson. Mr. Parker, will you give us your name?

Dr. Parker. Carleton H. Parker.

Mr. Thompson. Your address?

Dr. Parker. San Francisco.

Mr. Thompson. And your profession?

Dr. Parker. Executive secretary of the State commission of immigration and housing.

Mr. Thompson. How long have you held that position?

Dr. Parker. About a year.

Mr. Thompson. How long have you been on the coast here?

Dr. Parker. All my life.

Mr. Thompson. All your life. What position did you hold before that?

Dr. Parker. I was a student in Germany.

Mr. Thompson. Student in Germany. Have you made a study of the industrial problems on the coast, particularly with reference to seasonal labor?

Dr. Parker. I have.

Mr. Thompson. Will you state the condition as you view it?

Dr. Parker. The problem of seasonal labor, so called, in the State is at the same time a large percentage of California's problem of unemployment, and at the same time it has given birth to the newest labor difficulty that we have in California. California perhaps is becoming more seasonal in its demand for labor because of the growing importance of agriculture labor relatively in the State, and also the purely American type of agricultural worker is being replaced by the immigrant. You can't analyze the Wheatland affair and the riot that took place; you can not analyze the strike that has been in process for the last two months in the hop fields, nor can you touch the problem of the unemployed in San Francisco last winter without bringing into the analysis the seasonal character of California's demand for its labor. And I consider that that is one of the most important subjects to establish definitely. A number of the witnesses, I am sure, have been chosen to show in their testimony the maximum of their demand and the minimum, showing the seasonal character of the employment here. A study has been made recently in which I was very much interested, and 100 of the typical life stories contained in that history were taken out and segregated; and the following facts came out in the analysis, and I think probably illuminate the problems as well as anything else. Of these 100 cases that were studied—these were the migratory workers in California—of these statistics taken within the last month and a half, 42 per cent were found to be of foreign birth, 86 per cent were from outside of California. Of the foreign born, 21 per cent naturalized citizens and 31 per cent of the total number reviewed were aliens; 51 per cent had been in California less than six years.

Commissioner GARRETSON. That is, 21 per cent of all the total?

Dr. PARKER. That 21 per cent is of the total. As to their schooling, 55 per cent had left school before the age of 15, and of 26 per cent we were unable to get figures. It seems probable they had never been at school. Seventy-nine per cent of the total were below the age of 40 years; 54 per cent had been migratory and seasonal laborers for less than 10 years, and we were unable to get data for 16 per cent; 20 per cent had worked on an average less than 7 months in the year; 62 per cent worked less than 10 months. The best daily earnings of 36 per cent had never exceeded $3 a day. As to their occupations: 76 per cent had never been anything except common laborers, even the 24 per cent who were classed as skilled, these had in most parts fallen or been forced out of the trades they professed; 35 per cent were or had been members of labor unions, while 65 per cent were absolutely unorganized, knew nothing of any labor organization; 51 per cent sought what work they wanted or could get through the present system that we have, the haphazard private employment agency system.

The extent of the social unrest which has been typical of the California agricultural laborer for the past two years was shown by the fact that 42 per cent of these accidental individuals investigated expressed extremely radical political and economic opinions; 30 per cent professed to be seeking steady work and planning to steady down. Practically the remaining 70 per cent gave their occupation as floating laborers; had no ambition, apparently, or, at least, had no prospect of getting a steady job. Of nationalities—American born, 58 per cent; foreign born, 42 per cent; of the foreign born 6 per cent were Swedes, 5 per cent Italians, 5 per cent English, 1 per cent Austrian, 5 per cent French, 3 per cent Russian, 7 per cent Irish, 4 per cent German, and 1 per cent Finnish, Danish, Mexican, Bohemian, and Portuguese.

The political status of these men: 65 per cent were American citizens—United States citizens, 33 per cent aliens, and 2 per cent we could get no data on.

The ages range in this wise: 4 per cent were from 16 to 20 years, 19 per cent from 21 to 25, 22 per cent from 26 to 30, 12 per cent from 31 to 35, and 22 per cent from 36 to 40.

Then the per cent for the other age groups running up to 65—from 41 to 45, 46 to 55, 56 to 60 and 61 to 65, was 7 per cent, 4 per cent, 1 per cent, and 3 per cent. The men were massed between the ages of 21 and 40.

The years in the United States of those that were foreign born: 11 per cent were here under 6 years, 15 per cent between 6 and 10, and 5 per cent betwen 11 and 15, and it runs on up. It shows that these migratory laborers taken from these statistics were more Americanized than the normal industrial workers in the city; that is, they had—they almost all spoke English; we found very few who still spoke their mother tongue, and they were all the so-called American hobo type. And even Coxey's army had its little regiment—little company of Germans and a company of Italians; but I noticed that both those companies spoke English. They are either Americans purely or else they are aliens who have been in America long enough to assume all the characteristics of the American laborer. The years in California, if born out of the State: 51 per cent had been in California under 6 years; 22 per cent had been in California from 6 to 10 years.

These statistics are compromised by the fact that a good deal of the Californian population of this character has been a short time in the State. A number have been in California a long time; 11 to 15 years, 8 per cent; 32 per cent had been members of trade unions; 3 per cent members of the I. W. W.; 65 per cent were nonmembers, had no membership whatsoever.

Of the political and economic opinions: 42 per cent were radical, 16 per cent were conservative, 25 per cent indifferent, and 17 per cent would furnish no data whatsoever.

It is hoped that within a few months we shall have careful statistics covering 600 to 700 altogether. And when those statistics are completed they will be laid before your commission.

This, in a rough way, illustrates the—or gives really the cross-section of the problem of agricultural labor in this State. The fact that San Francisco is said to have in winter thirty-five to forty thousand men lying up until the earlier season, the first agricultural demand for labor occurs, is explained by the fact that along in November and December, especially in November, agricultural work practically ceases. The State being fundamentally an agricultural State, the industrial life of the State not being of tremendous importance, and the fact that the State is geographically isolated, means that we have to nurse our own casual labor class through the winter. Then there is a certain percentage, a certain number who drift over the boundaries of the State because the climate is mild. They come in from Nevada and come in from Oregon with the closing down of the lumber mills, especially in the southern part of the State; it receives a number of migratory workers, both tramps, who will not work, and casuals, who are thrown out of work by the seasonal employment of the Middle West.

We have no statistics for 1910 of the employment in the seasonal industries of laborers of this class. If we had the statistics, I am certain that we could show that California's agricultural life, as well as the canning of fruits and the drying of fruits and the packing of dried fruit almost closes off its demand for labor. I think we will find that a great deal of this labor stays on in the State and does not migrate; in fact, it has no place to go where there is winter employment. Any increase in unemployment due to weakening of the demand by Californian industries for labor simply adds its quota of unemployment to those who are normally in the city of San Francisco and the city of Los Angeles.

It was said that last winter there were thirty-five to forty thousand men not working in San Francisco, of whom five to six thousand were fairly destitute; there were from ten to fifteen thousand not employed lying up in the city of Los Angeles, and of these three to four thousand were destitute.

The city of Sacramento—in that city it was estimated there were from three to four thousand, although it is a small place, three to four thousand men without work, of whom probably from a thousand to fifteen hundred were destitute—that is, they were men who would drift into the unemployed armies. They would drift any place that would seem to give them a chance to have a place to sleep and something to eat.

The seasonal character of California's industrial demand also brings this danger, that where the fruit season fails in part we find a great many men on the road in the valley who have not obtained work, and that has been the experience this summer.

There has been a great deal of summer unemployment in California, and serious summer unemployment. These men who formerly reached the city of San Francisco with forty, fifty, or a hundred dollars saved up to winter through will reach San Francisco without that, and the employment-agency men, men who have had experience in the city for years, have made the forecast that San Francisco will experience a greater problem of winter unemployment this winter than she did last winter. I have found no contrary opinion to that. If we had an unemployed army last winter that was normal, an army that was to be expected considering the conditions, we will have a larger army this coming winter. And the statement is made by men who have no pronounced philosophy with regard to the temperament of the people that the men who will land in San Francisco this coming winter will be more agitated and will be temperamentally more threatening; so far as you can call unorganized unemployment an army, that it will be a greater problem in San Francisco this coming winter than it was last.

The Wheatland experience ties itself into this general problem, because it exposed the fact that California's traditional method of treating, housing, and feeding migratory workers was disastrously bad. That the accepted traditions in ranch life, the traditions that rule among contractors for the care of their men, are traditions that have very, very low standards. The commission with which I am connected has investigated now 641 labor camps in the State of California, which contain 41,058 workers. Of these 641 labor camps—lumber camps, construction camps, hop camps, berry camps, and highway camps—188 camps were bad. By bad I mean that there was little or no toilet facilities. If there were women there, there were probably no toilets especially for women. There was no chance for the workers to bathe. Each one of these camps, these 188, violated the State law with regard to the sleeping accommodations—the cubic-air law, that there should be 500 cubic feet of air for every sleeper. The kitchens were not screened; the dining rooms were not screened. In a great many of the bunk houses there was no wooden platform or wooden flooring. We found some camps with 100, almost 100, women and children with no toilets at all. Some of the camps were especially—some of the contractors' camps were filthy, evil, and dangerous beyond any description. Of the 641 camps, 293 camps were fair. These camps had some accommodations. Of the 641 camps, 155 were good.

The investigators who went through the labor camps in the State at the same time investigated as nearly as they could the attitude of the men, the temperament, the presence of any spirit with regard to labor camp conditions. And they found—the estimate was made by the investigators—that a good deal of the unrest, which has, in a way, convulsed California's agricultural workers this year, was due to the careless, indifferent housing of migratory, casual labor. And so the commission made a determined effort to establish a minimum of camp sanitation, which has been the principal work of the commission for the last year; and of the 641 camps, but two camps were found who refused to raise their sanitation up to the modest minimum that has been established by the commission.

There was no attempt made to make this minimum a part of the law, although there is a law (law 182 of the laws of 1913), which designated the State board of health as the body which shall enforce the minimum camp sanitation. I appeared in this investigation as a deputy of the State board of health, but no attempt was made to make this minimum a part of the law.

The problem of the agricultural worker, the problem of the migratory seasonal worker in this State, is a dual problem according to my analysis. In the first place it includes the consideration of seasonal irregularity or seasonal irregular demand for labor that is fundamental in California hiring, and holds danger from a definite economic standpoint.

The second phase of the problem is the general indifference and carelessness in the treatment of these workers. That is due in part to the fact that they are utterly disorganized or their organizations are militant organizations gathered together for some definite strike object, and not for a long campaign for better conditions, and secondly, because we have a careless California tradition of laissez faire—let things rest.

I suppose, as a class, the California rancher is really as kind and benevolent and generous a person as you will have as an employer, but it is hard to harmonize that character with the universal tradition of careless housing and careless feeding of the men who work in the fruits; of the housing of women and children in the seasonal occupations such as berry picking and canning; and the only way in which that can be remedied is probably by being shocked into a realization of what it means by such episodes as the Wheatland affair, or a long-sustained publicity program. That part can be taken care of, and, perhaps, will be.

The greatest danger to-day that the State of California faces is the fundamental and almost necessarily irregular quality of the demand for labor in the agricultural districts of the State, more so than any other State in the Union, I believe; and the witnesses, who will appear, seem to be all able to contribute their isolated evidence upon the irregularity of the demand and its seasonal quality—the fact that it disappears when winter comes on.

Now, if there are any detailed questions that you would like to ask I would be glad to answer them.

Chairman WALSH. I don't think so at the present time. We want, as I understand. just to get the general condition so that we can omit those questions specifically to the other witnesses. So, that unless there is some question some commissioner wishes to ask, or Mr. Thompson, you will be excused now. Call your next.

Mr. THOMPSON. Mr. Speed.

TESTIMONY OF MR. GEORGE H. SPEED.

Mr. THOMPSON. Give us your name.
Mr. SPEED. George H. Speed.
Mr. THOMPSON. Your address?
Mr. SPEED. No. 59A Thirteenth Street.
Mr. THOMPSON. In San Francisco?
Mr. SPEED. In San Francisco.
Mr. THOMPSON. Your occupation?
Mr. SPEED. Well, I work at any old thing at the present time; my trade is a hatter.
Mr. THOMPSON. Are you connected with the Industrial Workers of the World?
Mr. SPEED. Yes, sir.
Mr. THOMPSON. What position do you hold with them?
Mr. SPEED. Not any at present.
Mr. THOMPSON. What position did you hold with them?
Mr. SPEED. Well, I have been on the executive board, and also general organizer.
Mr. THOMPSON. How long were you general organizer?
Mr. SPEED. One year.
Mr. THOMPSON. In this part of the country?
Mr. SPEED. Well, I have been all over the country.
Mr. THOMPSON. How long have you been located in San Francisco and California?
Mr. SPEED. Well, I came to California in 1878.
Chairman WALSH. In what States has he acted as organizer for the I. W. W.?
Mr. THOMPSON. In what States have you acted as organizer for the I. W. W.?
Mr. SPEED. Well, in this State and throughout the United States.
Mr. THOMPSON. Throughout the United States, where, particularly——
Chairman WALSH. Every State?
Mr. THOMPSON. Every State?
Mr. SPEED. Yes; south and all over.
Mr. THOMPSON. Well, where was the main portion of your time, or, at least, how much time did you spend in this State in that work?
Mr. SPEED. Well, I have been ever since the organization has been started, I have been working for it for all I know how.
Mr. THOMPSON. Either officially or——
Mr. SPEED. Voluntarily and officially.
Mr. THOMPSON. During that work, have you come in contact with the agricultural problems of the State? Of course you have?
Mr. SPEED. Oh, yes.
Mr. THOMPSON. What is your opinion as to the kinds of labor needed in the agricultural fields here, you might say with reference to whether it should be skilled or unskilled, and the proportion of skilled and unskilled workers that are required?
Mr. SPEED. Well, the skill is being eliminated not only in that line of work but in all other lines, evidently, by the application of new devices.
Mr. THOMPSON. Did you hear the testimony this morning that 90 per cent were unskilled and 10 per cent skilled?
Mr. SPEED. I believe that is about correct, probably fewer skilled, as far as that is concerned, in agriculture.
Mr. THOMPSON. Did you hear what was said about the proportion of women and men in industry, too?
Mr. SPEED. Yes, sir; I heard about it.
Mr. THOMPSON. Well, were those statements made by Mr. Horst—Bentley and Horst—with reference to those figures about correct?
Mr. SPEED. Well, I don't know about the wage part of it. I think the wage part of it is incorrect.
Mr. THOMPSON. Well, what have you to say about the wage that is paid to unskilled labor in agriculture?
Mr. SPEED. I want to say wages are less to-day than they were 25 or 30 years ago.

Mr. THOMPSON. Well, compare to-day with two years ago.

· Mr. SPEED. And the output is greater and the wages less; that is, not in all industries, but especially in the logging industry. I know more about logging than I do about farming.

Mr. THOMPSON. Well, what is the wage paid for logging, for common labor in the logging industry?

Mr. SPEED. Well, it is about 50 to 60 per cent less now than it was 25 or 30 **years ago.**

Mr. THOMPSON. What is it now?

Mr. SPEED. About $26 to $30 and board a month—to $35.

Mr. THOMPSON. And board?

Mr. SPEED. Yes; the board is miserable board. Thirty years ago their board was 50 to 100 per cent better than it is to-day, and their wages 50 to 60 per cent higher. The conditions are worse now than they ever were.

Commissioner WEINSTOCK. Just one moment, please. May I ask whether those figures you are quoting now are estimates on your part?

Mr. SPEED. No; I have worked.

Commissioner WEINSTOCK. Or are the result of exact calculations?

Mr. SPEED. It is my experience.

Commissioner WEINSTOCK. Are we to take your figures as accurate figures or **as estimates?**

Mr. SPEED. Well, you are to take them this way: The wages 25 to 30 years ago in the logging camps were $50 a month and board, from that up to $150. To-day they are down to $26 and $30, up to $70. At work that I got $110 a month for and board, to-day they work it for $50 and board.

Commissioner GARRETSON. It is actual experience that you have gone through yourself?

Mr. SPEED. That I have gone through myself.

Commissioner GARRETSON. Yes.

·Mr. SPEED. And the price of the commodity has increased from 30 to 50 per cent higher to-day than it was then in the market—lumber.

Mr. THOMPSON. Talking of the conditions of the workers, Mr. Speed, take the housing. You say conditions are bad. Describe those conditions as you see **them.**

Mr. SPEED. Well, I have been in camps where there has been four to five hundred men packed together in a camp in tiers, four tiers high, with only an alleyway of about 2 feet between them, and then boards put on the rafters for the men to sleep on there.

Mr. THOMPSON. What camps were those?

Mr. SPEED. Camps on the Sacramento River.

Mr. THOMPSON. Well, what companies?

Mr. SPEED. Where they were building wing dams to protect the island.

Mr. THOMPSON. Do you know the names of the contractors?

Mr. SPEED. Well, the man who owned the island was Gen. Williams, Grand Island on the Sacramento.

Mr. THOMPSON. That work was being done for him?

Mr. SPEED. That work was being done for him.

Mr. THOMPSON. How long ago was that?

Mr. SPEED. Oh, that is quite a few years ago.

Mr. THOMPSON. Well, now, coming down to the present time, I mean substantially the last two or three years, what can you say with reference to the housing of the men in camps?

Mr. SPEED. Well, in camps——

Mr. THOMPSON. In your industry.

Mr. SPEED. In camps that is movable the housing is miserable; in many of those you have no place to sleep at all unless out in the open altogether, and there is no provision made to keep out flies or any thing like that. I have been in camps where we would have a big clean up in the morning and we could fill two or three dispans with flies every morning that would fall off the roof of the tent.

Mr. THOMPSON. You are speaking of lumber camps?

Mr. SPEED. No; construction camps.

Mr. THOMPSON. Well, railroad camps?

Mr. SPEED. Railroads and bridges, like that.

Mr. THOMPSON. Are any of these camps in existence now?

Mr. SPEED. Yes. Well, I haven't been out lately. Reports I get here from the boys say the camps is just as rotten now as ever.

Mr. THOMPSON. Take it within the last two or three years, can you name some camps specifically, the name of the road or the name of the contractor?

Mr. SPEED. No.

Mr .THOMPSON. Or the name of the lumber firm?

Mr. SPED. No.

Mr. THOMPSON. You can't?

Mr. SPEED. No; nor for the last two or three years, because I have been engaged in other work.

Mr. THOMPSON. What work have you been engaged in?

Mr. SPEED. Well, I have been traveling around.

Mr. THOMPSON. Traveling around?

Mr. SPEED. Been up north; Washington and through there.

Mr. THOMPSON. Who would know about the temporary conditions?

Mr. SPEED. Really the best way to get a really definite knowledge concerning the camp life is to get a lot of men that is working in the camps to-day.

Mr. THOMPSON. You can't give the information?

Mr. SPEED. No; because I am not working in the camps. If I was working in the camps I could give you it more in detail. I only can give you that which I get from them, because I am not working in the camps myself. But it would be possible to get men that is actually working in the camps, however.

Mr. THOMPSON. Now, you have heard the testimony of Prof. Parker?

Mr. SPEED. Yes.

Mr. THOMPSON. With reference to the proportion of men in a hundred that were foreign born and native born, and the different other matters in connection with the men?

Mr. SPEED. Yes.

Mr. THOMPSON. Have you anything to add to that statement, or is that about a bair estimate of the situation in this State as you know it?

Mr. SPEED. Well, yes; I think it is possibily a fair estimate of the conditions in this State as far as that is concerned. But I want to say this. Here is the way the conditions have been. There was a time in this State when the bulk of the workers were natives. The wages was decent or good, or the board was good. They were pretty much all natives. The employers sent their agents out and got in other peoples who did not understand English or the conditions here, and got them in at a lower wage and through them cut dawn the wages one-half from what they were formerly. When these people became acquainted with the conditions prevailing in the country and they make for better demands, then they turn them down and ask the natives to come back and take their place, and they use one against the other. And this is the means that they have employed to cut down the wages, and the wages have been cut down throughout the whole State, especially in agriculture and logging.

Mr. THOMPSON. You spoke of the wages 25 years ago. Are the wages continually being cut down now through this competition?

Mr. SPEED. Yes.

Mr. THOMPSON. Are they less this year than last year, and less last year than the year before?

Mr. SPEED. No, I could not say that, but I know that they are cut down considerably. For instance, when a man got for sawing $65 a month each man done his own filing. To-day one man does the filing for 12 or 14 men, and these 12 or 14 men that does the sawing, they get $26 to $30 a month, and one man gets $45 to $50 for doing the filing.

Mr. THOMPSON. You say they work the foreign-born or the newcomers against the old comers or the people that have been here a long time. You say they do that, and that reduces the wages all the time by that method?

Mr. SPEED. They induce them to go to their particular camps.

Mr. THOMPSON. I see.

Mr. SPEED. And then they induce them to buy a lot and build a little house on it. They want your family there now in fact. If a man goes into a camp single, as I have, and asks for work the first question they would ask me was, have you got a wife, and how many children. If I didn't have a wife I couldn't get a job; but if I had a wife and family I would have got a job, but would have never got out of the place unless I walked out. They would take everything back from me in the prices of food, rent, and so forth.

Mr. THOMPSON. That is, use the man who has a family?

Mr. SPEED. Yes.

Mr. THOMPSON. How do they carry out this other proposition?

Mr. SPEED. When they get him in that position he has to submit to the conditions imposed on him; he has no way out.

Mr. THOMPSON. How do these men who go from place to place get employment? Do they go to a town and ask for it, or are they sent by employment agencies?

Mr. SPEED. These migratory laborers—he is chasing all over the country looking for a job; he asks for his jobs.

Mr. THOMPSON. Some of those Prof. Parker was talking about?

Mr. SPEED. Yes.

Mr. THOMPSON. Are the same methods used to get the new settler that are used to get the old settler, or do they go around to the employment agency?

Mr. SPEED. I presume that the employment agency is sending some men; but there is a large body f men who won't go near an employment agency to get work; they won't go near it.

Mr. THOMPSON. Take those who get positions through the employment agencies; how do the employers, or the agencies, play off one of those groups against the other with reference to wages?

Mr. SPEED. The employment agents don't play off one. It is the employing fellows who play. If they can get a foreigner in who don't know the wages here, don't know the conditions, he necessarily works cheaper than the individual, the native; and they are induced to come into the place and they give them a lower wage.

Mr. THOMPSON. In other words, those that live at a given city where work is to do in the agricultural or other districts, compete with the people already there?

Mr. SPEED. They compete with the people already there.

Mr. THOMPSON. By reason of these inducements, the larger surplus of labor, that beats down the price?

Mr. SPEED. Yes. And the American hobo, as he is called, he is driven out and he becomes a hobo, and he is run out of the jobs over the country by the cheaper labor.

Mr. THOMPSON. When the hoboes leave one place and go to another place they are used, then, in the same operation of the man who is there, to run him out; is that the way it works?

Mr. SPEED. He is used for a particular purpose; of course they always hire the cheapest labor they can get.

Mr. THOMPSON. Then the man who comes there bids for the job against the man who is there?

Mr. SPEED. He asks for the job; he simply asks for it. If the wages suit he takes it, and if they don't, he won't.

Mr. THOMPSON. Well, what are the general methods used here in this State of connecting the man with the job?

Mr. SPEED. A great many of these construction camps get their labor through these employment agencies, these agents—that is the way they get a large number of their laborers. Some won't hire anybody unless he does come from an agency.

Mr. THOMPSON. That is, with reference to the construction camps, the way they get theirs?

Mr. SPEED. Yes. The chances are there is a rebate. For instance, in this city there was a job right on Howard Street where the boss would go to the employment agent and hire his men, and these men had to pay $2 or $3 for their jobs. They may last a day and then get discharged, and another hired the next day, and keep on. It stands to reason there was some deal between the company and the agent to have men come and go right alongside of them when men was going up and asking for a job and could not get it. That is so right in this city.

Mr. THOMPSON. Is that belief pretty prevalent among the workers here?

Mr. SPEED. A great many of them understand it that way.

Mr. THOMPSON. What effect does it have on their attitude toward employment agents?

Mr. SPEED. They got no use for them.

Mr. THOMPSON. Does it create unrest on their part?

Mr. SPEED. Yes; it has a tendency to do that.

Mr. THOMPSON. You said a great many of these workers, however, would not deal with employment agents. How do they get their work?

Mr. SPEED. They get it by simply going around and striking for it here and there and all over.

Mr. THOMPSON. From district to district in the State?

Mr. SPEED. Yes, sir.

Mr. THOMPSON. And taking the chance?

Mr. SPEED. Yes.

Mr. THOMPSON. What would you suggest as being a good way to handle that proposition so that these men would not compete with each other for a job?

.Mr. SPEED. The only way it can be handled so that they won't compete .with each other is, when they get sense enough, intelligence enough to organize and solidify their forces and compel those who need their help to go right to their organization and get them. That is the only solution to it, as I can see..:

Mr. THOMPSON. You think that if the State or National Government. would establish an employment agency that would keep track of the men demanded, the desire for work in different localities, the kind of work that was expected of them, that they could help in the situation?

Mr. SPEED. Well, it might help to the extent.of informing them where work was, but as a solution I don't believe legislation can solve that at all.

Mr. THOMPSON. I don't mean a solution, but I mean a remedy to apply as a help in this distribution of labor.

Mr. SPEED. It may do that, because it may be able to inform men where there is a certain line of work going on. That is about the only thing it can do.

Commissioner GARRETSON. From your standpoint it would be ,a measure that might be desirable, until the time came when, from your standpoint, that solidarity would take place?

Mr. SPEED. Well——

Commissioner GARRETSON. Would that be true before you were able to carry out your belief that all should be in one organization and compel the employer to come to them?

Mr. SPEED. Yes; I believe in making the employer——

Commissioner GARRETSON. Until that time would this plan help out?

Mr. SPEED. It would help to the extent of informing the men where jobs were.

Commissioner GARRETSON. That is it.

Mr. SPEED. And if they do that, that is all it possibly could do.

Mr. THOMPSON. A good deal of testimony has been given here, it seemed to me unanimous, that the work in this State, particularly the agricultural work, is seasonal.

Mr. SPEED. Yes, sir.

Mr. THOMPSON. Running from three weeks to five months. Have you given that phase of the labor situation any consideration?

Mr. SPEED. Not any more than to know that the average worker, the bulk of them, will work if conditions are favorable. They follow up the orange season in the South in the winter and follow up the line of work clear up into British Columbia. Here the·agricultural work and then on construction work, and so on, whichever line of work happens to come along at that time. It may be in the agricultural field, or it may be a construction camp putting in a power plant, etc. They follow it up wherever they strike it. They don't know where they are going, and they are traveling, looking for a job.

Mr. THOMPSON. What do you suggest might help the men get steady employment, or make the work less seasonal?

Mr. SPEED. I don't know as you could make it less seasonal, because as these materials ripen they come in their natural season; you can't change the season. We have to meet those as the season develops, and follow them up. They follow the various seasons up. The harvest for wheat, say, is here this month, and on the coast a month later, and after they get that through they follow it up at other places. The workers, as a rule, know when these seasons come about. They know just when to hit the various places, and they follow it up. They understand that part of it well themselves.

Mr. THOMPSON. They don't know exactly whether they are going to get a job or not?

Mr. SPEED. No, sir; they don't know.

Mr. THOMPSON. What could be done to help them?

Mr. SPEED. The only thing that could be done to my notion is. this: It depends on the workers, what must be done; the workers must do it; nobody can do it for them. That is my contention. They have to learn to do it themselves, and they are going to suffer until they do learn. The workers should learn to organize in respective districts, say Bakersville, San Francisco, Sacramento, Marysville, etc. These various localities should have a central organization, a bureau of information, where the men could go and be informed what various work is going on at the various localities, and keep in touch with every other locality so as to keep the men in touch with work through their organization. This devolves upon the workers themselves to carry out.

Mr. THOMPSON. If this can be done by another organization, there would be no objection to it?

Mr. SPEED. I think it can be done more effectively by the workers themselves.

Mr. THOMPSON. What is your opinion about the possibility of being able to organize the agricultural and migratory laborers into unions?

Mr. SPEED. Well, I think this: In the last two or three years while the average migratory worker has had no sense of organization whatever—the Japs and Chinese have a far better sense of organization than has the native American, and the result is when he eliminates the native out of a given locality he gets better conditions and wages than the native worker does. The native worker through the agitation that has been going on in the State during the last several years is commencing to wake up and realize the necessity of some form of organization in order to keep in touch and develop. He is commencing to realize that now.

Mr. THOMPSON. As he operated over the State the general organization would have to keep in touch with the work?

Mr. SPEED. Yes, sir.

Mr. THOMPSON. Suppose a national employment bureau should gather all that data and keep the men informed through the post office in each town, or through an office of its own, to that extent at least, they would furnish the same relief, wouldn't they?

Mr. SPEED. That would furnish relief, but you see the men would be dependent on some one else. What you want to do is for the workers to depend on themselves and not any one else, and that is a thing they want to be developing.

Mr. THOMPSON. Is the I. W. W. pretty well organized now, or how well is it organized among the agricultural and seasonal workers in this State?

Mr. SPEED. No, sir; the I. W. W.—while the sentiment of the great bulk and great number of the migratory workers is strongly with the I. W. W., it is a difficult proposition to organize that class of laborers because of the shifting tendency; but the sentiment among them is strongly in favor of the I. W. W. throughout the State.

Mr. THOMPSON. How can this I. W. W. sentiment and attitude of the workers be crystallized into action?

Mr. SPEED. That depends on development, and it is crystallizing slowly, slowly. I don't know how you can add to it. It depends on the men themselves how quickly they will come to a realization of it. Many of them see it but the continual shifting around breaks it up. Say, for instance, they have an organization and have committees to do certain lines of work, but before a week or two is oved they have drifted some place else and undone the work, because of the continual shifting. They have the idea and sentiment for organization, and improvement of their condition, and that is developing through the migratory workers. I believe it will develop an organization probably in the near future, but it is a proposition that is pretty hard to handle.

Mr. THOMPSON. The winter season is a season when there is very little work in the various lines.

Mr. SPEED. Yes, sir; very little work.

Mr. THOMPSON. How would you handle that situation?

Mr. SPEED. You mean relative to the unemployment?

Mr. THOMPSON. Yes.

Mr. SPEED. I believe under present conditions the unemployment problem is an unsolvable problem. It can't be solved under present economic conditions. I believe the only thing the unemployed worker can do, as they have nothing to lose but misery and they are up against it and everybody's hand is turned against them, I believe in them committing some petty offense and making the State look after them, because it seems only drastic action will compel action on the part of the State.

Mr. THOMPSON. Suppose that the State, instead of looking after them and putting them in jail for some petty offense, should establish some employment agencies all over the country, and should say to the men out of work here in the wintertime, "There are other localities where you can get employment"; would that be a help, too?

Mr. SPEED. You may have employment agencies, but if the employers won't employ men, what good is the employment agency, if nobody won't employ the men?

Mr. THOMPSON. I mean an institution run by the Government, where they. can accurately and truthfully tell the workers there is a demand for labor in other localities—in other States, for instance.

Mr. SPEED. The amount of labor and the amount of work for laborers—the surplus over and above the amount of work is enormous, and it would only furnish a certain number work; the balance would still be out of work. You have to find means to give every man an opportunity to work, and will the State do that?

Mr. THOMPSON. Have you made any study of the relative efficiency or lack of efficiency of agricultural laborers?

Mr. SPEED. No, sir; they are too darned efficient now, I think.

Mr. THOMPSON. Is there any statement you would like to make, Mr. Speed, to the commission?

Mr. SPEED. My idea is this, take it as a whole, this commission or any other commission can not solve the problem that is confronting the world; that is, the issue that is involved between labor and capital. That there is two economic classes whose interests are diametrically opposed to one another, absolutely so, and between these two classes a struggle must and will go on; and in that struggle there is no compromise nor arbitration or nothing that can solve or settle it; either labor has to come into its own or go down—one or the other. That is my impression.

That political power is a reflex of economic power, and those who control the economic power of the State control the political power of the State—and we have evidence of this in Rockefeller telling President Wilson he may as well go to the devil as far as Colorado is concerned, showing he had more power than the Government itself.

This working class, this migratory laborer, has no political power or influence. The only political power it could possess is by a thorough compact organization and forcing its measures upon that part of the people who control its lives through controlling its industries; and the solution of that is that the working classes has to go and organize itself for the purpose of fighting its way through,. so that it can control its own life by controlling the industries in which it is engaged instead of being the slaves of the other man. There is no equality before the law; there is no justice before our courts. I have been in different sections of the country, and this commission interviewed a man in Seattle by the name of Mack, and this man Mack had in front of his mill a little fort called Fort Mack with 8 or 10 men with sawed-off shotguns in front of it.

I saw a lady when a man was getting beat up by the thugs which he had employed—a lady came out of a barber shop and protested against the beating up of men, and she was arrested and put under a $1,000 bond for inciting to riot because she protested against the beating up of men. That was Mack up in Aberdeen.

I have seen 64 men put in jail and held 36 hours without charge. Discharged them and hold two. They tried to frame up a charge against them, and failing to do that they kidnapped them and run them out of town, and the chief of police of the town was right in the room where the men were that they kidnapped, backing up the thugs that did the kidnapping. And when we tried to get Anderson, of the Anderson Middleton mill, arrested, when he shot a boy in the back—many of us tried to get a warrant for his arrest, but we could not. Why? Because the man who was holding the office was in this position: He knew the workers around the camp that were on strike had no political power; he knew that they didn't control the convention or the county committee; he knew that the mill owners and banking interests controlled all this, and he says, "If I want to get my job again as county attorney I have to stand in with the push that can get me the job. These working men have no votes and no power, and if I go and prosecute this man I might as well leave camp and hunt for another job." Consequently, he refused to issue a warrant, and the worker had no power in this case.

This is from actual experience, and I have seen it repeated half a dozen times. So that the worker has no show at all. What does he do? The only thing he can do is to organize and get sufficient economic power and go to it.

Mr. THOMPSON. That is all.

Chairman WALSH. Do you want to ask any questions, Mr. Weinstock?

Commissioner WEINSTOCK. Yes, sir.

Chairman WALSH. Mr. Weinstock wishes to ask you some questions.

Commissioner WEINSTOCK. I take it you have been a student of all these economic problems, judging from the way you speak, and perhaps you can talk with some authority on the subject. Can you tell us, for example, how many wage earners there are in this country?

- Mr. SPEED. I should judge there were somewhere in the neighborhood, say, of twenty-five or thirty million.

Commissioner WEINSTOCK. Twenty-five or thirty million. Evidently you put a different estimate on the number than my friend to whom I just put this question and his opinion——

Chairman WALSH. I wouldn't make comparisons.

- Commissioner WEINSTOCK. Now, out of those twenty-five or thirty million, how many belong to the migratory classes of labor as far as you can estimate them?

Mr. SPEED. I am not able to tell that.

Commissioner WEINSTOCK. You don't know?

Mr. SPEED. No, sir; but I am satisfied of this, that the migratory laborer is ever on the increase. Many tradesmen are to-day boomers; they are thrown out of their trades and they are hitting it all over the country, many of them.

Commissioner WEINSTOCK. You mean skilled laborers?

Mr. SPEED. Skilled laborers?

Commissioner WEINSTOCK. Are being thrown into the ranks of unskilled labor?

Mr. SPEED. Yes, sir; thousands of them.

Commissioner WEINSTOCK. You think that the number of unemployed is increasing?

- Mr. SPEED. Yes, sir.

Commissioner WEINSTOCK. Do you think that they would increase in normal times, appreciating the fact that the last year or so has been abnormal? Do you think if we had normal times they would be on the increase just the same?

Mr. SPEED. Yes, sir; it seems to me I read a report of the labor commissioners in New York, Pennsylvania, and Massachusetts showing, under the best possible conditions, this country had in it upward of 500,000 men continuously unemployed in those three States. Under the most prosperous conditions the country had that. Now, with the efficiency system springing up and the continuous application of new devices elminating labor, the same as this machine in the hop fields, it is increasing that number.

Commissioner WEINSTOCK. Do you also give it as your opinion that wages have actually gone down in dollars and cents, in money?

Mr. SPEED. Yes, sir; I know they have in this industry in which I have worked.

Commissioner WEINSTOCK. That is the logging industry?

Mr. SPEED. Yes, sir. I believe it is true of other industries.

Commissioner WEINSTOCK. Would you say that is so of the agricultural and horticultural industries in this State?

Mr. SPEED. I think as far as agriculture is concerned the wages remain pretty nearly stationary.

Commissioner WEINSTOCK. In agriculture the wages remain pretty nearly stationary?

. Mr. SPEED. Yes, sir; there is not much rise or fall.

Commissioner WEINSTOCK. Well, I happen to know in my own personal experience, and I give you this for your information, that 25 years ago as a fruit grower the standard wage paid by myself in common with other people was $1 a day and board.

Mr. SPEED. Lots of them get that now.

Commissioner WEINSTOCK. Which was regarded as equal to a dollar and a half, and the wages paid to Asiatics was one dollar, out of which they fed themselves. To-day, as far as I know, the wages paid to white men is equivalent to two dollars a day; therefore there must have been in California horticulture an increase of 25 per cent in those years.

Mr. SPEED. You might have got that, but that don't stand good over the State. I was up in Sacramento a year or two ago just where one of the witnesses was speaking about canneries, and men were working there for a dollar and a half a day and boarding themselves. Lots of men on that island in that miserable kind of work, hoeing and digging potatoes, and so forth. The Japs were getting better wages than the whites were. Right on the Sacramento River.

Commissioner WEINSTOCK. That is, the wages paid to Asiatics were better than the wages paid to the whites?

Mr. SPEED. Yes, sir; right in that spud district—potato district.

Commissioner WEINSTOCK. You have expressed an opinion also, Mr. Speed, that legislation can not solve the labor problem.

Mr. SPEED. Yes, sir.

Commissioner WEINSTOCK. And do you feel legislation can not even mitigate the problem?

Mr. SPEED. Well, it may stave off a little while, but in the solution of the problem why legislation can't solve it because those who control the industries of a nation necessarily control the political policies of a nation. That is a moral certainty.

Commissioner WEINSTOCK. You believe that the employing classes control, for example, the legislation of the State of California?

Mr. SPEED. Undoubtedly.

Commissioner WEINSTOCK. If they do, how do you explain the fact that in recent years we have had the eight-hour day passed for women and children, and the minimum-wage law established, and the child-labor law established, which, on the face of it, would be against the interests of the employers? If the employing classes were in the saddle, how do you explain the passage of that kind of legislation.

Mr. SPEED. When they make that legislation they don't make it against their interests. They certainly wouldn't act only in accord with their own interests. When they do that they realize that it is to their own interests. How do they arrive at that? They figure out what is the cost of keeping the army of unemployed; what is the cost of educating the boys and girls; which is the cheapest to us? Which is the cheapest—to see that the children become educated and efficient and give the most to the employer, or let it go on as it is. Whichever is the cheapest, if they find by making certain legislation, that legislation will be passed. And they never do anything unless it accords with their economic interest. It would be foolish to do so.

Commissioner WEINSTOCK. Assuming that to be true, I take it you will admit it is also true that labor generally is in favor of the eight-hour day for women and children; that labor generally is in favor of the minimum-wage law; that labor generally is in favor of the child-labor law; that labor generally is in favor of the factory-inspection law and of other laws that have been in effect in California in recent years. Then, if that is so, the conclusion is forced upon us that upon those issues capital and labor are united.

Mr. SPEED. No, sir.

Commissioner WEINSTOCK. That they both agree.

Mr. SPEED. I hold this, that these laws are rarely enforced and most difficult of enforcement, and where there is no powerful economic class back of them, then the laws are violated with impunity.

Commissioner WEINSTOCK. Well, are we to understand, then, Mr. Speed, that the eight-hour law for women and children in the State of California is not being enforced?

Mr. SPEED. Not being enforced all over the State.

Commissioner WEINSTOCK. Not being enforced?

Mr. SPEED. No. Some of the women in this city in the hotels like we have here, we hear them squealing about the conditions under which they work now with the eight-hour law, how they are imposed upon.

Commissioner WEINSTOCK. Well, who would you hold responsible for that law, for example, not being enforced?

Mr. SPEED. I hold this—of course, to place the responsibility—I hold this, that the best law that was made is the law made by labor itself. The building trades like we have in this city has an eight-hour law, half holiday Saturday; they don't have to go before any court to inquire whether it is constitutional or unconstitutional. Labor established it. That is the best law there is. I hold this, that legislatures are the institutions where the members of the prosperity class can get together and adjust their prosperity group interest. I hold it is to the interest of the working class to organize, and in their union make their laws and enforce them on the job. That is the worker's parliament, in the union hall. There he should make his law, and enforce it on the job. just as the business men make their laws at Sacramento. There are two warring classes, and each of them should have a parliament of their own, and both should make their own laws and enforce them to the best of their power, and power in the last analysis determines everything.

Commissioner WEINSTOCK. You expressed the opinion, Mr. Speed, that the remedy for the condition of the migratory laborer, the agricultural laborer, lay in the direction of organization; that if the migratory and agricultural workers would organize, have a strong union, that then he would be in a condition to demand and secure better conditions and better wages.

Mr. SPEED. Yes.

Commissioner WEINSTOCK. You also pointed out that because of the worker being migratory in his character, that thus far it had not been possible to organize?

Mr. SPEED. Yes, been difficult to do so.

Commissioner WEINSTOCK. That because he is here to-day and there to-morrow, it is impossible to have him meet collectively?

Mr. SPEED. Yes.

Commissioner WEINSTOCK. Well, now, if that is an indisputable fact, how are you going to be any more successful in the future than you have been in the past, because those conditions will continue?

Mr. SPEED. Well, take, for instance, there is a local in Sacramento and locals in other places; those groups are developing and the members are traveling about, and you establish a nucleus here and a nucleus there, and they get in touch with other men, they get imbued with the ideas, and it takes time; but it has developed more in the last several years than any time prior to that. That is the reason I say the workers now, the migratory labor, is commencing to realize the necessity of organization, something he had no sense of in the past, evidently.

Commissioner WEINSTOCK. When was the effort first made to organize the migratory laborer? How old is that effort in California?

Mr. SPEED. Six, seven, or eight years now.

Commissioner WEINSTOCK. There has been a persistent effort during that period to organize?

Mr. SPEED. Yes; probably 10 or 12 or more thousand, but they necessarily drift here and there.

Commissioner WEINSTOCK. What is to show for this six, seven or eight years' effort to-day?

Mr. SPEED. Nothing more than the sentiment and feeling that is manifest among that class of labor when we go among them.

Commissioner WEINSTOCK. You mean a desire has been aroused?

Mr. SPEED. Yes; a desire has been aroused. But it has not crystallized into organization yet, only in a small nucleus here and there.

Commissioner WEINSTOCK. Has that been brought about by the I. W. W. or the American Federation of Labor?

Mr. SPEED. It has been made by the I. W. W. The American Federation of Labor is not able, in my judgment, in any way, shape, or form, to organize that class of labor, or can not touch it. They don't understand it.

Commissioner WEINSTOCK. And what advantage has the I. W. W. over the American Federation of Labor in that connection?

Mr. SPEED. The American Federation of Labor is controlled from above, makes agreements and time contracts with employers and all that sort of thing; whereas, in the other form of organization, initiative, self-reliance is all within the membership itself. Each branch local can act without fear of being called down or shut down upon. Consequently they have brought the question, treated that question in this way because the worker learns to get all he can, and consequently whenever you have organized all the workers together in one organization, they realize it is of more value to them than being divided into separate groups. They are not compelled to fight against each other to stay on a job in a strike, as the pressmen's strike here in Frisco, out 53 weeks, and the rest of the unions working in the same industry. They were just as responsible for defeating those men as the strike breakers who were on the job. I believe in the closed shop and the open union; every man, woman, and child ought to be eligible to the organization, and should be all organized.

Commissioner WEINSTOCK. Are they not under the American Federation of Labor?

Mr. SPEED. No.

Commissioner WEINSTOCK. Why not?

Mr. SPEED. Because they are organized in crafts. Those outside have been ignored as without skill.

I used to belong to the A. F. of L. I took part in the struggles of labor for 42 years.

Commissioner WEINSTOCK. Are we to understand, Mr. Speed, that the I. W. W. is not a federated body, that each local is supreme within itself?

Mr. SPEED. No. They are organized in just this way. The I. W. W. is or.̇ ganized industrially; all the men working in any given industry should belong to an organization of that respective industry. It is a unit of organization community should be the shop. The union ironworkers, the boiler makers, the pattern makers, the molders, etc., they are organized into crafts. All of these crafts have their contracts expire at different periods of time with the owners of that plant, so that when the contract expires with one union, they go out at the end of the time and ask for an agreement and the boss refuses, and they strike. The other unions all sympathize with them, they are working. men and sympathize with all the others; but they have made a contract, they have made agreements, and they are compelled to stay on the job and work with a scab that comes in and takes the other's place, but they don't want to do it. They are compelled because of the agreement they have made. We are opposed to that.

Our plan is that the unit of organiaztion shall be the shop, and that any particular branch of that unit of organization that has a grievance with the boss, submits it before the unit of organization for the indorsement of the unit. If the boss refuses to settle, instead of the boss issuing his ultimatum, and saying " Go to work Monday morning or we will put other men in your places," we will issue an ultimatum to him: " We will shut down your plant and every plant you have got, if necessary."

Commissioner WEINSTOCK. That is, you would not enter into agreements with employers?

Mr. SPEED. Not time agreements, no. That shackles you and compels you to help the boss of the shop when another one is fighting.

Commissioner WEINSTOCK. Is it or is it not to the interest of labor that there shall be industrial enterprises?

Mr. SPEED. Well, labor is capable of running the enterprises. Give it a show.

Commissioner WEINSTOCK. Well, do you think that labor and labor alone, without capital, could start and run an enterprise?

Mr. SPEED. What is capital but unpaid wages? [Laughter.]

Commissioner WEINSTOCK. That may be, but it is capital just the same.

Chairman WALSH. There must be no applause, or expression of approval or disapproval. Please bear that in mind.

Commissioner WEINSTOCK. Could you start an industry without capital?

Mr. SPEED. No; we have got the industries. All we want to do is take hold of them and run them.

Commissioner WEINSTOCK. How?

Mr. SPEED. By power. The boss runs everything to-day because he has got the power to do it.

Commissioner WEINSTOCK. Are we to understand from that that your phil̇ osophy is to go out and take possession of industry?

Mr. SPEED. When we get the power; certainly.

Commissioner WEINSTOCK. Without compensation?

Mr. SPEED. Why, they have been getting enough off of us all our lives. They didn't give us anything for it, either.

Commissioner WEINSTOCK. If you had the power to-morrow would you take possession of the Union Iron Works, without paying for them?

Mr. SPEED. Certainly. Undoubtedly labor built the Union Iron Works, produced all that there is in it, and fed and clothed the fellows that owns it, and educated them.

Commissioner WEINSTOCK. And therefore, in your opinion, the Union Iron Works belongs——

Mr. SPEED. To the labor that created it.

Commissioner WEINSTOCK. And you have a right, to-morrow, to take possession without compensating the employer?

Mr. SPEED. Undoubtedly, if we have got the power. Power is the thing that determines everything. Capital has got the power to-day, and it works men, women, and children in the factories, doesn't it? And exploits them, gives them a dollar a day, and they exact from them $3 and $4 a day in profits. They have got the power.

Commissioner WEINSTOCK. In other words, if anybody has the power, you would have him exercise it?

Mr. SPEED. Exercise it, yes. I hold this, in other words, everything that will advance the interests of labor is moral, is right. Everything that will advance labor is moral, I hold.

Commissioner Weinstock. No matter whether it is against the law of the land?

Mr. Speed. The fellow that owns the property makes the law, and consequently he makes the law in his own interest. And that is against me. If I obey his law, I cut my own throat. In other words, any act upon the part of the working class that will in any way conflict with or destroy the material welfare of the property-owning class, that is of necessity an illegal act in the eyes of the property-owning class. And when we see strikes and we see men out on strike, what do we find? We find them jailed the same as they were jailed up in Aberdeen. We find they hire 200 field detectives to beat men up, arrest a woman because she protested against one getting a clubbing, and put her under a thousand-dollar fine. They have kidnaped men, and the chief of police stands looking on to see the job done. That was moral and right in their eyes. We could not get them arrested. Now, there is the law from their viewpoint. They have the power to make the law, likewise they must have the power to break the law when it is convenient to their economic interest.

Commissioner Weinstock. Well, then, summing up your philosophy, Mr. Speed, it really amounts to this, if I understand it rightly, that in your opinion might makes right?

Mr. Speed. It certainly does make right. Sentiment, feeling, emotion—all those things is very fine, but it stands to reason the fellow that has got the big club swings it over the balance. That is life as it exists to-day.

Commissioner Weinstock. That is all, Mr. Chairman.

Mr. Speed. Whether they like it or not, that is the fact.

Chairman Walsh. Any other questions?

Commissioner Commons. I would like to ask some questions.

Chairman Walsh. Prof. Commons.

Commissioner Commons. You spoke about the superior organization of the Asiatics, didn't you?

Mr. Speed. I spoke that they had, to my mind, a better sense of organization than the native had up to the present time.

Commissioner Commons. Have you come in contact with their organizations, do you know——

Mr. Speed. Well, I don't know the form of their organization, but I have met with them and seen them and talked to members of it. And I know this, that while a good many people in the State object to the Jap and the Chinee, I want to say, as far as I am concerned, one man is as good as another to me; I don't care whether he is black, blue, green, or yellow, as long as he acts the man and acts true to his economic interests as a worker. Now, the Jap does act true; has acted largely true. I have seen strikes on this coast when the Japs refused to take other men's places, while the white man would take them. And the wheatland situation is developing that very thing. Even the Hindus would not go to work, but the American went to work.

Commissioner Commons. Well, you don't know how they organize at all, do you?

Mr. Speed. No; not into their form of organization, no.

Commissioner Commons. Do you know about their business agents or anything?

Mr. Speed. Oh, no.

Commissioner Commons. Or strikes?

Mr. Speed. No.

Commissioner Commons. Or anything?

Mr. Speed. No; I don't know about that. They are necessarily timid because of antagonism that is aroused against them. They are timid and secretive in that respect, and won't give you any inside information. But they certainly have organization, and they have solidarity. They act more solid together than do the natives.

Commissioner Commons. Do you know of any, have you come across any instances where the white workers take cooperative contracts the way the Asiatics do?

Mr. Speed. No, no.

Commissioner Commons. Do you think that is a——

Mr. Speed. No; the white is too individualistic as yet.

Commissioner Commons. Well, does your organization favor that kind of taking contracts under gangs?

Mr. SPEED. No, no; it has not done so, and I don't think it—possibly it would not develop that way either. I think the organization would organize the workers to enforce whatever they think was their just demands, make them and present them, and then use every effort possible to achieve them. I don't think that they would go into that kind of business.

Commissioner COMMONS. You don't think that is practicable for whites?

Mr. SPEED. Well, not as yet, anyway. I don't know what might develop.

Commissioner COMMONS. All right.

Chairman WALSH. Anything else?

Commissioner GARRETSON. Yes.

Chairman WALSH. Mr. Garretson would like to ask you a question or two.

Commissioner GARRETSON. Has your connection or discussion with the Hindu or the Chink led you to any trace of the fact that those men have twenty centuries of communal life behind them that make them peculiarly combined in their interests?

Mr. SPEED. That may be true. That may be true. Probably you are correct on that.

Commissioner GARRETSON. And all that is necessary to graft on it is the trade-union idea?

Mr. SPEED. Yes, sir.

Commissioner GARRETSON. To make it binding, because they have already got concert or action?

Mr. SPEED. They have got concerted action.

Commissioner GARRETSON. They have from that source, possibly?

Mr. SPEED. Yes, sir.

Commissioner GARRETSON. Your idea, I gather, is, that from the experiences that you have had, and possibly from a good many of the men whom you have talked with that have gone through it, that it is a feeling of contempt because of the fact that they can't get justice under it?

Mr. SPEED. No; personal experience with it.

Commissioner GARRETSON. Well, I say, that is part of the contempt for it?

Mr. SPEED. Well, it would be one of the factors.

Commissioner GARRETSON. Because you believe it is poorly applied?

Mr. SPEED. No; not only because of that, but because of the fact that it stands to reason that the class which has economic power in a given state or nation, necessarily that class determines the political policy of the nation. How can a man without anything, make law?

Commissioner GARRETSON. Leave the causes that lead up to it out. What has your experience been, that the law was applied to you fairly?

Mr. SPEED. No; they ain't no such thing as law to the workman; he has to get it when he is brought up before it, especially in labor disputes.

Commissioner GARRETSON. You mean that the law is made to control the laboring man, instead of for his benefit?

Mr. SPEED. Probably, not necessarily.

Commissioner GARRETSON. For the purpose of controlling him, laws are made in the interests of property?

Mr. SPEED. That is what laws are made for, and the working class are a propertyless class, as a rule. Necessarily, then, laws are against the worker because he wants to get property. He wants to get more of the product of his labor. Now, then, he runs up against that law that the property-owning class makes.

Commissioner GARRETSON. Have you ever had the idea that some of those laws might regard him as property?

Mr. SPEED. Well, yes; that is all we are now. We are commodities, and we are bought and sold just like a sack of spuds is to-day upon the market.

Commissioner GARRETSON. You hold that under the ordinary trade-union idea, that organizations, like the ordinary trade-union, really that their responsibilities, which they recognize and assume in the making of contracts or in the enactment of laws to which all are required to conform, really act as a fetter?

Mr. SPEED. Yes; I hold this, that a contract made between an employer and a worker is not binding, it is null and void, it won't hold good in law, it can be violated by either party with impunity, and it oftentimes is violated whenever the economic condition is such that the boss sees it is to his interest to do certain things, he can violate it if he wants to.

Commissioner GARRETSON. You hold that there is no obligation resting upon the employee to carry out any agreement?

Mr. SPEED. Of course, it is a moral obligation. If conditions change, it is often violated. It has been violated. And if you have got the power, you don't need the contract. If you haven't got the power, you can't enforce the contract.

Commissioner GARRETSON. That carries the question of legislation. If legislation is enacted that, on its face at least, is beneficial, as the eight-hour enactment and so on, do you believe that they can be maintained or applied without a strong organization of men behind them?

Mr. SPEED. I believe they have got to have a strong organization behind them to see that they are enforced.

Commissioner GARRETSON. That the individual would be powerless for their enforcement?

Mr. SPEED. Yes, sir; and oftentimes he would not dare to try to question it because of losing his job, he submits to indignities, and his time is stretched upon him because of his desire to hold the job. As an individual he is helpless.

Commissioner GARRETSON. You spoke of the fact that we ought to get men here that are employed in these camps to testify as to conditions. In your opinion, would there be any hesitancy upon the part of any man that might be summoned from there to testify, for fear of losing his position?

Mr. SPEED. No; because they are worth so little to them; I guess he would not in them lines.

Commissioner GARRETSON. You think that would exercise no influence?

Mr. SPEED. Very little on construction work.

Commissioner GARRETSON. Have you been here during the entire hearing, Mr. Speed?

Mr. SPEED. No; I have been here just to hear about four or five. I believe.

Commissioner GARRETSON. Are you familiar with the form of these employers' associations that exist up and down the coast?

Mr. SPEED. Well, I hold that the employers' association is formed correctly.

Commissioner GARRETSON. I see. You are familiar with their method of organization?

Mr. SPEED. Yes.

Commissioner GARRETSON. It is exactly the same as your own, isn't it?

Mr. SPEED. Yes.

Commissioner GARRETSON. Only applied to the employer instead of the employee?

Mr. SPEED. You see the employer, as an employer, organizes all the men in manufacturing, both in the manufacturing and in the distribution of goods into one organization. Consequently, they act jointly together; whereas labor, working in the same industry, is organized into 10, 12, or 14 different unions, and the result is that they make contracts expiring at different periods of time, which causes them to compete one against the other. Now, we want to see them act together and in unison.

Commissioner GARRETSON. Have you any sense of friendship with the average employers' association on account of similarity of methods?

Mr. SPEED. Oh, no; not because of that. I believe in being up to date in organization, not fossilized.

Commissioner GARRETSON. Has your experience led you to make any suggestion as to any class of industries that might be combined together for the purpose of bridging this recess between seasons of employment as they now exist? Have you any knowledge of local industry that would lead you to believe that the men pursuing one pursuit for four or five months of the year might be utilized in a certain other pursuit that would fit into the interval between?

Mr. SPEED. Well, they may; but there is so many of the unemployed. There is always plenty, so they run up against a snag.

Commissioner GARRETSON. Would that dispose of a certain amount of it?

Mr. SPEED. No; I don't think so.

Commissioner GARRETSON. You think not?

Mr. SPEED. No.

Commissioner GARRETSON. That is all, Mr. Chairman.

Mr. SPEED. There is always a certain amount of unemployed and a certain amount of work.

Chairman WALSH. That is all; thank you, Mr. Speed.

Call your next.

Mr. THOMPSON. Mr. Horst is here.

TESTIMONY OF MR. E. CLEMENS HORST.

Chairman WALSH. Mr. Horst, there are just two questions that Mr. Commissioner O'Connell wants to ask you.

Commissioner O'CONNELL. I want to know, Mr. Horst, about this method of employment through this leader, of these various nationalities, whatever term he may have—the man whom you deal with for them. Do you pay the men directly—your employees?

Mr. HORST. Well, with the Chinamen, you pay the Chinese head man.

Commissioner O'CONNELL. Yes; well, now——

Mr. HORST. And so with the——

Commissioner O'CONNELL. Do you know what the Chinese laborer gets from the head man?

Mr. HORST. The head man of the Chinamen makes his commission out of his men by supplying them their rice and other food. He makes a commission out of them that way, and in many cases we pay him a commission for getting the men.

Commissioner O'CONNELL. Well, now, first——

Chairman WALSH. Is your answer, then, that they pay the entire compensation per man to the man that earns it or not? Do you know?

Mr. HORST. No; we pay our wages to the man that furnishes the Chinamen.

Chairman WALSH. Well, how do you know that the one Chinaman gives the pay to each Chinaman in accordance with his deserts and what he has earned for each day? Do you know?

Mr. HORST. Well, I can't give you any evidence of it. We know that. the Chinamen don't cheat one another. If you are doing business with the head man, he pays his rate of wages. You pay the rate of wages to the head Chinaman, and he pays the men, and he charges to the employer from 50 cents to a dollar a head on the men that he secures, and then he makes another profit out of the men by furnishing them their food.

Commissioner O'CONNELL. Let me see, now, if we can't get at it.

Commissioner GARRETSON. This is a lump sum for each employment—that 50 cents—is it?

Mr. HORST. Yes, sir.

Commissioner O'CONNELL. If you pay, we will say, a dollar and a half a day, to cite a case, it may be more—two and a half a day, it don't make any difference—you pay this Chinaman a dollar and a half for each of the men that he hires out to you. You pay that in bulk to him. Now, you have no knowledge as to whether he pays them, the individual Chinaman, a dollar and a half or not, or whether he gives them a dollar and a quarter?

Mr. HORST. Oh, we know the Chinaman pays to his men the rate of wages that is agreed upon, because that is always common knowledge around the employees—around the place—the rate of wages that is being paid. That is all common knowledge. Every Chinaman knows the rate of wages we pay. Each man knows it.

Commissioner O'CONNELL. Then what does each Chinaman pay to him for getting him the job and keeping the job for him?

Mr. HORST. Well, the Chinamen don't pay the Chinaman anything for getting the job. We pay that to the head Chinaman.

Commissioner O'CONNELL. How much do you pay?

Mr. HORST. It runs according to the scarcity of the men. Sometimes 50 cents and sometimes a dollar.

Commissioner O'CONNELL. What, a week or a month?

Mr. HORST. No; for the job.

Commissioner O'CONNELL. For the job?

Mr. HORST. For the job.

Commissioner O'CONNELL. Now, this is on contract and these men then are coming and going all the time?

Mr. HORST. Well, the bulk of them stay. For instance, he will agree to furnish 50 hands, and if five drop out he will furnish another five to replace them.

Commissioner O'CONNELL. If five men drop out to-day and their names are taken off the rolls, and they came back next week again, he would get that same amount for the reemployment of them?

Mr. HORST. No; he gets the money once. If he furnishes 50 men, he gets $50. Now, if five drop out he gets another five men; he don't get any more.

Commissioner O'CONNELL. Suppose he sends the same Chinamen back?

Mr. HORST. The Chinamen all look alike. You don't pay any attention to their names, you count them.

Commissioner O'CONNELL. How about the Hindus?

Mr. HORST. Well, with the Hindus, with a number of them, it is the same way. With some of them you pay the individual man.

Commissioner O'CONNELL. Do you find the same honesty obtains among those?

Mr. HORST. No; the Hindus do not compare with the Chinamen.

Commissioner O'CONNELL. Then the Hindu is not liable to get so much for his day's work?

Mr. HORST. The Hindu efficiency is not as great as that of the average Chinaman. If you care to have the figures on the efficiency, so far as hop picking is concerned, I will be glad to furnish them to you.

Commissioner O'CONNELL. In the use of the hop picking machine, does your company own the patent rights of that machine?

Mr. HORST. We invented the machine and we own the machine.

Commissioner O'CONNELL. You have the patent rights of that?

Mr. HORST. Yes, sir.

Commissioner O'CONNELL. You don't build it for sale?

Mr. HORST. We let other people use it; yes.

Commissioner O'CONNELL. Do you build them for sale, have somebody build them for sale?

Mr. HORST. Yes, sir; yes, sir.

Commissioner O'CONNELL. That is all.

Commissioner COMMONS. Have you considered what might be done in the way of furnishing winter work for these migratory laborers?

Mr. HORST. Yes; I have considered that very fully.

Commissioner COMMONS. What ideas have you on that?

Mr. HORST. There is to-day not enough work for the people, for the laboring people. There is no way near enough, because we have got this season and last season up to the point of harvest and through the harvest with a surplus of labor, and without any increase in the rate of wages during harvest season. Now, that situation is wrong. There ought to be enough work in California to take care of all the labor during the entire time of the year up to the harvest season. Then during the harvest season that class of labor, surplus labor that is necessary, should be drawn from a class of people that does not work the whole year around, as, for instance, people from the cities, families that go out for an outing, and so on, or people that need to work only a month or two months in the year. That is the class of people that should furnish the excess load for the harvest time. Now, in order to get that class of people it would become necessary to pay high wages and give better housing conditions in the country. Housing conditions, though they have considerably improved, I do not think are good enough for the people—I don't think the housing conditions are good enough, but they answer the purpose because of the overplus of labor.

Commissioner GARRETSON. The labor is not as critical as it would be?

Chairman WALSH. One moment. Prof. Commons has another question to ask.

Commissioner COMMONS. Well, have you any idea what class of winter work could be established; have you figured it out on that basis?

Mr. HORST. Well, we have got to improve the whole general condition. We have got to do more farming. For instance, if a man wants to start out and plant peaches or prunes, or anything else, or raisins, why he is afraid to do it to-day; he don't know what the tariff is going to be, for instance, two years from now.

Commissioner COMMONS. In doing that, he is simply adding to the seasonal labor. What I am getting at is, how he is going to add to the winter labor.

Mr. HORST. No; I don't agree with you you on that, if you please. There remains this additional work supply to take care of the people now engaged in agriculture. There is the big surplus now. There must be more work supplied for the winter and spring. There must be more work. Now, when the harvest season comes around, you must get out a different class of people to come in for your harvest work. Now, that is done in a great many places. It is done on that line in a great many places where people will go out simply for the harvest. The way you have got it now, the harvest hands are the same people that do the work when it is not the harvest season. You haven't got a different class of people for the harvest season. That is, you get your surplus supply out of this class of people that you are using the rest of the year.

Commissioner COMMONS. That is all.
Chairman WALSH. Thank you; that is all.
Call your next.
Mr. THOMPSON. Mr. Hecke.

TESTIMONY OF MR. GEORGE HENRY HECKE.

Mr. THOMPSON. Mr. Hecke, will you give us your name and your address?
Mr. HECKE. George Henry Hecke.
Mr. THOMPSON. And your address?
Mr. HECKE. Woodland, Cal.
Mr. THOMPSON. Occupation?
Mr. HECKE. Fruit grower.
Mr. THOMPSON. Are you a fruit grower and adviser for the University of California?
Mr. HECKE. I am a fruit grower on my own account, and my position as farm adviser is a complimentary position given to me by the University of California, probably because I have been of some slight assistance to them in investigating and work in agricultural industry.
Mr. THOMPSON. How long have you been engaged in fruit raising in this State?
Mr. HECKE. About 22 years.
Mr. THOMPSON. Were you here this morning?
Mr. HECKE. I was here part of the time.
Mr. THOMPSON. Did you hear the testimony of Mr. Bentley and Mr. Horst, and this afternoon of Prof. Parker?
Mr. HECKE. I have heard part of it.
Mr. THOMPSON. With reference to the character of labor and the percentage of skilled and unskilled?
Mr. HECKE. Yes, sir.
Mr. THOMPSON. Of the sexes; of the nationalities?
Mr. HECKE. Yes, sir.
Mr. THOMPSON. Is there anything you would care to add to that, or was that statement about correct?
Mr. HECKE. No; not in particular. As a whole, those figures are correct.
Mr. THOMPSON. Is there anything that you would care to add to what they have said with reference to the method of getting the man connected with the job?
Mr. HECKE. Yes; I have. Before I received the synopsis of the questions likely to be asked, I had written out my ideas of what I would suggest in bringing the employer closer to the employee.
Mr. THOMPSON. Will you state it to us?
Mr. HECKE. With your permission, Mr. Chairman.
Chairman WALSH. Very good.
Mr. HECKE. One of the greatest difficulties encountered each harvest by workers and agriculturists alike is the inability of the man and the job to connect. Workers at the beginning of the season often are many miles away from the place of possible employment. And farmers are distant from the labor market, so-called. There is no properly regulated agency through which they can be brought together. If the worker applies to an employment agency he must pay a fee to get the job, and very often conditions are improperly, at times even untruthfully, presented to him, so, when he arrives at his destination, after paying his fee, he finds the situation other than expected. At the very commencement of his employment he may become dissatisfied, and at the first opportunity will quit and seek another place, facing the same disadvantages as in the beginning of his nomadic search. The farmer also suffers from the loss of time entailed in finding another man for the vacant job.
To ameliorate this condition, I would suggest the establishment by the State of employment bureaus at various centers of California. These bureaus would be the medium of bringing together the men and the job. Proper and adequate systems of regulation should be maintained, and accurate data would indicate where and in what numbers men were wanted. At times we find a surplus of labor in one section and a scarcity in another, and such central bureaus properly conducted would have a tendency to correct that condition. This system certainly would prevent the mulcting of workers who are dependent upon private labor agents to obtain work. Seasonal workers could be moved about the State from the beginning of the fruit harvest in the north until the picking

and .packing of the citrus fruit crop in the south, thereby affording almost steady and certainly remunerative employment. Properly registered workers could travel from one job to another, the State possibly arranging for a reduced railroad fare upon presentation of a certificate from such labor bureau. Such a system would be a great aid to the migratory worker and undoubtedly would result in men of that class realizing more fully their duty to themselves and to the State. Eventually, the man who is ablebodied, but who will not work, will be brought under the direct control of the State, and the deserving citizen out of a job would be given necessary assistance at a time when it would prove most helpful. Farmers would welcome such bureaus, because they would be able to save considerable time now spent in searching for help, and by cooperating with the State the competent worker would be helped to obtain virtually continuous employment. I have given this idea just in general, leaving the details for future consideration, but on the whole I believe both the worker and the agriculturist would be helped materially by the establishment of such bureaus.

This is only a somewhat preliminary statement. But I have been thinking that $18,000,000 are now being spent by the State of California on State highways, and about the same number of millions have been appropriated by California counties in building bridges for these highways, and it will only be a year or two when it will be necessary to have laterals built, and have repair gangs at work on the said highways; and I have been thinking that perhaps there might be a solution of giving work to the unemployed during the time that they can not work in the harvest, particularly during the winter time. It is State work, and some method could be found, I am sure, by which such employment could be given in certain parts of the State. In the mountainous regions it might not be possible on account of the rain and on account of the snow. In southern and central California it will surely be feasible to put the unemployed to work.

Commissioner COMMONS. The road work now is mostly done in the summer season—in the busy season?

Mr. HECKE. We have not so far had any highways, State highways. They are building at the present time throughout the year; started in about three years ago, I believe.

Commissioner COMMONS. It has been done in summer?

Mr. HECKE. It is done throughout the year, the building of new highways.

Commissioner COMMONS. Your idea would be to stop the work during the summer—during the harvest season?

Mr. HECKE. No; to continue the way we are doing now for the building of it; but I am sure that in due course of time considerable extra work will have to be done on those highways, and during that time and while building laterals and making repairs on the old highways—this might give us a solution for the employment of the migratory worker in winter.

Commissioner COMMONS. Have you knowledge that this matter is being taken up by any State?

Mr. HECKE. Not at the present time.

Chairman WALSH. Mr. Hecke, there are experts, gentlemen who have been brought before this commission, who are making a very earnest endeavor to invent means of bridging over the seasonal character of labor in different localities. Would it be asking too much of you to ask you to confine yourself to that one topic and to write out these suggestions and send them to our secretary?

Mr. HECKE. I should be very glad to do so.

Chairman WALSH. Thank you.

Commissioner WEINSTOCK. You offered one suggestion to tide over the mid-season and keep the highways repaired during the winter months?

Mr. HECKE. Yes.

Commissioner WEINSTOCK. But in California that is our rainy season, and is not practical, is it?

Mr. HECKE. I mentioned in certain mountainous counties it might not be practical, but the work could be done in such parts of the State where the winter work could be done to advantage.

Commissioner WEINSTOCK. Well, the work done, then, during the winter months?

Mr. HECKE. Yes.

Commissioner WEINSTOCK. Let the work accumulate and be done during the winter months?

Mr. HECKE. Yes.

Commissioner WEINSTOCK. In place of having it done during the summer?

Mr. HECKE. Yes; I think that in all your inquiries you are endeavoring to find some suggestions to give the seasonal unemployed an opportunity to work. It has occurred to me that this might be one of them.

Commissioner WEINSTOCK. In preparing the paper for this commission suggested by Chairman Walsh, would you be good enough to make calculations showing how many would be likely to be thus employed on the highways throughout the State?

Mr. HECKE. Mr. Weinstock, the highway commissioners would be better able to give figures on this more correctly than I possibly could. My work lies mostly in the agricultural lines. Nevertheless, I have given considerable study to labor conditions as an employer as well as a county and Federal official.

Chairman WALSH. Connect it with your own industry—with that with which you are familiar—but make it as exhaustive and technical as you can, because we want to group them along with some other suggestions that are being made, especially by men who are studying this subject. Cover your own subject, and then go as far as you feel you generously can in making a study of it, and give us your views.

Mr. HECKE. I shall be very glad to.

Commissioner WEINSTOCK. You have been a fruit grower for a number of years?

Mr. HECKE. Yes.

Commissioner WEINSTOCK. And you heard the statement made by the preceding witness, Mr. Speed?

Mr. HECKE. Yes.

Commissioner WEINSTOCK. He gave it as his opinion that wages have had a downward tendency.

Mr. HECKE. Yes.

Commissioner WEINSTOCK. What are the facts, from your experience with agriculture and horticulture in California?

Mr. HECKE. At the time I came to California the wages for winter work, as well as for harvest work, were $1 a day.

Commissioner WEINSTOCK. And board?

Mr. HECKE. And board; yes.

Commissioner WEINSTOCK. What are the wages to-day?

Mr. HECKE. At the present time the lowest wages paid for winter work is a dollar fifteen, but most generally a dollar and a quarter per day.

Commissioner WEINSTOCK. And board?

Mr. HECKE. And board. From the beginning of the plowing season to the end of the harvest the average wage would be nearer a dollar and a half.

Commissioner WEINSTOCK. And board?

Mr. HECKE. And board.

Commissioner WEINSTOCK. Mr. Speed was mistaken on that?

Mr. HECKE. Absolutely mistaken.

Commissioner COMMONS. What was the wage, and how long ago was that, you say?

Mr. HECKE. That was about 22 years ago. I came here as a laboring man.

Commissioner COMMONS. And during the plowing season, what was the wage then?

Mr. HECKE. One dollar a day. The wages throughout the year at that time were the same——

Commissioner COMMONS. Now, a dollar fifteen in winter and a dollar fifty——

Mr. HECKE. During the summer time, and board.

Commissioner COMMONS. During the rest of the year?

Mr. HECKE. Yes.

Commissioner WEINSTOCK. What are the wages paid to orientals and Asiatics?

Mr. HECKE. They have increased almost twofold, almost 100 per cent.

Commissioner WEINSTOCK. What were the wages then compared with what they are now?

Mr. HECKE. At one time, when I first came to California, we had Japanese as low as 80 cents a day.

Commissioner WEINSTOCK. They fed themselves?

Mr. HECKE. They fed themselves.

Commissioner WEINSTOCK. What are they getting now?

Mr. HECKE. From $1.60 to $2.

Commissioner WEINSTOCK. From $1.60 to $2?

Mr. HECKE. Yes; but they board themselves.

Commissioner WEINSTOCK. They board themselves. And while really when they are getting $2 a day they are getting substantially the same wage that the white worker receives who gets a dollar and a half plus board?

Mr. HECKE. Yes.

Commissioner WEINSTOCK. Now, all other things equal, taking the average fruit grower, the average farmer, to whom does he give the preference at the same price, to the Jap at $2, or white at $2?

Mr. HECKE. Why, to the white.

Commissioner WEINSTOCK. He gives the white man the preference?

Mr. HECKE. Yes.

Commissioner WEINSTOCK. For what reason? Is it sentiment?

Mr. HECKE. It is sentiment which has crystallized during the last few years. We have had an influx of Japanese, we have had an influx of Hindus, in California. We notice that the Japanese is acquiring our land; that they are increasing in numbers; they import women over here and are raising families; now, most of the thinking farmers of California have come to the conclusion that it must be absolutely necessary to keep California for the white men. It is this sentiment, that is prevalent, that induces the California farmer to give the preference to the white man.

Commissioner WEINSTOCK. How will the two races compare in efficiency?

Mr. HECKE. There are two classes of white men. There is one which has been spoken about here this morning as the genus hobo; the other one is the respectable white man who will come to work on the farm with the intention of becoming an employer himself, or have a steady position. Then there is another type of man, which works on farms temporarily because thrown out of a job in the city on account of bad industrial conditions. For instance, labor was rather scarce in the agricultural district up to 1912; during 1913 and 1914 conditions have changed, hence we find that a good many white men who used to be employed in the cities have naturally drifted to the country and are hunting work; but as soon as the conditions begin to better in the cities—as business is picking up—those migratory workers will go back to their old employment. They are only temporary. Then we have got some men who don't care to work—— .

Commissioner WEINSTOCK. Take it through the harvest season, are there many women and children employed in horticulture?

Mr. HECKE. In particular work, light work.

Commissioner WEINSTOCK. In picking and packing?

Mr. HECKE. Not so much in picking. The picking is all done by adult males, but in packing, in cutting, in canning, a number of women and children are used.

Commissioner WEINSTOCK. The statement was made here a few years ago that during the harvest season there was a great scarcity of harvest labor in the orchards and vineyards.

Mr. HECKE. Yes.

Commissioner WEINSTOCK. Does that situation still prevail?

Mr. HECKE. No; not now. It was true at the time.

Commissioner WEINSTOCK. But at this time there is an abundance of labor?

Mr. HECKE. At this time there is an abundance of labor.

Commissioner WEINSTOCK. And between the men and women and Asiatics there is an abundance of labor?

Mr. HECKE. Yes; there is enough labor to carry through this crop very nicely.

Commissioner WEINSTOCK. That is all.

Chairman WALSH. That is all. Call your next witness.

Mr. THOMPSON. Mr. Mills.

TESTIMONY OF MR. JAMES MILLS.

Mr. THOMPSON. Give us your name, business address, and business, please.

Mr. MILLS. James Mills, Willows; my business is developer, and orange and lemon grower, and prospective planter of deciduous orchards and nuts. I have holdings at Riverside, where I formerly lived. I am in the north for developing.

Mr. THOMPSON. How long have you been engaged in this line of work?

Mr. MILLS. Twenty-five years.

Mr. THOMPSON. Were you here this morning?

Mr. MILLS. Yes; I was.

Mr. THOMPSON. Did you hear the testimony of Mr. Bentley, Mr. Horst, and Prof. Parker this afternoon with reference to labor conditions?

Mr. MILLS. I did.

Mr. THOMPSON. And the division of the skilled and unskilled and other divisions?

Mr. MILLS. Yes.

Mr. THOMPSON. Are those statements about correct, or have you anything to add to what they said in that respect?

Mr. MILLS. Substantially correct, except I believe it would be varied in the citrous industry.

Mr. THOMPSON. Give us the condition in the citrous industry, then, please; that is, the amount of skilled and unskilled and foreign people.

Mr. MILLS The citrous industry was for many years laboring under a very great disadvantage, because of the fact that a large proportion of our fruit was spoiled in transit to market, thus bringing us very often a serious loss. The Federal Government undertook to determine just what the factors were that brought us this loss, this decay in transit. And it was ascertained that the conditions under which our fruit was picked, hauled, packed, and shipped brought about the decay and the consequent loss financially to the growers. We found that our labor was indifferent, and that the growers were largely indifferent, too, because they knew not where the difficulty was. Some did, and some, in every way possible, endeavored to educate their men.

Now, I cite this for this reason: We learned that we needed more expert labor even on the soil, in the orchard, in the picking, in the hauling, in the loading, in the assorting, brushing, packing, and loading into the cars. And it has called for a higher efficiency, and there has been considerable trouble in getting that higher efficiency in the orchards; as yet we have not succeeded, for the reason that there is not that conscientious conviction of duty amongst the men of to-day of all classes and in all nationalities, I believe, that would cause them, for the money paid, however much or however little, to give absolutely their best to their employers. It has been impossible for us to get the efficiency that we need—I think, plainly speaking, largely because we have not the morals the we had in our fathers' time. Times have changed, my children tell me. They have in this regard. In our packing houses we do get higher efficiency because there we use the best American labor. The women are the most efficient workers we have in the fruit industry, the most likely to give the highest efficiency. We used to use Chinamen. Necessarily we had to. Never until recent years have we used the Japs or the Mexicans in our packing houses. But now we largely use women in our packing operations, that is, in handling the fruit, wrapping it in the paper, placing it in the box carefully. And these women have been largely developed, and the farmer did not call for skilled help there. We now do call for skilled help and we have it in that particular field largely to our desires.

In the field, too, we find from investigation that the men in picking would cut the lemons or the oranges with their finger nails. We had to get them to prune their finger nails and wear gloves, because when the fruit was punctured, the spore in countless millions being around, immediately lodged in the moist portion of the rind and began to develop. And thus it went through the brusher increasing and on through the sweating house increasing, and necessarily 25 per cent of our fruit was ruined before it got to market.

Here again we developed a higher class of labor even amongst the Japs and the Mexicans who would listen. I should say that in the citrous industry that we have 50 per cent that might be called technical; not technical in the way that a manufacturer would call technical, but technical so far as agriculture and horticulture is concerned.

In irrigation, too—there we need specially the men. Personally, I have not found any other race than the Japanese who would give that attention to detail in irrigation that was required and properly use the water and properly irrigate the tree. And for that reason I have used no other labor in this particular branch of our work for 10 or 12 years, giving better wages for that than for most all the other work. That is technical work, and it needs very diligent attention every hour of the day and of the night, if we irrigate in the night, as sometimes we do.

In the other development, in the development I am doing now in the north, to get the best work we do need a high type of man. In the north I have found that it was impossible for us to get that type of laborer through whose efforts, for the wages paid, we get the best results. I should say that in the Sacramento Valley that the laborer, farm laborer, is about the poorest in this or any other land; that is, the old agricultural laborer.

We needed about 200 men when we began, and I venture the assertion that I had on the ranch, on the road, and going to and fro, three men for every man that I used. The average was five days' labor. Five days is the average that we got out of the type of laborer that we were using for development work during the last two years. Types of laborers, I am sorry to say, compel me to absolutely indorse all that Mr. Parker said about the conditions that surround labor in many of the camps—in the great majority of the camps everywhere where labor is used in California and perhaps in other States. Labor I find here has been degraded largely because of the conditions that surround it.

. I was in conversation with a lady who had a large property. We were talking about the labor conditions. Perhaps I digress. She condemned her labor. That they went to the saloons on Saturday night, and if they came back at all, they came back unfit to work Monday and Tuesday. I said to her, "Madam, you are the culprit, not your man. Go down, if you will, and look at the conditions that surround your labor, and you will get the seat of your trouble. If the man was a man he would necessarily become much of a brute if he remained in your place surrounded by the conditions that now surround him. His conditions are not equal to the conditions of your brute animals. Change the conditions. Put him in a good house, give him a place to bathe, give him a good bed, give him literature and music, let him know you are interested in him, and you will find you have got a new man; that he will do for you whereas now he does you."

A year afterwards I went to the ranch, and the manager, a brother, caught me by the arm and he said, "Mills, don't look at the ranch; look at what we did for our men." I said, "My brother, has it paid?" "Mills, we have never realized what fools we were. The same men are new men. For higher wages we are doing cheaper work."

. I merely recite this that you may know that I believe that the employers are to blame for the conditions which we find among our laborers, as are those who lead labor. I am persuaded that the labor element, too, are largely ill advised by their so-called leaders, that they are brought into the frame of mind that causes them to believe that they need not put forth effort, that they need not make sacrifices, that they need not practice thrift; that they need not practice self-denial in order to accomplish the things that should be accomplished in life in order to be somebody and do something for themselves and for their fellow men.

I verily believe and want to go on record in saying that I am confident that the labor men are largely ill advised by many of the so-called labor leaders, and that they are morally injured by listening to them, as well as injured by treatment on the ranches.

I have found during the 25 years, and particularly within the last 15 years, very many men among the white race who would not go to the ranch and work; and that is true much of the time even in California, and because they will not work we are compelled, absolutely compelled, to hire Asiatics, Mexicans, or Hindus and the Chinese where they can be gotten. I have never used any Chinese nor Hindus. I have used many Japs, necessarily so.

In the fruit interests of the south these last years we have never had an abundance of labor. I assure you, if you go among the ranches in the south when the peak of the load is on, that you will find the question of the surplus of labor is not in the great fruit region of the State. For 10 years I personally never had enough men to do my work. We needed 700 or 800 men at times. We always needed from 200 to 300 men, even at the quiet times, just with the irrigation and cultivation and pruning and spraying and fumigation and the other processes of horticulture needed to be done, and yet we never could get all the men we needed. In one year we threw away 50 carloads of good lemons because I could not get men to pick them when they should have been picked. Others, I am sure, you will find among the ranches of the south who have had the same experience. I do not know and I can not speak with authority as yet as to the north; I can only give hearsay evidence as to that; but as to the south there has not been a surplus of labor for many years. We have had to employ the foreigner, the Asiatic, because we could not get the white labor. We had to use the women and girls because we could not get men to do the packing house work; we needed them outside. We were glad we had to use the women, because we found they were superior in every way to any class of labor as packers of fruit. These women were paid by the piece, many of them earning from three to four dollars a day for several months in the packing season and taking a pleasant holiday when the peak of the load was over.

I do not know, Mr. Chairman, if I am directing my attention to the things you are anxious to get.

Chairman WALSH. You are doing it very well, I think, Mr. Mills.

Mr. MILLS. I would like to say here again, and I would like to impress it upon the commission, and through the commission upon the public, that it pays for the employer to be good to his workmen, and it pays to build even expensive mess houses, to give them good beds, to keep them clean, to give them even sheets and pillow cases, to give them the best of board, even though they lose money on their board.

I charge 75 cents a day for my board. I lose some $3,000 to $5,000 a year on my boarding house. And when my interested parties, stockholders and others, ask me why, I say I get it at the other end twofold.

A gentleman who was much exercised by my criticism of his methods came to my home several years ago to finally discuss the matter and look into my methods, and when I was through he says, " I will go you one better."

He went home and built a $10,000 bunk house and boarding house, library and reading room and put in it literature, daily papers, weekly journals, monthly journals· and books.

I was talking to his foreman shortly afterwards, after the completion of it, and there had been time for the men to realize what had been done, and he says, " You do not know what you have done for us. Our men go up town—I was up town recently, and the merchants of the town said 'What have you done?' ' What do you mean?' 'What have you done to your men?' 'Why, what is the matter with the men?' 'Why, formerly they cursed you, and now they bless you,'" and he told the story.

I always paid higher wages than my competitors. My people said once, " You must cut wages." I says, " I will do it if I am not doing my work cheaper than my competitors. Get in my machine and let us go to some big packing plant or orchard company and see what it does cost them to do these different kinds of labor, irrigation, fertilization, pruning, spraying, picking, hauling—all the details."

We went. We got the costs. We did not reduce wages. Our men were doing work for higher wages and less expense to us.

I think that the employers make a great mistake—perhaps, I am moralizing, but I would like to get this to employers—in that they do not observe the merits of the different men who work for them, be they what they may— what nationality they may be. That every man shall be treated according to his deserts. That if he succeeds in doing good work; that if he succeeds in serving his master—his employer—well and truly, that his wages shall be increased correspondingly. All these years have I maintained this. I have made no difference between the Jap and the Mexican, Englishman, Scotch, Irish, Scandinavian, German, or French. The man who succeeded, went up to the top. I hired no experts; I trained them, those who could be trained, those who would study, and in that way I have developed a spirit among my men of striving to excel.

One man that I had 12 years ago, at $65 a month, draws $4,000 to-day on the salary roll. He earns it; he earns more; he will get it. Men that come to me from Tennessee as teamsters at $1.75 a day, when I left them, were getting $150 a month, a house, a horse and buggy for himself, and a horse and buggy for his wife. They earn it and earn it well. I follow the same here. When I came into the Northland, I said to my stockholders, " There is one thing I shall not hear any dictation upon. I want to build the most comfortable quarters; I want music; I want literature; I want books." I have 1,000 volumes of books, and am adding to it in every library.

For my Mexican help, which I had to bring, I built quarters costing $7,000, with shower baths, with toilets, with sewer systems, with washing tubs for the women, with every convenience. I keep it clean. It is all cement. I wash it out, and that, wonderful to behold them, are as clean—cleaner than my white help, and they have the altars of their gods in every home on the ranch.

I merely say this because I would that employers took the attitude toward labor that would inspire labor to do better; that would inspire labor to seek a spirit to reach the top.

A man spoke to you this afternoon, but recently—I hope he is gone—he went
to work on a ranch in the Sacramento Valley 20 years ago for $1 a day and
his board. He had inspiration, aspiration, ambition, he served, he wrought
worthily, he saved, he became the foreman, he became the superintendent, he
became the tenant, he became the owner; and this any man can do—any man
of any race in California.

When I came to California and went to Riverside I was offered $1.25 a
day and board myself, or eat myself, as the Irishman would say. I got $1.50;
I picked grapes for $1.50; I packed oranges by the box; I picked oranges for
$1.50. I have never wanted a day's labor. I am persuaded, persuaded be-
yond a doubt, that every brother of mine, the white brother from any nationality, can find work in California if he truly wants it, if he don't just merely
claim he wants it. Every farmer in California would gladly prefer the white
man to the Asiatic; gladly, if he could get the same service from him as
he gets from the Asiatic. I am sorry to say that some of the highest forms
of labor that I have to perform in my duty as a developer, as a superintendent,
and as a manager, I give to the Jap. I pay them the wage for it, higher
wages than white men, because they will perform the work given them with
splendid energy and splendid success. Pruning my trees. I tried all classes
of labor and I finally came to the Jap, I gave him $2.50 and $2.75. I have
Japs working at less than $2, $2.10, $2.25, and $2.50. I give them a place
to live; I build them bathing places; I furnish them light.

I give my Mexicans $2, $2.10, $2.20, and on up, according to the time that
they stay with me; always increasing as the years go, in order to entice the
men to stay with me. Some of the men have been with me for 15 years.
I give the Mexicans in addition to the $2, $2.10, $2.20, a comfortable house—a
very comfortable house, more comfortable than he has ever before lived in.
I furnish them, as I told you, with a shower bath and a toilet, all cement,
all flushed out every day. I furnish the men and the women separately, and
give the women washtubs—every woman having washtubs for her washing.

I give them electric light. I give them garden room and irrigation water, in
addition to the $2, $2.10, $2.20. My white men I give $2.25, $2.50, $2.75 $3,
and on up, according to the work they are doing and the time they are with me.
My white men, who have remained with me for a year, I give, in addition,
two weeks holiday on time. If unhappily any shall take sick or be injured in
my employ, for the last 10 years I have paid all their hospital expenses; paid
all their wages, full wages, and paid the doctor. This in addition to their
wages. This because it paid me to do do it; this because I realized I got a
greater devotion from my men; this because I found that my men endeavored
to come back and give me as good as I gave, and they have.

True, there are times when we have heartburnings and when we get together
and discuss things sometimes with a little heat; but we generally get away
into a corner where no one will hear us and fight it out, and whoever is wrong
admits it and gets back to the job.

Again, let me say in the southland beyond the Tehachapi, never have I
known a time when the fruit men had more laborers than they needed. Again,
let me say at no time in the south in the last 15 years have I seen during
the winter months, and for eight months, have I seen a time when the white
man seeking labor, wanting it, and gladly performing it, could not get the work
and get it in preference to any of the Asiatic men, so many of whom we have
to use.

Men honestly out of work. There are men and we generally find work for
them, but there are a great many men in California who are not honestly out
of work. I speak from authority; I speak knowing what I speak about. I
have been in close touch with them as an officer of the law—and the law was
pretty severely handled here a while ago—as a judge of the court—I am glad
I am a farmer—I handled many of these men; handled them year after year;
went into their circumstances and their history, and I found that they went
from Riverside to Yuma, from Yuma to Texas, and from Texas to Kansas,
from Kansas to Dakota, from Dakota to Montana, from Montana on around
through Washington and Oregon to California again, around the circle. Some
men go around the house to get the sun, if sun is needed; to escape it, if it
is too hot. Thousands of these men every year go around the circle on the
brake beam.

I have repeatedly gotten work for hundreds; I have bought them shears;
I have bought them picking sacks and picking tools; I have got them the job,

and have had them arrested and brought before me from the box car the next morning, having sold their boots and their picking sack and their picking shears, and laughed at me for my trouble.

This is true. It is a condition in the country that is lamentable. How it can be remedied, I don't know. I have dwelt on it long and seriously, but I really don't know how these men can be saved to society and to themselves.

I prefer—the question is asked what labor I prefer. I prefer the white man.

Chairman WALSH. I think, Mr. Mills, not to hurry you, that that was involved in another question given you, and you have given us that fact.

Mr. MILLS. All right. Perhaps if I am too verbose, you will put questions to me.

Chairman WALSH. That is all right. We repeat sometimes in our outlines. It is our fault, and not yours.

Mr. MILLS. I don't know how to deal with the unemployed. When I was in the justice of the peace chair for many years and dealing with them, I gave it considerable thought and suggestion along the line Mr. Hecke dealt with; but not particularly that, because we had no highways at that time.

I do believe society owes it to labor to have some work somewhere at public expense. I do believe it will be cherper for society to set aside the money that is taking care of our unfortunates in our prisons and in our asylums and use that for some great public development.

I do believe that our pork barrel could be very well used to that end in some wise way. I do believe we have the men to-day in the Nation, being big and broad and sympathetic and noble of sentiment and soul, who would solve this question for us if our Government would give them the opportunity and the means afterwards to take care of labor.

I do believe there should be a fund in the States so set apart that the different counties may send their temporarily idle to those particular spots where public work is being done in several places in the State. There is much of public work, I am sure, that must be done at different times of the year. The railroad should be enticed to help in sending them from place to place cheaply, and those men who would not work for pay should be compelled to work without pay.

I think it is demoralizing in our prisons that men are allowed to be idle, because idleness is one of the great means of moral degradation among the people of this Nation or any nation.

The Turks have well said that the devil—whoever he is—finds work for idle hands to do, and idle minds, and I do believe—let me repeat it—that it behooves the State and State authorities wisely to determine this thing. They are those who should determine it. Wisely set aside money that will be wisely used by wise men to in a large measure settle this crying evil in our land.

Chairman WALSH. We will now adjourn until to-morrow morning at 10 o'clock.

Kindly resume the stand at 10 o'clock to-morrow morning, Mr. Mills.

(Whereupon, at 4.30 o'clock p. m., on this Thursday, the 27th day of August, 1914, an adjournment was taken to the following day, Friday, August 28, 1914, at 10 o'clock a. m.)

SAN FRANCISCO, CAL., *Friday, August 28, 1914—10 a. m.*

Present: Chairman Walsh, Commissioners Weinstock, Commons, Lennon, O'Connell, and Garretson; also William O. Thompson, counsel.

Chairman WALSH. The commission will please come to order.

Mr. THOMPSON. Mr. Mills.

Chairman WALSH. Call your next witness. Mr. Mills is not here.

Mr. THOMPSON. Mr. Hyde

TESTIMONY OF MR. GEORGE E. HYDE.

Mr. THOMPSON. Mr. Hyde, will you give us your name?

Mr. HYDE. George E. Hyde.

Mr. THOMPSON. And your business address and business, please?

Mr. HYDE. My business address is Campbell, Cal.

Mr. THOMPSON. And your business?

Mr. HYDE. I am a fruit packer and also a fruit raiser. I have a fruit ranch.

Mr. THOMPSON. How long have you been engaged in that industry in this State?

Mr. HYDE. I have been fruit raising 32 years in Santa Clara County.

Mr. THOMPSON. Were you here yesterday?

Mr. HYDE. Yes, sir.

Mr. THOMPSON. And you heard the testimony of the witnesses on the stand with reference to the division of the labor in the agricultural district, skilled and unskilled portions?

Mr. HYDE. Yes, sir.

Mr. THOMPSON. And also with reference to their sex, nationality, and the like?

Mr. HYDE. Yes, sir; I did.

Mr. THOMPSON. Have you anything to add in that respect to the testimony already given?

Mr. HYDE. Not particularly. I think that the percentages of averages were about correct, or nearly so.

Mr. THOMPSON. Did you hear also what was said with reference to the way in which help is procured?

Mr. HYDE. Yes, sir.

Mr. THOMPSON. And in the agricultural districts?

Mr. HYDE. I did.

Mr. THOMPSON. When needed?

Mr. HYDE. Yes, sir.

Mr. THOMPSON. Have you anything to add to that phase of the subject?

Mr. HYDE. No more than from my own experience as an employer of help in the packing of fruits, namely dried fruits—I also handle fresh fruits—would be that in our vicinity the help is procured by application on their own part, as a rule; knowledge generally disseminated with regard to the requirements of labor in certain places and with certain firms. Application is made for labor. The labor, of course, is only local help.

Mr. THOMPSON. It comes from the locality?

Mr. HYDE. Yes, sir; much of it.

Mr. THOMPSON. What kind of help do you generally need for that work?

Mr. HYDE. Well, there is a proportion of skilled, but mainly unskilled labor.

Mr. THOMPSON. Do you have any difficulty in getting your help?

Mr. HYDE. No, I haven't had any difficulty for four years there.

Mr. THOMPSON. What scale of wages do you pay these workers?

Mr. HYDE. The wages of unskilled men would be about $2. There have been a few hired as low as $1.75, but they were mainly old men who were not capable of doing heavy manual labor—some easy work. Very few of those at that price. Most of our help get two dollars and a quarter. They represent help that have worked in fruit before and have had some experience.

Mr. THHOMPSON. How long does your season last there?

Mr. HYDE. Well, it began this last season on the 16th day of June with apricots—the drying of apricots—which is one of Santa Clara's greatest crops of fruit, and it is still in full force, and will last probably to the 1st of December. At the present time there is no fresh fruit on hand to be handled, excepting cling peaches.

Mr. THOMPSON. During this time about how many men will you employ—the total help, men and women?

Mr. HYDE. Well, it varies greatly in the number, on account of the demand of the work. My largest pay roll—I had 350 enrolled. That was during the month of July. The proportion of males and females during that time was about equal, about 50 per cent of each.

Mr. THOMPSON. What respective work do the two sections do, and what wages are the women paid?

Mr. HYDE. The women, very few of them work by the day. I have two foreladies who work by the day, and they received for 10 hours $2.50 in the fresh fruits. In the dried fruits we are operating under the old law—the present State law, and they are employed only 8 hours. They receive the same wages for 8 hours that they did for 10, $2.50. The women mostly work piecework—the cutting of apricots and peaches, and the paring of apples and pears and coring them and all that kind of thing is piecework.

Mr. THOMPSON. What would be the earnings of a woman working a full week about, what would it vary?

Mr. HYDE. The inexperienced help that is working there for the first time while learning probably would not receive an average exceeding $7 a week; but our average pay roll on those who are experienced, even with the experience of a week or so, will run up to very nearly $12 a week. Many of the experienced helpers in the fruit earn from $21 to $23 a week—$3 a day or better.

Mr. THOMPSON. Of the people you employ, how many are employed throughout the year?

Mr. HYDE. Throughout the year—I only keep a clerical force in the wintertime. The foreman and manager and clerical force in the office are on the pay roll the year around.

Mr. THOMPSON. Do you know what work the people you engage do when they are not working for you? You say they come from the neighborhood.

Mr. HYDE. Campbell is a small hamlet of about 800 people, and most of the people that work for me have their own little places in town, their houses, and during the winter months the males work in the orchard—we are right in the midst of a big orchard country—pruning trees and hoeing and plowing and all the work required in agriculture. They begin the fruit work with cherries in the month of May, picking cherries. Those are picked for the market fresh, or for the canneries. Then they come to work for the packing houses. There are two or three canneries at Campbell, and one dried-fruit house.

Mr. THOMPSON. How much money will an able-bodied man make in the season, fairly skilled, say, during the entire season from June to December?

Mr. HYDE. You mean from June to December?

Mr. THOMPSON. Yes, sir.

Mr. HYDE. Well, take all the laboring men, I think they would average $2.25 a day. There are quite a few of our men get $2.50 a day; men who have charge of small divisions of the work get $2.50 a day.

Mr. THOMPSON. That would be true, of course, of men who work all the time. What would be the average work a man would have who is ready to work there? Would he have continuous work during those months?

Mr. HYDE. Oh, yes; practically continuous. Of course, we have a transient help that we have to depend on. It is a floating help that comes in there and lives around in the town looking for work, and they come around, we notice, practically every year, a great many of them.

Mr. THOMPSON. What proportion of those you employ are of this floating character?

Mr. HYDE. Probably in men, among the men—of course, there are not many women—but among the men there probably would not be more than—in the height of the season—half of them, probably.

Mr. THOMPSON. Do you know where these men go and what becomes of them after they get through with your work?

Mr. HYDE. I have had several conversations with the men because I took an interest in what they were doing, and I know they have a circuit that they follow practically every year. For instance, men that we discharged last week for being through with their work, told me they were going to Watsonville, that is in the lower part of the county, to pick apples, the apple crop being about ready to harvest; and after that they went to the southern part of the State in the citrus fruit in the wintertime.

Mr. THOMPSON. This floating help, which you say is about 50 per cent at the height of the season, do they come to town unbidden, or are they sent for?

Mr. HYDE. They come unbidden.

Mr. THOMPSON. They don't come through any employment agency?

Mr. HYDE. No, sir; I have never employed anyone through an employment agency in all my experience.

Mr. THOMPSON. Have you any knowledge or information with reference to the number of people out of work in this State during the wintertime?

Mr. HYDE. No, sir; I have not.

Mr. THOMPSON. Have you any views with reference to the organization of the workers?

Mr. HYDE. I have some views of my own that might, I think, possibly be carried out with good effect. I am not in a position to know what the feelings of the men are—the floating class, I mean—only as I talk with them. They seem to be, to my mind, a large part of them, more than desirous of traveling around from place to place. They are an uneasy class of people, and many of them don't even work out the time I would like to have them work; they will work a week or so, and when they have got a little money they will move on— ask for their money and move on to other places.

Mr. THOMPSON. How many people would you employ in order to keep a steady force during the height of the season? You say about half of your force is of a floating character. During the season how many men would you have to employ in order to keep that force up?

⁻ Mr. HYDE. I think the force that we have there now is fairly an average for the season, from the beginning of the apricots in June until the packing is over, the dried fruits.

We have at the present time a force of 50 men. Of that 50 men fully 40 of them are help that we depend upon every year, that live in town and that stay with us until the last piece of work is done. The other 10 men are men that we have generally been gradually weeding out from the floating class of help to get the best of them, those who seemed desirous of staying until the end of the work—the steady men. I think that class of men that I refer to now are honestly out of employment, through some cause or other, I do not know what. I have known in some instances, where they have told me. But they are out of employment, and they are desirous of working as long as we wish them to. They are men who under other circumstances, if placed right, would be steady men.

Mr. THOMPSON. Well, take the number of people you say you employ during the height of the season of a floating character; you say about half of your men—that would be about 175. Would that be right or would the 350 include all?

Mr. HYDE. Well, the 350 include all the help—men, women, and children.

Mr. THOMPSON. Then, it would be about 80 to 90 floating men that you would employ part of that time?

Mr. HYDE. From first to last, yes.

Mr. THOMPSON. Well, in order to keep that force of 80 to 90, how many men would you employ during the season?

Mr. HYDE. Well, there would be probably at the height of the season at least one-half of the 300 I spoke of; there would be 150 men—that is the height of the season. Then they gradually would dwindle down until we get at the present time a force of about 50 men.

Mr. THOMPSON. I mean those that are left at the end of the week's work; how many men would you have to employ in order to keep your force up?

Mr. HYDE. I didn't catch your question before. I didn't take any figures off the pay roll that I could supply that. I could not say how many men. I know that toward the last—well, say two weeks ago my foreman of the yard where most of the men that are employed, the floating class—and I mean by the yard the drying yard. We have got a drying yard there of 16 acres, and we handle all the way from two to three thousand tons of fruit a season in that yard. This year we have handled 1,200 tons of apricots alone in that one yard, which is a record for that yard. Those men, many of them, do not stay long enough to hold the job only a day or two. My foreman has been weeding them out and taking the best of them all the time, for there are plenty of others. In fact, we had as high as 20 applications a day for work from this floating class of men sitting there waiting for a job.

Mr. THOMPSON. What, in your opinion, could be done either by the growers or by the community to help out the seasonal character of the work and to extend the seasons longer or to make additional work?

Mr. HYDE. Well——

Mr. THOMPSON. To fit in.

Mr. HYDE. The industries of California are such that practically within the limits of California as a State there is work, it seems to me, for deserving men, men who are willing to work, practically the year around. The fruit work in our neighborhood, as I said, will last from—in cherries—I do not deal in cherries, but we have that fruit there to be picked—would last from the latter part of May until in the green-fruit picking, the 1st of October. During that time we have, as a rule, demands for labor oftentimes beyond the supply. This year the supply has been good, better than common for some reason, I don't know why. Frequently the packers and canners of the country are obliged to resort to advertising in the papers. I advertised in three papers early in the season, thinking I might have the usual demand for labor—rather the poor supply, I should say, of labor. But I found it was unnecessary. I took out the advertisements after a few days, because I had plenty of help applying all that time at the office.

Then, after they get through the fruit work there, as I stated before, they would many of them move on to Watsonville or other centers where they have apples, and then from there to the citrus parts of the State. Early in the season we have berries in Santa Clara County. That is a great berry country. The berries are sold around the cities of the bay. And the only time really that seems to be a very poor demand for agricultural labor outside of our own resident labor would be during the winter months, in the pruning and the care of the lands and orchards. We have labor, sufficient local labor, for that purpose, I think.

Mr. THOMPSON. What could be done, then, with the floating labor during these winter months to correct these things as testified to by Prof. Parker?

Mr. HYDE. Well, my idea would be to have established in different industrial centers of the State, under the auspices of the State—I was going to say—labor bureaus or bureaus of information, and for labor employment, the main object of which would be to gather knowledge of the requirements of the different sections of the State, not only in agricultural pursuits, but in mining lumbering and all pursuits for labor. And they would know, by having the laborers, the men who were floating, enrolled at these various agencies or bureaus, where they could be placed by definite information when they are needed. That would avoid an oversupply or glut of labor at any one particular point, and also it would work out for the benefit of the employer and for the employee. The employer would feel reasonably sure of his labor when he wanted it, and the employee would not be called upon to move from one part of the State to another, and probably find when he got to the new place that there were others ahead of him who had secured the places, causing him to move on to another place.

I think these laborers, as they apply to the different bureaus for work, should be enrolled; and if they are sent to other places, and fail to show up, I think it would be wise to strike them from the rolls as not being really honest in their intentions. Of course, there could be something that might arise to prevent them from getting there, but I mean to say ordinarily. I think that method would find work for practically all the floating class of help, except, possibly, in the wet winter months when the men are not working in the lumber camps and can't do anything, and when there is no fruit to be handled.

Mr. THOMPSON. Do you think that a Federal bureau or employment office, working along the same lines that you mention, would help in the situation, too?

Mr. HYDE. I should think it would work just as well as a State bureau, and probably better.

Mr. THOMPSON. With reference to the housing conditions of your people, how do you house your additional workers while they are there?

Mr. HYDE. Well, the additional workers are housed in town, in the little village where there are a great many furnished rooms belonging to people who have houses there, and several boarding houses, conducted by private individuals, not by corporations—any of them.

Mr. THOMPSON. Then, you don't have camps?

· Mr. HYDE. No, sir; a good many come in tents, and whole families will come there from other sections in tents, and live in the tents during the harvest.

Mr. THOMPSON. Have you tent cities around your ranches, then?

Mr. HYDE. I am referring now to the village of Campbell, where the tent cities are close to the canneries.

Mr. THOMPSON. What provision is made for the keeping of those people, the sanitary needs, and so forth, in the tent colonies, if you know?

Mr. HYDE. Well, of course, in the houses they have sanitary conditions which are looked over very often by the health officer of the county, and, apparently, must be satisfactory to him. Of course, as far as the tents are concerned you can imagine what the sanitary condition is in a tent as well as I can. It is a natural condition mostly.

Mr. THOMPSON. There is not any general or specific provision made to take care of these tent colonies which come there?

Mr. HYDE. No, sir.

Mr. THOMPSON. With reference to sanitary matters?

Mr. HYDE. The ground is rented to them by the owners of the ground, generally some large lot where trees are, and the tents are put up; and they are furnished with water. The ground rent is usually $1 to $1.50 a month for tent space and the use of the water.

Mr. THOMPSON. How do you view the possible spread of the Industrial Workers of the World among the agricultural laborers?

Mr. HYDE. Well, there have been Industrial Workers of the World there, I know, because they have made their presence known by signs that they have written on fences and various places, mainly in chalk. I never have met any of them personally. I do not know any of them. I do not think they have ever attempted to propagate their doctrines among the help there; at least I have never known of it being done. The most of our workers there in town belong to the socialistic class; they are Socialist voters, as shown by the vote of Campbell. And the best workers we have got are those same Socialists.

Mr. THOMPSON. With reference to the floating help, particularly now, how do you view their efficiency or lack of it, and what causes would you assign either for one or the other?

Mr. HYDE. Well, at the time that we were cutting apricots, in the month of July, when the crop is at the height of the season, we didn't refuse work to anyone. If we did not have a place for a man in the drying ground doing a man's work—our drying ground of course was full all the time—we would state to him that he could take a knife and cut apricots by the piece the same as girls and women do. And many of them did that, and we had six or eight of them that went through the whole season doing it. But many of them said they would not do it, it was a woman's work, and they would not do it. I naturally came to the conclusion that they did not want work very badly. I looked upon those men as being unreliable in their statements to me regarding their desire for work.

Mr. THOMPSON. With reference to the kind of work, that is, the work required, the degree of efficiency in the cutting, is that a thing which requires a degree of efficiency, or can anybody do it?

Mr. HYDE. I had a man in particular there that earned more than $2 a day every day he worked. Some earned as much as if they had been in the field and had worked out there at the same time. They, most of them, with the exception of two of them, never had done that work before. But they soon learned it and applied themselves to the work and became efficient enough to earn their $2. One man in particular came from Santa Paula and said he had cut apricots before. I never saw any faster work done in my life than he did. He was almost a machine. He made $3 a day every day he worked.

Mr. THOMPSON. I was speaking more particularly about the skill required in order to preserve the goods and do the right kind of work—it is not a skillful operation, is it?

Mr. HYDE. No; it is not skillful, because there are children doing the work.

Mr. THOMPSON. What proportion of your work in the products cover the skillful work?

Mr. HYDE. The only skilled labor we require is foremen of the various departments. We have a forelady there, and then there are some experienced workers that we call skilled workers that work in and around the fruit, dipping the fruit, processing it, and all that kind of thing, that they have to have some skill. But they are experienced help we have had every year.

Mr. THOMPSON. You spoke of a larger number of floaters this year. What is the cause of that, if you know?

Mr. HYDE. I don't know the reason. I didn't hear the men state any reason, either.

Mr. THOMPSON. That is all.

Commissioner COMMONS. I would like to ask if it is possible in your business to enlarge the winter season by taking on new kinds of work?

Mr. HYDE. Well, I think that it could be done, and it is being done by some of the canneries. Some of the canneries that make catsup, for instance——

Commissioner COMMONS. Make what?

Mr. HYDE. Catsup. Instead of making it during the season of fresh tomatoes they take the tomatoes and work them up into a pulp and put them in gallon cans, and then open them in the winter and work it up when the fruit is not ripe.

Commissioner COMMONS. Does that prove profitable?

Mr. HYDE. Yes, sir; it has a commercial value. It is a commercial article. Of course the demand for labor in our county has always been great during the season of harvest on account of the perishable condition and nature of the fruit and vegetables that must be handled when ready. Nature does not stop in her work either for laws or for men's demands. If the fruit is ready it must be handled, otherwise it will be lost. For that reason we have to work our help in the cutting of fruit, fresh fruit, not only ten hours a day, but oftentimes two or three hours in the evening to keep up with the work; and we hire not only women, but children—that is, as the law allows them, between the ages of 12 and 16, on vacation permits issued by the school-teacher or school trustee where the child goes to school. Those vacation permits we file away very carefully and keep them all. We won't allow a child to go to work until we have it so that we can show it at any time to any authority that has the power to ask for it.

Commissioner COMMONS. That is all.

Chairman WALSH. Is that all?

Commissioner WEINSTOCK. One question: Have you found, Mr. Hyde, in· the last year or two, a surplus of desirable white laborers during the season?   '

Mr. HYDE. Well, there is a surplus of white labor. Most of the floating class seems to be the white, and even Americans; and some of them are desirable, and some are not desirable.

Commissioner WEINSTOCK. Well, from your experience, about what proportion would you call desirable workers, and what proportion undesirable workers among the whites?

Mr. HYDE. Well, referring to the floating classes of help, I should say that from my experience in putting men to work and having them stay ·with the work, showing a desire on their part to work, I should say there would be about one-half. There are a great many among the floating class that don't really ever apply for the work. They simply stay there awhile and move on. . I don't know why.

Commissioner WEINSTOCK. What seems to be the weak spot in these undesirable white workers? What are their weaknesses and failures?

Mr. HYDE. I think it is their desire for liquor, judging by the use they make of the money they get. They will work two or three days and take the money, and I have seen them drunk afterwards in the town or village. In some instances these were men whom I was quite surprised to see; they had appeared to be straightforward men and good workers.

Commissioner WEINSTOCK. Is your community, for example, a dry community?

Mr. HYDE. Yes, sir; the fourth district of Santa Clara County has been dry for two years by vote.   -

Commissioner WEINSTOCK. What opportunity would they have for drinking?

Mr. HYDE. The nearest point is San Jose where they can get it; that is, where it is openly sold.

Commissioner WEINSTOCK. At the beginning of your testimony' you made the statement that you believed that California with its remarkable resources can afford work for the willing and deserving men the year round. But a little later in your testimony you pointed out that during the winter months there were many avenues of employment that were practically closed on account of climatic conditions—so that I take it you want to modify your statement to that effect.

Mr. HYDE. I would modify it this way, that in the winter months—the time there would be no agricultural work to do—that is, fruit—and when the logging camps or mines might be closed by rain or snow—I think in the cities there would be work to be carried on, or on the roads. I would say, too, that the bureau I mentioned I think ought to have the power—there should be some act at least passed so that this floating help could be employed on the roads some way. Keep up the highways. We have a fine system of highways being inaugurated, and unless there is work done on them all the time the little holes soon become bigger and the road is ruined. That is part of the work that could be done in the winter as well as any other time, perhaps better. When the ground is wet it works up better and makes a better road.

Commissioner WEINSTOCK. Were you present when Prof. Parker testified?

Mr. HYDE. Yes, sir; I was.

Commissioner WEINSTOCK. You probably recall that he made a'forecast that, in his judgment, owing to the diminished agricultural labor employed during the present summer, that there was a strong likelihood of the number ·of unemployed in the cities in the coming winter being greater than ever.

Do you share that opinion of Dr. Parker?

Mr. HYDE. I think he would be right for this reason: I don't know whether it is on account of the approaching fair—it worked the same way just before the St. Louis fair in 1904—but the working· people, the skilled people and unskilled men came in looking for work and thought there was going to'be plenty of work. That would make a large class that would form your unemployed army in the State.

Commissioner WEINSTOCK. From what you know of the agricultural conditions of the State this year, have there been as many men and women employed in agriculture as last year, and have they been able to earn as much money as last year?

Mr. HYDE. The crops of the State—that would be governed by the size of the crops. The crops of the State have been mainly good.

Commissioner WEINSTOCK. This year?

Mr. HYDE. The prune crop is not as heavy as last year. It will probably be a hundred million pounds as against a hundred and fifty to a houndred and seventy-five million pounds last year. This is a shorter crop. The crop in our country this season, according to the best estimates, is, I would say, 60,000,000 pounds of dried prunes. Last year it was over a hundred million pounds.

Commissioner WEINSTOCK. So that there has been 40 per cent less employment?

Mr. HYDE. Yes, sir. On the other hand the peaches in San Joaquin and Santa Clara districts is a greater crop than last year. The orange crop this coming winter will probably be as good as it was last winter, which was a real good crop. There seems to be no climatic disturbance to hit it in any way, and it shows up well now.

Commissioner WEINSTOCK. You think taking the State as a unit and taking all agricultural workers as a unit, they will have earned as much money and as many been employed as last year?

Mr. HYDE. I think there would be.

Commissioner WEINSTOCK. You think this probably has been a normal year?

Mr. HYDE. I think the wages have been better than they were last year.

Commissioner WEINSTOCK. Why?

Mr. HYDE. I don't know why, but I know the Japs, for instance, in our county to-day form a considerable portion of the labor, on the farms, I mean, not in the packing houses, for I don't know a single packing house in the county or cannery that hires Japs.

Commissioner WEINSTOCK. The Japs are used for outside work?

Mr. HYDE. Yes; used in the fields. They are making good pay, better than they had been getting, and they are getting the same pay, as far as my observation goes, that the white men get for the same work in the fields.

Commissioner WEINSTOCK. What effect, in your opinion, will the opening of the canal, and the present European war, after it has been ended, have on the conditions of the California agricultural worker—the future condition of the agricultural worker of the State? Do you think it is going to help it or hurt it?

Mr. HYDE. I think there will be more labor here. I think all those people in Europe that wish to escape such conditions as have been existing in Europe several years, to avoid conscription in the army and all that thing, as soon as they get money enough will come to the United States. There are many steamship companies that have been booking immigrants, even some months past, that will bring them right directly to this coast. It seems to me that we would have an overabundance of agricultural labor in the State.

Commissioner WEINSTOCK. You think that the surplus will be greater than the demand?

Mr. HYDE. I should think it would be. That is all conjecture, of course.

Commissioner WEINSTOCK. So that from that line of reasoning the outlook for the agricultural laborer in California is not as encouraging as it might be?

Mr. HYDE. He will have more competition.

Commissioner WEINSTOCK. That, of course, is likely to increase the ranks of the unemployed during the winter months, is it not?

Mr. HYDE. It would for a while, but from my observation of the European agricultural laborer, they are a people that quickly establish themselves on ranches of their own, or on leased places.

Commissioner WEINSTOCK. Become renters or owners?

Mr. HYDE. Yes, sir.

Commissioner WEINSTOCK. What opportunities are there in California, Mr. Hyde, from your knowledge and experience, for thrifty, industrious, sober white agricultural workers to establish themselves as renters or owners?

Mr. HYDE. I am glad you asked me that question, because I think there is every opportunity in the world for a man who is thrifty, determined to do what is required of the laborer, while he is laboring for wages, and also with a fixed determination to improve his own condition. There is every opportunity in the world for such a man to succeed.

Commissioner WEINSTOCK. What is the smallest amount of actual capital that that kind of worker, thrifty, industrious, sober worker must have before he can hope to become a renter in the fruit crop?

Mr. HYDE. It is not so much the capital in money; it is the capital that every man must have to succeed, in being able to show those about him, that are acquainted with him, that he is a reliable, thrifty man. I will relate one instance of a man that came to work for me in 1885. He was an Italian boy who could not speak a word of English. He came from one of the southern Provinces of Italy, and his possessions consisted of a couple of letters from his mother, and a cheap silver watch, and a few dollars in money wrapped up in a red handkerchief.

He made the motions to me that he wanted—it was in the wintertime—that he wanted to work in the vineyard. He was accustomed to that, he had lived on a small farm in Italy and probably knew more about that than anything else. He made a motion he wanted to hoe around the trees and vines. I put him to work. At that time the wages ran from $20 to $25 a month and board for agricultural laborers. The Chinese at that time were getting $1.15 to $1.25 a day and board themselves. I am only giving you this to show you the conditions. He went to work for me and worked five years, and at the end of the first year he spent $1.50 a week getting an education from a little boy that showed him how to read and write. He quickly learned, and to-day that man has two farms, and has a house costing $3,000. He always pays for what he gets so I know that it is paid for.

Commissioner WEINSTOCK. Are the opportunities to-day better or worse than they were at the time that this Italian came to work for you?

Mr. HYDE. I think they are better.

Commissioner WEINSTOCK. Could the same man do the same thing over to-day?

Mr. HYDE. He could with the same determination that that man had to succeed. He would not require any money to lease a ranch. He saved his money and he had several hundred dollars in money and married, in the meantime, a woman of Italian descent, born in this country, and got a small farm and worked hard and gradually on up until he has two farms of his own. I have seen the same thing done by the Norwegian and Swedish people. They are very thrifty, too, and soon get a good start. It is the same with the Danish people of our agricultural district.

Commissioner WEINSTOCK. How long have you been a fruit grower, Mr. Hyde?

Mr. HYDE. Since 1882. I went into that county with my blankets myself.

Commissioner WEINSTOCK. What were the prevailing agricultural wages at that time, for white workers?

Mr. HYDE. I was hired for $40 a month and board myself, at first.

Commissioner WEINSTOCK. About a dollar and a half a day, out of which you boarded yourself?

Mr. HYDE. I boarded myself.

Commissioner WEINSTOCK. That was the prevailing wage?

Mr. HYDE. It was not, it was better; but I was sick; I wasn't able to do a man's work, and I started to work keeping time and getting supplies for a big ranch.

Commissioner WEINSTOCK. What did the farm worker receive at that time?

Mr. HYDE. Dollar and a half a day and board himself.

Commissioner WEINSTOCK. Dollar and a half a day and board himself?

Mr. HYDE. Yes, sir; the agricultural white worker.

Commissioner WEINSTOCK. Did he get a dollar a day and board?

Mr. HYDE. A dollar a day and board.

Commissioner WEINSTOCK. What is the agricultural wage now?

Mr. HYDE. Two dollars to two and a quarter. Two and a quarter during harvest time, two dollars other times, and board themselves.

Commissioner WEINSTOCK. Out of which they board themselves?

Mr. HYDE. Yes.

Commissioner WEINSTOCK. That would be an increase of about 33⅓ per cent?

Mr. HYDE. Yes.

Commissioner WEINSTOCK. From a dollar and a half to two dollars?

Mr. HYDE. Yes.

Commissioner WEINSTOCK. You heard the testimony yesterday given by Mr. Speed?

Mr. HYDE. Yes, sir; not all of it.

Commissioner WEINSTOCK. In which he stated the agricultural wages were lower to-day than they were 20 years ago, and cited some instances on the

Sacramento River where they were paying less than they had in the past. Has your observation led you to agree with Mr. Speed on that?

Mr. HYDE. No, sir; I do not agree with him.

Commissioner WEINSTOCK. You think he is mistaken?

Mr. HYDE. I think he is mistaken as far as Santa Clara County is concerned, where I have more particular knowledge.

Mr. THOMPSON. That is all.

Chairman WALSH. That is all; thank you. Call your next.

Mr. THOMPSON. Mr. Mills.

TESTIMONY OF MR. JAMES MILLS—Recalled.

Chairman WALSH. Was there something else you had to say in conclusion?

Mr. MILLS. There was a great deal I will say, if the commission cares to hear it.

Chairman WALSH. Well, now, the commission cares to hear it, but we don't want you to cover any subject that has already been covered.

Mr. MILLS. It is all—I am not at all anxious to stay over, Mr. President; I am perfectly willing to go. I am interested in this thing——

Chairman WALSH. With the suggestion I have made, just proceed, please.

Mr. MILLS. I am perfectly—I am afraid, Mr. President, I may have too much to say for your time.

Chairman WALSH. That might be possible.

Mr. MILLS. It would probably be better for you to put specific questions to me.

Chariman WALSH. Well, I had thought personally probably you had finished, Mr. Mills; that is, you had covered the subjects and gone into them in great detail. As you understand, we have a large number of witnesses. Now you have gone over conditions very well and, as I recall, you have compared them, have you not, with former times? If there is anything that you think that is significant to the inquiry, of course we would be glad to have you state it as concisely as possible. I do not think of any questions I care to ask you, any specific questions.

Mr. MILLS. Then I am through, Mr. Chairman.

Chairman WALSH. Are you? Well, thank you, very much, Mr. Mills. Call your next.

Mr. THOMPSON. Mr. Griffen.

TESTIMONY OF MR. WYLIE GIFFEN.

Mr. THOMPSON. Your name?

Mr. GIFFEN. Wylie Giffen.

Mr. THOMPSON. Will you also give us your address and your business, Mr. Giffen?

Mr. GIFFEN. Fresno. I am engaged in the vineyard and orchard business.

Mr. THOMPSON. How long have you been engaged in that business?

Mr. GIFFEN. For myself about 12 years. I have been working in vineyards and orchards for about 26 years.

Mr. THOMPSON. You were here yesterday?

Mr. GIFFEN. Yes, sir.

Mr. THOMPSON. You heard the testimony that was given in reference to the conditions in agricultural lines?

Mr. GIFFEN. Yes, sir.

Mr. THOMPSON. What have you to add with reference to what has already been testified to? I just ask you that one general question, and you may state what you have to tell.

Mr. GIFFEN. Well, I think the ground was fairly well covered, and in the main it was in accordance with my own experience.

I think the solution of the seasonal labor problem in this State is the diversity of farming. What has made it in this State is because of the fact that in California we like to do the biggest things in the world. We like to have the biggest vineyards in the world. We like to have the biggest orchards in the world. We like to have the biggest wheat ranches in the world. And if we can't have the biggest, we like to have the next biggest. And that spirit has gone through all the people.

So, in planting a quarter section of land, instead of planting it to five or six crops, we plant it to one crop. And the result has been that we need a very large amount of labor for a short time in the year and only a few men the rest of the year, whereas if we would take the quarter section of land and, as we can do in most parts of California, raise six or eight different crops on it, we could keep—well, in my own case, instead of having 200 men, as I have now, I could have 40 men the year around and provide places for them to live with their families. I would get a very much higher grade of men, very much better efficiency. I could raise fruit cheaper than I can to-day, with a good deal more satisfaction to myself and a good deal more usefulness to the State, I think.

Mr. THOMPSON. Is there anything being done to spread this idea among the growers of the State?

Mr. GIFFEN. Not because of the labor problem or anything of that kind, but the very necessity of the thing will force us eventually to do that. As the competition becomes keener we will be forced to diversify. And, incidentally, we will make more money than we are making now. We may not make as much in some years, but in the average of the years we will make more money. While that process is going on there necessarily will be some suffering, I think, among the men who are performing the labor of the State.

Mr. THOMPSON. Well, how would you take care of it in the interim?

Mr. GIFFEN. I think the suggestion of a State labor bureau is a help, but not a very great help. It would be some help in connecting the man up with the job, but it would not be a solution of the problem by any means. I don't know; I don't think there is any solution—any real solution. There might be some help, but there is no real solution until we are raising a greater diversity of crops in each community.

Mr. THOMPSON. Anything further you would like to say, Mr. Giffen?

Mr. GIFFEN. No; I think I have nothing further to say in this.

Mr. THOMPSON. That is all, Mr. Chairman.

Chairman WALSH. Thank you very much, Mr. Giffen.

Mr. GIFFIN. I might say this: I think that the question of the advance in wages that Mr. Weinstock has raised—26 years ago I began work at $30 a month and furnished my own bed, and never worked for any less than that. But there was a few years after that, during the hard times, that wages were some less. And they are a little higher now, perhaps $5 a month higher. I don't think, though, that when you consider the purchasing power of a dollar— I don't have any figures—I don't know how much higher the things that the laboring man has to buy are than they were. I don't think the increase in wages has been near equal to the increase in the price of the things that he has to buy. In other words, the laboring man is not as well off, I think, as he was 25 years ago in this State.

Commissioner GARRETSON. If he had to buy the same amount of the same commodities with the money that he now has, he would have a less balance left with the money that he now earns, in your opinion, than he would have had from the former $30?

Mr. GIFFEN. I think a great deal less. I think that Mr. Speed is right in one thing. I would not agree with him at all in his ultimate conclusions. But personally I have come to the belief that it would be a good thing if farm labor could be organized. In fact, I think it is the only way that they will ever get what they are entitled to, and that the solution should come through organizations of their own rather than through legislation.

I have been forced to that belief against my own prejudices, because of the fact that the laborers, as I see them, that are organized, are the only people that have been able to raise their wages as the price of living has gone up. And the rest are suffering. It seems to me the only solution. And as an employer of labor, I would welcome the unionization of the common laborer, if it can be done. I don't know that it can be done.

Chairman WALSH. Prof. Commons.

Commissioner COMMONS. You spoke about the increased cost of living. If a man saves money now, will it require more for him to get a piece of property, or to get a lease, or to get into independent farming or growing?

Mr. GIFFEN. Yes.

Commissioner COMMONS. Than it did 20 or 30 years ago?

Mr. GIFFEN. Yes; it would require a good deal more money. Land has advanced in the last 10 or 15 years over most of California a great deal, and it would take a good deal more money.

Commissioner COMMONS. Well, you started in without anything yourself. How much more would you have to have now to start in with, to reach the position that you have now reached, than you did when you started in 20 or 30 years ago?

Mr. GIFFEN. I don't know. I would have to have something more; but it will always remain a fact that some few men in every community, under any conditions, and with any price of land, will get ahead. But the fallacy of that is—the old saying that there is always room at the top that was quoted here yesterday, I don't think is correct, as far as it affects the labor problem of this State or any other State; because, while there is one round at the top, there is only a very, very few men can get to the top. And, in the very nature of things most of the unemployed labor must remain at the bottom to do the world's drudgery, and you can't get away from that fact, it seems to me.

Commissioner COMMONS If they all got to the top wouldn't the condition be just the same as it is now at the top as it is at the bottom?

Mr. GIFFEN. Just exactly the same, because the drudgery must be done. And it is not the man that can get to the top—it is not that you can find in every community those who are able to forge their own way up—it is not those that you are interested in, or that this commission is interested in. It is the people that must always be the carriers of water and the hewers of wood who do the world's work.

Commissioner COMMONS. Well, according to your statement, he probably could not save as much now as he could then on account of the cost of living going up faster than wages. It would seem to me he would be required to save a great deal more in order to become an independent farmer than he would at that time, is that it?

Mr. GIFFEN. I think the conditions are continually making it more difficult for men to get something of their own in this State.

Commissioner COMMONS. Well, you think, therefore, that the increasing number of wage earners will go on, that the larger proportion of the population will be wage earners in the agricultural pursuits?

Mr. GIFFEN. I don't know whether I quite get that point. Just ask me that again.

Commissioner COMMONS. Well, that is too much of a prophesy, I suppose. It it not necessary to follow that out.

Chairman WALSH. Any other questions?

Commissioner WEINSTOCK. Yes. You made the statement a few moments ago, Mr. Giffen, that you welcomed the unionization of the agricultural worker. From the standpoint of the employer, what advantage would there be to you if agricultural labor was organized?

Mr. GIFFEN. Only this advantage, as I see it. I believe that labor will be better off. And in the end, what makes labor better off must redound to the betterment of all of us, I think.

Commissioner WEINSTOCK. You think, then, I take it, that it is the interest of the worker, from your point of view, that he shall organize?

Mr. GIFFEN. I think it is.

Commissioner WEINSTOCK. You think that by organizing he would better his conditions?

Mr. GIFFEN. I think that has been truly proven in the other industries. We do not do things, most of us—Mr. Mills, who was on the stand yesterday, has done some things that he didn't have to do. Most of us men that are employing labor, no difference what our hearts may dictate in these things, we are in competition with other people, and we don't do those things until we have to do it. Individually, the common laborer is not in position to force us to do it.

Commissioner WEINSTOCK. Of course the unionization of agricultural labor would lead to what is known as collective bargaining in place of the method that at present prevails, or individual bargaining. As an employer, if agricultural labor was organized, you would have to be prepared to deal with them collectively in place of dealing with them individually. Now, every man that comes to you, you make an individual bargain with him. Under union conditions, of course, you would bargain with one or two men for a large group of men, for all your men perhaps. Would that be a preferred condition from your point of view?

Mr. GIFFEN. I think there would be some disadvantages in it; but I am inclined to think the advantages would more than offset the disadvantages.

Commissioner WEINSTOCK. Tell me specifically what you would regard as the advantages and disadvantages from the employer's standpoint.

38819°—S. Doc. 415. 64-1—vol 5——56

Mr. GIFFEN. The disadvantages, as I see them, are that it probably lowers the efficiency of some particular men. It seems to me that union labor works that way anyhow. I haven't been drawn very closely in touch with it, but it seems to me that it is a leveler of men more than the system that prevails to-day; that there is not the opportunity for the individual man to get ahead. . , ,

Commissioner WEINSTOCK. You mean it tends to the dead level, to make the dead level?

Mr. GIFFEN. It brings the lowest up, and the highest down, to a dead level, I think.

Commissioner WEINSTOCK. Yes; that is the disadvantage.

Mr. GIFFEN. I think so.

Commissioner WEINSTOCK. And that is a disadvantage to the worker rather than to the employer, is it not?

Mr. GIFFEN. Yes, sir.

Commissioner WEINSTOCK. Now what is the advantage?

Mr. GIFFEN. In a degree it would be some disadvantage to the employer, too.

Commissioner WEINSTOCK. What advantage would there be in it to the employer?

Mr. GIFFEN. In a large amount of our work collective bargaining would be a very great advantage, and is carried out now to a certain extent, not, I think, because there is any union that amounts to anything. We employe large number of Japanese and Chinese and Hindus, and that is all collective bargaining in our picking. I have perhaps a hundred pickers, and I only see one man in that transaction; and it is very much easier for me than it would be to see a hundred men.

Commissioner WEINSTOCK. So that in your Asiatic labor you are under collective bargaining now?

Mr. GIFFEN. Yes, sir.

Commissioner WEINSTOCK. You find it advantageous?

Mr. GIFFEN. I think so; yes.

Commissioner WEINSTOCK. That is all.

Chairman WALSH. That is all. Thank you.

Mr. THOMPSON. Mr. Dale.

TESTIMONY OF MR. J. B. DALE.

Mr. THOMPSON. You have heard the testimony of the last day and to-day on the seasonal labor?

Mr. DALE. Yes, sir.

Mr. THOMPSON. In agriculture?

Mr. DALE. Yes, sir.

Mr. THOMPSON. What have you to add to what has already been testified to?

Mr. DALE. Well, as an organizer of labor, I want to say to you and to the commission that I believe, I am positive, that the agriculture labor farm hand, the nomad, can be organized through and by the American Federation of Labor. There are organizations now known as the United Laborers of America, in San Francisco, in Oakland, in Richmond, in Fresno, in Bakersfield, in Sacramento, in San Jose, and one established last evening in San Rafael, affiliated with the central labor councils of those cities, and chartered directly by the American Federation of Labor. The cards they give those men—say a man is in Fresno and he migrates to Sacramento or San Rafael—the card that is given him in Fresno admits him to work in San Rafael without any additional pay.

Now, as to the farm hand, I will have to ask you to excuse a personal allusion. A good many years ago I carried my blankets and I worked in California. And I belonged to the Knights of Labor in California. In Solano County, in the little town of Dixon, some 70 miles from here, I had to crawl up, sneak up the back stairs of the K. P. hall to attend the sessions of the Knights of Labor—before I was grown—I was a young man.

Now, through that section of the Knights of Labor in Dixon the conditions of the farm hands were bettered to this extent: A man that fed his men on poor food, had a poor team, poor harness, poor plow—he had an awfully hard time to secure help. A good many men in the community knew nothing about it, but the farm hands that made up that section of the Knights of Labor knew all about it. The gentlemen that just left the stand said that he believed that he was willing to cooperate in the organization of the farm hands.

Now, gentlemen of this commission, that is the only thing that is necessary—get that in your minds now—there is not another thing needed to organize that fellow and better his condition but to intelligently—but intelligent, consistent cooperation of the farmer himself. That will solve the problem, and those are the only two elements; those are the only two factions in society that can solve it.

Chairman WALSH. One minute, Mr. Dale. Would you say the view of this gentleman was typical of the fruit growers of California?

Mr. DALE. No; I do not believe that it is. I believe that he is as exception. I am very glad to listen to the exception. Now, there is no one thing that will solve the problem of labor but the men of labor. They are the only ones that can solve the labor question. The labor question is a practical proposition. A man can stand on the sidewalk, and he can sympathize with the fellow that is carrying the hod up the ladder. Sympathize! The only way that he can un- derstand the condition of the hod carrier is to get a hod of brick on his shoulder, start up the ladder; his knees will begin to knock together, his eyes begin to stick out, the skin will begin to come off the shoulder, and then he realizes what it is to carry a hod of brick up the ladder. Now, I simply use that to convey the idea to this commission that it is practically impossible for men who have never labored, for men that do not know what it is for the sweat to run down in their eyes——

Chairman WALSH. Excuse me. May I interpolate some questions? You say that you are an organizer of the American Federation of Labor in this particu- lar field?

Mr. DALE. Yes, sir.

Chairman WALSH. Farm labor. When did you begin your work?

Mr. DALE. Four years ago—a little over.

Chairman WALSH. Had the American Federation of Labor attempted any means to organize this casual laborer in California prior to that time?

Mr. DALE. Well, they had to this extent and in this way: They organized what is known as Federal unions. That takes in—say if there is a Federal union organized in San Rafael, and there are not enough plumbers in San Rafael to secure a charter from the international plumbers' organization—they are eligible to the Federal union until such time as there are seven members of the plumbers to secure a charter from this international. Then, according to the law of the American Federation of Labor, they must withdraw from the Federal union and secure a charter from their international.

Chairman WALSH. How many agricultural laborers were in unions of that kind four years ago, when you began to organize them?

Mr. DALE. Well, I don't know that there was but very few.

Chairman WALSH. Well, could you approximate the number?

Mr. DALE. No; I could not.

Chairman WALSH. Well, now, then, have you had any assistance in your ef- forts to organize this labor during the last four years?

Mr. DALE. I have had the cooperation of organized labor; yes, sir.

Chairman WALSH. But have you had any specific organizers who called upon men, setting forth the alleged advantages of organization and gave them the form?

Mr. DALE. Well, no; none outside of myself that——

Chairman WALSH. Please state now as briefly as you can how you go to do that work; what you do, we will say, day by day toward organizing these men?

Mr. DALE. The first work of an organizer when he gets into a city or town——

Chairman WALSH. I want to get what your work is in this particular field, not generally.

Mr. DALE. Is to secure applicants, of course.

Chairman WALSH. Where did you go, for instance, when you started four years ago to secure these applicants? What is your field of work?

Mr. DALE. My first work was in the city of Oakland.

Chairman WALSH. Is the city of Oakland a place where large numbers of this class of labor congregate?

Mr. DALE. Migratory men, yes, sir; quite a lot of them.

Chairman WALSH. Briefly now typify that as you can.

Mr. DALE. It took us a solid month, to begin with, to get seven men and $10 to secure a charter from the American Federation of Labor. This was in the month of June, I believe—yes, in the month of June; 1910.

On the following Labor Day, the first Monday in September—I am told, I do not know of this as I was not in Oakland—but there were between two and three hundred men of this organization in line marching with other organized labor.

Chairman WALSH. That was in Oakland?

Mr. DALE. That was in the city of Oakland.

Chairman WALSH. Was the organization confined to Oakland? Was the meeting place of that organization Oakland?

Mr. DALE. Yes, sir.

Chairman WALSH. Now, how many are in that now?

Mr. DALE. I think in the neighborhood of six or seven hundred men.

Chairman WALSH. In the neighborhood of six or seven hundred men?

Mr. DALE. Yes, sir; probably more than that, probably less.

Chairman WALSH. Now, where else has there been an organization of that kind perfected?

Mr. DALE. One in Fresno, one in Stockton, one in Bakersfield——

Chairman WALSH. How many in Fresno?

Mr. DALE. I left Fresno a week ago Friday—Friday a week ago—and I think they have about 150 men in their organization.

Chairman WALSH. How many have you organized in the four years of the efforts you have made?

Mr. DALE. In the neighborhood of 5,000 men.

Chairman WALSH. In the neighborhood of 5,000 men?

Mr. DALE. Yes, sir.

Chairman WALSH. Are you engaged in organizing——

Mr. DALE. Now, just a moment. I do not want to claim credit for organizing all those 5,000.

Chairman WALSH. Since you started organizing?

Mr. DALE. There is in the city of San Francisco now in the neighborhood of 2,000 men in the united laborers alone. Those men were in existence when I began the work, but they were chartered—they had a local charter, I believe—they are now chartered from the American Federation of Labor since this organization.

Chairman WALSH. That includes the 5,000?

Mr. DALE. Yes, sir.

Chairman WALSH. What means of collective bargaining is there for these 5,000 men?

Mr. DALE. The Fresno local have a business agent the same as the Japanese have—just one point I want to dwell on, if you will permit me here, and it is that the employer—why is it that the employer of labor will object to dealing with the business agent from the white, the Caucasian, race and yet are ready and willing to deal with the fellow from the others? Can you answer?

Chairman WALSH. I am trying to confine it to your organization.

Mr. DALE. All right.

Chairman WALSH. Now, what method of collective bargaining have you for these 5,000 that are now in the organization?

Mr. DALE. Simply as I tell you, Mr. Chairman, through their representative—their business agent—or the business agent of the building trades council, or the business agent of the Central Labor Council.

Chairman WALSH. Well, the fruit laborer, the laborer on the fruit farm—how many collective bargainings have you with employers?

Mr. DALE. Now, I want to say this, that there is not many agricultural—that is, men that work on the ranches, that belong to these organizations so far.

Chairman WALSH. How many do you think that belong to that organization, of the 5,000, are there that work on fruit farms?

Mr. DALE. Well, they work on fruit farms, quite a number of them; but they don't deal with their business agents—they don't deal through their organization, they work as individuals on the fruit farm.

Chairman WALSH. They have no advantage of collective bargaining?

Mr. DALE. No; not as an organization, it has not reached that point.

Chairman WALSH. You really say that so far as the fruit laborer himself is concerned, that there is no organization that deals directly, through collective bargaining, with employers in the State of California?

Mr. DALE. That is it.

Chairman WALSH. Do you think they need organization?

Mr. DALE. I certainly think they do; yes, sir.

Chairman WALSH. Please state any plans that the American Federation of Labor has for organizing these men as such—as laborers upon fruit farms?

Mr. DALE. It is simply the plan, Mr. Chairman, that I have outlined, charter them by the American Federation of Labor—give them a charter.

Chairman WALSH. But if you have not gotten collective bargaining in four years, would you, or would you not, say that your efforts to organize were successful?

Mr. DALE. The efforts for organizing those men have been directed to the cities where they deal with the building contractors, with the sewer contractors——

Chairman WALSH (interposing). Yes; but we are taking up the subject of agricultural labor. You have heard all the testimony, that there are great numbers of men that do that alone. That they began 20 years ago; some say conditions were better 20 years ago than they are now, that there were outlets to other fields, but that now these men are placed under disadvantages in various ways; that is, that the work is seasonal; that while the land might give itself to more intensive cultivation, diversified crops, that the employers are not giving it that attention, and that these men go from place to place; on the one hand they are said to be rendered migratory on account of their conditions; on the other hand the employers say that on account of their habits of life, and so forth, they are nomads. But the fact remains that there are great numbers of those men. You heard Mr. Speed here say that there is a persistent need—a demand for organization among those men. Then, you have heard this employer say that they could not establish approximate justice for themselves unless they were organized. Now, how would you go. to organize them to-morrow?

Mr. DALE. If the farmers in Fresno County will cooperate with me——

Chairman WALSH (interposing). Let us assume that for the moment Mr. Speed is correct, and that they are economically at sword's points, that they are adversaries; let us assume that your estimate of the condition is true; that this last gentleman was not typical; that the employing frint growers desired them to be disorganized and compelled to bargain individually, What do you say, assuming that we can not get cooperation now with the employers; what would you do?

Mr. DALE. I still stick to the ship, Organization—organize.

Chairman WALSH. Suppose, now, at the end of eight years, four years more, you still have not one organized as such, what would you do then?

Mr. DALE. Continue to organize; never quit. There is no other remedy. I want to leave this thought with you: There is no remedy between paradise and perdition for the men under heaven that do the world's work to get opproximate justice, except through the medium of organization—collective bargaining.

Chairman WALSH. You have heard testimony here to the effect that these workers should be organized into labor organizations outside of the American Federation of Labor. What has been your experience in regard to the effort that has been made to do that? As briefly as you can, state the possible outcome of it.

Mr. DALE. Well, I believe that that so far has proved to be a failure. I do not think it can ever be successful.

Chairman WALSH. Then, what would your opinion be; would it be that it is impossible to organize this class of labor through the American Federation of Labor? At least you can not get an organization in four years. Do you think it is impossible to organize it the way these men suggest? Such effort at organizing having been futile, is it your opinion that it is bound to be? What would you say?

Mr. DALE. I should say, as I told you, Mr. Chairman, I would continue to persuade those men to organize, to point out the benefits that have accrued to the men and women that have organized; tell them that it costs him just as much to buy a beefsteak or to get bacon and eggs for his breakfast as it does the organized man that get $5 a day—just as much for the unorganized man that works for $2. As soon as you can get that idea in his cranium, then you have got him. There is an organized opposition to the organizing.

Chairman WALSH. From whom?

Mr. DALE. From the employer and from certain elements of labor.

Chairman WALSH. Have you found any organized opposition generally to organizing the employees in other crafts?

Mr. DALE. Well, I have found opposition to the organizing of the migratory man, from the organized point; yes, sir.

Chairman WALSH. Is he or is he not more protected or less protected on account of the seasonal nature of his occupation than these men in these other crafts in which you have been more successful?

Mr. DALE. That is probably true in a large measure.

Chairman WALSH. Have you thought of any means by which you could improve, from your standpoint, on the efforts of organization?

Mr. DALE. I do not quite get you.

Chairman WALSH. Have you ever endeavored to organize these men right in the places where they were working?

Mr. DALE. On the ranches?

Chairman WALSH. Right on the ranches.

Mr. DALE. I have not.

Chairman WALSH. What would you think as to that method of organizing them?

Mr. DALE. I do not believe that would be successful.

Chairman WALSH. How do you present to these men these arguments that you say, Mr. Dale, in your opinion are the only things that can be presented to them?

Mr. DALE. Now, for illustration, if I may illustrate. A man joins the Odd Fellows, and the Odd Fellows haven't got any lodge in the country. It is usually in town. Those men, they are in the town or village, the agricultural worker that works, say, within a radius of 5 or 10 miles of the city of Fresno or the town of Dixon or the city of Sacramento—he lives in Sacramento or Fresno or Dixon. That is his home. Now, then, if I can persuade that fellow to join an organization organized in one of those towns and officered by citizens of the town that live in the town that work at common day labor for their livelihood, they have got a stable set of officers, men that live in that community, and an organization that a man can join. When a man wants to leave Dixon or leave Fresno or Sacramento, he takes his card and goes his way to another lodge, and he deposits the card, and he goes out in the country and finds work, and when he gets ready he comes back and gets his card just the same as the Odd Fellows do. That is my idea of organizing these men.

Chairman WALSH. Approximately, how many of these incidental laborers are there that are migratory? How many laborers first, I will ask you, are there in the fruit-growing industry, vegetable growing and canning?

Mr. DALE. I could not say that; it would simply be a surmise.

Chairman WALSH. Could you approximate it?

Mr. DALE. No, sir.

Chairman WALSH. Has there been any study made of it by your organization?

Mr. DALE. Yes, sir.

Chairman WALSH. You know whether there is a thousand or a hundred thousand?

Mr. DALE. You mean in the State of California?

Chairman WALSH. Yes, sir.

Mr. DALE. I presume probably a hundred thousand.

Chairman WALSH. How many of these hundred thousand that work on these farms would you say have post-office addresses or have voting places or homes?

Mr. DALE. Well, I would say a good many of them have no voting place.

Chairman WALSH. As a class they don't vote?

Mr. DALE. No, sir.

Chairman WALSH. And as a class they have no home or family?

Mr. DALE. That is true.

Chairman WALSH. How many of the hundred thousand are so situated?

Mr. DALE. Well, probably one-third of them.

Chairman WALSH. Do you believe an effective organization of those men can be made in the way you have indicated?

Mr. DALE. I think so.

Chairman WALSH. Well, has there anything occurred in the history of California to demonstrate that that might be so?

Mr. DALE. I related to you at the beginning of my statement that I belonged as a ranch hand to a section of the Knights of Labor. Of course, no one knew anything about it. The preacher in the little town denounced the Knights of Labor to this extent: That if there were more days of labor than Knights of Labor, the town would be better off. He was denouncing at the time the Knights of Labor. He didn't know who belonged to it.

Chairman WALSH. Have you any other suggestion to make along this line, that you have not already made here, and not already testified to; along the line of organizing this class of laborers?

Mr. DALE. Well, nothing, only keep at the work, that is all.

Chairman WALSH. Keep at the work?

Mr. DALE. Stay with it.

Chairman WALSH. Have you stated it as well as you can and as well as you care to state, all the efforts you have made or that have been made by your organization up to date?

Mr. DALE. I think the ground has been pretty fully covered.

Chairman WALSH. Anything anyone wants to ask him?

Commissioner WEINSTOCK. Yes; I want to ask him some questions.

Chairman WALSH. All right.

Commissioner WEINSTOCK. Has it not been the history of labor organizations that where the grievance—where there are grievances there is a stronger possibility of organization than where there are no grievances? In other words, if you go into a community where the workers are all contented and getting what they believe to be satisfactory wages with satisfactory working hours and satisfactory conditions, it is much more difficult to organize them than when you go into a community and find the workers discontented and believe they are underpaid and overworked; is that not so?

Mr. DALE. That is a fact.

Commissioner WEINSTOCK. Therefore the best evidence of organization; that is, the best evidence that there are grievances is where you find men ready and willing to organize?

Mr. DALE. Well, that holds true in a measure, Mr. Weinstock. Now, in some places in China, you know the conditions are indescribable almost. They never think of organizing; that is, they never think of making any particular protest. It is a good deal in the mind; it is a good deal in the intelligence of the individual.

Commissioner WEINSTOCK. Yet we know that the workers in China are the best organized workers in the world. I know, because I have been there and made an investigation. There are no strike breakers in China; there are no scabs, as they are called in this country, in China. Every member of the craft belongs to the guild, and it is an absolute union.

Mr. DALE. Yes, sir; they belong to the guild.

Commissioner WEINSTOCK. If you have been unable—I take it you are a good deal above the average as an organizer?

Mr. DALE. Thank you, sir.

Commissioner WEINSTOCK. Because you have the intelligence and the ability, and you understand the conditions. If with all your ability and with the American Federation of Labor behind you, you have been unable to organize the agricultural workers of California, even in a limited degree, that would indicate that if these conditions that you and I regard as grievances, are grievances, they seemingly are not so regarded by the workers themselves.

Mr. DALE. Well, the average man on the ranch does not stay long enough, you know. He comes and goes. He is so disgusted with himself and so disgusted with his life; he is so hedged in with it, he does not stay long enough only to get a few dollars, and he goes. That is the trouble, Mr. Weinstock; if this fellow was reached right—if the men who hire these men would only cooperate with organized labor, those fellows could be organized. We would have a million of those men organized within the next five years if the farmers would only help. The men that are not—the men that are crying they can't get help could get it, and it would be the medium of bringing them reliable help.

Commissioner WEINSTOCK. If that is the situation, then your missionary work should be done among the farmers rather than among the farm workers?

Mr. DALE. The farmers have got a union, and I believe they have a fraternal delegate to the American Federation, do they not, Brother Lennon?

Commissioner LENNON. Yes, sir.

Commissioner GARRETSON. So does the manufacturers' union.

Mr. DALE. But they don't send fraternal delegates.

Commissioner GARRETSON. Or they are not helping organize their employees?

Mr. DALE. No, sir; they are not.

Chairman WALSH. Anything else? Let us hurry through. Prof. Commons has some questions.

Commissioner COMMONS. What is your idea of this proposition others have been speaking about, about the organization of State employment offices?

Mr. DALE. I am not in accord with it at all. I believe the work should be done through the organization. I believe the man seeking help should deal with the white man, the same as he deals with the Jap, the Chinaman, or the Hindu—go to the representative of those men. I am thoroughly in accord with the statement made yesterday by Mr. Speed, that the best and only lasting legislation that the workingman or working woman will ever get is through their organizations, because the courts are not with us; they're against us.

Commissioner COMMONS. Seeing they are migratory and traveling about, wouldn't you have to have some stationary organization to send them to the various places?

Mr. DALE. Yes, sir.

Commissioner COMMONS. How would you operate that?

Mr. DALE. The labor employers of Fresno when they needed help, let them ring up the business agent, a Mr. Bush, of Fresno, at the present time. His telephone number is 1198. Let the employer ring him up and say, "Mr. Bush, I want so many white men. Can you furnish them?" Let him get in communication with that fellow instead of getting in touch with the Chinaman.

Commissioner COMMONS. Suppose you wanted the employers to deal with you in collective bargaining—the farmers, I mean. Why shouldn't you have the association of farmers join with you and establish a joint employment office? Why should you ask them simply to call on your business agent; why should you not have somebody acceptable to them also to call on?

Mr. DALE. The farmers have a farm union, I believe, now in the county of Fresno. I believe they meet occasionally, and we would be only too glad to cooperate with them. We will meet them just the same as we agreed to meet the business men of Stockton around the table.

Commissioner COMMONS. Would you establish with them a joint employment office?

Mr. DALE. That might be feasible; yes, sir. Probably would be.

Commissioner COMMONS. In which they would have just as much voice in controlling it as you would?

Mr. DALE. I don't know whether that would be practical or not. Of course, that matter is worthy of consideration; I will say that.

Commissioner COMMONS. If the State should pay the expenses of such office and let the union and the farmers——

Mr. DALE. You could not keep it out of politics.

Commissioner COMMONS. How?

Mr. DALE. You could not keep it out of politics, and the average trade-union, in my opinion, should shun the political arena as they would the bubonic plague.

Commissioner COMMONS. Suppose the farmers' union and this union of employees should select the staff that operated it. Wouldn't that keep it out of politics?

Mr. DALE. That would; yes, sir; if that could be done.

Commissioner COMMONS. And the State might subsidize it or pay the expenses.

Mr. DALE. Why put it under the ban of the State at all? Why not let organized labor control it?

Commissioner COMMONS. Let the two together pay the expenses?

Mr. DALE. Yes, sir.

Commissioner COMMONS. Let the employer pay the expenses.

Mr. DALE. Yes, sir; let it be their own institution individually, and let them be responsible to themselves and their members for the conduct and success or failure of the institution.

Commissioner COMMONS. That is all.

Commissioner LENNON. Mr. Dale, is the evidence of the sympathy of the workers with organization made manifest by membership in organizations?

Mr. DALE. I think so.

Commissioner LENNON. You do?

Mr. DALE. In a large measure; yes, sir—not wholly.

Commissioner LENNON. Are the employers of this State thoroughly organized?

Mr. DALE. As far as I know they are, Mr. Lennon. You mean the farmers and business men—the men who employ labor?

Commissioner LENNON. Yes, sir; that is what I mean.

Mr. DALE. I think they are. I think the men that buy labor are pretty thoroughly organized, and the fellows that sell it are not so thoroughly organized.

Commissioner LENNON. Do you undertake to organize the farm labor without going to where they are employed?

Mr. DALE. I aim to meet them in town, where they are on Sunday.

Commissioner LENNON. That is all.

Chairman WALSH. Just one other question: In talking about the organization of orientals it was stated here that the way the Chinese were operated there was one man who made the contract, and he received from the employer 50 cents to $1 a head, depending upon the demand for laborers, the scarcity or oversupply at the time, and that he made a profit by selling them provender. Did you or did you not mean you would be in favor of establishing that sort of system?

Mr. DALE. Certainly not; no, sir.

Chairman WALSH. That is all; thank you. Call your next.

Mr. THOMPSON. Dr. Parker.

Chairman WALSH. Let us call another witness besides Dr. Parker, because he covered part of it yesterday.

Mr. THOMPSON. Mr. Bell.

TESTIMONY OF MR. GEORGE L. BELL.

Mr. THOMPSON. Give us your name.

Mr. BELL. George L. Bell.

Mr. THOMPSON. Your business address?

Mr. BELL. 215 Underwood Building.

Mr. THOMPSON. And your profession?

Mr. BELL. Attorney.

Mr. THOMPSON. Are you connected with the Commission of Immigration and Housing of California?

Mr. BELL. Yes, sir; I am attorney for the commission.

Mr. THOMPSON. How long have you been in that position?

Mr. BELL. About seven months now.

Mr. THOMPSON. In that position did you represent the commission at the Wheatland trials—the so-called Wheatland trials?

Mr. BELL. Yes, sir.

Mr. THOMPSON. While you were there representing the commission did you have a chance to study the treatment of labor suspects by the authorities and others?

Mr. BELL. Yes, sir; I attempted to follow that during the course of the trial by interviewing all of the men.

Mr. THOMPSON. Will you tell us briefly the treatment as you viewed it?

Mr. BELL. In regard to the treatment of the migratory laborer and suspects held in that case, I think the best way to bring out my view is by citing two cases, if I may refer to some documents to refresh my memory on that. They are affidavits made to the commission at the time.

The case of a man by the name of Brady, for instance, who was a migratory worker, and came to Sacramento, Cal., about the 1st of September, which was the month after the riot at Wheatland, and, was arrested by a policeman, charged with having assaulted a Hindu. He was put in jail, booked on what is known as the secret blotter. The next day he was interviewed by some men, but the case of assaulting the Hindu was not referred to, and he was immediately puestioned and cross-examined in regard to whether or not he had been in the riot at Wheatland August 3. He stated at the time he had not been, but that he was in jail on August 3 in a town in Wyoming, and offered to prove that fact,·and suggested that the authorities wire to the authorities in Wyoming and ascertain the facts. They did not do so, and he was subsequently taken up to Marysville, where he was held in jail, and then transferred from one jail to another among the different counties, and never was examined before a court. Finally, he succeeded in getting a letter out to the sheriff in this town in Wyoming. The sheriff wrote back proof of the fact that he had been in jail in Wyoming on August 3 and had escaped. The authorities then said that they could not identify him as that same man. This man then offered to have his picture taken, and offered to give them two or three other ways in which they could identify him back in Wyoming. The authorities did nothing for several weeks after that, until finally he was dismissed after having been held 75 days.

Now, the affidavit of the man states that at no time during that period was he ever taken before a court or before any judge, and never had an examination.

Chairman WALSH. What is the provision of the California constitution relative to speedy and public trials?

Mr. BELL. He was held as a suspect in that case. The provision is ■at a man must, as soon as arrested, be taken before the police magistrate at the earliest possible moment thereafter.

Chairman WALSH. Is there any statute that would authorize holding a man 75 days without lodging a charge against him?

Mr. BELL. No statute that I know of.

Chairman WALSH. Upon what authority is it done?

Mr. BELL. Simply done because the man had no way of getting out of the situation.

Chairman WALSH. The man had no lawyer?

Mr. BELL. The man had no lawyer. He said he knew no lawyer. He had no acquaintances in California. He was finally dismissed on the motion of the district attorney, evidently, without being taken before the court.

The instance of another man at the same trial, a man by the name of Nelson, who was arrested in September, and finally released in January. His affidavit states that during that period he was never taken before any magistrate.

Those two instances are the only express instances of that sort of violation that I found at that trial.

Chairman WALSH. Is it or is it not a typical condition in industrial disputes?

Mr. BELL. I was going to say, I continued and talked with several other people who were present at the trial who were migratory laborers—wanderers. Many of them were members of the organization known as the I. W. W., and they related similar experiences in different States throughout the Union. They stated, and seemed to have facts to back up their statements, that it is a general custom whenever a crime is committed to go out and bag men.' To throw out the dragnet. And they claim that very often they are dragged in, in this net, and held as suspects, and the officials try to force them to appear as witnesses, by a series of examinations in which they say, "as a matter of fact, were you not present at so and so," and keep that up for hours, trying to force them finally to say they had been at a certain place and had seen a man commit the crime or themselves had been involved in it.

The generalizations I make from those instances are twofold. One in regard to vagrancy in general. It seems a general custom to throw out the dragnet among the vagrants—migratory laborers. If a man is wandering around without visible means of employment, he is arrested as a suspect, and in this condition, being without friends and without means and usually without organization, he has no means of getting counsel. In the first place, I think it shows the lack in our present judicial system of a public defender. Very few places have a public defender. As I understand the growth of the law, the district attorney was supposed originally to be a public prosecutor and public defender as well, but district attorneys as a rule now are more prosecutors than defenders. If there was some one who could appear for these men as public defender, whether they had a private attorney or not, I think it would relieve the situation a great deal.

Mr. THOMPSON. In those two cases was any protest made by any organization, by your commission or organized labor, against holding these men?

Mr. BELL. No protest was made by our commission, and, as far as I know, no express protest made by any organization of labor in these two particular cases.

Mr. THOMPSON. Do you know whether any notice was given to any officer or voluntary body of men of the fact that two men were held under such circumstances?

Mr. BELL. Mr. Nelson states that the Swedish consul was notified, and finally they sent an attorney to represent him. but the attorney was not successful in getting a hearing until—well, not at all, in fact. Why I don't know.

Mr. THOMPSON. Did you take the matter up with the state's attorney, or other officer who prosecutes in that county?

Mr. BELL. I discussed the matter with the district attorney and judge and other officers in Yuma County. They explained the situation by simply stating it was the usual practice in such cases; that here was a hard case in which it was impossible to find the men who were connected with the crime; that they had to throw out the dragnet; that they thought they had some evidence against this man; that some one else had said he was in Wheatland and connected with the murder.

Mr. THOMPSON. Did they seek to justify their action on legal grounds at all?

Mr. BELL. None that I heard them state. They simply said it was the only way they could hold him.

Mr. THOMPSON. Did you ask them upon what legal ground they could hold him 75 days?

Mr. BELL. I did.

Mr. THOMPSON. What did they say?

Mr. BELL. They said if they took him before a court they did not have legal evidence sufficient to hold him, yet they suspected the man and thought they were carrying out justice in holding him, because they had enough knowledge in their private information to justify them in holding him. They thought they were performing their duties to the community in holding him.

Mr. THOMPSON. But put it on no legal grounds?

Mr. BELL. No, sir.

Mr. THOMPSON. Just simply because they wanted to do so?

Mr. BELL. No explanation was made to me of any statute or law that would back up their position.

Mr. THOMPSON. Did you or anybody else draw attention to the fact that that amounted to imprisonment without trial or recourse to law?

Mr. BELL. Yes, sir.

Mr. THOMPSON. What did they say to that?

Mr. BELL. The answer was that the man could get out a writ of habeas corpus.

Mr. THOMPSON. Did they say how he could get that out without having an attorney?

Mr. BELL. They admitted that he would have to have an attorney.

Mr. THOMPSON. Did they state they would supply an attorney?

Mr. BELL. The district attorney stated to me in the case of Mr. Brady that he told him if he wanted an attorney he could get one.

Mr. THOMPSON. Did they offer to furnish an attorney?

Mr. BELL. Not as far as I know.

Mr. THOMPSON. Did they offer to place him in communication with any organization or individual who might furnish an attorney?

Mr. BELL. No, sir; not as far as I know.

Mr. THOMPSON. As a lawyer of this State, what was the situation with regard to the possibility of getting such a writ?

Mr. BELL. Well, the man was really helpless.

Mr. THOMPSON. What would you suggest might be done, seeing that is, as was stated by the county attorney, a customary matter? What could be done to amend it as a law so that the citizen or individual might have the benefit of the law?

Mr. BELL. I think the law is satisfactory as written on the books, which says a man shall be taken before a magistrate as soon as possible after arrest. The only trouble is that this law is not respected. As the district attorney suggested, the district attorney no longer acts as district attorney and defender also. I think it is necessary to have the office of public defender, as they have in Los Angeles County.

Mr. THOMPSON. Then you think that a public defender's office is necessary, so that in cases of this kind the men can be defended, because the officers do not carry out what the law commands the officers to do?

Mr. BELL. Yes, sir; and so that the man can get representation. It is the only way that he can get legal representation from the officers.

Mr. THOMPSON. You may go on with your statement now about the conditions as you found them there.

Mr. BELL. Well, that is all in a general way, my generalizations from those two specific cases. It seems to me that one trouble—I would enlarge a little on the vagrancy problem generally. The men with whom I talked blame this condition of affairs upon the general practice of putting men in jail as vagrants. A man goes into a town without any visible means of support, and nine times out of ten is "vagged," as the expression goes; he is arrested and put in prison as a vagrant for a period of from 15 to 30 days. They get into the county jail.

Mr. THOMPSON. That is without trial in those cases?

Mr. BELL. No, no. That is with trial. I am speaking generally with regard to the vagrancy laws. They are put into jail for a period of from 15 to 30 days. The jail is an insanitary place. Many of the county jails are in insanitary buildings. They are given no employment but simply lay and sleep in a little dark cell and have no physical exercise to speak of. The food they complain of generally. They claim that they come out covered with vermin and that their self-respect is lost. They all state that after a man has been put in prison as a vagrant several times he then becomes a professional vagrant. That is, the punishment encourages them to be vagrants.

Mr. THOMPSON. What evidence is generally sufficient to put a man in prison for vagrancy?

Mr. BELL. Well, generally if a man has no employment, and if he has no money on his person when arrested, that usually is sufficient evidence.

Mr. THOMPSON. On that same ground, probably all the migratory labor in the State would be affected, wouldn't it?

Mr. BELL. Well, except for the migratory laborer who has a few dollars in his pocket. But when the migratory laborer finally runs out of money, then he is a vagrant.

Mr. THOMPSON. And can be sent to jail?

Mr. BELL. And can be sent to jail.

Mr. THOMPSON. Now, that labor forms the great part of the labor in this State, doesn't it?

Mr. BELL. Yes; in the summer time it certainly does.

Mr. THOMPSON. What suggestion would you make for the changes in the law in that respect?

Mr. BELL. Perhaps not exactly a change in the law, but in the method of the confinement of the vagrant after he is convicted of vagrancy. I think that it is not a helpful thing to put a man in prison and simply keep him in confinement for 30 days. He creates nothing for the State, nor is he improving his own condition. It seems to me that the solution is to put the vagrant in some creative form of employment, for instance, the State farms, such as they have in Prussia and some districts of Germany, as I understand.

Chairman WALSH. What is a vagrant under the law of California, or is it defined by city ordinances in various places?.

Mr. BELL. It is defined by the State code.

Chairman WALSH. What is it?

Mr. BELL. Any man who has no means of support and no visible means of employement. There are several other definitions included.

Chairman WALSH. And that alone constitutes a man a vagrant, in California?

Mr. BELL. That constitutes a vagrant in California.

Chairman WALSH. Without having bad associates or anything else?

Mr. BELL. Without having any bad associates or being connected with any crime.

Chairman WALSH. Or an evil reputation?

Mr. BELL. No; as I understand the law.

Mr. THOMPSON. What good do you think that law is to the people of the State of California?

Mr. BELL. I think it is really of very little good now, as I generalize. Perhaps it is a good thing to get men off the streets that would finally, perhaps, get destitute if they wander without funds or employment for any length of time. It may protect the community to a certain extent in putting them in jail where they will not reach that destitute state. But on the other hand, as far as the creative work affected by such a law goes, I think it amounts to practically nothing.

Mr. THOMPSON. Then, in the cases you have named, it has been used really as an unfair weapon against the men?

Mr. BELL. It strikes me it has.

Mr. THOMPSON. Anything further you would like to say, Mr. Bell?

Mr. BELL. No.

Mr. THOMPSON. That is all.

Chairman WALSH. Anything else? That is all. Thank you, Mr. Bell. Call your next.

Mr. THOMPSON. Mr. Carlin.

TESTIMONY OF MR. W. H. CARLIN.

Mr. THOMPSON. Mr. Carlin, will you please give us your name?

Mr. CARLIN. W. H. Carlin.

Mr. THOMPSON. Your business address?

Mr. CARLIN. Marysville, Cal.

Mr. THOMPSON. Your profession?

Mr. CARLIN. Attorney at law.

Mr. THOMPSON. How long have you been practicing law there?

Mr. CARLIN. Since August 1, 1890.

Mr. THOMPSON. Were you the special prosecutor in the Ford and Suhr cases?

Mr. CARLIN. Yes.

Mr. THOMPSON. What have you to say with reference to those cases, and particularly with reference to the statement of unfair treatment to labor suspects by detectives and other officers of the law?

Mr. CARLIN. Well, I will give you my statement. Then I would like to have you—Dr. Parker is by your side there, and he is quite conversant with a good deal of it up there—and I would like then to be asked such questions as you think might enlighten the subject somewhat here.

I will say that this trouble occurred on the 3d of August, 1913. Marysville is not a very large city. I have a good deal to do, and although spoken to by the district attorney about possibly coming in to help him, nothing definite was determined upon until some time along in, probably—I would not be certain, October, probably, or maybe November. After some persuasion, realizing the work was not going to be very easy or very pleasant, I, at the request of the attorney general, agreed to go into the case, and I did. Up to about that time I did not pay so very much attention to what was going on, except what I learned through the newspapers. I had heard about detectives, and men being arrested. But from the time that I agreed to go into the cases, I realized that I would have to do something, and made myself more or less conversant with the whole situation.

I found this situation. The trouble occurred there on August 3, among a large number of people. The thing happened in a very, very short space of time, probably five minutes, maybe less, and the actors in the tragedy, if you wish to call it such, scattered or disappeared, went where they thought best to go; that the officers evidently—the arm of the State—found it a very difficult thing to ascertain who were guilty of the shooting on the ground. They, I am told, sought the assistance of certain private detective agencies to locate those who were there at the time, and through their assistance did locate some.

I may as well say in passing, if it is proper, and I guess that is one of the things you desire to know, that I deprecate—let me say first that I have never made a specialty of criminal law. The first 8 or 10 years of my practice I tried a good many cases as a young fellow starting in the country. We find it a means of getting acquainted, hoping that we will get out of it and drop out as quickly as possible and get at something that is more pleasant and more lucrative. And in that time I did try throughout the northern counties of the State—I mean by that Yuba, Sutter, Nevada, Placer, and Siskiyou, and a couple of others—several criminal cases, among them about 24 or 25 capital cases.

Now, I will say that I deprecate the use or the employment of private detective agencies in any criminal case. In fact, and I may say in these cases I tried, they were all on the part of the defense except two, and one is the one now under discussion. In fact, the ordinarily regularly appointed or elected State official—State or county—who is under bonds and under the sanctity of his oath, and so forth, is very likely in gathering evidence in a criminal case to become zealous, to form a theory or opinion, and, having formed it, to go to improper lengths in order to sustain it; in other words, to become a prosecutor with all the zeal, all the energy and enthusiasm which properly belongs to the man on the defense. And I say that is the case with the ordinary police officer, and I am speaking of the country as distinguished from the city, where I will always claim we have a better administration of justice than you can have in a large city. The atmosphere is clearer, I will say, and I think, from a local standpoint, cleaner, without any disrespect to any city, of course, even San Francisco. But now when you take a case, however, and put the gathering of evidence in the hands of a private detective agency or individual you multiply the dangers to the defendant immeasurably by doing so. He has not surrounding him any of the influences which tend to keep the regular officer within proper bounds. I desire to state this with all due respect to all detectives and private agencies, but I am speaking in a general way.

Now, coming to the point at issue: I inquired as to why private detectives were called into this so-called Wheatland riot case, and I was told from its very nature it was impossible for the regular officers of the county to hunt out and find the ringleaders at the time of the riot. They had scattered, and they had to be searched out; as the saying is, run down. And that was the cause of it. Well, when I went into the case, there was a large amount of evidence which had been gathered by the district attorney, a very careful and extremely conscientious gentleman. He had not had a very large amount of experience in criminal law, but endeavored to do the right thing at all times. I found this evidence and went through it. In so far as that which was gathered by the detective agencies was concerned, I considered it worthless, and their work worthless, except in so far as it tended to locate the individuals whom I believe were afterwards legally and completely and fairly proven guilty of the charge laid against them. That was, the finding of them was a benefit. The evidence they gathered was of little value. To illustrate: A man named Suhr, one of the men afterwards convicted, was said to have made a confession to certain detectives; and certain of the detectives, I believe, called at my office and told me what he was purported to have said. He was in jail at Yuba City, Sutter County, which is across the river from Marysville. I asked to be taken over there so that I could talk to him, telling these detectives at the time that I didn't place any reliance upon anything they might have gathered, and that in so far as I might be concerned in the handling of the cases I would not use any evidence which he or any other private detective obtained, unless, after an examination of the witness or the person in question, independent of anything that they had gathered, I found it was voluntary and entirely free from duress or improper influence. I went over with the agent and, I believe, the district attorney—yes; I know it—and interviewed Mr. Suhr in the court room, in the presence of the sheriff and several others, the detective being present—his name I did not get; I could not mention it now. I asked this man to give me a statement of what had happened to him, what he had done, and how far he had been mistreated, if at all. He talked to me for probably an hour. I let him talk on. Only once did the detective interrupt, and I then told him—the detective—that he must either sit back in the rear part of the room, remain silent, or leave the room. I heard no more from him during that examination. The witness went over the scenes at the hop field, told me that he had been present there. This is in the record, of course, and it is proper for me to state it now. And that he had fired certain shots at officers, and he saw officers fall.

He traced his own connection with Mr. Ford from the time of the shooting, or rather from a place in Stockton before going to the hop field, and showed to me that he came there for the purpose of an agitation, and that Mr. Ford came with him for the same purpose, undoubtedly. He stated nothing at all which would implicate Mr. Ford, other than that they came there together. The testimony which I took down was written out in longhand, but I never used it. I went into the trial of the case without using his statements to me. While they were voluntary, yet he was not represented by counsel for himself. At the time I told him, of course, of all his rights. But I didn't think it exactly the thing to do, and I kept that testimony in my office, and it never got before the jury. So when the cases came on for trial we eliminated all of the statements, confessions, or admissions, as you may term them, obtained by the detectives, and introduced the evidence taken from the witnesses on the ground, plus that of certain statements made by Mr. Suhr to the officers—that is, the local men—both in Marysville and in Yuba City. And those admissions were to the effect of doing certain shooting and being on the ground, but not nearly as complete or full as that which he gave to me.

Passing over, now, the details, there was a good deal said during the time of the trial about unfairness up there. The gentlemen who defended those men are present in this room. Under our law they were entitled to 20 peremptory challenges. I am not certain as to the number; Mr. Royce is over here [indicating], and Mr. Lewis is at the other side. But it is my impression they used 17, and they may have used 18. They didn't use all; I know that. They had peremptory challenges left after the jury was impaneled.

At the conclusion of the testimony and answering statements made by Mr. Bell as to a public defender, and purposely refraining from asking any commendation for myself, when the testimony was closed I was satisfied that two of the men were guilty beyond peradventure of a doubt—Ford and Suhr. I believed a third man was guilty, a man named Beck. A man named Bagan, there was just a little testimony to connect him with the crime, but it was so vague that it would have been a crime to have asked the jury to convict him.

In closing the argument, after it had been ably presented by Mr. Lewis for the defense, and after Mr. Royce, a very keen, careful lawyer, for the defense, had brought out all the testimony within his power, and in which trial the rulings of the court were absolutely fair, in closing the argument I practically requested the jury—I did request them—to acquit Bagan and intimated to them strongly that they should acquit Beck, because, while I believed him guilty, yet under our law I may state there was in my mind a reasonable doubt as to this man's guilt, and, that being there, I intimated to the jury that they should acquit him.

I believed the other two men guilty of murder in the first degree, without any mitigating circumstances, in my own mind. I believed they went there for the full purpose of working up an agitation—not to work, but to work up an agitation, and to do so entirely heedless and reckless of the consequences. But I don't believe that either man thoroughly appreciated just what those consequences might be, and that while under the law they are presumed to know the ordinary consequences of their own voluntary acts, yet there was that question in my mind about the excitement and the cause which they thought they were leading which mitigated it. And I begged the jury in my closing remarks not to take their lives.

The jury took me at my word and did not—gave them second degree—acquitted the other two men—acquitted Mr. Beck, I was told afterwards, after quite a long discussion and disagreement there.

Now, the cases are, of course, on appeal. That is a brief résumé of the situation there.

I might say this: The conditions—I will touch on this briefly—prevailing in the field we did not go into deeply. It did appear, however, that those men were agitators; that there were probably 10 to 15 brought there for that purpose. The conditions were not excellent. Dr. Parker investigated them thoroughly. I only got it from the testimony. The Durst Bros. had sent out, as was necessary in those cases, circulars asking for pickers to come, and they probably came there, more than they expected. They were not prepared for all that did come. But when the conditions were made known to Durst Bros. he did proceed—that is, Saturday, the 2d day of August—this was a matter that was not mentioned in Dr. Parker's report, and I think by inadvertence he omitted it. But attention was called to Durst by a committee sent up by the pickers. Mr. Durst stated then and there that he would at once remove those unsatisfactory conditions, all excepting a raise in wage from a dollar to a dollar and a quarter.

That was a fact which was proven by the testimony in the case, and the record is here. I brought it down with me. And that is the unquestioned testimony of the defense to show that Mr. Durst, as soon as they called it to his attention, stated, "I will remove those at once." The wage—and there was another claim of what they called the high-pole men which was not necessary—that is, the men to take down the vines from the higher wires—now, I am passing along here rapidly for you.

As to the men who were kept in jail up there, Mr. Bell is in error. Alfred Nelson was arrested, a complaint sworn to against him, given a preliminary hearing, held for a trial on a charge of murder. The other man, I don't know much about him. But let me say this to you: Before my coming into the case there had been several arrests made—well, maybe 5 or 6 to 10—8 or 10—along there. The law of our State entitles anyone arrested to be taken before a magistrate and have an examination. But it is upon his demand—his request. Of course, no officer should confine a man too long until he is given a hearing. But these men were arrested, and, as I am informed, I think correctly, no request made by any of them for an examination until Messrs. Royce and Lewis came into the case, primarily as the attorneys of one or two of the defendants, now, I can't say which. They can tell you.

Now, as I gather it, after their coming into the case, they got into communication with these other suspects. It was a single fight, of course. And they did the right thing. They, I think, unsolicited in many cases, got in connection with these other men, and that brought about hearings that had not before been asked for.

Now, none of these men were arrested as vagrants. I don't know that Mr. Bell intended to imply that the vagrancy charge was used here. Of course, I am passing upon it rapidly, and I know that the time is short. I desire to say that I can't give you the full definition of the term "vagrant" under our law. It is a long one. It is in the penal code, and it is easily obtained. Mr. Bell's statement to you would be misleading—of course, inadvertently made—without reading the section. Idleness and lack of visible means of support is only a portion of the definition. In each case that is qualified by other terms. Like an idle and dissolute person; a person without any fixed abode; and usually a person who lives about houses of ill fame, and places of that kind, in a general way. I won't try to give it to you. The penal code is there, and I never try to keep in mind all the sections of the code. But you can easily get it.

Now, leaving the cities, I will say to you that in the country communities of the State, that vagrant law is not used to oppress anybody. No idle person, no person out of employment, no person simply because he was not working, in my time—I left New York State in 1881 and have been here since that time—has been arrested in the section of the State in which I have lived, to my knowledge, unless he becomes vicious and dissolute. The usual person that this law is applied to is the man that comes into those towns or cities like Sacramento, Marysville, Red Bluff, Redding, Nevada City, and so forth, and who, without work—either without work or whatever the reason is—acquires vicious habits, associates with known criminals, is found in houses of questionable repute, lies around, and finally gets to the place where he lives off of the earnings of fallen women. That is the man upon whom principally is visited the vagrant law. And I think I am safe in saying that 99 out of 100, well, that is pretty strong, 80 out of 100, yes; it is more than that, it is 90 out of 100, if not more, of the vagrancy cases in the interior counties of this State—I am not talking of the large cities, I don't know anything about them—are men and women who have inhabited the tenderloin, as the saying is, until they become obnoxious, and men who have, by associating with them and living off of their earnings, become an eyesore to the community. These are the kind of people that are affected by the vagrant law.

Now, I don't know that there is anything further that I might add to it.

Mr. Thompson. Mr. Carlin, you stated that you saw Mr. Suhr in jail?

Mr. Carlin. Yes, sir.

Mr. Thompson. Across the river from Marysville?

Mr. Carlin. Yes, sir.

Mr. Thompson. How long had he been arrested before that, if you remember?

Mr. Carlin. Suhr had been in jail, of course, I can not give you the exact time, but I should say in Yuba City probably 8 or 10 days.

Mr. Thompson. During that time did you keep track of him in jail?

Mr. Carlin. No.

Mr. Thompson. What he did or who saw him?

Mr. Carlin. No; I wasn't connected with the prosecution directly at that time. I was just about to notify Attorney General Webb that I would take up the cases—except that I heard that he was in jail, and I believe that he was being visited by private detectives.

Mr. Thompson. Do you know to what process of sweating or other treatment that usually goes by that name, he had been subjected before you saw him?

Mr. Carlin. I have no knowledge, excepting what I gathered from the man's own statement to me, and what I had heard. Of course, my source of information would necessarily be biased, but they said none. In my talking to him he gave no evidence of being sweated.

He impressed me at that time and at all times that I saw him afterwards, as a man who realized that he had got into a bad scrape. He is a man of not very high mentality, rather the reverse—got into a bad scrape and felt a keen sense of remorse, one who was willing to take the blame himself. Almost every other word, if he got a chance, he would say something in behalf of his associate Ford, and intimate that, so far as he was concerned, why he didn't have much show.

Mr. Thompson. Referring to the case of the two men who were held in jail, Mr. Carlin, for some time as suspects, one of whom you say had been arraigned and held for further trial——

Mr. Carlin (interposing). Yes.

Mr. Thompson. Mr. Bell stated that those were simply two examples that were given of concrete cases, but that other cases existed, I would understand him. What would you say of the law, as it exists to-day, that leaves to those men simply this theoretical charge that they must know the law, and that does not provide an officer to tell them that they have a right to demand a hearing, or to have advice, or of their other rights of habeas corpus, and so on—writ of habeas corpus?

Mr. Carlin. In an abstract way I think that is a very—it might work out all right. Men in jail ought to have some one whose duty it would be—the fact—now, I want to put this exactly without any criticism, these cases which I am discussing, I am a biased witness on behalf of the defense. I want that understood here.

In these Wheatland cases the district attorney was coping with an unusual situation. Now, having said that—I believe it is the duty of the district attorney as he is now constituted, the moment a man is arrested, to go to him and say: "Here, now, it is your right to send for an attorney, demand a hearing, or send for him." Under our present law there is no provision for appointing an attorney for a defendant until he is arraigned in the superior court. There ought to be some provision made for giving him one immediately after he goes into jail. Yes, sir.

Mr. THOMPSON. You think that change should be made?

Mr. CARLIN. Unquestionably it should. But as to the reason, I might—of course, I don't need to say that—you all grasp it—but, of course, the officer of the law, as we must concede, must be given some latitude in arresting a suspect and in holding him; otherwise you will go too far on the other side and, as the saying is, paralyze the hands of the law.

The officer can not always be sure he is putting his hand upon the right man's shoulder, and therefore he must have the right to arrest him, detain him a reasonably long time, give a reasonable time for investigation. Of course, the supreme court will do that anyway upon a proper showing as it is now.

Mr. THOMPSON. Take this case here. Apparently there was a very serious riot growing out of certain industrial conditions which made many hundreds of men and women feel they were not being treated right. This riot, in the course of the riot, some people were shot and killed, and then according to the advice perhaps of private detectives, as this case would show, men are thrown into jail and not informed of their legal rights to demand an immediate hearing, and are kept there until 75 or 90 days go by, as happened in several cases; what, in your opinion, would be the natural effect on workers who have had a struggle of that kind, to find their leaders and others interested in their cause held in such manner.

Mr. CARLIN. I am glad I was reminded of that. That is one of the worst features of this case up there. Things of that kind which, as I say, the district attorney was powerless to prevent, has enabled good-thinking, well-meaning people, some of them who attended the trial and some of them who are here now to get a warped view of that whole case up there. They got the impression, and it was published throughout the press that men were thus thrown into prison and not granted a speedy hearing or trial, that they had been questioned by private detectives, sweated, and given the third degree, as the saying is, and all that sort of thing, and that got abroad. It got abroad throughout the State of California, and to quite an extent, so much so that letters have been coming into the governor's office and keep pouring in until quite a propaganda has been established throughout the State of California based on that. While the actual facts are that the men from the time that they were brought before the superior court got a very, very impartial trial; I will say, absolutely fair and impartial trial. Yet, because of this happening you will understand that thereby the work of the—that every bit of the work of the private detectives from that time we got started was thrown aside, none of it used except the bare fact of the arrest; that the men were from the time the trial started and before that, from the time we took charge of it, given full access to their attorneys. I might say one of the first things they did, of course, was to have Mr. Royce come to my office and give a free access to the county jail. I may say to you that Mr. Royce was in my office, visited, me, I might say, talked with me as prosecutor and defender should in a proper way during the whole trial of the case. Our relations were the most friendly throughout the trial and are to-day. I am glad to be able to say that is true.

Mr. THOMPSON. Do you know whether Suhr had been talked to by an attorney; his own attorney, before you spoke to him?

Mr. CARLIN. I don't think Suhr had any attorney. I asked him at the time if he wanted an attorney, and he intimated to me a desire to plead guilty. And I had such—I felt such a feeling of sorrow, heart-sickness, for Suhr. He seemed to act so—well, so thoroughly guilty, it seemed to me, that I told him he might have an attorney, and to get one, and fully advise him in the premises. And, as I say, for that reason, that was one; the other was the fact I never in any way used what he said to me during the hearing at all, and nobody ever got it.

Mr. THOMPSON. But at that time he did not seek an attorney?

Mr. CARLIN. No, sir; but he was then informed of his legal rights.

Mr. THOMPSON. Now, with reference to the other suspects, those that were not apparently tried, at least they were held in jail, as it has been stated.

. Mr. CARLIN. Well, now, I can't give the names of all of them. There were several held in jail. There was a Mr.—I don't know his name—they were represented by attorneys—yes; they were held in jail—I think there were three or four who had not been tried at the conclusion of the Ford-Suhr trials.

The cases against these men were alike. They were probably about as strong as that against the man Beck, to whom I referred, but stronger than against Bagan, but they were the cases. I had no doubt in my mind that the men were there. For example, I might say to you rapidly, the testimony was he was seen going away from the scene of the shooting immediately after, with a pistol in his hand. And there was a little more testimony of that kind. I have no doubt but that the men were there, but with five or six hundred or maybe a thousand people in that excited crowd, why it is pretty hard to get the evidence, but it was a question, if they were guilty, why let them be settled with in some other place.

Mr. THOMPSON. That is all, Mr. Chairman.

Commissioner O'CONNELL. I want to ask about this statement of Mr. Bell regarding the conditions of the jails through those counties, particularly the jail in which these men were locked, which he says were infested by vermin, and so forth.

Mr. CARLIN. Well, now, Mr. Commissioner, perhaps first—as I intimated— the first four or five years of my practice I was there in jail a great deal of the time—went up there, would go into the jail to see——

Commissioner O'CONNELL. I suppose you mean you went there of your own accord?

Mr. CARLIN. Yes; I got out when I rapped on the door for the sheriff. Yes; keep the record right, Mr. Reporter, I was not confined.

I since then have been in and out. I may say the places that I have been called into were Oroville, Nevada City occasionally, Auburn, Marysville a few times, Red Bluff, Downieville, Susanville, Quincy, Yuba City. Now, the jails in those places at the time I have been in them were in good condition. There are not very many prisoners, and the sheriffs are self-respecting, respected men; stand high in their communities, and have to do so to be elected, because the people in the country will not stand for anything that is not straight and clean. They are well fed. The prisoners are kept in good shape, the prisoners are clean, and in fact I have never heard a prisoner complain about the feed, that he was not fed properly, was not housed properly, or that there was any vermin or anything of that kind in the jails.

Commissioner O'CONNELL. Were you in the cell in which these men were located?

Mr. CARLIN. Yes; the whole jail.

Commissioner O'CONNELL. In the particular jail when you were talking with the prisoner, were you in the cell?

Mr. CARLIN. Yes; sometimes the sheriff takes them out to his office for me, and sometimes I would go in and sit down on a stool in the cell and talk with him right there.

Commissioner O'CONNELL. The cell in which, as was stated by Mr. Bell, was the vermin?

Mr. CARLIN. I didn't hear Bell's statement as to what place was infested by vermin.

Commissioner O'CONNELL. I understood him to say that it was where these men were located, in the jail, and incidentally others.

Mr. CARLIN. I am applying my testimony rather to the Wheatland situation, because I wasn't in any of the cells where those men were confined at all. All the work I did on that was done with—of course the attorney for the prosecution does not go in there; it is improper for him to do so.

Commissioner O'CONNELL. I understood your conviction of these two men was based upon largely the fact that they were discovered in this crowd, with firearms in their hands.

Mr. CARLIN. No, sir; I don't. I do not believe much in circumstancial evidence. There was this, Mr. Commissioner; they were shown to be here. The testimony conclusively showed that the ringleader, Mr. Ford, had at divers times been in haranguing the crowd, announced that—knowing that the officers were coming down there to——

Chairman WALSH. If it is all right, we will get a detailed statement of that, because the other side is not present, and I understand we have the record of the evidence.

Mr. CARLIN. I was going to say this, I do not believe in circumstantial evidence. That ought to answer you. I rather thought you didn't want——

Commissioner GARRETSON. What is the secret blotter?

Mr. CARLIN. The secret blotter? You will have to ask an officer. I imagine it is; probably I may be wrong—probably some book in the police station where the man may be taken in and his name either not written down at all, or that there is a book that is not disclosed. But I must say to you that if any such practice as that exists in California I have never seen it.

Commissioner GARRETSON. The statement was specifically made here, that the name was entered in the secret blotter.

Mr. CARLIN. I never heard of the term "secret blotter" before, except possibly once. And I know, sir, that no such thing as a secret blotter has happened in my experience in California.

Commissioner GARRETSON. Where they do exist, is not the charge always indefinite or minor in its character?

Mr. CARLIN. It certainly—certainly no humane officer that was allowed to have charge of a prisoner in California would enter a man's name on a serious charge upon a secret blotter.

Commissioner GARRETSON. Could a secret blotter exist legally anywhere?

Mr. CARLIN. No, sir; I don't think so. If there is such a law, I never heard of it.

Commissioner GARRETSON. You expressed a peculiar view on vagrancy laws. Has your experience been or your study in regard to the application of vagrancy laws on this continent—on the subject——

Mr. CARLIN. Well, sir, it is confined to California, and necessarily very limited, because in my practice vagrancy trials did not come up and I only know of it as it is applied in these interior counties.

Commissioner GARRETSON. Have you ever noticed over any wide range of territory the ordinary report that appears in regard to municipal courts and the man that vags, that they generally do it in country villages and municipal courts of that class?

Mr. CARLIN. I may say to you, I was called upon to defend some cases up in Butte County a short time ago where there was a claim made against the county for some eight or ten thousand dollars by an officer for arresting vagrants. They presented the question to the board of supervisors and suit was brought upon them and the board contested, and I was called in to assist in the defense. We defeated the claims, but if I may say so, the evidence showed this, with all respect to all concerned, that those vagrants were treated with much consideration. They were taken before a justice of the peace and a charge laid against them, and they plead guilty. They were discharged, fees entered up. They went back to a nice shady place they had along the creek where the water flowed coolly, smoothly, and pleasantly, a shady place, and slept there and prepared next morning and taken back again.

Commissioner GARRETSON. Isn't the ordinary man that is vagged the man who calls at the back door and asks for meals?

Mr. CARLIN. Yes; nine chances to one he is not vagged, he is fed.

Commissioner GARRETSON. Oh, he is fed and then vagged?

Mr. CARLIN. No; not vagged at all.

Commissioner GARRETSON. I believe that is true, but isn't that what makes up the bulk of vag reports in village municipal courts?

Mr. CARLIN. In a village, I think, using the term advisedly.

Commissioner GARRETSON. I am using that as against the city.

Mr. CARLIN. I understand, and that is my recollection from my eastern village of Malone, N. Y. It was a village. But that was often in eastern cities. In California, speaking of the interior, you will find that the ordinary man will go up to a back door, as you say, and the housewife or the servant, sometimes a Chinaman, or whoever it is, will ordinarily feed him, give him a meal, hand-out, as the saying is, of something, and he will go away. Very few, indeed, I can say, in my neighborhood around where I live, in my house, men come up and ask for something to eat.

Commissioner GARRETSON. And if there is, oh, we will say 100,000 municipal courts in existence in the States—that is a low estimate.

Mr. CARLIN. Yes.

Commissioner GARRETSON. If each one of those vag a man a week, in the time that we have described, does not the total—well, isn't it staggering?

Mr. CARLIN. Yes; and if they are vagged for the cause you have mentioned it ought to be prevented if there is any way to do so.

Commissioner GARRETSON. It ought to be what?

Mr. CARLIN. It ought to be prevented, if there is any way to do so.

Commissioner GARRETSON. Now, in regard to the other class that you refer to ordinarily being vagged under your practice, isn't it a fact that when the cadet who lives on the earnings of women reaches the stage where he can square himself that he is never vagged? Now, I am not speaking of the——

Mr. CARLIN. I am not speaking of the large cities.

Commissioner GARRETSON. Now, I am going to the large city, for that is where he flourishes.

Mr. CARLIN. I have heard that is the case, that if he is, as you say, promoted from a cadet, well, even——

Chairman WALSH. We are going to try to get a man from the large cities. I have only one question I wish to ask, and I think I can finish it with that. You y these men went to this place not to work?

MrsaCARLIN. That is the evidence we derived.

Chairman WALSH. Is there any prejudice in that community against a person going to a place of that kind to agitate any lawful thing?

Mr. CARLIN. No; not if you become once convinced that they agitate for the sake of improvement—not—of bettering conditions—not for agitation's sake.

Chairman WALSH. Who is to determine that?

Mr. CARLIN. It is best determined in this way: In this concrete case the testimony from the defense showed that the proprietor was—acquiesced, rather, in the demands except practically, or except that of higher wage.

Chairman WALSH. Prior to the advent of these men that you say wanted to agitate?

Mr. CARLIN. No. Immediately upon the demand being made, in my opinion, at the instance of those agitators.

Chairman WALSH. Is that what they were agitating for, better conditions, decent conditions?

Mr. CARLIN. Undoubtedly that is one claim they had.

Chairman WALSH. Was it a cause of prejudice against them?

Mr. CARLIN. In the arrests the large number of arrests and the employment of special counsel and the employment of detectives leading up to the trial——

Chairman WALSH. Was that a factor?

Mr. CARLIN. No; there was no prejudice at all because they agitated, but as to the subject matter of the agitation it was quite generally conceded——

Chairman WALSH. Mr. Carlin, I am trying to get your viewpoint. When you said that they were agitators pure and simple, that they didn't go there to work, did you mean by that that there was something reprehensible about it?

Mr. CARLIN. No, sir; except this far: That if those people, with whom I have no quarrel, would establish some standard, if they had one that is establishable and then agitate toward that standard, some point in view, grant it all, but I do not see that—I do believe that it is a dangerous proposition to contemplate the idea of a set of agitators going into a community to agitate, and we will say that they have their demands agreed to, conditions are improved as they ask, and then still keep on agitating—there, I say, is real danger, where the real danger comes in.

Chairman WALSH. Do you believe, then, there should be some body or some authority that should say to what extent the agitation should go, the time at which the agitators should withdraw as being satisfied that those conditions had been improved?

Mr. CARLIN. Mr. Honorable Commissioner, I don't think so.

Chairman WALSH. The fact connected with this particular agitation, then, leaving out, of course, any question of what this agitation was, that certain men went to a certain place, I know nothing about it except what I see in the reports, to protest by word of mouth against conditions that they conceived to be inimical to the welfare of society and especially of their class; and following that agitation the conditions were removed, very shortly following their agitation. Is that correct?

Mr. CARLIN. That is—yes. That is stated rather fairly. But the fact—better state it this way: That certain men went there to that place and agitated, and to find, in my opinion——

Chairman WALSH. Yes.

Mr. CARLIN. Subject matter for agitation.

Chairman WALSH. Well, they found it, then, when they got there?

Mr. CARLIN. They found certain matters; yes.

Chairman WALSH. Wouldn't it be fair to assume, then, as a lawyer, that they had definite and positive information that such things existed?

Mr. CARLIN. Well, all I know is this: The past 10 or 12 years conditions there at that place had not been—no fault found. Of course that dosen't say they did not exist. I admit that. But they—here is the situation—in these hop fields it would be impossible, and I say impossible—not impossible, but impracticable—even now conditions could not be established by the commission of which Mr. Parker is secretary, but what it would be the subject matter of agitation and improvement. I do not think you can establish a hop-picking field or a fruit-curing plant.

Chairman WALSH. Then you are in favor, of course, of constant agitation?

Mr. CARLIN. Certainly; even in the right way.

Chairman WALSH. You would not want to, or would you claim the right to tell another individual what was the right agitation, if the conditions were bad—now assuming the conditions were capable of improvement.

Mr. CARLIN. I certainly would not. We are discussing now, Mr. Commissioner, a question of polemics.

Chairman WALSH. Yes; that is going too far.

Mr. CARLIN. I am glad to do it, but there is absolutely no standard; and in the nature of things there would have to be a standard. We have to progress to that standard if one would be established. It would have to be changed. A standard for to-day would not be satisfactory for next year, probably.

Chairman WALSH. We consider it very proper in our profession, do we not, Mr. Carlin, to constantly agitate for improved conditions?

Mr. CARLIN. All the time.

Chairman WALSH. We deny the right, do we not, to any other person to say to us how far we shall go with our agitation, or what we shall condemn in proper respectful language as subject matters, do we not?

Mr. CARLIN. We do, sir.

Chairman WALSH. That is all.

Commissioner WEINSTOCK. Were these men prosecuted, Mr. Carlin, for having agitated, or were they prosecuted for having used violence?

Mr. CARLIN. They were—the question of their agitation, it was stated upon the trial, if not expressed tacitly, that their agitation was proper. It was not denied at the time. No attempt was made to go into the conditions there. It was not denied that conditions needed improvement. They were prosecuted solely because they advised violence which resulted in the taking of human life. I would like to say one thing, with the permission of the commission. I do not think it is necessary, and in view of the fact that the Durst people have been interested—for they are admirable gentlemen—I was called in by the attorney general of the State to assist him at that time—that I had never done any work for the Durst interests up to prior to my going in to prosecute these cases, not until afterwards. Since Mr. Manwell, the man who was killed, at the time I had been acting as attorney for the Durst interests, and therefore I had——

Commissioner WEINSTOCK. Was Mr. E. Clemens Horst up there?

Mr. CARLIN. There was a lawsuit arose between the two interests regarding the water right, which made it necessary for them to appoint Mr. Manwell to represent the Dursts, and myself the Horst interests, trying to establish our rights to certain water against the Pacific Gas & Electric Co. of San Francisco, and after Mr. Manwell's death I completed carrying on these cases. I desire to say that, in view of the fact that I was called in there by the attorney general, I was not called in because I had any connection with Durst.

Commissioner WEINSTOCK. That is all.

Chairman WALSH. I simply wanted to see if I understood this; I did not understand this case as well as I might, but I have read the entire record, and the purpose of my inquiry was from the fact that you stated at the opening of your examination that these men were there to agitate, not to work, and for no other reason.

Mr. CARLIN. Oh, no; none at all.

Chairman WALSH. We will now stand adjourned until 2 o'clock. Mr. Carlin, you will please return at that time.

(Whereupon, at 12.30 o'clock p. m., an adjournment was taken until 2 o'clock p. m. of the same day, Friday, August 28, 1914.)

Met pursuant to adjournment.
Present as before.
Thereupon, the following proceedings were had:
Chairman WALSH. You may call the next, Mr. Thompson. Mr. Carlin may be excused now. Mr. Garretson said that he would forego his questions.
Mr. THOMPSON. You are excused, Mr. Carlin.
Chairman WALSH. I am much obliged to you, Mr. Carlin. Mr. Garretson says he will forego his questions.
Call your next.
Mr. CARLIN. I may say to the commission, by the way, that Mr. Bell has here a copy of the penal code of this State, in which is contained the definition of vagrancy, and he says that he would like to present it.
Chairman WALSH. Very good. We will take that from Mr. Bell. Thank you.
Mr. THOMPSON. Mr. Bell now, Mr. Chairman.
Chairman WALSH. Yes; if you wish to, put Mr. Bell on.

TESTIMONY OF MR. GEORGE L. BELL—Recalled.

Mr. BELL. It is suggested that this is the easiest way of bringing this to an issue as to what the law is, if we can read this into the record.
The crime of vagrancy is described in the penal code, section 647. It reads as follows [reading]:
"1. Every person (except a California Indian) without visible means of living, who has the physical ability to work, and who does not seek employment, nor labor when employment is offered him; or
"2. Every healthy beggar who solicits alms as a business; or
"3. Every person who roams about from place to place without any lawful business; or
"4. Every person known to be a pickpocket, thief, burglar, or confidence operator, either by his own confession or by his having been convicted of either of such offenses, and having no visible or lawful means of support, when found loitering around any steamboat landing, railroad depot, banking institution, broker's office, place of amusement, auction room, store, shop, or crowded thoroughfare, car, or omnibus or at any public gathering or assembly; or
"5. Every idle, or lewd, or dissolute person, or associate of known thieves; or
"6. Every person who wanders about the streets at late or unusual hours of the night, without any visible or lawful business; or
"7. Every person who lodges in any barn, shed, shop, outhouse, vessel, or place other than such as is kept for lodging purposes, without the permission of the owner or party entitled to the possession thereof; or
"8. Every person who lives in and about houses of ill fame; or
"9. Every person who acts as a runner or capper for attorneys in and about police courts or city prisons; or
"10. Every common prostitute; or
"11. Every common drunkard,
"is a vagrant, and is punishable by a fine not exceeding $500, or by imprisonment in the county jail not exceeding six months, or by both such fine and imprisonment."
You notice that each one of these things are separate. Either or or. My contention was that it says under the first clause every person without visible means of living, except a California Indian, who has the physical ability to work and who does not seek employment, nor labor when employment is offered him; or
Second. Every healthy beggar who solicits alms as a business; or
Third. Every person who roams about from place to place without any lawful business.
Under those sections a man can be convicted if he is simply found in those positions.
Mr. THOMPSON. In the case you refer to, did they prefer those prosecutions under those clauses?
Mr. BELL. What is that?
Mr. THOMPSON. You referred to several prosecutions for vagrancy.
Mr. BELL. Yes, sir.
Mr. THOMPSON. Were they under those first three clauses?

Mr. BELL. The cases I called attention to were. In each of those cases they claimed that they were cases of men arrested for vagrancy. However, I do not make that claim to the two cases cited this morning. Those were not cases of arrests for vagrancy. Mr. Carlin misunderstood me. They were arrested as suspects, but it was brought out in conversation with others at the trial that they had been arrested for vagrancy.

Mr. THOMPSON. You also testified that a great number of vagrants were arrested.

Mr. BELL. Yes, sir.

Mr. THOMPSON. And held in jail under the first three clauses?

Mr. BELL. Under these clauses.

Mr. THOMPSON. That is all.

Mr. BELL. The other statute over which there was some dispute between myself and Mr. Carlin to be cleared up—in regard to how the law stands with reference to the right of an officer to bring a man before a magistrate—is defined by section 825:

" Defendant must be taken before magistrate without delay."

It then goes on: " The defendant must in all cases be taken before the magistrate without unnecessary delay, and after such arrest, any attorney at law entitled to practice in the courts of record of California may, at the request of the prisoner or any relative of such prisoner, visit the person so arrested. Any officer having charge of the prisoner so arrested who willfully refuses or neglects to allow such attorney to visit a prisoner is guilty of a misdemeanor. Any officer having a prisoner in charge, who refuses to allow an attorney to visit the prinsoner when proper application is made therefor "—

There are two different parties. The arresting officer is under a duty to bring him before the magistrate, and secondly, the man, if he knows the law, has the right to request the officer to bring him an attorney. Those two points will clear up the discussion of the statute.

I would like also to say with reference to two other points——

Mr. CARLIN. Didn't I understand you to say that any of the Wheatland people were held under those two sections?

Mr. BELL. No, sir. There was another statement in regard to the secret blotter. Mr. Carlin is correct in stating there is no such thing in legal understanding. There is no such thing as a secret blotter legally, but anyone who has had experience around police courts knows the phrase " the secret blotter," and also the phrase " small book." It is an illegal practice, but it does exist. They file the name on the secret blotter and subsequently destroy it if they don't hold the man.

Mr. THOMPSON. You mean to say that that illegal practice exists among people who are sworn to enforce the law?

Mr. BELL. That is what it seems. The other point was the question of insanitary jails. My report was made mainly—my statement was made mainly on the report of the State board of health with reference to the condition of the Woodland jail, and that report is now on file. In that report it was reported as being very dirty and also vermin infested, and they said that it should be destroyed. I don't know what action was taken. I also base my statement on an investigation of the Orville, Chico, and Marysville jails. I can say from my personal observation that those jails were very dirty. And the three jailers, at Chico, Orville, and Marysville, stated that they usually had vermin in the jails. Their explanation was that so many men came in covered with vermin that they could not keep the jails clean. I also found one man in the Orville jail who was infected with a venereal disease, but was not isolated, and was using all the washing facilities of the other prisoners. Those are the facts upon which I base that opinion.

Chairman WALSH. That is all.

Commissioner GARRETSON. I would like to ask a question.

Chairman WALSH. Commissioner Garretson would like to ask you some questions.

Commissioner GARRETSON. I want to ask you a question I didn't ask before: The secret blotter, does that exist in every police headquarters, as far as you know them?

Mr. BELL. I would not say every police headquarters.

Commissioner GARRETSON. Of any size?

Mr. BELL. Every police headquarters of any size, I may say, in my opinion, it does.

Commissioner GARRETSON. And is it used in the abuse of the detention law more than any other one agency?

Mr. BELL. Well, I would not say that. My opinion is that the greatest abuse would be of holding the men without bringing them before the magistrate. They may be legally entered in the proper blotter, but, perhaps, next to that, that is so.

Commissioner GARRETSON. Entries in the secret blotter are not, as a general rule, allowed to go any further?

Mr. BELL. Very seldom.

Commissioiner GARRETSON. I wasn't asking altogether on account of want of information of how it is handled, I wanted to learn how is was handled here. The other question is under the vagrancy law: Isn't it a fact under the vagrancy law as it exists to-day that any wandering workingman without money can be convicted thereunder, and is often convicted?

Mr. BELL. Yes, sir. Cases have come to my attention under those sections which I read, of men wandering about from place to place without any apparent business or means of support.

Commissioner GARRETSON. Without either money or means of identification?

Mr. BELL. Yes, sir.

Commissioner GARRETSON. From your investigation do you believe the men who are unjustly convicted under that act form continuous additions to the army of men who question the justness of law in general from those very facts?

Mr. BELL. It is my belief they do. They usually come out very bitter against the system under which they were convicted, especially men put in jail with long sentences, 90 days, when the only crime must have been having no means of employment or means of support.

Commissioner GARRETSON. That is all.

Chairman WALSH. That is all. Thank you.

Call your next.

Mr. THOMPSON. Mr. McKenzie.

TESTIMONY OF MR. A. B. McKENZIE.

Mr. THOMPSON. Will you give us your name?

Mr. McKENZIE. A. B. McKenzie.

Mr. THOMPSON. Your address?

Mr. McKENZIE. Martinez.

Mr. THOMPSON. You are a lawyer by profession?

Mr. McKENZIE. District attorney of Contra Costa County.

Mr. THOMPSON. How long have you been district attorney there?

Mr. McKENZIE. Four years.

Mr. THOMPSON. You were prosecutor in the so-called Wheatland riot cases?

Mr. McKENZIE. No, sir.

Chairman WALSH. He prosecuted one of these detectives, I believe, in another county.

Mr. THOMPSON. What connection did you have with the treatment of labor suspects, or what knowledge have you of it in your county?

Mr. McKENZIE. As a preface, I might say that our county, Contra Costa County, is peculiar in that the portion of it fronting on San Francisco Bay is dominated by what is called a labor-union county. The other half of the county is agricultural and commercial and is nonunion. Persons residing in Contra Costa County look at questions of this kind from both angles.

As regards the Wheatland riot case, I want to say that considerable discussion has been indulged in by the laboring and poorer classes. It is hard to get acquainted with the average labor-union man. It is hard to see into the innermost recesses of his heart until you get well acquainted with him and until you gain his confidence. This is merely preliminary to getting to the Wheatland case. They are beginning to believe—and that is probably on account of the advantage of education—the poorer classes are beginning to believe—that every man who is brought into this world and makes a reasonable effort to do what.is right and earn a living is entitled to a wife, a home, and children, and that he is entitled to a reasonable compensation to maintain that home and support that wife and educate those children.

Now, as far as this Wheatland case is concerned, before I discuss my connection with it, the criticism that has been made since the trial is this: They asked this question, that if the man who was killed, District Attorney Manwell, or Mr. Durst, had shot Blackie Ford under the same circumstances as they claim Suhr and Ford were implicated, would they have received the same treatment as these men have received?

Now, that is the thought that is permeating the minds of the laboring classes and poorer people. That is the real point at issue.

Now, I can appreciate that from the fact that I had special prosecutors in two cases in my county, and in two cases alone. Personally, I do not believe in special prosecutors. But the first case was one where a scab—what is commonly known as a scab—killed a union man arising from trouble over a strike in this county. I realized then—at least I suspected—what I know now, that in a county like ours, where those different interests are and different viewpoints at which they look at things, that unless you had a very clear case it would be impossible for any prosecuting officer to convict either a union man or a scab, for the reason that the jury would be composed of both elements, and unless it was a case that a jury could find nothing to ease their consciences it would be impossible to secure a conviction, and I realized when I prosecuted the first case against the scab the conditions that existed, and when they asked for a special prosecutor I said no at first. I told them that they were only wasting their money, and I didn't need it; but they were somewhat insistent, and I allowed them to employ a special prosecutor.

Subsequently I prosecuted a union man, and a corporation requested that their attorneys might assist in the prosecution of the union man; and, having in mind the fact that I had granted special prosecution when prosecuting the scab, why, I felt I would have to grant it in the other case.

So that is my connection with cases of special prosecution. But I would say that I don't believe in them at all; that if a district attorney is unable to prosecute the case, that he should call in a prosecuting officer from some of the other counties, or get assistance direct from the attorney general's office.

I think it was some time in September that I was going home late Saturday night, and I stopped to chat with a young man with whom I am acquainted, and he told me that the night previous that some Burns detectives had beaten up a man. He didn't just commence it in that way, but from what he said I asked him some questions and found out that that is what his story was. It was too late to do anything about it that night, but Sunday morning I went to my office at the courthouse, and the stenographer in my office happened to be there. She was busy with some other work, and I called up the sheriff's office and inquired about it, and told them to bring the man to my office. They brought this man up, Alfred Nelson, who has been mentioned here by previous witnesses. This was Sunday morning about probably 10 o'clock. When he came into my office he had a cut on the left side of his head probably 2 or 3 inches long. His eye was black; he had two bruises on his left cheek; and his lip was swollen and somewhat bruised. I afterwards learned from the physician who examined him that he was black and blue all over the shoulders and the leg, and I think some place else.

The man had a wild or haunted look in his eye, and seemed to be very much afraid. But I told him who I was and told him if he had been ill treated that it was my duty to punish anyone who had ill treated him, no matter who the person might be. And I asked him to tell me his story. He said he had been camping or sitting or staying on the country road near Gurneyville, and that this man Cradlebaugh, who was a Burns detective, and some other man came along and picked him up and stated he was under arrest for being implicated in the Wheatland riot. They took him to Gurneyville and put him in the lockup, which is a small wooden jail, I presume, of these little towns, and kept him there a few hours and took him from there to Santa Rosa and kept him over night there and took him from there to Sacramento. They kept him there a couple of nights; then they took him from there to San Francisco, and kept him there one night. Then they brought him to Martinez.

There was just the week had intervened from the time the man was arrested until he was assaulted at Martinez. He was brought to Martinez on Friday morning and taken to the sheriff's office, and his name was entered in the transient book or detinue book, or something of that kind, which is a book used for booking prisoners that are en route, by other officers. For instance, if a man was being conveyed from Los Angeles to San Francisco, and the officer in charge wished to rest at Stockton or Bakersfield, he would take his prisoner to the county jail and give him in charge of the sheriff over night, no charge being against him because there was no charge pending in that county, and they entered his name in this transient or detinue book, of which I believe all sheriffs' offices have one.

Commissioner GARRETSON. Record of transients?

Mr. McKENZIE. Transients; yes, sir. About half past 9 o'clock at night the man was put in jail, and those in charge of him told the jailer to feed him nothing but bread and water. However, the jailer did not follow his instructions in that particular or in any other that I know of. About half past 9 or 10 o'clock at night, this man Cradlebaugh came and asked the jailer for this Alfred Nelson that he wanted. And the jailer turned the prisoner over to him. The jailer considered that he had no authority or charge over the prisoner; justice must be done to him in that particular, that he did not consider him as being a prisoner of his; that he was simply put in jail for the accommodation of the officer who had him in charge, and that he could have him or do with him what he pleased; that the jailer was not responsible for his going in or his going out.

He took him to a saloon, and was joined by another by the name of O'Donnell, I think his name was. And the two of them asked this man—took this man to the Martinez Hotel. And they demanded he come through, and asked him: "Did you not see Blackie Ford shoot Mundell?"

Now, it seems that they started off early in the proceedings with the conviction that these men did, these certain men had committed this crime, that they were the men who had done the shooting, or committed the crime, and that they were hunting up evidence to substantiate that theory. This man said he knew nothing about it; that he told them the truth; that he had been there, but that he was some distance away when the shooting took place. And they swore at him and said: "If you don't come through we will shoot you," or something of this kind, and shoved a revolver in his face, and they proceeded to beat him up.

Now, I believe that that was not—that it was planned—of course, it was planned to take him out of jail and treat him that way. Not only that, it was proved conclusively at the trial that they had a piece of heavy rubber hose, which one of them took from a suit case, which was conclusive to me that they carried the implement along with them for the purpose of using it on these men.

When this man told his story Sunday morning, I telegraphed to the district attorney at Yuba County, at least telephoned, called up his office and got into communication with his deputy and told him what had happened. Mr. Stanwood—I believe is the district attorney's name, I believe it is Stanwood—was not available, and I talked with his deputy and told him what had happened, and requested either at that time or subsequently, either the sheriff of Yuba County or the district attorney's office to send the sheriff himself to get this man. The detectives wished to take him from Artemas, take away from there this Alfred Nelson—he was afraid, he told me he was, and his appearance supported that statement. And I did not wish these detectives, these men who had abused him, to take him away from our county. However, they did not send a regular officer for this man, and Mr. Mundell, who was the manager of the Burns agency on this coast at that time, came and got that man and took him away against my protest and against my wishes. However, the man was treated all right on the way up there, so he told me subsequently, so there was nothing wrong about that.

Now, Mr. Mundell or no one connected with the Burns agency, when this was called to their attention, ever said to me that this man had exceeded his authority at all. They proceed to justify and defend his actions, and to decry and impute all sorts of things to me.

I would say that in my opinion a great many public officials are overawed by a private detective agency. They lose their moral courage. Most men have some things about their private lives, or some things that they have been doing on the sly, that they don't care for the public to know. And for that reason I think that there are very few of them who care to run up against a powerful private detective agency. And for that reason they have had rather the whip hand. And they have been accustomed to calling down and going roughshod over public officials. That has been the policy of those people in this State. And in fact with this particular agency before this thing happened, I had a similar experience. They claimed that I was crooked, because I had dismissed a case; and that they were going to show me, and told me that they represented the American Bankers' Association, and all these things, and they would stand me on my head, and I don't know what they were not going to do, and talked to me in that manner—of course, it was over the telephone. And I talked back pretty vigorously myself.

Now, this man was—this Cradlebaugh was tried and he was convicted by a jury. He was sentenced to one year in the county jail and he was fined a thousand dollars, of which we got the thousand dollars—although he didn't have it—got it out of the bail money. They forgot to take it down in time.

Now, when Cradlebaugh had served half his sentence, I, in conjunction with the sheriff of Contra Costa County, admitted him to parole, as county parole commissioners. We treated him just the same as we would treat anyone else, no better or no worse. There was some criticism on the part of some people that we should not have paroled him. But we did. We treated him the same as anyone else. He behaved himself when he was in the county jail, and his conduct was such that he was entitled to parole. Now, that is about all there is to that case.

Chairman WALSH. Mr. Garretson would like to ask some questions.

Commissioner GARRETSON. Mr. McKenzie, you stated in the commencement of your testimony very succinctly, the question that was universally asked by the laboring man as to whether or not if the proprietor had done the shooting instead of an agitator having done it, would he have received the same treatment. What is your answer to that question?

Mr. McKENZIE. Well, personally I don't know whether I would have the moral courage to stand up against public opinion.

We are all comparatively weak; and men are in office, and they go out and ask people for votes, and they have their ear to the ground a good deal of the time, and are influenced by public opinion.

Commissioner GARRETSON. Do you really believe from your experience, not only as prosecutor, but as a lawyer and as a citizen, that there is any equality before the law of a man with a million and a man with a penny?

Mr. McKENZIE. With some people there is; yes.

Commissioner GARRETSON. As a general proposition, in the treatment he receives?

Mr. McKENZIE (after a pause). Well, the law is all right.

Commissioner GARRETSON. Oh! I won't question that. It is the application that I am talking about, that I want the opinion regarding.

Mr. McKENZIE. No.

Commissioner GARRETSON. There is not?

Mr. McKENZIE. No; I think there is not.

Commissioner GARRETSON. Well, now, predicated upon that, I assume that you have had a good deal of personal contact with men of all classes.

Mr. McKENZIE. Yes, sir; I have.

Commissioner GARRETSON. And especially with the substratum?

Mr. McKENZIE. Yes; with all kinds.

Commissioner GARRETSON. And you have found the same belief that you have expressed here, almost universal among those men?

Mr. McKENZIE. Yes. They don't express it exactly in the way I do.

Commissioner GARRETSON. No; but their belief is virtually what you have expressed, no matter how crudely they may express it?

Mr. McKENZIE. Well, yes. Now, here is another thing. They regard what we call these soap-box orators——

Commissioner GARRETSON. Yes.

Mr. McKENZIE (continuing). Just the same as this audience or the general public, or the educated public would regard this commission.

Commissioner GARRETSON. Yes.

Mr. McKENZIE. The general public believes that this commission is honestly endeavoring to do something to make the world a little better, or to improve conditions. Well, now, these other fellows, they have faith in these soap-box orators.

Commissioner GARRETSON. Yes.

Mr. McKENZIE. And they believe that they are trying to do something for them, and consequently when you interfere with them, why, they resent it.

Commissioner GARRETSON. They regard it as an invasion of their rights?

Mr. McKENZIE. Of their rights; that is it, exactly.

Now, I would wish to say this, that I belong to no labor organizations, or no Socialist Party, that I was brought up very conservatively and am somewhat conservative, but that my association and business training and so on has brought me into contact with all classes of people, and probably the fact that I have a large family of my own that I know full well—I am not a dreamer—will have to go out into the world to make their own living, that they can get nothing from me, makes me have more sympathy for the working class than the average man. Now, that is——

Commissioner GARRETSON. Now, one other question, Mr. McKenzie: You take the very man that you have described, who feels that his rights have been invaded, been circumscribed of either the right of free speech or of free existence in the person of even the soap-box orator. Now, is or isn't in your opinion that man a recruit to the army of unrest?

Mr. McKENZIE. I am satisfied of that. I am satisfied that every man that was treated ill by—that there was no use talking to him and asking him to respect the law. That would be foolish and idle, and no man with any sense would attempt to do it.

Commissioner GARRETSON. In other words, a man who suffers from the law becomes a hater of the law?

Mr. McKENZIE. Becomes a hater of the law, that is absolutely true.

Commissioner GARRETSON. That is all.

Commissioner WEINSTOCK. I take it, Mr. McKenzie, that your criticisms are not against the law, but against the administration of the law?

Mr. McKENZIE. Well, there are so many things against the administration of the law, among the agricultural classes, among the farmers, that the laboring union men are intolerant, they so speak of them and think of them. While, on the other hand, the man that has inherited a little property from his father is the most intolerant man in the world as a general thing.

Now, there is intolerance on both hands. I believe if these people would get together and discuss these matters, become better acquainted, respect the opinions of each other, they would get along very much better. That is the difficulty, they don't understand each other.

A man will be summoned on the jury. He will say yes; he is in favor of labor unions, he has no objection to them, but what he has in mind is that they must conduct themselves the way he says they should conduct themselves. That is his idea of being fair to them.

On the other hand, the labor union man says he has no antagonism against agriculturists and the farmers, or the employer, but that they must conduct themselves the way he says that they say he shall conduct himself. That is the condition that exists.

Commissioner WEINSTOCK. Your remedy then, Mr. McKenzie, I understand is this: Greater mutual contact and a higher degree of mutual tolerance, is that it?

Mr. McKENZIE. Well, now, that is one thing.

Now, Mr. Commissioner, there is a problem confronting us. The question is this, whether we are to follow the Darwinian theory of the survival of the fittest, or whether we are to become our brother's keeper. Now, it is either one or the other.

Now, in labor unions they fix a standard wage, as I understand it, and that was something that—that a man who can't do as much as another man can, receives the same compensation. Now, that is the principle that each man is his brother's keeper. And there is a principle that is there that it seems to me must be followed by society in general, and that is the difficulty with us, that if we come into this world endowed mentally and physically and we go out into the world and surpass our brother, we are all swelled up over it, so that there is room for a man who is industrious and sober and capable. We are brought into the world with certain defects, and we can't help that. But this man who is somewhat defective—that is, not mentally—may be making a greater fight than the other fellow to get along, and consequently he is entitled to a place in the world; or else you can take the other theory of the survival of the fittest and you crowd him to the wall. Now, it is either one or the other.

Mr. THOMPSON. Do they periodically vag at Martinez and other towns in your county, do you know?

Mr. McKENZIE. Not since the doing away with the fee system. When we had the fee system they would pay men to come into the county to be vagged; at least they said they did.

Mr. THOMPSON. That is, arrest men for vagging?

Mr. McKENZIE. Arrest men. Now, since they have done away with the fee system and the constables and the justices of the peace are paid a fixed salary we never have any vagging, because they get nothing for it. There are no vags arrested in our county.

Chairman WALSH. That is all, thank you.

Call your next.

Mr. McKenzie. I may say this, that this Alfred Nelson was not arrested on a charge of vagrancy. Furtherfore, the warrant was a John Doe warrant, which of course would keep the matter secret to a certain extent. And the charge was inciting a riot, which is a misdemeanor in this State.

Furthermore, the action in that case indicates that they were trying to keep the matter secret. In fact, I know that to be a fact that these men were taken around from place to place, and they didn't want the I. W. W.'s to know where they were, so that they could not get them out.

Now, that is the fact in this case.

I believe that these officers were acting conscientiously. I believe that the district attorney of Yuba County acted as he thought right and proper.

Commissioner Garretson. One question. We have had a statement of two members of the bar on these facts, and I shall be glad to have an expression from you, if you feel free to make it. Under the California Code must a man be brought to a speedy trial?

Mr. McKenzie. Yes; he must. Now, if I had nothing else to prosecute these fellows on, I would have prosecuted him for that. And I do not know but what he could have been prosecuted for kidnapping. There are plenty of ways to prosecute these men, if the prosecutor wishes to prosecute.

Mr. Thompson. Mr. Lewis.

TESTIMONY OF MR. AUSTIN LEWIS.

Mr. Thompson. Give us your name, address, and your occupation.

Mr. Lewis. Austin Lewis, Oakland, attorney.

Mr. Thompson. You are the attorney for the defense in the Ford-Suhr cases?

Mr. Lewis. One of the attorneys.

Mr. Thompson. One of the attorneys?

Mr. Lewis. Yes, sir.

Mr. Thompson. Will you state that case and the surrounding circumstances as you view them?

Mr. Lewis. Now, that would be a little long. I would like to know how to divide that. Supposing I take and testify first with regards to the circumstances attending the riot, the preliminary conditions.

Mr. Thompson. That is all right.

Mr. Lewis. This case at Wheatland was peculiarly an interesting case from a sociological standpoint in that it is one of the few cases on record in which agricultural laborers have spontaneously combined to improve their conditions.

The Wheatland case stands on a par in agricultural development with the Lawrence case in Massachusetts, and the Little Falls and all those factory-cases which have developed a mass action, which mass action is typical of the new activities of labor organization in this country, and not only in this country, but elsewhere. So the Wheatland case may be regarded, sociologically speaking, as a typical case. With the permission of the commission, I will enlarge a little upon that.

Here we got a hop ranch 150 miles away from San Francisco. Advertisements were sent out, painting the conditions of labor on that hop ranch as being attractive. And in response to those advertisements a large number of people, some 2,400 or 2,700 people came to get work upon that hop ranch. Now, Mr. Carlin stated in his testimony that more people came to the hop ranch than Mr. Durst had anticipated. I beg to differ from Mr. Carlin in that respect. Mr. Durst wanted more people there than he could find work for, because Mr. Durst worked under a bonus system, the rationale of which was as follows: A man went to work for and he got a dollar per hundred pounds of hops picked, with a 10-cent bonus; but that 10-cent bonus was only paid if the man remained at work the whole of the time that the hops were picking. For example, if a man went to work on Monday, if he picked 100 pounds of hops he had a dollar coming, and 10 cents bonus—Tuesday, Wednesday, Thursday, Friday, Saturday. At the end of the week he would have $6 coming for his 600 pounds, and he would have 60 cents at 10 cents a day bonus.

Now, supposing he was hired on Saturday, and did not like the job, did not like the conditions, he could go to Mr. Durst and draw down his pay; but he wouldn't draw $6.60. He would only draw $6. The 60 cents was forfeited, because he did not work the entire time of the hop picking. Now, when you consider that some 1,800 to 2,000 people were engaged in hop picking, and that even if there was only a bonus of 10 cents a day on each one of those people, it would amount to a very considerable sum that was actually stolen from them in the course of the hop-picking season. Well, these people came together. When they got to the Durst ranch they found the conditions, which I need not go into, I think you gentlemen are familiar with them. Mr. Parker made his report to you with regard to it——

Chairman WALSH. Does that report fairly cover it?

Mr. LEWIS. That report is an excellent report of the conditions on the Durst ranch.

Now, on Saturday—conditions grew worse and worse, and the children were covered with filth, and everything was in an intolerably insanitary condition; the camp was infested with flies, the people had not sufficient water to drink. As a result of that, what could only be described as a spontaneous action on the part of those people occurred. They held a mass meeting. In that mass meeting they drew up their list of grievances, and at that mass meeting there spoke Ford, who was a speaker. Suhr never spoke. An Assyrian speaker; a Spanish speaker, a Greek speaker, and various other nationalities, some seven nationalities. The action of the Japanese on that occasion was very remarkable. The Japanese came to Ford and Suhr, who were practically the leaders of that movement, and the practical leaders; that is, they were the intelligent American brains that conducted that movement. That is why they are in jail. The Japanese came and said: "Now, if we side with you boys and associate with you, we shall probably get you into trouble with union labor in the State of California, because union labor in the State of California does not like us Japanese. But we do not like these conditions on this ranch and we are not going to stand them, and we are going to move." And they did. They moved in a body. And ever since then, for the last three months they have published an advertisement in their Japanese paper calling upon all Japanese to abstain from taking a part in the hop industry until the grievances of which the hop pickers complain are ended, and until these two men that are in jail are released.

Now, on that Saturday the meeting was held when those grievances were formulated. Mr. Durst himself was present at that meeting. He said: "I can't talk to all of you men at once. You will appoint a committee to come to see me." And they appointed the committee, and they met Mr. Durst next morning. Now, Mr. Durst, as Mr. Carlin says, did make certain concessions, but by no means the concessions which have been mentioned. For example, Mr. Durst said that he would provide proper toilet accommodations. Well, the health inspector, besides Mr. Parker's commission, investigated afterwards, after this was all over, and found that the toilet accommodations had not been provided. Water was not provided in the field, and various other grievances were not remedied. But the question immediately came up on the matter of wages. And Ford said: "If you boys want to work for a dollar a day, you can work for a dollar. I won't. We want a dollar and a quarter per hundred pounds." Thereupon, the camp was picketed. The public meeting was held on the public place, which was hired by the hop pickers for their own use. The meeting, as the sheriff testified, was entirely peaceable. The meeting was invaded by a band of armed men, some of whom were not too sober, and shooting occurred which has given this affair all the publicity.

My opinion, as an investigator of social phenomena for about 25 years, is that the movement on the Durst ranch was a spontaneous movement; that it was not a movement due to agitation in any shape or form, because there could not have been any agitation. One very reputable witness has testified that there were 27 languages spoken on the ranch. The people did not begin to come in on the ranch until Thursday, and the public meeting was held on Saturday. So there was no room for agitation. It was a purely spontaneous uprising, and it was an uprising—a psychological protest against factory conditions of hop picking; that is, I regard the hop field as an open-air factory and not as, typically, an agricultural pursuit. And consequently you have got the factory psychology instead of the agricultural psychology, and that is the natural result; and the emotional result is the result of the nervous impact of the exceedingly irritating and intolerable conditions under which those people worked at that time.

Now, following that, after the trouble, the drag net, so to speak, was put out. Men were arrested incontinently, without reason in a great many cases; they were not only arrested in that way, but they were shut up and put away, so as not to be discovered. Men were in prison in Sacramento, in Oroville, in Yuba·

City, in Marysville, in Chico, and a man we found in Martinez in connection with this affair which occurred at Marysville.

.. Commissioner GARRETSON. Were those men held incommunicado?

: Mr. LEWIS. They were held incommunicado. It was almost impossible to discover the whereabouts of these prisoners. Had it not been for the fact that a small group of men in Sacramento discovered the whereabouts of Ford, I doubt very much whether those men would ever have had a chance of a fair defense in any way.

When I took charge of the case in September, or the last of August, we found that condition of affairs. Men were held detinue in many cases without complaint being lodged against them; in some cases the complaints were lodged against them; and in one case brought before the magistrate, when we sued out a· writ· of habeas corpus, we were threatened by the district attorney. He was discharged and then they placed a charge of murder against him. In some cases the district·attorney did place charges of murder against them, and did swear to charges of murder against them, although he himself was not present at Wheatland, and not personally cognizant of the occurrences at Wheatland. Men were brought up on preliminary examination. Some were discharged on preliminary examination. Two men, Beck and·Bagan, of whom Mr. Carlin spoke to you of·this morning, the grand jury refused to indict. But the·district attorney .himself swore a charge of murder against them and placed them on trial for their lives, although, as I say, the district attorney was not present at Wheatland at that time. In fact, speaking broadly, we found the whole course of justice thoroughly obstructed. We found every impediment placed in our·way to·the discovery of the whereabouts of prisoners. and to giving them a fair, full, impartial hearing at an early date.

We found the law of the State of California with regard to having the prisoners given a speedy hearing violated repeatedly. And, as far as the administrative end the Wheatland case is concerned, if you want my opinion on it, I consider it a scandal.

Now, to come down to another aspect: We found that not only while this was being done were men· not protected by the district attorney—helpless men a hundred and fifty miles away from anywhere that had no friends—not only did they get no counsel or friendly advice, but innocent men who were away from the scene of action were taken into jail, and, as Mr. McKenzie said, were maltreated by detectives, so that one man, Johnson—Allen Johnson—went to the lunatic asylum. Another man, Nels Nielson, whose arm was blown off, hanged himself. All down the line we found a tale of treachery and brutality to innocent men, whose misfortune it was to be migratory laborers. The general question came up in the course of the examination as to the treatment of migratory laborers.· And if you will pardon me injecting my personal opinion there, and I am saying so after considerable experience in investigation, I think that migratory laborers in the State of California are treated with a calloused indifference both to the law and to ordinary elemental justice. They are incontinently arrested, thrown into filthy, fetid jails without any power of recourse, and illy treated while in jail, and kicked out of jail. And any man who has made a study of this question and followed it will corroborate what I have said.

I am sure I could call scores, literally scores, of men in to substantiate my statement in that regard. Yet I don't think that the Durst ranch was exceptional; I don't think the Durst ranch was exceptionally bad. I don't think that obloquy should rest·on the shoulders of Mr. Durst in this matter. As I think the Durst ranch was not exceptionally bad, so do I also think the administration of justice in Marysville was not exceptionally bad. I think that it was typical of the attitude of district.attorneys to migratory labor throughout the State of California, and is productive of the intense feeling of hatred which exists in the minds of the migratory laborers to the administration of law in the State of California.

Now, while this was going on, another thing more dangerous, in my opinion, occurred. That was the use of private detectives in jail. The sheriffs allow—and this seems to be a general rule—the sheriffs allow the private detectives to come into the jail and to interview the prisoners, and indeed, in some instances, to maltreat prisoners in their own jails.

Now, let us take the case of Fresno, the case of Suhr in Fresno. I can speak of that in detail, because I went to see the sheriff of Fresno only a week or two ago, and went over the whole situation with the sheriff. So I know both sides of it, and can be fair to it. The sheriff said, "Suhr was not ill-treated in my jail." I said, "If that is the case, Sheriff, I want it to be known, because I don't want you to be falsely accused." I said, "Just what did happen in your jail?" He said, "This is what happened." He said, "They brought Suhr off the train to my jail aᵌ Fresno. They said 'We want to put this man over for the night; he is tired of traveling, and we want to put him over for the night.' " So he said, "Take him in." Then he said, "I wish you would take me up to the room." They took him into a room, and into the wall of that room they inserted a dictograph. Then they took another man and put him in the same room with Suhr. And that man lay with Suhr that night and disturbed him and kept him awake and proceeded to talk,,all the time the dictograph recording for the district attorney of Yuba County and the detective agency, the conversations which Suhr had with that man in that jail at that time. Now, I am only giving you that example. Mr. Royce knows more details, more close personal details, of the matter than I do. And that is typical. It is not exceptional. It is typical of the treatment to which those people are subjected at the hands of the authorities in the State of California. Of course ·with regard to the case itself, that is a matter of record, and it would not be professional for me to go into it, and I would not care to do that,

Mr. THOMPSON. Mr. Lewis, do you share the opinion of· Mr.·McKenzie· that the hiding of these men in various parts of the State was a justifiable hiding?

Mr. LEWIS. No, sir.

Mr. THOMPSON. To keep them from the I. W. W.?

Mr. LEWIS. No, sir; I do not justify it on any grounds.·

Mr. THOMPSON. Is there any law of this State which warrants the officials in doing that?

Mr. LEWIS. No, sir; it is purely extra legal.

Mr. THOMPSON. What is the name of the county where the men were put in prison under an affidavit by the State's attorney?

Mr. LEWIS. Why, Yuba County—two men were put on trial for their lives on the sworn complaint of the district attorney.

Mr. THOMPSON. That they had committed murder?

Mr. LEWIS. Yes, sir.

Mr. THOMPSON. And he was not a witness of the fact?

Mr. LEWIS. Yes,.sir; he was not a witness.

Mr. THOMPSON. Does the law of California permit that to ·be done?

Mr. LEWIS. In my judgment the law of California does not·permit it to be done.

Mr. THOMPSON. In your view that was an illegal action by the State's attorney?

Mr. LEWIS. In my view it was an action which strained the law to its very limits.

Mr. THOMPSON. In this whole proceeding, which seemed to· have arisen very quickly and seems to have been met by an equally quick action on the part of the various authorities, and particularly by the work apparently of private detective agencies, who do you hold responsible for this action of. arresting these men and separating them in the different counties of the State and holding men illegally?

Mr. LEWIS. Why the person I hold immediately responsible is Mr. Stanwood, district attorney of Yuba County. The people that I hold secondarily responsible is the public opinion of Yuba County, in support of which—in accordance with which Mr. Stanwood undoubtedly acted.

Mr. THOMPSON. Well, do you know whether he was the one who employed this agency or not?

Mr. LEWIS. I think he will admit that he was.

Mr. THOMPSON. What opinion do you hold with reference to the employment of private detective agencies in cases of this kind, and also in general cases of industrial trouble?

Mr. LEWIS. I think they ought to be abolished; they are a menace.

Mr. THOMPSON. Do you know whether such things are done in other countries or not?

Mr. LEWIS. I have never heard of it being done, and I could pretty positively testify it is done nowhere else in the world.

Mr. THOMPSON. That is all, Mr. Chairman.

Chairman WALSH. Do you want to ask any questions, Mr. Weinstock?

Mr. WEINSTOCK. Yes.

Chairman WALSH. Mr. Weinstock.

Commissioner WEINSTOCK. I find, Mr. Lewis, that there are some who are under the impression that these two men were prosecuted for being agitators. There are some who are under the impression that they were prosecuted for conspiracy. And there are some who are under the impression that they were prosecuted for resorting to violence. Now, what are the facts?

Mr. LEWIS. The facts are that the State bases its charge against them on the ground of conspiracy, that Mr. Carlin's basis of his charge against them is that of agitation, and that public opinion is left to guess with regard to the rest.

Commissioner WEINSTOCK. Well, what crime are they charged with?

Mr. LEWIS. They are charged with the crime of murder.

Commissioner WEINSTOCK. Then, they were prosecuted for murder?

Mr. LEWIS. They were prosecuted for murder, but the theory is that they used language which contributed to murder. There is no contention on the part of the prosecution that either of these men killed Mr. Manwell. In fact, there is no contention on the part of the prosecution that Ford ever had a gun. And they only base their contention with regard to Suhr having a gun on certain alleged declarations.

Commissioner WEINSTOCK. Well, under the law, Mr. Lewis, if I incite you to commit murder am I guilty of a crime?

Mr. LEWIS. Oh, yes; if you did incite me; yes.

Commissioner WEINSTOCK. What would be my crime?

Mr. LEWIS. Well, it might be conspiracy to murder, possibly it might be incitement to murder. If you took active part in it you would be a principal.

Commissioner WEINSTOCK. They were charged, then, with the crime of murder, because it was alleged that they had incited others to commit murder?

Mr. LEWIS. No; that wasn't categorically put. They couldn't put it that way. The theory of the prosecution was that their language was such as led ultimately to the murder of Mr. Manwell. They don't claim that they told anybody to kill Mr. Manwell. They don't claim that they told anybody to kill an officer.

Commissioner WEINSTOCK. That is all.

Chairman WALSH. Anything else? Commissioner Garretson?

Commissioner GARRETSON. No.

Chairman WALSH. Mr. Lennon.

Commissioner LENNON. I just want to ask one question: Does the law provide that criminal trials may be had either upon indictment by the grand jury or upon information?

Mr. LEWIS. Yes, sir.

Commissioner LENNON. That is so in some States.

Mr. LEWIS. That is it.

Commissioner LENNON. Yes.

Chairman WALSH. One minute, please. I want to ask you a question. You say that you have studied these conditions generally prior to this time?

Mr. LEWIS. Yes, sir; for a good many years.

Chairman WALSH. Have you observed the efforts or anything of these occasional workers to organize for the purpose of bettering their conditions?

Mr. LEWIS. Very closely.

Chairman WALSH. I would like you to briefly give a description of that development as you have observed it in the State of California, bringing it down to this attempt, if it be such, to organize by the I. W. W.

Mr. LEWIS. The development in the State of California of the migratory worker is a very interesting history, about seven years ago. We first of all got movements, small movements of the migratory workers to better the conditions. These took the form ultimately of the organization of locals, largely of the Industrial Workers. At the same time the American Federation of Labor, as Mr. Dale has already described, was endeavoring to organize the migratory laborer in the American Federation of Labor. And largely owing to the agitation of the American Federation of Labor in that respect, and the able articles and papers written, and the necessity of organizing the unskilled, together with the agitation of I. W. W. agitators and Socialists, a definite movement was launched tending to the organization of migratory unskilled labor in the State of California. That took up certain strategic positions. It did not prosper in the towns where the American Federation of Labor was strongly organized. But it cropped up first noticeably at Fresno, where there was a long and bitterly fought free-speech fight. Now, that free-speech fight was for the right of promulgating the doctrines of the new industrialists in the streets of Fresno, which is a strategic point for industrial labor, as it is at the foot of the San Joaquin Valley, and there are large ranches around and large construction works and those things, and there is a continual. stream of migratory labor coming in and going out of Fresno. That was an exceedingly bitter fight, with a great deal of trouble and imprisonment. and torture and that sort of thing. Then came succeeding that a fight at San Diego, which is historic, where there was a great deal also of torture and suffering. The result of these fights was that the tenets of the industrial union, or the Industrial Workers, became more popularized and their songs became known, which was the reason that such a large portion of the audience on the Durst ranch were able to sing the song called "Mr. Block," which they were all singing at the time that the sheriff's posse came in.

The I. W. W. locals were formed, as you may say, down the backbone of the State—Reading, Sacramento, Fresno, Bakersfield, Los Angeles, San Diego, San Francisco, Oakland, so on. From these locals there went out a continual stream of literature, and some of these locals employ what are called camp delegates. Now, a camp delegate is a man who goes from the local. onto the job. That is the essence of their form of organization, and that must be comprehended to really understand what occurred at Wheatland. These organizers do not organize like an A. F. of L. organizer who has headquarters in a town, as Mr. Dale described this morning. But they send their camp delegates on the job and these camp delegates go onto the job and get their members on the job, and forward contributions from the members to the headquarters in towns like Fresno and Sacramento; and that town is a central local from which radiate emissaries on the. job. the camp delegates, who are continually organizing on the job. Now, as a result of that, of course, there was a very widespread propaganda of what you might call industrial unionism. For instance, one of the professors at Stanford University, of the economics department, informed me that it was very noticeable to him that the tramps who camped for the night under the bridges in San Mateo and Santa Clara Counties would sing I. W. W. songs in the evening while they were camping there. Then they carried out masses of literature continually from their local headquarters. The result was that there was a permeation of the mass to a certain extent by this I. W. W. doctrine, at least a sufficiency of a permeation to enable them to take the leadership in a matter like that of the Durst ranch.

Chairman WALSH. Is there anything going on at the present time in the way of organization, or attempted organization. of these incidental workers?

Mr. LEWIS. Continually going on.

Chairman WALSH. In what way is the propaganda being spread at the present time?

Mr. LEWIS. Why, the propaganda of course is conducted through the two channels which I have mentioned, and is conducted in the regular way, although the educational, the purely what you might call doctrinaire side of the question, is being pushed more and more into the background, and the camp delegates are being used more and more freely and actual organization on the job proceeds more steadily.

Chairman WALSH. You heard the testimony of Mr. McKenzie?

Mr. LEWIS. Yes.

Chairman WALSH. I noticed you were sitting there.

Mr. LEWIS. Yes, sir.

Chairman WALSH. And the answers to the questions of Commissioner Garretson to the effect that he didn't believe that there was equality before the law, as I gathered it, but that public opinion was so strong in certain places that officials wavered in their duty?

Mr. LEWIS. Yes.

Chairman WALSH. Have you noticed in the trial of the cases, vagrancy cases and the like, this expression of class prejudice? For instance, if a jury was composed entirely of farmers, would a man of the class you have mentioned be insured a fair trial before that jury?

Mr. LEWIS. No, sir. Why, the matter of class prejudice is taken for granted. There is not a lawyer that is engaged in this call of cases but knows it and appeals to the class prejudice on one side or the other.

Chairman WALSH. Is there more or less solidarity of class feeling between workers in the State of California whether unorganized or such men as organized in the A. F. of L. and other organizations?

Mr. Lewis. Yes, sir; and very fast growing. As an example of this we may say that the support which the Industrial Workers have received in this fight has come from the American Federation of Labor, which theoretically is opposed to the Industrial Workers.

Chairman Walsh. In the qualification and selection of the jurors, is there a fair proposition of the workers who reside in the locality—does a fair proportion of the workers who reside in the locality appear upon the jury?

Mr. Lewis. No, sir; it can't, because there is a property qualification for jurors in the State of California.

Chairman Walsh. How many people are there in this county in which these defendants were tried, Ford and Suhr?

Mr. Lewis. Oh, I could not say how large the county is.

Chairman Walsh. Approximately?

Mr. Lewis. I don't know, 20,000—10,000 in the county.

Mr. Carlin. Forty-eight hundred voters.

Mr. Lewis. Forty-eight hundred voters. Thank you.

Chairman Walsh. Forty-eight hundred voters in the county?

Mr. Lewis. Yes, sir.

Chairman Walsh. How many were competent for jury service in the 4,800? Commissioner Garretson. On the property qualification.

Mr. Lewis. I could not tell you; I wouldn't know that.

Mr. Carlin. About 2,000.

Mr. Lewis. About 2,000 Mr. Carlin says, and he knows.

Chairman Walsh. I believe that is all. Thank you.

Commissioner Weinstock. One minute.

Chairman Walsh. Commissioner Weinstock would like to ask you some questions.

Commissioner Weinstock. You made a statement a few moments ago that the American Federation of Labor is opposed to the I. W. W. Can you tell this commission, if you know why the American Federation of Labor is opposed to the I. W. W.?

Mr. Lewis. Why, yes, sir; it is easy enough. The American Federation of Labor is opposed to the I. W. W. on two main lines. First of all, the American Federation of Labor admits that labor is a commodity, and consequently the American Federation of Labor is organized for getting the best price for the commodity, labor power, in the market at this time.

The I. W. W. is a revolutionary organization which denies the commodity side of labor and regards labor as a factor in production and is opposed to the present state of society and consequently the political organization constructed on it.

Commissioner Weinstock. You mean, then, the American Federation of Labor is not revolutionary, and the I. W. W. is revolutionary?

Mr. Lewis. I am sorry to say that is so.

Commissioner Weinstock. That is the distinction between them?

Mr. Lewis. I think so.

Commissioner Weinstock. The American Federation of Labor wants to better existing conditions in accordance with existing laws, and the I. W. W. wants to revolutionize the whole social condition?

Mr. Lewis. That is not quite a fair way of putting it.

Commissioner Weinstock. Put it your own way.

Mr. Lewis. The American Federation of Labor organizes men in their special crafts for the purpose of selling that craft labor for the best price possible in the market. The I. W. W. want to organize the mass of labor in antagonism to the existing capitalistic classes with the ultimate object of abolishing the existing capitalistic classes.

Commissioner Weinstock. Were you here yesterday, Mr. Lewis, when Mr. Speed testified?

Mr. Lewis. No, sir; I was not.

Commissioner Weinstock. And his final statement substantially was this—and I want to make sure he represents I .W. W. sentiment more than his own opinion, and I take it you are thoroughly familiar with I. W. W. sentiment—his final statement was to the effect that the I. W. W. attitude is that might is right; that anything that is good for labor is right, and anything that is bad for labor is wrong. Does that express the I. W. W. sentiment as you understand the I. W. W. sentiment?

Mr. Lewis. I think that is rather crude. but quite fair.

Commissioner Weinstock. I gather further from Mr. Speed's statement that the I. W. W. is opposed to entering into agreements with employers, and if that ngreement exists to break it if it suits the convenience of the workers to break it, regardless of their obligations. That is, that they don't respect their agreements.

Mr. LEWIS. In other words, they consider such agreement an armed truce.

Commissioner WEINSTOCK. Therefore they feel themselves at liberty to break it whenever it suits their convenience?

Mr. LEWIS. Yes sir; they regard it as an incident in warfare and not as a contract.

Commissioner WEINSTOCK. That is all.

Commissioner GARRETSON. One means of fighting the devil with fire?

Mr. LEWIS. Yes, sir.

Commissioner GARRETSON. My friend on the right has interpreted your opinion, and I want to see if I can correctly interpret another. Do you believe any form of organization among the class of labor that is engaged in agriculture can be successfully perfected unless you carry it to him?

Mr. LEWIS. No, sir; you can not.

Commmissioner GARRETSON. The machinery, that is.

Mr. LEWIS. You have got to go on the job.

Commissioner GARRETSON. Next, do I gather correctly your belief is this: It matters comparatively little by what name a movement may be called as long as it furnishes a mass form of expression.

Mr. LEWIS. That is the thought. I don't care what name you call it as long as you have the mass form of expression.

Commissioner GARRETSON. That is all.

Chairman WALSH. Commissioner Lennon would like to interrogate you, he says.

Commissioner LENNON. Where has the American Federation of Labor declared that they look upon labor as a commodity itself and should be so treated?

Mr. LEWIS. In every statement of the American Federation of Labor you find a demand for a fair day's wages for a fair day's work. They carry that on their banners in all parades. That is nothing but asking for a fair price for their commodity, to wit, the labor power.

Commissioner LENNON. What has been the field of activity of the American Federation of Labor in the trade-union movement—the general trade movement of the world?

Mr. LEWIS. What do you mean by field of activity?

Commissioner LENNON. As to the matter of protection of the right of labor because they are human beings and not being treated as commodities.

Mr. LEWIS. All right. Now, you have opened up a big question there. The American Federation of Labor and the English labor movement and the German labor movement and the French labor movement have all taken precisely the same lines, with slight variations but the same general line. They all organize the crafts for the specific interests of those crafts, and where they have taken the side of human rights in the broad sense they have taken them as liberals, using the term in the broad sense, and not as labor unions.

Commissioner LENNON. Well, they have taken—that is your answer?

Mr. LEWIS. Yes, sir. In other words, to put the thing sociologically and technically, the aspect of organized labor is petit bourgeois.

Commissioner LENNON. Upon what hypothesis do you make the claim that the American Federation is practically a craft organization?

Mr. LEWIS. On the construction of the American Federation itself; on the component crafts which go to make it up.

Commissioner LENNON. Are you aware of the fact that nearly one-third of the Federation is on industrial lines?

Mr. LEWIS. What do you mean by on industrial lines?

Commissioner LENNON. I mean where the industry is being combined in one organization; that the work is going on from time to time of consolidating unions in industries.

Mr. LEWIS. That makes no difference. That makes no difference. As a matter of fact, if you break down your compartments and make it a little larger it only covers the same lines. It is still craft lines. I am not using the word craft in contradistinction to industry or craft organization in contradistinction to industrial organization; I am using the word craft as skilled labor in contradistinction to unskilled or common labor.

Commissioner LENNON. Would you then indicate that it is your belief that the trade-union movement does not try to organize unskilled labor?

Mr. LEWIS. In my belief, the trade-union has not tried until recent years, and very recent years.

. Commissioner LENNON. That is true. We admit it.

Mr. LEWIS. And is now trying in vain.

Commissioner LENNON. That is all.

Commissioner WEINSTOCK. Just one more explanation. You pointed out that the American Federation of Labor seemingly regarded labor as a commodity by virtue of its public statement that it stands for a fair day's wage for a fair day's work?

Mr. LEWIS. Yes, sir.

Commissioner WEINSTOCK. And that the I. W. W.'s are not in harmony with that sentiment?

Mr. LEWIS. Yes, sir.

Commissioner WEINSTOCK. Well, may we infer from that, then, that the I. W. W. stands for a fair day's wage for an unfair days' work?

Mr. LEWIS. It stands for as much wages as we can get for as little work as possible.

Commissioner WEINSTOCK. We are to understand, then, Mr. Lewis, that the purpose of the worker in the I. W. W. is to be as absolutely unfair to the employer as possible?

Mr. LEWIS. The purpose of the worker in the I. W. W. is the abolition of the wage system, no matter who gets squeezed.

Commissioner WEINSTOCK. By what means?

Mr. ᴸEWIS. By such means as may suggest themselves.

Commissioner WEINSTOCK. By the use of force, if necessary?

Mr. LEWIS. That depends on what you mean by force. Force is of various kinds. There is the force of the militia and the force of starvation, which is the other side. To starve a man to death is using force against him as much as bayoneting him.

Commissioner WEINSTOCK. Did Mr. Speed in his statement yesterday express the ꞆI. W. W. sentiment as you understand it when he said that if the I. W. W. had the force and numbers they would take possession of the Union Iron Works and turn out the owners without compensation?

Mr. LEWIS. Why, sure. To the victor belongs the spoils.

Commissioner WEINSTOCK. In other words, you would justify force if you have the force?

Mr. LEWIS. Why, of course; in a state of war force is justified.

Commissioner WEINSTOCK. That is all.

Chairman WALSH. Commissioner O'Connell has a few questions to ask you.

Commissioner O'CONNELL. Are you a member of the I. W. W.?

Mr. LEWIS. No, sir; I am ineligible.

Commissioner O'CONNELL. You are not eligible?

Mr. LEWIS. No, sir.

Commissioner O'CONNELL. What is the eligibility?

Mr. LEWIS. Handwork or wagework. I am a practicing attorney.

Commissioner O'CONNELL. That is not hand work or wage work?

Mr. LEWIS. No, sir; it is not wage work.

Commissioner O'CONNELL. Mr. Commissioner Weinstock asked you a minute ago what the A. F. of L. position was against the I. W. W.?

Mr. LEWIS. Yes, sir.

Commissioner O'CONNELL. I don't suppose you are authorized to speak for the American Federation of Labor as to its position?

Mr. LEWIS. I am not authorized by the American Federation of Labor to do that, and I wouldn't attempt to do such a thing.

Commissioner O'CONNELL. In other words, you are not authorized to give the reasons of the A. F. of L.?

Mr. LEWIS. No, sir; not authorized. I said I was merely a student.

Commissioner O'CONNELL. Do you believe the organization's position on sabotage is right?

Mr. LEWIS. I have argued publicly against sabotage, not because I don't think it is right, but because I don't think it is effective.

Commissioner O'CONNELL. The organization, however, does?

Mr. LEWIS. That is rather broad. Possibly at the present time the dominant feeling of the organization might be in favor of sabotage as it might be in the confederation générale; but it is a changing sentiment, you can't tell.

Commissioner O'CONNELL. When the national officers appeared before this commission in hearings we havè held heretofore they expressed themselves very much in favor of sabotage.

Mr. LEWIS. The national officers generally typify the organization, but they don't typify changes in the organization.

Commissioner O'CONNELL. That is all.

Chairman WALSH. I notice you are on the program to-morrow on the ques- tion of unemployment, and if it is satisfactory to you and convenient, I will ask those questions now.

Mr. LEWIS. On unemployment?

Chairman WALSH. Yes, sir.

Mr. LEWIS. Yes, sir.

Chairman WALSH. Is there a problem of unemployment peculiar to the State of California?

Mr. LEWIS. Well, of course, that would be a rather hard question for me to answer, because I am not accustomed to industrial centers, having spent so many years in the State of California.

Chairman WALSH. Can you state precisely the problem as it appears in Cali- fornia, the problem of the unemployed?

Mr. LEWIS. There are two aspects of that problem, speaking offhand. I would rather have looked up some notes so as to speak more accurately, but speaking offhand, there are two aspects to that problem. One is the problem of the unemployment of the ordinary skilled laborer or the ordinary workman in town; the other is the unemployment caused by seasonal occupations.

Chairman WALSH. Have you any suggestions you could make to this com- mission—would you care to make some suggestions by which some better method might be devised for handling this migratory labor.

Mr. LEWIS. Well, I think the best way to handle the migratory labor problem would be to turn it over to the trade-unions. I think that the State makes a very fundamental mistake—special legislation, I don't know, might possibly— in overlooking the fact of the tremendous organization of union men which is such a valuable asset. Now, we have over 100,000 of our best picked people, members of trade-unions in the State of California with a tremendous amount of ability and actual experience in contact with the field; and I would much rather trust the organization with the handling of the unemployment question than I would any State department that I can conceive of.

Chairman WALSH. What, if anything, are those organizations doing in the State of California toward taking care of the situation of unemployment?

Mr. LEWIS. Those organizations have done a tremendous lot, although what they do is of such a nature it can't very well be made public; but, speaking as an outsider, last winter was a hard winter, and the organization of the American Federation of Labor in this State looked after their members wonderfully well, and, although many men of my own acquaintance got no work from October until March—many men that I know were out of work from October until De- cember—yet, owing to the self-denying effort of the members of their organiza- tion, they were able to put up a fairly respectable appearance and keep off the streets.

Chairman WALSH. What, if any, suggestion could you make, then, in the line of Government encouragement of that sort of activity?

Mr. LEWIS. I was reading the suggestions as sent to me through the mail, and instead of making a political affair out of it, what I should suggest would be that the Government frankly recognize the existence of trade-unions and that they utilize those trade-unions for social benefit; that is, they allow the trade- unions to start labor exchanges and that they make such allowances for the formation of those exchanges as may seem necessary under the circumstances.

Chairman WALSH. Such funds, you mean?

Mr. LEWIS. Such funds; yes, sir. Leaving the work of the system to the dis- cretion of the trade-unions and their responsibility to the public. I think one of the greatest mistakes at the present time is the nonresponsibility of labor to the public. Here we have a tremendous organization of a hundred thousand in this State, and that is speaking conservatively. They have all our destinies in their hands. We could not live if those men chose not to let us live, and yet those men have no public responsibility, in spite of the immense power which they exercise. Now, I think that power ought to be recognized and turned to public advantage.

Chairman WALSH. That is all. Prof. Commons would like to ask some ques- tions.

Commissioner COMMONS. Would you permit the employers' association to have any voice in that?

Mr. LEWIS. The unemployment question?

Commissioner Commons. In running this question you speak of, the unemployed·

Mr. Lewis. No, sir.

· Commissioner Commons. Why would you exclude the employers' association?

Mr· Lewis. Because I consider the·monopolization of the labor market by organized labor as the prime essential to any social advance.

Commissioner Commons. Your scheme, then, must necessarily mean an entire and complete organization of all labor in the State?

Mr. Lewis. Yes, sir.

Commissioner Commons. There is about how many besides a hundred thousand?

Mr. Lewis. Well, I suppose that, take it altogether, we have probably 500,000 men that work in the State. We have two-odd million population, and I think it would be fair to say we have about 500,000 workingmen.

Commissioner Commons. I presume in that event you would not install your plan, or could not, until all the 500,000——

Mr. Lewis. Oh, yes, you can; you can install it partially and so help the organization of labor tremendously. If you had a labor exchange in San Francisco and Fresno and Sacramento, union labor having control of those exchanges, then you could do much to increase the importance of the labor union, and consequently bring in more men.

· Commissioner Commons. Do you think the American Federation of Labor could be intrusted to take care of these migratory laborers?

Mr. Lewis. It would be metamorphosed; it is not a static concern.

Commissioner Commons. Suppose the employers of the State would refuse to hire people sent to them from exchanges controlled by the union?

Mr. Lewis. Well, then, it is a case of pull-devil-pull-baker. It is a tug of war. They can't refuse to hire all the labor in the State.

Commissioner Commons. I suppose you know how those offices are conducted in Germany—by the joint officers of the employers and employees.

Mr. Lewis. Yes, sir.

Commissioner Commons. What is your reason for objecting to a system like that?

Mr. Lewis. Because I object to the employer having anything whatever to say with reference to the organization and handling of labor. The employer is in control of the material instruments of production, absolutely. Labor has nothing to say with regard to that. The labor department—organized labor—should be absolutely in control of its factor of production, to wit, labor power.

Commissioner Commons. According to that, as I understand it, you mean the employer should have no choice in the people he employs?

Mr. Lewis. Certainly he should not.

· Commissioner Commons. Naturally, it would follow, then, he should have no voice in the control of the employment office?

Mr. Lewis. Yes, sir.

Commissioner Commons. That is all.

Chairman Walsh. Mr. Weinstock.

Commissioner Weinstock. As I understand it, Mr. Lewis, your constructive program on the question of unemployment would be to establish labor exchanges?

Mr. Lewis. Yes, sir.

Commissioner Weinstock. And to have those labor exchanges managed and controlled by organized labor?

Mr. Lewis. Yes, sir.

Commissioner Weinstock. What chance would that scheme have of succeeding in a community such as we find Stockton to be to-day, where the employers, .practically as a unit, are at war with organized labor? What chance would there be for those employers going to that labor exchange, managed and controlled by organized labor, to secure their. labor?

· Mr. Lewis. Why, there wouldn't be any, as things are now in Stockton.

Commissioner Weinstock. Then it would be a failure in Stockton?

Mr. Lewis. Everything is a failure in Stockton at present.

Commissioner Weinstock. Then, you would duplicate substantially the same conditions that prevail in Stockton in every industrial or agricultural communtiy where the employers are anti·union, would you not?

Mr. Lewis. Sure. I would put them up against it.

Commissioner Weinstock. Very well. Then, is not your plan and scheme sure to fail at a great many points?

Mr. LEWIS. Yes, sir; it would. All attacking armies do.

Commissioner WEINSTOCK. Then, what is the use of adopting a plan when you know the plan will not succeed?

Mr. LEWIS. Because the general plan marks such a complete advance that incidental failures are nothing compared to the recognition of the principle.

Commissioner WEINSTOCK. Well, don't you think that the chances for success would be far greater if California adopted the plan in connection with the proposed public-labor exchange that is followed in the State. of Wisconsin, with which you may or may not be familiar? Are you familiar with the system that is operated there?

Mr. LEWIS. No, sir; I could not place it in my mind now. That is what I wanted to look up my notes for.

Commissioner WEINSTOCK. We have the author of the system right here. I will try to explain it briefly, and if I am in error you can correct me, Professor. The State established the public exchange.

Mr. LEWIS. Yes, sir.

Commissioner WEINSTOCK. And organized a board.

Mr. LEWIS. Yes, sir.

Commissioner WEINSTOCK. This board has upon it an equal number of employers, I think, chosen by a group of employers, and an equal number of unionists, chosen by organized labor.

Mr. LEWIS. Yes, sir.

Commissioner WEINSTOCK. And this board jointly operates the public exchange or public labor exchange. Under those circumstances the conditions are kept neutral.

Mr. LEWIS. Yes, sir.

Commissioner WEINSTOCK. The employers, as I understand it, do not hesitate to send to these labor exchanges for their help, and, by virtue of this system, the private employment offices, many of them that have been very improperly and very unrighteously conducted, have been practically wiped out, and only last evening Prof. Commons informed me that the problem of unemployment, largely through the medium of these agencies, is no longer a problem in the State of Wisconsin. Is that correct, Professor?

Commissioner COMMONS. Substantilly.

Commissioner WEINSTOCK. Isn't that a better plan than the one you propose?

Mr. LEWIS. I don't think so, because I am exceedingly jealous of any interference on the part of the State with the individual laborers. That is one reason why I object very strongly to what we call the Lloyd George system of legislation. I object to any control by the State over individual labor. I think he should be master of his own labor, subject to the organization, and that his organization is paramount and takes precedence over everything else. Only in that way can you teach him good work, loyalty, and that class consciousness which is necessary to his behavior as a man.

Commissioner WEINSTOCK. That is all.

Chairman WALSH. That is all; thank you, Mr. Lewis.

Is Mr. Mundell here?

Mr. THOMPSON. He is not here now.

Chairman WALSH. Let Mr. Royce take the stand.

Mr. THOMPSON. Mr. Royce.

TESTIMONY OF MR. ROBERT M. ROYCE.

Mr. THOMPSON. Give us your name, address, and profession.

Mr. ROYCE. Robert M. Royce. My address is Fourteenth and Clay, Oakland, and my profession attorney at law.

Mr. THOMPSON. You are one of the attorneys for the defense in the Ford and Suhr cases?

Mr. ROYCE. Yes, sir; Mr. Lewis and I represented the defendants.

Mr. THOMPSON. In the defense of those cases did you come in contact with the holding of suspects by the authorities?

Mr. ROYCE. Yes, sir. I came in contact with it in every conceivable way.

Mr. THOMPSON. Will you tell us the facts in connection with the holding of suspects in that case?

Mr. ROYCE. It is a little difficult to get at this thing, but the system adopted by the district attorney of Yuba County was this: He would go to a justice of the peace and file a great number of John Doe complaints, charging people with various crimes, sometimes inciting riot, and sometimes murder. On these complaints John Doe warrants would be issued.

These John Doe warrants would be distributed or were distributed to various so-called deputy sheriffs or Burns detectives. Some of the latter were formerly made deputy sheriffs for the purpose of serving those warrants. They would take those warrants out over the State of California; arrest anybody they saw fit. They would confine those arrested in jails all over the State, as Chico— Chico was one—Orville, and Santa Rosa, and Martinez, and in·many other places. Cloverdale in one case.

When I first went to Marysville I found some 10 or 15 men in jail. Some of these men I was allowed to see and some I was not allowed to see. There was a certain group in the Marysville jail, and I went to Mr. Stanwood and asked him why he did not have a preliminary hearing. Well, he said he did not choose to have it.

Chairman WALSH. May I interrupt you? You have just barely started and Mr. Mundell is here, and we want to put him on a little out of .order. If you will kindly retire, we want to develop some things in view of Mr. Lewis's testimony before we put you on.

Mr. Mundell, if you will, please take the stand.

TESTIMONY OF MR. WILLIAM A. MUNDELL.

Mr. THOMPSON. Will you please give us your name, business address, and business?

Mr. MUNDELL. William A. Mundell; Merchants National Bank Building; owner of Mundell International Detective Agency.

Mr. THOMPSON. How long have you been engaged in that business in this city?

Mr. MUNDELL. About four years?

Mr. THOMPSON. Was your agency employed in the case ordinarily called the Wheatland hop case?

Mr. MUNDELL. Yes, sir; eventually. Primarily I was employed as manager of the Burns Detecvtive Agency. I was manager of the Burns Detective Agency when first employed.

Mr. THOMPSON. In those cases?

Mr. MUNDELL. Yes, sir. After I left there and opened up my own agency I continued the case.

Mr. THOMPSON. You continned the work you were doing for the Burns Agency?

Mr. MUNDELL. Yes, sir.

Mr. THOMPSON. Who first called you or the Burns Agency into this case, if you know?

Mr. MUNDELL. It was District Attorney Stanwood, of Yuba County.

Mr. THOMPSON. When you handled the case personally, did you continue working under him?

Mr. MUNDELL. Why, I was given the task of running down and arresting the men implicated in the murder of public officials at Woodland on August 3, 1913. I didn't work entirely under his direction.

Mr. THOMPSON. Did you work under his employment?

Mr. MUNDELL. I assumed charge of the case myself.

Mr. THOMPSON. Did you work under his employment?

Mr. MUNDELL. I did, if you consider the employment of the county of Yuba his employment. He was district attorney of the county.

Mr. THOMPSON. Did you work under the employment of anybody else?

Mr. MUNDELL. I did not.

Mr. THOMPSON. All the time you handled these cases you worked for the county of Yuba?

Mr. MUNDELL. Yes, sir.

Mr. THOMPSON. From the beginning to the end?

Mr. MUNDELL. Yes, sir.

Mr. THOMPSON. During that time how many detectives did you have assisting you in that work?

Mr. MUNDELL. Well, it varied from 12 to 15.

Mr. THOMPSON. Were they all working in the State of California, or go elsewhere?

Mr. MUNDELL. In other States, also.

Mr. THOMPSON. During that time did your men make arrests of people that they called suspects?

Mr. MUNDELL. Fourteen.

Mr. THOMPSON. What were the names of those 14, if you know now?

Mr. MUNDELL. I could not give you the names of the 14; I can give you the names of 3 or 4.

Mr. THOMPSON. Give us those you remember.

Mr. MUNDELL. Suhr, Cokely, Nelson, Johnson, Gleaser, and others whose names I don't recall.

Mr. THOMPSON. Were any of these suspects imprisoned in various counties?

Mr. MUNDELL. Yes, sir; all of them.

Mr. THOMPSON. Were any of them taken from one county to another?

Mr. MUNDELL. Yes, sir.

Mr. THOMPSON. Were they taken by you and your men?

Mr. MUNDELL. Sometimes; not always.

Mr. THOMPSON. In what cases were they taken by your men from one county to another and placed in the county prison?

Mr. MUNDELL. Why, I think when the men were first arrested they were put in the nearest jail as a safety precaution and afterwards transferred to Yuba County or Sutter County, which is across the river. It was not always possible to remove a man immediately to Yuba County upon his arrest, because the trains don't run regularly from all parts of the State.

Mr. THOMPSON. Did you take people from Yuba County to other counties?

Mr. MUNDELL. No, sir; except to Sutter County. We did not do that ourselves. Men were transferred, on account of the condition of the Marysville jail, to the Sutter County Jail and Yuba City.

Mr. THOMPSON. How long were people held in the other jails outside of Yuba County?

Mr. MUNDELL. I don't know—how long?

Mr. THOMPSON. Yes, sir; after their arrests as suspects.

Mr. MUNDELL. They were held until taken to Yuba County. The Yuba jail wouldn't accommodate all the people arrested, in addition to the people arrested for other crimes. Yuba County is a small county and has a small jail. The authorities in the various counties throughout the State were cooperating with the authorities in Yuba County in imprisoning these men.

Mr. THOMPSON. How long were men held in other counties before being brought to Yuba County?

Mr. MUNDELL. How long?

Mr. THOMPSON. Yes, sir.

Mr. MUNDELL. I can't say exactly. Some men were taken to other jails to be held until their hearing came up—until their trial came up—because there was no room for them in the Yuba jail.

Mr. THOMPSON. On what warrants were these men arrested?

Mr. MUNDELL. John Doe warrants for murder and inciting riot.

Mr. THOMPSON. When they were arrested and placed in the jail in other counties were they given a hearing immediately?

Mr. MUNDELL. That I don't know. I didn't follow the cases after the arrests. We had nothing to do with the administration of the law.

Mr. THOMPSON. Is that true of all the cases?

Mr. MUNDELL. True of all of what cases?

Mr. THOMPSON. Of the arrests of suspects, that you didn't follow them after you arrested them?

Mr. MUNDELL. I presume——

Mr. THOMPSON. Or your men?

Mr. MUNDELL (continuing). They got hearings as soon as the regular work of Yuba County would permit them to give them hearings. I know nothing of that; had nothing to do after the delivery of the men in Yuba County.

Mr. THOMPSON. No; but I didn't ask you that Mr. Mundell; I am asking you the question if your men dropped the cases immediately after the arrests. You say they did?

Mr. MUNDELL. That was the end of our work.

Mr. THOMPSON. Is that true of the case of Suhr?

Mr. MUNDELL. The case of Suhr?

Mr. THOMPSON. Yes.

Mr. MUNDELL. We went with Suhr until he was placed in the county jail of Sutter County.

Mr. THOMPSON. Then, in his case you did stay with him longer than being placed in jail?

Mr. MUNDELL. While he was en route only.

Mr. THOMPSON. While he was en route?

Mr. MUNDELL. Yes.

Mr. THOMPSON. Were your men with him while he was in the jail at Fresno?

Mr. MUNDELL. Some of the time.

Mr. THOMPSON. Did you place what is ordinarily called a stool pigeon in the cell with him while he was in the jail there?

Mr. MUNDELL. I did not.

Mr. THOMPSON. Did any of your men do it?

Mr. MUNDELL. I placed a man in the jail with him, in the cell. I don't recognize any man who gives evidence to support the laws of the country as a stool **pigeon.**

Mr. THOMPSON. Well, call him by any name which pleases you.

Mr. MUNDELL. Yes; if you will call him by his proper name, I will answer that question.

Mr. THOMPSON. Well, call him by any name which pleases you.

Mr. MUNDELL. One of my men was placed in the cell with Mr. Suhr; yes, sir.

Mr. THOMPSON. Did you also put in that jail a dictagraph?

Mr. MUNDELL. Two of them.

Mr. THOMPSON. Two of them?

Mr. MUNDELL. Yes, sir.

Mr. THOMPSON. And did your man keep Mr. Suhr awake most of the night, disturb him in his sleep, and endeavored to get from him a statement of his **connection with this——**

Mr. MUNDELL. No, sir.

Mr. THOMPSON. Will you say——

Mr. MUNDELL. Mr. Suhr went to sleep about 11 o'clock. Our work then ceased for the night.

Mr. THOMPSON. Will you state that that was not done?

Mr. MUNDELL. I will say that that was not done; yes sir.

Mr. THOMPSON. Were you there?

Mr. MUNDELL. I was there.

Mr. THOMPSON. Were you the man?

Mr. MUNDELL. I was not. I was in the bathroom of the jail next to his room.

Mr. THOMPSON. Next to the cell?

Mr. MUNDELL. Yes, sir; superintending the operation of the dictagraph.

Mr. THOMPSON. Could Suhr see where you were from the cell?

Mr. MUNDELL. He could not.

Mr. THOMPSON. Could he tell what you were doing?

Mr. MUNDELL. No.

Mr. THOMPSON. Could you see him?

Mr. MUNDELL. No, sir.

Mr. THOMPSON. Could you tell what he was doing?

Mr. MUNDELL. No, sir.

Mr. THOMPSON. Then, how do you know that he was not awakened?

Mr. MUNDELL. Because the man reported to me that he went to sleep at 11 o'clock. At 11 o'clock all talk ceased in the room.

Mr. THOMPSON. And that is your basis——

Mr. MUNDELL. I assume that if he were awake my man would have been talking to him.

Mr. THOMPSON. And that is your basis for making the statement?

Mr. MUNDELL. Yes; I think a very good basis.

Mr. THOMPSON. Did your people take Suhr to the Sutter Hotel in San **Francisco?**

Mr. MUNDELL. They did.

Mr. THOMPSON. Did you keep him there all night?

Mr. MUNDELL. All night.

Mr. THOMPSON. What was the reason for taking him to a private hotel instead of to the public jail in this city?

Mr. MUNDELL. We did'n care to have his whereabouts known at that time.

Mr. THOMPSON. To whom?

Mr. MUNDELL. To anybody.

Mr. THOMPSON. How long had he then been under arrest?

Mr. MUNDELL. Oh, he was arrested in Nelson Ariz., just as long as it took us to come up from there. I think the deputy sheriff who brought him up stopped at Los Angeles for a night, and stopped at Stockton, or rather at Fresno, for a night, and the next stop was in San Francisco. The stop was made here at the hotel pending the selection of the jail to place him in.

Mr. THOMPSON. You could have taken him to the public jail here?
Mr. MUNDELL. We could have, but we did not desire to.
Mr. THOMPSON. Did not desire to. Did you or your men inform him up to that time about his rights to employ counsel?
Mr. MUNDELL. I didn't talk to the gentleman at all.
Mr. THOMPSON. Did any of your men talk to him about that?
Mr. MUNDELL. I presume that they did.
Mr. THOMPSON. You think that they advised him about that?
Mr. MUNDELL. I don't know.
Mr. THOMPSON. When was he taken to the county jail at Alameda County?
Mr. MUNDELL. The following morning.
Mr. THOMPSON. How long was he kept there?
Mr. MUNDELL. I think one or two days.
Mr. THOMPSON. Were any of his friends notified of his presence there?
Mr. MUNDELL. Not that I know of.
Mr. THOMPSON. Did your men in charge of him keep him awake at night, walk him around, and insist upon his talking?
Mr. MUNDELL. I don't believe so. My men could not have been walking him around, because he was locked in the cell and they were outside.
Mr. THOMPSON. Are you sure that your men were not with him during the nights at the time he was at the Alameda jail?
Mr. MUNDELL. They were with him, but not in his cell. His cell was locked. They were outside.
Mr. THOMPSON. Well, in that case you didn't have a man with him in the cell?
Mr. MUNDELL. No, sir; at no time.
Mr. THOMPSON. Were your detectives continually with him in the Yuba City jail?
Mr. MUNDELL. Yes; practically so. He had attempted to take his life in the Alameda County Jail. We were guarding against him committing suicide.
Mr. THOMPSON. And that was the sole reason that you kept company with him?
Mr. MUNDELL. Absolutely.
Mr. THOMPSON. No other purpose?
Mr. MUNDELL. No other purpose; and that upon the direction of the district attorney of Yuba County, who was told that he had made an attempt to take his life in Oakland, in the Alameda County Jail.
Mr. THOMPSON. What became of Nelson, who was arrested?
Mr. MUNDELL. When? After he was arrested?
Mr. THOMPSON. Yes.
Mr. MUNDELL. Or eventually?
Mr. THOMPSON. Eventually.
Mr. MUNDELL. After he was arrested?
Mr. THOMPSON. Eventually.
Mr. MUNDELL. Eventually?
Mr. THOMPSON. Yes.
Mr. MUNDELL. The charges against him were dismissed because the county felt it had gone far enough in prosecuting Ford and Suhr. There were many men arrested that could not have been convicted.
Mr. THOMPSON. Was there another Nelson that was arrested?
Mr. MUNDELL. Yes, sir.
Mr. THOMPSON. What became of him?
Mr. MUNDELL. He committed suicide. However, he wasn't arrested by us. One of the men we didn't drive to suicide.
Mr. THOMPSON. Where did he commit suicide?
Mr. MUNDELL. I believe in the detention hospital of Yuba County. I would not be sure.
Mr. THOMPSON. Do you know whether he was removed from the hospital to the jail and placed in solitary confinement?
Mr. MUNDELL. I don't know.
Mr. THOMPSON. After his injury?
Mr. MUNDELL. We never had anything to do with that particular Nelson.
Mr. THOMPSON. Did you have a man working for you by the name of Cradlebaugh?
Mr. MUNDELL. At one time.
Mr. THOMPSON. In this work?
Mr. MUNDELL. Yes, sir.

Mr. THOMPSON. Did he have anything to do with a man by the name of Johnson and also with Nelson, who was arrested at Martinez?

Mr. MUNDELL. He took part in the arrest of both of them.

- Mr. THOMPSON. Do you know whether he had anything to do with assaulting either one of them?

Mr. MUNDELL. I do.

Mr. THOMPSON. Did he?

Mr. MUNDELL. Yes, sir; he assaulted Nelson. I presume you would like to know why.

Mr. THOMPSON. I will ask you that——

Mr. MUNDELL. You haven't asked me that. He assaulted Mr. Nelson because Mr.——

Chairman WALSH. Just one moment. He will ask you another question.

Mr. MUNDELL. Oh, I see. All right. I want to make everything perfectly clear.

Chairman WALSH. Certainly.

Mr. MUNDELL. That is all.

Mr. THOMPSON. Well, you may state.

Mr. MUNDELL. He was assaulted because he tried to escape frcm a room in the Martinez Hotel, in Martinez, Cal.

Mr. THOMPSON. What was the nature of the assault?

Mr. MUNDELL. He was struck over the head.

Mr. THOMPSON. With what?

Mr. MUNDELL. I don't know what with.

Mr. THOMPSON. With a weapon of some kind?

Mr. MUNDELL. I could not say. It wasn't brought out in testimony in the case in Martinez what he was struck with. He was supposed to have been struck with the open hand of the deputy, and to have fallen and struck his head.

Mr. THOMPSON. Did you hear the testimony to-day of Mr. McKenzie with reference to his condition?

Mr. MUNDELL. Yes.

(The transcript of certain proceedings occurring at this point were, by direction of the chairman, stricken from the record.)

Chairman WALSH. Say, one moment. We are conducting this under these rules——

Mr. MUNDELL. I understand.

Chairman WALSH. That no witness is allowed to characterize another witness or his motives.

Mr. MUNDELL. All right.

Chairman WALSH. Please bear that in mind in the future.

Mr. MUNDELL. I have heard Mr. McKenzie's testimony.

Chairman WALSH. One moment. That reference to Mr. McKenzie's testimony will be stricken from the record and not written.

Mr. MUNDELL. I have heard some statement by Mr. McKenzie.

Chairman WALSH. And if you have any facts to controvert Mr. McKenzie——

Mr. MUNDELL. I have facts, which is something Mr. McKenzie did not present.

Chairman WALSH. Now, then, we have told you to desist from that.

Mr. MUNDELL. Yes.

Chairman WALSH. If you have any facts to controvert anything Mr. McKenzie said, certainly state them. But don't characterize Mr. McKenzie or any other witness.

Mr. MUNDELL. Yes.

Chairman WALSH. What was your question, how far had we proceeded?

Mr. THOMPSON. Well, I will just ask him about the injuries. Did you see Nelson?

Mr. MUNDELL. Which Nelson?

Mr. THOMPSON. Nelson, the one that was hit by Cradlebaugh?

Mr. MUNDELL. At Martinez, I saw him.

Mr. THOMPSON. Did you see him after he was hit by Cradlebaugh?

Mr. MUNDELL. Yes; I took him, after he was hit by Cradlebaugh, from Martinez to Marysville.·

Mr. THOMPSON·. What were the nature of his injuries as you saw them?

Mr. MUNDELL. He had a scalp wound about an inch and a half long and a slight discoloration, I think, on the cheek bone or somewhere around there.

Mr. THOMPSON. What do you mean by " a slight discoloration on the cheek bone "?

Mr. MUNDELL. Well, slight, barely perceptible.
Mr. THOMPSON. Barely perceptible?
Mr. MUNDELL. Yes; barely perceptible.
Mr. THOMPSON. No other marks on his face or head?
Mr. MUNDELL. No; the man was examined by the county physician of Yuba County after he reached Marysville, which was the day following this assault.
Mr. THOMPSON. Who had him examined?
Mr. MUNDELL. The district attorney, Mr. Stanwood.
Mr. THOMPSON. What was the reason for his examination by a physician?
Mr. MUNDELL. I don't know. Perhaps Mr. Stanwood could tell that.
Mr. THOMPSON. Do you think that if his injuries had been very slight, as you have described them, that the district attorney would have had him examined by the physician?
Mr. MUNDELL. Yes; I think so, in the light of the fight that was being made against us at that time.
Chairman WALSH. I would not ask him any more on that.
Mr. THOMPSON. Did you arrest a man by the name of Gleaser?
Mr. MUNDELL. Gleaser?
Mr. THOMPSON. Gleaser.
Mr. MUNDELL. Yes; we arrested Gleaser.
Chairman WALSH. I would like to ask two or three questions here. Where was Mr. Nelson arrested, Mr. Mundell?
Mr. MUNDELL. Nelson was arrested on a ranch near Healdsburg, Cal.
Chairman WALSH. By whom arrested?
Mr. MUNDELL. By two of my men who were also deputies.
Chairman WALSH. How long was it after the occurrence on the Durst ranch that he was arrested?
Mr. MUNDELL. Well, I should say between three and four weeks. You see we were not called in on the case until about two weeks after this affair in Wheatland.
Chairman WALSH. Now, I want to avoid the details of the trial, if possible, and yet ask some questions surrounding it. Was he in the employ of the Burns Detective Agency at the time this occurred?
Mr. MUNDELL. Who, Cradlebaugh?
Chairman WALSH. Yes.
Mr. MUNDELL. Yes; he was.
Chairman WALSH. Now, who employed the Burns Detective Agency?
Mr. MUNDELL. The county of Yuba.
Chairman WALSH. What individual?
Mr. MUNDELL. The district attorney.
Chairman WALSH. Were the terms of the employment in writing?
Mr. MUNDELL. No.
Chairman WALSH. Was the contract consummated; have you performed all the duties; has the Burns Detective Agency performed all the duties it was hired to perform?
Mr. MUNDELL. Yes.
Chairman WALSH. And paid for?
Mr. MUNDELL. It has not been paid for.
Chairman WALSH. How is that?
Mr. MUNDELL. It has not been paid for the services as yet.
Chairman WALSH. Have any of the services been paid for?
Mr. MUNDELL. Not a dollar.
Chairman WALSH. Not a dollar?
Mr. MUNDELL. Not a dollar.
Chairman WALSH. Has the bill been rendered by the Burns Detective Agency?
Mr. MUNDELL. Yes; the demands were filed, I think, in January, February, and April of this year.
Chairman WALSH. Was the contract made through you, Mr. Mundell?
Mr. MUNDELL. The contract was made through me.
Chairman WALSH. Individually?
Mr. MUNDELL. Yes, sir; after I had procured an opinion from the attorney general's office to the effect that the district attorney had the legal right to employ such outside help.
Chairman WALSH. Where was your office at that time?
Mr. MUNDELL. In the First National Bank Building, San Francisco.
Chairman WALSH. And where did you have your interview with the prosecuting attorney or district attorney?
Mr. MUNDELL. In that office.

Chairman WALSH. In San Francisco?

Mr. MUNDELL. He came to see you?

Mr. MUNDELL. He came to see me after he had paid a visit to the office of the attorney general of the State of California.

Chairman WALSH. Was there any limitation placed upon the number of detectives that you were to hire?

Mr. MUNDELL. None whatever.

Chairman WALSH. Were there any instructions given to you by the district attorney as to the way you were to conduct the work in detail?

Mr. MUNDELL. No. The district attorney told me that effort had been made to get these men; that the peace officers had not been able to get them, they hadn't an organization which would reach beyond the confines of their county; they needed some agency with an organization which would reach throughout the country, and therefore he wanted us to arrest these men. He gave us two or three meager descriptions, and one or two names. That is all we had to work on.

Chairman WALSH. And does that substantially cover the details of the instructions given you by the district attorney? ·

Mr. MUNDELL. Yes; practically so; yes. At the time he came to me he didn't believe, and I doubted very much whether we could get these people, and I was told to go ahead for a few days, or a few weeks, and see whether any progress could be made. If so, then we would continue the work.

Chairman WALSH. What instructions, if any, were given to the men that went out to capture these men, or to attempt their capture?

Mr. MUNDELL. Why, the instructions given them were these, they were told the story of the riot up there, they were given descriptions of the men, they were told the type of men they were, and where they were most apt to be found. And the instructions were given them to "rope in" with them, gain their confidence, secure their stories of this affair, and to hunt particularly for these persons who were most wanted, Suhr and Ford, and others whose names were not known, but whose descriptions were given. And their instruction were, of course, upon arrests—upon locating a man who had any information at all in connection with these matters up there, to communicate with me.

Chairman WALSH. Now, did they do that, did they communicate with you——

Mr. MUNDELL. They did.

Chairman WALSH (continuing). Mr. Mundell, when a man was arrested?

Mr. MUNDELL. Oh, they communicated with me before his arrest. I ordered his arrest after they communicated with me, and after I had communicated in detail with the district attorney of Yuba County.

Chairman WALSH. Did they or did they not arrest every man that they found who had been on this ranch at the time of this occurrence?

Mr. MUNDELL. No; they did not. We found a great many romances in our travels. We found members of the I. W. W. who told stories about having taken part in this riot and having shot at people, or slugged people, whose stories we disproved. There were many of those we did not arrest.

Chairman WALSH. Did you arrest——

Mr. MUNDELL. We had to sift down their evidence and verify it so far as we could before an arrest was made.

Chairman WALSH. Did you arrest all of those people who you ascertained had been on the Durst ranch at the time of the occurrence?

Mr. MUNDELL. No, sir.

Chairman WALSH. Now——

Mr. MUNDELL. Not unless they were in a position to be defendants or act as witnesses.

Chairman WALSH. Now the matter of the treatment of Mr. Nelson culminated in this trial that was testified to here already?

Mr. MUNDELL. Yes, sir. ·

Chairman WALSH. Who, if any person, paid for this man's defense? Did the organization pay for it?

Mr. MUNDELL. Why, I paid for it myself mostly, personally—put up bail myself.

Chairman WALSH. How many regularly employed detectives did the Burns Detective Agency have at this time?

Mr. MUNDELL. Well, that varied, depended upon the amount of work that we were doing, anywhere from 25 to 75.

Chairman Walsh. Did you try——

Mr MUNDELL. In this particular office.

Chairman WALSH. And you drew them also from other places?

Mr. MUNDELL. Yes, sir. Yes; I brought a man from New York to work, on this case.

Chairman WALSH. Now, there was something that I think you were going to say in answer to a question, and I interrupted you, thinking that Mr. Thompson was about to read another question.

Mr. MUNDELL. I don't recall what that question was now.

Chairman WALSH. Well, if you recall it, you may make your statement. I don't want to shut you off. Go ahead.

Mr. THOMPSON. When was Gleaser first arrested?

Mr. MUNDELL. Gleaser was arrested in company with Alfred Nelson.

Mr. THOMPSON. Where and when?

Mr. MUNDELL. He was arrested as I have just described.

Mr. THOMPSON. Where?

Mr. MUNDELL. On a ranch near Healdsburg.

Mr. THOMPSON. In Yuba County?

Mr. MUNDELL. No; that is Sonoma County.

Mr. THOMPSON. Was he taken to Yuba County?

Mr. MUNDELL. Eventually.

Mr. THOMPSON. How old a man was Gleaser?

Mr. MUNDELL. Gleaser was 18 years old, so he said.

Mr. THOMPSON. Did he have his home in this State?

Mr. MUNDELL. The boy did not live with his parents, as I understand it. One of his parents was dead, and he didn't live with the other, and had been living with his uncle, who was a business agent of the molders' union in San Francisco, I believe, a man named Burton.

Mr. THOMPSON. While this young man was under arrest, were his folks, either his uncle or one of his parents, looking for him at that time?

Mr. MUNDELL. I believe so; yes.

Mr. THOMPSON. Then did you keep his whereabouts away from his people?

Mr. MUNDELL. I simply placed him in the jail. I had nothing to do with him after that.

Mr. THOMPSON. What jail did you place him in?

Mr. MUNDELL. Yuba City.

Mr. THOMPSON. Then when his people started looking for him, did you take him to the jail in San Francisco, in order that they should not find out where he was?

Mr. MUNDELL. No, sir.

Mr. THOMPSON. And then afterwards when you thought you had got them off the track, did you take him back to Yuba County Jail?

Mr. MUNDELL. You are assuming I answered the previous question in the affirmative. I did not.

Mr. THOMPSON. You may answer the question as you please.

Mr. MUNDELL. Yes; but your question is rather peculiar, too.

Mr. THOMPSON. I am not assuming anything. You may answer it as you please.

Mr. MUNDELL. Yes; it gave me that inference anyway. You said then I took him back. I didn't take him anywhere from Yuba County in the first place.

Mr. THOMPSON. And when you took him those places, if you did, did you tell him over his protest, that he either had the privilege of going with you or being held as a prisoner on a murder charge?

Mr. MUNDELL. At what time and what place?

Mr. THOMPSON. At any time.

Mr. MUNDELL. No, sir.

Mr. THOMPSON. At any place?

Mr. MUNDELL. Never at any time.

Mr. THOMPSON. Or any place?

Mr. MUNDELL. If you would name the place, I think I could probably enlighten you. I know, in a way, what you are trying to get at, but I don't know just what particular time and place you refer to.

Mr. THOMPSON. If at any time and place you made those statements to him——

Mr. MUNDELL. No, sir; never did.

Mr. THOMPSON. (continuing). I would like to have you tell us.

Mr. MUNDELL. No; I never made any such statement.

Mr. THOMPSON. That is all, Mr. Chairman.

Mr. MUNDELL. Gleaser always went willingly with us.

Chairman WALSH. That is all; thank you.

Call Mr. Royce.

TESTIMONY OF MR. R. M. ROYCE—Recalled.

Mr. ROYCE. Now, to take up this matter where I left off and going into the system under which these arrests were conducted, you see here are John Doe warrants. Here are complaints filed, charging John Doe with murder, or John Doe with disturbing the peace. And a John Doe warrant is issued, placed in the hands of a Burns detective, or some other officer, and under that anybody can be arrested. Now, people under such warrants were arrested all over the State and confined. When Mr. Lewis and I took up these cases and went up to Marysville, our first business, our first effort was to find out who our clients were. It was impossible to find out who was under arrest. The statute requires as soon as a person is arrested that he be forthwith brought before the nearest magistrate, and, if in the county, before the magistrate by whom the warrant is issued and bail fixed.

W would 'go to the justice of the peace in Marysville, and find there a great many John Doe complaints, which gave us no information. When we demanded of the justice of the peace that he fix the preliminary hearings on these John Doe complaints, he would say that there had been no warrants returned, and therefore he could not be certain that any warrants had been served.

When we went to the district attorney he would say he knew nothing about— he would refuse to tell me who John Doe was, any particular John Doe was, upon the ground that I was not John Doe's attorney. And if I should discover that a certain person was in jail, we will say in the county jail—in the city jail in Yuba, I would go to the jail and ask the chief of police to let me see that particular man, and he would say: "No; you are not his attorney, and I will not let you see him unless District Attorney Stanwood says so." I would then go to District Attorney Stanwood, and Stanwood would say: "You are not his attorney." Then I would say: "I wish to be his attorney, to see if he wishes an attorney." "No;" Stanwood would say, "you can't see him in jail unless he says he wants you to be his attorney." So the fellow in jail could not possibly get an attorney, any attorney, unless he would ask for some specific man, and then there was no method by which he could communicate with him even in that event. Now, the only way to get around that was to find out the name of the person in the jail and file a writ of habeas corpus and have the man brought into the superior court on a writ of habeas corpus; which, by the way, instead of being made returnable in 24 hours, or the next day, as is customary, would be returnable in a week, or in some cases longer; we could to get him into court on the writ of habeas corpus, and in that way see him. And in the case of two persons, Leonard and Copely, who had been in jail for months, three or four months, they were brought into the court room and kept on the opposite side of the room. And I had to shout across the room in the presence of the superior judge and ask if they wished an attorney to act for them, to which they said that they did; upon which it was generally admitted that I had a right to appear for them.

Now, we will take up certain individual instances. Take this man Johnson, that is a minor case. Now, Johnson was arrested in Martinez. He was not at Wheatland. He had never been in Wheatland. He was struck in the face, so he tells me, by the detectives, told to say that he was present at the time of the Wheatland shooting and that Ford shot Manwell. That is what he told me. He was brought up from Martinez, and he was brought up to Marysville, and he was put in the county jail, and he was in the county jail for a long time. And then as I was about to get out a writ of habeas corpus for him, I heard that he had been discharged. I then heard indirectly that he was up in the city and county hospital, or rather the county hospital. And I went up to the county hospital, and he was there and I got a statement from him.

At the same time this Nielson, the man who afterwards hanged himself, was in the city and county hospital, but I didn't know he was there, so I did not try to see him. I went down to San Francisco, I came back to Oakland, and I hadn't more than got here than I heard that Johnson was in the insane asylum. Just as soon as I left, Nielson, who was being kept in the hospital and his arm treated, was taken out of the hospital and taken back to the jail, and I am informed by other persons, was put in solitary confinement, and he hanged himself—his arm was shot off here [indicating].

Johnson was brought up before the superior judge of Yuba County charged with insanity and sent to Stockton. I wrote to Stockton, and I got a letter from the asylum, unsigned by anybody, saying he was there and they thought that he would soon be discharged.

3   °   D   41⁻ C4—   ˙ ⁻   ⁻

When the Suhr trial commenced and the articles appeared in the Bee, in regard to the treatment of Suhr, the day after those articles appeared, Johnson was incontinently turned out of the sanitarium in Stockton by the superintendent of it, climbed on the train and came down to our office, and we took him back to Yuba County again to produce him there as an instance of what was supposed to be an insane man.

Johnson was a migratory worker, and I asked him what he thought about it, and he said, " My nerves are rather shaken on account of the long imprisonment; my teeth needed fixing and," he said, " I think that going to the Stockton Insane Asylum, they had a good dentist there, my teeth were fixed up and I do not think I suffered very much on that account."

I thought that was an ingenious way of a migratory worker having his dental bill attended to.

We will take the case of Cokely; Cokely was in jail in Marysville for a long time. And I asked Mr. Stanwood's permission to see him. He refused, and I sued out a writ of habeas corpus and I dragged him before the superior court, and he is the man I had to ask if he wanted an attorney, cured to have me, clear across the court room. I found out his name from other people who were in the county jail being discharged.

Leonard was an old man. He was also arrested in this same way. And Leonard was, I think, my impression is that Leonard was with Cokely. There were some 30 or 40 of these names, and I get them a little confused.

After Cokely was brought up before the court, and I had become his attorney, he informed me that he was—that District Attorney Stanwood' said—although he was arrested and charged with inciting a riot—that if he employed me as his attorney, he would be charged with murder.

The prophecy came true: As soon as I became his attorney he was charged with murder : Mr. Stanwood swore to a complaint charging him with murder, and thereby rendering it impossible to get bail.

Take the next case. We took the case of Gleaser: I first heard of Gleaser, that he was in jail in Yuba City, opposite Marysville, and I heard all sorts of conflicting stories as to Gleaser—what he was charged with and what he was going to testify to. And, of course, I could find no—I could get no clear line on him because he was charged under one of these John Doe anonymous warrants, and so I could not tell. I could not identify him.

However, I found he was in jail with Suhr in the Yuba City Jail. I went there and asked to see him. I was refused. I was allowed to see Suhr, but was not allowed to see Gleaser. I was allowed to see Suhr afterwards.

I then sent for Gleaser's uncle. He lives here with his family, his wife and children. I believe he is business agent of one of the unions—the A. F. of L. unions. The boy lives with him, lived as one of his family. And I sued out a writ of habeas corpus. When I first sued out that writ of habeas corpus, I swore to the petition, took it up to Judge Mahon, of Sutter County: When I showed him the petition Judge Mahon said he didn't propose to issue it; there was something wrong with the form, something of that sort, and that he would not issue it. I told him that if he didn't issue it I would go down to the district court of appeals and get it; that I had already gone to the district court of appeals to force a hearing on the Suhr case, and that I would go down and get another writ of habeas corpus from the same court and get a hearing in the Gleaser case. Therefore he told me that I was guilty of contempt of court for talking to him in any such way as that, that the sheriff's office was his court room when he was in it, it was his chambers, and that he didn't care for the district court of appeals, and that I might as well understand that the grangers were handling those cases up there. That is what the superior judge told me.

He finally issued the writ, and he set it a week, I think it was, either a week or—I wouldn't like to be positive as to the number of days, but approximately it was a week after; for the hearing; which is a very unreasonable time to set a return on a writ of habeas corpus with the man only a few—in the same building as the judge.

I took the writ, took it over to the county clerk's office, had the county clerk put his seal on it. The judge had signed it in the presence of the sheriff; they were sitting on each side of the stove in the sheriff's office, the judge on this side and the sheriff on the other side, and I went into the office to turn the writ over to the county clerk, and I handed the writ, after he put his seal on, to the sheriff, in the presence of the judge: The writ was issued Monday, and the hearing came on Saturday, I think. When the hearing came on there wasn't any Gleaser. And the sheriff said—came into court and said—that the day after that writ had been issued, after it had been given to him, the district attorney, Stanwood, had sent over there to Yuba City, and had taken Gleaser away, and he didn't know what had become of him or where he had gone.

When I made the point that the writ of habeas corpus was issued to bring him into court, Judge Mahon said that the code provided that a writ of habeas corpus had to be served on the sheriff by the county clerk, and the fact that it was signed by the judge in the presence of the sheriff, the seal of the court put on it, and handed to the sheriff in the presence of the judge didn't make any difference. The service of the writ was void, and the sheriff was under no obligation to bring the man into court at all, and he didn't propose even to go into the question of what had become of him.

Upon the strength of that I went to the supreme court of the State for a writ of habeas corpus for this Gleaser. I directed the writ of habeas corpus to Mr. Stanwood, for the principal reason I couldn't find head or trace of Gleaser in any way. He wasn't in Yuba County, and he wasn't in Sutter County, and Mr. Stanwood said he didn't propose to tell me where he had gone. So I got the writ of habeas corpus out of the supreme court directed to Mr. Stanwood.

Mr. Stanwood came down before the court and testified that Gleaser had gone out of the office followed by Burns detectives, but he didn't know where he was.

Thereupon, I told the supreme court that the writ was directed to Mr. Stanwood, his agents and servants, and the Burns detectives were his agents and servants, and that, therefore, I asked the court to require the Burns detectives to bring him into court under that writ.

The court said, in substance—the record is printed—that Mr. Stanwood could not authorize the Burns detectives to do an unlawful act, and, therefore, if they had Gleaser they did not have him as Mr. Stanwood's agents and servants, and, therefore, they would not make the order requiring him to be brought before the court, and then discharged the writ, with permission to renew it if I could prove who had Gleaser in custody.

I proceeded to hunt around for Gleaser. We found that he was down at Gilroy Hot Springs, in charge of two Burns detectives. And so we sent his uncle down there, and he went to San Jose. He went to San Jose. He went there and sued out a warrant against the people who had Gleaser in charge for kidnapping.

They went out there. They arrested the man who had him, Gleaser, in custody. Gleaser ran away when the officers, as the officers came on the scene; he ran away up in the hills, and after the officer, the constable, had departed with the Burns detective, he came back, saw his uncle, and he told his uncle that he ran away because he was told by the Burns detective that the I. W. W.'s wanted to kill him. And he also told his uncle that he wished his uncle then would leave him alone, because the Burns detectives had given him clothes and were letting him fish and ride horseback, and that he was having a very good time. They promised him a suit of clothes and a job after the case was over if he would only stay with them and do as they told him.

Well, his uncle started back with his boy, and he got in as far as Fourth and Townsend Streets, San Francisco, when a detective from the chief of police's office in Oakland—I mean in San Francisco—came up to him and told him that Gleaser would have to go with him to headquarters—the police station.

So they took Gleaser to the police station and his uncle telephoned over to Mr. Lewis and myself, and I came over on the next boat. By the time I arrived at the police station Gleaser had gone again. Gleaser had gone again with the detective. The chief of detectives said Standwood had come down there, and that he told them not to bother with the charge of murder, but to let Gleaser go. So they let Gleaser go, and he had gone away with Stanwood.

Well, he went away, and we did not see any trace of him until after the trial was over, when he turned up and came home.

Now, we had trouble getting the testimony that Gleaser gave before the grand jury, because Mr. Stanwood had the idea that if all the testimony—that the investigation was not an investigation into the murder, the matter of killing of Manwell or the matter of killing Reardon, to say nothing of the killing of the two hop pickers, shooting off the arm of the third, which the grand jury never took any notice of, one way or the other, at all; their interest was entirely to the Reardon and Manwell matter.

And Mr. Stanwood took the position that they were concerned in the matter of whether Leonard killed Manwell, or whether Ford killed Manwell, or whether Nielson killed Manwell. That, therefore, the testimony—we were not entitled to the testimony of the grand jury in regard to the matter of Manwell, but only the testimony that referred to our particular client suspected thereof. At least that is the plea that he put forward in court and later.

Moreover, we had a dispute as to when we were entitled to the testimony. The statute provides that the defendant is entitled to the testimony taken before the grand jury at least five days prior to the hearing. Well, it is customary as soon as testimony is taken before a grand jury to write it up and let the defendant have it. So if a witness testifies before the grand jury in favor of the defendant, the defendant can go out and subpoena him. But if he has only got five days before the trial, particularly in a complicated case, such as this, practically he has to come into court and ask for a continuance. Five days is not sufficient time to use the testimony before the grand jury which is written up, for the benefit of all concerned, for the benefit of having all the knowledge that is possible in regard to an investigation into the matter.

Now, I have here the testimony of this fellow Gleaser before the grand jury. And he testifies here that Nelson said to him that he, Nelson, had told the Porto Rican to pick up the deputy sheriff's gun and to shoot, and that the Porto Rican did so.

I have the testimony here. It is official.

That was very important testimony for the defense to get, because as it turned out at the trial one of the witnesses for the prosecution and two of the witnesses for the defendant—and there wasn't anything to the contrary—testified that what occurred on that ranch was this, at the time of the shooting, and as there is no particular dispute as to this I may as well tell it.

One of the officers of the armed posse that went into that crowd got up close to Ford and drew his gun, and one of the posse fired a gun, revolver, into the air; this was Mr. Durst's testimony and the testimony of others. When he drew this gun, and some say fired the gun, one of the hop pickers, believed to be the Porto Rican, struck him over the wrist. He struck him over the wrist, and the gun dropped out of the officer's hand down onto the ground, and the testimony of several others there was that the Porto Rican reached over when the officer fell. There was absolutely no necessity for drawing the gun under our theory, because, as the sheriff and everybody else admits, the crowd was perfectly quiet.

Then Daken—a deputy sheriff—blazed over the crowd with his shotgun, and the Porto Rican picked up the revolver off the ground and shot Manwell.

Several witnesses for the prosecution testified that Manwell and the Porto Rican were face to face, about 2 feet apart, when Maxwell fell.

The uncontradicted testimony being that Ford ran away, as this fellow Gleaser also testified before the grand jury. Therefore, you see, Gleaser would have been a very useful witness for the defense. He was brought down to Marysville before trial, and the attorneys for the prosecution decided that his testimony was of no advantage to the prosecution, and we had no opportunity to subpoena him or to confer with him or to use his testimony before the defense. Now, that, in the main, is the story of Gleaser.

Commissioner WEINSTOCK. What became of the Porto Rican?

Mr. ROYCE. The Porto Rican was shot. He was shot. There is a dispute by whom, but he was shot and killed. He was dead.

Chairman WALSH. We will now adjourn until to-morrow morning at 10 o'clock. Kindly resume the stand at 10 o'clock.

(Whereupon, at 4.40 o'clock p. m., on this Friday, the 28th day of August, 1914, an adjournment was taken to the following day, Saturday, August 28, 1914, at 10 o'clock a. m.)

SAN FRANCISCO, CAL., *Saturday, August 29, 1914—10 a. m.*

Present: Chairman Walsh, Commissioners Commons, Lennon, O'Connell, Garretson, and Weinstock; William O. Thompson, counsel.

Chairman WALSH. The commission will please be in order.

Mr. THOMPSON. Mr. Royce, will you resume the stand?

TESTIMONY OF MR. R. M. ROYCE—Continued.

Mr. THOMPSON. You may proceed with your statement, Mr. Royce.

Mr. ROYCE. At the last session I intended to state generally the general system pursued by the prosecution in Marysville in the conduct of these cases. To, pick up one matter before leaving the Gleaser incident: I was informed, and there are affidavits on file in the habeas corpus and other cases which state that Gleaser was 16 years of age at that time. Mr. Mundell said that Gleaser stated to him that he was 18. But my information is that he is 16. It's a minor matter.

Now, taking up and going on with the procedure in Marysville, and I do not want to repeat anything that I have gone over before, it is sufficient to state that generally I was not allowed to see prisoners or suspects confined in the various jails, in the two jails in Marysville.

When I would go to the sheriff and ask permission I would be referred to the district attorney; and when I went to the district attorney I got no satisfaction. And on applying to the superior court, the Superior Court of Yuba County would state that it had no power to instruct the district attorney to allow me to interview witnesses and people confined in the jail, because the jail was in the control of the sheriff; and he had no power to command the sheriff to allow me to inspect the jail, because the prisoners confined in the jail, other than my own clients, were in the control of the sheriff, and he had a wide discretion as to how they should be treated, on the theory that they might be safely kept in prison.

Now, all those matters were embodied in an affidavit filed in the supreme court of the State. It is on record in the supreme court of the State. It was filed—I think it was in December of last year—asking for a writ of mandate against Mr. Stanwood, to allow me to interview these prisoners. The supreme court took that under advisement and held it under advisement until the conclusion of the Marysville trials. And after those trials had been concluded they then denied it nunc pro tunc, as of the time it was filed, and have expressed no opinion otherwise on the merits of the proceeding whatsoever.

I could go into a good deal of detail in regard to the various batches of prisoners, or various batches of suspects and witnesses that were imprisoned in Marysville, and applications for writs of habeas corpus and their discharge on same.

Chairman WALSH. Well, if you will just give it generally, for instance, Mr. Royce, that some were arrested against whom there was no evidence, some were arrested simply because they were there—if such were the facts, and, in that way, because we can't carry the details.

Mr. ROYCE. I understand; but I don't intend to go into the details any further; they can be assumed.

Chairman WALSH. Yes.

Mr. ROYCE. Now, the only other matter which—the only other two matters which I think are worthy of taking up as being of special interest is one matter that occurred during the trial, or just before the trial commenced, and the other is the Suhr matter.

The papers in Marysville and Wheatland were very unfavorable to the defendants. In fact there was a constant statement and assumption that a murder was committed, and the International Defense League, the committee interested in the defense of these folks—Ford, Suhr, and others—got up a pamphlet and sent it to Yuba County and had it distributed throughout the county for the purpose of overcoming, if possible, the statements contained in the local press, or neutralizing them.

The judge of the superior court called Mr. Lewis and myself before him in court, not in the presence of the jury, however, or of the panel, and said we were guilty of contempt of court in circulating any such document throughout Yuba County.

That night or the next morning the reporters, who had been denied by Mr. Stanwood access to the prisoners, published articles in certain papers, namely, and among others the Sacramento Bee; and among other statements published, was the statement of Mr. Dayton to the effect that Suhr had been badly treated, and commenting on the methods employed by District Attorney Stanwood.

The judge then brought us before him again—before the court sitting formally as a court—and stated that he had decided to take no action whatever in regard to the publication in the press, but that that certainly ought to stop while the trial was in progress—which opinion was certainly the correct one.

Now, to take up the Suhr matter: I first found Suhr in the jail at Yuba City, and he was very white and very nervous, and had a gash on his arm, and slight gashes on his neck where he had attempted to commit suicide, and I₁ had great difficulty in seeing him. I finally succeeded in getting in communica-, tion with him. Now, the story he tells me is this:

He told me he was arrested in Arizona; taken to some station in Arizona and put in a box car, which was used as a place of detention. He was then taken, if I recollect correctly, to Los Angeles, detained there about a day, and then he was taken to Fresno and placed in the Fresno Jail, and Mr. Lewis told the commission about what occurred at the Fresno Jail; and from there he was taken to San Francisco and taken to a hotel, and at that hotel a detective sat at his feet during the night with a loaded revolver in his hand, and every time he would try to sleep he would talk to him and keep him awake.

From there he was taken to the Alameda County Jail and placed in a cell, which, from his description, seems to have been one of these graded cages. He was kept there, as I understand from him, two or three days; I think three days only. And they told him that he must talk.

He said that when he laid down on the bed they pulled the bedclothes off, and he said that when he laid down on the floor they poked him with long pieces of squills of paper rolled up, and he said when he leaned up against the side of the wall of his cell they would bang on the outside of the cell and make a noise.

Finally they took him out of the cell, and they walked him around and around until finally he said he would talk.

Then he said he dictated to them a statement. I asked him what that statement was, and he said he could not recall what it was, because he was in such a condition that he did not know what it was, but he said something about shooting.

I went to Sheriff Barnett, of Oakland, and the sheriff told me that Suhr had not been mistreated in his jail, but that, to tell the truth, he thought he had been mistreated somewhere else. When I saw Suhr in the jail in Yuba City the sheriff there said, "He is technically in my jail, but really I consider him in the control of the Burns detectives." And when I went in to speak to Suhr there was a detective rolled up on a cot with his fact toward the wall, a few feet off, evidently—Suhr said to me, "That man is there to listen." I had not even noticed him. Finally I got Suhr out in the outer office—the sheriff's outer office—and the sheriff went out of the room and shut the door.. I tried to talk to Suhr, but the door into the inner part of the inner room where the Burns men, theoretically his guards, were, was opened about 2 inches. I walked over to see, and then it was drawn shut from the inside.

I complained to the sheriff about it and said it was a case of eavesdropping, and he said no such thing had occurred at all. Anything more that I say will be merely a repetition of what I have gone over already, and the time of the commission is limited, and I have nothing further to say in this matter.

Chairman WALSH. Thank you very much, Mr. Royce.

Commissioner GARRETSON. I would like to ask a question.

Chairman WALSH. Mr. Garretson has a question he would like to ask.

Commissioner GARRETSON. What is the qualification of jurors?

Mr. ROYCE. Why, the qualification of jurors in this State is that they shall be on the assessment roll.

Commissioner GARRETSON. They must pay taxes?

Mr. ROYCE. They must pay taxes; they must be on the assessment roll.

Commissioner GARRETSON. Then there is nothing—no man is eligible to jury service except a property holder?

Mr. ROYCE. That is my understanding.

Commissioner GARRETSON. In sufficient amount to pay taxes thereon, a man that is subject—all his property is subject to exemption would not be competent for jury duty?

Mr. ROYCE. I think there is no property of any consequence in this State that is——

Commissioner GARRETSON. Subject to exemption.

Mr. ROYCE. No.

Commissioner GARRETSON. That is all.

Chairman WALSH. That is all. Go ahead.

Mr. THOMPSON. Is Mr. Stanwood here? [No response.] He is the prosecuting attorney and asked the privilege to be heard.

Chairman WALSH. All right. Call your next.

STATEMENT OF MR. EDWARD B. STANWOOD.

COURTHOUSE, MARYSVILLE, CAL.,
September 1, 1914.

WILLIAM O. THOMPSON, Esq.,
Counsel for United States Commission on Industrial Relations,
San Francisco, Cal.

DEAR SIR: During the session of the commission on last Friday, August 28, I spoke to Col. Weinstock about certain misstatements in the testimony of Mr. George L. Bell on which I desired to be heard. He referred me to you and you informed me that I should have an opportunity to make a statement at the conclusion of the announced program of that day. However, adjournment was taken for the day before such opportunity was afforded me, and I have been unable to attend your subsequent sessions. I, accordingly, ask that this letter be filed and considered as my testimony in the matter. As no oath is administered to witnesses, I suppose there will be no technical objection to this course. Mr. W. H. Carlin was called, apparently, as the prosecution's representative at the hearing, but as he stated on the stand he had little knowledge regarding matters previous to the actual trial of the Ford-Suhr case. These earlier matters are particularly within my own knowledge.

Mr. Bell stated in his testimony Friday that one Alfred Nelson was arrested and imprisoned by the Yuba County authorities with no charge against him, and finally released without having had a hearing. This is incorrect. Alfred Nelson was arrested upon a warrant, a complaint having previously been filed against him. He was given a preliminary examination by a magistrate and was held to answer for murder before the superior court. An information was filed against him for murder, this being an alternative proceeding to the finding of an indictment under California law. After the conviction of Ford and Suhr the case against Nelson was dismissed, on my motion, as it was regarded as comparatively a weak one, though I was then and still am of opinion that he was guilty. Mr. Bell also stated that one Brady was arrested and imprisoned by the Yuba County authorities with no charge against him, and that Brady, when arrested, told me that he was in jail in Idaho at the time of the Wheatland murders, and offered to produce proof of this fact; that finally Brady "managed to get a letter out to the Idaho authorities," and that upon word coming from them, his release followed. This is incorrect. Brady did have a definite charge lodged against him, and he did not say a word to me when arrested, or until shortly before being released, about the jail episode in Idaho. On the contrary, he carefully concealed it, and tried to account for the time so spent in jail (as afterwards claimed) by saying that he used this time—about two weeks—in traveling by rail from a certain point in Idaho to another in Utah—a journey which can not possibly take more than two days. Brady was at all times free to send out letters, and did not have to "manage" in order to do so. When finally he did tell me of his jail experience in Idaho, investigation was made, and he was released.

It was a little difficult to ascertain from Mr. Bell's testimony just when he was referring to the Wheatland murder cases and when to conditions in general. He spoke of vagrancy charges being preferred. I will state that no vagrancy charges were preferred against anyone held in connection with the Wheatland cases. Mr. Bell also spoke of a "dragnet" being cast for all suspicious characters. There was no dragnet in the Wheatland cases. Everyone who was arrested was arrested on a definite charge based on evidence against him.

In all cases I have given careful personal investigation as much from the point of the defendant as of the people. This, I know to be the custom of the district attorneys I am acquainted with, and I believe it to be the general custom of district attorneys throughout California. The institution of a public defender is still in an experimental stage, but in my opinion there are two functions such an officer might fill—first, that of providing a defendant with counsel in the lower court, and second, that of relieving members of the bar from unpaid services in behalf of defendant. But there is no need of a public defender to protect the defendant from the district attorneys of this State. Give the district attorneys an elastic provision for extra assistance when needed and there will be no lack in efficiency either in favor of or against the defendant.

In Mr. Austin Lewis's testimony before the commission, on Friday, there was a statement especially calling for comment. He said that the officers who were assaulted at Wheatland "were none too sober." There is absolutely no truth to this whatever and no shred of evidence to support it. The exact contrary is the truth—namely, that the officers were absolutely sober, and moderate and conciliatory in their actions.

I heard only a part of Mr. R. M. Royce's testimony, and do not know whether it contained anything of sufficient importance to call for notice from me. In general, Mr. Lewis and Mr. Royce appeared in their testimony to be going over familiar ground. The judges of .the superior courts of Yuba and Sutter Counties and the district attorney of Yuba County were accused, as they have been before by the same gentlemen, of various kinds of arbitrary action, including in the case of the judges unfairness in habeas corpus proceedings and the " railroading " of an alleged sane person—Allan Johnson—to a State hospital for the insane. It is unfortunate that the judges in question had no opportunity to be heard by your commission on these matters. So far as I know, however, no weight has ever been attached by anyone to these accusations when previously made, and it is unlikely that they will make any different impression at this time.

Very .respectfully,

EDWARD B. STANWOOD,
District Attorney of Yuba County, Cal.

EXHIBITS.

E. CLEMENS HORST CO.,
San Francisco, December 15, 1914.

on on *Industrial Relations.*

your favor of December 7:
r of employees that we have on our hop ranches during
during the harvest season, during which time the num-
follows:

```
---------------------------------------         400
---------------------------------------          50
--------------------------------------          175
---------------------------------------         175
---------------------------------------         350
---------------------------------------         170
---------------------------------------         360
-------------------------------------- 1, 050
---------------------------------------         150
'olumbia ------------------------------ 1,200
h Columbia--------------------------- 1,400
                                        ------
-------------------------------------- 5,480
```

further information we will be pleased to furnish you

E. C. HORST.

5027

ENT IN CALIFORNIA

this subject, see pages 5079 to 5085.)

COMMISSION ON INDUSTRIAL RELATIONS.

SAN FRANCISCO, CAL., *Saturday, August 29, 1914—10 a. m.*
Present: Chairman Walsh, Commissioners Weinstock, Garretson, Lennon, O'Connell, and Commons. William O. Thompson, counsel.
Mr. THOMPSON. Mr. Lilienthal.

TESTIMONY OF MR. JESSE W. LILIENTHAL.

Mr. THOMPSON. Will you give us your name and your address and your profession, Mr. Lilienthal.

Mr. LILIENTHAL. My name is Jesse W. Lilienthal. I am an attorney at law, and president of the United Railroads.

Mr. THOMPSON. How long have you been located in San Francisco?

Mr. LILIENTHAL. Something over 20 years.

Mr. THOMPSON. And practicing law for many years here?

Mr. LILIENTHAL. During all of that time.

Mr. THOMPSON. How long have you been chairman or president of the United Railroads?

Mr. LILIENTHAL. Just one year to-day.

Mr. THOMPSON. You might state generally where that road operates, or those roads.

Mr. LILIENTHAL. Well, it operates principally in the city and county of San Francisco. It also has an interurban line running over into the county of San Mateo, altogether operating about 275 miles of road.

Mr. THOMPSON. How long have you been connected with the road other than as president?

Mr. LILIENTHAL. I never had any connection with it at all until I became president.

Mr. THOMPSON. Now, Mr. Lilienthal, you are also chairman of the Municipal Relief Committee of San Francisco, are you?

Mr. LILIENTHAL. I was during much of last winter when we were working on that matter.

Mr. THOMPSON. During that time, of course, and before, you had come in contact with the question of the unemployed here?

Mr. LILIENTHAL. Yes; more or less.

Mr. THOMPSON. Particularly in the wintertime?

Mr. LILIENTHAL. For many years.

Mr. THOMPSON. For many years?

Mr. LILIENTHAL. Yes.

Mr. THOMPSON. Will you kindly give us your opinion as to the causes of the periodical acuteness of the problems of unemployment in this State?

Mr. LILIENTHAL. Well, I think the conditions that obtained last winter were not particularly unusual, and are likely to recur each winter, principally, I think, from the periodical cessation of work in the logging camps and in the fisheries up north, resulting in men that have been accumulating a little money perhaps from the work they have been doing, seeking some place where it is pleasant to live, as it is in San Francisco in the winter, and where opportunities are afforded for enjoying one's self, and after a time getting rid of the savings, and then walking the streets, and most of them seek employment, of course, in something that is outside of their usual line. Is that the question? I do not mean to volunteer anything. Conditions, I think, are going to be very much aggravated in the immediate future.

Mr. THOMPSON. What do you consider the main contributing causes to this army of unemployment?

Mr. LILIENTHAL. Well, I can think of nothing else than what I have stated, so far as our past experience is concerned. Men are unable to work at certain

5031

occupations except for a certain number of months of the year, and then at the expiration of that time there being no use for them in that particular employment, they gravitate to other places and seek work of a different character, perhaps, from what they have been accustomed to, and find it or do not find it.

Mr. THOMPSON. Do you consider that the supply of labor in California to-day, leaving out for a moment the question of seasonal work, is too large.

Mr. LILIENTHAL. Under normal conditions I should not say so. I don't think we are at the present time under quite normal conditions, and there is evidence at the present time of an excess of labor, I think.

Mr. THOMPSON. Then the fact under normal conditions—the main contributing cause would be the seasonal character of the work?

Mr. LILIENTHAL. That is true in California, particularly in San Francisco.

Mr. THOMPSON. To what extent, if any, would the maladjustment of economic conditions—that is to say, in other respects—contribute to the army of the unemployed?

Mr. LILIENTHAL. Well, I think in the experience we had last winter the maladjustment is due purely to the circumstances I related—that a man, being deprived of his usual occupation, say, through no fault of his own, and having accumulated a little money, would naturally go to the place where it is pleasant to live, and perhaps where, because of the size of the community, there is unusual chance for finding other employment; I don't know any other case of maladjustment in this community.

Chairman WALSH. Has any study been made by you, or anyone connected with you, as to a means of bridging over these conditions here in California; that is, making the work less seasonal, or easier for the men to get at, or anything of that sort?

Mr. LILIENTHAL. Well, I think—I have not had the pleasure of attending the hearings, and I do not know whether the commission has been already informed—but I think perhaps a recital of the exact experience we had last winter would be interesting.

Chairman WALSH. I wish you would give it to us.

Mr. LILIENTHAL. If it has not been mentioned before.

Chairman WALSH. It has not been. You are the first witness on the subject.

Mr. LILIENTHAL. The city officials, early in the winter, were informed of the fact that a large number of people in San Francisco were unemployed and seeking employment. They had a certain fund—I think it was approximately $30,000 and no more—that, with the approval of the supervisors, could be applied to some such purpose as taking care of those who needed assistance, because of the unemployment. In the expenditure of the money they were absolutely governed by the conditions of the city charter, which provided that no city employee should be paid less than $3 a day or work more than eight hours a day.

And considering the limited size of the fund and the large number of people seeking employment and the attraction that these conditions afforded to others outside of the city, the city authorities very soon became convinced that they were not able to deal with the situation; and thereupon concluded to assemble a number of citizens who should occupy themselves with the matter as one of private philanthropy. And with that in view, a committee of 100 was selected by the appropriation committee of the board of supervisors, and that committee met at the city hall to organize and determine how they should deal with the situation. Very early in that session some one whose philanthropy was not under question at all, because of his record in the community, said that times were pretty hard; that we had a large number of people here to deal with—it was estimated to be about 7,500, and, of course, numbers of others dependent on those 7,500—and it was not likely that we could raise a very large sum; it behooved us, therefore, to husband our resources, cut our coat according to our cloth, and begin by giving a dollar a day to such as we could furnish employment to. That committee of 100 represented all classes—capitalists, employers, employees, heads of labor unions—all shades of opinion were represented.

And immediately upon the making of that suggestion I remember a very bitter opposition developed upon the ground that this was an insidious attempt to establish a wage which was not a living wage. And while protests were made that nothing of the kind was intended, it looked for a little while as if the entire movement would collapse, and it was only by the adoption of a resolution referring the entire question to an executive committee to determine the conditions under which such money as might be raised would be expended that, I think, the situation was saved. That executive committee recommended that the city should designate places where work might be done, and that the work should be done at such places; that men should be paid 20 cents an hour and not necessarily be employed the full day, but for such time as they did work that they should receive 20 cents an hour. And that method was adopted, and I think that saved the situation.

I refer to the matter as indicating, in the first instance, the unavoidable antagonism that develops when the matter is dealt with as a private charity, and, secondly, because when we made appeals to people of means to help us out in the situation, to furnish money that we needed to take care of the situation, over and over again we found a disposition of resentment because of the opposition shown at the outset on the plea that men should not be paid so small a wage as this 20 cents an hour.

As a matter of fact, however, we succeeded in raising some $40,000, and that, with the money the city had available, the $30,000, pretty well carried us through the worst of it. We would employ a man perhaps four hours and give him 80 cents, or 5 hours and give him $1. If he was a married man we would do better than that. But little by little, I think, we bridged over the worst. I mention these incidents because I think they are inevitable in any community, certainly in this community, when the matter is undertaken to be handled by private charity. I believe that answers the question.

Chairman WALSH. Have you given any thought to the probable methods of dealing ■ith this question of unemployment generally, Mr. Lilienthal, such as the establishment of some public agency by the Government of the United States or the State government?

Mr. LILIENTHAL. I have, Mr. Chairman.

Chairman WALSH. Kindly give us your views.

Mr. LILIENTHAL. I am not certain that I haven't some very radical notions about it. I start out with the idea that the man who is willing to work is entitled to have work from the point of view that under those conditions he and his family should not be permitted to starve. I purposely referred to those incidents of last winter, because I presumed it would be followed up by questions leading up to just this subject.

Private charity can't deal with the situation. In other words, I conceive it to be the duty of the State to take care of just such situations as developed here last winter. The State, as at present constituted, isn't in position to take care of the situation, so that calls for some remedial legislation. Primarily, I don't know why we should not provide a fund by the State, raised by taxation in the ordinary way, to take care of the unemployed—that is, those who are honestly seeking employment and can't find it because of special conditions— just exactly the same as the State takes care of the insane and sick, and so on. And I think, maybe, Mr. Chairman, it might be well to go one step further than that. It may be well to protect the employees—some of them need this protection—against the lack of thrift on their own part. I am not certain now that I am not going to suggest something that has not been suggested before, and perhaps I haven't thought it out thoroughly, but it is a horseback opinion and I give it for what it is worth.

In other words, it occurs to me that it might be well worth considering to require every employer of labor to set apart from the wages due his employee a certain per cent—what that should be I don't know—and having set it apart, to turn that per cent over to the State, constituting the State, in a sense, a savings bank for the employee, to the extent of the money that has been set apart, with the right on the part of some commission—just as we have railroad commissions and industrial accident boards and what not—to determine upon a proper presentation of a case by the employee to whom that money belongs and for whom it is reserved, and upon which he is entitled to get at least a moderate rate of savings bank interest—to determine, upon the application of the employee under the circumstances he presents, whether the whole or any part of that sum should be paid out to him.

Then for one thing we have saved up a little money for him, which under proper application to some State body constituted in the proper way, he may receive in times of need. I am not familiar in a general way with the unemployment insurance. It may be that the employer should be compelled in addition to that to contribute some per cent of his own and the State some certain per cent, as has been tried abroad; but I should say that that would depend on the best place to raise the money,—that is, raising it where it will constitute the smallest burden—and it may be it should not be from the employer, but simply an additional tax to be collected.

Chairman WALSH. Have you to any degree studied the cause or observed the effect of private employment agencies as at present run, on the seasonable labor and on the whole question of unemployment?

Mr. LILIENTHAL. I don't believe I am competent to express an opinion on that point. I know we have all kinds of employment agencies.

Chairman WALSH. You haven't studied them closely?

Mr. LILIENTHAL. Not closely.

Chairman WALSH. Have you thought anything——

Mr. LILIENTHAL. I welcome any kind of cooperation even from them; that would be my opinion, until we have some State body, such as is contemplated by the methods suggested before the commission.

Chairman WALSH. Have you heard the tentative proposal before the commission as to a system of free employment agencies?

Mr. LILIENTHAL. I think it is exactly right and should displace everything else. I don't want to discourage the Young Women's Christian Association, or the Young Men's Christian Association, or other proper charitable organizations from helping along as they do in emergencies to find employment; but whether or not they would be interfering with such agencies as this commission has in mind I don't know.

Chairman WALSH. Generally speaking, the plan looks feasible.

Mr. LILIENTHAL. Yes, sir; absolutely all right.

Chairman WALSH. That is all. Just a moment. Mr. Garretson would like to ask a question.

Commissioner GARRETSON. Your idea as presented, and if I gather it correctly, is that the State—I am not giving its political term here, but the body at large, the Nation—owes as much to the citizen as the citizen owes to the State?

Mr. LILIENTHAL. Yes, sir.

Commissioner GARRETSON. In the employment agency idea, I gather your idea is that employment agencies should be tolerated; that is, in the final adjustment of the scheme, that levies tribute upon the man seeking work?

Mr. LILIENTHAL. That is provided an adequate substitute——

Commissioner GARRETSON. I say, if your scheme was put into effect.

Mr. LILIENTHAL. Yes, sir; along the lines suggested.

Commissioner GARRETSON. On the line of private employment agencies, no scheme should be employed which makes the laborer pay tribute?

Mr. LILIENTHAL. I agree to that absolutely.

Commissioner GARRETSON. That is all.

Commissioner WEINSTOCK. Just one question: Are you at all familiar with the European system of unemployment insurance?

Mr. LILIENTHAL. Just generally. I don't believe I could enter into any discussion. I have read pamphlets about it.

Commissioner WEINSTOCK. From what you know about it, do you think it would apply to American conditions—that we could follow the example of Europe along those lines?

Mr. LILIENTHAL. I believe we could with proper enlightenment of the public once we made them understand it; but I would develop it along the lines I have suggested, which I think involves some difference, perhaps, from the way the scheme is worked out abroad. That is to say, I would make it a compulsory savings bank for the employee, not something that is kept away from him, but kept away from him for a time until he comes along and says to the proper State authorities, "I have been sick," or "I am out of work, and I need this money," and have a commission whose business it is to deal with just such questions say he should or should not have all or have part and not all.

Commissioner WEINSTOCK. You would require that the employee shall be called upon to contribute to a fund out of his wage?

Mr. LILIENTHAL. Yes, sir; and the employer should be required to contribute a certain per cent.

Commissioner WEINSTOCK. From the work.

Mr. LILIENTHAL. And turn it over to the State treasurer for disbursement by him for the benefit of the employee when the occasion requires.

Commissioner WEINSTOCK. Would you have the employer also contribute to that fund?

Mr. LILIENTHAL. There must, of course, be some supplemental contribution, and I meant to say before, that whether it should be done by the employer himself or through money raised by some other method of taxation that might be less burdensome I don't know—but the money should be raised. In other words, a stated fund should be there. I realize, I think, the spirit under which the workmen's compensation act was adopted here, the notion being that the employer should be compelled to do something and that he could recompense himself by higher prices on the things disposed of. I am not certain that in practice that always works out equitably to the particular employer. That is to say, it does with some and does not with others. It may be that would be the very best way.

Chairman WALSH. Have you given any thought to the suggestion that has been made by different publicists in different places of the State operating what is commonly known as State farms in which to bridge over the gap between the employing seasons?

Mr. LILIENTHAL. Well, I have got very strong opinions on that point, gentlemen. I don't see, particularly in a State like California, where we have vast tracts of land undeveloped and vast tracts of land held in private ownership unsubdivided, that the Government in the one instance should not prepare the land, make it fit for cultivation, and in the other instance, if necessary, by condemnation proceedings, make an enforced subdivision of these large tracts, and then do a little something perhaps along the lines of the land purchase act in England; select appropriate persons and put them on the land as tenants, like under a contract of purchase, with the right to acquire the land, under proper supervision, which will be perfectly practical considering the school of agriculture we have in this State of California; under proper superintendence, telling them that this land is most available for a certain purpose; the seed should be sown at a certain time and cultivation should be made at a certain time; but the man himself all the time getting the benefit of the work that he is doing and ultimately acquiring title to the land. I don't know why that is not entirely practical in California, but, of course, it is an ideal condition.

Now, some men don't want to become farmers. I don't mean to say that they should be driven upon the farm at the end of a bayonet. But all kinds of people would be glad to go if they only saw a way to finance themselves. And that is particularly important when we are all talking about the development of this State through the opening of the Panama Canal and talking of bringing in all kinds of agricultural immigrants who should be put upon the land.

Commissioner WEINSTOCK. Are you at all familiar with the Australasian system of dealing with that problem?

Mr. LILIENTHAL. Only very generally, Mr. Weinstock.

Commissioner WEINSTOCK. Well, briefly, it is this, and I would invite your opinion as to whether you think it could be made to apply to California or to other American States:

The Australasian Governments, Australia as well as New Zealand, does very much what you have outlined here, in buying up bodies of land that have been experted, the quality of which has been assured, issuing Government bonds to cover the purchase price, then cutting up these bodies of land into small parcels after they have been properly drained and improved under scientific management, selling those small parcels to selected colonists, men who in the judgment of the Government are fit mentally and physically to handle the proposition, calling upon them to pay an installment, I think, possibly as low as 10 per cent of the purchase price and not to exceed 20 per cent of the purchase price; making the balance payable on the amortization scheme—that is, in installments covering a period of from 30 to 50 years, so that the colonist is called upon to pay only as little as a half of 1 per cent a year on the principal, and not to exceed 1 per cent on the principal charged him, and on the interest on the deferred payments, charging exactly what the Government itself pays, which is the lowest world rate, plus, say, a half per cent for cost of administration; in addition to that, furnishing a trained instructor, an agricultural instructor who has had a college education, to live among the group of colonists and educate them agriculturally, to guide and direct them and be their friend and adviser and counselor; in addition to that, advancing a further amount, large enough to build a modern cottage constructed on scientific principles at the least possible cost, and making that likewise payable on the amortization scheme, covering a long period of years. Do you know of any reason why that same idea could not be transplanted on American soil successfully?

Mr. LILIENTHAL. I do not know why not; and that accords with my own idea, with one exception; I would not even, as we are dealing with the matter of unemployment here, I would not even exact the initial payment.

Commissioner WEINSTOCK. You would not?

38819°—S. Doc. 415, 64–1—vol 5——60

Mr. LILIENTHAL. No; let the man have it, because he can not acquire the title until he has paid for it. Give him a chance to get started, and if he is an industrious man give him a chance to get started on the land.

Commissioner WEINSTOCK. In other words, you would go as far as England, and you would follow the Irish peasant?

Mr. LILIENTHAL. I would.

Commissioner WEINSTOCK. Advancing the purchase price?

Mr. LILIENTHAL. Yes.

Commissioner GARRETSON. Does not the difference in the plan named and the one you have in mind consist largely in this fact, one is devised to attract colonists and the other to meet an existing condition that we have? We have people here, and we desire to take care of them; that is your idea?

Mr. LILIENTHAL. Yes. I think that is one way of taking care of them. They would not all want to become farmers, but a great many would under those conditions. I am satisfied of that from personal experience and talking with people out of work.

Commissioner GARRETSON. Is it not your idea, Mr. Lilienthal, that if that class of the floating population, the unattached population that we have who desire to go upon the land, went there, that would relieve the overplus that exists in other pursuits?

Mr. LILIENTHAL. No doubt.

Commissioner GARRETSON. And in other industries, as a rule?

Mr. LILIENTHAL. I have no doubt in the world of it.

Commissioner WEINSTOCK. Acting as a safety valve?

Mr. LILIENTHAL. As a safety valve.

Commissioner COMMONS. I would like to ask about this rate of pay; what was the actual effect or result, the city's limitation that it should pay not less than——

Mr. LILIENTHAL. $3 a day.

Commissioner COMMONS. That would be 37½ cents an hour. You actually used city money to pay 20 cents an hour?

Mr. LILIENTHAL. Oh, no. By that time we had exhausted the fund. But some of it was used in the providing of food. We had a soup kitchen here which was maintained by the city. But so far as the city paid any wages at all, they paid them conformably to the charter conditions. There was no violation of law.

Commissioner COMMONS. They kept up some of the soup kitchens out of that money?

Mr. LILIENTHAL. Yes; they did that; and that is where most of the money went. Then, we raised——

Commissioner COMMONS. I suppose the objection to paying less than that minimum wage came from the unions——

Mr. LILIENTHAL. Yes.

Commissioner COMMONS. The labor people?

Mr. LILIENTHAL. Yes.

Commissioner COMMONS. And their idea was that it would break down the minimum wage?

Mr. LILIENTHAL. Yes; that was the argument. And the answer was——

Commissioner COMMONS. Did you have any—what was the answer?

Mr. LILIENTHAL. I was going to say that the answer was that nothing of the kind is intended. The very object—the question was as to conserving the resources in hand. We succeeded ultimately in raising altogether about $40,000. We had approximately 7,500 people to take care of. That many were registered. Finally some dropped out when they were up against the actual conditions that we prescribed. We could not afford to do any better. And the idea was to bridge these people over the interval of time where they had no employment, so that we could at least keep them from starving. We were only trying to protect them so far as we could with the amount of money that we were able to get; there was no pretense that these men were amply compensated according to any fair standard, but it was a question of conservation. We did the best we could. We wanted to take care of all worthy persons who applied for assistance. We had only so much money. As I said before, we cut our coat according to our cloth.

Finally, I think, the view was asquiesced in by all persons, with one exception. I don't want to be wandering away from the subject, but perhaps that would be of some interest; that is, the so-called army of unemployment—

we had one branch of that army in San Francisco. I remember when we had gotten pretty well to the end of our fund—shall I speak of this, gentlemen?

Chairman WALSH. Certainly; you may proceed.

Mr. LILIENTHAL. We were waited upon at the city hall—the executive committee of the citizens and the appropriation committee of the board of supervisors always cooperated—we were waited on by Mr. Kelley, I think it was, who was the head of the branch of the army of the unemployed in San Francisco. He came to us and asked for money enough to send them across the bay to Oakland, the statement being that they were moving from place to place and did not have the means to get out of San Francisco. I did not attempt to speak for anybody but myself—I do not know that I ever have spoken for anybody but myself about that particular thing—but I said that I would not allow one single penny to be contributed for any such purpose, they were living in San Francisco, it was San Francisco's problem, and we must solve it here the best way we could.

Now, I said, if you men will go to work on the same conditions that the others went to work, the others of the unemployed who have been taken care of, we will make another effort, an additional appeal to the people for more funds, so that we can take care of you, as we have taken care of the others, and on the same basis. And his answer, with his fist pretty closely protruded into my face, was, " I dare you to go down south of Market Street to that army and make the same statement there that you have made to me." Well, I didn't go down, maybe, because of lack of courage on my part. Nothing came of that. But somehow this army managed to get across the bay to Oakland, and then they went from place to place, and it has been insinuated, I think, that the citizens' committee was instrumental in sending them out of San Francisco. That has done this committee a great injustice, and I am glad of the opportunity of stating that that is not the fact. We recognized that they were here; it was our problem, and we must deal with it the best way we could.

Commissioner COMMONS. Am I correct in this understanding, that all those who objected to this 20-cent rate, the lower rate than the standard, finally yielded except Kelley and the army?

Mr. LILIENTHAL. Oh, yes. We talked it over. We went to see the mayor after we developed our plans, and then we spoke to one or two gentlemen who were prominent among the unions, and we told them the purpose, that we did not know what else we could do, and it was simply giving them something to do to tide them over, and that we were making no claim that 20 cents was an adequate wage for labor. There was no pretense that that was an adequate wage; it was simply a case of so many people to take care of, and so much money to take care of them with, and we must do the best we could to alleviate the misery.

Commissioner COMMONS. Under your scheme of unemployment insurance have you an idea that it would obviate any such menace to the wage scale; that is, men would not be required to work at all; if they are unemployed they would be paid out of this employment fund, and could still remain idle, be furnished free living expenses over the period of unemployment? Is that your idea?

Mr. LILIENTHAL. No; that is not my idea at all.

Commissioner COMMONS. Is that your idea of the way out of this argument?

Mr. LILIENTHAL. No. My idea would be that the commission that might be appointed to handle the situation and distribute such funds as might be provided by the State should deal with the situation precisely as this committee did.

We started off with a registration of approximately seventy-five hundred. I happen to notice one or two gentlemen present who can give you more accurate figures that I can. I am only approximating it. We made the registration; we asked them, " Where do you live? What is your family? What have you done in the past? What are you seeking to do? We will put you to work at such and such a place, under such and such conditions, at 20 cents an hour. We won't give you anything but work," and we did not give anything but work. And I think that within a very few days the registration of seventy-five hundred, approximately that amount, dwindled down to twenty-five hundred; that is, just a third of the registration of men honestly seeking employment and willing to accept work under any condition, living or otherwise, just to get something to eat and to have a few cents to take home to the family to provide support.

Now, I would expect such a commission as I have had in mind to deal with the situation in the same way, and provide employment, and where employment· did not exist to at least provide bread and butter, on the notion that a man should not be allowed to starve who has the right attitude and is willing to work.

Commissioner COMMONS. What kind of work was that that was provided? ·

Mr. LILIENTHAL. Street work, the roughest sort of street work. We got permission from the Federal authorities to build a road out at the Presidio.' They built a road out there. And we got permission from the city authorities to build some. We were very anxious that these men should be employed. There was no attempt under any circumstances to change the ruling scale of wages. But when the work was done for the city, wholly for the benefit of the city or for the benefit of the Nation, there was no room for that implication; it was just that we had to have this kind of work somewhere. We did not want to dole out money.

Commissioner COMMONS. Of that seventy-five hundred at least five thousand were not willing to work?

Mr. LILIENTHAL. Under those conditions. They managed somehow to get along. I would expect any governing body dealing with the problem to do so with some discretion. We did not want to pauperize the people. I realized this; we did not want to do anything of that kind. We wanted to help the man to be thrifty, and to help him to do something to keep his family from starving.

Commissioner COMMONS. Do you think in this form of unemployment insurance there should be a provision for those who can work, that they should be required to work at less than the scale of wages in times of unemployment?

Mr. LILIENTHAL. Should not be required, no, sir; but I would refuse assistance if they asked for it, unless they accepted· the conditions imposed.

Commissioner COMMONS. Refuse their participation in the unemployment insurance if they did not work? That is the only ·provision you would take into account? Not merely their willingness, but their ability to work? There might be tradesmen, tailors, for instance, that could not work at that sort of work. That man would have to then be offered work in the trades that he was competent to work in.

Mr. LILIENTHAL. I am not sure that I would say that; I mean work that he was physically able to do. I can understand a man, for instance, with weak lungs, if you like, having some light occupation somewhere that he can survive under. If he is told to take a pick and shovel and break up the rock, he would succumb, but give him something that he was physically able to do, that he is qualified to do. I say yes. I answer the ·question yes.

Commissioner COMMONS. Has this matter ·of unemployment insurance been taken up by anyone else in an organized way?

Mr. LILIENTHAL. No.

Commissioner COMMONS. In California? ·

Mr. LILIENTHAL. No.

Commissioner COMMONS. Just a matter that you propose on your own initiative and without any organization that is attempting to bring about such a thing?

Mr. LILIENTHAL. Personally I really would like, at least, while I have the opportunity of sitting in this chair, of suggesting some things that I personally have done; that is to say, that I have had occasion to observe and try out, because, anyway, this is missionary work, and if it is good gospel we had better, spread it. For instance, in the United Railroads, I persuaded—I succeeded in persuading the insurance companies, quite a number, to fall in line and take all of my employees in a group and to insure their lives without any physical examination, and, of course, without any expense on the part of the employee.

That scheme went into effect the 1st of January of this year. Presently a man who undoubtedly could not have passed a medical examination on the part of these insurance companies, if he had applied in the usual way for a life insurance policy, drops down dead, weak heart, or a case of tuberculosis, or what not. And immediately there is $1,000 paid ·to his family. Now, I know what that has meant to that family that is concerned—no money saved, or very little, extra expenses to pay in view of the funeral—$1,000 there looks as big as a mountain to them.

And then in addition to that, and this is something that I am occupying, myself with just to-day really—we have here a very excellent institution, philanthropic of course, similar in character to other institutions throughout the country—you gentlemen are no doubt familiar with the character of it—which we call the Remedial Loan Association, the purpose of which is to loan money in moderate amounts to people who need it for the moment and who have something to put up by way of collateral; that is, a piano, or a chair, or a bracelet, or what not. But that has not yet come to a point—and it is a very young association with no opportunity to accumulate much of a surplus yet to extend its work to a credit business. That is to say, a man comes to them and says, ".I need-$20.". "All right, you can have it. What have you got to put up?." "Well, I haven't got anything to put up." And as we are conducting that association to-day he is refused the money.

We have discussed the matter of character credit, and we have concluded that we must wait a bit until we have a little more capital or surplus so as to care for the losses incidental to that kind of business.

If I can get the approval of my board of directors in the United Railroads— and of course that would apply only to our own employees—I propose to have a fund set apart for the benefit of our employees to be used in just that way by people who have not got anything to put up, but do need a little money to turn the corner. And I mention this matter this morning because I think that it might be a very interesting project for all employers of labor to be considering. I am not certain that it is germane to the subject, but in a general way it ■ffects the condition of the employee and his welfare.

Commissioner GARRETSON. Did you get the thread of that idea from the German mutuals?

Mr. LILIENTHAL. No. Frankly, so far as I am personally concerned, I have taken the credit for it myself.

Commissioner GARRETSON. That is purely a personal matter in a group, each man standing as a guarantor for his associates.

Mr. LILIENTHAL. That is just the question, as to whether it would be practicable. Take an organization such as ours—you might do it in a small way, you might get a little group together who would be willing to work together. But at all events I think the principle of it is right, and I hope we can somehow work out a plan that we will be able to put into operation in the United Railroads.

Commissioner GARRETSON. In evolving these ideas of social legislation, or whatever we might term them, in the course of formulating the idea, have you noted how many of the functions that you suggest are already performed by many labor unions on behalf of their own membership?

Mr. LILIENTHAL. Oh, I know there is a great deal of that done. Any work that I would be doing I would feel would be cumulative.

Commissioner GARRETSON. Both in life insurance and in pensions, too? That is, I am using pension in the term not applied to anything but disablement.

Mr. LILIENTHAL. I am very much interested to ask the commissioner if in cases of that kind the physical examination is dispensed with?

Commissioner GARRETSON. In the insurance; no.

Mr. LILIENTHAL. I know it is not in the regular life insurance.

Commissioner GARRETSON. But I mean in these fraternal insurances; in some it is and in some it is not. But in the pensions it is only used to establish absolute physical disability to earn, except in case of age. Where age brings inability then there is no physical examination necessary.

Mr. LILIENTHAL. I felt I had accomplished a great, good work when I got this insurance for the men without physical examination, because so many of them could not have stood examinations.

Commissioner GARRETSON. That is true. One thing I just wanted to call attention to: In the most of the unions that carry that form of benefits they make the man do it, which brings out your idea that the should be guarded against himself. They compel their members to conform to those.

Mr. LILIENTHAL. Protect them against lack of thrift on their own part.

Commissioner WEINSTOCK. Just one more question, Mr. Lilienthal: You express the opinion that, owing to the existing conditions, the situation of the unemployed is likely to be aggravated in the near fuure. I take it that that would not be local in its character; that that is likely to be the common condition all over the country.

Mr. LILIENTHAL. Yes.

Commissioner WEINSTOCK. Well, now, with the experience of the past as a guide, how would you meet the problems pending these ideal conditions that you and I and the rest of us hope for? With the experience of last winter behind you, if you have the same situation in an aggravated form to deal with, say, in this city, the coming winter, how would you handle it?

Mr. LILIENTHAL. It may be necessary to appeal to Gov. Johnson to call a special session of the legislature to deal with it. The public is less able to respond to-day; that is, these so-called people of means, because they are not in a very comfortable condition themselves. Times are very hard for everybody. I would not expect to be any more successful this winter in making an appeal than I was last winter. Conditions are apt to be worse. I am very confident they are going to be worse for a little while. And as I say, we must not let people starve. That is the problem, and it might be a question of starvation. As I say, in the case of men honestly seeking employment and willing to work under any old conditions just to make some food for their families——

Commissioner WEINSTOCK. Well, now, what could the State do even if the situation should become as acute as it may become—sufficiently acute to justify the governor in calling a special session of the legislature?

Mr. LILIENTHAL. Of course——

Commissioner WEINSTOCK. As I understand the law, all the State could do would be to proceed to make certain public improvements; but that would have to be submitted to the people, and the bonds would have to be voted upon.

Mr. LILIENTHAL. Well, we had one concrete instance last winter where we got very cordial cooperation from the governor. You may remember that there was an appropriation made of $70,000 looking to the building of a highway, conditioned upon obtaining a grant of right of way from the people through whose lands the highway was to be built. And in our distress here, looking for assistance where we could get it, we appealed to the governor, and he said, "Why, yes; if you can just straigthen out this right of way business I will put your men to work immediately." And we were met in a very broad spirit. I know I made the suggestion, perhaps that is one of some interest to the commission, that the rest of the State might resent the expenditure of this $70,000 in San Francisco; that is to say by the employment of people who were temporarily in San Francisco; because, whenever an appropriation is made for expense, every one in the State feels that he is entitled to some benefit from it.

The governor made no trouble on that score at all, although the question was put up to him directly. He said, "Straighten out this right of way and I will see you get your $70,000." Well, we were slow in getting that straightened out; people were reasonable enough about it, but a certain amount of timber was destroyed, and when we said, "Give us some money for the right of way," it was slow. By the time it was occomplished and the men were put to work the question was pretty well solved; that is, the period had been tided over, the men were leaving the city and going elsewhere, for instance, for the canning season.

But I can't think of any other way, Mr. Commissioner, except to find something to do to put the men to work on. Sometimes we must not allow a little thing like the constitution to stand in the way, you know. We have been told that before.

Commissioner GARRETSON. Not between friends.

Mr. LILIENTHAL. Not between friends.

Chairman WALSH. Is that all?

Commissioner GARRETSON. Yes.

Chairman WALSH. Thank you, Mr. Lilienthal.

Chairman WALSH. Mr. Scharrenberg.

TESTIMONY OF MR. PAUL SCHARRENBERG.

Chairman WALSH. Your name, please.

Mr. SCHARRENBERG. Paul Scharrenberg.

Chairman WALSH. Your business?

Mr. SCHARRENBERG. I am editor of the Coast Seamen's Journal, and secretary-treasurer of the California State Federation of Labor.

Chairman WALSH. Secretary-treasurer of the State federation of labor?

Mr. SCHARRENBERG. Yes.

Chairman WALSH. How long have you lived in San Francisco?

Mr. SCHARRENBERG. Well, I used to go to sea for many years, but I have been located here since 1898.

Chairman WALSH. You have been located here permanently since 1898?
Mr. SCHARRENBERG. Since 1898; yes.
Chairman WALSH. Away from the sea?
Mr. SCHARRENBERG. No. I used to go to sea up to 1901.
Chairman WALSH. In what capacity?
Mr. SCHARRENBERG. As a sailor.
Chairman WALSH. Have you observed so that you can give us an opinion, as to the cause of this periodical acuteness in the problem of unemployment, Mr. Scharrenberg?
Mr. SCHARRENBERG. Yes, sir; I have, to some extent.
Chairman WALSH. Were these questions submitted to you?
Mr. SCHARRENBERG. Yes, sir.
Chairman WALSH. While we are hurrying through, we would like to get what you have to say on the subject concisely, and if you can do it with the questions I would prefer you would. The questions are short, and you can just give the questions and answers to them as you have them, if you would kindly do so.
Mr. SCHARRENBERG. I note all these first questions are practically repeated later on.
Chairman WALSH. Wherever they are repeated just omit them, because repetition seems to have been necessary, and where you can answer them, that will settle it, of course.
Mr. SCHARRENBERG. The first question is: "Is the responsibility of unemployment individual or social?" Of course the answer to that is obvious; it is social.
Chairman WALSH. Would you like to give your opinion as to what figure those various factors cut in the problem: Maladjustment; total supply of labor over demand, if any; excess of the class which will not work; excess of the class which can not work; periodical and seasonal demand for labor.
Mr. SCHARRENBERG. You see that subject comes again in question No. 4.
Chairman WALSH. You are going to answer that later.
Mr. SCHARRENBERG. Yes; they are repeated there almost verbatim. This question No. 2 is answered, isn't it?
Chairman WALSH. Yes, sir; it is answered, that it is obvious it is social.
Mr. SCHARRENBERG. "Question No. 3. Is the extent of unemployment increasing?" The answer to that it, it surely is.
Chairman WALSH. Now, give your answer to the other question, question No. 4.
Mr. SCHARRENBERG (reading): Give your opinion as to the character of the men in the army of the unemployed. To what extent are the following classes represented: A. Men honestly out of work; B. Men who won't work; C. Agitators; D. Unemployable."
Now in Class A, the number of men honestly out of work I should think would be about 90 per cent, and the other 10 per cent are more or less unevenly divided in groups B, C, and D.
In California we have a situation somewhat different, perhaps, from other States. Every spring some three thousand or more of men, able-bodied men, leave this State to go to the Alaska fisheries. They return in the fall of the year, and many of them save their money, and many of them again do not; hence a great number of these immediately begin to look for employment, and they are thus added to the already unemployed within our midst. Then we have, of course, the problem of the agricultural workers, which has been dwelt upon in detail here. They work during the summer, and during the winter the farmers don't want them and don't care about them any more than I care about the European war. They all drift to the big cities, and the cities of San Francisco, Los Angeles, Sacramento, and Stockton have their problems of unemployment every winter. The construction worker may be added to that class because very little if any construction work is going on in the State during the winter season. So that element also becomes a problem of our cities.
With reference to the man who won't work, there may be such men, but my experience has been that this class is very small; there are so few of them that it becomes negligible.
Regarding agitators, of course, I am an agitator. Any man who is paid by a labor organization is an agitator. The gentlemen who are paid by the other side are respectable citizens.
The unemployable: Unfortunately, there is a group of men who for one reason or another are physically or mentally disqualified, and are unable to secure employment; but that group is very small. There are very few men

who are not able to do some kind of sustaining labor in this State if they are
given the opportunity.

Is that sufficient on that subject?

Chairman WALSH. I think it is. You have covered it very clearly and well.

Mr. SCHARRENBERG (reading). " Question 5. Give your opinion as to the effect
of the unemployed period of the individual. Are these periods factors of physical and moral degeneration?" The answer to that is also very obvious. Now,
I have been unemployed for short periods, and I know many men who have
been unemployed for long periods, and I know men who have been through
long strikes, and have been forced to be unemployed, and I know the results
which these enforced periods of unemployment have on men and women.

It is a bad thing to be unemployed; everyone admits that. The workingmen
know that as well as the gentleman who appeared here and stated that labor
should not be permitted to remain unemployed. It is a very bad thing, and if
we could arrange conditions so that all men could secure employment I think
we would move about 90 per cent toward the millenium.

"Question 6. Give your opinion as to the social loss through unemployment." It seems to me that the greatest social loss is that men refuse to become burdened with families. I have particular knowledge upon that subject
because of my affiliation and association with men who go to sea. Generally
speaking, men who go to sea do not earn sufficient to support a family with
any degree of ease and comfort, and as a consequence they no longer become
married. There are on this coast 5,000 sailors, men before the mast. I don't
think 5 per cent of those men are married. They would all like to get married.
I got married as soon as I became a union officer and earned sufficient money
to support a family. If I had continued going to sea I am sure I would never
have dreamed of assuming that burden. That is just an incident of similar
conditions throughout all strata of society. Men will not assume the burden
of family life when they do not see their way clear to support a family. There
are many other minor factors, but that seems to me to be the most important
and serious one.

The next question is: " To what extent are discontent and social unrest
traceable to unemployment?" Well, I should say to a very large degree. I
know, for example, that men who are classed as very radical agitators, or
I. W. W.'s, never work for any length of time. A man who has a steady job, a
permanent position, is very seldom classed as an agitator or as an " undesirable " or, as one who is termed here " discontented." He is usually satisfied.
Men who work all the year through, and who are assured of permanent revenue, they are usually willing to put up with a great deal. But the man who
only works occasionally, he finally gets into the frame of mind that it is immaterial whether he works or not. He reasons himself into that state of mind,
and, as a natural result, becomes dissatisfied with conditions generally. He
does not care, so to say. He don't care what happens. He has learned to make
a living by working once in awhile, and as far as he is concerned things can
go on. He will join in a strike or a revolt, but has not enough energy to bother
about the constructive work of unionism.

All these things that are going on up here at these hearings, for example,
are looked upon as " high-brow " arrangements, and a gathering of freaks, and
so forth. That is the way the men who only work occasionally feel about these
public hearings. I happened to overhear some of those remarks, and I made
it my business to delve into it a little further.

The next question: " Give your opinion of the following methods of eliminating and doing away with unemployment: A. Forcible breaking up of the
army of unemployed." I want to pay my respects to the man who compiled
this question. To do away with unemployment by breaking up the army of
unemployed. That, of course, is silly. It will not lessen unemployment or do
away with it if you break up every army of unemployed and every other army.

" B. Organized charity." Organized charity, as I know it, usually has its
hands full at all times of the year to take care of the ordinary human misery
that confronts us; and when we have periods of real distress, such as Mr.
Lilienthal described, organized charity is simply up against it, to use the language of the street. I think organized charity is totally inadequate to deal
with that subject.

" C. Farm colonies." Farm colonies would be all right provided you could
do all your farming in the winter. It so happens, however, that farm colonies
would have to do, almost all of their work during the summer, when there is
no serious problem of unemployment. Farm colonies won't do, because the

men who are unemployed are looking for employment during the winter when the farm colonies are closed up.

"D. Unemployment insurance." Unemployment insurance is all right. The trade-unions are doing some work along those lines, and I am inclined to think that the State ought to do something along the English system or along the system that is in vogue in Denmark, where the State annually contributes large sums to the trade-union treasuries.

Regarding State subsidies, however, I am fully conscious of the fact that Denmark is about four centuries ahead of California, because we will never be able to get any subsidy for the trade-union treasuries as long as we have any number of such gentlemen as appeared here from Stockton, denying us practically the right to organize. I might say in that connection that at the last session of our legislature, the trade-union movement of this State introduced a bill providing for a commission to investigate unemployment. We had in mind these various things. Three years ago we had a very severe winter here, and knew there were others coming. But that particular bill provided for an appropriation of $10,000, and it never got out of the finance committee of the senate; it stayed right there, notwithstanding our most eloquent and urgent appeals. There were too many commissions already, and the crusher had to be put on some commissions, and since unemployment was not a problem that particular winter, this particular bill was put on the shelf.

"E. Labor exchanges." Labor exchanges are all right. We need labor exchanges to distribute the workers. May I express the opinion that the workers can do that themselves very nicely if they are given the opportunity. I might again cite the seamen of this coast as an example of what others can do. About 30 years ago the seamen on the Pacific coast were unorganized. They were working then for approximately $17.50 to $20 a month, including board and lodging. They were the prey of every boarding-house keeper, clothing dealer, and others, and they were generally regarded as a hopeless class, a class that was ordained by God Almighty to be preyed upon by every one who wanted to. About that time, 29 years ago, they came to the conclusion—that is, some of the actual workers who went to sea at that time—that it was time to do something for themselves. There were then in existence numerous seamen's friend societies, ladies' seamen's friend societies, and others. The seamen's friend societies would receive their support from the boarding-house keepers and clothing dealers, who would prey upon the seamen while the societies in turn prayed for the seamen. That went on happily year after year. When the seamen finally decided to do something for themselves, the boarding-house men and that variety of vultures who lived upon them simply laughed, because through all the history it had been demonstrated that seamen could never do anything for themselves; that they were exactly in the position in which you find the migratory workers of to-day; they were hopeless and helpless.

However, history has shown that as soon as they determined to do something for themselves they succeeded. They built up their organization; they increased their wages and shortened their hours; they went on to Congress, educated public opinion, changed the maritime laws of this country, and only yesterday we received a telegram from Washington that the seamen's bill, which will make the seamen free men on all American ships all over the world, was passed unanimously by the House of Representatives.

All that has been done by the seamen's organization, by the economic organization of the men who go to sea. It is immaterial what name you call it. It may be labeled I. W. W.-ism, but it happens to be an American Federation of Labor organization.

As a matter of fact there is more of the I. W. W. system—more of the I. W. W. method—in the seamen's organization than of the other variety. We have a real "one big union," so called. It covers the entire Pacific coast. There are no locals. A man who is a member of that union can sail anywhere between here and the coast of Africa. That is the jurisdiction of the seamen's union of the Pacific coast, and, as I have tried to outline briefly, they have simply done wonders for themselves.

To-day they are occupying their own home down on Clay Street, 59 Clay Street. We moved in two weeks ago. This home was erected at a cost of $120,000, and if you gentlemen of the commission would like to see what migratory workers can do for themselves, I would like to take you down and show you the building and offices and everything connected with it.

I have for some years been of the opinion that what was done by these coast sailors—these so-called ignorant foreigners who make their living by going to sea—can surely be.done by the men who are classed as migratory or unskilled or common laborers. There is no reason in the world why it should not be done.

I have dwelt at some detail on that, Mr. Chairman. There are some questions here about labor exchanges that I would have to go into.

Chairman WALSH. I guess that was directed to have you give your opinion on the tentative proposition for a bill, which was submitted to you.

Mr. SCHARRENBERG. Yes, sir; they are itemized here. "To what extent is the present employment agency responsible for unemployment, and is stricter regulation required?" Now, with reference to that, my theory is that employment bureaus should be treated just as they have been treated by Congress with reference to the men that go to sea. We found when organizing the seamen's union—I wasn't old enough then and I didn't find it, but someone else did—that one of the principal objects which caused this preying upon the seamen was to secure the fee for getting him employment. The crimp is the man who furnishes employment to the seamen and gets the advance, and so forth.

We made representations to Congress, and Congress agreed with us, after years of trial, there was only one way to solve that problem, and that was to make it a crime to charge a seaman for securing him employment; and since that law has been on the statute books everything has gone along charmingly. The shipowners everywhere have been able to secure workers—competent and qualified men—and no one has made a living as a seamen's employment agent for many, many years; and I can see no reason in the world why similar laws should not be adopted in every State and thus legislate the employment agent out of business. We tried it in California some years ago. We tried to place a limit upon the fee the employment agent may exact from the worker. But that law was contested and brought up to the supreme court, and the learned justices held that an employment agent was a useful functionary in society; that he was like an agent who sells butter and eggs. We could not limit the price on butter and eggs, and consequently we could not limit the price upon the fee which some other agent charged for securing work for laborers. So it seems that we will have to do something with our constitution or our supreme judges before we can limit the fee, leave alone abolishing the employment agent altogether.

Now, the last question is: "Suggest methods of dealing with the problem of unemployment." I have noted here five different methods of dealing with that problem, and I want to say that they are not my suggestions. I am trying to represent the point of view of organized labor of this State on that subject. First in importance I would place a more thorough organization of all workers; and I might say in that connection I tried to outline such a plan in a minority report which I wrote on the Wheatland hop-fields situation.

Dr. Parker, of the California Commission of Immigration and Housing, supplied this commission with the majority report, and I wrote the minority report; and if there is no objection, I would like to give a copy to the stenographer.

Chairman WALSH. We would be glad to have you do so.

Mr. SCHARRENBERG. The outline of the plan is to have the system, by which the seamen have fairly well solved the problem, apply to the migratory and unskilled workers. Thorough organization of migratory workers would, I believe, aid in many things. It would have a tendency to make those men respect themselves and have some respect for the rights of others. It would make less of the kind of talk you have heard from one of the witnesses here who talked about organizing and solidarity, but who has never identified himself with anything that is really useful. I refer, of course, to the representative of the I. W. W. They are great on talking solidarity, but they absolutely object to working in cooperation or conjunction with anyone except those who belong to their little insignificant group. When men are organized.all I. W. W. theory fades away; it evaporates. No sanely organized man can ever continue under the banner of the I. W. W. I do not say this offhand, but I say it because all our history, all our experience, has proven that conclusively, and absolutely.

The second point in importance in solving the problem of unemployment is the single tax. In California we call it "home rule in taxation." There is now pending before the voters of our State a constitutional amendment—assembly constitutional amendment No. 7—which will give each county or subdivision in the State the right to determine its own method of taxation. In other words, it is a modified system of the single tax. That will enable the State—the citizens of the State—to go after the large landowner; break up the land monopolies and do the things that were outlined here in the discussion between Mr. Weinstock and Mr. Lilienthal.

The third method of solving the problem of the unemployed is to shorten the working day. We have also pending before the voters a proposition for a universal eight-hour day, and I was very pleased to hear that one of the hop growers who testified here thought that it was quite feasible, as far as his business was concerned. Of course, the workingmen of this State do not regard the employers' opposition to this measure as serious. They have learned that the employer will oppose nearly everything. When we proposed the eight-hour law for underground miners, they told us if we put that law on the statute books we would drive away California's basic industry, the pride of our State, the mining industry. And they kept on repeating that over and over again until quite a few of our statesmen at Sacramento believed them, but when the law was finally enacted—and it has been on our statute books some years—mining continued to go on, and they are to-day taking more gold out of the ground than ever before, and they are doing it under the eight-hour law.

Two years ago we went to Sacramento to try to establish the eight-hour day for women and children, and we were told the same thing. The managers of the large department stores in San Francisco charged up there in an army and assured everyone that they would have to close their doors, and from every section of our State we heard similar tales. That law has been in effect some two years, and the very men who were there predicting dire disaster are now entirely satisfied.

For that reason we think that the opposition to the universal eight-hour day will meet with a similar fate. The universal eight-hour day, as far as the farmer is concerned, will work out this way, in my opinion: He will be compelled to induce workers to settle on small tracts of land adjacent to his. Thus he will build up a population of white workers on the farms, who have a little piece of ground, say an acre or two of their own, and who can give a great deal of their time in tilling the soil of the large landowner. Of course, the large farm employer tells us that the eight-hour law will drive the white men out of the State and establish the Jap and Hindu, but they haven't anything to back up their theory in that regard. We feel that the universal eight-hour day is absolutely feasible and that it is practicable, and it will do away with a large share of the present problem of unemployment.

The fourth remedy for unemployment is restriction of immigration. We stand for the policy of the American Federation of Labor that there should be a literacy test; that all Asiatic immigration should be shut out, and so forth. You are all familiar with the policy of the American Federation of Labor on that subject, and you know that we have for years endeavored to keep out the horde of immigrants on the eastern borders and have failed. For the workers of California I want to say we absolutely indorse every effort made by the American Federation of Labor in restricting immigration, and we do this, not from a selfish point of view, but we feel, by keeping some of the workers in Europe—some of the independent roving spirits who come over here—they might be able to do something at home and revolutionize things over there and bring the workers of other countries up to our standard.

The final remedy I would suggest is to have all kinds of public work performed during the acute period of unemployment. That is very simple in our State. The acute periods of unemployment are always during the winter. We could have road work and construction work and all kinds of work done during the winter. All that is required for that is a sufficient amount of money.

I think that covers it.

Chairman WALSH. Well, Mr. Scharrenberg, the commission would like you to epitomize—you have given it here in writing—epitomize your migratory worker problem. You probably have it well in mind, and we are going to put this in the files. But they said they would like to hear it. I would, too. It is a very important point, and it will make your testimony here more complete, so far as that is concerned.

Mr. SCHARRENBERG. Well, Mr. Dale, who is the organizer for the State federation of labor, has testified here and told you what we have tried to do in organizing the migratory workers in California. I wasn't here, and I don't know just how far he went into that. Our plan is simply this: We want to organize all unskilled and unorganized workers, and we have started in by forming a nucleus of an organization in each one of the cities in California.

We have one in practically every city now. Then, our plan is to establish information bureaus at the headquarters of these respective little units, where the workers may go and secure the information regarding employment in a distant territory, or in the north or south of the State as the case may be. As these little units grow, of course, we are going to amalgamate them, get them closer together, and have what our friends, the I. W. W's, describe as one big union, with this one distinction: They want to absorb and take over the industry.

Now, we may have that notion in our heads also, but we are not foolish enough to talk about it morning, noon, and night. What we want just now is to get a little more, a little more to eat, and a little better conditions, and shorter working hours. And when we have that, then we want to ask for more again, and so on until we arrive at that happy picture that is painted by the soap-box orator. That is the only distinction between our plan of organizing the migratory workers and theirs. We have succeeded, notwithstanding what has been said here to the contrary—we have had some splendid success. And we have had this success, notwithstanding the position of hostility of all employers, whom we are trying to benefit, and nothwithstanding the hostile attitude of the I. W. W's. From both of these elements we have had constant opposition in trying to build up and in furthering a legitimate organization among migratory workers.

Now, if this migratory workers' organization in California should become permanently established and have some power, it would work out just about the way that the seamen's organization has worked out. The various branches from one end of the State to the other would supply each other with information regarding work and working conditions. Men would know where to go, where there is work, and where there is better work. As a natural result, conditions would be improved here and there. If there should be a ranch in some section of the State where conditions were intolerable, the workers would soon know about it and they would stay away from that ranch if there was any other place to go, and that would gradually remedy and improve things, just as it has revolutionized things for the so-called skilled workers.

Now that, in brief, is the plan that we evolved some years ago, and at which we are still working. The only thing that stops us is the lack of money and the lack of cooperation.

A great deal has been said about what is the American Federation of Labor going to do for the unskilled migratory worker. Now, the answer to that question is, What is the migratory worker going to do for himself? We can spend Rockfeller's fortune in an attempt to organize these men, but unless they want to be organized, unless they cooperate and realize that a man must do something for himself if he wants to succeed, we can never succeed in making anything out of them. That is the greatest problem that confronts us. We can organize men, we can get them together in a hall and tell them all these things, but they must work it out themselves. We can't do it for them. It is the old story of leading the horse to the trough, but you can't make him drink. Does that cover the point?

Chairman WALSH. I think it covers the point very well. Prof. Commons would like to ask you some questions.

Commissioner COMMONS. You heard what Mr. Lilienthal said about the use of the minimum wage in the matter last winter here?

Mr. SCHARRENBERG. Yes.

Commissioner COMMONS. What is the trade-union point of view of that proposition?

Mr. SCHARRENBERG. The use of the minimum wage?

Commissioner COMMONS. You remember the matter as he expressed it?

Chairman WALSH. Was it protested against?

Commissioner COMMONS. The proposition of the 20 cents an hour for public work, and the city scale was $3.

Mr. SCHARRENBERG. Yes. I was a member of that committee of 100, and the 20 cents an hour plan worked on this way: There is a lot of work to be done in San Francisco. For example, there is a lot of street work to be done, and the going wages here are $2.50 a day for that kind of work. Now, if our employers could secure labor for 20 cents an hour, some of them would find it to their advantage to immediately have all this work done that particular winter. Do you see the point, Professor?

Commissioner COMMONS. I see that.

Mr. SCHARRENBERG. No?

.Commissioner Commons. I do see that. I want to ask why did you finally yield to the argument and take the 20 cents?

Mr. Scharrenberg. We did not yield.

Commissioner Commons. I understood Mr. Lilienthal to say that all accepted except Mr. Kelley, of the army of the unemployed.

Mr. Scharrenberg. No; he was speaking about an interview that took place between an executive committee and a committee of the board of supervisors and a committee from the army of unemployed. He was not speaking about the trade-union movement in that connection.

Commissioner Commons. Actually, the thing did work out that men were paid 20 cents an hour for doing public work?

Mr. Scharrenberg. Yes.

Commissioner Commons. Was that still unsatisfactory—that practice? Did that still remain unsatisfactory to you and to the trade-unions?

Mr. Scharrenberg. We did not oppose it, because we did not want to be placed in a position as being on record against furnishing work to men who were starving. But we certainly did not encourage it. We did not wish to supply some of our benevolent employers with cheap labor and boost their plan along.

Commissioner Commons. I think he said they restricted it to public employment—to work that was not done for private employers.

Mr. Scharrenberg. Well, it does not work out that way.

Commissioner Commons. How do you mean?

Mr. Scharrenberg. There is no public work that does not have to be done. All our roads in San Francisco and vicinity have got to be improved, and they are going to be improved very rapidly, because this city is growing. The city of San Francisco pays $3 a day for eight hours for that kind of work, and here it was proposed to have all this done at the rate of 20 cents an hour. Now, in the very nature of things you could not expect any enthusiastic support from us for that kind of a plan.

Commissioner Commons. What is your plan? You say your plan is to have the public work transferred to the winter and not done in the summer?

Mr. Scharrenbreg. At going wages; yes.

Commissioner Commons. During the busy season?

Mr. Scharrenberg. Yes.

Commissioner Commons. But to have it done at the regular——

Mr. Scharrenberg. At the regular going wages..

Commissioner Commons. What do you call " going wages " for such work.

Mr. Scharrenberg. Why, it differs in various parts of the State. We tried to establish a minimum wage for employees of the State. We failed in that. The present wage that is paid for common labor in California for public work, I think, varies from $2.25 to $3 a day, depending upon the section of the State.

Commissioner Commons. That is determined by what authority—the city, county, or——

Mr. Scharrenberg. Oh, it is usually determined by the contractor who hires the men.

Commissioner Commons. I mean, where there are fixed wages, statutory wages?

Mr. Scharrenberg. Some of the subdivisions of the State, like San Francisco, have fixed a minimum wage; but the State has not. The work that I refer to, public work, would ordinarily have to be done by the State. No single city could solve that problem or undertake to solve that problem. It would not be fair for San Francisco to do the public work with Los Angeles lying idle. The unemployed would all come up here, as they did last winter.

Commissioner Commons. The matter of what the rate should be would be a matter of negotiation, I presume; is that it?

Mr. Scharrenberg. Yes; it might be.

Commissioner Commons. It might be $2.50, $2, or $3?

Mr. Scharrenberg. Depending some on the organized workers; yes.

Commissioner Commons. Then the only difference between your plan and his is on that minimum rate of pay that it shall be made in this dull season.

Mr. Scharrenberg. Mr. Lilienthal was only speaking about an emergency that confronted San Francisco. I was not speaking about San Francisco. I was speaking about the State, about an attempt to deal with the subject on a broad, comprehensive plan, having State work undertaken by authority of the legislature and the people. To make it perfectly fair, that certain public work, improvements of roads, and other things—the upkeep of roads—must be done every winter and left severely alone through the summer. That would give thousands of men who are thrown into the city during the winter an opportunity to continue at work when there is no other work to be had.

Commissioner COMMONS. Then, if I get the difference, it simply is, his was a proposition for temporary emergency relief?

Mr. SCHARRENBERG. Yes.

Commissioner COMMONS. And your plan is for a permanent method?

Mr. SCHARRENBERG. Yes; that is it.

Commissioner COMMONS. And if you want to have a permanent method, you want to maintain the minimum standards of wages?

Mr. SCHARRENBERG. At all times; yes.

Chairman WALSH. Commissioner Lennon would like to ask you some questions.

Commissioner LENNON. Mr. Scharrenberg, I am a little doubtful as to whether the record shows the expenditure of the money raised here last winter just as it ought to show, as I imagine it ought to show it, the money expended for the employment of the people who were here without work last winter; in so far as the $30,000 of the city fund was concerned, that was paid for at the rate of $3 a day, was it not?

Mr. SCHARRENBERG. We started in to do that, but soon quit.

Commissioner LENNON. Did they quit before they had expended the $30,000.

Mr. SCHARRENBERG. I think so. You see that $3 a day plan was proposed in one city only. It worked out something like this: The workers from not only in California but from Oregon, Washington, Nevada, and other States began to flow in here; they had heard about the milk and honey that was flowing in San Francisco. Three dollars a day and eight hours—those are ideal conditions among workers.

Commissioner LENNON. Then the payment of the 20 cents per hour began before the exhaustion of the $30,000 and before they began to use the $40,000 that had been contributed by the citizenship?

Mr. SCHARRENBERG. Yes; the committee, which worked under the auspices of the city, was carrying on some other relief work, soup kitchens, etc., and that used up the money without a technical violation of the charter.

Commissioner LENNON. You are secretary of the State federation, are you not?

Mr. SCHARRENBERG. Yes; that is a position that does not require all of a man's time, and brings in a nominal revenue.

Commissioner LENNON. How many members of trades-unions are there in the State of California?

Mr. SCHARRENBERG. Under the American Federation of Labor?

Commissioner LENNON. Yes.

Mr. SCHARRENBERG. Between 80,000 and 90,000.

Commissioner LENNON. Have you any idea as to the membership of the I. W. W. in the State of California?

Mr. SCHARRENBERG. No; I have not, and no one else has.

Commissioner LENNON. Is there as great effort made on the part of organized trades-unions in this State to organize the seasonal workers as there is to organize any other class of workers in the State?

Mr. SCHARRENBERG. Well, you see the workers in the State who are already organized, take the carpenters, for instance, they send out an organizer, and if they find a town in our State where the carpenters are unorganized, that man will go there and organize the carpenters; and the tailors, the sailors, and others, do that likewise.

Now, the migratory workers, seasonal workers, they have no one to do that, because they have no organization. The only legitimate effort that is made to do that was made by the State federation of labor, working in conjunction with the American Federation of Labor. The American Federation of Labor pays Mr. Dale, who was there, a salary of $20 a week, and the State federation of labor pays him the balance in traveling expenses. We have a fund set aside for that purpose known as the migratory labor fund, we do everything within our power, and to the limit of our financial resources.

I will dwell in brief upon the statement that was made here that the I. W. W. were quite numerous in the States that their doctrine had permeated the migratory workers. I have found, as I tried to explain a moment ago, that the only really good I. W. W. is the one who is out of work. You take the most rabid, radical I. W. W. and give him a nice, steady job, and he becomes a tame conservative. Of course, there are some exceptions. There are lawyers, college professors, doctors, and students who are I. W. W.'s because it is·

romantic, and it sounds nice to some to be called 'radical." In fact, I am inclined to think, and have been for some time, that there are more I. W. W.'s among college professors, lawyers, and students than there are among workers as far as California is concerned. And I claim to know as much about I. W. W.'s as any man in this hall, because I associate with them all of the time.

Men who go to sea, the 5,000 members of the organization to which I belong, have a habit of going into the country frequently. They do all kinds of work during the winter, and they always drift back to our headquarters here where I get their stories in detail.

Commissioner LENNON. You indicated to us in your talk the changed conditions as to wages that had taken place since the seamen's union had been organized. Can you indicate to us whether or not there is any difference between the wages now of the union seamen on the coast and any crews of nonunion seamen that go in and out of these ports on the coast, or are you so solidly organized that there are no nonunion crews?

Mr. SCHARRENBERG. Oh, no; there are some. There is the Pacific Mail Steamship Co., they employ Chinese, who receive $7 a month and board and lodging. The going offshore wages are $35 a month, and in the coastwise trade the going wages are now $55 a month. The overtime brings it up somewhat higher, but the regular wages are $55 a month under union conditions. Under nonunion conditions they are always $45 and less, and by comparison with the Atlantic coast, where the open shop prevails, the point comes out more strongly. Back there the wages are—well, they run between $25 and $35.

Commissioner LENNON. And here $45 and up?

Mr. SCHARRENBERG. Forty-five to fifty-five.

Commissioner LENNON. Are you sufficiently familiar with any other lines of ousiness in this section of the country to be able to indicate as to whether there is or is not a material difference between the wages of union and nonunion people in the industry or trade?

Mr. SCHARRENBERG. Well, I can give you an example. Take San Francisco and Los Angeles. The laundry workers of this city are organized. The laundry workers of Los Angeles are not organized. They have made several efforts, but they are practically unorganized. The maximum scale of the Los Angeles laundry workers is somewhat below the minimum scale of our laundry workers. And take the metal trades. The metal trades in San Francisco or in this section of the State work for eight hours, and they have a certain minimum wage. The men in the south, in Los Angeles, work nine hours and more, and very few of them receive the minimum that is received here by the metal workers. And there is no reason in the world why that should be so except for the fact that there is the closed-shop organization up here and the open shop and employers' domination down there.

Commissioner LENNON. Could you indicate to us as to the make-up of juries in trials in this State? This question was taken up by several witnesses. What show is there for wageworkers being called on juries; what is your experience; does it corroborate what has been stated?

Mr. SCHARRENBERG. Yes; there is not any at all. Now, I will give you an example. San Francisco has the reputation among our enemies as being a union-ridden city. Now, we have a grand jury in this community that is selected by the superior judges. Each judge selects, I think, 12 names, and the entire number of names is thrown into the box, and the grand jury is then selected. Now, for a number of years I have made it my business to look over that list of names and there has never been an instance when there were more than one or two—one year there were three wage earners—on that entire list of grand jury men that were thrown into the box to begin with. The jury system of California is a disgrace to our State. This is a progressive State. We are far ahead in social legislation and many other things, but as far as the jury system is concerned, it is shameful. We have the property qualifications, and it was practically admitted in the assembly at the last session of our legislature that the employers and the business men of California were not going to stand for any change, because they did not propose to put themselves at the mercy of workingmen serving on the jury. That was the statement made in the assembly of our State.

Commissioner LENNON. You are not considered competent, even in California?

Mr. SCHARRENBERG. No.

Commissioner LENNON. To serve on juries?

Mr. SCHARRENBERG. No.

Commissioner LENNON. That is all, Mr. Chairman.

Chairman WALSH. Any questions?

Commissioner O'CONNELL. Yes.

Chairman WALSH. Mr. O'Connell would like to ask you some questions.

Commissioner O'CONNELL. Mr. Scharrenberg, you are secretary of the State organization of the American Federation of Labor?

Mr. SCHARRENBERG. Yes, sir.

Commissioner O'CONNELL. And as such you are familiar with the policies of the American Federation of Labor?

Mr. SCHARRENBERG. I think I am; yes.

Commissioner O'CONNELL. You are also editor of the Seamen's Journal?

Mr. SCHARRENBERG. Yes, sir.

Commissioner O'CONNELL. And as such come in touch with the editorial policy and literary policy of the A. F. of L.?

Mr. SCHARRENBERG. Yes, sir.

Commissioner O'CONNELL. In yesterday's testimony of Mr. Lewis he was asked by Commissioner Weinstock, I think it was, if the A. F. of L. did not consider labor a commodity.

What is the policy and position of the American Federation of Labor, as you understand it, and the policy of your federation in the State of California, as to whether labor is a commodity?

Mr. SCHARRENBERG. Yes; I was very sorry to have Mr. Lewis make that statement, because it will discredit whatever else he has said. Anybody who knows anything, surely knows that labor, organized labor, has made a struggle for years and years and years to establish the fact that labor is not a commodity. All our anti-injunction bills pending in the various States, and pending in Congress, and our efforts to amend the Sherman antitrust law, have been based upon our efforts to make it absolutely clear that labor is life; that labor is not a commodity, that labor power can not be sold the same as goods, that it can not be divorced from the body. And I was very sorry to have Mr. Lewis, who is an I. W. W. sympathizer of remarkable broadness and openmindedness, make that remark.

Commissioner O'CONNELL. That is all.

Chairman WALSH. Anything else?

Commissioner WEINSTOCK. Yes. You were reciting, Mr. Scharrenberg, how seamen, by collective action, have been able materially to better their conditions in more recent times. And among other things, you pointed out that 29 years ago before they had become organized, their wages were from $17.50 to $20 a month and board.

Mr. SCHARRENBERG. Yes, sir.

Commissioner WEINSTOCK. May we ask what are the current wages now?

Mr. SCHARRENBERG. They are between $45 and $55 a month.

Commissioner WEINSTOCK. That is, the minimum is $45 and the maximum $55?

Mr. SCHARRENBERG. Yes, sir.

Commissioner WEINSTOCK. Plus possible extra time, I suppose?

Mr. SCHARRENBERG. Yes; that is a very material difference. In those days, before organization, men worked 12 hours a day and received no overtime. Now, men receive an average overtime of at least $10 per month, and they work only 9 hours instead of 12.

Commissioner WEINSTOCK. So that really their average earnings, including overtime, would be about $60?

Mr. SCHARRENBERG. Yes.

Commissioner WEINSTOCK. As against the maximum under the old conditions of $20?

Mr. SCHARRENBERG. Yes, sir; that is a very conservative figure regarding the overtime .

Commissioner WEINSTOCK. It really increased their earning power about 300 per cent?

Mr. SCHARRENBERG. Yes; fully that.

Commissioner WEINSTOCK. As the result of their collective action?

Mr. SCHARRENBERG. Yes.

Commissioner WEINSTOCK. Well, now, I can't quite reconcile those facts with the other statement you made, Mr. Scharrenberg. Doubtless you can explain it. You pointed out that under existing—that where formerly seafaring men could afford to marry and to have families, now they can't, and that family life, therefore, was diminishing among the seafaring men. Now, if they could afford to marry and have families on $20 a month, why can they not afford to do it when their earnings have increased 300 per cent?

Mr. SCHARRENBERG. I certainly did not make any such statement, Commissioner Weinstock, that the seamen could afford to marry, certainly not on this coast. If I made that statement, it was made in reference to conditions that prevailed say a hundred years ago when seamanship was looked upon as an honored profession, when a seamen was held in higher regard than a tailor or a carpenter or any other craftsman. I certainly had no reference to modern conditions.

Commissioner WEINSTOCK. I see. Well then, I misunderstood it.

Chairman WALSH. That is all, thank you, Mr. Scharrenberg.

Commissioner WEINSTOCK. Just one minute.

Chairman WALSH. Oh, excuse me, you have another question?

Commissioner WEINSTOCK. Just another question, Mr. Chairman.

Mr. SCHARRENBERG. All right.

Commissioner WEINSTOCK. I gathered from what you said that while as a representative of organized labor you did not see your way clear to oppose the policy adopted during the emergency of last winter in fixing a 20-cent-an-hour wage, you did not approve it for fear that it might lower the minimum?

Mr. SCHARRENBERG. No; for fear that some employers who are always looking for cheap labor would use this period of depression to have their work done at low wages.

Commissioner WEINSTOCK. I see. Well, now, having in mind the policy of the American Federation of Labor, and assuming that the committee of one hundred had given you sole power to act, and had placed the entire fund at your command, what would have been your way of handling the situation?

Mr. SCHARRENBERG. Well, Commissioner Weinstock, you are asking me a hypothetical question. I don't think that is quite fair. I am perfectly willing to map out a plan, and I have submitted a tentative program. But it takes time to work that out.

Commissioner WEINSTOCK. I was speaking purely, Mr. Scharrenberg, of emergency conditions.

Mr. SCHARRENBERG. Well, organized labor in this State is looking forward to those emergency conditions. We have gone to Sacramento year after year with our bills and measures approved by our organization for emergency relief, etc., and have been ruled out of order time after time. Then when these acute periods come on they are not of our making. We are always trying to do our best to help along our people, those who are within our own ranks. And, I might say, that of all the unemployed who were here in the city last winter there were very few trade-unionists. They were taken care of somehow and somewhere by their own people.

Commissioner WEINSTOCK. Well, you heard the statements made by Mr. Lilienthal, and I take it that it is based on careful thought, that in his judgment that same emergency is likely to be repeated this coming winter in a more acute form. Of course we can't hope that between this period and then that we can get legislation, so the same problem will face us and will have to be dealt with. Now, profiting by last year's experience, Mr. Scharrenberg, that, doubtless, will be duplicated all over the country, how would you handle it, given the same fund and the same conditions, except in a more acute form?

Mr. SCHARRENBERG. I haven't anything to suggest for any emergency that may arise within the next few years. It takes time, it takes laborious effort, thought, and study to dispose of those problems, because the average problem that the citizenship has to deal with fades into insignificance compared with this problem.

Chairman WALSH. Anything else?

Commissioner WEINSTOCK. Yes; just one other question. You expressed it as your opinion also, Mr. Scharrenberg, that you did not think the I. W. W. movement would prevail because the people are not in harmony with their ideas. Now, what do you regard as the weak spots in the I. W. W. doctrine; where will be their point of failure?

Mr. SCHARRENBERG. Where? There are so many.

Commissioner WEINSTOCK. Name the salient ones as they come to you.

Mr. SCHARRENBERG. Well, first of all, their system of organization is impossible, of course. They are only good for the purpose of stimulating unrest. That is very desirable. They are teaching our California employers, for example, that it might be to their advantage to do business with legitimate labor organizations. Some of them have already arrived at that conclusion. You may have noted the testimony of hop growers' that they have no more serious objection to legitimate labor organizations. And when the I. W. W. has prodded them into that frame of mind, why they have performed a very useful function, **and** then they die a natural death. Throughout history, you can take their case wherever you go, and you can't cite one single instance where they have ever accomplished anything permanent or lasting. They are just a flash in the pan; that is what they are.

Commissioner WEINSTOCK. Sort of an irritant?

Mr. SCHARRENBERG. Yes; a flare-up. And they do some little good things once in awhile, like Lawrence; and they did some other things up at Wheatland. I don't approve of the shooting, but the rest of the revolt up there was all right. But they never accomplish anything permanent. The camp inspection that you have heard of here—the law that provides for sanitation of labor camps—was not evolved or proposed by any I. W. W. That came from sanely organized labor. I myself gave that bill to Senator Flint up in the senate, and it was put through with the assistance and aid of organized labor. There was no I. W. W. or doctor or lawyer or college professor up there helping us along in getting those laws through. There never is.

Commissioner WEINSTOCK. You probably were present the other day when we had a representative of the I. W. W. testifying, and, if I remember correctly, he expressed it as his opinion that the worker need look for no betterment of conditions through legislation.

Do you think he was correct in that opinion?

Mr. SCHARRENBERG. Well, he is correct to this extent, that the workers who depend upon legislation alone to solve their problem, they are going to get left. But if they have a powerful organization behind to see that laws are enforced, then legislation is all right. In this State we have a very fine example of how that works out. At present we have a labor commissioner who is doing some real work. That office was created for the purpose of protecting labor, but until the present man got there it was a sinecure for political hacks, etc. They simply held down the job as a reward for services rendered, and the office of labor commissioner became a stench in the nostrils of workmen. At present everybody knows we have a labor commissioner in that office, and that man is doing really good work. He is a trade-unionist and he has the labor organizations of this State behind him, backing him. Generally speaking, in a community where labor is organized and able to take care of itself the laws are enforced. On the other hand, in a community without a labor organization the law usually looks very good on the statute books, but there is no one to enforce it. The district attorney knows all about it, but unless somebody comes to him and prods him up he leaves it alone. To have a labor law and to enforce it are two entirely different things.

Commissioner WEINSTOCK. You believe, then, that while legislation may be efficient, it is not sufficient unless there is public sentiment behind it to enforce it?

Mr. SCHARRENBERG. Unless there is organization behind it.

Commissioner WEINSTOCK. That is all.

Commissioner LENNON. That is all. Much obliged to you; that is all. Call the next.

Mr. THOMPSON. Mr. McLaughlin.

TESTIMONY OF MR. JOHN P. McLAUGHLIN.

Mr. THOMPSON. Mr. McLaughlin, will you give us your name?

Mr. McLAUGHLIN. John P. McLaughlin.

Mr. THOMPSON. Your business address?

Mr. McLAUGHLIN. 948 Market Street.

Mr. THOMPSON. Your business?

Mr. McLAUGHLIN. Labor commissioner.

Mr. THOMPSON. Of this State?

Mr. McLAUGHLIN. Yes, sir.

Mr. THOMPSON. How long have you been labor commissioner of the State?

Mr. McLAUGHLIN. Four years in March coming.

Mr. THOMPSON. What work do you cover as labor commissioner, briefly?

Mr. McLAUGHLIN. Enforcement of labor laws of the State of California, inspections, and the like of that.

Mr. THOMPSON. In your work as labor commissioner, do you come in contact with the unemployment problem?

Mr. McLaughlin. On two different occasions.

Mr. Thompson. Now, will you tell us what is your opinion of the main causes which contribute to unemployment, and what remedies would you suggest to relieve it?

Mr. McLaughlin. Well, I have a list of those questions, the same as Brother Scharrenberg had, I suppose.

Mr. Thompson. Will you take those questions and answers, such of those as you think you can say something on to the commission?

Mr. McLaughlin. On two different occasions I have been requested by the governor of the State to make an investigation of the unemployment situation in San Francisco, and on one occasion throughout the State of California. In 1911 the situation here was very acute. There has been no organization, however, of the unemployed, until along in the month of March, latter part of February, or the 1st of March, and several claims were made as to the number of unemployed. It was contended by many that there was between forty and fifty thousand in San Francisco. And the governor, to ascertain the facts, instructed the bureau to make an investigation.

We went carefully into that matter, as hurriedly as possible, and our figures placed it at that time, somewhere in the neighborhood of 25,000.

The situation had begun to relax, spring was at hand, construction work was opening up, and conditions were improving, so that shortly after the issuing or the publication of our report, why the situation had entirely cleared up. There are several elements that enter in. California is in a peculiar position in that respect by reason of the fact that her climate is an inducement to the unemployed to come here. Thousands of them come from all over the western coast; in fact, as far as the Middle West and East, to California, to winter. And the problem to my mind is one that will have to be taken care of by the National Government. It is not fair to burden the State of California with the problem as it exists. Take California as a whole, possibly if the men were separated all over the entire area they might be taken care of, but when they get together and congregate in any given community, the burden becomes too much. Several of these questions here can be answered, and possibly will assist in finding a satisfactory solution.

Maladjustment, to my mind, is not altogether responsible. The elements are what we have to contend with in that respect, and to do work—public work or any other kind of work in winter months is not very profitable if it is going to be considered from a standpoint of dollars and cents. On road building or anything else, if you have a week's rain, you could not put the men onto the ground again for a week after it ceased raining; and as, a matter of fact, they would have eaten up all they had earned in the time that they had been idle, so that there would not be much satisfaction to them, nor much good accomplished. In normal years we will take care of ourselves, but in abnormal years we will need possibly some assistance.

The existence of a class which will not work: There is such a class, but the percentage of it, I believe, is very, very small. I believe possibly at the outside that you would not get 2 per cent. That would fully cover it. It has come to my knowledge that there are a number of men that make it their business to hang around, for instance, where the employment agencies are situated; that make it a business of finding out how long a man has been on a job, and when he returned; the first thing you know, why he is off having a drink with him. The next day the worker is around with a black eye, drunk and broke, and what becomes of his money—why the other fellow has disappeared. There are men, I believe, who eke out an existence by taking advantage of the poor fellow that has gone out and made his stake in the country and has come back in the city to spend it.

The existence of a class that can not work: That is very true; there are some that are old and crippled that are not able to do the day's work that is demanded of men nowadays. The percentage of them is considerably larger than of those that will not work.

Periodical and seasonal work: The relation of the demand for labor between employment of a seasonal character, etc.

Our work here in California, as far as it affects our agricultural resources, is practically unlimited, and in summer months here the demand for labor is heavy. In our winter months, from November up until April, why there is practically no demand at all, so that all of that help naturally comes into our city. The same thing can be said of the mills and of the woods. There is very little logging done in the country in winter months, so that the result is that from the middle of November up until along about the 1st of April there is a dull spell. They don't do any more than they absolutely have to do. And the result is that there is a great deal more men unemployed at that time than any other season of the year.

Along with that, in San Francisco there is an element that is thrown on our community every winter that works in Alaska. Brother Scharrenberg figures it at 3,000. As a matter of fact, from actual tabulation, there is very near 7,000. There is very near 3,000 fishermen alone and there is over 4,000 what they call cannery hands. These men are thrown on this market every winter about the latter part of September and during the month of October. To my mind they make up the big bulk of the army of the unemployed. I have watched their parade through this city, and I recognized many among the number of those that were marching as men that were working in the canneries during the summer months.

The bureau that I am representing has been responsible for the passage of an act in the legislature that provided for our department supervising the paying off of these cannery hands. In the past it had been customary that these men were allowed to drink and gamble, and they were charged all kinds of exorbitant fees for positions, and a charge of $5 for a man to watch them while they were waiting to go aboard ship, and things of that kind, so that, as a result, when pay day came around for their season's work there were many of them didn't have anything coming, and there were few of them had much over $40 for their season's work.

We went to the legislature and had this bill passed, and took the matter up with the large canning concerns and asked for their cooperation, with the result that last winter, under the supervision of our department, the men who went to Alaska and did their season's work had over a hundred dollars apiece. The canneries would not permit of their spending over $20 the entire season for extras, cut out entirely their gambling and whisky debts, and this year we hope to increase that from $30 to $40, so that their earnings should be increased this year even larger than last year.

I believe that while the State of California is trying to handle this matter, it is a duty that probably belongs to the Federal Government, and this commission, if they did nothing else than to recommend that these men be signed on under the United States shipping commissioner. would prevent much of the injustice that is worked on them, and their efforts, so far as the visit to this coast, would not be in vain. It is a duty that belongs to them. The men are working in Alaska and are employed in California. While the question has not been raised as to the constitutionality of this act, the employers realized that something had to be done, and they were willing to do anything that was within reason to try to help improve conditions. I would like your commission to consider this phase of the situation. If you do, you will do considerable toward relieving the situation in California. These men, I might add, are not long ashore before they are broke. What they do with their money, I don't know. But the great majority of them live over on the north side of town, and they have quite a lively time there after a vessel arrives. And it lasts for a period of two or three weeks; then many of them seek employment as porters in hotels, and one thing and another of that kind, until the next season opens up. They are not thrifty. They are largely Mexicans, Filipinos, Porto Ricans, Japanese, and Chinamen.

For your information, I might explain how the work is done. The packing companies employ the fishermen themselves, who get so much for the run and so much per fish. These men are organized, and are well protected. The real packing of the salmon is let to a Chinese contractor who get so much per case for the pack. He, in turn, contracts with a Filipino boss for the men. He guarantees to furnish him so many men, and he is penalized if his men don't show, under a contract that was drawn up, and is generally signed by both parties. And for weeks in advance of a ship sailing, these men are gathered together from different points and housed in some boarding house. And it had been the custom, until such time as we stopped it, that these men were turned over to the Chinaman at so much per head. We have also stopped them from making a charge of $5 apiece to each man while they were down on the dock waiting to go aboard the ship, and several other charges which were not justified. That situation can be remedied considerably by your commission, by having those men signed on before the United States shipping commissioner. Last year there was one vessel that fought the efforts of our bureau. They went up to the justice court and secured somewheres in the neighborhood of a hundred·and fifty or two hundred attachments on every one of the men's money. The poor fellow that had gone to Alaska, he could not wait long enough to have that case tried in court, and as a result, to keep them from starving, we had to permit-them to accept what was offered. But I have taken the matter up with several judges, and I feel this year they will have a little more trouble in getting those attachments. If they were signed under the United States Shipping Commission,·that would not. be permitted.

Is the responsibility for unemployment individual or social? To my mind, there is no·doubt where the responsibility is. It is social. In a few individual cases it might be individual, as the result of drinking, and so on, but it is very small.

Is the extent of unemployment increasing? I am inclined to think so. The year 1911 was bad; 1912 we had ho trouble; 1913 was bad; and I believe 1914 is not going to be good.

· Of 1913, however, I want to say this in passing: I was a member of the committee of one hundred, with Brother Scharrenberg and Mr. Lilienthal. And to my mind, the number of unemployed in San Francisco was greatly increased as the result of a lot of publicity that the unemployed received.

It was published to the world that there was an effort to be made to give them three dollars a day and eight hours. And they came from all over the coast to accept of those conditions, with the result that San Francisco's number of unemployed, on one day that a tabulation was kept of the number of applications, increased something like to twelve ann fifteen hundred. Every other county was kindly urging them along to get to San Francisco to get $3 and eight hours, and when they got here, why they anchored here. It took quite a while to fianlly move them, but they eventually moved. That was the inducement that brought them in, and the condition in 1913 would not have been near as acute if it hadn't been published to the world that they were to get $3 and eight hours in San Francisco.

Commissioner LENNON. Mr. McLaughlin, the time for adjournment having arrived, the commission will adjourn until 2 o'clock.

Mr. THOMPSON. We have only got one more witness.

Commissioner LENNON. Only one more?

Commissioner WEINSTOCK. No; there is another one coming back this after-noon.

Commissioner LENNON. Tne commission will adjourn until 2 p. m.

Commissioner COMMONS. Two p. m. to-day?

Commissioner LENNON. Yes.

(Whereupon, at 12.30 o'clock p. m., on this Saturday, the 29th day of August, 1914,·an adjournment was taken until 2 o'clock p. m. of the same day.)

AFTER RECESS—2 P. M.

Met pursuant to adjournment. Present as before.

Chairman WALSH. The commission will please be in order.

Call the first witness now, please, Mr. Thompson.

Mr. THOMPSON. Mr. McLaughlin.

TESTIMONY OF MR. JOHN P. McLAUGHLIN—Continued.

Mr. THOMPSON. You may proceed with your statement, Mr. McLaughlin.

Mr. McLAUGHLIN. I was taking these questions as I went along and just making a statement that I thought would be of interest.

The fourth question, " Give your opinion as to the character of men in the army of the unemployed; as to the number of men honestly out of work."

In my judgment, 90 per cent of those men were honestly out of work; no question about it. Of the men who would not work, a very small majority of them—possibly 2 per cent.

Agitators: I would say possibly 1 per cent; of the unemployables, possibly 5 or 6 per cent, or thereabouts. So that most of the men would honestly claim—could honestly claim, anyway—that they were honestly out of work, when we are not in a position to offer them work. There is no doubt in my mind that every one of them was willing to work by reason of the fact that when work was offered to them they stood in line, and in the rain for hours at a time, to get a ticket that entitled them to the privilege of working four days a week at the almshouse or some place else.

On one occasion 500 men were assigned to the almshouse to work, and it rained, and rained hard; those men insisted on working in the rain for the purpose of securing 20 cents an hour for six hours. At that time they were deprived of admission to the free boarding house that was conducted at Fifth and Folsom Streets during the period of that employment. So that the men proved that they were honestly willing to work if work was offered.

As to the next question, it is not necessary to say anything on that. All of us know that if a man is idle or unemployed, it is not either good for him or society generally.

The next question is, "Your opinion as to the social loss through unemployment."

Brother Scharrenberg, I think, fully covered that. The social loss is enormous, for the reason that men can't and conditions won't permit of their marrying and taking on the burden of keeping a family. In fact, very few of this class of men attempt to take on that burden.

The next question is, "To what extent is the discontent and social unrest traceable to unemployment?"

I believe it is directly traceable to it. However, there is a good deal to be said upon that subject. Personally I believe that if most of these men were thrifty that they earn enough during the summer season to carry them all through the winter; but, unfortunately, many of them when they visit the city squander their money—some in drink, others gambling, and in other ways—and they become public charges.

"Give your opinion of the following methods of alleviating and doing away with unemployment":

First, forcibly breaking up the army of the unemployed: The best way to break it up is to give them something to do. That will break it up.

Second, organized charity: It has enough to do to take care of the regular residents of the city who are situated with us continuously and are men of families. It is too much to ask them to render assistance to the migratory group who assemble in this city every winter.

Farm colonies: Farm colonies to my mind are not practicable by reason of the fact that you can't do much on the farm in the winter months, this being the time we have the surplus of labor. It would be simply another form of charity, the same as a poor farm that you would send them to, where they would have nothing to do but remain at the State's expense. There is very little work, if any, that they could do during that particular period.

Unemployment insurance: That is a subject I haven't given a great deal of consideration to. I do believe where they are well organized in a city like this, for instance, it might possibly work out satisfactorily. A good deal of that kind of work is being done by some of the trade-unions independently. There is this to be said, however, in connection with that. If something could be done that would compel men to save part of their earnings during the summer months that they could draw upon and have for use during the dull period, to my mind it would go a long way to solving this question.

I know this, if all the money that is taken from these men on construction work and others in the form of taxation, was put into a common fund, that it would more than meet this situation.

The average one of these poor fellows that goes on to that work takes it at certain seasons of the year anyway, has to pay a poll tax, a road tax, a county hospital tax, and a company hospital tax. I have had a case of a man working 14 days; during that period he was taxed $8, leaving him to walk home after putting in 14 days labor.

But there are many other cases of that kind. I have taken up many cases with the auditors of the counties, they having collected a poll tax twice from the same individual. And that is permitted by the law at the present time. To my mind, if it was abolished, and the amount of money that was taken from these men who bear the bulk of that burden was put into a common fund, it would more than carry them over the dull period of the year. They, unfortunately, are carrying most of the burden in this respect because collectors have nothing to do but advise the contractor, "You have got so many men," and the amount is withheld from everybody's pay. Workers have no redress. The law permits of it. And particularly with reference to the road tax—he will have to pay a road tax in this county, and if he gets another job next week in another county he will have to pay a road tax again in the next county.

Several counties charge a hospital tax, and all of the companies charge a hospital tax, so that a man is doubly taxed for the same purpose.

· I had a bill introduced at the last session of the legislature—though for some reason or another it was overlooked in the rush of the adjournment—which provided that no contractor would be permitted to charge any employee a hospital tax unless he actually maintained a hospital with doctors and nurses in attendance. The reason for framing it in that way was that there were a good many objections from the men that were employed by the Southern Pacific Co. who were charged 50 cents per month. If the contractor kept a box of pills they would be lucky in most of these construction camps. But nevertheless the man is charged a dollar a month. If he only works one day, he has to pay the dollar just the same. If he worked the day of the 31st, and the 1st or the 2d, he would be charged $2. It is the grossest injustice that has ever been permitted, and there is absolutely no means of relief at the present time.

This bill did get out of the committee, but died on the third-reading file. If it had passed, I am satisfied we would have at least curbed some of the injustices that are being worked on these men in that direction.

Labor exchanges: To my mind labor exchanges will be beneficial, particularly so with interstate shipments. But as far as solving the problem, it is not going to do that. The establishment of free employment bureaus is not going to furnish the men with positions if there is no work to do.

All of these suggestions that are contained in the pamphlet that you gentlemen have published with reference to private employment agencies are practically being complied with in California to-day. All of the employment agencies of the State of California are licensed in the bureau of labor statistics, and when any complaint is made to that department both sides are given a hearing, and the employment agent invariably complies with the instructions from the commission.

I have only had one case where there was any question raised as to our right to tell them what to do, and thousands upon thousands of dollars have been returned in fees, together with railroad fares and expenses too numerous to mention, and hundreds of other positions furnished to those making complaints.

There is no harm or wrong particularly in labor exchanges. To my mind they will do good in that they will check up on many injustices that are affecting people at the present time, particularly the theatrical profession.

Your commission, I believe, has not had much time to look into that; but it has been my experience in the city that those following that profession are the most helpless of any that I have come in contact with. They are timid, they are afraid of blacklisting, and are absolutely at the mercy of the theatrical managers·and booking agents; and some of the stories that I have heard in connection with that would not be well to repeat here.

To what extent is the present employment agency system responsible for unemployment? I do not believe the present system is responsible for unemployment in any manner. It has been intimated many, many times, but so far I have not been able to get any documentary evidence where men will claim, or surmise, at least, that a certain foreman is standing in with the employment agent; but as yet I have been unable to get any evidence of that fact.

We amended our employment agency act at the last session of the legislature, compelling the return of the fee if a man works less than seven days on a job. It had been charged he would work a day or two and get discharged. So the limit of seven days' employment was put on.

I do not feel it would be fair for me to say the employment agent is in any degree responsible for unemployment.

Stricter regulations required: I think, as far as that is concerned, the regulations are ample at the present time. They have to turn in a regular monthly report of the amount of the business that is done, are under our control, and, to my mind, are doing as they are told with regard to all kinds of complaints that are called to our attention.

In that connection I may say our courts sometimes take a rather peculiar view of things. There was a certain agency in this State which, from information I received, was paying for the business he was receiving by compensating an employee of a large corporation here. And it was testified to by a sworn statement that he had not only accepted money but a diamond ring and other presents. I denied him a license, and I was brought before the court on a mandamus order, and the court frankly said that there was no harm; he did not see anything wrong in a representative of a corporation accepting presents from an employment office. I do not know how he might view it, but I am satisfied that he don't know all of the conditions or he would never have made such a ruling. To my mind it was wrong—grossly unjust—because the men had been traveling back and forth for that particular corporation·for several months as a result of the compensation he was getting from the employment office. However, I was compelled under order of the court to issue a license.

Suggestions and methods for dealing with the problem of unemployment: That is a big question. To my mind the problem of the unemployment is entirely a national question. It is not for the State to assume, nor is it·for the community or the municipality to assume.

Aside from the compulsory saving proposition, that you gentlemen might give some consideration to, you might also consider the proposition of the building of national highways by the Government, under bond issue or otherwise; this work to be prosecuted whenever there is the great surplus of labor in any section of the country; and I am frank in saying that I would not put it at a wage that would be an incentive for men to leave private employment to·go there. But it would be a refuge where, in times such as we have to meet in the winter months here, men could fined employment enough to keep the wolf from the door, surrounded by proper sanitary conditions and regulations, and the United States Government to finance it.

That, to my mind, is the best solution and the one that will give us the best results.

Of course, they would have to provide possibly some means of transportation to and from that work. Our labor exchanges, if they were put into effect, might advise men in California that there are a thousand men wanted in Utah, but they would not provide any means of transportation. And if they did provide the means of transportation they also would have to provide a means of transportation after the job was done, so they could get away from there; otherwise they would be stranded in Utah. So there is a matter to consider in connection with employment.

The national highway proposition, to my mind, is the one that is worthy of a great deal of thought and consideration, together with the problem or proposition of compulsory saving.

The question of immigration: The American Federation of Labor, as Mr. Scharrenberg has said, is on record, and I am thoroughly in accord with some restriction or regulation, whether by education or otherwise; because as long as this country has practically open doors the migratory laborers, the men that do the rough labor work in this country, are never going to be able to better their condition very much by reason of the fact that the men that are coming in are always ready and willing to take their places. Employers have no trouble finding men when they need them.

That, I believe, is about all I have to suggest in the matter.

Unemployment insurance, as I said, I have not given much thought and time to that. It may work out in places where men are well organized.

I might say further, if you will permit me, that prior to 1913 there was not any act on our statute books in California that gave anybody the right to insist upon camps being kept in a sanitary condition. That bill was introduced as a result of a visit that I made over to Blue Canyon investigating a complaint against an employment agent. And while on the job I saw several men go off with their blankets, and I interviewed them, and they told me that they were quitting; they had come up with the same shipment which I was investigating, and the reason that they quit was on account of the accommodations. They said they were willing to work, but the conditions that they had to put up with there, while they were nothing out of the ordinary, were more than they could stand. I inquired where they had been sleeping. They pointed to a tent upon a side hill, which I investigated, and I found these conditions: There was about a foot of snow on the ground at the.time. The water had been seeping in through under the tents. There was an old tin stove in the center of the tent, a hole in the roof, and wooden bunks built around of rough old lumber, double-deckers. There was not enough straw in those bunks to fill a man's hat. I asked the superintendent, " In the name of God, do you expect men to work 10 hours a day and sleep there at night? " He says, " Why, yes; I have been 18 years at the business, and it is as good as I have ever seen.' I said, " God help the rest of them." That was the first time I had had any experience of this kind. I immediately considered and had drawn up the bill that is at the present time on the statute books which regulates the condition of camps.

That same gentleman, superintendent on the job, after talking the matter over with me, showed me a pamphlet, that he had in his possession, of steel bunks, called a tiger bunk. I communicated with the company at Chicago and learned that they had an office or representative here on Fremont Street. They provide or furnish these steel bunks with a wire-woven mattress that will give reasonable comfort. And I have been told, and I have a letter in my possession from a contractor who insisted on putting them in, that it is the best money that he ever spent; that it not only increased the efficiency of his men, but it was cheaper in the long run by considerable.

That act, while it was introduced and originally read that it should be the duty of the labor commissioner to enforce it, for some reason or other it was switched to the board of health, about on the third reading file, and passed in that form. I called the governor's attention to it at that time, but it was too late to have it changed, and it was signed.

I took the matter up with the board of health and received their consent to put a deputy in the field to enforce the provisions of this act, with the result that we have in our northern section of the State—had succeeded up to the time the immigration and housing commission asked to do this work—installed six or seven thousand of these steel bunks in permanent lumber camps. We met with hearty cooperation from most of the lumber companies. Few of them offered resistance, and many of them expressed satisfaction that they have made the change.

The men themselves, I know, are considerably pleased at the result. At the present time this work is being done by the immigration and housing commission.

This bill originated in the bureau of labor, and was presented through Brother Scharrenberg, and indorsed by the State federation, and presented by him to some representative in the legislature.

We have taken on, or I have taken on since being appointed labor commissioner, the enforcement of the labor laws of California, irrespective of the fact as to whether or not it was specifically my duty. I found this, that the laws on the statute books that were left to the district attorney to enforce were seldom enforced. As the result I decided from the outset that every law that was on the statute book that affected labor in any manner, shape, or form, upon my receiving complaint, it would be my duty to enforce them. That I have done. We have, I guess, at the present time, some eight or nine different acts that specifically mention the duty of the labor commissioner, and aside from these others become the duty of the district attorney, but we have enforced them.

I believe at the present time in California that the labor laws, and I am speaking advisedly, are as well enforced, if not better enforced, than they are in any other State in the Union.

Our eight-hour law for women, when it was originally passed the first year— we had it amended at the 1913 session—it was the duty of the district attorney to see that it was enforced. The governor, at the time of signing the bill, called me into his office and advised me: "This bill don't specifically mention what department is to enforce it. I don't know anybody better able or more willing to enforce it than yourself, and I expect you to see it don't become a dead letter."

I believe it is a measure that will result in much good to the women of this State, and for that reason should be enforced. We had many, many prosecutions, with the result that at the present time, I believe, that and all other laws are fairly well observed in California. I believe, gentlemen, I have made a general statement.

Another thing I might mention. Possibly some one may bring it out. A duty I have taken on is the collection of wages. That, while it don't appear to be a big work, the fact is it takes up about 75 per cent of the work of our department. We have collected in a little over two years and a half about $125,000 in disputed wage claims. This act, however, unfortunately has been declared unconstitutional by Judge Ogden, of Oakland, and also a judge in Los Angeles County. These decisions have interfered with us at those two points and in several other places throughout the State where they have learned of the decisions.

Prior to that decision we are able, on the refusal to pay wages when earned and due, to bring the party before the district attorney and, if necessary, secure a warrant for his arrest, with the result we have settled thousands and thousands of claims. Altogether, we have received up to June 1, 1914, over 8,000 wage complaints, about 65 or 70 per cent of which were settled without our having resorted to civil action. So that that work in itself is a big work, and I don't know of many other States that have undertaken it. I don't know how long I will be able to continue it, because with these decisions that are being rendered it makes it almost an impossible task to do much with the fellow who is studiously trying to beat his employees.

The average employer you meet with is willing and more than willing to go more than halfway. These disputes arise over misunderstandings of one kind and another, and the employee is invariably told he can go and sue for it. A lawsuit we have found is not much of a boon to a man with an empty stomach, and in most of these cases where they come in with these complaints they are dependent upon what they have earned for their lodging and livelihood. So that it is a situation that requires immediate attention. We have done the best we can. It is impossible for me to satisfy all of them, and sometimes you might hear of some criticisms. I believe, gentlemen, I have made about as thorough a statement as is possible.

Chairman WALSH. Anybody wish to ask any questions?

Commissioner O'CONNELL. Yes.

Chairman WALSH. Mr. O'Connell has some questions to ask.

Commissioner O'CONNELL. Can you give us an explanation of the methods explained to us the other day of the contractor employing men in the vineyards and fruit ranches—as to the method by which they are paid and pay to those they contract for and with; orientals, largely, I mean?

Mr. McLAUGHLIN. Well, in the case of Japanese, there is generally a contract boss who goes around and secures the work; he will go on in advance and take contracts on this, that, and the other, and follow the crops possibly all over the State with all of his people. Sometimes they will work for day's pay, other times work so much per box, or so much per ton, so that they make different arrangements of that kind. It is a kind of peon system by which the man gets a certain per cent of the actual earnings of the group for conducting the business and looking after their welfare generally. He is the commissary man, attends to the correspondence, and does everything else for them. He is the boss of the whole group. That is the way that thing is handled with the Japanese.

Commissioner O'CONNELL. You are a member of organized labor?

Mr. McLAUGHLIN. Yes, sir.

Commissioner O'CONNELL. What organization?

Mr. McLAUGHLIN. Teamsters.

Commissioner O'CONNELL. Some of the gentlemen who were on the stand the other day, the ranch owners, told us that they paid their laborers, I don't know just the exact amount, $1.60 or $2 or $2.20, something like that, and they employed these contractors to furnish the labor, and they paid the contractor that amount per day for these men, and the contractor paid his men. Now, have you any knowledge as to what the contractor pays his men? Does he pay them the amount that the ranch owner pays him per man?

Mr. McLAUGHLIN. Less the amount agreed upon between them all, which, possibly, is 5 per cent or some amount of that kind for securing the business, the general conduct of their housing accommodations, and everything of that character. He attends to all of the business and gets a per cent of what they earn.

Commissioner O'CONNELL. Have you got any information as to what the profits of that man are—the contractor?

Mr. McLAUGHLIN. Not particularly.

Commissioner O'CONNELL. They told us that they paid him for each man he employed, and then he charged each man for his job, in addition to which he ran the commissary. You say in addition to that he gets a pro rata of the earnings?

Mr. McLAUGHLIN. That is the way that it has been explained to me.

Commissioner O'CONNELL. Nobody knows anything about what his combined income is?

Mr. McLAUGHLIN. No, sir; the Japs have a faculty of settling their own disputes. I want to say there is not a notionality on the face of the earth that we have less complaints from than the Japanese themselves. They settle their own complaints in some way that is agreeable to them. We have never had complaints one against another. We have had complaints by them against white persons, but none against Japanese.

Commissioner O'CONNELL. Do you suppose that is with any fear that they won't get proper treatment from the office?

Mr. McLAUGHLIN. No, sir; absolutely none. We have several of them in the employment agency business, and I have yet to receive a complaint against any of them. They have a credit system of their own. The man never pays for his job in advance, but always pays after he receives the work.

Commissioner O'CONNELL. Your department licenses the employment agencies?

Mr. McLAUGHLIN. Yes, sir.

Commissioner O'CONNELL. Have you had any experience with the employment agencies entering into the white-slavery business in any way?

Mr. McLAUGHLIN. We have at times had women come in and say that they were sent to a place that they didn't think was respectable. We have investigated a few of them, but didn't find there was any merit to them, but we have notified the employment offices to be very careful where they send their women help. We have at other times reported to the department of justice a certain office we thought possibly was sending women to a place that was not entirely respectable, outside of the State of California.

Commissioner O'CONNELL. Does the employment agent itemize each position he secures, where he sends the applicant, when he reports to you?

Mr. McLAUGHLIN. He did formerly, but we have recently changed that by reason of the fact there was not really anything accomplished by it. We have a form of receipt which gives all of the information that the office will require, and that has to be kept in duplicate, so that his book is a record of **everything.**

Commissioner O'CONNELL. Do the employment agencies furnish men during **times of strike?**

Mr. McLAUGHLIN. Not if they know it. There has been two arrests made in San Francisco for having done that, and they are very careful about furnishing men in time of strike. They nearly all have a little rubber stamp that they stamp on the back of the receipt, to which the gentleman has to affix his signature, that the situation has been thoroughly explained to him, and he knows there is a strike on the job and he is going of his own free will or something to that effect.

Commissioner O'CONNELL. Are those stamps usually legible?

Mr. McLAUGHLIN. Indeed they are.

Commissioner O'CONNELL. Sometimes stamps can be used that require a microscope to ascertain what they meant.

Mr. McLAUGHLIN. The best proof of their carefulness in this city is that I have had occasion, I guess, in the last year to have possibly half a dozen or a dozen men that come in who said they didn't know anything about the trouble. I sent for the employment agent, brought him up to the office, and he absolutely produced his receipt with the man's own signature that the matter had been thoroughly explained to him.

The employment agents of the State know my position relative to labor; they know I am not in sympathy with their going out of their road to furnish nonunion men to strike jobs. Two of them have been arrested and have been prosecuted, and they are not taking any chances.

Commissioner O'CONNELL. Do all forms of agencies employing people come under your observation. For instance, is there any detective association in the city of San Francisco or in the State that furnishes men in time of strike?

Mr. McLAUGHLIN. They are not licensed by us if they do. They are not furnishing help and charging any fee. The only man I can compel to take a license is a man who is charging a fee for the position. If a detective agency is furnishing labor gratuitously, why, that wouldn't come under my department. I could, however, take him up if he misrepresents conditions. The moving of persons from one part of the State to another under misrepresentation is punishable with very heavy penalty up to the extent of a $2,000 fine.

Commissioner O'CONNELL. Did you make any observations of that kind?

Mr. McLAUGHLIN. Whenever any complaints are made to the department.

Commissioner O'CONNELL. But complaints usually must be filed first before you would give the matter attention?

Mr. McLAUGHLIN. Oh, yes.

Commissioner O'CONNELL. Does it come under your personal observation or have you at all made any official investigations where there are agencies employing men in this city for the purpose of sending out, or even in the city, men to take the place of strikers?

Mr. McLAUGHLIN. They won't operate very long until somebody will report it. Even their employing them in private employment offices and not charging any fee, we have investigated and instructed them that they would have to tell these men the exact conditions under which they were being employed, and there isn't much of that. There has not been much occasion for it, to be candid with you.

The Stockton situation on now—there is one office in San Francisco which had an order, and he was instructed—reminded at least, and his receipts were shown that he had complied with the law.

They would, however, do this: Men were sent down to the Russ building,· where they were employed for the M., M. & E., of Stockton, and our deputy called there and notified them they would have to notify those men they· were going to a struck job, and he was satisfied that this was being done and· the men thoroughly understood the conditions under which they were being employed.

Commissioner O'CONNELL. Suppose there appears in your morning or evening paper an advertisement for a number of men, mechanics of various kind and workmen, to apply at a certain room in a certain hotel or a certain room in a certain building here, would your office take any notice of that?

Mr. McLAUGHLIN. If we noticed it, we sure would. If it happened to be called to our attention or if we seen it, we certainly would.

Commissioner O'CONNELL. What would you do in that case?

Mr. McLAUGHLIN. We would go down and offer the man some money for a job in the first place, and, if he accepted, he was immediately locked up. If he didn't accept it, and had some other motive in view—that is, one of trying to induce men to become partners in business or some get-rich-quick scheme or other—we would cite him to appear before the district attorney and explain his position. We have done that many, many times. We have had attorneys that went into the employment agency business, and accepted a fee from a deputy in our office, and he was locked up in 10 minutes afterwards. We have all the authority of the sheriff in cases of that kind.

Commissioner O'CONNELL. That is all.

Chairman WALSH. Mr. Commons has a question.

Commissioner COMMONS. Do you have your own prosecuting attorney for prosecuting cases?

Mr. McLAUGHLIN. We have an attorney in the department in this city.

Commissioner COMMONS. Does he conduct all cases of all kinds?

Mr. McLAUGHLIN. Prosecutions?

Commissioner COMMONS. Yes, sir.

Mr. McLAUGHLIN. Largely.

Commissioner COMMONS. You don't depend, then, on the district attorney or county prosecuting attorney?

Mr. McLAUGHLIN. Not in San Francisco.

Commissioner COMMONS. Well, over the State at large?

Mr. McLAUGHLIN. In the balance of the State we have to depend upon the county prosecutor.

Commissioner COMMONS. You have to depend upon the district or county prosecutor in the balance of the State?

Mr. McLAUGHLIN. Yes, sir.

Commissioner COMMONS. You say in the city of San Francisco one of your deputies is prosecuting attorney?

Mr. McLAUGHLIN. Oh, no; we have an attorney. There was an act passed at the last legislature that provided for the employment of an attorney for the department here.

Commissioner COMMON. That takes the place of the district attorney or prosecuting attorney of the county?

Mr. McLAUGHLIN. He represents the bureau in these prosecutions. Of course, his duty is not all confined to the city. A short time back we amended the eight-hour law for underground mines and tunnels to include railroad tunnels. The court held that the act didn't apply to them, and we amended at the last session of the legislature, with the result that after the law became effective, most of the construction companies immediately put the law into effect. Then they suddenly got the notion, I believe on account of some decision rendered in Utah or some place, that it was not constitutional, and they went back to the 10-hour day. We immediately notified them if they didn't desist we would arrest them, which we did, and one of the contractors was arrested in the vicinity of Colfax; he went up on a writ of habeas corpus, I having an understanding with the attorney for the construction company that if the superior court upheld the law he would go back to the the 8-hour day, and if it didn't, he reserved the right to work the 10-hour day until. finally decided by the supreme court. The superior court upheld the law. Our attorney had to go up there and prosecute that case. There is nothing to stop me from sending him to any part of the State I feel there is need for him.

Commissioner COMMONS. But you do depend upon the district attorney?

Mr. McLAUGHLIN. To a large extent.

Commissioner COMMONS. How do you find their cooperation?

Mr. McLAUGHLIN. Most of the attorneys do fairly well. Of course, you have this to contend with, and it is quite an obstacle in the enforcement of any law, you have the local political influence to contend with, and that makes it extremely hard to get them to be very active in the interests of the State if the man that is being prosecuted happens to be friendly with the party in power. In that case the best we can get possibly is a compromise with a plea of guilty with the fine remitted or an agreement from him that he will comply with the law in the future. If we get the result, we are not overanxious to send anybody to jail.

Commissioner COMMONS. Do you find in general that they take up the case in such way as you would do through your own attorney?

Mr. McLAUGHLIN. Yes, sir; they generally go in with considerable vim and vigor, but generally relax a little bit before the case comes to trial.

Commissioner COMMONS. Is that quite general?

Mr. McLAUGHLIN. Oh, I could say yes; very nearly general.

Commissioner COMMONS. What you mean to say is that at some stage of the game there is a compromise made in those cases?

Mr. McLAUGHLIN. Very often we are compelled to, and I don't know when you get the result that it can be considered really harmful. If a man has been brought to trial and put to considerable trouble, possibly the employment of an attorney and the like, he is going to be careful about what he is doing in the future.

Commissioner COMMONS. So that you are satisfied with the system as it is?

Mr. McLAUGHLIN. Well, it possibly could be improved, but I haven't got much complaint to offer in that respect. Of course, all our wage complaints—in the payment of wages we have been handicapped considerably as a result of the decision I spoke of a moment ago.

Take Alameda County: Judge Ogden rendered that decision, and immediately we were notified by the district attorney that we could not use his office any more for the collection of wage claims, so that makes it extremely hard to do anything over there. The same thing applies in Los Angeles County. There the district attorney, on account of a similar decision, won't do anything for us either. They have, however, down there, a public defender that we refer all these cases to, that we are unable to assist, and let him commence a civil action in their behalf. San Diego does fairly well. Sacramento does very good.

Commissioner COMMONS. What kind of work do you find that the claims come up, in farming or construction camps, or what?

Mr. McLAUGHLIN. Very few farming complaints. Some, but very few. · We have some complaints with construction camps, but as a rule when a man quits on that job they give him his time and he goes about his business and we don't have so much trouble with them. We will have more particularly complaints of hotels and restaurants and dishwashers and waiters and work of that kind. The bulk of those complaints I have mentioned is in this city and Alameda County, the bulk of them.

Commissioner COMMONS. The complaints then are not on account of large corporations?

Mr. McLAUGHLIN. We don't have very many complaints that after investigation we find there is much merit to against the big corporations. It is more the smaller employer.

Commissioner COMMONS. That is all.

Commissioner WEINSTOCK. You expressed the opinion in the early part of your testimony, in touching on the I. W. W. movement, that it consisted chiefly of so-called " highbrows," who wanted to shock their friends with their radicalism and a handful of straggling workers.

Mr. McLAUGHLIN. I think you have my testimony mixed with somebody else.

Commissioner O'CONNELL. That was Mr. Scharrenberg.

Commissioner WEINSTOCK. Was it Mr. Scharrenberg that made that statement. I thought it was you. How strong is the I. W. W. movement in California, from your observation?

Mr. McLaughlin. Well, if you judge from the amount of noise they make, you would think there was an awful lot of them, but I fail to see where there is many of them. There is no record that anybody can get. There is this about that: The percentage of agitators I have found during the unemployed situation, I guess, is about 1 per cent, and they are largely Germans, and the balance of them follow along in the gang. They have nothing else to do; they are unemployed; they are around to see the fun. That is the way the thing works out here. As far as getting an idea of the membership of the I. W. W., I think it is impossible almost to give you any accurate figure on that. I think their strength is greatly exaggerated.

Commissioner Weinstock. Do you think they are growing in the State of California in numbers? Is it an increasing or decreasing quantity?

Mr. McLaughlin. I am inclined to think it is increasing a little bit. I think it is increasing as a result of the unrest in the minds of a great many. You know you can't blame them much. I believe the I. W. W. is possibly serving a pretty good purpose. Brother Scharrenberg outlined that awhile ago. They are giving the other fellow something to think about. The one organization that is standing between the employer and the destruction of property and everything else, is the American Federation of Labor, and he is trying to knock that down. It will give him some food for thought that he had better get down on the ground possibly and do business with those he can do business with.

Commissioner Weinstock. You mean it is educating the employer to deal rather with the American Federation of Labor than the I. W. W.?

Mr. McLaughlin. Yes, sir.

Commissioner Weinstock. You offered two constructive suggestions to the commission to help solve this unrest problem. One was the construction of national highways at unattractive pay, so as not to take men away from legitimate avenues of industry, and the other one was that of compulsory savings. Now, if your idea should be carried out and if it should be possible to initiate a movement for the construction of national highways at unattractive pay, what is liable to be the attitude of organized labor on the question of unattractive pay? Is not organized labor likely to take the stand that the Government is establishing a low wage standard that is likely to be harmful to labor generally?

Mr. McLaughlin. Well, it is a question of what you might consider a low wage. There are a good many of us differ on that subject. I believe a wage of $2 a day, possibly, the minimum wage established by the State of California, is a low wage. Some other man might say $2 a day is a high wage.

Commissioner Weinstock. Take it with the unskilled labor generally, that is, the labor we find in the camps and on the farm and highways, would $2 be regarded as unattractive pay by them?

Mr. McLaughlin. It would be to keep himself on $2 a day, because he gets $2.25 or $2.50 on other jobs.

Commissioner Weinstock. The testimony that has been submitted by farmers is that the standard pay now in summer is a dollar and a half a day and board, and in winter, I think, something less than that. Now, take the maximum; of course, there are exceptional cases where they pay above that, but that is the average or standard. If that is the standard in summer, wouldn't $2 a day be, in fact, an attractive pay in winter in place of being an unattractive pay?

Mr. McLaughlin. I don't think so, not with the cost of living as it is. It has always been the rule in construction camps that the meals should be 25 cents. In times gone by it was a little less, and now they are getting it up to 30 and 35 cents, and they will tell you that they can't make any money at that. If a man pays 30 or 35 cents a meal he is not going to have a great deal left to clothe and keep himself on $2 a day.

Commissioner Weinstock. You pointed out, as I thought very effectively, that the situation of building highways during the winter months in order to absorb the surplus labor was not practicable, because highways could not be built in the winter except at almost prohibitive cost, on account of climatic conditions. Wouldn't that apply to the building of national highways just as well?

Mr. McLaughlin. Yes; but the National Government can better afford to meet the expense than can the local community or State.

Commissioner Weinstock. It would be in the nature of a subsidy?

Mr. McLaughlin. Exactly.

Commissioner Weinstock. Your idea is that the National Government could subsidize better than any one State?

Mr. McLAUGHLIN. And it is their duty to do it, in my opinion.

Commissioner WEINSTOCK. I presume a further reason is that if any one State attempted to do that the unemployed of all the other States would flock there and submerge them?

Mr. McLAUGHLIN. Yes. sir; particularly in California, where they have a pleasant climate.

Commissioner WEINSTOCK. And if the Nation does it, it is spread over the country?

Mr. McLAUGHLIN. If the Nation does it, it is spread over the country, and the work could be started all over the country.

Commissioner WEINSTOCK. On the question of compulsory savings, your other constructive suggestion, have you thought of any effective way of carrying that out? Have you thought of the machinery?

Mr. McLAUGHLIN. I haven't, possibly, given it a great deal of thought; it is hazy with me. Possibly it might be worked out in this fashion, and I think it should be done, if done at all, by the Federal authorities: That the employer should possibly pay 4 or 5 cents on the dollar, and the individual, say, pay 2 cents on the dollar or 4 cents on the dollar, whichever the amount may be that he would have to turn in, this amount to be deducted from the individual, and the other amount contributed by the employer, and these amounts would be turned in to some department that would hold them in reserve, subject to the call of the individual. That he would have some kind of identification. Or even a greater amount possibly than that. That he would have some system of identification whereby he could present it and get that money in any part of the country he might happen to be in.

Commissioner WEINSTOCK. Something like the postal-savings idea?

Mr. McLAUGHLIN. Something of that kind.

Commissioner WEINSTOCK. You wouldn't make that voluntary, but compulsory?

Mr. McLAUGHLIN. Well, that is, of course, a big question. I am satisfied there would be a lot of opposition to it, but I think it is a question of helping them protect themselves, that is all. Because I know this, that an awful lot of them will work long enough on the job to get a stake and then go to the nearest base of supply, the first town that has a saloon, and lay there a short while, get broke, and move on to the next place. That is what is occurring day in and day out with a lot of them. I want to say that that don't apply to some of our foreigners. Take our Italians and Greeks and Austrians; those men save money enough in the summer season to carry them over the winter. They are not a burden during this particular period we are discussing.

Commissioner WEINSTOCK. Who are—what nationalities?

Mr. McLAUGHLIN. Oh, they are largely of our own people; many Germans, many of them from our island possessions, principally Americans and Germans, I would say.

Commissioner GARRETSON. What is the temperamental difference between the Germans and Austrians?

Mr. McLAUGHLIN. I can't account for it. Nevertheless. they do save their money, and I had little trouble with them.

Commissioner WEINSTOCK. You think despite the fact that a system of compulsory savings would meet with opposition, that nevertheless it ought to prevail?

Mr. McLAUGHLIN. Yes, sir; I am inclined to say it should prevail. Something should be done to compel these men to keep enough of the money that they earn in the summer season to keep them in the winter season.

Commissioner WEINSTOCK. What machinery would you furnish to make these collections? If it was compulsory, you would have to have some machinery to do it.

Mr. McLAUGHLIN. That is a matter that would be worked out in detail by the department having supervision, whether our Postal Service or by compelling the employers to make a report as this commission now compels them. Your commission exacts that now, don't they?

Commissioner WEINSTOCK. The industrial commission?

Mr. McLAUGHLIN. Yes, sir.

Commissioner WEINSTOCK. Why, no.

Mr. McLAUGHLIN. Don't the commission insist on their paying a certain per cent on industrial insurance?

Commissioner WEINSTOCK. Oh, on industrial insurance. That is voluntary.

Mr. McLAUGHLIN. I know that, but they report that information to you.

Commissioner WEINSTOCK. For your information, it might be well to explain that in discussing this question of compulsory payment—that is done in Germany, where the Government collects from the employer and the employee and gives the cost of administration—in discussing that question with John Burns, labor cabinet minister of Great Britain, his statement was that the Parliament had seriously considered the question of duplicating that system in England, but on investigation they found that the cost of collection would be so heavy and the enforcement of the law would be so difficult that they abandoned the system, and, I take it, if it is difficult to enforce it in England——

Mr. McLAUGHLIN. It would be extremely difficult in a territory like this.

Commissioner WEINSTOCK. Where there is a great deal less respect for the law than in England, it would be almost impossible to do it in this country.

Mr. McLAUGHLIN. It would cost possibly a good deal more here.

Commissioner WEINSTOCK. That is all.

Commissioner GARRETSON. Let me ask one question of Mr. McLaughlin.

Chairman WALSH. Mr. Garretson would like to ask you some questions.

Commissioner GARRETSON. Do I gather from your attitude that you hold that if the State assumes a responsibility on behalf of a man that it also consistently can assume the right of compelling him to become a party to it?

Mr. McLAUGHLIN. Well, I don't want you to take me too far on that. I object to being compelled to do anything.

Commissioner GARRETSON. Compulsory; does that convey any other meaning?

Mr. McLAUGHLIN. I think possibly you could do that with a little education for a period. Try and educate these men up to what is for their own best interests; but when you tell a person he has to do something, after he has belonged to the trades-union movement, he objects.

Commissioner GARRETSON. Don't the trades-union movement say that very thing?

Mr. McLAUGHLIN. He gives you that right when he takes his obligation.

Commissioner GARRETSON. What I want to get is, if your idea of this same allegiance to the State carries that with it?

Mr. McLAUGHLIN. No, sir; I don't believe he would forfeit it as willingly to the State. The trade-union is doing more for him than the State at the present time.

Commissioner GARRETSON. It would be difficult, would it not, to make a compulsory plan of this kind effective, unless the power of the State is recognized to make him do it?

Mr. McLAUGHLIN. I will admit anything you attempt to do will be difficult to enforce. I was only trying to give you my views on the subject.

Commissioner GARRETSON. That is what we are trying to get.

Mr. McLAUGHLIN. I have given you the best that I have.

Mr. THOMPSON. Mr. Bogart.

TESTIMONY OF MR. HARRY R. BOGART.

Mr. THOMPSON. Kindly give us your name and your business address.

Mr. BOGART. Harry R. Bogart; 116 Lick Building, San Francisco.

Mr. THOMPSON. You are financial secretary of the Associated Charities of San Francisco?

Mr. BOGART. I am.

Mr. THOMPSON. How long have you held that position?

Mr. BOGART. I have been connected with the associated charities since the earthquake and fire.

Mr. THOMPSON. How many years is that, four or five years, now?

Mr. BOGART. Seven years.

Mr. THOMPSON. Seven years. In the work you have had to do as such secretary, of course you have come in contact with the unemployment problem of this part of the country?

Mr. BOGART. More or less.

Mr. THOMPSON. More or less. From that, have you any views as to its cause and as to what might possibly be done to relieve the unemployment?

Mr. BOGART. Well, I have thought a good deal of it; probably have some suggestions that, if worked out with some other suggestions, might be of value.

Mr. THOMPSON. You may either tell those generally, or you may answer the specific questions which were sent to you.

Chairman WALSH. If you can state it generally, we would be glad to have you do it, and as concisely as possible, Mr. Bogart.

Mr. BOGART. Well, Mr. Chairman, I would rather answer the questions as they 'were put down here.

Chairman WALSH. Very good. If you have thought them out or written them out, why, please do that.

Mr. BOGART. Give your opinion as to the cause of the periodical acuteness of the problem of unemployment. Of what importance are the following factors:

Maladjustment: Well, that is a problem that in a climate like California is pretty hard to adjust, for the reason that our unemployed, as a rule, in California during the winter months are not all people that belong to California. We get a great many from Oregon; we get a great many from Utah. And in that way it is a pretty hard thing to adjust.

The excess of the total supply of labor over demand: That was answered by the other one, because during the winter months in San Francisco we have a great many men that don't belong there. We have men that go to the fisheries—about 8,000 of them that go to the fisheries in April and come back here in October. We have men that work in the construction camps in Oregon that come here. We have them in Utah that come here because the climatic conditions in San Francisco are better than they are in the other States that they are leaving.

The existence of a class which will not work: That is a very small class. There is a class of men that won't work because they can't. They are disqualified, in fact, for the labor market.

In my connection as secretary of the Cooperative Employment Bureau, half of the men that apply to us there for meals and lodging are men that will work if they could get light work—work that they can possibly do; but about half of the men that come down there, to send them out to labor work would be absolutely foolish, because almost 50 per cent of the men can't do it. I should say they are in that condition either from lack of nourishment or from disease of some sort.

Existence of class which can not work: That has been increasing in San Francisco, as far as I have been able to find out. For instance, this is the first year in the existence of the city and county of San Francisco that our relief home and our city and county hospitals have been filled at this time of the year. There has always been room for 100 to 150 men in our relief home in San Francisco at this time of the year, and there has not been a vacancy during the whole of this summer.

Periodical and seasonal variations in demand for labor: There is a greater demand for labor in San Francisco during the summer than there is in winter. I do not know of any way, unless as Mr. McLaughlin said, work could be done on State highways. During the winter months that work on the State highways should be held off until the unemployment in the country, on the fruit ranches, farms, construction camps, etc., slows down, and then put these men onto that sort of work.

But there is another thing outside of that, conditions in California not allowing that(particularly in regard to the State law and the county law. They do not provide for a man to work that does not belong to the city or to the county or State.

For instance, in San Francisco, a man to work even in the sewer work, digging sewers under contract, is supposed to be a citizen of San Francisco and a voter. The same way with California. You can not work men on the highways of California unless he is a citizen of California; and 50 per cent of the men that we found last year in our unemployment work here were not men that belonged in California, but were residents of other States.

Is the responsibility for unemployment social or individual? Well, 2 per cent is very conservative. The social conditions are easily the cause of unemployment.

Is the extent of unemployment increasing? Well, it is increasing in the last two years. There is an increase in our work, both to the associated charities and the Cooperative Employment Bureau. In the last two years the associated charities, through its own activities and the activities of the Cooperative Employment Bureau, have spent over $45,000, something that it could have ill afforded to do on account of its financial condition, because last year there were about twenty-three or four thousand dollars of its own money, besides money that was used by the city, by the citizens' relief committee, used on the unemployed; but their money was used for the unemployed married man only, with a family.

Give your opinion as to the character of men in the army of the unemployed: To what extent are the following classes represented—men honestly out of work? Well, last winter our registration showed a little over 7,000, about 7,078 men, and of that number probably about 3,500 of them worked. The other 3,500 were always asking for free meals and free lodging. And that would have been carried on probably all during the winter if we had not made a restriction that the man that did not work did not eat. We so arranged the registration card and the card of identification that we gave him that he could not get into the kitchen or into the dining room for a meal unless his registration card showed that he had either applied for work or had been given four days' work.

We found very soon after that our meals dropped just one-half. Those men that dropped out were the men that formed Kelly's army. Those were the men that were quartered at Fifth and Howard Streets and did not work at any time for the 20 cents an hour—just one-half of them.

Men who won't work: Well, there is a class of men who won't work. For instance, San Francisco County, the city of San Francisco, contributes about $125,000 a year to the man that begs on the street. That is an estimate of the police department, that there is that much money collected by that class of men. They may call it work.

Commissioner WEINSTOCK. You mean men that receive alms that are handed out on the street?

. Mr. BOGART. That are handed out on the street.

Commissioner WEINSTOCK. One hundred and twenty-five thousand dollars a year?

Mr. BOGART. One hundred and twenty-five thousand dollars a year.

Commissioner WEINSTOCK. Distributed among how many men, approximately?

Mr. BOGART. Well, I should say every day in San Francisco that there is in the neighborhood of from 100 to 125 begging on the streets.

Commissioner WEINSTOCK. That would be a thousand dollars a year a man.

Mr. BOGART. At this time of the year. At this time of the year there is that amount of men. I do not know in the wintertime how many men there are, or how many men that the police think get some of that money, who go around from home to home, but that was the estimate given by the police.

Commissioner O'CONNELL. What method have the police department of gathering those statistics?

Mr. BOGART. I don't know.

Commissioner O'CONNELL. Have they a cash register somewhere on the street corner?

Mr. BOGART. I do not know. It was simply a question that we asked the police department, if they had any idea of the amount of money that was collected in the city of—county of—San Francisco, and they said about $125,000 a year.

Commissioner O'CONNELL. That was just a guess. No method of scientifically getting at that, is there; is it possible?

Mr. BOGART. I do not know that there would be any scientific method of getting at that.

Commissioner O'CONNELL. Does that include men and women?

Mr. BOGART. We particularly asked for men. Our question to them was, "What is the amount of money contributed annually to the man that begs on the street?" and the answer was, "Approximately $125,000 a year." There are men in San Francisco that have been in San Francisco for years making $2, $3, and $4 a day.

Commissioner O'CONNELL. Are they professionals?

Mr. BOGART. Yes.

Commissioner O'CONNELL. Do they get themselves up particularly in shape for that sort of thing; butter up their faces, apparently, tie up their arm, or fix up their knee, or something like that—walk on their knee?

Mr. BOGART. Well, no; they are really cripples. Take the hunchback, the man on crutches, the man with one arm off, an arm paralyzed, or some condition of that sort.

Commissioner O'CONNELL. Is it systematized; is there an organized society of professional beggars, men who hire men—make a specialty of that sort of thing?

Mr. BOGART. Well, there is in town here institutions that go around from home to home, from store to store, and ask for donations and subscriptions.

Commissioner O'CONNELL. I don't mean societies.

Mr. BOGART. I do not know what you call them; I don't know whether you call that begging.

. Commissioner O'CONNELL. We have heard in the larger cities where there are men who make a profession of preparing men to become professional beggars.

Mr. BOGART. Nothing of that sort in San Francisco that I know of.

·Agitators: We had two or three agitators here last year that probably kept the 50 per cent that did not work last year for the dollar and twenty; kept them from working.

Commissioner O'CONNELL. Who were they?

Mr. BOGART. Mr. Kelly, Mr. Thorn, and Mr. Buck, and probably two or three others. I know there were two or three others, I can't remember their names, that advised the men not to work for the dollar and twenty a day which was offered them, not as a wage, but as a relief measure. It was not offered; we told them when we started work that it was not offered to them as a wage. We offered it as a relief measure. We were not trying to make that man work for that wage, just simply enough to keep him together, by giving the man four· days' work altogether a week at $1.20 a day, so that it would tide them over until they could get work. Not that we wanted to do any work, for the fact of the matter is, the work that was done with these men at $1.20 could· have been done cheaper at $3 a day according to the report of the board of public works, because they did that by hand; they had no cars or dump wagons or anything of that sort, and the work was done with men.

Commissioner O'CONNELL. It wasn't a matter of economy to employ them for a $1.50 to $2 a day?

Mr. BOGART. According to the statement of the board of public works it was not; they could have done it cheaper for $2 a day. They could have had it done cheaper by contract.

Commissioner WEINSTOCK. You mean the cost per cubic yard would be less?

Mr. BOGART. That is the report made by the board of public works; yes.

Chairman WALSH. Proceed.

Mr. BOGART. As I said before, there is a large class of men that are unemployable from the standpoint of labor. We have had men that come down to us in the last three and a half years—we have handled down at our Cooperative Employment Bureau 8,181 different men—supplying them with their meals and lodgings and, whenever it was possible, placing them out in permanent employment. Of these 8,181 men 50 per cent of them were not fit for laboring work; neither were they fit for clerical work. A good deal of it was disease and a good deal of it was lack of nourishment—the sleeping underneath sidewalks and the sleeping along the railroad tracks, where they got all doubled up with rheumatism or crippled in some way—absolutely impossible for them to use the pick and shovel or any hard work of that sort.

But the State could put about 75 per cent of those men back on their feet so that they would make good laborers, if they had such a thing as a State farm or a State—well, yes, a State farm where these men could be taught to do some sort of work that they could get after they go out of there.

For instance, the man that is picked up in the streets of San Francisco for vagrancy is given 30 or 60 days at the county jail. The time he is out there at the jail he does not work at all; he just lays around and smokes cigarettes and has a good time at the jail, and comes out in exactly the same position.

If he was put on a State farm instead of in the jail and taught to use the pick and shovel, the pruning of trees, or some sort of agricultural work, and kept in there long enough—until the superintendent or the instructor out there said that that man was able to go out and do agricultural work or pick-and-shovel work—about 75 per cent of them could be made respectable citizens and an addition to society.

."Give your opinion as to the effect of the unemployed periods on individuals. Are these periods factors in the physical and moral degeneration?" Yes. Naturally a man being out of employment for any length of time, it is going to reduce his moral and physical welfare. If he hangs around, if he gets into a cheap lodging house or a cheap charitable place, where he gets no care or proper food, he gets in with a crowd of men that he is not in the habit of getting into; he is going to go down the same as the 50 per cent of those other men that we handle down at the wood yard.

"To what extent are discontent and social unrest traceable to unemployment?" That is answered in almost the one above. The man that is unemployed for any length of time of course is discontented. I would be, or anyone else would be that was out of a position for any length of time. He would get discontented with his condition. It is natural.

"Give your opinion of the following methods of alleviating or doing away with unemployment:"

Forcible breaking up of the army of the unemployed: Well, I don't believe that that would do any good. If they were doing nothing against the law, I don't believe that they should be broken up. I do think this, and I thought it last winter while this unemployed army was walking up and down Market Street saying things that should not have been said; I think that they should have been—the ones that said those things—taken out of the ranks and told to get away from there, not only by the city officials but by the men that were trying to do a certain good by their marching up and down the streets. There were things said last winter that possibly should not have been said.

Organized charity: Organized charity is not in a position to handle the unemployed problem—never has been, only in a temporary way. It does a good deal of work. It does about $16,000 or $18,000 of work—that is, the associated charities does—every winter in taking care of them.

Commissioner O'CONNELL. Can you tell us there, is that your total amount of work, $16,000 or $18,000?

Mr. BOGART. Amongst the unemployed, nble-bodied men that would be able to work if they had work.

Commissioner O'CONNELL. What does it cost you to distribute that; what per cent?

Mr. BOGART. Well, our auditor's report for 1912 showed that a little over 9 per cent of the receipts of the associated charities were used for administration and clerical service—everything that went into administration. The balance of it, 91 per cent—almost 91 per cent—was used for relief.

Commissioner O'CONNELL. That is, of your entire income?

Mr. BOGART. Yes. There is no more—it doesn't cost any more to administer the unemployed that we have here than it does the rest of our work.

Commissioner O'CONNELL. It costs you about 9 per cent to distribute your income?

Mr. BOGART. Yes.

Commissioner GARRETSON. Out of every dollar that you get in, 91 cents goes back?

Mr. BOGART. Goes into relief.

Commissioner GARRETSON. For the people to be benefited?

Mr. BOGART. Yes, sir. Our auditor's report shows that last year, and probably will show less this year.

Commissioner GARRETSON. Doesn't it really cost less to reach the unemployed than your other forms of work?

Mr. BOGART. Yes.

Commissioner GARRETSON. It comes largely to you?

Mr. BOGART. Yes. Our work amongst our sick class costs a great deal more, because the unemployed family will come to us and they will be given there their relief right direct without a lot of investigation, which is necessary with the sick and the planning for the sick.

Farm colonies: Well, there are two kinds of farm colonies that do good—that is, the one that I have spoken about to train the men to work. And then there is the other one. There are a great many families in San Francisco and all over California—in fact in the United States—who would probably go out onto the land if they had the opportunity.

I have four or five cases in mind now where we have taken Spanish families that were from in the Hawaiian Islands; that came over here from the Hawaiian Islands on account of the long hours of work over there, and got into San Francisco. They were agricultural people in their own country. These families were taken down, their transportation paid, and enough money given them for their first two weeks' provisions in Huntington, which is just outside of Los Angeles. These families—there were 21 of them taken down there, and there are 18 of them still there. That is two years ago. They are still there, and these farmers for whom they are working—it is in the beet-sugar industry—say that they haven't had a better class of workmen than these men with their families. They would not go away from there for anything. Some of them are getting two and a half and three dollars a day, with the free rent of their cottages, and enough ground to plant their own vegetables and truck gardens.

That shows that if they would go down there and do that on rented ground, or, rather, on ground for their wages, that if they had the opportunity to go out on a 10 or 15 or 20 acre tract of land, they would more than likely go. And every one of those you get out on a place of that sort you lessen the number of unemployed in your city.

Commissioner GARRETSON. Did you hear the testimony of Mr. Lilienthal this morning?

Mr. BOGART. I did; yes, sir.

Commissioner GARRETSON. Do you believe that the plan or idea that he advances is a tangible, practical one?

Mr. BOGART. The one——

Commissioner GARRETSON. Land tenure.

Mr. BOGART. Yes, I do. I think it ought to be done. For instance, we have now a committee composed of five or six different organizations working on a scheme for the temporarily unemployed this winter. That is a temporary plan of relief. We have another one working with the idea in mind of establishing or getting the State to establish State employment bureaus. This committee has been working for two months, every Thursday night, putting in a good deal of time on it. And we have discussed there at great length, and had somebody down from Sacramento to talk this farm colony over with us, and he has brought down a map showing the amount of available land in California and where it is located, etc. And it is very possible that within the next couple of months some sort of report will be ready to show what can be done on that land and the number of families that it will accommodate.

Commissioner GARRETSON. Will you furnish a copy, when it is made, to the commission?

Mr. BOGART. I can; yes.

Commissioner GARRETSON. Very glad to have it.

Mr. BOGART. Unemployment insurance: That is a problem that the secretary of the associated charities and myself have discussed a good deal. And we see a danger in it. We see a danger of the man that might and will probably take advantage of the fact that he will get a certain wage or a certain sum of money if he does not work. Yet it might be a good one with the family man if he was supposed to have paid into this unemployment fund a certain amount of money. For instance, if he was to pay in 7 cents on every dollar that he got, or 5 cents on every dollar that he got, and the employer that he was working for at that time put in half of that amount, or 4 cents when he puts in 7—that might possibly give the man the opportunity to tide himself over during the winter months. Of course that is something I am not able to answer very thoroughly now because we haven't gone into it far enough.

Labor exchanges: As I said before, a committee of five or six different organizations are trying to work out a plan similar to the one in operation in Wisconsin, a plan to handle the unemployed through a chain of employment bureaus throughout the State, conducted by the State. Because we think, and it was one reason why we established our cooperative employment bureau, we don't think a man that wants work should have to pay for his job. A man is entitled to work without having to pay $2 or $2.50 for his job, if the job is there for him to have. And that is one reason why we have been thinking and talking over these labor exchanges for the last two or three months.

Commissioner GARRETSON. The wider its field the more effective it would be?

Mr. BOGART. Sure. If you can get the bureaus all over the State, San Francisco at times may need at lot of men that Stockton might have, and Fresno might have, and vice versa.

Commissioner GARRETSON. Or all over the Union?

Mr. BOGART. Yes, sir.

"To what extent is the present employment-agency system responsible for unemployment?" Well, I can't say that it is responsible for very much unemployment, yet at the same time it is, for this reason: We have men come to us—if we were to pay the fees of men that could get jobs at the employment bureaus in San Francisco, it would require us to have a fund of about $45,000 or $50,000 a year. Men come to us by the dozens saying: "I see a job at Brady's I can get for $1.50 or $2, and the transportation is free. It is a job that I can do. It is milking cows, or something of that sort. Can you give me the $1.50 or $2 fee?" We did that, but we had to quit after awhile because we found that we had a chain of men there that would bankrupt us. So I think if a free labor bureau was established, that that part of the unemployment would be stopped.

Stricter regulation required: I think that the labor bureaus in San Francisco should be restricted a little more than they are. For instance, men are shipped all over the country. They ship men from here to Nevada during the summer months. They ship men from Nevada to San Francisco, or the vicinity of

San Francisco, on contract work. There must be some reason in doing that, whether it is on account of the fee they get, or whether it is to keep these men going to and fro on account of getting their fees, is another thing. But I think that the enforcement of laws stricter than that what they are on the employment offices, and looking into their dealings more thoroughly would be advisable.

Are State or Federal labor exchanges advisable? Well, I have answered that in my one above.

Suggest methods of dealing with the unemployed: There is not any method that I can suggest outside of the one that I have of the labor exchanges and the State farms, and the State training schools, you might·call them; outside of the one that has got to be handled this winter. There is a problem that we are coming to face this winter, and that was another reason that this committee has been working on the thing. We see it coming, and it is going to be almost the same question this winter as it was last winter, of getting these men to work for what we call a relief measure and not a wage.

It will be impossible in San Francisco at this time to raise a sufficient sum of money to put the men to work at more than 20 cents an hour. And I doubt whether we are going to be able to raise money in San Francisco to put the men to work for that money, unless we get something through our city treasury. Last winter a man worked four days at 20 cents an hour, six hours per day. He wasn't allowed to work the six days unless for some very good reason. If a captain of a police station or somebody we knew and could rely on came in and said, " You have got so-and-so working on this job; he has got a wife and seven children," well, in that case we would give the man more hours' work, and the full six days in the week.

Commissioner GARRETSON. In other words, you based it on subsistence instead of remuneration?

Mr. BOGART. Yes; exactly. That is about all, Mr. Chairman.

Chairman WALSH. That is all, thank you.

Mr. THOMPSON. Mr. Bonheim.

TESTIMONY OF MR. A. BONHEIM.

Mr. THOMPSON. Mr. Bonheim, Mr. Weinstock wishes to ask you some questions on the subject of unemployment.

Mr. BONHEIM. All right.

Commissioner GARRETSON. Better get his name into the record.

Chairman WALSH. Give the name.

Mr. THOMPSON. You might give your name and address.

Mr. BONHEIM. A. Bonheim; Sacramento.

Mr. THOMPSON. Your business?

Mr. BONHEIM. Merchant and banker.

Mr. THOMPSON. How long have you been located there?

Mr. BONHEIM. Thirty-eight years.

Mr. THOMPSON. Thirty-eight years. All right, Mr. Weinstock.

Commissioner WEINSTOCK. Have you any suggestions, Mr. Bonheim, that you can give this commission in the matter of dealing with the unemployed?

Mr. BONHEIM. Yes; but I can only go over the matter from the standpoint of Sacramento, not from that of San Francisco.

We had the experience of about 1,500 unemployed last year in January. The men that came at that time were men who wanted to work, and finally after they were given work on the levees of Sacramento they accepted it and worked faithfully.

In March, I think it was in March, about 2,500 people came from San Francisco. San Francsico, of course, claimed that they did not send the 2,500 men to Sacramento, but they admitted that they sent the 2,500 men and paid their passage from San Francisco to Oakland. Oakland in turn sent them to Benicia. Benicia sent them to Sacramento. Sacramento——

Chairman WALSH. Mr. Bonheim, would you please try to pitch your voice a little higher?

Mr. BONHEIM. Yes.

Chairman WALSH. I can barely hear you, and I know the audience out here would like to hear you.

Mr. BONHEIM. Sacramento in turn sent them to a small town of Roseville, which is in Placer County right adjoining Sacramento; also to Woodland, Yolo County. And as a result the committee in Sacramento arrived at the conclusion that this was not a problem for a municipality to solve, but a problem for the State and Nation in conjunction with each other cooperating.

Now, the solution that I would offer would be to go to the National Government and ask the National Government to pass a new law giving to the State the privilege of clearing and farming, say, 50,000 acres of land which at present belong to the forest reserve. The forest reserve, as I understand it, has in the neighborhood of 19,000,000 acres of land that is not being occupied and it is not for sale. The State or National Government also has in the neighborhood of 250,000 acres or more of land, of United States lands, which are held for purposes of settlement, which can be taken if people will live on them for three years and homestead them. But that land is not quite as good as the forest reserve land, which is about one-fifth of the State of California, and the State of California has in the neighborhood of 158,000 square miles. One-fifth of that is forest reserve, and that would be in the neighborhood of 19,000,000 acres.

Now, all that California would require would be in the neighborhood of 50,000 acres. That will require a law to give this land to the State of California, or to the committee formed here for that purpose, under the supervision of the railroad commission, say, or some Government commission to be appointed for that purpose. The problem must be divided into two propositions. First, to take care of the unemployed who move from town to town during the summer, who find ample employment in summer but none in winter. Now, clearing of lands is not farming. Clearing of lands can be done in November, December, January, February, and March, during the period that is wet and rainy, and when the climate for outdoor work is not quite as desirable as in summer. Clearing this land would mean to make it more valuable to the State, not wasting any money, not throwing away, as charity does, so and so much money, or wasting 9 or 10 or 20 per cent in distributing, but every penny spent would mean increasing the value of the land through the clearing.

Of course, this could be tried with one or two or three thousand acres. After clearing a thousand acres the unemployed, during those months, might also be employed for fencing it. Some of the mountain land might be terraced. It is excellent land for growing peaches, apricots, and applies, but particularly olives. The olive industry is a very profitable one.

So that the question of employing the army of unemployed would be solved by labor of that kind, which any man could do. Besides the lumber could be prepared. There is another industry. The wood could be cut and sold. After the land is cleared and fenced, select good men wanting to farm but without means to cultivate it. These could be assigned, say, to 20 acres of land. They could farm this tract and, for the time being, say for a period of five years, they would not be required to make any payments whatsoever. After five years the cost plus the interest of the land would be charged to the farmer, and he would pay, say, at the rate of 5 per cent a year for 20 years, the cost of the land, including interest, plus everything that was put on the land.

If the State takes hold of the proposition, there is no need of issuing bonds. But if the State does not wish to take care of the problem, it will be necessary to issue, say, $250,000 in bonds and sell these to the merchants and bankers of the State.

Following reasons would induce the capitalist to buy the bonds: First, it would be a matter of self-protection against a menace that will grow and grow and grow from year to year. In place of asking the merchants to pay for the bonds in coin, we should ask them to furnish the material which these men will require. For instance, a lumber firm would furnish a certain amount of lumber to build houses. A hardware firm would furnish the locks, the nails, and whatever hardware would be required. The seed man to furnish seeds; the nursery man to furnish the plants and the trees. In that way the system could be carried out with little cost and in a practical manner. In dividing the land, in place of selling it in rotation, sell every alternate 20-acre tract. Leave the adjoining tract to the one sold vacant, enabling you to give the farmer employment on the second tract, adding the expenditure to the cost of the second tract, which is being improved.

Secondly, if the farmer was successful and wanted to increase his acreage, say, in 10 years, he would be able to get 20 acres adjoining 10 years later, making it possible for him to own 40 acres, which would be quite an advantage and inducement to exert himself.

This is the plan quickly outlined, and I think it is practical for the solution of the problem to a certain extent. The problem of the unemployed is, of course, a serious question, and it requires considerable effort to meet it. I believe it can be met by giving the workingmen who move from week to week to different locations simple work they can do—work which requires very little experience and can be taught by a superintendent in one or two hours. In addition establish State employment offices. When these men arrive register them, stating their trade, their vocation, age, and capacity. As soon as the State employment offices can obtain a job for a blacksmith, send him immediately to the place where he is needed, and in that way reduce the number of unemployed from day to day.

Commissioner WEINSTOCK. Has it been ascertained definitely how many acres of land the Federal Government has in reserve, for example, in the State of California?

Mr. BONHEIM. Nineteen million acres.

Commissioner WEINSTOCK. Nineteen million acres?

Mr. BONHEIM. Yes, sir.

Commissioner WEINSTOCK. How much of that land, so far as you know, is arable?

Mr. BONHEIM. I am told three-fourths of it. I wouldn't want to state that positively. It would be necessary, perhaps, for the University of California to send two or three men from either Davisville or the agricultural station to examine it and report on it.

Commissioner WEINSTOCK. How far is that land located from transportation?

Mr. BONHEIM. A good part of it is within easy reach.

Commissioner WEINSTOCK. Is it within easy reach of railroad facilities?

Mr. BONHEIM. The railroad facilities are within 10 to 20 miles.

Commissioner WEINSTOCK. The idea, as I understand it, would be to have Congress set aside a certain portion of that land?

Mr. BONHEIM. Yes.

Commissioner WEINSTOCK. And throw it open to settlement under the direction of the State of California?

Mr. BONHEIM. Fifty thousand acres.

Commissioner WEINSTOCK. Fifty thousand acres?

Mr. BONHEIM. Out of 19,000.000.

Commissioner WEINSTOCK. That is, it is to practically present the State of California with 50,000 acres?

Mr. BONHEIM. Yes.

Commissioner WEINSTOCK. Without compensation?

Mr. BONHEIM. They don't ask any compensation now. Anyone can get this land by living on it for three years.

Commissioner WEINSTOCK. Then the State of California in turn is to issue bonds aggregating $250,000?

Mr. BONHEIM. Yes; they can; or a private corporation can issue bonds.

Commissioner WEINSTOCK. Issue bonds, say, of $250,000?

Mr. BONHEIM. Yes; by the State or a private corporation.

Commissioner WEINSTOCK. And this $250,000 is to be used in what way?

Mr. BONHEIM. Partially as an inducement to settlers to build homes, but mainly to furnish them the material they require to build them, and add that to the value of their land.

Commissioner WEINSTOCK. This land is to be sold in small parcels to prospective colonists?

Mr. BONHEIM. Yes.

Commissioner WEINSTOCK. At what valuation?

Mr. BONHEIM. At whatever it costs the committee or the State to clear and prepare it.

Commissioner WEINSTOCK. At actual cost?

Mr. BONHEIM. At actual cost plus 6 per cent interest.

Commissioner WEINSTOCK. To be paid back in small annual installments?.

Mr. BONHEIM. In 20 annual installments.

Commissioner WEINSTOCK. Over a period of 20 years?

Mr. BONHEIM. Twenty-five; the first five years no payments at all.

Commissioner WEINSTOCK. How are these colonists to be selected, by whom?

Mr. BONHEIM. They would have to be selected by a committee appointed for the purpose or by a commission.

Commissioner WEINSTOCK. That is, you pick out only the fit?

Mr. BONHEIM. Only those that bear a good reputation and are sturdy and strong and are willing to work. The motto must be: " Nothing without labor."

Commissioner WEINSTOCK. Now, how are these moneys to be paid back by the colonists in their annual installments?

Mr. BONHEIM. Either to the private corporation which issues the bonds or to the State, returning it to the State treasurer, if the State treasury advanced the money.

Commissioner WEINSTOCK. What would prevent these colonists from selling out their holdings to some land grabber?

Mr. BONHEIM. There would be a clause in the original agreement that would prevent it.

Commissioner WEINSTOCK. Well, if they wanted to drop out, what would they have to do with their holdings?

Mr. BONHEIM. Sell it to some one else—to the next comer.

Commissioner WEINSTOCK. And they would not be permitted to buy the adjoining property?

Mr. BONHEIM. No, not until after 10 years. They have to prove they are worthy of it. That gives the man an inducement to do good work and holds out some sort of a hope to increase his acreage right close by.

Commissioner WEINSTOCK. Now, the first step, according to your idea, as I gather it, is to employ the unemployed in the clearing of this land?

Mr. BONHEIM. Yes, sir.

Commissioner WEINSTOCK. Most of this land, I take it, is wooded?

Mr. BONHEIM. Yes, sir.

Commissioner WEINSTOCK. And how would you support these workers, by the clearing of the land?

Mr. BONHEIM. Sale of the wood.

Commissioner WEINSTOCK. Supposing that would be insufficient?

Mr. BONHEIM. Perhaps it would be necessary to furnish the farmers with lumber to build their homes, and if that was not sufficient income, take it from the bonds that are issued for the time being.

Commissioner WEINSTOCK. You mean subsidize the men?

Mr. BONHEIM. What would you call subsidizing?

Commissioner WEINSTOCK. Well, suppose the sale of the wood was not enough to pay for clearing the land, would you take the balance necessary from the sale of bonds?

Mr. BONHEIM. Yes.

Commissioner WEINSTOCK. Would yield a wage not to exceed a dollar a day?

Mr. BONHEIM. Yes.

Commissioner WEINSTOCK. And suppose it costs a man, if he had a family, $2 to $2.50 a day to live, how would you make up the difference between the dollar and the actual sum?

Mr. BONHEIM. From the sale of the bonds.

Commissioner WEINSTOCK. You are really subsidizing in this case.

Mr. BONHEIM. I would only pay them a sufficient amount to live on, as has been said here a number of times to-day. The idea is to find something to do for the unemployed to bridge over a certain time during the year, and that wage should not be so attractive as to make them wish to retain the work.

Commissioner WEINSTOCK. Well, but as I understand the plan as outlined, it is not merely to bridge him over a period, but the idea is to make these men permanent settlers there.

Mr. BONHEIM. That is the second class. That is, the members of the army of the unemployed, as it is named, are not men that would be likely to become farmers and remain permanent on the land.

Commissioner WEINSTOCK. Oh, I see. Then you differentiate and divide the unemployed into two classes?

Mr. BONHEIM. Two classes.

Commissioner WEINSTOCK. A, those who are temporary workers, and who would be utilized to clear the land.

Mr. BONHEIM. Virtually blanket men—carry their own blankets and go from farm to farm and from town to town.

Commissioner WEINSTOCK. And B, the class that would be chosen from the unemployed to become permanent settlers.

Mr. BONHEIM. You asked the question how they were to be selected. You could not select from the blanket men. You have to select from the sturdy, strong, and willing to work; men who have a good reputation and want to farm.

Commissioner WEINSTOCK. Is this the scheme that the witness who preceded you had in mind?

Mr. BONHEIM. Yes; I think so.

Commissioner WEINSTOCK. When he said it was under contemplation now?

Mr. BONHEIM. I don't think you can say it is under contemplation. It is simply submitted to the Commonwealth Club, who have taken it up and considered it, and have a meeting every Thursday night to discuss it.

Commissioner WEINSTOCK. And, I presume, have worked out a plan on paper?

Mr. BONHEIM. Yes.

Commissioner WEINSTOCK. And your first step, I take it, would be to get congressional action?

Mr. BONHEIM. No.

Commissioner WEINSTOCK. To set aside this land?

Mr. BONHEIM. No. The first step would be to ask the University of California to send several men out without expense to select land suitable for farming.

Commissioner WEINSTOCK. Exactly.

Mr. BONHEIM. Yes.

Commissioner WEINSTOCK. Assuming they have done that, what would be the next step?

Mr. BONHEIM. The next would be to interest our Congressmen, our Senators, Secretary of the Interior, and the President himself, who is very much interested in the matter, to overcome the question by adopting proper legislation.

Commissioner WEINSTOCK. To get Federal action?

Mr. BONHEIM. To get Federal action; yes.

Commissioner WEINSTOCK. Congress having passed the proposed act, sets aside how many—500.000 acres?

Mr. BONHEIM. No; 50,000 acres.

Commissioner WEINSTOCK. Fifty thousand acres? Then what would be the next step after that?

Mr. BONHEIM. The next step after that would be a decision by the State whether the State would undertake to take care of the financing of the plan.

Commissioner WEINSTOCK. To finance it?

Mr. BONHEIM. To finance it. Or whether it would be necessary to get a private corporation to do so. But either way it can be done without great difficulty.

Commissioner WEINSTOCK. That is all.

Commissioner GARRETSON. I want to ask one question on that last phase—private-corporation financing.

Mr. BONHEIM. Excuse me. Under the supervision of the railroad commission or some Government commission appointed——

Commissioner GARRETSON. Under whatever term——

Commissioner WEINSTOCK. State supervision?

Mr. BONHEIM. Yes.

Commissioner GARRETSON. Yes. Under State supervision, and men are chosen to go on there; failure results, because it has, as far as my knowledge goes—that is an untried experiment. It is reasonable to assume, is it not, that there will be a large percentage of failures on the part of those individuals chosen?

Mr. BONHEIM. You ask that?

Commissioner GARRETSON. Yes; I was asking.

Mr. BONHEIM. I hardly think so, because it is, you see, so extremely easy for them to meet their obligations that it is hardly possible to ever fail; but if one man makes a failure there will be some one else to step in his shoes.

Commissioner GARRETSON. Assume, though, that it might fail. I understood from your earlier testimony that there is not to be an open market for this man to dispose of any equity or vested right that may have grown up in him.

Mr. BONHEIM. No. Well, it would be necessary to make an agreement with each farmer, and that agreement could be made in any way that the commission would see fit——

Commissioner GARRETSON. Yes.

Mr. BONHEIM. I would not want to determine that to-day definitely.

Commissioner GARRETSON. You spoke of preventing the land-grabber?

Mr. BONHEIM. Yes.

Commissioner GARRETSON. From getting into the camp.

Mr. BONHEIM. Yes.

Commissioner GARRETSON. If there were a sufficient number of failures, would not that land fall into this corporation at charity prices?

Mr. BONHEIM. Well, I can't imagine, I can't agree with you, that there would be many failures. It seems to me almost impossible that there could be failure. A man can get 20 acres of land, say, for $1,200, that would include all interest and expenses, and only need to pay $60 a year. For first five years free, the first five years he makes no payments at all; after the first five years he begins to make his payments. That is for the purpose of giving the farmer an opportunity to get started. At the end of five years he ought to be on his feet.

Commissioner WEINSTOCK. Nothing for interest for the first five years?

Mr. BONHEIM. No.

Commissioner WEINSTOCK. The man would have to make no payment at the start?

Mr. BONHEIM. None whatsoever.

Commissioner WEINSTOCK. None whatever?

Mr. BONHEIM. No, sir.

Commissioner GARRETSON. It is fair to assume that a considerable percentage of the failures would not develop, might not develop until after the first five years was up. But even then, if any reasonable amount of lapses did occur, there would be quite a lot involved in it, wouldn't there?

Mr. BONHEIM. No; I think not. The supervision must be so strict that there can be absolutely no profit to any organization which undertakes it, or any commission that is appointed; there must be not a penny wasted, not a thing that would make it possible to be earned by private corporations, by a member of the corporation or by a member of the commission.

Commissioner GARRETSON. Or by the corporation itself?

Mr. BONHEIM. Or by the corporation itself.

Commissioner GARRETSON. No residuary interest?

Mr. BONHEIM. Absolutely none.

Commissioner GARRETSON. That is all.

Chairman WALSH. Thank you.

Mr. BONHEIM. You are quite welcome.

Chairman WALSH. The commission will now stand adjourned until Monday morning at 10 o'clock.

(Whereupon, at 3.50 o'clock p. m., on this Saturday, the 29th day of August, 1914, an adjournment was taken until Monday, August 31, 1914, at the hour of 10 o'clock a. m.)

STATEMENT OF MR. F. H. AINSWORTH.

FEDERATION OF FEDERAL CIVIL SERVICE EMPLOYEES,
San Francisco, Cal., August 31, 1914.

THE COMMISSION ON INDUSTRIAL RELATIONS,
San Francisco, Cal.

SIRS: I am constrained to address your honorable body in behalf of a class of workers from whom, I judge, you have had little if any testimony. I refer to the employees of the United States Government under the civil service. There is in this city an organization among such employees known as the Federation of Federal Civil Service Employees, and the purposes of the organization are to improve the condition of the civil service and to improve the condition of the workers. I will state at the onset that I believe there can be no substantial denial that these workers are part of the industrial population of the United States, and are entitled to all consideration accorded workers employed by private enterprise. To illustrate what I mean, I will say that, although the machinery of employment for this three hundred thousand or more group of workers is under what is known as the civil service, in practical operation their performance of duty and the standards by which they are judged are little different from those of private enterprise, noticeably those of large corporations.

This body of workers, from an industrial standpoint, has a different relationship to its employer than that of the private employee and employer, for the reason that said employer, the Government of the United States, does not wish to profit at the expense of the workers, and fundamentally may be termed a beneficent and benevolent employer. The reason that these workers complain is that inconsistencies, inequalities, and irregularities operate to their detriment in many cases through no intentional fault of their employer, the United States Government, but owing to lack of knowledge and indifference. It is true, this body of workers does not have to protect itself against the inclination of an employer who seeks to get as much profit as possible from the worker, but there is an element along that line that works hardship; that is where a subordinate chief, seeking to make a record for himself as an efficient and economical administrator, almost invariably does so at the expense of the lowest-paid and poorest equipped employee of the Government. When any plan for economy is discussed, almost invariably the lowest-paid man has to face a reduction of wages or a lengthening of his hours of labor, and he has no appeal.

I will not dwell at greater length upon this general situation, but I shall take the liberty of citing one condition, which is a complete illustration in itself and which may be duplicated in other branches of the service, I am convinced, a great many times.

I am inclosing herewith a number of letters constituting correspondence that I have had concerning a class of Government employees under the civil service known as customs guards. Some of these men are members of this organization and have sought, so far in vain, to receive some benefit by the act of March 15, 1898 (30 U. S. Stat. 316), which provides that Sundays and holidays are excepted from days of labor. As you will see by the correspondence, the Treasury Department apparently is not familiar with the law, because in the letter of May 2 the Assistant Secretary of the Treasury states that the customs guards are required to work every day in the year excepting 14 days' annual leave. Perhaps the most important part of this correspondence will be found in the letter from the Civil Service Commission under date of July 23, 1914, in which it disclaims any responsibility for the enforcement of the laws and regulations which it publishes under its own name and also any ability to assure those who enter the Government service that the conditions set forth in this publication shall be fulfilled. The Civil Service Commission disclaims any contractual relation, and if the position of the Treasury Department is correct there seems to be no obligation on the part of the Government either to fulfill its contractual obligations, if, indeed, such exist, or to live up to the law as far as its relationship to the civil-service employees is concerned. This is regarded as a remarkable situation, and I am not sure that I interpret the commission's letter correctly, because I believe that Congress would resent the intimation that its laws were not to be enforced.

This brings to my mind, and I submit it to the commission for such attention as you think it merits, a plan which I have long deemed feasible and which is taking hold of the minds of the people, especially in this city. In the city of Los Angeles there is what is known as a public defender. No doubt the commission is entirely familiar with the reasoning supporting the creation of such an office. There is a movement on foot to have one in this city, and from the results thus far obtained there is no question in my mind that the project will be of substantial service. I refer to that because my plan would be to create either a commission or a bureau, or possibly to extend the authority of the present Civil Service Commission, so that it would be the duty of the proper authority to report the nonobservance of a law in a case such as the one I have cited above. There has been in my experience numerous instances where those employees of the Government who had neither ability nor influence have been unjustly dealt with, principally to justify the claim of some individual regarding his particular administrative ability. So that if it would be possible to create a bureau or commission, either as an independent body or as a part of the Civil Service Commission, I believe a substantial reform could be accomplished, which by permitting the civil-service employees to know that they might submit questions of this sort to it would stimulate them to a more effective performance of their duties.

Any information that this organization or its officers and members have will be at the service of the commission should it desire to go into the subject.

Respectfully,

F. H. AINSWORTH, *President.*

EXHIBITS.

AINSWORTH EXHIBIT.

APRIL 16, 1914.

The SECRETARY OF THE TREASURY,
Washington, D. C.

SIR: During some reorganization of the customs department at this port certain conditions have arisen which members of this organization are interested in and which I therefore present for your consideration. Recently some changes have been made and some few positions abolished, owing, I am told, in part to the new tariff law, which does not require as many duties to be collected and therefore not as many employees as the old one; further, that an effort was being made along all proper lines to economize in every legitimate manner. As one result of this policy a number of positions have been abolished, and among them some known as " customs guards," and, in addition, those guards who have been retained are required to work in some instances 14 days without having a day off.

The purpose of this inquiry is to ask whether the necessities of an economical administration require a man to work eight hours a day for more than six days, when one day of rest should be given? It is my understanding that in all the branches of the Government service it is recognized that a man or woman should have one day off in seven, and I have no doubt that the particular situation that I refer to has escaped the notice of those who have charge of the matter, because it is relatively of small importance, and I take this method of making the inquiry and ask for such action as you deem proper.

Respectfully,

F. H. AINSWORTH, *President.*

TREASURY DEPARTMENT,
Washington, May 2, 1914.

Capt. F. H. AINSWORTH,
San Francisco, Cal.

SIR: The department is in receipt of your letter of the 16th ultimo, relative to the hours of service of the customs guards at San Francisco.

Customs guards at present are required at all ports to be on duty for eight hours daily, seven days each week, except that they are allowed 14 days' leave of absence each year. This has been the rule for a number of years. While the department has under consideration the readjustment of the force in such a manner as to give each guard one day off each week, at the present time the appropriation available is not sufficient to permit such action to be taken.

Respectfully,

WM. J. MALBURN,
Assistant Secretary.

MAY 12, 1914.

Hon. WILLIAM J. MALBURN,
, *Assistant Secretary of the Treasury,*
Washington, D. C.

SIR: I have the honor to acknowledge receipt of your letter of May 2, 1914, No. 100000/128, and I thank you for the information contained therein. The statement that customs guards are required to work eight hours daily seven days in the week throughout the year with the exception of 14 days' leave is new to me, and I am surprised that such a condition exists. I appreciate that the duty which the department feels necessary to impose is imperative and that the force is regulated by the apppropriation. Therefore I

5079

shall lay the matter before this association in order to ascertain whether it will take any steps to ask for an increase in appropriation, in order that sufficient employees may be hired to allow one day off in seven. In this connection, may I ask you whether I may refer to your letter as authority for the statement quoted regarding the duty expected?

Respectfully,

F. H. AINSWORTH, *President.*

———

TREASURY DEPARTMENT,
Washington, May 23, 1914.

Capt. F. H. AINSWORTH,
San Franciso, Cal.

SIR: The department is in receipt of your letter of the 12th instant, relative to the hours of service of the customs guards at San Francisco.

You are authorized to quote my letter of May 2, 1914, as authority for the statement regarding the duties of these employees.

Respectfully,

S. HAMLIN, *Assistant Secretary.*

———

JUNE 15, 1914.

UNITED STATES CIVIL SERVICE COMMISSION,
Washington, D. C.

SIRS: May I seek information for the benefit of the members of this organization and in an entirely helpful and instructive manner with reference to a situation which has come to my notice?

Owing to the fact that certain employees of the Government known as customs guards do not receive one day off in seven I addressed a letter to the Secretary of the Treasury asking why they should be required to work longer time than some other Government employees. In reply I received a letter stating that the customs guards are required to work at all ports 8 hours a day, 7 days a week, excepting that they have 14 days' leave of absence each year. I again wrote him on May 12, asking for authority to use his letter, such permission being received under date of May 23. Copies of all correspondence are attached herewith. My purpose in addressing the commission is to inquire as to what regulation has been authorized to modify the act of March 15, 1898 (30 U. S. Stat., 316), especially that portion which reads:

" Hereafter it shall be the duty of the heads of the several executive departments in the interest of the public service to require all clerks and other employees of whatever grade or class in their respective departments not less than seven hours of labor each day, *except Sundays and days provided public holidays by law or Executive orders.*"

I find the foregoing on page 15 of the Civil Service Act, Rules, and Executive Orders amended to June 2, 1913.

I also have the honor to inquire why " customs guards " are designated as such in the appropriation bill, but I do not find any reference to them in the manual of civil-service examinations.

Respectfully,

F. H. AINSWORTH, *President.*

———

UNITED STATES CIVIL SERVICE COMMISSION,
Washington, D. C., June 25, 1914.

Capt. F. H. AINSWORTH,
Federation of Federal Civil Service Employees, San Francisco, Cal.

SIR: In response to your letter of June 15, 1914, you are advised that the civil-service act and rules, which in general define the province of this commission, do not touch upon such matters as the hours of labor to be required of civil-service employees, and the commission therefore does not take action in regard to those matters, nor attempt to interpret the duty of the different departments with regard to them, its responsibility being limited to the interpreting of the statutes bearing the question in relation to its own employees. It may be stated, however, that the proviso following the portion of the statute which you quote from page 15 of the commission's pamphlet containing the civil-service act and rules appears to empower the heads of departments to further extend the hours of labor to be required.

. In regard to your other question, you are advised that "customs guard" is a recent designation given to the position formerly known as customs watchman, and is filled by appointment from the third grade, subclerical examinations for the customs service.

By direction of the commission.

Very respectfully,

JOHN A. McILHENNY, *President.*

FEDERATION OF FEDERAL CIVIL SERVICE EMPLOYEES,
Port of San Francisco, July 11, 1914.

UNITED STATES CIVIL SERVICE COMMISSION,
Washington, D. C.

GENTLEMEN: I beg to acknowledge receipt of your letter of June 25, 1914, advising in answer to my inquiry concerning section 7 of the act of March 15, 1898, that the commission has no authority to investigate or make inquiry concerning the manner in which this section of the law is administered. I therefore inquire what steps the commission would deem proper where any employee of the United States found that this act was not conformed to and who, as a consequence, was called upon to perform service different in character and for longer periods of time than his fellow, and to whom he should apply for redress. Per⬛ps it may be illuminating if I state in some detail the point of view from which this inquiry is made and my letter of June 15, 1914, was written.

The Civil Service Commission, operating as an agent of the Federal Government, has from time to time announced that certain vacancies existed and that they would be filled by examinations held under the auspices of the commission, and that those appointed would receive certain compensation and be employed under certain conditions; in other words, the commission issued a proposal for labor to be performed under certain conditions. The commission also issues from time to time reports and pamphlets defining and outlining the conditions of the civil service of the United States; thus when any person seeks employment and, conforming to the requirements of the commission, passes the necessary examination and accepts employment he also is a party to the contract—the second party. If the United States through the Civil Service Commission, the party of the first part to the contract, makes certain stipulations and undertakes in accordance with such stipulations to pay a certain remuneration to those who fill them, the employee, the party to the second part, fulfills his part of the contract by meeting the requirements. These publications of the Civil Service Commission define in part the stipulations of the party of the first part, indicate how examinations shall be held, how appointments shall be made, how promotions and demontions shall be made, how removals shall be made, how reinstatements and transfers shall be made, and in considerable detail are substantially the stipulations and requirements of the party of the first part.

One of these stipulations above referred to will be found on page 15 of a publication entitled "Civil Service Act, Rules, and Executive Orders, etc., Amended June 2, 1913." This document quotes a number of sections of the law, notably the civil-service act of 1883 and amendments thereto, all of which may reasonably be regarded as the contractual requirements of the party of the first part. There are also definitions and limitations which the party of the second part— the employee—may properly expect to be observed when in his favor as rigidly and as carefully as when in the Government's favor. This detail is headed "Statutes affecting leaves of absence and hours of labor," and states as follows:

"·SEC. 7. * * *· Hereafter it shall be the duty of the heads of the several executive departments, in the interest of the public service, to require of all clerks and other employees, of whatever grade or class, in their respective departments, not less than seven hours of labor each day, except Sundays and days provided public holidays by law or Executive order: *Provided,* That the heads of the departments may, by special order, stating the reason, further extend the hours of any clerk or employee in their departments, respectively; but in case of an extension it shall be without additional compensation: *Provided further,* That the head of any department may grant thirty days' annual leave with pay in any one year to each clerk or employee: *And provided further,* That where some member of the immediate family of a clerk or employee is afflicted with a contagious disease and requires the care and attendance of such employee, or where his or her presence in the department would jeopardize the health of fellow clerks, and in exceptional and meritorious cases, where a clerk or employee is personally ill, and where to limit the annual leave to thirty days in any one calendar year would work peculiar hardship, it may be extended in the discretion of the head of the department, with pay, not exceeding thirty days in any one case or in any one calendar year.

" This section shall not be construed to mean that so long as a clerk or employee is borne upon the rolls of the department in excess of the time herein provided for or granted that he or she shall be entitled to pay during the period of such excessive absence, but that the pay shall stop upon the expiration of the granted leave (30 Stat., 316, Mar. 15, 1898)."

The first element of the statute is that all clerks and other employees of whatever grade or class shall work not less than seven hours each day, a positive and mandatory condition which is imposed on the part of the Government and, as far as the writer knows, rigorously lived up to. This is clearly a requirement of the party of the first part imposing a duty upon the party of the second part, but there is a substantial limitation to this part of the section, and that limitation is that Sundays and days provided as public holidays by law or Executive order are excepted. That is a provision in favor and for the protection of the party of the second part. Why is not the party of the second part entitled to the same protection in the inforcement of the stipulation in his favor that the party of the first part has? There is a proviso attached to the whole paragraph, and that is that the heads of the departments by special order, this indicating by the well-known rule of construction that in the absence of special order the proviso shall not prevail, may extend the hours of work of any clerk. There is, however, no provision authorizing the heads of departments to direct those concerned to be employed on Sundays or holidays. Now, it seems to be clear from this act that Congress had in mind a fixed hourly value of labor, and by the term labor clerical as well as manual is meant, and also the intent not to demand labor on Sundays or holidays. There is no complicated wording involved; the statute is plain—" six days a week, not less than seven hours a day," but no work on Sundays or holidays. It is a well-known rule of construction that when the title of a statute and the text set forth in plain terms the purpose of the act, no limitation amounting to a nullification can be sustained in a construction. So that, again referring to the contractual aspect of the case in this particular respect, the party of the first part has said through Congress that it demands not less than seven hours' labor per diem of its employees for six days in the week, and, furthermore, that on special occasions or in emergencies heads of departments may by special order extend the hours of work, not, mark you, authorizing work on Sundays or holidays, but to extend the hours each day when labor is permitted, because it is obvious that Sundays and holidays being excepted the hours of labor could not be applied to those days.

Let us contemplate for a moment the statement of the Secretary of the Treasury regarding the customs guards. He says that they must work eight hours a day seven days a week all the year around. Is this not a clear violation of contract? Can there be any room for difference of opinion on that proposition? Has the Secretary of the Treasury or any authorized subordinate issued a special order extending the hours of work in this case from seven to eight a day? If so, where can such order be found? These are all proper questions by the party of the second part, by which he may ask for the same regard for his part of the contract as that which is paid to the party of the first part's part of the contract.

This act goes on to provide that the head of the department may grant 30 days' annual leave. In the case of the customs guards the head of the department apparently deems that the public service can spare only 15 days' leave for this particular group of employees. This act also provides for certain absence with pay on account of sickness, putting a limitation upon the total leave of about 60 days; and it is the opinion of the writer that all the provisions of this act hereinabove mentioned are fairly and reasonably kept by both parties to the contract, at least by the customs guards, who must work on Sundays and holidays, contrary, it would seem, to the specific mandate of this act.

The foregoing is argumentative in character and seeks to set forth the point of view from which this communication is addressed, and, having thus far discussed the matter, I ask in a helpful manner that your honorable commission would indicate how the customs guard, for instance, or any other employee who feels that he is not having his part of the contract as carefully observed as to the other party, may proceed in an orderly and respectful manner to seek redress. I also further ask if your honorable body can not be of some assistance to such a person, so that he would not be in the position, if seeking redress, of being charged with insubordination or of seeking to disrupt discipline. The case to point is probably one of the best illustrations that has come within the writer's knowledge of the helplessness of the employee to present "the case in which it appears he is not receiving what he might expect to receive, as indicated by the publications of the Civil Service Commission when inviting men and women to take employment. To return to section 7 of the act of March 15, 1898, is it not a fact that if the head of the department can ignore the expression "except Sundays and days provided public holidays by law or Executive order," he can also ignore any other portion of this section? These particular words have no preferential or limited significance, and if an executive officer can leave these words out of the law when he administers it, can he not with equal justice leave out any other words of any other law? And if he does this where shall the employee who is concerned seek redress?

It will be seen in this controversy that the Secretary of the Treasury himself practically ignores this law. How, then, shall these customs guards have their part of the contract enforced? I have asked this question in several forms to lead up to this proposition: Would it not be a reasonable function of the Civil Service Commission, and I do not know that such is authorized, to come to the assistance of this particular group of civil-service employees and say to the honorable Secretary of the Treasury that his letter and the service required of these men are not in accord with the law? These men themselves have one of several methods by which to approach the subject. They can associate themselves together and petition the Secretary of the Treasury; they can associate themselves together and petition Congress; or they can do this individually; but it will not be necessary for me to state that for them to associate themselves together is a thing improbable of accomplishment, because they are scattered over the United States and they have no means of getting together. If they prepare individual remonstrances, are they not likely to be visited with some discipline for presuming to say that their chief, the head of the department, does not obey the law? The same line of argument applies to the petition to Congress. It is true, without doubt, that if all the people in the United States affected by this particular legislation could be assembled in one place they would very shortly prepare a remonstrance and back it up with substantial representation, but they are helpless in that respect because scattered. They can not systematically and intelligently either protest to the Treasury Department or to Congress, and furthermore they are likely to be met with this statement: "If you do not like the place why do you not resign?" But that is not a fair statement nor a tenable position for the Government to take. As I stated above, the Government has entered into a fair contract with these men, and it is as much incumbent upon the Government to fulfill its part of the contract without pressure or petition by the party of the second part as it is for the party of the second part to fulfill its duty conscientiously and faithfully when not under the scrutiny of supervisory eyes; in other words, one of these customs guards, watching a vessel at night in stormy, cold weather when no one was near to detect him, and he should abandon his post and seek warmth and shelter from the storm when he was expected to be on duty, he would be justifiably censurable, although no one knew it, and I wish to say that so far as my observation goes no more faithful body of men serve the United States to-day than this particular group, whom I have had occasion to see in many parts of the United States. That being the case, why should the United States, and the Treasury Department, not fulfill its contract and allow them their Sundays and public holidays?

I am not overlooking the argument about the limitation of appropriations, but I held that to be no argument. If that argument is valid, and that section does not apply, the Secretary of the Treasury would be justified in keeping these men—and, in fact, all the men he has—employed seven days a week, 10 hours a day, because there is work for them to perform. I take the position, however, that the right of the humblest employee of the Government to his pay and to his hours off duty is just as sacred and binding as the power and limitation of the appropriation for the enforcement of the law; in other words, if an employee enters the service with the understanding that he shall work not less than seven hours a day six days a week and have his Sundays to himself, he has just as much right to have that provision rigidly guarded as the Government has to require that he perform 7, 8, 9, or 10 hours' duty each day faithfully; and, on the other hand, I believe that the Government has no more right to make him work an extra day, when there is no legal authority for it, than he would have to take an extra day's pay out of the Treasury. I can not emphasize too forcibly the tendency that is growing up in the Government service of administrative officers, well meaning and conscientious in their efforts, to seek to make a record in efficiency and economy by demanding longer hours and an ever-increasing amount of work from those in the service who are ill prepared to protect themselves; and I believe your honorable body will agree with me that the contractual right of the employee should be just as fairly enforced by the Government through its administrative officers as the contractual right of the party of the first part. I know there are many emergencies and unusual situations which frequently require unusual hours and extra service, and I wish clearly to be understood as not discussing those conditions; but I refer to the fixed conditions which this customs-guard situation illustrates, which, I believe, is one that should be changed, and I earnestly ask the commission to take up the matter or indicate how it believes the matter can be taken up, so as not to react upon these men themselves, so that they may have what it seems to me they are entitled to under the law.

There is one last illustration—crude, it is true, but somewhat to the point—that I wish to make in this connection: When the Government or any other organization seeks transportation on a railroad train or seeks to have freight hauled on a railroad train it expects to pay the railroad company for the service rendered to destination; and indeed if a man buying a ticket in Washington to, say, Columbus, Ohio, over the Pennsylvania Railway, sought to travel 100 miles beyond Columbus the Pennsylvania Railway would not carry him because he was an agent of the Government unless he paid for it. When the Government buys shoes for the Army it pays for every pair; when it buys horses for the Army it pays for every horse; when it buys armor plate for the Navy it pays for every pound. Why should it not pay for the unit of labor that it purchases from its employees? If the Government contracts with a man to work seven hours a day six days a week and then asks him to work 10 hours a day, should he not be paid just as much as if the Government buys 80 miles of railroad transportation from the Pennsylvania Railway and then pays for 20 miles extra when it has use for it?

Many civil-service employees, to my knowledge, have looked to the Civil Service Commission as a sort of protection, on the theory that being the arm of the Government through which they are employed and that which in many ways designates their working conditions, it might with some degree of justice act as their protector, if such is not too strong a term, when they have been discriminated against. A great many times during my 20 years in the civil service have I heard the expression used, "Why does not the Civil Service Commission make some effort to see that this or that law or regulation protecting our interests is enforced?" If the commission feels that it is powerless in this matter, would I be presuming in asking whether it would favor an amendment to the civil-service law clothing the commission with authority to investigate cases of alleged lack of enforcement and some authority to require the enforcement?

I wish at this time to tender to the commission any assistance or support that I may be able to give or that this organization may give, and to give assurance that these problems are the problems of men and women and their daily existence, and ask such assistance or advice as the commission may feel it can properly give, both on the general subject discussed and on the particular matter in hand.

Respectfully,

FRANK H. AINSWORTH, *President.*

UNITED STATES CIVIL SERVICE COMMISSION,
Washington, D. C., July 23, 1914.

Capt. F. H. AINSWORTH,
President Federation of Civil Service Employees, San Francisco, Cal.

SIR: In response to your letter of July 11, 1914, continuing previous correspondence, you are advised that the mere fact that a statute, such as that affecting the hours of labor of Government employees, is quoted in one of its publications does not make the commission responsible for its interpretation and enforcement. The pamphlet containing the civil-service act and rules, to which you refer, contains much matter inserted from the statutes and opinions of the Attorney General merely for the information of persons who may wish to refer to them in connection with certain civil-service matters. In its announcements of examinations also the commission merely states the entrance salaries which the particular department or departments expect to pay, along with any other matter furnished by the appointing officers for the information of applicants. It is in no way responsible as a party to the contract, as you suggest, that the expectations aroused by these statements shall be realized by those appointed. As stated in a previous letter, the commission can not offer advice as to the proper office or officials to whom to appeal to compel a department to comply with the hours-of-labor provisions of the statutes when it is believed they are being violated in a certain case. As previously explained, its province is in general defined and limited by the civil-service act and rules and the duties laid upon it by the President and Congress, and it can not undertake to rectify alleged abuses in departmental administration which are believed to be in contravention of other provisions of law.

By direction of the commission.

Very respectfully,

J. H. McIlhenny, *President.*

Lightning Source UK Ltd.
Milton Keynes UK
UKHW011845271218
334506UK00017B/1497/P